D1283735

Encyclopedia of Historic Forts

Encyclopedia of

HISTORIC FORTS

The Military, Pioneer, and Trading Posts of the United States

ROBERT B. ROBERTS

MACMILLAN PUBLISHING COMPANY
NEW YORK

Collier Macmillan Publishers
LONDON

Macmillan Publishing Company
A Division of Macmillan, Inc.
866 Third Avenue, New York, N. Y. 10022

Collier Macmillan Canada, Inc.

Library of Congress Catalog Card Number: 86-28494

Printed in the United States of America

printing number
1   2   3   4   5   6   7   8   9   10

Library of Congress Cataloging-in-Publication Data

Roberts, Robert B.
    Encyclopedia of historic forts.

    Includes index.
    1. Military bases—United States—Dictionaries.
2. Fortification—United States—Dictionaries.   I. Title.
UA26.A45   1987   355.7′0951   86–28494
ISBN 0-02-926880-X

Editorial and Production Staff

Charles E. Smith, Publisher
Elyse Dubin, Project Editor
Sylvia Kanwischer, Associate Project Editor
Pamela Nicely, Copyeditor
Linda Westerhoff, Proofreader
Morton Rosenberg, Production/Manufacturing Manager
Ann Marie Fernandez, Manufacturing Assistant

Contents

Illustrations

Preface

THIS LONG-NEEDED encyclopedic compilation, intended for serious scholars and researchers as well as general readers and school students, is the product of some forty years of private research—an effort to perpetuate and preserve America's four-century military history—beginning with French (1564), Spanish (1565), English (1607), Dutch (1614), and Swedish (1638) colonization in the New World.

Henri Pirenne, a noted Belgian historian, stated that "war is as old as humanity, and the construction of fortresses almost as old as war." It follows that no architectural structure had a longer history.

During the last year of World War II, "the Atomic Age began at exactly 5:30 Mountain War Time on the morning of July 16, 1945, on a stretch of semi-desert land about fifty airline miles from Alamogordo, New Mexico. At that great moment in history, ranking with the moment in the long ago when man first put fire to work for him and started on his march to civilization, the vast energy locked within the hearts of the atoms of matter was released for the first time in a burst of flame such as had never before been seen on this planet . . . an elemental force freed from its bonds after being chained for billions of years." (William L. Laurence, *New York Times,* September 26, 1945). The atomic bomb in two brief instants, later in the same year, largely destroyed two Japanese cities and decimated their populations, practically destroying many millenniums of advances in the art of fortification and the latest products of the centuries-long development of weaponry.

No effort will be made here to delineate in depth the fortifications of ancient times, the Greek and Roman eras, the Dark Ages, the Middle Ages, and the Renaissance in the Near East, Asia, and Europe. Briefly, for the purposes of this compilation, the preponderance of the defenses consisted of cities surrounded by battlemented walls, later ramparted and bastioned, and baronial and royal castles reinforced by carefully located high towers and deep moats.

Late in the seventeenth century, the art of permanent fortification, already greatly developed, became an even more critical element of warfare as the result of the genius of a French engineer, Sébastien Le Prestre Vauban (1632–1707). Vauban retained the traditional plan for a fortress—inner enclosure, rampart, moat, and outer rampart—but he extended the outworks as far as possible in order to force the enemy to begin his siege operations at a distance. He also insured that every defensive face was flanked and supported by the works behind and beside it, thus creating a vast polygon replete with great bastions at every angle interspersed with smaller ones in between, each of which was near enough to the next to provide supporting small-arms fire. He revolutionized the art of fortification. In addition to developing new successful siege strategies—directing some fifty of them—he constructed thirty-three new fortresses and improved almost three hundred others, fortifying all of France's frontiers. The perfection of Vauban's style was apparent in the design of Dunkerque (Dunkirk), on the English Channel in northern France, which is considered to have been one of his finest works. The city was protected by a formidable arrangement of bastions, curtains, ditches, ravelins, tenailles, redoubts, and hornworks.

Vauban had profound influence on both the theory and the practice of the art of defense in Europe and in the New World. In 1690, as a consequence of his influence, a corps of engineers was founded in France. Ultimately, this corps would be significant in America by providing experience with military architecture to men who would serve in the colonies as well as in the United States. On theory of defense, Vauban's first system formed the foundation of academic work in military architecture in France. The highly esteemed École Polytechnique made the precepts of this system the basis for its program on field and permanent fortification and attack and defense of fortified places. Eventually, the United States Military Academy at West Point, founded in 1802, developed a curriculum similar to that of the esteemed French school. Thus, European influence, particularly that of France, was ingrained into the art of defense in America from early colonial times through the nineteenth-century development of the country. [Willard B. Robinson, *American Forts: Architectural Form and Function* (1977), page 12].

During the Renaissance (1400–1600), several European nations were roused to initiate explorations in strange lands, launching voyages to the west, highlighted by Christopher Columbus' four historic crossings of the south Atlantic.

It was not, however, until the middle of the sixteenth century that any of these nations attempted to claim any section of the North American continent by settlement. France undertook colonization on the Saint Lawrence River as early as 1541; in the 1560s both France and Spain started colonization on the southeastern Atlantic seacoast [with Fort Caroline by the French on the St. Johns River in 1564 and St. Augustine by the Spanish in 1565]; later in the century England attempted to colonize the central coastal region [short-lived Fort Raleigh on Roanoke Island in present North Carolina].

Motivation to colonize North America derived from the desire for political freedom, material profit, acquisition of territory, or missionary zeal. Disagreement and competition over these objectives made conflict an inevitable part of colonial life and settlement. Consequently, for protection from natives and from other Europeans, fort building was a mandatory measure from the very beginning.

In colonial America political and physical geography were integrally related to defense. Spain and France both sought to maintain early land claims with forts that were strategically located to limit the expansion of other nations. Since communication was vital to colonization, strongholds were positioned to control harbors and natural interior highways. Forts were built at the mouths of rivers which emptied into the Gulf of Mexico and the Atlantic Ocean; inland, other defensive works appeared on large lakes and at points of confluence of major rivers. Thus, with the maintenance of comparatively few fortifications it was theoretically possible to control large sections of land.

The selection of appropriate locations for fortifications and the design and realization of works to occupy them required the services of individuals knowledgeable in the principles of the art of fortification. As the intensity of competition among nations became greater and as warfare became more methodical, the demand for skilled professional military engineers increased. [*Ibid.,* page 13].

In North America, during the latter part of the seventeenth century, the frontier fort surrounded by a log palisade became an integral part of warfare as Europeans pushed their settlements westward, accompanied by the spread of fur-trading empires. Indian wars in the Northeast, colonial wars, and a revolution for independence that forged a homogeneous people into a new nation, were followed by a British invasion (the War of 1812), a four-year American civil war, intermittent Indian wars in the West, a short-lived war against Spain in Cuba and the Philippines, and two twentieth-century World Wars that were fought almost wholly on foreign soil. They spawned the establishment of many thousands of defenses, in aggregate transforming America into the most internally fortified territory in the world, dating from 1562 when the French attempted their first fortification in the New World—a score of years after initially undertaking colonization on the St. Lawrence River—by erecting short-lived Charles Fort in the environs of present-day Parris Island in South Carolina.

The defenses were spread across the face of the United States (including Alaska and Hawaii), from coast to coast and border to border. They ranged from minimally fortified, temporary Indian frontier "private" and "public" forts and blockhouses, "garrison houses" in New England, "station" settlements in Kentucky and Tennessee, and stockaded trading posts in inland bastioned fortresses and brick-and-concrete-built coast defense installations. The sites of a number of frontier forts have been lost in the mists of history. Some of them, however, have been rediscovered in recent decades and converted into state parks, often enclosing reconstructions of the former posts. During World War II, populous urban centers in the United States were first protected by antiaircraft batteries, later supplanted by Nike missile sites ringing metropolitan areas.

For the purpose of assembling a convenient work of consistency, I have limited the compilation to military-type posts, eliminating U.S. Navy (including Marine Corps) and Air Force establishments, excepting those converted to or from U.S. Army use. I have intentionally omitted most federal arsenals, quartermaster depots, transitory encampments, and short-lived minor subposts. Also omitted are most settlers' frontier dwellings, crudely "fortified" during three centuries of intermittent Indian wars.

This work is arranged alphabetically, state-by-state and by post name within each state, for simplicity and convenience. Many of the posts listed are followed by italicized names in parentheses to indicate alternate identifications, suggesting original construction, modification, change in command, or official redesignation to honor an officer killed in action. Pioneer/civilian defenses and trading posts were usually named for the men who established them, with some of the posts ultimately taken over, either temporarily or permanently, by the U. S. Army for strategic reasons, leading to structure modification and armament reinforcement. In a number of instances, forts were officially abandoned or destroyed, after which new defenses were begun on or near the same site, at times resulting in redesignations. Posts followed by names in capital and small capital letters refer the reader to the main entry under which the post is discussed.

The usage of U.S., S.R., and C.R. indicates present-day federal, state, and county travel routes. USMA is the acronym for the prestigious United States Military Academy at West Point, New York.

Countless hours have been spent researching and compiling data extracted from numerous official federal reports and lists, manuscript and microfilmed post returns in the National Archives, and hundreds of historical accounts of military and trading posts published in state and county journals. A selected bibliography; a list of state archives and libraries for consultation; and an index of forts, which alphabetically lists all of the forts in this volume, serve as appendixes. A list of illustrations and a glossary of fortification terms are supplied in the front matter.

ACKNOWLEDGMENTS

I am indebted to the nation's state, county, and university libraries, too many to list here, for their generous cooperation through the years. My greatest gratitude, however, is expressed to the following historical repositories:

Library of Congress, National Archives, National Geographic Society, National Park Service, and U.S. Army Center of Military History, Washington; New-York Historical Society; New York Public Library; Public Archives of Canada, Ottawa; Royal Archives, Windsor Castle, England; U.S. Army Military History Research Collection, Carlisle Barracks, Pennsylvania; USMA Library, West Point, New York; and archival repositories in France, Mexico, and Spain.

In addition, many of these institutions provided me with the required illustrations to accompany this work.

Robert B. Roberts
Lehigh Acres, Florida
January 1986

The publisher gratefully acknowledges the kind assistance of Mr. Alan Conrad Aimone, of the U.S. Military Academy Library, who, since Mr. Roberts' death in November of 1986, has contributed significantly to the publication of this volume.

The Publisher

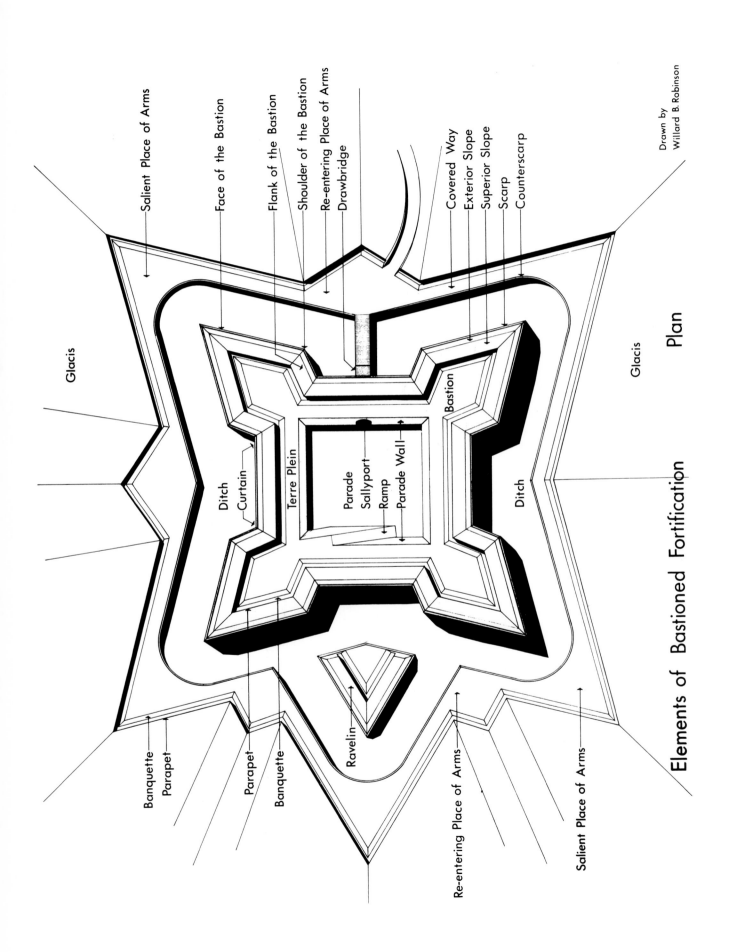

Salient Place of Arms

Face of the Bastion

Flank of the Bastion

Shoulder of the Bastion

Re-entering Place of Arms

Drawbridge

Covered Way

Exterior Slope

Superior Slope

Scarp

Counterscarp

Glacis

Glacis

Ditch

Curtain

Terre Plein

Parade

Sallyport

Ramp

Parade Wall

Bastion

Ditch

Banquette

Parapet

Parapet

Banquette

Ravelin

Re-entering Place of Arms

Salient Place of Arms

Drawn by
Willard B. Robinson

Plan

Elements of Bastioned Fortification

Glossary

ABATIS. A barricade made up of closely spaced, felled trees with pointed and interlaced branches facing the enemy.

ADOBE. The sun-dried brick used in Mexico, Arizona, California, and elsewhere for building houses and frontier defenses.

ADVANCED WORK. Any work of fortification located outside the glacis yet within reach of musketry or rifle fire.

ARTIFICER. Soldier-mechanic.

BANQUETTE. A continuous step or platform for riflemen at the base of a parapet.

BARBETTE. A wooden or earthen platform inside a fortification, on which cannons were mounted to permit firing over the rampart instead of through embrasures.

BASTION. A projecting work or blockhouse, usually located in an angle of the fort, to allow enfilading of the enemy along the wall or curtain.

BERM or BERME. The horizontal surface between the ditch and the base of the rampart.

BLOCKHOUSE. A traditional frontier defense, either detached or used as a bastion in a fort. Constructed of either rounded or squared logs, with an overhanging second story, the structure was loopholed for musketry or embrasured for cannon, or both.

BOMBARD. An early artillery piece that propelled stones or other projectiles.

BOMBPROOF. A structure designed to provide security against artillery fire.

BROWN BESS. Familiar name for an infantry musket first used by the British army at the beginning of the eighteenth century, replaced by the rifle more than a century later. "Brown" was derived from the color of the gun's stock, while "Bess" was apparently a corruption of "buss" from the outmoded blunderbuss.

CALIBER or CALIBRE. Measurement applied to the diameter of the bore of a gun.

CANISTER or CASE SHOT. Bagged or cased small metal pellets, loaded in cannon on top of a gunpowder charge; devastating at close quarters.

CARCASS. A sieved metal gun, loaded with rags soaked in a flammable liquid, that was set afire when shot from a mortar or howitzer; a firebomb.

CASEMATE. A bombproofed vault in a fortification wall for embrasured cannon, often used to quarter troops and store supplies.

CASTLE. A medieval-period fortified building or group of buildings. In nineteenth-century America the term also designated a type of seacoast fortification resembling a medieval shell-keep.

CAUSEWAY. An elevated roadway, usually over a ditch or moat, or occasionally a marsh or morass, leading to the fort's entrance.

CAVALIER. An elevated work for artillery to command the surrounding country; at times placed on the curtain or terreplein of a bastion.

CHEVAL-DE-FRISE (CHEVAUX-DE-FRISE, *pl.*). A barricade used on land or in the water, it was constructed of massive timbers with protruding iron-tipped poles. Its use by the Americans during the Revolution was a dismal failure.

CIRCUMVALLATION. An enclosing wall, rampart, or trench, or any system of these. The term may also be applied to a line of fieldworks.

CITADEL. A small but strong fort within, or situated to form a part of, a larger fortification or fortress. Usually located to command the area and other works surrounding it, it functioned as a place of refuge from which a defense could be prolonged after the main works fell.

COHORN or COEHORN. Originally of Dutch deviation (*coehoorn*), it was a small short-barreled howitzer.

COQUINA. A soft, whitish limestone made up of shell fragments, coral, and fossilized fish. Quarried, it is used as building stone, particularly in Florida.

COUNTERGUARD. A work made up of two faces forming a salient angle and located before bastions or ravelins, but separated from them, to protect their faces from artillery fire.

COUNTERSCARP. The outer wall or slope of a ditch or moat.

COVERED WAY or COVERT. An open corridor in the outer wall of a ditch (counterscarp) for riflemen, who were thus protected by an earthern breastwork.

CURTAIN. The wall of a fortification between bastions.

DEFENSIVE BARRACKS. Fortified quarters usually designed to serve as a citadel within a fort.

DEFILADE. A natural or man-made shield to protect either troops or a gun position in face of the enemy.

DEMIBASTION. A bastion with only one face and one flank.

DEMILUNE, HALF MOON, or LUNETTE. In early Renaissance defenses, an outwork consisting of two faces and a crescent-shaped gorge, constructed to protect a bastion or the fort's curtain. French engineers termed it a *demilune*. Half moons were replaced by ravelins in later-built fortifications.

DITCH. A wide, deep trench around a defensive work. The material from its excavation was used to form the ramparts. When filled with water, it was termed a *moat* or *wet ditch,* otherwise it was called a *dry ditch* or *fosse.*

DRAWBRIDGE. A bridge across a ditch or moat at the fort's entrance, manually raised or lowered.

EMBRASURE. An opening or slot in a curtain or rampart with its sides slanted outward to increase the angle of cannon fire.

EN BARBETTE. An arrangement for cannons in which they were mounted on high platforms or carriages so that they were fired over a parapet instead of through embrasures.

ENCEINTE. The enveloping works of a fortification consisting of the curtains, ramparts, and parapets.

ENDICOTT-PERIOD BATTERIES. In 1885, a group of men known as the Endicott Board was established by President Grover Cleveland under the chairmanship of Secretary of War William Endicott to cooperate with the Corps of Engineers in studying coastal defense needs and make recommendations for the development of a new system of defense. The board's combined Army, Navy, and civilian membership undertook an extensive analysis of the coastal defense situation and in 1886 released its findings with proposals that ultimately led to the erection of numerous concrete batteries, including the heaviest artillery rifles mounted on disappearing carriages.

ENFILADE. A sweeping fire from a line of troops or gun batteries.

ENVELOPMENT. An assault directed against an enemy's flank; in the case of attack against two flanks, it is called a double envelopment.

EPAULMENT. The immediate area where the curtain and a bastion meet.

ESCARPMENT. *See* Scarp.

FACE. In some five-sided seacoast forts, the designation for the sides of the enceinte that form a salient directed toward the main passage; also, the wall between bastions or salients.

FASCINE. A bound bundle of long branches or twigs, used in the construction of a rampart or an earthwork.

FIELD FORTIFICATION. Impermanently constructed works intended for occupation only for a short time during a campaign.

FIELD GUN. A cannon mounted on a mobile carriage for use in the field.

FLANK. The wall of a bastion between the curtain and the face.

FLANKED ANGLE. The angle formed by two faces of a ravelin or bastion. It is also called the "salient," the "point of the ravelin," or the "point of the bastion."

FLANKER. A projecting work from which the ground in front of adjacent walls could be defended.

FLECHE. A defensive outwork with two walls or faces forming a salient angle with an open ditch or gorge. *Fleche* is French for "arrow."

FLINTLOCK or FIRELOCK. A gun with a mechanism for firing the priming charge by striking a piece of flint on steel to produce sparks.

FORT. An enclosed land or seacoast defensive work, with walls or palisades and blockhouses or bastions. Manned by soldiers, it was armed with artillery such as cannons and howitzers.

FORTALICE. A small fort or its outwork.

FORTRESS. Generally, a town or city enclosed by fortifications.

FOSSE. *See* Ditch.

FRAISE. Pointed stakes in the rampart or berm, either horizontal or inclined.

FRONTAL ASSAULT. Equally distributed forces attacking along the whole front.

GABION. Wickerwork filled with earth and stone,

used to protect gun batteries; the Revolutionary equivalent of today's sandbag.

GLACIS. Sloping earthwork from either the covered way or counterscarp.

GRAPE or GRAPESHOT. The same as a canister, except that the balls were much smaller and more plentiful.

GRASSHOPPER. The nickname for the small three-pounder field gun, mounted on legs instead of the normal wheeled carriage. The name was derived from the action of the gun when fired. The grasshopper was the artillery piece commonly carried during field operations.

GUARDHOUSE. The headquarters for a fort's daily guard, it was also used as a structure to house prisoners.

GUARDROOM. A small enclosed structure located at or near the entrance of a fort.

HALF BASTION. *See* Demibastion.

HALF MOON. *See* Demilune.

HORNWORK. An outwork consisting of a pair of demibastions joined by a wall or curtain.

HOT SHOT. Cannonballs heated red-hot in a hot-shot oven and utilized for setting fire to wooden fortifications or timbered enemy ships.

HOWITZER. In use today, it is a short-barreled gun with the ability to fire shells at a high angle of elevation, particularly effective against targets within fortified enclosures or trenches.

INTRENCHED CAMP. A fortified army encampment located outside a fort but within range of its armament.

INTRENCHMENT. A fieldwork consisting of a ditch and an earthen parapet.

LINSTOCK. A cannoneer's forked rod or stick that held the slow-burning match to be applied to the prime charge in the touchhole of muzzle-loading cannon.

LOOPHOLES. Apertures or slots in defenses through which the fire of small arms or cannon could be directed at an attacking or besieging enemy.

LUNETTE. *See* Demilune.

MAGAZINE. A storage facility, usually bomb-proofed, for ammunition, armaments, goods, or provisions.

MAHAM TOWER. Devised by Colonel Hezekiah Maham, it was first used during the successful siege of Fort Watson, South Carolina, April 1781. Made of logs, the tower had a parapeted superstructure higher than the walls of the fort being besieged.

MANTELET. A mobile bulletproof screen to protect gunners.

MARTELLO TOWER. A free-standing masonry tower defense, usually erected along the coast to fight off invasion by sea.

MERLON. The section of fortification wall located between any two embrasures.

MINE. A subterranean tunnel excavated by besiegers under a fortification for the purpose of destroying a section of the work by explosives or other means.

MOAT. *See* Ditch.

MORTAR. In use today, it is a short-barreled gun with a large-caliber bore, able to propel shells at high angles.

MUSKET. The heavy smoothbore handgun of large caliber used throughout the eighteenth and nineteenth centuries.

PALISADE. A wall or curtain constructed of logs or stakes set perpendicularly in the ground, forming a defensive enclosure.

PARADE. A level area of the interior of a fortification where troops are assembled or reviewed while marching or drilling.

PARALLEL. A trench in the ground, parallel to the lines of a besieged fortification, for covering an attacking force.

PARAPET. An earthen or stone defensive platform on the wall of a fort.

PICKET. A pointed pole planted vertically in the ground.

PORTCULLIS. A reinforced grating, raised or lowered in vertical channels, to prevent entry through a fort's gateway.

POSTERN. A passage leading from the interior of a fortification to the ditch.

POUNDAGE. Term applied to guns that fired solid balls of a certain weight (four-pounder, ten-pounder, etc.).

RAMPART. A mass of earth formed with the material excavated from the ditch to protect the enclosed area from artillery fire and to elevate defenders to a commanding position overlooking the approaches to a fort.

RAVELIN. A V-shaped outwork outside the main moat or ditch.

REDAN. A V-shaped outwork, with its angle projected toward the enemy.

REDOUBT. A defensive outwork, usually square or polygonal, minus defensive flanks.

REENTERING or REENTRANT ANGLE. An angle pointing toward the interior of a fortification.

REVERBERATORY FURNACE. A kiln in which the fuel is not in direct contact with the metal; used for the production of hot shot.

REVETMENT. Support facing, masonry or earthen, of the rampart between the fort's wall and the ditch.

ROYAL. A small mortar.

SALIENT ANGLE. A projecting angle, the opposite of recessed angle or reentrant.

SALLYPORT. The gateway or postern of a fortification.

SAP. A deep narrow trench, protected by gabions, used as an approach to a besieged enemy's position or fortification.

SAPPER. British nomenclature for a military engineer.

SAUCISSON. A large fascine.

SCARP or ESCARP. The inner wall of the ditch surrounding a fort's ramparts.

SHELL. An explosive missile or bomb fired from a cannon.

SHOULDER BASTION. A bastion located at the conjunction of face and flank walls of a fort. This designation referred only to a particular type of five-sided seacoast defense that had the shape of two-thirds of a hexagon.

SLOW MATCH. A slow-burning fuse or match, consisting of a cord or rope usually soaked in saltpeter.

SORTIE or SALLY. A sudden attack on besiegers by troops from a defensive work. The principal objective was to destroy the siege works that had been constructed by the aggressors.

SPIKING A GUN. Rendering a muzzle-loading cannon useless by driving a spike deep into the gun's touchhole.

STAR FORT. An enclosed defense with a trace made up of a series of salient and reentering angles.

STOCKADE. A palisade or barricade, usually loopholed, for entrenchments, blockhouses, and bastions.

SWIVEL GUN. A small cannon mounted on a swivel support to permit wide movement of the weapon on a horizontal plane; usually mounted on a fort's parapet or in a blockhouse.

TENAILLE. A fieldwork with one or two reentering angles, planted in a ditch or moat between two blockhouses or bastions, immediately in front of the fort's curtain.

TERREPLEIN. A platform for cannon on a rampart behind the parapet; also, the level surface around a fieldwork.

TRACE. The ground plan of a fortification.

TRAVERSE. The defensive barrier placed across the terreplein to minimize enfilading by an attacking force.

TRUNNION. One of the two cylindrical projections on a cannon, one on each side, to support the gun on its carriage.

TURRET. A small tower located at an angle of a fortification or building; consisted of a revolving structure housing guns.

WATTLE AND DAUB. An interwoven network of twigs, sticks, branches, etc., daubed over with clay and mud; used in constructing rude huts.

Alabama

FORT ALABAMA. FORT JACKSON.

FORT ALEXANDRIA. A Confederate-built fortification, it was designed to defend the city of Mobile.

FORT ALEXIS. SPANISH FORT.

CAMP ANNISTON. Confederate forces established this camp and supply base at Anniston in Calhoun County.

CAMP ANNISTON (*Camp Shipp*). This post was established at Anniston in 1898 as a training center for recruits during the Spanish-American War. Renamed Camp Shipp during World War I, the camp was closed in 1922.

APALACHICOLA FORT. In Russell County, on the west bank of the Chattahoochee River, near Holy Trinity, it was a key Spanish outpost built about 1689 during the imperial struggle to control the Indians in the southeastern United States. The fort was destroyed by the Spaniards in 1691 because of the English threat. The moated palisade of the fort was rectangular, roughly 61 by 53 feet, with corner bastions. Constructed of wattle and daub, the palisade was reinforced by an exterior half-wall of clay. The well-preserved site is privately owned.

FORT ARMSTRONG. Historians have long disputed over the probable site in Cherokee County. The most logical locations are believed to be either on the north bank of the Coosa River, east of Cedar Bluff, or on the Etowah River near Coosa. According to local tradition, the site was a British base of operations during the Revolution. Fort Armstrong was built by General Andrew Jackson in 1813–14 during the Creek War and was garrisoned mostly by Cherokee Indians.

ARNOLD BATTERY. Mounting four 10-inch mortars, it was erected by Union forces in 1864 for the purpose of supporting the siege of Fort Morgan.

FORT AUTREY. Built by Alexander Autrey in 1816, it protected settlers in Conecuh County against bands of Creek Indians who had lost their lands by the Treaty of Fort Jackson in 1814. The stockade, later converted to a farm structure, was located on the Wolf Trail leading from Burnt Corn to Pensacola, Florida. No action is known to have taken place here.

FORT AUX ALIBAMOS. FORT JACKSON.

FORT BAINBRIDGE. Located on the old Federal Road in Macon County, it was a supply post 17 miles southeast of Tuskegee near the Russell County line. Built in January 1814 by Georgia troops under General John Floyd during the campaign against the Indians, the fort was named for Commodore William Bainbridge. After the war, Captain Kendall Lewis, a former U.S. Army officer, established his popular Lewis Tavern on the site, with his father-in-law, Big Warrior, a silent partner in the enterprise.

CAMP BALAAM. A temporary camp, in Russell County, established in 1836 during the Creek War.

FORT BELL (*Fort Belleville*). A defense against Indians built in 1817 and located on John Bell's land, the fort was about six miles from Fort Autrey, near Belleville, Conecuh County.

FORT BELLEVILLE. FORT BELL.

FORT BIBB. A stockade erected early in 1818 during the Indian uprising, it stood on old Federal Road, on the present site of Pine Flat, 15 miles west of Greenville in Butler County. The fort was built around the home of Captain James Saffold and named in honor of Territorial Governor William Wyatt Bibb.

FORT BLAKELY. A Civil War defense of Mobile built by the Confederates in 1864–65, it occupied the site of the dead town of Blakely in Baldwin County at the northern end of Mobile Bay. Blakely, once a rival of Mobile, was abandoned after two yellow fever epidemics and a severe financial depression. To Fort Blakely's south is the site of old Spanish Fort established by Bernardo de Gálvez. (See: SPANISH FORT.) Blakely's defenses consisted of a four-mile-long barricade of pine logs covered with mud and sand and fronted with dense abatis. With its flanks standing in Appalachee River's marshes, the fort boasted nine lunettes and was fortified by 35 artillery pieces in addition to siege mortars. The fort, holding 2,700 defenders, was commanded by General St. John Liddell, a West Point graduate and seasoned veteran of the Confederate campaigns in Tennessee. After subduing Spanish Fort, Union forces under Major General Frederick Steele appeared before Fort Blakely and commenced an eight-day bombardment. General E. R. S. Canby later joined in the siege with additional Union troops. On the afternoon of April 8, 1865, about 22,000 Federals launched the final assault through the shredded abatis and overpowered the defenders. A small number of Confederates effected escapes into the marshes, but some 2,300 others surrendered.

FORT BLUFF. Constructed by local citizens in 1861 atop a high hill near Hulaco in the eastern part of Morgan County, the defense had no official recognition by the Confederate government. No engagements took place at or near the fort during the war.

FORT BOWYER. FORT MORGAN.

FORT BROWDER. A stockaded fort built by Barbour County settlers, it was one of a number of such defenses in the region occupied by troops during the campaign to compel the Lower Creek Indians to evacuate their lands in compliance with the terms of the Treaty of Cusseta.

FORT BURNT CORN. A rude stockade built in 1817 by a retired major, Richard Warren, it served as a refuge for local Conecuh County settlers. The Battle of Burnt Corn was fought between Alabama volunteer militiamen and Indians on old Federal Road north of today's Evergreen.

CANAL BATTERY. A Confederate defense near Mobile.

CANBY BATTERY. A Union installation near Mobile.

FORT CARLOTTA. FORT CHARLOTTE.

FORT CARNEY. FORT HAWN.

CATO'S FORT. A small stockaded defense, the fort was located in Clarke County, on the west side of the Tombigbee River, about five miles south of Coffeeville, near the Choctaw-Washington County line. Erected in 1813 by settlers, it was abandoned very soon after the Creek War broke out.

FORT CHARLOTTE (*Fort Louis de la Louisiana; Fort Louis de la Mobile; Fort Condé de la Mobile; Fort Carlotta*). Erected by the French at Twenty-Seven Mile Bluff on the Mobile River, it was begun in 1702 by Louisiana's colonial governor, Sieur de Bienville, to guard the Mississippi's entrance and named Fort Louis de la Louisiana for Louis XIV. Designated as the capital of French Louisiana, it was considered

America's first "modern" city since it was not enclosed by walls, as were towns in Europe and Quebec in Canada, or located on an island, as were Charleston, Montreal, Jamestown, and New York. After a 10-year battle against the environment, flood waters invaded the fort and adjoining town for the second time and some 400 inhabitants were removed to the site of today's Mobile.

Fort Louis de la Mobile was built in 1711 and largely rebuilt in 1717, when it was renamed Fort Condé de la Mobile in honor of the French Bourbon family. The fort, the strongest French military work on the Gulf coast, was described in 1735 as constructed of brick, with four bastions measuring about 300 feet between their salients; there were demilunes, a ditch, a covered way, and a glacis. The fort occupied the block today bounded by Royal, Church, St. Emanuel, and Theater streets.

The Treaty of Paris in 1763, ending America's last French and Indian War, ceded France's North American possessions, with the exception of New Orleans, to Great Britain. The British occupied Mobile and changed the name of Fort Condé to Fort Charlotte in honor of King George III's young queen, Charlotte Sophia, former princess of Mecklenburg-Strelitz. The Spaniards seized possession of the fort, establishing it as a center of Spanish rule, and called it Fort Carlotta. In 1813 General James Wilkinson captured Mobile, dispossessed the Spanish, and garrisoned the fort with U.S. troops. General Andrew Jackson established his headquarters at Fort Charlotte, from which he led his troops to seize Spanish-held Pensacola. From Fort Charlotte also departed the forces that defeated the British in the Battle of New Orleans.

Peace was restored to the Mobile area by 1818 and land developers sought to demolish the fort, which occupied ground required for the expansion of the city's port. In response to the recommendation made by Secretary of War John C. Calhoun, Congress passed an act enabling the sale of the fort, consummated in 1820. Archeological excavations of Fort Condé were completed during the early 1970s, followed by the reconstruction of portions of the fort's walls and bastions in exactly the same locations as the original. The twin tunnels of Interstate 10 were constructed beneath the fort's foundations and were opened to traffic in February 1973. The reconstructed fort was opened to the public on July 11, 1976, during the nation's bicentennial celebration.

FORT CHINNABEE. CHINNABY'S FORT.

CHINNABY'S FORT (*Fort Chinnabee*). This small fort was located on the north bank of Big Shoal Creek close to the mouth of Wolfskull Creek, six miles east of Oxford, Calhoun County. An amicable Creek chief named Chinnabee built the fort about three miles north of his village in 1813.

FORT CLAIBORNE. A strongly built temporary fort, built by General Ferdinand L. Claiborne in 1813 as a supply base during the Creek War, stood on Weatherford Bluff or Alabama Heights in Monroe County, on the Alabama River near the mouth of Limestone Creek.

CAMP CLARK. Located on a site near Mobile, Camp Clark was a rendezvous for militiamen during the Spanish-American War.

FORT COFFEE. Located in Bullock County, the fort was established in 1836 as a defense against marauding Lower Creek Indians during the enforced evacuation of their ceded lands in southeast Alabama.

FORT CONDÉ DE LA MOBILE. FORT CHARLOTTE.

FORT CONFEDERATION (*Fort Tombécbee; Fort Tombigbee; Fort York*). One of the several forts built by the French in Alabama, Fort Tombécbee (the spelling varies in historical records) was built in 1735 as a military–trading post by Sieur de Bienville, governor of French Louisiana, near present-day Epes in Sumter County. Located above the confluence of the Tombigbee and Black Warrior rivers in Chickasaw-Choctaw Indian country, it served as an advanced base during the war against the English-allied Chickasaws, as a post for trade with the Choctaws, and as a check against British influence in the area. After the French and Indian War, the British renamed it Fort York and occupied it for five years until 1768, when it was abandoned.

Following the capture of Mobile by the Spaniards under Bernardo de Gálvez in 1780, the fort was renovated, named Fort Confederation (Confederación), and served as an outpost of Spanish influence. The Pinckney Treaty of 1795, known as the Treaty of San Lorenzo, forced the withdrawal of Spanish troops, who were replaced by Americans. In 1802 a treaty with the Choctaws was concluded at the fort whereby the Americans acquired their first cession of lands from the tribe. Here again in 1816, the Choctaws signed a second treaty providing for more land cessions. During the last year of the Civil War a

Confederate general, Nathan B. Forrest, established a lookout point at the old fort, the last time the site served militarily. Today earthworks three or four feet high outline what were the perimeters of old Fort Tombécbee. The two-acre site on White Bluff, 80 feet above the low water of the Tombigbee, is owned by the Alabama Society of Colonial Dames.

BATTERY CRAVEN. A Civil War fortified position near Mobile.

FORT CRAWFORD. Located about a mile from today's Brewton in Escambia County, across a creek on a rising eminence, this square work with two blockhouses at diagonal corners was built in 1817 on a site that was later occupied by the Downing-Shofner Industrial Institute. Fort Crawford was most probably established by Major General Edmund Pendleton Gaines in order to protect the region's settlers from numerous marauding Indians. One hundred regulars of the 7th U.S. Infantry, commanded by Major White Youngs, garrisoned the fort in 1818. It was maintained until 1819 and abandoned sometime before 1821.

CURRY'S FORT. Built on the east bank of the Tombigbee River, about four miles south of Jackson in Clarke County, it was a settlers' defense against Indian raiders. Colonel James Caller and his militiamen stopped at the fort, which was in use throughout 1813, while they were en route to Burnt Corn Creek where they fought and lost the first battle of the Creek War on July 25, 1813.

FORT DALE. This fort was located about five miles north of Greenville, near U.S. 31, in Butler County. It was established by Colonel Sam Dale in 1818 on the old Federal Road as a defense against Indian hostiles.

FORT DAUPHIN. Searching for a site more appropriate than Biloxi, Mississippi, for Louisiana's capital, the French, led by the Le Moyne brothers, d'Iberville and Bienville, selected an island at the entrance to Mobile Bay. On Dauphin Island they erected a fort and built a port in 1701. The fort, named Fort Dauphin, was established as a defense against probable English raiders. The depth of the island's port was originally more than 20 feet, but a violent storm in 1717 washed a sandbar into the harbor, reducing its depth to only 10 feet and severely restricting its usefulness as a port. Abandoned by the French two years later, it was, however, utilized by small watercraft until 1742. Hurricane Frederic on Sep-

tember 12, 1979, almost wiped out Dauphin Island and destroyed the two-lane bridge to the mainland, thus isolating the island's inhabitants from Mobile County. The bridge was replaced in early 1982.

FORT DECATUR. Located on the east bank of the Tallapoosa River, the fort was near the town of Milstead in Macon County. Colonel Homer Y. Milton and Carolina troops he commanded built the fort in March 1814. Tennessee's first governor, John Sevier, died at Fort Decatur on September 24, 1815, while he was arbitrating a boundary settlement between Georgia and the Creek Nation. He was interred on the site, but in 1888 his remains were removed and sent to Knoxville for reburial.

CAMP DEFIANCE. Located in the extreme southern part of Creek country in Macon County, the camp was established by General Elijah Clarke and elements of the Georgia Militia very early in 1814. General John Floyd, with 1,300 troops and 400 friendly Indians, rested at Camp Defiance on the night of January 26. Early the next morning his army was attacked by a large force of Indians. After much confusion during the action, the Indians were finally routed. General Floyd's loss was 17 killed and 182 wounded, with his allied Indians suffering five killed and 15 wounded.

FORT DEPOSIT. Located on the site of today's town of Fort Deposit in Lowndes County, it was erected by General Ferdinand L. Claiborne in 1813 as a supply base and a field hospital. The post was guarded by 100 men. Later Fort Deposit, situated on the old Federal Road, was used by local settlers as a haven of safety against Indian depredators.

FORT DEPOSIT. This supply base was located at the mouth of Honey or Thompson's Creek, on the south bank of the Tennessee River, in Marshall County. General Andrew Jackson and the Tennessee Militia established the post in October 1813 soon after the outbreak of the Creek War.

FORT EASLEY. The site of this fort was on Wood's Bluff, on the east side of the Tombigbee River, in Clarke County. A settlers' defense built in 1813, it enclosed about three acres. News arrived informing the inhabitants of the massacre at Fort Mims on August 30, influencing them to quickly evacuate Fort Easley.

FORT EUFAULA. One of the several forts that was garrisoned to enforce the terms of the 1832 Treaty of Cusseta that deprived the Creeks of their lands, it was erected in 1836 in Barbour County.

BATTERY FARRAGUT. Located near Mobile, it was probably built by Admiral David G. Farragut's fleet after the Battle of Mobile, August 5, 1864.

CAMP (ALBERT G.) FORSE. POST AT HUNTSVILLE.

FORT GAINES. The first defenses of this still-existing fortification, located at the eastern point of Dauphin Island at the entrance to Mobile Bay across from Fort Morgan, were completed in 1822. Records of the U.S. Corps of Engineers first mention Fort Gaines in 1819. Actual construction began in 1821, although it is not clear exactly what shape these first fortifications assumed. Work continued for many years, subsiding and being renewed as the state of war or peace prevailed. Some fortifications were completed by the early 1840s, and in 1846 the federal government allotted $20,000 for "laying out a new Fort Gaines," named in honor of General Edmund Pendleton Gaines. In 1848–49 Captain

Pierre G. T. Beauregard, later one of the most prominent Confederate Army leaders, was superintending engineer for the project. Plans for construction were drawn in 1850, and final approval and orders were signed by Jefferson Davis, then secretary of war under President Franklin Pierce. Fort Gaines, a regular pentagonal bastioned work with corner blockhouses, is 400 feet long on the west wall, 223 feet along the north and south walls, and 209 feet on the two eastern walls, with outer walls 22½ feet high. Included in the fort's defenses are Battery Stanton and Battery Terrett. In 1861 the fort was seized by Alabama troops, and held by the Confederacy until August 8, 1864, when it surrendered to Admiral David G. Farragut during the Battle of Mobile Bay. Inside the fort today is a Confederate museum, and just a few yards from the fort's entrance is a huge anchor and chain from the USS *Hartford*, Admiral Farragut's flagship.

FORT GAY. Built by Butler County settlers in 1818, it served as a defense during the Lower Creek uprising.

BATTERY GLADDEN. A lighthouse that was erected in Mobile Bay on the ruins of tiny, oval-shaped Battery Gladden, a Confederate-created

FORT GAINES. (Courtesy of the Mobile Area Chamber of Commerce, Mobile, Alabama.)

island near Fort Blakely that was intended to defend Mobile during the Civil War.

FORT GLASS. This small redoubt was located near the Alabama River, just south of Suggsville in Clarke County. Zachariah Glass built the defense, evacuated shortly after a local massacre, and its occupants took refuge in Fort Madison, which was only 225 yards distant.

CAMP GRAVELLY SPRINGS. This Union Army camp was located on Waterloo Road in Lauderdale County, about 15 miles west of Florence. The camp extended from the Springs to the Tennessee River. From this base of operations, General James Harrison Wilson began his raid into southern Alabama in March 1865.

FORT GULLETT. FORT HAWN.

FORT GULLETT. This small Confederate fort stood on Gullett's Bluff on the Tombigbee River about four miles south of Jackson in Clarke County. According to local tradition, it was built on the site of a pioneer fort. Constructed in 1862, Fort Gullett was designed to guard the vicinity's salt works from Union raids. The fort was abandoned during the last months of the Civil War.

GUNTER'S LANDING CANTONMENT. A Confederate defense established in 1863 on the Tennessee River in Marshall County.

FORT HAMPTON. Situated on the Elk River, occupying today's site of Harmony Church, this very early fort was 17 miles west of Athens in Limestone County. Colonel Reuben J. Meigs of the U.S. Army built the fort in 1809 to protect Indian lands from illegal squatters. He named it for General Wade Hampton, then stationed at Huntsville. Fort Hampton was abandoned in 1817 after the region's Indians ceded their lands to the United States.

CAMP HARDAWAY. A Civil War post said to have been established near Glenville, possibly today's Glenwood, in Crenshaw County.

FORT HARKER. Located south of the railroad depot in Stevenson, Jackson County, is the well-preserved earthen fortification built by Union troops and occupied from 1862 until the end of the Civil War. A rectangular defense, it was 50 yards square with walls rising as much as 14 feet. Records indicate it had seven barbettes, a powder magazine, and a bombproof. Four of its

gun platforms are still in evidence. A National Park Service excavation in 1976 uncovered a wooden tank in one corner, probably a reservoir for the fort. After the archaeological digging, the city planned to establish a small park around the fort.

FORT HAWKINS. Located on the Elk River in Limestone County, it was apparently a settler's house, stockaded and minimally fortified, in existence from about 1810 to 1812.

FORT HAWN (*Fort Carney; Fort Gullett*). Built on Gullett's Bluff overlooking the Tombigbee River, the defense was approximately six miles from Jackson in Clarke County. It was erected in 1813 by Josiah Carney, who came to this area from North Carolina in 1809. It is not clear whether this stockade was the same as Fort Gullett built around the home of the Gullett family. According to Owens' *History of Alabama*, vol. 1, pp. 614–15, this fort was the same as Fort Hawn. In any case the defense was abandoned early during the Creek War because of the presence of Indian war parties in the area.

FORT HENDERSON. Built in 1836, this fort was a settlers' defense during the Creek Indian uprising. It was located 15 miles below Fort Mitchell, on the Alabama side of the river.

CAMP (HILARY A.) HERBERT. Probably a Confederate post at Montgomery.

FORT HUGER. This Confederate battery, a thousand yards from Fort or Battery Tracy, and between one and two miles above Spanish Fort, was a work with four bastions, open at the north end, and garrisoned by Louisiana troops and Mississippi artillerymen. It was armed with 11 guns of various calibers. In the fort's center was a bombproof, 25 feet high, on which were mounted two 10-inch smoothbore Columbiads. A defense of Mobile, the work was evacuated and blown up by the retreating Confederates on the night of April 11, 1865, two days after General Lee's surrender at Appomattox Courthouse.

FORT HULL. This fort was constructed on the old Federal Road, about five miles southeast of Tuskegee in Macon County. Georgia militiamen commanded by General John Floyd built the fort during the winter of 1813–14. Fearing Fort Mitchell would be subjected to an attack by warring Creeks, Floyd took the bulk of his militia to that defense, leaving a small detachment to garrison Fort Hull.

POST AT HUNTSVILLE (*Thomas Barracks; Camp Monte Sano; Camp Wheeler; Camp [Albert G.] Forse*). In January 1864 the Post at Huntsville was established by the Seventeenth Iowa Volunteer Infantry, commanded by Colonel C. R. Weaver. The District of Huntsville, with headquarters at the post, was established by General Orders No. 12, Department of Alabama, August 8, 1865. The post return of December 1873 indicates that the name was changed to Thomas Barracks (abandoned on September 13, 1877). A post at Huntsville was reestablished and named Camp Monte Sano on July 7, 1888 (abandoned on December 5, 1888). On August 17, 1898, the 4th Army Corps established headquarters at Huntsville. The post was named Camp Wheeler, but it was subsequently renamed Camp Albert G. Forse on October 23, 1898, only to be abandoned in February of the next year.

FORT INGERSOLL. Established in 1836 and garrisoned by Georgia troops during the Indian troubles, the fort's site is now incorporated within Phenix City in Russell County.

FORT JACKSON (*Fort aux Alibamos; Fort Alabama; Fort Toulouse*). The first fort on Fort Jackson's site, situated about 3 miles south of Wetumpka in Elmore County and 12 miles northeast of Montgomery, was built by the French in 1717. It stood on the east bank of the Coosa River, less than a mile from its junction with the Tallapoosa River. At the beginning of the eighteenth century, the French established a colony on Mobile Bay. Governor Sieur de Bienville saw the need for trade outposts northeast of Mobile. In order to check the growing influence of the British, it was decided to build a fort on the eastern flank of the Louisiana colony. The location was deep in the heart of the Creek Confederacy; to the north were the Cherokees, to the west were the Choctaws, and to the northwest were the Chickasaws. Intensely hostile toward the British because of their brutality during the tragic Yamasee War (1715–16), the Creeks extended an invitation to the French to erect a trading post among the Alibamos (a tribe within the Creek Nation). With the goodwill and aid of the Indians, the French constructed their fort, first calling it Fort aux Alibamos or Fort Alabama, then renaming it for Comte de Toulouse, son of Louis XIV. A small garrison of 30 to 50 soldiers manned the fort. They cultivated the friendship of the Indians and traded extensively with them.

A mutiny disrupted the peace at the fort in 1722. The soldiers' discontent stemmed from boredom, isolation, shortages of food and supplies, and low pay. The rebellious soldiers imprisoned the officers, who managed to escape. With the help of friendly Indians they captured the mutineers and sent them to Mobile, where harsh punishment was administered. Strained conditions persisted at the fort, and in an attempt to relieve the unrest authorities permitted the soldiers to marry Indian girls. The fort was in general disrepair and plans were made for a new post. The French valued Fort Toulouse enough to spend half of their military budget for the whole Louisiana colony for its reconstruction. It was rebuilt about 1751 under the direction of François Saucier.

The French soon lost possession of the fort. The Paris Treaty of 1763, which ended the French and Indian War, dictated the transfer of all French possessions east of the Mississippi to the British, and the change in ownership of Fort Toulouse took place peacefully. Indian loyalty to the French, however, prevented the British from operating the fort. The fort was assigned a caretaker, but the English never manned it. By 1776 the fort had fallen into ruins.

Colonel Benjamin Hawkins, U.S. Indian agent to the Creeks, reported that only the moats and the cannon remained in 1796. Eighteen years later Andrew Jackson arrived at the fort during the Creek Indian War of 1813–14, which was fought simultaneously with the War of 1812. After defeating the hostile Creeks at Horseshoe Bend on April 27, 1814, Jackson returned and planned the reconstruction of Fort Toulouse. He left in April, and construction of Fort Jackson was completed by militia from the Carolinas under the direction of General Joseph Graham. General Jackson returned in July, and the following month the signing of the Treaty of Fort Jackson ended the Indian threat in the area. The pact opened 20 million acres of land to American settlers and isolated the Creeks from further influence from the British centered at Pensacola.

From Fort Jackson "Old Hickory" began a campaign against the British and Spanish which culminated with the Battle of New Orleans. After the victory, Jackson and some of his men returned to the fort. Elements of regular Army regiments remained to garrison the fort, and a small settlement called Jackson Town arose nearby. By the end of 1817 the town was abandoned as residents moved downriver to what later became Montgomery, the future state capital. After Fort Jackson fell into ruins, the site became farmland. The Alabama Historical Commission gained possession of the site in 1971 and archeologists began excavating the fort area—which is a National Historic Landmark—finding evidences of Fort Toulouse.

Archeologists have located evidences of the original log walls and other features, including the Fort Jackson powder magazine. Reconstruction followed the exact outlines of the 1751 fort, which was composed of vertical log bastions connected by horizontal double curtain walls filled with dirt, with the inserts of north and south gates. The structures within included the commandant's quarters, a chapel, storehouse, barracks, and a powder magazine. The 180-acre park occupies a scenic peninsula between the Coosa and Tallapoosa rivers where they join to form the Alabama River.

FORT JEB STUART. A Confederate-built defense of Mobile.

FORT JOHNSTON. FORT SIDNEY JOHNSTON.

CAMP (JOSEPH F.) JOHNSTON. A recruiting and training camp established in May 1898 during the Spanish-American War and located in the suburbs of Mobile.

FORT JONES. A Confederate fortification, near Roanoke, Randolph County; built in early 1865.

FORT JONESBOROUGH. In 1813 "Devil" John Jones and several settlers erected a crude stockade on the site of the early Jefferson County settlement of Jonesboro. In 1887 the Bessemer Land Improvements Company was formed, culminating in the founding of the "Marvel City," Bessemer, which incorporated the village of Jonesboro. The site of the fort is today a part of a foundry.

FORT LANDRUM. One of several forts erected in Clarke County by settlers during the Creek War of 1813–14, Fort Landrum was located 11 miles west of Fort Sinquefield.

LASHLEY'S FORT (*Leslie's Fort*). "Lashley's Fort" should be "Leslie's Fort," pronounced the English way. Nineteenth-century historians took it upon themselves to spell it erroneously. Alexander Leslie, Jr., a half blood, built the fort around his home in the fall of 1813. Its site was located about a mile from Talladega's present Court Square, on a knoll about 400 feet east of Sylacauga Highway. Leslie's father entered the Creek Nation as a Tory during the Revolution and served as secretary to the chieftain. In November 1813, many amicable Creeks sought refuge in Fort Lashley, which then was surrounded by 1,000 hostile Red Sticks (a Creek faction), who demanded their surrender. An Indian scout slipped out of the fort and made his way to Fort Strother, where General Andrew Jackson was informed of the situation. On November 9 Jackson's army of 1,200 infantrymen and 800 cavalrymen surrounded the hostiles. The ensuing battle resulted in 15 militiamen killed. The bodies of 299 Red Sticks were later counted.

FORT LAVIER. According to a Clarke County historian, the fort was located southeast of Suggsville, but the exact site is still uncertain. The fort was most probably built shortly before the Fort Mims massacre and was erected around the home of Captain Lawson Lavier. Shortly after the Kimball-James massacre on September 1, 1813, Fort Lavier was abandoned and the settlers hurriedly found shelter at Fort Madison.

LESLIE'S FORT. LASHLEY'S FORT.

FORT LIKENS. The only available information reports that it was located in "Brown's Lower Valley."

BATTERY LINCOLN. A Federal fortified position during the Civil War, it was located near Huntsville.

FORT LOUIS DE LA LOUISIANA. FORT CHARLOTTE.

FORT LOUIS DE LA MOBILE. FORT CHARLOTTE.

FORT MCCLELLAN. Located three miles north of Anniston, Fort McClellan is 90 miles west of Atlanta and 55 miles east of Birmingham. The Choccolocco foothills, part of the Appalachian Mountain chain, surround the post. A spur ridge of the foothills crosses the main post from north to south. The ridge first attracted military interest in 1898 during the Spanish-American War, when the mountains were discovered to form an excellent background for artillery firing. After several years of study, the War Department established Camp McClellan on July 18, 1917. The camp was named in honor of Major General George B. McClellan, general-in-chief of the U.S. Army from 1861 to 1862. The camp was a mobilization post used to quickly train men for World War I. By October 1917 there were 27,753 men training at the camp. The camp was redesignated Fort McClellan, a permanent post, on July 1, 1929. New construction went rapidly and later afforded the necessary accommodations for troop training during World War II. A 3,000-capacity internment camp for prisoners of war was built during 1943. Nearly 500,000 men were trained at Fort McClellan during World War II, including a company of Japanese-Americans. The installation was placed on inactive status June 30, 1947, with only a maintenance crew to roam the post. Beginning in 1950, when the post was reactivated, various Army elements were stationed there for training associated with advanced defense techniques. In 1954 the post became the first permanent home for the U.S. Women's Army Corps Center, until it was disestablished and its flag retired in 1978. On March 1, 1983, the post was officially redesignated U.S. Army Chemical and Military Police Centers and Fort McClellan.

CAMP MCCLENDEN. In 1836 this temporary camp was established 15 miles from Tuskegee, on the road to Columbus, in Macon County.

FORT MCCRARY. A Confederate fortified defense, Fort McCrary was located eight miles north of Roanoke in Randolph County.

MCDERMOTT'S BATTERY. A Civil War fortified position, it was located on the east shore of Mobile Bay and figured in the campaign against Fort Blakely in 1864 and 1865.

MCGREW'S FORT. Located near the Tombigbee River, this small fort was three miles north of Fort St. Stephens in Clarke County. Two brothers, William and John McGrew, British royalists during the Revolutionary War, settled on what became known as McGrew's Reserve, an old Spanish grant, shortly after 1800. They built a palisaded defense, which enclosed two acres of ground, in 1813 during the Creek uprising. Colonel William McGrew was killed in September of the same year in an ambush near Bashi.

BATTERY MCINTOSH. A Civil War defense of Mobile built by the Confederates.

FORT MADISON. Located near the Alabama River, a little more than a mile west of Suggsville in Clarke County, the fort stood 225 yards north of Fort Glass. With the aid of the soldiers in the Fort Glass garrison, the settlers erected the fort, enclosing a tract of land 60 yards square with 12-foot-high walls and an outside three-foot-deep ditch. Subsequent to the Indian attack on Fort Sinquefield on September 3, 1813, settlers from other Clarke County forts, including Fort Glass, sought refuge in Fort Madison. Widespread Indian depredations caused General Ferdinand L. Claiborne to shift 200 soldiers and 500 settlers from Fort Madison to Fort St. Stephens in Washington County. In order to alleviate the fears of the remaining settlers within the fort, 80 militiamen were dispatched to protect them. General Claiborne, however, shortly rescinded his order and returned the troops to Fort Madison.

FORT MIMS. This fort, famous in early-19th-century history, was situated approximately 12 miles north of Stockton in Baldwin County. During the summer of 1813 area settlers built a stockade surrounding the home of Samuel Mims, who operated a ferry on the Alabama River. A square fort enclosing an acre of ground, it had large, formidable gates in the eastern and western curtains. The structures within the fort included the Mims home, a fabric-weaving building, and several hastily built cabins. A blockhouse was begun but never completed.

Nineteenth-century historian Albert James Pickett stated that the fort at the time of the massacre there held 553 people, including 265 soldiers, with a significant number of the settlers being half breeds with close relatives who belonged to the hostile Red Sticks, a faction of the Creek Nation. General Ferdinand L. Claiborne in July 1813 sent Major Daniel Beasley to command the fort's garrison. On August 7 the general inspected the defense and directed Beasley to "strengthen the pickets and to build one or two additional blockhouses." The order was never carried out.

At noon on August 30 a thousand warriors, led by Chief William Weatherford (the "Red Eagle"), stormed through an open gate. The carnage within the fort lasted from two to three hours, sparing only 36 white survivors. Beasley had been among the first to meet death. The Red Sticks then set fire to the fort. On September 9 a burial detachment of soldiers and settlers arrived at the blackened ruins and interred the many dead. In 1955 the five-acre site was donated to the state of Alabama. In September 1972 the site was listed in the National Register of Historic Places. A year later the Alabama Historical Commission made a large grant to initiate archeological excavations in the area of the fort site. A monument erected by the United Daughters of the Confederacy marks the approximate site of Fort Mims.

FORT MITCHELL. The site of this defense in Creek Indian country stood a half mile from the Chattahoochee River and is incorporated within the town of the same name in Russell County. The fort was erected by General John Floyd during the 1813 Creek War and was named for David Bryde Mitchell, then governor of Georgia. It was garrisoned by U.S. troops until 1837. Late in the year 1817, the Creek Indian Agency was established there. In 1825 the Marquis de Lafayette of Revolutionary War fame visited Fort Mitchell while touring the South and was entertained by the Indians, who put on one of their exciting ballgames. Another famous visitor to the fort was Francis Scott Key, author of "The Star Spangled Banner." He was then (1833) a federal commissioner appointed to investigate Russell County complaints regarding squatters or intruders on ceded Creek lands. A small number of notorious duels were fought at or close to the fort. A duel fought in 1832 involved two Army officers, one a general and the other a major, ending with the death of the former. In accordance with the stipulations of the Treaty of 1832, the Creeks ceded 18,000 acres of their lands to the U.S. Government and moved west to what was then Indian Territory (Oklahoma). Very soon after their departure, the Agency went out of business.

CAMP MONTE SANO. POST AT HUNTSVILLE.

FORT MONTGOMERY. Located opposite the "cutoff" of the Alabama River, about 12 miles above the junction of that river with the Tombigbee River, the fort was two miles from the site of tragic Fort Mims in Baldwin County. It was erected in 1814 by Lieutenant Colonel Thomas H. Benton to serve as a defense against

Indians and as a supply base. The fort was apparently abandoned in 1818.

CANTONMENT MONTPELIER. FORT MONTPELIER.

CAMP MONTPELIER. FORT MONTPELIER.

FORT MONTPELIER (*Cantonment Montpelier; Camp Montpelier*). This post was located about seven miles northeast of Fort Montgomery in Baldwin County and about 10 miles from the Alabama River. Built by the 4th Regiment in 1817, it remained in use until 1820.

CAMP (JOHN T.) MORGAN. Established in 1915, the U.S. Army post was located at Anniston in Calhoun County.

FORT MORGAN (*Fort Bowyer*). Mobile Point, the site of Fort Morgan, is at the end of a scenic drive 22 miles from Gulf Shores, with the Gulf of Mexico on one side and Mobile Bay on the other. Considered one of the finest examples of brick architecture in America, it was designed by Simon Bernard, a French engineer and former aide-de-camp to Napoleon. After joining the U.S. Army in 1816, Bernard was in charge of developing national defense on the eastern and Gulf of Mexico coasts. His designs conformed to the theories of Marquis de Vauban, a fortification engineer who revolutionized fort construction in France. The five-pointed-star fort with its arches within arches is testimony to fine craftmanship

FORT MORGAN. Photograph of the front and west side, taken soon after the fort fell to Union forces in 1864. (Courtesy of the U.S. Naval Historical Center.)

FORT MORGAN. Aerial view of the renovated fort as it stands today. (Courtesy of the Fort Morgan Historical Commission.)

exhibited from 1819 to 1834. Flags flying today over Fort Morgan's entrance reflect the long history and many changes in the area.

In 1519 a Spanish explorer sailed into Mobile Bay, called "Ochuse" by the Indians, and mapped the bay. A succession of Spanish explorers followed, but it was the French who first colonized the area in 1702 on Dauphin Island, three miles across the channel. The British took possession from 1763 until 1780 and the area began to prosper, with Mobile the hub of commerce. When the American Revolution was in its fourth year, Spain joined the colonists against England, and Mobile Point again belonged to another nation. Bernardo de Gálvez, governor of Spanish Louisiana, sailed from New Orleans to Mobile in January 1780 with a fleet of ships. A storm wrecked the frigate man-of-war *Volante* in the shoals. Her guns were salvaged and a sand battery was established on Mobile Point. The rest of the armada sailed on to seize Fort Charlotte in Mobile. For 33 years Mobile Point was part of Spanish West Florida.

In 1813 the United States was again at war with England. President James Madison directed General James Wilkinson to take Mobile Point. Colonel John Bowyer's troops ousted the Spanish from the strategic point, and a small wood and sand fort was built near the site of Fort Morgan. General Andrew Jackson inspected the defense and sent Major William Lawrence with 161 men to garrison the fort, named for Colonel Bowyer.

The fort contained 17 pieces of armament, three buildings, and a powder magazine. The first British assault came from both land and sea on September 14, 1814. Despite repeated broadsides from the British fleet, the defenders repulsed the enemy. The victory gained by Lawrence and his gallant garrison was short-lived. A British armada of 28 ships returned on February 9, 1815, after suffering defeat in the Battle of New Orleans. They surrounded the fort and, after a three-day siege, the outnumbered garrison of Americans surrendered. The treaty ending the war returned Mobile Point to U.S. possession.

Congress realized the need for stronger defenses on the Atlantic and Gulf coasts. Plans were drawn for a brick fort to replace little Fort Bowyer. While the present fort was under construction in the 1820s, Fort Bowyer was destroyed by storms. In 1837, three years after the fort was completed, more than 3,000 Indians were brought down the Alabama River from Montgomery to Fort Morgan. After several months and many deaths, the Indians were again put aboard boats and were taken to Mississippi for the overland journey to Indian Territory, now Oklahoma.

On January 4, 1861, seven days before Alabama seceded from the Union, the governor of Alabama ordered the state militia at Mobile to seize Fort Morgan and Fort Gaines simultaneously from Federal forces garrisoned there. The fort remained part of the Republic of Alabama for five weeks before joining the Confederate States of America.

Fort Morgan, a critical fortification during the Civil War, was next to the last fort to fall at war's end. The fort was engaged in fiery action during the Battle of Mobile Bay on August 5, 1864, the famous engagement in which torpedoes were strung across the channel to prevent the entrance of the Union fleet. The Confederates' ironclad *Tennessee* and three wooden gunboats fought Admiral David Farragut's fleet of eight sloops of war and eight gunboats. The fort's guns inflicted serious damage, sending the monitor *Tecumseh* with 93 of her 114 men to the bottom. More than 3,000 cannonballs were hurled at the fort during the night of August 22. The white flag of surrender, ending three years of conflict, was raised above the fort. At 2:30 P.M. on August 23, 1864, Fort Morgan was once again the possession of the United States.

Years passed with only intermittent military caretakers and lighthouse keepers occupying the reservation. Then plans were drawn for the construction of coastal defense batteries. Battery Bowyer was the first to be built in 1895, followed by Battery Duportail. After the Spanish-American War, Batteries Thomas, Schenk, and Dearborn were completed, with wooden barracks, officers' quarters, a hospital, and other structures. Fort Morgan became an active training base for artillery corpsmen during World War I. After the war, the fort was abandoned. In 1927 the state of Alabama purchased the old fort to create a state park. Work by the Public Works Administration during the 1930s cleared away the debris of years of military use and abandonment to create the state park. In 1941 Alabama was advised that Fort Morgan was needed again as a military base. The Navy, Coast Guard, and 50th Coastal Artillery mounted guard against possible attack by German submarines. Horses and jeeps were used to patrol the beach from Fort Morgan to Alabama Point, 32 miles away. At the close of World War II, the reservation was returned to the state of Alabama.

The pentagonal fort, with five bastions, was named in 1833 for General Daniel Morgan, a hero of the American Revolution. Each of the five sides has seven arches, arches within arches, and arches at cross angles, with more than 150 arches in all. On each of the five sides are seven embrasures, with positions for small-arms fire on each side of the embrasures. A cannon positioned to fire over the counterscarp wall was mounted in each arch, with the barrels extending from the embrasures. Fort Morgan, operated by the Alabama Historical Commission, is a National Historic Landmark.

FORT MOTT. A defense against Indians erected in 1813 during the Creek War, and located in the same neighborhood as Landrum's Fort in Clarke County.

MOUNT VERNON ARSENAL. MOUNT VERNON BARRACKS.

MOUNT VERNON BARRACKS (*Mount Vernon Arsenal*). Situated about 28 miles north of Mobile on the west side of the Mobile River at the town of Mount Vernon, the arsenal was authorized by Congress in 1824 and completed in 1828. It served as an important assembly plant for guns manufactured elsewhere. Just prior to secession, the arsenal was seized by Alabama troops at the direction of Governor Andrew B. Moore. Its use was critical to the needs of the Confederacy. At war's end, it reverted to its former status as a U.S. arsenal. According to orders dated July 25, 1873, its designation was changed from Mount Vernon arsenal (which had been officially established on January 1, 1829) to Mount Vernon Barracks. The post, abandoned in December 1894, was deeded by Congress to the state of Alabama for public purposes.

BATTERY MOUTON. Erected in the vicinity of Mobile Point, this Union battery built in 1864 aided in the siege of Fort Morgan. The battery mounted four 30-pounder Parrotts.

FORT OKFUSKEE. FORT OKFUSKI.

FORT OKFUSKI (*Fort Okfuskee*). Situated on the Tallapoosa River, opposite the Upper Creek Indian village of Okfuskee, this garrisoned post—the only British military outpost ever erected in that section of the territory now known as Alabama—was 40 miles northeast of the site of French Fort Toulouse and 12 miles west of present-day Dadeville. To prevent any French competition among the Creeks, British traders erected the fort in 1735. Due to the fealty of many Creeks to the French, the enterprise proved to be unsuccessful. Meager references to Fort Okfuski indicate that the military trading post lasted only a few years. The fort's site is now under the waters of Lake Martin.

OLD SPANISH FORT. Built in 1799 by Bernardo de Gálvez, who captured Mobile in 1780, the Spanish fortification's remains, consisting of earthworks, are located on the northeast shore of Mobile Bay, near Daphne in Baldwin County. With Confederate-built Fort Blakely, the old fort was the last bastion in the Mobile Bay area to hold out against Federal troops and naval bombardment.

FORT OPELIKA. Though never having existed as such, there are Federal references to it in military post lists. During the last days of the Civil War, planters in east Alabama sent their slaves to labor on a proposed earthwork fortification at the town of Opelika in present-day Lee County, but apparently nothing definite was achieved. During the period 1872–75, however, there was a U.S. Army post established at Opelika.

OZARK TRIANGULAR DIVISION CAMP. FORT RUCKER.

FORT PAYNE. The town of Fort Payne in DeKalb County perpetuates the memory of a stockaded log blockhouse erected in 1836 during the Cherokee troubles. The fort was named for Captain John Payne of the U.S. Army, who was sent there to drive out the dispossessed Indians, large numbers of whom were eventually congregated and removed to Indian Territory (Oklahoma).

FORT PIERCE. This small defense against Indians two miles southeast of Fort Mims in Baldwin County was erected by John and William Pierce early in 1813 during the Creek War. Shortly after the Fort Mims massacre, Fort Pierce's occupants abandoned their fort and fled to Mount Vernon. Fort Pierce remained deserted until sometime in November, when General Ferdinand L. Claiborne garrisoned it with troops commanded by Lieutenant Colonel George Henry Nixon.

FORT POWELL. This Confederate defense occupied a sandbar just off Cedar Point and a little north of Heron Island, two miles north of Dauphin Island, at the western entrance to Mobile Bay. The fort was built by the Confederate Corps of Engineers to prevent passage of enemy shipping through the channel (today's Grant Pass) between Alabama's mainland and Dauphin Island. On August 4, 1864, during the height of the Battle of Mobile Bay, Admiral David Farragut ordered the *Chickasaw*, commanded by Lieutenant Commander George H. Perkins, to commence shelling Fort Powell. After being subjected to heavy cannonading, the fort's garrison escaped to the mainland the following night.

POWELL'S FORT. Situated three miles south of Fort Carney in Clarke County, this Indian defense was built most probably in 1813 during the Creek War. The fort was occupied by six families, two of them belonging to James and John Powell.

RANKIN'S FORT. Located in Washington County, Rankin's Fort was a sizable stockade defense during the Creek War. It was the most western of the Alabama-Tombigbee River group of forts erected in 1813.

RED FORT. SPANISH FORT.

REDSTONE ARSENAL. Nerve center of the U.S. Army missile rocket program, Redstone Arsenal's 38,658 acres are a combination of two adjoining arsenals built in 1941 to make conventional ammunition and toxic chemicals. The Tennessee River is the arsenal's southern border, with Redstone situated in the middle of the scenic Tennessee Valley. In addition, Huntsville (Madison County) bounds the arsenal to the east and north.

First designated center of missile research and development in October 1948, the arsenal at that time had dropped from World War II peak employment of more than 19,000 to a little-used government property with a work force of a few hundred. Most of its many buildings and facilities had been placed in standby. Some actually had been offered for sale. Hiring of technical and professional people for the new rocket mission began in early 1949. In April 1950, as the buildup continued, the Army moved its missile experts then working at Fort Bliss, Texas, to Redstone. This group included Dr. Wernher von Braun and more than 100 of his colleagues, who had developed the first ballistic missile during World War II and who later came to this country to work for the Army.

During the late 1950s, the Army team at Redstone pioneered many of the nation's first achievements in space exploration. Redstone experts orbited the free world's first scientific earth satellite, *Explorer I*; launched the first successful lunar probe; and first flew animals—two monkeys—into space and recovered them alive. In 1960 the Army's space team at Redstone was transferred to the National Aeronautics and Space Administration by order of President Eisenhower and formed the nucleus for the Marshall Space Flight Center of NASA, which still operates on the arsenal.

The Army commands on the post now are the successors of early Army missile activities here. Today Redstone houses the U.S. Army Missile Command and the U.S. Army Missile and Munitions Center and School. In nearby Huntsville are the Ballistic Missile Defense Systems Command; Ballistic Missile Defense Advanced Technology Center; Redstone Readiness Group; the Patriot Project Office; and Huntsville Division, U.S. Army Corps of Engineers. About 3,500 soldiers are assigned to the various Army commands at Redstone or in Huntsville. Together those agencies employ about 10,500 civilian government workers. The combined Army payroll exceeds $350 million annually. Army buildings, equipment, and utilities on Redstone Arsenal have a book value in excess of $525 million. Together with similar facilities of the Marshall Space Flight Center of NASA, they make the total government property investment at the installation in the neighborhood of one billion dollars.

FORT REPUBLIC. This settler-built Indian defense, erected in 1813 during the Creek War, was situated on an eminence in the center of St. Stephens in Washington County, one of Alabama's most historic settlements. In 1811 the citizenry changed the name of the settlement to St. Stephens, deleting the prefix "Fort." (See also FORT ST. STEPHENS.)

CAMP RUCKER. FORT RUCKER.

FORT RUCKER (*Ozark Triangular Division Camp; Camp Rucker*). This Army post is located 12 miles south of the town of Ozark in Dale County on land that was a part of the British colony of West Florida when the Declaration of Independence was signed in 1776. Opening in May, 1942, as the Ozark Triangular Division Camp, it was a training site for infantrymen who were destined to become fighting participants in World War II. The post was renamed Camp Rucker in June 1943 to honor General Edmund Winchester Rucker, a Confederate Army officer from Tennessee. Camp Rucker closed in 1946 after the war ended. It was on an inactive status until August 1950, when it was reactivated upon the United States entering the Korean conflict. The post housed the 47th Infantry Division until that unit moved to Fort Benning, Georgia, in May 1954. After reverting to mothball status again in June 1954, a month later the Army announced that the Aviation School would be moved to Camp Rucker from Fort Sill, Oklahoma. The advance contingent arrived in August, and formal command of the school in its new location was assumed September 1 by Brigadier General Carl I. Hutton. So Rucker had a new status and a new mission. Now instead of foot soldiers on the ground there were airplanes and helicopters in the sky. The post was redesignated a fort on October 26, 1955.

FORT ST. PHILLIP. Owens, *History of Alabama*, locates this undated post on the Mobile River, 20 miles above Mobile.

FORT ST. STEPHENS. In 1789, during George Washington's first-year occupancy of the presidency, Spain reinforced its possession of Alabama territory it had gained by the Treaty of Paris (1763) by erecting a fort on top of a limestone bluff (called *Hobucakintopa* by the Indians) on the west bank of the Tombigbee River. The site of the historic fort and adjacent town, founded by the French in 1714, is about nine miles from Leroy in Washington County and some 90 miles above Mobile. In 1795, when the fort was found to be rotting away, it was wholly rebuilt of cypress and housed an infantry garrison. It was learned in 1799 that the Spanish-occupied land was situated on the American side of the boundary. The fort and town were reluctantly turned over to American authorities. Lieutenant John McClary and elements of the 2nd U.S. Infantry marched from Natchez, Mississippi, and took possession of St. Stephens on May 5. The fort, however, was not then occupied by Americans. The government instead built Fort Stoddert on the Mobile River to the south. Archival evidence, however, suggests that Fort St. Stephens was garrisoned from 1805 to 1808. In 1804 St. Stephens became the site of the first American court in Alabama. The first chartered public school in Alabama, Washington Academy, was established here in 1811. During the same year, the town's citizens changed the name of the settlement to St. Stephens, deleting the prefix "Fort." Two years later, during the Creek War, another fort was built there and named Fort Republic.

SAND FORT. A Civil War battery, probably Confederate-built, situated near present-day Colbert Heights in Colbert County.

SAND FORT. Situated on the old Federal Road, this small defense was 15 miles west of Fort Mitchell and six miles northwest of Seale in Russell County. Essentially an earthwork of sand, it was appropriately named Sand Fort. It was built by General John Floyd and the Georgia Militia he commanded in 1814 as a rendezvous for his troops. A small garrison of troops occupied it during the Indian uprising of 1836.

FORT SANTA MARIA. A fortified settlement, it was founded on August 14, 1559, by Don Tristan de Luna, a Spanish explorer. It stood on either the east or west shore of Mobile Bay, not Pensacola Bay in Florida as mistakenly assumed by the Spaniard. It has been proved by qualified southern historians and cartographers that de Luna's descriptions are eminently true of Mobile Bay.

SELMA ARSENAL. Its site on U.S. 80 and State 22, in Selma, Dallas County, was occupied by one of the most critical supply depots in the Confederacy. The town possessed a naval foundry, rolling mill, armory, and powder manufactory. During the last two years of the Civil War, approximately half the cannon and two-thirds of the ammunition used by the Confederacy were made here. The arsenal property covered about 50 acres and employed about 6,000 men and women. General James Harrison Wilson's cavalry triumphed in the Battle of Selma on April 2, 1865.

FORT SHACKLEFORD. Tradition, hearsay, and suspect historical reportage have indicated the existence in Escambia County, directly north of Pensacola, Florida, of two forts of this name—one during the years of the War of 1812 and another a Civil War defense. Persevering research has failed to unearth definite data.

CAMP SHELBY. A World War II training camp, it was situated in or near Shelby, Shelby County.

CAMP SHERIDAN. Located about four miles north of Montgomery, Camp Sheridan was established during World War I as a National Guard camp. It was occupied by the 37th (old 16th) Division. The first inducted men reported October 1–15, 1917; the last, November 16–30, 1918. The camp was named in honor of General Philip H. Sheridan of Civil War fame, pursuant to General Orders No. 95, War Department, July 18, 1917. It was abandoned March 15, 1919.

CAMP SHIPP. Camp Anniston.

CAMP SIBERT. Even before the active participation of the United States in World War II, it became increasingly obvious to members of the General Staff that chemical expertise and training were to become important in modern warfare. The site selected for the Chemical Warfare Replacement Training Center was situated about seven miles from Gadsden in Etowah County. The camp was named for Major General William Luther Sibert, a long-time resident of Gadsden and first chief of the Chemical Warfare Service, who died in 1935. Camp Sibert was completed by its scheduled date, October 1, 1943, although 80 percent of it was already in use as early as February of the same year. Some 1,500 installations were erected, most of them constructed of prefabricated materials to house thousands of Army and civilian personnel. The project cost the government more than $16 million.

FORT SIDNEY JOHNSTON. A Confederate-built fortification, it was designed to aid in the defense of Mobile.

FORT SINQUEFIELD. This defense against Indians stood on the west bank of Bassett's Creek, about five miles southeast of Grove Hill in Clark County. A spring in a valley some 275 yards southwest of the fort furnished its occupants with a supply of water. About 90 feet northwest of the site are a number of unmarked graves. During the bloody Creek War (1813–1814) settlers in the environs built the fort, which was reported to have been smaller than Fort Madison near Suggsville. Very soon after the Fort Mims massacre, settlers scurried to Fort Sinquefield for their safety. Because of overcrowding within the fort, living there became intolerable, forcing the families of Ransom Kimball and Abner James to return to Kimball's large cabin home, about a mile from the fort. On September 1, 1813, Red Sticks (a Creek faction) suddenly attacked the cabin, killing 13 women and children, leaving six survivors to escape to the fort. Two days later soldiers from Fort Glass were dispatched to the still-smoking ruins of the Kimball cabin, where they recovered the victims' bodies and transported them by oxcart to Fort Sinquefield. They were interred in graves 90 feet from the walls of the fort. While the burial services were going on, about 100 Red Sticks attacked the mourners, killing one woman. The Indian hostiles then made for the fort's gate, but the guns of the 35 defenders drove them off, killing at least 20 warriors. The fort's occupants, in fear of a greater assault by Chief Weatherford and his 1,000 followers, evacuated the threatened haven and fled to the safety of Fort Madison.

SPANISH FORT (*Fort Alexis; Red Fort*). The site of this historic fort is evident in today's community of Spanish Fort on the east shore of upper Mobile Bay. While the British were battling Americans during the Revolution, opportunist Bernardo de Gálvez and his Spanish troops seized Mobile from the British occupants. The port city then became a Spanish base for operations against the British. Postponing a planned attack against Pensacola, capital of British West Florida, Gálvez built a fort on Mobile Bay to reinforce possession. After British and Hessian troops unsuccessfully attacked Spanish Fort on January 3, 1781, Gálvez in May captured the British capital on the Gulf.

Eighty years later, the site of Spanish Fort became a critical Confederate defense guarding against enemy penetration to Mobile from the Gulf. Seven miles from Mobile three strong redoubts—Spanish Fort, Fort Alexis, and Red Fort—linked together by rifle pits, stretched some 2,500 yards from the Appalachee River to Bayou Minette. At the base of the works was a deep ditch six feet in width, with its inner side next to the forts protected by telegraph wire fencing, an elaborate chevaux-de-frise, and a line of thick abatis, all backed up by heavy artillery.

Early in 1865 these forts were garrisoned by 2,500 men from General John Hood's army, under the commands of General Randall L. Gibson, General Bryan M. Thomas, and Colonel I. W. Patton. On March 27 General E. R. S. Canby, commanding 32,000 Union troops, invested the three forts. The Confederate garrison was reduced to 1,800 men when a number of companies were detached and sent to Fort Blakely. The outnumbered Confederates maintained a gallant, obstinate defense for 14 days. Canby at last launched a final assault on April 8, pulverizing the Confederate fort with 90 pieces of artillery while Union gunboats heavily shelled the rear. Resistance was no longer feasible. During the dark of night, the Confederates spiked their artillery and made their way across the marshes to wade out to the watercraft sent from Mobile to rescue them from certain capture. Early the next morning, Federal troops swarmed into the forts only to be greeted by empty rifle pits and dead guns.

CAMP SPRING HILL. An auxiliary drill camp in association with Camp Joseph F. Johnston, Camp Spring Hill was situated in Mobile's suburbs in 1898.

FORT STEVENSON. A Confederate defense, it was located at or near the town of Stevenson in Jackson County.

FORT STODDERT. This fort stood on the west bank of the Mobile River, about four miles south of the confluence of the Alabama and Tombigbee rivers. As soon as the Spanish evacuated the territory claimed by the United States, a fort was erected in July 1799 by Captain Bartholomew Schaumburgh of the 2nd U.S. Infantry and named in honor of Secretary of the Navy Benjamin Stoddert. The fort's construction, typical for the period, consisted of palisades and a blockhouse in each of the four angles. In February 1807 Aaron Burr was held prisoner for several days at Fort Stoddert before he was taken to Richmond to stand trial for treason against his country. Burr, disguised as a river boatman, had been arrested by the fort's commander, Lieutenant Edmund P. Gaines, who accommodated the prisoner in his home.

Alabama's first newspaper, the *Centinel,* was published at Fort Stoddert, with its first issue appearing on May 23, 1811. In July 1813, confronted by increasing violence from hostile Creeks known as the Red Sticks, General Ferdinand L. Claiborne marched with his army of Mississippi militiamen to Fort Stoddert, where he initiated assignments of troops to the growing number of settler-built stockades. A year later, when the general moved his headquarters, Fort Stoddert was abandoned.

FORT STONEWALL. This Confederate defense was built in 1864 at Choctaw Bluff on the Alabama River.

FORT STROTHER. The site of this temporary Creek War fort on the west bank of the Coosa River is located some four miles west of Ohatchee, opposite Charchee Creek's mouth in St. Clair County. After General Andrew Jackson easily attained victory in 1813 against Chief Weatherford's hostile Creeks at the Indian village of Tallassahatchee, he marched 30 miles to the Coosa River, where he built Fort Strother just prior to the Battle of Talladega. The fort enclosed a piece of ground about 100 yards square. Within the palisades were a hospital consisting of eight huts, a structure to house supplies, and 25 tents to lodge the soldiers. The fort's enclosure also served as a haven for about 100 hogs, which might otherwise have been stolen by marauding Creeks.

SULPHUR BRANCH TRESTLE FORT. This Union mountaintop fortification near Sulphur Springs Creek was located in the environs of Elkmont, about eight miles north of Athens in Limestone County. Federal forces constructed the fort in 1864 to protect a major trestle on the Alabama and Tennessee Railroad. The earthwork, garrisoned by the 9th and 10th Indiana Cavalry, featured two large blockhouses. After capturing the Union garrison at Athens, the Confederates, under General Nathan B. Forrest, attacked the trestle fort on September 25 with artillery, bombarding the position with deadly efficiency. The fort's commander was killed along with some 200 of his men. The Confederates stormed the fort, which then offered no resistance, and captured 973 men, 300 horses, two artillery pieces, and a large store of small arms and supplies. General Forrest took his army northward and continued his successful destruction of other bridges useful to the enemy.

TALLADEGA POST. The town of Talladega was occupied from May to October 1865 by Brevet Brigadier General Morgan H. Chrysler, 2nd Veterans of New York Cavalry, with 12 companies aggregating 1,090 men. In October the garrison was relieved from duty and ordered mustered out.

CAMP TAYLOR. Records only indicate that this post was located at or near Huntsville in Madison County.

THOMAS BARRACKS. POST AT HUNTSVILLE.

TIGHLMAN BATTERY. A Confederate-built defense of Mobile, it was constructed in 1863.

FORT TOMBÉCBEE. FORT CONFEDERATION.

FORT TOMBIGBEE. FORT CONFEDERATION.

FORT TOULOUSE. FORT JACKSON.

FORT TRACY. A Confederate-built defense, it was located near the mouth of the Tensas River in Baldwin County. The fort was evacuated on April 11, 1865.

TURNER'S FORT. This pioneer-built defense against the Red Sticks, the warring faction of the Creek Nation, was located near the northwest bend of the Tombigbee River, in the environs of West Bend in Clarke County. The small stockade, probably built during the spring of 1813, occupied ground adjacent to Abner Turner's home. The palisades were constructed of split pine logs, which were doubled in thickness for greater protection. Within the enclosure were two or three blockhouses. Just 13 men and boys guarded the small community's women and children. Early in September, as the Creek War escalated in violence, the settlers evacuated their fort and found a haven at St. Stephens.

FORT TYLER. Located on the west bank of the Chattahoochee River, this small Confederate-built fort was two miles west of West Point, Georgia, and just east of adjacent Lanett in Chambers County. In 1865, suspecting that Federal troops would make an effort to capture West Point, Confederate General Robert Charles Tyler crossed the river and built Fort Tyler, "a strong bastioned earthwork, 35 yards square, surrounded by a ditch 12 feet wide and 10 feet deep, situated on a commanding eminence" (*Battles and Leaders*, IV, p. 234). The earthwork, fronted by a dense abatis, was armed with two 32-pounders and two field guns. On the morning of April 16 Union Colonel O. H. LaGrange, commanding elements of Wilson's Raiders, attacked the fort and captured it. LaGrange suffered casualties of seven men killed and 32 wounded. General Tyler was killed along with 18 men of his command.

CAMP WHEELER. POST AT HUNTSVILLE.

FORT WHITE. This small pioneer-built defense stood a short distance northeast of Grove Hill in Clarke County, a town located on the Choctaw Indian boundary established by the British in 1765. The fort was erected prior to the summer of 1813. It is quite probable that it was abandoned shortly after the destruction of Fort Mims.

FORT WILLIAMS. The site of this Creek War fort was inundated many years ago by the backed-up waters created by the Mitchell Dam on the Coosa River. It stood at the mouth of Cedar Creek, near Talladega Springs, in southwestern Talladega County. Early in March 1814, General Andrew Jackson ordered Colonel Williams of the 39th Regiment to proceed down the river from Fort Strother with a load of supplies to prepare for Jackson's third campaign against the hostile Creeks. It took Jackson five days to cut a road to the mouth of Cedar Creek. There he joined the colonel and built a fort, naming it Fort Williams to honor his fellow officer, on March 22. Several days later, posting a guard over the supplies at the fort, Jackson led his men to Horseshoe Bend, where, on March 27, he severely defeated the Red Sticks faction of the Creek Nation and destroyed the power of the Creeks. On April 2 he returned to Fort Williams with his many wounded. It was reported that 54 men had been killed in the bloody battle. There were 156 wounded, many of them dying in the improvised hospital at the fort and then buried near the fort. Besides a commemorative monument near the fort site, there are rows of headstones bearing the names of 80 men who had died of their wounds.

CAMP WINN. In 1862, during the Civil War, the Confederates established Camp Winn, a post for the training of troops, at what was then a highly popular health spa called Shelby Springs in southern Shelby County. (The site today is a large cattle ranch located just off County Highway 25, between Columbiana and Calera.) The medicinal properties of the springs had so impressed the area's early settlers that Shelby Springs had been developed into a resort in 1839. In 1855 its popularity skyrocketed when a railroad spur was deliberately run to the site. A two-story hotel was erected with a walkway leading to the railroad depot. The resort's 2,700-acre grounds were sprinkled with many guest cabins. During the last year of the war, the spa's hotel and cabins were taken over by the Confederacy and transformed into a 350-bed hospital. In 1869 the resort was reopened. Between then and 1915, when the spa was permanently closed, three successive fires destroyed the hotels.

FORT YORK. FORT CONFEDERATION.

FORT ABERCROMBIE. FORT GREELY (Kodiak Island).

FORT ADAMS. An American trading station, it was established on the north bank of the Yukon River, at the mouth of the Tozi River, in 1868 or 1869.

FORT ALEXANDER (*Fort Alexandrovsk*). The Russians established a trading post at the village of Nushagak on the bay of the same name, six miles south of Dillingham, in 1818 or 1819. In 1834 the post was further developed with a stockade, a large blockhouse, and several other structures. The name of the trading station has been variously spelled Alexandrovsk, Alexandrovski, and, erroneously, Alexandra. The site is known today as Nushagak.

FORT ALEXANDER (*Fort Alexandrovsk; Alexander Redoubt*). This sizable fort was established at the mouth of the Kenai River on Cook Inlet at Graham Harbor by Grigory I. Shelikoff in 1785. The fort, 120 yards square, was enclosed in a 12-foot fence of pine logs and had two bastions. There were 22 buildings, of which the largest was the 35-foot-long barracks. The post commander lived in separate quarters. Russia's imperial arms were displayed over the fort's entrance, which was protected by two guns.

ALEXANDER REDOUBT. FORT ALEXANDER (Cook Inlet).

FORT ALEXANDROVSK. FORT ALEXANDER (Nushagak).

AMCHITKA POST. Established during World War II on January 12, 1943, it was located on Amchitka Island. The garrison consisted of 101 officers and 1,844 enlisted men.

CAMP ANCHORAGE. FORT RICHARDSON.

FORT ANDREAVSKY. A Russian fur company trading post, it was located on the right bank of the Yukon River, 13 miles below the mouth of the Milavanoff River, 849 miles from Fort Yukon, and 116 miles from the ocean. The fort was built in the form of a square—the buildings forming two of the sides and a stockade the other two, enclosing barracks, storehouses, a powder magazine and other structures—and was protected by a few pieces of artillery. It was erected about the year 1853. Two years later it was the scene of an Indian massacre. Part of the garrison was absent when the Indians attacked the remaining

Alaska

Russians, killing them with clubs and knives. When the others returned they fell upon the Indians and avenged the massacre. When Alaska was ceded to the United States in 1867, this post, with others, was abandoned.

ANNETTE ISLAND POST. Established during World War II on September 2, 1940, it was located on Annette Island. Its initial garrison consisted of 17 officers and 497 enlisted men.

FORT ARCHANGEL GABRIEL. FORT ST. MICHAEL.

FORT ARCHANGEL MICHAEL. FORT ST. MICHAEL.

ATKA POST. This World War II camp, located in the Andreanof Islands, was activated on September 16, 1942, with 25 officers and 707 enlisted men.

ATTU POST. CAMP EARLE.

FORT BABCOCK. Forts Babcock, Bulkley, and Brumback were created as part of the Alaskan defense program during the prewar and early World War II period. Named in honor of Colonel Walter C. Babcock, Fort Babcock was situated on Kruzof Island, opposite Sitka. Established in 1942, a battery mounting two 6-inch guns was begun the same year. The battery was abandoned on April 1, 1944, when 88 percent completed, due to the low priority of coastal defense construction during the latter stages of the war.

BETHEL POST. This World War II Army facility at Bethel was activated June 26, 1942, with seven officers and 305 enlisted men.

BIG DELTA POST. This World War II post at Big Delta was activated on June 24, 1942, with four officers and 74 enlisted men.

FORT BRUMBACK. Named in honor of Lieutenant Virgil J. Brumback, this World War II defense was located at Dutch Harbor and activated April 30, 1942. A battery was constructed on the post mounting four 155-mm. guns. But by early 1944 the post had been deactivated.

FORT BULKLEY. Named in honor of Colonel Charles S. Bulkley, U.S. Volunteers, the World War II defense was situated on Rugged Island, Resurrection Bay, at Seward, and established August 29, 1941, when a battery of two 6-inch guns was planned for the fort. This battery was abandoned March 29, 1944, when 90 percent completed.

CHILKOOT BARRACKS (*Fort William H. Seward*). Located at Haines on the Lynn Canal, the original post was established in 1898. The site, then known as Haines Mission, was the port of entry for about 500 domesticated reindeer transported there with Army assistance from Norway and Sweden during the same year. The temporary Army post was upgraded to a permanent installation by the War Department on March 3, 1904, and named Fort William H. Seward in honor of the secretary of state who purchased Alaska in 1867. Its first garrison, arriving on September 27, 1904, consisted of field and staff headquarters and Companies A, B, and C of the 3rd Infantry, commanded by Colonel Thomas C. Woodbury. The post's name was changed to Chilkoot Barracks by General Orders No. 54, War Department, December 13, 1922. Chilkoot Barracks was abandoned in June 1943.

CAMP CIRCLE CITY. On November 8, 1897, Major General Nelson A. Miles recommended to the secretary of war, Russel A. Alger, that a military expedition be dispatched to the Klondike to alleviate the deprivations of the miners there, most of them American citizens. A post was established at the small town and trading post of Circle City by a detachment of the 8th Infantry on September 30, 1898. Camp Circle City became a subpost of Fort Egbert, which was established at Eagle. Camp Circle City was abandoned on August 31, 1900.

FORT CONSTANTINE (*Fort St. Helens; Fort Helena; Fort Konstantine*). Located at the native village of Nuchek, Tshugatshian Bay, on Prince William Sound, southwest of Cordova near the mouth of the Copper River, this blockhouse redoubt was built in 1792.

COPPER FORT. The first successful attempt to ascend the Copper River was made in 1819 by Klimovski. He built a cabin on the left bank of the Copper just above the mouth of the Chitina River. The probable site of the trading post that was later maintained at the site is today's town of Chitina, north of the Chugach Mountain range.

CORDOVA POST. A World War II defensive position, this post, located at Cordova, was activated on March 15, 1942, with 21 officers and 443 enlisted men.

FORT COSMOS. Named in honor of the Cosmos Club of San Francisco, this temporary camp was established as the winter quarters of Lieutenant George M. Stoney's exploring expedition during the 1885–86 season. It was located in Alaska's northwestern region, near the Arctic Circle, which was thoroughly explored by Stoney, 1883–86. The site of Fort Cosmos was 330 miles up the Kobuk River from its mouth in Kotzebue Sound.

FORT CUDAHY. Baker's *Geographic Dictionary of Alaska* locates this post on the west bank of the Yukon, near the mouth of Fortymile Creek. It probably was active circa 1900.

FORT DAVIS. Established at the mouth of the Nome River, four miles southeast of today's Nome on Norton Sound, it was named in honor of Colonel (Brevet Major General) Jefferson Columbus Davis, of the 23rd Infantry, who was Department commander in 1867, when the United States purchased Alaska from Russia. The post was first garrisoned on June 28, 1900, by Companies A and K of the 7th Infantry. The post was abandoned in 1919.

FORT DELAROF. Also known as Delarof Redoubt, it was located on Unga Island in Delarof Harbor, in the Aleutian Islands. Established in 1833, it was described as having consisted of a small stockade.

FORT DERABIN. FORT NULATO.

FORT DURHAM. FORT STIKINE.

FORT DURHAM. FORT TAKU.

CAMP DYEA. Located at the mouth of the Taiya River three miles northwest of Skagway, this post was established by General Orders No. 5, Department of the Columbia, March 8, 1898, and garrisoned by troops from Companies B and H of the 14th Infantry. The camp was destroyed by fire on July 28, 1899, and abandoned. The garrison was ordered to proceed to Skagway to establish a new camp.

CAMP EAGLE CITY. FORT EGBERT.

CAMP EARLE (*Attu Post*). After the U.S. and Canada recaptured Attu Island in the far western Aleutians from the Japanese, Camp Earle was established and garrisoned by infantry. The post was activated on May 11, 1943.

FORT EGBERT (*Camp Eagle City*). Situated on the left bank of the Yukon River at the mouth of Mission Creek, about six miles west of the Canadian border, a settlement called Eagle was first established in 1874, later developing into a mining town of about 800 people. Here the Army established Camp Eagle City on June 19, 1899, in compliance with orders of the Department of the Columbia. Fort Egbert was established in accordance with General Orders No. 104, June 7, 1899, and garrisoned by troops of Companies A and L of the 7th Infantry, commanded by Captain Charles S. Farnsworth. The garrison was withdrawn on August 7, 1911, except for a Signal Corps detachment left to operate the telegraph.

FORT ETCHES. A base of operations for the employees of the Lebedoff Company, it consisted of a usual stockade, enclosing dwellings and storehouses. One side of the stockade was formed by an armed vessel of 70 tons, hauled on shore. It was located in an inlet on the western shore of Hinchinbrook Island, Prince William Sound, just southwest of today's Cordova. Its probable date was about 1787, when it was visited by a man named Portlock, who called the location Port Rose.

EXCURSION INLET POST. This World War II Army camp was located at Excursion Inlet west of Icy Point and north of the great Alexander Archipelago. The post was activated on October 5, 1942, with five officers and 218 enlisted men.

GALENA POST. Situated at Galena on the Yukon River, this World War II camp was activated on June 24, 1942, with one officer and 44 enlisted men.

FORT GEORGIYEVSK. Located on Kenai Bay, now Cook Inlet, this was a Russian trading post contained within a fortified earthwork, established about the year 1817.

FORT GIBBON. Situated near the junction of the Tanana and Yukon rivers, the site had been known by the natives as Nukluket, today's Tanana. It was surveyed and reported as a possible military site in 1869 by Captain Charles W. Raymond, U.S. Engineers, while on a journey to Fort Yukon. (The site had been earlier occupied by the trading post called Fort Adams). Fort Gibbon was established in compliance with General Orders No. 104, June 7, 1899, and garrisoned by Companies E and F of the 7th Infantry on July 25, 1899. It served as the headquarters for all of interior Alaska until it was abandoned in February 1923.

FORT GLENN. This World War II defense and the adjacent Cape Army Air Field occupied the northeastern end of Umnak Island in the Aleutians. They were activated on January 17, 1942. The aggregate cost of the construction there was estimated to have been $11 million.

FORT GREELY (*Fort Abercrombie*). Fort Abercrombie, named for Captain (later Lieutenant Colonel) William R. Abercrombie, a U.S. Army explorer in Alaska about the turn of the century, was a subpost of Fort Greely on Kodiak Island (not to be confused with the fort of the same name near Big Delta). Fort Greely on Kodiak Island, named in honor of Major General Adolphus W. Greely, was established for the defense of Kodiak's harbor, as was Fort Abercrombie, on April 2, 1943, in compliance with the War Department's General Orders No. 17. The first garrison arrived on April 3, 1941, consisting of six officers and 169 enlisted men. Construction had begun on February 1, with facilities planned to adequately accommodate 236 officers and 5,592 enlisted men. The first post commander was Lieutenant Colonel Malcolm F. Lindsey. Fort Greely finally evolved as an extensive Army base with a garrison of 11,000 men, adjacent to the Kodiak Naval Air Station. Fort Greely was discontinued on December 15, 1944.

FORT GREELY. This far-flung Army base is home to the Northern Warfare Training Center (NWTC) and the Cold Regions Test Center (CRTC). Fort Greely, 105 miles southeast of Fairbanks, lies within a central valley and hill area known as the "Great Interior." It is bordered by the Brooks Mountain Range to the north and the Alaskan Mountain Range to the south. The main post area is six miles south of the junction of the Alaskan (ALCAN) and Richardon highways, in the neighborhood of both Big Delta and Delta Junction. Fort Greely is known as "home of the rugged professional" and is a unique post. Although the main post is small, the entire reservation covers 677,000 acres, the Army's largest post in Alaska. It is used for Arctic testing of the Army's equipment and for training the finest Arctic soldiers in the world. The 172nd Infantry Brigade (Alaska) units utilize the vast lands for year-round field training exercises. The NWTC is an exclusive joint service school that provides training in Arctic survival, navigation of inland waterways, river crossing, military skiing, and mountaineering.

The Cold Regions Test Center is in its second quarter-century of service. Established in 1949, the center conducts tests of equipment and material under the stress of severe Arctic conditions. A wide variety of items have been tested at the center and many have been commercially adopted. Tests have included year-round evaluations of freeze-dried food, cold weather clothing, and Arctic oils and brake fluids. The interior of Alaska provides the center with several assets vital to this type of testing. Terrain and weather conditions at Fort Greely are typical of Arctic and subarctic areas around the world. The post was the second major Alaskan Army facility to be named for Major General Adolphus Washington Greely, Arctic explorer and founder of the Alaska Communications System.

GULKANA POST. This World War II Army base was established at Gulkana on the Copper River on July 9, 1942, with 11 officers and 254 enlisted men.

FORT HAMILTON. According to Baker's *Geographic Dictionary of Alaska*, Fort Hamilton was originally a village in the Yukon Delta, on the right bank of Apoon Pass, about 25 miles from its mouth. New Fort Hamilton was a supply depot and trading post of the North American Transportation and Trading Company, on the right bank of Kwikpak Pass, 20 miles above Old Fort Hamilton. Located on the lower Yukon River, it was 105 miles southeast of St. Michael.

FORT HAMLIN. A trading post on the south bank of the Yukon, 10 miles below the mouth of the Dall, it was a property of the Alaska Commercial Company and named for Charles Sumner Hamlin, assistant secretary of the treasury, 1893–97.

FORT HELENA. FORT CONSTANTINE.

FORT HIGHFIELD. FORT STIKINE.

JUNEAU POST. A World War II Army post, it was established at Juneau, Alaska's capital, on March 1, 1942, with a garrison of 20 officers and 547 enlisted men.

KASILOF RIVER POST. FORT ST. GEORGE.

KENAI REDOUBT. FORT ST. NICHOLAS.

FORT KENAY (KENAI). Situated at the mouth of the Kenai River on the east shore of Cook Inlet, 65 miles southwest of Anchorage, it occupied the site of the old Russian post known as Fort St. Nicholas or Paul's Fort. It was established in compliance with General Orders No. 7, March 24, 1869, and garrisoned by Batteries F and G of the 2nd Artillery, commanded by Brevet Captain John McGilvary. The one-mile-square post had officers' quarters, men's barracks, a guardhouse, a quartermaster and commissary storehouse, a blacksmith shop, a laundry, a bakehouse, stables, a company kitchen, and a hospital. The post was abandoned on August 13, 1870.

FORT KENNICOTT. This post, named for Robert Kennicott of the Western Union Telegraph Expedition (1866–67), was established near the village of Nulato on the Yukon River. Construction began in April 1866, but the post was not named until Kennicott's death on May 13. It was abandoned in the fall of 1866 as being too large and cold to be habitable over the winter.

KISKA POST. A World War II Army post, it was located on Kiska Island in the Aleutians and activated on August 15, 1943, with a garrison of 595 officers and 1,217 enlisted men. After their loss of Attu, the Japanese evacuated all their troops from Kiska Island late in July.

FORT KODIAK. Situated on the northeast coast of Kodiak Island at St. Paul's Harbor, close to the site of old Fort Pavlosk, Fort Kodiak was established in compliance with Special Orders No. 59, June 6, 1868, and first garrisoned by elements of Battery G, 2nd Artillery, commanded by Major John Tidball. The post was abandoned on August 13, 1870, pursuant to Special Orders No. 99, Department of the Columbia.

FORT KOLMAKOF (*Lukeen's Fort*). An old Russian trading post also known as Kolmakof Redoubt, it was situated on a high bluff in the village of Nulato on the north bank of the Kuskokwim River, about 200 miles above its mouth. Ivan Lukeen ascended the river in 1832 to this place, where he built a stockade, which for some years was known as Lukeen's Fort. Partially destroyed by the Indians in 1841, it was rebuilt by Alexander Kolmakof and took his name. It consisted of a stockaded blockhouse.

FORT KONSTANTINE. FORT CONSTANTINE.

FORT KOUTZNOU. Its proposed site was Admiralty Island near Sitka, where a U.S. Army post was to be built in 1867 shortly after the purchase of Alaska. Although the fort was never constructed, it was referred to in several official dispatches as Fort Koutznou.

FORT KUSSILOF. FORT ST. GEORGE.

FORT LEARNARD. FORT MEARS.

FORT LISCUM. Situated on the south shore of Port Valdez, four miles southwest of the city of Valdez, the post was established on February 12, 1900, in compliance with General Orders No. 14, Headquarters of the Army. The fort was named in honor of Colonel Emerson H. Liscum, who was killed in 1900 at the battle of Tientsin, China. The post was initially garrisoned by Company F of the 59th Infantry. Fort Liscum was the southern terminus of the Fairbanks-Valdez Military Road and in the very near environs of today's Trans-Alaska Pipeline terminal at Port Valdez. The post was abandoned on July 23, 1922.

LUKEEN'S FORT. FORT KOLMAKOF.

FORT MCGILVRAY. During World War II, by authority of War Department General Orders No. 17, April 2, 1943, a post of the Seward, Alaska, Harbor Defense at Gaines Head was designated Fort McGilvray, in honor of Captain John McGilvray, U.S. Army. McGilvray had enlisted as a private on June 20, 1853, rising to the rank of sergeant major in March 1863. In the following year he was commissioned a 1st lieutenant, and he was subsequently cited for gallantry in the Battle of Fisher's Hill, Virginia. Captain McGilvray retired from service in 1884 and died on January 23, 1902. The Fort McGilvray battery (no. 293), authorized for construction on February 10, 1942, consisted of two 6-inch shield-type guns. The battery was ordered abandoned on April 7, 1944, and was dismantled on March 4, 1947. One gun was shipped to the Harbor Defense, San Diego; the remaining guns and carriages were shipped to Black Hill Ordnance Depot.

MCGRATH POST. This World War II post, located at the town of McGrath on the Kuskokwim River, was activated on July 25, 1942, with two officers and 46 enlisted men.

FORT MEARS (*Fort Learnard*). Fort Learnard was a subpost of the harbor defenses of Dutch Harbor, and thus was probably a subsidiary of Fort Mears, with its history a part of the history of that installation. It was named in honor of Lieutenant (later Brigadier General) Henry G. Learnard, who had explored in Alaska with the Glenn expedition in 1898. Construction of Fort

Mears began on January 25, 1941, to accommodate 225 officers and 5,200 enlisted men. Its initial garrison strength was eight officers and 142 enlisted men commanded by Lieutenant Colonel Henry P. Hallowell. The fort was named in honor of Colonel Frederick Mears, who in 1914 had been a member of the Alaska Engineering Commission, which built the Alaska Railroad. Located adjacent to the Navy's installation at Dutch Harbor, Fort Mears and its airfield finally accommodated 11,300 men; the total cost of construction was about $12.6 million. The post was discontinued on April 5, 1945.

FORT MICHAEL. FORT ST. MICHAEL.

MIKHAILOVSKI REDOUBT. FORT ST. MICHAEL.

FORT MORROW. A World War II defense post located at Port Heiden, Fort Morrow was activated on January 17, 1942, with 51 officers and 1,348 enlisted men. It was deactivated at the end of the war, with no specific date noted.

FORT MORTON. Situated at the mouth of the Kobuk River, Hotham Inlet, in the Arctic Ocean, Fort Morton was most probably a winter camp established by Lieutenant George M. Stoney, U.S. Navy, or Lieutenant J. C. Cantwell, both of whom conducted extensive explorations of the Kobuk River region.

MOSES POINT POST. A World War II defensive installation, it was located about 100 miles east of Nome and began operations on August 18, 1942, with a garrison of 28 officers and 813 enlisted men.

FORT NAKNEK. FORT SUVAROV.

NAKNEK POST. A minor World War II facility, it was located at Naknek, Kvichak Bay, on the Alaska Peninsula. It was activated on May 22, 1942, with one officer and 14 enlisted men.

CAMP NENANA. Situated on the Nenana River, southwest of Fairbanks, this World War II post was garrisoned by an Army Transportation Service unit, a platoon, a medical detachment, and harbor craft personnel in charge of six riverboats. Major Howard Wakefield was the post's commander. The post's responsibility was to move cargo to downstream military stations, supplying particularly Galena's air base. The freight was brought to Nenana by the Alaska Railroad,

transferred to boats and barges, and taken by soldiers down the Tanana River into the Yukon, and ultimately southwest to Galena.

FORT NEW ARCHANGEL (*Fort Novo Arkangelesk*). Familiarly known as "Baranof's Castle," this Russian fortress was constructed of stone and logs by Alexander Baranof in 1804 on a rocky and wooded promontory in Sitka's harbor, protected by a water battery arranged in two parallel emplacements one above the other. The ordnance ranged from 80-pound mortars to three-pound falconets, aggregating some 60 guns. It was reported that the fort's arsenal also held 87 unmounted guns and tons of powder and shot. From 250 to 300 men constituted the garrison, which could be increased by Russian Imperial Navy sailors and marines when their ships were in port. The formidable fortress commanded the approaches to the harbor, the governor's castle-residence, and the settlement of Sitka, the capital of Russian America. When the Russians evacuated the fort, it was partially dismantled and then abandoned to the elements.

FORT NIKOLAYA. FORT ST. NICHOLAS.

CAMP NOME. This camp had a brief existence. In June 1900, Fort Davis was established two miles from the town and all the troops were moved there, the garrison consisting of Companies A and K of the 7th Infantry. This post was abandoned in 1921.

NOME POST. A World War II Army facility, it was activated on September 3, 1941, with a garrison of nine officers and 221 enlisted men.

NORTHWAY POST. This World War II camp, situated at today's Northway Junction, about 22 miles west of Canada's Yukon Territory border, was activated on June 11, 1942, with a miniscule garrison composed of one officer and 13 enlisted men.

FORT NOVO ARKANGELESK. FORT NEW ARCHANGEL.

NUKLUROYIT STATION. In the fall of 1868 a small group of Americans and French Canadians, with practically no capital, formed the Pioneer Company and established a trading post about a dozen miles below the confluence of the Yukon and Tanana rivers. Most of them had entered Alaska with the Western Union Telegraph Expedition or the Hudson's Bay Company. It was the first American establishment on the Yukon or anywhere in the interior of Alaska. The location had been used as an Indian trade rendezvous since time immemorial. Both Hudson's Bay Company agents and Ivan Pavloff's Russian traders from Nulato had come there each June to barter for furs. The Pioneer Company, however, lasted only a season or so. The manager of Parrott and Company, traders and owners of the *Yukon*, purchased the trading post.

FORT NULATO (*Fort Derabin*). This Russian fortified trading post was situated near the village of Nulato, located on the right bank of the Yukon River, about 100 miles from Norton Sound and 550 miles by river from the ocean. The dates cited in Baker's *Geographic Dictionary of Alaska* differ somewhat from those appearing in a Department of the Army report on the post. Built by the Russian Fur Company in either 1838 or 1841, the post was then the company's farthest outlying permanent trading station. The fort was described as large, with two sides and a part of the third formed by log structures, and the remainder a 16-foot-high log stockade with gun turrets, enclosing a sizable compound. Shortly after it was completed, the post was burned by Indians. It was rebuilt in 1842 by a Lieutenant Zagoskin of the Russian Imperial Navy, who was soon replaced by one Vasili Derzhavin, whose many acts of cruelty led to the massacre of the entire garrison by the Koyukuk Indians in 1851. The post was originally called Fort Derabin after its builder and first overseer. Some years later—date undetermined—the post was moved two miles farther upstream to Nulato. A United States military reservation, located between Nulato and St. Michael, was set apart by Executive Order on May 4, 1908, for use of the Signal Corps. But when it was later found to be useless for military purposes, it was transferred to the secretary of the interior for disposition. On May 25, 1921, also by Executive Order, 30.7 acres were reserved for a Signal Corps station.

FORT NUSHAGAK. FORT ALEXANDER.

OZERSKOYE REDOUBT. A Russian blockhouse, probably stockaded and minimally fortified, it was located on Baranof Island, at the outlet of Deep Lake in Sitka Sound, about 16 miles south of Sitka. It was attacked and burned by Stikine Indians in 1852.

PAUL'S FORT. FORT ST. NICHOLAS.

FORT PAVLOSK. Established by Baranof in 1792, the stockaded blockhouse was situated at Three Saints Bay, St. Paul's Harbor, Kodiak.

PAVLOVSKAYA REDOUBT. FORT ST. NICHOLAS.

FORT PEIRCE. By authority of War Department General Orders No. 17, April 2, 1943, a subpost of the Sitka, Alaska, Harbor Defense on Biorka Island was designated Fort Peirce in honor of Captain Charles H. Peirce, U.S. Army. Peirce enlisted as a private on June 10, 1846, and rose to the rank of captain on June 11, 1864. Between 1868 and 1870, he commanded elements of the 2nd U.S. Artillery Regiment at Fort Tongass, Alaska. On November 4, 1869, he was (temporarily) relieved of his command by general court-martial and cashiered from the service for drunkenness while on duty. Through the intervention of President Grant, Captain Peirce's sentence was remitted and he was restored to duty on January 18, 1870. He was mustered out of the service on December 31, 1870. The Fort Peirce battery, authorized for construction on February 10, 1942, consisted of two 6-inch shield-type guns. Further construction on the battery was abandoned on March 8, 1944, and it was dismantled on March 4, 1947. The guns and carriages were shipped to the Black Hills Ordnance Depot.

CAMP RAMPART. Situated on the south bank of the Yukon River, 61 miles northeast of Tanana, the post was established to protect public property in the town of Rampart, a supply center for miners during the 1898 Gold Rush. The camp was established on July 27, 1899, by authority of the commander of the District of North Alaska. A detachment of Company E, 7th Infantry, arrived by steamer to form the garrison, commanded by Lieutenant Benjamin J. Tillman. The camp was abandoned on August 1, 1901, in accordance with orders dated July 12, 1901.

FORT RANDALL. Subsequent to aerial surveys, the Army Corps of Engineers laid out an air base at Cold Bay in the eastern Aleutians, later named Fort Randall in honor of Major General George Morton Randall. He had enlisted as a private in 1861, served throughout the Civil War years, and risen rapidly through the ranks, having been cited for gallantry in various actions. He was also cited for action during the Indian wars in Arizona. Fort Randall was established on January 29, 1942, under the command of Colonel Edwin Jones, with a complement of 48 officers and 1,122 enlisted men. Along with Fort Glenn at Umnak and Dutch Harbor, Fort Randall constituted World War II's strategic air defense for the Aleutian Islands.

FORT RAY. At Sitka, where the U.S. Navy had operated a seaplane base since 1937, Fort Ray was established at a cost of about $10.6 million to provide coast and antiaircraft protection. The post was activated on March 21, 1941. Later there were several subposts of Fort Ray established in the Sitka area.

FORT RAYMOND. During the early months of World War II, Fort Raymond was established on Resurrection Bay near Seward; it was activated in April 1942 at an estimated cost of $7.9 million. The cost, however, included subpost seacoast batteries built in and around Seward.

FORT RESURRECTION. Built by Baranof on a tributary at the head of Kenai Peninsula's Resurrection Bay in 1792, it probably consisted of a stockaded blockhouse used as a trading post and factory.

FORT RICHARDSON (*Camp Anchorage*). Troops were stationed at Anchorage in 1919 for the purpose of protecting government property during the construction of the railroad. The Alaskan Engineering Commission had requested this protection and furnished quarters for the troops a mile north of Anchorage. By 1923 the railroad had been completed and the feasibility of establishing a permanent post in the vicinity was studied by the War Department. However, in November 1926 the post was ordered abandoned, and the troops moved out on December 4, 1926.

Built during 1940–41 on the site of what is now its sister installation of Elmendorf Air Force Base, Fort Richardson was established in 1947 as the headquarters of the United States Army, Alaska (USARAL), and was moved to its present location in Anchorage's environs in 1950. Fort Richardson, popularly known as "home of the Arctic soldier," then had barracks for 500 soldiers, a rifle range, a few warehouses, a hospital, and bachelor officers' quarters. Today it is an energetic community of more than 5,000 soldiers and 6,000 dependents. It spans 62,500 acres of land north of the port city of Anchorage. Fort Richardson was named for a pioneer explorer in Alaska, Brigadier General Wilds P. Richardson, who served three tours of duty in the rugged territory between 1897 and 1917. A native Texan

and 1884 graduate of West Point, he commanded troops along the Yukon, and supervised construction of Fort Egbert and Fort William H. Seward (Chilkoot Barracks) near Haines. He retired in 1920 after 40 years of service, much of it as one of the original Arctic soldiers.

FORT ROUSSEAU. By authority of the War Department's General Orders No. 17, April 2, 1943, the headquarters post of the Sitka, Alaska, Harbor Defense on Makhnati Island was designated Fort Rousseau, in honor of Brevet Major General Lovell Harrison Rousseau, U.S. Army. Rousseau joined the 2nd Indiana Infantry as a captain on June 22, 1846, was commissioned a colonel of the 3rd Kentucky Infantry on September 9, 1861, and served as a major general of volunteers during the Civil War, earning citations for gallantry during the war. On March 28, 1867, he received the commission of Brevet Major General and in that year received the transfer of Alaska to the United States. He died on January 7, 1869. The Fort Rousseau battery, authorized for construction on February 10, 1942, consisted of two 6-inch shield-type guns. It was eliminated from the Alaskan Defense Project on March 26, 1946, and dismantled on March 4, 1947.

FORT ST. DIONYS. This temporary post was a strongly built log palisade erected on Sitka Island by Lieutenant Zarevbo in 1831. The fortification served to repulse an attack by Hudson's Bay Company forces during a brief trade war in the early 1830s.

REDOUBT ST. DIONYSIUS. FORT STIKINE.

FORT ST. GEORGE (*Kasilof River Post; Fort Kussilof*). Established in 1786 by the Lebedef-Lastochkin Company, the stockaded post was situated on the east shore of Cook Inlet at the mouth of the Kasilof River, Kenai Peninsula, about 12 miles south of Kenai. The trading establishment came into the possession of the Russian-American Company in 1799 and was abandoned by the same company at some time prior to 1867, when Alaska was sold to the United States.

FORT ST. HELENS. FORT CONSTANTINE.

FORT ST. MICHAEL (*Fort Michael; Redoubt St. Michael; Mikhailovski Redoubt*). A stockaded post was ordered built by Baron Wrangel, governor general of Russian America, at present-day St. Michael on Norton Sound in the Bering Sea, above the mouth of the Yukon River. In compliance, Captain Michael Dmitrievich Tebenkof, an officer of the Russian-American Company, established the post in 1833, and it was named Redoubt St. Michael or Mikhailovski Redoubt. In 1836 the vicinity's Indians, Unaligmuts, attacked the fort but were successfully repulsed by the post's commander. The stockade and blockhouses, built of spruce, were erected on a bluff 30 feet above sea level and protected a sizable adjoining settlement. In 1897 historian Henry Elliot reported that "the stockade which once encircled it has long since been dispensed with, though the antique bastions and old brass cannon still stand at one or two corners as they stood in early times."

St. Michael was the site of a Signal Corps telegraph station from March 18, 1874, to June 30, 1886. The War Department ordered a post established there "to protect life and property," and a detachment of the 3rd Infantry arrived on September 17, 1897. On October 8, 1897, the garrison was increased by Companies A, C, E, and F, 8th Infantry, commanded by Lieutenant Colonel George M. Randall. Fort St. Michael was officially designated a Military Reservation on October 20, 1897, by Headquarters of the Army, to extend in a 100 mile radius of the flagpole. The post was abandoned in compliance with Special Orders No. 120, May 23, 1923.

FORT ST. MICHAEL (*Fort Archangel Gabriel; Fort Archangel Michael*). The first Russian settlement on Sitka Island, it was established by Alexander Baranof in 1799. The large palisaded blockhouse was armed with at least three brass guns and garrisoned by 200 Russians and a large contingent of Aleuts. In June 1802 the fort was attacked and destroyed by the Kolosh Indians, who methodically massacred the garrison. Other Russians found "only the half-melted barrel of a brass gun and a broken cannon" among the ruins. The fort was located some six miles north of today's Sitka.

REDOUBT ST. MICHAEL. FORT ST. MICHAEL (Norton Sound).

FORT ST. NICHOLAS (*Paul's Fort; Fort St. Paul; Kenai Redoubt; Pavlovskaya Redoubt; Fort Nikolaya*). Situated near the village of Kenai on the east shore of Cook Inlet, some 65 miles southwest of present-day Anchorage, it was established in 1791 by Grigor Konovalkov, commander of the Lebedef-Lastochkin Company's ship *St. George*. The post consisted of two large blockhouses, armed with 11 cannon: six 4-pound iron guns, four falconets, and one carronade.

Battery F, 2nd U.S. Artillery, after a shipwreck the previous year, successfully established Fort Kenay on April 17, 1869, occupying the site of old Fort St. Nicholas.

FORT ST. PAUL. FORT ST. NICHOLAS.

ST. PAUL POST. A World War II installation, it was located in the Pribilof Islands in the Bering Sea. It was activated on September 19, 1942, with a garrison of 38 officers and 719 enlisted men.

ST. PAUL ISLAND POST. One of the most remote Army installations, this post was located on St. Paul Island, 44 miles north of St. George Island, in the Pribilof Islands in the Bering Sea. It was established by Special Orders No. 3, Headquarters, District of Kenay, May 10, 1869, and garrisoned on May 22, 1869, by 15 men of Company G, 2nd Artillery, commanded by Lieutenant James L. Mast. The post was abandoned on September 10, 1870.

FORT SCHWATKA. This World War II installation west of Dutch Harbor was situated at Ulatka Head on Amaknak Island. It was named in honor of Lieutenant Frederick Schwatka, who led an exploring expedition on the Yukon River in 1883. The post was activated subsequent to an order dated March 22, 1943. All gun batteries planned were completed. On April 11, 1945, the post was placed in caretaker status.

FORT WILLIAM H. SEWARD. CHILKOOT BARRACKS.

SHEMYA POST. Located on Shemya Island, in the Near Islands group in the extreme western Aleutians, this World War II post was activated on May 29, 1943, with 236 officers and 4,565 enlisted men.

POST OF SITKA. Situated on the west coast of Baranof Island, some 95 miles southwest of Juneau, this post was never officially designated Fort Sitka, although it was often called so. It was garrisoned by American troops 11 days after the American flag replaced the Russian imperial standard. It was the site of the ceremonies officially transferring Alaska to the United States on October 29, 1867, and was Alaska's capital until it was moved to Juneau in 1900. The first American military post in Alaska, Sitka was also headquarters of the Military District of Alaska commanded by Brevet Major General Jefferson Columbus Davis (not to be confused with President Jefferson Davis of the Confederacy). The post was established in compliance with Special Orders No. 154, September 6, 1867, and garrisoned by Company F, 9th Infantry, and Company H, 2nd Artillery. Ordnance consisted of one battery of 12-pound field pieces and one battery of 10-pound Parrott guns. The troops occupied the old Russian barracks and other structures and manned the stockade and blockhouses separating the Indian village from the city proper. Sitka was abandoned on June 14, 1877, in accordance with General Orders No. 13, Headquarters Department of the Columbia.

CAMP SKAGWAY. Situated at the mouth of the Skagway River near the head of Taiya Inlet, some 90 miles northwest of Juneau, this post was established pursuant to General Orders No. 5, Department of the Columbia, on February 27, 1898. The Gold Rush had turned Skagway into an uproarious boomtown, and Companies A and G of the 14th Infantry were stationed there to preserve law and order and to protect public property. They were under the command of Captain Frank E. Eastman. Because of the Spanish-American war, two companies of troops of the 14th Infantry posted in the District of Lynn Canal (Camp Dyea and Camp Skagway) were recalled from Alaskan duty. The camp was abandoned on October 5, 1904, and the troops transferred to Fort William H. Seward at Haines.

FORT SMITH. A World War II harbor defense post on the north side of Kodiak Island, Fort Smith was named in honor of Brevet Captain John Hewitt Smith, U.S. Army.

FORT STIKINE (*Redoubt St. Dionysius; Fort Highfield; Fort Durham*). In accordance with an order by Baron Alexander Wrangel, a fortified log-stockaded blockhouse was erected on the northwest tip of Wrangell Island, near the mouth of the Stikine River, in 1834 by Lieutenant Dionysius Zarembo of the Russian-American Company to halt encroachments of the Hudson's Bay Company. Lieutenant Zarembo named it Redoubt St. Dionysius. In August 1833 the Hudson's Bay Company had sent an expedition to the Stikine River to locate a site for a trading post within British territory, about 10 sea miles up the river. A site had been marked and arrangements had been made with the Indians. In February 1834 the Indians reported that during the winter the Russians with about 80 men had come from Sitka and erected an establishment at Point Highfield. When the Hudson's Bay vessel *Dryad* arrived in June 1834, she was boarded

by a Russian officer with a proclamation signed by Baron Wrangel, threatening force if the *Dryad* attempted to enter the river. This was considered a violation of the convention signed at St. Petersburg in 1825, and official complaints were made. Finally, on June 1, 1840, Redoubt St. Dionysius was handed over to the Hudson's Bay Company on a 10-year lease; it was now known as Fort Stikine, but at times was called Fort Highfield because of the fort's proximity to Point Highfield. The post was maintained until April 15, 1849, when it was finally abandoned. James Douglas, a Hudson's Bay Company representative, who arranged the lease in 1840, called the post Fort Durham in his reports.

FORT SUVAROV (*Fort Naknek*). Apparently built by a Russian-American Company employee, the trading post was located near the mouth of the Naknek River on the north coast of the Alaska Peninsula, about 36 miles below Dillingham. Established in the 1830s, it was a stockaded blockhouse also called Fort Naknek.

FORT TAKU (*Fort Durham*). This trading post, though officially named Fort Durham, was usually called Fort Taku. In June 1840 the Hudson's Bay Company vessels *Beaver* and *Vancouver* were sent with men and supplies to establish a trading post on the Taku River. No suitable site was found on the river or on its inlet, but a safe harbor about 15 miles to the south was chosen. This is Taku Harbor, where the fort was located on Stockade Point. It was named Fort Durham after the earl of Durham, the governor-general of Canada. After touring the coast in 1842, Sir George Simpson, administrator of the Hudson's Bay Company's territory, decided that the fur trade in the region could be better handled by the steamer *Beaver*. An order was issued to take steps to abandon the short-lived post. In the spring of 1843 the men and stores were evacuated from the fort and landed on the south point of Vancouver Island, British Columbia, where Fort Victoria was built.

CAMP TANACROSS. At Tanacross on the Alaska Highway and the Tanana River, Exercise "Great Bear" was significant not only because 8,000 soldiers were involved, but also because this marked the first time in 13 years that Canadian troops had maneuvered in Alaska. In order to accommodate these troops, a massive construction job was performed by men of the 56th and 562nd Engineer Companies from Fort Richardson and the 18th Engineer Company from Fort Wainwright during December 1961 and January

1962. They built what constituted the sixth largest city in Alaska, Camp Tanacross. The tent city mushroomed as the engineers pitched 300 ten-man tents, 150 five-man tents, 50 general-purpose tents, and 14 mess halls under canvas. Camp Tanacross lived a short life and was gone by spring. During World War II, an Army post was established on the south bank of the Tanacross River opposite the town of Tanacross. It was activated on July 7, 1942, with an initial garrison of one officer and 20 enlisted men under the command of Captain Henry A. McKean.

FORT TIDBALL. A World War II harbor defense situated on Long Island near Kodiak, it was named in honor of Brevet Major General John C. Tidball, U.S. Army. It was established sometime in 1942 and abandoned in 1945.

FORT TONGASS. Named for the region's Tongass Indians, this Army post was situated on the west coast of Tongass Island, southeast Alaska, and close to the British Columbia border. Located south of Ketchikan, it was the most southerly of the American posts in Alaska. Dates for its establishment and abandonment vary. The fort was probably activated in June 1868 and garrisoned by Battery E, 2nd Artillery, possibly commanded by Captain John H. Smith. However, the publication *The Army's Role in the Building of Alaska* states that the garrison was commanded by Captain Charles H. Peirce. The post was abandoned in August 1870, and its garrison of 10 officers and 50 men was transferred southward. The Ketchikan Centennial Committee in 1966 believed that the fort was established on April 29, 1868, garrisoned by three commissioned officers and 50 enlisted men, and abandoned on October 7, 1870.

CAMP TREADWELL. In May 1907 a 10th Infantry detachment of two officers and 28 enlisted men performed guard duty over property of the Alaska Treadwell Gold Mining Company, because of a new gold strike. The soldiers' stay was short. The detachment was ordered to proceed to Fort William H. Seward in compliance with telegraphic instructions from the fort's commanding officer. The detachment evacuated the camp on May 15, 1907.

CAMP VALDEZ. A World War II rest and recreation facility, it was situated in the immediate environs of the city of Valdez on the coast southwest of Anchorage. It was ordered established in late March 1942, and activated a month later

with 20 officers and 547 enlisted men. The camp was garrisoned as late as 1968.

FORT WAINWRIGHT. On January 1, 1961, when Ladd Air Force Base in the environs of Fairbanks was transferred to the Army and renamed Fort Wainwright, it already had a notable history dating back to the days when Brigadier General Billy Mitchell campaigned for improved defenses in the state. Testifying before Congress in 1935, he stated: "I believe in the future, he who holds Alaska, holds the world, and I think it is the most strategic place in the world."

Construction finally began on a cold weather experimental station in 1939, and the following year Congress approved construction of an Army air field at Ladd. In September 1940 the first troops, about 50, arrived at Fairbanks. During World War II the installation was used as a troop dispersal point, as a point for delivery of lend-lease aircraft to Russian pilots, and as a link in Alaska's air defense chain. Following the war, the post resupplied and maintained the remote DEW (Distant Early Warning) radar sites and experimental ice islands in the Arctic Ocean. Two years after Alaskan statehood, the Army assumed command of the post. Since then, units varying in amount and size have been stationed at the fort. In the last 15 years, because of the large territory available for exercises, the post has been the site for some of the largest Army exercises, including Acid Test and a 400-mile-wide Jack Frost. The diverse Fort Wainwright combat support units and teams provide specialized arctic training and research on environmental cold.

The fort was named for General Jonathan M. Wainwright, a West Point alumnus with a 41-year-long career in the Army. His courageous defense of Bataan's fortress of Corregidor during the opening months of World War II had become legendary. A month after the fall of Bataan, General Wainwright joined his comrades in the ordeal of Japanese prison camps, which for him lasted three years and four months. He was finally liberated and in time he was to stand on the deck of the *Missouri* and witness the surrender of Japan. He was awarded the Medal of Honor.

WHITTIER POST. A World War II post, it was located at Whittier southeast of Anchorage. It was activated on October 3, 1942, with one officer and 15 enlisted men.

FORT WRANGELL. Situated on the north side of Wrangell Island, in southeast Alaska's Alexander Archipelago, this fort was established on May 5, 1868, in compliance with Special Orders No.

26, Military Division of the Pacific, and garrisoned by Company E, 2nd Artillery, commanded by Lieutenant J. H. Smith. The post was abandoned on September 27, 1870, in compliance with Special Orders No. 99, Department of the Columbia. The fort was reoccupied on August 13, 1874, and abandoned again on July 27, 1877. The Gold Rush influenced another reoccupation on May 24, 1898. Fort Wrangell was finally abandoned for good on May 12, 1900, in accordance with General Orders No. 9.

YAKUTAT POST. A World War II Army installation at Yakutat on the eastern Gulf of Alaska, it was activated on October 23, 1940, with an estimated 70 officers and 130 enlisted men.

YAKUTAT BAY FORT. In 1796 the Russian government authorized the building of a fort at Yakutat Bay in the eastern Gulf of Alaska. The Shelikof Fur Company accordingly built a fortified trading post here, and a number of convicts assigned by the czar were settled here.

FORT YUKON. Situated on the right bank of the Yukon River at its junction with the Porcupine, this temporary post was established on September 15, 1897, and garrisoned by a detachment of the 8th Infantry under the command of Captain Patrick Henry Ray. On November 8, 1897, Major General Nelson A. Miles recommended to the secretary of war that a military expedition be sent to the Klondike region with supplies to prevent starvation among the miners there, most of whom were American citizens. The expedition did not materialize until the following year, but in the course of preparation Captain Ray had been assigned to make the preliminary arrange-

ments. Fort Yukon was abandoned by the small garrison in January 1898.

FORT YUKON. This historic trading post was located one mile north of the Arctic Circle, on the most northerly point of the Yukon River, a couple of miles from its confluence with the Porcupine River. The fort was built in 1847 by Alexander Hunter Murray of the Hudson's Bay Company, about 115 miles west of the border between the company's trading regions and Russian-occupied America. Murray was fully cognizant of the fact that he was trespassing but felt reasonably safe since the Russians were hundreds of miles away. The site had already been selected two years earlier by chief trader John Bell when he explored the entire length of the Porcupine River to its confluence with the Yukon. To reassure himself should the Russians penetrate as far as his fort, which stood on the right bank of the river, Murray vowed to build "the best and strongest [fort] between Red River and the Polar Sea." His fort consisted of three large log structures surrounded by a stockade 100 feet square, with a fortified blockhouse in each of the four angles.

It took 17 years before the first Russian trader, Ivan Simonsen Lukeen, reached the fort from the sea. But before a sizable force of armed Russians arrived there, the United States purchased Alaska from the Russians. The year of purchase was 1867, but in 1864 the Hudson's Bay Company had already begun to build a new fort about a mile farther down the Yukon, because the river was undermining the steep bank on which Murray's fort stood. Strongly in doubt of England's sovereignty in the area occupied by

FORT YUKON. Artist's rendition of the Hudson's Bay Company's post. (Courtesy of the Alaska Historical Library.)

Fort Yukon, in 1869 the U.S. government dispatched 27-year-old Captain Charles W. Raymond, Corps of Engineers, to make a reconnaissance of the Yukon River and assess the status of the Hudson's Bay Company post. Raymond and his assistant, John J. Major, left San Francisco on April 6, 1869, and arrived at St. Michael on Norton Sound in the Bering Sea, above the mouth of the Yukon River, on July 1. They ascended the river in a small steamboat and arrived at Fort Yukon on the last day of July. Captain Raymond's observations were accurate and found that the fort was west of the 141st meridian and therefore occupied Alaskan territory. On August 9 he hoisted the Stars and Stripes over the fort and gave the Hudson's Bay traders notice to evacuate the property. The survey made by Captain Raymond is the first indication of the presence of the Army Corps of Engineers in the territory of Alaska—and it was not the last.

CAMP AJO. A Mexican border patrol post established about 1800 at Ajo, Pima County.

CAMP APACHE. FORT APACHE.

FORT APACHE (*Camp Ord; Camp Mogollon; Camp Thomas; Camp Apache*). Established on May 16, 1870, Fort Apache was located south of the Mogollon Plateau on the south bank of the east fork of the White River, near the present-day town of Fort Apache. Intended to put a stop to the raids perpetrated by the Coyotero Apaches, the post was first activated by a detachment of the 1st Cavalry, commanded by Major John Green, and named Camp Ord for Brigadier General Edward O. C. Ord. The post's name was changed to Camp Mogollon on August 1, 1870; to Camp Thomas, for Major General George H. Thomas, on September 12, 1870; and to Camp Apache on February 2, 1871. It became a permanent post in 1873, and on April 5, 1879, it was designated Fort Apache.

The land on which the fort stood had been formerly a part of the White Mountain Indian Reservation, but the parcel included within the grounds of the post was restored to the public domain January 26, 1877. It was designated a military reservation by Executive Order, February 1, 1877. In 1922 the Fort Apache military reservation was transferred to the secretary of the interior, since it was no longer useful for military purposes. The site is now occupied by an Indian school established by the Indian Service within the lands allotted for the Fort Apache Indian Reservation.

FORT ARAVAIPA. FORT GRANT NO. 1.

CAMP ARIVACA. A Mexican border patrol post established in Pima County about 1800.

CAMP ARIVACA JUNCTION. A Mexican border patrol post, it was established about 1800 near Arivaca, Pima County.

CAMP ASH CREEK. CAMP HENTIG.

FORT BADGER. Located in the immediate vicinity of the confluence of the Verde and Salado rivers, it was most probably established in 1866. Several citations have erroneously made it synonymous with early Fort McDowell. Fort Badger appears on a map dated 1866. No other references have been found.

FORT BARRETT. Established on May 31, 1862, by Lieutenant Colonel Joseph R. West, 1st Califor-

Arizona

nia Infantry, by order of General James H. Carleton, it was located in the Pima villages on the Gila River above its junction with the Salr River on the present Gila Indian Reservation. The fortification consisted of an earthwork at a flour mill and served as a subdepot and supply station. The post was named for 2nd Lieutenant James Barrett, 1st California Cavalry, who was killed in a skirmish with Confederate troops near Picacho Pass on April 15, 1862. Existing for less than two months, the post was abandoned on July 23, 1862.

CAMP BEALE'S SPRINGS. Located about 40 miles east of Fort Mojave and a few miles northwest of present Kingman, this post was established on March 25, 1871, during the period of Indian unrest in the Southwest. It was named for Lieutenant E. F. Beale, a graduate midshipman and lieutenant in the U.S. Navy during the Mexican War. At the close of the war, he resigned his commission and became an explorer, naming many localities in Arizona. The post was garrisoned by Company F of the 12th Infantry. Camp Beale's Springs was abandoned on April 5, 1874.

CAMP AT BEAR SPRING. Almost nothing is known about this post, occupied intermittently by either infantry or cavalry during 1863–64, possibly involved in Civil War conflicts in the Southwest. Located in Coconino County, Bear Spring, named by ex-Lieutenant E. F. Beale in 1859, is believed to be today's Elden Spring, about four miles northeast of Flagstaff.

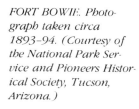

FORT BOWIE. Photograph taken circa 1893–94. (Courtesy of the National Park Service and Pioneers Historical Society, Tucson, Arizona.)

CAMP BENSON. A Mexican border post established about 1800 and located at Benson in Cochise County.

CAMP BISBEE. A Mexican border post established about 1800 and located at Bisbee in Cochise County.

CAMP BOUSE. A World War II desert training post during 1942–43, it was located east of Bouse in Mohave County.

FORT BOWIE. One of the earliest military posts in Arizona, it was established on July 28, 1862, by Major Theodore A. Coult, 5th Infantry, California Volunteers, on orders by General James H. Carleton. The post, with 412 feet of stone walls, was located in the Chiricahua Mountains on the eastern approaches to Apache Pass, south of today's town of Bowie. It was designed to protect all travel along the Tucson-Mesilla Road, guard the important spring nearby against Indians, and prevent Confederate penetration into the region. In July 1862, 11 companies of Union infantry, en route from Tucson to New Mexico, were attacked here by Apaches led by chiefs Cochise and Mangas Colorados. During the life of the post, numerous infantry and cavalry regiments had large detachments here. Originally called a fort, the post was later designated Camp Bowie, then Fort Bowie again on April 5, 1879. Named for Colonel George W. Bowie, 5th Infantry, California Volunteers, the post in 1868 was moved from its original site to a nearby hill. Abandoned on October 17, 1894, the military reservation was transferred to the Interior Department for disposition on November 14, 1894. About two years later the land was sold to local farmers at a public auction. The post's structures were sold on June 20, 1911. Little more than tottering stone walls remained of the fort when it was taken over by the National Park Service in

1964. Stabilization of the ruins began in 1967 to preserve the historic site. A marker is located on State 86 at the turnoff to Apache Pass Road.

BOWIE STATION. This post in Cochise County was established in January 1886 by Lieutenant Colonel Montgomery Bryant, 8th Infantry, with Companies A, B, D, E, H, and K and Troop M of the 4th Cavalry. The post was abandoned in June of the same year.

FORT BRECKINRIDGE. FORT GRANT NO. 1.

CAMP BRODIE. Established prior to World War I during the Mexican border difficulties, it was located near Prescott in Yavapai County.

FORT BUCHANAN (*Camp near Calabasas; Camp Moore*). Established on November 17, 1856, by Major George A. H. Blake, 1st U.S. Dragoons, with Companies B, D, G, and K, it was the first military post in the territory covered by the Gadsden Purchase. Planned to control the region's Apaches and protect southern Arizona's travel routes, such as they were, it was located on the Sonoita River about 25 miles east of the historic town of Tubac, near present-day Patagonia. First named Camp near Calabasas, it was soon renamed Camp Moore for Captain Benjamin D. Moore, 1st U.S. Dragoons, killed on December 6, 1846, during the Battle of San Pascual. On May 29, 1857, the post was designated Fort Buchanan in honor of President James Buchanan. "The site was unhealthful and the post was considered to be the worst situated and most poorly constructed in the Southwest. It consisted of a few scattered adobe buildings without even a stockade around them" (*Forts of the West*, pp. 6–7).

When Confederate forces entered Arizona from Texas, the fort's garrison evacuated and then burned the post's structures on July 23, 1861. The newcomers then occupied the ruins until May 4, 1862, when they learned of the approach of a large force of Union troops from California. The Union soldiers raised the Stars and Stripes over the blackened ruination, but General James H. Carleton, in command of the California column, decided that the site had no military value, and the post's remnants were surrendered to the elements. Six years later, to the day, Camp Crittenden was established to replace it in response to increased Apache unrest. An adobe post was constructed half a mile from the old fort.

CAMP CALABASAS (*Presidio near Calabasas*). Probably built in 1837, the presidio was located in the precincts of the old Papago Indian village of Calabasas, now one of Arizona's numerous ghost towns, in Santa Cruz County. Located on the land grant owned by Manuel Maria Gandara near the Papago village on the Santa Cruz River, about nine miles north of Nogales, the presidio was established by him, when he was appointed governor of Sonora, in order to defend his property against Apache incursions. The structures of stone were in such good repair that subsequent to the Gadsden Purchase, from 1856 to 1858, they were garrisoned by U.S. Dragoons, who named the post Camp Calabasas. In 1862, during the Civil War, the place was occupied temporarily by a Confederate force commanded by Colonel Benjamin S. Ewell. Two other posts were established in its environs: Camp Mason in 1865 and Camp Cameron from October 1, 1866, to March 7, 1867.

CAMP NEAR CALABASAS. FORT BUCHANAN.

POST AT CALABASAS. FORT MASON.

PRESIDIO NEAR CALABASAS. CAMP CALABASAS.

CAMP CAMERON. This temporary camp was situated on the northwestern base of the Santa Rita Mountain, some 16 miles northeast of Tubac and 45 miles southeast of Tucson. It stood on a dry, rocky mesa, on the bank of a clear mountain stream. The men were quartered in "A" tents, the officers in huts, which were constructed of stone, planks, logs, canvas, and rawhide. Established on October 1, 1866, the post was named for President Lincoln's secretary of war, Simon Cameron, who was an uncle of the Cameron brothers, well known cattle raisers in the region. The post was abandoned on March 7, 1867, with the troops moving first to Tubac, on account of Indian depredations there, and then to Camp Crittenden.

FORT CANBY. Established on July 23, 1863, this post was located about 28 miles southwest of Fort Defiance near the present town of Ganado. It was built by elements of the 1st New Mexico Infantry, with Colonel Kit Carson commanding, as a base for Carson's campaign against the Navajos. It was named for Brigadier General R. S. Canby, who preceded General James H. Carleton as commander of the Department of New Mexico. The post was abandoned on October 20, 1864, at the conclusion of the campaign.

CAMP CANYON DE CHELLY. The historic canyon was used as a temporary campsite by early exploration expeditions. From September 6 to September 10, 1849, a camp was established by Brevet Lieutenant Colonel John M. Washington two miles northwest of the mouth of the canyon, while negotiating a treaty with the Navajos. About the year 1700 the Navajo Indians, who were then concentrated in northern New Mexico, began to occupy Canyon de Chelly, which became one of the chief Navajo strongholds. Their raids continued into the American period. In 1864 a detachment of United States cavalry under Kit Carson campaigned against the marauding Indians in Canyon de Chelly. This was part of a military campaign that put an end to Navajo raiding by removing over 8,000 of them to a reservation in eastern New Mexico. This first reservation experiment failed, and after four years the Navajos were permitted to return to their homeland.

CAMP CHRISTIANSON RANCH. This was a temporary post established at the ranch, located east of Nogales in Santa Cruz County, during the border trouble with Mexico prior to World War I.

CAMP CLARK. WHIPPLE BARRACKS.

CAMP COCHISE. A pre–World War I border post established in Cochise County.

CAMP COLORADO. FORT MOHAVE.

CAMP COLORADO (*Camp Colorado River*). According to records in the National Archives, this post was first known as "Camp on the Colorado River." Located on the Colorado River, near the mouth of the Bill Williams River, this camp was established on the Colorado River Indian Reservation about 40 miles north of La Paz on November 25, 1868. The troops were withdrawn and the post abandoned in April 1871. One reference reports that the post's property was sent to Fort Mohave. Camp Colorado's garrisons consisted of Company H, 14th Infantry (1868–69), and Company G, 12th Infantry (1869–71).

CAMP COLORADO CHIQUITO. CAMP SUNSET.

CAMP COLORADO RIVER. CAMP COLORADO.

CAMP COOK'S RANCH. A pre–World War I Mexican border post near Lowell in Cochise County.

CAMP CRAWFORD. A temporary post established in the Chiricahua Mountains in Cochise County around 1800, it was named for Captain Emmett Crawford, famed for his military exploits against the Apaches.

CAMP CRITTENDEN. Established on March 4, 1868, to protect the area's settlers, Camp Crittenden occupied the former site of Fort Buchanan (abandoned in 1861) at the headwaters of the Sonoita River in present-day Santa Cruz County. Its first garrison consisted of Companies H and K of the 32nd Infantry and Troops C and K of the 1st Cavalry, which arrived from Camp Tubac, commanded by Captain Stephen G. Whipple, who established the post. It was named for Colonel Thomas L. Crittenden of the 32nd Infantry, who had recommended the site. The post was abandoned on June 1, 1873, because its site had proved to be unhealthful. The military reservation was transferred to the Department of the Interior for disposition on July 22, 1884.

CAMP CURTIS. Other than that it was established on Big Bug Creek, about four miles above Mayer, Yavapai County, nothing is known about the post's origin.

CAMP DATE CREEK (*Camp McPherson; Camp Skull Valley*). A temporary post on the left bank of Date Creek some 60 miles southwest of Prescott in Yavapai County, Camp McPherson was established January 23, 1867, to protect travelers along the La Paz–Prescott road. The post had been named for Brigadier General James B. McPherson, who was killed in the battle for Atlanta on July 22, 1864. In March 1867 the post was moved 25 miles north on the road to Prescott, for the protection of settlers in the area, and called Camp Skull Valley. The reason for this name was that three years earlier there had been a fight between soldiers and a sizable war party of Apaches in the valley; many Indian dead were not yet buried, so a detachment of troops returned to inter their remains. On May 11, 1867, the post was returned to Date Creek. The camp was shifted again to another situation on Date Creek on August 24, 1867, and finally, in 1868, to the south bank of the stream, when the post was renamed Camp Date Creek on November 23. Federal records for 1868 report that Captain J. W. Weir was then in command of Companies

H and I, 14th Infantry. The post was abandoned on August 30, 1873 (another reference says it was abandoned in 1874).

FORT DEFIANCE. On September 18, 1851, after several unsuccessful military campaigns by other leaders in the field against the large numbers of recalcitrant Navajos, Colonel Edwin Vose Sumner selected a site for a base of operations in Canyon Bonita, the first military outpost in Arizona, in Apache County close to the New Mexico line. Colonel Sumner, in the spring of 1852, again failed to engage the Navajos. He returned to Canyon Bonita and continued the task of building on the perimeter of a parade ground a number of structures including barracks, officers' quarters, and a stable, most of them of pine-log construction with dirt roofs but a few of adobe. The post was designated Fort Defiance. Several spirited skirmishes were fought in the vicinity during the 1850s. On April 30, 1860, Fort Defiance was unsuccessfully attacked by as many as a thousand Navajos. Because of the incidence of Civil War conflict in the West and Southwest, the post was abandoned on April 25, 1861. Fort Defiance had been garrisoned at different times during the 1851–61 period by elements of the 1st and 2nd Dragoons, the 2nd Artillery, and the 3rd, 5th and 8th Infantry. The fort, however, was reactivated for a short period in 1863, when Colonel Kit Carson was assigned to continue subduing the Navajos. He established Fort Canby, 28 miles to the southwest, as a base of operations and supply camp. In 1868 the fort became the site of the Navajo Agency. The grounds are today occupied by a large Navajo school and a hospital, with the town bearing the same name as the fort growing up around it. The only remains of the old fort are a three-story stone structure.

FORT DEFIANCE. Apparently a short-lived American stockaded affair, it was located four miles below Fort Yuma, which was located on the Colorado River opposite the mouth of the Gila River. According to John R. Bartlett in his *Personal Narrative*: "In 1849 a party of Americans dispossessed the Yuma Indians of the crude boat they used for a ferry boat; and drove them away and established a ferry across the Colorado river. They then built a fort which in contempt for the Indians they called 'Fort Defiance.'"

CAMP DEVIN. CAMP HUALPAI.

CAMP DON LUIS. A pre–World War I post to guard the Mexican border, it was located in Cochise County.

CAMP DOUGLAS. CAMP HARRY J. JONES.

CAMP EL DORADO. Intended to guard a mining enterprise, Camp El Dorado was established on January 15, 1867, on the west bank of the Colorado River near the entrance to El Dorado Canyon, near Mount Davis, and south of Callville in Mohave County. There are no maps pinpointing its location. Company D, 9th Infantry, garrisoned the temporary post until the cessation of mining operations at El Dorado. The military abandoned the post on August 24, 1867.

CAMP EL REVENTON. El Reventon, or Revanton, was a very well known ranch 35 miles south of Tucson and seven miles northeast of Tubac in Santa Cruz County. The old ranch, according to *Arizona Place Names*, was occupied in 1859 by Elias Brevoort, who had come to Arizona to be the sutler at the new Fort Buchanan. It was occupied as a military camp in July and August 1862 and again on April 14, 1864. The garrison was moved to Tubac on June 22, 1864. The military occupations, no doubt, were in connection with Civil War conflict in the area.

CAMP FLORILLA. A remote military outpost in 1864, it was reportedly established near Kin-li-chee in Apache County, not far from Fort Canby.

CAMP ON THE GILA RIVER. No precise location has been ascribed to this camp. It was established in the area then known as Arizona Territory on June 15, 1882, by Lieutenant Colonel W. Harvey Brown with Companies D, E, and G, 1st Infantry. The camp's last post return was dated November 21, 1882.

CAMP GLOBE. A pre–World War I post to patrol the Mexican border, it was established in the town of Globe, Gila County.

CAMP GLOBE. A World War I encampment at Globe, Gila County, it was occupied by units of the U.S. 17th Cavalry.

CAMP GOODWIN. FORT GOODWIN.

FORT GOODWIN (*Camp Goodwin*). The original Camp Goodwin, situated on the Gila River about 32 miles east of its later position, was established on June 11, 1864, as a temporary post until a permanent site was selected by Major Nelson H. Davis, assistant inspector general. A week later, the decision having been made, the camp was relocated south of the river in the Tularosa Valley, about seven miles west of today's town of Fort Thomas. It was established by Colonel Edwin A. Rigg with elements of the 1st Infantry, California Volunteers, in response to an order by General James H. Carleton. The post was primarily intended to be used in the campaign to subjugate the Apaches and offer protection for the area's settlements and travel routes. Named in honor of John N. Goodwin, Arizona's first territorial governor, the post was redesignated a camp instead of a fort. It took almost seven years to determine that the site was quite unhealthful, and the post was abandoned on March 14, 1871. Subsequent to its first garrison of California Volunteers, the other units posted at the camp included elements of the 14th, 21st and 32nd Infantry Regiments, and the 1st and 3rd Cavalry. Camp Goodwin then served for a period of time as a subagency for the San Carlos Apache Reservation. The military reservation was ultimately transferred to the Department of the Interior on July 22, 1884, for disposition.

CAMP GRANITE REEF DAM. A pre–World War I Mexican border post, it was located near Whipple Barracks.

FORT GRANT NO. 1 (*Camp San Pedro River; Fort Aravaipa; Fort Breckinridge; Camp Stanford*). The second military post in the territory comprising the Gadsden Purchase, it was established on May 8, 1860, about 56 miles north of Tucson. Various contradictory references for its establishment range from 1856 to 1860, although it was highly unlikely it could have been earlier than July 1859. Situated on the north side of Aravaipa Creek at its junction with the San Pedro River in Pinal County, it was for a brief time called Camp San Pedro River. The post was designed to restrain the Apache Indians and safeguard the emigrant wagon-train route traversing southern Arizona. It was established by Captain Richard S. Ewell with troops of the 1st Dragoons from Fort Buchanan. The camp was renamed Fort Aravaipa, then Fort Breckinridge on August 6, 1860, in honor of Vice President John C. Breckinridge. With the incidence of the Civil War's spreading theaters of conflict, the garrison was withdrawn, and the post was destroyed by fire on July 10, 1861, because of the arrival in Arizona territory of a Confederate force from Texas. The camp was reoccupied on May 18, 1862, by Lieutenant Colonel Joseph R.

West with units of the 1st California Volunteer Infantry. A week later, on May 24, the name of the post was changed to Fort Stanford for Governor Leland Stanford of California. The garrison was again withdrawn on June 29, 1862, and not permanently reoccupied until after war's end. In October 1865 a new camp was established on the San Pedro near Fort Breckinridge's site by Colonel Thomas F. Wright with elements of the 2nd California Infantry. On November 1 it was redesignated Camp Grant to honor General Ulysses S. Grant (the camp was never officially designated a fort, though it was so popularized by historians). Sometime during the following summer, the post was partially destroyed by river flooding and was rebuilt on the site of former Fort Breckinridge. The camp was abandoned on March 31, 1873, because of the prevalence of malaria among the troops. The military reservation was turned over to the Department of the Interior on July 22, 1884, for disposition.

FORT GRANT NO. 2 (*New Fort Grant*). In advance of the expected abandonment of the first Fort Grant on the San Pedro River, New Fort Grant was established on December 19, 1872, at the head of Grant Creek Valley about two miles from the western base of 10,713-foot-high Mount Graham and near today's town of Fort Grant in Graham County. The site, located on a mesa, had been selected by Major William B. Royall of the 5th Cavalry, who also built the post, which was intended to control the recalcitrant Apaches and to safeguard the area's settlers. Named Camp Grant in honor of General Ulysses S. Grant when it was established, the post was designated a fort on April 5, 1879. The garrison of infantry and cavalry troops was withdrawn in 1898 to serve in the Spanish-American War. After the war, however, the post was not reoccupied by a regular garrison. After it was abandoned on October 4, 1905, the installation was put in a caretaking status. The structures and the site were ceded to the state of Arizona in 1902 and are now occupied by a state industrial school for boys.

CAMP GRASSY CAMP. Established sometime in 1862, it was located three miles east of Grinnell's Station, six miles from Agua Caliente, on the Gila River, Yuma County.

CAMP GRIERSON. Very little is known about this post established in 1889 in the area then called Arizona Territory. National Archives records show that the post was garrisoned by elements of the 4th and 10th Cavalry and the 24th Infantry.

CAMP HARRY J. JONES (*Camp Douglas*). A military post, at one time garrisoned by as many as 15,000 troops, Camp Douglas was established in the environs of the city of Douglas, Cochise County, in 1910, beginning the long period of border strife with Mexico. The post was renamed Camp Harry J. Jones shortly after the soldier was killed on November 1, 1915, by a stray bullet. One of the units that operated in Arizona during 1917–19 around Douglas, Naco, Globe, and Nogales was the 17th Cavalry, which was constituted on July 1, 1916, at Fort Bliss, Texas, and formed from elements of the 1st, 6th, 8th, and 14th U.S. Cavalry Regiments.

The establishment of Camp Harry J. Jones was part of a larger military plan. A synoptic view of America's military involvement along its southern border is excerpted from the June 12, 1919, issue of the *Tucson Citizen*:

It's [a fence] 1,200 miles long, and while its posts are of wood and other building materials, its rails will be American soldiers. . . . It's a double row of cavalry patrol stations, barracks buildings and miscellaneous structures, stretching from Brownsville, Texas, on the Gulf of Mexico, to Arivaca, Arizona, on the edge of the great desert. At each of the fifty outpost stations one troop of cavalry—about 100 men—will be on guard all the time, patrolling the border between stations. Some distance back from these patrol stations will be another series of twelve posts which will constitute a sort of "second line of defense" against the Mexicans. These twelve posts will be larger, and each of them will serve as a base for four or five of the patrol stations on the boundary. The complete system will house 10,000 soldiers. . . .

The border has been split up into 12 patrol districts. . . . One of the main posts will be erected in each of these districts, following the line of the Southern Pacific railroad. Each post will be the base for four to six of the patrol stations. One troop of cavalry will be constantly on guard at the latter, which are located from 60 to 150 miles from the main posts, and each troop will be relieved and returned to its base once a month. . . . The desert wastes between Nogales and Yuma, Arizona . . . will be the only part of the border left unguarded by this line of defenses.

At the time the foregoing was published, there were about 10,000 soldiers on the border, all cavalry, with the exception of the 25th Infantry at Camp Stephen D. Little at Nogales.

Camp Harry J. Jones was abandoned in January 1933, and its troops distributed to other posts.

CAMP HENTIG (*Camp Ash Creek*). This camp was little more than a good level site with water and wood available which happened to be about halfway between San Carlos and Fort Apache on Ash Creek Flat. It was used as an overnight camping stop on the trip between the two points and was never an officially established military post. The only structures on the site were a corral and a shed. It was called Camp Ash Creek until a Lieutenant Hentig was killed at Cibecue in 1881. Then it was renamed Camp Hentig by the men of the 6th Cavalry stationed at Fort Apache.

CAMP HOLBROOK. This post was established in July 1882 by 2nd Lieutenant Louis P. Brant, with Company K of the 1st Infantry and Troop H of the 3rd Cavalry, during an Indian outbreak. The camp was situated at Holbrook in Navajo County.

CAMP HORN. A World War II post, Camp Horn was the training camp for the 81st Infantry Division in 1943. It was situated along the right of way of the Southern Pacific Railroad west of Gila Bend.

CAMP HUACHUCA. FORT HUACHUCA.

FORT HUACHUCA (*Camp Huachuca*). The fort is a product of the Indian wars of the 1870s and 1880s. In February 1877 Colonel August V. Kautz, commander of the Department of Arizona, ordered that a camp should be established in the Huachuca Mountains to offer protection to settlers and travel routes in southeastern Arizona while simultaneously blocking the traditional Apache escape routes through the San Pedro and Santa Cruz valleys to sanctuaries in Mexico. A temporary camp was established at the post's present location at the base of the mountains on March 3, 1877, by Captain Samuel Marmaduke Whitside with two companies of the 6th Cavalry. The site had been selected because it contained fresh running water and an abundance of trees, and had excellent observation in three directions and protective high ground essential for security against Apache tactical methods. The post became permanent on January 21, 1878, and was designated a fort in 1882.

In 1886 General Nelson A. Miles designated Fort Huachuca as his advance headquarters and forward supply base for the campaign against Geronimo. The Indian chief's surrender in August 1886 practically ended the Apache danger in southern Arizona. The Army closed more than 50 camps and forts in the territory, but Fort Huachuca was retained because of continuing border troubles involving renegade Indians, Mexican bandits, and American outlaws and freebooters. In 1913 the 10th Cavalry "Buffalo Soldiers" arrived, and they remained almost 20 years. The 10th Cavalry joined General John Pershing in the 1916 expedition into Mexico, and during World War I it was assigned the mission of guarding the United States–Mexico border.

By 1933 the 25th Infantry had replaced the 10th Cavalry as the main combat unit for the fort. The 25th in turn was absorbed by the 93rd Infantry Division during World War II. When the 93rd departed for the Pacific in 1943, the 92nd Infantry Division arrived at the fort for training and subsequent assignment to the European Theater. During the war years, the troop strength reached 30,000 men at the fort. At war's end the fort was declared surplus and transferred to the state of Arizona. It was reactivated during the Korean War by the Army Corps of Engineers. A new era began in 1954, when control passed to the chief signal officer, who found the area and climate ideal for testing electronic and communications equipment. The importance of the fort in the national defense picture grew steadily from that moment. In 1967 Fort Huachuca became the headquarters of the Army Strategic Communications Command (which became the Army Communications Command in 1973). Then, in 1971, the post became the home of the Army Intelligence Center and School. The arrival of the Army Communications Command and the Intelligence School made Fort Huachuca the major military installation in Arizona, and one of the most prominent in the Southwest. The original Fort Huachuca cantonment was declared a National Historic Landmark in March 1977 during a four-day centennial celebration. A rustic wooden sign and reconstructed artillery piece sit on the northeastern corner of Brown Parade Field, the center of post life during the days of horse soldiers. When Captain Samuel M. Whitside led his column of Company B, 6th Cavalry, into southern Arizona, he did not have the slightest prescience that the temporary post he was ordered to establish in the foothills of the Huachuca Mountains would survive to play a major role in the high drama of the western United States. The history of the U.S. Army in the Southwest is displayed at the Fort Huachuca Historical Museum, housing one of the most representative collections in the state.

CAMP HUALPAI (*Camp Devin; Camp Toll Gate*). Established on May 9, 1869, Camp Devin was situated on a mesa above Walnut (Mohave) Creek, one and a half miles southeast of Aztec Pass and about 40 miles northwest of Prescott, in Yavapai County. Located on the toll road between Prescott and Hardyville, the post was es-

tablished by Major William R. Price of the 8th Cavalry. Two weeks later the post was renamed Camp Toll Gate, then Camp Hualpai on August 1, 1870. Abandoned on July 31, 1873, the reservation was transferred to the Department of the Interior for disposition.

CAMP HYDER. Located in the World War II Desert Training maneuver area, Camp Hyder was close to the Maricopa-Yuma County line and several miles northeast from Aztec. The 77th Infantry Division was at Camp Hyder from April through September 1943. It was literally a city of tents extending two miles across the dusty desert. Each company had a double row of pyramidal tents, and in each tent were six cots, six straw ticks, 12 barracks bags, and several lizards and scorpions. Division headquarters was a semicircular row of pyramidal tents. But the camp eventually did obtain one structure when the officers of the 306th Infantry built an adobe club. Later the 305th Infantry also went into the mud-brick business and erected a larger club. All units had an equal share of 100°-plus heat, desert sand, cacti, snakes, and ground squirrels. Situated in the immediate environs of the town of Hyder, a water-stop in the heart of the Arizona desert on the Southern Pacific Railroad, the camp's troops learned to subsist on less of everything.

CAMP ILGES. A temporary campsite on the Verde River near Camp Lincoln (later Camp Verde), short-lived Camp Ilges was established by Captain and Brevet Major William H. Mills with detachments of Companies A and B of the 32nd Infantry, aggregating 111 men in late May or early June 1867. It was undoubtedly named for Colonel Guido Ilges, who served with distinction during the early Arizona Indian campaigns. The camp had been established while he was en route to Camp Reno for the purpose of scouting duty against the Apaches. The site was abandoned on June 13, 1867.

CAMP INFANTRY. CAMP PICKET POST.

CAMP JOHN A. RUCKER (*Camp Supply; Camp Powers*). This supply depot was established on April 29, 1878, and named Camp Supply by the troops in pursuit of marauding Chiricahua Apaches near the Mexican border. It was first located on a creek at the old San Bernardino Ranch in Cochise County. Shortly thereafter the post's name was changed to Camp Powers (a post office, called Powers, apparently named for a local rancher, was established here on March 3, 1891; its name was changed to

Rucker on June 20, 1891). When the camp was moved some six miles to a site on the upper end of the White River, the post was renamed, in April 1879, for Lieutenant John A. Rucker, who drowned on July 11, 1878, in an attempt to rescue another officer trapped by a flash flood. During 1879–80 the post was commanded by 1st Lieutenant J. H. Hurst, 1st Infantry, with Company D, 12th Infantry. The site was abandoned on November 4, 1880, and the troops removed to Fort Apache.

CAMP JOHNSON. This camp was established on October 1, 1862, by Captain William McCleave, commanding Company A, 1st Cavalry, California Volunteers, aggregating 101 men. They had moved from the east (Texas) side to the west (Arizona) side of the Rio Grande.

CAMP JONES. CAMP HARRY J. JONES.

CAMP LA PAZ. Established as a temporary camp and supply depot on April 20, 1874, the post was situated within the Colorado Indian Reservation at the old deserted Mexican town of La Paz on the left bank of the Colorado River. Companies F and G, 4th California Infantry, occupied several of the town's adobe buildings. The camp was possibly abandoned on May 23, 1875 (another reference reports the date as September 1875). Ten years earlier the town had been briefly occupied by a Civil War U.S. Army garrison. La Paz had its beginnings as a boom town when gold nuggets were found above ground on January 12, 1862. Hungry prospectors swarmed up the river and the town became an important steamer landing. But by 1870 the field was empty of pickings, avid prospectors moved on, and La Paz's 270 city blocks of adobe structures became a ghost town. In 1971 the National Park Service and the Indian council of the Mohave and Chemehuevis tribes jointly engaged in an archeological exploration on the 320-acre site, which was placed on the National Register of Historic Places.

CAMP LAGUNA. This post, a part of the California-Arizona Maneuver Area, activated during World War II, was a training ground for the 80th Division from December 1943 to February 1944. It is a part of today's Yuma Army Proving Ground located between U.S. 95 and the Colorado River.

LEE'S FORT. This year-round outdoor recreation center is located at Lee's Ferry in north central Arizona, on the left bank of the Colorado River. A scenic and history-saturated playground in the shadow of the Vermillion Cliffs, at the northern end of the Marble Canyon National Monument, this development is operated by the National Park Service. The name of the center, however, is no longer appropriate, since the ferry that operated here from about 1871 until 1928 disappeared long ago. Lee's Fort or Fort Lee would be more apt, considering that some of the stone buildings that constituted a Mormon frontier fort are still intact and have been restored by the National Park Service. Jacob Hamblin, a Mormon missionary, explorer, colonizer, and Indian agent, encountered the crossing in 1860 while seeking a way to transport Mormon followers across the river to future settlements along the Little Colorado. He recommended to the Church that the crossing be developed as a permanent ferry site, with a fort to protect it from the Indians.

Hamblin operated a crude ferry for about a year or so before Brigham Young, president of the Mormon Church, sent to the site John Doyle Lee, one of the most controversial figures in Southwestern history. He was then a fugitive from justice for his alleged role in the Mountain Meadows massacre of 1857, when an emigrant train from Arkansas and Missouri was ambushed by a party of white fanatics dressed as Indians or accompanied by Indians. About 120 men and women were killed and their children captured. Suspected as the ringleader, Lee was exiled by the Church and ordered to the ferry site, where he developed a ranch. Lee ran the ferry and the fort for only two years when a United States marshal tracked him down. He was tried twice, convicted in 1877, and then executed by a firing squad on the spot where the massacre had taken place. One of Lee's widows operated the ferry for several years until the Church took it over. It was sold in 1909 to a cattle company, and in 1916 it was sold to Coconino County.

CAMP LEWIS. Most probably established in 1865 on Fossil Creek in Yavapai County, the camp was situated near the head of the Verde River near its juncture with the Salt River and on the trail that led from Verde Valley to Tonto Basin. The post was named for Colonel Charles H. Lewis of the 7th Infantry, California Volunteers, who headed several expeditions against the Apaches in 1865 and 1866. The dates of actual operation of the camp are indefinite, but the camp is shown on several maps drawn between 1866 and 1870. It was most probably abandoned in 1870.

CAMP LINCOLN. FORT VERDE.

CAMP LINCOLN. Established in early 1864 near La Paz in Yuma County, Camp Lincoln was a subpost of Fort Yuma, 140 miles to the south. On August 15 in the same year, an official directive ordered Captain Sherman's Company F, 4th California Infantry, to abandon camp and return to its base.

CAMP LOEHIEL. A Mexican border post, probably pre–World War I, located just east of Nogales in Santa Cruz County.

CAMP LOWELL. FORT LOWELL.

CAMP LOWELL. A Mexican border post in Cochise County.

FORT LOWELL (*Post of Tucson; Camp Lowell*). Established as the Post of Tucson on May 20, 1862, by Lieutenant Colonel Joseph R. West, 1st California Infantry, this military post was originally located in the city of Tucson, where it occupied several successive sites. It was first active on a site in what is today's downtown district. First established as a supply depot for southern Arizona, the post had its responsibilities expanded to become a base of operations against hostile Apaches and a supplier of military escorts. It became a permanent post on August 29, 1866. On March 19, 1873, the post was moved seven miles to the southeast to a new site south of Rillito Creek, selected by Lieutenant Colonel Eugene A. Carr of the 4th Cavalry. It became Camp Lowell on August 29, 1866, and then on April 5, 1879, it was designated Fort Lowell, named for Brigadier General Charles R. Lowell, who was mortally wounded on October 20, 1864, at Cedar Creek, Virginia. Fort Lowell was abandoned on April 10, 1891. Impressive ruins, some reconstructed, commemorate the fort's site. The first step in the re-creation of the historical military base was the restoration of the commanding officer's quarters. The base is now owned and maintained by the Arizona Historical Society.

FORT MCCLEAVE. A detachment of troops from Fort Goodwin set out on a scouting mission through the Arizona territory's southeast region sometime between July 6 and 24, 1864. They proceeded down the Rio Bonito to the San Carlos, followed that stream for about four miles, and made camp for two or three days here, about 24 miles south of Fort Goodwin. The campsite was named Camp McCleave to honor Major McCleave, 1st Cavalry, California Volunteers, who had scored an impressive victory against Indians

at this place in 1863. The site was occupied by at least eight ancient cliff dwellings built of rock in an excellent state of preservation.

FORT MCDONALD. During an Indian scare in 1882, the people of Payson and Marysville in Gila County "forted up" to the east of Payson on a flat-topped sandstone butte about 100 feet high. The fort was named after William McDonald, for whom McDonald Mountain is named. The remains of the old fort were still very much in evidence as late as the 1930s.

CAMP MCDOWELL. FORT MCDOWELL.

FORT MCDOWELL (*Camp Verde; Camp McDowell*). Established on September 7, 1865, this post was situated on the west bank of the Rio Verde, about seven miles above its confluence with the Salt River and 45 miles southwest of Camp Reno. Its primary purposes were to restrain the Yavapai Indians and a number of Apache bands and to safeguard the trans-Arizona route. It was established by Lieutenant Colonel Clarence E. Bennett, 1st Cavalry, California Volunteers, with five companies of troops. Originally called Camp Verde for the river, it was soon renamed Camp McDowell to honor Major General Irvin McDowell.

The original size of the post reservation measured, from the center of the parade ground (525 by 435 feet), three miles north and south and two miles east and west. All the buildings, built along the sides of the parade ground, were of adobe, with earthen floors, mud roofs, and open fireplaces. On April 5, 1879, the camp was designated a fort. On June 18, 1890, a directive ordered its abandonment and the last of the garrison's troops, elements of the 4th Cavalry and the 9th Infantry, evacuated on January 17, 1891. Transferred to the Interior Department on October 1, 1890, the post became an agency for the Yavapai and Pima Indians. The last acreage in the military reservation was relinquished to the Interior Department on March 2, 1891, for an Indian school.

CAMP MCKEE. FORT MASON.

CAMP MCPHERSON. CAMP DATE CREEK.

CAMP MANSFIELD. Located about seven miles south of Fort Defiance in Apache County, the temporary camp was named for Brigadier General Joseph King Fenno Mansfield, who was mortally wounded on September 17, 1862, at Antietam.

MARICOPA WELLS POST. References are very sparse regarding this post's length of operations. From July 10 to 21, 1865, an expedition was made from Fort Bowie to Maricopa Wells in the vicinity of Maricopa, Pinal County. One reference believes the post's life lasted from 1865 to 1867, very possibly on an intermittent basis.

FORT MASON (*Post at Calabasas; Camp McKee*). Established on August 21, 1865, this post was located near Calabasas on the Santa Cruz River, Santa Cruz County, about 13 miles south of the old presidio town of Tubac. Replacing the Army's post at Tubac, the camp was important because it was situated on the main travel route to points in Sonora, Mexico. The camp, first called Post at Calabasas, then Camp McKee, was established by Colonel Charles W. Lewis, 7th California Infantry, on a site selected by Brigadier General John S. Mason, commander of the District of Arizona. On September 6, 1866, the camp was renamed Fort Mason, although it was never officially designated a fort. Less than a month later, on October 1, the post was abandoned because of the high incidence of disease among the troops, who were then moved to newly established Camp Cameron on a site 15 miles northeast of Tubac.

CAMP MIAMI. A Mexican border post located in Gila County.

FORT MILLIGAN. Located in Round Valley, a mile west of Eagar in Apache County, this was apparently a settlers' stockaded fort that served as a protection against hostile Indians. The probable date was sometime during the 1860s.

MISSION CAMP. A Butterfield Stage line station, garrisoned for a time in 1862 by Army troops, it was located 35 miles east of Yuma, in the vicinity of today's Welton, Yuma County.

CAMP MOGOLLON. Fort Apache.

CAMP MOHAVE. Fort Mohave.

FORT MOHAVE (*Camp Colorado; Camp Mohave*). Established on April 19, 1859, this post was situated on the east bank of the Colorado River at Beal's Crossing in Mohave County, near the head of the Mojave Valley opposite today's town of Needles, California. The camp's original purpose was to control the Mohave and Paiute Indians and to safeguard the emigrant travel route to California. Major William Hoffman, 6th Infantry, both selected the site and established the post. At first called Camp Colorado by the major, the post was named Fort Mohave on April 28, 1859, by Captain Lewis A. Armistead, 6th Infantry, the camp's commanding officer, who was responsible for erecting permanent quarters for the garrison. In accordance with a directive from Brigadier General Edwin Vose Sumner, the post was abandoned on May 31, 1861, with the garrison transferred to Los Angeles because of secessionist activities in southern California following the outbreak of the Civil War. The camp on the Colorado River was reoccupied on May 19, 1863, by two companies of the 4th California Infantry in compliance with an order by Brigadier General George Wright. Following the Civil War the post was designated Camp Mohave, but on April 5, 1879, it again took the name of Fort Mohave. Finally abandoned in 1890 in accordance with an order issued on May 23, 1890, the military reservation was transferred to the Interior Department on September 29, 1890, with the post's structures to be used for an Indian school. The school was closed by the Indian Service in 1935 and the buildings were demolished in 1942.

CAMP MOORE. Fort Buchanan.

FORT MORONI (*Fort Rickerson; Fort Valley*). During construction of the Atlantic and Pacific Railroad (later the Santa Fe), which arrived at Flagstaff in 1882, Fort Moroni was established seven miles northwest of the town. The log fort, 60 feet long, was used as the headquarters for the Moroni Cattle Company, managed by John W. Young, son of Brigham Young, leader of the Church of Jesus Christ of Latter-Day Saints and perhaps the greatest molder of Mormonism. Fort Moroni was named after the Mormon angel. The structure was also known as Fort Valley and Fort Rickerson, named for Charles Rickerson, treasurer of the Arizona Cattle Company.

CAMP NACO. This post was a Mexican border patrol station in Naco, Cochise County, in the Douglas district, and was active from 1911 to 1915.

NEW FORT GRANT. Fort Grant No. 2.

NEW POST AT BABOCOMARI. Camp Wallen.

NEW POST ON THE GILA. Fort Thomas.

NEW POST ON THE UPPER SAN PEDRO. Camp Wallen.

NEWELL CANTONMENT. Almost nothing is known about this post. A noted Arizona military historian and cartographer believes that Newell Cantonment, or Camp Newell, might also have been known as Camp Naco. If so, it was a temporary camp at Naco, Cochise County, from about 1910 to 1915.

CAMP NEAR NOGALES. This temporary camp was ordered by General Nelson A. Miles as a result of a shooting incident when Mexican troops crossed the border from Nogales, Sonora, and attacked civilian authorities in Nogales, Santa Cruz County, sometime during April 1887. The post was established by Captain J. M. Lee and Company D of the 9th Infantry. Archival sources suggest 1887 to 1911 as the dates for the camp, but there is a large gap in the post returns between September 1887 and 1911.

CAMP ON OAK CREEK. A temporary outpost of Fort Verde, this camp was established in June 1881 by Company K of the 12th Infantry and Companies H and L of the 6th Cavalry, and was abandoned the following month. Oak Creek Canyon, a scenic delight for tourists, is just south of Flagstaff in Coconino County.

CAMP O'CONNELL. A short-lived post, Camp O'Connell was established by 1st Lieutenant G. W. Chilson with two companies of the 32nd Infantry sometime in 1868 while en route to Camp Reno from Fort Goodwin. The camp was situated in the Tonto Valley, Gila County.

OJO DE LES LEMILAS POST. Very little is known about this apparently short-lived post except that it was established in about the year 1860 and was located some 100 miles northwest of Fort Defiance, probably in Navajo County.

CAMP ORD. FORT APACHE.

CAMP OVERTON. This post, established in 1903, was probably named for 1st Lieutenant Overton of the 6th Cavalry, who served tours of duty at Fort Grant and Fort Apache in 1881.

CAMP PAPAGO. A World War II prisoner of war camp, it was established in Papago Park about eight miles northeast of Phoenix, Maricopa County. It was activated September 16, 1943, as a camp for German naval personnel. The camp was closed in April 1946. It had had pre–World War II use as a National Guard cantonment and a Civilian Conservation Corps camp.

CAMP AT PATAGONIA. Apparently a short-lived post, it was located in or near Patagonia, Santa Cruz County, directly west of Fort Huachuca.

CAMP PEACH SPRINGS. Established in July 1894 by Company B, 11th Infantry, as an outpost of Fort Whipple, it was located at Peach Springs, Mohave County, in the extreme southern section of today's Hualapai Indian Reservation. The camp was abandoned the following month.

CAMP PICKET POST (*Camp Infantry; Camp Pinal*). Camp Infantry was established by General George Stoneman on November 28, 1870, at the Pinal Ranch in Mason Valley, near the headwaters of Mineral and Pinto creeks, six miles west of today's town of Miami and some 30 miles northeast of Florence in Pinal County. The camp, intended to protect miners in the area, was garrisoned by Companies A, E, G, and I of the 21st Infantry in the spring of 1871. Its name was changed to Camp Pinal on May 20, 1871. Less than two months later, on July 15, the campsite was abandoned and the post's troops were moved by General Stoneman a few miles west to Queen Creek, where, below Picket Post Butte, he laid out a new camp called Camp Picket Post. Compelled to contrive more effective measures toward restraining the marauding Apaches, General Stoneman began construction of a road leading from Camp Picket Post, near present-day Superior, into the Pinal Mountains. The road, permitting greater accessibility to Apache retreats, was known as "Stoneman's Grade." The camp was abandoned on July 24, 1871. By the year 1877 the site of the camp had grown into the mining village of Pinal, with a population of 2,500, and the nearby Silver King Mine was at its peak of production. Though the miners there were supposedly prospering, Martha Summerhayes, in *Vanished Arizona* (1873), wrote: "That blighted and desolate place called Picket Post. Forsaken by God and Man, it might have been an entrance to Hades."

CAMP PINAL. CAMP PICKET POST.

CAMP POMEROY. In November 1863 General James H. Carleton established a temporary camp in Coconino County. Named for Lieutenant Pomeroy, the camp consisted of a small guard, provisions, and a mule team. The mules were soon run off by marauding Indians. A new camp, however, was established on December 21, 1863, in the Chino Valley at Del Rio Springs and named for John A. Clark, the surveyor-general. Camp Clark eventually became Whipple Barracks.

CAMP POWERS. CAMP JOHN A. RUCKER.

PRESCOTT BARRACKS. WHIPPLE BARRACKS.

CAMP PRICE. Established in 1881, this temporary camp was named for Lieutenant Colonel Sterling Price, who earned plaudits for his service in the Mexican and Civil wars. The post was located in Cochise County just east of Camp John A. Rucker and situated in Texas Canyon at the southern end of the Chiricahua Mountains. Reports on the camp's garrison complements are contradictory. According to the National Archives listing of post returns, the camp was garrisoned from April to October 1882 by Captain Hugh G. Brown with Company E, 12th Infantry; Company A, 6th Cavalry; and Company C, Indian Scouts. Another reference, however, reports that during the same period Companies F and I of the 1st Infantry and Companies A, D, and I of the 6th Cavalry were posted there. During 1882–83 Captain C. G. Gordon, 6th Cavalry, was in command with one company, apparently making up the camp's last garrison. There was a military telegraph office in operation at the camp.

QUÍBURI PRESIDIO. Located in Cochise County, near the junction of the San Pedro and Babocomari rivers, Quíburi was an ancient Indian community founded in the mists of time before written history. When the Spaniards arrived there in the 1600s they influenced the local Sobaipuri Indians to defend themselves against the Apaches. Finally, in 1772, the Spaniards posted a garrison at the site, and in 1775 they built an adobe-walled fortress on the west side of the San Pedro. Evidences remain today of its thick walls, about 300 feet long, made of adobe brick supported by stone foundations. The structure had angular bastions in at least one of its corner angles. The soldiers' quarters lined the interior walls. The inevitable chapel stood against the south wall. The presidio stayed for about five years. But then, proving ineffective against the fierce Apaches, the presidio was moved back again to Las Nutrias in Sonora, not far from Terrenate, where it had been established originally. By 1789 the Spanish had abandoned the Quíburi site to the Apaches.

CAMP RAWLINS. In February 1870 the Army established a temporary camp in Williamson Valley, 17 miles southeast of Camp Hualpai and about 27 miles northwest of Prescott in Yavapai County. Named for General John A. Rawlins of Civil War note, it was a subpost of Whipple Barracks. Post returns show that from April 23 to August 12, 1870, it was garrisoned by Companies C and G of the 3rd Cavalry.

CAMP RAY. A Mexican border post, it was located in Pinal County.

CAMP RENO. An outpost of Fort McDowell, Camp Reno was established in October 1867 on Tonto Creek in the Tonto Valley near Reno Mountain. Named for General Marcus A. Reno, the post was garrisoned until February 1870 by three different infantry units: 1867–69, Companies D and F, 14th Infantry; 1869–70, Company A, 21st Infantry; and 1867–69, Companies A and B, 32nd Infantry. The camp, used as a staging area for expeditions against the Apaches, was commanded by General A. J. Alexander. Camp Reno was abandoned on March 8, 1870.

FORT RICKERSON. FORT MORONI.

CAMP RIGG. In 1864 the Army established a temporary camp on the north bank of the Gila River, about 40 miles east of Fort Goodwin in Graham County, and named it for Colonel Edwin A. Rigg, 1st California Infantry. An 1870 map shows Camp Rigg situated north of the Gila in Aztec Valley, apparently evidence that the post was still in existence then.

CAMP RIO GILA. Very little is known about this temporary camp. It was established sometime in 1867 and was located in or near Sacaton, Pinal County, on today's Gila River Indian Reservation.

CAMP RIO SAN FRANCISCO. An outpost of Fort Whipple, this temporary camp was established sometime in 1863 at an undetermined location.

CAMP RIO SAN PEDRO. A temporary camp, it was established near Redington in the extreme northeast corner of Pima County in 1859.

CAMP AT ROBINSON'S RANCH. On March 24, 1864, Captain G. T. Witham of the 1st Cavalry, California Volunteers, proceeded with Company M from ineffectual Fort Lowell and made camp on the Rillito River near the town of Rillito in Pima County, at or near Robinson's Ranch. The post was abandoned on September 15, 1864.

FORT ROCK. A defense against Indians built by settlers in 1864, it was located about 60 miles northwest of Prescott in Yavapai County.

FORT ROCK SPRING. Sometime in 1866 Captain John C. Cremony with Company B of the 2nd California Cavalry established a temporary camp while reportedly patrolling the Fort Mohave Road between Camp Cady on the Mohave River and Rock Spring. The post, if it ever existed, was located north of Truxton, seven miles northwest of Valentine in Mohave County. At least one reference says it was "probably never built."

ROCKY CANON CAMP. Established sometime in 1879, it was located somewhere in Arizona territory. One post return in a National Archives listing is dated as early as July 1857, reporting that Captain Alex B. MacGowan was there with Company D, 12th Infantry. A September 1879 post return, from the same source, shows that Company F of the 6th Cavalry was stationed at Rocky Canon.

CAMP ROOSEVELT DAM. A Mexican border post, it was located in Gila County.

CAMP RUCKER. Camp John A. Rucker.

PRESIDIO OF SAN AUGUSTÍN DE TUCSON. The establishment of Tucson as an effective Spanish settlement took place in 1776 when the garrison formerly posted at the Presidio of Tubac was ordered to take quarters here. Franciscan friar Francisco Tomás Garcés is generally credited with its founding on the west bank of the Santa Cruz River. An adobe-walled presidio, at first only minimally fortified, was soon begun on the site, accompanied by a church and an industrial arts school for the area's Papagos and Pimas. The name Tucson is derived from *Chuk Shon,* a Papago Indian term meaning "black base," no doubt referring to Signal Mountain, which is much darker at the base than at the summit. Tucson was most probably continuously occupied despite a century-long series of intermittent raids and depredations by the Apaches. Lieutenant Colonel Philip St. George Cooke, commanding the Mormon Battalion, took temporary possession of the presidio in 1846. Subsequent to the Gadsden Purchase (1853), Mexican troops still garrisoned the presidio until March 10, 1856. It was then briefly garrisoned by four companies of the 1st U.S. Dragoons.

CAMP SAN BERNARDINO RANCH. A Mexican border patrol post established in 1911 by ten cavalrymen from Douglas, it was located at John Slaughter's San Bernardino Ranch in Cochise County.

CAMP SAN BERNARDINO SPRINGS. A temporary encampment, it was located very close to the Mexican border, 18 miles east of Douglas, Cochise County, and was active sometime in 1883.

CAMP SAN CARLOS. Situated on the north side of the San Carlos River about a mile from its junction with the Gila, in Gila County, Camp San Carlos was officially established in the San Carlos Indian Reservation on May 29, 1873, by I Troop, 5th Cavalry, although the site had been intermittently occupied beginning in June 1872. The purpose of the camp was to confine the region's Indians to their reservations. From October 10, 1894, until September 30, 1898, it was a subpost of Fort Grant. From its inception until its closing in July 1900, Camp San Carlos was garrisoned at different times by as many as 16 infantry, cavalry, and Indian Scouts units. The last remaining San Carlos Indian Agency buildings were dynamited on February 16, 1930.

PRESIDIO OF SAN PEDRO. Located near the site of Camp Wallen and west of Fort Huachuca, this was a temporary camp established probably in 1878 on the west side of the San Pedro River, south of Babocomari Creek. Military correspondence refers to it by several names, none of them denoting the presence of a presidio there.

CAMP SAN PEDRO RIVER. Fort Grant No. 1.

CAMP SCHROEDER. A temporary camp in Navajo County, occupied by Company V, 8th Infantry, in 1858.

CAMP SKULL VALLEY. Camp Date Creek.

CAMP SMITH. A temporary camp, an outpost of Fort Goodwin, it was probably established by Major Smith on August 11, 1864, about two and a half miles north of the fort in Graham County.

CAMP AT SOLOMONSVILLE. The Arizona Pioneers Historical Society has a photo, numbered B–61, showing a military camp located near today's Solomon in Graham County, with no other information. Another reference dates the camp in 1867.

CAMP SOMERTON. A Mexican border patrol post established about 1800, it was located in Yuma County.

CAMP STANFORD. FORT GRANT NO. 1.

CAMP STEPHEN D. LITTLE. An Army post established in 1910 because of Mexican border troubles, it was located within the city limits of Nogales, Santa Cruz County. It was named for an Army private who was killed by a stray bullet. The camp was ordered abandoned effective January 1, 1933.

CAMP SUNSET (*Camp Colorado Chiquito*). The site of this intermittently used camp, located about six miles east of Winslow, Navajo County, was occupied by the military, Mormon settlers, and trappers. It was first established in 1858 as a temporary campsite and was in use until 1882, when the railroad came through. Historians generally believe that the camp was first made use of by Lieutenant Edward Beale and his camel expedition from Fort Defiance to Fort Mohave. In 1876 a small town was established here. One other reference says that a military camp was established here on the "Colorado Chiquito" (Little Colorado) River.

CAMP SUPPLY. CAMP JOHN A. RUCKER.

CAMP SUPPLY. A temporary camp for stored provisions, it was established by Colonel Kit Carson in 1863 while embarked on his campaign against the Navajos. It was located on the north bank of the Little Colorado River, about two miles east of today's Holbrook in Navajo County.

CAMP THOMAS. FORT APACHE.

CAMP THOMAS. FORT THOMAS.

FORT THOMAS (*New Post on the Gila; Camp Thomas*). Established on August 12, 1876, by Captain Clarence M. Bailey, 8th Infantry, on the site of the present town of Geronimo about a mile south of the Gila River, Graham County, the fort was located about seven miles above old Fort Goodwin. The site had been selected by Colonel August V. Kautz, 8th Infantry, for the purpose of removing the Chiricahua Apaches to the San Carlos Reservation. First called New Post on the Gila, it was named Camp Thomas on September 18, 1876, in honor of Brigadier General Lorenzo Thomas, who died on March 2, 1875. In 1878 the post was moved about five miles up the river to the site of the present town of Fort Thomas, a mining, cattle-raising, and farming community. The post was designated a fort in February 1882. Orders dated December 22, 1890, demoted the post from its independent status to become a subpost of Fort Grant. Although Fort Thomas was ordered abandoned on April 10, 1891, troops temporarily garrisoned the post until May 1892, the last having been Companies B, E and I of the 24th Infantry. The military reservation was finally transferred to the Interior Department on December 3, 1892, for disposition.

CAMP TOLL GATE. CAMP HUALPAI.

CAMP TONTO. In December 1864 Captain John Thompson of the 1st New Mexico Volunteer Cavalry established a temporary field post called Camp Tonto, located most probably somewhere within the confines of today's Tonto National Forest. He reported that on December 17 he led his troopers of Company K in a successful attack against a small band of 15 Indian warriors, killing 11 of them.

CAMP TUBAC. PRESIDIO OF TUBAC.

PRESIDIO OF TUBAC (*Camp Tubac*). The earliest white settlement in Arizona, the Presidio of Tubac was situated about 40 miles south of Tucson in Santa Cruz County. It was the most northerly Spanish military outpost of Primera Alta (the northern region of the province of Sonora, which included today's Arizona south of the Gila River) between 1752 and 1776. It was from Tubac that Juan Bautista de Anza set out in 1774 to open an overland route to California and ultimately found the colony that grew into the city of San Francisco. The Spanish established the presidio in 1752, on the site of a Pima Indian village, to protect Jesuit missionaries who had been driven from the area during a Pima rebellion the preceding year. Settlers, attracted by mining and agricultural possibilities, came north from Sonora and built the pueblo of Tubac and the Church of Santa Gertrudis de Tubac.

Because of frequent Apache depredations, Spanish officials replaced the Presidio of Tubac with one at Tucson. During the earliest years of American occupation, followed by the acquisition of Arizona by the United States, Tubac and Tucson were perhaps the only towns in the region. Camp Tubac was established by the U.S. Army first on July 20, 1862, when Troop D of the 1st Cavalry and a troop of the 2nd Cavalry occupied a temporary post near the old Spanish presidio. Intended primarily as a supply depot, the camp had been established by an order of Colonel Joseph R. West, 1st California Infantry. It was abandoned in compliance with an order issued by Brigadier General John S. Mason in August 1865, and the garrison was withdrawn to establish the camp that later became Fort Mason. Tubac was reoccupied in October 1866 when Fort Mason was abandoned. When Tubac was finally abandoned in 1868, the garrison was transferred to Camp Crittenden. All of Arizona in 1867, including Camp Tubac, was garrisoned by just 27 companies of troops. With the founding of Tombstone in 1879, as the result of a rich silver find there, Tubac's few able-bodied men decamped and sought their fortunes in the new El Dorado. Tubac became a ghost town and even a railroad's branch line did not awaken the place. The last nail was driven into Tubac's coffin when the main road was rerouted to bypass the old Spanish town in 1930, and only a few residents obstinately hung on. Then, in 1940, for no reason that anyone could fathom, Tubac was overrun by an influx of artists who stayed. In 1958 Tubac became a State Historical Monument.

POST OF TUCSON. FORT LOWELL.

TUCSON POST. Regularly garrisoned from May 18, 1862, until September 1866, the post was temporarily occupied in 1871 by Company L of the 3rd Cavalry and in 1872 by Company F of the 5th Cavalry. The dates and units of the regular garrison were: Company A, 3rd Artillery (1862); Companies C and D, 1st Cavalry, and Company G, 14th Infantry (1866); and Volunteers (1862–66).

CAMP AT TURKEY CREEK. An outpost of Fort Whipple, this temporary post in 1882 was located 17 miles southwest of Fort Apache in Gila County.

CAMP TUTHILL. Established in 1928 when the Arizona legislature provided monies for the project, Camp Tuthill was located south of Flagstaff in Coconino County. It was named after Dr. Alexander MacKenzie Tuthill, a brigadier general during World War I and commander of the Arizona National Guard. During summer encampments in August of each year while the post was active, it provided drills, target practice, and sham battles for the National Guardsmen. On April 11, 1955, Governor Ernest McFarland signed papers which transformed the camp into the Coconino County Park and Recreation Area.

FORT TYSON. Erected in 1856 near Quartzsite on the Mohave-Yuma county line, this settlers' defense against the Mohave Indians was named for Charles Tyson. In the Quartzsite cemetery is the grave of Hadji Ali, a Syrian camel driver known to the Americans as Hi Jolly. He came to the United States in the mid-1850s with a camel corps

which the Army hoped to use for desert transportation. The experiment failed chiefly because the Americans—and their horses—could not develop a liking for the camels.

FORT UTAH. The Mormons built an adobe fort in 1877 at the site of the present-day city of Lehi (named after one of the Prophets in the Book of Mormon), about three miles north of Mesa in Maricopa County. Built as a haven against Indian attack, the fort was formed by an extensive adobe wall enclosing a considerable tract of land.

FORT VALLEY. FORT MORONI.

CAMP VERDE. FORT McDOWELL.

CAMP VERDE. FORT VERDE.

FORT VERDE (*Camp Lincoln; Camp Verde*). The U.S. Army occupation of the Verde Valley was initiated near the junction of the Verde River and West Clear Creek, about 35 miles east of Prescott in Yavapai County, in response to the urgent requests by farmers whose cornfields were being raided by Tonto and Yavapai Apaches. With the influx of Anglo and Mexican miners into what had been an Apache hunting preserve, the Indians had begun a reign of terror against the mining camps. The first post, established in January 1864 by Lieutenant Colonel J. Francisco Chavez, 1st New Mexico Infantry, was originally situated on the west bank of the Verde River. It was primarily intended to provide protection for the farmers and the newly developed Prescott mining region. In the beginning an outpost of Fort Whipple, it was first occupied by Army regulars in September 1866. In a few years the site was judged unhealthful enough to dictate the moving of the post in the spring of 1871 to a new site four miles south and about a mile west of the Verde, a short distance below the mouth of Beaver Creek. Originally called Camp Lincoln for President Abraham Lincoln, the post was renamed Camp Verde on November 23, 1868, to avoid confusion with Camp Lincoln, Dakota Territory.

According to an informational release from the Fort Verde State Historic Park: The first military post, in 1865, overlooked the farms at West Clear Creek. The next camp was named Lincoln, one mile north of the present fort, and was used from 1866 to 1871. The present fort was the third post, built during 1871–1873. The more than 20 buildings arranged around the parade ground never had a wall around them, and the fort was never attacked. It served as a supply base and staging area for army operations. During much of its life, two companies of cavalry and two of infantry were stationed there.

The foregoing is at variance with other references, but in the main they are compatible. On April 5, 1879, to confirm its permanency, the post was designated Fort Verde. Finally, Fort Verde was ordered abandoned on April 10, 1890, in accordance with General Orders No. 43, Headquarters of the Army. The military reservation was transferred to the Interior Department on October 14, 1890. Elements of the 9th Infantry, however, continued to man the post until April 25, 1891.

CAMP WALLEN (*New Post at Babocomari; New Post on the Upper San Pedro*). Situated on Babocomari Creek on the Babocomari Land Grant, near the San Pedro River, about 15 miles west of Tombstone in Cochise County, this post had its beginnings as New Post at Babocomari or New Post on the Upper San Pedro. It was established on May 9, 1866, by the California Volunteers. Soon after the camp was activated, it was given the permanent name of Camp Wallen in honor of Colonel H. D. Wallen, commander of the Northern Arizona District. The first regular garrison consisted of Company G of the 1st U.S. Cavalry and Company E of the 14th Infantry. The Army took over Babocomari Ranch, erected tents, and used available buildings for a horse corral. The men of the garrison had much to complain about. In addition to their duties on the post and in the field in pursuit of thieving Apaches, the soldiers bitterly resented the lack of adequate quarters. The government refused to appropriate funds for construction on the post. A Mexican cattle herder on the ranch was induced to teach the soldiers how to fashion adobe bricks from raw materials. In a relatively short time they had made several thousand large, sun-dried bricks ready for building purposes. The men also went into the Huachuca Mountains for the timber required for rafters and lintels. From 1867 to 1869 Companies C and E, 32nd Infantry, garrisoned the post. In 1869 Company K, 21st Infantry, joined them. The camp was abandoned on October 31, 1869, and whatever reservation had been established during the life of the post was formally transferred to the Interior Department on April 22, 1874.

CAMP ON WALNUT CREEK. A short-lived post, it was located in Yavapai County, very probably near the site of Camp Hualpai (Camp Toll Gate), and established in 1881.

CAMP WHIPPLE. WHIPPLE BARRACKS.

FORT WHIPPLE. WHIPPLE BARRACKS.

WHIPPLE BARRACKS (*Camp Clark; Camp Whipple; Whipple Depot; Prescott Barracks; Fort Whipple*). Established on December 21, 1863, this post was originally named Camp Clark in honor of Surveyor-General John A. Clark and located in the Chino Valley at Del Rio Spring near the Verde River, about twenty miles north of Prescott. The camp, established by Major Edward B. Willis, 1st Infantry, California Volunteers, in compliance with an order of Brigadier General James H. Carleton, was intended to protect the new gold-mining district. The offices of Arizona's territorial government were operated from log cabins and tents here from January 22 to May 18, 1864, when the post was relocated on a site on the left bank of Granite Creek just northeast of Prescott. It was then renamed Camp Whipple, and designated Fort Whipple in 1870, in honor of Major General Amiel W. Whipple, who was mortally wounded on May 7, 1863, during the Battle of Chancellorsville. While a lieutenant in the Corps of Topographical Engineers in 1853, he had surveyed the route from Albuquerque, New Mexico, through the territory where the gold strikes were later made by prospectors.

Camp Whipple originally consisted of a large rectangular stockade constructed of strong undressed pine logs, with the crevices caulked with mud. The roofs of all the enclosed buildings were shingled. The men's quarters, kitchen, and bakery occupied one side of the parade ground, with the officers' quarters opposite. The other two sides were occupied by storerooms, guardhouse, adjutant's office, and laundresses' quarters. In the beginning, only one company of infantry was garrisoned here. During 1869 the post's buildings were torn down and rebuilt. On April 15, 1870, Fort Whipple became the headquarters for the Military Department of Arizona. On April 27, 1872, the corrals and stables of the adjacent depot were destroyed in a fire. The original site was abandoned for a new one nearby and the depot was completely rebuilt, completed in July. Whipple Depot became an independent command on October 13, 1870. On April 5, 1879, Fort Whipple and the depot, renamed Prescott Barracks, were consolidated and designated Whipple Barracks. The post was deactivated in March 1898 except for a caretaking detachment, but was regarrisoned in 1902. The garrison was withdrawn on February 25, 1913, and the post was again placed on a caretaking status. In 1922 the military reservation was transferred to the secretary of the treasury and reserved for use by the Public Health Service. The site is now occupied by a Veterans Administration hospital.

WHIPPLE DEPOT. WHIPPLE BARRACKS.

CAMP WILLOW GROVE. A temporary Army post, it was established on August 23, 1867, by 1st Lieutenant Levi H. Robinson and Company E of the 14th Infantry. It was located about 95 miles northeast of Fort Mohave and about 40 miles east of Beale's Springs in Mohave County. From 1867 to 1869 the post was garrisoned by Company E, 14th Infantry, with Captain G. R. Vernon in command; and for one year, 1868–69, Companies E, F, and K, 8th Cavalry, with Captain C. H. Lester in command. Most of their duties were devoted to operations against the hostile Hualapai Indians. The post was abandoned on October 12, 1869.

FORT WINSOR CASTLE. The picturesque, well-preserved Mormon fort at Pipe Spring, about 15 miles southwest of Fredonia, Mohave County, demonstrates the need felt by the pioneers for protection against the Indian tribes. Much credit has been given to the Mormons, who settled at Pipe Spring and many other places in the region, for the exploration, colonization, and development of this part of the Southwest under the leadership of Brigham Young. Pipe Spring is situated on a strip of northwestern Arizona that lies between the Utah state line on the north and the Grand Canyon of the Colorado on the south. Members of the Jacob Hamblin party, the first white men to visit Pipe Spring, camped at this spring in 1858. They had been sent out by Brigham Young to explore and report on the Colorado River country and to negotiate, if at all possible, a treaty of peace with the Navajos living on the south side of the river. Dr. James M. Whitmore and Robert McIntyre first settled Pipe Spring in 1863 as a cattle ranch. They built a dugout of juniper logs and earth to use as their headquarters. Both men were massacred by a band of marauding Navajos and Paiutes during the winter of 1865–66.

The Mormons acquired the estate, and in 1869 Bishop Anson P. Winsor arrived to build a fort and care for the cattle reserved for the support of the Church. By 1870 he had finished the fort, which was called Winsor Castle. Standing near the base of the colorful Vermillion Cliffs, it consisted of two 2-story red sandstone buildings, facing each other across a courtyard closed at the ends with high sandstone walls and heavy gates. There was a firing platform a few feet below the top of one wall. The north building was erected directly over the spring, and the water flowed through the south building, assuring a plentiful supply of good water at all times. Bishop Winsor left Pipe Spring about 1875, and the place was sold to private interests for a cattle ranch. For years it was an important cattle-buying and shipping point. Finally, the old fort and auxiliary buildings were acquired by the federal government, and in May 1923 Pipe Spring National Monument was established by presidential proclamation.

CAMP WRIGHT. Established in 1865, it was a temporary post located on the site of Fort Grant No. 1.

YUMA DEPOT. In 1864 a sizable quartermaster depot was built in the environs of Yuma on the east bank of the Colorado River half a mile below its junction with the Gila. By the time it was completed, the seriously flood-damaged structures of Fort Yuma on the California side of the Colorado had been repaired and renovated. Large quantities of stores were shipped to the depot from Fort Yuma. In April 1865 General James H. Carleton was informed of "fraudulent transactions" at the depot and measures were taken to correct the misappropriations. It continued to be the principal point for receiving supplies that were distributed to the region north of the Gila River. In 1867 fire destroyed the depot, but immediate steps were taken to rebuild. During subsequent years it quartered as many as 900 Army mules at one time. During its score of years of service, the depot had been garrisoned by troops of various units on a rotating basis. On December 16, 1885, both California's Fort Yuma and the Yuma Depot were abandoned and transferred to the Department of the Interior, which assigned the installations to the Yuma Indian Reservation on March 5, 1892.

YUMA POST. This intermittently garrisoned post was established on June 4, 1885, when Company M, 4th U.S. Cavalry, under the command of 1st Lieutenant D. N. McDonald, crossed over from Fort Yuma, California. Yuma was abandoned on December 16, 1885. The post was reoccupied on February 7, 1911 and again abandoned on January 26, 1913. It was again reoccupied in March, 1915 and finally abandoned on January 30, 1922.

FORT ARKANSAS. ARKANSAS POST.

ARKANSAS POST (*Poste de Arkansas; Fort Carlos III; Fort San Carlos; Fuerto San Estevan de Arkanzas; Fort Arkanzas; Fort Hindman*). The Arkansas Post National Memorial on the Arkansas River is located 7 miles south of Gillett and 20 miles northeast of Dumas in Arkansas County. Much of the early history of what is now the state of Arkansas focuses on this almost-forgotten historical outpost. Often called the "Birthplace of Arkansas," the post was the site of French and Spanish forts and trading stations, the stage for a minor battle in the aftermath of the American Revolution, a territorial capital, a prosperous river port, and a bloody Civil War battleground. Arkansas Post was the focal point for numerous confrontations between Indian and European cultures, and its colorful history spanned the reigns of several nations in the region.

René Robert Cavelier de La Salle first visited the region in 1682, hoping to establish an inland empire connecting French Canada and the Gulf of Mexico. The explorer made an extensive land grant and a generous trading concession to his lieutenant and trusted friend, Henri de Tonty. In 1686, about 32 years before the founding of New Orleans, Tonty had a trading post built on the Arkansas River some miles from its confluence with the Mississippi. The precise site of this first Poste de Arkansas has not been established, but it probably stood seven miles south of the present Memorial. In the late spring of 1687, Henri Joutel and the other survivors of La Salle's ill-fated Fort St. Louis on Matagorda Bay in Texas struggled wearily through the wilderness to the edge of the Arkansas River, where they discovered across the width of the river a large cross, and a short distance away from it the Poste de Arkansas, their salvation.

During the subsequent three-quarters of a century, the fortunes of the French post rose and fell dramatically. Although Indian raids and spring floods compelled several relocations, Arkansas Post continued to serve as both a military outpost and a trading station. The first white child of record born in Arkansas was brought into the world at Arkansas Post. She was Catherine Landrony, daughter of Joseph and Marie Landrony. The earliest known Arkansas vital records are those of the post, the originals of which are located in the Public Archives at Ottawa, Canada. In 1748 the post was rebuilt a few hundred yards to the northwest of the 1686 location and near today's Lake Dumond, which was then a part of the Arkansas River channel. By a secret 1762

Arkansas

51

treaty, Louis XV ceded all of Louisiana east of the Mississippi to Spain, which did not take actual possession until 1768, renaming the post Fort Carlos III or Fort San Carlos. During that year, Captain Philip Pittman of the British army visited there and described it:

The post is situated three leagues up the Arkansas, and is built with stockades, in a quadrangular form; the sides of the exterior polygon are about one hundred eighty feet, and one three pounder is mounted in the flanks and faces of each bastion. The buildings within the fort are, a barrack with three rooms for the soldiers, commanding officer's house, a powder magazine, and a magazine for provisions, and an apartment for the commissary, all of which are in a ruinous condition. The fort stands about two hundred yards from the water-side, and is garrisoned by a captain, a lieutenant, and thirty French soldiers, including sergeants and corporals. There are eight houses without the fort, occupied by as many families, who have cleared the land about nine hundred yards in depth; but on account of the sandiness of the soil and the lowness of the situation, which makes it subject to be overflowed, they do not raise their necessary provisions. These people subsist mostly by hunting, and every season send to New Orleans great quantities of bear's oil tallow, and salted buffalo meat, and a few skins. [*The Present State of the European Settlements on the Mississippi*]

Despite shifts to new sites along the river, the fort each spring suffered flooding. In 1779 it was again rebuilt on a site about half a mile south of the present remains of the village, which had retained its French name, Poste de Arkansas. In 1788 the river again rose over the banks and so undermined the fort's works that they were irreparable. The Spanish commandant ordered another structure built but on appreciably higher ground, on the site of today's Arkansas Post State Park. This, the last of the European-built forts on the river, and named by the Spaniards Fuerto San Estevan de Arkanzas, was completed in 1791. All that remains of this bastion of defense is a large brick-lined cistern. In 1803, at Napoleon's insistence, Spain retroceded the territory of Louisiana to France, and in the same year the United States consummated the Louisiana Purchase. The fort's name was then anglicized to Arkansas Post.

On December 31, 1813, Arkansas County came into being, with Arkansas Post designated as the county seat. Arkansas attained territorial status in 1819, with Arkansas Post as its capital. The first newspaper in Arkansas, the *Arkansas Gazette*, was initially published here during the same year. After the capital was moved to Little Rock, Arkansas Post rapidly declined. By 1830 its population had dwindled to 114 people. In 1861 the Confederates at Arkansas Post erected Fort Hindman and garrisoned it with 5,000 troops. On January 10 and 11, 1863, the fort was pulverized into helplessness and the village virtually destroyed by shelling from Union gunboats and land batteries in the Battle of Arkansas Post, the state's most crucial battle. Federal forces occupied the site for the remainder of the Civil War. When the railroads crippled traffic on the river, Arkansas Post became a ghost town. The final blow came in 1903, when the Arkansas River changed course and left the place high and dry.

Maps continued to mark the site where Arkansas Post had stood. The village's streets were taken over by weeds and the site of the last Spanish fort was gradually swallowed by a wilderness. The sites of the fort and village were all but forgotten until the Arkansas Legislature in 1929 set up the Arkansas Post State Park Commission. Appropriations were made and the government's Civilian Conservation Corps (the CCC) was assigned to work on the grounds. During the years much was accomplished on the site. On June 23, 1964, Arkansas Post became a memorial in the national park system.

The locations of the various Arkansas Posts, including the John Law Colony, are a matter of conjecture. No one knows the exact location of the French settlements, until the establishment in 1752 of the first fort on today's park site, and the erection of three Spanish forts between 1771 and 1778. Investigation of historical literature, however, reveals that Tonty's settlement in 1686 was several miles downstream, in the Little Prairie area near Nady and the Menard Mounds. All of the various posts' settlers had attempted to accomplish the mutually exclusive tasks of being close to the mouth of the Arkansas River, near the Indian towns for trade, and still avoiding the virtually annual spring floods. The present site is above high water, reasonably close to the Quapaw villages, but is at least 40 miles, as the river flows, from the river's mouth on the Mississippi.

CAMP BABCOCK. A Confederate camp, southwest of Fayetteville in Washington County, it was established prior to the bloody Battle of Prairie Grove fought several miles away in early December 1862. Here the Union forces under Generals F. J. Herron and James G. Blunt were repulsed by Confederate defenders.

CAMP BELKNAP. FORT SMITH.

CAMP BRAGG. General Sterling Price's major permanent Confederate encampment during the winter of 1863, it was located near Woodlawn, about 17 miles southwest of Camden.

FORT CARLOS III. ARKANSAS POST.

CAMP CARR. A Union post established in 1862 and named for Eugene Carr, a Federal cavalry officer, it was located on Big Sugar Creek in Benton County.

FORT CHAFFEE. Located on level prairie lands and in the rolling hills east of old Fort Smith, built by the Army in the early 1800s to deal with the Cherokees and Osages, Fort Chaffee was established beginning September 1941 and was officially activated in March 1942. The post, originally spread out over 90,000 acres during World War II, and later reduced to about 73,000 acres, was named for Major General Adna Romanza Chaffee, Jr., cavalry officer and first chief of the armored forces. Son of a former Army chief of staff, Lieutenant General Adna R. Chaffee, he formed the first experimental mechanized unit at Fort Knox, Kentucky, in 1928. The Arkansas base was a training center from 1941 to 1944, and then served as a personnel center until it was deactivated in 1946. Reactivated in 1948, it became the home of the 5th Armored Division. It was restored to training status in September 1950 and was redesignated as the U.S. Army Field Artillery Training Center. It was given permanent status by the Army in March 1956 and formally became Fort Chaffee. The post was again deactivated in July 1959 after a relatively short period of training soldiers for the Korean War. The post's reactivation once more came in October 1961 due to the Berlin crisis. It became an armor training facility again in 1962, and late that year was made an artillery training center for STRAC (Strategic Army Corps) units.

FORT CHARLES. A Confederate fortification established in June 1862 by Captain Joseph Fry at St. Charles on the White River, Arkansas County, its primary purpose—not achieved—was to prevent the passage of a Union gunboat fleet up the river.

CAMP CULLODEN. A temporary Confederate post, formerly located in the part of Carroll County that is now Boone County, near the town of Harrison, it was used by either Confederate or Arkansas state troops commanded by Captain John R. Homer Scott in 1861. The three companies of cavalry later moved to Camp Hardee in then Burrowsville, now Marshall, Searcy County. Captain Scott probably named the camp "Culloden" for the 1746 Battle of Culloden Moor in which the British decisively defeated Prince Charles Edward.

FORT CURTIS. Union forces constructed this fortification at Helena after the town's capture in the summer of 1862 by General Samuel R. Curtis. Companies D and F, 33rd Missouri Volunteer Infantry, manned the fort's three 30-pounder Parrotts, which played a leading role in the disastrous defeat of attacking Confederates on July 4, 1863. The field of battle was strewn with more than 2,000 dead and wounded Confederates. Most of the dead were interred by the victorious Federals, who took more than 1,000 wounded as prisoners. From January to March 1865, the site was reoccupied by Company D, 60th U.S. Colored Infantry, with Captain William A. Stuart in command.

FORT DAVIS. A Confederate defense, it was evacuated on April 13, 1861, later reoccupied, and finally captured by Union troops in December 1862. The fort's site has not been definitely located.

DE VALL'S BLUFF POST. At this site located on U.S. 70 east of Little Rock, Federal troops camped and then built an arsenal and a large barracks, which was later used as a courthouse, hotel, and opera house. Occupied from 1863 to 1865, the federal post was situated in Prairie County.

CAMP DODGE. On May 2, 1898, Governor Daniel W. Jones issued an order to establish Camp Dodge as a rendezvous point for Arkansas troops, consisting of two regiments of infantry, to enlist as U.S. volunteers. The site is on the corner of College Avenue and 17th Street in Little Rock. The camp was named for Dr. Roderick Dodge, whose estate owned the site, and was donated by the heirs to the state for military use.

ECORE FABRE TRADING POST. The site of this trading post is incorporated within the city of Camden, Ouachita County. A Frenchman, named Fabre, established a post in 1824 in the settlement of Ecore Fabre, later renamed Camden. In 1973 the Arkansas American Revolution Bicentennial Commission approved a grant of $5,200 to construct a replica of this trading post, the first structure in the community, on park property belonging to the city. The plan, however, to do a conjectural reconstruction was later abandoned.

FORT ESPERANZA. Situated on the west bank of the Mississippi River opposite Memphis, Tennessee, in Crittenden County, Fort Esperanza was erected in 1797 by the Spaniards. Two years earlier they had built Fort San Fernando de las Barrancas on today's site of Memphis, but pressure brought by the United States government compelled them to move across the river into Arkansas territory. The settlement that grew up around the fort was later called Hope Encampment, which later was renamed Hopefield. The town was set ablaze during the Civil War, and its remains and those of the Spanish fort were washed away by the river.

CAMP HARDEE. A temporary Confederate post established in late 1861, it was located near old Burrowsville, now Marshall, in Searcy County, and was utilized until the Pea Ridge campaign in early 1862. The post was named for then Major General William Joseph Hardee, a graduate of West Point in 1838.

HELENA BATTERIES. Two of the best-known battles of the Civil War were fought on July 4, 1863. While Federal forces repulsed the Confederates' northernmost advance at Gettysburg, rebel forces at Vicksburg finally capitulated to Grant's army after a prolonged siege. The coincidence of Union victories on Independence Day was made still more ironic by a third success in eastern Arkansas, at Helena on the Mississippi River. The Battle of Helena was a futile attempt by Confederate forces to recapture the river town from Federal occupation forces.

Commanded by Major General Benjamin Prentiss, Union troops had taken advantage of Helena's topography by building a series of fortifications on hills surrounding the city. Four hilltop batteries—A, B, C and D—overlooked the roads leading into Helena. When news came that Confederate forces, led by Lieutenant General Theophilus H. Holmes, were on the march against the city, the four batteries were strengthened in late June by the construction of a series of rifle entrenchments and abatis.

Costly mistakes by the Confederates, including leaving their artillery behind, were their undoing, although the Union defenders were outnumbered almost two to one. All the batteries were to be assaulted simultaneously, but lapses in communication defeated the plan. The Battle of Helena began with the rebels' attack on Battery D on Hindman Hill. Throughout the morning hours the battle raged. Finally Union guns forced the weary attackers into full retreat. The prearranged signal to retreat, however, never reached about 240 Confederate soldiers hidden in an isolated ravine. As the main force abandoned the area, this group of men was surrounded by Union troops and taken prisoner.

The strong Union fortifications, particularly Battery D, protected the Federal defenders well, as demonstrated by the number of casualties. While the Confederates suffered 47 killed and 115 wounded, only 5 were killed and 10 wounded behind the Union earthworks. On the crest of Hindman Hill are the well-preserved earthworks and rifle entrenchments of Battery D, covering about an acre of ground, partially covered with trees and undergrowth. Access to the Union battery is gained via Military Road, where two commemorative markers stand at the entrance. The other Helena batteries (A, B, and C), however, have been greatly altered since they were constructed in 1863.

FORT HINDMAN. ARKANSAS POST.

CAMP JOSEPH T. ROBINSON (*Camp Pike*). A military reservation about seven miles north of Little Rock, it was established in 1917 during World War I, when it was named Camp Pike. In 1918 it housed as many as 100,000 men. The post was named in honor of Brigadier General Zebulon M. Pike, discoverer of Pike's Peak, who was killed in action in 1813. The camp was established on July 8, 1917, to serve as a training base for the 87th Division, which remained here from August 1917 to June 1918. Construction commenced June 17, 1917, and continued through 1918. After the war the camp was retained as a permanent reservation, and since 1937 it has been known as Camp Joseph T. Robinson. The post was reopened in 1940 and activated the following year to accommodate World War II soldiers, with its area greatly enlarged and hundreds of new barracks erected. The post is now a state-operated camp used for the summer training of National Guard and Reserve troops.

FORT KAPPA. FORT ST. FRANCIS.

LITTLE ROCK ARSENAL (*Little Rock Barracks; Post of Little Rock*). The site of Little Rock Arsenal, contained within MacArthur Park at East Ninth and Commerce Streets, is on land acquired by the federal government in 1836. Situated on the north side of the park, the Arsenal is the birthplace of General Douglas MacArthur. Today the Little Rock Museum of Natural History and Antiquities is housed here. Just after Arkansas was admitted into the Union, Governor

James Sevier Conway pleaded with the War Department for the establishment of a military post at Little Rock as a protection against migrating Indians traversing the state. The War Department responded with an appropriation for an arsenal to be built at Little Rock. Lieutenant F. L. Jones selected the site, which is the same as that which makes up present MacArthur Park. Actual construction began in 1838, accompanied by the establishment of the Post of Little Rock, either adjoining the arsenal site or in its near environs, with quarters for two companies, officers' quarters in two buildings, a storehouse, magazine, guardhouse, and office buildings, all of brick; the hospital and other structures were built of wood. The Arsenal was completed in 1840.

In November 1860, with the secession movement near its height, the 2nd Artillery was transferred to Little Rock from Fort Leavenworth, Kansas, with Captain James Totten in command. After South Carolina seceded on December 20, 1860, Arkansas took steps to secure the Arsenal. On February 8, 1861, Captain Totten surrendered the structure, intact with all its artillery maintenance equipment, to Henry M. Rector, governor of Arkansas. While preparing to evacuate the city in 1863, the Confederates unsuccessfully attempted to burn down the Arsenal, a two-storied brick structure with two wings flanking an unusual octagonal tower. On July 25, 1873, the facility became Little Rock Barracks. It was abandoned as such on September 25, 1890. On April 23, 1892, the Arsenal and grounds were traded by the federal government for 1,000 acres of ground, north of the Arkansas River, which was owned by the city of Little Rock. The Arsenal was turned over to the city with the stipulation that the grounds be "forever exclusively devoted to the uses and purposes of a public park."

LITTLE ROCK BARRACKS. LITTLE ROCK ARSENAL.

POST OF LITTLE ROCK. LITTLE ROCK ARSENAL.

FORT LOOKOUT. Located at Camden, Ouachita County, this Civil War fortification was situated off Gravel Pit Road on the Ouachita River for the purpose of guarding the town from the north. Remains consist of rifle trenches and cannon pits.

FORT LYNN. All that is known of this post is its location at present Fort Lynn, Miller County, in the southwestern corner of the state.

CAMP MARMADUKE. Probably a Confederate post, it was established in 1862 in Washington County.

FORT MINOR. The site of this Civil War fortification, probably Confederate, has not been definitely established.

CAMP NELSON. The first Confederate regiments to reach Arkansas were stationed at Camp Nelson, located near Austin, Lonoke County. Named for Brigadier General Allison Nelson, the camp was established in the fall of 1862. Nelson served under General Thomas M. Hindman in 1862 at DeVall's Bluff on the White River and was given command of a brigade. Appointed a brigadier general on September 28 the same year, he was leading a division when he died of a fever at Camp Nelson on October 7 and was buried at Little Rock. General Henry E. McCulloch succeeded him.

FORT OSCEOLA. A temporary Confederate fort erected near the town of Osceola, Mississippi County, it was situated on Plum Point on the Mississippi River.

CAMP PIKE. CAMP JOSEPH T. ROBINSON.

CAMP PINE BLUFF. A Federal post established by the 1st Indiana Volunteer Cavalry, pursuant to an order of the Headquarters, Army of Arkansas, dated September 22, 1863, it was located at Pine Bluff in Jefferson County. A battle was fought here on October 25, 1863. The post was garrisoned by volunteer units during the Civil War and thereafter by elements of the regular Army. Camp Pine Bluff was discontinued on April 5, 1869. The last unit stationed at the post was Company D, 28th Infantry.

PINE BLUFF ARSENAL. Located in Jefferson County, it was an Army chemical warfare manufacturing facility during World War II and subsequent years.

FORT PINNEY. A Civil War defense, it was erected by Federal forces as an outpost of the Post of Helena immediately after their arrival at Helena on July 12, 1862. Situated on the bank of the Mississippi close to the town, it was commanded by Captain Benjamin Thomas, provost marshal, 63rd Colored Infantry.

POSTE DE ARKANSAS. ARKANSAS POST.

FORT RECTOR. A temporary fortification, it was erected during the Civil War. The site of this post, probably Confederate, has not been definitely established.

RED FORK FORT. A temporary fortification, it was reportedly located in "Arkansas Territory" in 1834.

FORT REITER. A temporary Confederate defense, it was situated on Reiter's Hill near Helena.

CAMP ROBINSON. CAMP JOSEPH T. ROBINSON.

FORT ROOTS. Established in accordance with an act of Congress, April 23, 1892, Fort Roots was located on the west side of the Arkansas River about four miles north of Little Rock. Construction on the 1,100-acre post began in 1893, and it was first garrisoned in 1896 by a 4th Cavalry detachment consisting of one officer and 22 men. It was designated Fort Roots on April 22, 1897, in honor of Brevet Lieutenant Colonel (Captain) Logan Holt Roots, Commissary, U.S. Volunteers, who served with distinction during the Civil War and died on May 30, 1893. Post construction was discontinued in 1898 when its garrison was ordered to Puerto Rico. A small garrison, however, was maintained at the incomplete post until World War I, at which time Camp Pike was established nearby. Fort Roots was converted to a post hospital in May 1917 and then designated a general hospital on October 1, 1918. Since 1921 the facility has been operating as a Veterans Administration hospital.

FORT ST. FRANCIS (*Fort Kappa*). The first fortification built by white men in the present Phillips County area was constructed in 1738 and 1739 on the St. Francis River, when the region was a part of huge French Louisiana. While France claimed the whole Mississippi Valley, based on La Salle's explorations, Pierre Le Sueur was dispatched to the upper Mississippi River in search of mineral wealth. In 1700 he and 25 men went up the great river and, after passing the Arkansas River entrance, found a smaller river on the west side of the Mississippi, which they named St. Francis. The main obstacle to French development of the Mississippi Valley was the British-allied Chickasaw Nation, which terrorized the French settlements and posts in what is present-day Mississippi. A long French military campaign was begun against the Chickasaws. A large detachment of soldiers was sent from New Orleans to construct a temporary fort and auxiliary cabins at the mouth of the St. Francis River, and, once

the fort was built, put it in a state of defense. The fort was planned as a general depot for military supplies and a refuge for the sick and wounded. The French, under the governor of Louisiana, Sieur de Bienville, spent the miserable winter of 1739–40 at Fort Assumption on the Fourth Chickasaw Bluff at Memphis, holding councils with the recalcitrant Indians but not achieving any progress toward peace. Running out of food, the troops were reduced to eating their horses. Disease was rampant and many soldiers died during the stalemated winter. Finally, in resignation, Bienville retreated to the civilized environs of New Orleans, leaving the Chickasaw problem to be resolved at a later date. When he left Fort Assumption with the remnants of his army in the spring of 1740, the fort was deliberately destroyed. Fort St. Francis was likewise razed by the army on its way south.

FORT SAN CARLOS. ARKANSAS POST.

FUERTO SAN ESTEVAN DE ARKANZAS. ARKANSAS POST.

FORT SMITH (*Camp Thomas; Camp Belknap*). The Fort Smith National Historic Site commemorates an important phase of America's westward development. In the midst of a busy, thriving city, also called Fort Smith, the National Park Service preserves the remains of two successive frontier forts and the celebrated Isaac C. Parker court as reminders of the day when civilization ended on the banks of the Arkansas River. Fort Smith's history had three phases: the small First Fort, 1817–34; the enlarged Second Fort, 1838–71; and the Federal District Court, 1871–96. In accordance with orders "to select the best site . . . and thereon erect as expeditiously as circumstances will permit, a stockade," Major William Bradford, Riflemen's Regiment, arrived at Belle Point on December 25, 1817, having been preceded by Brevet Major Stephen H. Long, Topographical Engineers, who had selected this rocky bluff on the right bank of the Poteau River near its junction with the Arkansas. Bradford had his 70 men initiate construction of a simple wooden stockade with two blockhouses, soon designated Fort Smith in honor of Colonel Thomas A. Smith, commander of U.S. forces west of the Mississippi. Work, however, proceeded very slowly, and it was not until February 1822 that the fort could be considered completed.

The fort's location, today immediately adjoining Oklahoma's eastern border, had been chosen to keep peace between the Osages and the Cherokees, to protect travelers and trading posts

FORT SMITH. (Courtesy of the National Park Service.)

in the area, and to prevent white men from encroaching on Indian lands. The post was located on land belonging to the Choctaw Nation in accordance with the Treaty of Doak's Stand (October 18, 1820). The so-called Choctaw Strip, including Fort Smith's site, was ceded to the United States on January 20, 1825. Until 1824 Fort Smith's soldiers were successful in preventing Indian uprisings. By then the frontier had shifted westward, and in April 1824 the fort's garrison moved some 80 miles up the Arkansas River to a point near present Muskogee, Oklahoma, where the troops established Fort Gibson. Only small detachments then intermittently garrisoned Fort Smith before it was finally closed on June 16, 1834. Its last garrison, troops commanded by Captain John Stewart, 7th Infantry, was removed to establish Fort Coffee in Oklahoma. Once abandoned, the old fort rapidly deteriorated and became ruinous. Its exact site remained lost until archeologists uncovered the fort's foundations in 1958.

In response to demands from inhabitants in western Arkansas for a resumption of military protection, Congress authorized the War Department to reestablish Fort Smith in 1838. Plans specified an impressive fortification to be located near the earlier fort. The military reservation was reestablished on July 27, 1838, by Captain Benjamin L. E. Bonneville and troops of the 7th Infantry, occupying a temporary camp while

the fort was being constructed immediately adjacent to the original Fort Smith site. The camp, first called Camp Thomas, was renamed Camp Belknap for Captain William G. Belknap, 3rd Infantry, who was superintending the construction. Actual work began in 1839, but the fort was never completed as first envisioned. By 1841 the danger of Indian uprisings had significantly lessened. Colonel Zachary Taylor, the new departmental commander, ordered construction halted on the partially completed pentagonal stone fort. The government modified its facilities to serve as a supply depot. Occupied by troops in May 1846, the new fort during the remainder of its active life served to equip and provision other forts in Indian Territory.

Both the Federals and the Confederates used the fort's supply and hospital facilities during the Civil War. Seized by Arkansas troops on April 24, 1861, the fort was retaken by Union troops commanded by Major General James G. Blunt on September 3, 1863. It was evacuated in December 1864, and reoccupied after the end of the war. The fort was permanently abandoned in September 1871, with its last garrison transferred to Fort Gibson. The military reservation was consigned to the Department of the Interior on March 25, 1871. In March 1885, however, a portion of the former reservation was ceded by the government to the town of Fort Smith. Today only the barracks and the commissary buildings remain. The barracks during the following years underwent a number of changes.

When Fort Smith was closed in 1871, its barracks became the home of the U.S. District Court for Western Arkansas. Its powers were perverted during the period of social and political unrest caused by the Civil War and Reconstruction, and it ultimately became totally corrupt. President Ulysses S. Grant remedied the situation by wisely appointing Isaac C. Parker to the judgeship. Although at the age of 38 Parker was the youngest member on the federal judicial bench, he had a sound legal background. For 21 years the court at Fort Smith handed out rapid and impartial justice. In sheer volume only, the record is astounding. Of some 13,400 cases docketed, 12,000 were criminal in nature, with 344 men accused of major crimes appearing before Judge Parker. Of the 160 men convicted, 79 were hanged. Only Sundays and Christmas halted the inexorable justice of the court. Finally, in September 1896, the court was dissolved. Parker was destined to outlive his famous court by only two months. With the passing of the Parker court, an epoch had terminated: the frontier had vanished.

FORT STEELE. A temporary Civil War fortification erected by Union troops and named for Brigadier General Frederick Steele, under whom they served, it was located a few blocks south and one block west of the Mount Holly Cemetery in Little Rock.

CAMP STEPHENS. Named for Alexander H. Stephens, vice president of the Confederacy, by the men of the 3rd Louisiana Infantry, Camp Stephens was established in July 1861 by Brigadier General Nicholas Bart Pearce when he moved troops from Camp Walker to train the Louisiana troops. The camp occupied land on both Little Sugar and Brush creeks and was located several miles southwest of the Pea Ridge battlefield on the Arkansas–Missouri border in the northwest corner of the state. Union forces took over the camp after the battle, fought March 7 and 8, 1862. Union general Samuel R. Curtis had moved to this camp "to get away from the stench of the battlefield." Today the exact location of the camp is not known. On September 30, 1962, the Pea Ridge Memorial Association dedicated a marker to commemorate the camp and placed it at Highway 72 and the Fairgrounds at Bentonville, near the general location northeast of the town.

CANTONMENT TAYLOR. In June 1821 troops were dispatched to provide protection for the trading factory located at the mouth of the Sulphur Fork of the Red River, just above the Louisiana-Arkansas line, in Miller County. During the following year, the post named Cantonment Taylor was constructed there by the soldiers and remained active until May 1824.

CAMP THOMAS. FORT SMITH.

CAMP (JESSE) TURNER. This World War II post, designed as a training ground for soldiers to operate railroads, was located on a hill just east of Van Buren in Crawford County. It was activated in 1942 and deactivated in 1945. Today the Crawford County Memorial Hospital and the Van Buren Housing Authority share the site located on Chestnut Street.

CAMP VINE PRAIRIE. Probably a temporary post established by the Confederates, it was located near Van Buren, Crawford County.

CAMP WALKER. A Confederate camp established in 1861 for the training of all recruits in northwest Arkansas, it was situated on elevated land about a mile and a half northeast of Maysville, Benton County. The post stood on the old Military Road from Fort Smith, Arkansas, to Fort Scott, Kansas, which had been built by the Army several years before the Civil War. The camp occupied a part of the land owned by the Benton County Harmonial Society, organized in 1860, and used some of the society's buildings for barracks. Camp Walker was also a training post for General Stand Watie's regiment of Cherokees and Creeks. In 1864 a fire destroyed the structures.

CAMP A. E. WOOD. CAMP YOSEMITE.

ADOBE MEADOWS CAMP. Established as an outpost of Camp Independence by Captain Rowe and a company of troops, the post was occupied during June and July 1862. It was located 25 miles from Aurora and 95 miles above Camp Independence (Inyo County).

ALCATRAZ ISLAND. When the Spanish first entered San Francisco Bay in 1775, a naval lieutenant, Don Juan Manuel de Ayala, named Alcatraz Island "Isla de los Alcatraces" (Island of the Pelicans). There are no records indicating its occupation by Spaniards during the 1775–1840 period. After the short-lived Bear Revolt in 1846, Mexico in 1848 ceded the island to the United States. The famous 12-acre precipitous rocky island, facing the Golden Gate, was declared a military reservation by an executive order on November 6, 1850. A part of the area's defensive system, along with Fort Lime Point, intended to guard the entrance to the bay, its first fortifications were begun in 1853 under the direction of Lieutenant Zealous Bates Tower, U.S. Corps of Engineers, and consisted in the main of a brick 200-by-100-foot citadel, batteries, two barrack structures for troops, and three cell blocks.

First garrisoned on December 30, 1859, the post was officially designated Alcatraz Island but was often referred to as Fort Alcatraz. By 1861 the fort had 85 cannon and a garrison of 130 men. The island became a detention camp for political prisoners during the Civil War. Later it was a disciplinary barracks for military prisoners, a prison for recalcitrant Indians, and then a P.O.W. facility for Spanish-American Philippines Islands prisoners and World War I conscientious objectors. Alcatraz Island had been privately owned when the War Department bought it because of its strategic location. It was used as a fort until the disastrous 1906 earthquake, when San Francisco jail inmates were transferred there for safekeeping. "The Rock," as it was popularly called, was an Army prison from 1907 to 1933, when title to the island passed to the Department of Justice.

The Federal Bureau of Prisons, an agency of the Justice Department, took it over and ran the establishment as a maximum security prison for incorrigible criminals until 1964, when it was shut down because of its progressively decaying condition and deteriorating assurances of incarceration. Asserting century-old treaty rights and planning to convert it into a center for Native American studies, a large group of militant American Indians occupied the island in defiance

California

of the federal government for 19 months ending in June 1971. Now a part of the Golden Gate National Recreation Area, Alcatraz Island has since emerged as one of San Francisco's most popular attractions for tourists and American history buffs under the aegis of the National Park Service.

CAMP ALERT. A Civil War encampment established in San Francisco and located between 24th and 25th, Mission and Folsom streets, near Bernal Heights, it was active from 1862 to 1865.

CAMP ALLEN. A Civil War–period post in Oakland, it had been established for the training of volunteers before they were sent east, chiefly to join Edward Dexter Baker's Pennsylvania regiment. Other men assigned to the camp found themselves serving monotonous guard duty at warehouses or on some of the islands in San Francisco Bay.

CAMP ANDERSON (*Post near Sacramento City; Post near Sutterville*). In mid-July 1849 Major Julius J. B. Kingsbury with a battalion of the 2nd Infantry established a post in a swamp south of Sutterville, about a dozen miles from Sacramento City, for the purpose of staging an advance to the Bear River to establish Camp Far West. The camp was named for 2nd Lieutenant Charles C. Anderson, 7th New York Volunteers, who had earlier commanded Fort Sacramento (Sutter's Fort) and died at San Francisco, September 13, 1847, from a fever contracted while on detached service at Fort Sacramento. A few days later the camp was moved to the levee next to Sutterville's landing site. Unhappy in California, the major shortly before September 17 turned the command over to Captain Hannibal Day and took an unauthorized leave of absence. On September 22, Captain Day and the battalion abandoned Camp Anderson and marched overland to the Bear River.

FORT ANDERSON. Located on the right bank of Redwood Creek about 27 miles northeast of Arcata, Humboldt County, this post was established in May 1862 by Captain Charles D. Douglas, 2nd California Infantry. Named for Colonel Allen L. Anderson, 8th California Infantry, the post was intended to safeguard the area between the creek and the Klamath River from Indian hostiles. There is no evidence that the post was ever officially designated a fort, although orders for its establishment and subsequent official correspondence so referred to it, as did a number of regional historians. Abandoned sometime in the late summer of the same year as it

was set up, the post was reestablished in February 1864 as Camp Anderson to renew the campaign against the Indians. It was finally abandoned August 9, 1866.

CAMP ANDRADE. A Mexican border patrol post, probably established prior to World War I, Andrade was the heading of an old canal at the border on the California side of the Colorado River, with Algodones, Baja California, on the other side.

POST OF ANGEL ISLAND. FORT MCDOWELL.

CAMP ANZA. This World War II training post, located six miles southwest of Riverside and about 55 miles east of Los Angeles, with construction beginning on July 3, 1942, and completed on February 15, 1943, was activated on December 2, 1942, as Headquarters, Arlington Staging Area, but was redesignated Camp Anza on December 12, 1942. On November 5, 1942, it was activated as a reception center, and was redesignated Special Training Center on September 9, 1943. Camp Anza was deactivated March 31, 1946.

CAMP ARCADIA. Established during World War I as an Army Balloon School, it was located on the site of the Baldwin Race Track at Arcadia, Los Angeles County, about 16 miles northeast of Los Angeles. In May 1919 it was designated Ross Field in honor of Lieutenant Cleo J. Ross, Air Service, who was killed near Brabant, France, on September 26, 1918. The airfield had been established on June 3, 1918.

CAMP ARMSTRONG. In 1861 Lieutenant Lynn and 30 men established a temporary camp on the Van Dusen Fork of the Eel River near Yager Creek in Humboldt County.

CAMP ATASCADERO. In compliance with General Orders No. 84, War Department, 1908, a temporary camp of instruction for troops from various posts was established for the month of October, 1908, at the Atascadero Ranch in San Luis Obispo County. The ranch was apparently not used in 1909. Troops were again scheduled for one month's training there, September 15 to October 15, 1910, after which the ranch was not used again as a military post.

CAMP BABBITT. Established on June 24, 1862, by two companies of the 2nd California Cavalry, one mile from the town of Visalia, Tulare County, the post was intended to maintain order in the area where rabid pro-Confederate partisans were creating unrest. The garrison was also engaged in putting down Indian uprisings in the Owens River Valley. The post was named for Lieutenant Colonel E. B. Babbitt, quartermaster general of the Pacific. On October 2, 1865, the post was relocated about a mile northeast of its first site. Various dates have been given for its abandonment, from late in 1865 to August 19, 1866.

FORT BAKER NO. 1. Established on March 23, 1862, the post was located about 23 miles east of Hydesville on the west bank of the Van Dusen Fork of the Eel River in Humboldt County. In compliance with an order by Colonel Francis J. Lippitt, the post was established by Captain Thomas E. Ketcham, 3rd California Infantry, to protect the area between the Eel River and the Mad River from Indian hostiles. The post, actually never designated a fort, was named for Colonel Edward D. Baker, 71st Pennsylvania Infantry, who was killed on October 21, 1861, in the Battle of Ball's Bluff, Virginia. Colonel Baker had resigned his California seat in the Senate in order to serve in the Union army. On September 7, 1863, the post was recommended for closure, to be replaced by Camp Iaqua. Fort Baker was abandoned before the end of the year. It was reportedly burned on May 11 or 12, 1864, by either Indians or Confederates.

FORT BAKER NO. 2 (*Fort Lime Point*). Located on the north side of the entrance to the Golden Gate and San Francisco Bay, adjoining Fort Barry and opposite Fort Winfield Scott, and about two miles south of Sausalito, Marin County, the fort's original works were constructed during the Civil War and intermittently garrisoned for a number of years. The fortification was named (Fort) Lime Point until April 29, 1897, when it was renamed in honor of Colonel Edward D. Baker, an ex-U.S. senator from California, who had been killed on October 21, 1861, in the Battle of Ball's Bluff, Virginia.

After its works were rebuilt in the 1890s, with its armaments modernized, the fort was permanently garrisoned for the first time by a company of artillery, aggregating 93 men and two officers. Eight batteries formed the fort's outlying works: Duncan, Kirby, Point Cavallo, Point Diablo, Spencer, Wagner, Wallace, and Yates. In 1904 the original reservation property was divided into two forts separated by the true north and south line running through Point Diablo. The name Fort Baker was retained for the eastern portion. The western, or Point Diablo segment, was named Fort Barry. Fort Baker became a subpost of Fort Winfield Scott on September 25, 1946, then became a subpost of the Presidio of San Francisco on January 1, 1950.

FORT AT BALLAST POINT. FORT ROSECRANS.

CAMP BANNING. CAMP CARLETON.

CAMP BARBOUR. FORT MILLER.

CAMP BARRETT. A temporary camp for a few months in 1898 for a regiment of California Volunteers, it was located at Fruitvale, now a part of the city of Oakland.

FORT BARRY. Located at the entrance to San Francisco Bay, near Fort Cronkhite in Marin County, it was named in honor of Colonel (Brevet Major General) William F. Barry, 2nd Artillery, who served in the Peninsular Campaign in 1862 as chief of artillery, Army of the Potomac, and died July 18, 1879. Established as a separate reservation of approximately 1,344 acres in 1904 from lands formerly a part of Fort Baker, it was for many years a two-company post of the Coast Artillery. Along with a number of auxiliary Endicott-period batteries—Guthrie, McIndoe, Mendel, O'Rorke, Rathbone, and Smith—Fort Barry was formerly a subpost of Fort Winfield Scott and is now a subpost of the Presidio of San Francisco.

CAMP (JOHN H.) BEACOM (*Camp U.S. Troops*). A semipermanent camp located at Calexico, Imperial County, it was formerly known as Camp U.S. Troops. Named in honor of Colonel John H. Beacom, 6th Infantry, the post was established for border patrol duties during the Mexican Revolution, 1911–20.

CAMP BEALE. A World War II training camp activated on March 15, 1942, and encompassing 86,488 acres, it was named in honor of Brigadier General Edward Fitzgerald Beale, who served in the Mexican and Civil wars and the Indian wars of the West, and died in California in 1893. The camp, located 13 miles east of the "twin cities" of Marysville and Yuba City, county seats of Yuba and Sutter counties, respectively, occupied part of Captain Sutter's lands, where gold was found that precipitated the famous Gold Rush. Camp Beale was deactivated in 1947.

FORT BEALE. FORT PIUTE.

BENECIA ARSENAL. Once the oldest and largest ordnance supply depot for the entire Pacific

BENECIA ARSENAL.
(Courtesy of the Benecia
Historical Museum.)

area, this arsenal adjacent to Benecia in Solano County was located 43 miles northeast of San Francisco and situated on the west shore of Suisan Bay and on the north bank of Carquinez Straits. The arsenal was established on August 25, 1851, more than two years after the Army founded Benecia Barracks there. The settlement of Benecia was apparently named for Francisca Benecia, the wife of General Vallejo, a California pioneer. The original reservation was acquired by purchase in 1849, 1854, and 1855. Activity at the arsenal began to be phased out in March 1961, when the Defense Department announced plans to close it. Finally terminated in 1964, the arsenal was declared excess and turned over to the Government Services Administration (GSA) for disposition.

BENECIA BARRACKS. A site adjoining Benecia in Solano County was selected in April 1849 for a Quartermaster's Department depot by Brevet Major General Persifor F. Smith and Commodore Thomas C. Jones after the facilities occupied in San Francisco proved unsatisfactory. The site was first occupied by two companies of the 2nd Infantry under the command of Lieutenant Colonel Silas Casey. In 1852 the post was designated Benecia Barracks. During the Civil War the Barracks was used as a rendezvous for California Volunteers. From December 18, 1865, to

November 17, 1866, it was left without a garrison. It was one of the four depots for congregating and instructing recruits for the general recruiting service announced in General Orders No. 46, 1969. Except for short intervals, the post served continuously until 1964. (See: BENECIA ARSENAL.)

FORT BENTON. Apparently occupied for a short period in 1849, this post was located just across the California line from Mineral, Nevada, north of Bishop, Mono County. The town is known as Benton, Benton's Hot Springs, or Benton's Station, the latter from the nearby location of a depot for the Carson and Colorado Railroad during the 1880s.

CAMP BIDWELL. FORT BIDWELL.

CAMP BIDWELL (*Camp Chico*). This camp, originally called Camp Chico, was established at Chico, Butte County, by Captain Samuel H. Starr with Company F, 2nd Cavalry, on August 15, 1863, and by Company A, 6th Infantry, on August 26, 1863. Available post returns are dated from August 1863 to May 1865.

FORT BIDWELL (*Camp Bidwell*). Although various dates have been given for the inception of this post (1863 to 1866), located at the present town of Fort Bidwell at the northern end of Surprise Valley in Modoc County, it was most probably established sometime in 1863. The post, strategically located in the northeastern corner of the state, was intended to hold in check the marauding Indians of northeastern California, southern Oregon, and western Nevada, and to protect the travel routes into eastern Oregon and Idaho. Originally called Camp Bidwell, it was named for Major John Bidwell, California Volunteers, a veteran of the Mexican War, and a pioneer California settler. Abandoned early in 1865, it was reestablished as a log-built two-company post on July 17, 1865, close to its original situation on a new site selected by Major Robert S. Williamson, Corps of Engineers. Major General Irvin McDowell, the department's commander, then referred to it as a fort, but officially it was designated as Camp Bidwell until April 5, 1879, when it became Fort Bidwell. (Records in the National Archives maintain that when the post was reestablished, it was designated "Fort" Bidwell by General Orders No. 44.) Although the post was still garrisoned until October 21, 1893, the military reservation had been transferred to the Department of the Interior on November 22, 1890. The property then became a government Indian school and the headquarters for the Fort Bidwell Indian Reservation. In 1930 the boarding school was discontinued and the military barracks, formerly used as Indian student dormitories, were torn down. The commanding officer's quarters, however, are still standing, and nearby is the old post's cemetery.

CAMP BISHOP CREEK. A temporary post, it was established sometime in 1863 near present Bishop, Inyo County. It was probably named for Samuel A. Bishop, a well-known rancher who came to California in 1849, served as an officer in the Mariposa Battalion in 1851, and resided in Owen's Valley from 1860 to 1863.

REDOUBT BITTER SPRINGS. Located on the Salt Lake Road in the Mojave Desert, San Bernardino County, this redoubt was a subpost of Camp Cady, established by Major Carleton, who waged a campaign against the Paiutes and Shoshones in the early 1860s.

BLACK POINT FORT. FORT MASON.

FORT BLANCO. FORT WINFIELD SCOTT.

BLUNT POINT CAMP. Batteries were established on Blunt Point on the southeastern tip of Angel Island in San Francisco Bay in 1863 to protect the approaches to the Mare Island Navy Yard. Blunt Point Camp was deactivated in 1865.

BOYLE'S CAMP. CAMP NEW SUPPLY.

CAMP BOYNTON PRAIRIE. Located east of Eureka in Humboldt County, the camp was active from March to July 1864. It was established by Captain Thomas Buckley, with Company C, 6th Infantry, and the 1st Battalion, Mounted Cavalry.

FORT BRAGG. Established on June 11, 1857, Fort Bragg was located about 50 miles south of Cape Mendocino and situated one and a half miles north of the Noyo River, at the present town of Fort Bragg, Mendocino County. It was established within the Mendocino Indian Reservation for the purpose of both controlling and safeguarding the area's Indians. Established by 1st Lieutenant Horatio Gates Gibson, 3rd Artillery, with a detachment from Company M, the post was named for Captain Braxton Bragg, 3rd Artillery, a Mexican War veteran and later a general in the Confederate Army. There was a period of agitation to have the post's name changed because of his disaffection, but the post retained the name during the Civil War. In September 1864 many Army units serving in the Humboldt district were ordered south. The steamer *Panama* left Humboldt Bay October 18, 1864, picked up the Fort Bragg garrison the next day, and arrived at the Presidio of San Francisco on October 20. This constituted the permanent evacuation and abandonment of the post. The Mendocino Indian Reservation was discontinued in March 1866, and the land opened for settlement several years later.

CAMP BURNT RANCH. A temporary camp established in 1864, Burnt Ranch has been identified only as having been located "30 miles north of Hoopa," in either Humboldt County or Del Norte County.

CAMP BURTON. A temporary camp, April 28 to May 19, 1855, near San Diego, it was established by Captain Henry S. Burton, commanding Battery F (G?), 3rd Artillery. He and his men had come from Monterey to set up a temporary position before occupying permanent quarters in the then abandoned Mission San Diego de Alcalá in Mission Valley.

CAMP NEAR BUTTE CREEK. A temporary camp in 1856, it was garrisoned on October 31, 1856, by Company D, 4th Infantry. No definite location has been found for this post.

CAMP CADY. Located about 20 miles east of Barstow, San Bernardino County, Camp Cady was posted on April 14, 1860—in compliance with an order by General N. S. Clarke—by Major Carleton with Company K, 1st Dragoons, aggregating 80 men, near the Mojave River Road. The encampment was called Camp Cady for Major Albemarle Cady, 6th Infantry, then in command of Fort Yuma. For three months the Dragoons quartered themselves in temporary shelters of brush and mud or dugouts similar to those used later by the region's miners. The makeshift quarters were finally replaced by permanent structures built by Army regulars. The post had a parade ground 300 yards square, with the buildings arranged along three of its sides. The buildings were of adobe, floored and shingle-roofed, plastered outside and plastered and whitewashed inside. The officers' quarters was the only structure with ceilings. Camp Cady served as the base for a whole series of camps, redoubts, and forts along the Old Government Road to Fort Mohave and the Salt Lake Road, with campaigns waged against the Paiutes and Shoshones. The post was abandoned on April 24, 1871.

CAMP CAJON. The vicinity of Camp Cajon (1847 and 1857–58) was 15 miles from Cajon Pass on the Devore cutoff, a mile and a half west of Interstate 15, San Bernardino County. Company C of the Mormon Battalion was posted to guard Cajon Pass in April 1847.

CAJON PASS CAMP. From the time of the Mexican War, when a company of the Mormon Battalion garrisoned Cajon Pass, until the Civil War, there were military camps around San Bernardino from time to time. The Mormon Battalion camp was near present-day Devore, possibly on Martin's Ranch, which was later used as an Army camp in December 1857 and January 1859 for a company of infantry.

CAMP CALEXICO. A Mexican border patrol post, it was established on April 24, 1914, by the Los Angeles battalion of the 7th California Infantry under Colonel W. G. Schreiber, "to protect life and property," half a mile north of Calexico, Imperial County.

CAMP CALHOUN. FORT YUMA.

CAMP CALLAN. Established by the War Department in 1940 as a training center for antiaircraft artillery, it was named in honor of General Robert E. Callan (1874–1936), a veteran of the Spanish-American War and World War I. The 1,644-acre training camp was located on Porrey Pines Mesa, a few miles from La Jolla, but within San Diego's city limits. On November 1, 1945, the War Department declared Camp Callan surplus property.

CAMP CAMPO. A Mexican border patrol post, the camp was located at Campo, near Palm City, San Diego County. It was probably established prior to World War I.

CAMPO'S STONE FORT. Situated in the village of Campo, San Diego County, less than a mile from the Mexican boundary, a building of massive construction has become a tourist attraction over the years. The stone and masonry walls of the first story are 4 feet thick and almost 3 on the second story. A tunnel more than 6 feet high originates within the fort and extends into the hill for 40 or 50 feet. At one time thick wooden shutters covered with iron made this border fortress formidable. The fort was built about 1885 by the brothers L. H. and S. E. Gaskill to defend against bands of outlaws and thieves.

CAMP CAÑADA DE LAS UVAS. FORT TEJÓN.

CAMP CAP-ELL. Located on Cappell Bay, on the west side of the Klamath River, 15 miles above Fort Ter-Waw and about 10 miles below the mouth of the Trinity River, in Humboldt County, this post in 1856 was a temporary summer camp of Company B, 4th Infantry.

FORT CAPE OF PINES. PRESIDIO OF MONTEREY.

FORT CAPE OF PINES. FORT POINT OF PINES.

CAMP CARLETON (*Camp Banning; Camp Prentiss; New Camp Carleton*). From the days of the Mexican War, when Mormon Battalion soldiers were posted at Cajon Pass, until the Civil War, there were military camps around San Bernardino from time to time. A Mormon post, Cajon Pass Camp, was near present-day Devore, probably on Martin's Ranch, which was later used as an Army camp in December 1857 and January 1859 for a company of infantry. In February the soldiers moved nearer San Bernardino and named their newly established post Camp Banning. When official designation was made, it was called Camp Prentiss. Between these two designations the troops went to Fort Yuma and the Mohave War and returned across the desert. Their camp is believed to have been situated in the environs of Valley College, near the intersection of Mt. Vernon Avenue and Mill Street.

When the men returned from their desert duty they established Camp Carleton on the north bank of the Santa Ana River, south of San Bernardino, in the vicinity of present Waterman Avenue. Camp Carleton was the largest of several to be maintained at various times in the city's vicinity. It was established in the fall of 1861 by Captain William A. McCleave and the 1st California Cavalry. In 1862 this camp's garrison moved to El Monte, 10 miles east of Los Angeles, and established New Camp Carleton.

CAMP CASS. Located at Red Bluffs, Tehama County, Camp Cass was originally an American Fur Company post. On May 26, 1859, Company A, 6th Infantry, arrived to occupy the camp until August 3, 1859.

CAMP CHICO. CAMP BIDWELL.

CHOUCHILLE CAMP. Named for a local Indian tribe, this temporary post was established sometime in 1856 in or near present Chowchilla, Madera County.

CAMP CLIPPER. A World War II Desert Training Maneuver Area post, it was located southwest of Needles.

COLUSA POST. A temporary post established in late 1864 or early 1865 at Colusa, Colusa County, it was occupied by Captain W. K. Knight with Company D of the California Volunteer Cavalry.

CAMP COOKE. A World War II armored division training center, it was located on the coast five miles northwest of Lompoc, Santa Barbara County. The 88,000-acre post, activated in 1942, was named in honor of Philip St. George Cooke, who led the Mormon Battalion to San Diego in 1847 and became a general in the Union Army. The post was inactivated on January 6, 1953. The site is today occupied by the Strategic Air Command's 100-square-mile Vandenberg Air Force Base, the nation's first operational missile center.

CAMP COSTER. Established in 1862 or 1863, after the founding of Camp Independence, it was located on or close to the south shore of Owens Lake, Inyo County.

CAMP COXCOMB. A World War II Desert Training Maneuver Area post, it was located east of Indio and occupied by the 7th Armored Division.

CAMP CRANE. Situated in Crane Valley (discovered in 1848 and named for the area's wild cranes), Camp Crane was most probably established as a temporary post in 1852 by troops from Fort Miller north of Fresno. In 1901 Crane Valley Reservoir, enlarged by the waters backed up by the Bass Lake Dam constructed in 1909, engulfed the site of Camp Crane.

CAMP CRESCENT CITY. Established in 1856 during the Red Cap War by elements of the 4th Infantry out of Fort Humboldt, this camp in Del Norte County was irregularly garrisoned until 1858.

FORT CRONKHITE. Located on the Pacific Ocean shore, north of Rodeo Cove, in Marin County, north of and adjoining Fort Barry, about three and a half miles west of Sausalito, it was named by General Orders No. 9, 1937, in honor of Major General Adelbert Cronkhite. Fort Cronkhite's original reservation consisted of about 800 acres, acquired in 1937. Throughout World War II the fort, one of the subposts of Fort Winfield Scott, was being continuously expanded by frame, brick, concrete, and steel construction of 108 structures and gun batteries.

FORT CROOK (*Camp Hollenbush*). Located on the north bank of the Fall River, one and a half miles from Glenburn and about seven miles above the Fall River's junction with the Pitt River, Shasta County, the fort was established on July 1, 1857, for the purpose of providing area protection from Indian hostiles. Originally called Camp Hollenbush for Assistant Surgeon Calvin G. Hollenbush, but later designated Fort Crook for 1st Lieutenant George Crook, 4th Infantry, the post had been established by Captain John W. T. Gardiner, with Company A, 1st Dragoons, and Company D, 4th Infantry. In May 1866 the garrison was withdrawn and replaced by a small detachment from Fort Bidwell, of which Fort Crook then became a subpost. The post was abandoned on July 1, 1869 (June 1, 1869, according to National Archives records). On February 15, 1881, the military reservation was returned to the public domain.

CAMP CURTIS. Today a California Historical Landmark, Camp Curtis was the headquarters of the Mountain Battalion of California Volunteers from 1862 to 1865, located one mile north of Arcata, Humboldt County. (Before its establishment, it was called Camp on Janes Farm.) In 1863 Captain George Ousley with Company B (34 men) of the Battalion first garrisoned Camp Curtis near Daby's Ferry and then moved to Fawn Prairie on the Hoopa Trail. A bronze tablet commemorating the camp's site was unveiled on October 5, 1930.

DABY'S FERRY POST. A detachment was dispatched in early June 1862 by Captain Eugene B. Gibbs, commanding Camp Curtis, to a crossing on the Mad River about three miles from Arcata, Humboldt County, and there established a temporary post to safeguard the area's settlers from further Indian incursions.

FORT DEFIANCE. In 1850 Lieutenant George H. Derby, on orders of Major General P. F. Smith, made a reconnaissance of the Colorado River. His map, dated December 1850, shows Fort Defiance on the California side of the river, about half a mile above the Mexican boundary. The remains of this nonmilitary installation are located four miles below Fort Yuma. According to John R. Bartlett's *Personal Narrative* (1852), "This is the spot where we first encamped, and were unable to reach the water. It was an old ferrying place, and the scene of a massacre by the Yumas the year before our visit." According to the War Department, a military post known as Fort Defiance, garrisoned by a lieutenant and 10 men, was also established at Pilot Knob to the northeast. The soldiers and ferrymen garrisoned the stockade that had been erected by the Glanton party.

FORT DEFIANCE (*Roop's Fort*). Enlarged into a fortified blockhouse in June 1854, Fort Defiance is Susanville's oldest structure, today a museum on Weatherlow Street. It was formerly the log-built trading post built by Isaac N. Roop in the spring of 1853 after he arrived on horseback from Shasta. In 1854 a border dispute, known as the Sagebrush War, erupted between California and Nevada, and the fort played a leading role in the bitter conflict, ultimately settled by a compromise. The boundary dispute was resolved when the California-Nevada line was run northward from Lake Tahoe, east of Honey Lake Valley. Hard feelings persisted until the California Legislature, on April 1, 1864, created Lassen County with its seat at Susanville.

FORT DENNY. A trading post built by Albert H. Denny, it was located at the upper end of Scott Valley, Siskiyou County, in 1851.

CAMP DOLORES. Late in 1850 southern California ranchers were subjected to a devastating raid by Chief Walkara and his Ute horse thieves and demanded protection from the authorities. Authorized by the governor, General J. H. Bean, militia commander, organized a company of 50 volunteer rangers to protect the frontier. At first stationed in Cajon Pass, they moved into the San Bernardino Valley and established Camp Dolores near the present Valley College. In April 1851 troops from Camp Dolores were called upon to defend José del Carmen Lugo's Rancho San Bernardino from a band of renegades, who were tracked down. A bloody battle ensued. When a coroner's jury found the killing of white men by the Indians justifiable, General Bean condemned the finding and shortly afterward broke up Camp Dolores and disbanded the rangers. A little later that year the Lugo family, weary of the hardships and dangers, sold Rancho San Bernardino to Mormon settlers.

CAMP DOWNEY. In mid-July 1861 the War Department requested California's Governor Downey to raise a force of volunteers, infantry and cavalry, to protect that part of the overland stage and mail route between the Sierras and the Rockies. Recruits were plentiful and they were sent to two training camps that had been established on the east side of San Francisco Bay, the infantry to Camp Downey and the cavalry to Camp Merchant. Camp Downey overlooked Lake Merritt in today's Oakland, on today's Seventh Avenue. The camp was established by Lieutenant Colonel J. R. West with the 1st Infantry, California Volunteers, on August 31, 1861. On September 15 Lieutenant Colonel West and Companies A, B, C, E, G, and H left the camp en route for Los Angeles.

CAMP DRAGOON BRIDGE. This post was established in August 1860 by 1st Lieutenant John Hamilton, 3rd Artillery, with Company I. On September 17 he left with 27 men of the company for the Presidio of San Francisco, leaving 2nd Lieutenant E. R. Warner in command. The post, apparently intermittently garrisoned, was reportedly in existence until sometime in 1863.

DRAKE'S FORT. In June 1579 Sir Francis Drake constructed a short-lived, crude fortification at Drake's Bay in the neighborhood of Point Reyes north of San Francisco. He had been compelled to make the landing in order to make ship repairs, presenting him with the opportunity to lay claim to the land, which he named Nova Albion (New England).

CAMP DRUM. DRUM BARRACKS.

DRUM BARRACKS (*Camp Drum*). Established as a five-company post in January 1862, and located one mile from Wilmington, now a part of Los Angeles, this post until December 1863 called itself Camp Drum; it was thereafter designated Drum Barracks. It was named by the War Department in honor of Lieutenant Colonel Richard Drum, assistant adjutant general of the Department of California. When it was built the Civil War was already being waged and the government considered California as a doubtful state on the question of slavery. The state's northern half was about equally divided in its sympathies, but the southern half, particularly the area around Los Angeles, where at least 75 percent of the Americans had come from slaveholding states, was strongly pro-Secession. It was determined that California must be held loyal to the Union. Captain (later General) Winfield Scott Hancock was sent to Los Angeles to establish a quartermaster's depot, ostensibly to have his troops fight the Indians. But there were no Indians in the area. The government spent more than a million dollars on Drum Barracks, a very large sum of money then, which judiciously expended could buy an appreciable amount of allegiance. While most other California posts were simple adobe structures roofed with corrugated iron, Drum Barracks was entirely different. The elegance of its officers' quarters impressed the inhabitants of Los Angeles.

Drum Barracks, however, soon became a staging station for troops in transit. On April 13, 1862, Colonel (later Brigadier General) James Henry Carleton led an army of more than 2,000 California Volunteers from the post to begin the longest and most difficult march of the Civil War. His route was through Temecula to Arizona and New Mexico and to the Rio Grande Valley, then being invaded by Confederate armed forces. Drum Barracks, intermittently occupied during the war, was finally abandoned on November 7, 1871.

FORT DUPONT. PRESIDIO OF SAN DIEGO.

EAST GARRISON. FORT MCDOWELL.

CAMP ON EEL RIVER. FORT SEWARD.

EL CASTILLO. PRESIDIO OF MONTEREY.

CAMP EL CENTRO. A Mexican border patrol post at El Centro, Imperial County, it was probably established prior to World War I.

EL PRESIDIO ROYAL DE MONTE REY. PRESIDIO OF MONTEREY.

ELK CAMP. Sometime in May 1862 the people in the small settlement of Elk Camp, about 15 miles northeast of Camp Anderson, Humboldt County, urgently requested government military protection. Sparse archival records and other sources indicate that a temporary post, garrisoned from Camp Anderson, was probably established within the settlement.

FORT EMORY. A subpost of Fort Rosecrans, Fort Emory was a World War II installation located at Coronado Heights, San Diego, designated a part of the city's harbor defense. Situated near the south end of San Diego Bay, adjoining the community of Imperial Beach, it was named for Brigadier General William Helmsley Emory in December 1942. Almost immediately after the post's completion, the installation was turned over temporarily to the U.S. Navy for its use. Originally it had been planned to mount a battery of 16-inch seacoast guns there, but these were never installed. Fort Emory, declared surplus on March 1, 1948, was taken over permanently by the Navy as its Communications Training Center. A few of the post's original structures and the concrete gun mounts still remain.

CAMP FAR WEST. FORT FAR WEST.

FORT FAR WEST (*Camp Far West*). A military post was established on September 28, 1849, on Bear Creek, located near present Marysville, Yuba County. The post was strategically placed to safeguard the travel routes to the area's mines. Until 1851 it was known as Camp Far West, then as Fort Far West. It was abandoned on May 4, 1852.

CAMP FAUNTLEROY. Special Orders No. 79, dated August 6, 1856, and received November 13, 1856, directed Major George Blaker, 1st Dragoons, with Companies F, H, and I (217 rank and file) to proceed first to Fort Tejón, Kern County, and then to the site selected for the temporary establishment of Camp Fauntleroy, where the troops arrived on November 29, 1856.

FEDERAL ARMORY. Located at the south end of Copperopolis, Calaveras County, this installation was the region's headquarters for Union troops during the Civil War. The Army's massive iron doors were reputed to have been by far the largest in the area.

CAMP FITZGERALD. A short-lived emergency post, it was established in early March 1852, about 30 miles south-southwest of Fort Yuma by Major Edward H. Fitzgerald when he and his 40 dragoons were attacked by some 200 Indians. The outnumbered soldiers, four of them killed in the action, retreated to a hill and dug in. The camp apparently lasted but one day.

CAMP FITZGERALD. Established in early June 1861, near Los Angeles, where it occupied three different sites, each abandoned on account of the lack of water and pasture for the horses, Camp Fitzgerald was first garrisoned by Colonel James Henry Carleton, 1st Dragoons, with Companies B and K, 1st Dragoons, and Companies F and I, 6th Infantry. Most of the 304 troops came from Fort Tejón, California, where Carleton was stationed until May 3, and Fort Mojave, New Mexico, between June 12 and June 27. The camp was named in honor of Brevet Major Edward H. Fitzgerald, 1st Dragoons, who died in 1860. On September 8, 1861, Companies F and I, 6th Infantry, numbering 118 men, left for Fort Yuma. On September 20 Carleton and his 1st Dragoons evacuated Camp Fitzgerald.

FONTANA BARRACKS. Used during the Spanish-American War as a troop center in San Francisco, Fontana Barracks was a temporarily converted packing and storage plant for the Fontana Packing Company.

CAMP FREDERICA. Established in 1850 by Major Albert S. Miller with a battalion of the 2nd Infantry, Camp Frederica was situated on the Stanislaus River in the present county of the same name. For many years historians, locating the camp as "150 miles east of Monterey," had confused the 1849 and 1850 summer encampments on the river, consolidating them as "Miller's Camp" or Camp Stanislaus (1849), located at or near Taylor's Ferry (modern Riverbank) on the north bank. Miller's post of 1850 was established following escort duty for Lieutenant George Derby, U.S. topographical engineer, who surveyed the coast's mountain range, seeking an easy transport route from Monterey to the central San Joaquin Valley. The military escort, from Monterey, primarily camped at Mission San Miguel Arcangel, San Luis Obispo County, until Derby completed his survey of the coast range. The first part of Derby's survey completed, the escort proceeded from Mission San Miguel and crossed over the coast range to the San Joaquin Valley. Following Derby's survey of the valley, he left the escort to write his report while Major Miller carried out the second part of his instructions, moving to the Stanislaus River and going into camp about seven miles from the Durham Ferry crossing on the San Joaquin River. Historians have made a number of conjectures regarding the derivation of the name "Frederica," without arriving at any conclusion.

CAMP FRÉMONT. Established on July 18, 1917, to serve as a training camp for the 41st Division, National Guard, consisting of troops from Washington, Oregon, Idaho, and Wyoming, it was located at Menlo Park, near Palo Alto, and named in honor of Major General John C. Frémont. Later, orders directed the organization of the division at Camp Greene, and the 8th Division was concentrated here. Construction began on July 24, 1917, and included 1,124 structures. The 7,203-acre reservation was ordered salvaged on December 19, 1918, and the buildings were sold at auction. The camp was abandoned in September 1919.

FORT FRÉMONT. FORT JURUPA.

FORT FRÉMONT. PRESIDIO OF MONTEREY.

FORT FRÉMONT PEAK. On Gabilan Peak (renamed Frémont Peak), Captain John C. Frémont built a fort in 1846, expecting stiff resistance from Mexican Californianos. After four days, when the battle did not materialize, he broke camp and left for Oregon. The state of California now maintains Frémont State Park, south of San Juan Bautista, Santa Cruz County.

POST AT FRIDAY'S STATION. Very little is known about this short-lived military post established in 1864 near Lake Tahoe, apparently situated on the California side of the lake.

FORT FUNSTON (*Laguna Merced Military Reservation*). Situated on Lake Merced, on the fringe of the Golden Gate, and located in the city and county of San Francisco, with its reservation line touching the San Mateo County border, Fort Funston was established in 1898 as the Laguna Merced Military Reservation. In 1917 it was renamed for General Frederick Funston. Most of the fort was declared surplus in 1950 and the city acquired 50 acres at the north end and, later, 117 acres east of Skyline Boulevard in the Lake Merced area. The remaining parcel, a 71-acre beach and bluff area west of the highway, was last militarily used as a missile site and is a park at the present time.

CAMP GASTON (Humboldt County). FORT GASTON.

CAMP GASTON. Situated on the west bank of the Colorado River about 45 miles north of Fort Yuma by land, Camp Gaston was established in 1859 by Captain Henry S. Burton, 3rd Artillery, to serve as a temporary supply post in connection with the new establishment of Fort Mohave, Arizona. Although it was abandoned as soon as the stores were moved to the new Arizona post, it intermittently served as an outpost of Fort Yuma and was garrisoned from time to time by small detachments as late as 1867. The camp was named in honor of 2nd Lieutenant William Gaston, 1st Dragoons, who was killed in action against the Spokane Indians on May 17, 1858.

FORT GASTON (*Camp Gaston*). Established on December 4, 1858, it was situated in the Hoopa Valley on the west bank of the Trinity River, some 14 miles above its junction with the Klamath River, Humboldt County. Located within the Hoopa Valley Indian Reservation, it was intended to both control the area's Indians and protect them against hostile depredations. The post was established by Captain Edmund Underwood, 4th Infantry, and named for 2nd Lieutenant William Gaston, 1st Dragoons, killed on May 17, 1858, during the campaign against the Spokane Indians. Originally called Fort Gaston, it was renamed Camp Gaston on January 1, 1867, and then redesignated Fort Gaston on April 5, 1879. Abandoned on June 29, 1892, the military reservation was transferred to the Department of the Interior on February 11, 1892, reserved for the use of the Indian Service.

GENERAL GILLEM'S CAMP. CAMP IN THE LAVA BEDS.

CAMP GIFTALER RANCH. Apparently a temporary military post established in 1863 on the ranch's property in connection with the Civil War conflict in the area, the camp was located some 14 miles southeast of Temecula in southwestern Riverside County.

CAMP GILLESPIE. A World War II paratrooper training base, it was established by the government on former farming land near El Cajon adjoining San Diego. Three 256-foot-high towers, used in conjunction with the training, were removed in 1954–55 after the county received title to the 700-acre field. The site is now Gillespie Field, a county airport.

CAMP GILMORE. CAMP MCDOUGALL.

CAMP GILMORE. In 1863 a post, named Camp Gilmore, was established about four miles north of Trinidad, Humboldt County, to protect the mail route. The camp was abandoned sometime in 1864.

GOLD BLUFFS POST. Other than its location between Klamath and Orick, Humboldt County, no definitive archival evidence has been found to confirm the existence of a military post there, reportedly established in 1863 and abandoned sometime in 1864. The site was discovered in the fall of 1850 by Hermann Ehrenberg and named Gold Bluffs because of the gold found in the sand washed down from the bluffs. The fact that it was the site of extensive mining operations over the years suggests that protection had been required and that a minimally garrisoned military post was provided.

CAMP AT GOOSE LAKE. Formerly called Pitt's Lake, Goose Lake in Shasta County was the site of a camp reportedly established in the spring of 1866 by Company F of the regiment called the Sacramento Rangers. According to the *Records of California Men in the War of the Rebellion*, p. 169, the Sacramento Rangers were organized at Camp Alert, then stationed at several locations in California and Nevada before taking post at Goose Lake. The original members were mustered out at San Francisco on September 24, 1864, but the company was again filled up, only to be finally disbanded at Sacramento on June 27, 1866.

CAMP GRANITE. One of the Desert Training Maneuver Area camps established in 1943 during World War II, Camp Granite was located about 45 miles west of the Colorado River. In June 1943 the 76th Field Artillery Brigade was at Camp Granite although the permanent camp had not yet been completed.

CAMP GRANT. Situated on the upper Eel River near Scotia, Humboldt County, Camp Grant was established in October 1863 by Captain John P. Simpson with Company E of the Mountain Battalion. Abeloe's revision of *Historic Spots in California*, p. 100, placed Camp Grant "on the Eel River, 3 miles east of Dyerville." Simpson and his troops captured 166 Indian hostiles, whom he placed on the Round Valley Reservation in 1864. Company E was mustered out at Fort Humboldt on June 14, 1865, apparently not long after Camp Grant was abandoned.

CASTILLO DE GUIJARROS. PRESIDIO OF SAN DIEGO.

FORT GUIJARROS. FORT ROSECRANS.

FORT GUNNYBAGS (*Fort Vigilance*). The sandbagged warehouse converted in 1856 to the use of the San Francisco Vigilantes as its armory and drill hall, Fort Vigilance, popularly nicknamed Fort Gunnybags, also served as the dictatorial group's headquarters. The vigilantes were ostensibly organized to establish law and order within the city, but they disbanded when it was determined that they were much worse than the supposed offenders. The site of the pseudo fort in San Francisco is on Sacramento Street, bounded by Front, Davis, and California streets.

CAMP HAAN. Located nine miles southeast of Riverside, Camp Haan was a World War II installation used principally as an Antiaircraft Replacement Training Center beginning in January 1941. Other miscellaneous operations included an Army Service Forces Depot and a Prisoner of War camp. The Southwest Branch, U.S. Disciplinary Barracks, was also authorized for activation at this post. The military reservation, a trapezoidal area about four miles long and three miles wide, comprised some 8,058 acres, and was named in honor of Major General William George Haan, who had a very distinguished Army career during World War I and was awarded a number of American and foreign government decorations. Camp Haan was declared surplus to Army requirements on August 31, 1946.

CAMP HALLECK. Established on a local racetrack at Stockton, San Joaquin County, in May 1861, the Civil War post was named for Henry W. Halleck, California's first secretary of state during its military government, 1846–50. Seven hundred men from the 3rd California Volunteers in Benecia were stationed here. On July 12, 600 men left the post on an overland march to Salt Lake City to establish Camp Douglas. Camp Halleck was abandoned sometime in 1863.

FORT HALLECK. PRESIDIO OF MONTEREY.

HANCOCK'S REDOUBT. FORT SODA.

HAY FORK CAMP. In 1864 a short-lived military post was established at Hayfork, Trinity County, to protect the mining operations there.

FORT HILL (Los Angeles). FORT MOORE.

FORT HILL (Monterey). PRESIDIO OF MONTEREY.

FORT HILL (*Fort Keysville*). An earthen fortification was erected in 1855 or 1856 by miners on a hill adjoining the town of Keysville (Keyesville), Kern County, in expectation of Indian attacks.

CAMP HOLLENBUSH. FORT CROOK.

CAMP HOLTVILLE. A Mexican border patrol post, it was located in the environs of Holtville, Imperial County, and probably established prior to World War I.

CAMP HOOKER. Established on August 21, 1862, near Stockton, San Joaquin County, by Captain J. B. Moore, 3rd California Volunteers, with four companies of troops, aggregating 174 men, the post was evacuated in October 1862.

FORT HOOPER. A trading post established on McAdams Creek in Siskiyou County in the spring of 1852, it was built by the father of Frank W. Hooper. No archival evidence was found to indicate the length of its existence.

CAMP NEAR HORNITOS. Apparently a short-lived military post established in 1865, it was reportedly located about 18 miles northeast of Merced.

CAMP HOT CREEK STATION. Probably a stage station on a travel route, located some 35 miles southwest of Fort Crook, it was garrisoned for a short period by a military detachment in 1862.

CAMP HOWARD. Captain Van A. Andruss, 1st Artillery, with seven batteries of artillery, aggregating 87 men, marched 130 miles from the Presidio of San Francisco north to Ukiah, Mendocino County, arriving on June 26, 1888, where they encamped for two weeks.

FORT HUMBOLDT. Established on January 30, 1853, by Captain Robert C. Buchanan, 4th Infantry, this post was situated on a 35-foot-high bluff overlooking Humboldt Bay at what was then Bucksport, presently a part of the city of Eureka. Intended to provide protection for the area's inhabitants from Indian hostiles, it served also as a supply depot for other posts in northern California. Ulysses S. Grant served here in 1854 as a 4th Infantry captain. In 1866 the garrison, except for one company of artillery, was withdrawn and the post then became a subdepot, maintained primarily to provide supplies to Fort Gaston. Department commander Brigadier General Irvin McDowell reported on September 14, 1867, that the company of artillery had been withdrawn and the post completely abandoned (one historical chronologist reports abandonment took place in 1866, in accordance with Special Order No. 243, Department of California). On April 6, 1870, the military reservation, now a state historic monument, was transferred to the Department of the Interior. The post hospital, completely renovated, was moved a short distance from its original site. Also still standing is the restored building which formerly housed the commissary's headquarters, now a museum.

FORT HUNTER LIGGETT (*Hunter Liggett Military Reservation*). Occupying land purchased by the Army from the William Randolph Hearst estate in late 1940 for World War II troop training, 164,000-acre Fort Hunter Liggett is adjacent to the town of Jolon, the site of the old Mission of San Antonio de Padua founded in 1771 by Father Junipero Serra. The fort is located halfway between San Francisco and Santa Barbara, and about 60 miles south of Fort Ord, of which it is a subpost. The post functions as a 7th Division maneuver area and a field laboratory of the Combat Development Experimentation Center (CDEC). Originally designated the Hunter Liggett Military Reservation, it was named in honor of Lieutenant General Hunter Liggett, who served during the Spanish-American War, and was chief of staff for General Pershing during World War I. In 1975 the reservation was redesignated a fort and was further developed for its present uses. The fort's main area, nestled in the San Antonio River Valley, is centered around an imposing structure called the Hacienda, built in the 1920s as headquarters for the Hearst ranch. Today it serves as an officers' club and guest quarters.

HUNTER LIGGETT MILITARY RESERVATION. FORT HUNTER LIGGETT.

FORT IAQUA (*Camp Jaqua*). The fort was established primarily as a Civil War post on August 5, 1863, on the travel route between Fort Humboldt and Fort Gaston, and its garrison attempted to reconcile differences between the area's settlers and Indians without significant success. The fort was reportedly situated on Yeager (Iaqua) Creek, about 18 miles east of the mouth of the Eel River, in Humboldt County. The post was abandoned on August 9, 1866.

CAMP IBIS. One of the temporary World War II camps forming the Desert Training Center, known after October 20, 1943, as the California-Arizona Maneuver Area, it was discontinued on April 30, 1944. Camp Ibis was constructed during the period of November 8, 1942–March 28, 1943. The 4th Armored Division, under Major General John S. Wood, was at Camp Ibis until June 1943, when its place was taken by the 9th Armored Division, commanded by Major General John W. Leonard. Most of the troops trained at Camp Ibis in desert survival, gunnery, and armored vehicle tactics were destined to join General George S. Patton's European command, far from a desert battlefield. The post was located near Needles, close to the point where the borders of California, Arizona, and Nevada meet.

CAMP INDEPENDENCE. FORT YUMA.

CAMP INDEPENDENCE. Situated in Inyo County on the north side of Oak Creek, about three miles from the town of Independence, in the Owens River Valley, on the eastern slope of the Sierra Nevadas, the post was established by Lieutenant Colonel George S. Evans, 2nd California Cavalry, on July 4, 1862. Never officially designated a fort, it was established to provide protection for the area's miners, who were troubled by Indian marauders. Temporarily abandoned in 1864, it was reoccupied in March 1865, due to renewed Indian depredations. The post was finally abandoned on July 5, 1877. The military reservation was transferred to the Interior Department for disposition on July 22, 1884. The building which served as the commanding officer's quarters was moved from its original site to its new setting on Edwards Street in Independence.

CAMP NEAR IONE CITY. CAMP JACKSON.

CAMP IRON MOUNTAIN. A World War II installation, one of a number established during the 1942–44 period, it was located in the Desert Training Maneuver Area, just north of Camp Granite, almost halfway between Indio and the Colorado River, south of Needles.

CAMP IRWIN. FORT IRWIN.

FORT IRWIN (*Mojave Antiaircraft Range [MAAR]; Camp Irwin*). Situated in the Mojave Desert, San Bernardino County, Fort Irwin is located 37 miles northeast of Barstow and 37 miles south of Death Valley. The Old Spanish Trail cut through the reservation en route to what is now Santa Fe, New Mexico, with Bitter Springs one of the stopovers. Captain John C. Frémont was the first member of the Army to visit Bitter Springs. Accompanied by Kit Carson, he passed through the present reservation in 1844. In 1846 the Army's Mormon Battalion was stationed in the area, with headquarters in the Cajon Pass area. In 1860 the Army returned to Fort Irwin's environs. During the Indian Wars, a unit patrolled the area and established a base camp on a hill overlooking Bitter Springs. There they constructed a small stone fort.

In the 1930s General George S. Patton used the area as a maneuver site for armored vehicles. Tank tracks from those maneuvers are still visible in places. In 1940 President Roosevelt established a military reservation of 1,000 square miles, in the area of present-day Fort Irwin, which was named the Mojave Antiaircraft Range. On November 4, 1942, the post was officially designated Camp Irwin in honor of Major General George Leroy Irwin, World War I battle commander of the 57th Field Artillery Brigade. The camp was deactivated in 1944, then reactivated in 1951 as a training center for combat units during the Korean War.

The post was designated a permanent Class I installation in August 1961 and was renamed Fort Irwin. During the Vietnam War many types of units, primarily artillery and engineer, were trained here and deployed to Southeast Asia directly from the post. In January 1971 the post was again deactivated and was placed in maintenance status under the control of Fort MacArthur. In 1972 full responsibility for the post was assumed by the California Army National Guard. Despite deactivation the post has served as a training site for the National Guard and Army Reserve elements since World War II. On October 16, 1980, the National Training Center was officially activated here, following years of planning and study at the Department of the Army, Headquarters, U.S. Army Forces Command and U.S. Army Training and Doctrine Command. On July 1, 1981, the fort was officially reactivated as an active Army installation.

CAMP JACKSON (*Camp near Ione City*). This post, located near Ione (formerly Ione City), Amador County, then in a gold-mining region, was established by Company D, 2nd California Volunteer Cavalry, in March 1865 and remained in garrison for three months.

FORT JANESVILLE. In 1860 settlers built a loopholed stockade, with a bastion or blockhouse in its southwest angle, less than a mile from the town of Janesville, Lassen County, after the Battle of Pyramid Lake. The site of the fort is now a California Historic Landmark.

CAMP JAQUA. FORT IAQUA.

CAMP JOHNS. A temporary post established by Nevada troops in the summer of 1864, occupying it during their expedition in July and August, it was located in the center of Susanville, adjacent to Roop's Fort, in Lassen County. Captain Almond B. Wells, with Company D, 1st Nevada Territorial Cavalry, from Fort Churchill, Nevada, set up a base camp here which they named Camp Johns. From this point, they toured the areas of northeastern California and northwestern Nevada. They returned to Fort Churchill on August 28.

FORT JONES. PRESIDIO OF MONTEREY.

FORT JONES. Established on October 16, 1852, this important 640-acre post was situated on the east side of the Scott River at the present town of Fort Jones (formerly Wheelock), Siskiyou County. The post was established by Major Edward H. Fitzgerald, with Companies A and E, 1st Dragoons, for the purpose of protecting the mining town from Indian depredations. The fort was named for Colonel Roger Jones, adjutant general of the Army, who died on July 15, 1852. On June 23, 1858, the post was evacuated by the garrison. In 1864 it was reoccupied for a short period by the California Mountaineer Battalion. The reservation was transferred to the Interior Department on May 27, 1870, for disposition.

FORT JURUPA (*Rancho del Jurupa Post; Fort Frémont*). Between 1852 and 1854 a military detachment of no more than 20 men occupied a gristmill on the Rancho Rubidoux property in the present community of Rubidoux, a suburb of Riverside, intended as a guard on the so-called eastern Indian frontier. When first established, the post was called Rancho del Jurupa; then it was shortened to Fort Jurupa. Later, sometime during its existence, it was renamed Fort Frémont. There is no record of any military action having occurred there during the period of occupation.

CAMP KEARNY. A temporary camp on the fringe of Monterey, it was established immediately after the New York Volunteers landed to take possession in April 1847.

CAMP KELLOGG. A Civil War post established sometime in 1861 by elements of the 5th California Infantry, who named it for their regimental commander, it was located in the Los Angeles suburb of Culver City. The post was abandoned in 1862.

FORT KEYSVILLE. FORT HILL.

KLINE'S RANCH POST. Probably a temporary Civil War post, it was established sometime in 1862 on ranch property in the vicinity of Los Angeles.

CAMP (JOHN T.) KNIGHT. The California State Archives reported that Camp John T. Knight, a temporary World War I post at Oakland, was named for John Thornton Knight, who was awarded the Distinguished Service Cross during the war for his outstanding service in the Quartermaster Corps. Despite persevering research, no more definite chronological data could be found.

CAMP KOHLER. A World War II Signal Corps Replacement Center, located in the environs of Sacramento, was dedicated on December 1, 1942. It was named for Lieutenant Frederick L. Kohler of Oakland, a Signal Corps officer, who was killed in China on March 14, 1942. On March 1, 1946, Camp Kohler was abandoned as a troop-training center. On March 19, however, it was announced that the post would be taken over by the Army Corps of Engineers. On September 26, 1947, plans were made to offer the post's buildings for sale to veterans.

FORT LAGUNA DE CHAPALA. A short-lived Mexican fortification, established in early December 1825 by Lieutenant Romualdo Pacheco with a cavalry force from the Presidio of San Diego, Fort Laguna de Chapala was located between the New River and Bull Head Slough, west of El Centro, Imperial County. The fort lasted only four months and was never regarrisoned. During the last week of December 1825, Lieutenant Pacheco's report from the fort predicted completion of the post in one month. By the end of January he was back in San Diego and apparently one Ignacio Delgado was left in charge of the fort. News arrived at the Presidio of an impending Indian uprising. In April Indians employed on the fort revolted and attacked the garrison.

Lieutenant Pacheco returned just in time with 25 cavalry lancers. Together with the fort's garrison they counterattacked. Mexican lances, sabers, and a few muzzle-loaders faced Indian arrows, spears, and clubs. Six troopers were killed while various others received arrow wounds; 28 Indians died in the battle. The first attempt at non-Indian settlement in the Imperial Valley was all but forgotten.

During the late 1950s a group of archeologists and historians, associated with the present Imperial Valley College Museum, began researches on the ruins of the Mexican fort. A recorded Mexican description of the fort reported it as having been 60 feet square and adobe-built. Measurements taken in 1958, however, revealed a structure about 100 feet square.

CAMP LAGUNA GRANDE. Sparse archival reports indicate that a Camp Laguna Grande, apparently short-lived, was established in 1862 at Elsinore, Riverside County.

LAGUNA MERCED MILITARY RESERVATION. FORT FUNSTON.

CAMP LATHAM. Located on Ballona Creek, on Ballona Ranch property, near the Culver City suburb of Los Angeles, a Civil War tent camp was established as a headquarters by the 4th California Volunteer Infantry in May 1862. During the June–September period, Companies F, G, and H of the regiment garrisoned Camp Latham. Sometime in September the troops evacuated the post and departed for Arizona to do battle with the Confederates.

CAMP IN THE LAVA BEDS (*General Gillem's Camp*). The National Park Service maintains the Lava Beds National Monument, a California Historical Landmark, the site from which the Army fought the protracted Modoc War. General E. R. S. Canby, commanding officer of the Department of the Columbia, was bitterly disappointed to learn that his army had been decisively repulsed, although they outnumbered the hostile Modocs seven to one. Canby replaced the commanding officer on the scene with Colonel Alvin C. Gillem (Brevet Major General during the Civil War), who, after being delayed en route, had to reorganize the forces under his new command. He moved the original camp to a new site closer to the Modocs' stronghold. The boundary line between Modoc and Siskiyou counties runs through the Lava Beds National Monument, locating Gillem's camp in Siskiyou County and the Modoc stronghold in Modoc County.

Near the Army camp is the site where two members of Indian agent Alfred B. Meacham's government-sponsored peace commission were treacherously shot dead on April 11, 1873, by Modoc leader Captain Jack and several of his men during a prearranged parley (Meacham, also shot, survived after being left for dead). Captain Jack and his Indian forces successfully resisted capture by U.S. Army troops from December 1, 1872, to April 18, 1873. The hostiles had taken refuge near the California-Oregon border in the region's desolate lava beds. Four of the involved Indians were ultimately found guilty of murder and hanged, as was Captain Jack, their leader, who went to the scaffold later, an unrepentant man.

CAMP LAWRENCE J. HEARN. The only indication that this post existed was found in the National Archives "Returns from Military Posts, 1800–1916," which placed Camp Hearn at Palm City, San Diego County, in 1916.

CAMP LEONARD. Located in the Kern River Valley, about 15 miles northeast of Keysville, Kern County, on the north bank of the south branch of the river, Camp Leonard was established in the late summer of 1863 by a company of the 2nd California Volunteer Cavalry to protect the region's mining camps from impending Indian marauders. During that year some 850 Owens Valley Indians left the Sebastian Indian Reservation because of the scarcity of food there, all intent on returning to their former homes. Camp Leonard, remaining operative for the remainder of the year, had been established to prevent their return.

LIGHTHOUSE POINT POST. Company I, 2nd Infantry, commanded by Captain Edward R. Theller, on orders dated August 1, 1864, was directed to take his troops to Lighthouse Point on the Samoa Peninsula, Humboldt Bay, in Humboldt County, to guard Indian prisoners kept there awaiting disposition. Another source indicated that the post was occupied in 1865.

FORT LIME POINT. FORT BAKER NO. 2.

CAMP LINCOLN (*Long's Camp; Fort Long; Lincoln's Fort; Fort Lincoln*). Variously called by several names, Camp Lincoln was established on June 13, 1862, at the Indian Agency near Crescent City, Del Norte County. On September 11, 1862, Major James F. Curtis moved the camp

some six miles to a clearing in a forest of redwoods in order to observe stricter impartiality in the Army's attempts to effect a peaceful reconciliation between the settlers and the Indians. The post was abandoned on June 11, 1869. The structure that formerly housed the commanding officer's quarters has been rebuilt on the site.

FORT LINCOLN. CAMP LINCOLN.

LINCOLN'S FORT. CAMP LINCOLN.

CAMP LIPPITT. Established on January 10, 1862, this short-lived post was located at Bucksport, now a part of the city of Eureka, Humboldt County. Established in compliance with the orders of Colonel Francis J. Lippitt, commanding the District of Humboldt, for whom the camp was named, it was garrisoned by the 2nd California Infantry, Captain Douglas commanding. The post, set up because of the lack of adequate facilities at Fort Humboldt to accommodate the augmented command, consisted entirely of rented buildings and lasted for only two months.

FORT LISCOM. CAMP LISCOM HILL.

CAMP LISCOM HILL (*Fort Liscom*). A log cabin post, occupied by a small group of California Volunteers, four of them members of the local Janes family, was established during April 1862 at Liscom's Hill to furnish escorts to travelers, express messengers, and supply trains. Liscom Hill was named for Charles Liscom, a well-known Humboldt County pioneer. After the Civil War the site was the location of Scottsville, formerly the Bates Ranch. Scottsville eventually joined Blue Lake as the latter town spread northward.

CAMP LOCKETT. Located at Campo, San Diego County, in the Milquatay Valley, Camp Lockett was a World War II Mexican border cavalry post established in 1941. It was named for Colonel James Lockett, awarded two Silver Stars for "gallantry in action against insurgent forces" in the Philippine Islands during the Spanish-American War. Later the post housed prisoners of war. Late in December 1942 Camp Lockett was placed on stand-by status for future use as a convalescent center. The entire camp was declared surplus on April 30, 1946.

LOCKHART'S FORT. A fort built by Sam Lockhart and other settlers in 1856, it stood on a hill near Fall River Mills, Shasta County. Here, for five days, Sam Lockhart and others were besieged by hostile Indians, whom they fought off.

FORT LONG. CAMP LINCOLN.

LONG'S CAMP. CAMP LINCOLN.

POST AT LOS ANGELES. FORT MOORE.

CAMP LOW. During the last days of the Civil War a gang of white marauders, led by two men named Henry and Mason, terrorized Santa Cruz and Monterey counties, robbing and murdering ranchers at will. The Army was determined to provide protection for the citizens by establishing a military post somewhere in Monterey County. The town of San Juan was selected as the post. The National Hotel was rented by the government to be used as a barracks and military supplies were stocked. The post was named Camp Low in honor of then California's executive officer. In December 1864 three companies, two infantry and one cavalry, under the command of Major J. S. Ceremony, marched into town and bivouacked on the plaza. In April 1865 a squad of cavalry came upon Henry and Mason in the mountains; shots were exchanged, but the outlaws escaped after a running fight. Sometime in May Ceremony and his men were ordered to Arizona to fight the Indians there, thus terminating Camp Low. The two outlaw leaders were subsequently tracked to Los Angeles County by a company of California Volunteers and killed while resisting arrest.

CAMP LYON. A Civil War mustering point for troops before being moved to the Presidio of San Francisco, it was established in September 1861 and named in honor of Nathaniel Lyon, California Volunteers brigadier general, who was killed on August 10, 1861, during the Battle of Wilson's Creek, Missouri. Located near present-day Hunter's Point on San Francisco Bay, the camp was most active during the years 1862–65.

CAMP LYON (*Fort Lyon*). A short-lived post established in March 1862 on Bremer Ranch property on the right bank of the Mad River, about 20 miles east of Arcata, Humboldt County, its primary purpose was to protect the area between the river and Redwood Creek from Indian hostilities. Established by Captain Charles Heffernan, 2nd California Infantry, it was named in honor of Brigadier General Nathaniel Lyon, who was killed on August 10, 1861, in the Battle of Wilson's Creek, Missouri. Although the post was never officially designated a fort, it was so referred to in the orders issued by Colonel Francis J. Lippitt, 2nd California Infantry, and in subsequent official correspondence. The post was abandoned toward the end of 1862.

FORT LYON. CAMP LYON (Humboldt County).

FORT MACARTHUR. Located just south of Los Angeles on the Palos Verde Peninsula in the community of San Pedro, 427-acre Fort MacArthur was named by General Orders No. 1, War Department, January 10, 1914, in honor of Lieutenant General Arthur MacArthur, father of General Douglas MacArthur. Land had been reserved for the fort in 1888 and construction began in 1914. The fort was the only major Taft-era construction within the continental United States, with Batteries Barlow, Farley, Leary, Lodor, Merriam, Osgood, and Saxton, buttressed by many antiaircraft guns, which are still defensive fixtures at this Pacific Coast bastion. It was first garrisoned by the 4th Coast Artillery Company from San Francisco's Fort Winfield Scott, which thereby became the 1st Coast Artillery Company, Fort MacArthur. During World War II the post was an active reception center. After the war it became an Army Reserve training center. Nearly two-thirds of the reservation was turned over to the General Services Administration (GSA) for disposal in 1975 following formal closure action. The middle reservation remains in Army control, and operating under a Fort Ord deputy post commander, it supports Reserve components in southern California.

CAMP MCCLEAR. There has been at least one indication that a "Camp McClear" was established on the Fresno River about the year 1851. There are, however, no archival records to confirm its existence.

CAMP MCCLELLAN. Established at Auburn, El Dorado County, in 1861, Camp McClellan was a mustering-in location for the 4th California Volunteers during the Civil War.

CAMP MCDOUGALL (*Camp Gilmore*). Established in 1861 to accommodate an infantry regiment, it was located at French Camp Slough about three miles south of Stockton, San Joaquin County. The California Volunteers during the Civil War were very active recruiting and training. Their post near Stockton was composed of tents for the rank and file, hospital, and kitchen. The campsite was reoccupied in 1863 and called Camp Gilmore.

FORT MCDOWELL (*Camp Reynolds; West Garrison; Post of Angel Island; East Garrison; North Garrison*). Located on Angel Island in San Francisco Bay, Fort McDowell and its antecedents had a long, interestingly varied history. The 640-acre Isla de Nuestra Señora de los Angeles was visited by Spaniards when the Portolá expedition entered the bay in 1769, but its first intensive exploration was made in 1775, the same year the Presidio of San Francisco was established, by Don Juan Manuel de Ayala, who named the island. The island was largely in agricultural and livestock use when President Millard Fillmore, on November 6, 1850, declared it a military reserve. Its first post, the West Garrison or Camp Reynolds, was established on September 12, 1863, and named in honor of Major General John F. Reynolds, who was killed at Gettysburg. The camp included two facing rows of buildings on the island's west shore, on a triangular site flanked by hills (two artillery batteries were built about 1900 south of Camp Reynolds, which had been partially restored). Abandoned in 1866 and reoccupied the same year, it was renamed Post of Angel Island.

The East Garrison was established as a military camp in 1899 at Quarry Point, which the California State Parks Department describes as "a large rocky point of sandstone jutting into San Francisco Bay," quarried into three descending flats. "The upper flat was a recreation field and tennis courts. The other two contained varied structures, many of which still exist." South of this point is the largest natural beach on the island.

On April 4, 1900, the Post of Angel Island was redesignated Fort McDowell for Major General Irvin S. McDowell of Civil War fame. The North Garrison, a 26-acre enclave on the northeast side of the island, was established in 1905 and used mainly as an immigrant station ("Ellis Island West") in the early 1900s. Japanese and German war prisoners were confined there during World War II. Recalcitrant Arizona Indians had been held in custody on the island much earlier in its development. During its history Angel Island has also served as a quarantine station. Since 1886 the government has been operating a lighthouse there. The Army discontinued the military post in October 1942 and four years later relinquished all control of the island. In 1965 the government ceded the island to California for use as a state park.

CAMP MACKALL. A temporary post located on Cash Creek in Round Valley, it was established by Captain J. W. T. Gardiner with Company A, 1st Dragoons, in April 1857. The post was apparently intermittently occupied until sometime in 1858.

CAMP MACQUAIDE. A World War II special gunnery and artillery training installation, the post was established on September 17, 1940, by the War Department in the coastal part of old Rancho San Andrés, west of Watsonville, Santa Cruz County, on Monterey Bay. It was named in honor of Joseph P. MacQuaide (or McQuaide), a chaplain in the Spanish-American War and in World War I. The site and some of the post's buildings are now occupied by the Monterey Bay Academy of the Seventh-Day Adventists.

MARE ISLAND POST. Established during the first year of the Civil War to guard against secessionist attacks, the Mare Island Navy Yard, adjacent to Vallejo in San Francisco Bay, had the U.S.S. *Independence* docked in its harbor for use as a barracks for 25 soldiers and occasional marines. The expected attacks did not materialize and the guard was suspended after four months in early 1862.

CAMP MARL SPRINGS. Located six miles northeast of Kelso, San Bernardino County, the post at Marl Springs in the Mojave Desert was first garrisoned by the Army as an outpost by troops from Camps Cady and Rock Spring on October 5, 1867, and was occupied continuously until May 22, 1868, at which time it was abandoned permanently. The number of troops stationed there was usually miniscule. The site apparently was never given official status by the Army except as an informal outpost of Camp Cady. Marl Springs, however, continued to be an important station on the travel route across the Mojave Desert, also serving as the site for several trading posts. Many deserted structures and ruins now occupy the site. Crumbling rock walls mark the site of the old Army post that was erected by John Drum and his troops in 1867.

CAMP AT MARTIN'S FERRY. A short-lived post established in March 1864, it was occupied for only two weeks during the Army's campaign against hostile Indians. It was located at Martin's Ferry on the Klamath River, about 13 miles west of Weitchpec, Humboldt County.

FORT MASON (*Battery San José; Fort Point San José; Black Point Fort*). The 68-acre Fort Mason reservation on San Francisco Bay, inside the Golden Gate, on Point San José, enclosed the site of the Spanish battery of five 8-pounder brass cannon, called Bateria San José, built in 1797. By the turn of the nineteenth century it was virtually abandoned. In 1850–51 the area was set aside by President Millard Fillmore for military purposes, but not until 1863 were troops quartered there, when the post was called Fort Point San José or Black Point Fort (the Spanish called it Punta Medanes, or Black Point). On November 25, 1882, it was officially designated Fort Mason in honor of Colonel Richard Barnes Mason, 1st Dragoons, who was military governor of California (1847–49). A logistical mission was assigned to the fort in 1898 when the Army Transport Service was created and troops were sent from here to the Philippines. During World War I a number of Fort Mason's guns were removed and shipped to Europe's battlefields.

The post's 13-acre complex of piers and warehouses saw service through two World Wars as the San Francisco Port of Embarkation. Fort Mason functioned as a military installation until 1962, when the Army gave up the lower fort to civilian use. In 1972 Congress made lower Fort Mason a part of the Golden Gate National Recreation Area (GGNRA), a newly formed urban national park encompassing several thousand acres of shoreline. By 1976 the National Park Service had received over 400 proposals for use of the site, including the suggestions of two citizens' advisory commissions. On the basis of these ideas, the Fort Mason Foundation was formed to administer a wide variety of programs at the fort. In January 1977 Fort Mason Center opened its doors to the public as a nonprofit, community-oriented, 300,000-square-foot, eight-building complex offering a broad spectrum of free or low-cost activities including education, performing arts, and visual arts.

CAMP MATTOLE. A temporary post located 24 miles west of Weott, Humboldt County, it was established in early 1864 by 2nd Lieutenant William W. Frazier, commanding a detachment of Company E of the 1st Battalion of Mountaineers, which was organized in 1863 for service against Indian hostiles in Humboldt County. Company E was raised by Captain John P. Simpson in Mendocino County and mustered into Army service at Fort Humboldt. Lieutenant Frazier and his men had several engagements with the Indians on the upper Mattole River during February 1864, killing 13 of them and capturing 21 prisoners.

CAMP MERCHANT (*Camp Merritt*). First established as Camp Merritt, then renamed Camp Merchant, this was a short-lived Civil War tent encampment established in 1863 and located near Lake Merritt in Oakland, on the east side of San Francisco Bay.

CAMP MERRIAM. Located on the hills just north of the Lombard Street entrance to the Presidio of San Francisco, Camp Merriam was established in 1898 to quarter and train volunteer soldiers from California, Iowa, Kansas, and South Dakota for service during the Spanish-American War. Near the Lombard Gate, at the junction of Lincoln and Ruger, is a marker identifying the area as the location of Camp Merriam's great tent city. Two old bronze cannon made in Spain in 1783 are located outside the Presidio's main gate. Captured by United States forces during the war with Spain, they bear inscriptions identifying them as "Arms of Charles III" of Spain.

CAMP MERRITT (Oakland). CAMP MERCHANT.

CAMP MERRITT (San Francisco). Established on May 19, 1898, as a rendezvous tent camp for troops intended for service in the war with Spain, and named for Major General Wesley Merritt, commander of the Philippine Expedition, it was originally located at the old racetrack encompassing the area bordered by Balboa and Fulton streets and 2nd and 3rd avenues in San Francisco. Cramped for space and short of tents, many of Camp Merritt's soldiers became victims of various diseases. On July 18 the Army ordered the camp abandoned, and troops not already shipped out were moved to the Presidio.

FORT MERVINE. PRESIDIO OF MONTEREY.

CAMP METTAH. A post established during the summer of 1872 to preserve the peace between the settlers and Indians in the area, it was located at the Metta Indian village situated below the juncture of Mettah Creek and the Klamath River, Humboldt County.

FORT MILEY. Located on an original 54-acre reservation acquired on January 23, 1893, on Point Lobos at the south side of San Francisco Bay's entrance, 12-acre Fort Miley was established in 1900. It was named for Lieutenant Colonel John D. Miley, U.S. Volunteers, who was killed at Manila in the Philippines in 1899. The fort was buttressed by Endicott-era Batteries Call, Chester Murphy, Livingston, and Springer, in addition to World War II's Battery No. 243. Today part of the

Fort Miley reservation is occupied by a large Veterans Administration hospital.

MILITARY POST AT GOAT ISLAND. Camp Yerba Buena Island.

CAMP MILLER. Fort Miller.

CAMP MILLER. A Spanish-American War training camp, it was established in 1898 within the Presidio of San Francisco.

FORT MILLER (*Camp Barbour; Camp Miller*). Established on May 26, 1851, Fort Miller was situated on the south side of the San Joaquin River in the foothills of the Sierra Nevadas, Fresno County, some 150 miles above Stockton. The fort's site is now covered by Millerton Lake, which is formed by the waters of the San Joaquin River and impounded by the Friant Dam. In 1944, when Friant Dam was completed and the waters of Lake Millerton would soon cover its original site, Fort Miller's blockhouse was dismantled and reconstructed in Roeding Park in Fresno. The post, established to protect the mining district, was primarily intended to control the area's Indians.

The first post on or near the fort's site was Camp Barbour, established purposely for the use of the three-man commission delegated to negotiate treaties with the Indians then in a state of armed rebellion. Established on April 14, 1851, by elements of the Mariposa Battalion, the camp was named for George W. Barbour, one of the three commissioners. There is still controversy over where the camp was situated. Most historians locate it on the site later occupied by Fort Miller. An alternate opinion, however, places it on the south bank of the San Joaquin, about 10 miles below that site. The regular Army post was established by 2nd Lieutenant Treadwell Moore, 2nd Infantry, and was originally called Camp Miller; it was designated Fort Miller in 1852, in honor of Major Albert S. Miller, 2nd Infantry. Abandoned in June 1858, it was reoccupied in compliance with an order of Brigadier General George Wright, the department's commander, on August 22, 1863. It was again abandoned on October 1, 1864, except for a company of the 2nd California Cavalry, which continued to garrison the post until December 1. In 1866 the government sold the fort's buildings at a public auction.

MILLER'S CAMP. Camp Stanislaus.

CAMP MINERAL KING. Camp Sequoia National Park.

MOJAVE ANTIAIRCRAFT RANGE (MAAR). Fort Irwin.

FORT MONROE. Located near Wawona, about a mile from Inspiration Point, Mariposa County, Fort Monroe was an old relay station converted in 1891 to a military checkpoint at the entrance to Yosemite Park. It was named for George F. Monroe, a stage driver for the A. H. Washburn Company in the 1880s.

PRESIDIO OF MONTEREY (*El Presidio Royal de Monte Rey; El Castillo; Fort Hill; Fort Jones; Fort Stockton; Fort Mervine; Fort Savannah; Fort Halleck; Fort Cape of Pines; Fort Frémont; Monterey Redoubt; Monterey Ordnance Depot; Monterey Barracks; Ord Barracks; Monterey Military Reservation; Ord Barracks*). No other military installation in the United States had as many changes in nomenclature as the two-century-old Presidio of Monterey. The military has played a role in the history of the Monterey Peninsula since 1770 when a small expedition led by Governor Gaspar de Portolá officially took possession for Spain of what is now central California. In compliance with instructions, his men immediately began construction of the Presidio. Portolá's actions were influenced by the Spanish fear that other nations, particularly Russia, had designs upon her New World empire. Spain moved to occupy that portion of the western American coast which she had previously neglected. Ripe for colonization and military fortification was the port of Monterey, which had been visited and charted a century and a half before by the Spanish explorer, Sebastián Vizcaíno.

Monterey became one of five presidios, or forts, built by Spain in what is now the western United States. Others were founded in San Diego, in 1769; San Francisco, in 1776; Santa Barbara, in 1782; and Tubac, Arizona, in 1784. The fortunes of the Presidio at Monterey rose and fell with the times: it has been moved, abandoned, and reactivated time and time again. At least three times it has been submerged by the tide of history, only to reappear years later with a new face, a new master, and a new mission—first under the Spanish, then the Mexicans, and ultimately the Americans.

The first Presidio of Monterey—El Presidio Royal de Monte Rey, Spain's initial military reservation in Alta California—was situated about one mile east of the present U.S. Army Presidio of

Monterey. The mission and chapel of the Royal Presidio still stands and appears as it did upon its completion in 1795. The old presidio's fort, surviving for 50 years, was located on Presidio Hill, a site now listed in the National Register of Historic Places. In 1771 Father Junípero Serra moved his principal religious activities from Monterey to his new mission in Carmel. Soldiers were stationed both there and at Serra's newer mission, San Antonio de Padua, at Jolon, now Fort Hunter Liggett's reservation. El Castillo (1792–1846), the fort of the first presidio at Monterey, began as an open V-shaped parapet of logs and adobe revetments enclosing a small wooden barracks. Adobe structures were added later. From 1792 to 1822, this fort was the *castillo*, or fortification, for the Spanish presidio. From 1822 to 1846 (the Mexican era), this was the principal fort protecting the city and harbor of Monterey. Other redoubts included small fortifications at Point Piños and above El Castillo on Presidio Hill, the site of Fort Mervine's ruins.

Monterey remained the capital of California during the Mexican era. Twice El Castillo fell from Spanish and Mexican control. On November 20, 1818, the French privateer Hippolyte Bouchard sailed into Monterey Bay with two vessels flying the flag of Argentina, then the United Provinces of the Río de la Plata. Bouchard easily took El Castillo the next day while half of his forces launched an attack by land. They sacked the town and dispersed the Spaniards. Bouchard's privateers sailed away on December 1. On October 20, 1842, the fort was taken by U.S. Navy Commodore Thomas Catesby Jones, commander of the Pacific Squadron, who mistakenly believed the United States and Mexico were then at war. El Castillo was renamed Fort Catesby (popularly called Jones' Fort in many journals of the day) and remained such for one day, until Jones learned of his error, apologized, and reinstated the Mexican standard.

On July 7, 1846, the naval forces of Commodore John Drake Sloat, commander of the Pacific Squadron, sailed into Monterey Bay. This time a state of war did exist. Perhaps remembering Jones' blunder four years earlier, Sloat chose to send his second-in-command to claim Monterey for the United States. Thus Captain William Mervine landed and ordered the American flag raised over the old Custom House. Instead of occupying El Castillo, the Americans built a new fortification on Presidio Hill above El Castillo. This fort, later named for Captain Mervine, was the first U.S. military reservation in Monterey. In 1902 this post was greatly enlarged into the Presidio of Monterey and the old fort fell into ruins. Today only one ravelin remains, which mounts five guns on Presidio Hill behind the Army's museum.

In the early American period, Monterey was still the capital of California; later, the capital was shifted to Benecia, and ultimately to Sacramento. Construction on Fort Mervine had been begun by an ensign from Sloat's command. On July 15, 1846, it was named Fort (Robert F.) Stockton in honor of the Pacific fleet commander who succeeded Sloat. On January 28, 1847, Company F, 3rd Artillery, arrived with orders to complete the permanent fort, which was designed by engineer Lieutenant (later General) Henry W. Halleck, and the post was renamed Fort Halleck. The fort's construction was superintended by Lieutenant Edward Ortho Cresap Ord and his second-in-command Lieutenant William Tecumseh Sherman, both men becoming distinguished generals during the Civil War. For a brief period during its early construction, the post was also known as Fort Savannah for Sloat's flagship. From August 1852 to February 1865, Fort Halleck was inactive, although for the first four years of this period the post had been designated the Monterey Ordnance Depot in title and function.

On February 17, 1865, the post was renamed Ord Barracks and reactivated for the last month of the Civil War. Two log barracks were constructed to accommodate Company B, 2nd Artillery, Company G, 6th Infantry, and Company B, 1st Battalion, California Volunteers. On October 18, 1865, Ord Barracks was deactivated and left in a caretaking status. On September 9, 1902, the 15th Infantry was ordered to take post at the Monterey Military Reservation and begin building a post to house an infantry regiment and a squadron of cavalry. The end of the Spanish-American War in 1898 saw a significantly sized force stationed here. The 15th Infantry, returning from the Philippines, was headquartered here and developed the fort further. On July 13, 1903, General Orders No. 102, Headquarters of the Army, officially designated the post Ord Barracks in honor of Major General Edward O. C. Ord. On August 30, 1904, by Presidential direction, General Orders No. 142, War Department, designated that in perpetuation of the name of the first Spanish military installation in Alta California, the post would be renamed the Presidio of Monterey.

From 1904 to 1910 a school of musketry operated on the post. From 1914 to 1917 a school for Army cooks and bakers was located here. Subsequently, the post was garrisoned by two squadrons of the 11th Cavalry and the 1st and 2nd Battalions of the 76th Field Artillery. These units remained at the Presidio until 1940. In 1941 it became a reception center for World War II inductees. The post was declared inactive in 1944, but was reactivated in 1945 as a staging area for troops being trained for occupation duty. In 1946 it became the home of the Army Language School, with the impetus for initiating foreign language instruction originating shortly before the outbreak of war with Japan in 1941, forerunner of the present Defense Language Institute Foreign Language Center at the Presidio, graduating more than 120,000 language specialists during the past four decades.

MONTEREY BARRACKS. PRESIDIO OF MONTEREY.

MONTEREY MILITARY RESERVATION. PRESIDIO OF MONTEREY.

MONTEREY ORDNANCE DEPOT. PRESIDIO OF MONTEREY.

MONTEREY REDOUBT. PRESIDIO OF MONTEREY.

FORT MONTGOMERY. In July 1846 Captain John Berrien Montgomery, commander of the U.S. sloop *Portsmouth* and the ship's marines, established the post at Clark's Point in what is now downtown San Francisco, immediately after the American occupation of San Francisco Bay in the first days of the war with Mexico. On July 20 the captain reported that "we are progressing very well with the new fort . . . and I have in view to erect a block house also, in a position to overlook the fort and command the town and hills in its rear" (*Forts of the West*, pp. 27–28). Although there are archival references to the fort, abandoned in 1847, there is no indication that it was ever officially designated Fort Montgomery. One historical chronologist places the fort's site in Portsmouth Square at Washington and Kearny streets. The Society of California Pioneers believes the site to be near the intersection of present Broadway and the Embarcadero.

FORT MOORE (*Fort Hill; Post at Los Angeles*). In 1846, at the outset of the war with Mexico, Captain Archibald H. Gillespie and other marines built a rudimentary barricade on Fort Hill in what is now downtown Los Angeles, but the Mexicans soon ejected the small American force. The Army returned in force and on January 12, 1847, erected a 400-foot-long breastwork on the same strategic site and named it the Post at Los Angeles. It was intended to control the city,

then the principal center of population in California. The site was agreed to, and plans were drawn by 1st Lieutenant William H. Emory, Corps of Topographical Engineers, in compliance with orders of Brigadier General Stephen Watts Kearny. Actual construction, supervised by Lieutenant Emory, began on January 12, 1847, but the fort plans were revised, and on April 23 a new, twice as large defense was begun on the same site. The work on the second fort, an earthwork embrasured for six cannon, was superintended by 2nd Lieutenant John W. Davidson, 1st Dragoons. The post (never completed), designated Fort Moore on July 4, 1847, by Colonel John D. Stevenson, 1st New York Volunteers, commander of the southern military district of California, was named for Captain Benjamin D. Moore, 1st Dragoons, killed in the battle of San Pascual, San Diego County, on December 6, 1846. Colonel Stevenson publicly read the Declaration of Independence at the dedication of Fort Moore. It was apparently a grand ceremony, with Companies E and G of the New York Volunteers, a detachment of the 1st Dragoons, and the Mormon Battalion drawn up in a hollow square around the specially erected tall flagpole. A band played and the fort's cannon roared a salute. The garrison was withdrawn in 1848 on orders of General William T. Sherman and the post abandoned the following year. The hill that accommodated the fort was removed in 1949, and its site, on Hill Street near Sunset Boulevard, is commemorated by a huge stone mural.

MORMON CAMP. FORT SAN BERNARDINO.

MORMON STOCKADE. FORT SAN BERNARDINO.

CAMP MORRIS. Apparently a temporary Civil War post established in San Bernardino on June 6, 1863, its garrison occupied buildings in the town in lieu of barracks. Camp Morris was abandoned on October 27, 1863.

NEW CAMP CARLETON. CAMP CARLETON.

FORT NEW HELVETIA. SUTTER'S FORT.

POST OF NEW SAN DIEGO. PRESIDIO OF SAN DIEGO.

CAMP NEW SUPPLY (*Old Supply Camp; Scorpion Point Camp; Boyle's Camp; Peninsula Camp*). The first supply depot established for the long protracted Modoc War in 1873, it is historically known as the Old Supply Camp or

Scorpion Point Camp to differentiate it from the new depot which soon replaced it nearer the town of Newell, northeast of the eastern edge of today's Lava Beds National Monument, in Modoc County. The Battle of Scorpion Point took place in the near environs of the camp, about six miles south of Newell (apparently named for Frederick H. Newell, the first chief engineer of the U.S. Reclamation Service).

Camp New Supply, alternately known as Boyle's Camp or Peninsula Camp, was established by Major William H. Boyle, one of General E. R. S. Canby's battalion commanders during the war against Captain Jack and his Modocs, after the Indians fled into the Lava Beds. Major Boyle suffered a thigh wound and did not finish the campaign. Late in the campaign the supply base served as a prisoner of war camp. (See: CAMP IN THE LAVA BEDS.)

NEWKIRK'S MILL POST. A short-lived military post established sometime in 1864, it was probably located near Fort Gaston in the Hoopa Valley, Humboldt County.

CAMP NOME LACKEE. FORT VOSE.

NORTH GARRISON. FORT MCDOWELL.

OLD SUPPLY CAMP. CAMP NEW SUPPLY.

CAMP OLNEY. A temporary Civil War post established sometime in 1862 by Lieutenant Hubbard with Company K, 2nd California Volunteers, it was located on the upper Mattole River, about 40 miles south of Fort Humboldt.

CAMP IN ONION VALLEY. A temporary camp established sometime in 1860, it was located on a site either near Downieville in Sierra County or in adjoining Plumas County.

CAMP ORD. FORD ORD.

FORT ORD (*Camp Ord*). This fort began as a maneuver area and field artillery target range for the 11th Cavalry and the 76th Field Artillery stationed at the Presidio of Monterey. The government acquired 15,324 acres near what is now the East Garrison area. The fort was originally known as the Gigling Reservation after a German family who once owned the land. Few improvements were made until 1938 when permanent buildings were constructed. In 1940 the reservation, then named Camp Ord in honor of Major General Edward Cresap Ord, fighter of Indians who had served at the Presidio and later commanded northern troops in the Civil War, was expanded to 20,000 acres. In the next two years additional land was acquired by the Federal government. The people of Salinas and the Monterey Peninsula bought 274 acres of sand dunes just south of the present city of Marina and donated them to the Army for use as firing ranges.

In August 1940 Camp Ord was designated a fort, and the 7th Infantry Division was reactivated, becoming the first major unit to occupy the post. The division left Fort Ord in 1943 for duty in the Aleutian Islands. During most of World War II, Fort Ord was a staging area for many combat divisions and units, including the 3rd, 27th, 35th and 43rd divisions. At one time more than 50,000 troops were on the post. Following the war, activity at Fort Ord slowed. In 1947 it became the home of the 4th Replacement Training Center, which provided the nucleus for the soon-to-be-reactivated 4th Infantry Division. This division ultimately moved to Fort Benning, to be replaced by the 6th Division, which remained until January 1956. It was replaced by the 5th Division which had returned from duty in Germany and a year later was deactivated. Fort Ord then became an infantry training center.

During the 1960s, Fort Ord again became a staging area for units departing for Asia. The post continued as a center instructing basic and advanced infantrymen. In 1974 the training center was deactivated, and Fort Ord again became the home of the 7th Infantry Division. The post has undergone extensive renovation and modernization since 1974. Clusters of World War II buildings still dot the post and serve as offices for the installation and unit activities. However, millions of dollars have been expended for new troop billets and family housing, and for medical, recreational, commissary and exchange facilities. New construction and renovation of facilities is continuing at present. Fort Ord, now a reservation of some 28,500 acres of rolling plains and rugged hills, sits on the northern shoulder of the Monterey Peninsula, extending eastward into the fertile Salinas Valley, with its western border, paralleling U.S. 1, adjoining the sand dunes and Monterey Bay. Two of Fort Ord's subposts are nearby. A few miles away, on a knoll in the city of Monterey, is the Presidio of Monterey. In the southeast corner of Monterey County, about 60 miles from the peninsula, is Fort Hunter Liggett, a rurally isolated inland training area.

ORD BARRACKS. PRESIDIO OF MONTEREY.

ORLEANS BAR POST. A temporary post, it was established in 1864 by Volunteer Mountaineers to safeguard the mining town of Orleans Bar, now Orleans, Humboldt County.

CAMP OTAY. A Mexican border patrol post, it was established prior to World War I by the California National Guard and located south of San Diego.

CAMP PAH-UTE SPRING. An Army outpost was established on November 27, 1867, at Pah-Ute Spring in the eastern Mojave Desert, San Bernardino County, by troops of Company D, 9th Infantry, from Camp Mojave. The post's buildings, erected by the infantrymen, were maintained until May 3, 1968.

CAMP PALM CITY. A World War I training camp was reportedly established at Palm City, San Diego County. No dates have been found for its length of tenure.

CAMP PARDEE'S RANCH. Beginning in 1858 and continuing throughout the years of the Civil War, troops frequently posted themselves at this favored ranch, situated on the old Trinity Trail between Eureka and the Trinity River, Humboldt County.

CAMP PARKS. Originally a naval base located 30 miles east of Oakland, Camp Parks first opened in 1942, and was named for Rear Admiral Charles W. Parks. After the war, Camp Parks, along with the Navy's adjacent Camp Shoemaker, became the Santa Rita Rehabilitation Center, the county prison farm. Except for about 500 acres subleased to the rehabilitation center, the Korean War reactivated the post as Parks Air Force Base, a basic training center. In July 1959 the base was deactivated and control of the reservation was given to the Army with the post again named Camp Parks. At that time the county negotiated a lease for about 900 acres of Camp Parks property for its rehabilitation center. Camp Parks, in an emergency, is capable of limited unit staging for mobilization, and trained soldiers could be processed for overseas movement in large numbers. At present, Camp Parks is a major site for Army Reserve Command (ARCOM) units from Fort Lawton, Washington.

PENINSULA CAMP. CAMP NEW SUPPLY.

CAMP AT PIERSON'S RANCH. A temporary camp established at Pierson's Ranch sometime in 1865, it was located near Colusa in Colusa County.

FORT ON PINE CREEK. A settler's fort built by Charles Putnam in 1861 at Little Pine, later renamed Independence, Inyo County, it was used as a refuge during Indian attacks in the Civil War years.

CAMP PINEDALE. A World War II post established on August 1, 1942, on the site of a Japanese internment camp near Fresno, Camp Pinedale began receiving soldiers selected for training as Army Air Force communications technicians in December of that year. By war's end, the post had trained 25,000 soldiers as electronic specialists and for allied army assignments—clerks, truck drivers, chemical warfare specialists, camouflage specialists, ordnance technicians, and cooks. The camp was deactivated in February 1947, when the Corps of Engineers assumed custody of the sprawling base and began preparations for the disposal of the post's buildings and other installations.

FORT PIO PICO. FORT ROSECRANS.

FORT PIUTE (*Fort Beale; Fort Piute Hill*). Established in late 1859 by Captain James H. Carleton, 1st Dragoons, this desert post was located near Piute Springs in the foothills of the Piute Mountain range, about 25 miles west of Fort Mohave, Arizona, and 10 miles north of Goffs, San Bernardino County, California, a few miles west of the California-Nevada border. Captain Carleton named the post Fort Beale for Lieutenant Edward F. Beale, U.S. Navy, who, in 1857–58, with his caravan of camels, explored the area for a wagon road. The fort, actually a subpost of Camp Cady, was one of a chain of military stations erected to protect the travel route from San Bernardino across the Mojave Desert to Fort Mohave. While the Piute post was misnomered a "fort," all the others were designated either "redoubt" or "camp," and all were strategically situated near sources of water. During the years of the Civil War, the posts were garrisoned by elements of the California Volunteers and evacuated at the end of the war. But local protests, stressing the critical need for the travel route and increasing mining activity in western Arizona, compelled the reoccupation of the posts in 1866. Upon reoccupation, the post was renamed Fort Piute or Fort Piute Hill, and was usually garrisoned by troops from Camp Cady, California. Fort Piute was abandoned sometime in 1868.

FORT PIUTE HILL. FORT PIUTE.

FORT POINT. FORT WINFIELD SCOTT.

CAMP POINT LOMA. FORT ROSECRANS.

FORT POINT OF PINES (*Fort Cape of Pines*). A redoubt built by the Spaniards before Mexico gained its independence, it was located on Point Pinos in what is now Pacific Grove, a city about two miles southwest of Monterey. In 1842 Eugene Duflot de Mofras drew his "Map of the Port of Monterey" and included the small redoubt. He wrote of "a small battery near Point Pinos, but few traces of this now remains." Americans, for many years, called this Spanish post Fort Cape of Pines, a misnomer.

FORT POINT SAN JOSÉ. FORT MASON.

CAMP POLLOCK. A temporary camp established sometime in June 1864, and lasting for about a month, as a base of operations for a regional reconnaissance, it was situated almost on the newly surveyed boundary line between California and Nevada. At the time the post was established the area was in Lake County, Nevada, but since the survey it has been divided between Washoe County, Nevada, and Lassen County, California. The camp was occupied by Captain A. B. Wells, commanding Company D, 1st Nevada Volunteers, during the expedition from Fort Churchill to the Humboldt River, by way of Smoke Creek Valley, Nevada, and Surprise Valley, California.

POOLE'S FORT. A stage station fortified in about the year 1850 by proprietor John Poole (or Pool), it stood at the ferry crossing of the Kings River, in the Y of the junction of the river and Wah-to-he Creek, about 20 miles southeast of Fresno.

CAMP PRENTISS. CAMP CARLETON.

EL PRESIDIO REAL. PRESIDIO OF SAN DIEGO.

EL PRESIDIO ROYAL DE MONTE REY. PRESIDIO OF MONTEREY.

CAMP RANCHO CUCAMONGA. Troops were camped on the grounds of this ranch, located near the town of Cucamonga, San Bernardino County, for two weeks, June 1 through June 15, 1864, because of civil unrest between Americans and Californios (Mexicans living in California) over the murders of John Rains, proprietor of the ranch, and Ramon Carillo, the paramour of Rains's wife Mercedes. Carillo had either directly or indirectly assassinated Rains on November 17, 1862, some 25 miles from his ranch. A year and a half later his widow married Carillo, who was murdered at Cucamonga on May 21, 1864, by friends of John Rains. Rancho Cucamonga, one of the most prosperous in the San Bernardino Valley, had been described as

the prettiest & most valuable ranche I have seen in the west. There are 160,000 grape vines in the vinyard & apples, appricots, pears, peaches, wild cherries, figs, English wallnuts & pomegranats in the orchard and springs that cover about 200 acres in an enclosed pasture of 500 acres, with good houses, cellars and out houses. [Diary of John W. Teal, ed. Henry P. Walker, *Quarterly Journal of History* 13, no. 1 (Spring 1971): 71]

RANCHO DE CHINO POST. A post was established on September 14, 1850, at Rancho de Chino, located near the Santa Ana River in the environs of the town of Chino, San Bernardino County, about 30 miles southeast of Los Angeles. The garrison, one company of the 2nd Infantry, occupied a leased ranch building at a monthly cost of $300. The post was intended to protect the general area from Garra Indian depredations and, particularly, to prevent their incursions via Cajon Pass. A current historian reports that the post was first garrisoned by the 1st Dragoons, an obvious factual error since the official report dated June 28, 1852, by the commander of the Pacific Division, specifies that the post was established by Captain C. S. Sovell, with Company A, 2nd Infantry, who was in continuous command until the abandonment of the post.

In addition to the regular troop garrison, the ranch was the rendezvous for 35 volunteers from Los Angeles and 15 from San Bernardino, who were mustered by General Bean of the California Militia to help put down the Garra uprising. Garra himself was finally captured, taken to San Diego, tried before a court martial, convicted, and executed. A son of Garra and another Indian were later convicted in a court martial for the murders of four Americans at Warner's Ranch along with other crimes, and they were shot at Chino in the latter part of December 1852. On September 17, 1852, the post was abandoned and the garrison transferred to the Robidoux Rancho on the Jurupa grant (Post of Rancho del Jurupa).

RANCHO DEL JURUPA POST. FORT JURUPA.

FORT READING. Established on May 26, 1852, this adobe-built, two-company post was located on the west side of Cow Creek, about two and a half miles from its confluence with the Sacramento River at the present town of Redding, Shasta County. Established by 1st Lieutenant Nelson H. Davis, 2nd Infantry, by order of Colonel Ethan Allen Hitchcock, 2nd Infantry, commanding the department, the post—often flooded during the rainy season—was primarily intended to protect the mining district from Indian depredations. The fort, one of the earliest posts in northern California, was named for Major Pierson B. Reading, paymaster of the California Volunteers during the Mexican war, and a pioneer settler in California. Although the garrison was withdrawn on April 1, 1856, the post was intermittently occupied until June 13, 1867, and completely abandoned on April 6, 1870. The fort's buildings were sold prior to the restoration of the reservation to the public domain on February 15, 1881.

CAMP AT RED BLUFF. A temporary post established during the summer of 1862 at the town of Red Bluff, Tehama County, it was garrisoned by one company of the California Cavalry.

CAMP REDWOOD. This camp was established in 1862 as a midway point between the communities of Trinidad and Elk Camp, Humboldt County, as a result of the bitter conflict between settlers and Indians in the region. Army regulars were posted at Camp Redwood to act as escorts for both supplies and travelers on what was then the Coastal Trail between the two towns.

REED'S RANCH POST. That it was established in 1862 southeast of Fort Humboldt was the only archival reference found.

CAMP RESTING SPRINGS. Located five miles east of present Tecopa, San Bernardino County, this desert outpost was intermittently occupied during 1859–60 by regular troops to protect a precious waterhole on the old Spanish Trail between Las Vegas and the Mojave River. It was the scene of an Indian massacre in 1844, avenged by Kit Carson and Alexander Godey of Frémont's expedition. A Mormon mail train was attacked here in 1854. There are still evidences of a stone redoubt and a corral at the site.

CAMP REYNOLDS. FORT MCDOWELL.

FORT RIGHT. CAMP WRIGHT (Mendocino County).

CAMP RILEY. On August 6, 1849, seven companies of the 2nd Infantry, commanded by Brigadier General Bennett Riley, the last military governor of California, arrived via transports at Monterey. Five companies were immediately shipped to San Diego. Two companies set up tents in the groves at Mission San Diego and the other troops went on to garrison Mission San Luis Rey. This encampment of the Boundary Commission was commanded by Major Samuel P. Heintzelman and was located at the southern end of San Diego Bay where today only salt flats exist.

CAMP ROBERTS. Situated midway between San Francisco and Los Angeles, Camp Roberts is located adjacent to U.S. Highway 101, twelve miles north of Paso Robles. Geographically, the camp is in the southern portion of the Salinas Valley, divided between Monterey and San Luis Obispo counties. There are 42,362 acres of which 1,203 acres are in the cantonment areas, and 41,336 acres are used for training purposes. The reservation has a satellite communications site that occupies a 20-acre enclave. The buildings on Camp Roberts are of World War II construction, many of which have been rehabilitated. The complex consists of nearly 1,000 buildings, including enlisted men's barracks, administration offices, mess halls, and recreation centers. The camp has a rated capacity for housing approximately 20,000 troops.

The camp was named for Corporal Harold W. Roberts, posthumously awarded the congressional Medal of Honor for sacrificing his own life to save that of a fellow soldier during the First World War. Originally surveyed for a cavalry post in 1902, the area received a favorable recommendation from the U.S. Army Corps of Engineers, but another location was selected. In 1940, construction of the present installation was begun. Camp Roberts was activated as a training center in March 1941, operating a 17-week cycle of infantry and artillery replacement training. Peak capacity was achieved during World War II with 36,000 troops on the post at one time. Deactivated in 1946, Camp Roberts reverted to caretaker status with a small garrison. In August 1950, however, the post was reactivated as the Korean War necessitated new activity on the training base. The post now became an Armor Replacement Training Center, with the 7th Armored Division as the resident command. Tens of thousands of men moved through the camp's training cycle and into combat until November 1953, when the installation again reverted to its role as home for a small year-round garrison with an infusion of National Guardsmen and Army Reservists. The California Army National Guard assumed control of the facility on April 2, 1971.

CAMP ROCK SPRING. An official Army post, Camp Rock Spring in the Mojave Desert, on the road from Camp Cady to Fort Mohave, Arizona, located near Kelso, San Bernardino County, was established on December 30, 1866. Post returns reveal that Lieutenant L. H. Robinson, 14th Infantry, with Company E, commanded the post from March 16, 1867 until January 2, 1868, after which it was maintained until May 21, 1868, as a small, intermittently occupied outpost of Camp Cady.

ROOP'S FORT. FORT DEFIANCE.

FORT ROSECRANS (*Fort Guijarros; Fort Pio Pico; Post at San Diego; San Diego Barracks; Camp Point Loma; Fort at Ballast Point*). The military reservation of Fort Rosecrans includes the site on Ballast Point in San Diego Bay of Fort Guijarros (called by the Spanish La Punta de los Guijarros ["The Point of Cobblestones"]) or Fort Pio Pico. The site, the probable landing place of Juan Rodríguez Cabrillo in 1542, was named by Vizcaíno in 1602, and it was so designated until early in the nineteenth century when English-speaking mariners appeared in Old San Diego (See: PRESIDIO OF SAN DIEGO). It was on this headland jutting out into the bay that Fort Guijarros, designed by Spanish engineer Alberto de Cordoba to mount 10 guns, was begun about 1797, under the direct supervision of the *commandante*, Manuel Rodríguez. Plans were made in 1798 to build a road from the Presidio of San Diego to the fort.

It was here that the so-called Battle of San Diego was fought on March 22, 1803, when the *Lelia Byrd*, an American brig commanded by fur smuggler William Shaler, was fired on by the fort's guns. The Americans, unaware of the Spanish edict prohibiting foreign trade, were in their innocence attempting to carry on a barter for furs. There was an exchange of cannon fire. The Virginia-built ship escaped out of the harbor but not before the fort's guns had damaged its hull. According to authorities on the Spanish period, the short skirmish was the only Spanish–American ship-to-shore artillery battle in California history. The cannon nicknamed "El Jupiter," cast in Manile in 1783 and used during this artillery duel, is now mounted on the site of old Fort Stockton on Presidio Hill. Fort Guijarros, constructed of Indian-made adobe bricks, stood at the foot of the hill which leads down to the sea from the later-established Fort Rosecrans barracks. The Ballast Point fort was abandoned in 1838 and had so deteriorated by the time American troops arrived to occupy San Diego that it was valueless.

The military reservation, designated Fort Rosecrans many years later, was first known as Post at San Diego and Camp Point Loma when it was established on February 26, 1852, at the southern end of the peninsula. The first American fortifications were located on Ballast Point close to the site of Fort Guijarros. An earthwork, begun in May 1873 for the purpose of protecting the entrance to San Diego Bay, was variously named Post at San Diego, San Diego Barracks and Fort at Ballast Point. The post was not designated Fort Rosecrans until 1899, when it was named for Brigadier General William S. Rosecrans of Civil War fame, who died on March 11, 1898. The Army built Fort Pio Pico, an Endicott period post, located on North Island in the bay, and included Battery Meed, mounting two 3-inch guns. One-half acre within the reservation on Point Loma was set aside in 1913 for the Cabrillo National Monument.

Fort Rosecrans was upgraded from time to time with additional fortifications. Its coastal batteries protected San Diego Bay during the Spanish-American War and both world wars. The Endicott period artillery emplacements included Batteries Calef, Fetterman, McGrath and Wilkeson, while Batteries Whistler and White were built during the Taft period. Fort Rosecrans was declared surplus on December 31, 1949. The military reservation was transferred to the Department of the Navy on July 1, 1959.

A large team of archaeologists, after a year of historical study, began on June 6, 1981, to explore the site of Fort Guijarros with the expectation of ultimately unearthing the eighteenth-century fort from its grave at the base of Ballast Point. The fort's site is within the Navy's Submarine Support Facility. One of the early finds during the digging was a number of redwood planks that formed the fort's esplanade, a sloping deck on which the fort's cannon rested. Other artifacts found include foundation boulders weighing up to 150 pounds each, bricks, floor tiles, bronze nails, and Spanish and Indian pottery. The explorations were continued during the summers of 1982 and 1983.

FORT ROSS (*Fort Rossiya*). This former Russian-American Company trading post, built on a shelf of land above the Pacific, 13 miles northwest of the mouth of the Russian River and 80 miles north of San Francisco, represented the farthest penetration south by the Russians. Fort Ross expressed the efforts of the company, a trade monopoly, with headquarters at Sitka, Alaska, to establish during the nineteenth century a base on the California coast for sea otter hunting and the development of agricultural supplies for Alaska.

In June 1812, a crew of 95 Russians and 40 Aleuts began to work on a stockaded redwood fort on an elevated coastal plateau overlooking a small harbor 30 miles north of Bodega Bay. The Russians now occupied a permanent trade base at Fort Ross and a harbor at Bodega Bay from which their needs in Alaska could be supplied. The fort was dedicated on August 13, 1812, as Rossiya, derived from the Russian word *Rus.* In 1821 the Czar issued an ukase closing the Pacific Coast north of San Francisco to all but Russian ships. The Russian government's attempt to control the region was responsible for that part of the Monroe Doctrine of 1823 which stated that the New World was no longer open to aggression by force and that European countries could not extend their holdings in it.

With the virtual extermination by ruthless slaughter of the sea otters and fur seals by the Russians, Americans, and British, the Russians increased their efforts in agriculture and manufacturing in their California colony, but without any marked success. By the end of 1839 the officials of the Russian-American Company ordered the colonists to sell out and return to Alaska. For several months, negotiations for the sale were carried on with both General Mariano G. Vallejo of Sonoma and Captain John A. Sutter of New Helvetia (Sacramento). Sutter's offer was finally accepted on December 12, 1841. He was to pay $30,000 in produce and gold for the movable property and other assets of the Russian colony. Between 1841 and 1844 Sutter's men took down a number of the buildings of the colony and removed the arms, equipment and livestock which the Russians had left.

After 1845 the fort area became the center of a large ranch, and the remaining buildings were used in various ways. The G. W. Call family purchased the fort and ranch in 1874. After the collapse of the Chapel of Fort Ross in the 1906 earthquake, the fort site was purchased by the California Historical Landmarks Committee of San Francisco and presented to the State of California in the same year. Restored in 1955–57, the stockade is built of hewn redwood timbers eight inches thick and 12 feet high. The maximum dimensions of the quadrangle it enclosed are 276 feet by 312 feet. The Russian Orthodox Chapel, built about 1828, was reassembled about 1917, but extensive termite damage and the effects of the weather made it necessary to do considerable repairing of the building in 1955–57. There are two blockhouses—a seven-sided one at the north corner and an eight-sided one at the south. Cannon ports on each of the walls of the two stories of each blockhouse could cover the walls of the fort and the landing on the beach below the fort. There were no musket ports. Both buildings have been restored. (See: SUTTER'S FORT.)

FORT ROSSIYA. FORT ROSS.

ROUND VALLEY POST. A temporary post situated in Round Valley in the northern part of the state, it was established sometime in 1892 by Captain William E. Daugherty with Company B, 1st Infantry, and a detachment of the 4th Cavalry, aggregating 78 men.

FORT SACRAMENTO. SUTTER'S FORT.

SACRAMENTO POST. A temporary encampment at Sacramento, it was established in July 1894 by Colonel William M. Graham, with a number of 5th Artillery batteries, two companies of the 4th Cavalry, Company E of the 1st Infantry, and three companies of Marines.

POST NEAR SACRAMENTO CITY. CAMP ANDERSON.

CAMP AT FORT OF SALMON RIVER. A short-lived military post, it was established in 1864 in present Siskiyou County.

CAMP SAN BERNARDINO. Post returns for Camp San Bernardino disclosed that it was established on February 11, 1858, pursuant to Special Orders No. 2, dated January 2, 1858, Headquarters Department of the Pacific. This camp was evacuated in June 1858. During August and September, 1861, troops of the 4th and 9th Infantry also garrisoned a camp near San Bernardino.

FORT SAN BERNARDINO (*Mormon Camp; Mormon Stockade*). In 1851 Mormons built a 300-by-720-foot, 12-foot-high stockade when the town of San Bernardino was threated by an Indian attack. The post, later renamed Fort San Bernardino, soon extended far beyond its original limits. In 1855 small elements of the Army were stationed here for a short time. The site is now occupied by the courthouse located on Arrowhead Avenue between 3rd and 4th streets in the center of downtown San Bernardino.

CAMP SAN DIEGO. A Mexican border patrol post was established at San Diego in March 1911 when Colonel Charles St. J. Chubb, with ten companies of the 30th Infantry, aggregating 703 men, arrived there on March 10. The command left the Presidio of San Francisco on March 7 in compliance with General Orders No. 21.

FORT SAN DIEGO. PRESIDIO OF SAN DIEGO.

GARRISON AT SAN DIEGO. PRESIDIO OF SAN DIEGO.

MISSION OF SAN DIEGO. PRESIDIO OF SAN DIEGO.

POST AT MISSION SAN DIEGO. PRESIDIO OF SAN DIEGO.

POST AT SAN DIEGO. FORT ROSECRANS.

PRESIDIO OF SAN DIEGO (*El Presidio Real; Castillo de Guijarros; Garrison at San Diego; Fort DuPont; Fort Stockton; Fort San Diego; Mission of San Diego; Post at Mission San Diego; San Diego Depot; Post of New San Diego; San Diego Barracks*). The site of San Diego, the oldest Spanish settlement in California, was probably first visited by a European in 1539 when Father Marcos de Niza, with an overland expedition, was searching for the mythical Seven Cities of Cibola. Juan Rodríguez Cabrillo, on September 28, 1542, made the first visit by sea after sighting Point Loma; his landing was probably near Ballast Point on the east side of Point Loma. In 1602 Sebastián Vizcaíno gave the name of San Diego Bay to its sheltered harbor. The friars in his party very probably celebrated California's first holy mass at Ballast Point near which the Spaniards later built Castillo de Guijarros. Settlement, however, did not materialize until 1769, when José de Galvez ordered colonization there. Two ships arrived in April, followed by two overland expeditions, the first under Fernando de Rivera arriving at San Diego on May 15, and the second under Governor Gaspar de Portolá, with Father Junípero Serra, arriving there on July 1, both expeditions driving herds of cattle. Father Serra said mass at the site on the same day before a gathering of 126 persons, survivors of 300 who had originally set out from Baja California by land and sea to occupy Alta California. After the *te deum*, Governor Portolá ceremoniously took possession of California for Spain.

Today's Presidio of San Diego commemorates the beginning of mission endeavor and European settlement in California. During the century that followed, the Presidio, its mission (completely restored in the early 1930s), and fortifications underwent a number of name changes, as control of San Diego passed from Spain to Mexico and ultimately to the United States. The religious ceremony of July 1, 1769, was followed by the formal founding of El Presidio Real (a fort until it was legally established as a presidio in 1774, now located in San Diego's "Old Town," surrounded by a modern American city) on July 16, adjoining the first mission in Alta California, San Diego de Alcalá. After a destructive Indian attack in August, the Spaniards erected a crude stockade on Presidio Hill to protect both the mission and the tiny colony. By the end of March 1770, the colonists had completed the stockade, mounted two bronze cannon, and built wooden houses with tule roofs.

The commandant's residence was situated in the center of the Presidio. On the east side of the square were a chapel, storehouses, and the cemetery; on the south side were the gate and guardhouse; and around the other sides were the soldiers' barracks. To remove his converted Indians from the destructive influence of the presidial garrison, Father Francisco Palou in 1774 moved the mission to a new site, six miles to the northeast, the present site of San Diego Mission. In 1778 the Presidio's original wooden walls and buildings began to be replaced with adobe structures. From 1795 to 1796 an esplanade, powder magazine, flagpole, and additional barracks were added to the Presidio, and Castillo de Guijarros—the harbor's first fortification—was erected on the east side of Point Loma. It included a battery designed to mount ten cannon, an adobe-built powder magazine, and barracks.

As the Spanish period drew to a close, the garrison of the Presidio increased, with 50 cavalrymen added in 1819 to the force of about 100 soldiers. The total Spanish population of San Diego and its near environs in that year was about 450, in addition to about 6,800 Indian neophytes. Under Mexican control, however, the size of the garrison and the condition of the Presidio declined rapidly after 1830. In 1831 the Mexican government withdrew the rest of the troops. In 1836 the Presidio was dilapidated and Fort Guijarros in ruins. In 1838, because of minor uprisings and general disturbances, an earthwork was built on Presidio Hill to protect the town.

By 1839 the Presidio was a complete ruin, with much of its stone and adobe removed to erect houses in the new pueblo of San Diego, founded in 1835.

When the United States occupied San Diego in 1846, neither the Presidio nor Castillo de Guijarros had any military value. But the 1838-built earthwork on Presidio Hill was incorporated in what was called Fort DuPont (for the captain of the sloop-of-war *Cyane*) and later variously known as Garrison at San Diego, Fort San Diego, or Fort Stockton (after Commodore Robert F. Stockton, who occupied the site later in the same year). In 1847, when the Mormon Battalion and its commander, General Philip St. George, were stationed at San Diego, they found that the Mission San Diego de Alcalá had been abandoned for at least a dozen years. Cooke settled his troops on open ground near the chapel. Later, a regular Army garrison used the chapel as a barracks, calling it Post at Mission San Diego.

Prior to the Civil War, San Diego became of military significance for a number of reasons, among them the disruptions caused by the Mexican war, the discovery of gold, and Indian depredations. Several new military posts in southern California were established. San Diego's chief contribution was as a depot from which supplies were distributed to Camp (later Fort) Yuma, 225 miles distant, and other posts in the southern department. In 1858–59, when Colonel Joseph K. F. Mansfield inspected the Department of the Pacific's military posts for the second time, he found the San Diego Depot unoccupied. Reoccupied in 1860, it was first called the Post of New San Diego and, later, San Diego Barracks, remaining continuously active until 1920.

The site of the Presidio of San Diego was rescued from complete oblivion in 1929 by the donation of a 37-acre parcel to the city of San Diego, to be used for park purposes. Presidio Park, formally landscaped, includes the Serra Museum as its principal architectural feature. Built in 1929, the museum houses a large collection of archaeological and historical memorabilia related to Spanish colonization and early California history. The museum's library contains both original and published records of the history of the city and the region. Most of the former site of the Presidio lies in front of the museum. Construction of the San Diego River dike and the Mission Valley Road had destroyed part of the site, and another small section of the site lies beneath a park road. In the center of the site stands the Junípero Serra Cross, erected in 1913, built from the many pieces of brick and floor tile found on the site. A number of fort plans relating to California's four presidios were discovered in 1982 in the Bancroft Library at Berkeley. The most valuable in the collection is the 1820 plan of San Diego Presidio. Archaeologists have been working on that site for more than 20 years without the guidance of a plan. Its availability should be of material assistance to the San Diego archeological program.

SAN DIEGO BARRACKS. PRESIDIO OF SAN DIEGO.

SAN DIEGO BARRACKS. FORT ROSECRANS.

SAN DIEGO DEPOT. PRESIDIO OF SAN DIEGO.

CAMP AT SAN FELIPE. A temporary post, it was established sometime in 1855 at San Felipe southeast of Watsonville, just over the border in Santa Clara County.

CAMP SAN FELIPE. This camp on the Butterfield mail route in San Diego County was occupied by General Stephen W. Kearny in 1846 on his march to San Diego and the Battle of San Pasqual. In 1865, Company D, 7th Infantry, California Volunteers, left Drum Barracks on April 4 en route for Fort Yuma and Tubac, Arizona Territory. On the ninth day out they were encamped at San Felipe.

PRESIDIO OF SAN FRANCISCO. As an outpost under the flags of Spain, Mexico, and the United States, the Presidio of San Francisco is one of the nation's oldest military reservations, consisting of about 1,500 acres occupying the northern-most point of the city's peninsula. Its long succession of changing garrisons has stood guard over the Golden Gate and San Francisco Bay since the first year of the American Revolution. It has been the headquarters for American military commands defending the territory west of the Rocky Mountains since 1857. At various times since the Spanish-American War it has directed troops that guarded America's interests in Alaska, the Panama Canal Zone, the Hawaiian Islands, China, and the Philippines. The Presidio today is the home of the Sixth Army command, comprising the eight western states of California, Oregon, Washington, Idaho, Montana, Nevada, Utah and Arizona. Within this organization are all regular Army, National Guard, and organized Reserve troops and installations in this area.

In 1776 the Spanish Viceroy of Mexico dispatched exploring expeditions northward along the California coast, establishing missions and military posts, and taking possession of the country in Spain's name. Captain Juan Bautista de Anza, who led the overland expedition to settle and fortify Yerba Buena (San Francisco), selected this strategic site on March 28, 1776. When first built it was a camp of approximately 200 yards square, surrounded by adobe walls.

Today's Presidio Officers' Club, the oldest building in San Francisco, was originally a low adobe brick structure, erected under the direction of Lieutenant José Joaquin Moraga, first *commandante* of the Presidio. Together with the old *iglesia* (church), which disappeared long ago, it was the first structure built on the Presidio site. As construction proceeded, it formed part of the stockade of the original Presidio enclosure, and served Spanish and Mexican *commandantes* as living quarters for half a century. The *commandencia*, with its bare earthen floors and paneless windows, was within the 14-foot-high adobe walls that protected the outpost. It required extensive repairs throughout the years, and when the Americans took over California in 1846, it was furnished as an Officers' Club. In 1933, the building underwent extensive remodeling and was restored as nearly as possible to its original appearance.

After the Presidio was completed in September 1776, it was frequently plagued by earthquakes, always a problem in the San Francisco

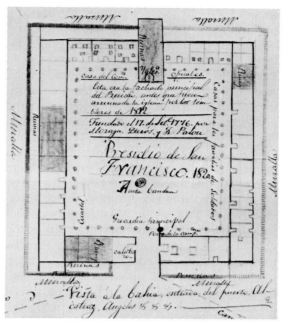

PRESIDIO OF SAN FRANCISCO. Spanish plan drawn in 1820. (Courtesy of the Bancroft Library, University of California, Berkeley.)

area. One quake, in 1812, damaged the enclosure and buildings and brought down several outer walls. Rebuilt, they were again largely in ruins by 1833. The Presidio was in continuous use by the Spaniards until it was taken over by the Mexicans when they gained their independence from Spain in 1822, and was garrisoned by them until the United States took forcible possession in 1846. The first regular American troops to enter the

PRESIDIO OF SAN FRANCISCO. Aerial view looking northward to the Golden Gate.

Presidio, a detachment of Marines, garrisoned it in July 1846. The Presidio was rebuilt and renovated, despite the exhorbitant prices for labor and materials brought about by the Gold Rush of 1849. During the Civil War, all regular Army units were withdrawn and sent to various theaters of war in the West while defense of the post was assigned to volunteer regiments from along the Pacific coast. After the Civil War, the Presidio became the headquarters from which many of the western Indian campaigns were directed during the 1870s and 1880s.

Letterman Army Hospital, the service's largest hospital west of the Mississippi, was constructed during the Spanish-American War on the grounds of the reservation, when the Presidio took on wartime responsibilities with a troop training program and served as a port of embarkation for the Philippines. Letterman served as a debarkation hospital in three wars, the Spanish-American War and World Wars I and II, and in the Korean conflict. During World War II, Letterman was the largest debarkation hospital in the nation, handling a peak load of 72,000 patients in one war year. The hospital was named in honor of Major Jonathan Letterman, Medical Director of the Army of the Potomac, one of the Union's armies in the Civil War. He organized the Army's first ambulance corps. During the years before and after the turn of the century, San Francisco's harbor defenses were strengthened, and many of the Presidio's subposts were rushed to completion. Fort Baker was established in 1897, Fort Miley in 1900, and Fort Barty in 1908. Fort Winfield Scott (Fort Point) was strengthened with coastal batteries. Alcatraz Island was an Army disciplinary barracks, and Angel Island became an Army retention quarantine station.

The Presidio's garrison at the turn of the century consisted of five companies of cavalry, with 350 men and 15 officers, five companies of the Coast Artillery, and four batteries of the Field Artillery, aggregating 1,160 men and 23 officers. The armament of the Presidio and its subposts numbered 20 guns and 32 mortars. The old muzzle-loading cannon that had been the mainstay of the defense installations protecting San Francisco Bay became obsolete in the latter part of the 1890s. The Army changed over to the then modern breech-loading rifle. Huge reinforced concrete installations to house the guns were constructed during the 1893–1908 period. Located at the southwest end of the Golden Gate Bridge are the old Batteries Godfrey, Boutelle, Marcus Miller, and Cranston.

Battery Godfrey was armed with three 12-inch guns mounted on barbette carriages. It was named in 1902 in honor of Captain George J. Godfrey, 22nd Infantry, who was killed at Cavite, on the Island of Luzon in the Philippines, on June 3, 1899. The guns were dismantled in 1946. Battery Boutelle was armed with three 5-inch, rapid-fire, pillar-mounted guns. It was named in honor of 2nd Lieutenant Henry M. Boutelle, 3rd Artillery, who was killed in action near Aliaga, Philippine Islands. The guns were dismantled in 1920. Battery Marcus Miller was armed with three 10-inch disappearing guns. It was named in 1907 to honor Brigadier General Marcus P. Miller, who served with distinction during the Civil War, the Indian campaigns, and in the Philippine Insurrection. The guns were dismounted in 1920. Battery Cranston was armed with two 10-inch disappearing guns. It was named to honor 1st Lieutenant Arthur Cranston, 4th Artillery, who was killed at the Lava Beds, California, on April 26, 1873, in action against the Modoc Indians, and is buried in the San Francisco National Cemetery. The guns were dismounted in 1943.

In addition, mounted in Batteries McKinnon and Stotsenbury were 12-inch mortars that provided high-angle fire for the protection of the Golden Gate and adjacent waters during the 1898–1946 period. Mortars of this type were used primarily against heavily armored naval vessels. The vertical plunge of the huge projectile would penetrate the deck and explode amidship. Battery McKinnon housed four 12-inch mortars in pits of two each. It was named in 1906 to honor Chaplain William D. McKinnon, 3rd Cavalry, who served with distinction during the war with Spain. Battery Stotsenbury was armed with eight 12-inch mortars. It was named in 1902 in honor of Captain John M. Stotsenbury, 6th Cavalry, who was killed in action on Luzon, Philippine Islands, on April 23, 1899.

When a major earthquake, followed by devastating fires, struck San Francisco in the early hours of April 18, 1906, Presidio troops under the command of General Frederick Funston reported to the city's chief of police to help keep order, assist refugees, and fight the many fires. A refugee camp was set up on Presidio grounds, and rations, tents, blankets, and medical attention were provided for thousands of the city's homeless. During World War I the Presidio was an officers' training facility for 11 western states, and troops drilled close by concentration camps housing enemy aliens. In World War II, the Western Defense Command was located at the Presidio, where the plans were formulated for the successful attacks on Japanese-occupied Attu and Kiska in the Aleutians.

Located at the Presidio today are Headquarters of the U.S. Army Garrison of the Presidio; Headquarters, Sixth U.S. Army; Letterman Army Hospital; Headquarters of the 6th Region, U.S. Army Air Defense Command; and Headquarters, Fifteenth U.S. Army Corps (Reserve), serving California, Arizona and Nevada. Since Lieutenant José Joaquin Moraga relinquished his command of the Presidio in 1785, at least 189 officers and one non-commissioned officer (a caretaker sergeant) have commanded the Presidio. Many of the Army's illustrious names are associated with the presidio. Major General Irwin McDowell, General William Tecumseh Sherman, Lieutenant General Philip H. Sheridan, Lieutenant General Hunter Liggett, Brigadier General Frederick Funston, and Lieutenant General Arthur MacArthur, the father of General Douglas MacArthur, all commanded the post at one time or another in their Army careers. General John J. Pershing, when in command of the 8th Brigade, was stationed at the Presidio in 1914 before leaving on his expedition into Mexico. It was here that his personal tragedy occurred, the death of his wife and three daughters in a fire which destroyed their home on the post.

The Presidio's old quadrangle is commemorated by bronze tablets placed there by the Daughters of the American Revolution in 1928. The old powder magazine at Sheridan Avenue and Anza Street is little changed since its construction by the Presidio's Mexican garrison in 1845. It has ten-foot-thick walls constructed of native stone. The walls are double, with an air space to ensure dryness of the powder within, and two narrow ventilation slots pierce the east wall near the magazine's heavy door. From the high hills of the Presidio, one obtains a spectacular view in every direction. To the southeast is the city of San Francisco; to the west, Fort Miley's flag and the Pacific Ocean, with the Farallon Islands far in the distance; to the northwest across the Golden Gate is Fort Barry; to the north is Fort Baker; to the northeast across San Francisco Bay is Angel Island; slightly to the east of Angel Island is Alcatraz Island; and to the east along the Bay's shoreline are the docks of Fort Mason. Today, the Presidio and all its San Francisco Bay coastal defense subposts are included in the Golden Gate National Recreation Area, established in 1972.

CASTILLO DE SAN JOAQUÍN. FORT WINFIELD SCOTT.

BATTERY SAN JOSÉ. FORT MASON.

CAMP SAN JOSÉ. A temporary camp at San José, Santa Clara County, it was established during April 1848 and abandoned on September 6, 1848. It was apparently reoccupied during the Civil War in 1863.

CAMP SAN LUIS OBISPO. Located five miles west of the city of San Luis Obispo, the camp was originally established as a National Guard camp in 1928. Shortly before World War II, the government took over the camp and built nearly all the buildings that exist today. During the war the reservation held some 15,953 acres and served as an infantry division training center. Inactivated in 1946, it was reactivated in 1951 as a Signal Corps training center. Inactivated again on November 15, 1953, part of the camp was used for National Guard and Reserve activities, with the remainder of the reservation utilized for cattle grazing and a minimum-security prison. Today, the camp is a major training site for ARCOM units from Fort Lawton, Washington.

SAN LUIS OBISPO POST. A temporary post, it was established sometime in 1864. No records of units involved have been found.

CAMP SAN LUIS REY (*Post at Mission San Luis Rey de Francia*). The Mormon Battalion camped at San Luis Rey in late 1846. Then the Army initiated small garrisons here to provide protection for travelers through the area. A camp was established on the San Luis River, about two miles from the coast and some 35 miles northwest of San Diego. It was abandoned on June 23, 1849. On April 18, 1850, however, a new post was established at Mission San Luis Rey. The troops were withdrawn in June 1852. The church and mission, just south of the U.S. Marines' Camp Pendleton, have been restored and the ruins of the soldiers' barracks are on the site located three and a half miles east of Oceanside. A military historian claims that only one site served both camps.

POST AT MISSION SAN LUIS REY DE FRANCIA. CAMP SAN LUIS REY.

CAMP SAN MIGUEL. An Army post established in 1849 at the Mission of San Miguel Archangel in San Luis Obispo County, it served as a base for 2nd Infantry escorts. The post was abandoned in 1851.

CAMP SAN PEDRO. A short-lived Army post established at San Pedro sometime in 1892, it apparently occupied a site very close to former Drum Barracks.

CAMP SANTA ANITA. Located east of Los Angeles and adjacent to Pasadena, Camp Santa Anita at Arcadia was opened March 27, 1942, as a relocation center for Japanese-Americans being evacuated from the West Coast. The last of the inmates left on October 27, 1942, and on November 30 the center was turned over to the Ordnance Corps for training purposes. The camp continued in this role until November 1944.

CAMP SANTA BARBARA. There were at least three temporary Army posts established at Santa Barbara. The first consisted of elements of Frémont's Rangers, who established their headquarters at the old St. Charles Hotel in 1846. The next year the hotel was the headquarters of the New York Volunteers, while their principal camp was located on the beach. The Volunteers were frequently stationed at Santa Barbara during the

PRESIDIO OF SANTA BARBARA. Spanish plan drawn in 1820.

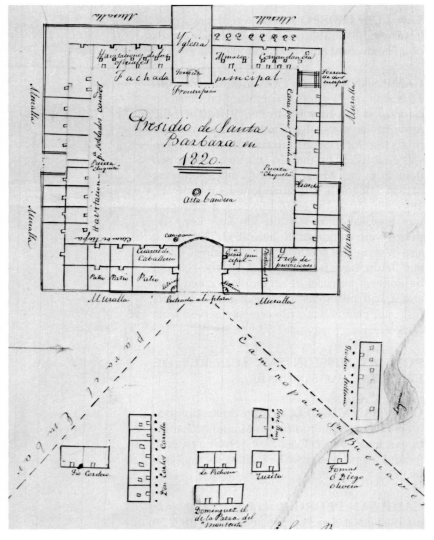

Civil War. Another garrison established camp in the town on April 8, 1848, and evacuated on September 8, 1848. Santa Barbara was reoccupied in January 1864 and abandoned during the following November.

PRESIDIO OF SANTA BARBARA. The fourth and last of the four presidios to be founded by the Spanish in Alta California was the Presidio of Santa Barbara, located on a small bay about half a mile from the later-built mission (since restored). Construction of the Presidio was begun on April 19, 1782, by 55 soldiers under the supervision of Governor Felipe de Neve, Captain Jose Francisco Ortega, and Father Junípero Serra. Its formal dedication took place two days later, on the Sunday after Easter. The initial edition of the Presidio was a temporary wooden stockade 60 yards square, enclosing a number of log huts that served as officers' quarters and barracks, accompanied by some irrigation works in preparation for small-scale farming. Two years later, the wooden structures began to be replaced by an 80-yard-square, adobe-walled, rectangular enclosure with adobe buildings lining the interior walls, all on stone foundations, and a bastion in the east and west angles. Most of the reconstruction was accomplished during the 1784–88 period.

In August 1793, the fort was finally completed. In 1826 the town, or pueblo, of Santa Barbara was formally established by the Mexican government, four years after it had won its independence from Spain. It had been reported that in the following year there were some 60 to 80 one-story adobe houses, each of which had its own garden, outside the Presidio's walls. By the time the Americans arrived in 1846 to take possession, the Presidio had become utterly decrepit. The American flag was raised above the Presidio's crumbling walls on August 1, 1846, by Commodore Robert F. Stockton. A small garrison occupied the Presidio until sometime in the late spring of 1848, when it was abandoned by the military and surrendered to the alcalde of Santa Barbara. A number of restored Spanish- and Mexican-built buildings were destroyed by the earthquake in 1925, but two pre-1790 buildings, formerly within the Presidio compound, survived, although considerably altered. The site of the Presidio is located in the area bounded by Gardem, Anacapa, Carillo and De la Guerra streets, in the heart of a modern American city.

CAMP SANTA CATALINA ISLAND. On January 1, 1864, Company C of the 4th Infantry, California Volunteers, commanded by Captain

B. R. West, occupied the island. The Army had established the post on the island with the idea of converting it into a reservation for Indians. However, when the proposal was abandoned, so was the Army post.

CAMP AT SANTA CRUZ. A "Camp of Instruction," it was established on July 15, 1887, by Colonel William R. Shafter, 1st Infantry, with Companies A, C, D, E, F, G, I, and K, and a detachment of the 1st Artillery, aggregating 326 men. The command had assembled at the Presidio of San Francisco, July 5, 1887, and marched, with intermediate stops, 90 miles to Santa Cruz.

CAMP SANTA ISABEL (YSABEL). Established in 1851 by the Army and used as a depot, it was located at Santa Ysabel, 60 miles east of San Diego, on the grounds of the *assistencia* there. The post was abandoned sometime in 1852.

CAMP SAN YSIDRO. A Mexican border patrol post in San Diego County, it was probably established prior to World War I.

SAN YSIDRO POST. Established on July 12, 1912, the post was garrisoned by 1st Lieutenant Ira A. Smith, 12th Infantry, with Company C, the command coming from Campo. The camp was abandoned on January 27, 1913, when the troops were ordered to the Presidio of Monterey.

FORT SAVANNAH. PRESIDIO OF MONTEREY.

CAMP SCHOFIELD. A temporary post, the camp was established by Troop M, 1st Cavalry, on August 6, 1883, in Marin County. It was evacuated on October 29, 1883, in compliance with Special Orders No. 131, Department of California, September 29, 1883.

SCORPION POINT CAMP. CAMP NEW SUPPLY.

FORT SCOTT. FORT WINFIELD SCOTT.

CAMP SEELEY. A World War II training post, it was established in the near environs of the town of Seeley, four miles east of El Centro, in the Imperial Valley. The post was some 65 miles east of Campo where its subpost, Camp Lockett, was located. Camp Seeley was named for the town which, in turn, had been named for Henry Seeley, a pioneer in the development of Imperial Valley.

CAMP SEQUOIA NATIONAL PARK (*Camp Mineral King*). The Sequoia and General Grant National Parks were occupied intermittently by troops, almost invariably cavalry, assigned from 1891 to 1913 to patrol the national parks and guard against depredations. The commanding officer was also acting superintendent of the parks. The first encampment was by Company K, 4th Cavalry, in obedience to Special Orders No. 30, Department of California, April 6, 1898. The various camps were known as Camp at the Summit, Camp Three Rivers, Camp Mineral King, Camp Big Red Hill, Camp Davenport's Place, Camp Washburn's Ranch, Camp General Grant Park, Camp Red Hill, Camp Millwood, Camp Giant Forest, Camp Weishan's Hill, Camp Wisher's Hill, Camp Old Colony Mill, Camp Kaweah, and Camp Sequoia. The most usual names were those of the nearest post offices—Three Rivers, Millwood, Kaweah, and Sequoia. The troops of Company C, 1st Cavalry, were the last recalled from the park by Special Orders No. 159, Western Department, August 26, 1913. The last acting superintendent and commanding officer was the late Hugh S. Johnson, then a 1st Lieutenant in the 1st Cavalry.

FORT SEWARD (*Camp on Eel River*). Located on the upper Eel River, 65 miles southeast of Humboldt, Fort Seward was established on September 25, 1861, by Captain Charles S. Lovell, 6th Infantry. The post was named for the then secretary of state, William H. Seward. Although it was actually abandoned in April, 1862, it has been variously reported as being abandoned in 1863 and 1866.

CAMP SHOEMAKER. Located 30 miles east of Oakland, this World War II installation was at one time a naval training and distribution center, adjoining Camp Parks. It was transferred to the Air Force for use in connection with the Parks Air Force Base in the 1950s and was subsequently transferred to the Army.

CAMP SIGEL. Company I, 4th Infantry, California Volunteers, was raised in Nevada City and mustered into the armed forces at Camp Sigel near Auburn, Placer County, on October 7, 1861. The company abandoned Camp Sigel in February 1862 and marched to Camp Union.

FORT SODA (*Hancock's Redoubt; Fort Soda Lake; Camp Soda Springs*). This desert camp, variously named for the dry soda lake in its vicinity, was first established south of Baker, San Bernardino County, in the spring of 1860 by men of the 1st Dragoons and called Hancock's Redoubt. Later, in the spring of 1867, an outpost was maintained there for a few weeks. Then, beginning on August 21, 1867, the site was manned almost continuously as an outpost of Camp Cady, 35 miles distant, until May 23, 1868, when it was abandoned by the Army permanently.

FORT SODA LAKE. FORT SODA.

CAMP SODA SPRINGS. FORT SODA.

CAMP SOLDIER'S GROVE. A temporary post established in 1864, it was located some 18 miles from Hyampom in Trinity County.

CAMP SONOMA (*Presidio of Sonoma; Sonoma Post; Sonoma Barracks*). Barracks were erected at the so-called Presidio of Sonoma by General Mariano Guadalupe, commander of the northern Mexico frontier forces and founder of the town of Sonoma. In June 1846 Americans, under the banner of California's "Bear Flag," staged a brief revolt against the Mexican rulers. Reinforced a few weeks later by more troops under Commodore John D. Sloat, the force took possession of California for the United States. Navy Lieutenant Joseph W. Revere, grandson of the American Revolution hero Paul Revere, was in command for a short period. A camp was established here on April 4, 1847, intermittently abandoned and reoccupied, and finally abandoned on October 16, 1851. A military post was established in 1852 and garrisoned for six years. Sonoma State Historical Park contains the old barracks and is located at Spain Street East and 1st Street East.

PRESIDIO OF SONOMA. CAMP SONOMA.

SONOMA BARRACKS. CAMP SONOMA.

SONOMA POST. CAMP SONOMA.

CAMP STANFORD. A Civil War tent camp established in 1863 in present Stockton, San Joaquin County, it occupied two square blocks of land in the then undeveloped perimeter of the city, which are now bounded by Rose, Acacia, Van Buren and Monroe streets.

CAMP STANISLAUS (*Miller's Camp*). The two summer encampments, Camp Stanislaus and Camp Frederica, both established by Major Albert S. Miller, 2nd Infantry, and located on the Stanislaus River, were confused by local historians, who have generally consolidated them as Miller's Camp. Camp Stanislaus (1849) was located at or near Taylor's Ferry (present Riverbank) and on the river's north bank; Camp Frederica was established about a year later but not on the same site. (See: CAMP FREDERICA.)

CAMP STEELE. On June 15, 1852, 1st Lieutenant Tredwell Moore of Company K, 2nd Infantry, led a detachment out of Fort Miller for the upper reaches between the middle and south forks of the Merced River. On June 20 he established temporary Camp Steele, named in honor of the acting assistant adjutant general of the Department of the Pacific, Frederick Steele, 2nd Infantry.

FORT STOCKTON. PRESIDIO OF MONTEREY.

FORT STOCKTON. PRESIDIO OF SAN DIEGO.

CAMP STONEMAN. Located on the San Joaquin River at Pittsburg, Contra Costa County, 40 miles northeast of San Francisco, this major overseas processing center during World War II and the Korean War was built five months after the attack on Pearl Harbor. On May 28, 1942, it was named in honor of Major General George Stoneman, Civil War leader and later elected governor of California in 1882. The camp was part of the San Francisco Port of Embarkation and a staging area for overseas assignment where 20,940 troops could be billeted on its 2,800-acre installation. In January 1946, the camp held more than 2,250 German prisoners-of-war. Totally deactivated on August 31, 1954, the land was sold to various state and county agencies and a number of private individuals.

CAMP STROWBRIDGE. FORT WOOL.

CAMP SUGAR LOAF. A temporary, intermittently occupied desert camp established in 1858, it was located just west of present Barstow, adjacent to the Mojave River, San Bernardino County.

CAMP SUMNER. A Civil War rendezvous for mustering troops and observing Secessionist activities, Camp Sumner was established late in 1861 on grounds adjacent to the Presidio of San Francisco for elements of the California Volunteers, and for a short time the 9th Infantry. The camp, functioning until sometime in 1865, was named in honor of the Department of the Pacific commander, E. V. Sumner.

CAMP SUSAN. Located at Susanville, Lassen County, Camp Susan was a temporary post established in the late spring of 1864 by Captain Malachi R. Hassett, 1st Nevada Territorial Infantry, for the purpose of protecting the travel routes in the town's environs. Scouting of the area was under the guidance of Lieutenant Andrew J. Close, who commanded a detachment of 30 men. In October the company was ordered to return to Fort Churchill.

SUTTER'S FORT (*Fort New Helvetia; Fort Sacramento*). A private trading post and fortified defense that became the foundation for modern Sacramento, it was established by a former Swiss army captain, John (Johann) Augustus Sutter, who is considered the founder of American agriculture in California. The post began as a wilderness barony flying the Mexican flag when in 1839 he accepted a 50,000-acre land grant in the rich Sacramento Valley by attesting his allegiance to the Mexican government. Sutter began his fort project in April 1840, naming it Fort New Helvetia (Switzerland), but referring to it at times as Fort Sacramento. A visiting scientist in 1843 described Sutter's fort as having "more the appearance of a citadel than an agricultural establishment." The scope and success of Sutter's enterprise were described in his own words:

Agriculture increased until I had several hundred men working in the harvest fields, and to feed them I had to kill four or sometimes five oxen daily. I could raise 40,000 bushels of wheat without trouble, reap the crops with sickles, thresh it with bones, and winnow it in the wind. There were thirty plows running with fresh oxen every morning . . . I had at the time twelve thousand head of cattle, two thousand horses and mules, between ten and fifteen thousand sheep, and a thousand hogs. My best days were just before the discovery of gold. [Kent Ruth, *Great Day in the West*, p. 30]

Ironically, the discovery of gold on his property on January 24, 1848, after he had built a sawmill on the American River, ultimately led to the death of his empire. His white employees deserted New Helvetia for the gold camps, hungry riches-maddened prospectors ruthlessly violated the hospitality of his fort, stole his cattle, ejected the area's friendly Indians, and finally appropriated his lands. Sutter, "who ruled his enclave in feudal splendor, died impoverished, a victim of his own enterprise."

Kit Carson and John C. Frémont were at the fort in 1844 during the beginnings of military maneuvering against the Mexican government's presence in California. They found the fort in early 1846 to be walled and bastioned, 15 to 18 feet high, quadrangular, and built of adobe. It mounted 12 pieces of artillery and could garrison a thousand men. The main buildings were grouped within an irregularly shaped area measuring approximately 425 by 175 feet. The ordnance came from Fort Ross, which Sutter had purchased from the Russian-American Company. With day-and-night sentinels, it was considered the largest and best fortified fort in California, which prompted the U.S. Army to take possession of the fort on July 11, 1846, when Sutter himself raised the stars and stripes above its walls. The Army garrisoned the fort during part of 1847 and thereafter intermittently until 1850.

During the following 15 years the fort rapidly disintegrated. By the mid-1860s it was almost obliterated, with only the large central building withstanding the assaults of neglect and vandalism. Since the peak of Sutter's enterprise, it had been used successively as a trading post and agricultural empire, gambling casino, a hospital, a warehouse, a residence, and finally, to its dishonor, as a stable, a chicken house, and a pigpen. From time to time, proposals were made to preserve the old building. Finally, in the 1880s, the first definite steps were taken to that end. The work of reconstruction was begun in 1891, with the intention of reconstructing the buildings and restoring the grounds as nearly as possible to their condition and appearance during the heyday of the fort. Today, the rebuilt property, located at 2701 L Street in Sacramento, is a California State Historic Landmark.

POST NEAR SUTTERVILLE. CAMP ANDERSON.

CAMP SWASEY. A temporary post established in 1862 by elements of the California Volunteers, it was located at Hydesville near Eureka, Humboldt County.

SYCAMORE GROVE CAMP. An intermittently used Army campsite situated on Martin's Ranch in San Bernardino County during the Mohave War, it was probably first occupied in 1847 by the Mormon Battalion. Sycamore Grove was also the site where the Mormon pioneers camped during the summer of 1851.

CAMP TAYLOR. Situated on the Pitt River at Fall River Mills in Contra Costa County, about eight miles southeast of Fort Crook, Camp Taylor was established on September 16, 1859, by Captain F. F. Flint, 6th Infantry, with Companies A and I, aggregating 62 men. The detachment had left Camp Cass, near Red Bluffs, on September 7, in compliance with Special Department Orders No. 94, dated September 1, 1859. The distance marched was 110 miles.

TECATE POST. A Mexican border patrol post at Tecate, San Diego County, it was established in March 1911 by Captain Theodore H. Koch with the 115th Company, Coast Artillery, aggregating 102 men, pursuant to General Orders No. 23, Fort Rosecrans, dated March 23, 1911. The post was active until November 1914.

FORT TEJÓN (*Camp Cañada de las Uvas*). Established on August 10, 1854, by 1st Lieutenant Thomas F. Castor, 1st Dragoons, to replace ineffectual Fort Miller on the San Joaquin River, Fort Tejón was located in the Cañada de las Uvas, about 15 miles southwest of the Tejón (Sebastian) Indian Reservation, near present Lebec, Kern County. The location had been selected by Brevet Major John Donaldson of the Quartermaster Corps, apparently with the approval of Lieutenant Edward F. Beale, U.S. Navy, who was named superintendent of Indian affairs for California in 1852. The post was intended to guard the pass through the Tehachapi Mountains, to control the area's tribes, and to protect the Indians on the reservation which had been established the previous year. In 1858, when the fort became a station on the Butterfield overland route, the garrison provided military escorts through the pass.

The post was considered comparatively small by Army standards, with an average garrison complement of 225 men. Adobe-built Fort Tejón was the principal military, political, and social hub of central California's vast area during the early American period. Fifteen of the officers who served there eventually became generals in the Civil War, eight Union and seven Confederate. While the fort was being constructed, the troops were encamped adjacent to its site, and their temporary quarters were called Camp Cañada de las Uvas. Lieutenant Beale, associated with all facets of Fort Tejón's history, made the post his headquarters. Serving as director of the large survey team planning a wagon road from Texas to California, he brought a caravan of 28 camels across the Southwest from a point near San Antonio to Fort Tejón in 1857. The experimental use of camels was so successful that Beale strongly recommended their continued use by the Army throughout the arid Southwest. The breaking out of the Civil War, however, in addition to other factors, put an end to his proposal. The fort was evacuated on June 15, 1861, by order of Brigadier General Edwin Vose Sumner. Fort Tejón was reoccupied on August 17, 1863, by California Volunteers in compliance with an order of Brigadier General George Wright. The permanent abandonment of the post on September 11, 1864, in accordance with a directive issued by Major General Irvin McDowell, was coincident with the termination of Tejón Reservation. The military reservation and its 25 structures then became a part of the Rancho Tejón, a Mexican land grant, purchased by Lieutenant Beale, who eventually increased his holdings to nearly 200,000 acres. Part of Fort Tejón's site is now a state historical monument and a number of the old fort's original buildings have been restored.

FORT TER-WAW. Established on October 12, 1857, by 1st Lieutenant George Crook, 4th Infantry, who suggested the name "Ter-Waw" (Yurok Indian for "beautiful place"), it was located in Del Norte County, on the north bank of the Klamath River, about six miles above its mouth, on Klamath Indian Reservation land and across the river from the reservation agency's headquarters. The post was evacuated on June 11, 1861, but reoccupied on August 28, 1861. River-flooded four times during the winter of 1861–62, with 17 of its 20 buildings undermined and washed away, plans were made to relocate the camp on a new site. However, during the following late spring, on June 11, Brigadier General George Wright countermanded the order to rebuild the post since any site on the river would be subjected to flooding. The post's troops were moved to the Smith River Valley where Camp Lincoln was being constructed six miles northeast of Crescent City.

TRINIDAD CAMP. A number of troops were stationed in the town of Trinidad, north of Eureka, Humboldt County, from July to October 1863, at which time they were moved four miles northward to Camp Gilmore.

CAMP TULARE. A temporary post on the Tulare Indian Farm located about three miles east of Portersville in Tulare County, it was established in 1871 by 1st Lieutenant William Vose, 2nd Artillery, with Company D, aggregating 105 men. The first post return was dated April 30, 1871. The camp was evacuated on July 30, and the troops marched nearly 100 miles to the Presidio of San Francisco.

CAMP UNION. Originally a training ground established in 1861 for California Volunteers, Camp Union at Sacramento became California's most prominent provider of troops for camps in the West throughout the years of the Civil War. A third of the state's 15,000 volunteers trained here. Toward the end of the conflict, the camp became a discharge or separation center for returning troops. The camp's first site, which had to be evacuated in October 1861 because of river flooding, is located across the Sacramento River from the old community of Suttersville, on what was once a race track. The second camp was across the river at what is now the intersection of Suttersville and Del Rio roads. Camp Union was abandoned in 1866.

CAMP U.S. TROOPS. CAMP (JOHN H.) BEACOM.

CAMP AND DEPOT VALLECITO. A stage station first occupied by Army troops in 1850, it eventually became an important supply center, which lasted until 1853, although it had been officially abandoned as a post. Its site, including the restored stage station, is the present Vallecito County Park, some 19 miles south of Scissors Crossing.

FORT VIGILANCE. FORT GUNNYBAGS.

FORT VISALIA. The town of Visalia, Tulare County, was first established in November 1852 when a group of settlers led by Nathaniel Vise erected a fort on the block now bounded by Garden, Bridge, Race and Oak streets. The town grew so rapidly that in the following year the county seat was moved from Woodsville to Visalia. It is not definitely known when the fort was finally dismantled; it was still standing in 1860.

FORT VOSE (*Camp Nome Lackee*). This post was established on January 4, 1855, on the Nome Lackee Indian Reservation formed in September 1854 on Thomes Creek about 20 miles west of Tehama. Originally situated in Colusa County, the reservation was relocated in Tehama County in 1856 when the county lines were redrawn. Elements of the 3rd Artillery were stationed at Nome Lackee until April 21, 1858, to provide local protection. In 1948 remains of the adobe-built fortification were still in evidence. The structure, approximately 100 feet square with walls about 10 feet high, was built primarily for the protection of reservation agency personnel. The reservation was the forerunner of the Round Valley Reservation; it was gradually displaced by the latter and was completely abandoned in 1861. The post was apparently renamed Fort Vose, possibly for Lieutenant William Vose, an artilleryman, who years later was attached to the 2nd Artillery.

CAMP WAITE. Troops maintained a camp on Antelope Creek, southeast of Red Bluff, Tehama

County, during 1865–66, to put down Indian unrest in the area.

CAMP WALTER R. TALIAFERRO. A semipermanent camp, it was established at San Diego as a Mexican border patrol post on March 31, 1916, by the 1st Battalion, less Company C, 21st Infantry, which arrived from its home base at Vancouver Barracks, Washington. Located on the grounds of the Panama-California International Exposition, the post was named for pioneer aviator 1st Lieutenant Walter R. Taliaferro who was killed in an aviation accident near San Diego on October 11, 1915. A flying field later established at Fort Worth, Texas, was also named for the lieutenant.

WARNER'S RANCH CAMP. CAMP WRIGHT.

FORT WASHINGTON. A settlers' log-and-earthwork Indian defense built about 1850 by Wiley B. Cassady and C. D. Gibbes, it was located about 10 miles below Fort Miller on the south bank of the San Joaquin River at the Stockton-Visalia stage crossing in Fresno County. It was reportedly washed away when the river overflowed in 1852.

CAMP NEAR WAWONA. CAMP YOSEMITE.

FORT WELLER. In response to urgent requests for the stationing of troops on the Round Valley and Mendocino reservations, for the purpose of protecting property from Indian depredations and to protect the Indians from retaliations, 1st Lieutenant William P. Carlin, 6th Infantry, with Company D, left Benecia Barracks on December 13, 1858, under orders to establish a post at or near the Nome Cult Indian Reservation in Round Valley, Mendocino County. Established on January 3, 1859, on the east bank of the Russian River in the Redwood Valley, the post was named for John B. Weller, governor of California. The post was abandoned in October of the same year.

WEST GARRISON. FORT McDOWELL.

CAMP WHISTLER. Established by Company B, 4th Infantry, on May 24, 1858, archival materials do not report location, date of abandonment, or for whom named.

WILMINGTON DEPOT. This Army depot, located at Wilmington, a short distance northeast of San Pedro, was established in 1861. It supplied Drum Barracks and Mojave Desert posts until 1870. The depot's site, one block long and two blocks wide, is bounded by C, Front and Canal Streets.

FORT WINFIELD SCOTT (*Castillo de San Joaquín; Fort Blanco; Fort Point; Fort Scott*).

On December 8, 1794, some 18 years after the Presidio of San Francisco was founded, the Spanish completed the fortification, El Castillo de San Joaquín, at what is now the southern terminus of the Golden Gate Bridge where Fort Point is located. The defense was also called Fort Blanco, derived from the Spanish name for the point, Punta del Cantil Blanco. The Castillo was built in the form of a horseshoe with a 10-foot-thick wall of palisades. Eight 17th-century bronze cannon, cast in Lima, Peru, were placed in the embrasures that pierced the fort's walls. Six of these cannon exist to this day: two flank the entrance to the Presidio Officers' Club; two others stand at the Presidio's main flagpole; and the remaining two are mounted at Fort Mason.

By the time the U.S. Army occupied the presidio in 1847, the Castillo was already in ruins. During 1853 the Army razed the old fortification, and the 107-foot-high cliff on which it stood was cut away to a solid rock foundation 16 feet above the water. Work on Fort Point began the same year. The engineer officers in charge of the work were, successively, Lieutenant Colonel James L. Mason, Major J. G. Barnard, Lieutenant Colonel R. E. DeRussy, and Major Z. R. Tower. In 1861 it was garrisoned by two companies of the 3rd Artillery. Fort Point, somewhat similar to Fort Sumter in its layout, is in the form of an irregular quadrangle, with a width of 150 feet, its longest side 250 feet, and 45 feet high, with seven-foot-thick walls. On November, 1882, Fort Point was renamed Fort Winfield Scott in honor of the lieutenant general. The fort was considered obsolescent in 1905 when construction was started on new structures on the hills a little to the south, above the fort, on the western portion of the Presidio reservation. This new site was fortified with 17 Endicott-period batteries: in alphabetical order, Baldwin, Blaney, Boutelle, Chamberlin, Cranston, Crosby, "Dynamite," Godfrey, Howe, Lancaster, McKinnon, Miller, Saffold, Sherwood, Slaughter, Stotsenburg, and Wagner.

In 1914 Fort Winfield Scott was deactivated. In World War II a battery of three-inch guns and a searchlight detachment manned the old bulwark in support of San Francisco harbor's defenses. Although all Fort Winfield Scott's batteries are unoccupied at present, the fort is still an active adjunct to the Presidio of San Francisco.

FORT WINFIELD SCOTT. Photograph taken circa 1900.

*FORT WINFIELD SCOTT.
Aerial view of the fort
at the southern base of
the Golden Gate Bridge.
(Courtesy of the U. S.
Army.)*

FORT WOOL (*Camp Strowbridge*). Located at the confluence of the Trinity and Klamath rivers, about 140 miles north of the mouth of the latter river, and on the northern edge of the Hoopa Valley Indian Reservation in Humboldt County, this temporary post established in 1855 was intended to control the warring Hoopa Indians. Very little is known about the post. Originally named Camp Strowbridge, most probably for its commanding officer, it was renamed Fort Wool, no doubt in honor of Major General John Ellis Wool, commanding the Department of the Pacific, who was credited with suppressing Indian disturbances in Washington.

CAMP WORTH. A temporary camp established in 1865 to house Indian prisoners-of-war, it stood on the peninsula between Humboldt Bay and the Pacific Ocean, about five miles from Lighthouse Point, Humboldt County.

CAMP WRIGHT (*Warner's Ranch Camp*). First established on October 18, 1861, on the grounds of Warner's Ranch, by elements of the 2nd Infantry, it was designed to protect the emigrant travel route between Arizona and California. Moved about November 23, 1861, to Oak Grove, also in San Diego County, the camp was reestablished by Major Edwin A. Rigg, 1st California Volunteers. The post was then renamed for Brigadier General George Wright. The camp was abandoned in December 1866.

CAMP WRIGHT. This temporary post was a Civil War mustering-in tent camp established near San Francisco in 1861.

CAMP WRIGHT (*Fort Right; Fort Wright*). In response to urgent requests for much-needed soldiers in Mendocino County made by George M. Hanson, superintendent of Indian affairs for northern California, troops were ordered to Round Valley on October 28, 1862. The unit chosen was Company F, 2nd California Infantry, Captain Charles D. Douglas commanding, which was ordered from Fort Gaston to Round Valley via Fort Humboldt and Fort Bragg. After protracted delays enroute, the troops arrived at their destination on December 11, 1862. According to National Archives records, however, the post's first garrison consisted of seven companies of the 9th Infantry, under the command of Captain F. T. Dent. A site was selected, and the new post was named Fort Wright, designated Camp Wright after the Civil War, for General George Wright, commander of the Department of the Pacific.

The post was located about one and a half miles northwest of the present town of Covelo. One of the principal duties of the camp's troops was the protection of the area's Indians and their interests from the depredations of bigoted and thieving whites. During 1863 and 1864 construction on the post continued with the building of log structures roofed with shakes designed for two officers' quarters, barracks, mess hall, bakery, hospital, guardhouse, storehouse and stables. In

1869 construction was resumed and continued for several years, including the building of a new adobe company barracks in 1869 on the south side of the parade ground, the same year a military reservation one mile square was established. Finally, because of the permanency of friendly relations with the reservation Indians, Camp Wright was ordered abandoned on June 10, 1875, and the troops left a week later. On July 26, 1876, the buildings and military reservation were transferred to the Interior Department for use and occupancy by the reservation's Indians, for whose benefit the land was later divided into 10-acre allotments.

FORT WRIGHT. CAMP WRIGHT.

YAGER CREEK CROSSING CAMP. Very little is known about this temporary post established in 1862 in the vicinity of Hydesville.

CAMP YERBA BUENA ISLAND (*Military Post at Goat Island*). This 116-acre island, nicknamed Goat Island, situated in San Francisco Bay, about two and a quarter miles northeast of the city, was originally intended for the installation of artillery batteries in defense of the bay. Established in 1868, it served however as a regular Army camp until 1880, when the island and the improvements built on it by the Army were transferred to the Navy Department.

CAMP YOSEMITE (*Camp near Wawona; Detachment at Yosemite National Park; Camp A. E. Wood*). This post was established on May 17, 1891, and called Camp near Wawona or Detachment at Yosemite National Park. Its first garrison consisted of Company I, 4th Cavalry, commanded by Captain A. E. Wood. Captain Abram Epperson Wood, the park's first superintendent, arrived with the troops on May 19 and continued in charge until his death in 1894. In 1901, the post was redesignated Camp A. E. Wood in his honor, but was renamed Camp Yosemite in May 1907. Each year the park's Army troops came in April or May and withdrew in the fall; during the winter months two civilian rangers attempted to patrol the area. For more than 23 years the Department of the Interior continued to call upon the War Department for assistance in administering Yosemite National Park. Finally, the National Park Service was created in 1916 and relieved the Army.

DETACHMENT AT YOSEMITE NATIONAL PARK. CAMP YOSEMITE.

CAMP YOUNG. World War II's command headquarters for General George S. Patton's huge Desert Training Center, established for the training of troops in desert warfare, was established sometime in 1942. It was located not far south of Indio, Riverside County, near the present junction of U.S. 10 and State 195, where the Cottonwood Springs Road runs up through the Joshua Tree National Monument.

CAMP YUMA. FORT YUMA.

FORT YUMA (*Camp Calhoun; Camp Independence; Camp Yuma*). First established on November 27, 1850, it was originally located in the bottoms near the Colorado River, less than a mile below the mouth of the Gila. In March 1851 the post was moved to a small elevation on the Colorado's west bank, opposite the present city of Yuma, Arizona, on the site of the former Mission Puerto de la Purísima Concepción. This site had been occupied by Camp Calhoun, named for John C. Calhoun, established on October 2, 1849, by 1st Lieutenant Cave J. Couts, 1st Dragoons, for the boundary survey party led by 2nd Lieutenant Amiel W. Whipple, Corps of Topographical Engineers. A ferry service, maintained by the soldiers for the survey party's convenience, also accommodated emigrants. Fort Yuma was established to protect the southern emigrant travel route to California and to attempt control of the warlike Yuma Indians in the surrounding 100-mile area. Established by Captain Samuel P. Heintzelman, 2nd Infantry, it was originally named Camp Independence. In March 1851, when the post was moved to its permanent site, its name was changed to Camp Yuma. A year later the post was designated Fort Yuma. In June 1851 the Army virtually abandoned the post because of the high costs incurred in maintaining it, and it was completely abandoned on December 6, 1851, when its commissary was practically empty of provisions.

The post, however, was reoccupied by Captain Heintzelman on February 29, 1852. In 1864 the Quartermaster Corps erected a depot on the left bank of the Colorado, below the mouth of the Gila River. When the extension of the railroad system obviated the need of a supply depot, Fort Yuma was abandoned (on May 16, 1883). The reservation was transferred to the Interior Department on July 22, 1884. Today, the site of the military reservation is occupied by the Fort Yuma Indian School and a mission.

CAMP ADAMS. On April 29, 1898, six days after the President's call for volunteers, Governor Alva Adams mobilized the entire force of the state's National Guard, which encamped in a tent city near Denver's City Park. Named Camp Adams for the governor, it was located northeast of the park, on the east side of Colorado Boulevard, between 25th and 26th avenues. On May 17 the camp was razed and the troops entrained for the first leg of their long journey to the Philippines.

BEN QUICK RANCH FORT (*Fort Washington*). In 1868 a minimally fortified stockade was built by rancher Ben Quick around his house for protection against marauding Indians. Also called Fort Washington, it was located at Palmer Lake about 20 miles north of Colorado Springs in the West Plum Creek Valley, whose residents "forted up" for a period during the same year.

BENT'S (NEW) FORT. FORT LYON.

BENT'S (OLD) FORT (*Fort William*). About nine miles east of present La Junta in Bent County, on the north bank of the Arkansas River in southeastern Colorado lie the remains of Bent's Old Fort, significant fur-trading post, important Indian rendezvous, and way station on the Santa Fe Trail for emigrant caravans. Situated in the heart of the Indian country and at the crossroads of key overland routes, the fort was a natural trading point. From establishment in 1833 to destruction in 1849 it was the chief point of contact between whites and the Indians of the southern Plains. With the advent of the Mexican War, it became in 1846 a military rendezvous and staging base for the American conquest of New Mexico.

Among the first to become interested in profitable trading with the Indians and Mexicans were the brothers Charles and William Bent and Céran St. Vrain, all of St. Louis. With experience gained in the Upper Missouri fur trade, the three men transferred their operations to the Arkansas River, where they built a small stockade near present Pueblo. Charles Bent originated the idea of a great trading establishment soon after the three men had formed a partnership. Finally, they selected a site on the north bank of the Arkansas, about 12 miles west of the mouth of the Purgatoire River. William Bent began work on the fort in 1828, first named Fort William by his brother, then later renamed Fort Bent or Bent's Fort. He used adobe construction, both because it was fireproof and because there was

Colorado

BENT'S OLD FORT. Front and aerial views sketched by Lieutenant James W. Abert. (Courtesy of the National Archives.)

ings between the Indians and U.S. government representatives. In 1846 Bent's Fort was chosen as headquarters for the Upper Platte and Arkansas Agency.

With the approach of armed conflict with Mexico, the United States designated the adobe trading post as the advance base for invasion of New Mexico, to soon become the rendezvous for General Stephen Watts Kearny's invading Army of the West. According to a National Park Service brochure, *Bent's Old Fort*, Lieutenant James W. Abert, a topographical engineer on John C. Frémont's 1845 expedition, sketched both an aerial perspective and a front view of the fort and described it:

The fort is composed of a series of rooms resembling casemates, and forming a hollow square, the entrance on the [north] side. A round tower on the left, as you enter, and another diagonally opposite, constitute the flanking arrangements. The outer walls, which are nearly two feet in thickness, intersect in the axes of the others, thus permitting their faces to be completely enfiladed; the outside walls of the enceinte and towers, pierced with loop holes, are continued four feet above the flat roofs which serve for the banquette, which being composed of clay cannot be fired by inflammable substances that might be cast upon it; the whole is built of "adobes," sunburnt brick, formed of clay and cut straw, in size about four times as large as our common bricks. The roofs are sustained by poles. On the [south] side is the cattle yard, which is surrounded by a wall so high as effectually to shelter them. The coping of the wall is planted with cacti, which bear red and white flowers.

The long-expected war opened on May 13, 1846. Two months later Kearny arrived at the fort with a force of 1,650 dragoons and Missouri volunteers. Closely behind rolled some 300 wagons of Santa Fe traders, which Kearny's column to all appearances was protecting. Here they remained until early August, then departed on their mission of conquest. After Kearny's army left Bent's Fort, government wagon trains congregated there in ever-increasing numbers. Government cattle overgrazed nearby pastures. Quartermaster stores piled up in the fort, and soldiers, teamsters, and artisans occupied its rooms. The Bents and St. Vrain had furnished an outpost for military expansionism and a very convenient substitute for the fort the War Department had failed to build.

little timber available on the plains for so large a structure. While more than 100 Mexican laborers fabricated mud bricks, Americans hauled in the timber required for the structure's roofs and gates. By 1833 the massive impregnable adobe fortress—180 by 135 feet with 15-foot-high walls—stood completed in the midst of an unbroken prairie.

From their location the Bents and St. Vrain for 16 years ran a trading empire extending from Texas into Wyoming, from the Rockies to middle Kansas. They also had major commitments in the Santa Fe trade, with large mercantile stores in Taos and Santa Fe, and conducted a lucrative trade with westbound caravans. As the principal outpost of American civilization on the southwestern Plains, Bent's Fort was a fairly self-sufficient establishment, employing some 60 persons—carpenters, wheelwrights, gunsmiths, and blacksmiths. Among the better-known figures of the West employed at the post at one time or another were Kit Carson, Lucien B. Maxwell, Baptiste Charbonneau, and Thomas O. Boggs. Because of its position in the heart of the Indian country, the fort was the logical place for meet-

The steady flow of soldiers across the Plains during the war, together with the influx of settlers, gold prospectors, and adventurers that arrived later, constituted a white tide that irrevocably changed the Great Plains. The company was caught in the middle between resentful Indians and invading whites. Indian warfare began seriously in 1847, and from then on the days of lucrative trading were gone. Meanwhile, Charles Bent, appointed governor of the newly won Territory of New Mexico, was killed in a revolt in Taos. This blow, together with the sharp decline in business, destroyed the firm. St. Vrain left for New Mexico, probably after selling his interest in the fort to William Bent.

The final blow to Bent's Fort came in 1849 when cholera, probably brought by emigrants, spread throughout the tribes. What little trade there had been dwindled to nothing, and William Bent, bitterly disappointed, had had enough. Loading his family and a few employees into wagons, he set fire to the storerooms and powder magazine and abandoned the fort. What had been the center of a giant commercial empire was left a blackened ruin, a monument to Manifest Destiny. He moved 38 miles down the Arkansas River to Big Timbers where within a temporary stockade he attempted to revive the Indian trade. In 1852–53 he built here a large stone trading post that became known as Bent's New Fort. (The first fort thus became known as Bent's Old Fort). But the trade never returned to its prewar volume. Bent stayed in business until the eve of the Civil War. After leasing the new fort to the Army, he retired to his ranch on the upper Purgatoire, where he died in 1869.

William Bent's work of destruction of his first fort was more symbolic than effective. After a decade of abandonment, the fort's renovated adobe walls in 1861 sheltered a stage station, the principal stop on the express route between Kansas City and Santa Fe. After railroads displaced the stage, Bent's old buildings served as cattle corrals. Gradually the fort collapsed and disintegrated. A number of the old adobe bricks were no doubt removed by ranchers and homesteaders and were used in the construction of other structures in the vicinity. Portions of the old walls still stand to this day, and elsewhere on the site there are only mounds to outline the fort's dimensions. The National Park Service administers and maintains Bent's Old Fort National Historic Site.

BOYD'S FORT. In 1859–60 Robert Boyd built a sod house, 20 by 60 feet, which stood close to the Cache la Poudre River. There he operated a ferry for the convenience of travelers. In 1865 Boyd rebuilt his house, which was protected by a small round sod fort on the northwest end of the property and a larger one east of the house. The house, along with a large sod corral, 200 feet square with walls seven feet high and two feet thick, is preserved to this day, several miles west of Fort Collins in Larimer County.

FORT BRECKINRIDGE (*Fort Mary B.; Fort Meribeh*). In 1859 a small party of travelers led by Charles Lawrence proceeded north through Hoosier Pass and found gold in profitable yields. A fort was built less than a mile below present Breckinridge in Summit County, practically astride the Continental Divide, and named the defense Meribeh in honor of the only woman member of the party. The fort, also called Mary B., consisted of several blockhouses with walls of green logs and earthen roofs constructed around a hollow square. Occupied as winter quarters during 1859 and 1860, it was found deserted in 1861.

BUFFALO SPRINGS POST. A temporary camp was established at Buffalo Springs in April 1865 when Captain N. J. O'Brien, Iowa Cavalry, with Company F, marched to the site from Julesburg on April 18. The captain's first post return was dated April 30, 1865.

CAMP CARSON. FORT CARSON.

FORT CARSON (*Camp Carson*). The largest World War II military camp established in Colorado, Camp Carson was named for the noted Kit Carson, nineteenth-century Far West scout and military leader. The site, six miles from Colorado Springs, was selected in 1941 to then comprise some 60,000 acres with plans calling for a post that could accommodate 30,000 to 40,000 troops. Construction began in early 1942 on a post laid out in triangular form and designed particularly for the training of a mechanized army. The massive building program called for 1,650 buildings, including 438 barracks to accommodate 74 men each; 17 station hospitals and a base hospital with 1,260 beds; 181 mess halls; 80 company administration and storehouse structures; 12 chapels and 5 theaters; and 44 officers' quarters, exclusive of buildings assigned as headquarters of the commanding generals and eight regimental commands. In August 1942 plans were initiated for an additional 375 buildings.

On January 1, 1943, a Prisoner of War Camp was established on the post for 3,000 POWs, with the first war prisoners, some 1,200 Nazis, brought to Camp Carson in July 1943. The prospect of many more POWs compelled enlarging the facility to handle 8,000. The first enlisted WACs arrived at the camp on May 20, 1943. A peak population of 43,000 troops was reached by the first quarter in 1944. After the war, the post became the summer quarters for mountain troops who wintered on the ski slopes at Camp Hale, a subpost of Camp Carson, located 150 miles west of Colorado Springs. During the subsequent years, regimental combat teams, such as the famous 11th Armored Cavalry (Blackhorse) Regiment, 1952–54, were stationed here. But continuously since mid-August 1954, when the post was given permanency by being designated Fort Carson, there has been an infantry division stationed there: the 31st (1954); 8th (1954–56); 9th (1956–62); the 5th (1961–70) and, since then, the 4th Division. For two years, 1959–61, Fort Carson was also the home of the 2nd U.S. Army Missile Command.

FORT CASS (*Gantt's Fort*). Two St. Louis fur traders, John Gantt and Jefferson Blackwell, built a small post in 1832 on the north bank of the Arkansas River, about five miles east of the mouth of Fountain Creek, in Pueblo County. Facts concerning the enterprise are few. The post was renamed Fort Cass for Lewis Cass, well-known frontier soldier, who replaced John H. Eaton as secretary of war under President Jackson. The post was abandoned some time prior to 1842 when J. P. Beackwourth erected Fort Pueblo at the confluence of the Arkansas and Fountain Creek.

FORT CEDAR POINT. Located in Elbert County, this post was established by Company B, 37th Infantry, on July 23, 1867. The soldiers occupied the ground surrounding a freight station on the Union Pacific Railroad. The name of the post was derived from the station's environs, a heavy cedar growth on the surrounding hillsides. It was from this vicinity that much of the timber used in building the first house in Denver in 1859 was brought. In 1868 the town, such as it was, consisted of a single house and a stable; the subterranean fort and canvas barracks occupied by Company F, 5th Infantry; a pile of posts that served as the "depot"; and a small camp of wood choppers. The post was abandoned on July 10, 1868, when the garrison consisting of Company F, 5th Infantry, left for Fort Riley, Kansas.

FORT CHAMBERS. The frequent Indian alarms in 1864 prompted settlers in the environs of Boulder Valley to take protective measures by building rude defenses on their property. The largest and best constructed was Fort Chambers, erected on the W. G. Chambers Ranch at the mouth of Boulder Creek where it enters the St. Vrain, four miles east of Boulder and northwest of Valmont in Boulder County. The rectangular sod and timber fort with reported 15-foot-high walls and round bastions or blockhouses protruding from each of the four angles, provided protection for as many as 75 families. Built by volunteers, it was frequently garrisoned by small military detachments. The date of its abandonment is not known.

CAMP NEAR THE CITY OF DENVER. FORT LOGAN.

CLINE'S RANCH POST (*Cantonment Uncompahgre*). This temporary post was established on Cline Ranch property near the Uncompahgre River on July 10, 1882, by Colonel E. Hatch and companies D, H, L, and M of the 9th Cavalry, companies D and F, 14th Infantry, some elements of the 26th Infantry, aggregating 451 men. The post was officially called Cantonment Uncompahgre when it was first established.

CAMP COLLINS. FORT COLLINS.

FORT COLLINS (*Camp Collins*). The first Camp Collins was established in the fall of 1863 by the 1st Colorado Cavalry on the Antoine Janis farm near the Overland stage station close to the town of Laporte on the Cache la Poudre River in Larimer County. Disastrously flooded on June 9, 1864, the post was relocated on higher ground in the present city of Fort Collins, the county seat, which developed around the post. Established by Captain William H. Evans with elements of the 11th Ohio Cavalry, the post was intended to protect the area's ranchers and settlers and travelers on the Overland Trail during the Indian war. The post took the name of Fort Collins on October 23, 1864, in honor of Lieutenant Colonel William Oliver Collins, 11th Ohio Cavalry, then commanding Fort Laramie, Wyoming. His son was 1st Lieutenant Caspar W. Collins, for whom Fort Caspar, Wyoming, was named. Abandoned in early 1867, the four-mile-square Fort Collins reservation was transferred to the Department of the Interior on July 16, 1872, and opened to settlement.

COLORADO CITY FORT. A settler-built log fort built in 1864 at the present city of Colorado Springs, the defense was abandoned in 1868 when danger of Indian attack had appreciably lessened. The fort's site is commemorated by a stone and plaque on Pikes Peak Avenue.

FORT CONVENIENCE. VÁSQUEZ'S POST.

FORT CRAWFORD (*Cantonment on the Uncompahgre*). Established on July 21, 1880, for the purpose of controlling and ultimately transferring the recalcitrant White River and Uncompahgre Ute Indians to Utah subsequent to the White River Agency Massacre, the post was located on the left bank of the Uncompahgre River about four miles north of the Los Pinos Indian Agency, near present Colona in Montrose County. Colonel Ranald S. Mackenzie, 4th Cavalry, at Fort Garland, was directed to proceed to the Uncompahgre Valley with a part of his command. The first troops arrived on May 25 and consisted of four companies of the 4th Cavalry, five companies of the 19th Infantry, and two companies of the 23rd Infantry. Constructed under the supervision of 1st Lieutenant Calvin D. Cowles, 23rd Infantry, the post was originally intended as a temporary supply camp or depot, called Cantonment on the Uncompahgre. On December 15, 1886, it was designated Fort Crawford in honor of Captain Emmet Crawford, 3rd Cavalry, who was mortally wounded on January 11, 1886, at Nácori, Mexico, while in pursuit of Geronimo, the wily Apache chief. With the probability of an Indian uprising dissipated, the post's garrison was gradually withdrawn. The last of Fort Crawford's troops left on December 31, 1890, one day after the reservation was transferred to the Interior Department, which held a public auction to dispose of the structures once comprising an elaborate military post.

CAMP CURTIS. Very little is known about this twice-used temporary campsite established somewhere in "Colorado Territory." The first troop detachment taking post here for 10 days ending April 30, 1860, was Troop B of the 1st Colorado Cavalry, aggregating 84 men, under Captain Samuel Logan. In November 1863, the campsite was again occupied for 10 days by 2nd Lieutenant Clark Dunn with elements of Troops B and C of the 1st Cavalry.

FORT DEFIANCE. In 1879 prospectors unlawfully entered the Ute reservation and found surface evidences of what promised to be a great mineral treasure. Desirous of continuing their search but dreading Ute retribution, the prospectors built a pine log fort and named it Fort Defiance. Its site in Garfield County is vaguely located. One account states that it was erected some 10 miles southeast of the prospectors' camp, later called "Carbonate City," probably today's Carbondale; another locates it some 20 miles west of the junction of the Grand and Eagle rivers; and a third report says it was 6 miles northwest of Glenwood Springs.

DENVER DEPOT. Established in 1859 and in operation throughout the Civil War years, the facility consisted of a large warehouse, used as a haven during the Indian uprising threats in 1864. The site of the post, abandoned in 1865, is on the northeast corner of Larimer and 11th streets in Denver. In 1864 the 1st and 3rd Cavalry, one company from each, were stationed at Denver.

DORA FORT. In 1848 and 1849 mountain men, including Kit Carson, pursued the warring Ute Indians across Mosca Pass, through Wet Mountain Valley, and up the Arkansas River, finally overtaking the Utes and inflicting a severe military lesson near Twin Lakes. The Ute defeat made them much more amenable to the Army's overtures for peace, at least for a few years. During the campaign a small fort was built as a supply base at the head of Grape Creek Canyon, near present Dora in Custer County. The fort was unsuccessfully attacked by the Utes on several occasions. The ruins of Dora Fort are covered by the waters of DeWeese Reservoir.

CAMP ELBERT. CAMP WELD.

FORT EL PUEBLA (*Milk Fort*). A relatively short-lived Bent County settlement of American fur trappers, Mexican mixed-bloods, and Indians, it was also called Pueblo de Leche (Spanish, Milk Town) and Milk Fort because of the unusually large herds of milk goats, sheep, cattle, horses, and mules owned by the town's residents. Fort El Puebla was found to be a flourishing community in 1839 when it was visited by Thomas J. Farnham, journalist and author. The fort consisted of a series of single-story adobe houses, built around an enclosed court that served as a night corral for livestock.

CAMP EVANS. The 3rd Colorado Cavalry occupied this temporary rendezvous campsite on the Platte River in 1864, located about two and a half miles northeast of Denver. The camp was named for the Governor of the Territory.

FORT FAUNTLEROY. FORT LYON.

CAMP FILLMORE. Named for the Colorado Cavalry's paymaster, the post was established by one company of the 1st Colorado Cavalry in 1864 in preparation for Colonel John Chivington's Indian campaign, which resulted in the infamous Sand Creek Massacre. The post was located on the Arkansas River 2 miles west of Boone and 18 miles east of Pueblo in Pueblo County. Between April and October 1865, the post was occupied by 1st Lieutenant Frank Morrell, 1st Colorado Cavalry, with Company F, aggregating 77 rank and file. The camp's abandonment owed to the establishment of Fort Reynolds on the south bank of the Arkansas in July 1867.

FORT FLAGLER. Shortly after the Meeker Massacre in 1879, when a general Indian uprising was feared, residents of Los Animas, Bent County, organized a town militia and built a short-lived stockaded log fort named for Henry M. Flagler, railroad magnate, whose Rock Island Railroad was extended through this region. The Army provided hundreds of troops who outposted the area in addition to garrisoning the fort.

FRAEB'S FORT. FORT JACKSON.

FORT FRANCISCO PLAZA. In 1862 Colonel John M. Francisco, who had served as sutler at Fort Massachusetts and Fort Garland, with Henry Daigre built Fort Francisco Plaza, a one-story structure enclosing three sides of a 100-foot square, on a land grant near the head of Cucharas Creek at the site of the present town of La Veta in Huerfano County. It had been constructed as an Indian defense, but the colonel never experienced problems with the Indians. When the Denver and Rio Grande Railroad ran a branch line through the area, the fort became its terminal. The structure served at various times as trading post, railroad depot, fortified defense, and rendezvous of trappers, prospectors, and military scouts, one of whom was Kit Carson who often visited his friend Colonel Francisco.

FRÉMONT'S FORT. The exploits of John Frémont, noted "Pathfinder of the West," engendered a number of fanciful stories regarding his explorations of the Rocky Mountain region. One of the most colorfully contrived was the so-called "Battle of Frémont's Fort." There was no "well-built structure with portholes for riflemen and thick adobe walls" as conjured by story-tellers. The "fort" is actually a cone-shaped plateau in the center of the Bijou Basin in Elbert County. In 1843 Frémont and his party of explorers were searching for a pass to the West through the Front Range of the Rockies when they were surprised by a large war party of Plains Indians. Frémont and his men fought their way to the plateau, impassable on three sides with sheer rock faces 15 to 25 feet high. The fourth side had only a narrow path leading to the top that could be easily defended by a small number of men. The "fort" proved unconquerable as the Indians were continuously repulsed with heavy losses. Finally the Indians retreated a short distance and waited, hoping to starve out the plateau's defenders. Sometime during the night, two scouts descended by ropes from the "fort" and made a desperate 70-mile dash for the small settlement that eventually became Denver. They safely reached their goal and returned with a rescue party that saved Frémont and his expedition from certain annihilation.

CAMP AT FREMONT'S ORCHARD. CAMP SANBORN.

GANTT'S FORT. FORT CASS.

FORT GARLAND. Established on June 24, 1858, to replace Fort Massachusetts six miles to the north, Fort Garland was located between Trinchera and Ute creeks in the San Luis Valley, at the present town of Fort Garland in Costilla County. The post's primary purposes were to control the Jicarilla Apaches and the Utes, protect the valley's settlers, guard the Sangre de Cristo (La Veta) Pass, and safeguard the passage of travelers on the road to Taos, New Mexico. The adobe-built post, named for Colonel John Garland, 8th Infantry, commanding the department, was established by Captain (later Lieutenant Colonel) Thomas Duncan with Company E, Regiment of Mounted Rifles, and Captain Andrew W. Bowman with Company A, 3rd Infantry. Fort Garland was the only military post in Colorado's southwestern region until the establishment of the first Fort Lewis at Pagosa Springs in 1878. Following the Meeker Massacre in 1879, about 1,500 troops were congregated at Fort Garland for the purpose of occupying the Los Pinos Agency in 1880, where Fort Crawford was established. Fort Garland was abandoned on November 30, 1883, when its garrison was transferred to the second Fort Lewis on the Rio La Plata. The post has been restored and is now a State Historical Monument.

FORT GEORGE. FORT ST. VRAIN.

FORT GERRY. A trading post at the junction of Crow Creek and the South Platte River, it was named for its factor, Elmer Gerry, adventurous grandson of Elbridge Gerry, a signer of the Declaration of Independence, governor of Massachusetts, and vice president of the United States (1813–14). The post (date of establishment undetermined) was abandoned in 1840, and another,

FORT GARLAND. (Courtesy of the Colorado Department of Public Relations.)

also called Fort Gerry, was built on the opposite, or south, side of the Platte and managed by Gerry and his two Indian wives.

CAMP GILPIN. Two Civil War encampments named for Colonel William Gilpin, first Territorial Governor of Colorado, were established in 1861. One was located in Quartz Valley, about a mile from Central City in Gilpin County, and the other at Golden to the east in neighboring Jefferson County.

GRAY'S RANCH STATION POST. A stage station located about four miles north of Trinidad, Las Animas County, it was used for a short time in 1864 as an outpost by U.S. troops.

CAMP HALE. Once the nation's highest Army post, situated a few miles west of the Continental Divide and located 17 miles from historic Leadville, Camp Hale's establishment had been probably planned from the beginning of America's military involvement in World War II, with construction initially completed in November of the same year. High in the Rockies, the camp was the cradle of one of the nation's most unusual fighting units, the 10th Mountain Division. Opened for troops on November 16, 1942, it could accommodate 15,000 men and 5,000 mules. After months of instruction in rock climbing, mule skinning, skiing, and the use of new materials and weapons tested at the 9,500-foot elevation, the 10th Mountain Division was ordered to Italy where it became a part of the Fifth Army commanded by General Mark Clark. Camp

Hale's primary mission of arctic training essentially over, the post was used sporadically until it was closed June 30, 1965. It had been idle and under caretaker status following the 1957 transfer of the Mountain and Cold Weather Training Command to Fort Greely, Alaska.

HENRY STATION. CAMP MONUMENT DELL.

FORT HUERFANO. About the year 1845 a small Mexican encampment was located by Charles Autobees, scout and trapper, at the mouth of the Huerfano River at present Avondale, which in 1861 became the county seat of Huerfano County (later transferred to Walsenburg). Fort Huerfano stood on the bank of the river about six miles south of Avondale. It was adobe-built with six-foot-high walls and heavy-timbered circular towers or bastions, pierced by portholes, on two diagonally opposite corners. It is not definitely known when the fort was first built or abandoned.

FORT JACKSON (*Fraeb's Post*). Probably the first of the Platte Valley fur posts, four of them built on a 15-mile length of the South Platte River, Fort Jackson was established in 1833 near present Ione in Weld County. Henry Fraeb and Peter A. Sarpy, agents for the Pratte, Chouteau Company of St. Louis, built the fort, first called Fraeb's Post and then renamed Fort Jackson. It is not definitely known whether the fort was named for the then president, Andrew Jackson, or for Gilbert Jackson, one of the employees there. Reports indicate that the post had shipped at least $10,000 worth of furs in just one season. In 1838 Céran St. Vrain bought the post but operated it for only one more season and then abandoned it.

JULESBURG POST. This military post was established on or about August 6, 1864, by Captain Wilcox with Company B, 7th Iowa Volunteer Cavalry. The garrison was relieved by Captain A. J. O'Brien with Company F of the same unit. With no barracks provided, it was reported that the troops suffered great discomfort. Julesburg, Sedgwick County, was named for Jules Beni who operated a trading post in the town's near environs.

POST AT JULESBURG STATION. FORT SEDGWICK.

FORT JUNCTION. Constructed in July 1864, this fort was situated at the junction of Boulder and St. Vrain rivers in Weld County. Because of the widespread Indian unrest in the region, the so-called Lower Boulder and St. Vrain Valley Home Guards had been organized in the spring of that year. The Federal government provided the militia with guns and ammunition. After the massacre of a local family on June 11, 1864, the Guards built the fort at the site of the junction as a refuge for settlers threatened by Indian attack. Sod-constructed, the fort measured 100 by 130 feet and was provided with two watch towers, probably placed at diagonal corners. After Indian hostilities abated, the fort served for a number of years as a way station for military officers, Army scouts, and other travelers.

POST OF JUNCTION. FORT MORGAN.

POST OF JUNCTION CITY. FORT MORGAN.

FORT LANCASTER. FORT LUPTON.

CAMP LAY. Nothing definite is known about this post. According to Dawson's *Place Names in Colorado*, it was named for a fur trapper named Lay who was the first white settler in the area and lived on Lay Creek in Moffat County. Another version reports that it was named for an early Army camp called Camp Lay, so named by a Lieutenant McCulloch in honor of his sweetheart, Peace Lay, who resided in Chicago.

FORT LE DUC. A short-lived, octagonal trading post constructed of pine logs, it was built by Maurice Le Duc during the 1830s near present

Wetmore in the extreme northeastern corner of Custer County.

FORT LEWIS NO. 1 (*Cantonment Pagosa Springs*). The first Fort Lewis, established on October 15, 1878, at Pagosa Springs, Archuleta County, in southwestern Colorado, was originally called Cantonment Pagosa Springs. The post was very soon renamed Fort Lewis in honor of Lieutenant Colonel William H. Lewis, 19th Infantry, who was mortally wounded during a fight with Cheyenne Indians at Punished Woman's Fork, Kansas, on September 28, 1878. Fort Lewis was occupied by the 15th Infantry and Company D of the 9th Cavalry. However, as a result of Lieutenant General Philip Sheridan's recommendation for a more centralized location, the post was relocated due to the White River Ute uprising in 1879 and probable difficulties with other Ute tribal branches. On October 8, 1879, the post at Pagosa Springs, in spite of its delightfully healthful situation, was abandoned and the garrison removed to a new site on the La Plata River. The site of Fort Lewis No. 1 is now a city park near the center of the town of Pagosa Springs.

FORT LEWIS NO. 2 (*Cantonment on the Rio Plata*). Fort Lewis No. 2 was established in July 1880 as a permanent post, situated on the right side of the La Plata River west of Durango, La Plata County, adjacent to the Southern Utes Los Pinos Reservation. The new post, although already officially designated Fort Lewis, was called Cantonment La Plata during its construction. Established by Lieutenant Colonel Robert E. A. Crofton, 13th Infantry, on a site selected by Colonel Thomas H. Ruger, 18th Infantry, the post was designed to prevent white encroachments into the Ute reservation, and provide protection for the Indian agency, the area's settlers from the Utes, and ongoing railway construction. Fort Lewis was abandoned in September 1891, and the military reservation with all its improvements was transferred to the Department of the Interior for Indian Service use on November 12, 1891. Not long after the Army moved out, the post was transformed into a school for Indians, who burned down many of the buildings, including most of the officers' quarters and men's barracks. In 1910 the reservation and all of its remaining structures were ceded to the state, which established the Fort Lewis Agricultural and Mechanical College.

FORT LINCOLN. Built in three days as a defense against Indians in August 1864, it was located at what was then the village of Huntsville, 19 miles south of Castle Rock, Douglas County. The irregularly shaped fort, "10 logs high," with all of its portholed cabins acting the role of bastions, occupied approximately a 100-by-100-foot piece of ground. At times during the remainder of Indian unrest, the fort was a day-and-night refuge for about 25 families and 150 men.

CAMP LIVINGSTON. A short-lived post established near Julesburg, Sedgwick County, it was so-named and used by Colonel Henry Dodge's troops in 1835.

FORT LOGAN (*Camp near the City of Denver; Fort Sheridan*). An act of Congress, proposed on February 17 and passed on February 28, 1887, approved the establishment of a military post in Denver's environs, only if the state would provide the necessary acreage. The state readily acquiesced. Construction was initiated late in the year under the supervision of Captain L. E. Campbell of the Quartermaster Corps. The site, three miles from Denver near the foothills of the Rockies, was selected by Lieutenant General Phil Sheridan. First occupied by Captain James H. Baldwin, 18th Infantry, he was soon followed by Major George K. Brady, assuming command on October 25, with two companies of troops of the same infantry unit. The next day temporary quarters, called "Camp near the City of Denver," were begun. A month later, Captain Lafayette E. Campbell, assistant quartermaster, arrived to supervise construction of a permanent post. It was not until July 25, 1888, however, before ground was actually broken for the first structure. Since its establishment in 1887, the post was called Fort Sheridan by both Denver residents and the troops. However, when the War Department was considering the official adoption of names for several new posts, Sheridan requested that his name be given to a fort on the shore of Lake Michigan near Chicago known as Fort Logan in honor of Major General John A. Logan, noted Civil War leader and Illinois politician. In accordance with Sheridan's request, the War Department interchanged the names. In any case, the post remained officially a camp until it was redesignated Fort Logan on April 5, 1889. During World War I it was a receiving station for enlistees and draftees, later becoming a center for the ROTC. In June 1927 the 2nd Engineers took over, replaced 12 years later by the 18th Engineers, who were shortly transferred to the West Coast. Fort Logan in 1939 became a subpost of Lowry Air Force Base. Seventy-five years after its establishment, Fort Logan's reservation

was deeded back to the state of Colorado for the establishment of a needed second state hospital for the mentally ill. New construction for the Fort Logan Mental Health Center began in February 1961, and the first patients were admitted in July of the same year.

FORT LOOKOUT. FORT ST. VRAIN.

FORT LUPTON (*Fort Lancaster*). Lieutenant Lancaster P. Lupton, a West Point graduate, who entered Colorado territory in 1835 with the expedition of Colonel Henry Dodge's Dragoons to the Rocky Mountains, appreciated the Platte River Valley's commercial possibilities. The fur trade at this time was being actively pursued in the Far West and he observed that the region of the South Platte, although often visited by trappers, had no permanent trading establishment, in sharp contrast to the Arkansas Valley where lucrative and influential Bent's Fort dominated the region. Lieutenant Lupton resigned his commission in 1836 and built Fort Lancaster on the east bank of the South Platte, two miles north of the present town of Fort Lupton, Weld County. His substantially built adobe trading post, 100 by 150 feet, was soon recognized as the first permanent settlement in northern Colorado. A year later he planted the area's first garden, growing a variety of vegetables, and initiated livestock raising on a small scale. Prospering for a time beyond expectations, his post outlasted all competition. The post, for a time named Fort Lancaster, was renamed by popular usage, using its founder's surname rather than his given name, and as Fort Lupton it became known.

By the middle 1840s, the lucrative days of the western fur trade had passed. In 1845 Lupton abandoned his fort and left for the East, returning home without the fortune he had hoped to acquire in the Rocky Mountains. The post remained unoccupied from 1845 to 1859. During Colorado's gold rush, the old fort was first converted into a corral for emigrant trains and then an Overland stage station for mail and express coaches. During the widespread Indian unrest in 1864 it became a refuge for pioneer settlers and was occupied for a short time by an Army detachment. The ruins of the old fort's adobe walls are now enclosed within a barn.

FORT LYON (*Bent's [New] Fort; Fort Fauntleroy; Fort Wise*). After William Bent in 1849 partially destroyed the great fort he had built in company with his brother Charles and Céran St. Vrain on the Santa Fe Trail, he moved five miles down the Arkansas River to Short Timbers Creek, where for a year he tried to restore some semblance of his former Indian trade business. But he moved again, some 40 miles down the river to a point about 8 miles west of Lamar, where in 1852–53 he built a new imposing fort of stone that became known as Bent's New Fort, on a high bluff overlooking the river. Although trade never returned to its former volume, Bent stayed in business until the eve of the Civil War. After leasing his fort to the Army in 1859, he retired to live with a daughter on his ranch on the upper Purgatoire River where he died in 1869.

The Army almost immediately named the fort Fort Fauntleroy for Colonel T. T. Fauntleroy of the old 1st Dragoons. But when the colonel joined the Confederates, the fort's name was changed to Fort Wise to honor Governor of Virginia Henry Alexander Wise. But he too joined the Confederate Army as a brigadier general, another embarrassment for the U.S. Army. And again the fort was redesignated, this time as Fort Lyon in honor of Nathaniel Lyon, killed at Wilson's Creek, Missouri, August 10, 1861, the first Union Army general to fall in the Civil War.

In 1864 Fort Lyon's garrison became involved in a disgraceful Indian massacre, one of the most tragic in the history of Indian warfare. Colonel C. M. Chivington, 1st Colorado Cavalry, arrived with his troops at Fort Lyon, influenced part of the fort's garrison to join his force, and very early on the morning of November 27, attacked unsuspecting, friendly Black Kettle and his Cheyennes who were camped at Sand Creek, not far from the fort. The resulting slaughter of men, women, and children has become variously known in American history as the Sand Creek Massacre and Chivington's Massacre. This act of treachery precipitated a long-enduring and widespread uprising of the Plains Indians that cost the government many millions of dollars to put down.

In 1866 the Arkansas River began to undermine the bank on which Fort Lyon stood, and a new sandstone fort was erected 20 miles upstream near present Las Animas, about 3 miles below the mouth of the Purgatoire River. The new Fort Lyon was established by Captain William H. Penrose, 3rd Infantry. Throughout the years of the Indian wars, Army regulars, state military volunteer units, and the so-called "Galvanized Yankees" garrisoned the key post on the Santa Fe Trail. It was at Fort Lyon that famous frontiersman Kit Carson died at the age of 59 on May 23, 1868. Buried there with full military honors, his body was later removed to Taos, New Mexico, for reinterment. Abandoned in October 1889, the Fort

Lyon Military Reservation was transferred to the Department of the Interior on January 20, 1890. In 1934 the former Army post was converted to a Veterans Administration hospital. Many of the old buildings, including the one in which Kit Carson had spent his last remaining hours, are still in use by the hospital.

CAMP MCINTIRE. A Colorado National Guard tent camp, it was established in 1896 at Leadville during a strike of miners marked by violence.

MCSHANE'S FORT. David McShane and his family arrived in the Monument area in 1865 to take up ranching about two miles from Palmer Lake, El Paso County. There, in 1868, close to his original log-constructed home, he built a stone fort as a protection against marauding Indians. In mid-August the Indians began a reign of terror, pillaging and murdering along Monument and Fountain creeks. The Indian defense built by McShane, one of the earliest pioneers in the region, was designed specifically to defend his home and property against attack by the Arapaho and Cheyenne Indians, who were at the time on the warpath against the Utes.

The ingenious circular fort was 12 feet in diameter, with its top 6 feet above ground and its floor 3 feet below the surface. The masonry consisted of stone mortared with a hardpan cement. With walls 2 feet thick, the roof of the fort was constructed of logs covered with a thick layer of earth, so that the Indians could neither penetrate its walls with bullets nor set it afire with flaming arrows. The walls were pierced by five portholes, four of them fitted with sliding blocks of stone to close the ports, with a piece of iron on the exterior of each block; the fifth port was actually a small window to admit light facing McShane's log cabin to the rear of the fort. An underground passage led from the house to this refuge and was closed by a double door on the wall's interior, so that when Mrs. McShane was alone with her children, she could resort to the haven in an emergency. Two years later, McShane built the stone residence to the rear of the fort, which still stands. The State Historical Society of Colorado placed an historical marker near the still evident remains of the fort.

MARCY'S CAMP. FORT REYNOLDS.

FORT MARY B. FORT BRECKINRIDGE.

FORT MASSACHUSETTS. The first United States military post in Colorado, it was established on June 22, 1852, on Ute Creek in the San Luis

Valley about six miles north of the present town of Fort Garland, Costilla County, in what was then New Mexico Territory. The fort was established by Major George A. H. Blake, 1st Dragoons, in compliance with an order by Lieutenant Colonel Edwin Vose Sumner, commander of the Department of New Mexico. The primary purposes of the post were to protect the valley's settlers, prevent depredations by the Utes and the Jicarilla Apaches to the south, and to guard the approach to New Mexico via the Sangre de Cristo (La Veta) Pass. There is no doubt the name of the fort was selected because Sumner was a native of Boston, Massachusetts. The site, proving to be swampy and quite unhealthful, compelled the abandonment of the post on June 24, 1858, and its replacement by Fort Garland.

FORT MAURICE. A French trader named Maurice, a former resident of Detroit, Michigan, established the first trading post on Adobe Creek, seven miles south of present Florence, Fremont County, in about the year 1830. The first agricultural settlement in the area was initiated near the mouth of the creek by a group of Mexicans who built 13 earth-roofed adobe houses on one side of an adobe-walled plaza. In 1838 the settlers, threatened by Arapaho and Sioux Indians, found refuge in Maurice's fort. The first American settlement on Adobe Creek was founded about 1840 by an association of hunters, trappers, and traders. Among the leaders of the company were such well-known men as Governor Charles Bent, Lancaster Lupton, Céran St. Vrain, Charles Beaubien, and L. V. Maxwell. The settlement apparently thrived until 1846 when the association was dissolved and the settlement broken up, and all the inhabitants, with the exception of Maurice, left for other more prosperous locales.

FORT MERIBEH. FORT BRECKINRIDGE.

MILK FORT. FORT EL PUEBLA.

CAMP MONUMENT DELL (*Henry Station*). Monument Dell, at present Monument, El Paso County, was most probably garrisoned between June 1 and November 15, 1869, by the 7th Cavalry, Captain Yates commanding. The post, eight miles north of Colorado City, was intended to protect the area known as "The Divide," the high ground near Monument, from Indian and Mexican depredations. Monument, formerly known as Henry Station, was named for the spectacular rock formation to the west.

FORT MOORE (*Valley Station*). Charley and Jim Moore, owners of Valley Station, located very near Sterling, Logan County, built a toll road and charged emigrant wagons one dollar each for passage. The road was apparently adjacent to today's site of the Platte River bridge. Garrisoned forts were established by the Army all along the route to protect emigrants. The probability is that one of the posts was designated Fort Moore for the Moore brothers. No definite date could be found for its establishment.

FORT MORGAN (*Post of Junction; Post of Junction City; Camp Tyler; Camp Wardwell*). Established on July 1, 1865, this post was situated astride the Overland Trail, one mile south of the South Platte River, at the present town of Fort Morgan, the county seat of Morgan County. It was largely built of sod with log reinforcement. Originally called Post of Junction and Post of Junction City, the post was designed to provide protection for both emigrants along the Trail and communications in general. When it was first designated Camp Tyler, then Camp Wardwell, the post had very uncomfortable makeshift barracks for the garrison. It was then the only military establishment between Fort Sedgwick and Denver, located about equidistant from each at what was known on the South Platte in staging and freighting days as the "Junction." Finally, in 1866 after a number of substantial buildings were erected, it was redesignated Fort Morgan in honor of Major Christopher A. Morgan, 1st Illinois Cavalry, who established the post and who died on January 20, 1866. The completion of the Union Pacific Railroad to Denver obviated the necessity for the fort, which was abandoned on May 18, 1868. Its garrison was transferred to Fort Laramie, Wyoming, and the Army post's buildings were sold at public auction.

MORMON COLONY WINTER CAMP. The largest white settlement before the Pikes Peak gold rush of 1858–59 was founded by Mormons near present Pueblo in 1846. The short-lived colony was incidental to the great Mormon migration westward from Nauvoo, Illinois. The main body of Mormons rested in Iowa during 1846 and did not continue further until the following year. One small group of Mormon proselytes, 43 people with 19 wagons, from Mississippi, however, did travel westward to the Rockies in 1846. They not only founded a settlement but had the distinction of having been the first Mormons to travel from the Missouri River west to the environs of Fort Laramie, Wyoming, almost a year in advance of the major official "Pioneer Band."

They arrived at Fort Pueblo, a trading post established four years earlier by a group of independent trappers.

Within a few days, the Mormons selected a site for their winter settlement on the south side of the Arkansas River some distance, perhaps "a half an hour's riding" from the fort. The temporary colony was described by a visiting Army lieutenant: "In the wide and well-timbered bottom of the Arkansas, the Mormons had erected a street of log shanties . . . built of rough logs of cottonwood, laid one above the other, the interstices filled with mud, and rendered impervious to wind or wet. At one end of the row of shanties was built the 'church' or temple—a long building of huge logs. . . . Most of [the Mormons] were accustomed to the life of woodmen, and were good hunters. Thus they were enabled to support their families upon the produce of their rifles" (Le Roy R. Hafen and Frank M. Young, "The Mormon Settlement at Pueblo, Colorado, During the Mexican War," *The Colorado Magazine*, no. 4, [1932]: 133.) In the late spring, on June 27, 1847, the Mormon group reached Salt Lake City, their goal, only three days behind the "Pioneer Band." Nothing remains of the Mormons' winter settlement near Pueblo, perhaps obliterated by river floods.

FORT NAMAQUA. In 1858 Mariano Modena came to southeastern Larimer County from the San Luis Valley with his Indian wife, five children, servants, and livestock. He staked out a squatter's claim and built a cabin near the forks of Buckhorn and Dry creeks, about four miles west of present Loveland. He later built a stone fort, called Fort Namaqua, for the protection of his family and property. In 1862 Namaqua became a station on the Overland Stage Line.

NARRAGUINNEP FORT. In 1885 ranchers located north of Dolores, Montezuma County, had their problems with the region's Indians, whom they accused of butchering their cattle. The controversy culminated in what became known as the Beaver Massacre in June when the ranchers killed 11 Indians. The Indians retaliated, murdering several settlers in the Montezuma Valley. A number of ranchers thereupon banded together at Narraguinnep Spring and erected a fort for their mutual protection. The fort was constructed of large pine logs, about three feet in diameter, with walls three logs high. Portholes were cut in the crack between the first and second logs on all sides. The roof was fashioned of pine poles topped with earth. The fort was in use for about two weeks, until the Indian threat had subsided. It was located in Narraguinnep Canyon, about 25 miles northwest of Dolores. The fort's remains, fenced in and maintained by the Forest Service, lie in today's Montezuma National Forest.

FORT NEPESTA. Sometime in the 1840s, a band of "free" trappers and traders, for the most part former American Fur Company employees, founded a trading post and an adobe fort called Nepesta (Spanish name for the Arkansas River) in Pueblo's environs. In 1854 Indians attacked the fort, massacred its occupants, and pillaged and partially dismantled the structure. The quadrangular foundations of the fort's adobe walls were still in evidence in the 1890s on the west side of Union Avenue, near the depot of the Atchison, Topeka, and Santa Fe Railroad.

CANTONMENT PAGOSA SPRINGS. FORT LEWIS NO. 1.

PIKE'S STOCKADE. The first construction of any kind by Americans in Colorado was that of Pike's Stockade, built in February 1807 by Lieutenant Zebulon Pike's 23-man expedition. This 36-foot-square breastwork of logs had walls 12 feet high surrounded by a moat or ditch. The party occupied the fort located near present Alamosa for less than a week while they unsuccessfully attempted to climb what is known today as Pike's Peak. The stockade has been faithfully reconstructed and is a popular tourist attraction.

CAMP POINT OF ROCKS. In 1862 Laporte in Larimer County was garrisoned by United States troops who were encamped at Point of Rocks a short distance west of the town. Their main duty was to control recalcitrant Indians in the area. In September 1864 the garrison was transferred to Fort Collins, established by Colonel William O. Collins, 11th Ohio Infantry.

FORT PUEBLO. The permanent settlement and designation of Pueblo is generally credited by historians to James P. Beckwourth. He arrived in the area in October 1842 and was soon joined there by other "free" trappers. "We all united our labors, and constructed an adobe fort sixty yards square (Dawson, *Place Names in Colorado*, describes it as a *circular* structure). By the following spring we gave it the name of Pueblo," a name probably conjured by Beckwourth himself (Kent Ruth, *Great Day in the West*, p. 36). The operations of the trading post, situated very close to the junction of the Arkansas and Fountain rivers, had varying success. The post's early visitors, among them George Frederick Ruxton, historian Francis Parkman, and Indian agent Thomas Fitzpatrick, were decidedly unimpressed by its usually rundown condition and its occupants. The post was continually occupied until 1854 although its population had decreased from the 150 reported in 1847 to about two dozen. Then, on Christmas Day, 1854, a band of Utes attacked the post and killed every man but one and carried off its sole woman and her two children. A commemorative marker for the fort is located south of the City Hall, and a replica of the trading post is in the El Pueblo Museum on South Prairie in Pueblo.

POST OF PUEBLO. FORT REYNOLDS.

CAMP RANKIN. FORT SEDGWICK.

REED'S SPRINGS POST. Nothing is known of this post except that it was located north-northwest of Ramah, Elbert County.

FORT REYNOLDS (*Post of Pueblo; Marcy's Camp*). Established on July 3, 1867, this Army post, 18 miles east of Pueblo, was situated on a plateau on the east side of the Arkansas River nearly three miles above the mouth of Huerfano River, in Pueblo County. It occupied a site previously selected by Colonel Randolph B. Marcy, inspector general, because the area's inhabitants needed protection. It was established by Captain Simon Snyder, 5th Infantry, with the garrison from the Post of Pueblo, north of the town, which was evacuated the previous day. The temporary camp set up by the garrison while the fort was being constructed was called Marcy's Camp. Upon the fort's completion, it was designated Fort Reynolds in honor of Major General John F. Reynolds, killed in action on July 1, 1863, at Gettysburg. Abandoned on July 15, 1872, the military reservation was transferred to the Department of the Interior for disposition on July 18, 1874. There is a marker for the old Army post on U.S. 50, one mile east of Avondale.

CANTONMENT ON RIO MANCOS. In September 1879 Colorado's military garrisons and inhabitants became alarmed by the massacre of Indian agent Nathan C. Meeker and 11 of his employees at the White River Agency in the northwestern part of the state. Fears were significantly heightened when Major T. T. Thornburgh, who was marching from Fort Steele, Wyoming, with a detachment of 150 men to the Agency, was ambushed and killed. Federal troops, in increasing numbers, entered Colorado both from the north and the east. Among them were four

companies of the 22nd Infantry commanded by Major Alfred Hough, who was ordered into the southern Ute country to keep this band of Utes under control and to march, if necessary, against the northern Utes who had perpetrated the massacre.

The 22nd Infantry troops reached Fort Garland on October 7, and proceeded from there to Alamosa on the Denver and Rio Grande Railroad. From this point the men proceeded on foot and marched 180 miles, reaching Animas, about three miles from present Durango, La Plata County, on October 22. The major wrote that "I have never campaigned through a country so beautiful—mountains, forest valleys, clear rushing waters, everything to make nature lovely, and here in Animas Valley we found quite a large settlement and a thriving town" (*Brand Book* 6 [1950]: 72). The troops remained garrisoned at their cantonment on the Mancos River for two months, apparently never seeing any action against the Utes during that length of time.

CANTONMENT ON THE RIO PLATA. FORT LEWIS NO. 2.

FORT ROBIDOUX (*Fort Uncompahgre*). Various dates, from 1825 to the late 1830s, have been rendered for the establishment of Antoine Robidoux's first trading post, situated on the left bank of the Gunnison River, near Delta, Delta County. The probable date falls between 1825 and 1828. The post, first called Fort Uncompahgre (Ute, "red water springs"), was located in the stretch of bottom lands near the junction of the Uncompahgre River with the Grand River. It consisted of a few rough log cabins enclosed within a quadrangle of palisades or pickets. It stood on a part of the Old Spanish Trail leading northward from Taos, New Mexico. Sometime during its 20-year existence, probably a few years after its establishment, it became known through common usage as Fort Robidoux. About 1846 or 1847, the Utes attacked and burned the fort and, so it was reported, killed all its occupants, the French trader Robidoux not among them. All evidences on the site were eradicated by settlers' ranching operations during the 1880s.

ROCKY MOUNTAIN ARSENAL. Established in 1942 and first opened on November 15, 1943, this important arsenal covers some 20,000 acres, located east of Derby and 12 miles northeast of Denver's business district. During World War II, the arsenal manufactured and assembled 87,000 tons of intermediate and toxic products and 155,000 tons of incendiary munitions. In 1945 it was placed in standby status. Reactivated during the Korean War, it began to produce incendiary and chemical munitions. A major new facility was constructed and placed into operation for the manufacture and filling of nerve gas. In March 1954 it became publicly known that the nerve gas was being manufactured there. The arsenal became a permanent installation on October 16, 1954.

FORT ST. VRAIN (*Fort Lookout; Fort George*). This historic trading fort, founded in 1837 by William and Charles Bent, and Céran St. Vrain, and known successively as Fort Lookout, Fort George, and finally Fort St. Vrain, was the first and largest of the South Platte River posts. It was situated at the confluence of the river and St. Vrain Creek, near Platteville, Weld County. The fort measured 125 feet long and 100 feet wide, with its 2-foot-thick adobe walls rising 14 feet. Located approximately halfway between Bent's Old Fort and Fort Laramie in Wyoming, it became a popular rendezvous for traders, trappers and emigrants. Marcellus St. Vrain, Céran's brother, managed the post for several years as an employee. The post was abandoned in 1844. When historian Francis Parkman visited it two years later, he found it "abandoned and falling to ruin." It has been reported that for a time during 1859 and 1860 a settlement existed at the site, commemorated by a granite marker erected in 1911.

CAMP SANBORN (*Camp at Fremont's Orchard*). Situated on the Overland Trail at Orchard in extreme western Morgan County, this military post, known originally as Camp at Fremont's Orchard, was garrisoned by the Colorado Mounted Militia, popularly named "Morgan's 100-Daysers," during the Indian troubles of 1864, when the post's garrison was enlarged by the addition of one company of the 11th Ohio Cavalry.

FORT SANGRE DE CRISTO (*Spanish Fort*). A Spanish military post, its official name unknown, was established in 1819 very near Oak Creek, a confluence of the Huerfano River, about 25 miles west of present Walsenburg in Saguache County. It was situated on a hill overlooking the creek and the valley traversed by the Taos Trail. Established in compliance with an order by Governor Facundo Melgares of New Mexico, the fort was intended to guard the Sangre de Cristo Pass against the possibility of an American invasion into Mexican territory. Abandoned in 1821, after the Adams-Onís Treaty established the in-

ternational boundary along the Arkansas River, it was known by Americans during its short-lived existence as simply Spanish Fort. Historians, however, have named it Fort Sangre de Cristo because of its proximity to the strategic pass.

FORT SEDGWICK (*Post at Julesburg Station; Camp Rankin*). Established as Post at Julesburg Station on May 17, 1864, the post was located a quarter of a mile from the right bank of the South Platte River about a mile east of the mouth of Lodgepole Creek, near present Julesburg, Sedgwick County. Purposely sited near several river crossings, including a branch of the historic Overland Trail and the creek's emigrant route, with the ford across the river about 500 yards below the post, it was intended to protect the travel routes and the area's settlers from Indian incursions. Pursuant to an order by Brigadier General Robert B. Mitchell, the district's commanding officer, the post was established by Colonel Christopher H. McNally, 3rd Volunteer Infantry. Upon completion of construction it was originally called Camp Rankin. The post was officially designated Fort Sedgwick on September 27, 1865, in honor of Major General John Sedgwick who was killed at Spotsylvania, Virginia, on May 9, 1864. The post's structures included two 25-by-100-foot adobe-built barracks, four officers' quarters, a guardhouse, and an adobe-built hospital. The fort was abandoned on May 31, 1871, after the area's Indians were considered to have been totally subjugated. On July 22, 1884, the 64-square-mile military reservation was transferred to the Department of the Interior for disposition.

FORT SHERIDAN. FORT LOGAN.

SPANISH FORT. FORT SANGRE DE CRISTO.

FORT STEVENS. Established in July 1866, Fort Stevens might be appropriately considered as Colorado's forgotten fort, located on the Apishapa River near present Aguilar, Las Animas County, about 20 miles north of Trinidad and 40 miles from the New Mexico border. Like most of the new posts in the West, it was established in response to area settlers' demands for protection. The short-lived post, September 4 to October 11, 1866, had been named in honor of Isaac Ingalls Stevens, former first governor of Washington Territory, who was killed in action in September 1862 during the Battle of Chantilly, Virginia. The post was garrisoned during its short life by Company G, 3rd Infantry, commanded by Captain and Brevet Colonel Andrew

J. Alexander, which had been temporarily posted on the Apishapa River prior to construction, and companies F and H of the 57th Colored Infantry, under Captain Jonathan Stuart (James Stewart?). Alexander's first task had been to locate a suitable site for the new fort. In accordance with his instructions from General James H. Carleton, Alexander met with Kit Carson, Colonel Herbert Enos, and Céran St. Vrain, a longtime Colorado resident, who had a large land grant in the Huerfano, Apishapa, and Purgatoire valleys. These men aided Alexander in finding a likeable site, finally selected on or before September 4.

During the last week of September, Alexander and his troopers rode to Trinidad to reason with the recalcitrant chief of a trouble-making band of Utes. The officer's seeming lack of sympathy for them incited the Utes into attacking a nearby ranch. In retaliation, Alexander ordered Company G to take the field against the Indians. During the brief skirmish which followed, the Indians suffered losses of 13 dead and a number of wounded, while the 3rd Cavalry lost one trooper. While thus engaged, other Utes attacked uncompleted Fort Stevens and attempted to raid the Army's horse herd there. But the men of the Colored Infantry repulsed the attack with accurate gunfire.

A week or so later Major General William Tecumseh Sherman, the new commander of the huge Military Division of the Mississippi, determined that a fort was not necessary at that location. Construction was immediately halted after orders to that effect were received from Headquarters at Santa Fe, and the troops and supplies already on the site were transferred elsewhere. Alexander was commended for his action by General Winfield Scott Hancock, and the skirmishes with the Utes, like Fort Stevens, passed into the annals of the West.

FORT TALPA. This short-lived adobe-built Spanish outpost was established in 1820 at Farisita, about 21 miles northwest of Walsenburg, Huerfano County.

CAMP TYLER. FORT MORGAN.

CANTONMENT UNCOMPAHGRE. CLINE'S RANCH POST.

CANTONMENT ON THE UNCOMPAHGRE. FORT CRAWFORD.

FORT UNCOMPAHGRE. FORT ROBIDOUX.

VALLEY STATION. FORT MOORE.

VALLEY STATION POST. During 1864–65, the only troops stationed along the 300-mile-long Overland Stage Line between Denver and Cottonwood Springs (now North Platte, Nebraska), were the small garrisons at Fort Sedgwick and Valley Station, now Sterling in southwest Logan County. Both were too weak to halt the depredations in the South Platte Valley. During one attack, Valley Station defended itself behind a breastwork of shelled corn. The Indians devastated a 75-mile stretch of the valley in six days. Ahead of them they drove more than 1,000 head of cattle, while in their wake they left burned haystacks and pillaged wagon trains. Few lives were lost because the valley's terrified whites found refuge at either Fort Sedgwick or Valley Station, where attacks could be easily repulsed by artillery fire.

FORT VÁSQUEZ. Varying dates have been offered by historians for the establishment of Fort Vásquez, from 1835 to 1838, located a mile and a half south of present Platteville, Weld County. The second of the fur posts in the Platte Valley, it was erected by Louis Vásquez and Andrew Sublette for the Rocky Mountain Fur Company, one of the more active competitors of Bent's Fort founded by the Bent brothers and Céran St. Vrain on the Arkansas River. In 1840 the fort on the South Platte River was sold to Locke and Randolph, who continued trading activities until frequent Indian depredations forced them to abandon the post two years later. The Indians then looted the fort of its remaining contents. There are historical indications that it was used as a base for U.S. troop movements during the Indian wars in the 1860s. In the late 1930s the old post was reconstructed, although not entirely as it was originally, by the Works Projects Administration. Standing on the original site at Platteville, the replica is a rather imposing structure with a 100-by-125-foot court enclosed by a 12-foot-high loopholed adobe wall, with its top lined with footpaths for riflemen. Each of its four angles are bastioned with towers. The reproduction is maintained by the Colorado State Historical Society. The South Platte River had changed course several times during the many intervening years, and the river now flows five miles farther to the west.

VASQUEZ'S POST (*Fort Convenience*). In 1832 or 1834, depending upon the authority referred to, fur trader Louis Vásquez built a stockade enclosing a rude cabin, trading house, shop, and corral, usually known as Fort Convenience. It was situated on what was then called Vásquez

Fort, now Clear Creek, on the outskirts of present North Denver. There was no settlement in the area until September 1858, two months after evidences of gold were found in Little Dry Creek, in present Englewood. Four years later, the trader abandoned his post and shifted operations to the South Platte River.

CAMP WARDWELL. FORT MORGAN.

FORT WASHINGTON. BEN QUICK RANCH FORT.

CAMP WELD (*Camp Elbert*). Established in September 1861 and abandoned in 1865, this Civil War camp, formerly known as Camp Elbert but renamed Camp Weld for Territorial Secretary Lewis L. Weld, had its site on the South Platte River at present West 8th Avenue and Vallejo Street, an area that was then adjacent to Denver. The 1st Regiment of Colorado Volunteers organized with 10 companies, who were mainly responsible for the defeat of the Confederates in New Mexico, were trained at this rather elaborate militia post. John P. Slough, a Denver lawyer, was commissioned its colonel. In 1864 two fires destroyed most of the camp, which was almost immediately rebuilt.

CAMP WHEELER. This short-lived tent camp was established in 1864 for the training of recruits for the Colorado Volunteers Regiment while Camp Weld was being rebuilt after two disastrous fires. The site is now occupied by Lincoln Park at 15th and Osage streets in Denver.

CANTONMENT ON WHITE RIVER. In response to the Meeker Massacre, this post was established on October 14, 1879, in compliance with telegraphic instructions from Headquarters Department of Dakota, October 1, 1879. The first garrison consisted of battalions of the 7th, 14th, and 4th Infantry and the 5th Cavalry, under the command of Lieutenant Colonel C. C. Gilbert. The post represented the headquarters of the Army contingent comprising 1,500 soldiers whose primary efforts were to control the Utes. The post was abandoned on August 7, 1883. Subsequent to the Army's departure, the post's log and frame buildings became the nucleus of the town of Meeker, Rio Blanco County, in northwestern Colorado. The town's courthouse occupied the center of the post's former parade ground. Three log structures north of it, now privately owned, were the officers' quarters, with one of the cabins serving as a museum.

FORT WICKED. A fortified ranch and station for the Overland Stage Line during the 1860s, it was located near Merino, Logan County. It was known as the American Ranch and Godfrey's Station, named for its factor, Holon Godfrey, before the Indian troubles broke out. During the bloody years of 1864 and 1865, Indians attacked every ranch between Fort Sedgwick near Julesburg and Fort Logan, a distance of 100 miles. When Godfrey's Station was attacked in 1865, his wife and daughter molded bullets and supplied him with powder while he maintained a continuous fire at the raiders. The repulsed Indians soon fled, carrying off their dead and wounded. Afterward the station was referred to as Fort Wicked, and Godfrey as "Old Wicked," because of the fierce, obstinate fight he put up.

FORT WILLIAM. BENT'S (OLD) FORT.

FORT WISE. FORT LYON.

BELCHER FORT. Often considered to have been a fort, this stone house was built by Andrew Belcher at Meriden, New Haven County, during King Philip's War (1675–76), and was probably used as both a home and a refuge. It reportedly had no windows, only portholes, and its sole heavy door was spiked for bullet-proofing.

BERLIN STOCKADE. In 1686 or 1687, Richard Seymour and other former residents of Farmington north of present New Britain moved to the precincts of today's Berlin, Hartford County, where they built a stockade in which all found shelter.

FORT BLACK ROCK. This Revolutionary War fort was authorized by Governor Trumbull and his Council on February 16, 1776, to be built on Grover's Hill, a headland on the west side of Black Rock harbor, incorporated within present Bridgeport, Fairfield County. West of the fort, on Ash Creek, was a bakehouse where several barrels of flour were made into bread every day during the war.

After the attack and burning of this Fairfield community on July 7 and 8, 1779, by the British a contemporary chronicler wrote: "Our fort yet stands; the enemy sent in a row galley to silence it, and there was constant firing between them all night; one or two attempts to take it were made by parties of troops, but it was most bravely and obstinately defended by Lieutenant Isaac Jarvis of this town, who had but twenty-three men beside himself. Many were killed on both sides; the number cannot be ascertained. They carried off some prisoners, but no persons of distinction" (Charles Burr Todd, *In Olde Connecticut: Being a Record of Quaint, Curious and Romantic Happenings There in Colonie Times and Later* [1906], p. 18). The fort was apparently maintained until after the end of the war.

FORT BLACK ROCK (New Haven). FORT HALE.

BRANFORD BLOCKHOUSE. Tradition reports that old Branford, New Haven County, was during its earliest days enclosed by a palisade five miles long. The first meeting house was a blockhouse, surrounded by cedar stakes for protection against Indian attack during worship services, while one or more settlers stood on guard. Elsewhere in the town was a fort built near the home of one William Bryan.

CAMP HAMILTON FORT. A New Haven Civil War encampment for the organizing of recruits,

Connecticut

it was established in May 1861 and had a short duration.

CONNECTICUT STATE CAMP. Located in Niantic, about seven miles southwest of New London, it is the state National Guard encampment. In use since 1873, the reservation is quite extensive. Originally occupying the campsite on a lease basis, the state purchased it outright in 1882. At one time it was customary to have it named for the state's adjutant general, changing as the incumbent changed, but for many years it has been named after the governor and subject to periodic change. It was used by Federal forces during the Spanish-American War and both world wars. They were, for the most part, state troops who were mustered into Federal service there.

DANBURY POST. Here, at Danbury in Fairfield County in August 1912, were held extensive National Guard war games while the troops were bivouacked in the city's environs.

FORT DECATUR. In the summer of 1813, Commodore Stephen Decatur erected a fortification on Allyn's Mountain in Gales Ferry on the Thames River, directly north of Groton, New London County. The fort was designed to protect Decatur's fleet from the blockading British armada anchored in Long Island Sound. His fleet consisted of his flagship the *United States*, a frigate, the sloop *Hornet*, and the British frigate *Macedonian* which he had captured earlier. Decatur had ordered the building of earthworks on the hill and had it armored with cannon. Because of British partisans in the area, who kept the enemy informed of Decatur's every move by the display of light signals, the commodore was unable to put to sea with his squadron for the remainder of the war.

FORT DEFENSE. A few days after the declaration of war by the United States against Great Britain on June 18, 1812, a meeting was held in Fairfield to organize a company of volunteers, who adopted the name of the "Mill River Sea Fencibles." Very soon after, an earthwork was constructed at the mouth of the town's harbor and was named Fort Defense.

DENISON'S FORT. Captain George Denison built a palisaded fort west of his home in Stonington during the earliest days of King Philip's War. In 1675 volunteers gathered there under his command to accompany him on the expedition to Kingston, Rhode Island, where the famous swamp fight with the Indians took place.

EAST FORT. LITCHFIELD FORTS.

ENFIELD STOCKADE. According to tradition, Enfield in Hartford County was the site of a stockade built as a refuge, most probably used during the years of the Indian wars. No time frame has been found for it. It stood on the east side of lower Enfield Street.

CAMP ENGLISH. A Civil War temporary encampment in New Haven, it was used for the organization of recruits into companies. It was abandoned shortly after its establishment in September 1861.

FORT FENWICK. FORT SAYBROOK.

FORT FOLLY. FORT NONSENSE.

FORT GOOD HOPE (*Fort Het Huys de Hoop; House of Hope; Fort Hartford*). On the site of present Dutch Point in Hartford's harbor on the Connecticut River, the Dutch erected their trading post fortified with two cannon called Het Huys de Hoop (House of Hope) or Fort Good Hope. A document from the West India Company based in New Amsterdam (New York), addressed in 1653 to the States-General of the United Netherlands (Holland), reported that "In the year, 1633, Wolter van Twiller, at the time Director in New Netherland, purchased the territory called Conittekock [Connecticut], situate on the Fresh [Connecticut] River of New Netherland, long before any other Christian Nation . . . [and] had Fort Hope built . . . [and] occupied by a garrison, who also made a bouwerie [farm] there and cultivated the soil. . . . This land was purchased from the [Pequots]."

In contrast to the Pilgrims at Plymouth and the Puritans at Boston, the Walloons in the New World were not congregated in one place. The Dutch West India Company desperately wanted to demonstrate that the whole territory claimed as New Netherland was being colonized. After eight families of Walloons were deposited at Manhattan's Bowery, two more families, with six unmarried men, and accompanied by Jacob van Curler, agent for Wolter van Twiller, were dispatched some 60 miles up the Fresh River. There, in June 1633, they began Fort Good Hope, constructed of yellow brick, the first European-built structure on the site of Hartford. Once Fort Saybrook, however, had been built by the English in 1635 at the mouth of the Connecticut River, Fort Good Hope was isolated and of no strategic value any longer. Soon the Dutch outpost was surrounded by vigorous, fast-growing English settlements, "a comely city, called Hartford, about a gunshot from Fort Good Hope on the Fresh River, together with divers other towns and hamlets."

GRANBY BLOCKHOUSE. During the earliest period of Granby's settlement, a blockhouse defense stood on Salmon Brook Street at the corner of Simsbury.

CAMP AT GRAPE VINE POINT. A temporary Civil War recruiting encampment in New Haven, it was abandoned very soon after its establishment in October 1862.

FORT GRISWOLD (*Groton Fort*). One of the most brutal incidents of the Revolution took place in 1781 at Groton's Fort Griswold, the last major engagement of the war in the north that culminated in a vengeful massacre of defenseless Patriot soldiers by an overwhelming force of British troops and Tories led by American traitor and turncoat Benedict Arnold. Now, every summer, many thousands of tourists climb the hill to the Fort Griswold State Park, commemorated by a 135-foot-high granite obelisk erected in 1830, for a curious examination of the stone and earthwork defenses. A plaque memorializes the death of the fort's commander: "On this spot, Col. William Ledyard fell by his own sword in the hands of a British officer to whom he had surrendered in the Massacre of Fort Griswold, Sept. 6, 1781."

Located in the town of Groton, Fort Griswold stands on the east side of the Thames River situated on a 120-foot-high grassy knoll nearly opposite the center of the harbor. In April 1775 a committee reported that strategic Groton Heights should be fortified. An acre and a quarter of land was purchased and a fort was begun on December 5, 1775. The name given to it in honor of Connecticut's Lieutenant Governor Matthew Griswold was not bestowed until a year later when it was still incomplete. In 1777 it was described as "an [embrasured] oblong square, with bastions at opposite angles, its longest side fronting the river. Its [12-foot-high picketed] walls were of stone, surrounded by a ditch." In 1778, finally, Connecticut militiamen completed the works, at times known as Groton Fort.

The town of Groton is situated directly across the Thames from New London, which during the war served as a home port for the privateer ships that constantly harassed the British on land and sea. Benedict Arnold's raid occurred in the closing months of the Revolution. It is believed that the primary, although wholly unrealized, objective was to divert General Washington, who was congregating his Continental forces in the Chesapeake Bay area for the siege of Yorktown. Without a doubt, another purpose was to destroy the privateer base. With a fleet of more than 30 ships and a force of about 1,700 men, Arnold sailed into New London's harbor on the morning of September 6, 1781. He formed his troops into two divisions. One of them, under his direct command, overran the New London defenses, including Fort Trumbull held by only 23 men,

FORT GRISWOLD. Stone and earthwork defenses. (Courtesy of the Connecticut Development Commission.)

FORT GRISWOLD. The Groton Monument. (Courtesy of the Connecticut Development Commission.)

and burned some 130 buildings before dark, destroying the town. The other division, a force of about 900 men, fought its way up Groton's heights to attack Fort Griswold, defended by about 160 men, including militiamen hastily summoned during the emergency. In addition to these two Patriot defenses, there was a smaller one on Town Hill that became known as Fort Nonsense.

Twice the attackers were repulsed. Finally the British gained entry into the fort after losing two of their ranking officers and 191 men. Colonel Ledyard ordered his men to lay down their arms. A British officer approached him and demanded, "Who commands this fort?" Ledyard replied, "I did, sir, but you do now," and in the traditional ceremony of surrender he handed over his sword. The British officer thereupon thrust the sword's blade through Ledyard's heart, precipitating a brutal indiscriminate massacre of the colonials, of whom 84 were slain, 40 suffered serious wounds, and the remainder were taken prisoner and terribly maltreated. The attack on Fort Griswold lasted only an hour.

During the postwar years, no serious efforts were made to rebuild or strengthen Fort Griswold, although Fort Trumbull at New London was rebuilt into a significantly strong defense. The War of 1812 found Groton in the same condition as most New England maritime towns. The war was not popular in New England but in no part of it was it so unpopular as in Connec-

ticut. Records, however, show that for at least three months in 1813 state militiamen were on duty at Groton and New London. The appearance off the coast of a large British blockading squadron brought hurried efforts to defend Fort Griswold and a company of volunteers manned the fort's gun emplacements. New London, Groton, and the Thames River were completely sealed off from active participation on the sea by the unceasing vigilance of the enemy fleet, which hovered off the coast until the end of the war.

FORT GRISWOLD. LITCHFIELD FORTS.

GROTON FORT. FORT GRISWOLD.

FORT HALE (*Little Fort; Fort Black Rock*). On the same site that held rudimentary defenses beginning in 1657 during New England's frequent Indian wars, a new fort was built in 1776 on the east side of New Haven's harbor. It stood on a natural rock formation, known as Black Rock, situated on the northern end of Solitary (Morris) Cove, about two miles opposite the city. The fortification was then called Fort Black Rock or Little Fort. At the time of the invasion by a division of Tories and Hessians led by General Tryon in early July 1779, it was commanded by a lieutenant with a garrison of only 19 men. Their gallant defense with the fort's battery of three guns prevented the enemy landing for a short time but culminated in a Patriot retreat and the destruction of the fort. A new elliptical-shaped fort of stone and brick was built on the site in 1809 and fortified with six guns. At the beginning of the War of 1812, it was garrisoned by 78 artillerymen and named Fort Hale in honor of the Revolution's martyr, Nathan Hale. The new name first appeared on a map published in 1813.

In 1861 the derelict fort was entirely demolished and replaced by a new earthwork fort. After the Civil War the fort was dismantled. In 1890 the fort site was ceded to the city of New Haven for the specific purpose of a park. On July 5, 1976, ceremonies were held at the site of Black Rock to mark the completion of the nine-year Fort Black Rock restoration project in Fort Nathan Hale Park. Monies from a number of sources, including the Department of the Interior and the National Park Service, funded the restoration.

FORT HARTFORD. FORT GOOD HOPE.

CAMP HAVEN. A temporary encampment established at Niantic, it was occupied from June to August 1898, by batteries A and C of the 1st Connecticut Artillery, commanded by Captain Francis G. Black.

FORT HET HUYS DE HOOP. FORT GOOD HOPE.

FORT HILL. A fort was built in 1675 two miles west of Woodstock in present Windham County by a company of settlers as a refuge for the community's women and children during King Philip's War. The hill also had served for a number of years as a lookout both before and after the war.

HOUSE OF HOPE. FORT GOOD HOPE.

FORT KILBOURN. LITCHFIELD FORTS.

LITCHFIELD FORTS (*North Fort; East Fort; South Fort; West Fort; Fort Griswold; Fort Kilbourn*). The bloody war that began in 1722 in Massachusetts between the settlers and the territory's eastern Indians incited the tribes in Connecticut to go on the warpath also. Since Litchfield was essentially a frontier town, forts and stockades were erected between 1720 and 1730 around five dwellings.

In August 1723, after a Litchfield inhabitant had been killed by Indians, a meeting was held and it was resolved to build four outlying forts to supplement the one which was built earlier on the site of the present courthouse. These forts were then built and two years later, on May 10, 1725, it was voted to build "one mount at each of the four forts." Joseph Kilbourn was ordered to build the mount on North Fort; Samuel Culver the mount on East Fort; Jacob Griswold the West Fort; and Joseph Bird the South Fort. The west one, named Fort Griswold, may have been located on Harris Plains; the north one, Fort Kilbourn, was possibly sited on what is now called Fern Road; the South Fort's probable location was in the town of Morris, south of Litchfield Center; the fourth, or East Fort, was certainly located on Chestnut Hill. During the last years of the Revolution, the Marquis de Chastellux in his *Travels* reported that "half a mile on this side of Litchfield, I remarked on the right a barrack, surrounded by palisades, which appeared to me like a guard-house; I approached it, and saw in this small enclosure ten pieces of brass cannon, a mortar and a swivel. This I learnt was a part of Burgoyne's artillery, which fell to the share of the state of Connecticut."

LITTLE FORT. FORT HALE.

LONG POINT FORT. During the Revolution, the inhabitants of Stonington, New London County, erected a water battery or fort in the southern part of the village of Long Point. Soldiers barracks were built in the same locality. No reports have been found to indicate whether Long Point Fort was involved in any action during the war. This fort eventually disappeared. Shortly after the War of 1812 broke out, Stonington's citizens erected another battery. On August 9, 1814, a British fleet appeared offshore and its commander sent a note ashore, saying, "Not wishing to destroy the unoffending inhabitants residing in the town of Stonington, one hour is given them from the receipt of this to move out of town." But the town's citizens replied that they would defend, though their armaments were limited to two 18-pounders and one 4-pounder. A three-day bombardment of the town followed. The men manning the battery at first had only enough ammunition for about one hour but that was amply replenished by New London to maintain a remarkable resistance that frustrated the enemy's design to destroy Stonington.

It was reported later that "in the three days' bombardment, they [the British] sent on shore sixty tons of metal and, strange to say, wounded only one man. They acknowledged they had twenty-one killed and fifty wounded, and further say, had we continued our fire any longer, they would have surrendered, for they were in a sinking condition" (Crofut, *Guide to the History and Historic Sites of Connecticut* 2:770 ff.). The British fleet, greatly disappointed, finally gave up the effort and sailed off to lick its wounds and perhaps find an easier prey. Volunteers from Mystic and Groton participated in the action.

LYMAN'S FORT. In 1744 at Torrington, Litchfield County, an eight-foot-high fort was built on Ebenezer Lyman's property in the western precincts of the town. It served, sometimes for days at a time, as a refuge from Mohawk Indians bent on depredations.

MANSFIELD BLOCKHOUSE. In 1704 the town of Mansfield Center in present Tolland County voted to fortify the dwellings of Joseph Hall and Peter Cross, located at the north and south ends of the town's main street. Some years later a blockhouse and stockade were also erected there. The remains of the blockhouse's foundations are still visible on the grounds of the General Cummings estate.

FORT MOLLY ROCKS. Despite the listing of this fort's ruins in the WPA's American Guide

Series, *Connecticut: A Guide to its Roads, Lore, and People*, as those remaining of a Civil War fort in Norwalk's harbor, no archival evidence has ever been found to substantiate its existence.

FORT NONSENSE (*Fort Folly*). During the Revolution in 1779, militia forces posted at New London were put to work erecting a fortification of timber and sod on Town Hill and had it further fortified by a breastwork and armed it with several fieldpieces. The town's inhabitants demonstrated their appreciation of the work by bestowing upon it the somewhat derogatory names of Fort Nonsense and Fort Folly. The fort had a small contributory role during Benedict Arnold's destructive assaults against Fort Trumbull at New London and Fort Griswold opposite at Groton on September 6, 1781.

NORTH FORT. LITCHFIELD FORTS.

NORWALK BLOCKHOUSE. The first settlers in present Norwalk erected a blockhouse or fort for their mutual defense on the plain east of the Silvermine River near Old Fort Point. A century and a half later, British troops under General Tryon raided and burned the town on July 11, 1779, and "then we could have used a fort."

CAMP AT OYSTER POINT. A temporary encampment established at New Haven in August 1862, it was used to recruit and organize one or possibly two regiments and then disbanded.

PARADE FORT. This fort at New London was established by order of the General Court in 1691. It was built some 16 rods from the edge of the water, at the foot of State Street, with its powder magazine and guardhouse on higher ground to the west, and was armed with six great guns from Saybrook, probably four- or six-pounders. In 1774 it had nine guns. After the September 6, 1781, conflagration precipitated by Benedict Arnold's forces attacking and destroying New London, the Parade Fort was never rebuilt.

PLYMOUTH TRADING HOUSE. WINDSOR BLOCKHOUSE.

CAMP PUTNAM. The Putnam Memorial State Park at Redding is the 252-acre memorial to the soldiers of the American Revolution who, under General Israel Putnam, established here their 1778–79 winter quarters, "Connecticut's Valley Forge." It is located at the intersection of Routes 58 (Black Rock Turnpike) and 107 (Park Road).

The location was strategically important to the Patriot cause as the troops would be available both for the defense of Connecticut's southeastern coast and also to return to the Hudson River highlands in case of attack there by the British.

FORT RACHEL. On one of West Mystic's granite crags, commanding the Mystic River's ship channel, some 40 feet above it, stood Fort Rachel, one of the town's defenses during the War of 1812. The fort's sole gun, a masked 12-pounder, provided adequate defense on more than one occasion against the British barges that sailed up the river during 1813 and 1814.

ROXBURY FORTS. The first settlers of Roxbury, in present Litchfield County, built stockaded log dwellings for protection as well as at least two detached forts at "Peace Farms" and atop Good Hill.

SABIN'S STOCKADE. This defense, date unknown, was located in the town of Pomfret, Windham County, standing on a hill near the northeast corner of the land belonging to a settler named Sabin.

SALISBURY FORTS. In May 1746 the General Assembly ordered a fort erected in the northwestern section of Salisbury, Litchfield County, located in the extreme northwestern corner of the state. In addition, a blockhouse was constructed on the west bank of the Housatonic River and another on the north side of Wononscopomuc Lake, just south of present Lakeville.

FORT SAYBROOK (*Fort Fenwick*). In early 1635, two years after the Dutch had founded their fortified trading post of Fort Good Hope at present Hartford, John Winthrop, Jr., son of the Massachusetts governor, dispatched a force of 20 men to occupy Saybrook Point commanding the mouth of the Connecticut River and there establish a settlement. It was named in honor of Lords Saye and Brooke who politically assisted him in obtaining a royal charter for a sizable patent encompassing this piece of land on the southern New England shore. The first step of the patentees in their new possessions was to build a fort, Connecticut's first, to serve as a nucleus for the new settlement. Lion Gardiner, a Scotsman, an accomplished engineer and "Master of Works of Fortification," with a dozen men was engaged to build a fort replete with ramparts, bastions, and a barracks, a work he never completed. In effect, the establishment of this English fort sealed the fate of the Dutch's Fort

Good Hope. Shortly after the fort was begun, a Dutch vessel entered the harbor but was driven off by the already mounted guns of Fort Saybrook.

The first Saybrook fort stood until the winter of 1647, when it caught fire, and all the buildings within the palisade were destroyed, with its commandant and his family barely escaping with their lives. The following year a new fort of stone and earth was erected nearer the river's bank. The waves of Pequot and Narraganset Indian warfare rolled about the fort for almost half a century. At times Indians besieged the fort and ambushed and killed members of the garrison while they were at work in the fields outside. During the early decades of the eighteenth century, the fort saw little military action and became progressively dilapidated. Early in the Revolution, efforts were made by the Connecticut authorities to renovate the fort's works but it was never put in a state of readiness.

During the War of 1812, because of its strategic position, the fort was partially reconstructed and renamed Fort Fenwick for Colonel George Fenwick who headed Saybrook's colony when it was first founded. ("Lady" Fenwick had died at Saybrook about the year 1648 and was buried on the bank of the river, supposedly within the enclosure of the wooden fort built by Gardiner in 1635). After the war the fort was abandoned. Evidences of Fort Saybrook remained until the 1870s, after which time all was swept away, together with the original contours of the site, as modern buildings were constructed in its near environs. In 1980 archaeologists under Dr. Harold Julie of the Department of Anthropology at Connecticut College, New London, conducted excavations at the suspected location of Fort Saybrook. Dr. Julie, after thoroughly investigating the site, found it had been destroyed by WPA's "make-work" projects in 1936.

SHAW'S FORT. This defense was erected about the year 1708 near the Southwick Road, about a mile north of Granby Street in the town of Granby, Hartford County.

SIMSBURY STOCKADE. The home of Simsbury's minister was palisaded, and within the stockade's walls was the well used by the garrisons posted there in 1675, 1690, and 1700. The well, when last reported, still exists and is marked by a tablet in a garden on Hopmeadow Street.

SOUTH FORT. LITCHFIELD FORTS.

FORT STAMFORD. Although the town of Stamford was not burned as were New London, Danbury, Norwalk, and Fairfield during the American Revolution, many of its inhabitants suffered deprivations through their losses of considerable property, particularly after Washington's Continentals surrendered New York to the British and retreated into New Jersey. Because of the town's proximity to British posts on Long Island and in New York, there was always the dread of still another foraging raid by either the enemy's regulars or Tories, with their primary objective focused on livestock—horses, oxen, cattle, sheep and pigs—used for transportation and to supplement their commissaries. It was not until Sunday, July 22, 1781, that there was a raid that resulted in wholesale kidnapping. About 40 Tories crossed Long Island Sound from Lloyd's Neck the night of July 21 intending to seize Reverend Moses Mather, a vociferous anti-Loyalist. They hid in a swamp not far from the Darien church and waited until afternoon services had begun. At approximately two o'clock, the Tories surrounded the church, summoned the minister down from his pulpit, and took him and about 50 men from the congregation as prisoners. The Reverend Mather was later among the more fortunate who returned, probably in an arranged prisoner exchange.

The bold raid compelled Connecticut authorities to speedily authorize the building of a fully garrisoned defensive fortification at Stamford. Construction, begun on October 4, 1781, was nearly completed in early December, at which time a plan of the fort was sent to Governor Trumbull. The fort's inside dimensions were approximately 135 by 165 feet, with the redoubts 30 by 30 feet. After the fort's completion, further steps were taken to secure the town against future enemy raids.

At war's end, the fort was considered surplus property, and the state, in desperate need of revenue, wasted no time disposing of it. On April 25, 1783, the state sold "the Fort at Stamford, all the Public Property, therein or thereto belonging . . . for the sum of £183:13:10" (Hartford, CT, *Public Records of the State of Connecticut* 5 [1943]: 93). After its transfer to a private purchaser, the fort passed into obscurity. In 1868, in a published history of Stamford, it was revealed that the fort then was still relatively well-preserved. After the death in 1970 of Mrs. H. Augusta Goodbody, whose estate encompassed the remains of Fort Stamford, steps were taken to facilitate the public purchase of the extensive property, which had a 7,400-foot frontage on the Mianus River. The great interest displayed by Stamford's people resulted in a local 1976 American Revolution Bicentennial celebration project to preserve the fort site, which occupies five acres in a particularly attractive tract of open country.

FORT STRATFORD. The town of Stratford on Long Island Sound, founded in the spring of 1639, according to one published authority (dated 1636 by archaeologists) on the banks of the Housatonic (Pootatuck) River, was originally known as Cupheag Plantation, representing one of Connecticut's earliest civilized enclaves. The entire settlement, for many years, was entirely enclosed by palisades. In the context of present geography, the site is located closely north of West Broad Street. Archaeologists employed by the town of Stratford in 1977 failed to definitely locate the palisade line, although several suggestive features were found.

TOWN HILL FORT. According to local tradition, an old fort on Town Hill in New Hartford, Litchfield County, protected early settlers from Indian raids.

FORT TRUMBULL. On October 2, 1775, acknowledging the absolute necessity of protecting New London against the British during the Revolution, the General Assembly ordered the work on an existing old fortification to be completed, stipulating that a platform be built for the accommodation of cannon and a powder magazine. On April 1, 1776, two companies of men were drafted to work on the fort. On April 10 application was made to Commodore Esek Hopkins for cannon to be emplaced there and at Fort Griswold opposite at Groton. In December the two

forts were named for the governor and lieutenant (deputy) governor of the state. Progress on their construction, however, was delayed because of the shortage of men. On July 18, 1777, Governor Trumbull and his Council ordered the completion of Fort Trumbull. Work resumed and the gun platform from the old fort was moved to Fort Trumbull. On March 25, 1778, William Ledyard, later killed by his own sword when Fort Griswold was captured, was appointed to command the forts at New London, Groton, and Stonington, with the rank of major.

Fort Trumbull, considered to have been a rather primitive work of stone and earth, facing north, east, and south, and entirely open to the west, proved to be of little or no service, as the fort had been designed to only withstand attack from the sea. Its garrison consisted of only 23 men when traitor and turncoat Benedict Arnold, with a British fleet of probably more than 30 ships and a force of about 1,700 men, sailed into New London's harbor on the morning of September 6, 1781. Arnold led one of his two divisions ashore and overran New London. Completely open on its land side, Fort Trumbull was easily taken, and its miniscule garrison, some of its men wounded, fled across the Thames to Fort Griswold. New London was put to the torch while Arnold's other division assaulted and captured Fort Griswold, where many of its defenders were grievously massacred.

In 1812 old Fort Trumbull was leveled and replaced by a much stronger work which, with Fort Griswold across the river, was sufficient to prevent entry of the British fleet into the harbor. The British then resorted to a continuous blockade offshore for the remainder of the war to effec-

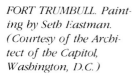

FORT TRUMBULL. Painting by Seth Eastman. (Courtesy of the Architect of the Capitol, Washington, D.C.)

tively bottle up Decatur's ships in the Thames River. In 1839 the War of 1812 fort was demolished and a third fort of granite was constructed. In 1902 Fort Trumbull's garrison consisted of two companies of artillery, aggregating 218 men, commanded by nine officers. In 1910 the fort was turned over to the Treasury Department for the use of the Revenue Cutter Service, later replaced by the U.S. Coast Guard. At present Fort Trumbull is maintained by the U.S. Navy as the Laboratory of the Naval Underwater Systems Center.

FORT TRUMBULL. To defend Milford, New Haven County, a battery surrounded with earthworks was constructed in 1776 on the west side of the harbor on West Point and a perpetually garrisoned post was established for the duration of the Revolution under the command of Captain Isaac Miles. The post was named in honor of Governor Jonathan Trumbull.

FORT UNION. During the War of 1812, Bridgeport was defended by a battery of guns on Grover's Hill, on the same site formerly occupied by Fort Black Rock during the Revolution.

WALLINGFORD FORT. In 1689 the people of Wallingford, New Haven County, voted to fortify the town's meetinghouse and surround it with a strong palisade.

FORT WATERBURY. In the town of Watertown (Litchfield County), originally a parish of Waterbury (New Haven County), there was a set or series of earthworks located at the "Horseneck," a bend of the Naugatuck River, constructed and manned periodically and somewhat indifferently by local militia. Its peak of activity occurred in 1781. These earthworks were called Fort Waterbury in honor of General David Waterbury, confirmed by at least one authority, one Joseph Wood, a Revolutionary War veteran who assisted in its construction.

WEST FORT. LITCHFIELD FORTS.

WETHERSFIELD FORT. According to a nineteenth century historian, a fort was built prior to 1640 and probably located "near and east of the present site of the state prison" on North Main Street in Wethersfield, Hartford County. Tradition maintains that an apartment house east of the prison occupies the site of the fort. In March 1675 it was voted that "the town be fortified round with a sufficient pallisadoe."

WINDSOR BLOCKHOUSE (*Plymouth Trading House*). Since Plymouth's settlers were evidencing strong interest in the economic possibilities of the Connecticut Valley, Edward Winslow in 1632 explored the region. The following year William Holmes established a trading post and built a fort on the site of Windsor on the left bank of the Connecticut River in present Hartford County, just north of the Dutch Fort Good Hope at today's city of Hartford. When the bloody Pequot war broke out in 1637, Windsor's settlers surrounded their dwellings with fortifications or palisades, consisting of strong high stakes or posts, set close together, and surrounded by wide ditches. In addition, a line of palisades for nearly a mile enclosed a considerable sized irregular parallelogram of ground. The Pilgrims had "out-generaled" the Dutch by settling north of them to secure the trade of the Indians residing higher up the river. The Dutch remonstrated but to no avail. According to Governor William Bradford of Plymouth Colony, the area around the English post at Windsor in 1634 was a terrifying spectacle in the spring of that year as "those Indians that lived about their trading house there, fell sick of the small pox and died most miserably." The Plymouth Trading House at Windsor prospered. In 1664 the English unseated the Dutch and extended their settlements throughout the Connecticut Valley.

FORT WOODRUFF. A fort of stone, nearly 16 feet square, was built about the year 1700 by Matthew Woodruff at Southington in present Hartford County. Elsewhere in the town, a fortified palisade enclosed a dwelling, possibly located at Newell's Corner. According to strong local tradition, another fort was built against a hill in the rear of a tavern at the north end of the town, on Queen Street.

FORT WOOSTER. On the site of a Quinnipiac Indian palisaded fort on Beacon Hill in present New Haven, a beacon was ordered built there in accordance with a town vote on November 14, 1775. The hill was the site of the earthworks captured by British General Tryon on July 5, 1779. During the War of 1812, a fort was built on the same site and named in honor of General David Wooster. Its site is northeast of former Fort Hale and above Townsend Avenue. The fort's remains are enclosed within today's Fort Wooster Park.

FORT ALTENA. Fort Christina.

CAMP ANDREWS (*Camp Hare's Corner*). The rural community of Hare's Corner, located near New Castle, was the site of a Civil War encampment, more correctly called Camp Andrews. Situated near the present junction of U.S. 13 and 40, it was named for Lieutenant Colonel John W. Andrews, 1st Delaware Volunteers. The period of September-October 1861 was occupied in drill. On October 20 the camp was evacuated and the troops left for the front.

CAMP BATTERY POINT. Fort DuPont.

CAMP BRANDYWINE. There were two different encampments called Camp Brandywine during the Civil War. The first, occupied from May 1861 until at least September 1861, was located on Kennett Pike approximately a mile and a half from Wilmington. The 1st and 2nd Delaware Infantry, in succession, were stationed there shortly after their organization. The second Camp Brandywine, established in September 1862 was occupied by about 500 troops who were assigned to the defense of the duPont mills. The camp was situated on Kennett Pike near Buck Tavern, about four miles from Wilmington. The camp is known to have been in existence as late as October 1864.

CAMP CAPE HENLOPEN. A permanent military installation that was active during World War I, the post was located by Delaware Breakwater Harbor in Sussex County on 140 acres acquired in 1873. The Delaware coastal defense was part of the Middle Atlantic Coast Artillery District.

FORT CASIMIR (*Fort Trefaldighet; Fort Trinity; Fort New Amstel*). Founded in 1651 with the building of Fort Casimir by the Dutch under Peter Stuyvesant on the site of a former Indian village, New Castle was the first town in Delaware to be laid out. It was the meeting place of all Colonial assemblies and the first state capital. Fort Casimir, named in honor of Count Ernest Casimir of Nassau, was situated on a spit of land known as Sand Hook, long since washed away by the river, below the end of present Chestnut Street. Deciding that it was time, after a number of threats, for the Dutch to regain control of the Delaware River and its trade, Stuyvesant arrived with an armada of 11 vessels and more than 100 soldiers, built the fort, and transferred the garrison from Fort Nassau on the Jersey shore to his new fort.

Delaware

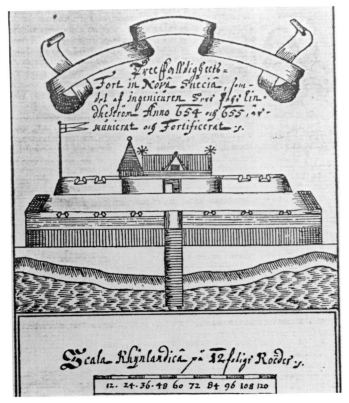

FORT CASIMIR. Drawing of the fort after its capture by the Swedes in 1653. (Reproduced in Delaware Tercentenary Almanack, 1938, by the Delaware Tercentenary Commission from Lindestrom's Geographia Americae. Courtesy of the Delaware Bureau of Archaeology and Historic Preservation.)

On Trinity Sunday, May 21, 1654, Johan Classon Rising, New Sweden's new administrator after Johan Printz's resignation as governor, captured the Dutch fort and renamed it Fort Trefaldighet or Fort Trinity. The Swedes held the fort only until August 26, 1655, when Peter Stuyvesant reappeared with several hundred soldiers and an armada of seven armed vessels. After its recapture by the Dutch, Jean Paul Jacquet was appointed vice-director of the territory on the Delaware and assumed command of the fort in December. On December 25, at his request, the colony's Council examined the fort and found extensive water damage in its walls and batteries. In 1658, under a new Delaware territorial directorship, some renovating and rebuilding were made on the fort, particularly to the director's residence within, and a new guardhouse was constructed.

When ownership of the colony was transferred from the West India Company to the Burgomasters of Amsterdam in 1656, it became known as New Amstel, a suburb of Amsterdam. In 1664 a British armada appeared off Manhattan Island's Battery and, after threatening to bombard New Amsterdam, forced capitulation by the Dutch of all New Netherlands and renamed it New York. Sir Robert Carr, appointed to oversee the transfer of the Delaware River settlements to British rule, renamed the Dutch-Swedish town New Castle. In 1673 the Hollanders recaptured New Netherland, which they renamed New Orange. But the following year it was returned to Great Britain in accordance with the terms of the Treaty of Westminster.

Under British control, a few new defenses, for the most part blockhouses, were erected and old Fort Casimir was gradually obliterated. In 1682 the territory of Delaware was conveyed to William Penn by James, Duke of York, and New Castle was Penn's landing place when he first set foot on American soil the same year. Lord Baltimore contested this transfer, and the boundary disputes were not resolved until the survey, conducted by Charles Mason and Jeremiah Dixon, Englishmen, who surveyed it in 1763–1767, and are now celebrated as the Mason-Dixon Line. The spire atop the State (Court) House, Delaware's Colonial capitol and first state house, was used as the radius of the 12-mile circle that formed the northern boundary of Delaware and part of the Mason and Dixon Line. This later became the dividing mark between Delaware and her sister slave states and the free states to the North. The Delaware River within this radius, to the low water mark on the opposite shore, is part of the state.

CHENEY CLOW'S FORT. The arrival of British forces under Major General Sir William Howe in Philadelphia in September 1777 emboldened the area's Loyalists, and in 1778 several hundred of them banded together under the leadership of Cheney Clow, a rabid Tory, and built and manned a fort that stood atop a bluff near present Kenton in Kent County. The people on Delmarva Peninsula, especially those in the isolated central portions of Kent and Sussex counties, and adjacent areas of Maryland, were either completely indifferent to the causes of the war or confirmed Loyalists in sentiment. The British withdrawal from Philadelphia in May 1778 left outspoken Tories defenseless in the face of certain Patriot retribution. Cheney Clow's fort was hurriedly abandoned, and overt Loyalism in the region evaporated.

At a place called Jordan Branch, apparently near the Pennsylvania line, a fort was erected by Tories in March 1778, where reportedly a thousand or more partisans were posted. A strong force of Patriot volunteers was stationed for three months in the fort's vicinity to sever the lines of communication between the Tories and the British in Philadelphia. In June the Tories, starved out by the Patriots, abandoned their fort and dispersed. Cheney Clow, after being tried for treason and acquitted in 1782, was rearrested and indicted for having shot a member of the posse that had apprehended him. He was finally convicted and hanged.

FORT CHRISTINA (*Fort Altena*). The first Swedish expedition to the New World made its landing on or about March 29, 1638, on a riverside site near the foot of present East 7th Street in Wilmington. It built Fort Christina, New Sweden's first fortification, around which was founded the first permanent white settlement in the Delaware River Valley and the nucleus of the aspiring colony. Peter Minuit, the Hollander who reputedly bought Manhattan Island to thereby establish New Amsterdam, headed the expedition of the New Sweden Company, which sent him from Sweden in December 1637 to establish a foothold in the New World. His assigned destination was the Minquas Kill, which on his arrival he renamed the Christina River in honor of Sweden's young queen. The expedition of 50 men, in two vessels, landed at a natural pier of rocks that jutted into the Minquas Kill about two miles above its confluence with the Delaware. Near the landing site, Minuit erected Fort Christina to protect the settlement and serve as the administrative and commercial center of the colony.

The fort, in which the earliest religious services of the colony were held, remained the principal center of Swedish settlement even during the period 1643–53, when Governor Johan Printz ruled from his residence and fort on Tinicum Island, about 15 miles north on the Delaware River. When New Sweden—poorly armed, bereft of reinforcements, and perenially inadequately provisioned by the home country—fell to Peter Stuyvesant and the Dutch from New Amsterdam in the relatively bloodless conquest of the Delaware River Valley in 1655, the Dutch posted a miniscule garrison at Fort Christina, which they renamed Fort Altena. The settlement around Fort Christina remained predominantly Swedish despite its annexation to New Netherland. In 1664, when the English armada forced the West India Company to surrender its colonial territorial holdings in New York, New Jersey, Pennsylvania, and Delaware, English soldiers garrisoned Fort Christina (Altena), but the Swedes remained in what was once the capital of New Sweden. They prospered and their settlement spread along the banks of the Christina to ultimately become the city of Wilmington.

The two acres comprising Fort Christina State Park include the still-existing natural wharf of rocks that was the site of the first landing and near which was the heart of the first Swedish settlement in North America. The ledge of rocks

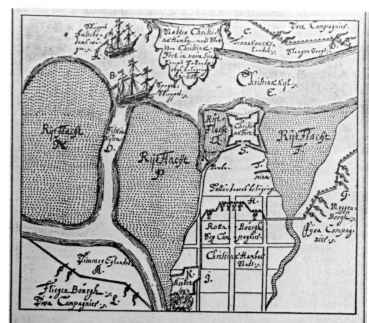

Fort Christina Under Siege By Stuyvesant

This plan, drawn by the Swedish engineer, *Pehr Martensson Lindestrom,* shows Fort Christina (S) and the village Christinahamn (I) as they appeared in 1655 during the siege of the fort by the Dutch under *Pieter Stuyvesant,* governor of Manhattan. Two of the Dutch ships, the *Waag* (A) and the *Spegel* (B) are shown anchored at the mouth of Fiske Kyl (Brandywine, O). Surrounding the fort are the siege-works; an earthwork (D) on Tennaconck's land (C), across Christina Kyl or River (E), with 4 guns manned by 3 companies, and other batteries of logs, Mosquitoburg (G) with 6 guns and 4 companies, Ratburg (H) with 6 guns and 6 companies, and Flyburg (L) on Timber Island (M), with 4 guns and 2 companies. These were so named by the Dutch according to the pests peculiar to each. In advance of these appear a mine (T) and in the rear the Dutchmen's kitchen (K). The little harbor (R) is to be seen at the left of the fort.

The plan shows the strategic value of the position of Fort Christina at that time, close to the end of a tongue of fast land terminating at the Rocks, a natural wharf, and flanked by marshes (N, P, Q, F). The river having since been bulkheaded and the marshes filled in, these strategic advantages have disappeared.

is partially visible because the natural formation has been covered by a plaza that surrounds a striking monument, a shaft designed by the later Swedish sculptor Carl Milles. It is constructed of black Swedish granite and surmounted by a stylized representation of the *Kalmar Nyckel* (Key of Kalmar), one of the two vessels in the initial expedition.

FORT DELAWARE. Situated on 178-acre, oval-shaped Pea Patch Island, a flat mud bank in the Delaware River midway between the Delaware and New Jersey shores, Fort Delaware eventually replaced an earthwork defense built there during the War of 1812 and purposely obliterated in 1821, and a wooden fortification that was erected between 1814 and 1824.

In 1813 the State of Delaware ceded the island to the Federal government for the purpose of erecting fortifications on the island to protect the Delaware River and adjacent land areas. In 1814 100 soldiers and 30 laborers began building new works, wharves and dikes, an intermit-

FORT CHRISTINA. (Reproduced in Delaware Tercentenary Almanack, *1938, by the Delaware Tercentenary Commission from Lindestrom's* Geographia Americae. *Courtesy of the Delaware Bureau of Archaeology and Historic Preservation.)*

tently interrupted project carried on until 1824, when the fort was near completion. In February 1831, a large part of the timber-built fort burned down. Despite many repairs made in 1833, the fort was dismantled shortly thereafter. In the interim a controversy rose over whether the island belonged to New Jersey or Delaware. After the dispute was finally resolved in Delaware's favor, Congress in 1847 made a $1 million appropriation to construct a large, modern, masonry fort. During the course of protracted construction, Congress was compelled to provide an additional million dollars to carry on the project. The massive, pentagon-shaped, granite-built fortification, covering six acres midway between the center and the southern end of the island, was not completed until 1859. Within are three three-story brick buildings, each placed against a separate curtain. The fortress was first occupied by Federal forces in February 1861.

Ironically, although Fort Delaware was designed for 252 guns and mounted 131, it served in the main as a military prison throughout the years of the Civil War. After the Battle of Kernstown, Virginia, in early 1862, about 200 of General Stonewall Jackson's men were brought to the fort as the first Confederate prisoners of war. By June of 1863, there were about 8,000 prisoners on the island; two months later there were 12,500, incredibly crowded under terrible conditions. As many as 331 of them died of cholera in one month. All the Confederates captured at Gettysburg were also held at the fort. About 2,700 of the prisoners died during their incarceration, with more than 2,000 of them buried at Finn's Point on the New Jersey side of the river. Fort Delaware remained garrisoned until 1870 when it was deactivated.

Fort Delaware was reactivated during the Spanish-American War when emplacements for three 12-inch disappearing guns were built at a cost of more than a half-million dollars, and reactivated again in 1917 during World War I. In 1944, finally, the fort was declared surplus property by the government and turned over to the State of Delaware. The fort, now an attraction for tourists and history buffs, is within the jurisdiction of the Delaware Park Commission, and the Fort Delaware Society aids in its preservation.

CAMP DUPONT. A Civil War mustering-in tent-camp located on the outskirts of Wilmington, it was situated near Brandywine Springs and Camp Brandywine on the farm of the Wilmington Agricultural Society, in the vicinity of 11th and Greenhill streets. The first few regiments were mustered in during the summer and fall months of 1861 and sent to several camps for training. Both names, at different times, were later successively given to a third encampment, created in September 1862, located on the Kennett Pike near the Buck Tavern, about a mile from the DuPont powder yards. (See: CAMP BRANDYWINE.)

FORT DUPONT (*Camp Battery Point; Camp Reynolds*). First established during the early years of the Civil War as a Fort Delaware auxiliary coastal defense battery, two miles northwest of Delaware City, it was initially named Battery Point. The post was renamed Camp Reynolds in 1863 in honor of General John Fulton Reynolds, who was killed at Gettysburg by a Confederate sharpshooter. Between 1872 and 1876, more guns were mounted there. In 1897, in preparation for the building of a modern masonry fortification, the battery's outmoded guns were removed from the site. The present installation was established in 1898 on a 320-acre reservation acquired by purchase in 1871. One of the few Army installations named in honor of a Navy man, it was designated Fort DuPont in tribute to Admiral Samuel Francis duPont, a Delaware hero of Civil War fame. Construction, begun in 1899, was completed in 1902, when its armaments consisted of two 8-inch and two 12-inch breech-loading rifles and sixteen 12-inch breech-loading mortars. Until 1922 it was manned by elements of the Coast Artillery, and from that date until the beginning of World War II it was predominantly an engineering post, occupied as the headquarters of the 1st Engineers. Expanded during World War II as an Army aviation engineering base, the fort was decommissioned on December 31, 1945. In 1946 the military reservation and its 65 buildings were given to the State of Delaware, which converted the installation into the Governor Bacon Health Center, opened on October 28, 1948.

CAMP HARE'S CORNER. CAMP ANDREWS.

FORT HOARKILL. FORT SWANENDAEL.

CAMP HOKESSIN. A temporary Revolutionary War encampment reputed to have been established by British General Sir William Howe on September 8, 1777, it was located on the "Lancaster Road," near the Pennsylvania border, at or near present Hockessin, northwest of Wilmington, New Castle County.

FORT MILES. Situated on the sand dunes at Cape Henlopen at the entrance of Delaware Bay, Fort Miles and the town of Lewes, two miles west, are steeped in the history of the nation. Lewes, called the "Birthplace of Delaware," was founded in 1631 by Dutch colonists, who called their settlement Zwaanendael. (See FORT SWANENDAEL.) Though short-lived, this early colonization was the basis of William Penn's claim that the territory was a part of Pennsylvania and not of Maryland as claimed by the Calverts. In 1682 the Duke of York deeded all the Delaware country south to Cape Henlopen to William Penn. Within the city of Lewes is so-called 1812 Park, established on the site of a battery built during that war.

Fort Miles was situated on a parcel of ground that was originally granted by Penn, then Governor of Pennsylvania, to the people of Lewes. Nearly 200 years later, in 1872, the original site of the military reservation was ceded by the citizens of Lewes and Sussex County to the Federal government. Named in honor of General Nelson Appleton Miles, commanding general of the U.S. Army from 1895 to 1903, Fort Miles was constructed during the early days of World War II as a regular installation for coast defense and manned by the Coast Artillery. After the war it became an anti-aircraft training center for both Army regulars and Reserve components. Inactivation of the post was announced on December 17, 1958, about a month after it was disclosed that a huge casemate secretly constructed during the war under the sand dunes at Fort Miles would be turned over by the Department of the Army to the Sussex County Civil Defense. The existence of the 3,761-square-foot casemate, which during the war housed mine field controls, a communications system, and a filtered air system for the elimination of poisonous gases, had not previously been made public.

NAAMAN BLOCKHOUSE. Situated on the Delaware River in Claymont on the Philadelphia Pike, it was built in 1654 by Johan Rising, the last governor of New Sweden. The blockhouse, the oldest structure in the State of Delaware, is attached to the Robinson House, a noted tearoom-restaurant built about 1723, which hosted a number of famous military men during the Revolution. The blockhouse is a smallish, two-story, loopholed structure with a hip roof and thick stone walls, originally built to protect the mills and farms along Naaman's Creek.

FORT NEW AMSTEL. FORT CASIMIR.

FORT OPLANDT. FORT SWANENDAEL.

CAMP REYNOLDS. FORT DUPONT.

FORT SAULSBURY. Situated near Slaughter Beach on lower Delaware Bay, and located about six miles east of Milford, Sussex County, Fort Saulsbury was a Coast Artillery defense installation on an 162-acre reservation, established during World War I in response to a proposal by U.S. Senator Willard Saulsbury. The post was actually named in honor of his father, also a former senator. The post, deactivated in 1946, is now privately owned.

CAMP SMITHERS. A Civil War encampment established for the training of four companies of the 1st Delaware Cavalry during the autumn of 1862 and winter of 1862–63, it was located at "Brandywine Hundred," near Wilmington. The camp was probably named for Nathaniel B. Smithers, a prominent Delaware Republican of the period.

FORT SWANENDAEL (*Fort Oplandt; Fort Zwaanendael; Fort Hoarkill; Fort Whorekill*). The Delaware Bay and River region had been known to Dutch traders since Henry Hudson's discovery of the Bay in 1609 and his favorable report on its fertile coastal shores to his employers, the Dutch East India Company. The Dutch had also learned very soon after their arrival in the New World that there were numerous whales in the Bay that could be captured close to shore. This provocative information led Captain David Pietersen de Vries, an adventurous but skilled seaman and navigator, and a group of patroons to plan an expedition to colonize the Delaware Bay region and establish a whaling station.

In late 1629 Giles Houset, agent for the planned colony, purchased land on both sides of the Hoorn Kill (present Lewes Creek), the site of the present city of Lewes, in preparation for the planting of the colony. On December 12, 1630, the first expedition to colonize lands on the "Bay of the South [Delaware] River" sailed from the Texel in Holland. The expedition consisted of merely two vessels, the 300-ton ship named the *Walvis* (Whale), which was armed with 18 guns and commanded by Captain Peter Heyes, and a small yacht. The smaller vessel went off course and was apparently taken by the French the next day. The *Walvis*, however, completed the voyage. She had aboard a cargo of yellow Dutch brick, cattle, provisions, and 28 colonists, besides the crew. The expedition arrived in America in the spring of 1631 and established their settlement on the land purchased by Houset a year and a half earlier.

The colonists erected a combination dwelling and storehouse constructed of the yellow brick brought from the Netherlands. In addition, they built a small "cook house." A fortified, double-bastioned palisade surrounded the structures. The settlement was called by several names—Fort Oplandt ("Upland"); Fort Zwaanendael ("Valley of the Swans"); and Fort Hoarkill and Fort Whorekill, for its situation on the creek. The name "Swanendael" was a somewhat anglicized form of Zwaanendael. Five other Dutchmen, most probably from New Amsterdam, joined the group of colonists. In September, Captain Heyes of the *Walvis* returned to his homeland and reported to De Vries that all was well with the colony. On May 24, 1632, Captain de Vries, with 50 men to augment the Zwaanendael colony, sailed from Holland in the *Walvis*. Upon their arrival in Delaware Bay on December 6, however, they learned that all the colonists had been massacred by the Indians. Through diplomatic questioning of the local Indians, Captain de Vries learned that the tragedy grew out of a misunderstanding between the two cultures. There was nothing but ruination where the settlement stood. Although the palisade was still in place, the buildings within the enclosure had been almost entirely burned. Scattered about within the fort and in the near environs were the skeletal remains of men and animals. All 33 men had perished.

The Zwaanendael Museum in Lewes, a replica of the ancient Town Hall in Hoorn, Holland, was erected by the State of Delaware in 1931 to commemorate the 300th anniversary of the founding of Fort Zwaanendael, the first Dutch settlement on Delaware soil. In May 1964 Sussex County archaeologists announced that the southern bastion of the fort had been uncovered. The four-sided bastion was found to measure 17 by 20 feet. This discovery implemented the unearthing of the stockade's post molds in 1952. The diggings had been planned on the basis of the map drawn by Captain de Vries himself more than three centuries earlier.

TALBOT'S FORT. This fort, situated on the present site of Christiana, west of New Castle, was built in 1684 by Colonel George Talbot, a cousin of Lord Baltimore, to defend the latter's claim to territory along the Delaware River as a part of the original 1632 Maryland grant. The fortification was garrisoned for two years by Maryland soldiers and Catholic partisans, supplied and provisioned by the Maryland Council, during the bitterly contested boundary dispute with William Penn. Lord Baltimore's Catholic-oriented charter was abrogated by a Protestant revolt in 1689.

CAMP TOWNSEND. Reportedly located some two miles south of New Castle, this World War I encampment was probably a temporary National Guard summer training ground, named in honor of Governor John A. Townsend.

FORT TREFALDIGHET. FORT CASIMIR.

FORT TRINITY. FORT CASIMIR.

CAMP TUNNELL. Named for Governor Ebe Walter Tunnell and established at the outbreak of the Spanish-American War in 1898, Camp Tunnell was located on the eastern end of Middletown, New Castle County.

FORT UNION. During the War of 1812, there was much concern demonstrated for the protection of the city of Wilmington and the mills in its environs. James A. Bayard, the first of five Bayards to represent Delaware in the U.S. Senate, joined citizens in the building of Fort Union in 1813 on the site of old Fort Christina, erected by the Swedes in 1638.

FORT WHOREKILL. FORT SWANENDAEL.

FORT ZWAANENDAEL. FORT SWANENDAEL.

BATTERY ALEXANDER. A Washington defense, it was situated at the end of Alexander Road.

CAMP ANDERSON. No definite location has been found for this Civil War encampment established in 1865.

ARMY WAR COLLEGE. FORT LESLEY J. MCNAIR.

BATTERY BAILEY. Established in present Westmoreland Park, a large percentage of its remains is still evident.

FORT BAKER. This earthwork was located east of the Anacostia River, between Forts Meigs and Stanton, about one mile east of Uniontown, D.C. Begun late in 1861, this strong point was designed, along with other works in its vicinity, to protect the crossing of the Anacostia River and the Navy Yard. Constructed by elements of various state regiments, the fortification had a perimeter of 492 yards. Its armament consisted of three 8-inch siege guns, two 24-pound howitzers, and eight 10-inch Parrott rifled guns, all embrasured; on its parapets were mounted seven 24-pound smoothbore guns. The defense was named in honor of Colonel Edward Dickinson Baker, 71st Pennsylvania, who was killed at Balls Bluff, Virginia, on October 21, 1861.

CAMP BARCLAY. A Pennsylvania volunteer cavalry encampment, it was located near Columbia College on Meridian Hill, about three miles north of the White House. Established on December 12, 1861, by companies A, B, C, and F of the 6th Pennsylvania Cavalry, the camp was named in honor of Clement C. Barclay of Philadelphia.

CAMP BARRY. An artillery encampment during the Civil War, it was located about one mile northeast of the Capitol, in the vicinity of the intersection of Bladensburg Turnpike and Benning Road. Established in August 1861 by the 1st Pennsylvania Artillery, while awaiting equipment and assignment, it was named in compliment to Major William F. Barry, then chief of artillery of the department. According to National Archives records, the post was established in 1862 and not wholly abandoned until July 12, 1865.

FORT BAYARD. One of Washington's defenses during the Civil War, Fort Bayard was located about two miles east of Fort Sumner at River Road and Western Avenue, N.W., in the District of Columbia. Construction began late in 1862 in

District of Columbia

accordance with plans designed by Colonel Barton Alexander, Engineers, to provide additional strength to the northern lines of the city's defenses. It was situated on a knob of rock, and was perfectly elliptical in trace, having a perimeter of 123 yards, with its parapet revetted with vertical posts and surrounded by a line of abatis. Its armament consisted of two 12-pound smoothbore howitzers and four 20-pound Parrott rifled guns mounted on platforms in embrasures. The fort was named in honor of Captain G. D. Bayard, 4th Cavalry, and brigadier general of volunteers, who died on December 14, 1862, from wounds received in action at Fredericksburg, Virginia. Fort Bayard was occupied until the close of hostilities, when it was dismantled and abandoned.

BATTERY BENSON. A Washington defense during the Civil War, it was located on the site of present 4805 Fort Sumner Drive.

BATTERY (RIGHT) BROAD BRANCH. A Washington defense, it stood on a site 400 yards east of the present Tunisian Embassy. There is evident a large percentage of the battery's remains.

CAMP BUFORD. A camp established in 1863 for the defense of Washington, no archival references have been found on its location.

FORT BUNKER HILL. This Civil War defense of Washington, erected in the fall of 1861 by the 11th Massachusetts, was named after Boston's famous old Revolutionary fort. It occupied an important position in the line of defense between Fort Totten and Fort Lincoln, on the east side of Sargent Road between Perry and Otis streets. During the investment of the city by troops under General Jubal Anderson Early in the summer of 1864, the fort was garrisoned by Company B, Maine Coast Guards, a detachment of the 2nd Company, New Hampshire Heavy Artillery, the 150th Ohio National Guard, and Battery G, 3rd Artillery. There was a battery to its left at 12th and Perry streets; another in front of present 1330 Perry Street; and still another to the fort's right at 15th and Monroe streets.

CAMP CADWALLADER. A temporary Union encampment established during the Civil War, it was situated on Kalorama Heights, about two miles from what was then the center of the city of Washington.

CAMP CALDWELL. Camp Caldwell was a temporary encampment in the environs of Washington during the Civil War.

BATTERY CAMERON. A defense of Washington during the Civil War, it occupied what is now 1900 Foxhall and Reservoir, about one mile above Georgetown.

CAMP CAPITOL HILL. A temporary Civil War encampment, it occupied ground on what was known as Capitol Hill.

BATTERY CARROLL. A Washington defense, the center of Battery Carroll's work occupied what is now 3720 Horner Place, S.E.

FORT CARROLL. Located about a half mile north of Fort Greble on the hills on the eastern side of the Potomac, this large and well-built Washington defense was begun in September 1861. It ultimately mounted 13 guns and 1 mortar.

CARVER BARRACKS. Carver Barracks existed during 1861–62 in the District of Columbia.

CHAIN BRIDGE BATTERY. A Washington defense, this battery stood at the District of Columbia end of the Chain Bridge.

FORT CHAPLIN. Named for Colonel Daniel Chaplin, Artillery, this Washington defense was situated east of the Eastern Branch about one mile southeast of Benning's Bridge.

CLIFFBURN BARRACKS. Located at Mount Pleasant in the District of Columbia, the barracks was a temporary camp established during the Civil War. This was a Depot Camp and Veteran Reserve Corps Camp.

CAMP COCHRAN. Camp Cochran was a temporary Civil War post situated near Washington.

FORT DAVIS. A Washington defense during the Civil War, Fort Davis occupied a site north of present Alabama Avenue and across from the Fairfax Village Shopping Center. The fort was considered as an outwork to Fort Baker.

FORT DERUSSY. The substantial remains of Fort DeRussy, one of Washington's defenses during the Civil War, still stand near the fork of Oregon Avenue and Military Road in Rock Creek Park. This fort commanded the valley of Rock Creek. It was constructed in 1861 by the 4th New York Heavy Artillery and named for its commander, Colonel Gustavus A. DeRussy. Its armament consisted of 11 guns and mortars, including a massive 100-pounder Parrott rifle.

CAMP DUNCAN. Camp Duncan was a temporary post established during the Civil War and located in the eastern section of Washington.

FORT DUPONT. A Washington defense during the Civil War, Fort Dupont was situated south of the Eastern Branch of the Potomac, "about two miles southeast of Washington City," on the northeast corner of Massachusetts and Alabama avenues in a very scenic picnic grounds area. During the war Alabama Avenue was called Old Fort Road because of the many fortifications situated on the important thoroughfare. The remains of the fort still evidence the embrasures for its guns.

ENGINEER RESERVE OFFICERS' TRAINING CAMP. A temporary post established during World War I and located within the city of Washington, it was probably a part of what is now Fort Lesley J. McNair.

CAMP FENTON. This was a temporary camp of instruction established at Washington during the Civil War. No dates or location of this post have been found.

FORT FOOTE. A defense of Washington during the Civil War, Fort Foote was located six miles below Oxon Hill at the end of Fort Foote Road.

CAMP FRY. A temporary defense of Washington during the Civil War.

FORT GAINES. This defense of Washington was located on grounds now encompassed by American University at Ward Circle, N.W.

FORT GOOD HOPE. FORT WAGNER.

CAMP GRAHAM. A temporary Civil War post, it was situated some four miles north of the city of Washington.

FORT GREBLE. Occupying the southern extremity of the plateau east of the Potomac, with its site on present Nichols Avenue, S.E., this large and strongly built Civil War defense was named in honor of Lieutenant John T. Greble, killed at Big Bethel, Virginia, on July 10, 1861. The fort had an armament of 17 guns and mortars. The fort site was turned over to the Chief Signal Officer, U.S. Army, sometime in 1868.

CAMP HARLAN. A temporary Union post, it was established during the Civil War and situated on North Seventh Street.

CANTONMENT HOLT. Established during the Civil War near Washington, it was established by Captain Alfred Pleasonton, 2nd Cavalry, with nine companies of men of the 2nd and 4th Cavalry, aggregating 563 men. They took post in January 1862. The first garrison return was dated February 4, 1862.

FORT HUMPHREYS. FORT LESLEY J. MCNAIR.

CAMP JAMES. This was a Civil War encampment in or near Washington established in 1861.

BATTERY JAMESON. The remnants of this powerful battery built in the defense of Washington are located in the Fort Lincoln Cemetery.

JERSEY CAMP. A temporary Civil War post, it was situated on Meridian Hill, north of Washington.

FORT KEARNEY. A Civil War defense of Washington, Fort Kearney was built by Colonel Fowler's 15th New Jersey Regiment and was garrisoned during May 1864 by detachments of the 151st and 163rd Ohio National Guard. The fort, named for General Philip Kearney, who was killed at Chantilly, Virginia, on September 1, 1862, was situated between Forts Reno and DeRussy and served admirably as a connecting link between the two.

BATTERY KEMBLE. A Civil War defense of Washington, this battery was located on an elevation on Ridge Road (Nebraska Avenue), near Chain Bridge Road. It was named for Gouveneur Kemble of Cold Springs, New York, a former president of the West Point Foundry. The battery's two 100-pounder Parrott rifles were intended to sweep the Chain Bridge and the heights of Virginia beyond.

KENNEDY'S HILL FORT. This Washington defense during the Civil War was situated on the present site of Chaplin Street and Hilltop Terrace.

CAMP KEYSTONE. A Washington encampment during the Civil War, it was located near Tennallytown (Tenleytown), in the vicinity of present American University.

BATTERY KINGSBURY. A Civil War defense in Washington, all that is known is its general location, east of Fort DeRussy.

CAMP LACEY. A Civil War encampment in Washington, it was established in 1861.

CAMP LEACH. A temporary camp at American University, Washington, it was established late in 1917 for the training of specialized Army Engineers, and named in honor of Colonel Smith S. Leach. The 11-acre facility was subsequently used by Chemical Warfare. It was abandoned in January 1919 and ordered salvaged.

FORT LESLEY J. MCNAIR (*Fort at Turkey Buzzard; United States Arsenal at Greenleaf's Point; Washington Arsenal; United States Barracks; Washington Barracks; Army War College; Fort Humphreys*). An historic land area in the nation's capital, now known as Fort Lesley J. McNair, this site has a history of active military duty longer than most of today's active Army posts. It has grown from "28 acres, 2 roods and 31 poles" on Greenleaf's Point set aside by George Washington as a military reservation from the land acquired for the Federal City in 1790 to its present 89.5 acres through acquisition and by earth fill in areas once covered by marshes and shallow water.

Old records do not disclose the exact date of the first military work, but Major Pierre C. L'Enfant, designer of the Federal City, evidently intended it to be the site of a fort as a part of his

FORT LESLEY J. MCNAIR. (Courtesy of the U.S. Army.)

city plan for Washington. Several old maps, some as early as 1792, show the area as a military fortification. The first fortification here is believed to have been in 1794—a one-gun battery mounted behind earth breastworks. Major L'Enfant selected Greenleaf's Point as the site for a "great military works, to secure the city from invasion." First mention of the battery divulges that it was under the command of Captain Andrew J. Villiard, a Frenchman who had served under the Marquis de La Fayette during the American Revolution.

Once a narrow, irregular finger of land at the mouth of the Anacostia River where it empties into the Potomac, the post now has an almost quadrangular-shaped land area. It has a formal smooth contour bounded by sturdy stone seawalls along the waterfront and thick brick walls separating it from the city. A map of the area dated 1792 details Tiber Creek joined to St. James Creek by a canal. The canal and creek separated the southwest extremity of Washington City into Buzzard and Greenleaf's Points. Therefore, its first name, "Fort at Turkey Buzzard."

Throughout the years the post has had various names. Until it was named Washington Arsenal in 1857, it had been the United States Arsenal at Greenleaf's Point. In February 1881 it became United States Barracks, and later the same year, Washington Barracks. In 1927 it was redesignated Army War College. In 1935, in honor of Major General Andrew A. Humphreys, the post was redesignated Fort Humphreys. In 1939 it was again named Army War College. During World War II, for administrative convenience and since the command of the post was separate from the college, the titles Army War College (Post) and Army War College (School) were used. In 1948 the post was given the name now used in honor of the commander of the Army ground forces during World War II, Lieutenant General Lesley J. McNair, who was killed at Normandy, France, on July 25, 1944.

Three colleges now operate at Fort McNair—the National War College, the Industrial College of the Armed Forces, and the Inter-American Defense College. The first class at the National War College convened in August 1946. It produces government officials qualified through previous careful selection and a year's study at the College, to engage in the formulation and the implementation of national security policy, particularly in the politico-military field. The Industrial College of the Armed Forces conducts advanced courses of study in the economic and industrial aspects of national security, from the viewpoint of both national and world affairs. The Inter-American Defense College, which formally opened on October 9, 1962, is an advanced studies institute for senior officers of 19 member nations of the Inter-American Defense Board, with a curriculum including the study of the international situation and world blocks, the inter-American system and its role, strategic concepts of war, and a planning exercise for hemispheric defense.

FORT LINCOLN. Fort Lincoln is situated on an eminence, one of the first points fortified on Washington's northern line of defense commanding the Baltimore & Ohio Railroad and the Baltimore Turnpike, where Commodore Joshua Barney set up his guns in defense of Washington during August 1814. Fort Lincoln was named in honor of President Lincoln. The site is now occupied by the Boys' Industrial School. A bastioned fortification with four faces, Fort Lincoln was more than adequately armed, mounting two 8-inch siege-howitzers, six 32-pounder seacoast guns, one 24-pounder siege gun, three 24-pounder seacoast guns, four 12-pounder field guns, and eight 6-pounder field-guns *en barbette*, with two 24-pounder field howitzers *en embrasure*. In addition to these smoothbores, there were also a 100-pounder Parrott and four 20-pounder Parrotts.

LINCOLN BARRACKS. Lincoln Barracks was established sometime during the Civil War. No historical data has been found to precisely date or locate it.

CAMP LOCHIEL. A Civil War encampment, this post was situated on Red Hill in Washington's Georgetown section. Its site was formerly occupied by the Mt. Alto Hospital. The Signal Camp of Instruction moved into Camp Lochiel, completed it, and used it throughout the war.

LOWELL BARRACKS. Other than mention of this post in the National Archives Microcopy No. 617, "Returns from U.S. Military Posts, 1800–1916," as having been established in 1866, no other data on it has been located.

BATTERY MAHAN. A Washington defense during the Civil War, it stood to the rear of present 3938 Benning Road, near Minnesota Avenue.

BATTERY MANSFIELD. This Civil War defense stood about 125 yards north of 5100 Massachusetts Avenue.

FORT MANSFIELD. This Civil War fortification occupied the present site of 5110 Worthington Drive.

CAMP MARSHALL. A temporary Civil War encampment established in 1863.

BATTERY MARTIN SCOTT (*Fort Scott*). Constructed in August 1861, this Civil War defense stood on a bluff above the Chain Bridge and commanded the opposite Virginia shore. It mounted one 8-pounder howitzer and two 32-pounders. These guns were later replaced by two 6-pounder James rifles on field carriages.

FORT MASSACHUSETTS. FORT STEVENS.

CAMP MEAGHER. No historical data could be found on this temporary Civil War encampment.

CAMP MEIGS (*Camp Ordway*). Located within the city limits of Washington, Camp Meigs occupied about 81 acres of ground at Florida Avenue and 5th Street, N.E. It was named in honor of Major General Montgomery Meigs, quartermaster general of the Army, 1861–1882. The site was originally used for the mobilization of the National Guard and known as Camp Ordway. It was leased in September 1917 to serve as a training camp for special units of the Quartermaster Corps. Approximately 25,000 men passed through this camp. Designated as a separation center for the District of Columbia in November 1918, it discharged approximately 7,000 men by March 15, 1919. Camp Meigs was abandoned sometime in 1920.

FORT MEIGS. A major defense of Washington during the Civil War, having a perimeter of 500 yards, it was located on the north side of Bowen Road approximately midway between Bowen Avenue and Benning Road in the extreme eastern corner of the District. According to David V. Miller's *Defenses of Washington During the Civil War*, "The 1864 Military Map of Northeast Virginia shows this fort to be within the District Line," [but a] careful check of the Official Coast and Geodetic Survey map will show the fort to have been located" in Prince Georges County, Maryland. The fort was named for Major General Montgomery C. Meigs, quartermaster general of the Army. The fort had an auxiliary battery, called Redoubt Rucker, located at the intersection of Bowen Road and Benning Road, and linked to the main work by a covered way.

BATTERY MORRIS. A defense of Washington during the Civil War, Battery Morris was located at the southeast corner of Rhode Island Avenue and 20th Street, north of Fulton Place.

CAMP OHIO. A temporary Civil War post established in 1863, it was located some six miles from Tennallytown (Tenleytown), in the District of Columbia.

CAMP ORDWAY. CAMP MEIGS.

BATTERY PARROT. The site of this defense of Washington is located at present 2300 Foxhall Road. A few remains are still evident on the site.

FORT PENNSYLVANIA. FORT RENO.

CAMP RAPP. A temporary post established during the Civil War, it was located at "Kendall Green," in the northern suburbs of the city.

CAMP RELIEF. A temporary Civil War encampment, it was situated on 7th Street, N.W., probably in the vicinity of present Mt. Vernon Square.

BATTERY RENO. A defense of Washington during the Civil War, it was located at the intersection of Gramercy Road and 39th Street, N.W.

FORT RENO (*Fort Pennsylvania*). Located northeast of Tennallytown (Tenleytown), this major Civil War defense occupied a commanding position "at a point where the dividing ridge between the Potomac and Rock Creek narrows so as to expose the slopes in both directions. It commands the three roads which unite at Tenallytown." When originally built, it was called Fort Pennsylvania, but was renamed Fort Reno in honor of General Jesse Lee Reno who was killed in action at South Mountain, Virginia, in September 1862. When first constructed, the fort lacked a good view of the approaches from the north. Improvements, however, made the work much more strategically important. To strengthen the position, a battery for eight guns was constructed on an advanced point of the ridge, about 300 yards northward, with a magazine and an enclosed gorge. This was connected with the work by a double line of rifle-trenches, with a flanking battery. The fort's site is located at Nebraska Avenue and Grant Place, N.W.

REYNOLDS BARRACKS. The National Archives No. 617 Microcopy, "Returns from U.S. Military Posts, 1800–1916," very briefly noted that Reynolds Barracks was active during the 1866–68 period, without specifying where in the District of Columbia it was located.

FORT RICKETTS. A defense of Washington during the Civil War, this battery was intended to sweep the deep ravine in front of Fort Stanton. Its site is located at Fort Place and Bruce Place, S.E. The fortification was also called Rickett's Battery.

BATTERY (LEFT) ROCK CREEK. A defense built during the Civil War, its site is on West Ross Drive in Rock Creek Park, north central Washington. There is evident a large percentage of the battery's remains.

ROSSEL BATTERY. A Washington defense during the Civil War, Battery Rossel was a substantially constructed work designed for eight field guns and a magazine. It occupied the ground between Forts Reno and Kearney.

REDOUBT RUCKER. FORT MEIGS.

FORT SARATOGA. A minor Civil War work, Fort Saratoga was a lunette with a 100-foot-long face and a stockaded gorge, and served as the connecting link between Forts Bunker Hill and Lincoln. The site of the fort built early in the war lies in a recreational (horseshoe pitching) area in the center of the block behind 1821 Jackson Street, S.E.

FORT SCAGGS. A Civil War circular fortification, its site is located at present 3950 Ames Street, N.E.

CAMP SCOTT. CAMP WINFIELD SCOTT.

FORT SCOTT. BATTERY MARTIN SCOTT.

SEDGWICK BARRACKS. No archival information could be found on this apparently temporary Federal facility in Washington.

CAMP SHEARER. A temporary Civil War encampment, it was located near Fort Baker, east of the Anacostia River.

BATTERY SILL. A Federal-built defense, it was situated to the west of the end of Nicholson Avenue. Another battery, to the right of Battery Sill, was located at present 1615 Manchester Lane, N.W.

BATTERY SIMMONS. A Civil War defense, it occupied the ground at the present intersection of Bayard and Allen streets.

FORT SIMMONS. A defense of Washington, Fort Simmons occupied a site near the present intersection of Berkeley and Crescent streets.

CAMP SIMMS. A District of Columbia National Guard facility, it was most probably established during World War II. Camp Simms, a 24.4-acre tract in southeast Washington, was put up for sale by the Federal government during the summer of 1983. District officials were hopeful for a deal which would allow the development of a shopping center and low-income housing units at the site. The facility, idle for some time, has 18 low-rise brick and concrete-block structures, including two small office buildings, located in Congress Heights.

FORT SLEMMER. A small, but well-situated strategic fortification, armed with only three 32-pounder smoothbore guns and an eight-inch howitzer, Fort Slemmer's site is behind Marist College and in front of the St. Joseph Statue. The Civil War defense was named for Lieutenant Adam Jacoby Slemmer who gallantly refused to surrender Fort Pickens in Pensacola Bay after Florida seceded from the Union (he was promoted to Major, 16th Infantry, on May 14, 1861, for his resourcefulness). The 26th New York Infantry occupied Fort Slemmer in February 1862 and accomplished much toward the completion of its works.

FORT SLOCUM. This well-armed Civil War defense was located between Forts Stevens and Totten. It was constructed in the fall of 1861 by the men of the 2nd Rhode Island Regiment and named in honor of Colonel John S. Slocum, their commander, who was killed during the first Battle of Bull Run, July 21, 1861. The fort's armament consisted of 22 guns and three mortars. The site of Fort Slocum is near the intersection of Oglethorpe and 3rd streets, N.W.

BATTERY SMEAD. Situated in Washington's Rock Creek area, as were several other batteries, this Civil War defense was located at the present site of St. Johns College High School, with a portion of the fortification standing on the west side of the street approximately between 5420 and 5452 N.W. 27th Street. The battery was named in honor of Captain John R. Smead, 5th Artillery, who was killed on August 30, 1862, at Centreville, Virginia. The last remains of the battery, includ-

ing its magazine, were leveled by a bulldozer in April 1958.

FORT SNYDER. This Civil War defense was considered an outwork of considerable Fort Stanton and "guarded the head of one branch of the ravine." It was located in the vicinity of Fort Place, S.E.

CAMP SPRAGUE. A temporary Civil War encampment established in 1861, it was occupied by the 1st Rhode Island Infantry.

FORT STANTON. Major General J. G. Barnard's report on Washington's defenses delineates Fort Stanton's strategic importance: "Fort Stanton occupies the nearest point of the ridge to the Arsenal and Navy Yard, and overlooks Washington, the Potomac, and Eastern Branch. It is a work of considerable dimensions, well built, and tolerably well armed." The remnants of the fortification are still in evidence on Fort Place, S.E.

FORT STEVENS (*Fort Massachusetts*). The outbreak of the Civil War in the spring of 1861 found the nation's capital without adequate defenses. The presence of Confederate forces

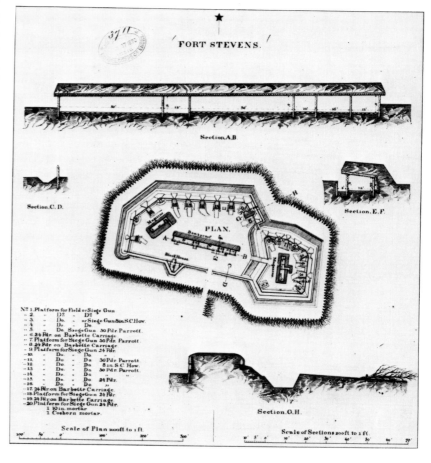

FORT STEVENS. (Courtesy of the National Archives.)

across the Potomac in Virginia finally dictated the need of large scale defenses. Records indicate that during the period 1861–65 a great ring of forts, batteries, and rifle trenches were constructed around the entire perimeter of the District of Columbia, with the addition of fortifications in adjacent areas of Maryland and Virginia. One of the earliest major forts built was Fort Massachusetts in August 1861 along the 7th Street Road (Brightwood Avenue) to defend the principal approach to the capital from the north. It was constructed by General D. N. Couch's forces composed of the 7th and 10th Massachusetts, the 2nd Rhode Island, and the 36th New York regiments.

It was later determined that Fort Massachusetts was inadequate as originally built. It was substantially enlarged in early 1863 and armed with mostly 24-pounder guns and mortars, in addition to five 30-pounder Parrott rifled guns. It was then renamed Fort Stevens in honor of Brigadier General Isaac Ingalls Stevens who was killed in action at Chantilly, Virginia, during the late summer of 1862. Fort Stevens was subjected to the brunt of the major Confederate attack, led by General Jubal Early, on July 11 and 12, 1864. Although powerfully built, the fort was undermanned. The opportune arrival of reinforcements, however, compelled General Early to abandon his attempt to capture Washington. President Lincoln stood on the fort's parapet watching the battle, much to the discomfort of Union officers present. This is the only known occasion when an American President was under fire of enemy guns while in office. Union losses at Fort Stevens numbered 72 killed and 207 wounded, with 40 of the dead, mostly from New York and Massachusetts, buried in Battleground Cemetery, established in 1864. Monuments were later erected here in honor of the men who participated in the battle to preserve the nation's capital.

In 1937–38, Fort Stevens was partially restored by the National Park Service with the assistance of Civilian Conservation Corps (CCC) labor. The fort's eastern magazine is now occupied by Emory Chapel; the western magazine, however, was reconstructed. Fort Stevens Park is located at Piney Branch Road (13th Street) and Quackenbos Street, N.W.

CAMP STONEMAN. A cavalry depot during the Civil War, it was located on Giesboro Point on the Potomac. The site is now incorporated within the Bolling Air Force Base, just south of Washington's U.S. Naval Station.

CAMP STONEMAN. A temporary encampment established during the Civil War, it was situated on Meridian Hill near 7th Street, N.W.

CAMP SULLIVAN. A temporary Civil War encampment.

CAMP TENNALLY. A temporary encampment established during the Civil War, it was situated in Tennallytown (Tenleytown), northwest Washington.

BATTERY TERRILL. This Civil War defense was located to the north of Fort Kearney's site. The remains of Battery Terrill are within a circular drive in front of the Peruvian Embassy on Garrison Street, just above Scott Circle. The battery was named in honor of Brigadier General William R. Terrill, who was killed at Perryville, Kentucky, on October 8, 1862.

FORT THAYER. Fort Thayer, a Civil War defense, was a minor work forming a connecting link between Forts Bunker Hill and Lincoln. It was a lunette located to control a spacious ravine that could offer cover to an approaching enemy. The fort was named in honor of Colonel Sylvanius Thayer, an engineering expert, who was called the "father" of the United States Military Academy. The site of the fort is located south of Irving Street between 24th and 25th streets, S.E. There was also a battery to the right of Fort Thayer at the intersection of Irving Street and South Dakota Avenue.

TODD BARRACKS. Reportedly a Civil War facility in Washington, nothing has been found to substantiate its existence.

FORT TOTTEN. At the end of the Civil War in April 1865, Washington's defenses consisted of 68 enclosed forts and batteries, with an aggregate perimeter of 13 miles, armed with 807 guns and 98 mortars mounted. There were emplacements for 1,120 guns, 93 unarmed batteries for field guns, 35,711 yards of rifle trenches, and three blockhouses surrounding the nation's capital. This front extended for 37 miles, with 32 miles of military roads. One of Washington's more important defenses was Fort Totten, begun in August 1861 to command the approaches to the capital from the north. Named in honor of General Joseph G. Totten, chief of engineers, the fort occupied a high point in advance of the Soldiers' Home. The fort's total armament consisted of two 8-inch howitzers, three 30-pounder Parrott rifles, eight 32-pounder seacoast Columbiads, four 6-pounder James rifles, one 10-inch siege mortar, one 24-pounder Coehorn mortar, and one 100-pounder Parrott rifle that was emplaced to sweep the sector from Fort DeRussy to Fort Lincoln. The fort was also furnished with a number of magazines and bombproofs. Fort Totten's site is enclosed within Fort Totten Park on Fort Place, off North Capitol Street. Also inside the park are the remains of Battery Totten.

FORT AT TURKEY BUZZARD. FORT LESLEY J. MCNAIR.

UNITED STATES ARSENAL AT GREEN-LEAF'S POINT. FORT LESLEY J. MCNAIR.

UNITED STATES BARRACKS. FORT LESLEY J. MCNAIR.

BATTERY VERMONT. The site of this Civil War defense is located at or near the intersection of Palisades Lane and Manning Place, N.W.

FORT WAGNER (*Fort Good Hope*). A defense of Washington, Fort Wagner's site is within the grounds of the Stanton School, bounded by Alabama Avenue, Good Hope Road, and 25th Street.

WASHINGTON ARSENAL. FORT LESLEY J. MCNAIR.

WASHINGTON BARRACKS. FORT LESLEY J. MCNAIR.

WASHINGTON POST. This post was situated at the nation's capital, on the right bank of the Potomac River. It was almost entirely garrisoned by elements of the 8th Infantry. Companies F and G were here in 1861; companies B, F, and G in 1862; and the entire regiment in 1864.

CAMP WINFIELD SCOTT (*Camp Scott*). Only the location of this Civil War encampment was gleaned from archival references, placing it at "Franklin Square."

WISEWELL BARRACKS. A Civil War facility, location and dates are unknown.

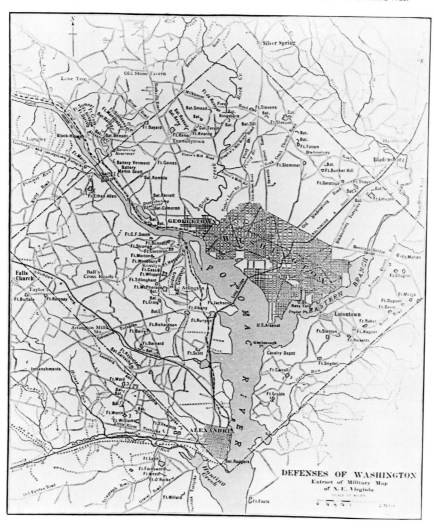

Defenses surrounding Washington during the Civil War. (Courtesy of the National Park Service.)

CAMP NEAR ADAMS. According to National Archives records, this temporary post was established sometime in January 1827 by Captain Francis L. Dade, with Company K, 4th Infantry. Another citation reports that four companies of the 4th Infantry and one company of the 4th Artillery, aggregating 58 men, garrisoned the camp during February. "Adams," reportedly between "Fort Duval, East Florida and Tallahassee," has not been identified.

FORT (T. B.) ADAMS. Located on the north bank of the Caloosahatchee River in Hendry County, opposite Fort Denaud, this short-lived post was established on December 5, 1838, by Company K, 1st Infantry. Later in the same month, the post's garrison was augmented by the addition of seven companies of the 2nd Infantry, with Captain Abercrombie in command. Apparently Fort T. B. Adams was not garrisoned after the spring of 1839.

ADDISON BLOCKHOUSE. FORT DUNCAN McRae.

ADVANCED REDOUBT (*Fort Redoubt*). Beginning in 1829 the U.S. Army Corps of Engineers' coastal defense program reached Pensacola, and during the next 15 years Fort Pickens (1829–34), Fort McRee (1834–39), and Fort Barrancas (1839–44) were constructed. These fortifications were designed to protect the new Navy Yard (now Naval Air Station Pensacola), Pensacola Harbor, and the city of Pensacola itself. In 1845 the last link in this chain was begun 1,000 yards north of Fort Barrancas. Because it was built to protect the rear of Fort Barrancas from land attack it was called "The Advanced Redoubt of Fort Barrancas."

"Redoubt," as this bastion came to be known, was not developed in the orderly progression enjoyed by the earlier forts. First, the lack of funds plagued the project. Later the Civil War drained off both labor and money. Then the fall of Fort Pulaski on Cockspur Island, Georgia, to Federal rifled cannon in 1862 rendered masonry fortifications obsolete, thus dooming Redoubt to be forever incomplete. The project was officially abandoned in 1870.

During the next 50 years, Redoubt moldered under the advancing mat of vegetation, and by the 1920s it was all but invisible. WPA workers during the 1930s cleared away the plant and tree growth and restored several portions of the fort. The bright red brick of the Redoubt was again very much in evidence. In 1971 Congress

Florida

authorized the establishment of Gulf Islands National Seashore as a unit of the National Park System. A portion of the Seashore includes the 48 acres at the Naval Air Station Pensacola, on which Fort Barrancas and the Advanced Redoubt are located. In 1975 a waterproofing contractor was employed to stabilize and waterproof large areas of Redoubt. Hand-made brick and well-researched historical construction methods were used during the project. In the summer of 1976, the Youth Conservation Corps began whitewashing the interior of the newly stabilized fortification. Redoubt is once more ready for the march of many feet over its drawbridge.

FORT ALABAMA. FORT FOSTER.

FORT ALAFIA. Located about 20 miles from Tampa Bay and 4 miles west of the Polk County line in Hillsborough County, Fort Alafia was established on August 29, 1849, by 1st Lieutenant and Brevet Major John C. Pemberton, 4th Artillery, with companies A and E. On May 9 the post was moved one mile closer to Tampa and nearer the Alafia River. Companies A and G, 7th Infantry, were then its garrison. On October 25, 1850, the artillery contingent then garrisoning the post was ordered to Key West, apparently abandoning the post. Although called Fort Alafia, it was never so designated officially.

FORT ALAQUA. This blockhouse, situated one mile south of present Portland, Walton County, was built in 1836 or 1837 near the mouth of Alaqua Creek, during the height of the Creek Indian war in West Florida. The fort was for a time commanded by Colonel George Hawkins of Marianna who was wounded in one of the battles fought near the blockhouse.

FORT ALLIGATOR (*Fort Lancaster*). During the Second Seminole War, seven or more forts were built at various times in the area of Columbia County. Fort Alligator, named for its proximity to Chief Alligator's village, was built in 1835 at the then-named town of Alligator. The defense, also called Fort Lancaster, stood on the site of the present northeast corner of Madison and Marion streets in Lake City. The fort's alternate calling was named for Captain Joseph B. Lancaster of the Florida Volunteers.

CAMP AMELIA. With the outbreak of the Spanish-American War, Fernandina once again entered the military picture. Although never quite completed, Fort Clinch and its surrounding reservation land were occupied by some 10,000 volunteers. Located on Amelia Island, Camp Amelia was established as a temporary post to accommodate the overflow of recruits.

AMELIA ISLAND BLOCKHOUSE. After establishing Savannah, General James Edward Oglethorpe turned his attention southward and constructed a number of fortifications in opposition to the Spaniards in Florida. Among the fortified posts was the blockhouse he had built on Amelia Island and garrisoned with Darien Highlanders, in preparation for his invasion of the Spanish province.

FORT ANCHUSA. This Spanish fort located at the entrance of Pensacola Bay, near the present site of Fort Barrancas, was built in 1696 by Count Don Andres de Arriola pursuant to royal instructions in order to protect the territory from French encroachments. It was a square bastioned work enclosing a few dwellings. It was named Anchusa from the ancient name given Pensacola Bay (doubtless from the *anchusa*, or cowslip, a plant that abounded in the vicinity). Captured by the French in May, 1719, Fort Anchusa was recaptured by the Spaniards the following month, only to be recaptured by the French in September. The fort and the surrounding territory reverted to Spain by the treaty of 1721. No indication has been found to establish when the fort was abandoned or destroyed.

FORT ANDREWS. Located four miles southwest of Hampton Springs on the Suwannee River in Taylor County, Fort Andrews was intermittently occupied from December 1838, when it was originally established, to May 25, 1840. Its first garrison consisted of a detachment drawn from companies A, F, and I, 6th Infantry, which withdrew several weeks later. The post was reoccupied on March 2, 1839, by Company I, 6th Infantry, commanded by Lieutenant H. W. Wharton. By Special Orders No. 2, dated May 25, 1840, the garrison was removed to Fort Gamble because of widespread sickness among the troops. The post was most probably named for Captain George Andrews. Shortly after the fort was evacuated, the Indians came and burned everything left behind.

FORT ANN. A Second Seminole War fort, Fort Ann was established by 1st Lieutenant James R. Irwin with one company of the 1st Artillery in November, 1837. Named by Irwin for "the prettiest girl in Pennsylvania," the post was situated at the Haulover, a narrow neck of land between the Mosquito Lagoon and the Indian River, the portage where Indians and traders hauled their watercraft to change water passage. The fort had been intended to control use of this portage. Fort Ann was abandoned in April, 1838. Its site is now part of the NASA Reservation, Titusville. During the Civil War, two small Union camps were established on either side of the Indian River at the Seminole War sites of Fort Ann and Camp Hernandez. The camps remained until the collapse of the Confederacy.

FORT ANNUTTEELIGA. A temporary fort erected during the Second Seminole War, this post was probably located about halfway between Tampa Bay and the Withlacoochee River, a few miles north of Brooksville, in what is now Hernando County. Established on November 30, 1840, by companies D, F, G, and K, 6th Infantry, Captain William Hoffman commanding, the fort was intended to check Indian hostilities in the area and to protect settlers in the event of an Indian attack. On March 25, 1841, companies F, G, and K were ordered from the post, leaving Company D to garrison it. On May 2, 1841, the post was abandoned, in compliance with Special Orders No. 30, Headquarters Army of Florida, dated April 25, 1841. The post took its name from the Indian name for the hammock near which it was located.

CAMP APALACHICOLA. After Federal naval forces scored successes in the Gulf of Mexico, recapturing Confederate-held ports, including the mouth of the Apalachicola River in early April 1862, it was decided to establish a military post at Apalachicola to command the bay and the entrance to the river. The 161st New York Infantry and the 82nd Colored Infantry were selected for this purpose, to leave Mobile with a stop en route at Pensacola. The Confederate defenders had left to fight at Shiloh, along with the body called north from Pensacola, which in turn was taken early the following month.

FORT APALACHICOLA. FORT GADSDEN.

APALACHICOLA ARSENAL (*United States Arsenal; Mt. Vernon Arsenal; Chattahoochee Arsenal*). The structural nucleus of the Florida State Hospital is a group of substantial buildings originally erected in a wilderness by the United States Government to serve as an arsenal for the storage of arms and ammunition. The four-acre brick-walled arsenal enclosure is situated to the north of Highway 90 in the town of Chattahoochee, Gadsden County.

The arsenal was authorized in 1832 but not completed for several years. The work appears to have made steady progress, despite difficulties encountered in retaining artisans in the face of the high wages being paid in the boom towns of Apalachicola and St. Joseph. On October 6, 1837, its building superintendent, 1st Lieutenant John Williamson of the 1st Artillery, stated that the work had progressed sufficiently so that the facility would be available at short notice for the purpose intended, and that the remaining buildings would be completed during the coming winter. Apparently the arsenal was in full operation by the spring of 1838.

On January 6, 1861, four days before Florida formally seceded from the Union, the Quincy Guards, a militia force, proceeded to the Apalachicola River and seized the Federal arsenal at Chattahoochee, then containing one six-pounder iron cannon, 5,122 pounds of powder, 57 flintlocks, and some 173,000 cartridges, although much higher figures, unsubstantiated, had been quoted. The Confederacy then operated the facility as a "Camp of Instruction" for thousands of recruits. At war's end, the Federal government transferred the arsenal from the Ordnance Bureau to the Freedman's Bureau in 1866. A bill was introduced at the 2nd session of the 41st Congress to donate the arsenal to the State of Florida for educational purposes. This was approved on December 15, 1870, about a year after the arsenal was to be used as a prison, although it was then judged to be in almost complete disrepair, vandalized by both sides during the war. Between 1870 and 1876, when the facility was transformed into a mental institution, the great deal of repair and renovation was performed on the arsenal's structures.

Of the four extramural structures, only the arsenal's large magazine survives. The vaulted magazine, with walls 5 feet thick, had originally but a single entrance on the south side and, at a distance of 20 feet, was entirely surrounded by a brick wall about 15 feet high. The magazine's original hip roof was replaced by a flat concrete roof, and new entrances have been cut on the north and east sides of the enclosing wall, which in addition is now pierced by numerous windows. The Florida State Hospital is one of the largest institutions of its kind in the United States. Many improvements and additions were made to the complex in the course of many years.

The arsenal, when first authorized, had been designated United States Arsenal. During its construction it was renamed Mt. Vernon Arsenal for the small adjacent community that had been so named in 1832 when it was given a post office. Then the facility was redesignated Chattahoochee

Arsenal for the town in which it was located. Finally, it was renamed Apalachicola Arsenal because of its close proximity to the Apalachicola River.

FORT ARBUCKLE. A Third Seminole War fort established on January 23, 1850, Fort Arbuckle was located at the northeast end of Lake Arbuckle, about a mile east of Frostproof, Polk County. Its site is now within the Avon Park Bombing Range.

FORT ARBUCKLE. A temporary Third Seminole War post, it was located on Lake Ishtopogah, 12 miles east of Fort Clinch and 75 miles east of Tampa Bay, in Highlands County. Reportedly established on January 23, 1850—a date coincident with the establishment of Polk County's Fort Arbuckle—by Company H, 1st Artillery, and Company K, 7th Infantry, it was probably named in honor of Colonel Matthew Arbuckle, 7th Infantry. The post was occupied by the same troops until May 16, 1850, when it was abandoned.

CAMP ARMISTEAD. If this Seminole War post ever existed, it was probably a short-lived outpost on the trail between Fort Armistead, farther to the south, and Fort Brooke. The latitude and longitude shown for the post in the Army's list of Florida forts plots it on an island in the Braden River, Manatee County.

FORT ARMISTEAD. A substantial Seminole War Army installation, headquarters of the 1st Infantry Regiment and the military district of Southwest Florida for about six months in 1840 and 1841, it was established at Sarasota on November 13, 1840, by companies A, C, F, I, and K, 1st Infantry, commanded by Major G. Dearborn. The post was named for Colonel and Brevet Major General W. K. Armistead, 3rd Artillery, commander of the Army's forces in Florida. The post's garrison in April 1841 consisted of 11 Field and Staff officers, companies A to K of the 1st Infantry, with 15 officers, aggregating 483 men, and Troop F of the 2nd Dragoons, with three officers, aggregating 59 men.

The Sarasota post was hurriedly abandoned on May 5, 1841, because of the incidence of a yellow fever epidemic, complicated by acute diarrhea and typhoid fever, which swept through the garrison killing many of its soldiers. Nearly half of 476 survivors were ill and unfit for duty. The garrison was withdrawn and sent to Horse Key in the Cedar Keys group to regain its strength. Fort Armistead's precise site is not known but local historians believe that a part of the military installation was located near the present intersection of Coconut Avenue and 5th Street, east of the Municipal Auditorium, in Sarasota.

CAMP ARMSTRONG. CAMP SMEAD.

FORT ARMSTRONG. A temporary Army fort established on December 18, 1836, located on the site of the Dade Massacre, it was a short distance east of the Withlacoochee River, about 50 miles northeast of Tampa Bay, in what is now Sumter County. According to data in the Adjutant General's Office, the post had been established in the autumn and not in the winter of 1836. It was established by a brigade of Tennessee Volunteers under the command of Colonel Robert Armstrong and apparently served as a rendezvous for troops arriving in that vicinity during the winter of 1836–37. In the spring of the last-named year the post was abandoned.

FORT ARRIOLA. Situated on Deer Point, the westernmost tip of the peninsula where the town of Gulf Breeze is located in Santa Rosa County, Fort Arriola was a gun battery built and manned by Confederate forces sometime in December 1861. Colonel Harvey Brown, commanding the Union troops at Fort Pickens, wrote Brigadier General Lorenzo Thomas, adjutant general, that for the past several weeks the Confederates had been constructing a battery there, and were emplacing 10-inch Columbiad guns in it. The battery apparently was abandoned in early May 1862, when the Confederates evacuated Pensacola.

FORT ARRUINADO. The name of this Spanish-built fortification located at the entrance to Pensacola Bay is variously phonetically spelled. One historical chronologist believes the small fort was located on the east end of Santa Rosa Island. It was no doubt an auxiliary to Fort Barrancas. Several old Spanish maps, particularly one drawn in 1787, describe the fort as a *redoubt de la Bateria de campagnia*. Notes in the file of Florida forts in the library of the University of South Florida, describe a "Fort Arunado (Arunnado, Ayenlade)" at the east end of Santa Rosa Island, with its establishment taking place in 1719. The fort's name is no doubt derived from the Spanish word *arruinar* ("to destroy").

FORT ASPALAGA. FORT BARBOUR.

FORT ATKINSON. A temporary Army post during the Second Seminole War, located on the Suwannee River in the northeast corner of

Lafayette County, about a mile from the town of Day and three miles west of old Charles' Ferry, it was established on January 18, 1839, by Company C, 6th Infantry, Lieutenant James Monroe commanding. The post was named in honor of Colonel Henry Atkinson, 6th Infantry. The same troops occupied the fort until July 6, 1839, when it was abandoned.

CAMP AUGUSTA. According to "A Map of the Seat of War in Florida, 1836," this post was established on the west side of the St. Johns River, opposite Picolata, in Clay County. No specific date has been found for this post.

FORT AULD LANG SYNE. FORT DRANE.

FORT AYACHIN. According to Chatelain's *Defenses of Spanish Florida, 1565 to 1763*, Puente's map of 1769 shows to the south and west of Fort Mosa a work which may have been Fort Ayachin, which is located on at least one map of the late Spanish period at the edge of the marsh that faces the St. Marks or Tolomato River. It was earlier recorded by the Spanish engineer, Pedro Ruiz de Olano, in 1740, in a map entitled "Plano del Sitio de la Florida," a copy of which is in the Library of Congress.

FORT AYAVALIA. A Spanish-built fortification, established about 1700, it was located five miles northwest of Hampton Springs in Taylor County, "on the lower Aucilla river." Its site is now apparently covered by U.S. 98, according to available coordinates.

FORT AYS. A Spanish-built blockhouse erected about the year 1567, it was located one mile east of Oslo, Indian River County, an area once inhabited by the Ais Indians.

CAMP BAKER. John Jackson Dickison, Florida's noted Civil War Confederate guerrilla leader, bivouacked with his troops at Camp Baker, south of Waldo, Alachua County, during the closing weeks of the war.

FORT BANKHEAD. Located on Key Biscayne, Dade County, this post was established on April 5, 1838, after the evacuation of Fort Dallas, by Company C, 1st Artillery, commanded by Captain L. B. Webster. It was named in honor of Lieutenant Colonel James Bankhead, 3rd Artillery. Occupied for only a short time by the artillerymen, it was abandoned in May, 1838. The famous 2nd Dragoons, commanded by Lieutenant Colonel William S. Harney, were next to occupy

the fort, a large parade ground with rows of tents enclosed by a wooden stockade, established in the shadows of the old Cape Florida Lighthouse. The dragoons broke camp for the last time sometime in August 1842, but two Navy schooners, the *Wave* and the *Phoenix*, remained until 1844 to aid stricken vessels wrecked on the reef.

FORT BARBOUR (*Fort Aspalaga*). A Second Seminole War post, Fort Barbour was established May 16, 1841, on the Apalachicola River near Aspalaga Landing, about four miles west of Greensboro, Gadsden County. It was named in honor of Major P. H. Barbour for his meritorious service in the war (the major was later killed on September 21, 1846, during the Battle of Monterey in Mexico). Fort Barbour was abandoned June 26, 1842.

FORT BARKER. This post was situated on the right bank of the Steinhatchee River, Lafayette County, about 20 miles from Fort Frank Brooke. Fort Barker was established February 1, 1840, by Major John Garland and abandoned on September 17, 1840.

FORT BARNWELL (*Fort Columbia*). Established March 21, 1836, on the east bank of the St. Johns River near its mouth, at Old Volusia, Volusia County, this post was named for the Barnwell district in South Carolina, where troops had been raised to fight in the Second Seminole War. The stockade was erected by Captain Elmore's Columbia Volunteers, and in compliment to them the post was also called Fort Columbia. It is not known when this Army post was abandoned.

FORT BARRANCAS (*Fort San Carlos de Austria; British Royal Navy Redoubt; Fort St. Charles; Fort San Carlos; Bateria de San Antonio; Water Battery; Fort San Carlos de Barrancas; Fort Siquenza; Fort Prince*). The history of fortifications on the *barranca* site goes back nearly three centuries to April 1693, when Spanish cartographer Don Carlos de Siguenza y Gongora entered Pensacola Bay to chart it for future settlement. Siguenza recognized the importance of the high bluff (named La Barranca de San Tomé) and declared, "There is no place better adapted for defending the entrance of the bay with necessary fortifications than Siguenza Point [site of present-day Fort Pickens on Santa Rosa Island] and Saint Thomas bluffs."

The complex history of the fortifications that once occupied the site of Pensacola's present

FORT BARRANCAS. The Spanish fort and the American fort on the barranca *site. (Courtesy of the Florida State Archives.)*

Fort Barrancas and its near environs had for years confused both historians and history buffs. Nearly identical Spanish names, anglicized variously by British and American occupants and aggravated by the multiplicity of names and dates labeling many engineering drawings and maps, further deepened the confusion.

Carlos II was the last of the Hapsburg kings in Spain. For nearly two centuries (1516–1700) the Austrian Hapsburg family ruled Spain, and when a colonial fortification was established near Pensacola in 1698–99, the new fort was named San Carlos de Austria to honor the Hapsburg ruler. A score of years later, France and Spain were at war and additional colonial defenses were erected. In 1719 the Spanish built a rudimentary stockaded fort on Siguenza Point at the west end of Santa Rosa Island and named it Principe de Asturias ("Prince of Asturias," for the old province in northeast Spain). Although not on the mainland in the vicinity of Fort Barrancas, the Asturias fort is included within this chronological exposition to illustrate its similarity in nomenclature to the first named defense, both of which were captured and razed by the French in 1719 during the colonial war for domination in the Gulf region. (Fort Pickens, built in 1829–34, occupies the site of Fort Principe de Asturias).

Strategic Pensacola, with its excellent harbor, was retroceded to Spanish control in 1722, then turned over to England in 1763 at the end of the French and Indian War (the Seven Years' War), only to be regained by the Spanish by the force of arms in 1781. During the 1790s a new San Carlos fort was built by the Spanish, standing west of the site of the 1796 Bateria de San Antonio (Water Battery), in front of later erected Fort Barrancas. To the rear of the battery and on the bluff, the Spanish then constructed a log-and-earth fortification named San Carlos, situated within the ditch of the earlier British Royal Navy Redoubt, built in 1780. After the successful Spanish siege of Pensacola in 1781, the British forts were taken over and renamed. The British fort on the *barranca* was designated San Carlos (St. Charles).

In 1821 Florida was ceded to the United States. Little was left of the second Fort San Carlos, but the brick-built Bateria de San Antonio remained and was repaired by U.S. engineers in 1840. Fort Barrancas was next constructed (1839–44) on the site of Fort San Carlos with a brick-lined tunnel connecting it to the old Water Battery. To further confuse the issue of names, many engineer-drawn plans and maps label the combined work as Fort San Carlos de Barrancas. Still later, all existing works came to be popularly known as Fort Barrancas (the American work) and Fort San Carlos (the Spanish Bateria de San Antonio or Water Battery). The initial Spanish fortification, Fort San Carlos de Austria, was located to the east of these works; its site has not been firmly established.

Constructed in the shape of a parallelogram on the 30-foot-high bluff, 440 yards from the edge of the bay, 10-acre, brick-built Fort Barrancas formed the southern anchor of the land defense perimeter of the Navy Yard. All that remained was to build the northern anchor. This final work was to be the Advanced Redoubt of Fort Barrancas. Construction of the Redoubt dragged on over some 15 years, from 1845 to 1859, with several years seeing virtually no work accomplished due to the deprivation of appropriations during the Mexican War and subsequent years. By the Civil War, however, the fort was complete but without permanent platforms or the guns to place upon them. (See: ADVANCED REDOUBT.)

On January 10, 1861, Florida seceded from the Union to join what would soon become the new Southern Confederacy. Nearly all Federal property in the state was seized by secessionists, with a notable exception at Pensacola. A force of 50 United States regulars, under the command of Lieutenant Adam Slemmer, plus 30 sailors and two Navy ships, left the *barranca* forts and Navy Yard on the mainland and occupied Fort Pickens on Santa Rosa Island (see: FORT PICKENS). Rebel troops took control of all other installations in the area, but without Fort Pickens under their control, they could not effectively use the harbor and Navy Yard. An uneasy truce was negotiated between North and South to forestall bloodshed. When the Civil War finally began in mid-April 1861, Fort Pickens was reinforced and supplied by sea, while the Confederate Army of Pensacola, some 8,000 strong, held a four-mile-long fortified position from Fort McRee to the Navy Yard. Over the long, hot summer of 1861, both sides labored to strengthen their defenses. Heat and disease took a heavy toll of the men.

In September Federals from the fleet raided the Navy Yard. In October Confederates raided the island, destroying the camp of the New York 6th Volunteer Infantry. On November 22 and 23, both sides engaged in an artillery duel exchanging some 6,000 shot and shell over the bay. Neither side suffered extensively, although fires compelled the rebels temporarily to abandon Fort McRee. Fort Barrancas had its flagstaff shot away and its walls slightly scarred, but casualties were light due to the strong walls and long range. A second bombardment on January 1, 1862, was equally ineffective in driving the antagonists from their defenses. In May 1862 the Confederates pulled out of Pensacola to strengthen other field armies and Union forces reoccupied all the harbor installations. Fort Barrancas would see no further combat.

After the war, Fort Barrancas was used only intermittently, with its troops garrisoned at Barrancas Barracks, established in the early 1850s, a quarter of a mile to the east. Army garrisons occupied the post continuously until the end of World War II when the harbor defenses were declared surplus to national security needs. In 1971 Fort Barrancas was transferred to the National Park Service, which undertook the restoration of the fort and Water Battery in 1978–80. The restoration required 90,000 new bricks at a cost of $1,200,000. Old Fort Barrancas is now contained within the reservation grounds of the Naval Air Station, established in 1914. There are 11 guns on exhibit at Fort Barrancas, none of them mounted. They are of English, Spanish, French, and American origin and all but the U.S. Seacoast 42-pounder are naval pieces. Today's Gulf Islands National Seashore encompasses all of Pensacola's surplus military and active naval installations.

FORT BARRINGTON. A temporary fortification erected by the British during their early occupation of Florida, it was established in 1765 near King's Ferry on the St. Marys River, Nassau County.

FORT BASINGER. A Second Seminole War fort established December 23, 1837, by Colonel Zachary Taylor, it was named for Lieutenant William E. Basinger, 2nd Artillery, who was killed in the Dade Massacre. It was situated on the west bank of the Kissimmee River, 17 miles above its mouth at Lake Okeechobee. Serving as a temporary supply post in the chain of forts extending from Tampa to Lake Okeechobee during Taylor's campaign against the Indians in the region, Fort Basinger consisted of a pine-log palisade, with blockhouses and lookout towers in the northwest and southeast angles. The fort was abandoned at the end of the war. Its name survives in the town of Fort Basinger, Highlands County, a mile and a half from the site of the fort.

BATERIA DE SAN ANTONIO. FORT BARRANCAS.

BATTERY POINT FORT. A Confederate-built fortification established during the Civil War to guard the passage of the Apalachicola River, Battery Point is located one-half mile from the Torreya State Park entrance. On the point are the remains of old entrenchments, gun emplacements, pits, and an ammunition magazine. Steel tracks, still embedded in the river's clay bank, served to convey donkey carts, which hauled freight from the landing.

FORT BATTON ISLAND. Situated opposite the town of Mayport and the mouth of the St. Johns River, Batton Island was the site of a small fort or blockhouse built by the Spanish about the year 1567 to guard Fort San Mateo against a surprise attack from the sea. The fort was apparently attacked and destroyed by Dominique de Gourgues in 1568 as part of his revenge for the slaughter of the French Huguenots by the Spanish at Fort Caroline.

FORT BAYARD. The only notices of this military post appear on John Lee Williams' "Map of Florida," 1837, marked as "Bayard," almost coincident with an unnamed fort on the 1843 "Map of the Seat of War" by Humphreys and McClelland. The map coordinates would place "Fort Bayard" opposite Picolata in Clay County.

CAMP BEAUREGARD. Confederate forces commanded by General Joseph Finegan went into permanent camp on February 13, 1864, at Camp Beauregard, near Olustee on Ocean Pond, a few miles east of Lake City and about 50 miles west of Jacksonville. The Confederates at once threw up entrenchments at this campsite selected by the general because of its protected position between two small lakes, with each flank protected by marsh and open water. Finegan's total effective force consisted of some 4,600 infantry, less than 600 cavalry, and 12 guns manned by artillerymen.

FORT BIENVENUE. A temporary Army post during the Third Seminole War, Fort Bienvenue, also known as "southern Fort Alafia," was established sometime in January 1850. Both posts, about one mile apart, were located about four miles west of the Polk County line in Hillsborough County.

BATTERY BIGELOW. FORT DADE (Tampa Bay).

FORT BIRCH. Apparently a temporary Army post established on or about March 5, 1839, it was located on Lake Ashby, about 15 miles west of New Smyrna in Volusia County. A map, drawn by Lieutenant J. W. Phelps, 2nd Artillery, shows the fort situated on the west side of the lake and on the east side of the road to Fort Mellon.

BLACK CREEK ARSENAL. FORT HEILEMAN.

CAMP BLANDING. A major Army training post during World War II, now a state-operated post for the training of the Florida National Guard, Army reservists, and regular Army units, it is located in Clay County, 10 miles east of Starke and 20 miles southwest of Jacksonville. The 125,194-acre reservation, named for Lieutenant General Albert H. Blanding in 1939, provided extended field training for seven infantry divisions and three field artillery brigades, in addition to the basic training of two infantry divisions. A postwar utilization study by the Corps of Engineers, dated September 1945, determined that the post was unsatisfactory for use as a permanent post, principally because of poor housing.

CAMP BLODGETT. A temporary Army encampment on the west bank of the Withlacoochee River, Marion County, it was established on the site of Scott's battle, March 29, 1836.

FORT BLOUNT. The earliest recorded settlement of the area that is now the city of Bartow in Polk County took place in October 1851, when Riley R. Blount, a native of Beaufort, South Carolina, with his family and a number of black slaves, some 21 persons in all, established residence a mile west of today's court house. First known as Pease Creek, the community's name was changed to Fort Blount after the settlers erected a blockhouse as a defense against the Indians during the Third Seminole War. The town's name was changed in 1867 to Bartow in honor of Confederate General Francis Bartow, the first general on either side to be killed in the Civil War. The site of the blockhouse is believed to be in the immediate vicinity of the intersection of Church Street and Floral Avenue. In February 1975 it was announced that a Bicentennial project of a library/museum would be established at the site of Fort Blount.

BLOUNT'S FORT. A temporary Army post named for Seminole Chief John Blount, established sometime during the Second Seminole War, it was located on the east bank of the Suwannee River, about two miles from the Georgia line, in Columbia County.

FORT BLUE SPRINGS. FORT NO. 13 (East Florida).

FORT (VIRGINIA) BRADEN. Located 16 to 18 miles southwest of Tallahassee at "Holland" on the Ocklockonee River, Fort Braden was established on December 31, 1839, by 1st Lieutenant S. B. Thornton with Company G, 2nd (Howe's) Dragoons. Post returns call this post Fort Virginia Braden. In February 1840 the post was commanded by Captain S. Eastman, 1st Infantry, with Company G. A month later, it was commanded by Lieutenant C. A. May, 2nd Dragoons. The post was abandoned on June 7, 1842, and its troops are believed to have moved to Camp Wardell.

"FORT" BRADEN CASTLE. Located near the confluence of the Manatee and Braden rivers in Manatee County, Braden Castle was built by one of the region's most prominent sugar plantation owners, Virginia-born Dr. Joseph Addison Braden. Construction of his massive tabby-built mansion began in 1845 on his 1,100-acre plantation. The two-story edifice, with four chimneys and eight fireplaces, often served as a refuge for the area's settlers during the Third Seminole War and was attacked on more than one occasion. The property was engulfed by fire in 1903, leaving nothing but the crumbling walls of the mansion and ruins of a nearby sugar mill.

FORT BRADY. The only notice found of this apparent Army post appeared on an 1839 Florida war map.

BRANCH'S FORT. This fort came into being during the Indian scare of 1849 and probably consisted of a fortified homestead built by Dr. Franklin Branch. It was located near the Manatee River at the foot of present 13th Street East in Bradenton, Manatee County.

CAMP BRENNAN. No location could be found for this short-lived Army post. According to National Archives records, it was situated somewhere in "Middle Florida" and was established in January 1842 by Captain Gustavus Dorr, 6th Infantry, with Company A, in compliance with Special Orders, dated December 15, 1841, issued at Tampa. The troops were apparently here for less than a month.

CAMP BRISBANE. During the Second Seminole War, U.S. troops took possession of General Joseph M. Hernandez's plantation called St. Joseph's, located on the Matanzas River in St. Johns County, and fortified its buildings.

BRISTOL BLOCKHOUSE. The only reference to this defense, apparently built by settlers, indicates that it was located in the town of Bristol, Liberty County.

BRITISH FORT. FORT GADSDEN.

BRITISH ROYAL NAVY REDOUBT. FORT BARRANCAS.

FORT BROADNAX. A Second Seminole War fort, it was established on March 28, 1836, by Colonel William Lindsay and located north of Brooksville, near Floral City, Citrus County. The post was named for an Army inspector general in Florida, Captain John H. Broadnax.

FORT BROOKE. The first settlement of the present city of Tampa was made on January 20, 1824, with the construction of a log fort by four companies of the 4th Infantry, commanded by Colonel George Brooke, in compliance with orders dated November 5, 1823, Office of the Adjutant General, Washington, D.C. Known originally as Cantonment Brooke until 1835 and thereafter as Fort Brooke, it was situated near the mouth of the Hillsborough River at the head of Tampa Bay. The post was established after the Treaty of Camp Moultrie had provided for a reservation for the Seminoles in south-central Florida in 1823.

FORT BROOKE. (Courtesy of the Florida State Archives.)

A principal post during the Second Seminole War, it became a rendezvous for friendly Indians and an embarkation point from which Seminoles were removed westward to Indian Territory.

Leaving from Fort Brooke and heading for Fort King near Ocala, Major Francis Dade and more than a hundred men of his command met death in the Wahoo Swamp near the Withlacoochee River on December 28, 1835. Fort Brooke served as the headquarters for General Edmund Gaines in 1836 during his Indian campaign. As late as 1841, the garrison's complements aggregated 680 officers and men. The post was regularly occupied until 1860. After the Civil War, Fort Brooke served as a seasonal camp for the garrison at Key West Barracks. The post was abandoned about December 21, 1882, in compliance with Special Orders No. 120, Department of the South, dated December 13, 1882. The site of Fort Brooke, on the southwest corner of Platt and Franklin streets, is indicated by a bronze plaque.

FORT (FRANK) BROOKE. Situated at Dead Man's Bay near the mouth of the Steinhatchee River and near Stephensville, Taylor County, the post was apparently established sometime in November 1838 and abandoned in June 1840.

FORT BROOKS. A temporary post established sometime during the Second Seminole War, it was situated on the left bank of the Ocklawaha River, north of the mouth of Orange Lake Creek, near Kenwood, Putnam County.

FORT BROOME. A Third Seminole War post named for Governor James E. Broome, Fort Broome was located about two miles southeast of Dade City, in a section then known as Tuckertown, in Pasco County.

CAMP BROWN. A temporary post established during the Civil War by Union forces when the New York 6th Zouave Volunteers arrived about June 26, 1861, Camp Brown was located on Santa Rosa Island, Pensacola Bay. In effect "Billy Wilson's Camp," the post was established by Colonel William Wilson, 6th New York Volunteers, with eight companies of men, apparently in mid-July. The post is presumed to have been named for Colonel Harvey Brown, then commanding at Fort Pickens. The camp and all its improvements were burned by the Confederates during the Battle of Santa Rosa Island. The Union troops then apparently moved into or nearer Fort Pickens. By May 1862, however, the unit moved to the mainland and occupied Pensacola, evacuated by the Confederate troops who were urgently needed in northern theaters of war.

FORT BROWN. Located on the St. Johns River, 10 miles east of Palatka, this temporary post was established on February 24, 1840, by 1st Lieutenant W. A. Brown, 3rd Artillery, with Company E. General Orders No. 45, September 19, 1840, ordered the abandonment of the fort and the occupation of Fort Searle at Picolata. The post was then abandoned on September 30, 1840.

CAMP BROWNE. A temporary post situated on Black Creek, near Palatka, probably in Putnam County, it was established on March 20, 1842, by Captain William Overton Kello, 8th Infantry, with Company C. The post was probably named in honor of General Jacob Browne, formerly "general-in-chief" of the Army. The post was abandoned sometime in August 1842.

FORT BUCKEYE. Very little is known of this temporary post. It was apparently established prior to 1850 near Steinhatchee Springs in Lafayette County. Fort Buckeye is marked on several maps as being located at Latitude 29 degrees, 48 minutes, Longitude 83 degrees, 15 minutes.

FORT BUENA VISTA. Situated on the east side of the St. Johns River, this apparently temporary post was established sometime in 1812, about six miles north of Rollestown and one mile south of "Little Grove Plantation," a property belonging to General Joseph M. Hernandez.

FORT BULOW. In 1783 Spain reacquired control of Florida by treaty with England, and during this last period of Spanish occupation the policy of encouraging settlement was continued with the aid of Spanish land grants. One such grant was made in 1812, when the Acting Governor of Spanish East Florida transferred 4,000 acres of land to John Russell of the Bahamas. Although Russell had sufficient slaves to develop and work the plantation, little was accomplished before his death in 1815. In 1821 Russell's heirs sold the property to wealthy plantation owner and former member of the South Carolina Legislature, Charles W. Bulow, who began the effective development of the plantation, operating it until his death in 1823. The property passed to his son, John Joachim, but was managed by trustees of the estate for the next five years until he reached his majority.

Bulowville soon became one of the more prosperous plantations in East Florida with 300 slaves, 1,200 acres planted in cotton, and 1,000 acres in sugar cane. The plantation consisted of the stone sugar works, sawmill, assorted service buildings, and 40 houses for the slaves. All of these structures were destroyed together with the grand mansion, a two-storied house with veranda all around. John Bulow's fortunes ended with the outbreak of the Second Seminole War in December of 1835. In an effort to protect the plantations south of St. Augustine along the St. Johns and Halifax rivers, a detachment of Florida militia, under the command of Major B. A. Putnam, was sent out from St. Augustine. His objective was to defend the area from Seminole depredations and so he selected a strategic base of operations—Bulowville. John Bulow objected so vigorously to the occupation that he is reported to have shelled Major Putnam and his troops with a four-pound cannon.

Major Putnam and his men fortified Bulow's home with bales of cotton and constructed a fort in front of the mansion. Bulowville was occupied from the night of December 29 until January 23, 1836, when General Joseph M. Hernandez ordered it abandoned because of insufficient defenders. The troops and those refugees who had congregated there abandoned the plantation and went to the safety of St. Augustine, about 40 miles north of Bulowville. The exact day the Seminoles entered the deserted plantation and destroyed it is not known, but the Indians did a thorough job as evidenced by the ruins, standing today much as they did a century and a half ago. The Florida Department of Natural Resources, Division of Recreation and Parks, maintains and operates the Bulow Plantation Ruins historic site.

BURNSED BLOCKHOUSE. One of the last relics of its kind in Florida—a blockhouse built by pioneers as a defense against Indian attack—still stands in the backwoods of Baker County near S.R. 154. It is located about a dozen miles north of MacClenny and Glen St. Mary, near the town of Taylor and the North Prong of the St. Marys River. The blockhouse had been ascribed in 1940 by the Florida State Board of Planning to a pioneer named Burnsed who erected it in 1837 during the Second Seminole War. Descriptions of the defense and its location have led others to suggest that this same blockhouse had been built by one Carl Brown. In any case, the blockhouse standing on the crest of a hill commands a good view of the surrounding country. It was built of hand-hewn pine logs, dovetailed at the corners, and assembled by wooden pegs, with

walls of extraordinary thickness incised by "peepholes" and rifle loopholes.

FORT BUTLER. Located near the town of Astor in Lake County, on the west bank of the St. Johns River opposite Volusia, Fort Butler was established on November 5, 1838, by a body of 2nd Dragoon troops, numbering 75 officers and men (mostly of Company K) under the command of Captain E. S. Winder, and named in honor of Colonel Robert Butler, 4th Infantry. Two days later they were reinforced by companies A and C of the same regiment, and on the 13th by Company E of the 2nd Dragoons, and companies B and I of the 2nd Infantry. The post consisted of a crude log stockade and barracks for the garrison. The fort was one of the military installations designed to protect the river, which served as an important artery of communication with the garrisons in central Florida. On the opposite bank, near the frontier settlement of Volusia, stood Fort Call. The fort was apparently abandoned on April 27, 1839, when Captain Winder (the post's only commander) and his troops marched against the Indians.

During the Civil War, Federal forces were posted at Fort Butler across the St. Johns River at Volusia to protect the western approach to the important river crossing there. Sometime in May 1864, Captain J. J. Dickison, Confederate guerrilla leader, and his 2nd Cavalry crossed the river and raided Fort Butler, taking 88 infantrymen and 6 cavalrymen prisoners, with arms and equipment.

FORT CABEN. Drake's map (1840) indicates a Fort Caben, misspelled Caven in a few references. Apparently in existence prior to 1840, it was probably a Second Seminole War post situated two miles west of St. Johns Park, just within the lower hook of Crescent Lake, Flagler County.

CAMP CALL. Established on or about July 15, 1836, by companies E and G, 4th Infantry, at Suwannee Old Town, Dixie County, Camp Call was reinforced several days later by companies A, D, and I, at which time Brevet Lieutenant Colonel (Major) William S. Foster assumed command. The last post return, dated October 1836, shows that the post was then commanded by Brevet Major Henry Wilson, 4th Infantry.

FORT CALL. This Army post situated on the St. Johns River, south of Lake George, at Volusia, was established on December 10, 1836, by Brevet Major (Captain) J. L. Gardner with Company A,

4th Artillery, and Company H, 3rd Artillery, plus a detachment of Creek volunteers. Fort Call's last post return, dated February 1838, indicates that the post was then commanded by 1st Lieutenant R. H. K. Whiteley, 2nd Artillery. The post was actually abandoned on March 22, 1838.

FORT CALL. Located in Union County, about four miles northwest of Worthington Springs and about five miles east of the junction of the Santa Fe River and Olustee Creek, Fort Call was most probably named for Florida's Territorial Governor Richard Keith Call. No specific date has been found for the post's establishment. Since it was named for a Florida territorial governor, Fort Call had to be established prior to 1845.

FORT CAPRON. Situated on the west side of the Indian River, opposite the river's inlet at St. Lucie, St. Lucie County, Fort Capron was established in March 1850 by Captain Erastus A. Capron of the 1st Artillery. One of the last Seminole War forts to be abandoned in Florida, Fort Capron was evacuated on June 14, 1858, and Captain Abner Doubleday, the post's last commander, with Company E, 1st Artillery, marched to Fort Kissimmee as ordered.

FORT CAROLINE. Plan drawn by a settler in 1564. (From Laudonniere and Fort Caroline: History and Documents, *by Charles E. Bennett, 1964. Courtesy of University of Florida Press.)*

FORT CARLOS. Reportedly located on the "north central waterfront of Old Fernandina," Nassau County, it was established by the Spanish prior to 1763.

CARLOS BLOCKHOUSE. A map indicates that Pedro Menéndez de Avilés, the founder of St. Augustine, had a blockhouse built on the Bahama Channel near Key Biscayne, Dade County.

FORT CAROLINE (*Fort San Mateo*). When Fort Caroline was founded 10 miles east of present Jacksonville, there was no other European colony on the North American continent north of Mexico. By planting this colony, France hoped for a share of the New World claimed by Spain. The French colonizing effort forced Spain to act and brought on the first decisive conflict between Europeans for the area now included in the continental United States. At Fort Caroline the battle between France and Spain for supremacy in North America was joined.

The Fort Caroline National Memorial represents an important part of Florida's heritage and the story of America's beginning more than 400 years ago. The establishment of Fort Caroline was not an isolated historical event, for its construction in 1564 by the French brought about the establishment of St. Augustine, some 35 miles to the south, by the Spanish in 1565. Thus came into being the first permanent settlement in Florida and the United States.

French interest in the New World, especially Spanish Florida, resulted largely from the desires of Admiral Gaspard de Coligny, France's Protestant leader and friend of Catherine de Medici, the Queen Mother. Coligny had several reasons for wanting to colonize Florida: to establish a base from which French ships could raid Spanish treasure galleons; to establish a point of entry and seat of commerce in the New World; and, perhaps most importantly, to found a French colony in which the Huguenots (Protestants) could worship freely and safely.

Although the religious wars in France between the Catholics and Huguenots (Protestants) began in 1562, Coligny in that year outfitted an expedition to Florida. In April 1562 a French party led by the Huguenot Jean Ribaut (Ribault) landed at the mouth of the St. Johns River, and on May 1 he erected a monument and continued by sea to Port Royal Sound (South Carolina) to establish a short-lived settlement named for the King of France. Civil War in France prevented reinforcement and, after much suffering, the survivors built a crude craft and crossed the South Atlantic to home. Spain, learning of this French intrusion into their previously uncontested domain, sent an expedition to drive out the French, but found the fort and settlement already abandoned. (See: CHARLESFORT [S.C.].)

With the Peace of Amboise in 1563—a truce in the French religious wars—a little fleet of three vessels assembled at Havre-de-Grâce to transport some 300 people to the New World. Of this number, 110 were sailors, 120 soldiers, and the rest artisans, servants, and a few women—but no farmers. Most of them were Huguenots. The commander was René de Laudonnière, a skilled mariner who had been with Ribaut on the 1562 voyage. On June 25, 1564, the expedition anchored off the St. Johns River. For the site of the colony, the French selected a broad, flat knoll on the river shore about five miles from its mouth. With Indian help they erected a triangular fort of earth and wood which enclosed several palm-thatched structures. Other houses were built on the meadow outside the fort. In honor of King Charles IX, the colony was named Fort Caroline.

The French depended upon the area's Indians for food, but intertribal enmity very often prevented the colonists from obtaining an adequate quantity. Other troubles plagued the French colonists. Discontent increased when Laudonnière refused to permit any large-scale explorations for gold and silver until the fort and settlement were strengthened. Toward the end of the year, mutineers absconded with a vessel and sailed southward. After taking a Spanish treasure ship and plundering a Cuban village, they were finally seized by the Spaniards, who then learned firsthand about the French colony. That winter 66 other mutineers seized two barks built by the colony's artisans and captured three Spanish vessels, before they were cornered off Jamaica by a Spanish squadron. Some were hanged as pirates, but 26 escaped and made their way back to Fort Caroline, where the ringleaders were shot.

During the winter and spring of 1564–65, the Indians withdrew as usual to the forests and hunted for their food until their new crops of corn and beans ripened. Without Indian assistance, the French were close to famine. The settlers decided to repair a vessel and return to France. Just at this time, the English slave trader John Hawkins sailed into the St. Johns to refill his water casks. The French traded cannon and powder for supplies and one of Hawkins's four ships. The French were ready to abandon the colony, waiting for a favorable wind.

As the mutineers had proved, the French colony was a threat to Spanish commerce. The Spanish treasure fleets had to sail past Fort Caroline, following the Gulf Stream seaway to the Azores and home. In addition, Fort Caroline was a possible base for attack against the Indies. The Spaniards considered the fort a nest of pirates on Spanish land. A Spanish armada left Cadiz for Florida in June of 1565. But another fleet was already on the high seas. Jean Ribaut had left France with reinforcements—soldiers, gentlemen, and artisans with their families—for Fort Caroline. He had been apprised of the armada being readied at Cadiz by Pedro Menéndez de Avilés, Spain's foremost admiral, who had specific orders to explore and colonize Florida, and to drive out settlers of other nationalities.

Ribaut reached Fort Caroline on August 28, just as the colonists there were about to sail for France. Cargoes went into the storehouses and there was no more talk of leaving. The same day, Menéndez was off the coast with his fleet, searching for the French. A few days later he found the French ships anchored at the mouth of the St. Johns. He tried to board them, but they cut their anchor cables and escaped. Menéndez sailed down the coast a few leagues and on September 8th established the colony destined to live through the centuries as St. Augustine.

Despite advice to the contrary, Ribaut decided to attack the Spanish. It was a fateful mistake during the then hurricane season. A storm blew up and drove the fleet many leagues southward, to be ultimately forced ashore and wrecked. Menéndez learned of the storm-driven dispersal of the French fleet and guessed that most of the soldiers were aboard the ships. He seized the opportunity to attack Fort Caroline. With 500 men, guided by Indians and a French prisoner, he marched through the storm toward the French fort where there were about 240 people. Because of the storm the sentries had been sent to their quarters. At dawn the Spaniards attacked the unguarded settlement. During the confusion, someone opened the fort gate and the enemy poured in. Laudonnière attempted to rally his men but they were overwhelmed. He and some others got over the walls and fled to the woods. Menéndez shouted orders to spare the women and children, but the men were all killed. In an hour it was over. The day was September 20, 1565. The Spaniards had massacred 132 and captured about 50 women and children. Menéndez posted a garrison at the fort and returned to St. Augustine.

Ribaut's shipwrecked men, perhaps 500 of them, survived and escaped Indian ambushes, only to face Spanish soldiers when they marched up the coast. Hungry and quite helpless, 350 of them surrendered. Menéndez had them killed. The site of the brutal massacre still bears the Spanish name *Matanzas* ("slaughters"). Destruction of the colony caused a furor in France. The interests of the French and Spanish royal families were such that friendly relations had to be maintained. Revenge was left to others.

Dominique de Gourgues, a 40-year-old Frenchman from a distinguished Catholic family, had no love for Spain. He set sail from Bordeaux with three vessels and 180 men, ostensibly on an expedition for slaves, but secretly determined to avenge his compatriots. He landed north of the St. Johns and enlisted Indian allies. Two blockhouses near the river mouth were captured, and the Frenchmen moved on Fort Caroline, which had been renamed Fort San Mateo by the Spaniards. Its garrison fled to the forest where the Indians were waiting. Very few Spaniards escaped to St. Augustine. Fort San Mateo was put to the torch. Thus was the grievous insult to France wiped out in blood on April 14, 1568. On May 3 Gourgues set sail for home from the St. Johns and was probably halfway to France when Menéndez, who had departed from San Lucar, Spain, on March 13, arrived back in Florida. The Spanish leader immediately set to work to rebuild Fort San Mateo.

In 1586, when Sir Francis Drake attacked and burned St. Augustine, most of the presidio's population fled to Fort San Mateo, which escaped a similar fate when bad weather discouraged an English attack against the settlement. Documents reveal that San Mateo was still being maintained as a fort and mission as late as 1669, though its importance had steadily declined. The first international conflict between the two white peoples in what is now the United States occurred at the site of Fort San Mateo.

During British possession of Florida (1763–83), another settlement was developed with a defensive earthwork on St. Johns Bluff. More gun batteries were installed on the bluff during the Civil War and the Spanish-American War. The site of Fort Caroline no longer exists. The plain and part of the bluff it had occupied were washed away after the river channel was deepened in the years following 1880. As a part of the 400th anniversary observance of the colony's founding, the National Park Service reconstructed the walls of Fort Caroline, basing the project on a sixteenth-century sketch by Jacques Le Moyne, the colony's artist and cartographer. The memorial, established on January 16, 1953, is located about 10 miles east of Jacksonville and five miles west of Mayport.

FORT CARROLL. Situated on the south shore of Lake Hancock, three miles north of present Bartow, Polk County, Fort Carroll was established on January 22, 1841, by elements of the 8th Infantry commanded by Captain T. P. Guynn. The post was named in honor of Sergeant Major Francis Carroll of the 7th Infantry, who was killed, along with 2nd Lieutenant Walter Sherwood, on December 28, 1840, while escorting a Mrs. Montgomery, the wife of a 7th Infantry lieutenant, from Micanopy to Waccahoota. Fort Carroll was abandoned shortly after its establishment due to health conditions, and the troops were transferred to Fort Cummings near today's Haines City. During the 1960s the site was being developed as a phosphate mine.

FORT CARTEL. Fort Quartel.

CAMP CARTER. A temporary post established in 1838, it was located near the Welaunee and Waukeenah plantations in Jefferson County. The camp was occupied by elements of the 6th Infantry and a number of dragoons.

FORT CASEY. A temporary Army post established on January 3, 1850, and abandoned on December 13, 1850, Fort Casey was located on east central Cayo Costa Island near the entrance to Charlotte Harbor, Lee County.

FORT CASS. Established sometime during the Second Seminole War, it was located on the Suwannee River at or near White (Mineral) Springs, Hamilton County. The post was also used as a hospital camp.

CEDAR KEY POST. An important military station, located on the Gulf near Waccasassa Bay in Levy County, Cedar Key was used by the military from 1839 through the Civil War years. Eventually the site of a fort, hospital and depot, Cedar Key was first occupied on October 16, 1839. In 1840 it was garrisoned by Headquarters and eight companies of the 8th Infantry, and by companies E, I, and K, 8th Infantry, in 1843. In November 1842, during an unusually long period of storms, Gulf waters rose 27 feet at Cedar Key, completely inundating the island and sweeping away all the government property. Seized by the Confederates during the Civil War, it was raided in force by Federal naval vessels. Cedar Key was then a terminus of the Florida Railroad and a center for blockade running. On January 16, 1862, a landing party entered the town of Cedar Key and destroyed the railroad depot, railroad wharf, seven freight cars, four schooners, warehouses, and the abandoned Confederate defenses.

CAMP CENTER. Reported as having been located "at Lewis' Settlement near Key Biscayne" (Motte, *Journey Into Wilderness*, p. 237), Camp Center may be a reference to Fort Bankhead, which was a naval installation during the Second Seminole War. It was a temporary depot that later moved to the mainland as Fort Dallas.

FORT CENTER. Established on January 25, 1856, and abandoned September 17, 1857, Fort Center was located on Fisheating Creek near the western extremity of Lake Okeechobee, two miles south of Lakeport, in Glades County.

CHARLES FERRY POST. A temporary encampment in 1842, this post was located at Dowling Park near the Suwannee River, Suwannee County.

CHATTAHOOCHEE ARSENAL. APALACHICOLA ARSENAL.

FORT CHIPOLA. Company E, 3rd Infantry, commanded by Captain Jefferson Van Horne, left Fort Stansbury on November 2, 1841, and marched to the Chipola River where, on its east bank, they established Fort Chipola on November 9. The post, located near the town of Chipola, Calhoun County, was abandoned June 27, 1842.

FORT CHISHOLM. Reports on this post indicate it was established sometime in 1836 and located about three miles east of where the Fort King military road crossed the Tatsala River, Pasco County.

FORT CHOKONIKLA. The name of this Second Seminole War post has a variety of spellings. Situated at the confluence of Paynes Creek and the Peace River, near Bowling Green, Hardee County, Fort Chokonikla (Indian word for "burned house") was established on October 26, 1849, a half-mile north of the Kennedy-Darling Trading Post, and abandoned July 18, 1850.

FORT CHRISTMAS. The Second Seminole War broke out in December 1835 when a war party led by Chief Micanopy massacred Major Francis Dade's entire command en route from Fort Brooke at Tampa to Fort King where the city of Ocala now stands. During the next two years, a chain of forts was built across middle Florida from Fort Brooke to Fort Mellon at Sanford. Located on a creek east of present State Road 420, two and a half miles north of the present town of Fort Christmas and about 22 miles east of Orlando in the extreme eastern part of Orange County bordering on the St. Johns River, Fort Christmas was established on Christmas Day at what was formerly Powell's Town, a temporary Seminole village occupied by noted Seminole Chief Osceola, known variously as Powell.

General Abraham Eustis selected the site because of its proximity to the St. Johns, an important traffic artery. Leading a large detachment of troops and a caravan of 70 wagons and 1,000 horses, General Eustis had an 80-foot-square palmetto-log stockade built, with two 20-foot-square diagonally placed blockhouses. When construction was completed at the end of a week, the fort was garrisoned by two companies of troops. After the fort was abandoned sometime in 1845, a series of forest fires totally obliterated the works. The fort's precise site is unknown. Today a faithful reproduction of Fort Christmas, dedicated on December 17, 1977, occupies the approximate ground where the original had stood.

FORT CHURCH. Several references locate this post at Fernandina, Nassau County, citing the coordinates of Latitude 30 degrees, 45 minutes, and Longitude 81 degrees, 30 minutes. It is possible that the fort's namesake was Albert E. Church, a 1st lieutenant in 1836.

FORT CLARKE. Located about eight miles west of present Gainesville, on the old Micanopy-Newnansville Road, Alachua County, this post was established sometime in 1836 and named for Lieutenant Henry Clarke, 5th Infantry. No indication has been found for its date of abandonment. A National Archives citation reports that a "Fort Clarke" was occupied during February 1840 by Captain Gustavus Dorr, 6th Infantry, with Company A.

FORT CLARKE. There are scanty references to this post, reportedly located on the Ocilla River, about six miles northeast of Mandalay, Jefferson County.

CLAY LANDING BLOCKHOUSE. Only one reference was found, indicating that this defense was established on August 31, 1837, and located about 10 miles south of Fort Fanning, on the Suwannee River, Levy County.

CAMP CLIFFORD J. R. FOSTER. CAMP JOSEPH E. JOHNSTON.

CAMP CLINCH. This post was established on January 13, 1850, a little more than a mile east of Tampa, by Major George Andrews, 7th Infantry, with Company I of the same unit, and Company A, 1st Artillery, aggregating 112 men. The garrison was employed in building a bridge between Tampa Bay and Fort Meade. The post's last return is dated May 1850.

CANTONMENT CLINCH. Occasionally called a "fort" by historians, Cantonment Clinch was located about three miles west of Pensacola at Bayou Chico, "on the road to Barrancas." Named for Duncan Lamont Clinch, then a colonel and the commander of the 4th Infantry, it was established in 1823 (first post return dated July) and deliberately placed outside the town because the former English barracks had been burned down and because an outbreak of yellow fever was feared. The site had been a cantonment or encampment for General Andrew Jackson's troops during his campaign against the Spanish in 1814 and again in 1821 during the formalities of transferring the territory of Florida into American possession.

Situated on an elevation, the cantonment consisted of 10 large log-built houses, each one designed to accommodate a company of men, arranged in a row under one roof. Fronting the long line of barracks was a spacious parade with a flagpole in its center, opposite to which were the officers' quarters. Each officer had a house, which stood opposite to the barrack of his own soldiers. On the right wing was the Colonel's house, placed in a garden surrounded by a palisade. It was built of wood, two stories high and furnished with a piazza below and a gallery above. The cantonment had its front towards the bay. It was abandoned on October 21, 1834.

FORT CLINCH NO. 1. Located on the north bank of the Withlacoochee River, about 10 miles from its mouth, in Levy County, and named for Colonel Duncan Clinch, the fort was established on October 22, 1836, and abandoned June 25, 1842. Shortly after its evacuation, the fort was burned down by the Indians.

FORT CLINCH NO. 2. An Army fort consisting of six or seven buildings within a stockade, Fort Clinch No. 2 was located at Keen's Cove, Lake Clinch, about a half mile west of Frostproof's city limits on present S.R. 630. Named for General Duncan Lamont Clinch and garrisoned by companies I and K, 7th Infantry, and Company A, 1st Artillery, it was established on January 13, 1850 (a National Archives citation reports the date as February 13), and abandoned June 8, 1850.

FORT CLINCH NO. 3. Named for General Duncan Lamont Clinch, noted for his meritorious services during the War of 1812, Florida's Seminole Wars, and the War with Mexico, handsomely restored Fort Clinch on Amelia Island, Nassau County, was begun in 1847 to safeguard the entrance to Cumberland Sound, which receives the outflow of both the Amelia and St. Johns rivers. The never fully completed pentagon-shaped masonry fortification, a major link in the chain of Atlantic coastal defenses, had been specifically designed to take prolonged cannonading by the smoothbore artillery of the time.

The appearance of rifled guns, however, changed this situation entirely. Rifling, the spiral grooving of a weapon's bore to impart a stabilizing spin to its projectiles, . . . had been brought to a reasonably workable level only in the decade or so preceding the Civil War. . . . The introduction in large numbers of such artillery during the Civil War soon furnished a clear demonstration that rifled cannon, even the fairly primitive muzzle-loading varieties of 1861–1865, were capable of accomplishing quickly and easily what smoothbores could achieve only after long tedious bombardments—the reduction of vertical walls to rubble. . . . [The Civil War] produced some of the most momentous technical changes in the history of warfare. . . . It may be said that the impressive and very costly masonry forts protecting the harbors of the United States were almost overnight and without exception relegated to obsolescence. [Lewis, *Seacoast Fortifications of the United States*, pp. 66–67]

Though far from complete at the outbreak of war, Confederate forces seized Fort Clinch in 1861 but abandoned it the following year when they were attacked by joint Union land and sea forces. Designed to mount 70 pieces of heavy ordnance, not one gun was in place. About April of 1861, however, a battery of four- to six-pounder cannon was temporarily installed in the fort. Construction on the fort was halted in 1867. During the Spanish-American War, it was improved and strengthened to some extent. The State of Florida in 1936 acquired 695-acre Fort Clinch from the Federal government for development as a park. During World War II, the fort served in a small way as a communications and security post.

CAMP COBB. A small but important Civil War post, named in honor of Brigadier General Howell Cobb, Confederate commander of the District of Middle Florida, Camp Cobb was established by the Confederacy at Quincy, Gadsden

County, to protect the area's cattle herds and the facilities that produced vital salt to preserve the supplies of meat required for soldiers constantly on the move.

CAMP COBURN. An Army post established in 1863 as the encampment for the 15th Maine Volunteers, Camp Coburn was located inside the walled compound of the U.S. Hospital near Pensacola and just east of Fort Barrancas.

FORT COLUMBIA. FORT BARNWELL.

FORT COMFORT. FORT CONCORD.

FORT CONCORD (*Fort Comfort*). Originally named Fort Comfort, Fort Concord was a blockhouse, probably privately erected during the Second Seminole War. It was located at the north end of Lake Concord, Seminole County.

FORT CONNOR. Apparently situated on or close to the Oklawaha River, Fort Connor was possibly established during the Second Seminole War. It was located between the community of Connor and the town of Grahamsville, Marion County.

FORT COOPER. A Second Seminole War defense, situated on the Fort Dade Road, Hernando County, it is located by coordinates Latitude 28 degrees, 15 minutes, and Longitude 81 degrees, 28 minutes. Fort Cooper was occupied in 1841 by companies B, D, and E of the 8th Infantry and named for Adjutant General S. Cooper.

FORT COOPER. A Second Seminole War post established just south of present Inverness, Citrus County, Fort Cooper was built and defended for a period of 16 days, from April 1 to April 18, 1836, by the 1st Georgia Battalion of Volunteers under the command of Major Mark Anthony Cooper. The troops had been en route to Fort Drane to unite with other troops for a new campaign against the Indians. During that period, the fort was under attack for 13 consecutive days by several hundred Indians. The Georgia frontiersmen, unschooled in civil engineering or military fortification construction, chose to erect a square-shaped work as the most appropriate for their purpose and marked off the defense's dimensions. Redoubts broke the palisade symmetry along two walls. A two-story blockhouse, designed to house their six-pounder fieldpiece, interrupted the picket work on a third side. The work proceeded quickly, and by the fifth day, the men were able to effectively defend themselves with rifle fire and cannon shot. After successfully repulsing the attacks, the fort was abandoned by the troops. Apparently not reoccupied on a regular basis during the rest of the war, it was thereafter used only for overnight stops or brief visits. The fort eventually collapsed or was burned by the Indians. Fort Cooper's site is located on a broad, low bluff on the west bank of Fort Cooper (Holathlikaha) Lake, between the lake's edge and the 40-foot contour of the bluff.

FORT CRABBE. Most probably established during the Second Seminole War, Fort Crabbe was located on the New River in present Bradford County, according to war maps in the National Archives.

FORT CRANE. Located southeast of present Gainesville and seven miles north of Micanopy near Rochelle in Alachua County, Fort Crane was a temporary fortification erected by the area's settlers as a defense against Indian attack and apparently maintained from about 1830 to 1840. According to a National Archives citation, it was first occupied by the military on March 20, 1837, by 1st Lieutenant J. H. Winder, 1st Artillery, while commanding a detachment of the Artillery unit and a number of Dragoons.

FORT CRAWFORD. Already existing in early 1850, Fort Crawford was apparently an outpost on the military road running east from Manatee to central Florida. Local tradition holds the post was located on the high ground south of the Manatee River between Fort Crawford Creek and Little Fort Crawford Creek, about 12 miles east of Manatee. No specific dates have been found for this post.

FORT CRÈVECOEUR. Early in 1718 Governor of Louisiana Jean-Baptiste Lemoyne de Bienville received orders to occupy St. Josephs Bay in present Gulf County. Though fully cognizant that the territory was claimed by Spain, Bienville sent his brother, Chateaugúe, to establish a post there. On May 12, 1718, a French force occupied the shore along the bay. The report submitted to the governor by his brother on his return to Mobile was that he had built a fort on the mainland just opposite modern St. Joseph Point and named it Fort Crèvecoeur, specifying a stockaded four-bastioned defense garrisoned by 50 men. The Spanish immediately protested the invasion. Bienville conferred with his colonial council and decided to abandon the fort to avoid a confrontation. By August 20, 1718, the French had evacuated the fort after attempting to destroy it.

The French departure was reported by Captain José Primo de Rivera, commandant of Fort San Marcos de Apalache, who had visited St. Josephs Bay to see what was taking place there. After the Spanish authorities were advised of the French evacuation, Primo was ordered to take command of the bay and garrison the fort with an officer and 12 men. During the intermittent hostilities between the French and the Spanish along the Gulf coast between 1719 and 1721, the fort was evacuated on a few occasions. Despite Spanish orders issued on September 20, 1721, to abandon St. Josephs Bay as "useless, weak and incapable of being put into a state of defense," a garrison was still there in the spring of 1722. It was finally and permanently abandoned, and the garrison, with the building materials of the fort's structures, evacuated to Pensacola. No evidence has been found to suggest Spanish reoccupation of the bay. Fort Crèvecoeur's site is located a little more than six miles west of Point St. Joe on U.S. 98.

FORT CROOM. FORT CRUM.

FORT CROSS. Two locations have been claimed for this Second Seminole War post: eight miles west of Dade City, Pasco County, and on the upper reaches of the Withlacoochee River, near Brooksville, Hernando County. The locations are about 15 air miles apart. The post was initially established on December 25, 1838, by Lieutenant George W. F. Wood, 1st Infantry, with Company I of the same unit, and Company G of the 2nd Dragoons. The fort was abandoned in either May or June 1842, when the war terminated.

FORT CROSS. In 1855, a decade after Florida was admitted into the Union as a state, hostilities with the Indians broke out again in what has generally been considered as the Third Seminole War, with most of the action taking place in the lower peninsula, some of it in the Everglades Park area. A new Fort Cross was established on January 14, 1857, on Palm Point or Middle Cape Sable, Monroe County, by Company H, 4th Artillery, and Company F, 5th Infantry. Fort Cross, situated "within a few paces of the Mexican Gulf upon a prairie about two and a half miles in length," was located about four miles northwest of Fort Poinsett. Fort Cross was evacuated on June 21, 1857, and its garrison transferred to Fort Dulaney.

FORT CRUM (*Fort Croom*). Misspelled "Croom" on occasion in Florida history, Fort Crum was a defense erected and occupied by settlers early in the Second Seminole War. It was located near the west end of Paynes Prairie, about six miles from Micanopy, southwest of Gainesville, Alachua County. Brigadier General N. Towson, U.S. Army Paymaster, was notified on May 24, 1840, that "Ft. Crum had been taken by the Indians, and all the occupants, save one, killed . . . Fort Crum lies about six miles from Micanopy, & has of late been occupied by an association of citizens, having plantations in that vicinity" (John B. Opdyke, ed., *Alachua County: A Sesquicentennial Tribute* [1974], pp. 11–12). The defense's citizen garrison was intermittently strengthened by state militiamen. No notice has been found to indicate when the fort was finally abandoned.

CAMP CUBA LIBRE. A temporary Spanish-American War training post located at Jacksonville, Camp Cuba Libre occupied three sites, two of them outside the city's limits. The first site, located between Ionia Street and the railroad, and between 3rd and 8th streets, was chosen primarily because of its proximity to transportation facilities. General Fitzhugh Lee, nephew of Robert R. Lee, commanded the 7th Army Corps here. Beginning with the first arrivals on the evening of May 22, 1898, by June 8 eight regiments, representing more than 9,000 men, had arrived. On June 4 General Lee had designated the camp as Cuba Libre. Early in July an epidemic of typhoid fever began to sweep through the camp, which was saturated with heavy rains during June and July. The original site was abandoned and the troops moved to the vicinity of 5th and Silver streets on July 29. Though the camp was planned for a maximum of 20,000 men, in September the number reached 31,000. A later move was made to the high ground north of the cemetery, near Phoenix Park and Cummer's Mill. The final closing of Camp Cuba Libre was on January 11, 1899, when its last soldier departed.

FORT CUMMINGS. Established on January 22, 1839, Fort Cummings was located on Lake Alfred, about a mile and a half outside the town of the same name and about 16 miles southwest of Davenport in Polk County, some 70 miles east of Tampa Bay. Named in honor of Colonel Alexander Cummings, 4th Infantry, the fort was a link in the chain of forts set up in central Florida to protect the route from Fort Brooke at Tampa to Fort Mellon at Sanford. The post's first garrison consisted of detachments of the 1st and 2nd Infantry and 3rd Artillery. The fort's last occupants were Headquarters and companies A, E, I, and K, 8th Infantry. Fort Cummings was abandoned on March 22, 1841.

FORT DABNEY. Situated on the west bank of the Suwannee River, less than a mile from Suwannee Old Town, Dixie County, Fort Dabney was probably established in late 1835 or early 1836 on the property of either the old Cottrell-McQueen Plantation or on a plantation in the same area owned by another grower named Dabney. The post was occupied by Florida militiamen from January 15 to June 18, 1836.

FORT DADE. On December 28, 1835, a battlefield off what is now U.S. 301, near today's Bushnell in present Sumter County, was the site of the major battle that precipitated the Second Seminole War. Major Francis Langhorne Dade, 4th Infantry, and a detachment of several officers and 102 men had left Fort Brooke at Tampa with their destination Fort King at Ocala. On the morning of the 18th, they were marching along the bank of the Withlacoochee River near present Bushnell when they were ambushed by a large Seminole war party commanded by chiefs Alligator, Juniper, and Micanopy. Major Dade and 106 of his men were killed while the Indians, estimated to have numbered about two hundred, had casualties of three killed and five wounded. The only survivor of the Dade detachment was severely wounded Private Ransom Clarke, who was left for dead and crept from the field of battle after dark and made his way back to Fort Brooke to report the tragedy.

On December 23, 1836, Brigadier General T. M. Jesup, in command of troops in Florida, ordered the construction of Fort Dade at the point where the road between Fort Brooke and Fort King crossed the Withlacoochee River. It was established in January 1837 on the left bank of the river, about 40 miles northeast of Fort Brooke and 13 miles from the Dade battleground, by elements of the 1st and 3rd Artillery, 4th Infantry, and a detachment of the Marine Corps, under the command of Major George Birch, 4th Infantry. During the following summer, the location was found to be unhealthy. The post was temporarily abandoned for the summer and thereafter intermittently occupied until its final abandonment on November 20, 1849.

FORT DADE (*Battery Bigelow*). In 1898, when war with Spain seemed certain, the people of Tampa petitioned Congress to build fortifications at the mouth of Tampa Bay for their protection. However, it took the efforts of influential Henry Plant and Florida's railroad builders and land developers to push the project through Congress, which took quick action. Work was begun on defensive works on Egmont Key and Mullett Key (occupied by Fort De Soto). On the south end of Egmont Key, 35 miles southwest of Tampa, stood 378-acre Fort Dade, with auxiliary Battery Bigelow. The fort was known as U.S. Military Reservation until 1900, when it was renamed in honor of Major Francis L. Dade, 4th Infantry, who was killed with almost his entire command by Seminole Indians, December 28, 1835.

The fort at the turn of the century had an artillery garrison aggregating 6 officers and 154 men. At the main work, the armament then consisted of two 8-inch guns, two Armstrong rapid-fire 6-inch guns, and one 12-pounder brass canon. There were emplacements for four rapid-fire 15-pounders, of which three were completed. Near the north point of Egmont Key, a sandbag battery with two fieldpieces was constructed to guard the entrance to the ship channel until such time when a concrete-and-sand fortification could be built. The battery on the north end contained two 10-inch disappearing guns. About a hundred yards to its south was another containing four 10-inch guns on barbette mounts. A hundred yards farther south of this was still another battery of two 14-inch guns. Three-quarters of a mile still farther south was another battery of 14-inch guns, one of which is now on view in Plant Park in Tampa. On the south end stood Fort Dade.

A narrow-gauge railroad was built to serve and connect all of the gun positions. The three-foot-gauge railroad had a steam locomotive and a string of flat cars for its rolling stock. Parts of the old roadbed can still be seen. In several places there are rails embedded in the concrete floor of what were once magazines and warehouses. Several miles of brick-paved streets and sidewalks are still to be found among the ruins of officers' quarters, barracks, houses, warehouses, and auxiliary structures. Fort Dade was officially abandoned in 1936 but was reactivated during World War II, when it was strengthened by the addition of modern weapons. It was occupied until 1946, when it was permanently abandoned.

FORT DALLAS. Situated on a comparatively high bluff near the mouth of the Miami River, on the inner shore of Biscayne Bay, Dade County, Fort Dallas was established by the Army in late January or early February 1838 (some regional historians date the post from 1836). The fort was named for Commodore Alexander James Dallas, then commander of the Caribbean fleet, as requested by General Winfield Scott. A National Archives microfilmed citation (included in a synopsis of the post's occupations), however, says that the post was named for Vice President George M. Dallas, who was not inaugurated until 1845. The first troops were withdrawn in March 1838. Reoccupied February 5, 1839, the garrison was again withdrawn the following June, only to be again reoccupied October 22, 1839. Companies F and G of the 8th Infantry formed its garrison in 1841 and early 1842. On February 1, 1842, Fort Dallas was turned over to naval authorities for the use of the Navy. On October 20, 1849, the post was reoccupied by the Army, its garrison withdrawn December 31, 1850, and then reoccupied four years later on January 3, 1855. Fort Dallas was permanently abandoned on June 10, 1858. The fort is commemorated by Fort Dallas Park in downtown Miami.

CAMP DANIELS. Records of the War Department in the National Archives indicate that Camp Daniels was established on May 29, 1855, by three companies of the 2nd Artillery. The post, located some 200 yards from Fort Myers in Lee County, was abandoned on December 7, 1855.

CAMP DARLEY. According to M. M. Cohen's *Notices of Florida and the Campaigns* (1836), Camp Darley was located on "Darley's Plantation," apparently in Volusia County not far from Ormond. The plantation was damaged or destroyed by the Seminoles and was occupied by Company A, Second Brigade of Florida Militia, under Major Putnam about November 20, 1836. It was briefly used as a headquarters by General Joseph Hernandez and abandoned by Putnam a few days later because it was found unsuitable as a military position. Putnam's troops marched to Bulowville which became the operational center for that area.

FORT DAVENPORT. One of the line of forts between Tampa (Fort Brooke) and Sanford (Fort Mellon), Fort Davenport was situated on Reedy Creek opposite the mouth of Davenport Creek, two miles northeast of Loughman and one mile north of the Polk County line in Osceola County. Apparently originally established on January 9, 1839, a month later on February 9, elements of the 3rd Artillery and the 2nd Dragoons, commanded by 1st Lieutenant F. O. Wyse, 3rd Artillery, garrisoned the post, with Colonel William

Davenport in overall command. Fort Davenport was abandoned November 1, 1839.

DEADMAN'S BAY POST. A Confederate fortified position during the Civil War, apparently established to observe Union gunboat activity, the post was located on the shore of Deadman's Bay in Taylor County.

FORT DEFIANCE. FORT MICANOPY.

FORT DENAUD. The first Fort Denaud, named for a French-Indian trader, Pierre Denaud (Deynaud), on whose land the fortification stood, was established on the Caloosahatchie River during the late fall of 1837 by Captain B. L. E. Bonneville, 7th Infantry. He erected a blockhouse two miles from the river at the present town of Denaud, a few miles east of the Lee County line in Hendry County. At the same time, Colonel Persifor F. Smith, Louisiana Volunteers, had been directed to take his men to Fort Denaud and scour the area from there south of Cape Sable. Forty-five men of Smith's command and Company I, 1st Infantry, under Lieutenant S. N. Plummer, remained at the fort. Later Fort Denaud was reinforced by five companies of infantry commanded by Major William Hoffman, 2nd Infantry, from Fort Dulaney. In May 1838, the fort was abandoned after a peace parley with the Indians. During the winter of 1840–41, the post was reoccupied and abandoned not later than 1842. Again reoccupied on January 22, 1855, the site was abandoned May 28, 1855, because of unhealthful conditions due to heavy spring rains and upriver flooding. The troops were moved to Camp Daniels adjacent to Fort Myers in late May, 1855. In February 1857, Fort Deynaud was reestablished by Captain John A. Brown and Company M, 4th Artillery, on a new site two miles southwest on the opposite bank of the river. The post was permanently abandoned on May 16, 1858.

CAMP DEPOSIT. According to Thomas Wilhelm's *History of the Eighth Infantry*, vol. 2, Camp Deposit was a temporary post or depot in the Big Cypress Swamp, probably located in Collier County, and occupied by Company I, 8th Infantry, in 1841.

CAMP DEPOT NO. 1. There are two citations, 15 years apart, for possibly the same post. Wilhelm's *History of the Eighth Infantry*, vol. 2, reports that the depot was "situated in Southern Florida, about 30 miles east from Oyster Bay, and near Fort Keais; occupied by Companies C and E in 1841." A National Archives citation reports that this depot, located in the Big Cypress Swamp, was occupied on March 27, 1856, by Brevet Major (Captain) Louis G. Arnold, 2nd Artillery, with Company L, 1st Artillery, and Company C, 2nd Artillery, aggregating 181 men.

CAMP DEPOT NO. 2. Captain and Brevet Lieutenant Colonel William Chapman, 5th Infantry, with three companies, aggregating 234 men, occupied the depot in the Big Cypress Swamp in May 1857.

FORT DE SOTO. The city of Brooksville, Hernando County, was originally known as Menendez, named for the noted founder of St. Augustine. According to Bowe's *Pictorial History of Florida* (1965), the first settlers arrived here in 1845 after Fort De Soto was established nearby as a protection against Indian attack. The fort soon became a trading post and a new community, called Pierceville, was developed. The name of the town was changed to Brooksville on January 10, 1871.

FORT DE SOTO. Fort De Soto Park consists of six islands or keys: Madelaine Key, St. Jean Key, St. Christopher Key, Bonne Fortune Key, Scratch Key, and the main island, Mullet Key. In aggregate, they total 884 acres with more than 7 miles of waterfront. Until the construction of the Pinellas County Bayway's bridges and causeway, historic Mullet Key, 12 miles south of St. Petersburg in the Gulf of Mexico at the mouth of Tampa Bay, was accessible only by boat. Mullet Key gained its historical importance more from Ponce de Leon's explorations in 1513 than from Hernando de Soto's possible association with the Bay area.

Except for the local Indians and several early pioneers and fishermen, the keys remained undisturbed until 1849, when they were explored by U.S. Army Engineers led by then obscure Lieutenant Colonel Robert E. Lee, who was favorably impressed with Mullet Key's strategic location at the mouth of Tampa Bay. He later recommended that several of the keys be reserved for purposes of coastal defense. During the Civil War, Mullet Key was garrisoned by Federal forces as blockade headquarters for the area and a refuge for Union partisans. In 1889 the War Department transferred the island to the Treasury Department to be used as a quarantine station for vessels entering Tampa Bay.

Construction of the initial armament for Fort De Soto was begun in the fall of 1898, based on the plans drawn by Robert E. Lee. Eight 12-inch mortars guarded the entrance to Tampa Bay, but the guns were never fired at any enemy. A cessation of hostilities between the United States and Spain had been declared on August 12, 1898. Some of the gun emplacements are still in evidence. General Orders No. 43, War Department, officially established the permanency of the fort on April 4, 1900 and named it in honor of Hernando de Soto. From 1900 to 1922, the fort was manned by various detachments of the Coast Artillery. During World War I, as a subpost of Fort Dade, the fort was also activated as a Coast Artillery Training Center.

On September 13, 1922, the quartermaster general was instructed to offer the post for sale. However, disposition of the fort reservation was not actually consummated then. Pinellas County first acquired Mullet Key, with the exception of Fort De Soto, by purchase from the government on September 29, 1938. With the approach of World War II, the War Department again took possession of the island, and for several years it was used as an Air Force Gunnery and Bombing Training Center during Fort De Soto's status as a subpost of MacDill Field in Tampa. On August 11, 1948, Pinellas County made final purchase of Mullet Key, including Fort De Soto and all the auxiliary islands, with the stipulation that the properties were to be used only for park and recreational purposes. The Bayway road to Fort De Soto Park was completed on December 21, 1962, and the area officially dedicated on May 11, 1963.

CAMP DICKISON. A Confederate post located at Waldo at the present intersection of U.S. 301 and State 24 north of Gainesville, Camp Dickison was established sometime in 1864 by noted guerrilla leader Captain J. J. Dickison as a headquarters for his Second Florida Cavalry.

CANTONMENT DINKINS. A temporary post situated on the east bank of the Suwannee River in either Lafayette or Dixie County, it was established by then Captain Francis L. Dade on November 24, 1826. Nine years later, the officer, then a major, was killed on December 28, 1835, with almost his entire command near Bushnell, the principal incident precipitating the Second Seminole War.

FORT DOANE. A temporary Second Seminole War post situated on the edge of the Big Cypress Swamp in present Collier County, Fort Doane was located about 6 miles west of Immokalee, 2 miles west of Lake Trafford, and some 20 miles east of Estero Bay. It was occupied during 1841 and 1842 by companies B, C, D, E, and I, 8th Infantry.

FORT DOWNING. Situated on the Suwannee River, nine miles from the mouth of the Santa Fe River, in Lafayette County, Fort Downing was established on January 30, 1840, by Lieutenant L. P. Graham with Company C, 2nd Dragoons. Lieutenant Graham relinquished command of the post on May 21, 1840, to Lieutenant O. P. Roudoux who escorted the command out of the post the same day because of the unhealthiness of the site. The fort was later burned by the Indians.

FORT DOZIER. A privately built defense erected in 1856, it was located somewhere in Polk County.

FORT DRANE (*Camp Lang Syne; Fort Auld Lang Syne; Fort Old Lang Syne*). The site of Fort Drane was Auld (Old) Lang Syne, the 3,000-acre sugar plantation belonging to Colonel Duncan Lamont Clinch, located about 20 miles northwest of Fort King and 8 miles south of Micanopy, near present Irvine southwest of Orange Lake in Marion County. In November 1835 Colonel Clinch decided to attack the recalcitrant Seminoles under Osceola in their villages along the Withlacoochee River and ordered that his plantation be readied as a base of operations for the campaign. The first troops to arrive established camp on the property, then called Camp Lang Syne. Construction of the defenses was superintended by Captain Gustavus S. Drane of the Second Artillery, for whom the fortification was later named. An area of 150 yards in length and 80 yards in width was enclosed by a 12-foot-high palisade. A square blockhouse was erected in the fort's eastern angle and armed with a small cannon. Later, another blockhouse on which two cannon were mounted was built at the north end of the palisade that was loopholed for 300 rifles. Colonel Clinch's two-story plantation home served as the officers' headquarters while the enlisted men pitched their tents in long rows within the fort's enclosure. Additional forces arriving later were compelled to camp outside the fort's walls.

On Christmas Eve, 1835, Richard Keith Call, Territorial Governor of Florida, arrived at Fort Drane with 560 mounted volunteers from the Tallahassee area, and together with other volunteers and Colonel Clinch's force of some 700 men, marched to the Withlacoochee River where, on the last day of the year, the first organized battle of the Second Seminole War took place. The disastrous Battle of the Withlacoochee was the first of the Army's defeats contributing to the failure of the 1835–36 campaign. The Indians under Osceola, although outnumbered and later driven into retreat, emerged victorious, inflicting many casualties among the troops, with scores of men wounded and four killed. Colonel Clinch, tired and dispirited, retired with his men to Fort Drane, which became an improvised hospital for the many wounded and others who had become ill with severe fever.

In June 1836 the regulars were withdrawn from Fort Drane to Newnansville and the post was abandoned. Shortly thereafter, Osceola's Indians burned the fort and adjacent buildings and occupied the site. During the following October, Tennessee Volunteers ejected the Indians and occupied the site. Fort Drane was never rebuilt.

FORT DRUM. Situated on the east side of Fort Drum Creek, 2 miles south of the town of Fort Drum, and located about 20 miles directly north of Okeechobee, Fort Drum was an intermittently occupied Army post first established and garrisoned in 1849. On May 28, 1850, after a satisfactory parley with the area's Seminoles, the post was evacuated. In 1856 Fort Drum was reoccupied by Florida militia who remained until about 1861 or the outbreak of the Civil War.

FORT DULANEY. Located at Punta Rassa, Lee County, Fort Delaney was established on November 28, 1837, by Captain William Dulaney with companies D and E of the Marines, a detachment of dragoons, and a company of artillerymen. They had arrived on the U.S. Steamer *Iris* from Tampa (Fort Brooke), leaving there on November 23. Also aboard were companies A, D, G, and H, 2nd Infantry, commanded by Major William Hoffman. The infantrymen went up the Caloosahatchee River toward "the scene of activity." After a peace parley during the spring of 1838, Fort Dulaney and Fort Denaud on the Caloosahatchee were evacuated in May. At the beginning of the dry season in 1841, Fort Dulaney was reestablished. The post had to be completely rebuilt because the original structures had either been destroyed or vanished. Lumber was brought down the Caloosahatchee, and a new stockade, barracks, storehouses and a temporary hospital were begun. While Fort Dulaney was being reconstructed, it became a receiving point for Seminole Indians agreeable to accepting a government bounty and consenting to be transported westward to Indian Territory.

On October 19, 1841, before the last structures were completed, the post was washed away by a particularly vicious hurricane. The garrison then consisted of four companies commanded by Captain H. McKavitt, all of whom had to resort to tying themselves to the upper limbs of trees. Two men, however, drowned. All the buildings, provisions and supplies were swept away. And where the post had stood, the steamer *Iris* had taken its place, high and dry. The next day the men were moved to high ground. The fort was not rebuilt until 15 years had gone by. In November 1856 Fort Dulaney was reestablished by Captain John McCown, who commanded Company H of the 4th Artillery, and operated fully garrisoned until the early summer of 1858, during which time efforts were made to track down a small band of Seminoles still in hiding deep in the Everglades. Fort Dulaney was permanently abandoned about June 2, 1858.

FORT DUNCAN MCRAE (*Addison Blockhouse*). A picturesque structure built of coquina rock, the Addison Blockhouse was erected sometime between 1807 and 1825 for use as a kitchen, adjacent to a frame dwelling. The buildings stood on the former Carrickfergus Plantation, which was developed starting in 1807 by John Addison (on what is now known as the Addison Grant), to whom absolute title was granted by the Spanish in 1816. The blockhouse is located about "a three-mile-walk" (much closer by boat) from the 712-acre, scenic Tomoka State Park, also once part of plantation property granted one Richard Oswald by the English Privy Council more than two centuries ago. Tomoka State Park is bounded by the Halifax River on the east and the Tomoka River on the west, several miles north of Ormond Beach, Volusia County.

Very early in 1836, probably in January, Seminole Indians attacked and burned the dwelling and blockhouse then owned by Duncan McRae. A month later South Carolina troops arrived and built earthworks around the ruins of the Carrickfergus kitchen. Named Fort Duncan McRae for its owner by the troops, it was used for about a month and was involved in a defensive battle with Seminoles, during which three soldiers were killed.

CAMP DUNLAWTON. A large sugar plantation, Dunlawton was situated on the Halifax River about 25 miles south of the Bulow Plantation, in Volusia County. After a number of large plantations in the Halifax River country were attacked and pillaged by the Indians within one month's time, Major Benjamin A. Putnam marched two companies of Florida Militia to Dunlawton. On January 11, 1836, his outnumbered men were attacked by King Philip's Indians and compelled to retreat northward, suffering 2 killed and 15 wounded. Camp Dunlawton was put to the torch by the Seminoles.

FORT DUNN. Very little is known of this post. It was apparently situated near the Indian River at the intersection of the Military Road and Fort Dunn Creek, in Martin County.

FORT DUVAL. A temporary fortification ordered by the War Department at the request of Territory Governor William Pope Duval, Fort Duval was established on a site a quarter of a mile from the Indian agency near Silver Springs, Marion County. The post was established in November 1826 by Captain Francis L. Dade, 4th Infantry, with companies B, H, and K of the 4th Infantry and companies A and D, 4th Artillery, aggregating 52 men. The post's last return is dated December 1826.

FORT EAGLE. Erected during the Second Seminole War, it was located about 10 miles southeast of Live Oak, Suwannee County. No other information has been found to indicate date of establishment.

FORT ECONFINEE. Located five miles above the mouth of the Econfinee River, Taylor County, temporary Fort Econfinee was established by Captain Jacob Brown with two companies of the 6th Infantry on March 10, 1840. The post was abandoned May 21, 1840.

CAMP EDGEFIELD. A short-lived post established on February 22, 1836, five miles southwest of Summer Haven, St. Johns County, it was named in honor of the district of the same name in South Carolina. The camp, occupied as the temporary headquarters of a regiment of volunteers, was abandoned two days later, on February 24.

EGMONT KEY POST. An outpost of St. Francis Barracks, Egmont Key Post was established in July 1899 by 2nd Lieutenant William F. Stewart, Jr., with Company A of the 1st Artillery. The last post return, dated January 1900, shows that its commandant then was 1st Lieutenant H. E. Smith, 1st Artillery.

FORT ELENA. According to old Spanish records, a Fort Elena had been built as a defense on Talbot's Island, Duval County.

CAMP EUSTIS. A temporary tent encampment situated just south of St. Francis Barracks, St.

Augustine, Camp Eustis was established on February 14, 1836, and served as a training ground for the 1st South Carolina Volunteers, commanded by Colonel Brisbane.

EVERGLADES POST. A temporary encampment, the post was established in the Everglades Swamp on February 16, 1857, by Captain John C. Robinson with companies B and F, 5th Infantry. No indication has been found to determine the date the post was abandoned.

FORT FANNING (*Fort No. 9 [East Forida]; Fort Palmetto*). Originally known as Fort No. 9 and Fort Palmetto, Fort Fanning was situated on the left or east bank of the Suwannee River, about 23 miles above its mouth, in either present Dixie or Levy County (the county line runs along the river). Located near Suwannee Old Town, the post was established on November 30, 1838, and soon renamed Fort Fanning for Lieutenant Colonel A. C. W. Fanning of the 4th Artillery. The post was abandoned February 22, 1843.

FERNANDINA POST. A long-occupied post on Amelia Island, Nassau County, it was first occupied in January 1818, with Major James Bankhead of the Artillery its first commander. The post's last occupants consisted of the 3rd Division, 4th Army, commanded by Brigadier General S. H. Carpenter. The post was abandoned September 1, 1898, when the troops departed for Huntsville, Alabama, via Atlanta, Georgia, a distance of some 700 miles.

CAMP FINEGAN. The largest Confederate encampment in the St. Johns area, some 40 miles west of Jacksonville in Baker County, it was commanded by Brigadier General Joseph Finegan. In February 1864 Union forces under Brigadier General Truman Seymour invaded Jacksonville and marched westward to capture the towns of Baldwin and Sanderson, near the present Olustee Battlefield Historic Memorial. With inadequate forces to stem the Union advance, General Finegan evacuated the camp and left it to be occupied by Union troops.

FORT FLORIDA. Situated on the east bank of the St. Johns River, one and a half miles south of DeBary, Volusia County, Fort Florida was a depot built on the site selected by General Winfield Scott during his reconnaissance between April 24 and 29, 1836. The site, now private property, is on Fort Florida Road off Highway 17 and 92.

FORT FLOYD. The location of this post, erected by Zachary Taylor's forces in January 1838, is undetermined. It most probably was located in East Florida and served to complete the chain of forts across the peninsula from Tampa Bay to Indian River Inlet, with Fort Pierce the eastern anchor of the line.

CAMP FORBES. This post was located near Chattahoochee in Gadsden County. No other data have been found to indicate date of establishment.

CAMP FOSTER. A World War I training post, it was located on the St. Johns River, about 10 miles from Jacksonville. In 1939 the camp and adjoining properties were purchased by Duval County for the $15-million Southeastern Air Base of the United States Navy. It has been reported that in 1946 the original campsite was used by the National Guard.

FORT FOSTER. This post is indicated on an 1864 U.S. Coast Survey map of Jacksonville and vicinity. Fort Foster was most probably a temporary Civil War defense erected by Union forces after their invasion of the area.

FORT FOSTER. Named for Lieutenant Colonel William S. Foster, 4th Infantry, and established by the Army on March 24, 1837, on Rattlesnake Hammock, nine miles from Naples in Collier County, in the direction of Immokalee, Fort Foster was an oval-shaped stockade with a small creek running through an edge of the site. The fort stood on the old Indian trail from Henderson Creek northward to Bonita Springs and Fort Myers in Lee County. Intermittently occupied and abandoned at least twice, the post was permanently abandoned during July 1838.

FORT FOSTER (*Fort Alabama*). The indecisive Battle of Withlacoochee in December 1835 convinced the government that a major force was required to defeat the hostile Seminole Indians and effect their removal from Florida to Indian Territory in the West. General Winfield Scott, one of the Army's ranking commanders, was sent to the peninsula with orders to achieve this objective. The general had received his orders in late January 1836, but he was not ready until early March. He established his headquarters at Picolata, about 20 miles west of St. Augustine, and began planning his campaign.

Learning that most of the Seminoles were hiding in the country west of the Ocklawaha

River, south of the Withlacoochee River, and north of Tampa Bay, General Scott divided his command into three columns, which he called "wings." Colonel William Lindsay commanded the center wing, a regiment of Alabama volunteers, joined at Tampa Bay by a battalion of Florida militia under the command of Major Leigh Read and a company of Louisiana volunteers commanded by Captain Henry H. Marks. While impatiently awaiting delayed orders from General Scott, Colonel Lindsay decided to march and construct a stockade on the Hillsborough River where it was crossed by the main road from Tampa Bay's Fort Brooke, 25 miles distant, to Fort King. The command did not arrive there until March 17. The troops spent three days building a stockaded fort that Scott named Fort Alabama. Major Reed of the Florida Battalion was left in command of this post, and the remainder of the force returned to Fort Brooke on the 20th. Lieutenant Colonel William S. Foster of the 4th Infantry, in a letter to Roger Jones, Adjutant General of the Army, reported that the fort's pickets were of unequal length, "from 12 to 20 feet in height," adding that the magazine was built of "large logs hewn square." He did not mention the other structures within the stockade.

The receipt, finally, of General Scott's orders on the 21st, however, compelled Lindsay to take his force, return to Fort Alabama, and replace the Florida Battalion with Captain Marks' small garrison of Louisiana volunteers, which included about 30 sick and wounded. Lindsay, with the remainder of his troops, left the Hillsborough River fort on March 23. A few days later, an estimated force of 300 to 400 Indians attacked the fort. One soldier was captured, immediately killed and scalped. The Indians continued the attack for two hours, wounding two other men. In the meanwhile, General Scott was finding it practically impossible to coordinate troop movements in the almost impenetrable Florida wilderness and ruefully concluded, in anticipation of the summer rains and heat, to abandon the campaign.

On April 25 Lindsay, acting on Scott's directive, ordered Colonel William Chisolm of the Alabama volunteers to remove the troops at Fort Alabama, destroy the post, and salvage all movable supplies. On April 27 the post was evacuated after it was booby-trapped by a barrel of gunpowder in the magazine. Logs from the fort were thrown over 60 yards, and two Indians were killed. After fighting a pitched battle with the Seminoles en route, Chisolm's troops reached the safety of Fort Brooke. Before the end of 1836, soldiers returned to the site of Fort Alabama and began the construction of a new stockaded fort that soon became known as Fort Foster.

The government turned to the quartermaster general of the Army, Brevet Major General Thomas Sidney Jesup. On November 4, 1836, Acting Secretary of War Benjamin F. Butler, sent a letter to Jesup directing him to assume command of all operations in Florida, instructing him to occupy the "whole country between the Withlacoochee and Tampa Bay" and establish posts to effect the occupation. On November 28, Order No. 18 was issued by Jesup, directing that "Lieutenant Colonel Foster with the Infantry, the 3rd Artillery including Captain Lyon's Company, and the Washington City Volunteers, will reestablish Fort Alabama. A strong picket work with blockhouses at the opposite angles will be constructed without delay."

On November 30, "320 strong," they marched out of Fort Brooke and gingerly edged their way north along the road to Fort King to the Hillsborough River to the site of Fort Alabama. Sentries were immediately posted. Work parties were quickly organized and given specific assignments in the construction. One party was directed to erect "Blockhouse No. 1" and another was assigned the task of building "Blockhouse No. 2." Lieutenant H. Prince, 4th Infantry, was appointed project engineer, and also "put up the pickets of the Fort, a most laborious job," according to Colonel Foster. The job of building "the commissary store, magazine, . . . and the bridge," was assigned to Lieutenant Wall of the Artillery. Completion of the two two-story square blockhouses—45 feet to a side—provided relatively comfortable quarters in addition to their primary role as sentry posts. Archival records contain statements made by a few of the participants that there were *three* blockhouses. The only explanation of this is that they were referring to the commissary or storehouse, located in the center of the compound. The other interior structure was the powder magazine, approximately 8 by 15 feet and probably less than 10 feet high.

On December 22, with the fort near completion, Colonel Foster and a part of the work force were transferred to the Withlacoochee to initiate the construction of another supply depot. Just before Christmas Day, General Jesup arrived to "examine the state of the works," which he found satisfactory, and named the newly erected defense Fort Foster for the colonel. Fort Foster, continuously occupied by a garrison that was being adversely affected by the unhealthiness of the site, underwent a number of Indian attacks, both sides suffering casualties. Fort Foster was not the only interior depot plagued by sickness and disease, and General Jesup was sensitively troubled by the reports from post commanders.

After a meeting with principal Seminole chiefs, General Jesup agreed to ask the government to allow the Indians to remain in southern Florida. The general had apparently admitted to the impossibility of forcing emigration on the Indians. During the peaceful interlude, while awaiting a reply from Washington, Fort Foster's garrison was hopeful of evacuating the desolate site. A month later the government sent Jesup a sharp note rejecting his suggestion. The war was renewed. In April 1838 Fort Foster's garrison was surprised to learn that General Jesup had been relieved and that General Zachary Taylor had been selected to replace him.

On May 15, 1838, shortly before leaving Florida, General Jesup recommended to the new commander that the garrisons of Fort Dade and Fort Foster be evacuated before the advent of the unhealthy summer season. Taylor apparently concurred and before the end of the month the post was abandoned. Colonel Foster died a year and a half later, November 26, 1839, at Baton Rouge, Louisiana. Fort Foster remained unoccupied by Army troops throughout the rest of the war. It was briefly reoccupied September 23, 1849, by a garrison commanded by Captain and Brevet Lieutenant Colonel R. H. Ross, 7th Infantry, when it appeared that the Seminoles were about to go on the warpath again. The crisis, however, quickly dissipated and the post was abandoned October 13, 1849 (another official citation reports that Fort Foster was reoccupied by a detachment of the 8th Infantry). A century and a half later, restored Fort Foster is visited by many hundreds of Florida history buffs and tourists who participate in tours from the Hillsborough River State Park.

FORT FOWLE. A temporary fort or blockhouse, situated on the east side of the Ocklawaha River, six miles east of present Ocala, Marion County, Fort Fowle was established in 1839 during the Second Seminole War and named for Lieutenant Colonel John Fowle, 6th Infantry. Its purpose was to guard the bridge constructed by the Army at the crossing now called Sharpe's Ferry.

FORT FRASER (*Fort Frazer*). Reportedly located on the old Fort King road, Fort Fraser was established on or about December 20, 1837, by Brevet Major Henry Wilson, 4th Infantry, with elements of the 1st Infantry, 4th Infantry, 2nd Artillery, and Missouri Volunteers. The post was

most probably named in honor of Captain Upton S. Fraser (Frazer) who was killed in the Dade Massacre, December 28, 1835. The last post return was dated April 1838 when its commander was Captain John Munroe, 4th Artillery.

FORT FRASER. Situated at the southwest corner of Lake Hancock, southeast of Plant City, Polk County, Fort Fraser was established by Lieutenant Colonel William S. Foster (after whom Fort Foster, Hillsborough County, was named) on December 31, 1837, when it was occupied by his command, the 4th Infantry. During January 1838, the post was used as a commissary depot by Assistant Commissary Lieutenant McClure. No date is given in official records for the post's final abandonment. It had been named for Captain Upton S. Fraser (Frazer), killed in the Dade Massacre.

FORT FRAZER. FORT FRASER.

REDOUBT FRIBLEY. JACKSONVILLE FORTS.

FORT FULTON. There is a discrepancy concerning the location of this fort. Most historians, however, concur that it was named for Captain William M. Fulton of the 2nd Dragoons, the post's commandant, and established on February 21, 1840, and abandoned July 1, 1840. The most probable site appears to have been on the right bank of Pelicier Creek, near Matanzas Inlet, either in the southeast corner of St. Johns County or in the northeast corner of adjoining Flager County.

FORT GADSDEN (*British Fort; Fort Nichols; Negro Fort; Fort Apalachicola*). Located 6 miles southwest of Sumatra, Franklin County, Fort Gadsden State Park commemorates the site of violence and devastation that once enveloped Prospect Bluff. There the accumulated debris of more than a century and a half settled on the remnants of earthworks and a network of trenches that once were part of a fort overlooking the Apalachicola River, 16 miles upstream from the city of the same name.

The first fortification on the bluff on the river's east bank was built in the fall of 1814 by Lieutenant Colonel Edward Nichols of His Majesty's Marines as a rallying point to encourage the Seminole Indians to ally themselves with England against the United States in the War of 1812. While it was being constructed, the fort was called merely "British Fort" or "British Post," but it was soon renamed Fort Nichols for the colonel. Abandoned after 1814, it was occupied by a band of free Negroes and Seminoles who hijacked river traffic and aided runaway slaves from upriver plantations. In 1816 the defense was known as "The Negro Fort." Its location in Spanish Florida did not stop General Andrew Jackson from ordering its destruction because of its threat to American commerce on the Apalachicola River.

Alerted to the impending attack, women and children from Indian villages along the river had taken refuge in the fort when Lieutenant Colonel Duncan L. Clinch left Fort Scott (on the Apalachicola, just above the Georgia line) on July 17, 1816. He descended the river with 116 men in boats and was joined by 150 friendly Creek Indians. Two gunboats from Apalachicola rendezvoused with Colonel Clinch on the 23rd. The Negro commandant of the fort had taken the position that he had been left in command by the British and that any American vessel attempting passage would be sunk. Colonel Clinch ordered the gunboats to move up at the break of dawn on the 27th. A "hot shot" cannonball fired from one of the gunboats landed in the magazine of the fort, which was literally blown apart by the tremendous blast. Colonel Clinch later reported that "the explosion was awful and the scene horrible beyond description—the war yells of the Indians, the cries and lamentations of the wounded." Of the approximately 300 men, women, and children in the fort at the time of the attack, just 30 survived the explosion.

In 1818 General Jackson led a land force down the Apalachicola and directed Lieutenant James Gadsden, Engineer Corps, to build a new fortification on Prospect Bluff as a supply depot or base. Originally called Fort Apalachicola, the new work was renamed Fort Gadsden by General Jackson who was impressed by the lieutenant's zeal. A garrison was maintained at the fort, despite Spanish protests, until Florida was ceded to the United States.

Fort Gadsden remained neglected until the Civil War, when the Confederates in 1862 recognized the strategic value of Apalachicola and its upriver fort. The town of approximately 3,000 was the largest exporting and importing post in Florida, since the Apalachicola River and its tributaries led to plantations in Florida, Georgia, and Alabama, the South's breadbasket. On May 27, 1863, a Federal gunboat slipped past Confederate obstructions in the river and captured a small vessel loaded with 50 important bales of cotton at the fort. Confederate troops garrisoned Fort Gadsden until July 1863, when malaria drove them out of the river's lowlands. With the end of the war, Fort Gadsden receded into near oblivion. Years later it became a part of the vast Apalachicola National Forest. In 1961 the Florida Park Service leased 78 acres on Prospect Bluff for its development as a state park encompassing the site of Fort Gadsden.

GAINESVILLE POST. In compliance with General Orders No. 36, Department of Florida, dated November 1, 1865, this post was finally established in April 1866 by Captain James Cullen with Company F, 7th Infantry. The post was abandoned by Company C, 7th Infantry, on April 6, 1869, when its commander was 1st Lieutenant W. W. Armstrong.

FORT GALE. Only sparse records were found regarding this post, reportedly located somewhere in Putnam County. National Archives records on military installations locate Fort Gale at coordinates Latitude 29 degrees, 25 minutes, and Longitude 81 degrees, 45 minutes.

FORT GALT. Located at "Alafia Bridge," 20 miles east of Fort Brooke at Tampa Bay, temporary Fort Galt was established on January 19, 1857, by Captain and Brevet Major John B. Scott, 4th Artillery, with Company I, which consisted of 82 men. The post was named for Captain Patrick Henry Galt, 4th Artillery, who died on January 9, 1851. The post's last return was dated February 1857.

FORT GAMBLE (*Fort Welaunee*). An Army post established at "Fort Welaunee," a plantation located 30 miles southeast of Tallahassee near Wacissa, Jefferson County, Fort Gamble was first occupied on August 24, 1839, and abandoned on February 18, 1843.

FORT GARDINER (GARDNER). Located on the Kissimmee River near the north bank of Lake Okeechobee, Polk County, Fort Gardiner or Gardner was established by General Zachary Taylor on December 8, 1837, and named for Captain George Washington Gardiner, 2nd Artillery, who was killed in the Dade Massacre on December 28, 1835 (an erroneous National Archives citation reports that the post was named for Captain John Gardner, 4th Artillery). No archival evidence has been found to date the fort's abandonment.

FORT GAREY'S FERRY. FORT HEILEMAN.

FORT GATES. Apparently established sometime in 1835 as a supply post, Fort Gates was situated on the west bank of the St. Johns River, four miles south of the mouth of the Ocklawaha River, and located between Welaka and Lake George, "with a beautiful view of the lake." No date has been found for the post's abandonment.

FORT GATLIN. Lieutenant Colonel A. C. W. Fanning, with four companies of the 4th Artillery, arrived in the area of the present city of Orlando and began building Fort Gatlin on November 9, 1838, naming the post in honor of Dr. John S. Gatlin, who was killed in the Dade Massacre. Fanning departed on the 15th, taking with him three companies, leaving one company under 1st Lieutenat F. E. Hunt as a garrison. The last post return was dated June 1839. Fort Gatlin was briefly reoccupied in October 1849 by Captain I. Vogdes, 1st Artillery, with two companies of men. On March 27, 1924, the Orlando chapter of the Daughters of the American Revolution unveiled a granite marker near the site of the fort, on what is now Gatlin Avenue.

FORT GEORGE. FORT ST. GEORGE.

FORT GEORGE (*Fort San Miguel; Fort St. Michael*). Originally built by British forces under the command of General John Campbell in 1779, Fort George was continuously garrisoned to defend Pensacola, the capital of British West Florida. By 1781 Bernardo Gálvez, continuing his campaign to destroy fortified British enclaves along the Gulf coast, had already achieved impressive victories, including the capture of British forts at Baton Rouge, Natchez and Mobile. Fort George on Palafox (Gage) Hill at Pensacola, next on Gálvez's list to be taken, was besieged by land and sea for two weeks, April 24 to May 8, 1781, bombarded day after day.

On the morning of May 8, a Spanish shell penetrated Fort George's powder magazine, exploded, and sent flaming debris in every direction, killing many of the garrison. Finally, at three o'clock in the afternoon the British ran up the white flag of surrender. Early the next morning the formal articles of capitulation were signed. The number of British prisoners taken was 1,113. The garrison had consisted of about 1,600 men, of whom 300 had succeeded in escaping to Georgia, 56 deserted, and 105 were killed by the powder magazine blast. The overall number of 1,600 did not include the men killed during the siege. The Spanish army lost 74 men killed and 198 wounded, and its fleet had 21 killed and 4 wounded.

The Spanish in 1783 dismantled and reconstructed Fort George, renaming it Fort San Miguel (Fort St. Michael). Constructed of earth and timber, the fort soon fell into complete disrepair after the bombardment by General Andrew Jackson in 1814. Early in the nation's celebration of its Bicentennial, the City of Pensacola undertook the project of transforming the fort site into a minipark. A number of archeologists made a nine-month investigation of the site and their excavations revealed significant remains of both the British and Spanish forts.

CAMP GEORGIA. A temporary post during the Second Seminole War, Camp Georgia was probably established sometime in 1836 at or near Tampa, in the vicinity of Fort Brooke.

FORT GIBSON. A privately built Indian defense near Fort Meade on Pease Creek, Fort Gibson was constructed about the year 1850 near present Lake Gibson and north of Lakeland, Polk County.

FORT GILLELAND. The December 24, 1835, issue of the *Jacksonville Courier* reported that "upwards of 200 people had assembled at Newnansville where the Court House . . . is turned into a fort, and the Jail into a blockhouse." Outside the towns and fortified stockades, East Florida was a deserted countryside. Most of the settlers and their families, during these first few months of the Second Seminole War, had "abandoned their homes and assembled at the different places where the inhabitants . . . erected, or are erecting forts for protection."

Fort Gilleland, misspelled in history as Gilliard and Gilliaud, was established at Newnansville, Alachua County, on July 15, 1837, by Brevet Major James A. Ashby, 2nd Dragoons, with elements of the 2nd Dragoons and the 4th Artillery. The post return dated October 1838 reveals that the post was commanded by Major T. T. Fauntleroy, 2nd Dragoons. A Captain Gilleland, for whom the post was named, was killed by Indians on June 4, 1837 near Itchetucknee Springs while en route from Suwannee to Newnansville.

FORT GILLESPIE. Reportedly located three miles east of old Newnansville, Alachua County, no archival material has been found to date the post's establishment or abandonment. National Archives records show the fort's coordinates as Latitude 29 degrees, 50 minutes, and Longitude 82 degrees, 15 minutes.

CAMP GONZALES. A temporary Confederate post located on the old Pensacola Railroad, 15 miles above Pensacola, Camp Gonzales was probably established sometime in 1864. A small

Federal force left Fort Barrancas on July 21, 1864, and on the morning of the following day, after a march of 30 miles, attacked the Confederate post, then garrisoned by companies C, E, and I, 7th Alabama Cavalry, approximately 120 men each. They had completed, only two days earlier, a new fort named Hodgson, considered by them to be very strong, but the vigorous attack by the Union forces overran both the camp and the fort.

CAMP GORDON JOHNSTON. A World War II post, serving as a base for amphibian assault training, it was situated on James Island 4 miles east of Carabelle, Franklin County, 54 miles south of Tallahassee. The post had been named for Colonel Gordon Johnston, U.S. Cavalry, who saw action in three wars and earned many decorations for heroism and meritorious service, including the Congressional Medal of Honor. His last assignment was chief of staff, 2nd Division, at Fort Sam Houston, where he died as a result of injuries suffered in a polo accident in 1934.

CAMP GRAHAM. A temporary encampment or fort probably established on the Withlacoochee River near Dunnellon, Marion County, and named for General Graham, it served as Major Leigh Read's supply depot during the Second Seminole War. No definite dates have been found for this post.

FORT GREEN. A Third Seminole War defense, Fort Green was probably originated as a privately built post, one of several established along the Peace River during the Billy Bowlegs tribal uprising period, 1855–56. The post, intermittently garrisoned by U.S. troops, was located near present Fort Green, Hardee County, east of Tampa Bay.

FORT GRIFFIN. Established on January 30, 1840, by Captain Thomas L. Alexander with Company C, 6th Infantry, Fort Griffin was reportedly situated on the west bank of the Suwannee River, eight miles from its mouth, in present Dixie County. Another citation reports its location as three miles south of the town of Eugene. Named in honor of Lieutenant George H. Griffin, 6th Infantry, who died in Florida in October 1839, the post was abandoned on June 8, 1840.

FORT GUANA. Reportedly located nine miles north of St. Augustine, about two miles from South Point Verde Beach, St. Johns County, this Spanish defense was built in the late 1700s. During the 1790s it was commanded by Ensign Isaac Wheyler. Sometime in 1795 it was attacked by a detachment of Georgia militia who captured and looted the fort and took the ensign prisoner. No subsequent history has been found.

FORT HALLIMAN (*Fort McLemore; Fort Holloman*). Situated on the south bank of the Withlacoochee River, about three miles north of the present town of Citronelle and 12 miles from the river's mouth, in Citrus County, Fort Halliman was established as Fort McLemore in early April 1836 in compliance with General Winfield Scott's order to erect a supply base on the river. Major John McLemore, with a detachment of 100 men escorting a boatload supply of pickled beef and corn, built a small stockaded log blockhouse. By April 5th the blockhouse was completed. Major McLemore left the supply base under the command of Captain M. K. Halliman with a garrison of 40 men.

Shortly after his departure from the blockhouse, Major McLemore was killed while en route with most of the command to Old Town on the Suwannee River. After General Scott had ordered the fort built, he apparently forgot its existence and the men who garrisoned it, thus earning the blockhouse the sobriquet of the "Forgotten Blockhouse." Continuously besieged by at least 500 Seminoles beginning on April 12, the fort withstood more than 20 frontal attacks while the garrison's commissary was steadily being depleted. Sometime during the siege, Indian fire arrows burned off the blockhouse roof. Captain Halliman was killed, along with several other men, while attempting to extend the defense's stockade to a pool of fresh water. The fort's command was taken over by Lieutenant L. B. Walker.

Finally, 3 men on the night of May 10 managed to escape by raft down the river to the Gulf and got word to Tallahassee of the fort's plight. A volunteer rescue force of 95 men led by Major Leigh Read proceeded by boat from St. Marks to the mouth of the Withlacoochee, thence upriver under the cover of darkness, and safely brought away the men still remaining, who had been reduced to surviving on miniscule rations of corn. Ill-fated Fort Halliman was one more incident in the list of misfortunes that defeated General Scott's campaign of 1835–36 to subdue the Seminoles.

FORT HAMER (*Fort Llamar*). Named for General Thomas L. Hamer, brigadier general of volunteers, Fort Hamer (misspelled in several histories as "Llamar") was established in November 1849, with Brevet Lieutenant Colonel R. H. Ross, 7th Infantry, assuming command on December 20, 1849, accompanied by one company of the infantry and two companies of the 4th Artillery. Located near the mouth of the Manatee River, about five miles east of the Braden River, in present Bradenton, Manatee County, the post was abandoned November 24, 1850, after having served as a base of operations in the area. One of Bradenton's local roads is still named for the fort. Although the road lies *north* of the river, the fort was *south* of the Manatee near the west end of Upper Manatee River Road. A Presbyterian conference center now occupies Fort Hamer's site which had been held as a military reservation until the 1870s.

BATTERY HAMILTON. JACKSONVILLE FORTS.

FORT HAMILTON. Situated on the east bank of the Aucilla River near Surman's Station in Madison County, Fort Hamilton was established on or about August 14, 1841, by 1st Lieutenant Lewis Craig with Company D, 3rd Infantry. In compliance with Special Orders dated November 22, 1842, the post was apparently abandoned sometime in January 1843, the date of its last post return.

HANCOCK CREEK POST. No location has been found for this temporary post established on November 15, 1849, by Captain Henry Little, 7th Infantry, with one company each of the 7th and 8th Infantry. National Archives records show only one post return.

FORT HANSON. Located 13 miles southwest of St. Augustine at the headwaters of Deep Creek, St. Johns County, and named for Lieutenant Colonel John M. Hanson, Florida Volunteers, Fort Hanson was established on an undetermined date by 1st Lieutenant R. H. K. Whiteley, 2nd Artillery. The post's last return was dated June 1840.

FORT HARLEE. Located on the Santa Fe River, between present Hampton and Waldo, Bradford County, Fort Harlee was established in March 1837 by Major John Harlee (National Archives: William W. Harlee) and men of the South Carolina Volunteers. The post consisted of a stockaded pair of diagonal blockhouses, barracks, and auxiliary structures. According to two National Archives citations, the post was garrisoned by Lieutenant John H. Winder, 1st Artillery, with elements of the 1st, 2nd, and 4th Artillery, and abandoned in November 1838.

FORT HARNEY. Located in Brevard County near the town of Heath, Fort Harney was established sometime in 1837. No other official citation has been found, except that the post was named for William Selby Harney, noted Army officer during the Second Seminole War.

FORT HARNEY. In May 1839, the Seminoles in South Florida were offered the benefit of bartering their furs and hides for the white men's manufactured goods at a government-built trading post on the Caloosahatchee River in present Lee County, provided the Indians would agree to stay within the confines of an area bounded by Charlotte Harbor, the Peace River, Lake Okeechobee, and east along the Caloosahatchee to the Gulf. Lieutenant Colonel William Selby Harney was chosen to pick the site for the proposed post. With a detachment of dragoons and several non-Army men he established the promised trading post at a place on the river known today as Harney Point.

The Seminoles strongly suspected that the post was a lure, to entrap them for forced migration to Indian Territory in the West. At the break of dawn on July 22, 1839, a large party of Indians under Billy Bowlegs and Chief Chekika attacked the trading post and killed 18 of the post's garrison of 30 men. Lieutenant Colonel Harney, clad only in his underwear, escaped through a window and dove into the Caloosahatchee to swim to the safety of a vessel moored in the middle of the river.

Burned by the Indians, Fort Harney was not rebuilt by the Army. Some months later Chief Chekika was shot dead by an Army private during another battle. Today's Cape Coral Bridge spans the river close to Harney Point, the site of short-lived Fort Harney.

FORT HARNEY. Reportedly situated some five miles southwest of St. Augustine, and probably named for Lieutenant Colonel William Selby Harney, no additional data has been found to substantiate its existence.

FORT HARREL. Situated at the head of the New (Acotofia) River, reportedly near the intersection of present Collier, Dade, and Monroe counties, temporary Fort Harrel was probably established in 1837 to cut off suspected communication between the Seminoles and Cubans on the southwest coast. No further official citations could be found to determine the stockade's chronological history.

FORT HARRIET (*Fort Harrioliz*). Located at the source of the eastern tributary of the Ocklocknee River, some 17 miles northwest of St. Marks, Leon County, Fort Harriet (misspelled in at least one reference as Harrioliz) was established on March 13, 1840, by Captain George C. Hutter with one company of the 6th Infantry. Fort Harriet was abandoned September 3, 1840.

FORT HARRIOLIZ. FORT HARRIET.

FORT HARRISON (*Fort William Henry Harrison*). Established at the present city of Clearwater on the Gulf of Mexico, Pinellas County, as a recuperation center for wounded and malaria-infected troops, Fort Harrison was first occupied by Major William Hoffman, 6th Infantry, with eight companies, on April 1, 1841. A large log structure was built on the site situated at present Harbor Oaks, at the intersection of Druid Road and Orange Place. The officers' quarters occupied a nearby site on today's Turner Street. The post was named in honor of President William Henry Harrison. A post return shows receipt of General Orders No. 7, dated April 1841, announcing the death of the president. Various units arrived during the same month. Fort Harrison's last post return, dated September 1841, shows that companies B, C, F, G, and I, 6th Infantry, aggregating 189 men, were transferred to Fort Brooke at Tampa on September 6, 1841. Fort Harrison was permanently abandoned October 26, 1841. About the time the fort was abandoned, the government exercised its Armed Occupation Act and offered 160 acres of land to any private citizen who would settle in the scenic area.

FORT HARTSUFF. Serving as a link in the chain of posts established between Fort Meade and Fort Myers to protect the region's settlers during the Third Seminole War, Fort Hartsuff was situated on the Peace River (Pease Creek) on the site of today's town of Wauchula, about 10 miles east of Fort Green, Hardee County. The post was named for Lieutenant George L. Hartsuff, a topographical engineer.

FORT HARVIE. FORT MYERS.

FORT HATCH. JACKSONVILLE FORTS.

FORT HEILEMAN (HEILMAN) (*Fort Garey's Ferry; Black Creek Arsenal*). Established on May 5, 1836, as Fort Garey's Ferry and situated at the junction of the north and south forks of Black Creek near present Middleburg, Clay County, this post served as an Army Quartermaster supply depot and workshop. On July 4, 1836, Captain Merchant, the commanding officer at Garey's Ferry, renamed the post Fort Heil[e]man in honor of Brevet Lieutenant Colonel Julius F. Heilman who had been recently killed in action. In 1837 the fort became an ordnance depot, called alternatively Black Creek Arsenal, popularly known as the "Arsenal of the South." Fort Heileman was apparently discontinued as a depot in 1840 and permanently abandoned on June 18, 1841.

CAMP HERNANDEZ. A temporary post established in 1836 by Brigadier General Joseph M. Hernandez on the Indian River, about seven miles north of present-day Titusville, Brevard County, Camp Hernandez served as a cavalry camp and a base for 500 Tennessee Volunteers. General Hernandez energetically carried out a series of campaigns against the Indians along the coast. Among the important Seminole chiefs he captured were Osceola and King Philip.

FORT HIGGINSON. JACKSONVILLE FORTS.

CAMP HILL. According to Thomas Wilhelm's *History of the Eighth Infantry*, vol. 2, Camp Hill was a temporary post located in "East Florida" and named for Captain James M. Hill, 8th Infantry, who died at Baltimore, Maryland, on January 29, 1849. The post had been occupied by Company I in 1842.

FORT HITCHEPUCKASASSA. FORT SULLIVAN.

FORT HODGSON. A short-lived Confederate defense located about 15 miles north of Pensacola, Fort Hodgson was built in July 1864 by companies C, E, and I, 7th Alabama Cavalry, posted at nearby Camp Gonzales. A detachment of Union troops left Fort Barrancas at Pensacola on July 21, 1864, and on the next morning attacked and captured both Camp Gonzales and newly established Fort Hodgson.

FORT HOGTOWN. An Indian defense erected by settlers, Fort Hogtown was built at the beginning of the First Seminole War by the Spring Grove Guards, volunteers from Hogtown (Gainesville) and Spring Grove, the then county seat, four miles to the west. The fort was located in the vicinity of today's Westside Park at Northwest 8th Avenue and 34th Street in present-day Gainesville.

FORT HOLLOMAN. Fort Halliman.

FORT HOLMES. A privately built stockaded and fortified defense erected in early 1781 by prosperous plantation owner David Holmes, it was located some 15 miles from Pensacola, the capital of then British-occupied West Florida. To further protect his property, Holmes armed his 60 black slaves and white retainers. Pensacola's military commander, General John Campbell, admitted to the probability of an imminent attack by Spanish forces under Bernardo de Gálvez and erected Fort George on an elevation a half-mile behind the town, supporting it by two more defenses, the Queen's Redoubt and the Prince of Wales Redoubt, in the outlying area to guard the approaches to the town. Dreading the loss of well-stocked storehouses within Pensacola and on the farms, most of the citizenry lent assistance on the defenses and a few affluent plantation and farm owners hastily stockaded their estates in anticipation of the Spanish invasion primarily designed to repossess the Floridas.

FORT HOLMES. A temporary post during the Second Seminole War, Fort Holmes was located on Deep Creek, 11 miles southwest of Palatka in Putnam County. In compliance with General Orders No. 9, Headquarters Army of the South, the post was established in "Square No. 5, East Florida" on February 9, 1840, by 2nd Lieutenant C. Hanson with Company D of the 7th Infantry. The post was abandoned August 3, 1841.

FORT HOOK (*Fort No. 2*). A short-lived post, originally designated Fort No. 2, it was erected during the Second Seminole War and was located near the present town of Fellowship, about 12 miles west of Ocala's Fort King, Marion County. Fort Hook was apparently established in March 1839 by Captain William Ionett with Company I, 1st Infantry. The last post return was dated April 1839.

FORT HOOKE. A Fort Hooke was established somewhere in Monroe County. No other military data has been found to substantiate its existence.

FORT HOOKER. Apparently a privately built defense located on the Peace River (Pease Creek), about 16 miles north of Fort Meade in Polk County, Fort Hooker was erected about 1850 during the early stage of the Third Seminole War. Similar to other such posts, Fort Hooker was intermittently garrisoned by Florida Volunteers who were headquartered at Fort Meade. One of the last official citations regarding the fort showed that 24 Volunteers were stationed there on January 3, 1856.

CAMP HOPE. According to one National Archives citation, Camp Hope was established in October 1822 at an undisclosed location in northern Florida by Colonel Duncan Lamont Clinch, commanding companies A, B, C, D, E, F, H, and K of the 4th Infantry. Camp Hope's last post return was dated March 1823. Another National Archives note specifies a "Camp New Hope" located in "East Florida" and "garrisoned January 1813 by U.S. Troops."

CAMP HOSPITIKA. A National Archives citation reports that this temporary Second Seminole War post was situated on the Caloosahatchee River, in either Lee or Hendry County, and garrisoned by companies A, E, and G, 8th Infantry, in 1841.

FORT HOUSTON. On the afternoon of March 4, 1865, a large flotilla of Union-commanded vessels landed about 1,000 troops near St. Marks, consituting one of the largest Federal raids directed against Florida Panhandle's ports, and began to march into the interior, with Tallahassee its obvious objective. When Tallahassee's citizens first heard of the Union invasion, they immediately proceeded to throw up substantial breastworks on the edge of town where the old Plank Road from Newport entered Tallahassee. Here they expected to surprise the Union forces should they come by way of the Plank Road, but instead the battle took place at Natural Bridge, and Fort Houston was not involved in the Union-Confederate confrontation. Fort Houston's site is about 1,000 feet east of the present Tallahassee Country Club House, with part of the site marked today by a row of large live oaks on the circle drive around Duval's Pond. The fort was described as having been square-shaped, with each side about 160 feet in length. During the many subsequent years, trees grew up within the interior of the fort's battery and in all of its four trenches.

FORT HOWELL. Only one brief citation was found on this temporary post during the Second Seminole War, reportedly located some 10 miles east of Everglades City in present Collier County.

FORT HUDSON. Apparently a short-lived Second Seminole War fort, Fort Hudson was reportedly located some 15 miles from St. Augustine. Its coordinates were given as Latitude 29 degrees, 27 minutes, and Longitude 81 degrees, 35 minutes. According to the *Army and Navy*

Chronicle, 1840, p. 331, the fort was "burnt," apparently by Indians.

FORT HULBERT. A Second Seminole War defense, Fort Hulbert was located in Taylor County, about 3 miles from the coast and about 15 miles northwest of Deadman's Bay. It was established on February 2, 1840, by 1st Lieutenant L. C. Easton with companies B and C of the 6th Infantry and named for Lieutenant William Hulbert, 6th Infantry, who was killed May 21, 1839. Fort Hulbert was abandoned June 13, 1840.

CAMP HUNT. Camp Hunt was a temporary Confederate post established in 1862 in northeast Florida. No other citation has been found to further define its geographical position.

CAMP HUNTER. A temporary Second Seminole War post, Camp Hunter was reportedly located in the Everglades, northeastern Monroe County. It was established in February 1840 by 1st Lieutenant N. W. Hunter with Company F of the 2nd Dragoons (see: FORT HUNTER). The last post return was dated June 1840.

FORT HUNTER. A temporary Second Seminole War post, Fort Hunter was located on the St. Johns River at Rollestown, the site of Denys Rolle's plantation, one and a half miles south of Palatka, Putnam County. According to a National Archives microfilmed citation, the post was apparently established about 1840 and occupied by Company F, 2nd Dragoons, "Captain" Hunter commanding. A contradiction is evident since this unit of the 2nd Dragoons was supposedly then occupying Camp Hunter in the Everglades during the same period.

INDIAN KEY POST. Located about halfway between Miami and Key West, Indian Key in 1836 became the county seat of newly formed Dade County, which then extended from the west end of Bahia Honda Key in the Florida Keys to Lake Okeechobee and westward to the Hillsborough River (the county seat shifted to Miami in 1844). The importance of the settlement on Indian Key is evidenced by the reports of the customs inspector who recorded 637 ship arrivals there in 1834 and 703 the following year. Indian Key became the site of an infamous Indian massacre on August 7, 1840. Chief Chekika, the Seminole war leader who a year earlier had led the attack against Fort Harney on the Caloosahatchee River and killed 18 of its 30 occupants, commanded a flotilla of 17 canoes and raided Indian Key, killing Dr. Henry Perrine, early

Florida's noted horticulturist, and six others. They looted and burned the well-stocked warehouse and wharf belonging to Jacob Housman, who had been the architect of the settlement's prosperity, and a number of other structures, thus terminating the key's importance.

Colonel William S. Harney, then posted at Fort Dallas, enthusiastically "accepted the assignment to seek out and eliminate Chekika and his band. On December 4, 1840, ninety men in sixteen canoes left the fort and made their way across the Everglades, surprised Chekika on his island hideout, and killed him. Harney had developed a technique that made it possible to follow the Indians to their most remote hiding places. This raid produced one of the first accounts of a trip across the southern Everglades" (Charlton W. Tebeau, *A History of Florida*, p. 167).

Indian Key subsequently became the site of at least two intermittently occupied Army posts, one in 1856 in compliance with General Orders No. 18, Department of Florida, dated June 20, 1856, and in 1869 when companies B and D of the 3rd Artillery commanded by Brevet Lieutenant Colonel (Captain) E. R. Warner established a post there on the night of July 31, 1869, abandoned sometime in September.

CAMP IZARD. A Second Seminole War post established in early March 1836, in response to emergency circumstances, Camp Izard was situated on the Withlacoochee River about 25 miles from its mouth and several miles east of Dunnellon, Marion County. General Edmund Gaines, leading more than a thousand Louisiana Volunteers, had embarked on his Indian-hunting campaign from Fort King on February 26, 1836. Marching in three columns, about a hundred yards apart, they reached the river the next day. While seeking a fordable crossing, they came under heavy Indian fire from the opposite bank. The soldiers made camp for the night. Early the next morning they gingerly proceeded down the river for perhaps another three miles where they came upon the ford. Before Gaines could get a man across, the Indians, numbering between 1,100 and 1,500 warriors under chiefs Osceola and Alligator, attacked in force. Lieutenant James Farley Izard was instantly shot as he entered the stream intending to lead across an advance detachment. Shot through the head, Lieutenant Izard was the first soldier mortally wounded in the battle. He clung to life for five days, at the end of which he was interred in one of the bastions erected by the soldiers.

The Seminoles surrounded Gaines's force,

besieging them for two weeks as they were compacted into a 250-yard-square quadrangle enclosed by log breastworks. In tribute to Lieutenant Izard's valor, General Gaines designated the impromptu post Camp Izard. During the evening of the siege's first day, Gaines wrote a message to Brigadier General Duncan L. Clinch, urgently requesting reinforcements. The following day, Gaines dispatched another message to Clinch, stating that he would hold the position until aid would arrive. The soldiers, finally out of Army rations, were reduced to eating their horses. They had run out of shot for their six-pounder cannon and were firing rocks and nails at the Indians.

The siege ended when General Clinch arrived with a reinforcement of 500 men. When they showed up, Gaines was parleying with the Seminoles at their request. The Seminoles offered to lift the siege and retire across the river provided the general would guarantee that they could abide there in peace despite the arbitrary treaties. Gaines responded that he did not have the authorization to make such a grant, but promised to present it to the proper officials. Camp Izard was thereafter occupied intermittently during the remaining years of the war.

CAMP JACKSON. A temporary Confederate post, probably established in 1864, Camp Jackson was situated at the old trestle on the St. Marys River in Nassau County, from which point the railroad ran to Camps Milton and Baldwin, 12 miles west of Jacksonville in Duval County.

FORT JACKSON. Located 12 miles southwest of Ellaville, Madison County, Fort Jackson was established on November 11, 1838, by Captain T. L. Alexander with Company C of the 6th Infantry. A month later Alexander and his command were replaced by Lieutenant William D. Berrien with Company K, 6th Infantry. Fort Jackson's last post return was dated August 1840. The site of the post was apparently the place where General Andrew Jackson made peace with the remnants of the Creek Nation on August 9, 1814.

FORT JACKSONVILLE. As settlement of the Florida peninsula increased, the Seminole Indians were gradually but inexorably driven southward. Finally a general demand was voiced to get rid of the Seminoles altogether, and they were enticed into an agreement to emigrate to Indian Territory in the West. Some of the chiefs, among them the celebrated Osceola, did not sign the pact and absolutely refused to migrate.

Government efforts to enforce the removal precipitated the Second Seminole War, the longest and costliest Indian war in the nation's history. The first hostilities occurred during the last week of December 1835, when Chief Osceola and 20 warriors killed General Wiley Thompson and others at Fort King, (present-day Ocala), and Major Francis Dade's command of more than a hundred men was massacred near today's Bushnell in Sumter County, two almost simultaneous events.

Florida's governor issued a proclamation urging people to build defenses in every community. A blockhouse was built in Jacksonville, probably in early 1836, at the present northeast corner of Ocean and Monroe streets. A structure strongly constructed of logs, it was a large square room elevated high above the ground on a pedestal-like base. Entrance into the fort was through a door in the floor of the upper story. Portholes were provided for firearms on all sides and in the floor. The blockhouse stood at what was then the frontier of the town, with all else north and west of it a barren waste. During its 15 years of existence, the blockhouse served the community first as a defense against Indian attack and then as a place for worship. Throughout the war, Jacksonville was an Army supply depot, a subcommissary to the chief post at Middleburg. The ninth town in Florida Territory to be incorporated, Jacksonville was a stronghold for refugees during the Second Seminole War. In 1840 there were less than 600 inhabitants in the community.

JACKSONVILLE FORTS. Florida in 1860 was in political upheaval heightened by vociferous agitation demanding secession from the Union. The result of the presidential election of November 7, 1860, in which not a single Floridian voted for Lincoln, was more than most Southerners could endure. On November 30 Governor Madison Starke Perry signed the bill calling for a secession convention, which met on December 22 to select delegates. On January 10, 1861, the convention declared all political and legal ties between Florida and the United States severed. On Thursday, February 28, the state convention at Tallahassee unanimously ratified the provisional constitution of the Confederate States of America.

In January 1861 enthusiastic Southern partisans had taken over much of the Federal property in Florida, including Fort Marion (Castillo de San Marcos) in St. Augustine on January 7, and Fort Clinch on Amelia Island the following day. By summer several small forts had been built, including one at Jacksonville Beach, named Fort Steele, a work constructed of palmetto logs.

Located a mile east of Mayport, it served to protect the entrance into the St. Johns River. Other forts erected in the Jacksonville area early in the war included Yellow Bluff Fort, situated on a triangular-shaped peninsula projecting into the St. Johns at Dames Point; a fort at St. Johns Bluff, five miles east of New Berlin; and breastworks on Talbot Island. Late in the war, Confederate forces established a heavily fortified encampment at McGirt's Creek about 12 miles west of Jacksonville and named it Camp Milton in honor of Florida's Civil War governor.

On February 24, 1862, because of Confederate military reverses in Tennessee, General Robert E. Lee ordered all available Confederate forces in East Florida to proceed to Tennessee at once. On February 28 Commodore Samuel Francis DuPont sailed from Port Royal with 26 ships and on March 4 landed Marines and Infantry on Amelia Island, immediately occupying Fernandina and Fort Clinch. Six days later St. Augustine's Fort Marion surrendered. The post established at Fernandina consisted of the 97th Pennsylvania Volunteers Regiment, six companies of the 4th New Hampshire Volunteers, and Company E of the 4th Artillery, commanded by Brigadier General H. G. Wright.

During their third occupation of Jacksonville in March 1863, Federal forces built two forts within the city. Fort Higginson, named for Colonel T. W. Higginson, commander of the Union 1st South Carolina Volunteers, and designed to protect the railroad terminus, was at the present intersection of Broad and Bay streets. Fort Montgomery, named for Colonel James Montgomery, commander of the Union 2nd South Carolina Volunteers, stood further along the railroad's right-of-way. According to a contemporary newspaper account, "a large forest of pine and oak trees" was cut down, and some 50 small buildings, mostly inferior dwellings, were demolished during the construction of the two forts, with all the work performed by black troops.

The fourth and final occupation of Jacksonville, in February, 1864, was conceived by Major General Q. A. Gilmore commanding at Port Royal, South Carolina, and was sanctioned by President Lincoln. The plan was to occupy Jacksonville with a sizeable force and establish a supply base there. The federals hoped to push into interior Florida, capture Lake City, and the railroad across the Suwannee, and thus control the eastern approaches to Tallahassee. They wanted to sever Florida and thus destroy the vital food supply lines to the other Confederate states. Florida had become the "Breadbasket of the Confederacy" and was shipping a vast quantity of pork, beef, molasses, corn, potatoes, and other foodstuffs, to the Confederate

military. The federals hoped that the Unionists in East Florida could organize a loyal state government, and to put this part of the plan into operation Lincoln sent John Hay as his personal representative to Jacksonville. Hay, however, was not very successful; the federals consistently overestimated their strength in Duval County. [Samuel Proctor, "Jacksonville During the Civil War," *Florida Historical Quarterly* 41 (April 1963): 353]

Most of the Union forces did not linger in Jacksonville. They fanned out north, west, and south, taking it for granted that the region's Confederate forces had been seriously depleted. But the rebels had secured significant reinforcements and on February 13 established a strong position near Olustee, on Ocean Pond just east of Lake City. A week later, on February 20, the two opposing armies were engaged in a major battle there. The Battle of Olustee resulted in severe losses on both sides, with the Federals ultimately routed and pursued as far as McGirt's Creek. Hundreds of wounded were brought back to Jacksonville, where private dwellings and churches were hurriedly converted into hospitals. The Federals at once built fortifications in expectation of a Confederate assault against the town.

A chain of breastworks, supported by seven batteries, was constructed from Hogan's Creek to the present vicinity of Union and Beaver streets, then west to Davis Street, and southwest to McCoy's Creek. In addition, Yellow Bluff on the St. Johns was fortified, and Mayport was posted with a strong garrison. Hurried reinforcements brought the aggregate total of Union troops in Jacksonville to about 12,000, which included six Negro regiments. An official Union report dated March 15, 1864, describes the seven batteries along the line of breastworks: Redoubt Sammon, four guns; Battery Myrick, occupied by field guns as the occasion may require; Redoubt Fribley, five guns; Battery McCrea, two guns; Redoubt Reed, four guns; Battery Hamilton, nine guns; Redoubt Moore, described "as having been all cleared of trees and placed near the cemetery." In addition, the Federals erected Fort Hatch, apparently within Jacksonville's precincts, location undetermined.

Union commanders in crucial Northern theaters of war requested reinforcements, and orders were issued for a gradual evacuation of Jacksonville. Every day during the five weeks between April 8 and May 15, Union transports loaded with troops were moving down the St. Johns to the Atlantic. About 2,000, mostly Negro troops, remained to garrison the town. On the night of May 31–June 1, they attacked and took heavily fortified Camp Milton at McGirt's Creek, compelling the Confederate defenders to disperse to Baldwin and Whitehouse to the west. In June 1864, the Post of Jacksonville was commanded by Brigadier General William Birney, U.S. Volunteers, with a garrison consisting of 6 companies of the 75th Ohio Mounted Volunteers; 4 companies, 107th Ohio Volunteers; 10 companies, 3rd Colored Troops; companies B and D, 4th Massachusetts Cavalry; and Company A, 3rd Artillery. On July 26, 1864, all of these troops were withdrawn and, except for minor raids from the St. Augustine and Fernandina garrisons, there was no further military activity in Jacksonville during the remaining months of the war.

JAMES ISLAND POST. Established sometime in June 1838 by companies B, F, and I of the 6th Infantry, commanded by Captain George C. Hutter, the post was located south of Tallahassee. The detachment evacuated on August 13, 1838, in pursuit of fugitive Creek Indians supposedly hiding in the swamps of the Ochlockonee and Sopchoppy rivers.

FORT JEFFERSON. The seven Dry Tortugas Islands and the surrounding shoals and waters in the Gulf of Mexico are included in the Fort Jefferson National Monument, off the beaten track but famous for the area's bird and marine life. Like a strand of beads hanging from the tip of Florida, reef islands trail westward into the Gulf

FORT JEFFERSON. (Courtesy of the National Park Service.)

of Mexico. At the end, almost 70 miles west of Key West, is the cluster of coral keys called Dry Tortugas. In 1513 Ponce de Leon named them Las Tortugas ("The Turtles") because of "the great amount of turtles which there do breed." The later name Dry Tortugas warns mariners that there is no fresh water here.

Spain's treasure-laden ships, braving shipwreck and pirates, sailed past the Tortugas. Not until Florida became part of the United States in 1821 were the corsairs driven out. Then, for additional insurance to a growing nation's commerce in the Gulf, a lighthouse was built at Dry Tortugas, on Garden Key, in 1825. Thirty-one years later, the present 150-foot light was erected on Loggerhead Key. In the words of the naval captain who surveyed the Keys in 1830, Tortugas could "control navigation of the Gulf." Commerce from the growing Mississippi Valley sailed through the Gulf to reach the Atlantic. Enemy seizure of Tortugas would cut off this vital traffic, and naval tactics from this strategic base could be effective against even a superior force.

During the first half of the 1800s, the United States began a chain of seacoast defenses from Maine to Texas. The largest link was Fort Jefferson, hexagonal, fully bastioned, half a mile in perimeter, and covering most of 16-acre Garden Key. From foundation to crown its 8-foot-thick walls stand 50 feet high. It has three gun tiers, designed for 450 guns, and a garrison of 1,500 men. The fort was begun in 1846 and, although work went on for almost 30 years, it was never completed. The U.S. Engineer Corps planned and supervised the building. Artisans imported from the North and slaves from Key West made up most of the labor gang. After 1861 the slaves were partly replaced by military prisoners, but slave labor did not end until Lincoln's Emancipation Proclamation in 1863.

To prevent Florida's seizure of the half-complete, unarmed defense, Federal troops hurriedly occupied Fort Jefferson on January 19, 1861, but aside from a few warning shots at Confederate privateers, there was no action. The average garrison numbered 500 men, and building quarters for them accounted for most of the wartime construction. Little important work was accomplished after 1866, for the new rifled cannon had already made the fort obsolete. In addition, the engineers learned that the foundations rested not upon a solid coral reef, but upon sand and coral boulders washed up by the sea. The huge structure settled and its walls began to crack.

For almost 10 years after the Civil War, Fort Jefferson remained a prison. Among the prisoners incarcerated there in 1865 were the so-called "Lincoln Conspirators"—Michael O'Loughlin, Samuel Arnold, Edward Spangler, and Dr. Samuel A. Mudd. Knowing nothing of President Lincoln's assassination, Dr. Mudd had set the broken leg of the fugitive assassin, John Wilkes Booth. The innocent physician was convicted of conspiracy and sentenced to life imprisonment at hard labor. Normally, Tortugas was a healthful post, but in 1867 yellow fever invaded Garden Key. From August 18 to November 14, the epidemic raged, striking 270 of the 300 men at the fort. Among the first of the 38 fatalities was the post surgeon, Major Joseph Sim Smith. Dr. Mudd, together with Dr. Daniel Whitehurst from Key West, worked day and night to fight the scourge. Two years later Dr. Mudd was pardoned.

Because of hurricane damage and another fever outbreak, Fort Jefferson was abandoned in 1874. During the 1880s, however, the government began a naval building program, and Navy men looked at this southern outpost as a possible naval base. From Tortugas's harbor the battleship *Maine* weighed anchor for Cuba, where she was blown up in Havana Harbor on February 15, 1898. Soon the Navy began a coaling station outside the fort's walls, bringing the total cost of the fortification to some three and a half million dollars. The big sheds were hardly completed before a hurricane smashed the loading rigs.

One of the first naval wireless stations was built at the fort early in the 1900s, and during World War I, Tortugas was equipped for a seaplane base. But as the military moved out again, fire and storms and salvagers took their toll, leaving the "Gibraltar of the Gulf" the vast ruin that it is today.

FORT JENNINGS. Situated on the Waccasassa River, near today's Otter Creek, Levy County, Fort Jennings was established sometime during the Second Seminole War and named for Lieutenant Henry Jennings, Georgia Volunteers, killed in Florida, December 26, 1837.

FORT JONES. A temporary post probably established during the Second Seminole War, Fort Jones was located on the eastern bank of the Aucilla River in western Madison County, near present-day Lamont, Jefferson County.

CAMP JOSEPH E. JOHNSTON (*Camp Clifford J. R. Foster*). Named in honor of Confederate General Joseph E. Johnston, who had been quartermaster general of the U.S. Army in 1860, Camp Johnston was established as a Quartermaster Corps training and mobilization post

on October 13, 1917. In September the government had taken over the Black Point campsite of the Florida National Guard, located 12 miles southeast of Jacksonville. During World War I, as many as 27,000 men were encamped here. A total of 405 units were organized, of which 360 special technical units were sent overseas. The cantonment of 825 buildings on the 3,036-acre reservation was closed on June 28, 1919, after which time the training site reverted to the Florida National Guard. It was later named Camp Clifford J. R. Foster for General Foster, adjutant general of Florida. In 1939 the land was deeded to the Department of the Navy and is now part of the Jacksonville Naval Air Station.

FORT JOSEPHINE. An intermittently occupied Third Seminole War post, Fort Josephine was established in late 1857 and was located between Avon Park and Sebring, Highlands County.

FORT JUPITER. Situated on the south bank of the Jupiter River about three miles from the mouth of Jupiter Inlet, Fort Jupiter stood on the point formed by the junction of the river and Jones Creek in Palm Beach County. The post was established on January 25, 1838, by General Thomas S. Jesup, who suffered a disfiguring facial wound the day before when crossing the Loxahatchee River with his forces against Indian resistance. During that year more than 600 Indians were made prisoners at Fort Jupiter, in an apparent violation of a truce, and transported to Tampa, a shipping point for the migration of Seminoles to Indian Territory in the West. Fort Jupiter was abandoned sometime in 1842.

Fort Jupiter was reestablished on a new site on February 21, 1855, by Company D, 1st Artillery, commanded by Brevet Major (Captain) Joseph A. Haskin. The post's new location was on the south side of the Loxahatchee River, about three miles from Hobe Sound and a half mile from Old Fort Jupiter to the west. Its post return dated August 1855 reveals that Fort Jupiter was abandoned in September, with its garrison transferred to Fort Capron. Fort Jupiter was reoccupied on April 14, 1857 (a National Archives citation dates the reoccupation in March 1857) by Captain Joseph Roberts, 4th Artillery, with Company D. Under instructions dated February 27, 1857, Captain Roberts was ordered to select a healthy position near Jupiter Inlet. After an examination of the country in the neighborhood of the Inlet, he decided to reoccupy Fort Jupiter. The post was abandoned on September 9, 1857.

FORT KANAPAHA. FORT WALKER.

FORT KEAIS. Established by forces under General Persifor S. Smith in 1838, the historically accepted location of Fort Keais (variously misspelled) is about 30 miles west of the Everglades, on the eastern edge of a large stand of cypress now known as the Camp Keais Strand in the Big Cypress Swamp, 10 miles south of Immokalee, Collier County.

FORT KEMBLE. Established as a temporary post in 1839 by the Navy to protect woodcutters working along the banks of the Miami River in Dade County, Fort Kemble was located near the temporarily deserted Fort Dallas and occupied by Marines commanded by Lieutenant Thomas T. Sloan, USMC.

KENNEDY MILLS POST. Reportedly located in northern Florida, this briefly occupied fortified post was established by the Army in 1813. According to a National Archives citation, Kennedy Mills was evacuated and afterwards burned by the Indians in September of the same year, after the fall of Fort Mims in Alabama.

KEY BISCAYNE POST. An intermittently occupied island post in Dade County, this post was originally established in 1838 and evacuated the same year. It was reoccupied in 1841 by a detachment of Company E, 8th Infantry, which captured a number of Indians.

KEY LARGO POST. Company B of the 1st Artillery, commanded by Captain John M. Brannan, left Fort Dallas in Dade County on February 9, 1857, to reconnoiter the upper Florida Keys and arrived on February 26 at Key Largo, which they briefly garrisoned.

KEY WEST BARRACKS (*United States Barracks*). This post, repeatedly abandoned and reoccupied for more than a century, was first established as United States Barracks on January 2, 1831, by Company H, 4th Infantry. It was located at Key West on the west shore of the island and served as a garrison for Fort Zachary Taylor, the seacoast artillery fortification begun in 1845. Occupied continuously from January 25, 1893, until after World War II, Key West Barracks was finally declared surplus by the War Department on July 22, 1947. (See: FORT TAYLOR.)

CAMP KING. A temporary post located east of Fort King, it was occupied by Companies E and H, 8th Infantry, in 1840.

CAMP KING. FORT KING.

CANTONMENT KING. FORT KING.

FORT KING (*Camp King: Cantonment King*). Established more than a century and a half ago on a small elevation near today's S.E. 39th Avenue (Fort King Road) in present Ocala, Marion County, Fort King was one of the more important military outposts during the U.S. Army's campaign to remove Florida's Indians to a barren wasteland in the West. Situated adjacent to a Seminole Indian agency established in 1825, it was named for Colonel William King and first occupied in March 1827. Outside its stockade, on December 28, 1835, Seminoles led by Chief Osceola ambushed and killed General Wiley Thompson and four others. On Christmas Day, 1835, Major Francis Langhorne Dade and his command of 111 men bivouacked on Fort King Road (known originally as the Military Road), which stretched 125 miles from Fort Brooke (Tampa) to Fort King. Three days later, on December 28 (coincident with the murder of General Thompson) near Bushnell in Sumter County, about 20 miles north of their Christmas campsite, Major Dade and all but one of his men died in a Seminole ambush. This battle largely served to precipitate the Second Seminole War.

To erect a protective barrier between the Seminoles and the whites, it was determined to establish a military post on the southern frontier of Alachua. In February 1827, two companies of the 4th Infantry commanded by Captain James M. Glassell proceeded south from Micanopy in compliance with orders of Colonel Duncan L. Clinch to erect a fortification close to the juncture of the road to Fort Brooke and the north boundary of the Seminole reservation. The troops camped on a knoll about a mile from the Indian agency, a site now within the eastern section of Ocala. Captain Glassell named the campsite Cantonment King, or Camp King, soon redesignated Fort King, in honor of Colonel William King, the 4th Infantry's former commander.

An area 152 by 162 feet was cleared and enclosed by a stockade constructed of split logs. Heavy timbered gates were set in two sides of the stockade, with a 14-foot-square blockhouse in one of its angles. A large barracks, divided into four 25-foot-square compartments, was erected for the enlisted men, while the officers' quarters consisted of two separate buildings, each about 20 by 50 feet. The remainder of the post's enclosure was taken up by a munitions magazine, kitchens and mess halls. Fort King's garrison was withdrawn on July 1, 1829, but was reoccupied three years later when plans were formulated to convince the Indians to emigrate to a new reservation in the West. But the Seminoles rebelled against deserting their homeland, and war ensued. Fort King, except for brief periods, was occupied from 1832 to March 25, 1843, when it was abandoned.

FORT KINGSBURY. This post was located at the northeast end of Lake Monroe near present Enterprise, Volusia County. Established during the Second Seminole War, it was named for Lieutenant Charles E. Kingsbury.

FORT KIRKLAND. Its probable location was five miles north of Coestview, Okaloosa County.

FORT KISSIMMEE. Located on the Kissimmee River on territory now included in Highlands County, about 15 miles south of S.R. 60, the fort site lies within the Avon Park Bombing Range. During World War II, the Air Force put a bridge across the river at the fort site. Fort Kissimmee was established on January 30, 1850, by Company M, 2nd Artillery, and served as a base for scouting operations until abandoned on June 23, 1850. The post was reoccupied March 23, 1852, but was again abandoned May 20, 1852. On January 6, 1857, the post was reoccupied by Brevet Major (Captain) John C. Pemberton, 4th Artillery, with companies E and F. The post was finally permanently abandoned in May 1858.

LAKE CITY POST. According to a National Archives citation, this post in Columbia County was active during 1867–68. On March 27, 1867, in compliance with Special Orders No. 25, 1st Lieutenant F. C. Grossman, 7th Infantry, with Company B, was removed from this post to St. Augustine, leaving 15 men as its garrison. The last post return was dated August 1868.

LAKELAND POST. This post was established May 16, 1898, by Brigadier General S. B. M. Young, U.S. Volunteers, with elements of the 1st and 10th Cavalry, numbering 926 men. The last Lakeland Post return was dated August 1898.

FORT LANCASTER. FORT ALLIGATOR.

FORT LANE. Established December 13, 1837, by Brevet Major Greenleaf Dearborn, 2nd Infantry, with companies F and K, Fort Lane was located on the west shore of Lake Harney, two miles east of Geneva, Seminole County, and named in honor of Lieutenant Colonel John F. Lane, Creek Volunteers, who died in Florida in 1836. Fort Lane's last post return was dated February 1838.

CAMP LANGFORD. A Confederate post located near Jacksonville and active during 1861–62, Camp Langford was intermittently used as a base of operations by Captain J. J. Dickison, the noted guerrilla cavalry leader.

CAMP LANG SYNE. FORT DRANE.

FORT LAUDERDALE. The first Fort Lauderdale was located near the forks of the New River about a mile from its mouth, on the present site of the city of the same name in Broward County. The square, stockaded two-story blockhouse was constructed in March 1838 by Major William Lauderdale with a contingent of Tennessee Mounted Volunteers and Company D of the 3rd Artillery commanded by Lieutenant Robert Anderson, the same officer who, as a major, surrendered Fort Sumter during the first days of the Civil War. Major Lauderdale conducted several expeditions into the Everglades from this post before it was abandoned later in the year. In the configuration of the city's geography today, the site of this first fort lies between 4th Place and the river, midway between Southwest 8th and 9th avenues.

On February 14, 1839, Captain William C. Davidson, with Company K of the 3rd Artillery, arrived to reoccupy the post but found that it had been burned by the Indians. The captain chose a new site on the beach at the head of the New River Inlet, a short distance southeast of the first fort site, and erected a new fortification. This site is now incorporated within the Bahia Mar Yacht Center on S.R. A1A. The second Fort Lauderdale was abandoned about February 15, 1842, when the Second Seminole War ended.

FORT LAWSON. Located about four miles southwest of Palatka, Putnam County, Fort Lawson was established sometime in May 1839. Fort Lawson was a picket work with one blockhouse, with a lake on the north and south side of it. It was commanded by a sergeant of the 7th Infantry with six men. The post was apparently abandoned in either late November or early December, 1839.

FORT LAWSON. Located northeast of Ivan, on the road between Tallahassee and St. Marks, and situated on the St. Marks River just south of the Leon County line, in present Wakulla County, Fort Lawson was a log stockade erected about the year 1840 and named for Surgeon General Thomas Lawson.

CAMP LAY. In the spring of 1863 Florida's governor impressed slaves in West Florida to construct Confederate defenses along the Apalachicola River. A number of Florida Negroes were impressed into direct Confederate service. The Confederate Congress provided on February 17, 1864, for the impressment by states of 20,000 free Negroes and slaves for menial service in the Confederate Army. The war department fixed Florida's quota at 500. Free Negro laborers were conscripted first. The exact number is unknown, but free Negroes were sent to Camp Lay, near Madison (Madison County), in the fall of 1864. At the camp they were clothed, given physical examinations, and then delegated to work details. The impressment of slaves began in December 1864, and the same routine was followed, except that slave owners were informed in writing. Slaves were then entered into Confederate service and paid a sum not exceeding $25 per month.

CAMP LINCOLN. Established in early December 1861, Camp Lincoln was located about one mile east of Fort Pickens on the western end of Santa Rosa Island in the Gulf of Mexico. The cantonment was garrisoned by the 6th New York Volunteer Infantry (Wilson's Zouaves) until they occupied Confederate-evacuated Pensacola the following May. The post had been established by Colonel William Wilson, with seven companies of the 6th New York Volunteers.

FORT LINDSAY. Apparently established sometime in March 1836 by Colonel William Lindsay, the post was located on or near the Withlacoochee River, near present Brooksville, Hernando County, in the vicinity of Fort Broadnax. Colonel Lindsay (Lindsey) was killed in action before the end of the Second Seminole War.

LITTLE FORT. A fortification built by the British sometime in 1763, soon after Spain's cession of Florida to Great Britain, it was located on the Matanzas River about four miles south of St. Augustine.

LIVE OAK POST. Company G, 8th Infantry, established a temporary post in 1870 at Live Oak in Suwannee County.

LIVINGSTONE FERRY FORT. Reportedly established on August 21, 1837, on the Suwannee River at "Livingstone Ferry," its precise location has not been determined.

FORT LLAMAR. FORT HAMER.

FORT LLOYD. Located 7 miles northeast of Lake Okeechobee in present Okeechobee County, Fort Lloyd was established during General Thomas S. Jesup's winter campaign of 1837–38 against the scattered bands of Seminoles in South Florida. To support that campaign new posts were needed adjacent to the Okeechobee region. Troops under General Abraham Eustis marched southward, reaching a point about 20 miles west of Fort Pierce, where Fort Lloyd was erected, most probably in early 1838, completing a chain of fortified depots stretching across the peninsula from Charlotte Harbor on the Gulf to Fort Pierce. The road finally constructed from Fort Lloyd to Fort Pierce to alleviate logistical problems roughly follows today's S.R. 68.

FORT LOUTHERS. One citation dates its establishment in August 1837 north of Jacksonville in Duval County.

CAMP MCCALL. A temporary post "about one day's march from Fort Brooke" at Tampa, Camp McCall was established and occupied by Company I, 8th Infantry, in 1842.

FORT MCCLELLAN. A Union-built defense on Palafox Hill in Pensacola where old Fort George was located, Fort McClellan was erected in late 1862 and used by Federal forces during most of 1863.

FORT MCCLINTOCK. Located on or near Lake McClintock, six miles southwest of Lake Tohopekaliga, Fort McClintock stood on the road from Fort Maitland to Fort Brooke at Tampa. Established during the Second Seminole War, this fort was named for Major William L. McClintock, 3rd Artillery.

FORT MCCLURE (*Camp Wendell*). About a half-day's march from Fort King at Ocala and located about a mile and a half south of today's intersection of S.R. 35 and 468 on the Withlacoochee River at Warm Springs Creek, Sumter County, this temporary post was apparently established in either late 1838 or 1839, when it was named Camp Wendell. Abandoned sometime in 1839, the post was reoccupied in 1842 by Company B, 8th Infantry, which renamed the post Fort McClure in honor of Lieutenant James McClure, 1st Infantry.

MCCORMICK BLOCKHOUSE. In about the year 1840, James McCormick, owner of a ranch located about 10 miles west of Jacksonville, erected a blockhouse on his property as a defense against Seminole attack. During this period of time, the government was congregating Indians at the fort in St. Augustine preparatory to sending them west to Indian Territory. The blockhouse was attacked at least once by Indians.

FORT MCCOY (*Fort McKay; Fort Mackay*). A fort equipped with blockhouses in the angles and enclosed within a stockade of palmetto logs, this fort was established in 1838 or 1839. It was first named Fort McKay or Mackay in honor of Lieutenant Albert (Alfred?) D. McKay, 1st Artillery, who drowned in St. Johns Bay on December 7, 1836. The fort was located on the west bank of the Ochlawaha (Oklawaha) River, northeast of Ocala, in Marion County. The name of the post was changed to Fort McCoy, and the present town of the same name occupies the site of the fort.

FORT MCCRABB. Located on the right bank of the Suwannee River near Suwannee, Dixie County, Fort McCrabb was established on January 31, 1840, several miles northwest of Fort Fanning. The post was abandoned September 19, 1840.

FORT MCCRAE. This fort was built in March 1836 on the old Acdison Grant on the west side of the Tomoka River, Volusia County. It was a little blockhouse of coquina rock surrounded by an eight-point star moat and a stockaded earthen embankment. Ten acres of the McCrae site belongs to the state of Florida. The stockade had been built around the detached stone kitchen of the McCrae dwelling, which experienced one Indian attack. The ruins are on the old Carrickfergus Plantation.

REDOUBT MCCREA. JACKSONVILLE FORTS.

FORT MCINTOSH. Built by the British during the American Revolution, Fort McIntosh was located on the south bank of the St. Marys River, on the old Oakland Plantation just south of King's Ferry on the old Kings Road, Nassau County. The Battle of Cabbage Swamp was fought near the fort in June 1778 when a force of 300 Americans attacked British rangers under Colonel Thomas Brown. A large detachment of British regulars arrived and extricated the rangers.

FORT MACKAY. FORT MCCOY.

FORT MCKAY. FORT MCCOY.

FORT MCLEMORE. FORT HALLIMAN.

FORT MCNEIL. Built in 1837, Fort McNeil was located on today's S.R. 532, north of the Taylor Creek Bridge, in Orange County. A stockade with blockhouses at diagonal corners, it was established December 28, 1837, and named in the memory of 2nd Lieutenant John Winfield Scott McNeil, USMA graduate, who was killed in action near Dunlawton, September 11, 1837. He was the son of General John McNeil and nephew of Franklin Pierce, 14th President of the United States.

FORT MCRAE (*Fort McRee*). A stockaded depot established between February 18 and 24, 1838, by Major Riley of the 4th Infantry, it was named for Major Archibald McRae, occasionally misspelled McRee, Florida Volunteers, located about five miles north of the present town of Port Mayaca on the east side of Lake Okeechobee, Martin County. Apparently abandoned during the same year, it was reoccupied and rebuilt in early 1857 and abandoned June 11, 1857.

FORT MCRAE. FORT MCREE (Escambia County).

FORT MCREE. FORT MCRAE (Martin County).

FORT MCREE (*Fort McRae*). Named for War of 1812 veteran Lieutenant Colonel William M. McRee (at times misspelled in historical reports as McRae), Corps of Engineers, construction was begun in 1833 on the brick casemated fortification situated on Foster's Bank, now a tongue of the mainland at the entrance to Pensacola Harbor, opposite Fort Pickens. Apparently completed in 1842, the fort was never permanently occupied and no returns of it are on file. Fort McRee was seized by Florida and Alabama troops on January 21, 1861, prior to the actual outbreak of the Civil War. It was partially destroyed while occupied by the rebels during the engagement with Fort Pickens, November 22, 1861. The Confederates abandoned the fort on May 10, 1862.

In later years two Endicott-era auxiliary batteries were built: Battery Slemmer, named in honor of Lieutenant Colonel Adam J. Slemmer, 4th Infantry, who was in command of Fort McRee in 1861 when it was seized, and Battery Center, named in honor of Lieutenant J. P. Center, Adjutant, 6th Infantry, who was killed in the Battle of Okeechobee, December 25, 1837. Added during World War II was Battery No. 233. Sweeping tides and pounding surf destroyed the fort. Ruins of the original brick foundations are still visible at low tide. The present channel flows across the fort's old parade ground.

FORT MACOMB. Named for General Alexander Macomb, chief of engineers, and located on the Suwannee River "about three miles below the foot of the rapids," in Lafayette County, Fort Macomb was established April 16, 1839, and abandoned February 5, 1843.

FORT MACOMB (*Fort No. 1* [Middle Florida]). Located 10 miles north of St. Marks, near the river of the same name, Leon County, the date of its establishment has not been determined. Fort Macomb was abandoned on or about February 8, 1842.

MADISON BLOCKHOUSE. The town of Madison in Madison County was one of the earliest permanent English settlements in Florida and was called Newton when South Carolina planters first settled here. In the center of the town's park, known as Confederate Square, is a memorial to Confederate soldiers, erected on the site where in 1835–42 a blockhouse stood as a defense and refuge during the Second Seminole War. Madison was a Confederate stronghold during the Civil War.

FORT MAGNOLIA. Today a ghost town, Magnolia was located on the west bank of the St. Johns River, about a half mile north of present Green Cove Springs, Clay County. Magnolia Point, a small peninsula jutting into the river, was the site of the town and the fort built by Union forces under Brigadier General J. P. Hatch during the Civil War.

FORT MAITLAND. Originally one of a chain of forts established across central Florida during the Second Seminole War, Fort Maitland was built during the first days of November 1838 on the west shore of what is now Lake Maitland, adjacent to the city of Maitland, Orange County, by Lieutenant Colonel Alexander C. W. Fanning. The fort was named in honor of Captain William Seton Maitland, 3rd Artillery, a West Point graduate, who was seriously injured in the Battle of Wahoo Swamp, receiving a wound from which he never fully recovered. He committed suicide by drowning in the Ashley River near Charleston, South Carolina, on August 19, 1837. Fort Maitland was apparently abandoned in 1842 at the close of the Seminole war.

CAMP MALCO. A temporary post established on January 16, 1857, by companies B and C, 5th Infantry, it was located near the head of the Malco River, near the Pavillion Keys, Monroe County.

FORT MANATEE. According to a National Archives citation, Fort Manatee was "situated on the southern shore of Manatee Inlet, near Grant's Pass, in Manatee County. Company B, 8th Infantry, visited this place on a tour of observation in 1841."

FORT MANDARIN. A blockhouse defense located on the east bank of the St. Johns River, almost opposite present-day Orange Park, Duval County, Fort Mandarin was established on or about August 31, 1837, by General T. S. Jesup and garrisoned by Florida Volunteers.

FORT MANY. Located about 16 miles southeast of Tallahassee, near Wakulla Springs, in Wakulla County, Fort Many was established August 13, 1841, and named for Colonel James B. Many, 3rd Infantry. The post was abandoned June 6, 1842.

MARIANNA FORT. The Battle of Marianna in Jackson County on September 27, 1864, is commemorated by a monument in Confederate Park. The town was then defended by forces largely composed of invalided or wounded Confederate soldiers and boys. There were 60 casualties, killed and wounded, among the Home Guards, with another 100 or more captured by Union troops. Prior to the battle, the town held several hundred Union prisoners who, along with Negro slaves, had been put to work on fortifications in expectation of the arrival of artillery.

FORT MARIA SANCHEZ. Mention is made of this Spanish fortification in St. Augustine in Clarence Edwin Cater's multi-volumed *Territorial Papers of the United States*, vol. 22, p. 201, relating to the "Inventory of Public Property" delivered by the Spanish Engineer shortly after Spain ceded Florida to the United States in 1821. Included in this inventory was Fort Maria Sanchez, adjacent to a powder magazine. No other citations have been found to substantiate the fort's existence.

FORT MARION. CASTILLO DE SAN MARCOS.

CAMP MARSHALL. Located on the Escambia River in 1814, Camp Marshall was a supply depot for Major Urich Blue's forces who were in pursuit of hostile Red Stick Creeks in West Florida.

MARTELLO TOWERS. At the beginning of the Civil War, the government fortified Key West with two Martello Towers to supplement Fort Taylor. The town's residents were enthusiastic Confederate partisans, but Key West was held by

Federal forces throughout the war. The two circular brick towers, called East Martello Tower and West Martello Tower, between Reynolds and White streets, were built in 1861 and located on Roosevelt Boulevard facing the sea. The military purpose of the two Key West towers was to secure the island and the land side of Fort Taylor by interdicting the fire of vessels covering an amphibious landing. West Martello Tower was modified and used throughout World War II and is now deteriorating. East Martello Tower was converted into a museum and art gallery.

CAMP MARY DAVIS. Located near Tallahassee in Leon County, this camp was established in 1861 as a Confederate assembly point for new troops.

FORT MASON. A stockaded post erected in 1837 on the north shore of Lake Eustis, between Eustis and Tavares, Lake County, Fort Mason was built by forces under Major Richard Barnes Mason. Another citation reports that the post was located some three miles north of the lake. The date of the post's abandonment has not been determined.

FORT MATANZAS. The decisive scenes of the Spanish-French struggle for the possession of Florida occurred within and in the near environs of the Fort Matanzas National Monument, where in 1565 about 300 French soldiers and sailors, all Huguenots (Protestants), were put to death. Here Spain achieved potential control of the entire continent of North America and actual domination of the Southeast for nearly two centuries. The lower Matanzas River inlet just south of Anastasia Island, about 14 miles from St. Augustine, was considered highly strategic by the Spanish, and by 1569 a wooden blockhouse for 50 soldiers was built there. From this date forward, there was always a military post at the inlet. The blockhouse, assaulted several times during piratical raids and English invasions, had to be either rebuilt or renovated for the next century and a half.

Soon after discouraged General Oglethorpe raised his siege of St. Augustine on July 20, 1740, the governor of the Spanish colony finally took the advice given him by Spanish engineer Arredondo in 1736 and began the construction of Matanzas Tower, a strong bastion built of coquina rock quarried on Anastasia Island. Before the end of 1742 the tower was completed. Marshy Rattlesnake Island, the site of the tower, was naturally defensible and only a short cannon shot from the channel entrance. Construction had been difficult. Long piles had to be driven deep

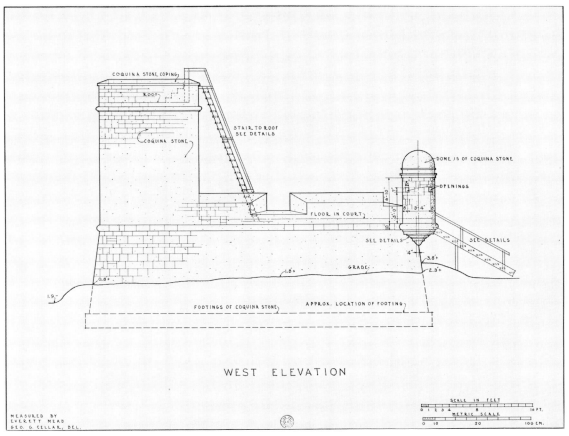

FORT MATANZAS. West elevation. (Courtesy of the Library of Congress.)

FORT MATANZAS. View from the lower Matanzas River inlet. (Courtesy of the National Park Service.)

into the mud to support the courses of coquina stone. Oglethorpe returned in 1743 and was close enough to see the shining white tower and the six cannon mounted on its rampart. He wisely gave up the idea of assaulting the tower, and so again sailed away, never to return.

The English finally gained Matanzas Tower, along with the rest of Florida, by treaty in 1763. After their previous experiences, they too regarded Matanzas as the key to St. Augustine, and in addition to the 30 soldiers and a pair of iron 18-pounders at Matanzas, they stationed two galleys in the harbor. No attacks came during the 20 years the English occupied Matanzas, but during the American Revolution, Spain made plans to capture Matanzas and advance upriver to the most vulnerable side of Castillo de San Marcos at St. Augustine. These plans, however, never came to fruition, and at the Treaty of Paris in 1783, the English retroceded Matanzas and the remainder of Florida to Spain. By then, Spain could no longer afford to maintain her many remote outposts. Matanzas soon began to fall into disrepair, and when the Spanish soldiers sailed away from Florida for the last time, the interior of Fort Matanzas was already in ruins.

Florida was ceded to the United States in 1821, and Matanzas became the property of the U.S. Army. But the fort had little military value to the government and was soon forgotten. During the Civil War, blockade runners operated in its vicinity, and after the war Matanzas Inlet became a port of entry, with a custom house on Anas-tasia Island nearly opposite the fort. This activity hardly lasted a decade, however, and the old tower and its vicinity were abandoned. A long and colorful history had terminated. The fort ruin, designated a National Monument by presidential proclamation on October 15, 1924, was transferred from the War Department to the National Park Service in 1933.

FORT MEADE. Located on the Peace River (Pease Creek), 46 miles southeast of Tampa Bay and adjacent to the present town of Fort Meade, Polk County, Fort Meade was established December 19, 1849, and named for its first commander, Lieutenant George Gordon Meade, who gained prominence at the Battle of Gettysburg in the Civil War. The post was established by companies A, D, and H, 1st Artillery; Company H, 3rd Infantry; Company H, 4th Infantry; and companies B, H, I, and K, 7th Infantry. Thomas Jonathan "Stonewall" Jackson was stationed here in 1851. Abandoned on November 14, 1854, Fort Meade was reoccupied March 13, 1857, and then again abandoned September 20, 1857.

FORT MELLON (*Camp Monroe*). Situated on the southwest shore of Lake Monroe, in the present city of Sanford, Seminole County, this post was originally called Camp Monroe when established in December 1836 by Lieutenant Colonel A. C. W. Fanning with four companies of the 4th Artillery. The post's name was changed to Fort Mellon in memory of Captain Charles

Mellon, killed when 300 to 400 Indians attacked the fort on February 8, 1837. The community that eventually grew up around the fort was first called Mellonville, later renamed Sanford. Fort Mellon was abandoned on or about June 15, 1837, on account of the high incidence of sickness among its troops. The post was soon burned by the Seminoles. Orders dated November 4, 1837, directed its reoccupation. The fort was found to be completely in ruins. The houses of the officers, hospital, blockhouses, and everything combustible, had been burned by the Indians. The troops set to work to build a number of large warehouses and blockhouses that would serve as a depot for provisions. Fort Mellon was finally abandoned May 27, 1842.

FORT MICANOPY (*Fort Defiance; Fort No. 7* [East Florida]). This early Second Seminole War fort, known originally as Fort Defiance and Fort No. 7 (East Florida), was the scene of several bloody engagements with the Seminoles under Chief Osceola. Situated on Lake Micanopy, Alachua County, Fort Defiance was apparently established in December 1835 by Florida militia under the command of General Richard Keith Call. On or about April 30, 1836, the post was taken over by U.S. troops under Major Julius Heil(e)man, then overall commander in the area. On July 24, Lieutenant Colonel Ichabod Crane assumed command of northeastern Florida. He sent Major B. K. Pierce with a detachment from St. Augustine on August 15 to evacuate the troops and supplies from Fort Defiance, which was virtually in a state of siege. The post was temporarily abandoned on or about August 24, 1836, but was soon reoccupied as Fort Micanopy. Companies I, H, and K, 8th Infantry, garrisoned the fort in 1842. When Fort Micanopy was finally abandoned on February 13, 1843, it was occupied by Company H, 8th Infantry.

CAMP MILLER. A fortified Confederate post located near Waldo, Bradford County, Camp Miller was guerrilla cavalry leader Captain J. J. Dickison's headquarters during October 1864.

FORT MILLS. Located near today's LaCrosse, about 10 miles above Fort Gilliland at old Newnansville, Alachua County, Fort Mills was established in September, 1836, and named for Colonel William J. Mills, Florida Volunteers.

CAMP MILTON. An important fortified Confederate camp established in 1862 in compliance with orders of General W. M. Gardner, it was named for Florida's Governor John Milton. The post, with its lines of fortified breastworks, officers' barracks, mess halls, and a large tent city, was located on McGirt's Creek, 12 miles east of Jacksonville. Evacuated and reoccupied twice, Camp Milton was finally destroyed by Union forces from Jacksonville on July 26, 1864.

FORT MITCHELL. The Republic of East Florida was established in 1811 in the vicinity of Fernandina, despite tacit disapproval by the Spanish, and a constitution was adopted on July 17, 1812. On January 25, 1814, the Republic of East Florida was ceded to the United States at a convention held at Fort Mitchell, situated on Lake Bryant, Marion County, about 18 miles east of Ocala. The fort, named for Governor David B. Mitchell of Georgia, was a two-story blockhouse erected in January 1814 by Georgia militia Colonel Buckner Harris with 150 settlers to protect an American settlement in defiance of Spanish officialdom. The settlement collapsed after Harris was killed by Indians and the settlers returned to Georgia. The fort was burned shortly afterward by possibly the same Indians.

FORT MITCHELL. Located on the left bank of the south branch of the Fenholloway River, six miles north of Sadler, Taylor County, Fort Mitchell was established on February 2, 1840, by Captain E. Backus, 1st Infantry, with Company G, and abandoned May 28, 1840.

FORT MOCCASON BRANCH. Located east of the St. Johns River, about 20 miles southwest of St. Augustine, this temporary post was established sometime in 1837 near present Orange Mills, Putnam County.

FORT MONIAC. Situated on the North Prong of the St. Marys River, about a mile from the Georgia border, in Baker County, Fort Moniac was a small, hewn-log defense established June 24, 1838, and named in honor of Lieutenant David Moniac, a Creek Indian, 6th Infantry of Creek Volunteers, a West Point graduate, who was killed at the Battle of Wahoo Swamp on November 21, 1836. The fort was abandoned September 7, 1842.

CAMP MONROE. FORT MELLON.

FORT MONTGOMERY. One of two temporary Union posts established to guard Jacksonville's railroad terminal in March 1863 during the third Federal occupation of the city, Fort Montgomery was named for Captain James

Montgomery, 2nd Union South Carolina Volunteers.

REDOUBT MOORE. JACKSONVILLE FORTS.

CAMP MORGAN. Located in the Cedar Keys, a group of islands at the mouth of the Withlacoochee River, in Levy County, Camp Morgan was occupied on August 10, 1841, by 1st Lieutenant Thomas Hendrickson, 6th Infantry, with companies D and K. In 1842 it was garrisoned by Lieutenant Colonel E. A. Hitchcock and three companies of the 3rd Infantry and companies I and K, 8th Infantry.

CAMP MORRIS. Situated on the north end of Lake Topopekaliga in Osceola County, Camp Morris was established November 21, 1849, by Major George Andrews, 7th Infantry, with Company I, and companies A and H of the 1st (2nd?) Artillery. The post was abandoned December 18, 1849.

FORT MOSA (*Negro Fort*). For years during the early decades of the 1700s, fugitive black slaves from Georgia and the Carolinas had sought refuge in Spanish Florida. A Spanish royal decree promulgated in 1733 stipulated that these fugitives from slavery were to be considered free. In 1739 Governor Manuel de Montiano established a settlement two miles from St. Augustine for freed blacks and their families and directed that the community be fortified. Montiano called the Negro settlement Gracia Real de Santa Teresa de Mose. During subsequent years this name was shortened or abbreviated to Mosa. The Spanish appreciated this affront to their enemies to the north and the economic burden it put on English plantation owners. When General James Oglethorpe invaded Florida the next year, Fort Mosa became a battleground during his siege of St. Augustine.

The English Army, estimated to have numbered 2,000, including about 1,000 allied Indians, appeared before Fort Mosa late in May 1740. Cooperating with it were six men-of-war, equipped with heavy cannon and landing parties for siege operations. After Oglethorpe attacked and captured the Negro fort in a bloody engagement, he conducted a reconnaissance of St. Augustine's inner defenses. The general was compelled to institute a siege which lasted for several weeks and ended in an English defeat. While Oglethorpe was overseeing the landing of units on Anastasia Island, the Spanish seized the initiative to surprise the enemy occupying Fort Mosa and recapture the post, killing many of its defenders. After it

had been retaken, it was repaired and Negro troops again occupied it. It was hence known as the "Negro Fort," and was so designated on many maps after 1740. When Spain ceded Florida to Great Britain in 1763, Fort Mosa was described as a sizable village of thatched huts with a chapel and the fort with two cannon-mounted bastions, surrounded by a moat. In 1775 the British dismantled Fort Mosa.

CAMP MOULDER. Located in the Pavillion Keys, Monroe County, about 120 miles southeast of Fort Myers, Camp Moulder was established on February 17, 1857, by 2nd Lieutenant Thomas Wilson, 5th Infantry, with companies C and E. The post was apparently abandoned on or about February 28, 1857.

FORT MOULTRIE. One of the redoubts on the Cubo or inner defense line built by the Spanish to defend St. Augustine, it was located just west of the Castillo de San Marcos. This defense was named Fort Moultrie during the British occupation of St. Augustine.

FORT MOULTRIE. The plantation of Lieutenant Governor John Moultrie at Buena Vista during the British occupation, Fort Moultrie was located on the Matanzas River about four miles south of St. Augustine. Buena Vista was fortified in the early days and later a regular fort was constructed here, occupied as one of St. Augustine's outposts. Here, in 1823, was executed the Treaty of Fort Moultrie between the government and the Seminole Indians. Alleged infractions of this treaty were among the causes leading to the Second Seminole War, 1835–42.

MT. VERNON ARSENAL. APALACHICOLA ARSENAL.

CAMP MURAT. This post, possibly located in what is now Taylor County, was established on June 6, 1840, by Captain Jacob Brown, 6th Infantry, with companies A, C, E, and H, aggregating 154 men. Captain Brown's staff arrived here on June 6 while the units arrived on June 20. Camp Murat was probably abandoned on or about August 19, 1840.

CAMP MURPHY. Jonathan Dickinson State Park, situated on the west side of U.S. 1 between Stuart and Jupiter, Martin County, was the site of Camp Murphy during World War II. Here Army, Navy, and Marine personnel were given specialized radar instruction.

FORT MYAKKA. A fortified blockhouse or stockade of the Third Seminole War, Fort Myakka was located on the Myakka River some 40 miles southeast of Tampa Bay in the vicinity of Myakka City near the border of Manatee and Sarasota counties. The post was established November 16, 1849, by Brevet Major (Captain) Gabriel I. Rains, 7th Infantry, with companies A and G. A National Archives citation locates the post 15 miles southeast of Fort Chokonikla and 15 miles northeast of Fort Crawford on the Manatee River. Fort Myakkas was abandoned March 22, 1850.

FORT MYERS (*Fort Harvie*). The construction of Fort Harvie on the Caloosahatchee River in today's city of Fort Myers, Lee County, some 20 miles up the river from the Gulf of Mexico, was brought about by the destruction of Fort Dulany at Punta Rassa at the river's mouth on October 19, 1841, during a particularly fierce hurricane, during which the soldiers lashed themselves to the upper limbs of trees. Two men drowned. Captain Henry McKavett, the fort's last commandant, reported that the fort was utterly destroyed and would have to be completely rebuilt. He was instructed to abandon the Punta Rassa site, proceed up the Caloosahatchee, and establish a new fortification at a place more im-

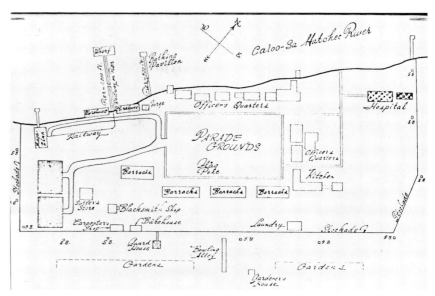

mune against violent storms. The site Captain McKavett selected ultimately became the downtown section of today's bustling city of Fort Myers.

Captain McKavett returned to Punta Rassa and on November 4 brought his garrison up the river and immediately commenced construction of a new defense, named Fort Harvie in memory of 1st Lieutenant John Marshall Harvie, a West Point

FORT MYERS. Plan drawn in 1856. (Courtesy of the Southwest Florida Historical Society.)

FORT MYERS. Drawing of the guardhouse in 1856. (Courtesy of the Southwest Florida Historical Society.)

FORT MYERS. Colonel Abraham C. Myers. (Courtesy of the Southwest Florida Historical Society.)

graduate, who died of malaria in the Cedar Keys on September 7, 1841. During the winter McKavett and elements of his garrison took part in an expedition against the well-hidden Seminoles in the Big Cypress Swamp. One of the participants was Captain Abraham Charles Myers. During the same winter, Fort Harvie was a busy place with barracks, storehouses and a small hospital in the process of being erected. The post very soon became the base for all military operations south of the river. With the end of the Seminole War, however, the short-lived fort was abandoned on March 3, 1842, and burned by Seminoles a short time later.

The tenuous peace was ruptured by a small number of widely spaced acts of violence during 1849. Washington soon became aware of Florida settlers' vehement demands for Army protection. The War Department directed Major General David E. Twiggs to renew military steps against the fractious Indians. The naming of the new post Fort Myers was directly related to the betrothal of General Twiggs' daughter Marion to Colonel Abraham C. Myers. The general thought it was required of him to simultaneously please his daughter and honor a distinguished fellow Army officer. They were wedded in Florida and their first offspring was named John Twiggs Myers, who later became a brigadier general in the Marine Corps.

Upon the outbreak of the Civil War, General Twiggs and Colonel Myers, both Southerners, enlisted in the Confederate Army. Myers was for some time quartermaster general of the Confederate States of America. His service to the

rebel cause, however, was summarily ended when Jefferson Davis was informed that Marion Twiggs Myers had incautiously made the observation at a social soiree that Mrs. Davis looked like a "squaw." Put in limbo by President Davis, Myers went to Europe with his wife after the war and lived there for 11 years, almost as expatriates. He returned to America, retired from the military in 1877, and died at Washington in 1889. According to one record, Myers may have made only one visit to the site of the fort named for him and that was in 1841 when he apparently passed through Fort Harvie en route up the Caloosahatchee.

Within the week following the receipt of his orders, Major Ridgely was sailing up the Caloosahatchee to the blackened ruins of Fort Harvie. He too decided that the place was a very fine location for the new post. Fort Myers was officially established on Wednesday, February 20, 1850, when his men, Company D of the 1st Artillery and Company A of the 4th Artillery, began landing supplies for construction. The fort, one of the finest and largest posts established during all the bloody years of the Seminole Wars, boasted two groups of officers' quarters, four barracks for enlisted men, an administration building, a three-story hospital in the northeast corner of the stockade, storehouses, blacksmith shop, stables, a bakery, laundry facilities, a sutler's store, and servants' quarters. The first buildings constructed were palmetto-thatched, and more than a year passed before these structures were renovated with more durable materials. In addition there was a 1,000-foot-long wharf to accommodate the steamers and sailing vessels that brought both visitors and supplies to the post. The amenities even included a bowling alley. All the framework for the buildings was made of yellow pine. Some of this sturdy timber was found more than three-quarters of a century later when the last fort structure was demolished. The wood was just as sound as when it was first cut in 1850. The fort spanned about eight blocks along the riverfront in today's geographical context of downtown Fort Myers.

As violence between the whites and Indians increased to full-scale war, forts abandoned a dozen years earlier along the Caloosahatchee were reconstructed, and Fort Myers was heavily reinforced. Expeditions into Indian-occupied lands announced in no uncertain terms that the whites had come to stay. By mid-1856 a total of 57 large and small structures had been built within the stockade. Included was a new blockhouse-guardhouse built of Florida heart pine erected just outside the southeast wall of the stockade. It was considered adequate to be defended by 30 men against Indian attack.

Fort Myers, evacuated on May 31, 1858, was reestablished in December 1863 by several companies of Federal troops commanded by Captain James Doyle, who had a log-and-earth breastwork thrown up around the fort. It was from here that he sent out frequent raiding parties against Confederate camps in the interior, appropriating the rebels' cattle, supplies and munitions. The post was continuously garrisoned until June 1865, when it was finally abandoned. In the following year, the first permanent settlers arrived and established themselves within the fort, which was gradually dismantled for its valuable building materials by subsequent pioneering families.

BATTERY MYRICK. JACKSONVILLE FORTS.

FORT NANCY. Located on the south edge of present Gainesville at Boulware Springs, Fort Nancy was a privately built blockhouse erected by "Bud" Higginbotham and area settlers during the Indian troubles of 1856–58 and named for Mrs. Nancy Higginbotham. The fort was destroyed by Federal troops as they marched against Gainesville on August 17, 1864.

BATTERY NASSAU. A temporary defense erected by Confederate troops, it was located at Fernandina on Amelia Island.

NEGRO FORT. FORT GADSDEN.

NEGRO FORT. FORT MOSA.

FORT NEW BUENA VISTA. A fortified blockhouse erected in 1836, it was located opposite Palatka, Putnam County.

CAMP NEW HOPE. A U.S. Army encampment located on Hollingsworth's Plantation on the St. Johns River, Camp New Hope was established on or about October 12, 1812, during the Patriots War. Its site is located near the old Cowford Crossing, which later developed into the present-day city of Jacksonville. The post was used particularly by Colonel Daniel Newnan during his campaigns. His troops also had available a blockhouse on Davis Creek near today's Federal Point.

NEWNAN'S FORT. East Florida in 1812 was involved in what became known as the Patriot Revolution, instigated and supported by the U.S. government. It was ostensibly a revolt by American settlers on Spanish grants. U.S. Army troops entered Florida in support of the rebellion but not in sufficient numbers to influence the Spanish to evacuate St. Augustine. In order to bring the war to the Spanish-allied Seminoles, Colonel Daniel Newnan led a volunteer military force against the Alachua Seminoles under King Payne and engaged them on the east side of today's Newnan Lake on September 17, 1812. Newnan's force, mauled by the Indians, erected "a tolerable breastwork of logs and earth, with portholes." This fort protected the men during the whole week following as they fought both the Indians and mounting hunger. King Payne was killed during the battle. The volunteers finally extricated themselves and retreated to the northeast.

FORT NEWNANSVILLE. Probably the most important military post at old Newnansville (named for military leader Daniel Newnan) in present-day Alachua County, Fort Newnansville was a fortified haven for the settlers fleeing from their plantations and farms after the Second Seminole War broke out in 1835. The town's population, swelled by hundreds of refugees, rose to more than 1,500 people, making it then one of Florida's larger communities.

FORT NEW SMYRNA (*Fort Smyrna*). A Second Seminole War fort, also called Fort Smyrna, situated on the west side of Mosquito Lagoon, part of today's Intercoastal Waterway, below Mosquito Inlet, it was located near the present city of New Smyrna, the site of the settlement founded in August 1768 by Scottish physician Andrew Turnbull, in Volusia County. The post was apparently first established in 1835 by the 2nd Dragoons. It was reestablished on February 18, 1852, by Company L, 2nd Artillery, and abandoned November 10, 1853.

FORT NEW SWITZERLAND. Situated on the east bank of the St. Johns River, opposite the mouth of Black Creek, at the present-day town of Switzerland, St. Johns County, this blockhouse was most probably erected by the area's settlers in July 1835.

FORT NICHOLS. FORT GADSDEN.

FORT NICHOLS. Apparently erected in 1850, Fort Nichols was located about two miles south of the old Nichols phosphate mine near the town of Mulberry, west of Bartow, Polk County.

FORT NOEL (*Fort No. 3* [Middle Florida]). Florida historians have attributed this fort's location to several different northern counties. Fort

Noel, also known as Fort No. 3, was most probably situated on the east bank of the Aucilla River near the present-day town of Lamont in Jefferson County and presumably named for Captain Thomas Noel, 6th Infantry, who established the post in late March, 1839. Fort Noel's last post return was dated January 1842.

FORT NO. 1. General Zachary Taylor, commander of Florida's forces during part of the Second Seminole War, formulated the plan to lay off the whole of the northern half of the Florida peninsula into 18-mile squares with a small, 20-man garrisoned post in the center of each square. His idea was put into operation during 1839, believing that it was the only way to crush the Seminoles.

FORT NO. 1 (East Florida). According to a National Archives citation, this post was located 11 miles from the Indian River. It was ordered abandoned by General Orders No. 45.

FORT NO. 1 (Middle Florida). FORT MACOMB (Leon County).

FORT NO. 2 (East Florida). FORT VINTON.

FORT NO. 2 (Middle Florida). The only citation found for this post locates it in "Leon County, south of the Rose P.O., on the St. Marks River."

FORT NO. 2. FORT HOOK.

FORT NO. 3 (East Florida). This post was apparently located in Levy County and situated on Waccasassa Bay near the mouth of the river of the same name.

FORT NO. 3 (Middle Florida). FORT NOEL.

FORT NO. 4 (East Florida). Company K, 7th Infantry, commanded by 1st Lieutenant D. P. Whiting, arriving from Fort Clinch, established this post in the Cedar Keys on April 19, 1839. The fort's last post return was dated June 1841 when it was commanded by Captain Jacob Brown, 6th Infantry, with Company E.

FORT NO. 4 (Middle Florida). The only citation found for this post indicates that it was located in the vicinity of the town of Sirmans in Madison County, close to the northern boundary of Taylor County. The post's coordinates were given as Latitude 30 degrees, 24 minutes, and Longitude 83 degrees, 34 minutes.

FORT NO. 5 (East Florida). A citation reports that this post was located about four miles west of Lake Delaney, in the north end of the Ocala National Forest, Marion County.

FORT NO. 5 (Middle Florida). The location of this post was given only by its coordinates, Latitude 30 degrees, 9 minutes, and Longitude 84 degrees, 20 minutes, very possibly placing it in Wakulla County, south of Tallahassee.

FORT NO. 6 (East Florida). FORT RUSSELL (Alachua County).

FORT NO. 7 (East Florida). FORT MICANOPY.

FORT NO. 7 (Middle Florida). This temporary post was located between the mouths of the Fenholloway and Econfina rivers, near the Gulf, in Taylor County.

FORT NO. 8 (East Florida). FORT WACCASASSA.

FORT NO. 8 (Middle Florida). A reliable citation places this fortification near the city of Perry, Taylor County. Its coordinates were Latitude 30 degrees, 10 minutes, and Longitude 83 degrees, 27 minutes.

FORT NO. 9 (East Florida). FORT FANNING.

FORT NO. 9 (Middle Florida). This post was located near the town of Mayo in Lafayette County. Its coordinates were Latitude 30 degrees, 5 minutes, and Longitude 83 degrees, 15 minutes.

FORT NO. 10 (East Florida). This post was situated near the south bank of Lake Grandin near the town of Hollister, 10 miles west of Palatka, Putnam County.

FORT NO. 10 (Middle Florida). Located near the mouth of Spring Warrior Creek, east of the Fenholloway River, in Taylor County, its approximate bearings were Latitude 29 degrees, 50 minutes, and Longitude 83 degrees, 45 minutes.

FORT NO. 11 (East Florida). Located at present-day Keystone Heights, northeast of Gainesville, in Clay County (just east of the Alachua County line), Fort No. 11 was reportedly situated between a pond and Lake Geneva. It was established March 21, 1839, by Company H, 2nd Infantry, commanded by Lieutenant H. W. Wessells. The post was reinforced on April 1 by a part of

Company E of the 2nd Dragoons. Fort No. 11's last post return was dated June 1840, at which time the post was commanded by Lieutenant D. Davidson, 2nd Infantry. The fact that Fort Harlee was already in the extreme northwest corner of Square No. 11 did not stop General Zachary Taylor from placing a second post in the same square.

FORT NO. 11 (Middle Florida). Reportedly located in present Taylor County, this post's bearings were Latitude 29 degrees, 46 minutes, and Longitude 83 degrees, 31 minutes.

FORT NO. 12 (East Florida). Located about nine miles east of present-day Alachua on the old Bellamy Road, Alachua County, Fort No. 12 was established by 1st Lieutenant James W. Anderson with Company D of the 2nd Infantry, aggregating 61 men. Lieutenant Anderson married a Newnansville girl and was later killed in action in the war with Mexico. General Orders No. 18, issued at Fort King on May 20, 1840, received June 2, 1840, ordered "the white flag to be raised at all posts east of the Suwannee."

FORT NO. 12 (Middle Florida). This temporary fort's coordinates were reported as Latitude 29 degrees, 49 minutes, and Longitude 83 degrees, 11 minutes, probably placing its site in present Lafayette County.

FORT NO. 13 ([East Florida] *Fort Blue Springs*). An unnamed fort shown on several maps at Blue Springs, situated between present-day High Springs and the town of Bell, Gilchrest County, was most probably the same as Fort No. 13. The post was located on the critically needed military road linking Fort White on the Santa Fe River with Fort Gilleland at old Newnansville. No dates have been found for the post.

FORT NO. 13 (Middle Florida). This post was probably located on the north shore of Deadman's Bay near the mouth of the Steinhatchee River and "west of Stephensville," Taylor County. Its bearings have been reported as Latitude 29 degrees, 40 minutes, and Longitude 83 degrees, 29 minutes.

FORT NO. 13 DISTRICT POST. According to a National Archives citation, this post was apparently located in Taylor County and established April 30, 1839, by Captain H. Day, 2nd Infantry, with companies F and K, aggregating 54 men.

This post may be identical with Fort No. 13 (Middle Florida), Taylor County.

FORT NO. 14 (East Florida). Located "at the head of Kingsley Pond," near Kingsley, Clay County, a citation reports this post was abandoned June 8, 1840.

FORT NO. 14 (Middle Florida). Reportedly situated on California Creek in Dixie County, its bearings appear to have been Latitude 29 degrees, 36 minutes, and Longitude 83 degrees, 15 minutes.

FORT NO. 15 (East Florida). Located on Swift's Creek, about four miles "northeast of Providence P.O.," Union County, Fort No. 15 was established by Captain M. S. Howe with Company G, 2nd Dragoons, on April 15, 1839, and abandoned sometime in June 1840. Its last post return was dated May 1840.

FORT NO. 15 (Middle Florida). No information could be found on this post.

FORT NO. 16 (East Florida). Contradictory citations place this post in either Suwannee County or Columbia County, but more probably in the former, about eight miles west of O'Brien, not far from the Columbia County line. The post was established in the latter part of April 1839 by Captain Silas Casey with Company C, 2nd Infantry, arriving from Fort White. The post was probably abandoned in the late spring of 1840.

FORT NO. 17 (East Florida). Located south of the Suwannee River near the town of Mayo, Lafayette County, Fort No. 17 was established during the last week of April 1839.

FORT NO. 18 (East Florida). This post was established sometime in 1839 near the town of Sanderson, Baker County.

FORT NO. 19 (East Florida). Located close to the present intersection of the Columbia, Baker and Union county lines, this post occupied a site very near today's town of Lulu, Columbia County.

FORT NO. 20 (East Florida). Situated on the south bank of the Suwannee River, about five miles west of White Springs, Suwannee County, Fort No. 20 was established on or about June 30, 1839, by Captain J. B. Kingsbury, 2nd Infantry, with Company E, aggregating 50 men.

FORT NO. 21 (East Florida). A citation reports this post's bearings as Latitude 30 degrees, 20 minutes, and Longitude 83 degrees, 10 minutes, placing its site within present Hamilton County.

FORT OCILLA (AUCILLA). Established in July 1843, this fort was situated between the Aucilla and Wacissa rivers near the town of Lamont, two miles west of old Fort Gamble, Jefferson County.

FORT OCKLAWAHA. Located near Apalachicola in Franklin County, the post's coordinates were reported as Latitude 29 degrees, 45 minutes, and Longitude 84 degrees, 55 minutes.

FORT ON OCKLOCKONY RIVER. A usually reliable source indicates that this post was located about 30 miles from the sea, near the "Smith Creek P.O.," in either Liberty or Wakulla County. A National Archives citation reports that the post was "20 miles from the sea; captured from Spaniards by Governor Moore of South Carolina in 1704. In the strife the Governor of Apalachee, Don Juan Moxia and the greater part of the garrison of 400 men were slain and the fort burnt to ashes."

FORT OGDEN. Established sometime in 1841 probably by companies A, D, E, and K, 8th Infantry, the post was named for Captain E. A. Ogden, 8th Infantry (later assistant quartermaster), who died August 30, 1855 at Fort Riley, Kansas. Fort Ogden was located near the Peace River, at or close to the present-day town of Fort Ogden, De Soto County.

FORT OLD LANG SYNE. FORT DRANE.

FORT PAGE. A Second Seminole War fort, Fort Page was reportedly located in the vicinity of today's town of Wellborn in the northeast corner of Suwannee County.

PALM CITY DEPOT. Early in the year 1838, General Thomas S. Jesup ordered a depot established on the St. Lucie River for supplying operations to the south. Designation on an 1843 Army map locates the post in the vicinity of today's All American Boulevard in Palm City, Martin County. Archaeological explorations have failed to disclose the depot's remains because of the construction of the St. Lucie Canal.

FORT PALMETTO. FORT FANNING.

FORT PARKER. Historical citations locate this post on Cook's Hammock, north of Steinhatchee, 33 miles from Fort McCrabb, in Lafayette County.

FORT PEATON. A Confederate post in 1864, Fort Peaton was reportedly located about seven miles from St. Augustine.

PENSACOLA BARRACKS. The British occupation of Pensacola during the American Revolution demanded the need for barracks for their soldiery. Finally acting on plans made as early as 1772, two separate sets of barracks were built. One, formerly the residence of British Governor Peter Chester, was rebuilt as a barracks in 1778 for the Loyalists from Pennsylvania and the German Waldeck troops. The building, measuring 50 by 20 feet, burned during the last Spanish period sometime before 1813. Its site is directly behind the present headquarters of the Pensacola Historical Society. The other barracks, a three-story structure measuring about 156 by 40 feet, stood at the corners of Zarragossa and Tarragonna streets, a half block from the Society's building. The barracks was apparently fortified by the addition of two blockhouses; one was 31 feet square and two-storied, with brick floors and foundations, and the other, also two-storied, was 22 feet square. The original structure had been modified for use as a barracks and was mostly destroyed in the 1820s.

PENSACOLA BLOCKHOUSE. Constructed by the Spanish during their final occupation of Florida, this blockhouse stood on or near present Plaza Ferdinand (Square of Ferdinand) in downtown Pensacola. After the cession of Florida to the United States, the blockhouse was used as a customhouse.

FORT PENTON. Situated in Lake County, 19 miles from the Indian River, Fort Penton was established January 31, 1856, by Company L of the 3rd Artillery. According to a National Archives citation, it had been redesignated Fort Penton from Fort No. 2 in February 1850.

FORT PEYTON. A wooden fort and blockhouse established July 17, 1837, it was named for 1st Lieutenant Richard H. Peyton, a West Point graduate, the post's commander, and situated on the right bank of Moultrie Creek, about five miles southwest of St. Augustine. The celebrated Seminole leader, Chief Osceola, was en route to the fort under a flag of truce when he was treacherously seized on October 20, 1837, in accordance with orders of General Thomas S. Jesup. The violation of the truce is commemorated by a historical marker about a mile from the site of the fort. Fort Peyton was abandoned in July 1840.

FORT PICKENS. Named in honor of Brigadier General Andrew Pickens of the South Carolina State Troops during the American Revolution, Fort Pickens was built by the U.S. Army Corps of Engineers beginning in 1829 and completed in October 1834. Contracted slaves labored on the fortification, using some 21.5 million bricks, most of this material made locally and brought by barge to the island. Plans for the fortification of Pensacola Harbor were projected in 1822 in anticipation of the selection of Pensacola as the principal U.S. Naval Depot on the Gulf of Mexico. These plans resulted in the construction of Fort Pickens on the western tip of Santa Rosa Island, Fort McRee (1835–39) on the western end of Perdido Key, and Fort Barrancas (1839–45) and its Advanced Redoubt (1845–59) on the mainland. Together these forts were to secure the approaches to Pensacola Bay and the U.S. Navy Yard from foreign invasion. Fort Pickens, along with Fort Barrancas and the Advanced Redoubt are the only remaining relics in this area of a coastal defense system rendered obsolete by the invention and development of rifled cannon, armored battleships and the advanced technology of late nineteenth-century warfare.

Completed Fort Pickens was pentagonal in shape, with a bastion at each of the five corners. Each bastion was a fort in itself, having its own guns and magazine. These bastions projected from the regular line of the fort walls so that they could set up a cross-fire with the facing bastion and prevent the enemy from attacking the fort walls. The fort was complete with covert ways (protected passageways), a dry ditch, and flanking outworks. Its brick walls were 40 feet in height and 12 feet in thickness, and were embrasured (portholed) for one tier of guns in bombproof casemates, while one tier of guns was *en barbette* (mounted on top of the walls). The peacetime garrison of the fort was set at 100 men, to be increased in time of war to 1,260 men. The armament of the fort was to consist of 252 guns of various types and calibers. This fort was one of the few in the South from which the United States flag was never hauled down during the War Between the States. It was under intermittent cannon fire from its companion forts McRee and Barrancas, both of which were in Confederate hands. Fort Pickens foiled an abortive land attack by the Confederates before the

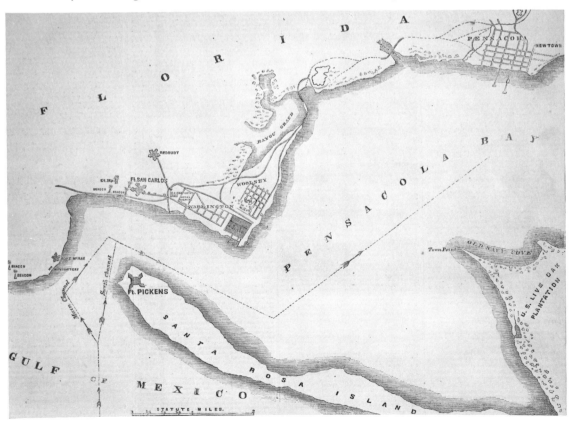

FORT PICKENS. Forts surrounding Pensacola Bay in 1861. (Courtesy of the Florida State Archives.)

attackers came close to the walls of Fort Pickens. This attack became known as the Battle of Santa Rosa Island.

On January 10, 1861, Florida left the Union to join what would soon become the new Confederate States of America. Most of the Federal property in the state was seized by secessionists, with a notable exception occurring at Pensacola. A force of 50 U.S. Army regulars, under the command of Lieutenant Adam Slemmer, in addition to 30 sailors and two Navy ships, left the Barrancas forts and Navy Yard on the mainland and occupied Fort Pickens. The many years of non-occupation had caused the fort to fall into a state of disrepair, compelling the Federal troops to work around the clock in an effort to make Fort Pickens defendable. In the meanwhile, rebel troops took control of all other installations in the area, but without Fort Pickens under their control, they could not effectively use the harbor and the Navy Yard. An uneasy truce was negotiated between North and South to forestall bloodshed.

On April 12, 1861, a few hours after the Confederates fired on Fort Sumter, Union troops landed on Santa Rosa Island breaking the truce. In October 1861, Confederate troops attacked the 6th New York Volunteer Infantry camped approximately one mile east of Fort Pickens. The Confederates destroyed most of the Union encampment before retreating under pursuit of regulars from Fort Pickens. The only time the forts themselves came under fire occurred on November 22–23, 1861, and January 1, 1862, when Confederates at Fort Barrancas and several other positions along the mainland exchanged artillery fire with Union artillerists at Fort Pickens. By May 1862, events outside Florida ended Confederate efforts to hold coastal Florida as they evacuated the Pensacola area. Soon afterwards Union forces reoccupied all the harbor installations. Although Fort Pickens would see no further combat, it served out the remainder of the war as a prison for military and political prisoners.

Between October 1886 and May 1888, Fort Pickens served as a prison home for approximately 50 Chiricahua Apache men, women, and children. The Indians had been removed from their former lands in New Mexico and Arizona Territories following the last of the U.S. wars against the Apaches in the Southwest. Included among the prisoners were Geronimo and Naiche, the son of Cochise. For 18 months the Apaches at Fort Pickens performed maintenance jobs around the fort and entertained curious visitors from the mainland. The Indians lived in the officers' quar-

ters on both the north and south sides of the fort and were generally well treated. The Apaches finally left Pensacola for Mount Vernon, Alabama, in 1888, where they lived for six years before being moved to a reservation at Fort Sill, Oklahoma, in 1894. Geronimo died in 1909 and is buried at Fort Sill.

By the late nineteenth century, American sea-coast forts of brick or stone masonry and earth had become obsolete. Consequently, a new phase of sea-coast defense began which continued well into the twentieth century. This new system of reinforced concrete structures continued the tradition of American strong, yet passive coastal defense. President Grover Cleveland called for a review of the coastal defenses. Headed by William C. Endicott, secretary of war, the review board was composed of Navy and Army officers as well as civilians. The purpose of the board was to submit recommendations for a program that would update such defenses by taking advantage of the technological revolution in weaponry. During the years 1887–96, detailed plans for the defense of 23 key harbors, including Pensacola, were prepared based upon the Endicott Board reports. It was 1893 before the final report for the Pensacola Harbor defenses was reviewed and approved. These plans provided the basis for additional changes and adaptations made over the next 40 years. Today many of the structures initiated by this plan still remain.

The reinforced concrete batteries and other historic structures contained within Gulf Islands National Seashore illustrate the evolution of the nation's coastal defense, spanning 150 years (1797–1947) of military history. Each concrete battery played a key role in the overall defensive plan. The batteries are constructed of steel reinforced concrete and were manned during the Spanish-American War, World War I, and World War II by the men of the Artillery and Coast Artillery Corps. The headquarters and post were at Fort Barrancas on the mainland adjacent to the Naval Air Station. The Fort Pickens area served as a subpost and by 1938 was being called the largest Army post in Florida and one of the largest Coast Artillery training centers in the United States.

There are nine concrete batteries on Santa Rosa Island. In chronological order of completion they are:

Battery Pensacola. Located in the center of Fort Pickens, Battery Pensacola was begun in 1898 and completed in 1899. It mounted two 12-inch rifles on disappearing carriages capable of firing 1,070-pound shells approximately eight miles. The battery was declared surplus in 1933, with its guns removed in 1934 and its carriages sold for scrap in 1942.

Battery Van Swearingen. The threat of war with Spain prompted the immediate construction of this battery in 1898. Two 4.7-inch guns were mounted on pedestal carriages and turned over to the Artillery on June 29, 1898. By 1917 the guns were obsolete and dismounted. The battery was named for Captain Joseph Van Swearingen, who was killed in action against the Seminole Indians during the Battle of Okeechobee on Christmas Day, 1837.

Batteries Cullum and Sevier. Although these structures appear to be one large complex, they are two separate structures. Completed by 1898, the complex housed four 10-inch rifles on disappearing carriages and was originally designated Battery Cullum in honor of Brigadier General George W. Cullum. Because of the size and complexity of the structure, it was divided into two separate batteries, each having its own fire control equipment. In 1916 General Order No. 15 was issued designating emplacements Nos. 1 and 2 as Battery Sevier, honoring John Sevier, pioneer, soldier and first governor of Tennessee. Emplacements Nos. 3 and 4 continued to be known as Battery Cullum.

Battery Worth. Completed in 1899, Battery Worth housed eight 12-inch mortars in two gun pits. Although the battery lost half of its armament in 1918 in accordance with the War Department policy to reduce weaponry mounted in the nation's older emplacements, the other four mortars remained active until 1942. The battery is named in honor of Brevet Major General William J. Worth, who was the first to plant the U.S. Flag on the Rio Grande in 1847.

Battery Payne. Constructed in 1904, the design and mission of this battery were identical to Battery Trueman. The battery is named for 1st Lieutenant Matthew M. Payne of Virginia, who served in both the War of 1812 and the Mexican-American War. Ten months after V-J Day, the two three-inch guns and carriages were marked for disposal.

Battery Trueman. Named for Alexander Trueman of Maryland, who died of wounds received in action with Indians near Fort Recovery on June 2, 1792, this battery was positioned on the western end of Santa Rosa Island north of the harbor entrance. The battery was built in 1905 and mounted two three-inch rapid-fire guns designed to defend the channel and submarine minefield against fast torpedo boats and minesweepers. In June 1946 the guns were dismounted and turned over to the Post Salvage Officer for disposal.

Battery Cooper. Built in 1905, Battery Cooper mounted two six-inch guns on disappearing carriages. During World War I (1917), the guns were removed for use on railway mounts in France. The carriages remained until 1920, when they were declared obsolete and salvaged. In 1937 four emplacements for 155mm guns were constructed around Battery Cooper and designated Battery GPF, remaining part of the Harbor Defense Project until the spring of 1945, when it was disarmed. The battery is named Battery George Cooper in the memory of 2nd Lieutenant George A. Cooper, killed in action in the Philippine Islands, on September 17, 1900.

Battery Langdon. Constructed in 1917, the battery was completed in 1923 and mounted two 12-inch guns *en barbette*. The battery is named in honor of Loomis L. Langdon, who served at Fort Pickens on three different occasions. The attack on Pearl Harbor brought major structural changes to Battery Langdon during 1942–43. Massive concrete casemates, with walls 10 feet thick and 17 feet of overhead masonry, were added to protect the guns and crews.

Battery No. 234. Because of overwhelming German victories in 1940, a special War Department board convened to prepare a new master plan for coastal defenses that resulted in plans for two new six-inch gun batteries for the Pensacola Harbor Defense Project. An identical emplacement known as Battery No. 233 was constructed on Perdido Key. The six-inch guns had curved shields of cast-steel four to six inches thick, providing protection against machine gun and light artillery fire. By the time the batteries were completed in the autumn of 1943, the war favored the Allies, and there was not a high priority for arming the batteries. Although the batteries did receive their shields and barbette carriages in 1946, the six-inch guns were never received.

In addition to the concrete batteries on Santa Rosa Island, there are three more batteries on the eastern end of Perdido Key. They are Battery Slemmer, completed in 1899 mounting two 8-inch breech-loading rifles; Battery Center, completed in 1900 mounting four 15-pounder Driggs-Seabury rapid-fire guns; and Battery No. 233, identical to Battery No. 234 on Santa Rosa Island.

In May 1947 the War Department declared the Pensacola Harbor defenses surplus to the nation's needs and ordered them deactivated. With the end of World War II, and subsequent advances in military technology and weaponry, it was concluded that America's national defense should be concerned with attacks from the air and not from the sea. The era of coastal defense had passed and the Coast Artillery Corps was disbanded, replaced by the use of guided missiles and nuclear weapons.

FORT PICOLATA. At the "Pass of the Salamatoto River" (so named for a nearby settlement), probably on the site of present-day Picolata, where the St. Johns River significantly narrows, was a natural crossing used by the Indians. Here, soon after 1700, the Spanish built two outposts, called the "Ferry Forts," opposite each other—first Fort Picolata on the east bank (in St. Johns County) and then Fort San Francisco de Pupo on the west bank (in Clay County)—about 20 miles west of St. Augustine. Probably no more than palisaded sentry boxes when first built, they were designed to command the strategic crossing.

Fort Picolata was temporarily abandoned sometime in 1706 when the English were continuing their campaign of purging the Spanish mission system in northern Florida. Sometime between 1714 and 1716, Fort San Francisco de Pupo was built opposite Fort Picolata. When the Spanish engineer, Antonio de Arredondo, visited the ferry crossing in 1737, the two posts were in an advanced stage of dilapidation. On January 7, 1740, Fort Picolata was captured and burned to the ground by James Oglethorpe's troops during his first invasion of Florida. After Oglethorpe was repulsed for the second time in 1743, the Spanish began a general rebuilding of the defenses throughout their province, including the complete reconstruction of Fort Picolata with a 30-foot-high tower.

Fort Picolata was intermittently garrisoned during the British occupation of Florida (1763–83). In November 1769 Governor James Grant of East Florida held a conference at the fort with the chiefs of Indian tribes to establish boundaries. In 1744 naturalist William Bartram visited Fort Picolata and found it dismantled and deserted, though there still remained a 30-foot-high square tower surrounded by a deep ditch. The upper story was open on each side, with battlements that had formerly been mounted with eight 4-pounders, two on each side. The works were constructed with hewn stone cemented with lime.

Early in the Second Seminole War, a wooden blockhouse was built on or very close to Fort Picolata's site. The town of Picolata became a supply depot, the location of an Army hospital and a base for operations against the Seminoles. A regular Army post was established here on March 7, 1836, by Lieutenant Colonel James Bankhead, 3rd Artillery, commanding a garrison of 254 men. During the Civil War, Picolata's fort was enlarged and occupied by Union troops. Its location was about a mile north of today's Magnolia Landing and 20 yards from the river. A state historical marker commemorating Fort Picolata is located at the intersection of S.R. 13 and S.R. 208 on Picolata Road near Green Cove Springs.

FORT PIERCE. Constructed as a part of General Thomas S. Jesup's winter campaign of 1837–38 against the scattered bands of Seminoles in South Florida, Fort Pierce was situated on a high bluff on the west bank of the Indian River, about four miles south of the now closed Indian River Inlet, in St. Lucie County. Construction of the palmetto log blockhouse, named for Brevet Lieutenant Colonel Benjamin Kendrick Pierce, brother of the 14th President of the United States, was accomplished by elements of the colonel's command, the 1st Artillery, during the first days of January 1838. The post was apparently temporarily abandoned late in the following summer. General Zachary Taylor, Jesup's successor, reported in July 1839 that he had ordered Fort Pierce rebuilt and reoccupied. Precisely what units occupied the post and for how long they may have remained from the summer of 1839 to early 1841 is unknown, although it is probable that the fort was garrisoned on a more or less permanent basis. Following the order declaring an end to hostilities in August 1842, Fort Pierce was abandoned.

FORT PILATKA. Located about 18 miles west of St. Augustine at Palatka, Putnam County, on the left or west bank of the St. Johns River, Fort Pilatka served as an important military depot during the years of the Second Seminole War. Eight blockhouses, a large hospital, barracks and stables were erected there in 1840.

CAMP PINCKNEY. A temporary Confederate post and storage depot during 1864, Camp Pinckney was located near the St. Marys River "on Little Front Creek, between Orange Bluff and Calico Hill," in Nassau County.

FORT PIRIBIRIBA. Apparently a defense built by the Spanish after Carolina Governor James Moore's invasion of Florida in 1702, the four-bastioned wooden fort was situated at the mouth of the St. Johns River in the immediate vicinity of today's Jacksonville. A map and accompanying translation are evidence that it was erected after January 1703 and existed until at least June

1705. No indication has been found to define the meaning of the fort's name.

FORT PLACE. The predecessor of the present-day town of Wewahitchka, Gulf County, Fort Place was built in the early 1830s as a refuge from hostile Indians. It consisted of a hewn-log blockhouse equipped with portholes for firearms and was enclosed within a two-acre stockade.

FORT PLEASANT. Situated on the right or east bank of the Econfinee River, 22 miles from its mouth, in Taylor County, Fort Pleasant (or Pleasants) was established on November 12, 1838, by 1st Lieutenant Charles S. Lovell, 6th Infantry, with Company E, arriving from Micanopy. The post was abandoned November 27, 1842.

FORT PLENTIFUL. Very little is known about this post, reportedly located "between Warm Springs and the Hernando County Court House," Hernando County. A Resolution of the Legislative Council, dated February 28, 1844, constitutes the only source found for its location.

FORT POINSETT. Established October 16, 1839, by Surgeon General Thomas Lawson with 248 men on East Cape (Cape Sable), the southeastern extremity of the United States, in Monroe County, this post was named for Secretary of War Joel R. Poinsett. The post was abandoned March 21, 1843.

FORT PORT LEON. A temporary Second Seminole War post, it was reportedly located about five miles southeast of St. Marks at Port Leon, Wakulla County. The town of Port Leon, situated on the east bank of the St. Marks River, existed for only two years, 1841–43, when a hurricane and tidal wave wiped it out. During the Civil War, a gun battery was established on or near its site.

FORT POSA. An unverified citation locates this Spanish defense on Anastasia Island, just south of St. Augustine, St. Johns County.

CAMP POWELL. A temporary Confederate post located near the Perdido River in Escambia County, it was occupied in 1864 by one company of cavalry.

FORT PRESTON. The only citation found locates this blockhouse at Spring Garden, Volusia County.

FORT PRESTON. Situated on the left bank of Apalachicola River, "13 miles from Aspalaga," or southwest of Blountstown, Calhoun County, Fort Preston was established in February 1840 by Captain E. D. Bullock, commanding Company E, 2nd Dragoons. The post's last return was dated February 1842.

FORT PRINCE. Fort Barrancas.

PRINCE OF WALES REDOUBT. Fort Sombrero.

FORT PRINCIPE D'ASTURIAS. Fort San Carlos de Austria.

CAMP PRINGLE. After its evacuation of the Pensacola Navy Yard in 1862, the 1st Florida Regiment was stationed for a time at the Confederates' Camp Pringle on the Escambia River above Pensacola. The soldiers at the camp suffered a serious visitation of the measles shortly after the arrival there by the 1st Florida troops.

FORT QUARTEL (*Fort Cartel*). Established by the Spanish in about the year 1575, this defense was reportedly located one mile north of Anastasia Island on the north bank of the Matanzas River, near St. Augustine.

QUEEN'S REDOUBT. Fort San Bernardo.

QUESADA BATTERY. Erected by the Spanish in or about 1793 at the mouth of the St. Johns River north of St. Augustine, the battery was designed to prevent the passage up the river by enemy vessels. At one time the Quesada Battery had boasted two cannons, a two-story barracks, and a large powder magazine. The battery was apparently abandoned sometime prior to the Patriots War in East Florida.

FORT READ. Fort Reid.

FORT REDOUBT. Advanced Redoubt.

FORT REED. Fort Reid.

REDOUBT REED. Jacksonville Forts.

FORT REID (*Fort Read; Fort Reed*). Established by Lieutenant Colonel William S. Harney on July 7, 1840, the post's command was taken over by Captain George A. H. Blake, 2nd Dragoons, with companies A, B, F, and K. The post was named in honor of Robert Raymond Reid, Florida's fourth Territorial Governor and located on Lake Monroe adjacent to the present-day city of Sanford, Seminole County. The post was probably abandoned at the conclusion of the Seminole War in 1842 and temporarily reoccupied on November 4, 1849, by elements of Company D, 1st Artillery, which evacuated December 17, 1849. Between the first and second occupations, Fort Reid's blockhouse was intermittently used and maintained by the area's settlers as a defense against Indian attack.

CAMP ROBERTS. Established by Union troops from Vermont in June 1862, Camp Roberts was located at Warrington in southern Escambia County. The town had been burned by Confederate forces before abandoning it a month earlier.

CAMP RODGERS. A temporary camp established during the Spanish-American War, Camp Rodgers was located at Ybor City, adjacent to Tampa.

FORT ROGER JONES. Established March 17, 1839, at the "Ocilla Ferry" (Aucilla River), north of today's Highway 90, Jefferson County, Fort Roger Jones was first occupied by Captain E. G. Mitchell with Company F, 1st Infantry. Captain Mitchell became ill and was replaced by Lieutenant W. W. Pew of the same regiment. The post's last return was dated May 1839.

CAMP ROGERS. Established during the winter of 1856–57 near Deep Lake, Collier County, some 60 miles southeast of Fort Myers, Camp Rogers was situated on the edge of the Big Cypress as a temporary headquarters from which raids were made in every direction. There is no indication when this post was abandoned.

CAMP ROGERS. Located at Ybor City, adjacent to Tampa, this post was established on May 21, 1898, as a camp of the Battalion of Siege Artillery of the Army's field forces for the Spanish-American War. The first organization selected for the Siege Train was Battery K, 5th Artillery. This unit departed August 19, 1898, and the post was abandoned the following day.

CAMP ROMANO. A temporary camp, similar to and near Camp Moulder, this post was established sometime in early February 1857 on or near Pavillion Keys in the Gulf of Mexico, Monroe County, about 120 miles southeast of Fort Myers.

ROSE'S BLUFF PATRIOT CAMP. A citation reports that this camp, situated on a bluff on the south bank of the St. Marys River in Nassau County, was for a time during 1778 the headquarters of American-born British-allied partisan troops during the American Revolution.

FORT ROUGH AND READY. The only clue found relating to this post's location was found on an 1856 map, indicating that it was situated near Rye Bridge, on the south side of the Manatee River, in Manatee County.

FORT RUSSELL. A temporary post situated on Key Biscayne, Dade County, this post was most probably established on February 28, 1839, by Major Sylvester Churchill, 3rd Artillery, with three companies of the same regiment, and one company of the 2nd Infantry. The post was named for Captain Samuel L. Russell, 2nd Infantry, killed on the same day on the Miami River. Fort Russell's last post return was dated September 1839.

FORT RUSSELL. Situated on Orange Lake Creek, about five miles from Fort Brooks and near the present-day town of Orange Springs, Marion County, Fort Russell was established on March 31, 1839, by Captain W. W. Morris with Company E, 4th Artillery. The post was named in the memory of Captain Samuel L. Russell, 2nd Infantry, killed on February 28, 1839, on the Miami River near Key Biscayne. The post was abandoned in September 1842.

FORT RUSSELL (*Fort No. 6* [East Florida]). Originally known as Fort No. 6 (East Florida), this post was named in the memory of Samuel L. Russell, killed near Key Biscayne on February 28, 1839. The post was reportedly located near the town of Island Grove, Alachua County.

RUSSELL'S LANDING POST. A National Archives citation locates this post near Fort Pierce, St. Lucie County. Active from December 1849 through March 1850, the post was garrisoned by Brevet Colonel Justin Demick, 1st Artillery, with elements of the 1st, 2nd, and 3rd Artillery, aggregating 346 men.

ST. ANDREWS BAY POST. Captain George C. Hutter, 6th Infantry, with companies A, B, and G, established this post located in Bay County on January 27, 1839. The post was abandoned August 26, 1839.

FORT ST. AUGUSTINE. Reportedly located about nine miles northeast of Fort Macomb, east of Tallahassee, this post was established by Captain Gardiner with Company E, 1st Infantry.

ST. AUGUSTINE ARSENAL. The site of the former barracks that housed English, Spanish, and U.S. troops is located at 82 Marine Street in St. Augustine.

FORT ST. BERNARD. FORT SAN BERNARDO.

FORT ST. CHARLES. FORT BARRANCAS.

ST. FRANCIS BARRACKS. (*State Arsenal*). These coquina rock walls were once part of the chapel and Convent of Our Lady of the Immaculate Conception established by Franciscan missionaries in 1573. Thatch-roofed wooden buildings on the site were burned in 1599, rebuilt, and again destroyed by fire in 1702 when English Carolinian forces burned St. Augustine. Reconstructed of coquina in 1735–55, the buildings were converted to military use during the British occupation of Florida, 1763–83, and also used by the Spanish for military purposes during 1784–1821, and by the United States from 1821 until 1900 when the garrison was withdrawn.

The reservation was leased to the State of Florida in 1907 for use as the headquarters of the National Guard. Fire again destroyed the interior in 1915, leaving only the coquina walls standing. The administrative offices were moved to adjacent buildings on the reservation. In 1921 the property was donated to the state and the buildings renovated and reconstructed for use as the headquarters for the Military Department, State of Florida. The coquina-walled structure is located at 108 Marine Street in St. Augustine.

FORT ST. FRANCIS DE PUPO. FORT SAN FRANCISCO DE PUPO.

FORT ST. GEORGE (*Fort George*). In 1736 General James Oglethorpe, in preparation for an eventual assault against St. Augustine, occupied San Juan Island nearly opposite the mouth of the St. Johns River and renamed it Fort George Island in honor of King George II. He built a fortification named Fort St. George or Fort George, primarily an earthwork enclosed within a palisade. The work was situated near Mt. Cornelia, on which he emplaced cannon pointed toward the southern shore of the St. Johns River. On the northern end of Fort George Island, some 17 miles northeast of Jacksonville, stands the Kingsley Plantation House, begun in 1817 when Zephaniah Kingsley bought the island, the oldest surviving plantation house in Florida.

ST. JOHNS BLUFF BATTERY. A survey of the St. Johns River in March 1898 resulted in the decision to construct emplacements for eight-inch breech-loading rifles on St. Johns Bluff, and construction of the works was begun early in April. The fortifications were designed to defend the city of Jacksonville and the entrance to the river from attack during the Spanish-American War. The battery was dismantled in October 1899 and the guns sent to Pensacola. The ruins of the battery lie off Fort Caroline Road, near the site of Fort Caroline built by the French in 1564.

FORT ST. MARK. SAN MARCOS, CASTILLO DE.

FORT ST. MARKS. FORT SAN MARCOS DE APALACHE.

FORT ST. MICHAEL. FORT GEORGE.

FORT ST. MICHAEL. FORT SAN MIGUEL.

FORT ST. ROSE. FORT SANTA ROSA.

REDOUBT SAMMON. JACKSONVILLE FORTS.

FORT SAN ANTONIO DE PADUA. Located on the southeast shore of Charlotte Harbor on the Gulf of Mexico, Fort San Antonio was established near the principal village of Chief Carlos's Calusa Indians. Fifty Spanish soldiers under Captain Francisco de Reinoso sent there by Pedro Menendez erected a blockhouse in May 1567, intended to protect the Florida Keys and the Bahama Channel sea-lanes. The Indian village soon thereafter became the site of the mission established by Jesuit Father Juan Rogel, a conversion effort that failed. When the blockhouse's garrison was denied food during the late months of 1568, the Spanish captured a number of minor Indian chiefs, charged them with treachery, and executed them on or about December 17, 1568. The Calusas immediately adopted a scorched earth policy, and the Spanish soldiers were left hopelessly destitute of food. The fort was abandoned during the last days of the same month. The Calusas wasted no time burning the blockhouse.

FORT SAN BERNARDO (*Queen's Redoubt; Fort St. Bernard*). Formerly the Queen's Redoubt in Pensacola built by the British sometime between 1778 and the spring of 1781 during their 20-year occupation of Florida, it was renamed Fort San Bernardo after the Spanish regained possession of the territory. The fort, a semicircular network of batteries connected by trenches, was situated several hundred yards northwest of Fort George which stood on a hill on the north side of Pensacola. The forts were in complete disrepair when General Andrew Jackson attacked Pensacola in 1818.

FORT SAN CARLOS. Built at old Fernandina on Amelia Island in Nassau County during the Second Spanish Period (1783–1821), Fort San Carlos was most probably erected during the year 1816. The town of Fernandina was situated on a peninsula or neck of land defended by a strong picket and two blockhouses that enclosed the whole town. On the harbor side was Fort San Carlos, which mounted eight guns, and which commanded the anchorage, reaching as far as the middle line of the waters or boundary of the United States. In the "Old Town" section of today's Fernandina, at the foot of Estrada Street, are some of the remains of Fort San Carlos.

FORT SAN CARLOS. FORT BARRANCAS.

FORT SAN CARLOS DE AUSTRIA. FORT BARRANCAS.

FORT SAN CARLOS DE BARRANCAS. FORT BARRANCAS.

FORT SAN DIEGO. Located just east of present-day Palm Valley, about 20 miles north of St. Augustine, Fort San Diego was the palisaded and fortified ranch owned by Diego de Espinosa, one of the more affluent residents in St. Augustine's environs. To protect his property from Indian incursions, Espinosa had provided the ranch's main building with defensive works during the early 1700s, certainly before 1736. A 1703 Spanish citation is the earliest reference to the San Diego Ranch. Espinosa's defenses consisted of a palisade of cedar posts about 15 feet high, with two diagonal bastions, and regularly fortified with five falconets (light cannon), increased to 11 cannon in 1740 when General James Oglethorpe and his army invaded north Florida. In May of that year, the English captured Fort San Diego, garrisoned it with their own troops, and went on to besiege St. Augustine.

FORT SAN FERNANDO. The Spanish in 1686 built this fort on Amelia Island in the area known as Old Town in Fernandina. In September 1702 Governor James Moore of South Carolina, leading a force of English and allied Indians, invaded north Florida, overran Amelia Island, and captured Fort San Fernando, culminating in the complete depopulation of the island.

FORT SAN FRANCISCO DE PUPO (*Fort St. Francis de Pupo*). Soon after the turn of the eighteenth century, most probably between 1714 and 1716, the Spanish erected Fort San Francisco de Pupo on the west bank of the St. Johns River in Clay County, opposite its twin outpost of Fort Picolata, about 20 miles west of St. Augustine and a few miles below present-day Green Cove Springs on the same side of the river. The fort was captured and destroyed by General James Oglethorpe's invasion forces in 1740. Rebuilt by the Spanish, the original wooden structures of both so-called "Ferry Forts" were replaced by palisaded, square two-story, 30-foot-high coquina towers, surrounded by deep ditches. Their upper stories were open on all four sides and armed with two swivel guns to a side. During the British occupation of Florida (1763–83), they were intermittently garrisoned by small detachments of troops. (See: FORT PICOLATA.)

FORT SAN JUAN. Some of the guns of French Fort Caroline (renamed Fort San Mateo) captured by Pedro Menéndez in 1565 were used to arm new Spanish forts on or close to the mouth of the St. Johns River. One of the defenses erected was Fort San Juan on Little Talbot Island, several miles north of Mayport in Duval County. In April 1568 retribution visited the Spanish. Dominique de Gourgues, French patriot, sailed secretly from France with 180 followers with the object of revenging the Fort Caroline massacre. With the aid of several hundred Indians, the French first seized the island, and after reducing Fort San Juan, fashioned scaling ladders to assault Fort San Mateo. (See: FORT CAROLINE.)

FORT SAN JUAN DE PINOS. CASTILLO DE SAN MARCOS.

FORT SAN LUÍS DE APALACHE. A noted fort and a mission known as San Luís de Talimali, situated on an elevation just west of present-day Tallahassee, were established by the Spanish military authorities and Franciscan friars in 1640. An extensive, palisaded, and fortified town in the form of an irregular parallelogram with bastions in its angles and a blockhouse, approximately 90 by 60 feet, in the center, and the whole surrounded by a moat, Fort San Luís served as the headquarters for seven missionary settlements in the Tallahassee area. In January 1704 an army of 50 Carolinians and 1,000 allied Creek Indians led by Colonel James Moore invaded West Florida, destroyed five of the Apalachee missions, and demoralized the whole province. After two more missions were destroyed in June, the Spanish in

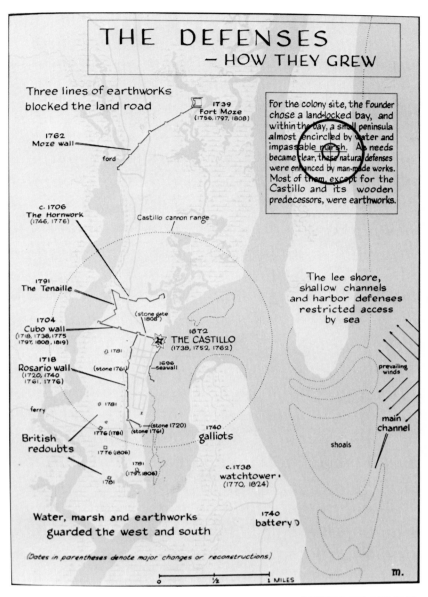

July evacuated Fort San Luís and blew up the fort and blockhouse.

CASTILLO DE SAN MARCOS (*Fort San Juan de Pinos* [Pinillo]; *Fort St. Mark; Fort Marion*). The most representative Old World city in America, St. Augustine has the distinction of being the oldest European settlement on the basis of continuous existence in the continental United States. Architecturally, it is a great repository of interesting historical detail, with the magnificent Castillo its most celebrated structure, the final replacement for a century-long series of nine wooden forts (the sixth was named Fort Juan de Pinos or Pinillo). Established 42 years before the English settled Jamestown and 55 years before the Pilgrims founded Plymouth Colony, St. Augustine was already 210 years old when the first shots of the American Revolution were fired at Lexington and Concord.

Today, guarding the city of St. Augustine against vanished enemies, the Castillo de San Marcos recalls an important part of Florida's exciting heritage. For generations this fortress has stood as a symbol of the long struggle among European nations for control of Florida and dominance in the New World. As the sixteenth century arrived, these often vicious struggles for military, economic, and religious power continued. Nation fought nation, royal families quarreled and battled among themselves, civil wars raged and Catholic fought Protestant. This was a part of the heritage of Europe and, for good or bad, this heritage was brought to the New World. Here and on nearby waters, Spaniard, Frenchman, and Englishman would fight as they had in Europe for centuries. All would eventually lose out to an energetic new nation, but they were to leave their indelible mark on our early heritage.

With the exception of the land which is now Brazil, all of the lands in the New World belonged to the Spanish Empire. These lands of the non-Christian world belonged to Spain by virtue of Columbus's discovery in 1492, by decree of Pope Alexander VI in 1493, by treaty in 1494, divine right and legal possession. England and France had all but been excluded; but both were growing in strength and national ambition in the sixteenth century and were gazing enviously at the wealth Spain was reaping from her New World possessions. It was to be France that would first startle Spain out of her complacency and challenge, on Florida's northeast coast, Spain's New World monopoly.

Fifty years after discovery in 1513, Spain still had neglected to establish a colony in Florida. When the French built Fort Caroline near the mouth of the St. Johns River on Spanish-claimed territory, it touched off the first armed conflict between European powers in North America. But, more importantly, while ejecting the French from Fort Caroline and Florida and attempting to protect her treasure-laden galleons sailing along the coasts of Florida from the New World to the Old, Spain founded St. Augustine, about 35 miles south of the French colony.

The Spanish settlement at St. Augustine faced a precarious future. The English settled Jamestown in 1607, and by 1670 had spread southward to the Carolinas. St. Augustine had already been attacked and destroyed by English raiders from the sea, and assault by land appeared inevitable. To meet this increasing English threat, the Spanish began construction of the Castillo de San Marcos in 1672. Though the city, which existed for the fortress, would again be destroyed

CASTILLO DE SAN MARCOS. Map showing the development of the defenses from 1672 to 1791. (Courtesy of the Eastern National Park and Monument Association.)

CASTILLO DE SAN MARCOS. Artist's conception of the building of the castillo. (Courtesy of the Eastern National Park and Monument Association.)

from the north, but citizens of the newly created nation, who were determined that Florida should be a part of that creation. In 1821, when Spain ceded Florida to the United States, the colors of Spanish Empire were lowered for the last time from above the Castillo. Renamed Fort Marion in 1825 in honor of General Francis Marion, Revolutionary War leader, the fortress served as a military post and prison stockade through the Spanish-American War. In 1942, by Act of Congress, the original name of Castillo de San Marcos was restored to this famous landmark.

FORT SAN MARCOS DE APALACHE (*Fort St. Marks; Fort Ward*). Eighteen miles south of Tallahassee, in south-central Florida's Panhandle, two rivers—the St. Marks and the Wakulla—meet to form a wide, deep harbor six miles above the entrance to Apalachee Bay from the Gulf of Mexico. At the strategic juncture of the two rivers is a comparatively narrow peninsula or headland upon which, in the year 1679, the Spanish built the first Fort San Marcos de Apalache, the site of the present-day town of St. Marks in Wakulla County. The fort was built of logs coated with lime to give the appearance of stone. Three years later, in 1682, the fort was attacked by pirates and so severely damaged that it had to be abandoned. Plans were made for a new fort in 1683 but apparently were not carried out.

Despite the increasing raids made against the Tallahassee area's 14 Franciscan missions by British colonials and their Indian allies from English colonies to the north, Spain failed to strengthen her Florida provinces or reestablish the post at St. Marks. In 1704 English forces, led by Colonel James Moore of Carolina, invaded Apalachee Province and systematically began the destruction of the missions there. A second wooden fort was built at St. Marks in 1718, and in 1739, construction on the third Fort San Marcos de Apalache was initiated. This fort was to be a permanent Spanish strong point, built of limestone quarried in an area across the Wakulla River. Work on the fort, however, progressed slowly, and by 1763, when England gained possession of Florida from Spain by the Treaty of Paris, ending the Seven Years' War, the fort was but half completed. During the years 1763–83, when British troops occupied Fort San Marcos (anglicized to Fort St. Marks), a number of significant improvements were made on the fortifications. The fort was reoccupied by the Spanish in 1787, four years after they regained possession of Florida.

by English colonial armies, the impregnable Castillo survived repeated attacks and sieges.

By treaty with Spain in 1763, England at last gained control of the Castillo, renamed Fort St. Mark, and Florida. British possession was to last only a brief twenty years, but much would happen during that time. In 1775 England's colonial offspring in the north rebelled against English rule, and by 1783 a new nation had been created by revolution—the United States. But while battles for independence were being fought at Bunker Hill, Lexington and Concord, and King's Mountain, sparsely settled Florida remained loyal to England.

In 1783 Florida was retroceded to Spain, and the flag of Spain once more flew above the ramparts of the Castillo de San Marcos. Now it was not the English who threatened Spanish Florida

CASTILLO DE SAN MARCOS. Wall, ramparts, and moat. (Courtesy of the National Park Service.)

CASTILLO DE SAN MARCOS. Aerial view. (Courtesy of the National Park Service.)

In 1792 William Augustus Bowles, a disgraced British officer turned pirate, with a small number of whites and about 300 Seminoles, captured Fort St. Marks. His success, however, was short-lived, for the Spanish returned with seven men-of-war from Pensacola and recaptured the fort. In 1818 General Andrew Jackson captured the town and the fort but later withdrew. Three years later, Florida was ceded to the United States. In 1861 Confederate troops seized the fort and renamed it Fort Ward. For four years a Federal fleet blockaded the mouth of the St. Marks River. Finally, on May 12, 1865, Federal sea and land forces attacked and captured St. Marks and Fort Ward. Today the stabilized limestone remains of Fort San Marcos de Apalache at St. Marks constitute a National Landmark maintained by the State of Florida.

FORT SAN MATEO. FORT CAROLINE.

FORT SAN MIGUEL. FORT GEORGE.

FORT SAN MIGUEL (*Fort St. Michael*). During the War of 1812, the British occupied Pensacola and its excellent harbor as their base for operations against New Orleans and Mobile despite the protests of the Spanish governor, who attempted to maintain strict neutrality. The British had seized the guardians of the bay, Fort Barrancas and Fort St. Miguel, which they immediately anglicized to Fort St. Michael, hoisted the English standard, and took over the governor's own house.

FORT SAN NICHOLAS. In 1740 the Spanish under Governor Manuel de Montiano, in anticipation of an attack by the English under James Oglethorpe, built still another blockhouse on the south bank of the St. Johns River in today's South Jacksonville, not far from Fort San Mateo. Its site, located at the strategic ford at the foot of present Liberty Street, had been named Wacca Pilatka ("cows crossing over") by the Indians, but called the Ferry of San Nicholas by the Spanish. The fort was situated about a mile east of the early twentieth-century South Jacksonville ferry landing. No indication has been found that the British had garrisoned the Spanish fort during their 20-year occupation of Florida. The little thriving settlement established at the ferry crossing was called Cowford, the forerunner of modern Jacksonville.

When the Spanish returned in 1784 they reestablished and refortified Fort San Nicholas, surrounding it with a moat 100 feet square. The officers' quarters and barracks were located outside the moat. In 1796 John Houston McIntosh, former Revolutionary War officer, led a band of unsavory adventurers from Georgia in an attack against Fort San Nicholas, destroying it in revenge for Spanish mistreatment and appropriation of his lands in the area. Despite his depredations, he and the Spanish arrived at an amicable settlement, and the fort was rebuilt. In 1812, during the Patriots War, aroused Americans captured and destroyed the fort. And again it was rebuilt. During the last years of the fort's existence, after the cession of Florida to the United States in 1821, Fort San Nicholas was maintained principally to prevent smuggling, but bribery was routinely accepted as the normal way of conducting business. During World War I, the fort site was a part of the property used as a shipbuilding facility, about 1,500 feet north of the river. The only memorial to the fort's existence is a gray stone marker about three miles east of U.S. 1 in Jacksonville.

CAMP SANDERSON. The site of Sanderson in Baker County was used by both Union and Confederate soldiers as a camp during the campaign of 1864. The camp was used as a Confederate supply depot, but it was abandoned on February 9, 1864. From the 9th to the 13th, it was held by Federal troops and used as a base for raids on Lake City and Gainesville. On February 20 the site was used as a springboard by Federals attacking Olustee. During the retreat from the battle there, the camp was retaken by the Confederates.

FORT SANDERSON. Located at old Garey's Ferry in Clay County, Fort Sanderson was established by 2nd Lieutenant C. Hanson, 7th Infantry, with Company D, on July 12, 1840, and named in memory of Lieutenant James S. Sanderson, 7th Infantry, killed by Indians on May 19, 1840. Fort Sanderson was abandoned February 1, 1841.

FORT SANTA LUCIA DE CANAVERAL. In compliance with an order of Pedro Menéndez de Avilés, founder of St. Augustine, about 200 soldiers commanded by Captain Juan Velez de Medrano built a fort in 1568 in the immediate vicinity of present-day Jensen Beach, opposite Hutchinson Island, St. Lucie County. The fort very soon after its completion was besieged by Indians. So many of its garrison were killed that the survivors mutinied, abandoned the fort, and returned in great haste to St. Augustine.

FORT SANTA MARÍA. No citations have been found to indicate when this fort was established. Fort Santa María, situated in the north central part of Amelia Island, Nassau County, was reportedly a Spanish military headquarters until 1686.

FORT SANTA MARÍA DE GALVE. A citation based on Roberts and Jeffrey's map of 1763 reports that this Spanish fort was located on the mainland opposite the west end of Santa Rosa Island in Pensacola Bay, with no indication when it was established. In 1693 two groups of soldiers, cartographers among them, mapped the area between Fort San Marcos de Apalache at St. Marks and Pensacola Bay. One of the mapmakers changed the name of the bay from Santa María de Filipino de Ochuse to Santa María de Galve, named for the then viceroy of Mexico. At the same time they were also calling the bay Penzacola for a small Indian tribe that lived on the shore of the bay.

FORT SANTA ROSA (*Fort St. Rose*). Situated on the western end of Santa Rosa Island in Pensacola Bay, this blockhouse built by the Spanish in 1722 was apparently intended to protect the village of Santa Rosa de Punta de Siguenza. On a few British maps the fort was designated as Fort St. Rose. It was destroyed by a hurricane in November 1752. During the British period (1763–83), a signal battery possibly occupied the same site. Sometime after 1698, Andrés de Arriola reportedly built a battery called Santa María de Galve (not to be confused with the mainland post of the same name) in the immediate vicinity of Fort Santa Rosa's site.

SAN VICENTE FERRER BATTERY. The Spanish built additional fortifications at several places on the St. Johns River north of St. Augustine, intended to prevent enemy vessels from approaching the province's capital. By the time George Mathews had launched his Patriots War (1810–12) invasion, two of them, the Quesada Battery at the river's mouth and the San Vicente Ferrer Battery a few miles up the river on its south bank, had been largely abandoned. San Vicente Ferrer had two barracks buildings for permanently garrisoned troops and an auxiliary structure to house transient militia. (See: QUESADA BATTERY.)

FORT SCOTT. Established on the site of Chattahoochee's Arsenal, Gadsden County, in 1816, it was named in the memory of Lieutenant Richard W. Scott, 7th Infantry, killed by Indians.

FORT SEARLE. Situated about six miles east of Picolata, St. Johns County, Fort Searle was established December 20, 1839, by Captain William M. Fulton, 2nd Dragoons, with Company B, relieved by Lieutenant Edward O. C. Ord, with Company H, 3rd Artillery, on February 20, 1840. The post was abandoned June 19, 1841.

CAMP SEWARD. A temporary Civil War post occupied by Union troops from Vermont, Camp Seward was situated on the western tip of Santa Rosa Island, a short distance south of Fort Pickens.

FORT SHACKLEFORD. Established in 1855, about 20 miles south-southwest of the southern end of Lake Okeechobee, Hendry County, on the edge of the Big Cypress Swamp, Fort Shackleford was abandoned less than a year later and burned by the Indians.

FORT SHANNON. Established on the left bank of the St. Johns River at Palatka, Putnam County, in May 1838, this fort was one of the major quartermaster depots in Florida during the Second Seminole War. Named for Captain Samuel Shannon of Quartermaster Department, it operated under General William J. Worth until he assumed command of the armies in Florida. Its military facilities included a large barracks, blockhouses, hospital, and stables for more than 400 horses. Established as a trading post in 1821, Palatka was burned in 1836 by the Indians. During the fort's existence, the rebuilt settlement was military in appearance, being under total Army control. Winfield Scott, Zachary Taylor, and William Tecumseh Sherman were stationed here. Fort Shannon was abandoned August 24, 1843.

CAMP SHELDON. A temporary post located 10 miles from Smyrna, Volusia County, it was garrisoned in 1852 by a detachment of the 2nd Artillery.

FORT SHERRARD. Unlocated, this temporary Second Seminole War post was reportedly situated somewhere in "Middle Florida." It was established April 22, 1839, by 2nd Lieutenant F. Van Liew, 6th Infantry, with 20 men. The post was abandoned December 10, 1839.

FORT SHERROD. Unlocated, this temporary post was established in compliance with Special

Orders No. 37, dated March 13, 1842, by Captain N. W. Hunter, 2nd Dragoons, commanding companies H and K, 2nd Dragoons, and Company H, 7th Infantry. Its last post return was dated May 1842.

FORT SIMMONS. Situated on the south bank of the Caloosahatchee River, about six miles below old Fort Denaud (Deynaud), Hendry County, Fort Simmons was established November 5, 1841, by part of the former garrison of Fort Dulany at Punta Rassa which was obliterated by a hurricane in October. Fort Simmons was abandoned in March 1842.

FORT SIMON DRUM. Situated between Lake Trafford and Immokalee in Collier County, near the Big Cypress Swamp, Fort Drum was a stockaded work named for Captain Simon Drum, 4th Artillery, and established sometime in March 1855. Intended as a depot, it was garrisoned by small detachments from Forts Myers and Denaud. Fort Drum's last post return was dated April 1856.

FORT SIQUENZA. FORT BARRANCAS.

CAMP SMEAD (*Camp Armstrong*). A temporary post located on the south bank of the Manatee River, about 40 miles south of Tampa Bay, near present-day Manatee in Manatee County, it was established as Camp Armstrong on September 2, 1856, by Company K, 2nd Artillery, with Captain Harvey A. Allen in command. In December 1856, the name of the post was changed to Camp Smead. The post's last return was dated May 1857.

CAMP SMITH. The only citation found for this temporary post locates it near Fort Drane, southwest of Micanopy, Marion County.

FORT SMYRNA. FORT NEW SMYRNA.

FORT SOCRUM. A privately erected post erected sometime in 1856, Fort Socrum was located on or near the present Bethel Church on Providence Road, north of Lakeland, Polk County.

FORT SOMBRERO (*Prince of Wales Redoubt*). Probably built between 1778 and the spring of 1781 at Pensacola by the British during their occupation of Florida, the Prince of Wales Redoubt was renamed Fort Sombrero after the successful siege and seizure of the city by the Spanish in 1781. The fort soon became a ruination because of lack of maintenance by the victors.

FORT STALLINGS. A short-lived blockhouse located on Davis Creek near present-day Bayard in southern Duval County, Fort Stallings was established in 1812 during the Patriots War (1810–12).

FORT STANLEY. Unlocated, Fort Stanley was established in August 1839 by Company A, 1st Infantry, commanded by Lieutenant R. S. Granger.

FORT STANSBURY. Located on the Wakulla River, nine miles above St. Marks, and 12 miles south of Tallahassee, in Wakulla County, Fort Stansbury was established March 15, 1839, during the period when most of the area's plantations were stockaded against Indian attack. It was named for General F. E. Stansbury, who commanded a brigade at the Battle of Bladensburg and distinguished himself in the defense of Baltimore against the British during the War of 1812. The post was abandoned April 5, 1843.

FORT STARKE. A short-lived post situated at the mouth of the Manatee River, atop one of the largest Indian mounds in the state in Manatee County, Fort Starke was apparently established on or about November 25, 1840, by companies B, E, and F, 1st Infantry, commanded by Captain A. S. Miller. Its last post return dated December 1840, the post was actually abandoned sometime between January 5 and January 16, 1841. The fort's site was most probably used for an outpost during the Civil War.

STATE ARSENAL. ST. FRANCIS BARRACKS.

FORT STEELE. On January 10, 1861, the Secession Convention held at Tallahassee adopted the Articles of Secession. On April 18, Florida formally joined the Confederacy. Governor John Milton dispatched the Jacksonville Light Infantry to Mayport (Duval County) to establish Fort Steele, named in honor of the Infantry's commander, Dr. Holmes Steele. The fort's defenses were maintained until sometime in March 1862, when exigencies of the war demanded the stripping of Fort Steele's armaments.

CAMP STILWELL. An Army Reserve training center was dedicated on March 7, 1962, at Palatka in Putnam County. It was named in honor of General Joseph W. Stilwell, World War II commander of the China, Burma, and India theaters. The general, a graduate of West Point, was born at Palatka in 1883, and before his death in 1946 commanded the 10th Army and the 6th Army.

FORT SULLIVAN (*Fort Hitchepuckasassa*). Located just northwest of the town of Socrum and a mile and half west of the Polk County line in Hillsborough County, this fort was first established as Fort Hitchepuckasassa, named for the Indian village the post occupied, soon renamed Fort Sullivan in honor of recently deceased Wade Sullivan, assistant surgeon of the Army's Medical Staff. The fort was established on January 20, 1839, by Captain Hezekiah Garner with Company G, 3rd Artillery. General Zachary Taylor decided to abandon Fort Sullivan, and Special Orders No. 128, dated October 25, 1839, directed that its garrison proceed to Fort Brooke at Tampa Bay.

FORT TARVER. Shown on old maps to be approximately located about three and a half miles southeast of Gainesville and situated on the north side of Paynes Prairie (Alachua Lake), Fort Tarver occupied a site on the extension of present-day Southeast 15th Street. The post was apparently established sometime in 1839. A National Archives citation specifies post returns for May, August, September, and October of the same year.

FORT TAYLOR (*United States Barracks; Key West Barracks*). The island of Key West was first occupied by government forces in early 1822, after Lieutenant Matthew C. Perry of the U.S. Navy was ordered on February 7 to take possession. On March 25, the American flag was formally hoisted over the island. In 1826 the naval base was moved from Key West to Pensacola to take advantage of its fine harbor. On January 2, 1831, the Army established United States Barracks on the north shore of the island, the facility later renamed Key West Barracks. On May 10, 1836, Lieutenant Benjamin Alvord, later Paymaster General of the Army, arrived on Key West with Company B, 4th Infantry, and temporary quarters were erected to house the troops. The makeshift accommodations were removed in 1844, when six buildings for officers' quarters and two for enlisted men and a guardhouse were constructed, in time for the beginning of construction on Fort Zachary Taylor the following year. In 1892 three more structures for officers' quarters were erected, and in 1906 the facility was significantly enlarged with additional quarters to accommodate a much expanded garrison.

Fort Taylor was begun in 1845 at the southeast corner of the former naval base and was ready for occupancy in 1861 when the Civil War erupted. Built in the shape of a trapezoid and three-tiered, the fort's seaward curtains were 255 feet long and its land face measured 495 feet. A double-casemated brick fortress on the Vauban design, Fort Taylor's planned armament consisted of 106 guns, mortars, and howitzers of various calibers on the first and second tiers, with 36 more on

FORT TAYLOR. Painting of the Key West fort by Seth Eastman. (Courtesy of the Architect of the Capitol, Washington, D.C.)

the parapet. It was situated on a sandy shoal about a quarter of a mile from shore and boasted four bastions and four curtains, three of them commanding the water approaches to Key West.

In 1861 the government began the building of two Martello towers along the shoreline, one near the extreme northeastern end of the island, and the other approximately two miles closer to the town. But the new rifled ordnance developed during the war obsoleted their defensive usefulness. Strongly garrisoned Key West, in possession of the Federals during the entire war, was one of the primary reasons for the end result in the war. Fort Taylor underwent a complete modernization between 1898 and 1905, constructing a new battery and magazine called Osceola on the parade ground and reducing the three-tier height to one level to make the fort less vulnerable. Throughout its many years of existence after the Civil War, it was repeatedly abandoned and reoccupied. For a century and a quarter the fort was entirely surrounded by water, but about the year 1965 its surrounding area was dredged and landfilled by the Navy. On December 7, 1968, Fort Taylor was recognized as a National Historic Landmark. (See: KEY WEST BARRACKS.)

FORT TAYLOR. Situated on the north bank of Wolf Creek, a mile west of Lake Winder, in the northeast corner of Osceola County, Fort Taylor was established in December 1837 by troops under Colonel (later Major General) David E. Twiggs. No definite data has been found to indicate when it was abandoned. The fort site assumed a nonmilitary importance when Assistant Surgeon S. Forry in 1838 explored a 12-foot-high, 30-foot-diameter prehistoric Indian mound about 200 yards to the south, uncovering from its surface a treasure of relics, including a number of European origin.

FORT TAYLOR. An 1857 map indicates a Fort Taylor located about six miles south of Brooksville in Hernando County.

FORT TAYLOR. An unverified citation locates another post of this name in Brevard County, west of Cape Canaveral near upper Merritt Island.

FORT TEGESTA (TEQUESTA). In 1567, two years after he founded St. Augustine, Pedro Menéndez sent Captain Francisco de Reinoso and Father Juan Rogel to establish a fort and a mission at the main village of the Tegesta (Tequesta) Indians in the Miami River–Biscayne Key area, near the present-day city of Miami. By 1570 the post was wiped out by the rebellious Indians. Another citation places the Tegesta fort site at Cape Sable in Monroe County.

FORT THOMPSON. A temporary post located on the south bank of the Caloosahatchee River, near the mouth of Lake Flirt and present-day LaBelle, Hendry County, Fort Thompson was established November 23, 1854, by the garrison of evacuated Fort Meade consisting of companies C, I, and L, 2nd Artillery, commanded by Brevet Major Lewis G. Beach. The post was named in honor of Lieutenant Colonel Alexander R. Thompson, killed in the Battle of Okeechobee, December 25, 1837. The post was abandoned January 22, 1855.

FORT TOCOBAGA. In 1567 Pedro Menéndez, during his explorations along Florida's Gulf coast, established a tenuous alliance with the Tocobaga Indians at their principal village on Tampa Bay. The blockhouse erected on the northern side of the bay by a detachment of Spanish soldiers who also garrisoned the fort lasted less than a year. The Indians rebelled, slaughtered the garrison, and burned the blockhouse.

FORT TONYN. Situated at the junction of Peter Creek and the St. Marys River, near today's town of Kings Ferry in Nassau County, Fort Tonyn was a Revolutionary War defense erected in 1776 by East Florida's British forces designed to command the southern part of the colony of Georgia. The fortification was named for Patrick Tonyn, the last British governor of Florida. On July 2, 1778, the fort was evacuated and partially destroyed by its garrison in the face of advancing American troops under General Robert Howe, who took possession the next day and unearthed a great quantity of British stores and baggage buried beneath the barracks.

UNITED STATES ARSENAL. APALACHICOLA ARSENAL.

UNITED STATES BARRACKS. KEY WEST BARRACKS.

FORT VAN COURTLAND. A temporary Second Seminole War post, Fort Van Courtland was situated at the head of Kingsley Lake, in western Clay County.

FORT VAN SWEARINGEN. Located about 14 miles northwest of present-day Indiantown, 6 miles northeast of Lake Okeechobee, Martin

County, this temporary post was established by Captain B. Beall, 2nd Dragoons, and named for Captain J. Van Swearingen, 6th Infantry, killed in the Battle of Okeechobee, December 25, 1837.

FORT VINTON (*Fort No. 2* [East Florida]). Known originally as Fort No. 2, East Florida, this post was situated on the Indian River 20 miles northwest of Fort Pierce, Indian River County, and established on April 7, 1839, by Captain G. W. Moore, 7th Infantry, with Company I, aggregating 45 men. The post was renamed Fort Vinton on February 25, 1850, in the memory of Captain John Rogers Vinton, 4th Artillery, killed in the Battle of Vera Cruz, Mexico, in 1848. Fort Vinton was abandoned May 22, 1850.

FORT VOLUSIA. Situated on a large shell mound on the east bank of the St. Johns River, three miles south of Lake George, in the northwest corner of Volusia County, Fort Volusia was established on February 28, 1836, by Captain Elmore's company of South Carolina Volunteers and Lieutenant Irving's company of artillery. Fort Volusia was apparently abandoned and reoccupied several times until about 1857, when it was briefly occupied by a company of Volusia volunteers.

FORT VOSE. Located about a mile east of the Aucilla River, 24 miles from its mouth and 32 miles from Tallahassee, in Madison County, Fort Vose was established November 5, 1841, apparently by 2nd Lieutenant William B. Johns with Company G, 3rd Infantry, and named for Lieutenant Josiah H. Vose, Jr., 3rd Infantry. Fort Vose was abandoned June 5, 1842.

FORT WACAHOOTA. Located about nine miles southwest of Micanopy in northern Marion County, Fort Wacahoota was established by Lieutenant William Alberts with Company H, 2nd Infantry, in May 1840 and abandoned September 1842 at the end of the Second Seminole War.

FORT WACCASASSA (*Fort No. 8* [East Florida]). A number of citations indicate two posts of this name, both apparently erected during the same time frame, and both most probably located in Levy County. A National Archives citation is contradictory, first reporting that Fort Wacasassa was situated near the mouth of the Waccasassa River, about 30 miles northeast of Cedar Keys Post, and that it was established March 17, 1839, by Captain J. J. Abercrombie, 1st Infantry, and abandoned February 20, 1843. The report goes on to say that it was situated on the west bank of the river near Fort Fanning. Another National Archives citation reports that the post at the mouth of the river was established by Captain J. J. Abercrombie, with Company K, 6th Infantry.

Opposing citations state that Fort Waccasassa, originally Fort No. 8, East Florida, was located at the head of the river near the town of Archer in the southwest corner of Alachua County, close to the Levy County line. This is supported by another source that locates the fort about seven miles north of Bronson in the northeast corner of Levy County, quite close to the Alachua County line. This report states that the post consisted of barracks and blockhouse, a cookhouse, and blacksmith shop, all surrounded by a 250-by-350-foot stockade, and that it was established by a Lieutenant Barruta. It is believed that Fort Waccasassa was reoccupied during the Third Seminole War and again during the Civil War.

FORT WACISSA. A temporary Second Seminole War post first established by a militia expeditionary force in 1838, and later garrisoned by regular Army troops, Fort Wacissa was reportedly located south of so-called Fort Welaunee (Robert Gamble's plantation) and near the junction of the Wacissa and Aucilla rivers, Jefferson County.

FORT WADE. Unlocated, a National Archives citation reports that this post was named for Captain Richard D. A. Wade, 3rd Artillery.

CAMP WALBACH. Situated near the site of Fort Myers in Lee County, Camp Walbach was a short-lived post established on December 27, 1856, by Captain Thomas Williams with Company L, 4th Artillery, and named for Colonel Walbach, 4th Artillery. The post was abandoned on January 1, 1857.

FORT WALKER (*Fort Kanapaha*). Originally known as Fort Kanapaha, this temporary post was located west of Orange Lake, between Micanopy and old Newnansville, Alachua County. It was established on or about July 7, 1838, by Captain (?) William M. Fulton with Company B of the 2nd Dragoons. The post was renamed for Captain William H. T. Walker, 6th Infantry. The post was abandoned sometime in August 1838.

FORT WALLABOUT. The only information found appears on an 1839 Florida war map, showing this post as having been located just south of Fort Walker, in Alachua County.

CAMP WALTON. FORT WALTON.

FORT WALTON (*Camp Walton*). The resort town of Fort Walton Beach in Okaloosa County stands on the site of a fort named for Colonel George Walton, who was secretary of West Florida during Andrew Jackson's governorship (1821–22) and the son of George Walton, a signer of the Declaration of Independence. During the Civil War, a fortified Confederate post, originally called Camp Walton, was constructed in 1861 to guard the East Pass entrance to Santa Rosa Sound and garrisoned by a company of Florida militia called the "Walton Guards." The post was abandoned following the Confederate evacuation of Pensacola in 1862, and its garrison, elements of the 1st Florida Infantry, was assigned to duty on the Tennessee front.

FORT WARD. Situated on the south bank of Olustee Creek, above its mouth on the Santa Fe River, this temporary post was established in 1835 or 1836 near the present-day town of Providence in Union County.

FORT WARD. FORT SAN MARCOS DE APALACHE.

WARNER'S FERRY STOCKADE. A fortified Indian defense erected during the Second Seminole War by local plantation owners, the post was situated on the east side of the Withlacoochee River, in the area between the town of Bellville and the Georgia state line, in Hamilton County.

WATER BATTERY. FORT BARRANCAS.

FORT WEEDMAN. Located about seven miles west of St. Augustine, Fort Weedman was established sometime in 1837. It apparently was still active in 1840.

FORT WEKIWA. The only citation found for this post locates it on the left bank of Spring Creek, about one mile above its mouth, in Levy County.

FORT WELAUNEE. FORT GAMBLE.

CAMP WENDELL. FORT MCCLURE.

FORT WESTCOTT. This post has been variously located as "in the Everglades, 15 miles northeast of Chatham Bay" and "18 miles east of the Ten Thousand Islands," in Monroe County. Its coordinates have been reported as Latitude 25 degrees, 30 minutes, and Longitude 80 degrees, 50 minutes.

FORT WHEELOCK. Situated on the southwest side of Orange Lake, south of Micanopy, in Marion County, Fort Wheelock was established July 7, 1840, and named for Lieutenant Thompson B. Wheelock, 1st Dragoons. The post was abandoned March 22, 1842.

CAMP WHIPPLE. This temporary post located on the Peace River in Charlotte County was established on January 10, 1857, by troops of Company H, 5th Infantry, from Fort Myers. The detachment was part of a task force designed to oversee the resettlement of Seminoles on reservation land in Southwest Florida. During their short-lived stay on the river, the troops surrounded their campsite with earthworks. The post was evacuated March 1, 1857, when Company H returned to Fort Myers.

FORT WHITE. Situated on the left bank of the Santa Fe River, about four miles west of present-day Fort White, Columbia County, this post was probably established in late December 1837 or early January 1838. The post was abandoned June 26, 1842, for reasons of "bilious fever," no doubt related to malaria, among the troops.

FORT WILLIAM HENRY HARRISON. FORT HARRISON.

FORT WILLIAMS. Apparently a temporary Civil War post, Fort Williams was reportedly located "on the river on the mainland side of Port Orange," Volusia County.

FORT WINDER. A temporary Seminole War post, Fort Winder was located on or near the Peace River in southwest DeSoto County.

CANTONMENT WINFIELD SCOTT. A National Archives citation reports that the cantonment was established August 24, 1841, by Captain Benjamin L. Beall with Company I, 2nd Dragoons. "This post is situated one mile east of the Natural Bridge on the Santa Fe River and on the road from Newnansville to Charles's Ferry." The post was abandoned sometime in May 1842.

FORT WOOL. Established during the Second Seminole War, this post was situated on the west bank of the Suwannee River, about 10 miles from its mouth, in Dixie County, and was apparently named for General John E. Wool.

CAMP WORTH. Named in honor of Colonel William J. Worth, 8th Infantry, temporary Fort Worth was located near Fort Cooper and occupied by companies B, D, and E, 8th Infantry, in 1841.

YELLOW BLUFF FORT. Located on the north side of the St. Johns River, just off Heckscher Drive (S.R. 105), on the New Berlin Road in Duval County, Yellow Bluff Fort was one of two major Confederate fortifications on the river (the other being St. Johns Bluff) to control the passage of enemy gunboats up the river to Jacksonville. The placement of an earthwork fort on the 90-foot-high bluff was originally suggested or designed by General Robert E. Lee in November 1861 while surveying coast defenses. Later, in February 1862, he recommended to Brigadier General J. H. Trapier that the proposed Yellow Bluff fortification be used as the main defense before Jacksonville. Before this could be fully effected, Union forces attacked and reduced Fort Steele and the fortifications on St. Johns Bluff, causing the evacuation of Yellow Bluff by the Confederates. It was later reoccupied by rebel forces under Captain J. J. Dickison, refortified, and withstood repeated attacks by Federal gunboats. In March of 1864, Union forces again occupied Yellow Bluff when the Confederates evacuated the works, and established a signal station there, used until the end of the war. (See: JACKSONVILLE FORTS.)

FORT ADVANCE. This post was established by General Elijah Clarke in early 1794 on the west side of the Oconee River, opposite the mouth of Town Creek, in what is now Wilkinson County. At the time the fort was built, the Oconee was the state's boundary and west of the river was Indian territory. In an attempt to form an empire of his own in the territory reserved to the Indians, in defiance of the state and Federal governments, Clarke built and garrisoned at least six forts in the area. His dream was short-lived, however, and all his posts were destroyed in the latter part of 1794.

FORT ALERT (*Trader's Hill Post*). Located about four miles southwest of Folkston in Charlton County, at the head of navigation on the St. Marys River, Trader's Hill was one of the more important trading centers in the Southeast. A fort was established here in November 1812 as a refuge for settlers during the Indian wars and defended by U.S. troops who named the stockade Fort Alert. The fort or a replacement was also used during the Creek War, 1835–36.

FORT ALLATOONA. Situated atop the hill on the Etowah River to the east of old Allatoona, near Cartersville, Bartow County, Fort Allatoona was a star-shaped defense erected by Union troops under General Sherman during his advance on Atlanta in late 1864. The town of Allatoona had been captured and fortified by the Federals to protect the river bridge, part of the rail line which enabled the general to supply his army. On October 5, 1864, 3,000 Confederate troops under General Samuel Gibbs French, sent to destroy the bridge, attacked the fort defended by 2,000 Federals under General John Murry Corse. The battle was costly and indecisive. The besieging Confederates suffered 799 casualties while the defenders lost 706 men. General French, not wishing to risk an all-out attack, withdrew before the fort was reinforced.

ALLATOONA PASS FORT. A temporary Confederate defense erected by Georgia militia troops in the fall of 1864 during the Union army's advance on Atlanta, the fort was located several miles from Fort Bartow, near Cartersille, Bartow County.

ANDERSONVILLE PRISON. CAMP SUMTER.

FORT ARGYLE. Situated on the west bank of the Ogeechee River on the present grounds of Fort Stewart in Bryan County, Fort Argyle was established in 1733 under the direction of General

Georgia

James Oglethorpe to command one of the main passes by which enemy Indians had been invading South Carolina and to give protection to Savannah settlers from anticipated raids by the Spanish from Florida. The palisaded fort, measuring 110 feet on each side, was garrisoned by Rangers and named in honor of the Duke of Argyle, friend and patron of General Oglethorpe. The Ranger troop organization was disbanded in 1747. Ten years later the fort was reportedly a ruination.

FORT A. S. MILLER. An 1839 war map shows this temporary post located on the northwest side of the Okefenokee Swamp, on the northeast side of the Suwannee Creek, probably in what is now Ware County. This fort was built along with some 20 others in the Okefenokee area under the orders of General John Floyd. The fort was most probably abandoned at or even before the end of the Second Seminole War.

CAMP AT ATHENS. Designated only as "Camp at Athens," this post was occupied by the headquarters of the 1st and 2nd Brigades, 3rd Division, 2nd Army Corps, in 1898. Since this division was never fully organized, only one brigade was encamped at Athens, Clarke County. The brigade consisted of the 15th Pennsylvania Volunteers, the 102nd New York Volunteers, and the 3rd New Jersey Volunteers.

CAMP ATKINSON. A temporary recruiting and training post established in 1898 during the Spanish-American War, Camp Atkinson was located in or near Atlanta.

POST OF ATLANTA. By General Orders No. 10, Department of Georgia, March 1, 1866, the name of the District of Allatoona was changed to the Post of Atlanta to be commanded by Captain L. Beckwith, 13th Connecticut Volunteers. At about the same time, McPherson Barracks was built at Atlanta and occupied until December 1881 when the post was abandoned. Several other posts have also been located in Atlanta. In 1866 steps were taken for the erection of a large permanent post at this point which developed into the Infantry School at Fort Benning. (See: FORT BENNING and MCPHERSON BARRACKS.)

FORT AUGUSTA (*Fort Cornwallis*). The site of present-day Augusta on the Savannah River, Richmond County, was selected by two fur traders as a trading post to be nearer the Indians than old Savannah Town (in today's Beech Island), seven miles below Augusta. To protect them and the area's settlers, General James Oglethorpe in 1736 built Fort Augusta, named for a royal princess, maintaining a garrison there until 1767. Here he met Cherokee and Chickasaw chiefs in 1739 to pacify them after a smallpox epidemic. In 1750 the first St. Paul's Church was built "under the curtain of the fort." In 1763 the chiefs of five Indian nations met at the fort with the governors of Georgia, North and South Carolina, Virginia, and the King's representative and signed a treaty of peace. Ten years later, in 1773, Cherokees and Creeks here ceded two million acres in north Georgia.

During the Revolution, the British in 1779 seized Fort Augusta, enlarged it and renamed it Fort Cornwallis in honor of the general. The fort was captured on September 14, 1780, in a surprise attack by the Americans, who soon abandoned it to the British. In May 1781, an attack led by General Andrew Pickens and Lieutenant Colonel Henry "Light Horse Harry" Lee, aided by the use of a Mayham Tower, forced ultimate capitulation by the British commander, Lieutenant Colonel Thomas Brown, and his garrison of 300 men, with the surrender taking place on June 5, 1781. Thereafter, Augusta and most of Georgia remained in American hands until the end of the war. In 1786 the fortifications were removed and a new and larger church was built. The present-day intersection of 6th and Reynolds streets is the site of the fourth edition of St. Paul's Church.

AUGUSTA ARSENAL (*United States Arsenal*). For a period of 128 years until its abandonment in 1955, a United States Arsenal was located on a tract comprising approximately 70 acres lying just north and west of the city of Augusta. An "arsenal at Augusta" to aid the State in "resisting invasion" was originally provided for by President George Washington in 1793. In 1816 a U.S. Arsenal was established on the Savannah River where the King Mill is now located, but the garrison having been wiped out in 1819 by "black fever," it was removed to the present site in 1827 and consisted of two sets of officers' quarters, an enlisted men's barracks, and a storehouse connected by a loopholed wall. On January 24, 1861, five days after Georgia seceded, it was surrendered to Georgia troops with its garrison of 80 men commanded by Captain Arnold Elzey, who later served in the Confederate army. During the Civil War, the arsenal manufactured a variety of ordnance for the Confederate forces. The arsenal's site is on Walton Way, between Katherine Street and Monte Sano Avenue, in Augusta.

FORT BARNUM. A small militia-held fort built in 1840 during the Second Seminole War, Fort Barnum was located in the northwestern part of the Okefenokee Swamp.

FORT BARRINGTON (*Fort Howe*). Its site located approximately 12 miles northwest of the present-day city of Darien, McIntosh County, Fort Barrington was a fortified stronghold whose origin dates back to Colonial times. The fort stood on the northeast side of the Altamaha River on old Barrington Road, an important trade route between the Carolinas and Florida in the early 1700s, which became a well-traveled route for military forces before and during the Revolution. The fort had been built in 1751 as a defense against the Indians and was so named in honor of Lieutenant Colonel Josiah Barrington, a kinsman of General James Oglethorpe. Described as a 70-foot-square wooden structure, with a bastion in each of its angles and a two-story barracks-storehouse in the center topped by a lookout tower, Fort Barrington was captured in 1777 by the British and renamed Fort Howe. The fort, the scene of several battles and skirmishes, was apparently recaptured by American forces in the spring of 1778. The site of the fort, long deceased, was occupied by Confederate troops during the Civil War.

FORT BARTOW. Situated on a hill to the east of Cartersville, Bartow County, Fort Bartow was erected in the fall of 1864 by General Sherman's forces to protect the railroad bridge over the Etowah River during his campaign against Atlanta.

BEARD'S BLUFF FORT. This fort, a stockaded defense manned by a company of Light Horse, stood on the Altamaha River in the western part of Long County, near present-day Ludowici. One of the more important posts built on Georgia's southern frontier during the first year of the Revolution, it was the scene of frequent skirmishes with British-allied Indians. During one of these engagements, in December 1776, a number of men were killed and buried in unmarked graves near the stockade.

FORT BEAULIEU. An important Confederate defense of Savannah on the Vernon River, Fort Beaulieu was strongly fortified, provided with one 8-inch and two 10-inch Columbiads and three 32-pounder and two 42-pounder guns. On December 14, 1864, Admiral John Dahlgren's Union fleet began the bombardment of this fort and also Fort Rose Dew on the Ogeechee River.

By the 21st, these two works and all other Savannah defenses had been abandoned by General William Hardee, who had held Savannah's long defense line for nearly two weeks against General Sherman's invasion army, which numbered nearly four times as many men.

CAMP BENNING. FORT BENNING.

FORT BENNING (*Camp Benning*). Located south of Columbus on U.S. 27, Fort Benning is known as the "Home of the Infantry." It is here that the famed U.S. Army Infantry School was established and through the years emerged as the most influential infantry center in the modern world. Its progenitor was the "Infantry School of Instruction," proposed in 1826 by Major General Edmund P. Gaines, at Jefferson Barracks at St. Louis. The Infantry School, however, failed to endure and was officially closed on November 24, 1828. In 1892 the Fort Riley School for Cavalry and Field Artillery was created. Later this school was split into two separate fields of study, but no school was established for the Infantry. Because of his concern over the marksmanship of infantrymen, Lieutenant General Arthur MacArthur persuaded the Army to establish the School of Musketry at the Presidio of Monterey, California, on February 21, 1907. This may be considered the beginning of the present Infantry School, and the event that led to the creation of Fort Benning. In January 1913 the School of Musketry was transferred from Monterey to Fort Sill, Oklahoma.

With the outbreak of World War I, it was determined that Fort Sill was not adequate for the training of both the Infantry and Artillery. A separate camp for training the Infantry had to be established. After many sites were considered, the city of Columbus and its near environs were ultimately selected. The first troops from Fort Sill arrived on October 6, 1918, and occupied a temporary camp three miles east of town on Macon Road. The next day the camp was officially opened and named in honor of Confederate General Henry Lewis Benning, a native of Columbus. The search for a permanent location for the camp settled on a plantation site south of Columbus. On February 8, 1922, the post was designated Fort Benning.

The post enjoyed a construction boom in the mid-1930s as a result of Federal work projects during the Great Depression. The boom continued into the 1940s with the eruption of war in Europe. Troop strength swelled with the arrival of the 1st Infantry Division and the establishment of Officer Candidate School and Airborne training. Since its inception, Fort Benning grew from its original 97,000 acres to 187,000 acres, of which about 12,000 are in Alabama. The post secured its final vestige of permanence during the 1950s. Today, Fort Benning is the undisputed representative of Infantry doctrine, tactics, and weapons.

FORT BOGGS. A Confederate defense of Savannah, Fort Boggs was situated on Brewton Hill on the Savannah River, about a mile east of the city. Mounting 14 guns, the fort was considered "one of the finest field works constructed on either side during the war," but, as with the other Confederate works in Savannah's semicircular line of defenses, it was evacuated December 19th and 20th, 1864, during General Sherman's famous "March to the Sea."

FORT BROWN. During the first days of the Civil War, state authorities began the construction of a strong earthwork as one of Savannah's later semicircular line of defenses. Fort Brown was located at or near the old Roman Catholic Cemetery. Before the fort was completed, it was turned over to the Confederacy which armed it with 11 guns. Fort Brown was most probably evacuated December 19, 1864, during General Sherman's "March to the Sea." The fort's works gradually disappeared after the restoration of peace.

BRUNSWICK POST. This Army post, located at Brunswick on the Turtle River in Glynn County, was established on April 14, 1870, by Brevet Major F. D. Ogilby with companies B and E, 8th Infantry. The post was abandoned sometime in September 1870.

FORT BUFFINGTON. One of the so-called "Cherokee Removal Forts" established between 1830 and 1838, Fort Buffington was a stockade located near the village of Buffington in eastern Cherokee County. The stockade was probably named for Joshua Buffington, a prominent mixed-blood Cherokee who lived on the Etowah River in present Forsyth County.

BURNT FORT. This old fort was located on the Satilla River, 12 miles from Folkston, Charlton County. The defense dated back to the pre-Revolutionary period when there was a constant danger of Spanish incursions from Florida.

FORT CAMPBELL. This "Cherokee Removal Fort" was located in Forsyth County and established for the purpose of congregating the Cherokees for their ultimate removal in 1838 to Indian Territory in the West.

FORT CARNES. WOFFORD'S STATION.

FORT CARR. Bloody and ruthless guerrilla warfare from 1779 on raged along the Savannah River above Augusta. Fort Carr, a Revolutionary War fort situated on a creek in the northern part of present McDuffie County, had been seized by a large detachment of British Tories. An American detachment invested the fort on February 10, 1779, and were at the point of successfully forcing capitulation when word arrived that a Tory army of 800 men was marching from Fort Ninety-Six in South Carolina to reinforce the British-held fort. The Americans lifted the siege and retreated toward the river. This action was a preliminary to the Battle of Kettle Creek four days later.

CARR'S FORT. Brunswick in present Glynn County was first settled by Mark Carr, who came to Georgia in 1738 with General James Oglethorpe's regiment. Carr was granted 500 acres on which he established a plantation. The several tabby buildings he erected in 1739 stood nearby and were occupied as a military outpost. In 1741 Spanish-incited Indians from Florida raided the plantation, caused a great deal of damage, and killed or wounded a number of the soldiers while others were taken as prisoners. A marker commemorating Mark Carr's fort stands at the intersection of Union Street and 1st Avenue in Brunswick.

FORT CEDARTOWN. One of the "Cherokee Removal Forts" established in 1838, this stockade was located at Cedartown, the present county seat in west central Polk County.

FORT CHASTAIN. A "Cherokee Removal Fort" established sometime between 1830 and 1838, Fort Chastain was located in Towns County in the northeastern corner of the state.

FORT CLARKE. During the spring of 1793, Governor Edward Telfair ordered a number of forts built along the Oconee River for the protection of the frontier against Creek Indian incursions. One of the forts was located at Scull Shoals in northern Greene County and was named in honor of Georgia's Revolutionary War leader, General Elijah Clarke. The fort consisted of a two-story blockhouse equipped with a door five inches thick. The blockhouse was surrounded by a rectangular, 11-foot-high palisade, 29 yards long and 19 yards wide. The fort was completed on April 29, 1793, and first garrisoned by a detachment of the Greene County militia. No records exist of Fort Clarke after 1794. The site later became the home of Governor Peter Early. Scull Shoals is now part of the Oconee National Forest, protected and maintained by the National Park Service.

CAMP CLYATT. A short-lived post established during the Creek War in 1836, it was located on the farm owned by Samuel M. Clyatt, Lowndes County's first commissioned surveyor. The farm probably stood a few miles east of the present town of Clyattville.

FORT COLERAINE. Located on the north bank of the St. Marys River, at the point where Camden and Charlton counties join, Fort Coleraine was probably established in 1793 and garrisoned until about 1796 to guard the frontier between American territory and Spanish-occupied Florida.

CAMP CONRAD. A brigade of 3,500 troops was stationed at Camp Conrad in Columbus during the winter of 1898–99 in training for the Spanish-American War. The campsite occupied the ground between 3rd and 6th avenues and 29th and 33rd streets.

FORT CORNWALLIS. FORT AUGUSTA.

BLOCKHOUSE NEAR COWETA. In 1689 the Spanish built a blockhouse near Coweta, the principal village of the Muscogee or Creek confederacy, on the opposite side of the Chattahoochee River from today's city of Columbus. A garrison was maintained there until 1691, when the needs of St. Augustine required the withdrawal of the fort's small garrison.

CAMP CRAWFORD. FORT SCOTT.

CAMP CRAWFORD. FORT SCREVEN.

FORT CUMMING(S) (*Old Indian Stockade*). Another in the series of "Cherokee Removal Forts," Fort Cumming (or Cummings), popularly known as the Old Indian Stockade, was established in 1835 or 1836 at present-day Lafayette in Walker County. The stockade was a large enclosure of upright logs, with a rifle tower or bastion in each angle. A company of Georgia Volunteers guarded the congregated Cherokees until their removal to Indian Territory in 1838.

FORT DAHLONEGA (*Fort Lumpkin*). Another of the so-called "Cherokee Removal Forts," Fort Dahlonega, also known as Fort Lumpkin (named for the county) was located in or near Dahlonega, the county seat. The stockade was probably established sometime between 1835 and 1838.

FORT DANIEL. At Fort Daniel on Hog Mountain, about 12 miles northeast of Duluth, Gwinnett County, began the original Peachtree Road to the village of Standing Peachtree on the Chattahoochee River. This old route was opened to haul military supplies to the river and floated downriver to General Andrew Jackson's and General John Floyd's troops, converging on the Indians during the Creek War of 1813–14. Built in late 1813 or early 1814, Fort Daniel was a stockade probably established to guarantee the safety of the supply line and to serve as a staging area for the troops. All the land to the west and northwest of the Chattahoochee was Indian country.

FORT DARIEN (*Fort at New Inverness*). Laid out by General James Edward Oglethorpe in 1736, a fort was built on the first high bluff of the Altamaha River to protect the new settlement of New Inverness, established in 1735 by Scottish Highlanders. The fort was first known as the "Fort at New Inverness," later renamed Fort Darien. It was a large fortification, with two bastions and two half-bastions, and defended by several cannon. From the time of its founding until the Battle of Bloody Marsh in 1742, the town was in constant jeopardy by invading Spaniards from Florida. After the war with Spain, the fort was no longer needed and fell into ruins. During the Revolution, the fort was rebuilt and fortified and saw action against British forces.

FORT DEARBORN. A temporary fortification erected and occupied by U.S. regular troops during the Second Seminole War, Fort Dearborn was located at the western edge of the Okefenokee Swamp, at the confluence of Suwannee River and Suwanoochee Creek, about a mile north of the Echols County line, in Clinch County. The state governor had urgently requested protection for the settlers in the lower Georgia counties who were being constantly harassed by Indian raids. The fort was named for Major G. Dearborn who commanded its garrison. The site was known as "Old Dearborn" for many years after both the military and Indians had left the area.

FORT DEFENSE. FORT MORRIS.

FORT DEFIANCE. In May 1794 General Elijah Clarke turned his attention to the Indian country west of the Oconee River where he attempted to form a state, or perhaps an empire of his own. He and his followers took possession, erected Fort Defiance, drew up a written constitution for a government, and began the work of settlement, all his labors expended in defiance of the state and Federal governments. Fort Defiance, one of at least six such posts he established, was situated six miles above Fort Advance in Wilkinson County. In September 1794, finding that most of his army of followers had deserted his cause, Clarke recrossed the Oconee. By order of the state government, all his short-lived forts were destroyed. Clarke's dream of a trans-Oconee republic was sometimes referred to as the "Oconee War." (See: FORT ADVANCE.)

FORT EARLY. Frequent flagrant border violations by white settlers and unjust treaties had created an atmosphere of deep mistrust that finally erupted into the Creek Indian War of 1813–15. Not all the Creeks had allied themselves to the British against the United States. The anti-American ones among them were called "Red Sticks" and it was against them that most southern states arrayed their forces. On January 4, 1814, two and a half months before General Andrew Jackson defeated a large body of Creeks at the Battle of Horseshoe Bend in Alabama, Governor Peter Early appointed General David Blackshear commander of all Georgia troops on the frontier.

In December, after new hostilities had begun, General Blackshear began his campaign against the Creeks by establishing a large breastworks on the left bank of the Flint River, about 12 miles south of present-day Cordele in Crisp County. In December 1817 his works were occupied by Major Thomas Woodward and a large detachment which "put up a little stockade-work, and called it Fort Early," which evolved into an important fortified supply depot and troop staging point. This was the very first time the general's old breastworks were so named. General Jackson arrived at Fort Early on February 26, 1818, with 900 Georgians, two companies of Tennesseans, and a large detachment of Indians. From there he proceeded to Fort Scott and then into northern Florida to pursue the Indian campaign. The first of the so-called Seminole Wars was then being waged there. After the summer of 1818, nothing more was officially recorded concerning Fort Early.

FORT EBENEZER. In 1757 William DeBrahm, His Majesty's Surveyor General for the Southern District of North America, erected a fort at the old town of Ebenezer, 25 miles above Savannah, in present Effingham County, intended primarily to protect the German settlement from Indian attack. The defense was again fortified in 1776 by the Continentals during the Revolution. After its capture by Colonel Archibald Campbell and his troops on January 2, 1779, it was occupied by the British until early 1782. The town, suffering many hardships, was again fortified by earthworks, and some of its public and private buildings were converted to British army use. Ebenezer literally became a thoroughfare for British troops passing between Savannah and Augusta. During the first week of July 1782, when the town was again occupied by General Anthony Wayne's Continentals, the Georgia Legislature met there and established it, albeit for a short time, as the actual capital of Georgia. No notice has been found to indicate when Ebenezer's fortifications were abandoned or dismantled.

FORT EDWARDS. Opposite the courthouse in Watkinsville, the county seat of today's Oconee County, was the two-story Eagle Hotel, a rectangular structure. In 1789 the building was used as a blockhouse defense against the Cherokees and called Fort Edwards.

FORT FIDIUS. Erected in 1793 for the protection of the Georgia frontier, Fort Fidius was situated on the north bank of the Oconee River, the border between Indian country and the white settlements, at Milledgeville, Baldwin County. At one time it was occupied by the largest Federal garrison south of the Ohio River. In 1797 the government replaced this fort with Fort Wilkinson on the west side of the river on Indian land.

FORT FLOYD. Located near the northeast corner of the Okefenokee Swamp, Fort Floyd was established on November 15, 1838, by Major Gustavus Loomis with Company C, 2nd Infantry, and occupied until September 25, 1839, when it was abandoned.

CAMP FORREST. Named in honor of Lieutenant General Nathan B. Forrest, C.S.A., who served with distinction in the Civil War, Camp Forrest was first known as Main Camp in the Chickamauga and Chattanooga National Military Park. The original cantonment was constructed in 1917 for the use of Regular Army units. A portion of the area was assigned to the Corps of Engineers for mobilizing and training units and replacements in May 1918. Camp Forrest was combined with Fort Oglethorpe, January 31, 1919.

FORTVILLE FORT. Near present-day Haddock in Jones County stood Fortville, a town so named because a strong blockhouse was built there to provide protection for the early settlers.

FORT FREDERICA. Established in 1736 on St. Simons Island, one of Georgia's famous Golden Isles, the fortified settlement of Frederica became General James Oglethorpe's military headquarters, both as a defense and a base for offensive operations against the Spaniards in Florida during the Anglo-Spanish conflict of 1739–48. The fort at the time claimed the distinction of being "the largest, most regular, and perhaps most costly" British fortification in America. The first group of Frederica settlers—116 men, women, and children—arrived in February and March, 1736. Quickly they built a fort on the bluff overlooking a sharp bend in the inland waterway. Less than a hundred miles from the Spanish stronghold at St. Augustine, Frederica was circumvallated by the English to constitute a strong buffer against Spanish aggression. The town was platted on a rectangular form inside of a fortified polygon, surrounded by a moat and ramparts. Oglethorpe, who planned Savannah, also a fortified town, proceeded to enclose the whole town. Fort Frederica was designed as half a hexagon with two bastions and two half-bastions and towers. The walls were of earth faced with timber and were from 10 to 13 feet high. Surrounding the walls was a moat 10 feet wide.

Oglethorpe himself superintended the work of construction and taught the men to dig the ditches and to turf the ramparts. There were two large magazines, 60 feet in length and three stories in height included within the stockade. The barracks were at the north end of the town, where they occupied quarters 90 square feet. Over the gateway rose a tower, while on either side there were bastions two stories in height, and 20 feet square, each equipped with heavy guns. To furnish adequate water supplies, a well was dug within the fort.

A citadel was constructed on the bank of the river at the base or western side of the polygon, with the main gate of the fort in the middle of the top of the form at the end of 75-foot-wide Broad Street, Frederica's main thoroughfare. A four-bastioned earthwork, the citadel was originally revetted with sod, but in 1739 the unstable sod was replaced by blue clay. Six other

FORT FREDERICA. (Courtesy of the Georgia Department of Community Development.)

narrower streets ran parallel to Broad, with Barracks Street intersecting them all. The settlers, to improve the town's appearance and provide shade, planted orange trees along the streets.

Within a month after the settlement's founding, the guns of Fort Frederica commanded all water approaches to the site. As Frederica grew, so did Oglethorpe's concern for its safety. The town stood on land claimed by Britain, France, and Spain. Should war come, it would be in a dangerous position. Consequently, Oglethorpe returned to England and secured command of a 650-man regiment of British regular troops. These soldiers manned the defenses of Frederica and several other British posts in coastal Georgia. The arrival of the regiment assured the immediate survival of Frederica and, at the same time, changed its nature. The military payroll provided a new source of income for the artisans and craftsmen of the town; Frederica quickly became a martial community. Even then, with Anglo-Spanish relations in turmoil, it was no place for the fainthearted.

The problems between Great Britain and Spain erupted in 1739 in the War of Jenkins' Ear. Spain now saw her opportunity to regain both

Georgia and South Carolina. Military operations in the Georgia-Florida area culminated in the Battle of Bloody Marsh on St. Simons Island, where Oglethorpe's outnumbered troops defeated a Spanish invasion force on July 7, 1742. Never again was Spain a major threat to Georgia. The War of Jenkins' Ear ended in 1748. No longer needed, Oglethorpe's regiment was disbanded the following year, destroying the town's economy. The shopkeepers and tradesmen of Frederica, lacking the support of a military payroll, moved elsewhere. The town could not survive the loss.

The "Great Fire" of 1758, which destroyed most of Frederica's buildings, proved to be the town's death blow. The few remaining soldiers withdrew from the fort in 1763, and Frederica—born of need and nurtured by war—no longer existed as a living place. But posterity did not forget Frederica. The remains of the fort's citadel were acquired in 1903 by the Georgia Chapter of the Colonial Dames of America, and the work of preservation was begun. It was continued by the Fort Frederica Association, which acquired eight acres. This tract, together with that held by the Colonial Dames, was donated to the Federal government. Fort Frederica National Monument, a dozen miles from Brunswick, was established on September 10, 1945. Today a causeway links St. Simons Island with the mainland. Archaeological excavations have uncovered house foundations, storehouses, blacksmith's shop, the King's powder magazine, the guardhouse, and the town gate. Still visible are the remnants of the "wet Ditch," two-thirds of a mile long. Near a number of masonry remnants of the fort are the ruins of a tower that was part of the soldiers' barracks. The burying grounds are the last resting place for many who died at Frederica—English, Spanish, and Indian. Remaining numberless and anonymous in the shade of Spanish moss–covered trees, the unmarked graves are today represented by only four raised tombs and a vault.

FORT FUTCH. Governor William Schley in 1836, in response to the killing and pillaging perpetrated by hostile bands of Indians along the frontier, ordered all the settlements to erect forts for their protection. One of the defenses was erected in present Cook County on Futch property at the Withlacoochee River ferry.

FORT GAINES. There were three forts so named within and in the environs of the present-day town of Fort Gaines in Clay County. On April 2, 1816, a detachment of 100 troops of the 4th Infantry erected a small stockaded fortification, with two blockhouses at diagonal corners, atop a bluff on the east bank of the Chattahoochee River near the Creek Nation's boundary. Today's town of Fort Gaines grew up outside the fort's palisades. The post, named for General Edmund P. Gaines, was garrisoned until sometime in 1819. In early May 1836, during the bloody Creek War, militia troops built the second Fort Gaines near the town to protect its inhabitants. By mid-May the community was flooded with refugees from the Roanoke massacre several weeks earlier. By the summer of 1836 a number of successful short battles with Creek hostiles in the Fort Gaines area assured the survival of the garrison town. The third Fort Gaines was built during the Civil War. In response to urgent local requests, the Confederacy's War Department ordered a fort built two miles south of the town on a high bluff overlooking the Chattahoochee. An imposing arsenal was constructed of lumber and sand and linked with deep trenches interspersed with artillery batteries. Below the cliff, breastworks were built near the river, providing an outer defensive perimeter. Manned by the Fort Gaines militia, the arsenal was maintained until the end of the war without having been engaged in any action.

FORT GAMBIA. Located about one mile east of Rome, Floyd County, Fort Gambia was a rather small Confederate defense built during the Civil War, designed to protect the city from attack from the northeast.

FORT GEORGE. FORT MORRIS.

FORT GEORGE. In late 1761 John DeBrahm, the Surveyor General of the Southern District of North America, laid out and superintended the construction of Fort George on Cockspur Island in the mouth of the Savannah River, opposite the entrance to the channel on the north side of Tybee Island. According to DeBrahm's later description, it was a small embrasured redoubt, 100 feet square, with a blockhouse or bastion 40 feet square and 30 feet high to serve as a magazine, storehouse and barracks, adequate to hold 50 men, "more to stop vessels from going up and down in time of peace, than vessels which had a mind to act in a hostile view." The fort was under construction by the following spring. In November the Assembly ordered improvements on the fort consisting of brickwork and palmetto puncheons around the perimeter of the earthworks. In January 1763 the governor ordered the fort be notified that all ships coming from Charleston must be quarantined for 10 days. The fort was armed with 11 guns and four mortars. In the spring of 1772, when Fort George was considered to be a total ruin, there were only three men and one officer left, "just to make signals." The fort was completely dismantled in 1776 to deprive the British of any benefits it might offer, and its guns were removed to Savannah where they could aid in the defense of the city.

CAMP GEORGE H. THOMAS. This camp was established in accordance with orders of the War Department, March 25, 1902. It was located within the Chickamauga National Park, a mile and a half from the town of Lytle in Walker County and was first occupied by the 7th Cavalry. The post was appropriately named in honor of Union General George Henry Thomas, "The Rock of Chickamauga," for his distinguished service during the Civil War. Camp Thomas was discontinued in October 1904, when the garrison was transferred to the newly established post near Cloud Springs, later designated Fort Oglethorpe.

FORT GILLEM. The final orders for the inactivation of the Atlanta Army Depot came in 1973 with the decline of American involvement in the Vietnam War and the nationwide reorganization of the depot system. On June 28, 1974, the colors of the U.S. Army Forces Command were unfurled in front of the old depot headquarters and the installation was renamed Fort Gillem in honor of Union General Alvan C. Gillem. The history of the depot was first linked with Fort McPherson when it was activated as a quartermaster depot of the IV Corps, Headquarters, Fort McPherson. Fort Gillem is located 10 miles from downtown Atlanta, in nearby Forest Park between State Highways 42 and 54, in Clayton County. The post is Fort McPherson's nearest Army neighbor and its subpost. Fort Gillem is home station to the Second U.S. Army and other units associated with criminal investigation, recruiting, and distribution.

CAMP GILMAN. A temporary post located near Americus, Sumter County, and active during November-December 1898, it was commanded by Major William Cogswell, acting brigadier surgeon.

FORT GILMER. One hundred yards east of U.S. 411, south of Chatsworth, in either Gilmer County or Whitfield County, is the site of Fort Gilmer, built in 1838 and garrisoned by troops to enforce the removal from this region of the remaining Cherokee Indians under terms of the New Echota Treaty of 1835. One of seven such forts erected in the Cherokee Territory, the post was the temporary headquarters of General Winfield Scott, under whose command the removal was effected. The reluctant Indians were congregated here and guarded until their westward march, "The Trail of Tears," began later in the same year.

FORT GILMER. Named in honor of Governor George Gilmer, this post was established in 1838 on the western edge of the Okefenokee Swamp on the west side of the Suwannee River, just below the mouth of Suwanoochee Creek, in present Echols County, a short distance above the Florida line. During the spring of 1838, Governor Gilmer began receiving reports from the state's southern counties of Indian attacks and depredations. He wrote to both General Zachary Taylor, then commander of Florida's forces, and to Secretary of War Joel R. Poinsett, requesting aid. General Taylor responded by arranging for Federal troops—two companies of infantry and two companies of Dragoons—to be sent from Florida. He posted one company of each at Fort Gilmer. The general, in the meantime, sent Major Henry Dearborn to the frontier to establish a ring of forts around the Okefenokee, accompanied by instructions to have their troops make regular patrols of the area. Fort Gilmer was probably garrisoned until sometime in 1841.

CAMP GORDON. Camp Gordon was named in honor of Lieutenant General John Brown Gordon, C.S.A., who also served as governor of Georgia. Camp Gordon was established July 18, 1917, to serve as a replacement and training camp for the 82nd Division, National Army. Construction began June 18, 1917, and continued through 1918. The post was located in the Chamblee area in DeKalb County, 14 miles north of Atlanta. In 1920 orders were issued for the sale of the post's real estate and buildings. Camp Gordon was finally abandoned September 1921.

FORT GORDON. The home of the U.S. Army Signal Center, Fort Gordon is the largest communications and electronics training facility in the free world. Located 15 miles southwest of Augusta, the post covers more than 55,000 acres of rolling countryside encompassing four counties. The post was activated 12 days after the Pearl Harbor attack in December 1941 as Camp Gordon, named after the Confederate Lieutenant General John Brown Gordon who also served as Georgia governor and U.S. senator. During World War II, Camp Gordon served as a divisional training base for the 4th Infantry, the 26th Infantry, and the 10th Armored Division, three units which eventually fought in Europe in General George S. Patton's Third Army. The 10th Armored Division still maintains Fort Gordon as its home, although the division is no longer active.

After the end of the war, Camp Gordon served as a personnel separation center until 1948 when the Southeastern Signal School was established at the post. In the same year the Military Police school was moved to Camp Gordon and remained until 1975 when it moved to Fort McClellan, Alabama. After being designated a permanent military installation in 1956 and becoming Fort Gordon, in 1974 the Army consolidated the bulk of its communications training here. The U.S. Army Signal Center and Fort Gordon trains more soldiers than any other branch training center of the United States Army.

CAMP GRAHAM. FORT SCREVEN.

FORT GREEN. Four forts were erected in 1813, 10 miles apart, along the western border of Pulaski County through the efforts of General David Blackshear acting on the orders of the governor. Fort Green was one of these stockaded defenses built for the protection of the frontier.

FORT GREENE. After the Revolution, new defenses were needed for the Savannah River. In 1794–95 Fort Greene, named in honor of the Revolutionary leader, General Nathanael Greene, was erected on Cockspur Island at the mouth of the river. The life of this fort ended tragically in 1804, when a vicious equinoctial gale completely demolished its battery and barracks.

CAMP GREENLEAF. Established in May 1917 at Fort Oglethorpe for the training of medical personnel, the post was named in honor of Brigadier General Charles R. Greenleaf, Marine Corps, who served meritoriously during the Spanish-American War. The camp was discontinued as a separate post in September 1919 and absorbed by Fort Oglethorpe on February 6, 1919.

GREENSBORO FORT. One of the first forts erected in Greene County, this fort was burned by the Indians in 1787. During the early years of its settlement, Greensboro (Greensborough) and Greene County suffered many hardships because of the many depredations committed by the Indians who occupied the country west of the Oconee River, about eight miles from the town. Most tragic was the destruction of Greensboro and the massacre of its inhabitants in 1787, when

the town consisted of 20 log cabins, a log-built courthouse, and a fort.

FORT GRIERSON. Located approximately at the present intersection of 11th and Reynolds streets in Augusta, Richmond County, this temporary fortification was named for British Lieutenant Colonel James Grierson during the temporary occupation of the town by his forces from May 1780 to June 1781. After a rendezvous between Colonel Richard Henry (Light Horse Harry) Lee, approaching from Sand Bar Ferry with General Elijah Clarke, and General Andrew Pickens and his troops coming from the north and west, Fort Grierson was invested. After sustaining vigorous attacks by the Americans, Grierson attempted to escape with his garrison to Fort Cornwallis (site of present-day St. Paul's Church). Very few British escaped. Grierson was captured and, while a prisoner, was shot by an unknown Georgia rifleman.

FORT GUNN. FORT ST. TAMMANY.

FORT HALIFAX. FORT WAYNE.

FORT HAMMOND. Nothing is known of this post except that it was located somewhere in Liberty County, according to the Adjutant General's *Journal of 1794.*

FORT HAMMOND. Reportedly a temporary Civil War defense located at Allatoona Pass near Cartersville, Bartow County, no definitive data has been found to substantiate its location. Fort Hammond may possibly have been another name for Fort Allatoona. (See: FORT ALLATOONA.)

CAMP HANCOCK. A temporary camp for the training of National Guard troops, Camp Hancock was established July 18, 1917, adjacent to the city of Augusta and named in honor of Major General Winfield Scott Hancock, veteran of the War with Mexico and the Civil War. Camp Hancock was designated as a demobilization center, December 3, 1918, ordered salvaged January 2, 1919, and abandoned and turned over to a caretaker detachment, March 27, 1919.

CAMP HARRIS. A remount depot during World War I, Camp Harris was located four miles northwest of the city of Macon.

FORT HARTFORD. The Blackshear Trail was opened by General David Blackshear in 1814, from Fort Hartford at Hawkinsville in present Pulaski County to Fort Early, for the purpose of fighting the war more effectively against the rebellious Creek Indians.

CAMP HASKELL. This temporary post, possibly established by the Confederacy during the Civil War, was located at or near the city of Macon.

CAMP HASKELL. Reportedly located at or near the city of Athens, Camp Haskell may have been a temporary Confederate post during the Civil War.

FORT HAWKINS. Today's city of Macon had its origin with the establishment of important Fort Hawkins in 1806 on the east side of the Ocmulgee River, 35 miles southwest of Milledgeville. A westward outpost, trading center, station for negotiating with the Indians, and assembly point for the troops engaged in the Battle of New Orleans during the War of 1812, Fort Hawkins was named for Colonel Benjamin Hawkins, federal commissioner to the Indians, who had selected the site on a commanding elevation near the river. A stockade enclosing 14 acres was constructed of hewn posts 14 inches thick and 14 feet in height, embedded 4 feet into the ground. Every other post had a round hole for musket firing. Within were two two-story log blockhouses, 28 feet square, on stone foundations. Smaller log structures were used as living quarters and trading rooms. The post was abandoned in 1817. Its site, at the southwest corner of Maynard and Woolfolk streets in Macon, is now occupied by a reproduction of one of the blockhouses, constructed in 1938 by the Nathaniel Macon Chapter of the D.A.R.

HEARD'S FORT. FORT WASHINGTON.

FORT HENDERSON. A temporary fort during Florida's Second Seminole War, Fort Henderson was located about two and a half miles west of Coleraine in Charlton County, near the Florida border. The post was named in honor of Brevet Brigadier General Archibald Henderson, Colonel of Marines, distinguished for his services during the war. The post was most probably abandoned in 1842, at the conclusion of the war, when it was occupied by Company D of the 8th Infantry.

FORT HETZEL. One of the series of "Cherokee Removal Forts," this stockade was probably established between 1835 and 1838 and located in northern Fannin County.

CAMP HOBSON. Also known as the "Camp at Lithia Springs," Camp Hobson was a temporary recruiting camp on the Chautaqua Grounds at Lithia Springs, Douglas County. A subpost of Fort McPherson, it was established August 2, 1898, by recruiting detachments from the 7th, 8th, 21st, and 25th Infantry Regiments. The camp appears to have been abandoned about September 16, 1898.

CAMP HOPE. A tempoary rendezvous point for 3,600 Georgia troops called up by the Federal government in September 1813 to fight Indian hostiles during the War of 1812, Camp Hope was located near Fort Hawkins on the Ocmulgee River, the site of today's city of Macon.

FORT HOSKINS. A "Cherokee Removal Fort," Fort Hoskins was established sometime between 1830 and 1838 in present-day Murray County.

FORT HOWE. FORT BARRINGTON.

FORT HUGHES. A dependency of Fort Scott, the site of short-lived Fort Hughes, established November 24, 1817, is now incorporated with today's Chason Park on the east side of the Flint River in the city of Bainbridge, Decatur County. The fort was named for bugler Aaron Hughes killed during the attack against Fowl Town (Fowlstown), a large Indian village, on November 23, 1817, by 300 men of the 7th Infantry. After the skirmish, a temporary stockade was established three miles north of Fowl Town and named for the dead bugler. The post lasted but four or five days.

INSTRUCTION CAMP. In compliance with General Orders No. 84, a Camp of Instruction was established at Chickamauga in Walker County, and specified troops were detailed to train there during July 1908 and again in July 1910.

FORT IRWIN. General Jared Irwin, with his three brothers, John, William, and Alexander, all veterans of the Revolution, built a fort near Union Hill in Washington County, for the protection of the area's settlers against Indian attack. General Irwin died March 1, 1818.

FORT JACKSON. Located on the south side of the Savannah River, about three miles south of the city of Savannah, Fort Jackson was begun in 1808 and completed in June 1812. Named in honor of General Andrew Jackson, the masonry-built fort was garrisoned immediately by state and U.S. troops. During the 1820s, 1840s, and again in the 1870s, additions and modifications were made to the fort. State militia and Confederate partisans seized Fort Jackson in March 1861. Confederate forces held it until General Sherman's famed "March to the Sea" forced the evacuation of Savannah and its defenses in December 1864. On December 19, orders were issued for the spiking of Fort Jackson's heavy guns and the destruction of gun carriages and ammunition. Fort Jackson's garrison, along with troops from other defenses, were evacuated by land and sea. After years of caretaker status following the Civil War, Fort Jackson was abandoned in 1905. The site, formerly operated by the State of Georgia until 1975, was taken over by the Savannah-based, nonprofit Coastal Heritage Society.

FORT JAMES. The peninsula formed by the confluence of the Broad and Savannah rivers, in present Elbert County, is the site of Fort James, one of Georgia's last Colonial forts. A land court at Dartmouth, renamed Petersburg in 1786, which grew up around the fort built in 1775, was held to assign parcels of land to new settlers from September 1773 through June 1775. Fort James was described as a "four-square" stockade, with salient bastions at each angle, surmounted by a blockhouse, and guarded by a number of swivel guns emplaced one story higher than the curtains that were pierced by loopholes. The stockade, covering about an acre of ground, enclosed the commandant's house, officers' quarters, and barracks for the garrison. Fort James, only one mile above Fort Charlotte on the east side of the Savannah in South Carolina, was apparently held by Loyalists until sometime in 1776. It is uncertain exactly who occupied Fort James during the hectic years of the Revolution or for what period of time it was garrisoned. The fort was most probably abandoned soon after the war had ended.

FORT JAMES. This fort, built in 1797 to defend the frontier during the Indian wars, was situated on the west or south bank of the Altamaha River, 50 miles above Darien, in Wayne County. The fort was abandoned about the year 1802.

FORT JAMES. The only information found on this post indicates that it was a Civil War defense situated on the Ogeechee River.

FORT JOADA. During his explorations in 1566–67, ordered by Pedro Menéndez, the founder of St. Augustine, Captain Juan Pardo and 300 Spanish soldiers penetrated what is today western Georgia and somewhere in the west central part of the state built a fortified blockhouse, most probably within or in the environs of an Indian village, called Fort Joada.

BATTERY JONES. Beginning close to U.S. 17 near Savannah and extending about 500 yards north along the left bank of Salt Creek, astride the old Savannah-Darien (Ogeechee) Road, strong earthworks were constructed by Confederate engineers to prevent Union forces using this approach to the city. Designated Battery Jones, the earthworks mounted three 32-pounders and four 12-pounder guns. Battery Jones was garrisoned until the night of December 20th, when vastly superior Union forces under General Sherman forced the evacuation of Savannah by Confederate forces to spare it from a destructive bombardment by General Sherman's heavy siege guns. The guns of Battery Jones were rendered useless and its garrison was withdrawn, first to Savannah and then across the Savannah River into South Carolina.

FORT JONES. A stockaded fort built in 1836 during the Creek War, Fort Jones was located about two miles south of Florence, Stewart County. After the massacre at Roanoke and the town's destruction by fire, frightened surviving settlers found refuge in the fort's blockhouse, built of upright, skinned logs with high windows for gun holes. The fort was built under the supervision of Major H. W. Jernigan and garrisoned by a company of Stewart County citizen soldiers.

JONES' FORT (*Fort Wimberly*). In 1733 Noble Jones built a small wooden fort, replaced in 1741 by a 30-foot-square tabby fort armed with four cannon, on the southern end of the Isle of Hope, overlooking Skidoway Narrows, about 10 miles south of Savannah, in present Chatham County. Jones's plantation was known as Wormsloe, today a state-owned historical site.

KENNESAW BLOCKHOUSE. Located in the town of Kennesaw, Cobb County, across from the railroad station, stood the frame-built, two-story Lacy Hotel, leased by George M. Lacy in 1859 as an eating-house for passengers on the state-owned railway, until June 9, 1864. On April 12, 1862, the Andrew Raiders seized the locomotive "General" while the train crew and passengers were breakfasting at the hotel. Fortified by a stockade, the structure served as barracks for a Federal garrison from June 9 to October 3, 1864, when it was captured by Confederate forces.

Reoccupied by Federal troops, it was maintained as a blockhouse until abandoned by them on November 14, 1864.

KERR'S FORT. A Revolutionary War defense, Kerr's Fort was located in eastern Wilkes County near Petersburg.

FORT KING GEORGE. Located one mile southeast of Darien, McIntosh County, the site of Fort King George sits on a high bluff overlooking the Altamaha River. The first fortification on Georgia soil, it was built by the English under Colonel John Barnwell of South Carolina in 1721, about 12 years before the Georgia colony was founded by General James Oglethorpe. The fort served as a barrier against the Spanish in Florida, the French in the interior, and their Indian allies. The fort experienced no major fighting, although there were occasional skirmishes between its garrison's troops and Spanish soldiers accompanied by allied Indians.

Fort King George's principal fortification was a strong, plank-sided blockhouse with a jutting third story. Its outworks consisted of an earthen wall, with only one of its sides palisaded, in the shape of an irregular triangle, and a palisaded moat. During the six years the fort was garrisoned, more than 140 British soldiers died of various illnesses because of the defense's unhealthful situation between the river and a marsh, influencing many others of the garrison to desert. In January 1726 the blockhouse and barracks burned, and a temporary barracks was erected. In September 1727 when Yamassee Indians instituted a series of attacks against the frontier, Fort King George was evacuated, and its garrison moved to Fort Beaufort to guard South Carolina's southern settlements. The fort thereafter remained without a garrison, except for two men employed as lookouts until 1734, when the fort was permanently abandoned. Its site today is a Georgia State Park maintained by the Georgia Historical Commission.

KNOX'S FORT. A defense against Indian attack, this fortification was built by Samuel Knox in 1786, shortly after he settled in Wilkes County.

FORT LAMAR. The only information found indicates that this was a frontier fort located in Madison County.

FORT LA MOTTE. This post, reportedly located on the perimeter of the Okefenokee Swamp, was most probably a defense erected during the Second Seminole War.

FORT LAWRENCE. The government's old Indian reservation occupying a tract of land about five miles square spanning the Flint River in present Crawford and Taylor counties was protected by Fort Lawrence, which was built by United States Indian Agent Benjamin Hawkins, who took charge of the agency there about the year 1800. The fort, often garrisoned by U.S. troops, was described as 180 feet square, palisaded, with two blockhouses, two hospitals, two storehouses, barracks, and other auxiliary structures. Several important treaties with the Indians were concluded at the agency. On November 15, 1827, a treaty was signed giving the state full title to the remaining Creek lands between the Flint and Chattahoochee rivers. Two earlier treaties were concluded there in November 1804 and April 1817.

FORT LAWRENCE. General David Blackshear in 1814 cut a trail through the wilderness from Fort Hartford at Hawkinsville to Fort Early on the Flint River. Four forts were erected in 1813, 10 miles apart, along the western border of Pulaski County, including stockaded Fort Lawrence.

LAWSON'S FORT. "Mount Pleasant," at Louisville, Jefferson County, was built by Roger Lawson in 1759 on land granted him by the British Crown. At the rear of the house may be seen the remains of his old fort erected for defense against Indians who had killed two of his sons. Lawson, distinguished during the Revolution, gave the land for the city of Louisville and for the old Louisville Academy, one of the state's first schools. His father, Hugh Lawson, was among those chosen to select a site for the first capital of Georgia. The house has been owned by only three families in more than 200 years.

FORT LAWTON. This Confederate prison, five miles north of Millen, Jenkins County, was established during the late summer of 1864 to relieve the overflow pressure on the prison at Andersonville (Camp Sumter). A square stockade, enclosing about 42 acres, the interior was divided by streets into divisions. The Union prisoners constructed their own huts from the branches of the trees used in building the stockade. By November of the same year, it held about 10,000 men. General Sherman's Union troops during his "March to the Sea" in late 1864 relieved much of the prisoner congestion and vengefully devastated much of Millen, burning the town's railroad station and the hotel, and pillaging houses.

The site of the prison is today occupied by the 1,100-acre Magnolia Spring State Park.

FORT LEE. A Confederate defense of Savannah, Fort Lee was situated on the Savannah River south of the city.

LOVEJOY'S STATION. On November 15, 1864, Confederate forces under General G. W. Smith built temporary fortifications here, 13 miles north of present-day Griffin, Spalding County, in preparation for an anticipated engagement with General Sherman's army during its "March to the Sea." The Union forces, however, had taken a different route in the direction of Macon.

FORT LUMPKIN. FORT DAHLONEGA.

LUMPKIN BLOCKHOUSE. The first courthouse in Lumpkin, in present-day Stewart County, was built of logs in August 1830 and used as a blockhouse during the Creek Indian War of 1836.

FORT MCALLISTER. A major Confederate earthwork defense of the city of Savannah about 12 miles to the north, Fort McAllister was situated on Genesis Point at the mouth of the Ogeechee River, built in 1861–62 to close the river to enemy ships. The fort mounted 11 siege guns, 12 field-pieces, and 1 ten-inch mortar. Below it piles and torpedoes obstructed the channel. When Union naval attempts failed to take the fort in December 1864 during Sherman's "March to the Sea," land forces under Brigadier General William B. Hazen were ordered to cross the river and take the fort from the rear. On the afternoon of December 13, after a difficult deployment, Hazen assaulted the fort, and in less than half an hour, his three brigades swarmed over the works and overpowered Major George W. Anderson's small garrison of 230 Georgians, who reportedly fought gallantly to the end. A few days later, the city of Savannah fell to Union forces.

FORT MCCRANIE. There are three sites of forts located in Cook County. In 1836 Governor William Schley, after the disastrous battle and massacre at Roanoke on the Chattahoochee River, when numerous bands of Creek Indians were roaming through south Georgia's frontier, ordered all settlements to erect forts for their protection. One of the defenses, Fort McCranie, was built on Bushy Creek. It was near this fort that the fiercely fought Bushy Creek Battle took place on June 19, 1836, in which the companies of all three forts (forts Futch and Morrison were the other two) took part. The bloody fight culminated in a terrible slaughter of Indian men, women, and children.

FORT MCCREARY. One mile north of Omaha, Stewart County, is the site of Fort McCreary, erected for the defense of the frontier along the Chattahoochee River. During the Creek Indian War of 1836, it was garrisoned by U.S. troops and Georgia Volunteers. The site is now owned by the Roanoke Chapter of the D.A.R.

CAMP MCDONALD. At Big Shanty Depot, east of Kennesaw, in Cobb County, about 30 miles north of Atlanta, were the parade grounds and tent city of Camp McDonald, one of the earliest camps in the state for the training of citizens for the Confederate Army. Established June 11, 1861, by Governor Joseph E. Brown, the camp closed in the late fall of the same year but reopened in 1862 and 1863 to train more troops for the Confederacy. Sham battles and parades held here attracted large and appreciative audiences.

FORT MCINTOSH. Built in 1776 on the northeast side of the Satilla River, west of the present-day town of Tarboro, Camden County, it was named for Colonel (later General) Lachlan McIntosh. It was a small stockade, 100 feet square with a bastion at each angle and a blockhouse in the center. In 1777 Captain Richard Winn, commanding a small garrison, was forced to surrender the fort when attacked by a much great force of British regulars, Tories, and Indians.

MCKAY'S (MACKAY'S) TRADING POST. Located on the Savannah River, about a mile and a half below Augusta, McKay's (Mackay's) Trading Post, also known in history as the White House, played an important role in the Indian trade and the Revolution. Built about 1758 by Thomas Red, a Virginia planter, it was operated by Robert McKay (Mackay) for nearly a decade prior to the opening hostilities of the Revolution. McKay, a Scot, was popular with the Indians, and his trading post was often the stage for important negotiations between Indians and whites.

In September 1780 the White House was besieged by Colonel Elijah Clarke and a band of Patriots intent upon recapturing Augusta. British troops and allied Indians, commanded by Colonel Thomas Brown, had retreated to this building. After a four-day siege, during which the British, deprived of water, were nearly at the point of surrender, reinforcements arrived from Fort Ninety-Six. The Americans withdrew, leaving 29 of their wounded behind. Thirteen Patriots were hanged in the stairwell of the White House while Colonel Brown, who lay wounded, could watch their dying. The rest were delivered to the Indians to be tortured and killed. The site of the trading post was purchased by the Richmond County Historical Society and deeded to the state of Georgia. It is now operated by the Georgia Historical Commission.

CAMP MCKENZIE. Located in Augusta, Camp McKenzie was established in 1898 as a recruiting and training post for the Spanish-American War. The camp apparently closed in early 1899.

FORT MCLANE. An Army post, one of the cordon of forts built around the great Okefenokee Swamp to confine the recalcitrant Indians within its jungles, was established sometime during the First Seminole War. Fort McLane was possibly located in present-day Ware County, on the northwest perimeter of the swamp.

FORT MCPHERSON (*McPherson Barracks*). General James Birdseye McPherson, for whom the post is named, graduated July 1, 1853, from the Military Academy at West Point. He was first in his class and became the first graduate in the history of the Academy to be retained as an instructor. During the Civil War his activities in the Battles of Jackson and Vicksburg earned him promotion to Brigadier General in the Union Army. He is credited with being the first to use land mine warfare. In 1864 he became Major General of the XVII Corps and moved to Huntsville, Alabama, for the drive on Atlanta. In less than a week after the first engagements on Atlanta's outskirts, he was killed in the front line when he attempted to outrun a Confederate patrol.

Fort McPherson, home of Headquarters U.S. Army Forces Command, is a 505-acre post located four miles southwest of downtown Atlanta. The mission of the post is to furnish garrison, administrative, and logistical support to Headquarters, United States Army Forces Command, and to supervise activities at its subinstallations, Fort Gillem, Georgia, and Fort Buchanan, Puerto Rico. The fort was established in 1867 on the grounds where Spelman College is now located. A 10-company post was constructed on the site and was named "McPherson Barracks" in honor of General McPherson. Congress in 1885 approved $15,000 for the purchase of a site for a permanent post southwest of the city. More land purchases were authorized the following year and the present reservation was acquired. On May 4, 1889, Fort McPherson was designated a permanent Army station.

At the outbreak of the Spanish-American War in 1898, Fort McPherson was garrisoned by the 5th Infantry. It also became a depot for the training of the 29th U.S. Volunteers. During World War I the post served as a prison camp for German prisoners of war. Activities were greatly expanded with the passage of the Selective Service Act of 1940 and the outbreak of World War II. The fort functioned as an induction and reception center during this emergency with hundreds of men being processed daily. In December 1947 Headquarters Third United States Army, which had been located in downtown Atlanta, was transferred to Fort McPherson. Headquarters U.S. Army Forces Command was activated, with headquarters at Fort McPherson, effective July 1, 1973. In December 1982 the Third U.S. Army was reactivated at Fort McPherson and became the Army component headquarters for the U.S. Central Command.

MCPHERSON BARRACKS. FORT MCPHERSON.

FORT MACON. Although the city of Macon had been occupied by the 176th N.Y. Volunteers since the summer of 1865, this post was permanently established in March 1866 when Lieutenant Colonel John A. Bogart with elements of the 103rd U.S. Colored Infantry relieved the N.Y. Volunteers. Fort Macon was abandoned on August 6, 1868. The post was reoccupied briefly by the 7th Cavalry in December 1898.

FORT MATHEWS. Located about two miles south of today's U.S. 278 at the Oconee River and situated in the fork of the Oconee and Appalachee rivers, Fort Mathews was built in 1793 and named for Governor George Mathews. From this fort observations were made of the illegal activities of General Elijah Clarke and his land-hungry followers as they built forts for the protection of Clarke's "Trans-Oconee Republic" on lands reserved to the Creeks. The report to Governor Mathews led to the arrest of General Clarke. All of his fortifications were destroyed. (See: FORTS ADVANCE and DEFIANCE.)

FORT MEANS. Another of the so-called "Cherokee Removal Forts," Fort Means was built sometime between 1830 and 1838 in the southeastern corner of Floyd County.

FORT MERCER. A Confederate-built Civil War defense of the city of Savannah, Fort Mercer mounted nine guns.

FORT (A. S.) MILLER. This post was reportedly located near the city of Dalton in present Whitfield County. No data has been found to support its existence.

CAMP MILNER. Most Georgia troops for the Confederate Army were mobilized in and near Griffin, Spalding County. Camp Milner, the cavalry camp, was named for Ben Milner, prominent businessman who gave financial aid toward equipping troops from his county. The infantry camp, Camp Stephens, was north of the town on McIntosh Road. Camp Milner became Camp Northen, named for ex-Governor William J. Northen (1890–94), in 1898, when it served during the Spanish-American War as a mobilization center and training camp for the National Guard. Later a fairgrounds, it is now the city's Municipal Park. (See: CAMP NORTHEN.)

CAMP MITCHELL. Named in honor of Major William G. Mitchell, this temporary camp was established near Atlanta in September 1884 for use of the garrison of Pensacola's Fort Barrancas during the yellow fever season in the South. Early in December the troops were returned to their station at the Florida fort.

FORT MITCHELL. In 1814 General David Blackshear blazed a trail through the wilderness from Fort Hartford at Hawkinsville to Fort Early on the Flint River. Fort Mitchell was one of the four stockaded forts erected in 1813, 10 miles apart, along the western border of Pulaski County for the protection of the frontier.

FORT MONTPELIER. Located on the Oconee River, a half mile below the town of Montpelier, Baldwin County, the post was erected in 1794 during the Creek Indian troubles.

MOON'S STATION POST. A Federal stockade, garrisoned by 84 officers and men of the 14th and 15th Illinois Infantry, it was located 50 yards from the railroad's Moon Station, two miles north of Kennesaw in Cobb County. On October 3, 1864, it was assaulted by Confederate forces.

FORT MORRIS (*Fort George; Fort Defense*). Old Sunbury (now a dead town) on the Midway River in Liberty County, 11 miles east of Midway on U.S. 17, was at one time a leading port rivaling Savannah in commercial importance. Built during the first year of the Revolution to guard the port, Fort Morris was an irregular shaped, quadrangular enclosed earthwork reportedly 275 feet in length along the waterfront. Surrounded by a parapet and a moat, with a parade occupying about an acre of ground within the enclosure, the fort was defended by more than 25 varied pieces of ordnance. It was named in honor of Captain Morris, who commanded the company of artillery which first occupied the fort early in 1776.

Colonel John McIntosh was commanding the garrison on November 25, 1778, when Colonel L. V. Fuser, with 500 British ground troops supported by armed vessels in the river landed at Sunbury and demanded the immediate surrender of the fort. Colonel McIntosh, with 127 Continentals, some militiamen and Sunbury citizens, less than 200 in aggregate, replied, "Come and take it." The British troops, after several unsuccessful attacks, retreated to their ships. The Continental garrison retained Fort Morris until January 9, 1779, when it was taken by a 2,000-man British force commanded by General Augustine Prevost after a short siege. Prevost renamed the fort Fort George for the king. During the War of 1812, the fort was rebuilt and renamed Fort Defense and manned by a body of mostly students. The fort, however, played no active role in the war. Today, remains of the fort's breastworks and embrasures are still in evidence.

FORT MOUNT PLEASANT. Situated east of the town of Clyo, Effingham County, on a bluff fronting the Savannah River, is the site of Mt. Pleasant, a former Uchee Indian village and English trading post. During Georgia's early days, a small garrisoned fort was maintained there by the Colonial government and commanded by Indian trader Captain Thomas Wiggin.

FORT MUDGE. One of the number of temporary forts and blockhouses cordoning the Okefenokee Swamp built in 1813 by Generals John Floyd and David Blackshear to contain the rebellious Creeks, Fort Mudge was located on the northern perimeter of the swamp, about nine miles south of Fort Floyd.

FORT MUSE. This temporary post was reportedly located on the perimeter of the Okefenokee Swamp, as noted on an 1839 Florida war map. No other data has been found to substantiate its existence.

NEAL'S FORT. A fort of this name was reportedly located near the town of White Plains in Greene County.

FORT NEW ECHOTA. One of the so-called "Cherokee Removal Forts," established between

1830 and 1838, Fort New Echota was a hewn-log blockhouse located in central Gordon County.

FORT AT NEW INVERNESS. FORT DARIEN.

CAMP NEAR NEWNAN. A temporary camp was established September 19, 1898, near Newnan, Coweta County, by 1st Lieutenant W. C. Rafferty with 151 men of Battery D, 1st Artillery. The post was abandoned on November 19, 1898.

FORT NEWNAN. One of the series of "Cherokee Removal Forts" established after 1830, Fort Newnan was located in today's central Cherokee County.

CAMP NEWPORT. A Confederate post established in the summer of 1864, Camp Newport in South Newport was occupied by Lieutenant W. L. Mole commanding Company F of the 3rd South Carolina Cavalry for the purpose of guarding McIntosh County's coast. On the night of August 18, the post was attacked by Federal troops who came up the South Newport River. Less than 20 men of Company F escaped death or capture. In addition, the Federals burned the bridge over the river.

NICOLLS' OUTPOST. Late in the War of 1812, probably in the late summer or fall of 1814, not long after the British force under Colonel Edward Nicolls had erected the "Negro Fort" at Prospect Bluff, the colonel established a fortified outpost at or near the confluence of the Chattahoochee and Flint rivers. The probable site lies within today's Seminole County.

CAMP NORTHEN. On April 23, 1898, President McKinley called on Governor W. Y. Atkinson for two regiments of infantry and two batteries of light artillery for service in the Spanish-American War. On May 4 Camp Northen, named for the ex-governor, was established at Griffin, the site of former Camp Milner, in Spalding County. The camp's commander was Colonel Oscar J. Brown, a regular Army officer, serving as Colonel of the Regiment of Georgia Volunteers. Camp Northen was probably abandoned sometime in November of the same year.

NORTON'S STATION (*Fort Repose*). This post, also known as Fort Repose, was established March 25, 1842, by Captain Henry McKavett, 8th Infantry, with Company E, "near Blunt's Ferry," on the Suwannee River in Clinch County. The post was a day's march from Fort Moniac. Norton's Station was at times called North's Station in historical citations.

FORTS NOS. 7, 8, 9. These are three of the forts in the interior line of defenses built by General W. T. Sherman's Federal engineers during September and October 1864. Their purpose was to shorten the original line of Confederate fortifications by several miles in order that the city could be held by a relatively smaller force. Fort No. 7 was on the grounds of the present Morris Brown College of Atlanta University. The area is bounded by Hunter, Tatnall, Walnut, and Beckwith streets, some distance to the west of the far end of the campus. It was closest to Hunter and Tatnall streets. Fort No. 8 was in the northwest angle of Fair and Walnut streets. Fort No. 9 was approximately on Larkin Street between Walnut Street and old Davis Street, now Northside Drive S.W.

OGLETHORPE BARRACKS. During the American Revolution, the area of the military barracks, located a short distance south of Savannah, was the scene of heavy fighting in 1778 and 1779. When Savannah was attacked by the British on December 29, 1778, a small contingent of Georgia militia was stationed east of the barracks. Colonel George Walton, a signer of the Declaration of Independence, was severely wounded near here while attempting to rally his militia during a sharp encounter with British Light Infantry troops. During the siege of Savannah in 1779 by American and French forces, the brick barracks were dismantled by the British defenders who left standing only the lower portion of the south wall. Under the direction of the noted British military engineer, Captain James Moncrief, the remains of the barracks were converted into a strong fortification, known as a hornwork, which dominated the center of the Royalist lines around Savannah.

Oglethorpe Barracks at Savannah was established in 1821 and abandoned in January 1851 after being irregularly garrisoned. Prior to the actual outbreak of the Civil War, the post was seized by Georgia troops in January 1861. The city was captured by Federal forces under General W. T. Sherman in December 1864, at which time the barracks were reoccupied. At the close of the war, volunteer forces were replaced by regulars for its garrison. This post, sometimes known as Oglethorpe Barracks, was abandoned on April 23, 1879, in compliance with Special Orders No. 63, Headquarters, Department of the South, April 11, 1879, at the end of the Reconstruction period. In 1884 the Federal government built new military barracks, officially designated Oglethorpe Barracks, on this site. They were razed in 1889 when the DeSoto Hotel was erected.

OLD INDIAN STOCKADE. FORT CUMMINGS.

CAMP ONWARD. This post was established during the Spanish-American War at Savannah on October 23, 1898, upon the arrival of the 7th Army Corps. The camp appears to have been abandoned when a detachment of the 2nd Cavalry withdrew on May 25, 1899, in compliance with telegraphed instructions.

PEACHTREE FORT. Since the majority of the Creek Indians were allied to the British and the Cherokees loyal to the United States during the War of 1812, it was decided to locate a fort beyond the Georgia frontier at the Indian village of Standing Peach Tree on the Chattahoochee River, the boundary line, in present Fulton County. Lieutenant George R. Gilmer (later twice governor of Georgia) was sent to the village with a small force in 1814 to erect a fort there. It was built on an elevation north of and at the mouth of Peachtree Creek and garrisoned for several months. The Creek Indian village spanned both sides of the river at the mouth of the creek. Because of its strategic position at a ferry on the river and where several Indian trails converged, Standing Peach Tree evolved as an important trading center between 1830 and 1840.

FORT PERRY. A half mile east of S.R. 41, about 12 miles north of Buena Vista, Marion County, lies the site of Fort Perry, adjoining the Old Federal Road. A stockaded fortification with blockhouses, completed in October 1813, the post had been ordered erected by General John Floyd as he led 400 Georgia militiamen to fight the hostile Creeks, the "Red Sticks," across the Chattahoochee River on Alabama territory. The fort was named in honor of Oliver Hazard Perry, naval hero of the War of 1812.

FORT PETERSON. One of the earliest Indian defense forts in Coffee County was erected by the settlers near the home of John Peterson in or near the town of Huffer, about five miles northeast of Douglas. The fort's stockade enclosed a two- or three-acre tract of land. Within were a number of small houses for the accommodation of refugee families.

FORT PICKERING. The site of historical Coleraine on the border of Camden and Charlton counties was marked in 1912 by a large, suitably inscribed granite boulder, erected by the D.A.R. to commemorate the signing of the "Treaty of Peace and Friendship" on June 29, 1796, between the president of the United States and the representative chiefs of the Creek Nation. After the pact was ratified by Congress, the government erected a rather pretentious fortification in the town on the St. Marys River for the protection of the settlement's inhabitants from both the Indians and the Spaniards across the border in Florida. The fort was no doubt named for then Secretary of State Timothy Pickering.

FORT PIKE. In 1814 General David Blackshear cut a trail through the wilderness from Fort Hartford at Hawkinsville to Fort Early on the Flint River. A year earlier, four forts had been erected, 10 miles apart, along Pulaski County's western border, by order of the governor through General Blackshear. One of these stockaded forts was Fort Pike.

CAMP PINCKNEY. An important supply depot and settlement and boat loading on the St. Marys River, near Folkston, Charlton County, the post proved useful during the campaigns against the Indians during the early years of the Second Seminole War. The depot was most probably named for Captain Thomas Pinckney of South Carolina who camped here with his men during the campaign against the Creeks.

FORT AT POINT PETER. A fort at this location was established by the Georgia government during the War of 1812. After it was attacked by British forces, compelling the fort's evacuation by the outnumbered American defenders, the British burned the fort.

FORT PREVOST. FORT WAYNE.

FORT PRINCE WILLIAM (*Fort William*). Situated on the southern end of Cumberland Island, Georgia's southernmost coastal island, Fort Prince William (or William) was most probably completed in April 1740 by James Oglethorpe to command Cumberland Sound, the entrance to the Amelia Channel, the St. Marys River, and the inland waterway approach to Fort Frederic to the north. On the northwest end of Cumberland Island stood Fort St. Andrews, erected by General Oglethorpe in 1736 in preparation for an attack against Spanish Florida.

FORT PULASKI. The Fort Pulaski National Monument commemorates the end of a distinct chapter in the ever-changing development of military science. Its massive walls, built with approximately 25 million bricks over a period of nearly 20 years, still bear the historic scars of a 30-hour bombardment by Federal artillery on April 10–11, 1862, demonstrating for the first time the tremendous battering power of the newly developed rifled cannon. Surrender of the "impregnable" fortress by the Confederates, who had seized it at the outbreak of the Civil War, served notice to military engineers that the day of brick citadels had passed forever. Today, the structure is not only a memorial to the fortitude of its defenders, but also to the valor of Count Casimir Pulaski, Polish friend of America during the Revolution, who was killed during the siege of Savannah in 1779 and whose name the fort bears.

Situated at the mouth of the Savannah River, Cockspur Island had played a significant role in the military defense of coastal Georgia. In the past two centuries, three forts had been built on this small marshy island. Fort George, a palisaded log blockhouse and earthen fortification, was begun in 1761 by the Colonial government to defend Savannah's harbor and enforce customs and quarantine laws. This early fortification, partially destroyed by storms, was dismantled in 1776 by the Americans to deprive its use by approaching British forces. After the war, new defenses were required for the Savannah River, and the government in 1794–95 erected Fort Greene, named for General Nathanael Greene. The great equinoctial gale of 1804 completely demolished its battery and barracks. A quarter of a century elapsed before Cockspur Island was again selected as the site of a fortification to command the South Atlantic coast and the Savannah River valley.

Brigadier General Simon Bernard, Napoleon's famed military engineer, developed preliminary plans for the new fort in 1827, and work was begun two years later under the supervision of Major Samuel Babcock. Robert E. Lee's first appointment after his graduation from West Point in 1829 was to Cockspur Island, where he assisted with the early work on the fort until 1831. In 1833 the new fort was named Pulaski in honor of the Count. Construction on the fort continued intermittently from 1829 to 1847. It was an enormous project. Lumber, lime, lead, iron, and other building supplies were bought both in the North and South in large quantities. Nearly a million dollars was spent on Fort Pulaski, but in one important respect it was never finished. Its armament was to include about 140 cannon, but at the beginning of the Civil War only 20 cannon had been mounted, and even those were not in a serviceable condition.

FORT PULASKI. (Courtesy of the National Park Service.)

During the tumultuous days that immediately preceded the outbreak of the war, Fort Pulaski had not been garrisoned by Federal troops, but in anticipation Georgia's governor ordered it seized on January 3, 1861. Georgia seceded from the Union on January 19, and on March 20 the fort was transferred to the government of the Confederacy. While cannon and munitions were being brought by the Confederates to Cockspur Island in the fall of 1861, a large Federal military and naval force was moving southward by sea, capturing and blockading ports along the Atlantic coast. From a base on Hilton Head Island, South Carolina, about 15 miles from Cockspur, the Federal attack on Fort Pulaski was planned.

Federal batteries of the new rifled cannon, together with regular smoothbore cannon, were set up on Tybee Island, opposite the fort, early in 1862. Early on the morning of April 10, when the Federal forces were ready, the Union commander, Major General David Hunter, sent a demand to the island for the fort's unconditional surrender. Receiving a refusal, the Federals immediately began a 30-hour bombardment, during which the southeastern angle and wall of Fort Pulaski were successfully breached, forcing the fort's commander to surrender about 2 P.M. on April 11. The supposedly impregnable fort fell, and with it were captured 385 officers and men, 48 cannon, and a large quantity of supplies.

Savannah, one of the principal seaports in the South, was thus cut off from all foreign trade. Since the fort was never relinquished by the Federals, it was an effective unit in the blockade that was eventually to throttle the economic life of the South. Its casemates also served as military and political prison in 1864–65. The siege of Fort Pulaski, moreover, was a landmark in military history. The breaching of the fort's massive brick walls by projectiles from rifled cannon demonstrated for the first time that the old type of brick and masonry fortifications could not withstand the fire of modern guns. In 1880 Fort Pulaski was abandoned as an active post, and while temporary defense measures were taken within the structure and on the island during the Spanish-American War, no occasion arose to use these defenses against the enemy. Fort Pulaski National Monument consists of Federal lands on McQueens and Cockspur Islands, embracing 5,364 acres, and is administered by the National Park Service.

RAILROAD BLOCKHOUSE. Allatoona Creek, spanned by today's modern bridge between Emerson and Acworth on old U.S. 41, Bartow County, was the site of a Federal blockhouse, garrisoned by companies E, F, and I of the 18th Wisconsin Infantry to guard the strategic bridge of the state-owned railroad. On October 5, 1864, Confederate forces burned the bridge and the blockhouse, capturing 84 officers and men. In 1949 the railroad was rerouted northward and in 1950 the creek was flooded, its water impounded by the Allatoona Dam.

CAMP RECOVERY. Established for the accommodation of soldiers convalescing from fevers to which Fort Scott's garrison was subject, Camp Recovery was a temporary, seasonal encampment on the elevated area about two and a half miles southeast of the fort. The site, in present Decatur County, cannot be identified with precision. The following inscription is incised on the base of the granite monument erected in commemoration of the camp: "Erected on the site of Camp Recovery near which are buried officers and soldiers of the United States Army who died during the Indian Wars in the Flint and Chattahoochee river country, 1817 to 1821."

FORT RED CLAY. Reportedly one of the "Cherokee Removal Forts" established between 1830 and 1838 somewhere in northern Georgia, no data has been found to indicate this stockade's location.

FORT REPOSE. NORTON'S STATION.

FORT ROME. Another of the "Cherokee Removal Forts" built sometime between 1830 and 1838, Fort Rome was located in Floyd County.

FORT ROSA. According to a National Archives citation, Fort Rosa was a short-lived post established by Lieutenant R. P. Campbell's Company H of the 2nd Dragoons, which left Fort Shannon, East Florida, October 12, 1841, arrived at Fort Henderson (Georgia) on October 14, and reached Norton's (North's) Station on October 19, where they established Fort Rosa. Lieutenant Campbell arrived October 28 to assume command.

FORT ROSE DEW. A small Confederate-built earthwork defense of Savannah on the Ogeechee River, Fort Rose Dew was subjected to heavy bombardment by Admiral Dahlgren's fleet on December 14, 1864. By the 21st, this work and all other fortifications in Savannah's line of defenses had been abandoned by Confederate forces under General Hardee, outnumbered four to one by General Sherman's army.

FORT ST. ANDREWS. Erected in 1736 on Cumberland Island by General James Oglethorpe, Fort St. Andrews stood on a high neck of land on the north end of Georgia's southernmost coastal island. Surrounded by a palisade and a ditch, the fort had earth-filled double walls of timber. Two companies of Oglethorpe's Regiment were reportedly stationed there until 1742, when the Spanish were disastrously defeated in the Battle of Bloody Marsh on St. Simons Island.

ST. CATHERINES ISLAND PRESIDIO. In April 1566, after Pedro Menéndez de Avilés founded St. Augustine, he began to establish Franciscan missions protected by fortified presidios on Georgia's mainland coast and on the bordering barrier islands. The establishment of the presidio on St. Catherines Island and the consummation of an alliance with Guale's (Georgia) chief marked the beginning of the long Spanish period in Georgia's history. In 1670 an English vessel, apparently mistaking St. Catherines's harbor for Charles Towne, newly established by the English, in South Carolina, landed a small party, which was at once attacked. Seven men were killed, and three men and two women captured and taken to St. Augustine.

Within 10 years after its founding, Charles Towne had built up a comparatively sizable military force of Englishmen and allied Indians to undertake the destruction of Spanish Florida's military outposts and missions. In 1680, 300 English-led Indians, furnished with new firearms, descended on the Spanish mission-presidios. The fort on St. Catherines Island, provincial headquarters of Guale, was subjected to the worst treatment. By 1686 the island had been completely abandoned by the Spanish.

FORT ST. SIMONS. On the southern end of St. Simons Island, seven miles from Fort Frederica, General James Oglethorpe built a small fortification, which became known as Fort St. Simons, to partially command the entrance to Jekyl Sound. The men's barracks were located in the very near environs of the fort and their foundations are buried underneath the garden plots of today's plush hotels.

FORT ST. TAMMANY (*Fort Gunn*). This was a federal-built fort established sometime about the year 1787, possibly existing as long as the outbreak of the War of 1812. It was located in the town of St. Marys overlooking the St. Marys River. Another name it was known by was Fort Gunn.

FORT SAN PEDRO. Established by the Spanish on Cumberland Island about the year 1569, four years after the founding of St. Augustine, Fort San Pedro seems to have existed until about the year 1702. In the sixteenth and early seventeenth centuries, the island was the site of two important Franciscan missions to the Indians: San Pedro y San Pablos de Poturiba on the northwest end of the island and San Pedro Mocama near its southern extremity. Cumberland Island was called San Pedro by the Spanish while the region's Timucuan Indians knew it as Tacatacuru.

FORT SANTA ELENA. In 1567 Captain Juan Pardo made a second round of explorations into the country's interior to expand Spain's domination, in compliance with orders of Pedro Menéndez de Avilés, the founder of St. Augustine. Pardo's lieutenant, Hernando Boyano (Moyano), with a party of soldiers, reached Chiaha, the principal town of the area's tribe, in the neighborhood of present-day Columbus. Here the lieutenant, while awaiting the arrival of his chief, built a fort with the consent of the natives. Boyano named his fort Santa Elena.

SAPELO ISLAND PRESIDIO. Despite disappointments and obstacles, Franciscan missionaries expanded their mission system in America's Southeast, particularly between 1605 and 1655. During that period, the mission of San Buenaventura was established on St. Simons Island, Santiago de Ocone on Jekyl Island, and San José de Zápala on Sapelo Island, bringing the aggregate number of thriving missions within present-day Georgia to nine, with two more in South Carolina. Several of the island missions were long protected by garrisoned tabby-built presidios—on Amelia, Cumberland, Sapelo, and St. Catherines islands. A 1760 map of Sapelo Island in present McIntosh County has a notation to the effect that a "Spanish Fort," the presidio, was situated on the northwest end of the island. The mission and the fort may have been established as early as 1566, when St. Catherines Island was garrisoned. In 1680 a series of Indian Wars was begun against the Spanish when the Cherokees and Creeks allied themselves with the English at Charles Towne in South Carolina and, led by English soldiers, attacked the missions in Guale (Georgia). One by one presidio-protected missions were devastated. In all likelihood, Sapelo Island was evacuated by the Spanish before the year 1686.

FORT SAVANNAH. FORT WAYNE.

FORT SCOTT (*Camp Crawford*). In the spring of 1816, in compliance with orders of Major General Andrew Jackson, Brigadier General Edmund P. Gaines directed Lieutenant Colonel Duncan L. Clinch to erect a fort on the lower Flint River in order to restrain the hostile Creeks, the "Red Sticks." In June Clinch arrived with a detachment of the 4th Infantry and established a camp on the west or right bank of the Flint River, just above its confluence with the Chattahoochee, about a mile west of S.R. 310, south of present-day Bainbridge in Decatur County, calling the post Camp Crawford. Construction of a fort there was begun in September. The defense was designated Fort Scott, possibly in honor of Lieutenant R. W. Scott, killed at the site before the fort's completion. Temporarily evacuated in December, the fort was almost at once plundered by the watchful hostiles. In the spring of 1817, Fort Scott was reoccupied by Captain S. Donoho and a company of artillerymen, reinforced later in the same year. Fort Scott was abandoned in September 1821, after the cession of Florida to the United States and a semblance of peace had been established on the frontier.

FORT SCREVEN (*Camp Graham; Camp Crawford*). Located on Tybee Island, Chatham County, about 18 miles southeast of Savannah, this post was established on March 18, 1898, and named Camp Graham by Captain John M. K. Davis, 1st Artillery, who garrisoned the camp with Battery F of that regiment. The name was changed to Fort Screven in honor of James Screven, colonel and brigadier general of the Georgia Militia who was killed at Midway Church in 1778 during the

Revolution. Construction on the fort was completed in 1901, when its armament consisted of 20 guns of various calibers. The fort was designated headquarters of Savannah's coast defenses, but ceased to be a Coast Artillery post in compliance with General Orders No. 8, War Department, February 27, 1924. Fort Screven was declared surplus on October 21, 1944.

SHERRILL'S FORT. This fort was a private blockhouse built by a settler named Sherrill on his farm on a creek east of present-day Union Point, in either Greene or Taliaferro County. The only record found of any activity there was that of an Indian attack in January 1774. The blockhouse was most probably built in 1773 when the land on which it stood was not opened to settlement until then.

FORT (HINAR) SIXES. One of the "Cherokee Removal Forts" erected between 1830 and 1838, Fort Sixes was located in Cherokee County.

REDOUBT SPRING HILL. The Central of Georgia Railroad Depot in Savannah occupies the site of the Spring Hill Redoubt, part of the forts and entrenchments built by the British during their occupation since December 29, 1778. Here was fought, on October 9, 1779, one of the bloodiest battles of the Revolution. After a siege of three weeks, the allied forces of American Continentals and French Grenadiers on the morning of October 9 stormed the fortifications manned by British redcoats, Scotch Highlanders, Hessians, and Cherokee Indians. Despite the valorous attack by the allies, they suffered heavy losses within their ranks, among them mortally wounded Count Casimir Pulaski. The disparity in the number of casualties testifies to the American-French disaster. The allies lost between 800 and 1,000 killed and wounded, most of them French. The defenders lost between 50 and 100 killed and wounded. Utterly beaten, the Americans returned to Charleston while the French sailed off with their fleet.

CAMP STEPHENS. The site of Camp Stephens, named for Alexander H. Stephens, vice-president of the Confederacy, is located about a half mile from Old U.S. 41, on Mackintosh Road in Griffin, Spalding County. The majority of Georgia's Confederate troops were mobilized here and at Camp Milner, the cavalry center, on the site of today's Griffin Municipal Park.

CAMP STEWART. FORT STEWART.

FORT STEWART (*Camp Stewart*). Named for General Daniel Stewart, Revolutionary War hero, Camp Stewart was established as an antiaircraft training center in June 1940, located 40 miles southwest of Savannah and 1 mile from Hinesville, Liberty County. In 1941, before construction had been completed, the camp opened and housed thousands of troops in a temporary tent city. During World War II, Camp Stewart was one of the largest troop training centers in the nation. It was determined in 1953 that the post could also be made available as an armor training center. In March 1956 the 280,000-acre reservation was redesignated as a fort and made a permanent installation.

CAMP SUMTER (*Andersonville Prison*). The early history of Andersonville National Cemetery is to a considerable extent the inevitable sequel of the grim events that transpired some 300 yards to the southeast in a stockaded area of 28 acres known variously as the Confederate State Military Prison, Camp Sumter, its more proper name, and more familiarly as Andersonville Prison. In 1863 when the course of the war and a growing shortage of food supplies in the Virginia area made apparent the necessity for the removal of the great body of Union prisoners of war from the Confederate prison camps near Richmond, Brigadier General John H. Winder, superintendent of military prisons for the Confederacy, had agents and surveyors, among whom was his son Captain W. S. Winder, look for a suitable site more distant from the theater of war. A site near Anderson in Georgia was finally decided upon. There in November 1863 Confederate soldiers with a labor force of Negro slaves requisitioned for the work from plantation owners of the area began clearing the tall Georgia pines that covered the area about a mile east of the Anderson railroad depot.

Through the winter of 1863–64, the work continued. Lofty pines were cut into 20-foot-long logs and planted five feet into the ground, forming an almost impregnable double stockade about the area. An inner stockade enclosed an area roughly 1,540 feet long and 750 feet wide, and was in turn enclosed by another stockade enclosing some 15 (later 26) acres. Sentry boxes were placed at intervals along the top of the inner stockade. A stream of water, a branch of Sweetwater Creek, ran through the prison yard dividing it roughly in half. Two entrances to the stockade, the North Gate and the South Gate, each protected by a double stockade, were provided on the west side. Forts equipped with artillery to suppress disturbances within the prison were located at each corner of the outer stockade. Other structures adjacent to the prison included a bakery and cookhouse and a hospital stockade 600 by 300 feet which contained 22 sheds mostly without sides. These structures were erected about three months before Andersonville Prison was abandoned.

General Winder appointed Captain Henry Wirz, a Swiss physician, as superintendent of the prison. The first contingent of Union prisoners arrived from Belle Island, Virginia, on February 15, 1864. From that time until April 1865, nearly 50,000 men were to be confined within the stockade. The largest number of prisoners incarcerated at any one time was over 33,000 men. More than 900 prisoners died every month during the 13 months' existence of the prison. The greatest death toll on any one day occurred on August 23, 1864, when 97 prisoners died. Andersonville Prison ceased to exist in April 1865, and the grounds were appropriated by the United States.

Many of the early national cemeteries were established at or near battlefields of the Civil War, or in the vicinity of military hospitals established by reason of the exigencies of war. No such circumstances dictated the location of Andersonville National Cemetery. The initial interments in the area that became the Cemetery were of those who died in the nearby prison camp. With the dissolution of the prison, the area 300 yards north of the prison that had been used as a burial ground for deceased prisoners was likewise appropriated by the United States government. It was established as a National Cemetery on July 26, 1865. There are 12,912 graves in the National Cemetery there, but estimates place the number of deaths at a much higher figure.

FORT TATNALL. One of the Army posts built on the perimeter of the Okefenokee Swamp to contain the Indian hostiles, Fort Tatnall was built by General John Floyd and his troops on November 10, 1838, to be used as a supply depot. He named it after one of his men. The picket fort was located on the midwestern side of the swamp, northwest of Fort Gilmer.

FORT TATNALL. A small Civil War battery situated on a small island in the Savannah River, it was located between Barnwell Island (also known as Smith Island)—on which also stood Fort Lawton—and Fort Jackson and Fort Lee on the bank of the river south of Savannah.

FORT TELFAIR. A palisaded defense with a pair of diagonally placed blockhouses, named for Governor Edward Telfair, Fort Telfair was built in 1790 during the protracted war against the Creek Indians. It was situated on strategic Beards Bluff on the east side of the Altamaha River immediately below the mouth of Beards Creek in present-day Long County. In 1793, when a large-scale Creek invasion was anticipated, Fort Telfair was heavily reinforced with additional state militia. A number of early records stressed the importance of Beards Bluff; between 1776 and 1814, many posts and garrisons were established at the site in response to Indian attacks or threatened military action from the Anglo-Spanish occupants of Florida. Fort Telfair was abandoned about 1795 but was regarrisoned in 1814 by state militia during the final confrontations with the recalcitrant Creeks. With the advent of peace on the frontier, maintenance of the fort could not be justified and it ultimately fell into ruins.

TILTON BLOCKHOUSE. This blockhouse, located just north of the town of Tilton in Whitfield County, was garrisoned in an emergency by 300 men of the 17th Iowa Veteran Volunteer Infantry. On October 13, 1864, a large force of Confederate troops of Stewart's Corps, Army of Tennessee, attacked the blockhouse with artillery and, after a battle lasting several hours, the Union garrison surrendered.

CAMP TOCCOA. A temporary World War II training post located near the city of Toccoa in Stephens County, Camp Toccoa was activated on January 8, 1943, and declared surplus on February 15, 1944.

TOLOMATO PRESIDIO. The ruins of the Tolomato mission established by Pedro Ruiz in 1595 and rebuilt by Franciscan missionary Diego Delgado in 1605, with a number of additions between then and 1680, are located on the so-called "Mansfield Place," also known as "the Thicket," five miles northeast of Darien, on Pease Creek, in McIntosh County. The mission-presidio reportedly consisted of at least seven buildings, included a fortress and an adjoining barracks. Just across Doboy Sound is Sapelo Island, also garrisoned by Spanish soldiers beginning in 1605. The English at Charles Towne (in present South Carolina), founded in 1670, aggressively campaigned to obliterate the Spanish mission system. By 1686 all of the missions and associated presidios in Georgia were abandoned by the

Spanish, who perennially suffered from a manpower shortage.

FORT TOMPKINS. An Army post of this name was reportedly located about eight miles west of Coleraine in Charlton County.

CAMP TOWNSEND. A temporary post established in October 1836 during the Creek War, Camp Townsend was located in present Lowndes County.

TRADER'S HILL POST. FORT ALERT.

FORT TWIGGS. Built in 1793 at the mouth of Shoulderbone Creek on the Oconee River in then Greene County, now Hancock County, Fort Twiggs was a critical link in the chain of defenses on the state's turbulent frontier to combat the hostile Creeks. The fort, completed in early May, 1793, consisted of "One Blockhouse twenty feet square in the Clear, as Also one Covered Bastion fifteen Square feet (Each) being About Ten feet in the Lower Story and Six in the Upper . . . with Portholes, the Same Being Enclosed with a Stockade of twenty one yards Square" (Forts Committee, Department of Archives and History, "Fort Twiggs," *Georgia Magazine* 2, no. 1 [1967]: 28). It was reported that the fort was capable of mounting 11 pieces of ordnance. The need for Fort Twiggs lessened as the Indian troubles in the Oconee River region abated. The fort was abandoned in April or May 1796.

FORT TWIGGS. This fort, located near Tarversville in Twiggs County, was erected in 1813 to protect the county's inhabitants during the War of 1812. Fort Twiggs was 100 feet square with two blockhouses in diagonal corners, enclosed by an eight-foot-high stockade. It was garrisoned by 20 men under the command of Colonel (later Major General) Ezekial Wimberly. The fort was the only one of the three forts ordered for the county to be completed.

FORT TYLER. Situated on an elevation overlooking the town of West Point on the Chattahoochee River, in the extreme southwest corner of Troup County, Fort Tyler had the distinction of being the last Confederate fort to yield to Federal forces during the Civil War, a full week after General Lee's surrender at Appomattox. A strong bastioned earthwork 35 yards square, surrounded by a ditch 12 feet wide and 10 feet deep, the fort was protected by an abatis and mounted two 32-pounders and two fieldpieces. The fort was named for and commanded by Confederate General Robert C. Tyler, who had lost a leg at the Battle of Missionary Ridge. On Easter Sunday, April 16, 1865, Fort Tyler was attacked by a brigade of Federals under Colonel O. H. La Grange. After a desperately fought battle lasting several hours, during which General Tyler was killed, the fort surrendered. Ruins of the fort on the hill are yet in evidence.

UNITED STATES ARSENAL. AUGUSTA ARSENAL.

FORT WALKER. In 1835 the Second Seminole War erupted in Florida. The long conflict was to have a considerable effect on Georgia's southern frontier, which included large sections of the Okefenokee Swamp, in which Seminoles found relatively safe havens and settled. From their hidden haunts, they emerged to attack and pillage isolated white enclaves. It was not until 1838 that the situation became a major concern, although Federal troops were called in two years earlier to alleviate fears along the Georgia border of the swamp. It was determined by the governor to call up militia units to encircle the entire swamp with a chain of forts to contain the Indian hostiles until larger contingents of Federal troops made their appearance. In early November 1838, General John Floyd established Fort Walker, a link in the chain, farther into the wilderness of Okefenokee Swamp on "Chepucky Island," northeast of Fort Tatnall.

FORT WALKER. The southeastern salient of Atlanta's inner line of fortifications built during the summer and fall of 1863, Fort Walker was named for Major General William H. T. Walker, killed in the battle for Atlanta on July 22, 1864. The fort site is atop the hill near the Atlanta Avenue and Boulevard entrance to Grant Park, and some remains of the fort's breastworks are still evident.

CAMP WARE. A temporary post established in 1838 during the Second Seminole War, Camp Ware was located northwest of the Okefenokee Swamp at Waresborough in Ware County.

FORT WARRENTON. This post was established at the town of Warrenton, Warren County, by Major John Van Voast on May 13, 1869. Fort Warrenton's first garrison consisted of companies D and G, 18th Infantry. The post was abandoned January 31, 1871, in compliance with General Orders No. 1, Headquarters, Military District of Georgia, January 25, 1871.

FORT WASHINGTON (*Heard's Fort*). Located near the headwaters of Fishing Creek on the present site of the city of Washington, Wilkes County, Heard's Fort was begun on New Year's Day, 1774, as a protection against Indians by Stephen Heard, described as a Virginia aristocrat, who settled there in 1773. In 1780, when the British threatened Augusta, Fort Heard was designated by the governor and Council as a place of meeting for transacting business of the government. The site was probably selected because Heard was at that time acting governor. After the Revolution, Heard's Fort was renamed Fort Washington, which has the distinction of being the first town in the United States to have been named for George Washington.

FORT WAYNE (*Fort Savannah; Fort Halifax; Fort Prevost*). The site of Fort Wayne at the present-day northeast corner of East Bay and East Broad streets in the city of Savannah is now occupied by the Municipal Gas Plant. Fort Halifax, also known as Fort Savannah, was built on the same site, or very near it, in 1750–60. Its planked double walls were filled with earth and featured a caponier (a crosswise-built work in the ditch to sweep it with flanking fire) on each of its four corners. By 1773 the fort was in such disrepair that it was considered of little use. When the British took Savannah in 1779, they rebuilt the fort and renamed it Fort Prevost in honor of General Augustine Prevost.

During the War of 1812, when British Admiral George Cockburn's fleet was raiding up and down the southern coastline, the Americans completely rebuilt the fort with buttressed brick walls encircling a high bluff overlooking what was once a marshy plain and renamed the defense in honor of General Anthony Wayne. The fort was reportedly constructed on the original site of the ten-acre Trustee's Garden.

FORT WAYNE. This fort was built near the present-day city of Brunswick, Glynn County, in October 1821. It was abandoned in June 1823.

CAMP WHEELER. This post was established during World War I about seven miles southeast of Macon, as a camp for the training of the 31st Division (National Guard), and named in honor of Lieutenant General Joseph Wheeler, C.S.A., later major general during the Spanish-American War. The National Guard occupied the camp from August 1917 to September 1918. The camp was ordered salvaged January 30, 1919, and officially closed April 10, 1919, although camp headquarters was maintained until November 1919. According to a September 19, 1945, press release and a National Archives citation, Camp Wheeler was abandoned as surplus property on January 19, 1946, in compliance with War Department Circular No. 405, October 29, 1945.

CAMP WILDE. A temporary Second Seminole War post, Camp Wilde was probably established in 1838 near Fort Floyd at the northeast corner of the Okefenokee Swamp.

FORT WILKINS. This protection against Indian attack was reportedly established in the early 1800s on the Oconee River.

FORT WILKINSON. The site of Fort Wilkinson, probably named for General James Wilkinson, lies atop a bluff overlooking the Oconee River, three miles south of Milledgeville, Baldwin County, and a few miles north of Fort Fidius. Established in 1797, the fort was an important regularly garrisoned frontier post until it was replaced by Fort Hawkins in 1806. On June 16, 1802, a treaty was signed here with the Creek Indians by which Georgia acquired all the territory between the Oconee and Ocmulgee rivers plus a tract south of the Altamaha River.

FORT WILLIAM. FORT PRINCE WILLIAM.

CAMP WILLIAM H. TAFT. Among the eight Camps of Instruction planned during the summer of 1908, one was established at Chickamauga Park. The troops trained here consisted of units of the Cavalry, Infantry, Field Artillery, Hospital Corps, and Signal Corps. The post became known as Camp William H. Taft. The camp was again used for the same purposes during the summers of 1909 and 1910.

FORT WIMBERLY. JONES' FORT.

WOFFORD'S STATION (*Fort Carnes*). After the end of the Revolution, William Wofford moved from North Carolina to Franklin County in Georgia and on December 21, 1792, bought a 400-acre tract of land. Wofford probably built his fort immediately after acquiring the land. After Wofford's Station had been in existence for a few years, it became known as Fort Carnes, probably named for Colonel Thomas Peters Carnes of the Franklin County Militia, elements of which frequently garrisoned the post. The last reference to the fort was dated in 1796.

WOOD'S FORT. Some years after the Revolution had ended, General Solomon Wood, veteran of the war, built his home on a high hill overlooking a wide expanse of country east of Bartow in Jefferson County. Near his hilltop home General Wood built a blockhouse for the protection of his family and neighbors. It was reported that when there was a threat of Indian attack, a large bell, loud enough when rung to be heard for a distance of two miles, would summon all within hearing to find shelter within the blockhouse.

CAMP WRIGHT. Confederate Brigadier General Marcus J. Wright was assigned to command the Post of Macon after being seriously wounded in the Shiloh and Chickamauga battles. He established Camp Wright on the outskirts of Macon, with his headquarters on the second floor of the railroad car sheds on the site. The post served as Macon's Confederate headquarters from early 1864 until the end of the war in the spring of 1865.

WRIGHT'S FORT. In 1774, during a rash of Indian depredations, or at the outbreak of the Revolution, Jermyn and Charles Wright, affluent landowners in both Georgia and East Florida, and brothers of Georgia's Governor Sir James Wright, erected a strong wooden stockade on their principal plantation situated on the north side of the St. Marys River several miles from its mouth. Known as Wright's Fort, the fortified plantation for a time was a strongpoint guarding the Wright brothers' three separate plantations on the river, more than 100 slaves, and the property of Loyalist neighbors. Garrisoned Wright's Fort was occasionally attacked by detachments of American partisans from both sides of the river.

WRIGHTSBORO FORT. On the site of Wrightsboro's Methodist Churchyard in McDuffie County, Edmund Grey (or Gray), a pretending Quaker, in 1754 founded the town of Brandon, named for one of the movement's leaders. In December 1768 Quakers Joseph Mattock and Jonathan Sell were awarded a grant of 40,000 acres by Governor Sir William Wright, reestablished the town, and renamed it Wrightsborough in the governor's honor. By the year 1775, more than 60 Quaker families had settled there. During the Revolution the town's fort, Fort Wrightsboro, was commanded by Captain Thomas White.

FORT YARGO. According to various historians, this remarkably preserved log-built blockhouse was erected in 1793 or even earlier. Fort Yargo's location was reportedly three miles southwest of the present-day town of Winder in Barrow County. Old archival records indicate that the fort was one of four forts built by the Humphries brothers to safeguard pioneering settlers from the Indians. The other three defenses were listed as having been located at Talassee, Thomocoggan (today's Jefferson), and Groaning Rock (now Commerce). Fort Yargo today is a State Park.

CAMP (S. B. M.) YOUNG. A temporary camp of this name was reportedly located at Augusta, probably sometime during the Civil War. Samuel Baldwin Marks Young, a Pennsylvanian, was a Federal Army officer who served throughout the war and was mustered out in 1865 with the rank of brigadier general. He eventually became a major general in 1901.

ALEXANDER REDOUBT. FORT ELIZABETH.

FORT ARMSTRONG. Built in 1907 on a 96-acre site on Kaakaukukui Reef in Honolulu Harbor, about midway between Diamond Head and Pearl Harbor, Fort Armstrong was first occupied by the 1st Company, Coast Artillery, Military Department of California. During World War II, Fort Armstrong was put under the control of the Army Port and Services Command. The post housed thousands of soldiers during their stopover in Hawaii en route to the war in the Pacific. It was also used as the headquarters for handling prisoner-of-war matters.

Fort Armstrong was named after a Hawaii-born officer, Brigadier General Samuel C. Armstrong (1839–93). General Armstrong fought valiantly in the Battle of Gettysburg in 1863 as a captain of the 125th New York Regiment. When the war ended in 1865, he was discharged at age 26 as a brigadier general. Fort Armstrong in 1974 was returned to the state of Hawaii, and the site is now part of Honolulu's dock resources. The major unit at the post, the Pacific Ocean Division, Corps of Engineers, moved to Fort Shafter.

BARCLAY REDOUBT. FORT ELIZABETH.

FORT BARRETTE. The military reservation at Kapoloi was announced as a permanent military post and designated Fort Barrette in honor of Brigadier General John D. Barrette, on November 23, 1934. In 1948 it was on a caretaker status as a subpost of Fort Kamehameha.

FORT DERUSSY. Beginning in 1904 the Waikiki military reservation was acquired through 12 separate purchases and condemnations. By 1915 the Army owned 72 acres of land fronting on Waikiki Beach. The area was not originally intended for use as an Army Recreation Center. The Coast Guard wanted a chain of forts built around the island, and the Army Engineers were put to work in 1908 followed by detachments of the Coast Artillery Corps in 1909. It was that year that the work of construction really began. First a burrow pit was dug behind the reef; then a suction dredge was used to transfer 250,000 cubic yards of coral and sand to fill the land that had for years served as duck ponds for Hawaiian royalty. This work took almost a year.

That same year the War Department issued General Orders No. 15 naming the post Fort DeRussy in honor of Brevet Brigadier General Rene E. DeRussy who died in 1895. He was known as one of the Army's most brilliant designers of fortifications during the Civil War and

Hawaii

FORT ARMSTRONG. Photograph taken circa 1926. (Courtesy of the U.S. Army.)

served as superintendent of the U.S. Military Academy from 1833 to 1838. Emplacements for 14-inch artillery guns were built at Fort DeRussy but sat idle until they were replaced by antiaircraft guns at the start of World War II. During the war Fort DeRussy served as a seacoast defense installation, provided housing for soldiers, was the site of a camouflage school, and was the home of a military police headquarters. Shortly after World War II, a headquarters of the U.S. Armed Forces Institute, a correspondence school for servicemen, was established there.

On June 8, 1942, the Fort DeRussy Recreation Center was opened with billeting accommodations for 25 enlisted men. By 1945 the center was able to billet 300 enlisted men and 109 officers. Over 1.5 million military people used the center's facilities during the war. The post was redesignated as an Armed Forces Recreation Center in June 1949. In 1966 a Vietnam Rest and Recuperation (R & R) Center was established at Fort DeRussy. A total of 494,140 military personnel had arrived on R & R flights from Southeast Asia to meet 402,425 dependents when the program ended on June 30, 1974.

The 14-story Hale Koa (House of Warriors) was formally opened in October 1975. Its cost of approximately $20.5 million was paid for from profits of nonappropriated fund activities at no cost to the taxpayer. The center today serves an active U.S. military population in Hawaii of some 50,000 with a total of some 75,000 dependents. An open post, its green acres on Waikiki Beach are enjoyed by Hawaii tourists and residents. Nearly two million people now visit the post annually.

FORT ELIZABETH (*Alexander Redoubt; Barclay Redoubt*). The Russian flag was raised over the island of Kauai in 1816 when Dr. Georg Anton Schäffer (anglicized to Scheffer), a German medical doctor in the Russian service under Governor Alexandr Baranov of Russian America (Alaska), built a fort at Waimea on the island's southwest shore, after he and his men were expelled from Oahu (see: HONOLULU FORT). He contrived the establishment of the fort by signing a secret pact with King Kaumualii who had appropriated the cargo of the Russian sealing ship *Bering* wrecked in Waimea Bay a year earlier. The document, apparently a form of recompense, virtually put the island under Russian rule. It was Governor Baranov's desire to obtain valuable sandalwood as compensation for the *Bering*'s cargo and obtain a monopoly of Kauai's sandalwood. He envisioned the establishment of a trading post on one of the islands, believing that the Hawaiian Islands would be a good source of provisions for Russian America and a convenient place to winter the Russian sealing ships and crews. Dr. Schäffer himself dreamed of extending the Russian Empire to include the entire Hawaiian Islands.

Dr. Schäffer began the construction of the Russian fort at the mouth of the Waimea River on September 12, 1816, with the labors of many islanders furnished by King Kaumualii. Built of stone plentiful in the area of the site, the formidable fort was in the form of an irregular eight-pointed star or octagon, 350 to 400 feet in diameter, with its walls enclosing about three acres and facing the sea 20 feet high, 30 feet thick at the base, and gradually diminishing to

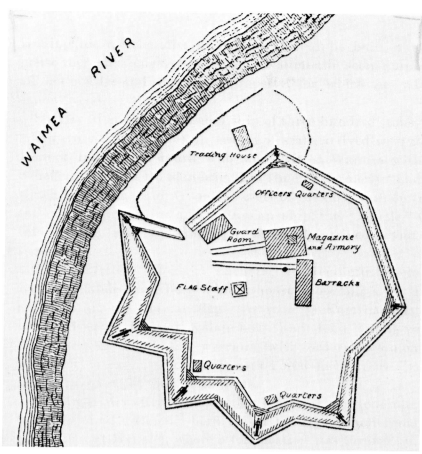

FORT ELIZABETH. Plan of the old Russian fort, drawn in 1885 by Lieutenant G. E. G. Jackson, R.N., for the Hawaiian Government Survey. (Courtesy of the Library of Congress.)

15 feet at the top. The fort's powder magazine was underground, protected by a super-thick lehua log and dirt bombproofed roof. Mounting 40 guns on its ramparts, the Russian fort was designated Elizabeth in honor of Czar Alexander I's consort. On October 8, 1816, a ceremonial seven-gun salute was fired and the Russian Imperial flag was raised above the fort's walls. Coincident with this auspicious event, King Kaumualii made a grant to Dr. Schäffer of the entire land area comprising the Hanalei Valley in the northern part of the island. Dr. Schäffer almost immediately took possession by constructing two redoubts or earthworks named Alexander and Barclay on the flanks of the valley.

King Kamehameha I of Oahu, who had been organizing the unification of all the islands, pressured Kaumualii into evicting the Russians from Kauai. Baranov was notified of the eviction and Dr. Schäffer departed from Hawaii for Russia on the earliest available ship by way of Canton, China. The Russian flag was reportedly replaced sometime in early 1817 by the Hawaiian standard by Captain Alexander Adams, commander of Kamehameha's vessel *Kaahumanu*. The Russian-built fort was the only Hawaiian fort to fire its guns in anger and that was during the preliminary struggles that culminated in the last major battle to enforce Hawaiian unification, the Battle of Wahiawa, Kauai, in 1824. The fort, garrisoned by Hawaiian soldiers until 1853, saw no further action. From about 1854 to 1860, the fort was occupied by a few caretaking men whose principal duty was to fire a salute each year in honor of the king's birthday. In 1864 the Hawaiian government ordered the fort dismantled. Thirty-eight of its guns were shipped to California where they were sold; the other two guns remain buried in the silt of Waimea Bay after they sank when a boat accidentally capsized.

HALEHUI BATTERY. After King Kamehameha I conquered the island of Oahu in 1795, he made strenuous efforts to unite the segments of his newly won kingdom. He moved from his original residence at Waikiki in 1809 to Honolulu (then known as Kou) where, on the harbor's waterfront, he erected an elaborate palace, on a site near today's intersection of Nimitz Highway and Queen Street. The king's compound, with the palace its largest structure and named Halehui, was surrounded on its land side by a palisade. Facing the sea was a battery of 16 carriage guns, which were formerly emplaced on the decks of his recently acquired 200-ton ship, the *Lelia Bird*. Other buildings within the enclosure included a powder magazine and a guardhouse. Close by, possibly outside the palisade, were two large stone-built storehouses that held imported goods from "Western" nations, principally Great Britain and America.

Kamehameha displayed the British flag in front of Halehui. His use of the British flag began on February 25, 1794, when he "ceded" the island of Hawaii to Captain George Vancouver, who represented Great Britain. (The cession was never accepted or ratified by the British Government.) Use of the powerful British flag during the Pax Britannica, when the British ruled the seas, undoubtedly prevented many unpleasant episodes with foreign ships. The Hawaiian flag was developed during the War of 1812 between Great Britain and the young United States: the crosses on the blue field retained the friendship of Great Britain; the red, white, and blue stripes recognized the United States; and the eight stripes represented the eight major islands of the Hawaiian group. [Walter F. Judd, *Palaces and Forts of the Hawaiian Kingdom* (1975), p. 24].

HAWAII ARSENAL (*Hawaiian Ordnance Depot*). A permanent installation located three miles from Honolulu, the original reservation was acquired in 1914 and designated Hawaiian Ordnance Depot in 1915. The installation was enlarged by the construction of 12 one-story shop buildings beginning in April 1917. On September 17, 1918, the 83-acre post was redesignated Hawaii Arsenal. The Arsenal manufactured harness and leather goods and repaired, maintained, stored, and distributed ordnance property for all of the Hawaii Territory's troops.

HAWAIIAN ORDNANCE DEPOT. HAWAII ARSENAL.

HONOLULU FORT. During the summer of 1816, two Russian trading vessels, the *Ilmena* and the *Kadiak*, arrived in Honolulu Harbor. Aboard were Dr. Georg Anton Schäffer, a German medical doctor in the service of the Russian government, and about 80 men. They had been sent to the Islands by Governor Alexandr Baranov of the Russian-American Company (Alaska) for two main purposes: to obtain compensation for appropriated cargo from a wrecked Russian vessel in Waimea Bay, Kauai, the previous year, and to establish a trading post on one of the main islands. The Russians wasted no time. They began to construct a blockhouse trading post near the harbor's entrance and hoisted the Russian Imperial flag over the site. King Kamehameha I, who had conquered Oahu Island in 1795, was then visiting the Island of Hawaii. He learned of the intrusion and sent two of his war leaders with a regiment of soldiers to evict them. The Russians, awaking one morning to find themselves surrounded by an army of weapon-carrying warriors, precipitately left the harbor and sailed westward to Kauai Island. (See: FORT ELIZABETH.)

Kalanimoku, one of the king's warrior leaders, dismantled the partially built blockhouse and began building a fortress on the same site. This fort was known to the Hawaiians as Kekuanohu (the Thorny Back, because of the bristling guns on the walls) or Kepapu (the Gun Wall). The site of the fort, located less than a mile inland of the channel's entrance into the harbor, is at the foot of today's Fort Street near its intersection with Queen Street. The fort's position allowed an enfilading fire from any of its guns against any unamicable vessel entering the channel. The part of the fort facing the harbor's entrance stood on the water's edge and had curved surfaces to deflect cannon fire. The historic fort was a rectangular structure about 340 feet long and 300 feet wide, with walls 12 feet high and 20 feet thick at the base, with its main entrance on Fort Street. The expertise required to understand the use of the great guns was furnished by George Beckley, a British sea captain who had elected to remain in Honolulu and became the fort's first commandant. The fort's complement of ordnance, beginning with about 40 cannon, was augmented in subsequent years. It was reported in 1849 that Honolulu Fort mounted 70 brass and iron cannon, ranging from 4-pounders to one 32-pounder, with 6-pounders by far in the majority. The guns, mounted *en barbette* on the walls, had been obtained over the years from various visiting ships.

Possession of Honolulu Fort was temporarily lost by the Hawaiian kingdom on three occasions, but without bloodshed. First, there was a minor abortive internal power struggle in 1830. The second instance occurred when Great Britain took over and ruled the kingdom for some five months in 1843. The third and last takeover was when two French warships sailed into Honolulu Harbor and their commander, Rear Admiral de Tromelin, presented a long list of demands to the king, demands which could not be satisfied without surrendering the kingdom's sovereignty. To enforce his demands, the admiral landed a force of men that spiked the fort's guns, seized the custom house and other government buildings, and perpetrated various depredations throughout Honolulu. After the French consul was removed 10 days later, the matter was settled.

It became evident in 1850 that Honolulu, its harbor crowded with Pacific whalers and ships trading in the California gold rush, required additional wharfage space. After it was determined that Honolulu Fort was not a necessary part of the Hawaiian kingdom's military establishment with its peaceful policies, it was demolished in 1857. The 1,500 cubic yards of coral blocks that made up its walls were used to extend the land out onto the shallow reef in the harbor and became a 2,000-foot retaining wall. [Walter F. Judd, *Palaces and Forts of the Hawaiian Kingdom* (1975), p. 59]

HONOULIULI MILITARY RESERVATION (*Camp Molakoli*). Located at Ewa in southwestern Oahu, west of Barber's Point Naval Air Station, Honouliuli is 17 miles from downtown Honolulu and equidistant from Schofield Barracks. The reservation (formerly Camp Molakoli) was established during World War II in 1942 and consisted of 2,531 acres, including a gunnery range. It was utilized as a base campsite for the antimechanized company personnel in conjunction with a shore-to-sea antitank gunnery range, which had been leased from the Campbell Estate by the Army. The reservation's acreage was turned back to the state of Hawaii, and the site of the former gunnery range is now occupied by the Standard Oil Refinery. Prior to its redesignation, Camp Molakoli took part in the

action on December 7, 1941, while Pearl Harbor's installations were being attacked by Japanese planes.

IOLANI BARRACKS. Originally located adjacent to Iolani Palace and across Palace Walk, now Hotel Street, in Honolulu, this medieval-appearing military barracks, adorned with battlemented square towers and embrasured parapets, was erected in 1871. The two-story structure was first designed in 1866 by Theodore C. Heuck, a German carpenter who became an architectural designer. The site had been formerly occupied by the Chief's Children's School from 1839 to 1851.

Utilization of Iolani Barracks over its many years has been very diversified. During the monarchical period, it accommodated troops of the Royal Guard. The Citizens' Guard occupied the Barracks during the provisional government (1893–94), followed by Hawaii's National Guard. Subsequent to Hawaii's annexation to the United States, Iolani Barracks was taken over by the War Department and used by the Quartermaster Corps until 1917. In 1931 the Barracks was ceded to the Territory of Hawaii and taken over three years later by the Hawaii National Guard for the second time and occupied throughout World War II as its state headquarters. After the military organization moved its quarters to Fort Ruger in 1950, the Barracks was occupied by various governmental agencies. Finally, in 1965, Iolani Barracks was physically moved to the grounds of Iolani Palace, surrendering its original site for the new state capitol building.

FORT (BATTERY) KAMAKAHONU. During the latter years of his life, King Kamehameha I in 1813 established his royal residence on Kailua Bay's waterfront, Island of Hawaii. The shore adjacent to the stone-enclosed compound was protected by a crescent-shaped battery of 16 cannon, probably the same ordnance that had guarded Halehui Palace at the entrance to Honolulu Harbor. The site of the battery is now occupied by the King Kamehameha Hotel.

FORT KAMEHAMEHA (*Fort Upton*). Fort Kamehameha, at Queen Emma Point, is located adjacent to Hickam Air Force Base near the entrance to Pearl Harbor Naval Base. Constructed in 1909 as part of Pearl Harbor's Coast Artillery defenses, it was originally named Fort Upton in honor of Major General Emory Upton who attained general officer rank at age 25 during the Civil War and served as commandant of cadets at the U.S. Military Academy from 1870 to 1875.

In late 1909, at the suggestion of Archibald Cleghorn, father of Hawaiian Princess Kaiulani, the name was changed to honor Kamehameha I, the greatest warrior-king in Hawaiian history. Discontinued July 1, 1949, the post today serves as an Army family housing area.

KAPALAMA MILITARY RESERVATION. The home of the Army Transportation Terminal and associated warehouses used by the Army Quartermaster Corps, the reservation is located on the shore of Honolulu Harbor.

LAHAINA FORT. Because of occasional disturbing confrontations with obnoxious foreign seamen at Lahaina, Maui, High Chief Hoapili built Lahaina Fort to safeguard the port. Very similar to Honolulu Fort in design, but on a smaller scale, it was situated on the waterfront in the center of Lahaina Town. Completed in 1832, built of blocks of coral quarried from the reef in the harbor, the quadrangular fort enclosed about an acre of ground, with its longest wall, approximately 275 feet, facing the sea. With walls at least 15 feet high and just as thick, its sea wall was embrasured for 20 guns. The varied ordnance of 21 to 30 cannon was principally used to fire 21-gun salutes in honor of the King's birthday. Lahaina Fort, never having fired a shot in anger, was demolished in 1854, with its guns disposed of three years later as sold scrap at Honolulu.

CAMP MCCARTHY. A National Guard post during World War I, Camp McCarthy was located on the grounds of the capitol in Honolulu.

CAMP MCKINLEY. A temporary post established in August 1898 as the first American military camp to be located in the Hawaiian Islands, it occupied ground on what was the race track in present Kapiolani Park near Honolulu. Maintained through most of the Spanish-American War, it was garrisoned by the 1st New York Volunteer Infantry and four companies of the 2nd volunteer Engineers. The New York Volunteers left the camp in September 1898, apparently to take post in the Philippine Islands. In 1902 the camp's garrison consisted of two companies of Artillery, aggregating 240 men and 11 officers. It was reported then that there was no ordnance on the post but that two 3.2-inch and two Gatling guns had been ordered.

CAMP MOLAKOLI. Honouliuli Military Reservation.

CAMP OTIS. This post was established by military orders on September 6, 1898, next to Camp McKinley, on what was then the race track (no longer in existence) in present Kapiolani Park near Honolulu and used expressly for all the expeditionary forces during the Spanish-American War. These troops were returned home in April 1899.

PEARL HARBOR MILITARY STATION. A temporary installation located at the United States Naval Station, it was established in 1918 to provide shelter for detachments guarding the naval base. It was garrisoned by the 1st, 3rd, and 5th Companies of the Coast Artillery.

FORT PUNLOA-PUNCHBOWL. PUOWAINA BATTERY.

PUOWAINA BATTERY (*Fort Punloa-Punchbowl*). To support Honolulu Fort's defenses a mile away, the ridge of Puowaina (the small extinct volcano today called Punchbowl, the site of the National Memorial Cemetery of the Pacific) was fortified with as many as 14 large cannon (Lord Byron reported eight 32-pounders there in 1825), surrounded by protective stone walls. The battery's powder magazine was constructed of adobe bricks. On October 22, 1851, about 40 prisoners escaped and took refuge within Puowaina Battery's stone walls. After breaking into the magazine, they loaded three of the largest guns. But they had forgotten to bring anything to light the slow matches to set off the cannon. Soldiers and police stormed the fort and scattered the escapees into the countryside, where all but two were captured the next morning.

FORT RUGER. In 1906 Fort Ruger was the first of five Army subposts established on Oahu, occupying a 755-acre site on the slopes of Diamond Head Crater, six miles southeast of Honolulu. Among the units that served at Fort Ruger were the 105th and 159th Companies, Coast Artillery (1909); 3rd Balloon Company (1920–21); and Headquarters, South Sector, Hawaii Defense Command (1947). Fort Ruger includes part of Diamond Head Crater, which presently contains a National Guard Armory and accommodates a rifle range. In ancient Hawaii Diamond Head was a burial ground, and some of the oldest graves on Oahu are located on the western slope of the dormant volcano.

In January 1950 the Hawaii Military Department, Territory of Hawaii (changed in January 1960 to Hawaii State Department of Defense)

moved its headquarters to Fort Ruger, where it remains today. In 1955 over 500 acres of post lands were returned to the state of Hawaii. In 1974 some 51 acres were sold to the state, with proceeds used for site development at Aliamanu Military Reservation for construction of 2,600 quarters for Army, Navy, and Marine Corps families. Under present plans, Army land at Fort Ruger will become one 11-acre site holding the Army Cannon Club and its related recreational and parking facilities.

Fort Ruger was named in honor of Major General Thomas H. Ruger, who served as superintendent of the Military Academy, from which he was graduated in 1854, from 1871 to 1876; and as commandant of the Command and General Staff College at Fort Leavenworth, Kansas, from 1885 to 1896. At age 29 he was appointed a brigadier general of volunteers in the Civil War, and in 1868 he served as provisional governor of the State of Georgia.

SCHOFIELD BARRACKS. The largest Army post in Hawaii, Schofield Barracks was constructed in 1909 on 15,000 acres. Initially the base for the Army's mobile defense forces on Oahu, between World Wars I and II it housed the Army's Hawaiian Division, which was reorganized in the fall of 1941 into the 24th and 25th Infantry Divisions. Much of the time since 1945, it has been home for combat troops held in reserve for emergencies in the Pacific area.

Lieutenant General John M. Schofield (1831–1906), whose foresight established the Army in Hawaii, won the Medal of Honor in the Civil War. In 1868 he served as secretary of war under President Andrew Johnson. From 1876 to 1881, he was superintendent of the U.S. Military Academy at West Point, and in 1888 was appointed commanding general of the U.S. Army. Today, the 25th Infantry Division is the major occupant at Schofield Barracks.

FORT SHAFTER. In 1903 plans were under way to build a permanent Army post centrally located in Honolulu to replace Camp McKinley in present Kapiolani Park. A 1,300-acre site was selected in the foothills of the Koolau Mountains, above Honolulu Harbor, and named in honor of Major General William R. Shafter (1835–1906). Winner of the Medal of Honor in the Civil War, General Shafter commanded the Fifth Army Corps in Cuba during the Spanish-American War. In 1898 his command captured the Cuban capital at Santiago, in one of the major engagements of the war.

Construction of Fort Shafter, oldest Army post

in Hawaii, began in 1905 and was completed in 1907. From 1947 until December 31, 1974, when the unit was inactivated, Headquarters, U.S. Army Pacific, occupied Fort Shafter. The geographic area over which U.S. Army Pacific forces and activities were deployed encompassed an area of more than 12 million square miles containing 25 nations and a third of the world's population. In 1974 Headquarters, U.S. Army Support Command, Hawaii, moved to Fort Shafter from Schofield Barracks. Also located at Fort Shafter are the Pacific area headquarters of several Army agencies and activities, including the Pacific Ocean Division of the Army Corps of Engineers.

The Army also uses several areas for training purposes. The largest of these is Pohakuloa, 115,000 acres on the Island of Hawaii, situated on the lava beds between two old volcanoes, Mauna Loa and Mauna Kea. Tripler Army Hospital, near Fort Shafter, is the largest hospital in Hawaii and is available to all military services in the Pacific Area and veterans. Fourteen stories tall, with many underground levels, Tripler has 1,500 beds. Construction started toward the end of World War II and was activated in 1945 as an Armed Forces General Hospital.

FORT UPTON. FORT KAMEHAMEHA.

FORT WEAVER. This military reservation at Keahi Point on the Island of Oahu was named Fort Weaver in honor of Major General Erasmus M. Weaver, who died November 13, 1920. During the Japanese attack against Pearl Harbor on the morning of December 7, 1941, Fort Weaver, located on the opposite side of the harbor's entrance from Fort Kamehameha (next to Hickam Air Force Base), opened fire at 8:10 A.M. with small arms, and 20 minutes later resorted to firing from a fixed three-inch battery, joining in the general antiaircraft action by Honolulu Harbor's other defenses.

CAMP BOISE. BOISE BARRACKS.

FORT BOISE. BOISE BARRACKS.

FORT BOISE. Erected originally by Thomas McKay in the fall of 1834 to meet the competition offered by Fort Hall farther up the Snake River, Fort Boise stood on the east bank of the Snake where it had its junction with the Boise. Originally McKay's private venture, with a guarantee, dated October 14, 1834, that the Hudson's Bay Company would cover any losses, the new fort definitely became a company post by 1836. Managed from 1835 to 1844 by François Payette, Fort Boise was staffed mostly by Owyhee employees the greater part of the time. When James Craigie took over after Payette retired, the post continued to maintain its reputation for unusual hospitality to travelers who came by along the Oregon Trail. As was the case of Fort Hall, the fur trade declined within a few years, and Fort Boise became more important as a salmon fishery than as a fur trading center. Constructed, like Fort Hall, of adobe, Fort Boise sustained much damage in the great flood of 1853. Only partially rebuilt after the flood, the post could not be maintained following military retaliation after the Ward Massacre of 1854. Indian hostility forced the Hudson's Bay Company to abandon the fort. When the U.S. Army followed up with a military Fort Boise after the gold rush to the Boise Basin, the new post was established up the river where the city of Boise was founded.

BOISE BARRACKS (*Camp Boise; Fort Boise*). In 1834 the Columbia Fishing and Trading Company of Boston established a trading post at Fort Hall in the Idaho country as a rendezvous for the trappers and traders of the expedition led by Nathaniel J. Wyeth, which had entered the region the previous season. The Hudson's Bay Company, which during that period monopolized the Northwest's fur trade, immediately took steps to counteract the enterprise of the newcomer and established a rival post named Fort Boise, located on the Snake River near the mouth of the Boise River, about 50 miles west of Boise City. In 1836 Fort Hall, with its property and business, was sold to the Hudson's Bay Company. Fort Boise was maintained for about 20 years but after a devastating flood in 1853 and the Indian outbreak in the vicinity in 1854, it was permanently abandoned.

In compliance with General Orders No. 6, War Department, 1860, the establishment of a military post in the neighborhood of Old Fort Boise was ordered and an examination was made

Idaho

FORT BOISE. View of the inside of the fort. (Courtesy of the Public Archives of Canada.)

by the military authorities of the country between Walla Walla and the Great Salt Lake, but no further steps were taken in the matter until 1863. On June 28, 1863, a detachment of the 1st Oregon Cavalry encamped near the later site of Boise Barracks and began the construction of temporary troop barracks. The post was established to protect emigrant trains against the Snake River region's Shoshone Indians. The post was first designated Camp Boise, but soon redesignated Fort Boise.

During the Bannock War of 1878 and the Sheepeater campaign of 1879, Fort Boise served as a base of operations in Idaho's final Indian wars. On April 5, 1879, the fort was redesignated Boise Barracks, where Army units were stationed until 1912. More than one notable military figure was stationed at the post, including General Jonathan Wainwright, who served there early in his military career. Soldiers returned to the post in 1916 preparing for the Mexican border campaign, and the barracks saw military use again from 1942 through 1944. In the meantime, a veterans hospital occupied the main part of the grounds from 1920 on. Finally, on March 14, 1944, the property not needed for the hospital was ordered turned over to the state of Idaho, effective on or about April 15, 1944.

CAMP BOISE RIVER. A temporary Army post, this post was established August 15, 1855, at the abandoned Hudson's Bay Company's Fort Boise at the confluence of the Snake and Boise rivers. The post was maintained for six weeks, apparently in connection with the Indian outbreak in the area.

CAMP BUFORD. This post, located in present-day Owyhee County, was established by L. H. Marshall on the Bruneau River near its junction with the Snake River in the summer of 1866 to furnish protection for settlers and emigrants.

CAMP COEUR D'ALENE. FORT SHERMAN.

FORT COEUR D'ALENE. FORT SHERMAN.

CAMP CONNOR. Established May 23, 1863, Camp Connor was located east of Soda Springs on the north bank of the Bear River in present-day Caribou County. The post was established to safeguard the overland emigrant route and the settlement of apostate Mormons. Established following the Battle of Bear River by Captain David Black, 3rd California Infantry in compliance with orders of Brigadier General Patrick Edward Connor, the post was named for the general. Properly called Camp Connor, the post was never officially designated a fort. The post was ordered abandoned February 24, 1865, but the troops remained until near the end of April when they departed for Salt Lake City.

CAMP DEFIANCE. This post "on the supposed waters of the Bonaventura" is the description of a trading post locality mentioned by William L. Sublette in his application for a trading license for the year 1832.

EAGLE ROCK BRIDGE GAP. A temporary post located at or near Idaho Falls in Bonneville County, it was established by Captain I. M. Hamilton, 5th Cavalry, commanding companies H and

I, 5th Infantry, and a detachment of the 14th Infantry. The post was established on September 30, 1878, apparently in connection with the outbreak of the Bannock War.

FORT FRANKLIN. Erected in 1860 by the Mormons on their land allocation located at what became the town of Franklin in present-day Franklin County, Fort Franklin stood about 1 mile north of the Utah border and 7 miles south of Preston. The fort had been built because of overt Indian hostility. The Indian warlike activities were finally cut short by the Battle of Bear River, fought 12 miles north of the fort. Fort Franklin was abandoned sometime in 1863.

FORT GALLOWAY. Three forts, each small, were built shortly after the town of Weiser in present-day Washington County was founded in 1863. The fort stood on the Weiser River four miles east of the town. The Indian defense was named for Tom Galloway, one of the original settlers and builder of the first frame house in Weiser in 1865. Two years earlier he had constructed the town's first log cabin.

FORT HALL. When the Rocky Mountain Fur Company declined to do business as a partner with pioneer fur trader Nathaniel J. Wyeth, the Boston representative of the Columbia Fishing and Trading Company decided to establish his own post near the junction of the Portneuf and Snake rivers in present-day Bannock County. Built originally of cottonwood logs set on end 15 feet high, with two bastions at diagonal corners, the 80-foot-square fort was completed on August 4, 1834. He named the fort in honor of Henry Hall, the senior member of the Boston firm that sponsored Hall's expedition. In 1836 the Hudson's Bay Company bought the post for $8,179.94 and promptly enlarged and reconstructed it with sun-dried adobe bricks. "For the next decade and a half its whitewashed walls were a welcome sight to countless wagon trains. Here, 1,300 miles from Independence and with two-thirds of their journey behind them, travelers could catch their breath, repair their wagons, and decide whether to swing southwest across Nevada to California or northwest along the Snake and Columbia to Oregon" (Kent Ruth, *Great Day in the West*, p. 54). The Hudson's Bay Company finally abandoned the fort in 1856. Intermittently, for short periods, during 1859 and 1860, Fort Hall was occupied by U.S. troops and the Oregon Volunteers, who continued efforts to protect the emigrant trains.

FORT HALL. Established May 27, 1870, in compliance with an order dated March 15, 1870, this post was proclaimed a military reservation October 12, 1870, by President U. S. Grant. Lieutenant Clinton B. Sears, after completing a survey for a post to protect the stage and freight route, located the site where Lincoln Creek flows out of the canyon 12 miles east of the Snake River and 15 miles from the Fort Hall Indian Agency, May 19, 1870. Captain James E. Putnam, 12th Infantry, established the post and became its first commander. On February 27, 1883, when the troops were no longer needed, the barracks were transferred to the Department of the Interior and used as an Indian school. The buildings eventually were moved to Ross Fork Creek. Located about 25 miles northwest of the ruins of the Hudson's Bay Company trading post of the same name, military Fort Hall was about 9 miles from the town of Blackfoot, Bingham County.

HENRY'S POST. Situated on Henry's Fork of the Snake River, a few miles southwest of St. Anthony in present-day Fremont County, Henry's Post was the earliest American fur trading establishment west of the Continental Divide. Andrew Henry led a party of Missouri Fur Company trappers up the Missouri, where they encountered trouble with the Blackfeet after building a small fort at Three Forks, the junction of the Jefferson, Madison, and Gallatin rivers, in present-day Montana, during the summer of 1810. Leaving Montana territory and entering Idaho during the same year, he erected a post on the south side of the North Fork of the Snake River at a point about five miles downstream from the present-day town of St. Anthony. The temporary fort or post consisted of a few log-built structures that Henry and his party used as a headquarters while trapping and hunting until the spring of 1811, when they abandoned the post and left Idaho territory.

CAMP HOPE. A temporary post established in July 1894 in the town of Hope, on Pend Oreille Lake, in Bonner County, Camp Hope was used by troops to deal with the violence brought on by railway strikes.

CAMP HOWARD. This was established on August 12, 1877, two miles west of Mount Idaho in Idaho County, by troops operating against recalcitrant Nez Percé Indians. Camp Howard consisted of nine officers' quarters buildings, two 32-by-25-foot barracks, and more than a dozen other structures, all log-built. The point of departure for Lieutenant Henry Catley and his troops during the Sheepeater War of 1879, Camp Howard was abandoned on either March 23 or July 11, 1881, depending on the authority cited. Two other Camp Howards were also in use: one was situated on Doumecq Plain and the other on the Lolo Trail.

HOWE'S CAMP. Established by Major Howe on the Portneuf River near Fort Hall in mid-June 1860 to provide protection for emigrant trains, the camp was abandoned in later September 1860.

HULL HILL FORT. Three forts, each small, were erected shortly after the town of Weiser was founded in 1863 in present-day Washington County. All established as protections against Indians, one of the forts was situated on Hull Hill.

JOHN (REID) REED'S HOUSE. Situated south of the mouth of the Boise ("Reed's") River, this trading post was established by an expedition from Astoria led by John Reed sometime in 1813. In 1819 Donald McKenzie of the North West Company rebuilt and occupied the abandoned post. In 1836 Thomas McKay erected Snake Fort on the same site as a private venture. (See: REED'S POST.)

KINVILLE'S POST. Michael Kinville built a temporary trading post on the Kootenai River near Bonner's Ferry in present-day Boundary County. No data has been found to indicate definite date of establishment of the North West Company enterprise, but it reportedly was maintained for a time between 1810 and 1812.

KULLYSPELL (KALISPELL) HOUSE (*Thompson Trading Post*). Built in the fall of 1809 by David Thompson and Finnan MacDonald at the eastern end of Lake Pend Oreille, near the mouth of the Clark Fork River, this pioneering trading post was located near present-day Hope in Bonner County. Kullyspell House, also called Thompson's Trading Post, a North West Company enterprise, was the first post established west of the Rocky Mountains in the United States. The post gave the Montreal fur traders a base among the Kalispell or Pend d'Oreille Indians (two names for the same Salish band) when Thompson extended the Canadian fur trade south from the upper Columbia, which he had reached two years earlier. Spokane House, built in 1810 west of the present city of Spokane, soon replaced Kullyspell House. Thompson decided on November 14, 1811, to have the Kalispell Indians remove their fur trapping operations from the original establishment on Lake Pend Oreille to Spokane House.

CAMP LANDER. After Cyrus H. Walker, with Company B of the Oregon Volunteer Cavalry, left Camp Wallace in Camas County on July 12, 1865, to select the site for Camp Lander, an order to establish the post was issued on September 6. Walker and his troops established the camp October 6 at the junction of the Salt Lake–Virginia City and Boise roads, three miles southeast of Old Fort Hall in Bannock County to protect emigrants along the Oregon Trail. Elements of the Volunteer Cavalry patrolled the Trail for about six months. Another citation reports that the camp was located "on Snake Creek a little north of Fort Hall," using remnants of the trading post as their shelters. Ordered abandoned May 12, 1866, Camp Lander was replaced in 1870 by Fort Hall.

CAMP LAPWAI. FORT LAPWAI.

FORT LAPWAI (*Camp Lapwai*). Established August 6, 1862, this post was situated on the left bank of the Lapwai River, a tributary of the Clearwater, about three miles above its mouth, near the city of Lewiston on the Washington border. The post's primary purpose then was to protect both the whites and Indians from perpetrating acts of violence against each other. Aggravating the tense situation was the encroachment of miners on the Nez Percé Reservation. The post was established by Major Jacob S. Rinearson, 1st Oregon Cavalry, with Company F, in compliance with an order of Brigadier General Benjamin Alvord. Originally called Camp Lapwai, the post was designated a fort in 1863. When Company F was ordered to Fort Dalles to be mustered out, Fort Lapwai was abandoned because there were insufficient troops to garrison all of the department's posts. Fort Lapwai was reoccupied by Company E, 8th Cavalry, in November 1866. When the Nez Percé War broke out, companies F and H, 1st Cavalry, were dispatched from the fort to assist in the suppression of the rebellion, but were beaten by Chief Joseph's Indians at White Bird Creek on June 17, 1877. Again evacuated the following month, the post was reoccupied in November 1867. Fort Lapwai's garrisons also had an active part in the Bannock and Sheepeater campaigns of 1878 and 1879. Finally abandoned in 1884, the reservation was transferred to the Department of the Interior for the use of the Indian Service. The last unit to occupy Fort Lapwai was Company B, 2nd Infantry.

FORT LEMHI. On June 18, 1855, a group of 27 Mormons dispatched by Brigham Young to instruct the Indians in "the arts of husbandry and peace," established Fort Lemhi (Limhi in the Book of Mormon) near the 1805 Lewis and Clark campsite about 25 miles southeast of Salmon in Lemhi County. The pioneers had traveled 380 miles across the trackless wilderness in 22 days with 11 wagons, 46 oxen, 7 horses, and many head of cattle. There were two sections to the fort: a log-built stockade 16 rods square enclosing 25 cabins and an adobe-walled corral of the same size. Representing the first attempt to establish a permanent settlement in Idaho, Fort Lemhi was the site of the Northwest's first irrigation project. For a number of reasons, primarily continuous confrontations with the Nez Percés, the agricultural experiment and Mormon mission failed. The Mormon capital at Salt Lake City sent a relief party in early 1858 and the Saints abandoned Fort Lemhi in either late March or early April.

CANTONMENT LORING. Often referred to as Fort Hall because of its proximity to the old Hudson's Bay Company's Fort Hall trading post, three miles up the Snake River, Cantonment Loring was established August 5, 1849, at The Dalles in Bannock County by Lieutenant Colonel William W. Loring with two companies of the Oregon Mounted Riflemen. The post, originally intended to be a permanent installation for the protection of the Oregon Trail, was abandoned May 6, 1850, because of the scarcity of forage in the area and its long distance from sources of supply.

CAMP LYON. Established on June 27, 1865, by companies A, B, and D, 1st Oregon Cavalry, and a detachment of Company D, 1st Oregon Infantry, from Fort Boise, Camp Lyon was located in the Jordan Valley on Jordan Creek, Owyhee River's northernmost tributary, less than a mile from the Oregon line, in Owyhee County. Its nearest town was Sheaville just across the state line. The post was abandoned on April 27, 1869.

MACKENZIE'S POST. This short-lived trading post was established by Donald MacKenzie, one of the Astorian partners, on the Clearwater River, above present-day Lewiston in Nez Perce County, sometime in the late summer or fall of 1812. He returned to Astoria, January 13, 1813, with news that the War of 1812 had broken out. During the period March 31–June 12, 1813, he returned to the Clearwater post to bring out the season's fur catch and abandon the post.

CAMP MINIDOKA. The Minidoka Relocation Center, or Camp Minidoka, at the town of Hunt in Minidoka County, was established in 1942 to house 10,000 Japanese-Americans moved from the Northwest Pacific coastal areas. The 946-acre camp area included a 600-bed hospital, schools, library, churches, ball fields, and other elements of a small town, but all the buildings were of military-style construction and were behind high barbed-wire fences with guard towers manned by Army troops. The camp closed in October 1945, and today only concrete foundations and the ruins of a guard station and the visitors reception center remain.

CAMP OSBURN. Occupied December 2, 1899, Camp Osburn in Shoshone County was garrisoned during the period of martial law which ended April 11, 1901.

CAMP REED. Established on July 13, 1865, by 2nd Lieutenant James L. Cussey, 1st Oregon Cavalry, with Company E and a detachment of infantry, Camp Reed was located on Rock Creek near modern-day Twin Falls, Jerome County, for the purpose of guarding the stage and emigrant road. The post was ordered abandoned on May 12, 1866.

REID'S (REED) POST. Located at the junction of the Boise and Snake rivers in the vicinity of present-day Parma, in either Payette or Canyon County, this temporary trading post was established by John Reid (Reed) to trap during the winter of 1813–14. Not long after this winter post was built, a Bannock Indian band wiped out Reid's party there. The only survivors, Madame Pierre Dorion (an Iowa Indian) and her children, were compelled to make the hazardous trip over the Blue Mountains to the Columbia River, where they brought the news of John Reid's death and the ruin of his winter post early in January 1814.

CAMP REYNOLDS CREEK. Captain Harry C. Egbert, 12th Infantry, with companies B, C, D, F, and K, established a temporary post on Maggie Creek in Idaho County on June 11, 1878.

FORT RUSSELL. When the Nez Percé War broke out in June 1877, Latah County's settlers sought safety in temporary forts and stockades hastily constructed as defenses against Indian raids. The first stockade erected was built to the rear of John Russell's house in the town of Moscow. The fort remained as a haven during the Bannock and Sheepeater wars of 1878–79. The fort's site lies on B Street in the 800 block in Moscow.

FORT SALING. One of three small forts erected shortly after the town of Weiser in Washington County was founded in 1863, Fort Saling stood on Mann Creek and was commanded by John Saling.

FORT SHERMAN (*Camp Coeur d'Alene; Fort Coeur d'Alene*). Located on the north shore of Lake Coeur d'Alene at the point where the Spokane River exits from the lake, this post was established April 16, 1878, by Lieutenant Colonel Henry Clay Merriam, 2nd Infantry, in compliance with an order of Brigadier General Oliver Otis Howard, commanding the department. Established to safeguard the area's settlers from hostile Indians, it was originally called Camp Coeur d'Alene and designated Fort Coeur d'Alene on April 5, 1879, then redesignated Fort Sherman on April 6, 1887, in honor of General William T. Sherman. The fort was ordered abandoned March 5, 1900, and evacuated in September 1900. Two of the post's original officers' quarters buildings still remain on the site in present-day Coeur d'Alene.

SKITSWIST POST. A temporary trading post established in 1812 by an Astor expedition, it was located on Lake Coeur d'Alene in Kootenai County.

SMITH'S CAMP. A temporary post established in May 1864 by Samuel P. Smith, intended to protect emigrants, the post was situated near the mouth of the Raft River, just north of present U.S. 86 and southeast of Lake Walcott.

CANTONMENT SOLDIER. Camp Wallace.

CAMP STEVENSON. Established May 3, 1898, within the Boise Barracks Reservation, the post was a congregation point for the Idaho Volunteers prior to their departure for the Philippines on May 19, 1898, during the Spanish-American War. The post was designated Camp Stevenson in honor of Territorial Governor Edward A. Stevenson. A number of later established camps, bearing different names, were located there also.

TETON PASS CAMP. A temporary post established August 3, 1895, by Major William H. Bisbee, 8th Infantry, with five companies of men aggregating 310 men, Teton Pass Camp was located in Teton County.

THOMPSON TRADING POST. Kullyspell House.

CAMP THREE FORKS (*Camp Winthrop*). Established during the Snake War on September 26, 1866, by Brevet Lieutenant Colonel John J. Coppinger with 200 men, in compliance with an order of Major General Frederick Steele, the post was situated on Soldier Creek at the southwestern base of South Mountain (then known to the Army as Mount Winthrop), near the south fork of the Owyhee River and south of the present-day town of Triangle, in Owyhee County. Because of the pressures brought to bear by the war, it took but six weeks to construct of fir logs a large barracks, two sets of officers' quarters, a 64-by-20-foot, 14-foot-high quartermaster storehouse, and other structures. Originally named Camp Winthrop, the post was designated Camp Three Forks in April 1867. The post was abandoned on October 23, 1871.

CAMP WALLACE (*Cantonment Soldier*). In compliance with an order dated June 26, 1865, this post was established on June 30, 1865, by Captain Joel Palmer on Big Camas Prairie at or near the later town of Soldier in Camas County, to protect emigrants and the area's settlers. The post was abandoned September 20, 1865.

CAMP WARDNER. This post was established at Kellogg, Shoshone County, on May 2, 1899, during the Coeur d'Alene miners' strike. The post's garrison was moved on December 2, 1899, to the town of Osburn to establish Camp Osburn.

FORT WEISER. German trapper and prospector Jacob Weiser reportedly built an Indian defense in 1865 at the confluence of the Snake and Weiser rivers. The fort, named for himself, was apparently the precursor of the town of Weiser in Washington County.

CAMP WINTHROP. Camp Three Forks.

FORT ALLISON. The vicinity of Russellville in Lawrence County was settled in 1809 or 1810 by Kentucky Baptist families, with the Allison clan conspicuous among them. They erected a fort in the spring of 1812 on Samuel Allison's property.

ALTES FORT. FORT LA FOURCHE.

ALTON (CAMP) POST. A military prison in operation during 1862–65, Alton Post was located at or near the town of Alton in Madison County.

CAMP ANNA. A Civil War encampment, this post was located at or near the town of Anna in Union County.

FORT APPLE RIVER. A fortified stockade, enclosing at least one two-story blockhouse, erected during the Black Hawk War, this fort was located near the present town of Elizabeth, about 12 miles east of Galena, in Jo Daviess County. On the night of June 24, 1832, about 150 Indians led by Black Hawk attacked the fort, then occupied by 22 men (mostly miners) and 23 women and children. Their spirited defense forced the Indians to withdraw after committing depredations and driving off horses and cattle. The fort continued as a settler's refuge until the close of the war.

FORT ARMSTRONG (*Rock Island Arsenal; Rock Island Barracks*). Rock Island's military history goes back to the close of the War of 1812, shortly after which Fort Armstrong was built there. Construction of the post, primarily intended to both keep hostile Indians in check and prevent British traders from operating on American territory, was begun on May 10, 1816, at the lower end of the island situated in the Mississippi River between the present cities of Davenport, Iowa, and Rock Island, Illinois. Established by Colonel George Davenport (for whom Davenport was named) in compliance with an order of Brevet Brigadier General Thomas A. Smith, Regiment of Riflemen, the post was located immediately to the east of the Sauk (Sac) and Fox Reservation on the Iowa side of the river. Many of the activities associated with the Black Hawk War of 1832 took place in the post's vicinity.

Fort Armstrong, named in honor of former Secretary of War John Armstrong, was described as having been situated on the lower extremity of the island where the shoreline consisted of 30-foot-high perpendicular cliffs of limestone.

Illinois

Two sides of the quadrangular fort were protected by the cliffs. The two blockhouses were two stories high, their second stories being placed diagonally upon the first. The faces were made up principally by the rear walls of the barracks and storehouse, which were about 20 feet high and furnished with two rows of loopholes. The works were constructed principally of timber and the lower part of the blockhouses, including lower embrasures, were stone. The stone magazine measured 70 square feet, with walls 4 feet thick. A government Indian factory was established at the post in the spring of 1822, shortly before the factory system was ended, and was terminated on December 31, 1822. Fort Armstrong was abandoned on May 4, 1836. A reconstructed blockhouse near the end of Government Bridge over the river marks the site of the fort. (See also ROCK ISLAND ARSENAL.)

FORT ARMSTRONG. A frontier fort erected in about the year 1812, Fort Armstrong was reportedly located in the vicinity of Allendale, Wabash County.

FORT ASCENSION. FORT MASSAC.

BARCROFT PLACE FORT. A defense erected during the War of 1812, it was located at or near Barcroft Place in Jackson County.

FORT BARNEY. William Barney, who had emigrated from western New York, built an Indian defense in 1811 in the vicinity of Allendale, Wabash County.

FORT BARTHOLOMEW. An Indian defense, this frontier fort was erected in 1832 by General Thomas Bartholomew five miles northwest of Pleasant Hill, McLean County.

BARTLETT'S BLOCKHOUSE. A blockhouse erected by Joseph Bartlett during the War of 1812 in Pin Oak Township, Madison County, it remained standing until about 1834 when he tore it down, moved it nearer his residence, and converted it into stables.

BECK'S BLOCKHOUSE. Paul Beck, one of Madison County's earliest residents, built his blockhouse about three miles east of Edwardsville. Most probably erected in 1811, it proved to be a popular refuge during the Indian troubles associated with the War of 1812.

FORT BEGGS. The home of Methodist minister S. R. Beggs, located at Plainfield, Will County, was converted into a fort in 1832 in anticipation of Indian attacks during the Black Hawk War.

FORT BELLEFONTAINE. Five families, residing near Bellefontaine, now part of Waterloo in Monroe County, united and built a blockhouse in early 1787 and surrounded it with a palisade.

CAMP BISSELL. A Civil War recruiting and training camp, Camp Bissell was established in 1861 "near Belleville and Caseyville" in St. Clair County. The post was probably named in honor of William H. Bissell, the first Republican governor of Illinois who practiced law in the county.

BLACK (BLOCK) ISLAND FORT. According to a National Archives citation, this fortification, armed with six guns, stood on an eminence atop one of the Black Islands in the Mississippi River, "about 130 leagues above the mouth of the Ohio River." A sketch of the fort appeared in an 1854 newspaper.

CAMP BLUM. A temporary Civil War assembly point for recruits, Camp Blum was located within the precincts of Chicago and established during the early months of the war.

BOONE'S FORT. Jonathan Boone, a brother of Daniel Boone, established a land claim on August 24, 1814, near the town of New Haven, Gallatin County, and soon after erected a stockade on the bank of the Little Wabash River. The stockade reportedly enclosed a considerable tract of land on which were constructed additional protections.

FORT BOULTINGHOUSE. A fort built during the War of 1812 by Daniel Boultinghouse in the northern part of then White County. He was killed by Indians on the prairie named for him, near his home and fort, in 1813.

FORT BOWMAN. FORT CAHOKIA.

CAMP BRADLEY. A briefly used World War I training post, Camp Bradley was established at Peoria in late 1918.

BRASHEAR'S FORT. Located at or near Harrisonville, Monroe County, Brashear's Fort was a frontier defense in use from 1786 to 1795.

CAMP BUREAU. A Civil War training facility, Camp Bureau was established in 1861 on the county's fair grounds at Princeton, Bureau County.

The camp was in use at least through 1862 primarily for infantry troops.

CAMP BUTLER. A Civil War concentration camp for Illinois Volunteers, Camp Butler was established in August 1861 and used until June 1866. It was located six miles east of Springfield and named for William Butler, then Illinois State Treasurer. Here about a third of the Illinois regiments were mustered into Federal service and later discharged. It was at this camp that Ulysses S. Grant offered his services. He became drill officer during the early months of the war, whipping into shape many regiments of infantry, artillery, and especially cavalry. His usefulness became so apparent to superior officers, that within a year after he left Camp Butler he was winning plaudits as commander of the Army of Tennessee. After the capture of Fort Donelson, Camp Butler was used also as a prison camp, housing at one time as many as 3,600 captured Confederates. Its site is now a national cemetery.

FORT BUTLER. Located near the site of the present village of St. Jacob in Madison County, Fort Butler was an Indian defense built in 1812 and used as a refuge for 11 families of this and adjoining townships. It was never attacked.

FORT CAHOKIA (*Fort Bowman*). The oldest town in Illinois, Cahokia on the Mississippi River was founded in 1698 when a mission was established here by the Seminary of Foreign Missions among the Cahokia and Tamaroa Indians, the only Mississippi Valley settlement not under Jesuit jurisdiction. The Seminary today is represented by Laval University at Quebec. In 1733, when the town's French settlers felt themselves threatened by the region's Indians, they built a wooden fort and garrisoned it with 20 men. By the terms of the 1763 Treaty of Paris, all of the French possessions in the Mississippi Valley, excepting New Orleans, passed into British control. Cahokia became a center of considerable trade and a depository of British arms for distribution among their allied Indians during the early years of the Revolution in the Valley. The British fort in Cahokia was most probably the former old stone-built Seminary mission.

The year 1777 was a bloody one for the American settlements along the frontier, because of the British-inspired Indian raids. Twenty-six-year-old George Rogers Clark of Kentucky felt that aggressive action was needed by the Americans. . . . The government of Virginia empowered him to raise the necessary army and with great secrecy Clark and his small force captured Kaskaskia by surprise on 4 July 1778. He im-

mediately sent his trusted officer, Captain Joseph Bowman, with some forty men and a party of Kaskaskians, to take the villages to the north. Cahokia was peacefully occupied on July 6. In Cahokia Bowman found an old stone house built in 1763 to serve as the parish house which the British had later used for a barracks. Bowman occupied the building, repaired it, and it became known as "Fort Bowman." However minor the part it played during the war, it was nevertheless the westernmost post of the American government. . . .

With Spain's declaration of war on England in 1779, a new phase began in the war in the West. The British immediately planned a vast strategy for capturing the valley, sending a British and Indian army to attack St. Louis and Cahokia on 26 May 1780. Their defeat ended the last serious British attempt to conquer the region. . . . When the war ended Clark had achieved his original objectives. . . . But the Creoles of the Illinois villages, as the pawns in the international struggle, were bankrupt and embittered. . . . Cahokia never recovered. The growth of St. Louis, the decline of the fur trade which had long sustained the village, all combined to relegate the village to the status of a quiet, country village. [*Old Cahokia*, ed. John Francis McDermott 1949, "Affairs at Fort Bowman, 1778–1780" ed. Charles van Ravenswaay, pp. 232–33]

CAMP CAIRO. A temporary Civil War encampment, it was established in 1861 at or near Cairo on the Mississippi River.

CARLYLE FORT. Hill's Fort.

FORT CAVENDISH. Fort Chartres.

FORT CHAMBERS. Erected by Nathan Chambers on his property in either 1811 or 1812, his fort was located one mile south of today's Summerfield, St. Clair County, and provided a refuge from Indian depredations for neighboring families.

FORT (DE) CHARTRES (*Fort Cavendish*). Fort de Chartres State Park, 20 acres in area, occupies the site of a former French fortress in the fertile valley commonly known as the American Bottom, 4 miles from Prairie du Rocher, in the northwest corner of Randolph County, close to the Mississippi River. The fort was the seat of military and civil government in the Illinois country for more than half a century.

Shortly after Father Marquette and Joliet traversed the Mississippi in 1673, La Salle explored the region through which it flowed and laid claim to the entire valley in the name of France. The fertile soil in the bottom lands east of the river below the mouth of the Missouri and the pervading belief among the French that

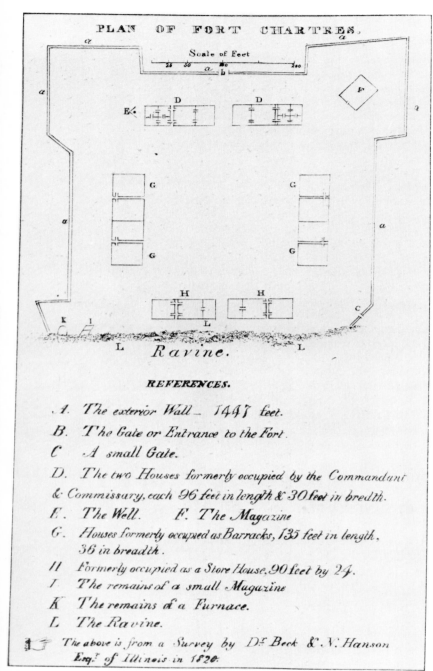

PLAN OF FORT CHARTRES.

Scale of Feet

REFERENCES.

A. The exterior Wall — 1447 feet.

B. The Gate or Entrance to the Fort.

C. A small Gate.

D. The two Houses formerly occupied by the Commandant & Commissary, each 96 feet in length & 30 feet in bredth.

E. The Well. *F.* The Magazine

G. Houses formerly occupied as Barracks, 135 feet in length. 36 in breadth.

H. Formerly occupied as a Store House, 90 feet by 24.

I. The remains of a small Magazine

K. The remains of a Furnace.

L. The Ravine.

The above is from a Survey by Dr. Beck & N. Hanson Engr. of Illinois in 1820.

FORT (DE) CHARTRES. Plan drawn by Dr. Beck and N. Hanson for a survey in 1820. (Courtesy of the Illinois State Historical Library.)

the bluffs in the region contained gold and silver drew many settlers. The hills, however, failed to yield precious metals in appreciable amount, and the people turned to agriculture and the fur trade.

With colonization came the necessity for some form of civil and military rule. In the autumn of 1718, Pierre Duqué de Boisbriant, who had been appointed commandant of the Illinois country, arrived at Kaskaskia with instructions to erect a permanent military post. He selected a site 18 miles north of Kaskaskia on the east bank of the Mississippi and built a strong

wooden stockade, reinforced on the interior with the earth excavated for the moat. This was the first Fort de Chartres, completed in 1720, and named for the son of Philip, duke of Orléans, regent of France. Exposed to the flood waters of the Mississippi, the fort quickly fell into disrepair. It was rebuilt in 1727, but by 1732 it was so dilapidated that Robert Groston, sieur de St. Ange, the commandant, built a new fort bearing the same name at some distance from the river. By 1747 this too had fallen into a condition beyond repair, and the garrison was withdrawn to Kaskaskia.

In 1751 the French again planned a strong fortification. The government selected Kaskaskia as the site, but the engineer in charge, Jean Baptiste Saucier, chose a location near the old fort. Construction was begun in 1753, and three years later the structure was substantially completed. The stone blocks were quarried and numbered in the bluffs about three miles to the east and transported across the lake to the fort in boats and on rafts. The massive stone walls, 18 feet high and more than 2 feet thick, enclosed about 4 acres. From the 15-foot-high arched gateway a railed, stone stairway led to a platform above. Within the walls stood a two-story building, guardhouse, chapel, government house, coach house, pigeon house over the well, two buildings for officers, two long barracks, powder magazine, kitchen and bake ovens, and four prison cells all arranged around the parade grounds. The massive fort remained the pride of Louisiana and New France for many years. It was capable of accommodating 400 men, although its garrison rarely exceeded half that number.

When the Treaty of Paris in 1763 ceded all French possessions east of the Mississippi, with the exception of New Orleans, French domination in North America was at an end. French garrisons held the post until October 10, 1765, when English troops took possession. Renamed Fort Cavendish, the fort was the seat of British military and civil rule in the Illinois country until 1772 when it was abandoned and destroyed. Almost a century and a half later, in 1915, the site was acquired by Illinois as a state park. The fort was reproduced according to plans drawn after careful research and study. On the original foundations of the stone structure have been erected custodian's quarters and a museum, the latter holding relics directly associated with the former French stronghold. Also reconstructed were the magazine, combined guardhouse and chapel, and the arched gateway, contributed by the Daughters of the American Colonists.

FORT CHECAGOU (*Fort St. Joseph*). During the early days of French exploration and colonization, they built Fort St. Joseph where Chicago's "Loop" is today. On a French map drawn in 1683 is marked "Fort Checagou." According to traditions handed down by regional historians, the fort was said to have been abandoned after the French and Indian War in 1763.

CHILTON'S FORT. Located about two miles west of the present town of St. Jacobs, Madison County, Chilton's Fort was built during the early days of the War of 1812 when British-allied Indians had begun a series of widespread depredations in the region. The fort, never attacked, provided a haven for the area's pioneering families who had emigrated from Kentucky and Tennessee.

FORT CLARK. FORT KASKASKIA.

FORT CLARK. This fort, named for explorer William Clark, was built on the right bank of the Illinois River in 1813 on the site of present-day Peoria, which bore the name of the fort until 1825. Fort Clark was garrisoned until about 1817. Two years later it was completely destroyed by Indians.

FORT COMPTON. Built by Levi Compton in about the year 1810 on Coco Creek in the vicinity of Allendale, Wabash County, the Indian defense was reportedly large enough to accommodate a hundred families and boasted such amenities as dwellings and granaries.

FORT COUNCIL. This Indian defense was reportedly erected in 1813 on the "Starkey place" by "Hardy Council" and located in what was then White County.

CRANE'S FORT. Apparently an Indian defense erected by a pioneering family, Crane's Fort was located somewhere in present-day Carroll County.

FORT CRÈVECOEUR. In 1673, René Robert de La Salle, intrepid French explorer, established Fort Frontenac on Lake Ontario. On two trips back to France, he obtained title to a seigniory in Canada, a license to trade in furs, and authorization to erect additional posts and find a water passage to the Gulf of Mexico. In 1678 he and a party of men, including his trusted lieutenant, Henri de Tonty and Père Louis Hennepin, arrived at Niagara Falls. There, in 1679, above the falls they built a blockhouse fort, Fort Conti, to guard Lake Ontario, and constructed a vessel to transport them through the Great Lakes.

Overcoming one obstacle after another, La Salle led the men to the site of Green Bay to trade, from which point he sent the boat, loaded with furs, back to Niagara for supplies. He then traveled by canoe down Lake Michigan and around its southern tip to the mouth of the St. Joseph River, where he built semipermanent Fort Miami. After waiting in vain about three months for the supply boat, he ascended the St. Joseph to the site of South Bend, crossed the Kankakee portage, and descended that river to the Illinois River, which he followed to Lake Peoria, arriving in January 1680. Here he built Fort Crèvecoeur, the first white habitation in Illinois, on a low knoll with a ravine on either side, situated on the left bank of the river below the lower end of the lake. The stockade of 25-foot-high, 1-foot-thick palisades enclosed two barracks, a small cabin that served as both living quarters and a chapel for the priests in the party, and a forge. The fort was named Crèvecoeur in honor of the Dutch stronghold that capitulated in July 1672 when Tonty served as a minor officer under Marshal Turenne.

La Salle set out with several men for his base at Fort Frontenac for needed supplies, leaving Tonty in charge of Fort Crèvecoeur. The explorer en route spent several days at an Indian village near Starved Rock at the lower rapids of the Illinois River, a cliff of yellow sandstone that struck him as being a natural fortress. Some days later he sent Tonty an order to examine the locality to assess its worth as a future stronghold in case of need. During the absences of both La Salle and Tonty, the Frenchmen posted at Fort Crèvecoeur mutinied. News of the calamity was contained in a letter from Tonty who wrote that most of his men had wrecked the fort, pillaged its storehouse, and fled.

During the winter of 1691–92, after La Salle's death by assassination, Tonty revisited Lake Peoria and built a new fort named St. Louis, commonly called Fort Pimiteoui. It was located on the right bank of the Illinois River, about a mile and a half from the lower outlet of Lake Peoria, a short distance from the site of the first fort. Despite assiduous archaeological explorations, the site of Fort Crèvecoeur has not been determined.

FORT CRIBS. In 1832, during the Black Hawk War, almost a dozen stockades were erected in present Marshall and Putnam counties. One of these, located about three and one-half miles north of Hennepin, was known as Fort Cribs because of the large number of corn cribs around the fort, inside the stockade as well as out. At times the fort sheltered as many as 100 people during the Indian scares.

CROSS ROADS FORT. An Indian defense, this fort was located at a village known as Old Fort in McDonough County.

CROZAT FORT. During the early days of French colonization in the Mississippi Valley, Antoine Crozat was granted a monopoly of working and exploiting precious metal mines. A number of his followers built a "fortlet" in the bottom lands near the Mississippi River about 15 miles above Kaskaskia.

FORT DARLING. In compliance with orders of Secretary of War Simon Cameron in the late spring of 1861 to occupy Cairo at the junction of the Mississippi and Ohio rivers, five regiments of Union troops were put to work erecting fortifications there. They built barracks, cleared parade grounds, and mounted guns for the establishment of Fort Darling, which was then occupied by the 1st and 2nd Illinois Light Artillery. A Confederate attack never came, and Fort Darling garrison's duties were chiefly confined to the prevention of contraband traffic on the river.

FORT DARNELL. An Indian defense erected in 1832 during the Black Hawk War, this fort stood on Benjamin Darnell's farm in Roberts Township, in then La Salle County (now Marshall County). The exact dimensions of this fort near Sandy Creek are not known, but it must have been of considerable size, since it enclosed sufficient cabins to accommodate at least 70 people besides wagons and other implements of husbandry.

CANTONMENT DAVIS. FORT EDWARDS.

FORT DEARBORN. Built in 1803 by Captain John Whistler on the windswept west shore of Lake Michigan where the Chicago River empties into the lake, Fort Dearborn occupied a site today incorporated within Chicago's famous "Loop" section. The basic design of the fort, named for Secretary of War Henry Dearborn, was much like that of earlier forts in the East and of others erected in Illinois, such as Fort Armstrong and Fort Clark.

In opposite corners of a 12-foot-high stockade of logs were two towering blockhouses. One, armed with two cannon, protected the lake (east) and south sides of the fort; the other blockhouse, with one cannon and a large stand of muskets, protected the north (river) and west sides. The stockade's gates opened to the south. Just inside them stood the hospital and the barracks, while on the west and east sides, against an inner palisade, were the commandant's residence and the officers' quarters. On the north side of the parade was the stone (brick) magazine. The fort's well was located under a covered walk which led to a dock or wharf on the river.

On August 15, 1812, after nine relatively peaceful years, Fort Dearborn's garrison was making last-minute preparations to abandon the fort. Six days earlier Captain Nathan Heald, the post commander, had received an urgent letter from Brigadier General William Hull, commander of American forces in Michigan Territory. Hull's letter was a positive command to evacuate the fort immediately and to proceed to Fort Wayne in Indiana. The captain was informed that this was necessary because there were not sufficient provisions to supply the fort.

Arms and ammunition, except for side arms, were thrown down the well and the whisky supply dumped into the river. Blankets, calicoes, broadcloths, and paints were divided among the 30 Miami Indians who accompanied Captain William Wells arriving from Fort Wayne to assist Captain Heald in the evacuation. The area's Potawatomi Indians, although evincing anger because of the ruination of the ammunition and liquor, reluctantly agreed to be an escort for the small group of soldiers, settlers, and their families. "At 9:00 a.m. the procession moved out of the fort. Captain Wells with 15 of his Miami band led the group, while the other Miami brought up the rear. Between them were 55 regular soldiers, 12 militiamen, nine women, and 18 children. . . . The Potawatomi accompanied the procession as an escort, riding in a column some distance to the right" (*Illinois History* 12, no. 7 [1959]: 171).

The column of Indians passed to the right of the sand dunes in the line of march and disappeared from view, hurrying to a prearranged place about a mile and a half from the fort.

"There were over 500 Indians and fewer than 100 in the procession, including the children. After only 15 minutes of fighting, almost one-half of the regulars and all the militiamen were dead. Twelve of the children and two women also were killed. . . . Some of the wounded prisoners were immediately slain, and others lost their lives later through torture and starvation"

(*Illinois History* 12, no. 7 [1959]: 171). The Potawatomi then vengefully proceeded to destroy the fort.

After the end of the war, the government was urged to rebuild the fort on the same site where only the brick remains of the powder magazine served as a stark reminder of the tragedy. On July 4, 1816, Captain Hezekiah Bradley arrived with 116 soldiers and Fort Dearborn's reconstruction followed. This second fort fell into disrepair after the Black Hawk War of 1832 and was abandoned in December, 1836. Twenty years later the fort was completely dismantled except for one small structure which was ultimately destroyed in the great Chicago fire of 1871. Today a reproduction of the fort stands near Lake Michigan on 26th Street, about three miles south of the original fort site in the immediate area of Prairie and 16th streets.

FORT DEFIANCE (*Camp Prentiss*). First called Camp Prentiss, for Union General Benjamin M. Prentiss, when Union forces began its construction on Cairo Point in 1861, Fort Defiance commanded the strategic confluence of the Mississippi and Ohio rivers, guarding against any Confederate ship that might get through the blockade. One block south of it were the drill grounds and array of barracks for the great army that General U. S. Grant assembled here. Nearby, at 609 Washington Avenue, was the headquarters of the Western Flotilla during the struggle to control passage of the Mississippi. Today, the Fort Defiance State Park on the Point contains a reproduction of the Civil War fort. The city of Cairo is perhaps the only walled city in the United States. It is surrounded by levees, and entrance to the city is through gates that can be closed against floods.

CAMP DEMENT. A temporary Civil War encampment at Amboy, Lee County.

FORT DEPOSIT. FORT WILBOURN.

FORT DES MIAMIS. FORT MIAMIS.

CAMP DES PLAINES. A World War II facility located on the west side of Route 66 in Grundy County, southwest of Joliet, Camp Des Plaines was established to house laborers brought in from Jamaica and the Barbados because of the labor shortage. Later it was used to accommodate special Army guards sent to guard the Illinois Waterway. The camp was activated in the fall of 1942 and used until 1945, and dismantled in 1948. The camp was named for the river that flows south through Joliet to join the Illinois and Kankakee rivers.

FORT DIXON. By an order dated May 22, 1832, General Henry Atkinson made Dixon's Ferry (Dixon in Lee County) on the Rock River his headquarters and base of operations during the Black Hawk War. Fort Dixon, erected on the north side of the river, consisted of two loopholed blockhouses within an earth and sod breastwork, four and a half feet high, abutting on the river bank near the west line of what is now North Galena Avenue. The northeast blockhouse was at least four times as large as the other, which probably held the fort's powder magazine. The structures stood for many years after the war. In the park on Fort Dixon's site is the Lincoln Monument, a bronze statue sculptured by Leonard Crunelle, depicting Abraham Lincoln attired in a captain's uniform.

FORT DOOLITTLE. The first school house in Pekin, Tazewell County, was built in 1831. It was located on 2nd Street between Elizabeth and St. Mary's streets. At the breaking out of the Black Hawk War the following year, the one-story school was palisaded and converted into a fort.

CAMP DOUGLAS. An extensive Federal Civil War encampment, first a camp for the instruction of recruits, then a camp for Confederate prisoners, Camp Douglas was established in Chicago in 1861 and soon became one of the two principal places for the mustering of Illinois regiments (the other being Camp Butler at Springfield). The 60-acre camp was then located between 31st Street and College Place, and Cottage Grove and Forest avenues. It covered the land through which has since been opened Calumet, South Park, Vernon, and Rhodes avenues, between 31st and 33rd streets. The camp's main gate was at what is now 32nd Street and Cottage Grove Avenue. To the south of the camp was the old university, to the west and north was prairie land, clumps of trees, and thinly scattered houses, which have all long since given way to the march of progress.

Camp Douglas remained as a camp of instruction until after the battle of Fort Donelson in February 1862 when by official order it was prepared for the reception of prisoners taken from Island No. 10. Nearly 9,000 prisoners—weak, worn-out, sick, and wretched—came to Chicago in the first lot. In November of 1863 a nearly successful attempt to escape was made. A number of the prisoners removed the boards from the floor of their barracks and digging down a few feet ran a tunnel under the fence and one by one silently crept through and out and fled into the darkness. Some 70 or more of them had escaped before the discovery of their plans, and about 50 of them were afterward recaptured.

In 1864 Chicago figured dramatically in one of the most daring plans devised by Confederate leaders. The plan called for the Confederate prisoners at Camp Douglas to break out of prison on the eve of the presidential election. But an informer, who while a prisoner had been privy to the prisoners' grapevine, and who had since escaped, related the details of the plot to the commandant. Federal agents on the night before the election, November 7, arrested some of the conspirators at a fashionable Chicago hotel and at the home of another near the camp where a veritable arsenal of weapons was found.

At the opening of the year 1865, the camp held 17,880 prisoners. In February the release began and continued irregularly until August 1865, when all but about 200 who were too ill to be moved had been discharged, and the office of Camp Douglas as a prison camp was closed. The barracks, fences, and improvements were torn down. The sale of the government property began on November 24, 1865, and continued until all was sold.

CAMP DOUGLAS. A temporary Civil War encampment "near Jonesboro Station" at Anna in Union County.

CAMP DUBOIS. On December 13, 1803, the Lewis and Clark Expedition set up a winter base camp where the Wood River emptied into the Mississippi River. The site is on the Illinois bank, some 23 miles upriver from St. Louis and opposite the mouth of the Missouri River. The camp, near the present towns of Wood River and Hartford in Madison County, was established in Illinois territory for several reasons, principally because St. Louis was then technically a French possession, although actually governed by a Spanish commandant, and because both the French and Spanish in St. Louis were suspicious of American intentions. The camp was named "Dubois" because its site was located at La Rivière Dubois, as the local French called the Wood River. On May 11, 1804, seven voyageurs arrived from St. Louis. They had been engaged to help paddle the exploration party up the Missouri River as far as the second winter encampment in North Dakota. On May 14 the 40 men in the

party, led by Meriwether Lewis and William Clark, abandoned their camp and set off on their great adventure.

CAMP DUBOIS. A temporary Civil War camp at or near Alton in Madison County.

CAMP DUBOIS. A temporary Civil War camp, established in December 1861 at or near Anna in Union County.

CAMP DUNCAN. A temporary Civil War camp at or near Jacksonville, Morgan County was established in 1861.

CAMP DUNNE. A temporary Civil War encampment in the suburbs of Chicago.

FORT DU PAGE. In 1832, during the first days of the Black Hawk War, a group of settlers in present Du Page County constructed a 100-foot-square fort with two blockhouses, covered with "shakes," in diagonal corners. The fort, defended by 50 well-armed men, was not actually attacked, but a number of confrontations with hostile Indians took place in its environs.

DUSABLE TRADING POST. A Negro and Chicago's first settler, Jean DuSable was also the first to recognize the commercial advantages of the location, having enough faith in its possibilities to establish a successful trading post near the mouth of the Chicago River. Today this pioneer's settlement has grown into the trading post of the world. DuSable, a Haitian, came all the way up the Mississippi in about 1779. The elaborate home he built was located at the present site of the Wrigley Building on the north bank of the Chicago River at Michigan Boulevard. He established a lasting friendship with the Potawatomi living in the area, or Eschikagou, as the Indians called it. He courted an Indian girl, joining the tribe in order to marry her and then sanctifying the marriage when a Catholic priest entered the region. They had two children, one a boy named after his father, and a girl named Suzanna, whose birth is considered the first recorded birth in the Chicago area. DuSable died at St. Charles, Missouri. Today a plaque marks the site in Chicago where his home stood, a high school in the city was named in his honor, and a memorial society exists to revere his memory.

FORT EDWARDS (*Cantonment Davis*). In the fall of 1815, a detachment of the 8th Infantry under Colonel Robert C. Nicholas ascended the

Mississippi in keelboats, with the purpose of establishing a fort at or near Rock Island, to control the Sacs and Foxes. The troops, however, were stopped by ice at the mouth of the Des Moines River in November and built rudimentary huts for winter quarters on the east bank of the Mississippi, calling their camp Cantonment Davis, which the next year evolved into Fort Edwards, at the present city of Warsaw, Hancock County, to secure the area against the Potawatomi Indians. Intermittently garrisoned, the post was finally abandoned in July 1824.

CAMP ELLIS. A World War II training post was established in December 1942 at Bernadotte, near Ipava and Table Grove, on the Spoon River in Fulton County. The camp, named in honor of Sergeant Michael B. Ellis, World War I hero, was originally designed to activate and train supply units for overseas war zones. In addition, a prisoner of war facility was established at the post, officially designated Camp Ellis, Illinois, Prisoner of War Camp, and was first used for a thousand German prisoners who reached the camp in August 1943. Camp Ellis was abandoned in 1950, its buildings dismantled, and the salvageable lumber sold.

CAMP ELLSWORTH. A Civil War encampment located in the suburbs of Chicago.

FORT FOOTE. A War of 1812 Indian defense built by a member of the large Eaton clan, Fort Foote was located in Crawford County.

CAMP FORD. A Mexican War recruitment camp at or near Springfield.

FORT FRANCOIS. FORT LA FOURCHE.

CAMP FREMONT. A Civil War encampment located in Chicago's suburbs.

CAMP FRY. A Civil War post established in February 1864, Camp Fry, like Camp Douglas, was a Chicago-located training camp at first, then a prisoner of war facility. The stockaded camp was located on the site now occupied by the Broadway-Clark-Diversey intersection on Chicago's north side.

FORT GAGE. FORT KASKASKIA.

FORT GALENA. A Black Hawk War defense, Fort Galena was an extensive 14-foot-high stockade enclosing a centrally placed blockhouse and another in one of the angles, in addition to three fortified residences. The fort, located in the center of the town of Galena, Jo Daviess County, was begun during the last week of May 1832. The defense was intermittently garrisoned by Army troops.

CAMP GEISMAR. A World War I encampment adjoining Fort Sheridan.

CAMP GOODE. A temporary Civil War encampment in Coles County.

CAMP GOODELL. A temporary Civil War training post at Joliet in Will County.

CAMP GRANT. A Civil War recruitment and training camp, Camp Grant was located on U.S. 45 at Mattoon, Coles County. General U. S. Grant mustered in the 21st Illinois Infantry here in June 1861. The camp's original flagpole now stands in front of the U. S. Grant Motor Inn.

CAMP GRANT. A temporary Civil War encampment, it was established in 1861 at Jacksonville in Morgan County.

CAMP GRANT. A 3,338-acre Army post four miles south of Rockford, Winnebago County, Camp Grant was established July 18, 1917, and named in honor of General Ulysses S. Grant to serve as a training camp for the 86th (Black Hawk) Division. A cantonment of 1,515 buildings, it had a troop capacity of 42,819. Camp Grant was designated as an infantry replacement and training camp on April 1918 and as a demobilization center on December 3, 1918. Following World War I, Camp Grant was used as a training camp for the Illinois National Guard. In World War II, the site was reclaimed by the federal government and used as a reception center and a medical replacement center. Subsequent to the war, the property was never used again by the state and was eventually disposed of by the federal government.

FORT GREATHOUSE. Erected in 1811 as an Indian defense on Greathouse Creek, in section 30, township 1 south, range 13 west, in Wabash County, the fort was occupied almost continuously by settlers' families until 1815.

GREEN'S FORT. FORT JONES.

FORT HAMILTON. An Indian defense named for William S. Hamilton, the fort was located at Wyota in Stephenson County.

CAMP HAMMOND. A temporary Civil War encampment established in 1861, it was located at or near Aurora, Kane County, and named for the president of the Chicago, Burlington, and Quincy Railroad.

FORT HANDY. A frontier Indian defense located in Clark County.

FORT HANNA. Probably an Indian defense erected during the War of 1812, it was built by John Hanna in what was then White County.

CAMP HARDIN. A temporary Civil War encampment established in 1861 at or near Villa Ridge, Pulaski County.

CAMP HAVEN. Formerly a subpost of Fort Sheridan, 164-acre Camp Haven on the shore of Lake Michigan had been used for antiaircraft artillery practice. The post was permanently closed in October 1959.

CAMP HAYDEN. A temporary Civil War encampment, Camp Hayden was cited by a Springfield newspaper as being located "near Fort Willard at Muddy Creek."

FORT HENLINE. An Indian defense erected during the Black Hawk War in 1832 by John Henline, the fort was located near Lawndale in what was then McLean County, now Logan County.

FORT HENNEPIN. An Indian defense erected in 1832 during the Black Hawk War, it was built a year after the town of Hennepin was founded on the Illinois River in Illinois County. The fort occupied a site on the east side of Front Street and stood for nearly 10 years after.

CAMP HERRING. A World War I ordnance camp at the Holt Manufacturing Company plant in East Peoria, Camp Herring was established in October 1917 and named for Major Harry T. Herring.

FORT HIGGINBOTHAM. An Indian defense erected on a site now incorporated within Joliet in Will County.

CAMP HIGHWOOD. FORT SHERIDAN.

HILL'S FORT (*Carlyle Fort*). First known as Carlyle Fort, this Indian defense was erected in 1811 by John Hill on the east side of Shoal Creek at or near the town of Carlyle in present Clinton County.

FORT HORN. The earliest white settlement close to the present city of La Salle was Fort Horn at old Illinoistown, now part of Peru, La Salle County. It was constructed between 1825 and 1828 and located on the north side of the Illinois River near the mouth of the Little Vermilion. The fort was built by a contracting partnership, Horn and Wilbur, two men engaged in furnishing supplies to the newly formed government of the state of Illinois.

CAMP HOUGHTALING. A Civil War artillery encampment near Cairo, Camp Houghtaling was established in 1861 by Captain (later major) Charles Houghtaling of the noted 1st Illinois Artillery.

FORT ILLINOIS. FORT ST. LOUIS NO. 2.

FORT JEFFERSON. "A fort was erected by Colonel George Rogers Clark, under instructions from the Governor of Virginia, at the Iron Banks on the east bank of the Mississippi, below the mouth of the Ohio River. He promised lands to all adult, able-bodied white males who would emigrate thither and settle, either with or without their families. Many accepted the offer, and a considerable colony was established there. Toward the close of the Revolutionary War, Virginia being unable any longer to sustain the garrison, the colony was scattered, many families going to Kaskaskia" (Newton Bateman and Paul Selby, *Historical Encyclopedia of Illinois* [1901]: 171).

FORT JOHNSON. In compliance with orders of General Benjamin Howard, a fort was established in late September 1814, during the War of 1812, by Brevet Major Zachary Taylor on a high bluff on the eastern bank of the Mississippi opposite the mouth of the Des Moines River, near present Warsaw in Hancock County. Taylor named the fort, a defense of the approaches to St. Louis, in honor of his Kentucky friend, Colonel Richard M. Johnson, whom contemporaries credited with killing the famed Shawnee Chief Tecumseh at the recent Battle of the Thames in Canada. Late in October, learning of the death of General Howard, Taylor was forced to burn his fort and return to St. Louis to assume command of all American forces in Missouri Territory.

FORT JOHNSON (*Fort Ottawa*). First known as Fort Ottawa, Fort Johnson was erected in the spring of 1832 during the Black Hawk War on a bluff on the south bank of the Illinois River, in what is now a residential area of Ottawa in La Salle County. Abraham Lincoln was at the fort during its early days. On May 27, 1832, Captain Lincoln and a detachment of his men reached Ottawa from Rock River where they were mustered out of service. Lincoln, however, reenlisted and was sworn by Lieutenant Robert Anderson, later in command of Fort Sumter during the Civil War. Lincoln was mustered out by Anderson at Ottawa on June 16.

FORT JONES (*Green's Fort*). Originally known as Green's Fort, built by a James Green(e) from Kentucky, then renamed Fort Jones, it was built probably in 1807. The fort was located on the east side of Shoal Creek, about eight miles southwest of present Greenville in Bond County.

JORDAN'S FORTS. Two forts were built in 1811 by Francis (Frank) and Thomas Jordan, two of the seven Jordan brothers in present Franklin County. One was located in Frankfort (named for Frank Jordan) and the other about three miles southwest of the present town of Thompsonville, eight miles from Frankfort.

FORT KASKASKIA (*Fort Gage; Fort Clark*). Fort Kaskaskia State Park, comprising 201 acres in Randolph County near Chester, was established in 1927 as a memorial to the early French and American pioneers who brought civilization to the Illinois wilderness. Of the town of Kaskaskia, which was once "Commercial Queen of the West," the first capital of Illinois, the seat of government during territorial days, and one of the Mississippi Valley's principal settlements of the French, nothing remains today. Across the river are the earthworks and foundations of the old fort and the old Pierre Menard Home at the base of the hill on which the fort stood.

Kaskaskia, founded in 1703, soon attracted a sizable number of settlers and traders to eventually become a major river port. In 1733, on an elevation overlooking the town, the French erected a rudimentary wooden stockade, called Fort of the Kaskasquias. A local tradition, passed on by several regional historians, but not substantiated in major historical works, says that the French government three years later had appropriated a large amount of money to replace the slight work with a substantial fortification.

During the French and Indian War, the inhabitants, in fear of a British attack, petitioned for a fort and offered to furnish the materials. Their petition was granted, and Fort Kaskaskia, built of heavy palisades enclosing four blockhouses, was located on the bluff above and across from the town. There it stood until 1766, when Kaskaskia's people destroyed it rather than have it occupied by the British, to whom control had passed in 1765.

When the first British troops arrived, under the command of Captain Thomas Stirling, Fort Chartres became British headquarters. By 1772, however, Fort Chartres was no longer a safe situation because of the encroaching waters of the Mississippi. Captain Hugh Lord, then commandant, removed the headquarters to Kaskaskia where he and his troops occupied the old Jesuit Seminary (in 1763 the Jesuit order had been suppressed and its property confiscated by the French government). Captain Lord fortified the Jesuit structure by surrounding it with a stockade on which were emplaced several pieces of ordnance. It was named Fort Gage in honor of General Thomas Gage, commander of British forces in America. In 1776 Captain Lord was ordered to proceed with his troops to Detroit, leaving his fort in the care of Philippe de Rocheblave, a former French citizen, but with no garrison. George Rogers Clark and his soldiers made a surprise attack on Fort Gage on the night of July 4, 1778. The fort was at once renamed Fort Clark, and the Americans occupied the town throughout the remainder of the Revolution. In 1844 a disastrous Mississippi flood destroyed most of Kaskaskia, and in 1910 another flood completely obliterated the town site.

KELLOGG'S FORT. An Indian defense named for Oliver W. Kellogg, it was located at or near Pearl City, Stephenson County. Kellogg blazed the then important trail in 1827 from Fort Clark at Peoria to Dixon's Ferry across the Rock River and from there to Galena by way of the southwest corner of Stephenson County.

KELLOGG'S GROVE FORT. A blockhouse fort erected in 1832 during Black Hawk's War, it was located about a mile southeast of present-day Kent, near Pearl City, Stephenson County. The blockhouse stood among a group of cabins, one of them the home of trailblazer Oliver W. Kellogg, for whom the village was named. On June 24 about 200 of Black Hawk's (or Chief Neapope's) warriors unsuccessfully attacked the fort at Apple River, and on the following day occurred the Battle of Kellogg's Grove, the war's last Indian-white encounter on Illinois soil. The 150 men garrisoning the blockhouse and cabins during the protracted spirited action prevented the Indians from obtaining desperately needed supplies.

KINZIE'S TRADING POST. Quebec-born John Kinzie, Indian trader and reputedly Chicago's first white settler, established a trading post in 1804, most probably located on or close to either the Chicago River or Lake Michigan. Kinzie's post was not the first in the area—Jean DuSable's trading enterprise preceded Kinzie's by about a quarter of a century (see: DUSABLE TRADING POST). Kinzie later established other posts on the Rock, Illinois, and Kankakee rivers.

KIRKPATRICK'S FORTS. In the year 1811, three different forts at different locations were erected in Madison County by three Kirkpatrick brothers—James, Frank, and Thomas. James Kirkpatrick's fort was about three miles southwest of Edwardsville. To the southeast was Frank Kirkpatrick's fort. Thomas Kirkpatrick erected his fort in Wood River on a point of land, north of his home, about 300 yards from Cahokia Creek, at the end of present O Street, just off North Main.

FORT LA FOURCHE (*Altes Fort; Fort Francois; Vieu Fort*). An old French fort was probably located on the north side of the Ohio River and the east side of the Mississippi. Tradition has ascribed several alternate names to it. It was marked as "ancient fort" on D'Anville's map of 1755 and several other French maps. Several Illinois historians have expressed the opinion that Fort La Fourche and Fort Massac may have been one and the same, although the latter was established in 1757 on the Ohio River, about 40 miles above its confluence with the Mississippi.

FORT LA HARPE. Reputedly the oldest pioneer fort built in present Hancock County at or near today's town of La Harpe, it was erected by a Frenchman named Bernard de La Harpe. No date has been indicated.

FORT LA MOTTE. A frontier Indian defense, Fort La Motte was erected in 1812 on the creek of the same name in Crawford County.

CAMP LATHAM. A Civil War encampment established 1861 at or near Lincoln in Logan County.

CAMP LINCOLN. Civil War recruitment and training post at Springfield, Camp Lincoln was the state's National Guard headquarters.

LITTLE FORT. A frontier Indian defense at Waukegan, Lake County.

LOFTON'S BLOCKHOUSE. An Indian defense erected during the War of 1812, Lofton's Blockhouse was located in the American Bottom, in present Nameoki Township, Madison County.

CAMP LONG. A temporary Civil War encampment in the suburbs of Chicago.

CAMP LOWDEN. A temporary state mobilization camp established during World War I at the State Fairgrounds, two miles north of Springfield.

CAMP LYON. A temporary Civil War encampment at or near Geneva, Kane County, Camp Lyon was established in 1861.

CAMP MCALLISTER. A temporary Civil War encampment established at or near Cairo in 1861.

CAMP MCCLERNAND. After General Grant displaced General Benjamin M. Prentiss at Cairo in 1861 by appointing Brigadier General John Alexander McClernand to replace him, the area around the St. Charles Hotel near Cairo's point was named Camp McClernand.

FORT MCHENRY. Built by Captain William McHenry in the summer of 1812, the fort was located in what was then White County.

FORT MASSAC (*Fort Ascension*). Located on the north bank of the Ohio River, 38 miles from its confluence with the Mississippi, and 1 mile southeast of Metropolis, the original Fort Massac, first named Fort Ascension, was erected by the French in 1757 (completed on June 2), to prevent British encroachment into the lower Ohio Valley. The only known attack upon the fort was made in the fall of the same year by a large band of Cherokees. In 1759 and 1760, the fort was significantly rebuilt and renamed Fort Massiac in honor of the French minister of marine, the marquis de Massiac.

At the end of the French and Indian War, when the French ceded the region east of the Mississippi River, excepting New Orleans, to England, the French abandoned the fort. It was soon largely destroyed by Indians, and its ruins were left untouched by the British. In 1794

General Anthony Wayne rebuilt the fort to guard against Spanish aggression and slightly anglicized its French name to Fort Massac. During the following tumultuous score of years, the fort survived the confederated Indian uprising led by the great Tecumseh and his brother, the Shawnee Prophet, and became a popular stopover for an ever-increasing number of soldiers, travelers, and prospective settlers entering the Ohio River Valley. Around the fort there developed a settlement, now the town of Metropolis.

The fort and its surrounding ground were occupied by at least one regiment of infantry during the War of 1812. Evacuated at the end of the war, its small caretaking unit finally abandoned the fort in 1817. Some of its structures were stripped of their timbers to fuel the first steamboats on the Ohio River. Congressional investigations of fort sites between 1841 and 1844 resulted in the selection in 1850 of Fort Massac, completely renovated, as a factory-fort, with the addition of foundries and machine shops capable of producing a great assortment of supplies required by the nation's military and naval services.

During the Civil War, the fort was intermittently occupied by Federal troops. The old fort and its grounds remained neglected from 1864 to 1903, when little more than the site remained. The Daughters of the American Revolution undertook its preservation and made possible some reconstruction. The state of Illinois maintains the area now as a State Memorial.

CAMP MATHER. A temporary Civil War encampment established in 1861 at Chicago or its suburbs.

CAMP MATHER. A temporary Civil War encampment, Camp Mather was located at Shawneetown, Gallatin County, just west of the Ohio River.

CAMP MATHER. A temporary Civil War encampment established on Peoria's Fairgrounds in 1861, Camp Mather was most probably named for Thomas S. Mather, the Illinois adjutant general.

FORT MIAMIS. (*Fort des Miamis*). Reportedly a French trading post established shortly after the turn of the eighteenth century, it was located at the mouth of the Chicago River, on the site of modern Chicago.

FORT MONTEREY. A blockhouse fort probably erected during the first months of the War of 1812, Fort Monterey was reportedly located on the Illinois River 20 miles from its mouth in Calhoun County.

MOORE'S BLOCKHOUSE. A blockhouse fort used as an Indian defense was erected by George Moore on his farm in 1808 or soon after. It was located not far from the present town of Wood River in Madison County.

CAMP MULLIGAN. A temporary Civil War encampment situated in Chicago's suburbs.

FORT NAPER. Captain Joseph Naper and his brother, originally from Ashtabula, Ohio, erected a trading post in 1831 near the Du Page River. During the first days of the Black Hawk War the following year, the post was fortified as a haven for the inhabitants of the Naper Settlement, now the town of Naperville in Du Page County.

NAT HILL'S FORT. An Indian defense of this name was reportedly situated a few miles above the mouth of Goshen (Doza) Creek in St. Clair County.

FORT NONSENSE. Apparently a temporary defense, it was located at Joliet in Will County.

FORT OTTAWA. FORT JOHNSON.

FORT PAINE. FORT PAYNE.

CAMP PAROLE. A Civil War encampment located in Chicago or its suburbs.

FORT PATTON. In 1829 John Patton and his family, with the help of other whites and several Kickapoo and Delaware Indians, erected his cabin in the Pleasant Hill section of Lexington Township, southeast of the town of Lexington, in present McLean County. When it was built it is said there was not another house between it and Chicago, then consisting of Fort Dearborn and a few traders' cabins. In 1832, during the Black Hawk War, a blockhouse was erected 12 feet from the cabin, and in 1840 the original cabin and the blockhouse were joined together. Still in existence, the structure is being maintained by the McLean County Historical Society.

FORT PAYNE (*Fort Paine*). In order to additionally safeguard the inhabitants of the Naper Settlement, now Naperville in Du Page County, during the height of the Black Hawk War of 1832, General Henry Atkinson detailed a Captain Paine (Payne) of Joliet, with a company of 50 volunteers from Danville, to erect a fort there. They built a stockade of about 100 feet square, surrounded by pickets, with two loopholed, shingled blockhouses in diagonal corners. (See: FORT NAPER.)

FORT PEORIA. FORT ST. LOUIS NO. 2.

PIGGOTT'S FORT. This was "a blockhouse built by James Piggott and others, at the foot of the bluffs, in Monroe County, where the road from Waterloo to Cahokia, unchanged since then, crosses the rivulet, named by the early French inhabitants of the American Bottom, *Le Grand Ruisseau*, where it emerges from the bluffs, a mile and a half directly west of Columbia in that county" (Illinois State Historical Society, *Transactions for the Year 1902*, p. 204).

FORT PIMITOUI. FORT ST. LOUIS NO. 2.

PRAIRIE MARCOT BLOCKHOUSE. A blockhouse erected by Lieutenant John Campbell during the War of 1812, it was reportedly located on the west bank of the Illinois River about 19 miles above its mouth in present Calhoun County.

CAMP PRENTISS. FORT DEFIANCE.

FORT RAMSEY. Probably a blockhouse Indian defense, it was erected by members of the Ramsey family in 1811 or 1812, reportedly located in Wabash County.

CAMP REINBERG. A temporary World War I encampment, Camp Reinberg was located at or near Palatine, Cook County.

ROCK ISLAND ARSENAL. FORT ARMSTRONG.

ROCK ISLAND BARRACKS. FORT ARMSTRONG.

FORT RUSSELL. Many blockhouses were erected in Illinois during the War of 1812, most of them defenses against attack by the Indians who were allied with the British. There were at least 22 such blockhouse-forts between old Kaskaskia and Alton in Madison County, with the largest and strongest of them being Fort Russell, just northwest of present Edwardsville. The fort was built by Governor Ninian Edwards and named for Colonel William Russell of Kentucky, who commanded ten companies of Rangers, organized by an act of Congress, to defend the western frontier against the British and Indians. Four of these companies were allotted to the defense of Illinois. At least five cannon were removed from Fort Chartres to arm Fort Russell. The only Army regulars stationed at the fort were there during spring of 1812 and constituted the garrison for only a few months.

FORT STE. ANNE. Erected in 1719 by the French, Fort Ste. Anne was reportedly located somewhere between Kaskaskia and Cahokia, the two oldest communities in the state.

FORT ST. JOSEPH. FORT CHECAGOU.

FORT ST. LOUIS NO. 1 (*Fort St. Louis de Rocher; Fort St. Louis des Illinois*). After La Salle established Fort Crèvecoeur in January 1680 at Lake Peoria, he left it under the command of his trusted lieutenant Henri de Tonty while he returned north to obtain additional supplies. En route up the Illinois River, he noted along its southern bank a range of irregular sandstone bluffs, culminating in a natural abutment rising perpendicularly to a height of 126 feet and accessible on only one of its sides. La Salle immediately recognized it to be a veritable fortress. He did not forget the site.

In 1682, after his momentous voyage of discovery down the Mississippi to the Gulf of Mexico, he and Tonty with their party turned northward. Later, in December of the same year, he and Tonty met at a large Indian village near the present town of Utica on the north bank of the Illinois River, in today's La Salle County, nearly opposite the sandstone cliff, known to the Indians as Starved Rock (Le Rocher). La Salle determined to establish there a base for his administration and development of the upper Mississippi Valley. He put his men to work on a storehouse of stunted pines, surrounding it with a strong palisade of timbers which had to be laboriously dragged up the steep ascent of the bluff. The fort was completed during the winter. In honor of his king, La Salle named his stronghold Fort St. Louis, variously known also as Fort St. Louis du Rocher and Fort St. Louis des Illinois. By right of his royal patent or license, the explorer ruled the fort and its environs as a seigniory.

In 1687 La Salle was assassinated by one of his own followers along the Gulf Coast in Texas. With his death, the fate of Fort St. Louis on Starved Rock was sealed. Because of strong Iroquois pressure in the Illinois country, the fort was practically abandoned in 1691. Tonty, however, maintained some connection with the fort until 1702, although it was only intermittently occupied until then. French traders reportedly were residing on "Le Rocher," as it was called, in 1718. Charlevoix, passing here in 1721, found only ruined palisades. Thus the fort sank into oblivion. Today, about six miles west of Ottawa, Starved Rock State Park is dominated by the pinnacle of Starved Rock itself and preserves some of the sites of the Indian communities that clustered around the fort.

FORT ST. LOUIS DES ILLINOIS. FORT ST. LOUIS NO. 1.

FORT ST. LOUIS DU ROCHER. FORT ST. LOUIS NO. 1.

FORT ST. LOUIS NO. 2 (*Fort Pimitoui; Fort Illinois; Fort Peoria*). Commonly called Fort Pimitoui, and at times referred to in old regional histories as Fort Illinois and Fort Peoria, Fort St. Louis No. 2 was situated on the right bank of the river or lake, probably near the narrows at the head of lower Peoria Lake. It was erected during the winter of 1691–92 by Henry de Tonty and François Dauphin de La Forest, who had acquired the concession or charter formerly held by La Salle, assassinated in Texas in 1687. The French and Indians moved here from Starved Rock, site of the first Fort St. Louis. Pierre de Liette, who was here with his cousin, Tonty, wrote that the Indians were settled "at the end of the lake on the north shore." Jesuit Father Jacques Gravier reestablished here the Mission of the Immaculate Conception, not later than April 1693. Tonty and La Forest were deprived of their concession in 1702.

CAMP SCOTT. Established as a staging area in 1861, Camp Scott was located near the town of Freeport, Stephenson County, on the site of Freeport's present senior high school.

FORT SHERIDAN (*Camp Highwood*). Activated in 1887 in response to urgent requests of Chicago business leaders during labor unrest marked by violence, the post was established on the shore of Lake Michigan 25 miles north of the city. It was first occupied on November 8 by two companies of the 6th Infantry. Originally called Camp Highwood for the town adjacent to the post, it was designated Fort Sheridan in 1888 in honor of General Philip Sheridan, who died that year. The general, then Commander of the Army, had been sent here to restore order dur-

FORT SHERIDAN. (Courtesy of the U.S. Army.)

ing Chicago's labor riots. Fort Sheridan's tower, a famous landmark on the lake built in 1891 as a barracks, was originally 227 feet high, but after its complete renovation in 1940, its height was scaled down to 167 feet and used to store a huge water tank.

In 1917 Fort Sheridan became the site of a large training camp in addition to facilities for two officers' training camps. From 1918 to 1920, the post served principally as a general hospital for the rehabilitation of wounded soldiers. During World War II, Fort Sheridan's Reception Center processed about 500,000 men after a mobilization center was constructed on the southern part of the post. The first soldier to be discharged on the basis of accumulated overseas credit points was processed here on May 10, 1945. Fort Sheridan has been commanded by all ranks, from sergeant to major general. In addition to technical branches of the Army, infantry, cavalry, and artillery units have been stationed here.

CAMP SIGEL. A temporary Civil War encampment located in the suburbs of Chicago.

CAMP SKOKIE. A World War II military police and prisoner-of-war camp, Camp Skokie was located near the towns of Skokie and Glenview, just north of Chicago. A War Department release, dated September 19, 1945, listed the camp as surplus property as of November 15, 1945.

CAMP SMITH. A temporary Civil War encampment near Cairo.

CAMP SONG. A temporary Civil War encampment located in Chicago's suburbs.

STARKEY'S FORT. A blockhouse defense built by Hardy Council in 1813 in then White County.

FORT SUMTER. Named for the South Carolina Civil War fort, the site of this defense is now part of the town of Highland in Madison County. No data has been found to indicate date of establishment.

CAMP TANNER. A Spanish-American War training encampment activated in May 1898, it was located on the State Fair Grounds outside of Springfield and named in honor of Governor John R. Tanner. Troops trained here included the 1st Illinois Cavalry, a militia unit expanded from a battalion, and several regiments of infantry.

TANQUARY'S FORT. A blockhouse defense built by Captain William McHenry in the summer of 1812, it was located in then White County.

CAMP TAYLOR. A temporary Civil War encampment in or near Springfield.

FORT TAZEWELL. Probably erected in 1811 or 1812, it was named for the county and located at or near the town of Pekin.

FORT THOMAS. On or about May 20, 1832, during the Black Hawk War, two companies of Mounted Rangers entered Bureau County and built a blockhouse surrounded with barricades 15 feet high constructed of heavy timber slabs set in the ground. There were about 140 men in the battalion, and they remained here on duty until the war was over. The fort was named for

Henry Thomas on whose property it stood, four miles north of Wyanet.

FORT TOUGAS. In 1803 or 1804, Joseph Tougas (or Tugaw), a Frenchman, and his family emigrated from Vincennes, Indiana, to the site of present St. Francisville, Lawrence County, where he was its first permanent settler. In 1812 he built a stockaded fort on his property as an Indian defense. The enclosure was some 12 to 14 feet high, within which were a number of log dwellings for the use of neighboring families. In two diagonal corners of the stockade were watchhouses or blockhouses to command the surrounding area.

CAMP TYLER. Most probably a temporary Civil War encampment, Camp Tyler was located within or near Chicago.

VIEU FORT. FORT LA FOURCHE.

CAMP WEBB. A temporary Civil War encampment located in the suburbs of Chicago.

FORT WILBOURN (*Fort Deposit*). A supply depot and mobilization center for the processing of Illinois volunteers, Fort Wilbourn (also spelled Wilburn or Willburn) was erected in 1832 during the early days of the Black Hawk War. First called Fort Deposit, it was located on the south side of the Illinois River opposite Peru, La Salle County. Here, on June 16, 1832, Abraham Lincoln reportedly enlisted in the Mounted Rangers as a private. Lincoln was later appointed captain of a company that did not participate in any action against the Sauk Indians.

FORT WILKINSON. CANTONMENT WILKINSONVILLE.

CANTONMENT WILKINSONVILLE (*Fort Wilkinson*). Established in January 1801 at Metcalfe Landing on the right bank of the lower Ohio River, near its confluence with the Mississippi, in present Pulaski County, Cantonment Wilkinsonville (also known as Fort Wilkinson for General James Wilkinson) was intended to protect this frontier against French encroachment on American territory. Its situation, however, proved unhealthy and the post was abandoned in 1802.

FORT WILLARD. A temporary Civil War defense erected by Union troops, this fort was cited by a contemporary Springfield newspaper as being located near Camp Hayden at Muddy Creek.

FORT WILLIAMS. A War of 1812 blockhouse located on "the east side of Big Prairie" in what was then White County, the defense was erected by Aaron Williams in 1813.

WILSON'S FORT. An Indian defense erected during the War of 1812, Wilson's Fort was reportedly located in present Randolph County.

CAMP WOOD. A temporary Civil War encampment established in 1861 at or near the town of Quincy, Adams County.

FORT WOOD. A year after John Wood emigrated from Kentucky in 1809, he and his neighbors erected an Indian defense at or near Friendsville, near Lancaster, Wabash County.

CAMP YATES. A temporary Civil War encampment established very soon after the fall of Fort Sumter in South Carolina, Camp Yates occupied the Sangamon County Fair Grounds several miles west of Springfield. The camp organized and trained a number of Illinois regiments for service on the Union front in Missouri or at Cairo on the Mississippi River. Ulysses S. Grant served at Camp Yates as drill master and mustering officer. After farmers west of Springfield vehemently complained of the disappearances of their chickens, pigs, fruits, and vegetables, a new campsite was selected on Clear Lake and named Camp Butler, six miles northeast of the city. In August 1861 the troops were moved there. (See: CAMP BUTLER.)

FORT AIKMAN. An Indian defense, most probably a blockhouse, was erected in 1813 on John Aikman's property, located on the southwest quarter of section 10, township 2, range 7, in present-day Daviess County.

CAMP ALLEN. A Civil War encampment, occupied by various Indiana regiments, it was located southwest of the Main Street Bridge, opposite Swinney Park, in Fort Waynem, and named for the county.

CAMP ANDERSON. CAMP STILWELL.

CAMP ANDERSON. A temporary Civil War encampment occupied by the 13th Indiana Volunteers, it was located near Anderson in Madison County.

CAMP ANDERSON. A Civil War encampment established in March 1864 at Michigan City in LaPorte County, it was named for Colonel Edward Anderson and occupied by both infantry and cavalry regimental units.

CAMP ANDY JOHNSON (*Camp Joe Bright*). A Civil War training encampment, first called Camp Joe Bright, Camp Johnson was located at or near Jeffersonville on the Ohio River in Clark County.

ARMSTRONG STATION. Situated on the north bank of the Ohio River in what is now Clark County, at the mouth of Bull Creek, about 18 miles above Louisville, Armstrong Station was a blockhouse built here between 1786 and 1790 by Colonel John Armstrong to prevent Indian raiders from crossing the river at this point.

CAMP ATTERBURY. Established on March 6, 1942, as a temporary training post during World War II and named for Brigadier General William Wallace Atterbury, director of transportation in World War I, Camp Atterbury is located 30 miles south of Indianapolis near the town of Edinburg. Construction of the post began in February 1942, and by July troops were moving in. Ultimately, it became the largest training center in Indiana. On December 31, 1946, the camp was placed in inactive status, reactivated August 24, 1950, and inactivated again on June 30, 1954. The 31st Infantry Division was posted here from April 1952 until the camp closed, when the troops were moved to Fort Carson, Colorado. In 1958 Camp Atterbury was the Personnel Center of the Fifth Army Service Command. Today Camp At-

Indiana

terbury is an inactive post used for summer Army Reserve training.

BALLOW FORT. An Indian defense erected in 1812, Ballow Fort was situated in the northwest quarter of section 9, township 2, range 7, in Daviess County.

CAMP BATTELLE. FORT WILLIAM HENRY HARRISON.

CAMP BATTELLE DES ILLINOIS. FORT WILLIAM HENRY HARRISON.

FORT BEANE. The site of old Fort Beane, at Reynolds Street and S.R. 2, in Goshen, Elkhart County, was occupied by an uncompleted fortification begun sometime during the Black Hawk War. The plans for the Indian defense were drawn by Captain Henry Beane. The town's settlers gave up finishing the fort when their fears of an Indian attack proved groundless. The uncompleted structure remained a landmark in Goshen for many years.

FORT BENJAMIN HARRISON. Established by an act of Congress on March 3, 1903, Fort Benjamin Harrison remained nameless until 1906, when President Theodore Roosevelt named the installation after his predecessor and friend. Located about 12 miles northeast of downtown Indianapolis, the post was originally intended as a station for one regiment of infantry and laid out in the form of a large horseshoe, with a parade ground in the center bordered by barracks, headquarters, and bachelor officers' and married officers' quarters.

During World War I, the fort operated as an officers' training camp. Following that war, and until World War II, it was known as an infantry post, housing at one time or another the 10th, 11th, 20th, 23rd, 40th, 45th, and 46th Infantry regiments. During World War II, some 200,000 men were processed through the reception center and sent to other posts for basic training. In addition, the fort was home for the Finance Replacement Training Center, part of the Army Finance School, the Army Chaplain's School, a Cook and Baker's School, the Military Police Disciplinary Barracks, and a prisoner of war camp for German and Italian prisoners.

In June 1947 the fort was placed on the inactive list, and only a small housekeeping detachment remained until the Indiana Military District headquarters moved from Indianapolis in September. In 1948, the Army released control to the Air Force, and the name was changed to Benjamin Harrison Air Force Base. The 10th Air Force was headquartered here until 1950, when the Army regained control of the installation. Initial elements of the U.S. Army Finance Center moved here from St. Louis in early 1951 and ground was broken for Bldg. 1, the Army's largest administrative building. It was completed in 1953, and the remaining segments of the Finance Center moved here to take occupancy of the building.

Gates-Lord Hall was completed in 1957 to house the Adjutant General and Finance Schools. The Defense Information School joined them in 1965, having moved from Fort Slocum, New York. In 1973 the post was removed from the managerial control of the Continental Army Command and placed under the control of the newly organized U.S. Army Training and Doctrine Command (TRADOC), with the designation of the U.S. Army Administration Center. At the same time, the Adjutant General and Finance Schools were merged and became the U.S. Army Institute of Administration. In July 1980 the post was reorganized and renamed the U.S. Army Soldier Support Center. The Institute of Administration became the Institute of Personnel and Resource Management.

CAMP BLOOMINGTON. A temporary Civil War post established in June 1863 and occupied by the 71st Infantry, the camp was located at Labertews Grove, north of Bloomington in Monroe County.

FORT BOYD. During his campaign against Tecumseh and his Indian confederacy, five days before the Battle of Tippecanoe, General William Henry Harrison had a blockhouse built near the mouth of the Vermilion River, near present Waterman, Vermilion County, on November 2, 1810, and named it for one of his men, Colonel John Parker Boyd of the 4th Infantry.

FORT BRANCH. Built in the spring of 1811 as an Indian defense because of the threat of attack by bands of Tecumseh's hostiles, Fort Branch was a strong stockade enclosing two 30-by-40-foot two-story, loopholed blockhouses on opposite sides of the palisade. The fort, built across a branch of Pigeon Creek, was located near the present-day towns of Fort Branch and Princeton in Gibson County.

CAMP BRIDGELAND (*Camp Bullock*). Originally called Camp Bullock when it was established in November 1861, this Civil War training post was renamed for Colonel J. A. Bridgeland and located four miles north of Indianapolis on the banks of Fall Creek. The camp was first occupied by the 20th Infantry while it was being reorganized, later replaced by the 2nd Cavalry.

CAMP BULLOCK. CAMP BRIDGELAND.

BURNSIDE BARRACKS. A cantonment established in the outskirts of Indianapolis in the fall of 1862 as an Encampment of Instruction for a period of two weeks, the site was reoccupied in 1864 by the 28th Infantry, which established a hospital. The site is located at 7th and Tinker (now 16th) streets.

CAMP BUTLER. A temporary Civil War encampment named for Lieutenant Colonel T. H. Butler and located at Cannelton, Perry County, it was occupied from December 1862 to February 1863 by elements of the 5th Cavalry.

CAMP CARRINGTON (*Camp Murray*). Established in March 1862 as a temporary encampment named Camp Murray in the northwestern outskirts of Indianapolis, near present West 15th and Missouri streets, the site was reoccupied in 1864 as Camp Carrington, replacing Camp Morton as the major training ground for central Indiana regiments. It was considered the largest and best arranged camp in the state.

FORT CLARK. The settlement at Clarksville on the Ohio River, opposite Louisville, Kentucky, had as its nucleus a stockade called Fort Clark, presumably named for George Rogers Clark. Within a short distance of its protecting walls, the cabins of the settlers were clustered.

FORT COLEMAN. An Indian defense erected in 1812 south of Conner in Daviess County.

CAMP COLFAX. A temporary Civil War encampment, occupied August and September 1861 by the 9th Indiana Volunteers, it was located just outside the town limits of LaPorte, LaPorte County.

CAMP COLUMBUS. A temporary Civil War post occupied for the month of March 1864 as an organizational camp for the 120th Infantry.

CAMP EMERSON. A Civil War encampment named for Colonel Frank Emerson and located on the old State Fairgrounds at Madison, Jefferson County, it accommodated the 67th, 82nd, and 100th Infantry regiments.

FORT FINNEY. FORT STEUBEN.

FORT FLORA. An Indian defense erected by settlers in 1813 and named for David Flora, one of the original founders of the town of Washington, in present Daviess County, it occupied a site at the present intersection of Main and East Second streets.

CAMP FLOYD. CAMP NOBLE.

CAMP FREMONT. A temporary Civil War encampment named for General James Fremont, it was established in December 1863 in the vicinity of Fountain Square, east of Virginia Avenue and south of Prospect Street in Indianapolis. The 28th Colored Regiment was stationed there.

CAMP GIBSON. A temporary Civil War encampment located on the Fairgrounds in Princeton, Gibson County, Camp Gibson was occupied by the 58th and 65th Infantry Regiments from December 1861 to August 1862.

CAMP GILBERT. A temporary Civil War encampment, occupied September 1862 by Company B, 81st Infantry, it was located at Port Fulton, Clark County. The site of the camp may have been the location of the Jefferson General Hospital, opened February 1864 and closed the last of 1866.

CAMP GRAHAM. A temporary Civil War encampment named for Colonel F. W. Graham, it was located at or near Mt. Vernon, Posey County, and established in January 1863 for Company K, 5th Cavalry.

CAMP GRAY. This was a temporary Civil War post located eight miles from the city of Madison, on the Ohio River, in Jefferson County.

CAMP GREENCASTLE. A temporary Civil War encampment occupied during September 1861 by the 59th Infantry, it was located at or near the town of Greencastle in Putnam County.

CAMP HANOVER. A temporary Civil War encampment located six miles below the city of Madison on the Ohio River, Jefferson County.

CAMP HARRISON. A Civil War encampment, established probably on February 27, 1862, with the posting there of the 61st Infantry of Indiana Volunteers, it was located in or near Terre Haute.

CAMP HARRISON (*Camp McClellan*). A Civil War encampment originally called Camp McClellan for General George McClellan, it was temporarily occupied during June 1861 by the 8th, 10th, and 11th Infantry regiments. The site, at Irvington, near Indianapolis, was later reoccupied as Camp Harrison (named for Colonel T. J. Harrison) in August 1861 by the 39th Infantry and the 8th Cavalry.

CAMP HEFFREN. A temporary Civil War encampment named for Horace Heffren, it was established for the organization of the 50th Infantry in September 1861, located at Seymour, Jackson County. Horace Heffren was then a lieutenant colonel in the regiment. He resigned his commission, then became active in the Sons of Liberty (Knights of the Golden Circle), and finally was arrested and tried by the government.

CAMP HOLLOWAY. A temporary Civil War encampment established August 13, 1862, for the 4th Cavalry, at or near Indianapolis.

FORT HOPKINS. An Indian defense, built in the summer of 1810 near the old Archer Cemetery, northwest of the city of Princeton, Gibson County.

CAMP JOE BRIGHT. Camp Andy Johnson.

CAMP JOE HOLT. A temporary Civil War post in or near Indianapolis, it was most probably named for Secretary of War Joseph Holt under President Buchanan.

CAMP JOE HOLT. Located on the west side of Jeffersonville in Clark County, this major Indiana Civil War camping site was used by many regiments on their way south to the theaters of war. It was situated just above the Big Eddy on the Ohio River bank opposite Louisville. The historic camping ground extended back from Front Street to Todd Street, and north past Montgomery Street almost to the railroad and Cane Run Creek. It derived its name from General Joseph Holt, secretary of war under President Buchanan. Lovell H. Rousseau, a prominent lawyer of Louisville, accepted a colonel's commission from President Lincoln and began to organize his regiment across the river on Indiana soil. Rousseau, who later was promoted to major general, established the post at Jeffersonville and named it "Camp Joe Holt" for the prominent and eloquent Kentuckian. After the camp ceased to be used as a rendezvous, a hospital was established on the site and maintained until early in 1864. The camp, however, was used almost continually until the close of the war.

CAMP JOE WRIGHT. A temporary Civil War encampment established in November 1861 by the 36th Infantry, it was located on the Bright Farm outside Port Fulton in Clark County and named for the U.S. senator from Indiana.

FORT JONES. A frontier Indian defense erected in the spring of 1813, Fort Jones was located about a mile and a quarter south of the town of Washington in Daviess County.

KEKIONGA TRADING POST. A trading post established by the English about 1778 at an old Indian village, it was located at the head of the Maumee River near present Fort Wayne.

CAMP KIMBALL. A temporary Civil War encampment established in June 1861 and named for Colonel Nathan Kimball, it was located in or near Indianapolis.

CAMP KNOX. A Civil War encampment for recruits and training, Camp Knox was established in July 1861 on the old Fairgrounds near the present intersection of 2nd Street and Niblack Boulevard in Vincennes. The number of men encamped there varied from time to time from a mere squad to 15 full companies.

FORT KNOX. The defense of Vincennes from the time of the formation of the Northwest Territory until Indiana Territory became a state, Fort Knox occupied two and probably three sites in and about Vincennes. The first fort of that name was built by Major John Hamtramck, who came to Vincennes in July 1787 with General Josiah Harmar, who was then in command of U.S. troops stationed in the Northwest Territory. Hamtramck was left in command with orders to erect a fort there. His fort was located on the river on the north side of present Buntin Street and named in honor of General Henry Knox, then secretary of war.

This fort was maintained until 1803, when the government acquired title to 83 acres of land on a wooded knoll about three miles above Vincennes. The tract was purchased from Toussaint Dubois, a noted Indiana trader, for whom Dubois County was named. Here a new fort was built overlooking the river. Among the commanders of the fort was Captain Zachary Taylor, who was in and about Vincennes from 1811 to 1815. On March 16 of the latter year, his daughter Sarah Knox Taylor, was born in Vincennes. She afterwards became the first wife of Jefferson Davis. In 1812 Acting Governor of Indiana Territory John Gibson, was given orders to move the fort back to town. There was a controversy over the site to be selected, and just where it was finally placed is not known. In 1816 the garrison abandoned the new site, and all military stores that could be moved were taken to Fort Harrison at Terre Haute.

CAMP LAFAYETTE. A temporary Civil War encampment, established August 15, 1861, and occupied by the 4th Cavalry, the post was located in or near Indianapolis.

CAMP LAZ NOBLE. A temporary Civil War encampment named for Indiana's adjutant general, it was established in August 1862 on the Whitewater Canal on the east side of Lawrenceburg, Dearborn County.

LETTSVILLE BLOCKHOUSE. An Indian defense erected by settlers in about the year 1811, it was located on Prairie Creek in the present-day village of Lettsville, Daviess County. Many Lett descendants still reside in the county.

CAMP LEWIS. A temporary Civil War encampment named for Colonel Andrew Lewis, it was established in August 1862 near Evansville, Vanderburgh County.

CAMP LINSAY. A temporary Civil War post established in December 1863, it was located one-half mile south of Terre Haute on the road to Mt. Vernon.

CAMP LOGAN. A temporary Civil War encampment, it was established in December 1861 for the organization of the 46th Indiana Volunteers. Two contradictory locations have been given for its site: (1) near Bates and Franklin streets, and (2) at 3rd and Ottawa streets in Logansport, Cass County.

CAMP LOGAN. A temporary encampment established in August 1862 and occupied by the 68th Infantry, it was located at or near Greensburg, Decatur County.

CAMP MCCLELLAN. CAMP HARRISON.

FORT MIAMI. FORT WAYNE.

CAMP MITCHELL. A Civil War encampment named for U.S. Representative William Mitchell, it was an organizational camp for the 12th Cavalry and 129th Infantry established in the spring of 1863 and located at or near Kendallville in Noble County. The camp was active until the close of the war.

CAMP MORRIS. CAMP WALLACE.

CAMP MORRIS. A temporary Civil War encampment named for General Thomas Armstrong Morris, it was established September 1861 on the White River, on the south side of West Washington Street, in Indianapolis.

CAMP MORTON. Probably the largest and best known of Indiana's Civil War installations was Camp Morton, named in honor of Governor Oliver P. Morton. Occupying a 36-acre tract, formerly known as Henderson's Grove, which had been purchased by the state for its new fairgrounds, the post was established in April 1861 to receive and train the first Indiana volunteers. In February 1862 the installation was converted into a prison camp. Before it closed in June 1865 Camp Morton imprisoned more than 15,000 captured Confederate soldiers. The encampment was located on what was then the outskirts of Indianapolis, occupying land between present 19th and 22nd streets, and between Talbott and Delaware to Central Avenue.

CAMP MOUNT. A Spanish-American camp, it was established on the State Fairgrounds near Indianapolis on April 25, 1898. The men were housed in tents or barns belonging to the Fairgrounds. It was named for then Governor James A. Mount. The post occupied part of the Fairgrounds, which extends from 38th to 42nd streets and from the Monon Railroad, east of Winthrop, to the boulevard along Fall Creek.

CAMP MT. VERNON. A temporary Civil War encampment, it was established in 1861 on Mt. Vernon's old fairgrounds in Posey County.

CAMP MURRAY. CAMP CARRINGTON.

CAMP NOBLE (*Camp Floyd*). A temporary Civil War post, Camp Noble was an artillery camp on the northern limit of the city of Indianapolis. It occupied ground to the west of Camp Burnside and served as a training center for the 17th and 23rd Batteries.

CAMP OAK GLEN. A temporary Civil War discharge camp established in June, 1865, it was probably situated near the present intersection of West and Georgia streets in Indianapolis.

CAMP ORTH. A temporary Civil War encampment located near Battle Ground and Lafayette in Tippecanoe County, Camp Orth served as a training ground for the 104th and 116th Regiments of Indiana Volunteers.

FORT OUIATENON. A small but prosperous trading post established by the French in 1717, the first white settlement in present Indiana, Fort Ouiatenon was located on the west bank of the Wabash River opposite a large village of Wea Indians, near today's Lafayette in Tippecanoe County. The fort grew in importance to the French regime in Canada because of its key position between the regional capitals of Quebec and New Orleans. At its height, the fort and its surrounding villages possessed several thousand inhabitants.

In 1760 Fort Ouiatenon and all the other French posts in the Mississippi Valley and in French Canada were turned over to the British as a consequence of the last of the French and Indian Wars. But the British did not have the same friendly rapport with the local tribes that they had enjoyed during the French partnership. It was principally because of this reason that the fort's new commander, Lieutenant Edward Jenkins, had no defense against the effects of Chief Pontiac's widespread Indian rebellion. After two short years of British rule, Fort Ouiatenon fell in the course of the uprising. However, un-

FORT OUIATENON. Elevation and plan drawn in 1745. (Courtesy of the Public Archives of Canada.)

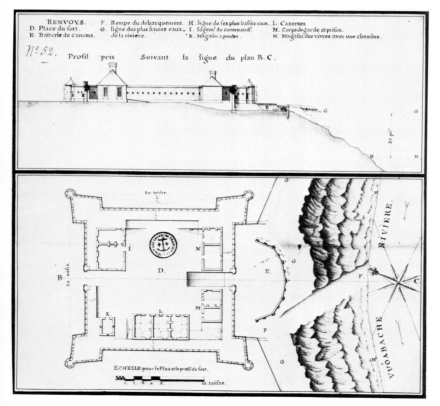

like many of the other posts taken during the war, Ouiatenon was captured without bloodshed and destruction. Its small garrison surrendered peacefully after Lieutenant Jenkins had been lured to one of the villages and there held hostage. It is said that the British were spared subsequent bodily harm only through the efforts of influential French settlers who had continued to trade in the region.

Fort Ouiatenon was later the scene of a council that would eventually bring an end to the hostilities. The stockade on the Wabash was never regarrisoned. Consequently, Ouiatenon was claimed by the French traders and trappers who had remained about the post with their Indian friends. The region, however, was nearly trapped clean by this time and the once lucrative trade diminished. During the American Revolution, the settlement witnessed some minor intrigues as the two principals in the conflict contended for the loyalties of its native inhabitants. George Rogers Clark easily took control of Ouiatenon from his base at Vincennes.

In the 1780s native unrest in the area was on the increase as white settlers encroached ever farther onto the frontier. The decaying stockade was used by Indians and British agents as a staging ground for raids on American settlements in Ohio and Kentucky. Continued attacks upon these new white enclaves caused President George Washington to wage an extensive military campaign in the Old Northwest. Finally, in 1791, after several disastrous defeats at the hands of the Indians, an expeditionary force under the command of General Charles Scott succeeded in destroying Ouiatenon and dispersing its inhabitants. The stockade, the surrounding villages, and the corn fields were all burned to the ground, depriving the Indians of homes and crops.

Periodic floodings of the Wabash would soon mask the charred remains of this formerly prosperous trading post. Lying buried in silt, Ouiatenon went unnoticed as later pioneers entered the region to found the city of Lafayette. Many claimed knowledge of the old fort's site along the river, but these reports were often confused and contradictory. In time, even these memories dimmed, and the exact location of Fort Ouiatenon was lost. In 1909 the local chapter of the Daughters of the American Revolution erected a monument along the South River Road, marking the ground on which the fort was then believed to have stood. Years later in 1930, Dr. R. B. Wetherill of Lafayette, having previously purchased this land, financed the construction of a replica blockhouse on the site. That structure still stands as the focal point of Fort Ouiatenon

Historic Park. Modern archaeological explorations, however, conducted after the middle of this century definitely located the site of the old French trading post.

FORT PALMER. An Indian defense erected in the spring of 1813, Fort Palmer was "built across Main Street, in the town of Washington," Daviess County.

FORT PATRICK HENRY. FORT VINCENNES.

CAMP PETTIT. A temporary Civil War encampment established August 1862 and named for Colonel J. U. Pettit, it occupied farmland south of the Wabash River, near the city of Wabash. The 75th Infantry was stationed here.

FORT PURCELL. An Indian defense, built in 1812, reportedly stood "in the Purcell neighborhood," Daviess County.

CAMP REYNOLDS. A temporary Civil War encampment established January 1862 and named for General Joseph J. Reynolds, the camp was garrisoned by the 53rd Regiment. It was located on the Jeff Snider farm near Rockport, Spencer County.

CAMP (JOE) REYNOLDS. A Civil War encampment established in 1862 and named for Major General Joseph J. Reynolds, it occupied ground lying between the canal and the White River, about a mile and a half from Camp Carrington, in Indianapolis. The 15th, 20th, and 99th Indiana Volunteers were trained here.

CAMP ROBINSON. A Civil War encampment named for Lieutenant Colonel W. J. Robinson, it was located on the west bank of the White River, occupying a site now at the south end of the Thomas Taggart Riverside Park on Cold Spring Road in Indianapolis. The 11th and 30th Infantry regiments were stationed here in September–October 1861. Sometime in 1864 the 11th Infantry reoccupied the camp to be reorganized.

CAMP ROSE. A temporary Civil War encampment occupying the old Fairgrounds near South Bend in St. Joseph County, it was named for Colonel David G. Rose. The camp was apparently used for the organization and training of the 73rd, 87th, and 99th Indiana Volunteers during August and October 1862.

CAMP ROSS. A temporary Civil War camp occupied by companies A, B, and I of the 83rd Infantry during August 1862, Camp Ross was located at or near Greensburg in Decatur County.

CAMP ROSS. A temporary Civil War camp occupied by Company C of the 39th Infantry during August 1861, it was located in or near Portland, Jay County.

CAMP RUSHVILLE. A temporary Civil War camp occupied by the 52nd Infantry during January 1862, it was located near Rushville, Rush County.

FORT SACKVILLE. FORT VINCENNES.

FORT ST. PHILIPPE. FORT WAYNE.

CAMP SAMPLE. A Civil War prisoner of war camp located near Lafayette in Tippecanoe County.

CAMP SCOTT. A temporary Civil War encampment named for General Winfield Scott, it was established sometime in 1861 for the training of the 1st Cavalry, and the 28th and 42nd Indiana Volunteer Infantry regiments. Its exact site near Evansville, Vanderburgh County, is not known.

CAMP (THOMAS A.) SCOTT. A 79-acre World War II encampment established on May 15, 1942, for the training of the 750th Railway Operating Engineer Battalion, it was named for Thomas Alexander Scott, fourth president of the Pennsylvania Railroad and organizer of the first military railroad service in the country. The camp was located at the southeast edge of Fort Wayne, opposite the International Harvester Company plant and between the trackage of the Pennsylvania Railroad and the road known as Wayne's Trace. On November 19, 1942, the 1564th Service Unit replaced the Engineer Battalion at the camp. On November 1, 1944, Camp Scott was converted to a prisoner of war camp. In a press release dated September 19, 1945, the War Department declared the camp surplus property as of November 15, 1945. In the summer of 1946, Camp Scott was converted to an emergency veterans' housing, which was closed October 15, 1949.

CAMP SHANKS. A Civil War installation named for Colonel J. P. Shanks in or near Indianapolis, Camp Shanks was open 1862–64 operating as either an organizational or training camp for the 6th, 7th, and 11th Cavalry.

CAMP SHERMAN. A temporary Civil War encampment named for General William T. Sherman, it was located east of Jeffersonville at Port Fulton, Clark County. The 36th Infantry was there during November 1861.

SMITH'S FORT. At the beginning of the War of 1812, settler George Smith converted his frontier cabin home into a fort as an Indian defense. It was located near Richmond in Randolph County.

FORT STEUBEN (*Fort Finney*). In 1786, in compliance with an order issued by Governor Patrick Henry of Virginia, Captain (Major) Walter Finney on August 12 evacuated his fort (Fort Finney, Ohio 1785) at the mouth of the Miami River on the Ohio, and moved his troops down the river to a point just below Louisville, Kentucky. Here on August 23 his men began to build a new Fort Finney on the north bank of the Ohio about three-quarters of a mile above the rapids. It was located in what is now the lower end of Jeffersonville in Clark County. The fort was renamed Fort Steuben in 1787 in honor of the Revolutionary War hero. Fort Steuben appears to have been a small, square-shaped work of timber and earth, with a deep trench cut from its south side to the river. This was covered with logs and earth, creating a tunnel through which water could be obtained and by which escape could be effectuated should the occasion arise. After the fort was abandoned in late 1791 by U.S. troops, it was garrisoned, apparently until sometime in 1793, by territorial militia.

CAMP STILWELL. A Civil War installation named for Colonel T. N. Stilwell and located at or near Kokomo in Howard County, Camp Stilwell was active 1863–64 and garrisoned by the 113th and 130th Infantry.

CAMP STILWELL (*Camp Anderson*). A temporary Civil War encampment first called Camp Anderson, then renamed for Colonel T. N. Stilwell, it was located on the grounds of the country club near Anderson, Madison County. Established in September 1861, it served as a training post for the 34th Indiana Volunteers.

CAMP STREIGHT. A temporary Civil War encampment named for Colonel A. D. Streight, it was located at the present intersection of Central Avenue and 11th Street in Indianapolis. It was opened October 1861 for the training of the 51st Indiana Volunteers.

CAMP SULLIVAN. A Civil War encampment named for its commandant, Colonel J. C. Sullivan, it was located on the old Fairgrounds, now the Military Park in Indianapolis. Occupying the site of a Mexican War Camp, it was opened first as a camp of rendezvous for the first regiments in 1862, then became the training camp for men drafted into service. It remained a draft camp for two years.

CAMP (BILL) TAYLOR. A temporary Civil War encampment named for Captain William Taylor of Company E, 10th Infantry, and activated September 1861, it was located on West Washington Street (near Camp Morris) in Indianapolis.

CAMP TIPPECANOE. One of the few Indiana camps to be active throughout most of the Civil War (1861–64), Camp Tippecanoe was located south of 4th and Kossuth streets in Lafayette, Tippecanoe County. It served as a training ground for at least seven Indiana Volunteer Regiments and one artillery battery. A new cast aluminum marker was erected in 1979 to mark its site at the top of the 4th Street hill to replace the one that had been stolen in 1973.

FORT TURMAN. A blockhouse defense erected in 1810 by Benjamin Turman soon after he and his family had emigrated from Virginia, Fort Turman was located near Big Springs in the vicinity of present Sullivan in Sullivan County. A citation reports that Turman's blockhouse was used as a temporary command post by General William Henry Harrison during his march northward to the Battle of Tippecanoe.

CAMP VAJEN. A temporary Civil War encampment named for John H. Vajen, Indiana quartermaster general (1861–62), Camp Vajen was probably located on the site of the present Vajen Building on Meridian Street, in Indianapolis. The camp was activated July 1861 and occupied by the 21st Regiment.

CAMP VALPARAISO. A temporary Civil War installation, it was located on the Fairgrounds at Valparaiso, Port County, for the reorganization of the veterans of the 9th Infantry, in February 1864.

CAMP VANDERBURGH. A Civil War training encampment located at Evansville's Old Fairgrounds, on Pigeon Creek, Vanderburgh County, it was active 1861–62 and occupied by the 25th and 42nd Regiments.

CAMP VIGO. Located in Terre Haute, this temporary Civil War training camp was active circa 1862. It was named for Francisco Vigo, an early settler.

FORT VINCENNES (*Fort Sackville; Fort Patrick Henry*). The oldest town in Indiana, Vincennes still retains remnants of its French inheritance. The date of its initial settlement is not known, but a French trading post may have been located at the site as early as 1683. It is definite, however, that settlers were residing there by 1727. Francois-Marie Bissot, sieur de Vincennes, was commissioned to construct a fort there, as part of a chain of posts to counteract the expansion of the English. He completed his fort on the east bank of the Wabash River in 1732. It was then variously known as Au Poste, Post Ouabache (Wabash), and Post St. Francis Xavier. Vincennes led an expedition against the Mississippi Chickasaws but was captured and burnt at the stake on Palm Sunday, 1736. To honor his memory, the town was renamed Vincennes and the fort designated Post St. Vincennes or Fort Vincennes.

After the French and Indian War, the British took over the settlement and occupied the small French fort, by this time quite dilapidated. During the Revolution, the British, acknowleding the threat posed by Colonel George Rogers Clark's victories at Cahokia and Kaskaskia, sent Lieutenant Governor (Colonel) Henry Hamilton from Detroit to Vincennes. He found it lacking a well, barracks, platform for small arms, or even a lock to the gate. Over the winter he built a guardhouse and barracks for four companies, sunk a well, erected two large blockhouses with loopholes and embrasures mounted with 5 cannon each. The new fort, completed in February 1779, was an 11-foot-high stockaded quadrangle: the side next the river was 275 feet in length; the side facing the village's main street was 190 feet; the side fronting the church 210 feet; and the side facing the southwest, 150 feet. Hamilton named the strong work Fort Sackville in honor of George Sackville, better known as Lord Germain, British secretary of state, and planned in the spring to destroy Clark and his army of frontiersmen.

Colonel Clark, however, accomplished the unexpected by taking his miniscule army on a 160-mile march in the dead of winter, undergoing multiple hardships in the wilderness, and surprised the British garrison at Vincennes, forcing Hamilton to surrender on February 25. Clark, in possession of Vincennes, renamed the British defense Fort Patrick Henry for the governor of Virginia. In recognition of Clark's exploits and the winning of the Old Northwest, an imposing national memorial was erected on the site of the fort, dedicated June 14, 1936, by President Franklin D. Roosevelt.

CAMP WABASH. A Civil War encampment named for the county in which it was located, Camp Wabash, open 1862–65, was the training ground for the 89th, 101st, 118th, and 153rd Indiana Volunteer regiments.

FORT WABASH. A number of references have been found to indicate the presence of a French palisaded fort at the junction of the Wabash and Ohio rivers, in present Posey County. Some historical authorities cite an approximate date of 1750 but, in aggregate, the references are contradictory and inconclusive.

CAMP WALLACE (*Camp Morris*). Originally named for General T. A. Morris, this short-lived Civil War encampment accommodated the 10th and 11th regiments during April–May 1861, and was located at the foot of what is now Reitz Hill, in Evansville, Vanderburgh County. A reference indicates that the camp was moved from Camp Morris to Camp Wallace on May 15, pointing to two locations, because the former was swampy. Camp Wallace was named for Colonels Lew and John Wallace.

CAMP WAYNE. A temporary Civil War encampment established July 1862 for the 19th Battery, Camp Wayne, named for the county, was located at or near Cambridge City.

CAMP WAYNE. A large Civil War encampment named for the county, it was located on the old Fairgrounds, now the Bellview area, south of the city of Richmond. Active May 1861–64, it served as a training center for the 5th, 16th, 36th, 57th, 69th, 74th, and 124th regiments.

FORT WAYNE (*Fort St. Philippe; Fort Miami*). For nearly a century and a half, the place where the St. Marys and St. Joseph rivers join to form the Maumee River, 150 miles southeast of Chicago, was one of the most strategically important in the American Midwest. It was the center of a great system of waterways connecting Canada and the Great Lakes with the Mississippi Valley. By utilizing the 9-mile-long portage between the Maumee and the Little River, which flows into the Wabash, explorers, traders, and military men were able to journey almost 2,500 miles through the center of the continent from

Canada to New Orleans, with the only other major portage, 14 miles long, at Niagara Falls.

Historians still differ regarding the time of the establishment of the first French fortification on the site of the present city of Fort Wayne, known for a long period as Post (Fort) Miami or Fort St. Philippe. Possibly as early as 1680 the French had a trading post on the right bank of the St. Marys, converted into a military post in 1722. The site is now occupied by the Sherman Avenue Bridge. Throughout America's frontier history there has been a proliferation of same-name fortifications to perplex and exasperate historians and archivists. Fort Miami is a case in point. There were at least five forts in the Old Northwest Territory named Fort Miami or Miamis.

Four trading/military posts—two French and two American—were built within the present geographical limits of the city of Fort Wayne. The site of the original Fort Miami, located near the ruins of the old aqueduct, was abandoned for a location on the east bank of the St. Joseph River at Delaware Avenue and St. Joseph Boulevard. This new French fort, erected in 1750, was the post surrendered to the British in 1760 shortly before the close of the French and Indian War.

The first American post, built in 1794 and named for Anthony Wayne after his victory at Fallen Timbers, was located across the St. Marys from the old Miami village of Kekionga and the remains of old Fort Miami, at the present intersection of Clay and Berry streets. The rapidly constructed fort was gradually improved and enlarged within the next half dozen years and served until 1815, successfully withstanding an Indian siege in 1812. During the winter of 1815–16, a new and much more commodious Fort Wayne was built on an adjoining tract of land, the site of which is in Old Fort Park at Main and Clay streets. This post was abandoned in 1819. The last remaining original structure was occupied by nameless human derelicts until it was torn down in 1852.

Through the dedicated efforts of many of Fort Wayne's citizens, the fort has been reconstructed on a plot of ground less than a quarter of a mile from the original site. The reconstruction is a faithful recreation of the post erected by American troops under the command of Major John Whistler in 1815–16, "perhaps the most sophisticated all-wooden fort ever built in North America." The structures within this reproduction consist of the enlisted men's barracks (a museum), officers' quarters, north blockhouse, commanding officer's residence, hospital storehouse, magazine, south blockhouse, and the post gardens.

FORT WILLIAM HENRY HARRISON (*Camp Battelle; Camp Battelle des Illinois*). After Shawnee Chief Tecumseh left on August 5, 1811, with a party of 24 warriors on his mission to the south to expand his confederacy, General William Henry Harrison congregated his force of 1,000 Army, militia and volunteers, and sent them 65 miles up the Wabash River from Vincennes to the Indian town of Battelle des Illinois, near present Terre Haute. On October 6 the general joined his troops encamped on a bluff overlooking the river and put them to work on a 150-foot-square palisaded fort with two-story blockhouses in three of its four angles, as part of his campaign against Prophetstown at Tippecanoe, occupied by Tecumseh's brother and his warrior disciples. When the fort was completed on October 28, the troops named the defense for their commander.

Ten days later Harrison's army and the Shawnee Prophet's warriors were engaged in the Battle of Tippecanoe. Although the Americans suffered heavy losses, the Indians were decisively defeated. In early September 1812, Fort Harrison was attacked by a sizable party of Indians under Tecumseh. The fort's small garrison, crippled by sicknesses, was effectively commanded by Captain Zachary Taylor. Despite one of the fort's blockhouses being burned to the ground, the Indians were sent into full retreat when the garrison was reinforced by Kentucky militia troops. Fort Harrison was finally abandoned in 1818 after peace was established in the region.

CAMP WOOD. A temporary Civil War encampment, probably located in the suburbs of Indianapolis, was established in July 1861 and named for the 17th Regiment's mustering officer, T. J. Wood.

CAMP ATKINSON. FORT ATKINSON.

FORT ATKINSON (*Camp Atkinson*). Established May 31, 1840, on the left bank of the Turkey River above today's town of Fort Atkinson in Winneshiek County, Fort Atkinson was intended to both speed the enforced migration of the Winnebago Indians from Wisconsin and to protect them from the Sioux, Sac and Fox, on their new reservation in the river valley. The post was established by Captain Isaac Lynde, 5th Infantry, in compliance with an order of Colonel Henry Atkinson, 6th Infantry, who commanded the department. During the summer and autumn months of that year, heavy loads of building materials were hauled by teams of horses, mules and oxen some 50 miles from Prairie du Chien to the site selected for the planned fort. By the following spring, the complex of erected buildings assumed the form of a substantial fortification.

Originally a camp during its construction period, the new post was designated Fort Atkinson in 1841. To effectively keep the Winnebago from wandering back to their ancestral homes in Wisconsin, a company of Dragoons arrived on June 24, 1841, to supplement the fort's infantry garrison. In 1846, when the post's garrison accompanied Colonel Watts Kearny of the 1st Dragoons on the expedition to Santa Fe, Fort Atkinson was partially regarrisoned by volunteers. The fort was abandoned on February 24, 1849, after the Winnebago were moved to a new reservation in north central Minnesota. In 1853 the post's buildings were sold at public auction for $3,521. Then, in 1860 the military reservation was turned over to the Interior Department. Today's five-acre Fort Atkinson State Park on the bluff overlooking the Turkey River includes a part of a two-story barracks, officers' quarters, blockhouse, and magazine, all restored from Fort Atkinson's original complex.

FORT BELLEVUE. FORT MADISON.

CAMP BLACK HAWK. A temporary Civil War cavalry training camp, it was located near Davenport in Scott County.

CAMP BURNSIDE. A temporary Civil War recruiting and assembly post for the 23rd Infantry, with most of its members from Polk, Story, and Dallas counties, Camp Burnside was active for a short period during the fall of 1862, located near Des Moines.

CEDAR FORT. REDWOOD POST.

Iowa

CHEROKEE BLOCKHOUSE. This Indian defense, most probably built at the expense of the town's inhabitants, was erected in 1862, shortly after the Sioux massacre at New Ulm, Minnesota. The town of Cherokee's blockhouse was built of one-foot-square timbers and sheathed with walnut shingles.

FORT CLARKE. FORT DODGE.

CORRECTIONVILLE STOCKADE. An Indian defense erected shortly after the Sioux massacre at New Ulm, Minnesota, it was most probably built at the expense of Correctionville's settlers. This Woodbury County fort, with a stockade of split logs enclosing buildings of foot-square heavy timbers, boasted a 60-foot-deep well lined with hackberry wood.

CAMP CORSE. Most probably a temporary encampment established sometime in 1909 near Des Moines, it was named in honor of Brigadier General John Murry Corse, the hero of the Battle of Allatoona Pass during the Civil War.

COUNCIL BLUFFS BLOCKHOUSE (*Camp Kearn(e)y*). In 1837 Potawatomi Indians were moved into Council Bluff's environs, and a troop of Dragoons under Captain D. B. Moore, in compliance with Colonel Stephen W. Kearny's orders, established a blockhouse, named for their commander, in August of the same year to protect them from the Sioux (another citation reports it was established by Kearny's Dragoons in the spring of 1838). The soldiers occupied the blockhouse until November when they were ordered to Fort Leavenworth. The following year, Father Pierre Jean de Smet arrived on May 31, and for the next three years conducted a mission, using the blockhouse as a church, after Colonel Kearny granted him unrestricted occupation of the defense for his work. The site, at East Broadway and Union Street in the city of Council Bluffs, is marked by a large boulder and a bronze tablet.

FORT CROGHAN (*Camp Fenwick*). Five years after Captain D. B. Moore built a blockhouse on the site of Council Bluffs (see: COUNCIL BLUFFS BLOCKHOUSE), another federal post was established on May 31, 1842, on the left bank of the Missouri, midway between the mouths of the Boyer River and Mosquito Creek, near the southwest corner of the present city of Council Bluffs. Intended to prevent hostilities between the Potawatomi and Sioux Indians and the trafficking of whisky, it was established by Captain John H. K. Burgwin, 1st Dragoons. Originally

designed as a temporary post, it was first called Camp Fenwick for Colonel John Roger Fenwick, 4th Artillery, then renamed Fort Croghan in November, in honor of Colonel George Croghan, one of the two Army's inspector generals. Spring floods forced the abandonment of the fort's buildings, but troops remained in the vicinity until the fall of 1843, when they departed for Fort Leavenworth.

FORT DEFIANCE (*Fort Ingham*). Erected shortly after the bloody Sioux Minnesota uprising in August 1862, Fort Defiance was located on the west fork of the Des Moines River at the town of Estherville in Emmet County. It was established by Captain William H. Ingham with troops of the Northern Iowa Border Brigade, for whom the substantially built defense, the largest in the region during the emergency, was later renamed. The fort was garrisoned by Army troops during 1863–64 in compliance with orders of Brigadier General Benjamin Alvord. The Sioux, pursued by strong volunteer columns, with the aid of federal troops, retreated westward into the Dakotas, giving up intentions of crossing the state line into Iowa territory. More popularly remembered as Fort Defiance, the fortification, a 132-foot-square strong stockade enclosing portholed shingle-roofed buildings with black walnut sidings, included a large barracks and a guardhouse. In recent years a 53-acre area, including the site of the old fort, was set aside as the Fort Defiance State Park, and a replica of the post stands at its entrance.

CAMP DES MOINES. FORT DES MOINES NO. 1.

FORT DES MOINES NO. 1 (*Camp Des Moines*). Established May 19, 1834, and located on the Mississippi River a few miles above the mouth of the Des Moines River at Montrose in Lee County, Fort Des Moines was intended to supervise the Sac and Fox Indians and prevent encroachment by whites on their lands. On a site selected by 1st Lieutenant George H. Crosman, 6th Infantry, the post was established by Lieutenant Colonel Stephen Watts Kearny, 1st Dragoons. Originally a camp, the post was designated a fort in 1835, with its name selected by Secretary of War Lewis Cass. Abandoned in 1837, with its last troops leaving on June 1, the post's buildings were sold to private individuals, and the town of Montrose grew up around its site. A granite boulder with an affixed bronze tablet now marks the site of the old barracks.

FORT DES MOINES NO. 2 (*Fort Raccoon*). Established on May 20, 1843, the second Fort Des Moines was located at the junction of the Des Moines and Raccoon rivers, at the present city of Des Moines, for the purpose of preventing whites from overrunning the lands of the Sac and Fox Indians. The post, established by Captain James Allen, 1st Dragoons, was named Fort Raccoon by the captain, but the War Department disallowed the name and the fort was designated Fort Des Moines by Major General Winfield Scott. Gradual abandonment of the fort began early in 1846 as the troops escorted the Sac and Fox Indians to their new reservation in Missouri according to treaty stipulations. On March 10 or 12, the post's last troops were withdrawn for service in the Mexican War.

FORT DES MOINES NO. 3. Located four miles south of the site of Fort Des Moines No. 2 and centered around the present intersection of Army Post Road and Southwest 9th Street, the land for the third Fort Des Moines was contributed by the city in 1900 to the Federal government for the establishment of a cavalry post, authorized on April 4, 1900. Construction of brick buildings (some intact to this date) was immediately begun on a treeless pasture. Formal dedication took place on November 13, 1903, after it was named to perpetuate the memory of old Fort Des Moines.

Two companies of Negro infantrymen were the first occupants of the new fort. Later, elements of the 2nd, 6th, and 11th Cavalry were stationed there until World War I. In June 1917 the post became an Officers Training School for Negro troops. In 1918 the fort was converted into a base hospital for convalescing soldiers. From 1920 until World War II, the 14th Cavalry shared the post with a Field Artillery unit. In 1942 Fort Des Moines became the first training center for the Women's Army Auxiliary Corps (WAAC), later the Women's Army Corps (WAC), and became famous as its home. More than 170 new buildings were constructed to house the 65,000 enlisted women and 7,000 officers trained there. In May 1946 Fort Des Moines officially ceased to exist as an Army installation to become a temporary housing project. In 1958 however, the U.S. Army regained possession of the fort. Today occupied by the Iowa Sector of the XIV Army Corps, Fort Des Moines is mainly a U.S. Army Reserve Training Center, also used as a facility for several government military agencies.

DES MOINES RIVER POST. In 1838 Nicollet established an American Fur Company trading post between two lakes that he designated "Tchan Hassan Lakes," apparently located in Emmet County.

CAMP DISAPPOINTMENT (*Camp No. 4*). During the early summer of 1861, Colonel Grenville M. Dodge, commander of the 4th Iowa Infantry, established Camp Kirkwood near the outskirts of Council Bluffs. News of a Confederate troop invasion influenced the colonel to organize an expedition. As the infantrymen moved southward toward the Missouri border, they established camps along the route. Camp No. 1 was pitched on a slope near Brush Creek in Fremont County. Camp No. 2 was near Sidney; Camp No. 3, 25 miles to the east; and Camp No. 4, at Clarinda in Page County, where it was learned that the column of Missouri troops had disbanded. The apparent futility of the march led the Iowa soldiers to rename their post Camp Disappointment. Later, the 4th Iowa Regiment was transferred to Rolla, Missouri, where the Federals retrenched after the Battle of Wilson's Creek, abandoning a huge section of the state to the Confederates.

CAMP DODGE. A Civil War recruiting and training encampment for the 29th Iowa Infantry, it was established by Colonel Thomas H. Benton, Jr., and named in honor of Colonel Grenville M. Dodge. Camp Dodge was located a little south of Camp Kirkwood, on the outskirts of Council Bluffs.

CAMP DODGE. A World War I encampment established on the site of the former Iowa National Guard's campgrounds at Herrold, about 12 miles northwest of Des Moines, the post was named Camp Dodge in honor of Civil War Major General Grenville M. Dodge by Secretary of War Newton D. Baker. Formally opened in August 1917 as a training camp for the 88th Division, Camp Dodge had a capacity for about 42,000 men, chiefly from Iowa, central Illinois, Minnesota, and North Dakota. On December 3, 1918, the camp was designated as a demobilization center.

FORT DODGE (*Fort Clarke*). Established on August 2, 1850, by Captain Samuel Woods, 6th Infantry, Fort Dodge was located on the east bank of the Des Moines River opposite the mouth of Lizard Creek, near the present town of Fort Dodge. First named Fort Clarke for Colonel Newman S. Clarke, 6th Infantry, the post was designated Fort Dodge for Colonel Henry Dodge. It was intended to suppress the thieving activities of the Sioux Indians in the area. The post was abandoned on June 1, 1853. In 1854 William Williams, the fort's former sutler, bought the post barracks and the surrounding site and laid out the town of Fort Dodge.

CAMP ELLSWORTH. The first Civil War encampment in Iowa was established in May 1861, located just north of the town of Keokuk in Lee County, on more than 200 acres of land. Men of the 1st Iowa Infantry were mustered into service there on May 14, 1861.

CAMP FENWICK. FORT CROGHAN.

CAMP FRANKLIN (*Camp Union*). A Civil War encampment established in August 1861, by Colonel Addison H. Sanders, it was located just southwest of Dubuque "at the upper end of the bottom land adjoining Lake Peosta." First called Camp Union, the post was renamed Camp Franklin about a year. The camp was apparently discontinued sometime in early January of 1863.

CAMP FREMONT. In 1861 the old Johnson County Fairgrounds, today a part of the Iowa City airport, was occupied by Camp Fremont, the Civil War assembly point for the 10th Iowa Infantry.

CAMP HALLECK. A Civil War encampment established at 5th and Johnson streets in Keokuk sometime in 1861, it was occupied by the Iowa 15th Infantry until March 25, 1862, when it embarked on the *Jeanie Deans* for its new quarters at Benton Barracks at St. Louis, Missouri.

CAMP HARLAN. CAMP MCKEAN.

HART'S BLUFF POST. Early in the history of Council Bluffs, it was known as Hart's Bluff, named for a white man of unknown origin, who according to tradition traded with the Indians at this point before 1824. Francis Guittar settled permanently on the site in 1827 when he was appointed agent of the Hart's Bluff Trading Post of the American Fur Company.

CAMP HENDERSHOTT. A temporary Civil War post established as a rendezvous for the 6th and 7th Iowa Cavalry regiments, Camp Hendershott was established on October 10, 1862, and located between 13th and Locust and Ripley and Scott streets in Davenport, Scott County.

CAMP HERRON. A temporary Civil War encampment established on August 25, 1862, to accommodate the 31st and 32nd Infantry Regiments, Camp Herron was located "in Le Claire's addition between Farnam Street and Churchill's addition" near Davenport, Scott County.

CAMP (JOE) HOLT. A temporary Civil War established on September 23, 1861, on the old Fairgrounds at Davenport, between 13th Street and Northern Avenue (Kirkwood Boulevard), Perry and Rock Island streets, Camp Holt was used as a rendezvous area for the 2nd Cavalry.

FORT INGHAM. FORT DEFIANCE.

IOWA LAKE STOCKADE. Very soon after the disastrous massacre perpetrated by the Sioux at New Ulm, Minnesota, during the summer of 1862, Iowa's settlers made hurried preparations to withstand an Indian invasion. Blockhouses and fortified stockades were erected, and volunteers, soon known as the Northern Iowa Brigade, were organized for the state's defense. At Iowa Lake in Emmet County, citizens constructed a formidable defense.

The seven buildings . . . were made of rough timber . . . built in a row extending for 160 feet along the west end of the enclosure. Stables containing two tiers of stalls . . . formed the east side. On the north was a sod fence eight feet high and five feet thick at the base, with portholes. On the south was a fence of upright timbers, with a gate. Bastions at the northwest and southwest corners completed the stronghold. [Jacob A. Swisher, *Iowa: In Times of War*]

CAMP JOHN A. T. HULL. A temporary encampment established in September, 1910, by Brigadier General Fred A. Smith on the outskirts of Des Moines, Camp Hull's last post return was dated October 1, 1910. The short-lived post accommodated elements of infantry, cavalry, field artillery, and the Corps of Engineers, aggregating 2,108 men.

CAMP KEARNEY. CAMP MCCLELLAN.

CAMP KEARN(E)Y. COUNCIL BLUFFS BLOCKHOUSE.

CAMP KINSMAN (*Camp Roberts*). A Civil War training encampment for the 8th and 9th Cavalry established in July 1863, it was first named Camp Roberts for General B. S. Roberts, commandant of the camp, then later renamed Camp Kinsman. The post was located on Duck Creek near the Oakdale Cemetery at Davenport in Scott County. After the camp's closing, its buildings were used for the establishment of the Iowa

Soldiers' Orphan Home at 2800 Eastern Avenue, where a stone marks the site of the old camp.

CAMP KIRKWOOD. A temporary Civil War encampment established in the summer of 1861 by Colonel Grenville M. Dodge, commanding the 4th Iowa Infantry, Camp Kirkwood was located on the outskirts of Council Bluffs north of Mosquito Creek.

CAMP KIRKWOOD. A temporary Civil War recruiting encampment established in September 1862, at or near the town of Clinton, in the county of the same name, Camp Kirkwood accommodated elements of the 26th Iowa Infantry, who drilled there under the command of Colonel Milo Smith. After a relatively short training period, the troops were moved to St. Louis and then to Helena.

CAMP LAUMAN. A temporary Civil War recruiting and training encampment established for troops of the 34th Infantry, Camp Lauman was located near the town of Burlington in Des Moines County. Established in the late summer and occupied until October 15, a period of two months, Camp Lauman was scourged by a measles epidemic that sickened more than 600 men.

CAMP LINCOLN. On August 11, 1862, Adjutant General N. B. Baker announced the establishment of several new camps, one of which was Camp Lincoln at Keokuk in Lee County, first occupied by the 19th Iowa Infantry. After that unit was moved to the south, the camp was occupied by the 30th and 36th Infantry in turn. In the fall of the same year, a smallpox epidemic at the camp took the lives of about 100 men of the 36th Iowa.

CAMP MCCLELLAN (*Camp Kearney*). Camp McClellan, established August 8, 1861, was the most important of five camps in the Davenport area, since it was located near the Mississippi, which provided southward transportation. The 8th, 11th, 13th, 14th, and 16th Iowa Infantry regiments regularly rendezvoused here.

Partitioned by a fence from the post proper on its north side, Camp Kearney was a stockade established in early December 1863 in compliance with General John Pope's orders for the confinement of the Sioux Indians who participated in the massacre at New Ulm, Minnesota, in 1862. The Indians were apparently housed there for the remainder of the war. Camp McClellan was active throughout the Civil War years, and many Iowa troops were mustered out of service there. Its site, now within Davenport's city limits, is maintained as a park area.

CAMP MCKEAN (*Camp Harlan*). A temporary Civil War rendezvous encampment for the 4th Iowa Cavalry, Camp Harlan was activated in October 1861 at Mount Pleasant in Henry County. The 4th Cavalry remained here until February 22, 1862, when it was moved to St. Louis. In the fall of 1862, the 25th Iowa Infantry used the Mount Pleasant campsite, which was then named Camp McKean, until early in November when these troops were moved to the south. Some time after their departure, the barracks burned down. The site of the camp is now marked by a boulder and bronze tablet.

CAMP MCKINLEY. During the war with Spain, 1898–99, the Fair Grounds at Des Moines, deeded to the state on June 26, 1885, were used for the mobilization of the National Guard. Four regiments—the 49th, 50th, 51st, and 52nd infantries—rendezvoused at the camp. Altogether 5,859 Iowans were mustered in or trained at Camp McKinley.

FORT MADISON (*Fort Bellevue*). The first fortified structure erected on Iowa soil, Fort Madison was established on September 26, 1808, on the west bank of the Mississippi River on the site of the present city of Fort Madison. Intended to control the Sac and Fox Indians and to serve as a government Indian factory or trading post, the fort was established by 1st Lieutenant Alpha Kingsley and troops of the 1st Infantry from the St. Louis garrison, and named for then Secretary of State James Madison. The post was sometimes referred to as Fort Bellevue. Throughout the post's existence, its garrison was harassed by the Indians of the upper Mississippi, who considered the fort a violation of their treaty rights. On the night September 3, 1813, during the War of 1812, Fort Madison was under heavy Indian attack. Unable to obtain reinforcements and low on provisions, the troops secretly dug a trench from one of the blockhouses to the river close by where the boats of the garrison were tied. The post was hurriedly abandoned that night and was burned by the departing garrison. All that remained of the fort was a blackened chimney, which became known as the Lone Chimney in Iowa history. The chimney was reconstructed and now stands on its original location between the river and U.S. 61.

FORT MARIN. A trading post built about the year 1739 by Paul de la Marque, sieur Marin, it

FORT MADISON. A plan of the fort superimposed on a view of the site as it appears today. (Courtesy of the W. A. Sheaffer Pen Co., Fort Madison.)

was located opposite the mouth of the Wisconsin River, in present Clayton County.

CAMP NO. 4. CAMP DISAPPOINTMENT.

PETERSON FORT. A defense erected by the settlers of Peterson in Clay County shortly after the massacre at New Ulm, Minnesota, in 1862, it was intended to protect the town from Sioux invasion. The blockhouses and officers' quarters were built of oak and ash timbers 10 inches square, roofed with maple boards.

CAMP POPE. A temporary Civil War encampment named for General John Pope, it was established in the summer of 1862 for the rendezvous of the 22nd Iowa Infantry commanded by Colonel William M. Stone. Later, in the fall of 1862, the post was occupied by the 28th and 40th Regiments. The site of Camp Pope is now located within the limits of Iowa City, Johnson County.

FORT PURDY. An Indian defense erected by the settlers of Denison, Crawford County, during the Indian scare associated with the 1857 Spirit Lake Massacre, Fort Purdy was located on the property of John Purdy not far from the town's courthouse square. In a five-day siege in 1857 near Estherville, a band of renegade Sioux Indians laid waste an entire settlement, the bloodiest Indian massacre in Iowa history. Today, there is a monument bearing a tablet listing the 40 victims of the massacre, located near their burial site.

FORT RACCOON. FORT DES MOINES NO. 2.

CAMP RANKIN. A temporary Civil War encampment established as a rendezvous for the 3rd Iowa Cavalry in the fall of 1861, it was named Camp Rankin in honor of Colonel J. W. Rankin, a resident of the town of Keokuk, Lee County, near which the post was situated on a bluff. The cavalry left Camp Rankin on November 11 and, within a few days, was replaced by troops from the 15th Iowa Infantry. The camp was abandoned on or about November 25, to be replaced by a new camp, called Camp Halleck, established at present 5th and Johnson streets in Keokuk.

REDWOOD POST (*Cedar Fort*). A trading post, also known as Cedar Fort, it was established by Jean Baptiste Faribault, noted trader for the Northwest Company, who maintained the post for four years during his dealings with the region's Sioux Indians. The post was situated on the Des Moines River, "about two hundred miles above its mouth," being in what is now the central part of Iowa, on Raccoon Fork in present Polk County.

CAMP ROBERTS. CAMP KINSMAN.

FORT SANFORD. Established in early October 1842, Camp Sanford was located on the left bank of the Des Moines River near the present town of Ottumwa in Wapello County. Established by Captain James Allen commanding troops of the 1st Dragoons dispatched from Fort Atkinson, the post near the Sac and Fox Agency was intended to oust squatters from the Indians' lands. With the permission of John Sanford of the American Fur Company, the men were housed in eight log cabins belonging to the trading company. Officers' quarters and stables were built by the troops. Captain Allen named the post Camp Sanford in acknowledgment of the courtesy extended to the military. One citation reports that the War Department rejected the name of the post because of its temporary status and officially designated it Sac and Fox Agency. Fort Sanford was occupied until May, 1843, when the troops were moved up the river to the mouth of Raccoon Creek, to erect a new Fort Des Moines.

CAMP STRONG. In response to President Lincoln's request for additional troops, Governor Samuel J. Kirkwood commissioned Eber C. Byam of Linn County to form the so-called "Iowa Temperance Regiment"—"men who touch not, taste not, handle not spirituous or malt liquor, wine or cider." They were mustered in as the 24th Iowa Infantry and sent to Camp Strong on Muscatine Island near the town of Muscatine on the Mississippi River, where the troops of the 35th Infantry had also rendezvoused.

TESSON POST. Montrose, Lee County, on the Mississippi River, is the site of one of the earliest permanent settlements founded in Iowa. Here, Louis Honoré Tesson, a French-Canadian, established a trading post in 1799 and planted apple orchards, the first in the state.

CAMP TUTTLE. A temporary Civil War encampment was established at Oskaloosa, Mahaska County, on October 1, 1862, for the mustering into service of the 23rd Iowa Infantry, comprised mostly of men from within the county. The post was named Camp Tuttle in honor of Colonel J. M. Tuttle of the 2nd Iowa Infantry. The troops abandoned Camp Tuttle on November 20, when they were marched to Eddyville, and ultimately to Keokuk, St. Louis, and Helena.

CAMP UNION. CAMP FRANKLIN.

CAMP WARREN. A Civil War encampment established in July 1861, Camp Warren near Burlington in Des Moines County was literally built from the ground up by troops of the 1st Iowa Cavalry, who had been transferred from Keokuk.

CAMP YOUNG. On June 18, 1916, President Woodrow Wilson issued a call for defense troops to man the Mexican border where troubles had erupted. In response, Troop D of the 1st Iowa Cavalry marched to Iowa City from West Branch, and then to Camp Young, near North Liberty in Johnson County, apparently in preparation for an eventual move to the Mexican border.

CAMP ALERT. FORT LARNED.

FORT ATKINSON (*New Post on the Arkansas; Fort Expedient; Fort Sod; Fort Sodom; Camp Mackay; Fort Sumner*). Established on August 8, 1850, the original post was located about six miles west of present Dodge City (Ford County) and situated on Walnut Creek, close to the point where the Santa Fe Trail crossed the Arkansas River. Intended to oversee the activities of the area's Indians and safeguard the vital Trail, the post was established by Lieutenant Colonel Edwin Vose Sumner, 1st Dragoons, and named in honor of Lieutenant Colonel Aeneas Mackay, deputy quartermaster general, who died on May 23, 1850. Because its walls were built entirely of prairie sod, partly covered with poles and canvas, the post was dubbed "Fort Sod" or "Fort Sodom," at times referred to by its nickname, "Fort Expedient." Captain William Hoffman, 6th Infantry, probably supervised the erection of the temporary post.

The War Department in the spring of 1851 ordered Colonel Sumner to proceed with the construction of a permanent fort. The post was rebuilt of adobe bricks beginning in early June, on or adjoining the original site, and was called New Post on the Arkansas or Fort Sumner until June 25, when it was designated Fort Atkinson in honor of Colonel Henry Atkinson, 6th Infantry, who died on June 14, 1842. A garrison of 90 men of the 6th Infantry and about 20 Dragoons occupied the fort. Evacuated on September 22, 1853, temporarily reoccupied in June 1854, the fort was permanently abandoned on October 2, 1854. The scarcity of grass and fuel (the nearest wood was 13 miles away) and the difficulty of obtaining adequate supplies and provisions were the major reasons for the fort's abandonment. The post's structures were demolished to prevent their use by Indians. Its site was temporarily occupied as a campsite in 1865 during a campaign against the area's recalcitrant Indians.

FORT AUBREY (*Camp Wynkoop*). Established early in September 1865 by companies D and F, 48th Wisconsin Infantry, commanded by Captain Adolph Whitman, who were soon joined by Company M of the 2nd Cavalry, this temporary dugout-type fort, large enough to accommodate a 300-man garrison, was situated at the head of Spring Creek less than three miles north of the Arkansas River, about four miles east of the present town of Syracuse in what is now Hamilton County. The post was intended to protect the mountain branch of the important Santa Fe Trail during the Indian troubles of

Kansas

1865–66. First called Camp Wynkoop, the post was soon renamed Fort Aubrey for Francis X. Aubrey, French-Canadian trader and explorer, the first man to take a wagon train from the Missouri River to Santa Fe, who was killed in a Santa Fe saloon on August 18, 1854. The site of the fort had been originally recommended by Aubrey. The post was abandoned on April 15, 1866, after Indian hostilities in the area had abated.

CAMP BATEMAN. According to one citation, Camp Bateman was established in October 1857 by elements of the 6th Infantry, under command of Lieutenant Colonel George Andrews, and located at "Cincinnati," near Fort Leavenworth in Leavenworth County. A National Archives record, however, reports that the post was established on February 28, 1858, by companies A, D, E, G, H, and K, of the 6th Infantry. The post was abandoned May 8, 1858.

FORT BAXTER. On October 6, 1863, William Quantrill's large force of guerrillas attacked Union-held Fort Baxter, a sod and log enclosure situated on the edge of Indian reservation lands and located near Baxter Springs in Cherokee County. The post was then being rebuilt by its garrison consisting of two companies of the 3rd Wisconsin Cavalry and one of the 2nd Kansas Colored Infantry. Immediately after killing 9 and wounding 10 of its defenders, the guerrilla leader and 250 of his men rode out to waylay an approaching headquarters column escorting Major General James G. Blunt.

Since many of Quantrill's Raiders were attired completely or partially in Union uniforms, the general assumed they were an honor guard from the fort. When the distance between the two forces narrowed to 60 yards, the guerrillas opened fire, killing about 80 of Blunt's 100 troopers, including all the members of the band, and wounding 8 others who escaped. General Blunt and a Mrs. Chester Thomas, wife of an Army contractor, jumped from their buggy and mounted horses to escape in a wild race to safety. The guerrillas, losing but 3 men killed and 4 wounded, were quite jubilant. They went on to massacre 150 Union Indians and Negroes who were gathering ponies between Baxter Springs and the Canadian River. On October 12 they entered the Confederate lines and joined General H. Cooper and his Indian soldiers on the Canadian.

BEAR CREEK REDOUBT (*North Redoubt*). Constructed in the fall of 1870 in conjunction with one similar in design near the Cimarron River to the south, Bear Creek Redoubt, otherwise known as the North Redoubt, was established in order to provide protection and a convenient resting place for military mail coaches and freight wagons traveling the road between Fort Dodge and Camp Supply. The Redoubt was located just north of Ashland in Clark County. The fort's remains are in an excellent state of preservation, evidenced by a square depression enclosed by three-foot-high walls.

CAMP BEECHER (*Camp Wichita; Camp Davidson; Camp Butterfield*). This post was established on June 11, 1868, on the Little Arkansas River a short distance from its mouth, where it joins the Arkansas River about a mile from the city of Wichita. Established as a temporary defense against the Cheyenne Indians, the camp was first called Camp or Fort Wichita, then renamed Camp Davidson. In October its name was changed to Camp Butterfield, and to Camp Beecher in November, for Lieutenant Fred Beecher, nephew of preacher Henry Ward Beecher who was very concerned about the struggle in Kansas as a free-state. The post was abandoned in October 1869.

FORT BELMONT. About two miles west of Buffalo, in Wilson County, is the site of what was once a military post and stagecoach station, garrisoned until after the Civil War. Relatively little is known about this obscure post, most probably erected in either 1860 or 1861, except for the historic fact that close to the site are the graves of Osage chieftain Hapo, who had fought for the North during the war, and his daughter.

FORT BISSELL. A hurriedly erected stone stockade, enclosing a number of cabins, was erected in the spring of 1873 by Phillipsburg's settlers when the commander of Fort Hays sent a military scout to warn them that warring Apaches might be expected any hour. The Apaches, however, did not attack the community. Although the fort site is about three miles from the center of town, a replica of Fort Bissell (not an exact match) stands a half mile west of Phillipsburg and encloses two of the original cabins.

FORT BLAIR. FORT SCOTT.

FORT BROOKS. Established in August or September 1864, Fort Brooks was located on the north bank of the Republican River in present Cloud County (then Shirley County). A log blockhouse, serving as headquarters for the defense of the area against hostile Indians, it was constructed by Shirley County's militia.

CAMP BULL CREEK. Established in August 1856 in Miami County, near Paola, by proslavery forces from Missouri, Camp Bull Creek had a very brief existence. On August 31, upon learning that they were to be attacked by antislavery forces, the camp was hurriedly abandoned and the proslavery troops retreated to Missouri.

CAMP BUTTERFIELD. CAMP BEECHER.

CARLYSLE STAGE STATION. One of the refuges on the Smoky Hill route, it was intermittently garrisoned by Army detachments during 1865–66. The station was located between Gove and Orion in Gove County.

CASTLE ROCK CREEK STATION. A stage station, intermittently garrisoned by a detachment of troops during 1865–67, situated on the Smoky Hill stage route, it was located in eastern Gove County, about a mile east of scenic Castle Rock.

FORT CAVAGNOLLE (*Fort de Cavagnial*). Anglicized from the French *de Cavagnial,* Fort Cavagnolle was New France's westernmost outpost, erected in 1744 or 1745 and located on the Missouri River opposite the Salt Creek Valley in Leavenworth County. Usually garrisoned by French marines, it was an 80-foot-square stockade with a bastion in each of its four angles, enclosing the commandant's residence, powder magazine, guardhouse, barracks, and a trader's house for his employees. Intended as a protection for French fur traders and a defense against Indians, Fort Cavagnolle apparently served until about the year 1764, when the Spanish took it over during its final days. Other citations report the fort was abandoned before 1760.

CAMP CENTER. FORT RILEY.

CHALK BLUFFS STATION. Intermittently garrisoned during 1865–67, this stage station was attacked and destroyed in 1867 by Cheyenne Indians, one of the incidents that precipitated the Plains Expedition that year. The station was located on S.R. 23 on the left or east side of the Smoky Hill River in Gove County.

CHOUTEAU'S TRADING POST. GIRAUD'S TRADING POST.

CIMARRON REDOUBT (*South Redoubt*). Also known as South Redoubt and Deep Hole, Cimarron Redoubt was constructed in the fall of 1870 in conjunction with one similar in design to the north near the headwaters of Bear Creek in order to provide protection for military mail coaches and freight wagons traveling the road between Fort Dodge and Camp Supply. Cimarron Redoubt and its companion, Bear Creek Redoubt, came into existence as a military response to counteract a threat to military communications. Located in Clark County, south of the Cimarron River, the redoubt was used by early settlers of the county. It became a general store in 1876, and from May 1881 until April 1887 it was officially established as a post office. At some undetermined date after the latter year, the redoubt was abandoned.

CAMP CRAWFORD. In response to the eruption of Indian wars in the fall of 1868, a state of emergency was declared by Kansas Governor Samuel Johnson Crawford, who issued a call for recruits to form a volunteer army. Men arrived from all over the state and were first quartered in the two legislative halls in Topeka's old state house on Kansas Avenue north of 5th Street. On October 21, 1868, Camp Crawford was established and named for the governor. Supplies, camp and garrison equipage, clothing, and arms arrived from Fort Leavenworth, and very soon the camp was a city of white tents, extending north and south, approximately from 2nd to 5th streets.

CRISFIELD POST. In anticipation of Cheyenne Indian troubles, a temporary camp was established at Crisfield in Harper County on July 8, 1885. The post was established by Colonel Henry Morrow, 21st Infantry, who commanded elements of four infantry and two cavalry regiments, an aggregate of 1,305 men. The camp was abandoned on September 4, 1885.

CAMP CROGHAN (*Cantonment Martin*). The first military post in Kansas, Cantonment Martin was established in 1818 when Kansas was an unknown portion of the Louisiana Territory. The military cantonment, established by Captain Wyly Martin of the Rifle Regiment, came into existence as a base of supplies and winter quarters for Major Stephen H. Long's historic scientific expedition on 1819–20 into the Rocky Mountains. It was located on Cow Island (known to the French as Isle de Vache) in the Missouri River within the confines of present Atchison County, about 10 miles north of where Fort Leavenworth would later be established. Major Long and his explorers reached Cantonment Martin on August 18, 1819, on the *Western Engineer,* the first steamboat to go up the Missouri River. Before leaving Cow Island, Major Long held a peace conference with Osage and Kansa Indians who were later known as Kaws. The Indians admitted to depredations against the military but promised to be peaceful in the future. White Plume, Kaw ancestor of Vice President Charles Curtis, was one of the chiefs who signed the agreement. Cantonment Martin was occupied until Long's exploring expedition returned in October 1820. The camp was then abandoned until 1826, when it was temporarily occupied as Camp Croghan by troops of the 1st Infantry commanded by Captain George Croghan.

CAMP CUYLER. This post apparently existed for only the month of July 1858 and was located near Fort Scott in southeast Kansas. The post was established by Captain N. Lyon, 2nd Infantry, with companies B and D of the 2nd Infantry and Company E of the 3rd Artillery, aggregating 48 men.

CAMP DAVIDSON. CAMP BEECHER.

FORT DE CAVAGNIAL. FORT CAVAGNOLLE.

FORT DODGE. Established on September 9, 1865, Fort Dodge was located on the left bank of the Arkansas River on the Santa Fe Trail, a few miles east of present Dodge City. A military camp had been established there in 1864 by Major General Grenville M. Dodge. It was situated near the intersection of the "dry" and "wet" routes of the Trail and between the two points where the Indians frequently crossed the river—the Mulberry Creek Crossing, about 15 miles to the east, and the Cimarron Crossing, some 25 miles to the west. The post was intended to protect the Santa Fe Trail and to serve as a base of operations against Indian hostiles. The most westerly of the large forts on the Trail, it was established by Brigadier General Washington L. Elliott, in compliance with an order of Major General John Pope, commander of the department, and most probably named for Colonel Henry Dodge, 1st Dragoons, not for General Dodge. After the post was abandoned on October 2, 1882, the military reservation was transferred to the Interior Department on January 12, 1885. Part of the post's grounds, including two of the old adobe barracks built in 1864, is now occupied by the Fort Dodge Soldiers' Home. When first laid out, the new town of Fort Dodge had been called Buffalo City. But since Kansas already had towns named Buffalo and Buffalo Station, the Postmaster General in Washington rejected the name.

The frontier town was then renamed Dodge City for the fort five miles away, which ultimately became an important cattle market and shipping point on the trail from Texas and one of the wildest cowtowns in the West.

FORT DOWNER. DOWNER'S STATION.

DOWNER'S STATION (*Fort Downer*). Fort Downer, more properly Downer's Station, was an outpost on the Smoky Hill route to Colorado's gold fields. It was located south of the town of Wakeeney in Trego County, about 50 miles west of Fort Hays. Established as a Butterfield Overland stage station in 1865, it was used as a military post during 1867–68, first used by 1st Lieutenant Joseph C. Coffman, with Company H of the 37th Infantry. The post's name was derived from the creek, which was named for James P. Downer, a Civil War veteran and a member of the team that surveyed the Smoky Hill stage route. General George Custer used this stage station and intermittently occupied military post as a base for his 1867 Plains Expedition, eventuating in his courtmartial on a number of charges. The post was abandoned on May 28, 1868.

CAMP DRYWOOD. A temporary Army post established sometime in 1871, it was intended to protect the railroad south of Fort Scott from Indian hostiles. It was located in the general area of the village of Englevale in Bourbon County, about 1 mile west of U.S. 69 and 16 miles south of the fort.

FORT ELLSWORTH. FORT HARKER.

FORT EXPEDIENT. FORT ATKINSON.

CAMP FLETCHER. FORT HAYS.

FORT FOLLY. A roofless log stockade erected in 1864 as a protection against General Sterling Price's Confederate raiders, its site is commemorated by a plaque imbedded in the sidewalk in front of the National Bank at the corner of Kansas Avenue and 6th Street in Topeka.

CAMP FORSYTH. FORT RILEY.

FORT FRANKLIN. A blockhouse located about three miles southeast of Lawrence in the city of Franklin in Crawford County, it was occupied by proslavery men who were subsequently attacked and defeated by free-state forces on August 12, 1856. The blockhouse adjoined the then post office.

CAMP FUNSTON. FORT RILEY.

GIRAUD'S TRADING POST (*Chouteau's Trading Post*). Long before Kansas was organized as a territory, a settlement was established in 1834 at the village of Trading Post in present Linn County, by Pierre Chouteau, Jr., and Company of St. Louis, holder of a license to trade with the Indians then in the vicinity. Chouteau and Michael Giraud established the post, known alternately as Chouteau's or Giraud's Trading post, as agents for the Northwestern Fur Company. Giraud headed the establishment for some years. Trading Post, located on the (Marais des) Cynges River, about four miles from the Missouri state line, was the scene of the May 1858 "Marais des Cynges Massacre," in which five free-state men were murdered and five wounded by a proslavery gang from Missouri.

CAMP GRIERSON. A campsite on the Santa Fe Trail on the west side of the Little Arkansas River where the Trail crossed it, it was established in 1866 by Colonel George Custer and named for a fellow officer in the 7th Cavalry. A log stockade was erected as a temporary protection.

GRINNELL SPRINGS STATION. Another of the short-lived Butterfield Overland stage stations on the Smoky Hills route, it was located about 10 miles west of Castle Rock Station and 9 miles east of the Chalk Bluffs Station, all in present Gove County. The station was intermittently garrisoned by an Army detachment until 1867.

CAMP HALPINE. A very temporary Civil War encampment, Camp Halpine was located near Osawatomie, Miami County, in February 1862, and occupied by the 8th Kansas Volunteers.

FORT HARKER (*Fort Ellsworth*). Established in August 1864 by troops of the 7th Iowa Cavalry under the command of 2nd Lieutenant Allen Ellsworth, the post was named for the lieutenant and was intended to safeguard the more isolated frontier settlements. Originally located on the left bank of the Smoky Hill River where the Santa Fe Trail stage route crossed the river, it stood about three miles east of the present town of Ellsworth. In January 1867 the post was shifted one mile to the northeast to a site now occupied by the town of Kanapolis. The newly located post was used as a base for the distribution of supplies to military posts farther west and as a staging area for operations against Indian hostiles in 1868–69. Originally called Fort Ellsworth, it was designated Fort Harker on November 11,

1866, for Brigadier General Charles G. Harker, killed on June 27, 1864, during the Battle of Kenesaw Mountain in Georgia. After the railroad was extended to Denver, it was determined that there was no further need of the post and it was abandoned on April 2, 1873. On July 12, 1880, the military reservation was transferred to the Interior Department for disposition.

FORT HAYS (*Camp Fletcher*). Established on October 11, 1865, this post originally was located on Big Creek, about 15 miles southeast of its later site, and first named Fort Fletcher in honor of Governor Thomas C. Fletcher of Missouri, then designated Fort Hays on November 11, 1866, for Brigadier General Alexander Hays, killed on May 5, 1864, in the Battle of the Wilderness in Virginia. On June 5, 1867, Big Creek overflowed and flooded the post, destroying most of its buildings. On June 22, 1867, a new post was established on higher ground south of Big Creek and half a mile south of the present town of Hays in Ellis County. Fort Hays had been primarily designed to protect the employees of the Kansas Pacific Railroad from Indian hostiles. In November 1889 the post was abandoned due to the cessation of Indian troubles in the region. The military reservation was transferred to the Interior Department on November 6, 1889, and in turn to the state by Congressional enactment on March 28, 1900. It was at Fort Hays that "Buffalo Bill" Cody acquired his nickname while supplying buffalo meat for railroad crews. Part of the reservation site is now occupied by the campus of Fort Hays State College. South of Hays in Frontier Historical Park are the original limestone-built blockhouse and the post's guardhouse.

FORT HENNING. FORT SCOTT.

HENSHAW'S STATION. A stage station on the Butterfield Overland line, it was the first stop east of Fort Wallace on the Smoky Hill route. Intermittently garrisoned by a detachment of Army troops, the site of Henshaw's Station is located one mile east of McAllaster in Logan County.

CAMP HOFFMAN. This camp was in existence from at least July 1867 to November 14, 1867. It was located on White Rock Creek in present Jewell County in north central Kansas. Its garrison consisted of Company K, 3rd Infantry, and Company B, 10th Cavalry. The camp's post return for October 1867 reported that it had received orders to evacuate the site and establish a temporary post at Lake Sibley on the Republican River, about three miles northwest of present Concordia, Cloud County. The following month's post return showed that the command left Camp Hoffman on Lake Sibley on November 14, 1867, to march to Fort Riley.

FORT INSLEY. FORT SCOTT.

FORT JEWELL. Constructed on May 13 and 14, 1870, and located at the town of Jewell in north central Kansas, this post was erected by a hastily congregated home guard of settlers, captained by William D. Street, in response to a circulated rumor that the Cheyennes had again gone on the warpath. Fort Jewell consisted of a sod enclosure 50 yards square with walls 4 feet thick and 7 feet high. The area's pseudo-militia garrisoned the post until June 28, 1870, by which time the Indian war scare had dissipated, and a company of the 3rd Artillery replaced the militia, occupying the fort until the early fall.

CAMP KIRWIN. Established on July 10, 1865, this short-lived stockaded encampment was located near the confluence of Bow Creek and the North Solomon River in present Phillips County. It was established by Lieutenant Colonel John S. Kirwin, 12th Tennessee Cavalry, and a company of Tennessee volunteers, primarily intended to escort and protect a survey party. The post was abandoned on September 3, 1865. Its site, less than two miles southwest of Kirwin, now lies beneath the impounded waters of the Kirwin Dam Reservoir. Six years later, in response to an Indian war scare, the inhabitants of the settlement named for the Tennessee officer erected a 90-by-50-foot stockade within the town.

FORT LARNED (*Camp on Pawnee Fork; Camp Alert*). Established on October 22, 1859, by Captain Henry W. Wessels, 2nd Infantry, the post was originally located about three miles east of its permanent site on the Pawnee River above its confluence with the Arkansas, at present-day Larned in Pawnee County. One of the more important posts established to safeguard the Santa Fe Trail, it also served as a regional center for the distribution of annuities, as stipulated by treaty, to the Indians. First called Camp of Pawnee Fork, the post's name was changed to Camp Alert on February 1, 1860. When it was moved to its new site a few months later, and reconstructed of stone on a much larger scale, the post was designated Fort Larned in honor of Colonel Benjamin F. Larned, paymaster general of the U.S. Army, on May 29, 1860.

During the Indian war of 1864, the post was garrisoned by two companies of the 2nd Colorado Cavalry, one company each of the 11th and 12th Kansas Cavalry, and a battery of the 9th Wisconsin Artillery. During its existence the fort was besieged by Indians on at least five different occasions. The agency for the Arapaho and Cheyenne Indians was located at Fort Larned until 1868. Upon the completion of the Santa Fe Railroad, marking the end of the Santa Fe Trail, the fort was abandoned on July 19, 1878, except for a small caretaking detachment that protected the quartermaster supplies until arrangements could be made for their removal. On March 26, 1883, the Army transferred jurisdiction over the military reservation to the Interior Department.

The Santa Fe Trail Center, located just west of Larned, contains the fort's parade ground surrounded by a number of well-preserved buildings, renovated and maintained by the National Park Service. About 12 miles to the northeast is 100-foot-high Pawnee Rock, a state monument, one of the celebrated landmarks on the old Santa Fe Trail.

CANTONMENT LEAVENWORTH. FORT LEAVENWORTH.

FORT LEAVENWORTH (*Cantonment Leavenworth; Camp Lincoln; Fort Sully*). More than 150 years of military service make Fort Leavenworth one of the nation's oldest active Army posts west of the Mississippi River. Even though the post has never been attacked, its garrisons have witnessed thousands of soldiers, surveyors, emigrants, Indians, preachers, students, and officials pass by. On March 7, 1828, Army orders directed Colonel Henry Leavenworth to leave Jefferson Barracks, Missouri, with a complement of troops to ascend the Missouri River and select a site for a fort on the left bank of the river within 20 miles of the Little Platte River. Four companies of the 3rd Infantry left Jefferson Barracks that year to join Colonel Leavenworth, who selected a site within the prescribed area.

Calling the site Cantonment Leavenworth, the War Department approved the location and ultimately promoted Leavenworth to brigadier general. Unfortunately, that promotion came after he was already dead from an illness complicated by injuries suffered during a fall from his horse. He was buried temporarily in Indian Territory (Oklahoma), and his remains were later moved to his home in Delhi, New York. Eventually, Leavenworth was reinterred in the National Cemetery at the fort.

The Mexican War brought the post into national prominence for the first time. Fort Leavenworth became headquarters for one of three armies organized for operations in Mexico. Following the war the post became the main depot and cavalry supply station for all military establishments in the west. During the Civil War, Camp Lincoln was established on post as a reception and training station. Union volunteers were mustered in, equipped, and prepared for battle. These same volunteers returned to be mustered out as their enlistments expired. When news that Confederate General Sterling Price had swept out of Arkansas into Missouri with 10,000 men, fear of attack on the fort and nearby town of Leavenworth grew rapidly. People, including military officers, believed Price would certainly attack and seize the fort. Earthworks were quickly constructed on the ridge west of the National Cemetery and named Fort Sully. But Price's forces never reached Leavenworth. They fled back south after defeat at Westport, Missouri, which is now part of Kansas City.

While Civil War veterans were still being mustered out here, Fort Leavenworth entered a new era. For the next 30 years, the Army's chief mission was control of the Indian bands on the Western plains. Between 1865 and 1891, the Army could count at least 1,067 combat engagements with Apaches, Modocs, Cheyennes, Utes, Nez Percés, Comanches, Kiowas, Kickapoos, and other tribes. Construction of the railroads across the Plains helped bring civilization to the region. Indian troubles lessened, and so did Fort Leavenworth's mission as supply base for Army campaigns in the West. As a result, the post continued to change.

The U.S. Disciplinary Barracks was built here, which gave one new role to the post. But it was the reorganization of the Army ordered by President Ulysses S. Grant that permanently changed Fort Leavenworth in more dramatic fashion. General William T. Sherman established "The School of Application for Infantry and Cavalry" here in 1881. That school eventually evolved into what is known now as the U.S. Army Command and General Staff College, the largest activity currently located on post. It was also during the late nineteenth century that other facilities became established on post.

With the advent of World War I, Fort Leavenworth became a training camp for draftees and newly commissioned officers. When the Civilian Conservation Corps (CCC) Act was passed in 1933, a reconditioning camp was established on post for CCC enrollees. During World War II, 318,000 selectees were processed through the post's induction station, and 385,000 men went through the Reception Center. The post's Separation Center discharged 147,000 soldiers. The Army War College was located here for a brief period from October 1950 to June 1951. It was then moved to its permanent home at Carlisle Barracks, Pennsylvania.

Exhibits blending pioneer and Army life help the Fort Leavenworth Museum depict the role the fort played in the opening of the West. The museum is located in Andrews Hall on Reynolds Avenue, directly across from the Command and General Staff College.

CAMP LEEDY. A recruiting camp established in 1898 for use during the Spanish-American War, it was located at the old Fairgrounds at 17th Street and Topeka Avenue, in Topeka.

CAMP LINCOLN. FORT LEAVENWORTH.

FORT LINCOLN. Located 12 miles north of Fort Scott and about 3 miles northwest of the present town of Fulton, on the Little Osage River, Bourbon County, Fort Lincoln, named for the President, was built by James H. Lane, leader of the Free State movement in Kansas and major general of the militia, in August 1861. The structure, 80 feet long and strongly built of logs, was primarily used to confine Confederate prisoners of war. It was garrisoned by several companies of Negroes, but the Federal government would not accept them as soldiers. The fort was abandoned in January 1864.

FORT LOOKOUT. Situated on a high bluff commanding the Republican River Valley, Fort Lookout guarded the military road from Fort Riley to Fort Kearney, Nebraska. The strongly built two-story structure performed regular Army duty before 1868, when it was abandoned by the regulars. State militia used the blockhouse during the Indian war of 1868. Following their withdrawal, the old fort was used as a rendezvous and refuge for settlers of the White Rock and Republican valleys during the Indian scares of the early 1870s.

CAMP MACKAY. FORT ATKINSON.

FORT MCKEAN. A temporary encampment occupied by Company C, 3rd Wisconsin Cavalry, from July to December 1864, Camp McKean was located near Fort Scott in Bourbon County.

CAMP MAGRUDER. Located near Fort Leavenworth, Camp Magruder was a temporary camp for recruits under command of Lieutenant Colonel

George B. Crittenden during July and August 1860.

FORT MANN. Established, most probably, in April 1847, Fort Mann was located on the north bank of the Arkansas River, about eight miles west of present Dodge City, because of the Army's need of a post roughly equidistant from Fort Leavenworth and Santa Fe for the repair of wagons and the replacement of animals. In compliance with an order issued by Captain William M. D. McKissack, assistant quartermaster, the post was erected by Captain Daniel P. Mann, master teamster, for whom it was named, and a corps of 40 teamsters. The fort consisted of four large log houses, connected by angles of timber framework in which were cut loopholes for cannon and small arms. The diameter of the post was 60 feet, with walls 20 feet high. Fort Mann was intermittently occupied by U.S. troops. It was abandoned in 1850 when Fort Atkinson (Camp Mackay) was established.

CANTONMENT MARTIN. CAMP CROGHAN.

MEAD TRADING POST. Located in the present city of Wichita was the trading post erected by James R. Mead with the aid of Jesse Chisholm in 1864. This section of Sedgwick County in the Arkansas Valley was then a hunter's paradise. During a period of only three weeks, assisted by two employees, he killed 330 buffalo, saved 300 hides and 3,500 pounds of tallow, and realized for their labors the sum of $400. Probably the first settler who built within the limits of Wichita Township, Jesse Chisholm, a half-breed, came here with a band of Wichita Indians in 1864 and built a cabin and trading post on the creek named for him. In the spring of 1865, Chisholm blazed a trail from his ranch to the present site of the Wichita Agency on the Wichita River, a distance of 220 miles. This trail subsequently became known as the "Chisholm Trail."

FORT MONTGOMERY. At the outbreak of the Civil War, citizens of the Eureka (Greenwood County) neighborhood constructed Fort Montgomery, named for Colonel James Montgomery, a free-state leader and colonel of the 10th Kansas Infantry, as a fort for home guards. When they disbanded at the close of the war, the fort was occupied by a detachment of the 15th Kansas Cavalry. During the Indian scares of 1864–69, it was used as a rallying point for Greenwood County's settlers.

FORT MONUMENT. MONUMENT STATION.

MONUMENT STATION (*Fort Monument; Fort Pyramid*). Established in November 1865, Monument Station was located in Gove County on the Kansas Pacific Railway route, between Forts Hays and Wallace. It was originally a station of the Butterfield Overland Dispatch stage and mail route. A detachment of troops, in compliance with an order of Major General Grenville M. Dodge, served as a garrison to protect the station from Indian depredations. The post was also referred to Fort Monument and Fort Pyramid because of its proximity to some monument-shaped rocks. The troops were withdrawn in June 1868.

NEW KIOWA POST. This short-lived post was located near the town of Kiowa, Barber County, on the extreme southern border of Kansas. The camp was established to protect the area's settlers from possible attack by Indians from Oklahoma. The threat of attack, however, was just a scare, and within several weeks in August and September 1885, the troops were withdrawn and returned to Fort Leavenworth and Fort Riley.

NEW POST ON THE ARKANSAS. FORT ATKINSON.

NORTH REDOUBT. BEAR CREEK REDOUBT.

CAMP ON PAWNEE FORK. FORT LARNED.

CAMP PHILLIPS. A World War II encampment, Camp Phillips was established in the latter part of 1942 and named in honor of Colonel William A. Phillips, one of the co-founders of the city of Salina, Saline County, in 1858. The post was used as a training center until its closing in the fall of 1944.

CAMP POND CREEK. FORT WALLACE.

POND CREEK STATION. This Butterfield Overland stage station on the Smoky Hill River route should not be confused with Camp Pond Creek, the prior name for Fort Wallace. The station, located just west of the town of Wallace, was intermittently garrisoned by a detachment of U.S. Army troops during 1865–66 to protect it from possible Indian attack and depredation. The station was attacked in June 1867, by about 300 Cheyennes commanded by Chief Roman Nose, who drove off its whole herd of livestock. The original stage station has been restored and moved to a park at the eastern side of Wallace.

FORT RILEY. Watercolor painted by Hermann Stieffel in 1873. (Courtesy of the New York Historical Society, New York City.)

FORT PYRAMID. MONUMENT STATION.

FORT RILEY (*Camp Center; Camp Funston; Camp Whitside; Camp Forsyth*). Fort Riley, which today ranks next to Fort Leavenworth in importance, was established on May 17, 1853, on the north bank of the Kansas River close to the strategic junction of the Republican and Smoky Hill rivers. The post was established by Captain Charles S. Lovell with companies B, F, and H of the 6th Infantry, on the site recommended by Colonel Thomas T. Fauntleroy, 1st Dragoons (later named the 1st Cavalry), believing that it would eliminate the need of other Army installations in the region. The post was first known as Camp Center because it was assumed to be very near the geographical center of the United States. On June 27, 1853, it was designated Fort Riley in honor of Major General Bennett Riley (after his death 18 days earlier), who led the first military escort along the Santa Fe Trail in 1829 and later served with distinction during the War with Mexico.

Construction of the permanent cavalry post by hundreds of civilian workers was begun in June 1855 under the direction of Brevet Major Edmund A. Ogden, 8th Infantry. On the night of August 1, several workers and officers' wives developed cholera, and in the next few days the epidemic spread rapidly. Major Ogden contracted the disease and died on August 3, leaving the new installation temporarily without a commander. During the next five days, between 75 and 100 had died and were buried—most in unmarked graves—in the southeast corner of the Fort Riley Cemetery. About 150 soldiers and workers mutinied and deserted. The main body

of 6th Infantry troops, fortunately, was away from the post on a summer campaign.

In the fall of 1866, the now famous 7th Cavalry, the "Garry Owens," was organized at Fort Riley. The regiment was authorized by Congress in July and formed at the post in September under Lieutenant Colonel George A. Custer. A brevet major general of Cavalry at the age of 25 during the Civil War, Custer was brilliant but erratic. At the same time that he made the 7th into one of the best fighting units on the frontier, he made several tragic errors. One occurred in the summer of 1867 when there was a second epidemic of cholera at Fort Riley, where Mrs. Custer was residing. Custer left his command and rode across Kansas to be with his wife. He

FORT RILEY. Monument commemorating the tragedy of Wounded Knee, in which Big Foot's band of Sioux fell to the 7th Cavalry. (Courtesy of the U.S. Army.)

FORT RILEY. General George Custer's home. (Courtesy of the U.S. Army.)

was court martialed and relieved of command until called back by Major General Philip Sheridan, who needed Custer for his Indian campaign. Sixty-seven at Fort Riley died in the epidemic.

With the U.S. entry into World War I, Fort Riley's size doubled, tripled, and quadrupled quickly as the post was converted into a training center for thousands of men. Even before Congress had declared war, construction began on the "14th National Army Cantonment," Camp Funston (named for Major General Frederick Funston), the largest semipermanent training center in the country, located on the eastern part of the reservation. At a cost of $10 million, it was built almost overnight (July 10–September 1, 1917) by thousands of civilian workers. Camp Funston eventually covered over 2,000 acres, and was 2 miles long, with 29 miles of paved streets. After the war, Camp Funston was gradually dismantled. By 1925 almost all traces of the great training post had disappeared.

War spread rapidly across Europe in 1939 and 1940, and mobilization and reorganization of the Army began the year before Pearl Harbor. Camp Whitside, established on Fort Riley's reservation in 1924 as a National Guard camp, was expanded between 1940 and 1942 for use as the cantonment hospital. The expansion program involved retraining and re-equipping a new mechanized cavalry. Camp Forsyth, named after the 7th Cavalry's Colonel James W. Forsyth, was constructed in 1940 on the Republican Flats, on the left side of the reservation, and in 1941 the Cavalry Replacement Training Center was established there. In the course of the war, 150,000 horses and mechanized cavalrymen were trained at Camp Forsyth.

One of the nation's greatest military installa-

tions, Fort Riley is located about 2 miles east of Junction City and 14 miles west of Manhattan, home of Kansas State University. Part of the reservation lies in Geary County and part in Riley County. The reservation is presently over 100,000 acres in size. Fort Riley is now the home of the 1st Infantry Division (MECH), a correctional activity at Camp Funston, Third ROTC Region, and an NCO Academy.

RUSSELL SPRINGS STATION. Another of the Butterfield Overland Dispatch's stage stations on the Smoky Hill River route, Russell Springs Station in present Logan County was intermittently occupied during 1865–66 by a detachment of U.S. Army troops.

CAMP SANGER. Located about two miles west of Fort Riley's east gate and occupying the approximate site of the old Territorial capital at Pawnee, now known as Pawnee Flats, on the edge of the military reservation, Camp Sanger was a temporary encampment active 1902–3 and named in honor of Assistant Secretary of War William Cary Sanger. Maneuvers on a large scale were held at Fort Riley and in its environs in October 1903, and involved Camp Sanger's 12,000 troops.

FORT SAUNDERS. Consisting of a strongly built log structure with some breastworks and other defenses on the property of James P. Saunders, a proslavery advocate, Fort Saunders was located on Washington Creek about 12 miles southwest of Lawrence, Douglas County. The so-called fort was captured by the free-state militia on August 15, 1856. The fort was probably built only a few weeks before this date.

CAMP SCOTT. FORT SCOTT.

FORT SCOTT (*Camp Scott; Fort Blair; Fort Henning; Fort Insley*). Officially established on May 30, 1842, on the Marmaton River, a tributary of the Osage, Fort Scott was located about eight miles west of the Missouri line in Bourbon County. The post was intended to safeguard the critical military road between Fort Gibson, Oklahoma, and Fort Leavenworth. Its site had been recommended in 1837 by a mission that included Colonel Stephen Watts Kearney of the 1st Dragoons, and finally selected on April 9, 1842, by Captain Benjamin D. Moore, 1st Dragoons, and Assistant Surgeon Jacob Rhett Motte. Sergeant John Harrison, with a contingent of 19 men from the 1st Dragoons, was left to erect the post's first barracks built of hewn walnut timber. The command of the post was assumed by Captain Moore when he arrived on May 30 with the garrison from evacuated Fort Wayne in Oklahoma.

First named Camp Scott in honor of Major General Winfield Scott, the post was officially designated Fort Scott when permanency was assured in 1843 with the construction of new structures. Fort Scott was practically abandoned in April 1853, when its garrison was disbanded and distributed to Fort Riley and other posts in the region. Two years later the post's buildings were sold at public auction. The adjoining town of Fort Scott, however, was intermittently occupied by troops during the guerrilla warfare that was being waged between small armies of proslavery and free-state partisans prior to the outbreak of the Civil War. With slave territory to the east and free-state Kansas territory to the west, the town of Fort Scott was in the center of the prewar conflict that gave the state the epithet of "bloody Kansas." The fort itself was not reactivated until March 29, 1862, when it was occupied by Colonel Charles Doubleday with elements of the 2nd Ohio Cavalry.

Blockhouses, stockades, and breastworks were erected in 1862 at the fort and at strategic points around the town. Three of the new defenses at the fort were two-story blockhouses named Fort Blair, Fort Henning, and Fort Insley. Fort Scott also served as a depot of large quantities of supplies for the use of troops stationed as far south as the Red River. The post was again abandoned at the end of the war and reoccupied in October 1869 as the headquarters for campaigns in the southeastern part of the state. Fort Scott was finally abandoned in 1873. Several buildings of the old fort, including a renovated Civil War blockhouse and Headquarters House, a former officers' quarters converted into a museum, stand in Carroll Plaza, Fort Scott's original parade ground.

FORT SIMPLE. In accordance with the home-guard movement during the Civil War, the state capital at Topeka erected a wooden stockade at the intersection of 6th and Kansas avenues in 1863. Intended as a defensive refuge from guerrillas, it was never forced to defend itself. The stockade was dismantled at the end of the Civil War.

SMOKY HILL STATION. One of the Butterfield Overland Dispatch's stage stations on the Smoky Hill River route, it was a circular, sodded, fortified dugout easily defensible against Indian attack. The station, intermittently garrisoned by a small detachment of troops during 1865–67, was located about seven miles southeast of the town of Russell Springs in Logan County.

FORT SOD. FORT ATKINSON.

FORT SODOM. FORT ATKINSON.

FORT SOLOMON. Built early in 1864 as a defense against Indian attack, Fort Solomon in Ottawa County was the only shelter for the majority of the people in the county from the summer of 1864 to the spring of 1865. It consisted of log houses, arranged in the form of a square and enclosed by strong palisades. The fort was never forced to undergo an Indian siege.

SOUTH REDOUBT. CIMARRON REDOUBT.

FORT SULLY. FORT LEAVENWORTH.

FORT SUMNER. FORT ATKINSON.

CAMP THOMPSON. A temporary encampment located near Fort Leavenworth, Camp Thompson was established by Lieutenant Colonel George Andrews, 6th Infantry, with companies A, D, G, and K, on April 29, 1858. The post was abandoned May 7, 1858.

FORT TITUS. A fort built by proslavery partisans from Georgia and South Carolina, it was located on the farm belonging to Colonel H. T. Titus, about two miles from Lecompton in southern Jefferson County. After this contingent of proslavery adherents were a party to the sacking and burning of Lawrence led by William Quantrill's Raiders, they retreated to Fort Titus, where some 600 free-staters attacked with cannon and destroyed their fortified base of operations.

CAMP VAN DORN. A briefly occupied encampment located on Prairie Dog Creek in Phillips County, Camp Van Dorn was established in July of 1859 by Company G of the 1st Cavalry. Prairie Dog Creek was the scene of a battle in the 1860s.

FORT WALLACE (*Camp Pond Creek*). The last and westernmost frontier military post of any permanency in Kansas, Fort Wallace was established in late September, 1865. After two changes of a site, the post was finally located at the junction of Pond Creek and the south fork of the Smoky Hill River, about two miles southeast of the present town of Wallace and near what was the Pond Creek Station on the Butterfield Overland Dispatch route to Denver. Originally named Camp Pond Creek, the post was designated Fort Wallace on April 18, 1866, in honor of Brigadier General William H. L. Wallace, who was mortally wounded on April 10, 1862, in the Battle of Shiloh, Tennessee.

First garrisoned by Army regulars commanded by Captain Edward Ball, 2nd Cavalry, in March 1866, Fort Wallace was intended to protect the Smoky Hill stage route, provide military escorts, and control the area's Indians. It was from Fort Wallace in September 1868 that a relief force was sent to the scene of the Battle of Beecher Island, where a little band of soldiers held out for nine days against 1,000 Indians. Fort Wallace was officially abandoned on May 31, 1882, but a small number of troops still occupied the post until September. Two years later the military reservation was transferred to the Interior Department for disposition. The fort's cemetery, enclosed by limestone walls and commemorated by an inscribed monument, is about two miles southeast of the town of Wallace, while a museum and the restored Pond Creek Station building are located at the eastern end of the town.

CAMP WHITSIDE. FORT RILEY.

CAMP WICHITA. CAMP BEECHER.

CAMP WYNKOOP. FORT AUBREY.

FORT ZARAH. Established on September 6, 1864, on the left bank of Walnut Creek, less than three miles from its confluence with the Arkansas River, the post was located about three miles east of the present town of Great Bend, Barton County. Fort Zarah was primarily intended to safeguard the Walnut Creek Crossing on the Santa Fe Trail and furnish escorts for both military and civilian wagon traffic. The post was established by Major General Samuel R. Curtis, who named it for his son, Major Henry Zarah Curtis, assistant adjutant general of Volunteers, killed on October 5, 1863, at Fort Baxter during William Quantrill's massacre. Unusual on the western frontier, the post was a single two-story, sandstone-built structure, 120 by 52 feet, with towers or blockhouses at diagonal angles, providing ample room for the troops, their horses, a storehouse, a kitchen, and a well. The lessening of Indian depredations and the decreasing use of the Santa Fe Trail dictated the abandonment of the post on December 4, 1869. The military reservation was transferred to the Interior Department on March 25, 1871, for disposition. Today the three-acre Fort Zarah State Park, marked by Civil War cannon, incorporates the fort site.

FORT ALBERT SIDNEY JOHNSTON (*Fort Lytle*). Also known as Fort Lytle, and marked as Fort Lytle on a few maps, Fort Johnston was a formidable Confederate defense of Bowling Green, constructed during October and November 1861. The fort was located on Vinegar Hill, otherwise known as Copley Hill, one of the four elevations commanding the approaches to the city. Vinegar Hill, so called because it was owned by a disreputable recluse named Betsy (Sally) Vinegar, is now the site of Western Kentucky University. Five weeks after General Simon Bolivar Buckner occupied Bowling Green on September 18, 1861, General Albert Sidney Johnston, commander of the Confederate Army of the West, moved his headquarters to the city, and began the erection of this fort, built entirely of native rock. He evacuated Bowling Green on February 14, 1862, because of the advance of Union forces from the west, and marched his army toward Nashville, ending Confederate control of the city and its environs. General Ormsby Mitchel and Union forces occupied Bowling Green the next day, and for the remainder of the war, Federal troops held Fort Johnston.

CAMP ALLEN. Named for Captain Thomas Allen, commanding Company B of "Morgan's Squadron," Camp Allen was a Confederate encampment located five miles south of Bowling Green. The camp was abandoned on February 12, 1862, when Confederate forces began the evacuation of Bowling Green in the face of the advance of Union troops from the west toward the city.

FORT ANDERSON. Named for Major Robert Anderson, who surrendered Fort Sumter at the outbreak of the Civil War, Fort Anderson was erected at Paducah, McCracken County, in compliance with General Grant's orders in 1861. On March 25, 1864, Fort Anderson was attacked by Confederate forces under General Nathan B. Forrest. During and subsequent to the battle, a number of warehouses were burned and about 60 houses destroyed. The Confederates lost 300 men before withdrawing that night, thus climaxing Forrest's memorable raid seeking horses, ammunition, and medicines. The site of Fort Anderson is on Trimble Street, between 4th and 5th streets, in Paducah.

CAMP ANDY JOHNSON. A temporary camp of Home Guards located near Barbourville, Taylor County. Civil War Union sympathizers organized for protection and in August of 1861 established a camp, named for Vice President Andrew Johnson

Kentucky

under President Lincoln. On September 19 the camp was destroyed by Confederate forces commanded by Colonel J. A. Battle.

ARMSTRONG'S STATION. Established in 1788 in southern Kentucky.

ARNOLD'S STATION. Erected by John Arnold in 1783, his station was located west of the Kentucky River, about three miles above Frankfort.

ASHTON'S STATION. ESTILL'S STATION FORT (1781).

BAGDAD POST. A temporary post located at Bagdad, Shelby County, about 52 miles from Louisville, it was established in March 1871 by Company I, 7th Cavalry, commanded by Captain Myles W. Keogh. Bagdad was occupied by the same troops until September 1871, when the post was abandoned.

BAILEY'S STATION. Established most probably in 1791, Bailey's Station was located nearly three miles south of Maysville on the Ohio River, and one mile from the town of Washington, Mason County.

FORT BAKER. Built most probably during the first year of the Revolution, Fort Baker was located about five miles west of Mt. Sterling, Montgomery County. Little Mountain Town was the first name given to the settlement which grew up around Enoch Smith's cabin erected in 1775. He surveyed the townsite in 1793 when it was renamed Mt. Sterling.

FORT BAKER. A temporary Confederate fortification, it was built on what was known as Baker's Hill near Bowling Green in early 1862 by General Simon Bolivar Buckner.

BALLARD STATION. TYLER'S STATION.

BARDSTOWN FORTS. Mapped with fortifications and outlying cabins by Filson on his 1784 map, the town of Bardstown, on a branch of the Salt River, was then a part of Jefferson County. The pioneer settlement is now the seat of Nelson County.

BARNETT'S STATION. Settled by Colonel Joseph B. Barnett in or before 1790, his fortified homestead was located about two miles from Hartford, the seat of Ohio County.

BASLEY'S STATION. Located near Washington in Mason County, Basley's Station was settled before 1793.

BEAR GRASS CREEK STATIONS. There were six important fortified pioneering stations located on the banks of Bear Grass Creek in 1780 with a population of about 600 men. By 1785 the number of stations and the population of the settlement in Jefferson County had doubled.

CAMP BEAUREGARD. A large temporary Confederate encampment, named in honor of General P. G. T. Beauregard and occupied by Mississippi troops commanded by Brigadier General James L. Alcorn, it was established near Mayfield in Graves County. The camp was abandoned at the end of December, 1861, and occupied a week later by troops under Union General C. F. Smith.

FORT BEAUREGARD. A Confederate fortification situated on the east bank of the Mississippi River, Fort Beauregard was one of the defenses of Columbia, Hickman County, and located a few miles to the north of the town. Constructed late in the fall of 1861 by the Confederates under General Leonidas Polk who, having seized and occupied Columbus in September 1861, began immediately the most extensive preparations for its defense, so formidable that Columbus came to be known in official reports as the "Gibraltar of the West." Formidable works consisting of tiers of batteries fronted the river, while batteries and parapets behind strong abatis of fallen timber encompassed the town on the land side. Fort Beauregard was in the outer line of these defenses, to the north of the town, and received its name in compliment to Confederate General P. G. T. Beauregard. The fall of Forts Henry and Donelson and the positioning of Grant's forces in the rear of the city rendered the point untenable, and on March 2, 1862, General Polk evacuated Columbus and its defenses, having previously removed their armament. Federal forces retained undisputed possession of the town until the close of the war, and its elaborate system of defensive works soon became mere piles of earth.

CAMP BEECH GROVE. Established on the north bank of the Cumberland River by Confederate General Felix K. Zollicoffer in November 1861, by the middle of December the camp contained about 9,000 Confederate troops. It was abandoned after the Confederate defeat at Mill Springs (or Logan's Cross Roads) in January 1862.

When Union forces entered the entrenchments on January 20, they found the camp surrounded by a breastwork over a mile in circumference with a deep ditch in front. They counted over 500 houses. Left behind were hundreds of wagons, about 1,200 horses and mules, harness, saddles, sabres and guns, as well as 10 cannon.

BELL STATION. No definite dates have been found for this station located a half mile from Paint Lick Creek and about three miles from the present town of Paint Lick in Madison County, close to the Garrard County line.

CAMP BEN SPALDING. A temporary Civil War encampment, date indefinite, located in Marion County.

BIG SANDY BLOCKHOUSE. A frontier defense, it was erected by Charles Vancouver in 1789 at the forks of the Big Sandy River in the vicinity of present Louisa, Lawrence County.

FORT BISHOP. A temporary Civil War defense erected in 1864 by Union troops, it was located near Louisa, Lawrence County, and named in the memory of Captain William Bishop, 100th Ohio Infantry, mortally wounded at Dallas, Georgia, on May 28, 1864.

BLACK'S STATION. Located on Clear Creek in what was then Fayette but is now Jessamine County, Black's Station was built before 1794 on a knoll on the north side of a road from the Harrodsburg Pike to Troy.

BOOFMAN'S STATION. This early fortified station was built by John and Jacob Boofman on a fork of Boone's Creek in Fayette County in 1776, on land surveyed for them in 1775 by John Floyd.

BOONE'S STATION. The fort and adjacent settlement established by Squire Boone before 1780 were situated on Brashear's (Clear) Creek and located close to present-day Shelbyville. (See: PAINTED STONE STATION.)

FORT BOONESBOROUGH. About a year after James Harrod and a group of Pennsylvanians built little Fort Harrod in what is now Mercer County, the first large palisaded fort in Kentucky was built at Boonesborough in the spring of 1775 by Daniel Boone, the trailblazer of the famous Wilderness Road, and a party of men, locating it a little below the mouth of Otter Creek, south of the Kentucky River, in present Madison County. They were sponsored by Colonel Richard Henderson of North Carolina, who organized the Transylvania Company with other land speculators for the purpose of colonizing Kentucky. In possession of a purchased grant, possibly illegal, from the Cherokee Indians, Henderson laid claim to a vast tract of territory named Transylvania.

The fortification, begun as a small stockade, was greatly enlarged in 1776 by the extension of strong palisades to encompass the entire settlement and significantly strengthened by the addition of blockhouses in its angles. The oblong-shaped fortification measured about 250 feet in length and 150 feet in width. Occasional threats, minor attacks, and seizures of settlers by Indians kept the fort's garrison in a constant state of readiness. On the night of September 6, 1778, British and Indians laid siege to Boonesborough, and for the next 10 days attempted repeatedly and unsuccessfully to subjugate the frontier by demanding negotiation, by storming the fort, by setting it on fire, and even by tunneling underneath it. Boonesborough's survival was important to the larger Western struggle. What little is left of Boonesborough today is commemorated by Fort Boonesborough State Park, a small resort with one of the few sand beaches on the Kentucky River, located southeast of modern Lexington.

BOSLEY'S STATION. Established prior to 1793, Bosley's Station was located about a mile above the main fork of Wells Creek near Washington, Mason County.

BOSWELL'S STATION. A short-lived frontier post, it was built and occupied by John Boswell where Burlington, seat of Boone County, now stands. Date has not been determined.

BOWMAN'S STATION. Located about six miles east of Harrodsburg, Mercer County, Bowman's Station and village were established by 30 families under Colonel Abram Bowman in 1776. A National Archives citation reports the date as 1779.

CAMP BOYLE. A temporary Civil War encampment, Camp Boyle was established in 1861 at or near Columbia, Adair County.

FORT BOYLE. A temporary Civil War fortification erected by the 50th Ohio Infantry in 1863, the Union defense was located on "Muldraugh's Hill," in Marion County.

BRADSHAW'S STOCKADE. A defense against Indian attack, the stockade was located about a mile north of Mt. Sterling, Montgomery County. Date undetermined.

BRASHEAR'S STATION. Located just below Floyd's Fork of the Salt River on the Bardstown-Louisville Trail, it was settled in 1779 in what is now Bullitt County.

CAMP BRECKINRIDGE. Established during World War II as an infantry division training center, accommodating 40,000 men at one time, Camp Breckinridge was named in honor of Confederate General John Cabell Breckinridge, who was vice president of the United States during 1856–60. The post was located one mile east of Morganfield, Union County. The 36,000-acre camp during the war housed many German and Italian prisoners of war who worked on nearby farms and in a cannery. The post was closed at the end of the war but reactivated during the Korean War. It returned to inactive status January 1, 1954. From then on, it was used for summer training of about 4,500 Reserve and National Guard troops.

FORT BRECKINRIDGE. A temporary Confederate-built Civil War defense named for General John Cabell Breckinridge, it was established in 1864 in Pulaski County.

BRYAN'S STATION. Occasionally misspelled as Bryant's Station in early regional histories, Bryan's Station was located five miles northeast of Lexington, Fayette County. The first log cabin here was erected on the south side of North Elkhorn Creek by Joseph Bryan, a son-in-law of Daniel Boone, in 1776. The formidable stockade built in 1779 lacked the one essential to withstand a siege: its water supply was outside its walls, a spring downhill from the fort, some distance away.

In 1782 the American Revolution was long over, except for occasional minor military confrontations in the hinterland where Indians, sometimes led by British commanders, still feuded with American pioneer settlements. One of the last raids was made by about 500 Indians, along with 30 Canadian Rangers, led by Captain William Campbell. He was assisted by Simon Girty, known on the frontier as the "Great Renegade." The intent of their foray into central Kentucky was to attack and destroy Bryan's Station, which they reached on August 16. Two men of the garrison effected an escape to warn neighboring stations. It was the women of the

fort who saved the day by bringing water to the besieged garrison from the spring down the hill. Bryan's Station was thus supplied with enough water to hold out until reinforcements—some 500 men assembled from Lexington, Boonesborough, Harrodstown, and Logan's Fort, and already en route—would arrive. Only one attack was made, and that was repulsed. On the night of August 17 the Indians retreated to Blue Licks, where pursuing frontiersmen, Daniel Boone and his son Israel among them, engaged them in what became known as the Battle of Blue Licks. The Indians cleverly devised an ambuscade and annihilated the Kentuckians, outnumbered three to one. Daniel Boone escaped by swimming the river, but his son was killed. General George Rogers Clark later avenged the defeat by setting out from Cincinnati with an army of 1,000 men to completely rout the Shawnees and their confederate tribes. The Bryan Station Memorial was erected around the celebrated spring to commemorate the memory of the courageous women who risked their lives.

BRYNE'S STATION. Erected by Edmund Bryne, the station was located on the North Fork of the Licking River in what is now Mason County (date undetermined).

BUCHANAN'S STATION. Located about a mile west of Germantown in what is now Bracken County, the date of its establishment has been undetermined.

CAMP BURGESS. A Civil War encampment established by Union forces, Camp Burgess was located on the south side of what was known as Vinegar Hill at Bowling Green. Today Western Kentucky University occupies the hill and the considerable area to the south and west of it. The camp, established in 1862, was occupied by 70th Indiana Infantry.

CAMP BURNHAM. A temporary Civil War encampment established in 1861 by Confederate forces, Camp Burnham was located one mile south of Bowling Green.

CAMP BURNSIDE. A temporary (Union) Civil War post reportedly in Lincoln County.

CAMP (FORT) BURNSIDE. Most Federal encampments established in the area of the headwaters of the Cumberland River were consolidated into the camp that was established at Point Isabel and named Camp Burnside for Union General Ambrose Everett Burnside, so designated as early as January 1864. It became a major staging area for the East Tennessee campaign of 1863. General Burnside envisioned making the area surrounding Camp Burnside a defensive stronghold to prevent the numerous Confederate incursions into Kentucky. By August 1864 most military units had abandoned the area. The small village did not retain the name "Point Isabel" but changed to "Burnside." By 1950 the town of Burnside was moved by the government to higher ground after Wolf Creek Dam was completed on the Cumberland River. The old town is under water, but part of the high ground forms an island, now General Burnside State Park in Pulaski County.

BURNT STATION. Located on or near Simpson's Creek in what is now Nelson County, its date has been undetermined.

BURNT STATION. As distinguished from the above, it was located about four miles east of Lexington, Fayette County, on the Winchester Pike. It was probably built about 1780 or 1781.

BUSH'S STATION. This fortified pioneer establishment, erected by Captain William Bush, was centered in Bush's Settlement on the north side of the Kentucky River in what is now Clark County, near Boonesborough. Its approximate date is 1780.

CALDWELL'S STATION. According to John Filson's map, Caldwell's Station is shown adjacent to Irvine's Station, at the head of the Salt River, west of Danville, Boyle County.

CAMP CALVERT. A temporary Civil War post, the camp was located in eastern Kentucky, most probably in the area of Cumberland Gap.

CAMP CAMPBELL. FORT CAMPBELL.

FORT CAMPBELL (*Camp Campbell*). The site of this Kentucky-Tennessee military installation was selected in the summer of 1941. Construction was initiated the following February, and within a year the reservation had been developed into a 105,592-acre training installation. Activated in the summer of 1942, the post was named on September 23, 1942, in honor of Brigadier General William Bowen Campbell, Union officer during the Civil War and the last Whig governor of Tennessee. The state lines of Kentucky and Tennessee cut through the post, with most of its acreage lying in Montgomery and Stewart counties across the border in Tennessee.

Fort Campbell, however, is identified as being in Kentucky because of its legal post office address.

The post's first occupant was a cadre of 1 officer and 19 enlisted men from Fort Knox. During the next three years, until the end of World War II, the post served as the training ground for the 12th, 14th, and 20th armored divisions, Headquarters IV Armored Corps, and the 26th Infantry Division. During the spring of 1949, the 11th Airborne Division returned from occupation duty in Japan and was stationed at the post until early 1956. In the meanwhile, in April 1950, the post became a permanent installation of the defense establishment and was redesignated Fort Campbell. In late 1956 the 101st Airborne Division, famed for its participation in Europe during World War II, was reorganized at Fort Campbell as the Army's pioneer pentomic division, making full use of the post's seven DZs (drop zones) and 47 ranges. It remains Fort Campbell's major resident.

CAMPBELL'S STATION. Located on Dry Ridge in what is now Grant County, about three miles north of Williamstown, Campbell's Station was established prior to 1792.

CANE RIDGE STATION. Established by James Sandusky, or Sodowsky, as he was frequently called, in 1786 or 1787, it was located in what is now Bourbon County.

CAPTAIN CRAIG'S STATION. According to John Filson's map of Kentucky in 1784, this station was located on the trail leading to the southwest from Lexington to the mouth of Dicks River, probably in present Fayette County.

CARPENTER'S STATION. Erected in 1780 on the Green River between the Salt and Dicks rivers, Carpenter's Station was located about two miles west of Hustonville in Lincoln County.

CARTWRIGHT'S STATION. Established in 1779, its location has not been determined in Washington County.

CASEY'S STATION. Settled by Colonel Casey three miles west of Stanford in what is now Lincoln County, "on the waters of the Hanging Fork of Dicks River," no date has been determined for its establishment.

CASSIDY'S STATION. No date has been determined for Michael Cassidy's Station in Fleming County.

CAMP CHARITY. A temporary Confederate Civil War encampment, located 10 miles east of Bardstown, Nelson County, it was established by Captain (later General) John Hunt Morgan for recruiting troops into the 2nd Kentucky Cavalry in September 1861. A marker on U.S. 62 indicates the camp's site.

FORT CLARK. One of the encircling forts erected for the defense of Louisville during the Civil War, it was named for Lieutenant Colonel Merwin Clark, 183rd Ohio Infantry, killed in the Battle of Franklin, Tennessee, November 30, 1864. The Union fort was begun January 2, 1865, and completed February 1, 1865. It was located between Forts Karnasch and Southworth in the southwestern perimeter of the city, near Paddy's Run, on a slight elevation between two gullies. In the context of today's Louisville geography, Fort Clark's site is in the immediate vicinity of 36th and Magnolia streets.

CLARK'S STATION. Lewis' Station.

CLARK'S STATION. Built by Robert Clark on Clarke's Creek in 1784, it was located near Paris, the seat of Bourbon County. Originally Huston's Station, Paris was established in 1789 and named Hopewell. Later, it was called Bourbon Court or Bourbonton, then finally Paris.

CLARK'S STATION. An early pioneer settlement, probably erected before November 1779, it was developed and fortified by George Clark. Located on Clark's Run Creek, a branch of Dicks River, southeast of Danville, Boyle County, it was one of the first stations built in the vicinity of the forts at Harrodsburg and Stanford.

FORT CLAY. A temporary Civil War defense on the outskirts of Lexington in Fayette County, no definite date has been found of its establishment. A marker at the west end of West High Street's viaduct indicates the site.

CLEAR'S STATION. Situated in what is now Bullitt County, its date of establishment is undetermined.

CAMP CLIO. The first Union encampment established for recruiting purposes in southern Kentucky, Camp Clio was established by Colonel W. A. Hoskins in September 1861, in compliance with orders of General George Thomas. It was soon determined that the base was too near Confederate areas of influence south of the Cumberland River. General Thomas moved his operations across to the north bank of the river, in Pulaski County, in October of 1861.

CAMP COFFEY. A temporary Civil War post, it was located 19 miles south of Richmond in either Jessamine or Madison County.

CAMP COLLIER. A temporary Civil War encampment at or near Lexington.

CAMP COLLINS. A temporary Civil War post at or near Warsaw, Gallatin County.

COLLINS' STATION. Located on Rockcastle River, its exact site and date of establishment are unknown. The Rockcastle River runs through or forms boundaries of Pulaski, Laurel, and Rockcastle counties.

FORT COLONEL CHURCHILL. A temporary Civil War defense at Cumberland Gap in Bell County.

COLONEL COX'S STATION. According to John Filson's 1784 map, this station was situated on Chaplain's Trail leading from Bardstown to Louisville, on the north side of Rolling Fork Creek of the Salt River, in what is now Nelson County.

COLONEL SHELBY'S STATION. Located on a branch of the Dicks River, just southwest of Knob Lick, in the Green River country, the station was probably situated in what is now northern Metcalfe County.

CONSTANT'S STATION. This early fortified habitation was located less than a mile from Strode's Station in Clark County.

COOK'S STATION. Erected in 1790, this minimally fortified cabin home was the first of record to be erected on the site of Russellville, seat of Logan County in southwestern Kentucky.

COOK'S STATION. This fortified station, as distinguished from the above, was built early in 1792 in the bottoms of Main Elkhorn Creek, in one of the three present (Pike, Franklin, and Woodford) counties. The station was the scene of a bloody Indian raid later the same year.

COOPER'S STATION. Erected, date undetermined, on Cooper's Run in Bourbon County, it was located two miles southwest of Kiser.

CAMP (H. C.) CORBIN. A temporary Civil War encampment located at or near Lexington, Fayette County.

CORN ISLAND FORT. The fort on Corn Island was built during the late spring of 1778 by George Rogers Clark, who brought 150 militiamen from Fort Redstone, Pennsylvania, down the Ohio River to the island, just offshore from the present site of Louisville. With him came a few families—the exact number is unknown—as settlers. The fort was erected to provide shelter to the settlers and to protect Clark's military stores. It was from this fort that Clark initiated the conquest of the Illinois territory. After rejecting the mouth of the Kentucky River as unsuitable for a fortification in accordance with his needs, he explored the Falls of the Ohio and inspected several sites in that area. Upon observing that Corn Island was not flooded when the river rose, he decided to locate the fort there. During the late fall or early winter of the following year, the Corn Island fort was abandoned for a new fort on the shore. It was erected at the foot of present-day 12th Street in Louisville, and called, simply, Fort-on-Shore.

FORT COVINGTON. A Civil War fortification erected in the environs of Covington, Kenton County, it was situated approximately opposite Cincinnati across the Ohio.

COX'S FORT. Colonel Isaac Cox (Coxe), with a small band of settlers, built a fort in 1775 on Cox's Creek, near Bardstown in Nelson County.

FORT CRAIG. A Union-built Civil War star-shaped defense of Munfordville in Hart County, defended by slightly more than 4,000 Federals commanded by Colonel John T. Wilder, it was surrendered to General Braxton Bragg's Confederate forces on September 17, 1862, after a two-day siege.

CRAIG'S STATION. Established on North Elkhorn Creek in Fayette County by Lewis Craig in 1780, it was located near or between Bryan's Station and Grant's Station.

CRAIG'S STATION. Situated on a tributary creek of Dicks River in then Lincoln, now Garrard County, it was established by Rev. Lewis Craig in 1780 at a point a few miles east of present-day Lancaster.

CRAIG'S STATION. This post was located five miles from the present town of Versailles in what is now Woodford County and erected by Elijah Craig in 1783.

CRAIG'S STATION. Russell's map of 1794 shows this station as having been situated near the juncture of the Little Barren and Green rivers, near the present-day site of Munfordsville, Hart County. Its date has been undetermined.

CRAIG'S STATION. No definite date has been found for this station established two miles east of Danville in Boyle County.

CRAIG'S STATION. As distinguished from any of the above, this Craig's Station was built by Joseph Craig on South Elkhorn Creek on the old turnpike to Lexington in Fayette County.

CREW'S STATION. Located one mile northwest of the village of Foxtown and about six miles northwest of Richmond in Madison County, it was built by David Crew(s) in the fall of 1781.

CAMP CRITTENDEN. A temporary Civil War encampment in Marion County.

FORT CRITTENDEN. A temporary Civil War defense located at or near Lexington.

CRITTENDEN BARRACKS. A U.S. Army facility established in 1866 at Louisville.

CURTIS STATION. Date undetermined, this station was located about two miles southwest of Washington in Mason County.

DAVIS' BLOCKHOUSE. Built by James Davis and John Montgomery in 1782, it was located in northeastern Christian County.

FORT DEFIANCE (*Sevier's Station; New Providence Blockhouse*). This old stone-built blockhouse, built in 1788–89 by Colonel Valentine Sevier, stood near or at present-day New Providence, Calloway County, several miles north of the Tennessee border. First known as Sevier's Station, it was later called New Providence Blockhouse after the establishment of the town. After repulsing a costly Indian attack here on November 11, 1794, Colonel Sevier wrote the following letter to his brother, John Sevier:

Dear Brother: The news from this place is desperate with me. On Tuesday, 11th Nov. last, about 12 o'clock, my station was attacked by about 40 Indians. On so sudden a surprise, they were in almost every house before they were discovered. All the men belonging to the station were out save only Snyder and myself.

William Snyder, Betsy, his wife, his son John, & my son Joseph were killed in Snyder's house. They also killed Ann King & her son Jas., and scalped my daughter Rebecca. I hope she will still recover. The Indians have killed whole families about here this fall. You may hear the cries of some persons for their friends daily. The engagement commenced at my house continued for about an hour, as the neighbors say. Such a scene no man ever witnessed before. Nothing but screams & the roaring of guns, & no man to assist me for some time. [*The American Guide* (1949), p. 959]

During the Civil War, Confederate forces occupied the blockhouse and renamed it Fort Defiance.

FORT DE WOLF. A Civil War defense located at or near Shepherdsville, in Bullitt County.

FORT DERUSSEY. During the first year of the Civil War, the town of Columbus (formerly Clarksville) on the Mississippi River regained national prominence. Being then both a rail and river shipping center, Columbus was a prize for both sides. Since the Federal plan for the conquest of the South required control of the Mississippi, the Confederates, in order to checkmate that strategy, violated Kentucky's neutrality, seized and heavily fortified the bluffs, known to French explorers as the Iron Banks for their iron deposits, just above Columbus late in the summer. Under the direction of General Leonidas Polk, the Confederates erected Fort DeRussey, equipping it with batteries of 140 cannon arranged on four elevations—40, 85, and 97 feet above the water and crowning the crest of the 200-foot-high bluff. One of the guns in Fort DeRussey's array of artillery was the largest breech-loading cannon in use at that time. It was a mounted eight-inch rifled Dahlgren gun, firing 128-pound cone-shaped projectiles. It was named "Lady Polk," in honor of the commander's wife.

In addition, in order to prevent Union gunboats from moving down the river, a great chain more than a mile long was stretched across the Mississippi to Belmont, also held by Confederate forces, on the Missouri side of the river. With links weighing 15 pounds each, it was attached on the Kentucky shore to a six-ton anchor imbedded deep into the side of the bluff. A camp located on the river bank about a mile south of the town's railroad depot was occupied by elements of the 1st Mississippi Cavalry.

After attacking Belmont on the west side of the Mississippi, General Grant realized that Columbus was impregnable. He swung eastward and captured Forts Donelson and Henry, Confederate outposts on the Cumberland and Ten-

nessee rivers, respectively. Surrounded, General Polk was compelled to evacuate Columbus. Before retreating the Confederates spiked all their cannon and rolled them into the river. Today, the Columbus-Belmont Battlefield State Park is located on the bank of the Mississippi, at the old site of Columbus.

CAMP DICK ROBINSON. Established in 1861 over the protests of Beriah Magoffin, then governor of Kentucky, Camp Dick Robinson was the first Federal recruiting station south of the Ohio River. It was located south of Nicholasville in Jessamine County.

DOUGHERTY'S STATION. Established about 1780, this station was situated on Clark's Run, one and one-half miles from Danville, Boyle County.

DOVER STATION. No date has been determined for Dover Station located on the Dicks River in now Garrard County.

DOWDALL'S STATION. Built on the Salt River before 1784, Dowdall's Station was probably located in northeast Hardin County.

CAMP DUMONT. A temporary Civil War encampment, Camp Dumont was located near Shelbyville, Shelby County.

DUTCH STATION. Established in 1779 or 1780 on Bear Grass Creek in Jefferson County, it was frequently called Low Dutch Station.

ELIZABETHTOWN POST. A post was established at Elizabethtown, Hardin County, on March 29, 1871, by Company F, 4th Infantry, in compliance with Special Orders No. 61, Department of the South. The post was occupied by troops until March 7, 1873, when Troop A, 7th Cavalry, was withdrawn in obedience to Special Orders No. 13, Military Division of the South.

ELLISTON BLOCKHOUSE. The name of the first settlement on the Ohio River, just above the mouth of the Kentucky River, was Port William, incorporated within the present-day site of Carrollton, Carroll County. A blockhouse was built here in 1786 or 1787 by Captain Elliston and followed by the establishment of the town in 1792.

FORT ELSTNER. The forts flanking Fort McPherson at Louisville were built to accommodate up to 600 infantrymen and 150 artillerymen. Beginning at Bear Grass Creek, Fort Elstner, named for Brevet Brigadier General George Ruter Elstner, was between Frankfort Avenue and Brownsboro Road in the vicinity of Bellaire, Vernon, and Emerald avenues. The fort was built sometime after August 1864.

EMERSON'S STATION. Built in April 1776 by Ash Emerson, the station was located on a branch of Dry Run of North Elkhorn Creek in central Scott County.

FORT ENGLE. A Union-built Louisville defense, Fort Engle was located in the vicinity of Spring Street and Arlington Avenue. The fort was constructed sometime after August 1864.

ESTILL'S STATION. Built by Captain James and Samuel Estill in 1780, their station was located five miles southeast of Richmond in Madison County.

ESTILL'S STATION FORT (*Ashton's Station*). Most probably the same as Ashton's Station, a pioneer fort referenced in Daniel Boone's 1782 autobiography, Estill's Station was settled by Captain James Estill in 1781. It was located on Muddy Creek, three miles south of what is now Richmond in Madison County. What is known as Estill's Battleground is located on Hingston Creek, about two miles below Small Mountain. Here Captain Estill and his men were ambushed, defeated, and killed by Indians in the spring of 1782.

FISHER'S GARRISON. Sometimes referred to as Fisher's Station, the post was erected by Stephen Fisher, date undetermined, a short distance from Danville in Boyle County.

CAMP FLAT LICK. A temporary Civil War post located at or near the town of Flat Lick, Knox County.

FLEMING'S STATION. Established by Colonel John Fleming in 1790 in what is now Fleming County.

FORT-ON-SHORE. In the late fall or early winter of 1779, the fort on Corn Island was abandoned for a new fort on the mainland. It was built at the foot of present-day 12th Street in Louisville and given the unaffected name of Fort-on-Shore. (See: CORN ISLAND FORT.)

FRANKFORT POST. In compliance with Special Orders No. 60, Department of the South, the Headquarters and companies G and K, 4th Infantry, established a post at Frankfort, on March 30, 1871. It was discontinued June 3, 1876, when its garrison consisting of Company K, 16th Infantry, was withdrawn to Newport Barracks.

FRANKLIN POST. In compliance with Special Orders No. 130, Post of Louisville, Company F, 2nd Infantry, was relieved from duty at that post on December 11, 1866, and proceeded to Franklin, Simpson County, where it established a new post. It was abandoned pursuant to Special Orders No. 119, Military District of Kentucky, November 15, 1867, and Company F, 2nd Infantry, returned to the Post of Louisville, arriving there on November 19, 1867.

CAMP FRAZIER. A Civil War encampment established by Union forces, Camp Frazier was located near Cynthiana, Harrison County. On July 17, 1862, General John Morgan's raiders defeated the Home Guards in the Battle of Cynthiana, burned the depot and its military supplies, and destroyed Camp Frazier. Morgan again defeated a Federal force here June 10–11, 1864, but Union reinforcements arrived the next day and drove off the raiders. Most of the town's business section was destroyed. On June 12 Morgan was badly defeated by Union troops under Major General Stephen Burbridge. On September 4, 1863, Morgan was surprised and killed at Greenville, Tennessee, by Federal troops.

BATTERY GALLUP. Named for Captain G. A. Gallup, 13th Kentucky Infantry, killed in action near Lovejoy's Station, Georgia, September 1, 1864, this Union-built Louisville defense was completed by March 1, 1865. It was situated between Forts Southworth and Clark, on the southern edge of the Kentucky State Fair Grounds, at Gibson Lane and 43rd Street.

FORT GALLUP. This was a fort reportedly built prior to the Civil War and located on a hill at Louisa, Lawrence County, opposite Fort Gay in West Virginia.

CAMP GILBERT. A temporary Civil War encampment located near Louisville, it was established February 19, 1862, by Captain John Mendenhall, 4th Artillery, with 650 rank and file.

CAMP GILL. A temporary Civil War post at Olympa Springs, Bath County.

GIVENS' STATION. REED'S STATION.

CAMP GOGGIN. A temporary Civil War encampment near Somerset, Pulaski County.

GOODIN'S FORT. Located on the north bank of the Rolling Fork of Salt River, midway between the future towns of Nelsonville and New Haven in Nelson County, the fort was built by Samuel Goodin in 1780 not long after he arrived with his family from Fayette County, Pennsylvania. Goodin's stockaded fort occupied a strategic position as a link in the cluster of early stations encircling future Bardstown, and throughout the perilous years it offered a haven to those settlers scattered over the 12 unprotected miles lying between it and the early forts to the west that became Elizabethtown and Hodgenville. The largest known group to be protected within the stockade at one time consisted of the women and children of the 25 or more Catholic families who migrated from Maryland in 1785.

GRANT'S STATION. Located on North Elkhorn Creek in Bourbon County, five miles from Bryan's Station, the fortification was erected by Colonel John Grant of North Carolina and Captain William Ellis of Virginia, in September, 1779.

FORT GRIDER. A Confederate-built defense of Bowling Green, located on Grider's Hill, it was begun in December 1861 or January 1862.

HAGGIN'S BLOCKHOUSE. Located on the Licking River, a mile and a half above the present town of Cynthiana, Harrison County, it was erected before 1782.

FORT HALLECK. This Confederate-built fortification at Columbus in Hickman County was abandoned after Union forces captured Forts Donelson and Henry.

CAMP HAMILTON. A temporary Civil War post at or near Lexington, Fayette County.

HAMILTON'S STATION. A stockaded cabin built by Robert Hamilton about 1790 or earlier, it stood on the Shelbyville Road a few miles west of Frankfort.

HARDIN'S FORT. On the site of present-day Hardinsburg, seat of Breckinridge County, Hardin's Fort was built in 1780 by Captain William Hardin, soldier and frontiersman, and a member of one of the first families to settle in Kentucky.

HARMAN'S STATION. East Point in Floyd County, which lies directly across Levisa Fork of the Big Sandy River, is the site of Harman's Station, the first fort in Big Sandy Valley, built during the winter of 1787–88. The bottoms between East Point and Prestonburg were used as camping grounds by Union forces under General James A. Garfield during the Civil War.

HARRISON BATTERY. A Union-built defense of Covington and Newport, its armament consisted of three 12-pounder fieldpieces as of November 1862.

HARRISON'S STATION. This pioneer settlement was established prior to 1786 at a point about two miles from Harrison's Fort and about three miles from the present-day town of Cynthiana, Harrison County.

FORT HARROD. The first defenses erected in Kentucky by early pioneering settlers were forts Harrod, Boone, and Logan. James Harrod of Pennsylvania in March 1774 advertised that he would lead a party to lay claims to lands in Kentucky, which he had visited in 1773. The 30 men congregated in response to Harrod's call were piloted down the Ohio to the mouth of the Kentucky River, and up that stream and the Licking River to the site of Harrodsburg in present Mercer County, first beginning its occupation on June 16, 1774. They at once began the building of a palisaded village, with the rear of their log cabins forming its walls.

Lord Dunmore's War of 1774 was about to break out. Daniel Boone and Michael Stoner, both highly skilled woodsmen, were sent to Kentucky to warn pioneering settlers in the region. The infant settlement of Harrodsburg was temporarily abandoned until the year following when James Harrod returned and reestablished the fortified settlement. For years thereafter, Harrodsburg served as a major refuge and strongpoint for the influx of homesteaders moving through the Cumberland Gap down Daniel Boone's Wilderness Road and coming by flatboat down the Ohio River. The Pioneer Memorial State Park, at Lexington and Warwick streets in Harrodsburg, contains an authentic reproduction of the old fort, stockade, blockhouses, and cabins.

FORT HEIMAN. An auxiliary fortified Confederate position in support of Fort Henry across the Tennessee River, Fort Heiman was late in building and uncompleted when Fort Henry fell on February 6, 1862 to Union forces. Fort Heiman's site, now flooded by Kentucky Lake, is memorialized by a marker at the junction of S.R. 121 and Fort Heiman Road in Calloway County.

CAMP HENRY KNOX. FORT KNOX.

FORT HILL. The eighth fort erected by Union forces in defense of Louisville, Fort Hill was completed by March 1, 1865. Located on Goddard Avenue between Barrett and Baxter streets, the defense was named for Captain George W. Hill, 12th Kentucky Infantry, who was killed in action in front of Atlanta, Georgia, August 6, 1864.

HINKSTON'S FORT. Major John Hinkston, a native of Pennsylvania, and a noted scout and frontiersman, in 1775 led a company of settlers into Kentucky and erected a fortified station on the South Fork of Licking River, reportedly one and a half miles above Higgins' Blockhouse, near present-day Paris in Bourbon County. It was apparently abandoned in July 1776 because of frequent Indian depredations in the region. Four years later, in 1780, Hinkston returned with his family to Kentucky. Shortly after the reestablishment of his blockhouse-station, he was captured on June 24 by a large British-Indian force under Colonel Henry Bird, which also attacked and captured Ruddle's Fort in the same area. According to Jillson's history, Hinkston's Fort and Ruddle's Fort were one and the same, originally established by Isaac Ruddle, but other historical references cite two different establishments. (See: RUDDLE'S FORT.)

FORT HOBSON. A temporary Civil War defense located near Glasgow, Barren County.

FORT HOLT. Colonel John Cook, with 20 companies of men of the 7th and 28th Volunteer Infantry, 1 company of Dragoons, and 1 company of Artillery, established Fort Holt on the Ohio River, opposite Cairo, Illinois, in Ballard County. The post was apparently evacuated in January, 1862.

CAMP HOPELESS CHASE. A temporary Civil War post near Pikeville in Pike County.

FORT HORTON. A Union-built Louisville defense, Fort Horton was erected after August 1864. It was located at the intersection of Shelby and Merriweather streets. Bullets were found at Fort Horton's site as late as 1915.

CAMP HOSKINS. This was the fortified Union camp that Colonel W. A. Hoskins established when he abandoned Camp Clio. The new campsite was in the Waitsboro area, near Somerset, Pulaski County, along the north bank of the Cumberland River. Confederate shelling of this camp from the opposite river bluffs caused it to be moved to the top of the hill. The new location was called Camp Goggin.

HOY'S STATION. Established by William Hoy in the spring of 1781, his fortified station was located on the west side of the Lexington Turnpike, about six miles from Richmond in Madison County. An Indian attack against the station prompted a retaliatory force, which resulted in the defeat of a small force of men under Captain Holder near the Upper Blue Licks on August 12, 1782.

FORT HUTCHINSON. A temporary Civil War defense near Mt. Sterling, Montgomery County.

IRVINE'S STATION. This station, probably fortified, was established by Colonel William Irvine in 1778 or 1779 a short distance south of Richmond, Madison County.

FORT JEFFERSON. Erected in 1780 by George Rogers Clark, it represented his last outpost of civilization in the West. The short-lived fortification, named in honor of Thomas Jefferson, then Governor of Virginia, was situated on an elevation on the east side of the Mississippi, five miles below Cairo, Illinois, at the mouth of the Ohio River. Located near Wickliffe, Ballard County, it stood in what was then Chickasaw country. The presence of the fort aroused Indian resentment, culminating in the cementing of an alliance between the Chickasaws and the British. Fort Jefferson was abandoned a year later because it provided little or no protection for the progress of western settlement.

FORT JONES. A Civil War defense at or near Colesburg, Hardin County, it was attacked by Confederate raiders on February 18, 1865.

FORT KARNASCH. One of the Union Army's 10-mile-long line of defenses of Louisville, Fort Karnasch, built after August 1864, occupied ground on Wilson Avenue between 26th and 28th streets.

BATTERY (PHIL) KEARNY. A Union-built defense of Covington and Newport, with an armament of one 32-pounder and one 24-pounder smoothbores as of November 1862, the fortification was located between Fort Whittlesey and Battery Shaler.

KELLER'S STATION. Keller's Station was built before 1780 on Bear Grass Creek near Louisville.

KENNEDY'S STATION. Established by John and Joseph Kennedy prior to 1779, this station was located near or on Silver Creek in Madison County.

CAMP KENTON. This Civil War encampment was established by Union Lieutenant William Nelson in the fall of 1861 near Maysville, Mason County, after General George Thomas succeeded him in command at Camp Dick Robinson.

KENTON'S STATION. Situated three miles southwest of what was then Limestone, now Maysville, and within a mile of Washington, in Mason County, it was established in 1784 by Simon Kenton, one of Kentucky's most noted pioneers. The town, on the south side of the Ohio, was settled in the same year by the erection of a blockhouse by Edward Waller, John Waller, and George Lewis of Virginia.

KILGORE'S STATION. Located in 1782 near what is now the southern boundary of Logan County, on the south side of the Red River on the Kentucky-Tennessee line, it was successfully attacked by Indians during the same year.

CAMP KING. A Civil War post near Covington, Kenton County.

BATTERY (J. L. M.) KIRBY. A Civil War defense of Covington and Newport, and of Cincinnati, Ohio.

CAMP KNOX. FORT KNOX.

FORT KNOX (*Camp Henry Knox; Camp Knox*). Located some 30 miles south of Louisville, Fort Knox, the "Home of Armor," has served as a U.S. military reservation since 1918. During this time it has played an integral part in the training of active duty and reserve members of the Army. Its history involves not only the reservation but also the surrounding area, rich in Civil War lore.

In 1903 large-scale Army maneuvers took place near Stithton, which was located in and around what is now the traffic circle on post. At that time Congress was considering the area as a site for a military installation, but it was not until the United States became involved in World War I that 10,000 acres were leased in January 1918. Before then the U.S. Army had a small field artillery corps and no training areas. During World War I, four artillery training centers were established, including one at Stithton. The new artillery cantonment was named Camp Henry Knox (shortened to Camp Knox) in honor of Major General Henry Knox, the Revolutionary War chief of artillery.

On June 25, 1918, $1.6 million were allocated to purchase 40,000 acres. In July construction began on the camp facilities. However, the signing of the Armistice and reduction of the Army during 1921–22 curtailed construction activities. The camp was then closed as a permanent installation, and from 1922 to 1932 it was used primarily as a training center for the Fifth Corps area, Reserve officers, Citizens Military Training Camps (CMTC) and National Guardsmen. In 1925 it was designated as Camp Henry Knox National Forest, but this status ended in 1928, when two infantry companies were assigned to the camp. Fort Knox has been most closely identified with Armor and the Armored Force.

The first commander of the Armored Force was Colonel Daniel Van Voorhis. Fort Eustis, Vir-

FORT KNOX. Headquarters. (Courtesy of the U.S. Army.)

FORT KNOX. VIP head-
quarters. (Courtesy of
the U.S. Army.)

ginia, was selected as the site for the experimental force, but the area lacked the necessary
maneuver terrain. It was decided that the size
and varied terrain of Camp Knox was more
suitable for organizing and training the
"Mechanized Cavalry Brigade." In November
1931 the first elements of the Armored Force
began moving into Camp Knox. It was here that
the new vehicles and concepts were tested. Staff
officers, Colonel George S. Patton, Jr., among
them, met and decided that the Army had to
start a unified development of armored units,
separate from Cavalry and Infantry. The German
blitzkrieg of Poland and France led to new
thoughts on the uses of Armor and provided
additional impetus for the formation of armored
units.

On January 1, 1932, Congress designated Fort
Knox as a permanent garrison. Later the Treasury
Department selected a portion of Fort Knox as
the site for the gold depository, and in 1936 the
U.S. Bullion Depository was completed. In July
1940 the Armored Force was created with the
Headquarters, I Armored Corps; 1st Armored
Division; Armored Force Board; and a comparatively small Armored Force School, centered at
Fort Knox. The school opened with a cadre of
155 officers and 1,458 enlisted men; by May 1943
there were more than 700 officers and 3,500
enlisted men. The school itself used more than
500 buildings. During this time construction activities rapidly expanded the post. In 1940 there
were 864 buildings; by 1943 there were 3,820, a
rate of 160 buildings a month. By 1943 the total
acreage had increased to 106,861 acres.

Since then Fort Knox has remained the site
for the Armor Center. To commemorate Fort
Knox's past, the Patton Museum of Cavalry and
Armor was established in 1949 to preserve historical materials relating to cavalry and armor

and to make these properties available for public
exhibit and research. The museum has been
recently expanded and is presently the most-
visited Army museum in the United States. Today,
Fort Knox is the largest single stateside Army
activity, and the biggest industry in the state of
Kentucky. The installation serves more than
110,000 persons, including active Army personnel and retirees and their family members and
Reserve personnel. It has the largest operating
budget of any Army installation.

BATTERY KYLE. A Union-built Civil War
defense of Covington and Newport, established
in 1862.

LANDFORD BLOCKHOUSE. Standing
behind the courthouse in Mt. Vernon, Rockcastle
County, is Landford House, built in 1790 as a
blockhouse defense against Indians.

LEBANON POST. The military history of this
post began about November 17, 1861, when
Brigadier General George H. Thomas established
at Lebanon, in Marion County, the headquarters
of the 1st Kentucky Brigade, Department of the
Cumberland. The post was occupied, except for
intervals, throughout the Civil War. On July 12,
1862, the post was captured by Brigadier General
John Morgan's raiders. On July 5, 1863, the post
was again attacked by Morgan to secure the ammunition depot at Lebanon. The town was held
by the 20th Kentucky Infantry for seven hours.
Morgan burned the town to force the regiment's
surrender.

The Post of Lebanon was abandoned in the
summer of 1865, apparently by Company B, 23rd
Volunteer Reserve Corps Infantry. Special Orders
No. 114, Post of Louisville, October 24, 1866,
ordered a detachment from various companies

of the 2nd Infantry to be stationed at Lebanon. The post appears to have been formally organized on August 21, 1868. It was abandoned on October 29, 1876, by a detachment of Company K, 2nd Infantry, as directed by Special Orders No. 150, Department of the South.

BATTERY LEE. A Union-built Civil War defense of Covington and Newport, and of Cincinnati, Ohio.

FORT LEONIDAS. A Confederate-built fortification whose location has not been determined.

LEWIS' STATION (*Clark's Station*). Originally settled by George Clark in 1785 or 1787 on the site of present Lewisburg, seven miles from Maysville, in Mason County, it was abandoned probably sometime in 1788. It was resettled a year later by George Lewis.

LEXINGTON STATION. The town of Lexington, founded in 1776, was developed by Colonel Robert Patterson and others. About April 1, 1779, a blockhouse was erected against Indian attack, with its first improvements consisting of three rows of cabins, the two outer serving as a part of the walls of the fortification.

LIBERTY FORT. Located on the Salt River in Mercer County, it stood about three-quarters of a mile below McAfee Station.

LITTLE FORT. TWITTY'S FORT.

LOCUST THICKET FORT. Settled prior to 1780 by James Estill on a 1,000-acre tract in Madison County, embracing both Mud and Otter Creeks, it was located within one mile of the Little or Twitty's Fort.

LOGAN'S FORT (*St. Asaph's Fort*). Frequently called St. Asaph and Logan's Station during Kentucky's colonial period, Logan's Fort was erected in 1775 by Colonel Benjamin Logan and other pioneering settlers, about a mile west of the present-day town of Stanford in Lincoln County. It was located about 10 miles from Boonesborough and 20 miles from Harrodsburg. Colonel Logan was a native of Virginia who played a prominent part in the early development of Kentucky. A noted Indian fighter, he served in numerous campaigns of this period. Logan's Fort had been described as "an oblong square formed by the houses making a double street, [and] at the angles were stockaded bastions."

FORT LYON. On Pinnacle Mountain near Corbin are the ruins of Civil War Fort Lyon, held in turn by both Union and Confederate forces.

FORT LYTLE. FORT ALBERT SIDNEY JOHNSTON.

MCAFEE'S STATION. James McAfee, possibly one of the men who accompanied James Harrod during his initial pioneering expedition to Kentucky, established a station on the Salt River about six or seven miles below the present site of Harrodsburg.

MCAFEE'S STATION. This settlement is not to be confused with the one named above. It was erected by William McAfee about one mile west of Harrodsburg at the mouth of Town Branch, in Mercer County.

MCCLELLAND'S FORT. This large station and fort, occupying a part of the present city of Georgetown, the seat of Scott County, was founded in 1775 or 1776, depending on the historical source cited, by John, Alexander, and William McClelland. The fort stood beside what has been known since pioneering days as the "Royal Spring," which to this day is still flowing at the rate of 20,000 gallons an hour, furnishing the city's entire water supply, as well as supplying power for some of its manufacturing plants. The fort, 12 miles north of Lexington, underwent a long and disastrous siege by a large party of Indians on December 29, 1776. John McClelland was badly wounded and died a week later. After the attack the station was abandoned but reoccupied in 1784 as Lebanon. In 1790 it was incorporated as Georgetown, Virginia, in honor of President George Washington. The fort served for many years as a refuge and shelter for pioneers emigrating farther west.

BATTERY MCKEE. This was a Civil War defense of Covington and Newport, and of Cincinnati, Ohio.

MCKINLEY'S BLOCKHOUSE. Located on the old Buffalo Trace south of Washington in Mason County, it was built by James McKinley in 1785.

BATTERY MCLEAN. A Union-built Civil War defense of Covington and Newport, it stood on Locust Hill in late 1862.

MCMILLIN'S FORT. Built in 1779, it was located in either northern Bourbon or southern Harrison County.

FORT MCPHERSON. Between August 1864 and the end of the Civil War, 11 forts and 12 batteries were built by Union forces, with the city of Louisville contributing $12,000 toward the cost and an army of forced laborers. The line of fortifications was about 10 miles in length, extending from Bear Grass Creek and the Ohio on the east, to Paddy's Run and the Ohio on the west, and angled to cover with overlapping fire every turnpike leading into the city. The forts were named for Union officers killed in battle. Fort McPherson, the key works in the center, was built to accommodate up to 1,500 infantrymen and 300 artillerymen. It occupied a large site in the vicinity of Preston Street, bounded by Barbee, Brandeis, Hahn, and Fort streets.

BATTERY MCRAE. A Union-built defense of Covington and Newport, its armament consisted of four 12-pounder fieldpieces, as of November 1862.

CAMP MADISON. A temporary Civil War encampment, its location in Franklin County has been undetermined.

MARTIN'S (STATION) FORT. This pioneer station fort on the Licking River was attacked, captured, and pillaged by a force of British and Indians, commanded by Colonel Henry Bird, during the last week of June 1780. The attack was made after Hinkston's Fort was taken.

MAULDING'S FORT. The site of this stockaded fort, built in 1780 on the Red River, is located 10 miles south of Russellville in Logan County. It was named for the James Maulding family, which emigrated from Virginia and later significantly participated in the development of Russellville.

CAMP MILL FARM. A temporary Civil War post near Lexington.

FORT MITCHEL. A Union defense of Covington and Newport located on the west side of the Licking River, Fort Mitchel was built by and named for General Ormsby McKnight Mitchel in 1862. General Mitchel died of yellow fever on October 30, 1862, at Beaufort, North Carolina. As of November 1862, the fort's armament consisted of one 30-pounder Parrott, and two 24-pounder and two 32-pounder smoothbores.

MONTGOMERY'S (STATION) FORT. Located on the headwaters of the Green River, 12 miles from Logan's Fort in Lincoln County, the station was established by William Montgomery in 1780.

CAMP MOORE. A temporary Civil War post near Columbus, Hickman County.

MORGAN'S STATION. Established at the confluence of Spencer and Slate creeks prior to 1793, Morgan's Station was located about seven miles east of Mt. Sterling, in present Montgomery County. On April 1, 1793, a force of Indians captured the station and carried away 19 prisoners, all women and children.

FORT MORTON. This Union-built defense of Louisville, erected after August 1864, was named for General James St. Clair Morton and located at 16th and Hill streets in Louisville.

MOUNT VERNON POST. A post at Mount Vernon, Rockcastle County, was established April 11, 1871, by Company D, 7th Cavalry, commanded by Major J. G. Tilford. The post was discontinued and the troops removed to Crab Orchard, October 9, 1871, in compliance with Special Orders No. 209, Department of the South. Crab Orchard Post was abandoned December 25, 1872, when its then garrison consisting of Company B, 4th Infantry, was transferred to Little Rock, Arkansas.

MUD GARRISON. A fortified settlement midway between Bullitt's Lick and the Falls of the Salt River, it was established during or shortly prior to 1778. It occupied a part of the present townsite of Shepherdsville in Bullitt County. Mud Garrison, fortified by two rows of stockades, was occupied by families of salt makers.

CAMP NELSON. One of the foremost concentration camps for Federal troops and munitions during the Civil War, Camp Nelson was located near Hickman's Bridge, in the vicinity of Nicholasville, Jessamine County. The cemetery there has the graves of 3,000 Union soldiers, more than 500 of whom had lost their lives at the Battles of Perryville and Richmond.

FORT NELSON. The establishment of Louisville was not made until the spring of 1778, when young George Rogers Clark brought 150 militiamen and a small number of families down the Ohio River to Corn Island, just offshore from the site of the future city. A fort was erected on the island to provide a temporary home for the settlers and to protect Clark's military stores. In 1779 they moved to the mainland and built a

FORT NELSON. Drawing of the fort as it looked upon completion in 1782. (Courtesy of the Filson Club.)

blockhouse fort of logs, called simply Fort-on-Shore, thus creating a new settlement.

In 1780 the Virginia Legislature passed an act for establishing the town of Louisville, named in honor of Louis XVI of France, which was then furnishing military aid to the Americans during the War of the Revolution. A stronger fort was constructed in 1781–82 and called Fort Nelson in honor of Governor Thomas Nelson of Virginia. The fort occupied an acre of ground along the Ohio shore, on present Main Street between 7th and 9th streets. A block of granite bearing an inscribed bronze tablet on the northwest corner of Main and 7th streets commemorates the fort. Plans to build a reproduction of Fort Nelson in the small park at Main and 7th streets were shelved by the Louisville Landmarks Commission after concerns were expressed that the replica would constitute a safety hazard and was inconsistent with Fort Nelson Park's original purpose as an open space.

CAMP NEVIN. This was a temporary Civil War post nine miles below Elizabethtown in Hardin County.

NEW HOLLAND STATION. The existence of this early fortification in Jefferson County is well substantiated, but the precise date of its establishment and its location remain undetermined. It is believed it was erected before 1784.

NEWPORT BARRACKS. Located at the juncture of the Ohio and Licking rivers, the site of Newport Barracks is now occupied by the Newport City Park. In the late eighteenth century, when Cincinnati was called Losantiville, forts were necessary for the protection of the city's inhabitants. Losantiville had its Fort Washington; Newport had no fort. On application to the War

Department, the Newport Barracks Post was formed in late July 1803. The post was first occupied on May 22, 1806, by Ensign J. W. Albright and 13 enlisted men of the 1st Infantry.

The barracks were erected on more than five acres of land outside Newport and cost one dollar—possibly the first one-dollar transaction ever made by the government. The little army post met many needs during the hectic years that followed. In 1811 it was used as a supply depot for munitions and provisions for General Harrison at Vincennes. The 4th Infantry under General Boyd trained there for six months before going into battle at Tippecanoe. In 1812 the post served as the first prisoner of war camp housing British prisoners. During the Mexican War it was a rendezvous for volunteer soldiers who had enlisted west of the Allegheny Mountains.

The unpredictable Ohio, a flood menace for centuries, caused abandonment of the Newport post and establishment of Fort Thomas on ground high above the river. The Newport reservation was inundated during the historic Ohio flood of 1884. After several floods, General Philip Sheridan made a survey for the War Department and that decided that the 111 acres of land overlooking the Ohio River and about four miles from Newport in the highlands of Campbell County was a fine spot for a new Army post. By an act dated July 31, 1894, the facility was relinquished to the city of Newport. Newport Barracks was finally abandoned on November 10, 1894, by Company E, 6th Infantry, and the reservation was actually transferred to the city on January 1, 1895, for park purposes. (See: FORT THOMAS.)

NEW PROVIDENCE BLOCKHOUSE. FORT DEFIANCE.

NORTH BATTERY. A Union-built defense of Cincinnati and Covington.

CAMP NORTHWEST. A Confederate Civil War post located near Huntersville, Clinton County.

OLD BATTERY. A Union-built Covington-Newport defense located on the west side of the Licking River, the fortification was actually constructed but not used.

CAMP OWENTON. A Civil War recruiting post, probably temporary, it was established at or near the town of Owenton, in Owen County.

PADUCAH POST (*Van Schrader Barracks*). This post was established as a rendezvous for recruits at Paducah in McCracken County on April 3, 1865, in accordance with General Orders No. 20, Headquarters Department of Kentucky, of the same date. It was also known as the Van Schrader Barracks and was situated one and a half miles from the city, due west and about three-quarters of a mile from the Ohio River. It was evacuated by the withdrawal of troops on May 8, 1869, but was reoccupied by Company D, 4th Infantry, on March 27, 1871. The post was abandoned with the departure of Company G, 4th Infantry, January 14, 1873.

PAINTED STONE STATION. Also known as Boone's Station, it was located just north of the present town of Shelbyville, and established prior to 1780. The important station was Squire Boone's military base during the summer of 1780.

PAINT LICK STATION. Paintsville, seat of Johnson County, occupied the site of this station, an old trading post.

PATTERSON'S FORT. Lexington is shown by John Filson on his map of 1784 as a fortification surrounded by numerous dwellings in the heart of the Elkhorn country. According to tradition, John Maxwell and a group of hunters camped at a spring on the site of the metropolis in the summer of 1775, and named it for Lexington, Massachusetts, where the first battle of the American Revolution had just been fought. The first blockhouse or fort at Lexington was built by Colonel Robert Patterson and his men who had come from Harrod's Fort for that specific purpose on April 17, 1779. Lexington eventually became the central town in the Bluegrass country, "the Athens of the West."

FORT PEQUOD. Probably a temporary Civil War defense, it was located about two miles west of Portersville, Clay County.

BATTERY PERRY. A Union-built Civil War defense of Covington and Newport.

PHILLIPS' FORT. Located on the north side of Nolin Creek, about one and a half miles from present-day Hodgenville, Larue County, it was established by Philip Phillips, a surveyor from Pennsylvania, about 1780 or 1781.

FORT PHILPOT. Union-built after August 1864, Fort Philpot was located in the vicinity of 7th Street and Algonquin Parkway, in Louisville.

CAMP POUND GAP. A Confederate post, it was situated at Pound Gap, on the summit of Cumberland Mountain, near the town of Jenkins, Letcher County. The camp was attacked by General James Abram Garfield (later the twentieth president of the United States) on March 14, 1862. The Confederates' barracks, huts, and military stores were burned, forcing them to retreat into Virginia.

FORT (COLONEL) RAINS. A Confederate fortification built and manned by Tennessee troops commanded by Colonel (later Brigadier General) James Edwards Rains, during the winter of 1861–62, it was located at Cumberland Gap in Bell County. General Rains was killed almost instantly during the Battle of Murfreesboro at Stones River, Tennessee, on December 31, 1862.

REED'S STATION (*Givens' Station*). Givens' Station was located about a mile southwest of Danville, Boyle County, and established prior to February 1780. Later, after John Reed came into its possession, it was renamed Reed's Station.

FORT RENO. By August 20, 1864, Union-built Fort Reno, erected adjacent to Camp Clio, was four-fifths complete. Located near present-day Burnside (named for Fort Burnside), Pulaski County, the fortification contained two embrasures and two barbette platforms. Its parapet was 153 feet long, and its magazine 14 feet long and 7 feet high.

RUDDLE'S FORT. Misnamed as "Riddle" by John Filson on his map of 1784, this fort was located on the east bank of the South Fork of the Licking River in Bourbon County, about seven miles from present-day Paris. The fort was established by pioneer Isaac Ruddle in 1777. It was captured and destroyed in June 1780, by British and Indians commanded by Colonel

Henry Bird, originating in Detroit. (See: HINKSTON'S FORT.)

ST. ASAPH'S FORT. LOGAN'S FORT.

SALT RIVER GARRISON. A minimally fortified post established on the lower Saot River, it was located near present-day Salt River, Bullitt County.

SANDUSKY FORT. Located on Pleasant Run in what is now Washington County, this fortified station was established by James Sandusky, or Sodowsky, in 1776. About 10 years later he removed to and established Cane Ridge in Bourbon County. (See: CANE RIDGE STATION.)

CAMP SANGER. A temporary Civil War post, it was located at or near Lexington, Fayette County.

FORT SAUNDERS. A Union-built Civil War defense of Louisville erected after August 1864, it was located in present-day Cave Hill Cemetery and situated between Fort Hill on the south and Fort Engle on the north.

FORT SAYLES. A fortification built by Union forces and completed before August 20, 1864, it was located near Fort Burnside at what was formerly known as Point Isabel, now the town of Burnside in Pulaski County. Fort Sayles had two embrasures and two barbette batteries, with a parapet 151 feet long and a magazine 27 feet long, 6 feet 3 inches wide, and 7 feet high. A continuous rifle pit, 6,500 feet long, extended from the fort to the bluffs of the Cumberland River.

CAMP SECESSION. Probably a Civil War Confederate encampment, it was located at "Ellicott's Mills," near Cairo, Illinois, in Ballard County.

SEVIER'S STATION. FORT DEFIANCE.

BATTERY SHALER. Constructed by Union forces, Battery Shaler served as a strong defense for the Covington-Newport sector and the Ohio River. As of November 1862, its armament consisted of three 12-pounder fieldpieces and two 32-pounder smoothbores, requiring in addition two 30-pounder Parrotts and one 32-pounder smoothbore.

BATTERY SIMONS. A Civil War defense of Munfordville, Hart County.

SLATE BLOCKHOUSE. Erected in 1788 in the vicinity of Slate Creek Furnace, it was located in what was then Bourbon but now Bath County.

BATTERY SLAYTON. A Civil War defense of Munfordville, Hart County.

BATTERY SMITH. A Union-built defense of Covington and Newport, Battery Smith's armament consisted of four 12-pounder fieldpieces as of November 1862.

CAMP (C. F.) SMITH. A Union encampment located at or near Louisville and named for General Charles Ferguson Smith, this post was established on February 22, 1862, by Captain John Mendenhall, 4th Artillery, with 424 men. Camp Smith's armament consisted of two 12-pounder howitzers, one Rodman siege gun, two Rodman rifle guns, and other ordnance.

FORT (C. F.) SMITH. This Union-held position was not a fort in the sense of structural defenses, only extensive breastworks and rifle pits. They were begun by Confederate forces in September 1861, and completed by Union troops after the Confederates evacuated Bowling Green on February 15, 1862, and held by them until the end of the war. Fort Smith, named in honor of General Charles Ferguson Smith, was located on what was then called College Hill because it was the site of the proposed Methodist College. Today the eminence is known as Reservoir Hill and occupied by the Bowling Green-Warren County Hospital.

FORT SOUTHWORTH. The last Union-built Louisville defense in the 10-mile-long line was on Paddy's Run, a short distance from the Ohio and named Fort Southworth. Built after August 1864, Fort Southworth was largely intact as late as 1936. The city of Louisville built its new sewage disposal plant on top of the fort.

FORT SPRING. This was possibly a Civil War defense located at "Fort Spring," in Fayette County.

SPURLOCK'S STATION. Built in 1791 by John Spurlock, this station was situated "in the big bottoms opposite the mouth of Middle Creek of the Levisa Fork of Big Sandy." A settlement gradually grew here and soon became known as Preston's Station, later Prestonburg. In 1799 it was declared the county seat of Floyd County, which then comprised practically all of the territory in eastern Kentucky.

STRODE'S STATION. Misspelled "Stroud" by John Filson on his 1784 map, Strode's Station was established by Samuel Strode in 1779 about two miles from present Winchester, Mason County. It became a point of considerable military importance during the early Indian wars. In 1780 it was besieged by a large party of Indians but the station's garrison repulsed the series of attacks.

TANNER'S STATION. A military post on the Ohio River in Boone County, almost opposite Lawrenceburg in Indiana, Tanner's Station was situated on the site of the present town of Petersburg. The station was established in 1785 two or three miles below the mouth of the Miami.

TANNER'S STATION. This station, as distinguished from the above, was located about six miles northwest of Richmond, settled by John Tanner in 1787, in Madison County. The station was built a year later.

CAMP TAYLOR. A World War I post located on the southern outskirts of Louisville, the site for Camp Taylor was selected by the government on June 22, 1917. The first building was begun the next day under the supervision of Major Frank E. Lamphere, constructing quartermaster.

TAYLOR BARRACKS. A temporary post at Louisville, Taylor Barracks was established in July 1871 by Colonel Samuel D. Sturgis, 7th Cavalry, with eight companies, comprising cavalry, infantry, and artillery units, aggregating 320 men.

TECUMSEH POST. Occupied from December 1856 to February 1857, the Post of Tecumseh was established by Captain Franklin F. Flint, 6th Infantry, with Company A, aggregating 68 men.

FORT TERRILL. A Union-built defense of Munfordville, Hart County, during the Confederate siege in September 1862, Fort Terrill was located just southeast of Fort Willich.

FORT THOMAS. Built in 1889 and 1890 on a site selected in 1887 by General Philip Sheridan high above the Ohio to replace frequently inundated Newport Barracks, Fort Thomas, located about three miles from the city of Newport, was named in honor of Union general George H. Thomas, who distinguished himself by rescuing Union forces from total defeat at the Battle of Chickamauga. The post was first occupied on August 15, 1890, by two companies of the 6th Infantry, later reinforced by two additional companies of the same regiment from Fort Porter, New York. The post's first commanding officer was Colonel Melville Cockran. Over the next half century and during three wars, despite intermittent abandonments, Fort Thomas served as an induction center, replacement depot, and military hospital for wounded convalescents. In 1946 the post was converted into a Veterans Administration Hospital Rehabilitation Center, covering about 116 acres of the former reservation.

THOMAS' STATION. Built as a frontier post in the fall of 1784 by William Thomas on 400 acres of land bought from John Kennedy on Kennedy's Creek, a branch the Licking River, the station was located in what is now Bourbon County.

TWITTY'S FORT (*Little Fort*). This blockhouse, at times known as the Little Fort, was established about five miles south of present-day Richmond, Madison County. During its colonial period, it was often referred to as the "first fort," having been built in 1775, but it was actually preceded by James Harrod's Station erected in 1774.

TYLER'S STATION (*Ballard Station*). Situated about three miles east of Shelbyville in Shelby County on Tick Creek, this station was named for Captain Robert Tyler, who established it in 1781. Later this important fortified station was occupied by Bland Ballard.

CAMP (JOE) UNDERWOOD. A temporary Union encampment, located about 25 miles from Cave City, Barren County, Camp Underwood was attacked by Confederate forces on October 24, 1861.

FORT UNDERWOOD. A Confederate-built defense of Bowling Green, occupying what was known as Underwood's Hill, Fort Underwood served as General Albert Sidney Johnston's headquarters until February 1862, when he evacuated the town after the downfall of Forts Donelson and Henry.

VANCOUVER'S FORT. A formidable blockhouse fort, it was erected in the fork of the Big

Sandy River near the present town of Louisa, Lawrence County, in 1789 by Charles Vancouver. It was occupied less than a year when the activities of Shawnee and Delaware Indians in the area became life-threatening. The group of settlers garrisoning the fortification were compelled to abandon the station on foot after their horses were stolen.

VAN METER'S FORT. Erected prior to 1790 in what is now Hardin County.

VAN SCHRADER BARRACKS. PADUCAH POST.

CAMP WADSWORTH. This was a temporary Civil War encampment at or near Hazelgreen in Wolfe County.

FORT WALLACE. One of several fortifications proposed by Union officers to be built along the Cumberland River in the vicinity of present-day Burnside in Pulaski County, by August 20, 1864, the only work performed was the clearing of some six acres of timber. Apparently the fortification was never completed.

FORT WEBB. One of several Confederate fortifications built for the defense of Bowling Green during the first year of the Civil War, it was evacuated and abandoned along with the others when General Albert Sidney Johnston found the town untenable after the downfall of forts Donelson and Henry in February 1862. Fort Webb's site is located next to the Bowling Green Country Club off Beech Bend Road and contained within Fort Webb Park.

FORT WHITTLESEY. Built by Union forces during 1862, Fort Whittlesey was an earthwork fortification located about two and a half miles southeast of Newport. It was probably named for Colonel Charles Whittlesey, 20th Ohio Infantry, and chief engineer, Department of the Ohio.

CAMP WICKLIFFE. A temporary Union encampment located northeast of Hodgenville, Nelson County, Camp Wickliffe was occupied by elements of the 4th Division, Army of the Ohio, from January to March 1862. It was under the command of Major General William Nelson.

BATTERY WIGGINS. A Union-built defense of Covington and Newport, and of Cincinnati, Ohio.

CAMP WILDCAT. Located near London in Laurel County and established by Union forces in 1861, Camp Wildcat was attacked on October 12, 1861, by Brigadier General Felix Kirk Zollicoffer with seven regiments and a light battery. The Wildcat battleground was the opening action of the Civil War in Kentucky. The camp, manned by the 7th Kentucky Infantry under the command of Brigadier General Albion Schoepf, occupied a natural fortification known as Wildcat Mountain. The Kentucky regiment repulsed the Confederates' first attack, providing enough time for the arrival of reinforcements that threw back later attacks. The site today includes deteriorated trenches and dugouts, a cliff overhang used as a Union hospital area, and a small cemetery with the empty graves of two Union soldiers.

FORT WILLIAM. Established in 1785 at the present-day town of St. Matthews, just east of Louisville, by William Christian and his wife, Anne, a sister of Patrick Henry, was Fort William, one of the earliest stone houses in Kentucky. A famous tavern standing on Harrod's Trace to the Falls of the Ohio, Eight Mile House was the base from which Colonel Christian directed the defense of Jefferson County.

FORT WILLIAMS. The site of this Civil War fort built in the spring of 1863 by Union forces is west of the Glasgow Municipal Cemetery, between the cemetery and U.S. 31-E Bypass, Barren County. It was attacked on October 6, 1863, by Confederate Colonel John M. Hughes and his 25th Tennessee Infantry, surprising the Union troops under Major Samuel Martin. More than 200 horses were captured, part of the fort burned, and 142 men taken prisoner, later paroled.

FORT WILLICH. A Union-built defense of Munfordsville, Hart County, it was surrendered along with other fortifications after a three-day siege by General Braxton Bragg's Confederate forces in September 1862. The Federal garrison of slightly over 4,000 men under Colonel John T. Wilder surrendered their arms.

CAMP WOLFORD. This camp and base of operations was established by Colonel Wolford and the 1st Kentucky Cavalry in November 1861, near Somerset, Pulaski County. It was established at this particular point because here was the fordable area of the Cumberland River; Confederate raiding parties had made it a favorite highway into central Kentucky. The camp was used as part of a staging area for General Ambrose Burnside's East Tennessee campaign in 1863. Camp Wolford was little used thereafter.

FORT (GEORGE) WOOD. Situated just north of Munfordsville, Hart County, Fort Wood was a Union three-gun battery overlooking the town.

WORTHINGTON'S FORT. Located four miles west of present Danville, Boyle County, this fortification was built by Captain Edward Worthington in 1779. He had been wounded at McClelland's Fort in December 1776 during an Indian siege and had moved to Harrodsburg, from which he later traveled to the Danville area and erected his fort. He had been one of George Rogers Clark's officers during the Northwest Campaign.

CAMP YOUNG. Established at West Point, Bullitt County, as a maneuvers camp in August 1903, Camp Young was used by troops from the departments of the East, the Lakes, and Missouri, together with militia from Ohio, Indiana, and Kentucky. They were assembled there under the command of Major General John C. Bates. The post does not appear to have been occupied after January 1904.

CAMP ZACHARY TAYLOR. This post was established early in World War I at Louisville as Camp Taylor for the 82nd Division and named in honor of Major General Zachary Taylor, president of the United States. On September 15, 1917, the name of the camp was changed to Camp Zachary Taylor. The post was abandoned on July 11, 1921.

PRESIDIO DE LOS ADAES (ADAIS). This long-enduring Spanish fort, properly known as the Presidio de Nuestra Señora del Pilar de los Adaes, was located in Natchitoches Parish on a site less than 2 miles northeast of Robeline and about 14 miles west of Natchitoches, garrisoned by the French. Concerned by the threat of French encroachment into Spanish-claimed territory, the Spaniards in 1716 had established San Miguel de Linares Mission among the Adais Indians. In 1719 the mission was attacked and destroyed by a French force from Fort St. Jean Baptiste de Natchitoches. The Spanish returned with a large expedition that arrived on August 29, 1721, at a new site near the wrecked mission. By the first week of November, they had completed a hexagonal fort, about 150 feet to a side, enclosing a small number of shingle-roofed adobe buildings used as officers' quarters, barracks, magazines, storehouses, and a chapel, protected by an initial garrison of 100 men and six brass cannon. A new mission, San Miguel de los Adaes, was established on a hill less than a mile away.

For the next half-century, the presidio was an important outpost and the capital of the frontier province of Texas, the seat of 13 Spanish governors until 1773, when the fort was abandoned. The site's strategic importance was still recognized in 1806 when a preliminary treaty was signed there between Ensign Joseph María Gonzáles and Captain Edward Turner of the U.S. Army, by which the former agreed to retreat to Spanish-owned Texas and to cease dispatching Spanish patrols across the border into the United States. This treaty led to the formal establishment, a few weeks later, of "neutral ground" between Texas and the United States by General James Wilkinson and Spanish Lieutenant Commander Simon de Herrera. The two nations honored the boundary for just 14 years. Today, only a few unidentified mounds of earth are visible on the ridge where the presidio stood. Of the 40 acres or so encompassing the presidio, mission, and village sites, about 9 acres are publicly owned as a historical park. In 1933 the National Society of the Daughters of American Colonists and the state of Louisiana had commemorated the site with appropriate markers. Excavations on the site were begun in 1979 by a team of archaeologists, led by Dr. Hiram Gregory of Northwestern State University.

CANTONMENT ALEXANDRIA. CAMP BEAUREGARD (World War I).

POST OF ALEXANDRIA. CAMP CANBY.

Louisiana

ALGIERS BARRACKS. POWDER MAGAZINE BARRACKS.

AMITE BARRACKS. A small British military installation located on the east side of the Amite River close to its junction with Bayou Manchac, Amite Barracks was cited in the capitulation agreement signed by Colonel Alexander Dickson and Spanish Governor Bernardo de Gálvez at Baton Rouge, September 21, 1779, surrendering West Florida to the Spanish. The post and its garrison of 16 men were included in the surrender pact.

AMITE POST. A temporary encampment of U.S. troops, it was located in or near Amite City in present Tangipahoa Parish and occupied from February 1868 until February 1869 by 3 officers and 71 enlisted men of the 1st Infantry under the command of Lieutenant Branagan. The post was reestablished in pursuance of Special Orders No. 5 dated January 7, 1868. Apparently its last occupants consisted of Company E, 1st Infantry, under Brevet Major Robert H. Offley.

ANNUNCIATION SQUARE CAMP. This so-named open area in New Orleans was used as a campsite by both Confederate and Union troops during the Civil War. During the one-month period between March 25 and April 25, 1862, six companies of the Confederate Guards Regiment were encamped on the square. Elements of the 18th New York Regiment camped on the square during January 1863.

CAMP ASHBY. A temporary Civil War post established in December 1862, it was garrisoned by elements of the Mississippi Cavalry Battalion commanded by Lieutenant Colonel C. C. Wilbourn, which was then operating in the Port Hudson area. The exact location of Camp Ashby is yet undetermined.

CAMP (CANTONMENT) ATKINSON. This post, named for General Henry Atkinson, the first adjutant general of the U.S., was located on the Calcasieu River, near the present town of Lake Charles. It was established in April or May 1830, and abandoned on January 2, 1832.

ATTAKAPAS POST. When the United States acted to occupy the Louisiana Purchase after its acquisition in 1803, a garrison was established at old Attakapas, in or near present-day St. Martinville. The post was regularly garrisoned from 1804 to 1808, when it was evacuated, only to

have troops stationed there again in 1818 and 1819.

FORT BABCOCK. A small hill fortified with log breastworks located on the west side of Sandy Creek at Port Hudson, the defense was erected by Union forces and named for Lieutenant Colonel Willoughby M. Babcock, 75th New York Volunteer Infantry, during Federal operations in the area in the spring of 1863. Colonel Babcock was later killed in Virginia's Shenandoah Valley.

FORT BALISE. The original fort of this name was built by the French in 1722 at the mouth of the Mississippi River. Its name was derived from the French *balise*, meaning "beacon," because the French had set up a seamark for the guidance of ships seeking the mouth of the river. The southeast pass at the mouth was the only practicable entrance for vessels drawing 14 feet and, to preserve it as well as to improve it, a high mole built of piles was thrown up that preserved the channel from the extreme point of the mainland to the sea. Here, in that year, the French established a water battery, a military post, storehouses, a powder magazine, and a chapel, on the bank formed by these piles. They usually maintained at the post a garrison of 50 men, as well as pilots and a few sailors. The spot originally occupied was the little flat island called Toulouse by the French, about a half-mile in circumference, with their buildings erected at the extreme edge of the Gulf shore beyond the bar. The magazine and part of the fortifications were later swept into the river. In 1768 a new *balise* or *balize* was established by Don Ulloa and chiefly used as a pilot station. Its site is now the village of Balize in Plaquemines Parish, but by reason of the enormous sedimentary deposits from the Mississippi River, it is some three or four miles from the seashore and the mouths of the river.

CAMP BANKS. Established in December 1862 by Union forces, Camp Banks was located on a field probably adjoining the old race track, very near the present intersection of Government and 18th streets in Baton Rouge. Probably named for Union general Nathaniel Prentiss Banks, former governor of Massachusetts, the encampment was occupied in rotation by Maine, New York, and Massachusetts troops, on an intermittent basis, until about August, 1863.

FORT BANKS. Probably unnamed when first erected by the Confederates, this enclosed fieldwork of earth was situated on the right bank of the Mississippi River less than a mile below LaBranche's Canal and above the Parapet defense line. It was constructed in either late 1861 or early 1862 in compliance with orders of Major General Mansfield Lovell, Confederate commander of the New Orleans sector. The defense was apparently designed for 90 men and six 32-pounders. After it was captured by David Farragut's sea forces in April 1862, the rebel defense was named Fort Banks in honor of Union General Nathaniel P. Banks of Massachusetts and incorporated within the chain of Federal defenses around New Orleans.

CAMP BAPTISTE. A temporary Confederate encampment, it was probably located near the Blood River in Livingston Parish in April 1865.

CAMP BARATARIA. An American encampment during the War of 1812, it was established on or about December 12, 1814, below New Orleans by a company of Louisiana Drafted Militia.

FORT AT BARATARIA. FORT LIVINGSTON.

CAMP BARRI CROQUANT. This Civil War encampment, located on the north side of Bayou Maria Croquant about two and a half miles south of Port Barre, in St. Landry Parish, was established in late 1863 to accommodate Union general Geoffrey Weitzel's division of the XIX Corps.

FORT BATON ROUGE (*Fort Richmond; Fort New Richmond*). Known in histories by such unofficial names as Fort Richmond or New Richmond by the British (actually names for the town of Baton Rouge), and Fort San Carlos or St. Charles while in Spanish possession, this fort on a Tory-owned plantation on the east bank of the Mississippi River was built in July–August 1779 by the British under Lieutenant Colonel Alexander Dickson as a strategic defense when rumors of war with Spain were prevalent. It was considered one of the more important English posts on the river during their control of West Florida subsequent to the 1763 Treaty of Paris. The site was just south of today's Pentagon Barracks, in the immediate vicinity of the intersection of Boyd Avenue (Spanish Town Road) and Lafayette Street. The dirt-built fort had *chevaux-de-frise* or palisade-protected parapets of packed earth about 18 feet wide, surrounded by a 9-foot-deep ditch, and mounted 13 cannon of various calibers.

On May 8, 1779, while the American Revolution was still raging, Charles III of Spain formally declared war against Great Britain and authorized Spanish subjects in America to participate in the hostilities. Spanish forces, originating in New Orleans, led by the Province of Louisiana's Governor Bernardo de Gálvez, consisted of some 500 soldiers, more than 600 militiamen, nearly 200 Indians, an American agent with several of his countrymen, and less than 100 negroes and mulattoes. The British defense was manned by some 400 regulars, British and German, about 100 militiamen, and about 100 men, white and black, from surrounding plantations.

The Spanish force arrived at Baton Rouge on September 12, 1779, and immediately besieged the fort. For about a week they secretly emplaced artillery in the woods to the east of the fort, in the vicinity of today's intersection of North Boulevard and Lafayette Street. After an effective three-hour bombardment on the morning of September 21, Lieutenant Colonel Dickson capitulated. Gálvez compelled the British commander to sign an agreement surrendering both the fort and other British posts in the lower Mississippi Valley, including Fort Panmure at Natchez. Dickson's letter from the fort to his superior officers on the day of its surrender was headed "Redoubt at Baton Rouge."

During the period of Spanish occupation, the fort was officially referred to as the "Fort at Baton Rouge," while American surveyors, after the Louisiana Purchase, called it Fort San Carlos or St. Charles. Significantly improved in the beginning and then renovated from time to time, the fort was described as being star-shaped with six points and mounted at one time as many as 16 cannon, 12 of them dominating the river. From time to time, however, the fort's works were reduced to utter dilapidation. The Baton Rouge fort remained in Spanish possession, regularly garrisoned, for some 30 years, until September 23, 1810, when West Florida revolutionaries seized it and ejected the Spaniards from the area.

After the cession of Louisiana in 1803, the United States government persistently asserted its claim to all the Gulf Coast region east of the Mississippi to the Perdido River, but for diplomatic reasons took no action to occupy West Florida until the Baton Rouge revolution of 1810 compelled President James Madison to take decisive measures toward American sovereignty. In 1810 the fort at Baton Rouge was commanded by young Lieutenant Louis de Grandpre, son of the fort's first Spanish commandant, and had a garrison of less than 50 men. Shortly after the seizure and establishment of the soon-aborted Republic of West Florida, W. C. C. Claiborne, governor of the Orleans Territory, acting upon presidential orders, took possession of the province of West Florida, including the fort at Baton Rouge.

BATON ROUGE ARSENAL. The U.S. Ordnance Department in 1816 selected Baton Rouge as the location for an ordnance depot to both conveniently supply troops within the city and the posts on the Mississippi and Red rivers. The site selected two years later was on the left bank of the Mississippi River just above the ruins of the British fort seized and occupied by the Spanish in 1779. Simultaneously, barracks to accommodate about 1,000 men were to be constructed based on plans drawn by Lieutenant James Gadsden. Congress appropriated monies for a two-story ordnance structure and a powder magazine, begun in 1819, on the river bank on the north side of what later became the Pentagon Barracks complex. The ordnance warehouse's foundations, however, were defective, compelling the demolition of the building in 1828. Most of the Arsenal buildings stood east of the 3rd Street extension.

Generally administered as a separate facility from adjoining Pentagon Barracks, the Arsenal over the years grew until it became the largest in the South. The Arsenal's largest structure was constructed in 1829 adjacent to 3rd Street but it was destroyed by a vicious storm after the Civil War. Although no ordnance was manufactured there, the depot stored great quantities of cannon, small arms, and ammunition. During the war with Mexico, the Arsenal served as a major supply depot for the military units involved in the conflict. When Governor Thomas Moore on January 10, 1861, compelled the surrender of the Arsenal to state forces, the depot held many pieces of ordnance and large quantities of small arms, which eventually equipped most of Louisiana's volunteer regiments. The Arsenal was first operated by the state and then by the Confederacy during the first year of the Civil War, until Baton Rouge was occupied by Union forces in May 1862.

At the end of the war, the Arsenal began to store the ordnance and military equipment removed from dismantled fortifications. In 1870 a public sale was held to dispose of the huge surplus of weapons, equipment, and general military stores, including 335 cannon. In June 1871 the Arsenal's personnel were withdrawn and the facility was placed in the care of the Infantry and Quartermaster Corps for their use. During the 1880s many of the Arsenal's buildings, including two powder magazines built in 1838 and 1850, were leased to Louisiana State University. The 1838 powder magazine, today generally called the Arsenal, is now used as Louisiana State museum. The other magazine, however, was demolished when the new Capitol was erected in 1931. (See: FORT WILLIAMS.)

BATON ROUGE BARRACKS (*Pentagon Barracks*). Troops posted at Baton Rouge after the area's occupation by the United States were first accommodated in the old Spanish barracks on the bank of the Mississippi and in additionally erected frame structures on the north side of the river. In 1816, after the end of the War of 1812, Baton Rouge was selected as the site for a major ordnance depot and adjoining barracks adequate to house 1,000 troops. After Lieutenant James Gadsden, U.S. Army engineer, had selected the sites for the two complexes, he drew the original plans for their construction. Lieutenant Gadsden years later attained fame when he negotiated the Gadsden Purchase from Mexico. The set of plans chosen called for the construction of five main structures arranged in the form of a pentagon.

After materials were congregated in 1818, construction was begun the following year on a site just north of the ruins of the old Spanish fortification. An assistant quartermaster superintended the erection of the four barracks structures, which still exist at the present time as the Pentagon Barracks. A commissary warehouse on the bank of the river in conjunction with the ordnance storehouse on its north side completed the fifth side of the pentagon. Completed in 1821, it was torn down during the same year when it was learned that its construction did not conform with specifications. The structure was never replaced. During this same year, a yellow fever epidemic caused the deaths of 91 soldiers of the 1st Infantry which was employed for much of the construction work. The dead were interred in the old Spanish cemetery on North Street, its site now occupied by the State Department of Education Building.

During the early years of Florida's Second Seminole War in the 1830s and the War with Mexico a decade later, most of the Army regulars were withdrawn from brick-built, galleried Baton Rouge Barracks for duties on the war fronts. On January 10, 1861, Governor Thomas Moore authorized the state militia to seize the Barracks and adjoining Arsenal, both garrisoned by small elements of the 1st Artillery, commanded by Captain Joseph Haskins. During the war, the buildings were occupied successively by state, Confederate and Federal troops. After the Battle of Baton Rouge, August 5, 1862, Union forces built extensive fortified earthen embankments to enclose the grounds of the Arsenal and the Barracks, naming the works Fort Williams in the memory of Union General Thomas Williams who was killed in the battle.

Federal troops continued to occupy the Barracks during the South's reconstruction period. One of the post's commanders during this time was Captain (later Major General) Arthur MacArthur, father of General Douglas MacArthur. Baton Rouge Barracks was deactivated on June 6, 1879, and left in charge of a caretaking unit until 1886, when the complex was turned over to Louisiana State University. In the 1920s the university moved its quarters to a new location, transferring title to the old reservation to the state. In 1966 complete renovations were undertaken on the historic complex, now used to accommodate state offices. (See: FORT WILLIAMS.)

CAMP BAYOU BOEUF. A Confederate post established by elements of the 13th Texas Cavalry in October 1862, it was located somewhere in central Louisiana.

BAYOU DE SAIR REDOUBT. A Federal defense situated on the west side of Lake Pontchartrain below Pass Manchac in St. John the Baptist Parish, it was established and occupied on June 9, 1864, by Company F, 7th U.S. Heavy Artillery.

BAYOU DES ALLEMANDE POST. FORT AT GERMAN COAST.

BAYOU DUPRE REDOUBT. A small American redoubt erected during the War of 1812, it was situated on the east side of the Mississippi River, on Bayou Dupre in St. Bernard Parish.

BAYOU FOURCHE REDOUBT. FORT GUION.

BAYOU GENTILLY REDOUBT. A Civil War defense for New Orleans and located in Orleans Parish, its armaments were removed before May, 1865.

BAYOU LAFOURCHE CAMP. CAMP HOPKINS.

BAYOU MAZANT (MAXTENT) REDOUBT. This defense was established by the British in 1815 at the junction of Bayou Mazant (Bayou Villere) and Bayou Jumonville (Bayou Ducros)

in St. Bernard Parish to protect their retreating forces.

CAMP BAYOU PORTAGE. This Confederate post, occupied by the 2nd Louisiana Zouaves Battalion, was located on the side of the bayou, a short distance north of Lake Dauterive in St. Martin Parish. Federal cavalry captured the camp on November 23, 1863.

CAMP BEACH CREEK. A temporary Confederate encampment located eight miles west of the town of Homer in Claiborne Parish, it was occupied by W. P. Lane's Texas Rangers from Marshall, Texas, in November 1862.

CAMP BEAL. A Confederate cavalry encampment in January 1863, Camp Beal was located on the Plank Road 10 miles south of Clinton.

CAMP BEAUREGARD. A temporary Confederate artillery encampment, occupied in December 1862 by Watson's Louisiana Battery, Camp Beauregard was located near Port Hudson, in East or West Feliciana Parish.

CAMP BEAUREGARD. A Confederate post in or near Clinton, East Feliciana Parish, it was captured by Union forces under General Albert Lee in 1864.

CAMP BEAUREGARD (*Cantonment Alexandria; Camp Hunter*). Named in honor of General Pierre G. T. Beauregard, C.S.A., who was distinguished for services in the Mexican and Civil Wars, Camp Beauregard is located on the former site of the first University of Louisiana, on the east side of the Red River, in Rapides Parish, about five miles northeast of Alexandria and two miles east of Tioga. Originally called Cantonment Alexandria when first planned in April 1917, it was renamed Camp Beauregard on July 18, 1917, four days before actual construction began. The post served as a training camp for the 39th Division of the National Guard, which occupied the camp from August 1917 to July 1918. The post was designated a demobilization center December 3, 1918, ordered salvaged February 1919, and closed March 18, 1919. In 1920 the Louisiana Legislature authorized its purchase for a National Guard camp, to be known as Camp Hunter, apparently named in honor of the then state adjutant general, Allen T. Hunter. The name of the camp soon reverted to Camp Beauregard.

The old reservation continued to be used by the National Guard of Louisiana as a summer training and maneuver area until the outbreak of World War II, when Camp Beauregard was again used extensively to congregate and train large numbers of recruits. The post was deactivated September 7, 1945, by direction of the Office of the Adjutant General, Washington, D.C., became surplus property on April 1, 1946, and its lease to the federal government terminated April 15, 1947. By then, however, the Louisiana National Guard had been reorganized and was once more using Camp Beauregard. In 1971 a major renovation program was begun, replacing nearly every building on the post with a modern structure.

FORT BEAUREGARD. PROCTOR'S LANDING TOWER.

FORT BEAUREGARD. A Confederate enclosed casemated earthen fort situated on a hill behind Harrisonburg, Catahoula Parish, Fort Beauregard was one of four forts stretching for two miles below the town and more than a mile above, designed to protect Monroe from Federal gunboats that might come up the Ouachita River. A formidable defense, it was built in the early spring of 1863. On May 10, 1863, four Union gunboats came up the river and anchored within sight of the fort. The Federals under Commodore C. E. Woodworth demanded unconditional surrender, and when rebuffed, began exchanging cannonades with two 32-pounders in the fort. Withdrawing and returning the following day for another engagement for about one and a half hours, the only damage to the fort was the breaking of some parapets while the fort was subjected to about 120 shells.

On September 4, 1863, a Federal column led by Brigadier General C. C. Crocker advanced on the fort but found that it had been evacuated that morning by the 40 Confederates under Lieutenant Colonel George W. Logan. Working through the night, the Confederates had destroyed the casemates, supplies, and larger guns, and withdrew with their horses, mules, wagons, and 3-inch guns. The Federals entered the fort and continued the destruction, spiking four 32-pounders and two 6-pounders and taking two other 6-pounders with them.

CAMP BENJAMIN. A Confederate post established late in 1861 and named for Secretary of War Judah P. Benjamin, it was located on Gentilly Road in Orleans Parish east of the Pontchartrain Railroad. In January 1862 a brigade of infantry from five regiments, commanded by General Daniel Ruggles, occupied the camp before departing for the theater of war in Tennessee.

BERRY'S BASTION. NEW ORLEANS (FRENCH) FORTIFICATIONS.

CAMP BERTONNIERE. A fortified camp in Orleans Parish, located on the Bertonniere Plantation on the Chef Menteur Road, it was established by the Americans after the British invasion in December 1814. Records and correspondence indicate it had two battery emplacements, with breastworks on both sides of Bayou Sauvage and a ditch-surrounded, 18-by-36-foot platform in front of the defense.

FORT BERWICK. A Confederate fort completed in late July 1861, Fort Berwick was located in St. Mary Parish, about four miles from Brashear City, at the north side of the junction of Wax Bayou and the Atchafalaya River. An earthen fortification, quadrangular in shape, with parapets five feet high on three sides, its rear protected by seven-foot-high palisades, loopholed for musketry, the work was surrounded by a moat six feet wide in front and three feet in the rear. On the front face two 24-pounder pivot guns were mounted to command the outlet of Wax Bayou. The garrison consisted of two companies, one of infantry and one of sappers and miners, an aggregate of 171 men, which replaced Company E, 4th Louisiana Infantry, in February 1862. In April 1862 Major Edward Fry, commanding Forts Berwick and Chene, was ordered to abandon the forts after having destroyed their heavy guns and carriages.

BERWICK CITY BATTERY. A report dated June 1, 1864, from the chief engineer of the Department of the Gulf says that the Federals in 1863 had built a very large, strong *tête-de-pont* (bridgehead) on the west side of Berwick Bay in St. Mary Parish, later describing it as having its flanks on the river and enclosing a 20-foot-high mound designed for a pivot gun.

BATTERY BIENVENU. Located at the strategic confluence of Bayou Bienvenu and Bayou Maxent or Mazant (present-day Villere), St. Bernard Parish, this long-enduring American fortification, first constructed in 1815, underwent a series of modifications over the subsequent 50 years, significantly enlarging and strengthening the work. Henry S. Latrobe, engineer, was directed to plan and build a battery there. The battery was designed to mount one 24-pounder and two 18-pounder cannon upon the withdrawal of the

British from the area. Situated in the crotch of the two bayous, its guns were pointed down Bayou Bienvenu. It has been noted that several of the early engineering plans lodged in the National Archives name the fortification Battery Maxent.

In December 1826, after plan modifications, construction was begun on an earthern fort intended for twenty 24- and/or 32-pounders with two 13-inch mortars, manned by one artillery company. The defense was unoccupied during Florida's Second Seminole War and the Mexican War. Through the years, until the end of the Civil War, a number of modifications, armament changes, and renovations were made. The district engineer's report of August 14, 1915, describes the remnants of the work as "an open work, a 'pan coupe' of about 600 feet length of trace, the capital pointing down the straight reach of Bayou Bienvenu just below its junction with Bayou Maxant. The work is surrounded by a moat which connects with Bayou Bienvenu. . . . The gorge is closed by four brick buildings, apparently a magazine, a barracks, a four-room set of officers' quarters and a guardhouse—in a general state of dilapidation. The roof remains on the barracks but all woodwork is gone. The other buildings are crumbling."

CAMP BIRD. The Confederate camp of the 9th Battalion of the Louisiana Infantry was apparently established in September 1862, located "3 miles from Baton Rouge," near today's intersection of Greenwell Springs Road and North Foster Drive.

FORT BISLAND. This extensive earthen fortification, originally constructed by Confederate forces in February 1863, was on or near the plantation home of Dr. Thomas Bisland, a sugar planter and physician, situated on the main road between Pattersonville and Centerville in St. Mary Parish, and stretched on each side from Bayou Teche to the swamp. The plantation, called "Fairfax," was known during the last years of the Civil War as Camp or Fort Bisland and was occupied at different times by both Confederate and Union forces. During the early months of 1863 several skirmishes were fought on the grounds and through the house itself.

CAMP BLANCHARD. A temporary intermittently occupied Confederate post, named for Brigadier General Albert G. Blanchard, it was located near Lecompte in Rapides Parish and was in use during the fall of 1862 and the spring of 1863.

CAMP BLANCHARD. A temporary encampment, named for Governor Newton G. Blanchard of Louisiana, it was used by 700 men of the Louisiana National Guard, August 3–12, 1904. It was located on the Bogue Falaya River, a little more than a mile north of Covington, St. Tammany Parish.

CAMP BOEUF. A temporary Confederate post, occupied by elements of the 28th Louisiana Volunteers during October 1863, it was located near Cheneyville in Rapides Parish.

CAMP BOGGS. A temporary camp, about five miles from Lecompte, Rapides Parish, it was occupied by the Confederate Guards Response Battalion in mid-July 1864.

CAMP BOGGS. This Confederate camp, first consisting of tents and then replaced by log cabins for quarters, was located one and a half miles south of Shreveport. Named for Brigadier General William Robertson Boggs, once in command of the Baton Rouge Arsenal before the Civil War, Camp Boggs was established in 1864 and served until sometime in May 1865. Part of the garrison's duties was devoted to guarding a nearby prisoner of war enclosure.

FORT BON DIEU FALLS. A citation in Milton Dunn's *History of Natchitoches* reports that the French in 1712 established this fort on the Red River near today's Montgomery in Grant Parish.

BONNET CARRE POST. A Federal post on the east side of the Mississippi River in St. Charles Parish, it was garrisoned from December 1862 until May 1865 by various Union units. It was evacuated on May 22, 1865.

FORT BOURBON. Built during the latter part of 1793 or the early part of 1794 during the Spanish administration of Francisco Luis Hector, baron de Carondelet, Fort Bourbon was located on the right bank of the Mississippi River, below New Orleans and opposite Fort San Felipe (St. Philip), about one mile above the later Fort Jackson, and established to protect the approaches to New Orleans. The fort, an earth and timber work, was wrecked by a hurricane on July 20, 1795. Rebuilt a short distance away, the new fort built of earth and planking was badly damaged by a hurricane in 1796. Repaired from time to time, it was continuously garrisoned by 10 to 15 men until about the time of the Louisiana Purchase in 1803. Four years later it was reported to be a complete ruination. The site of the fort is now submerged in the river.

FORT BOURGOGNE. NEW ORLEANS (SPANISH) FORTIFICATIONS.

FORT BRASHEAR (*Star Fort*). With the fall of New Orleans to Union forces on April 25, 1862, Confederate control in Louisiana virtually ended. Fortifications at Berwick Bay (Brashear) and other Gulf Coast points were abandoned, their garrisons withdrawn, works dismantled, and armaments thrown into the water (many of them later salvaged). Federal forces erected two sizable forts and several smaller works here in the fall of 1862. Fort Brashear, within the southern limits of present Morgan City, Terrebonne Parish, was a four-sided bastioned work with strong profile. Its artillery consisted of five 32-pounders (two of them not mounted), one 42-pounder, three 24-pounders, and two 12-pounder howitzers, and was equipped with good magazines. The length of the interior crest of the parapet was 465 yards and could adequately garrison 450 soldiers, later enlarged to accommodate 800 men. By January 1865 the fort (presently known as Star Fort), had one 48-pounder, three 32-pounders, three 24-pounders, and two 12-pounder howitzers. The fort site is now occupied by a Presbyterian Church.

CAMP BREAUX. Located near Port Hudson, this post was occupied by the 30th Louisiana Infantry from August 10, 1862, until May 6, 1863. The camp was named for Colonel Gus A. Breaux, the unit's commanding officer.

FORT BUCHANAN. Situated opposite the entrance to the Teche River and about a mile north of Fort Brashear, this Federal fort was named for Captain Thomas McKean Buchanan, who commanded a fleet of Union gunboats in the area. A strong dirt fort, its armaments consisted of six guns in 1863. Approval for its dismantling was given on June 14, 1864.

FORT BUHLOW. A Confederate-built dirt fort near Alexandria in Rapides Parish, Fort Buhlow stood on the east bank of the Red River on the north side of U.S. 71. Construction on the defense and its twin, Fort Randolph, about 500 yards away on the south side of the highway, was begun in June, 1864. They were designed as defenses against an expected third Federal invasion up the Red River Valley. The forts were named in honor of the construction engineers Christopher Meyer Randolph and Lieutenant A.

Buhlow, his assistant. The forts saw no action. After the war ended, they were turned over to General F. J. Herron's Union forces on June 3, 1865, and were subsequently demolished for their lumber and brick, despite being in very good condition. In October 1928 patriotic societies placed historical markers at the sites of the two forts.

FORT BURTON. FORT BUTTE A LA ROSE.

FORT BUTE (*Manchac Fort; Fort at the Iberville*). This fortification, sometimes called Manchac Fort and Fort at the Iberville, was built by the British in 1766 about 400 yards north of Bayou Manchac or the Iberville River at its junction with the left bank of the Mississippi River, in Baton Rouge Parish. The fort was named for John Stuart, 3rd Earl of Bute, England's premier at the time of the signing of the Treaty of Paris in 1763, ceding Florida to Great Britain. The fort has been described as a stockaded work designed to comfortably accommodate a garrison of 50 men and possibly 200 men should an emergency occur. Contemporary drawings show a rectangular fort with half-bastions. In 1767 its situation was described as being about a quarter of a mile from Point Iberville at the junction of the two rivers and approximately 100 yards from the Mississippi. The fort site has since been eroded by the river.

When Britain's colonies along the Atlantic seaboard became rebellious, the British were forced to concentrate their troops there and at Pensacola. Fort Bute was abandoned in September 1768, with its armament of six guns and munitions moved to Pensacola. Although the fort's gun emplacements were destroyed, its barracks remained in good condition. Early in 1778, when the British were apparently preparing to refortify Fort Bute, an American detachment under Captain Willing seized the fort. On March 22, not long after the American occupation, a force of 20 British Rangers led by Colonel John Stuart surprised the Americans, killed 3, wounded 5, and took 13 more as prisoners. The remaining Americans fled across the river, and the British column retired to the Amite River.

On July 1, 1778, British orders were issued to construct a permanent fort and a sizable barracks to accommodate 300 soldiers on a new site near old Fort Bute. On October 7, 1778, the commander of Spanish Fort St. (San) Gabriel across Bayou Manchac from Fort Bute reported that the British had demolished the fort they had begun and were rebuilding it nearer the Spanish fort (the middle of the bayou marked the boundary between British and Spanish West Florida). Instead of erecting a brick work as planned, the new fort turned out to be a palisaded dirt fort, fortified by six guns and garrisoned at first by at least one company of men.

After Spain formally declared war against Great Britain on May 8, 1779, Spanish Florida's Governor Bernardo de Gálvez in August led a force of about 1,400 men up the Mississippi to attack the British at Baton Rouge and Fort Bute. On September 6 they arrived at Bayou Manchac and learned that the British had withdrawn most of Fort Bute's garrison and removed all of its guns to Baton Rouge. Early the next morning a Spanish force took Fort Bute, capturing two lieutenants and 20 enlisted men. Florida was retroceded to Spain after the American Revolution and Fort Bute, its name retained, was held as a Spanish post until 1794 when it was abandoned.

CAMP BUTLER. A Union post located near Lake Providence in East Carroll Parish, it was established or occupied in May 1863 by the 1st Kansas Infantry, Major W. J. Roberts commanding.

FORT BUTLER (*Fort Donaldsville*). A Federal fortification constructed of logs and dirt at Port Barrow, Ascension Parish, it was situated on the north side of Bayou Lafourche opposite Donaldsville at the point where the bayou has its junction with the Mississippi. Named for General Benjamin F. Butler, the fort was begun in November or December 1862, and by the end of January 1863 all of its armament was mounted. It was commanded by Colonel Richard C. Holcomb, 1st Louisiana (Federal) Volunteers. The fort was described as having three bastions on its west side and two near the levee, thus protected on one side by the Mississippi and the other by Bayou Lafourche. A deep, brick-lined moat surrounded the star-shaped work mounting six 24-pounders. The earth parapet was high and thick and covered with thick turf. The sides flanking the river and bayou were further strengthened by a strong log stockade extending from the levee to the water. Built to accommodate 600 men, the fort was held by only 180. On the morning of June 28, 1863, Confederate forces led by General Thomas Green assaulted the fort which was then garrisoned by several companies of the 28th Maine Infantry, Major Joseph D. Bullen commanding. "The Confederates greatly outnumbered the Federals but found themselves unable to cross the moat on the east side between the fort and the levee, suffering" more than 250 casualties before retreating. The

Union defenders lost but 25 casualties. A little later three Federal gunboats bombarded the Confederates who were occupying exposed positions on the levee. Near the still evident ruins of the fort is a cemetery in which are buried, mostly in long trenches, the remains of several hundred Union and Confederate soldiers who lost their lives at the fort.

FORT BUTTE A LA ROSE (*Fort Burton*). A Confederate redoubt in St. Martin Parish on the west end of Cow Island at the point where the Atchafalaya River, Cow Island Bayou and Bayou a la Rose meet, it was erected in November 1862 and supplied with two 24-pounder cannon. This strategic point, if it could be held, would give the Confederates free use of the upper Atchafalaya and a way of transporting salt and other supplies to Vicksburg. The fort was also called Fort Burton, possibly named for Lieutenant Colonel W. D. Burton who commanded the Lafourche regiment. On April 20, 1863, four Federal gunboats, supported by several companies of the 16th New Hampshire Infantry, forced the fort to surrender. Sixty men of Burton's regiment and two old 32-pounder seige guns were captured (one citation reports that one of the guns was a 24-pounder). The New Hampshire troops garrisoned the fort until May 30, 1863, when the Federals destroyed the works and burned nine barracks buildings west of the fort, leaving the magazine intact probably because of a defective fuse.

CAMP CAFFREY. A Spanish-American War camp in St. Tammany Parish on the Tchefuncta River, about a mile above Covington, it was opened on May 18, 1898, to accommodate the early recruits of Colonel Duncan H. Hood's Regiment of Immunes. The camp was named for U.S. Senator Donelson Caffrey who facilitated authorization of the regiment's organization, which was mustered in on June 15, 1898, with 45 officers and 950 enlisted men.

CALCASIEU LAKE REDOUBT. A Confederate battery on Calcasieu Lake, reportedly "forty miles from Lake Charles," it was established in November or December 1861 and manned by an 82-man company. One 24-pounder and one 6-pounder formed the battery, surrounded by a breastwork, and designed to prevent Federal detachments from raiding southwest Louisiana's cattle ranches.

CANTONMENT CAMINADA. A National Archives citation indicates that the 2nd Battalion of Louisiana Volunteers, commanded by Major

H. D. Peire, occupied Caminada Island, Jefferson Parish, during the summer of 1813.

CAMP CANBY (*Post of Alexandria*). During the Reconstruction period, U.S. troops maintained a post at Alexandria from June 1865 to January 1875. The Post of Alexandria was garrisoned on May 7, 1873, by companies C and D, 19th Infantry, who were quartered on the grounds of the Louisiana State Seminary and Military Academy in Rapides Parish, several miles northeast of Alexandria. The site is now occupied by a Veterans Administration Hospital. The encampment was designated Camp Canby by the post's commanding officer, probably in honor of Brigadier General Edward R. S. Canby, who was assassinated by Indians while negotiating peace terms with them. Headquarters of the Post of Alexandria was transferred from Alexandria to the camp on February 20, 1875. Camp Canby was abandoned May 23, 1877.

CAMP CARROLL. This War of 1812 encampment, occupied by the 2nd Division of Tennessee Militia, commanded by Major General William Carroll, from December 1814 to March 1815, was located in the present Carrollton section of the city of New Orleans.

CAMP CARROLLTON. CAMP ROMAN.

CAMP CARROLLTON. During the occupation of Louisiana by Federal troops, many infantry and cavalry units encamped in or near Carrollton, now part of New Orleans.

CAMP CHALMETTE. During the Civil War a number of first Confederate and then Union army units established camps on the old Chalmette Battlefield, just below New Orleans, in St. Bernard Parish. The last occupation was apparently that of a Federal post from January to May 1865. The site dates back to the War of 1812, when it was the scene of one of the last battles of the war, fought on January 8, 1815. The Chalmette Monument, more than 100 feet high, together with surrounding grounds, including a huge cemetery, is now a National Historic Park, visited by millions of people since its inception.

CHARLES' BASTION. New Orleans (French) Fortifications.

FORT AT CHEF MENTEUR. Fort Macomb.

FORT CHENE. This small Confederate earthwork battery was begun in May 1861 at Mossy Point at the junction of Bayou Chene and Bayou Shafer in St. Mary Parish. Completed in August 1861, the fort had a small barracks constructed of rough planks, a ditch-surrounded glacis, and a stockade. Reports indicate that the fort in September 1861 mounted two 24-pounder pivot guns, and in December, one rifled 32-pounder and four 24-pounders mounted *en barbette*. One citation says that a 64-pounder Dahlgren was also mounted there in December. When New Orleans fell to Union forces in April 1862, the fort's guns were spiked and the garrison removed to Camp Moore. The Federals then occupied Fort Chene until it was abandoned on June 10, 1863. Confederate units later in the month reoccupied the fort but abandoned it in July 1863.

CHOISEUL'S BASTION. New Orleans (French) Fortifications.

CAMP CLAIBORNE. A temporary camp, "seven miles east of New Orleans," it was occupied by regular Army troops from August to November 1804 to escape the yellow fever epidemic gripping the city.

CAMP CLAIBORNE (*Camp Evangeline*). A World War II training camp, first called Camp Evangeline, it was renamed for William C. C. Claiborne, Louisiana's first governor. It was located in the Evangeline Division of the Kisatchie National Forest, about 17 miles southwest of Alexandria, in Rapides Parish. Construction began in 1940 on the site about two and a half miles long and one and a half miles wide, encompassing some 3,100 acres. The first units to arrive for training in December 1940 were companies E, G, and H of the 22nd Infantry. Nearly a half million troops trained at Camp Claiborne before it was deactivated on December 15, 1945. A portion of the camp was used to accommodate prisoners of war. More than 7,000 buildings on the post were sold at a public sale in March 1947.

FORT CLAIBORNE. On March 22, 1804, three months after the United States had taken possession of Louisiana on December 20, 1803, General James Wilkinson reported that Lieutenant Edward G. Turner with a detachment of troops were en route to Natchitoches to take over Fort St. Jean Baptiste, the Spanish post (originally built by the French) on the Red River. In a letter dated May 1804 to Governor W. C. C. Claiborne, Turner reported that he had taken possession of the Natchitoches post on April 26. On August 4 Tur-

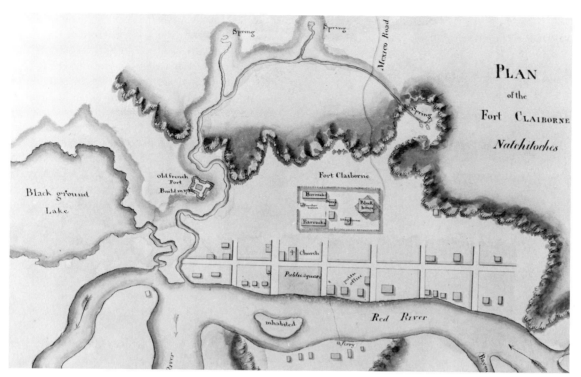

FORT CLAIBORNE.
(Courtesy of The Historic
New Orleans Collection
Museum/Research
Center, ACC. NO. 1970.
2. 17.)

ner reported to General Wilkinson that he was constructing a new fort on a site about 300 yards from the river in the center of the rear of Natchitoches village, a short distance from the old French fort. Turner's fort, named for Governor Claiborne, occupied a site of about two acres and consisted of a palisade enclosing two barracks buildings on the south end. On the opposite end was a two-story blockhouse, with its upper story turned 90 degrees. Although some reports indicate the fort was abandoned in 1822, orders were issued in June 1819 to evacuate the post and transfer its troops to new Fort Selden about eight miles away. It was further reported that Fort Claiborne was evacuated in July 1819 and demolished.

CAMP CLARK. This Federal encampment of the 6th Michigan Infantry, established August 5, 1862, when Confederate forces attempted to retake Baton Rouge, was located at the intersection of present Government Street and Perkins Road (17th or 18th Street). The post was named for Lieutenant Colonel T. S. Clark of the Michigan regiment.

CLINTON POST. This post located at Clinton in East Feliciana Parish was occupied from July 1, 1876, to April 1877 by elements of the 13th U.S. Infantry.

CAMP COBB. Located near Greenwell Springs and the Amite River in East Baton Rouge Parish,

Camp Cobb was occupied for several months in the summer and fall of 1855 by nearly the entire Baton Rouge garrison to avoid the threat of the yellow fever pestilence in the city.

COLFAX POST. A U.S. Army post was maintained at Colfax, Grant Parish, from April 1873 to January 1876 because of political unrest during the Reconstruction period. The post was occupied intermittently by several different infantry and cavalry units. A citation reports that plans for barracks and officers' quarters had been drawn but apparently not put into effect.

FORT CONCORDIA (*Vidalia Post*). Vidalia, the seat of Concordia Parish, was the first settlement founded by Europeans on the western bank of the Mississippi between Pointe Coupée and the mouth of the Arkansas River. About the year 1786, to counteract British influence at Fort Panmure (formerly Fort Rosalie) at Natchez, Spanish Governor Antonio de Ulloa established a post opposite the fort formerly occupied by Spanish forces. It was abandoned until Don José Vidal on April 21, 1798, obtained a grant of land from the Spanish government and established a settlement there in 1801, including a minimally fortified "strong house" or palisaded blockhouse and a barracks, variously called Concord Post, Post of Concordia, and Post of New Concordia. Vidalia was one of the shipping points to which Texas trail drivers brought large herds of longhorn cattle to the Natchez market during the first half of the nineteenth century.

CONDÉ'S BASTION. NEW ORLEANS (FRENCH FORTIFICATIONS.

FORT COQUILLES. FORT PETITE COQUILLES.

CAMP CORBIN. A Spanish-American War encampment on the grounds of the New Orleans Fair Grounds where the 1st Regiment of Immunes were trained. This regiment was later sent to Cuba as the 9th U.S. Volunteers.

CAMP COTTON. A Confederate camp located near Cheneyville in Rapides Parish, it was established or occupied in November 1863.

COTTON PRESS QUARTERS. Several large cotton warehouses and yards in New Orleans were used as quarters by both Confederate and Union troops during the Civil War.

CAMP (POST) COUSHATTA. This post was established at Coushatta in Red River Parish on October 4, 1874 by Company E, 3rd Infantry, commanded by Lieutenant William Mitchell, because of political problems in the area. It was abandoned November 13, 1876, by Company G, 3rd Infantry.

CAMP (FORT) COVINGTON. This post, located in the town of Covington in St. Tammany Parish, was named for either the town or in honor of General Leonard Covington, who was mortally wounded in the Battle of Chrysler's Fields in Canada in 1813. The post was intermittently occupied by units of the 1st Infantry in 1817 and 1818.

CAMP COVINGTON. A Civil War encampment at Covington, it was intermittently occupied during 1862 by Confederate artillery, infantry, and cavalry units.

CAMP COVINGTON. A citation reports that a Spanish-American War training camp was located at Covington, St. Tammany Parish, in 1898.

CAMP CUSTER. This camp, located at Marksville, Avoyelles Parish, was occupied by Company H of the 156th Infantry for several months during the flood of 1927.

D'ABBADIES' BASTION. NEW ORLEANS (FRENCH) FORTIFICATIONS.

FORT DARBY. This War of 1812 defense located near Dalacroix on Bayou Terre aux Boeufs, which constitutes the boundary between the parishes of St. Bernard and Plaquemines, was situated at the junction of the bayou with Lake Lery. It was built by and named for the geographer, William O. Darby, with construction beginning February 8, 1815. Designed to prevent enemy incursionists from coming up Bayou Terre aux Boeufs, it was an earthen redoubt surrounded by a ditch and its rear protected by palisades. The fortification mounted two 9-pounders. With the declaration of peace, the redoubt was dismantled.

CAMP DAUTERIVE. A Confederate post, it was located at Dauterive's sugar house, about a mile from Grand Lake, in Iberia Parish, and occupied by two battalions of troops from December 1862 to February 1863.

CAMP DAVIS. According to a National Archives citation, Camp Davis was an earthen battery mounting two guns on Calcasieu Pass in Calcasieu Parish and manned from August 1861 to April 1862 by Company G, 21st Regiment of Louisiana Infantry, commanded by Captain J. C. Batchelor.

FORT DE LA BOULAYE (*Fort Iberville; Fort on the Mississippi; Fort Louisiana; Fort Vieux*). This fortification, known in history by several names, was the first French military outpost in the present state of Louisiana. It was established on February 1, 1700, to counteract Spanish and English intrusions into the region. Pierre le Moyne, sieur d'Iberville, landed a party of soldiers on a low ridge along the east bank of the Mississippi River, about 50 miles above its mouth, where his men constructed a 28-foot-square wooden blockhouse and equipped it with six cannon, six- and eight-pounders. Iberville left an 18-man garrison under the command of his brother, Bienville, to hold the fort. Little is known of their experiences, but by 1707 the fort was abandoned because of Indian threats. Nevertheless, Louis Juchereau de St. Denis, who later attained prominence in the Natchitoches area, was on amicable terms with the Indians and remained at the fort for several years.

It is not known when the name Fort de la Boulaye was first given to the fort. Neither has it been definitely determined for whom it was named, although two possible suggestions have been offered by historians. One is that it was named for Chevalier Claude Agnan Guérin de la

Boulaye, a native of Orléans, France, who was the son of the commisionaire generale d'Orléans; the other, more probable, was Louis Hyancinthe Plomier, sieur de la Boulaye, inspector general of the French navy in 1697. No physical traces of the fort remain above ground. In the early 1930s four New Orleans historical archaeologists achieved virtually certain identification of the fort site on the basis of geographical evidence and the discovery of hand-hewn cypress logs. The site is now on the east side of the Mississippi, about 4,000 feet from the present bank of the river, about two miles north of Phoenix in Plaquemines Parish.

FORT DE RUSSY. A Confederate strongpoint on the south side of the Red River about three miles north of Marksville, Avoyelles Parish, the fort was named for Colonel Louis De Russy who had been appointed on November 1, 1862, to oversee the construction of defenses on the river to prevent Federal shipping toward Alexandria, about 30 miles away. Descriptions indicate that it was a square redoubt, each side about 100 yards in length, with half-bastions. Equipped with three ironclad casemates, reports vary regarding Fort De Russy's large complement of ordnance when it was taken, for the second time, by Federal infantry assault on May 14, 1864. The Federals, aided by gunboats, blew up the fort's magazines, largely destroyed its ramparts, tore apart its embankments, and carried off all the armaments and munitions.

FORT DESPERATE. A Confederate defense on a hill near Foster Creek at Port Hudson, erected in late December 1862, it earned the name "Fort Desperate" because of the repeatedly unsuccessful attempts by the Federals to take it during the siege in 1863.

FORT DONALDSVILLE. FORT BUTLER.

DONALDSVILLE P.O.W. CAMP. Located at Donaldsville in Ascension Parish, this was a World War II prisoner of war facility that accommodated more than 400 prisoners who were put to work in the sugarcane fields.

DUPRE TOWER (*Philippon Tower; Martello Castle*). This unusual fortification is situated at the entrance to Bayou Dupre (Bayou Philippon) on the south shore of Lake Borgne in St. Bernard Parish. Tower Dupre, at times called Philippon Tower, is more popularly known today as the Martello Castle because of its two-story

hexagonal form. Its lower level was loopholed for musketry while the upper story was designed to mount six howitzers. Although planned in 1821 as one of several fortifications to protect New Orleans' eastern approaches, construction on it did not begin until 1827, and it was completed in July 1830. A year later a storm severely damaged the fort and reconstruction postponed the installation of guns and the garrison until 1833.

While the fort and battery were later designed to mount 24 guns, with a peacetime garrison of 50 men, it was manned by only three men from Fort Macomb. The Second Seminole War in Florida and the Mexican War compelled the withdrawing of all the garrisons from Lake Borgne's forts and the tower was placed in the keep of a single caretaker. Continuously in need of repairs, the fort was significantly renovated and strengthened in 1848, 1852, and 1855. Tower Dupre played no important role during the Civil War, although the Confederates garrisoned it in 1861 with Company B, 21st Infantry, to man the five 24-pounders then in the fort. Captain J. T. Plattsmier was in command there with Company E of the 21st Infantry in April 1862 when the fall of New Orleans to Union forces caused the evacuation of the fort. After peace was established, additional monies were spent to again repair and renovate it. By the year 1883, Tower Dupre was deemed useless and surplus. The ground around the fort, now owned by a St. Bernard businessman, had become so eroded that the tower is at present entirely surrounded by water and somewhat preserved by the additions of a roof and a pier.

CAMP EVANGELINE. CAMP CLAIBORNE.

CAMP FOSTER. Named for Governor Murphy J. Foster, this Spanish-American War training encampment was located on the New Orleans Fair Grounds and was occupied by the 1st and 2nd Louisiana Volunteers, with the former quartered in the large brick building on the grounds, the 18th and 23rd U.S. Infantry, and the 5th U.S. Cavalry.

GALVEZTOWN FORT. Situated on land originally settled by English in 1778, this Spanish defense was located on the right bank of the Amite River about two and a half miles from Port Vincent, on the joint boundary of Ascension, East Baton Rouge and Livingston Parishes. In 1779 Bernardo de Gálvez, then acting governor of the Spanish Province of Louisiana, ordered a plan for a fortification at Galveztown opposite Fort Graham, the palisaded defense the British were erecting on the east side of the Amite River while refortifying the entire water route leading to their other posts at Mobile and Pensacola. The Spanish post's commander had started the construction of barracks in December 1778. In June 1779 two 4-pounders were emplaced there. A month later Galveztown Fort was strengthened by building additional barracks in front and log palisades on all sides.

After Spain's declaration of war against Great Britain, militia troops from Galveztown Fort in September 1779 took possession of Fort Graham across the river, blocking the waterway, while Governor Gálvez and his army were capturing Fort Bute and the British fort at Baton Rouge. It was recommended in 1793 that Galveztown Fort, then mounting 10 guns, be replaced by a brick fort because of its strategic location. Plans were prepared in 1797 delineating the old fort, shown as irregularly shaped with five bastions, and the proposed replacement. The plans, however, came to naught as the United States acquired the area through the Louisiana Purchase but did not make use of the old Spanish fort, which apparently became a ruination in time.

FORT AT GERMAN COAST. (*Bayou des Allemande Post*). During 1747–49 settlers of the German Coast on the east side of the Mississippi River above New Orleans were being subjected to destructive raids by the Choctaws and other Indians in the region. In December 1748 Governor Vaudreuil determined to establish a post there. Later, in 1749, while he dispatched 30 soldiers and 60 allied Indians to the area, he had Saucier, the French cartographer and engineer, draw plans for a fortified stockade and a map indicating the location for it. The fort, also known as the Bayou des Allemande Post, was built sometime during the latter half of 1749 or early in 1750 and a one-company garrison was placed therein, replaced every two months. Captain Philip Pittman, English officer, in his 1770 report on the European settlements on the Mississippi, says the small French defense, retained by the Spanish, was located approximately in the center of the German settlements, on the east side of the river, and garrisoned by 1 officer with 12 enlisted men (later replaced by militiamen) when he visited it between 1766 and 1768.

FORT GRAHAM. Acquiring West Florida from France by virtue of the 1763 Treaty of Paris formally ending the last of America's French and Indian Wars, the British began fortifying the water route from the Mississippi River to Mobile and Pensacola by way of Bayou Manchac (Iberville River), the Amite River, and Lakes Maurepas and Pontchartrain. In early 1779, British engineer J. J. Graham began building a stockade on the east side of the Amite River near its junction with the Iberville, at a point opposite Galveztown Fort maintained by the Spanish. The site of the British post, however, was soon inundated by flood waters and the stockade, named Fort Graham, was erected on a new site nearby. On August 30 of the same year, Spain having declared war, the fort was abandoned by the British before Spanish troops from Galveztown Fort captured it early in September, taking some British prisoners. (See: GALVEZTOWN FORT.)

FORT ON GRANDE TERRE ISLAND. FORT LIVINGSTON.

GREENVILLE BARRACKS (*Sedgwick Barracks*). This Federal post, also known as Sedgwick Barracks, was established in the summer of 1864 in the town of Greenville, now a part of today's uptown New Orleans. Continuously used until late in 1874, it was occupied in rotation by elements of a number of infantry, artillery, and cavalry units.

FORT GUION (*Bayou Fourche Redoubt*). A Confederate water battery erected in 1861 on lower Bayou Lafourche, Fort Guion was occupied in February 1862 by companies A and F of the combined 22nd and 23rd Louisiana Volunteer Regiments, aggregating 8 officers and 93 enlisted men with two 32-pounder cannon. After the taking of New Orleans by Union forces, the redoubt was abandoned.

CAMP HAMILTON. A U.S. Army post, probably an Indian defense, at times called a fort, Camp Hamilton was established in September 1804 near Opelousas, in the vicinity of Bayou del Puent, in St. Landry Parish, by Captain Jonathan Bowyer with elements of the 2nd Infantry. The post was abandoned after several years of occupation.

CAMP HARAHAN. CAMP PLAUCHE.

CAMP HARNEY. For a period of several pre–Civil War years, Camp Harney served as a summer encampment for the Baton Rouge Barracks garrison. It was located on the Comite River eight miles east of Baton Rouge. Named for U.S. Army Surgeon B. F. Harney, a brother of noted Brigadier

General William Harney, the site of the camp was occupied during the first year of the war, in September 1861, by two companies of the Confederate 1st Louisiana Cavalry.

HIGHLAND STOCKADE. A Federal strongpoint on the Highland Road, considered during the war to have been located seven miles below Baton Rouge, it was occupied in June 1864 by the 4th Wisconsin Cavalry, aggregating 391 men, rank and file. On July 29, 1864, six companies of the 14th New York Cavalry, then occupying the post, were attacked by a force of Confederate guerrillas.

CAMP HOPKINS (*Bayou LaFourche Camp*). This War of 1812 outpost was established on lower Bayou LaFourche in October 1814 by Captain Charles R. Hick's company of Louisiana militia. The camp was probably named for Brigadier General Stephen A. Hopkins, commander of the 2nd Brigade of the 1st Division.

CAMP HUBBARD. This Federal camp, scene of a mutiny on August 30, 1863, was located at Thibodaux in Lafourche Parish and named for an officer of General Godfrey Weitzel's staff at

Port Hudson. The units there during 1863 and 1864 were the 8th Vermont Infantry, the 9th New York Infantry, the 3rd Brigade of the 1st Division, and the 2nd Rhode Island Cavalry, elements of which were reassigned to the Federal 1st Louisiana Cavalry despite their vehement objections. Two men of the Rhode Island regiment were courtmartialed, convicted of mutiny, and shot by a firing squad.

FORT HUMBUG. FORT TURNBULL.

FORT HUMBUG. YELLOW BAYOU REDOUBT.

CAMP HUNTER. CAMP BEAUREGARD.

FORT IBERVILLE (Plaquemine's Parish). FORT DE LA BOULAYE.

FORT AT IBERVILLE (Iberville Parish). FORT ST. (SAN) GABRIEL.

FORT AT THE IBERVILLE (Baton Rouge Parish). FORT BUTE.

FORT JACKSON. This historic fortification was born of necessity. It was true that Fort St. Philip,

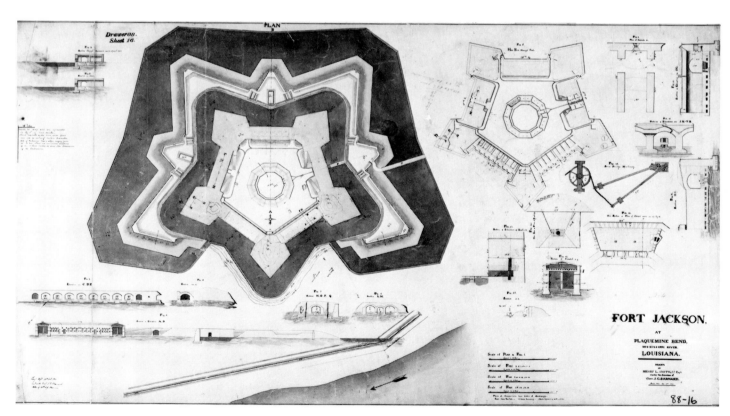

FORT JACKSON. (Courtesy of the National Archives.)

located on the east bank of the lower Mississippi River, had repulsed the British fleet after a nine-day bombardment in 1815 and had prevented it from joining Lieutenant General Sir Edward Pakenham's land forces attacking New Orleans. General Andrew Jackson, hero of the Battle of New Orleans, in his report to Secretary of War J. C. Calhoun, strongly emphasized the need of additional fortifications to protect the mouth of the river from possible Spanish attack. It was largely because of his recommendations that the government began the construction of Fort Jackson in 1822.

Fort Jackson was not the first fortification to be constructed on the west bank of the river. Earthen and timber breastworks dated back to the mid-1700s. Among the earliest references to fortifications at Plaquemines Bend is one dated 1746, when this site was recognized by the French as ideal for defenses. Sailing vessels, compelled to tack to negotiate the bend and sailing against a four-mile current, would be easy targets for land batteries. Later, in 1792, Baron de Carondelete, Spanish governor of Louisiana, constructed Fort St. Philip, then called Fort San Felipe. On the opposite, or right bank, he erected a redoubt that he named Fort Bourbon, which became the cornerstone of the west bank fortification from which Fort Jackson eventually evolved. Fort Bourbon was destroyed by a hurricane in 1795 and Carondelet ordered it rebuilt. The British attempt in the War of 1812 demonstrated the need of a major fort on the site previously occupied by the highly vulnerable Fort Bourbon, now submerged under the river.

Construction of Fort Jackson, named after Andrew Jackson, began in 1822 and was completed and occupied in 1832. The total cost of construction was $554,500. It is situated 32 nautical miles from the Gulf of Mexico, 22 miles from the lighthouse at the head of the passes, and 65 miles in a southeasterly direction from New Orleans, on the west bank of the river in Plaquemines Parish. Built in a regular star-shaped pentagon, the fort's walls were 25 feet above the water line of the moat that completely surrounded it. These walls were constructed of red brick and were 20 feet thick. The gun foundations were reinforced with red and gray granite. Two curtains facing the river were casemated for eight guns each. In the center of the fort there was a defensive barracks intended as a bombproof shelter accommodating 500 men. Fort Jackson's foundations were made of three layers of cypress logs topped by cypress two-by-fours used as a leveling device, made airtight by being submerged in water.

Upon its completion, Fort Jackson was garrisoned by a small force until February 9, 1842, when it was declared a military reservation by executive order of President John Tyler. With the coming of the Mexican War, it became imperative that Forts St. Philip and Jackson be readied for any emergency. On June 1, 1846, Governor Isaac Johnson of Louisiana ceded the lands to the government. Both forts remained garrisoned with relatively few soldiers until seized by Louisiana forces on January 8, 1861. Confederate engineers had a difficult task to ready the forts to defend the lower Mississippi River. Though original specifications allowed for 93 gun emplacements, Fort Jackson had much fewer guns available for immediate use. During the epic battle with Flag Officer David Farragut's Union fleet, there were only 69 guns at Fort Jackson and 45 at Fort St. Philip.

With New Orleans their target, Union forces had to get past Fort Jackson and the smaller Fort St. Philip situated diagonally upriver. In April 1862, 21 Federal mortar boats pounded the two citadels for nearly six days and nights, but could not silence the Confederate batteries. Then, at 2 A.M. on April 24, Farragut's 17 wooden gunships began to run the gauntlet of the forts. The Federals hurled a total of 8,100 projectiles at the Confederate positions, with Fort Jackson taking most of the punishment. It is recorded that the fury of the battle could be heard in the streets of New Orleans. An eyewitness, General Benjamin F. Butler, who commanded the Federal troops waiting to follow in transports, described the action:

The crash of splinters, the explosion of boilers and magazines, the shouts and cries, the shrieks of scalded and drowning men; add to this the belching flashes of guns, blazing rafts and burning steamboats, the river full of fire, and you have a picture of the battle that was all confined to Plaquemines Bend. [*New York Times*, 28 October 1962]

Thirteen Union ships got through, and New Orleans, the South's greatest city, surrendered on April 29. Two days later General Butler began the Federal occupation. The capture of the city was one of the first major victories for the Union and a blow from which the Confederacy never recovered. With the captures of Vicksburg and Port Hudson the following year, the entire Mississippi was in Northern hands and the South was split in two.

Fort Jackson's cannon were never again fired in anger, although two big coastal guns were installed there during the Spanish-American War. The installation was used as a training base during World War I, and in 1927 a New Orleans couple bought the fort as government surplus for $20,204. They donated it to Plaquemines Parish in 1960, the same year the Department of the Interior classified Fort Jackson and Fort St. Philip as national historical monuments. In 1961 the Plaquemines Parish Commission Council began the restoration program to transform the abandoned fort and its 82-acre reservation, which had become a veritable jungle with mud-filled tunnels infested with snakes, into an historical mecca for history buffs and tourists and recreational center.

JACKSON BARRACKS (*New Orleans Barracks*). Originally established in 1834 as New Orleans Barracks, and located on the left bank of the Mississippi about five miles below the city, extending from the highway to the river, between Delery Street and the St. Bernard Parish line, the post was designed in the manner of an Indian defense, with a high surrounding wall and four towers provided with rifle slots and embrasures for small cannon. It served as an embarkation point for troops assigned duty in Florida's Second Seminole War (1835–42). The post was turned into a general hospital during the War with Mexico. Temporarily abandoned in 1853, it was seized by Louisiana troops in January 1861 and reoccupied by Union troops on May 1, 1862. After the Civil War, in 1866, the post was renamed Jackson Barracks in honor of Andrew Jackson. In January 1922, the post was turned over to the state of Louisiana for its use. During World War II it was reoccupied by Federal troops, declared surplus October 31, 1946, and again turned over to the state. The historic reservation of approximately 85 acres, containing some 80 buildings renovated over the years, is now maintained by the state for the use of the Louisiana National Guard.

CAMP JEANERETTE. A World War II prisoner of war camp for about 500 men, the stockade was located near the town of Jeanerette in St. Martin Parish.

FORT JENKINS. A Confederate defense of Shreveport, it was situated on a hill on the site of the old Schumpert Hospital.

CANTONMENT JESUP. FORT JESUP.

FORT JESUP (*Cantonment Jesup*). A U.S. Army post established in May 1822, it was located in Sabine Parish about six miles northeast of the town of Many situated on S.R. 6, the old road from Natchitoches to Nacogdoches, Texas. The post was named in honor of Virginia-born Thomas Sidney Jesup, who achieved a long and distinguished career in the U.S. Army. Originally known as Cantonment Jesup, it was officially designated Fort Jesup by order of the War Department dated June 3, 1833, although the post was never considered fortified. Located near the western boundary of Louisiana, Fort Jesup was intended to guard the line between U.S. and Spanish territory. The post was evacuated in January 1846 and all of its buildings and improvements were put up for public sale. The Fort Jesup State Commemorative Park now occupies the site.

FORT JOHNSTON. A Confederate defense of Shreveport, this fort was named for General Albert Sidney Johnston and was located near the present intersection of Clay and Webster streets in the northwest section of the city.

KERLIREE'S (KIRKIRE'S, KERLEREC) BASTION. NEW ORLEANS (FRENCH) FORTIFICATIONS.

FORT KIRBY SMITH (*Fort Smith*). A Confederate enclosed earthen defense of Shreveport, this fortification was sometimes called Fort Smith. Named for General Kirby Smith, it was located across the Red River from the city of Shreveport on a plantation then owned by a Mrs. Mary D. C. Cane, now a part of present-day Bossier City, known as Cane City during the Civil War. The Fort Smith Memorial Park was dedicated on June 9, 1936, at the fort site where tangible remains of the fort's earthworks are still evident.

CAMP LEROY JOHNSON. This post, originally established in 1940 by the U.S. Army Air Corps, was located in New Orleans, on the south shore of Lake Pontchartrain on a 161-acre tract of land bounded by Franklin Avenue, Leon C. Simon Drive, and the Inner Harbor Navigation (Industrial) Canal. Originally known as the New Orleans Army Air Base, on November 25, 1947, it was renamed in honor of Sergeant Leroy Johnson, 126th Infantry, of Oakdale, Louisiana, a World War II hero who was posthumously awarded the Congressional Medal of Honor, having been cited for throwing himself on two grenades during an assualt on Leyte in the Philippines.

The camp had more than 100 temporary buildings that housed 1,500 men at peak times of operation. Signal Corps and Quartermaster Corps units were trained on the post. Later it was used as a staging area for the Port of New

Orleans. In 1951 Camp Leroy Johnson became a permanent transportation training center. In its final years, it served as a replacement center and a training center for Army Reserve units. The post was officially closed on June 30, 1964, by the Department of Defense.

FORT LITTLE TEMPLE. This Confederate post, misnomered a "fort" in General Mansfield Lovell's report of December 5, 1861, to Secretary of War Judah Philip Benjamin, was actually a small water battery buttressed by earthen embankments, palisaded and surrounded by a ditch. The redoubt was located about 24 miles south of New Orleans, at the junction of Bayou Perot and Bayou Rigoletts in Jefferson Parish. The battery of two 24-pounders was manned in January 1862 by Company B, 22nd Louisiana Infantry, aggregating 3 officers and 82 men. Because of the imminent fall of New Orleans to the Federals, it was abandoned on April 27, 1862, after its guns were spiked. The Confederate redoubt may have occupied the same site or location as the American defense established in 1814–15 during the War of 1812.

CAMP LIVINGSTON (*Camp Tioga*). This 48,000-acre World War II post, originally called Camp Tioga because of its proximity to the village of that name, was located about 14 miles north of Alexandria, within the Kisatchie National Forest in Grant and Rapides Parishes. In October 1940 the War Department designated the training post Camp Livingston, named for either Edward Livingston who served as U.S. senator from Louisiana and later as U.S. secretary of state, or more probably, for his brother Robert R. Livingston, one of the government's negotiators of the Louisiana Purchase in 1803.

Construction began September 16, 1940. At its peak, more than 14,000 men were employed. The post, when accepted as complete on March 31, 1941, included 708 buildings in addition to 6,765 tents, all linked by 22 miles of concrete- and asphalt-paved streets. The camp's hospital area occupied 9 acres with 81 buildings connected by 2 miles of corridors. The first arrivals for training were 218 officers and men of the 106th Cavalry of the Illinois National Guard. Camp Livingston was deactivated November 7, 1945. In October 1947 about 4,500 buildings were sold. On October 30, 1957, the government transferred 12,500 acres of the reservation to the state of Louisiana for use of the National Guard.

FORT LIVINGSTON (*Fort at Barataria; Fort on Grande Terre Island*). The remains of this tabby- and brick-built fort, known as Fort at Barataria or Fort on Grande Terre Island until 1833, when it was named Fort Livingston for Edward Livingston, secretary of state under President Andrew Jackson, are located in Jefferson Parish at the southwest end of the island at the mouth of Barataria Bay. The island had been intermittently occupied for military purposes as early as 1814. American military authorities had long recognized the need for a defense at the site to prevent enemy naval forces from invading Louisiana via Barataria Bay. In 1813 engineer Bartholemy Lafon drew up a plan for a fort here. Four years later General Simon Bernard, head of the Board of Fortifications, selected the specific site. In 1822 the government appropriated monies for the collection of materials for the fort on Grande Terre Island, but no further action was taken at this time. In 1834 the island was sold to the state of Louisiana by its owners, Étienne de Gruy and his wife, and the state in turn ceded it to the federal government the same year.

According to a number of National Archives citations, the fort was apparently started as early as 1835, but work progressed so slowly that it was not completed until 1861. In the interim, however, although not regularly garrisoned, what had been built was kept in a state of repair. At the outbreak of the Civil War, it was seized by Louisiana militia forces. Evacuated by Confederate forces on April 27, 1862, the fort was not reoccupied by Federal troops until February 26, 1863. Following the war, Fort Livingston was no longer garrisoned. It was turned over to the Quartermaster Department in 1888 and put in charge of the keeper of the 55-foot-high, octagonal brick lighthouse that had been built on the island in 1856. After the hurricane of 1893, which partly destroyed the fort's works, it was not rebuilt. The military reservation, turned over to the state of Louisiana in 1923, was retained.

FORT LOUISIANA. FORT DE LA BOULAYE.

CAMP LOVELL. This large Confederate encampment at Berwick City in St. Mary Parish was situated on the right bank of the lower Atchafalaya River and named for General Mansfield Lovell. Probably established in 1861 by the 4th Louisiana Volunteers, the camp could accommodate 1,000 men. In March 1862 the 26th Louisiana Volunteers was organized at the camp and left on April 20 to aid in the defense of threatened New Orleans. After the downfall of the city and the Confederate loss of control of the lower Mississippi, the site of the camp was most probably occupied by Federal forces.

FORT MACOMB (*Fort at Chef Menteur; Fort Wood*). Located in Orleans Parish, Fort Macomb is situated on the south bank of Chef Menteur Pass, which links Lake Pontchartrain and Lake Borgne, and between today's U.S. 90 and the Louisville and Nashville Railroad. The fort was called Fort at Chef Menteur until 1827, when it was renamed Fort Wood for Lieutenant Colonel Eleazer Derby Wood, who was killed in action in 1814 near Fort Erie. In 1851 the fort was designated Fort Macomb in honor of Major General Alexander Macomb, veteran of the War of 1812.

Begun in 1822 and completed in 1827, Fort Macomb with its twin, Fort Pike, five miles distant, guarded the major approaches to New Orleans. The posts were the initial two to be erected by the government after the War of 1812 as the first priorities in a complete plan for coastal defenses. Mississippi's delta historically controlled access to the American interior and the Mississippi Valley, and control of this entrance was considered critical. Forts Macomb and Pike were the first American forts built to contain all the features of the casemated bastion, borrowed from traditional European defense principles. Unlike most other American coastal forts, they were not altered by later additions.

Garrisoned until 1871, Fort Macomb was occupied by Confederate forces from January 14, 1861, until reoccupied by Federal troops on August 18, 1862, having had no combat role in the Civil War. Possession of the remains of the fort and its reservation was long a controversial issue. The Louisiana State Parks and Recreation Commission on February 24, 1966, granted the Fort Macomb Development Commission a long-term lease of the 16 acres comprising the fort site, despite vehement objections by a number of preservationists. In 1981, however, the state of Louisiana paid a large sum of money to regain possession of Fort Macomb.

FORT AT MANCHAC. FORT ST. (SAN) GABRIEL.

MANCHAC FORT. FORT BUTE.

MARTELLO CASTLE. DUPRE TOWER.

FORT MIRÓ (*Ouachita Post*). Originally called Ouachita Post, this Spanish village was established in 1785 by Juan Filhiol and a group of settlers from New Orleans and located on the Ouachita River at Prairie des Canots, the present site of the town of Monroe in Ouachita Parish. Erection of the fort was begun on September 8, 1790, at which time or shortly thereafter it was named Fort Miró for Estevan Miró, then governor of Louisiana. It is believed that the site on which the fort was built is located on or near South Grand Street, probably between Calyso and Oak streets. After the Louisiana Purchase, the fort was officially transferred to Captain Daniel Bissell, 1st Infantry, on April 17, 1804. In possession of the United States, the town was first garrisoned by troops commanded by 1st Lieutenant Joseph Bowman, 2nd Infantry. Because the Spanish fort was considered the private property of the former civil commandant, the American post was located about 400 yards below Fort Miró and consisted of a number of log barracks enclosed within a stockade. In May 1819 the steamboat *James Monroe* came up the Ouachita, the first of its kind ever to ascend the stream. After a joyful delegation of residents visited the vessel and shared the captain's hospitality, it was unanimously decided to honor both the vessel and the president of the United States, for whom it was named, by changing the name of Fort Miró to Monroe.

FORT ON THE MISSISSIPPI. FORT DE LA BOULAYE.

CAMP MOORE (*Camp Walker*). Named for Governor Thomas O. Moore, this camp was one of Louisiana's principal Confederate induction and training centers. When Camp Walker at the Metairie Race Track in New Orleans proved inadequate to house and train the large numbers of volunteers that asembled shortly after the outbreak of war, it was decided to establish a new camp in the pine woods across Lake Pontchartrain, at Tangipahoa, 78 miles above the city, on the Jackson Railroad (now the Illinois Central Gulf Railroad). On May 12 a large detachment was sent to lay out the new camp. Within three days practically all of Camp Walker's troops had been moved to Camp Moore.

In this camp the greater part of the state's volunteer regiments and battalions were congregated, organized into 10-company regiments, and trained. Raided several times by Federal troops in 1863 and 1864, Camp Moore was completely devastated on the morning of November 30, 1864, by a force of 5,000 Union cavalry with 12 pieces of artillery, commanded by Brigadier

General J. W. Davidson, on an expedition from Baton Rouge, via Tangipahoa, to the Pascagoula River. The cavalrymen dispersed the Confederate conscripts and burned the camp and all its many outbuildings, ending its prominent role in the war. The Camp Moore Cemetery, commemorated by a tall monument, contains the graves of between 400 and 500 mostly unknown Confererate soldiers who died at the camp during a measles epidemic between August and November, 1861.

FORT (JOHN M.) MORGAN. CAMP PARAPET.

FORT MORGANZA. A heavily fortified Federal post, designated as a "fort" on a National Archives plan of the camp, it was located on the west bank of the Mississippi River near Morganza in Pointe Coupée Parish. The plan delineates bastions at the post's west corners and at its sides where they crossed the levee. Numerous Federal corps and regiments, aggregating as many as 20,000 troops, were encamped at Morganza beginning in May 1864. It was reported on January 15, 1865, that Fort Morganza had thirteen 24-pounder siege guns, three 30-pounder Parrott guns, one 12-pounder siege gun, one 12-pounder howitzer, and four 12-pounder fieldpieces. The post was abandoned in May 1865.

FORT NATCHITOCHES. FORT ST. JEAN BAPTISTE.

NEW ORLEANS ARSENAL. During the first decades of the nineteenth century, a major part of the ordnance in New Orleans had been stored in rented buildings. During the 1820s, much of the ordnance then at hand was moved to the Baton Rouge Arsenal. The need for an independent New Orleans Arsenal became apparent in the 1830s. Situated directly behind the historic Cabildo in New Orleans is the Arsenal, constructed as a state armory from plans drawn in 1839. With facades of striking Greek Revival design, it was used from 1846 until the Civil War by the Orleans Artillery. In 1860 the Arsenal was used as the headquarters for General P. G. T. Beauregard, adjutant general of Louisiana. During the early months of the Civil War, the Confederates used it to store military supplies, and after the occupation of the city in 1862 by the Federals it became a military prison. During the Reconstruction period the Metropolitan Police occupied it, and it became their haven after precipitately retreating in a riverfront battle on September 14, 1874. In later years, it was used by the reorganized Orleans Artillery and as a state arsenal. On March 15, 1914, it was transferred to the Louisiana State Museum.

NEW ORLEANS BARRACKS. JACKSON BARRACKS.

CAMP NEW ORLEANS FAIR GROUNDS. Early during the Spanish-American War, in April and May 1898, the 18th and 23rd Infantry and the 5th Cavalry used the New Orleans Fair Grounds as an encampment before leaving for the war fronts in the Philippines and Cuba via San Francisco and Mobile.

NEW ORLEANS (FRENCH) FORTIFICATIONS. Other than erecting fortifications at Bayou St. John, at English Turn, and the Balize to obstruct enemy naval ships from penetrating to New Orleans, the French did relatively little in providing defenses within the city or in its immediate environs. Following the Natchez massacre at Fort Rosalie (Mississippi) in 1729, a palisade or enceinte was erected around the city, with small blockhouses at the corners, and excavation was begun for a moat that was never completed because of the lack of slave labor. In 1731–32 a small powder magazine, enclosed by high walls and mounting six-sided towers at each corner, was built on the east bank of the Mississippi River near the present intersection of Decatur and Iberville streets. The magazine was destroyed by fire on December 8, 1794.

Because of military reverses during the French and Indian War in the Ohio Valley and in Canada, the French were forced to fortify New Orleans against British forces coming down the Mississippi. Governor Kerlerec of Louisiana requested engineer De Verges to draw up plans for fortifications and a moat to completely surround New Orleans. The extant plan shows an embankment with nine bastions along its ramparts, identified as Conde's, Kirlires (Kerlerec), St. Louis, Choiseuel's, Orleans, Redan of the Bayou, Berry's, D'Abbadie's, and Charles' bastions. The Spanish later built Fort St. Louis and Fort St. Charles on the approximate sites of St. Louis Bastion and Charles' Bastion. Captain Philip Pittman, in his *European Settlements on the Mississippi* (1770), reports that these defenses were merely a chain of banquetted stockades only useful against Indian or slave attack. He further reported that the city "square [Place d'Armes] is open to the river, and on that side are twenty-one pieces of ordnance, *en barbette*, which are fired on public rejoicings."

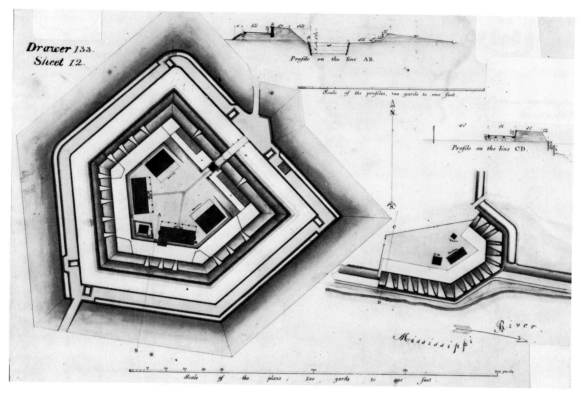

Drawer 133.
Sheet 12.

Profile on the line AB.

Scale of the profiles, 100 yards to one foot.

Profile on the line CD.

Mississippi   River.

Scale   of   the   plans   200   yards   to   one   foot.

NEW ORLEANS (SPAN-ISH) FORTIFICATIONS. Plan of Fort St. Charles drawn in 1817. (Courtesy of the National Archives.)

NEW ORLEANS (SPANISH) FORTIFICA-TIONS. When the tide of victory turned against her in North America, and her defeat elsewhere in the world became a certainty, France in 1762 quickly consigned western Louisiana to her ally Spain by the secret Treaty of Fontainebleau. Then, by the Treaty of Paris the following year, she surrendered the rest of her North American possessions to Great Britain. A few months after Lieutenant General Alexandre O'Reilly arrived in the newly established Spanish Province of Louisiana, he reported that the palisades and very minor works erected by the French in 1760 were utterly useless. But little was accomplished then to correct the deficiency of adequate for-tifications, although an English visitor to New Orleans in 1773 reported that there were 18 six-pounders on carriages near the city gates and more than 100 cannon of various calibers in the city's artillery park.

In the early 1790s, Governor Carondelet, in anticipation of a French attack, ordered the con-struction of Fort St. Philip at Plaquemines Bend down the Mississippi and the encirclement of New Orleans with fortifications. The task of draw-ing up plans for the New Orleans defenses was consigned to Gilberto Guillemand, whose work was approved by the governor on November 8, 1792. The plan consisted in the main of five redoubts linked by embankments stretching around the city and fronted by moats except

along the river. The largest was Fort St. Charles, located at the foot of today's Esplanade Avenue. The second was Fort St. John, located on North Rampart Street between Esplanade Avenue and Barracks Street. The third redoubt, Fort St. Fer-dinand, was located in what is today's Beauregard Square. The fourth, Fort Bourgogne, occupied the present-day intersection of North Rampart and Iberville streets. The fifth and last, Fort St. Louis, stood at today's intersection of Canal and North Peters streets. In addition, the Spanish es-tablished a number of batteries at various strategic points in and around the city.

After the purchase of Louisiana was formally consummated, General James Wilkinson's troops took possession of the territory on December 20, 1803. The general's Order Book on that day specified the assignments of troops to stand guard the first night at these five New Orleans forts: Fort St. Charles, 40; Fort St. Louis, 38; Fort Bourgogne, 11; Fort St. Ferdinand, 11; Fort St. John, 11. During the previous February, General Wilkinson was made cognizant of the dilapidated and defenseless condition of the Spanish redoubts. Fort St. Charles had fifteen 12- and 18-pounders on rotted carriages, Fort St. Louis had no ordnance at all, and the other three in the rear of the town were utterly defenseless.

In 1806, in compliance with War Department directives, plans were made to refortify New Or-leans, including the rebuilding or renovation of the five Spanish forts. In June 1812, when the war with Great Britain broke out, congressional legislation instigated by Louisiana's two senators in response to requests by the city's authorities ordered the abandonment of Forts St. Louis, Bourgogne, St. Ferdinand, and St. John. Fort St. Charles, however, continued to serve as troop quarters and as an ordnance depot. In 1819 new troop quarters and a new arsenal depot were being erected at Baton Rouge. Two years later orders came through to effect the demolition of Fort St. Louis. No tangible above-the-ground remains of these forts are evident today.

FORT NEW RICHMOND. FORT BATON ROUGE.

CAMP NICHOLLS. Located in City Park, New Orleans, Camp Nicholls was named in honor of Civil War veteran and former Louisiana Governor F. T. Nicholls. The tent camp accommodated the 1st Louisiana Infantry in 1916 before it departed for Alexandria and then the Mexican frontier for border patrol duties. The camp, enlarged by additional leased land, was reestablished on April 20, 1917, after the declaration of war against Germany, by the Washington Artillery. The 1st Louisiana Infantry, for the second time, was encamped there. When Camp Beauregard was established five miles north of Alexandria in August 1917, these units were transferred there from Camp Nicholls. Later other regimental units, including 11 Coast Artillery companies, were trained at the camp.

NORWOOD PLANTATION FORT. YELLOW BAYOU REDOUBT.

OLD OAK FORT. YELLOW BAYOU REDOUBT.

OUACHITA POST. FORT MIRÓ.

CAMP PARAPET (*Star Fort; Fort [John M.] Morgan*). When Federal forces began their occupation of New Orleans in the spring of 1862, they assigned the composite name of Camp Parapet to the heavily fortified breastworks, also known as the Parapet Line, fronting the string of Union camps on the east side of the Mississippi River, today's Causeway Boulevard. During the summer of 1861, the Confederates made plans to erect a line of breastworks, to be fortified with up to 50 pieces of heavy ordnance, to safeguard New Orleans from possible Federal attack. During the late summer, the fortifications already erected from the river to the swamp were described as being an extended parapet nine feet high fronted by a 30-foot-wide moat six feet deep. The Confederate line of breastworks had not been completed when Commodore Farragut's fleet showed up before New Orleans on April 25, 1862. Faced with the enormous task of evacuating all their troops, armaments, and ammunition by railroad, the Confederates did not have the time to remove the guns on the Parapet Line and made efforts to spike the guns and burn the carriages. Farragut's report dated May 6, 1862, says that only 29 guns were then on the Confederate line.

Their occupation of New Orleans assured, Union forces at once began significant improvements on the Parapet Line, including the addition of redoubts and forts, manned and strongly fortified by heavy ordnance incorporating former Confederate guns until the end of the war. Beginning on the bank of the Mississippi where Fort John M. Morgan, a principal redoubt on the Parapet Line, guarded the riverfront, the fortifications extended nearly directly north for about a mile and a half to end in the swamps. Guarding the line's north end was 10-pointed, heavily armed Star Fort with a magazine in its center. After May 22, 1865, when demobilization of the Federal army was already in progress, Camp Parapet and its line of fortifications were gradually dismantled for the removal of their armaments. Remains of gun emplacements were still in evidence during the early decades of this century.

PENTAGON BARRACKS. BATON ROUGE BARRACKS.

FORT PETITE COQUILLES (*Fort Coquilles; Fort Rigolets*). At times called Fort Coquilles or Fort Rigolets (a name also applied to Fort Pike), Fort Petite Coquilles ("little shells") was erected by the United States on the east end of Lake Pontchartrain, on the south side of Pass Rigolets, the larger of the two channels connecting it on the west with Lake Borgne on the east, in Orleans Parish. The site of the fort, now under water, is less than a mile west of Fort Pike State Park. General James Wilkinson, succeeding General Wade Hampton, who first suggested a fortification at that strategic location during the last weeks of December 1812, ordered the construction of Fort Petite Coquilles, planned and superintended by New Orleans engineer Bartholemy Lafon. His plan and the sketch by William T. Poussin in 1817 of the fort as completed, show it as a parallelogram with two full bastions at the west end, a partial or half-bastion at the southwest corner, and a semicircular battery extending beyond the north rampart on the side facing Lake Pontchartrain. The fort contained two sets of troops barracks and one set of officers' quarters, besides auxiliary structures and a magazine. The fort's complement of ordnance varied from time to time during its short history. An ordnance report dated January 31, 1815, indicated that there were then three iron 24-pounders, five iron 18-pounders and one brass 9-pounder. In June 1816 it was reported that the fort mounted eleven guns of different calibers. General Wilkinson in his *Memoirs* was of the opinion that the construction of Fort Petite Coquilles was a major factor in defeating the British plan to capture New Orleans in 1814–15.

The War Department's Fortification Board in 1817 decided on a new fort at Pass Rigolets, selecting a site three-quarters of a mile east of Petite Coquilles. Construction on it began in 1819. The new fort, at first called Fort at the Rigolets, Fort Rigolets, and even Fort Petite Coquilles—which it was replacing—was eventually designated Fort Pike. The confusion of names led to uncertainty regarding the precise dates when the old fort was abandoned and the new one garrisoned. The last post return for Fort Petite Coquilles is dated November 1827, while Fort Pike's initial post return is dated January 1828. A hospital was constructed on or in the immediate environs of the ruins of Fort Petite Coquilles in the 1840s.

PHILIPPON TOWER. DUPRE TOWER.

FORT PIKE (*Fort Rigolets*). This fort, 30 miles east of downtown New Orleans was at first called the Rigolets Fort and Fort Petite Coquilles. Fort Petite Coquilles was actually a fort about three-quarters of a mile to the east, which was replaced by Fort Pike. Fort Pike was named in honor of General Zebulon M. Pike, who explored a large part of the Louisiana Territory. It is located in Orleans Parish on the west bank of Pass Rigolets where it borders U.S. 90 and is preserved in the Fort Pike State Park. The fort and its predecessor guarded the nine-mile-long pass that connects Lake Pontchartrain with Lake Borgne. The Fortifications Board of the War Department in 1817 had determined that Fort Petite Coquilles was too far from the pass for its guns to adequately control the strategic waterway and proposed a new larger and stronger fort, selecting a site on the west side of Pass Rigolets where the channel was about 3,700 yards wide. The plan of the fort drawn in 1817 was signed by engineer General Simon Bernard and his able assistant Captain William T. Poussin.

Construction on the fort, built on a foundation of cypress logs sunk in the marsh, over which lies a layer of cemented shells, began in 1819 and was not accepted as complete until February 19, 1827, when it was considered ready to mount its armaments and be occupied by a garrison. The triangular brick fort with an arc of casemates to mount 13 guns fronting the pass had an additional 20 emplacements for other armament, the complement of which varied from time to time. In 1849 plans were drawn for a second brick story to be added to the citadel's works. Intermittently fully garrisoned, Fort Pike was seized by Louisiana troops on the night of January 10, 1861. The Confederate garrison occupying the fort had been augmented to five companies by the time Farragut's Federal fleet ran the gauntlet of Forts Jackson and St. Philip and reached New Orleans on April 25, 1862. The Confederates evacuated the fort on April 26, and Union forces repossessed it on May 4, occupying it until the end of the war.

Fort Pike's last garrison was withdrawn on May 22, 1871, and the post was left in the charge of an ordnance sergeant. The War Department's report for 1882–83 named Fort Pike in its list of forts to be abandoned. In 1884 Fort Pike was turned over to the Quartermaster Department for disposal. In 1921 a part of the reservation was given to the Department of Commerce for a lighthouse facility. The remainder of the reservation, including the citadel, was acquired by the state of Louisiana on February 9, 1928, and on November 15, 1934, Govenor O. K. Allen created the Fort Pike State Park on a 125-acre tract.

FORT PLAQUEMINE. This was a Federal earthen fortification located in Iberville Parish and situated on the west side of the Mississippi River at its junction with Bayou Plaquemine. The work, begun in the spring of 1864 and completed in June of the same year, was manned by 22 officers and 540 enlistees of the 8th U.S. Heavy Artillery. According to a newspaper article, Lieutenant John C. Palfrey selected its site and built the fortification, which mounted four 20-pounder Parrott rifles. In compliance with an order of the Department of the Gulf dated June 9, 1865, Fort Plaquemine was evacuated and its ordnance removed to Baton Rouge.

CAMP PLAUCHE (*Camp Harahan*). This World War II training post, originally called Camp Harahan, was located on the east side of the Mississippi River on the north side of Jefferson Highway, between the town of Harahan and the Huey P. Long Bridge, in Jefferson Parish. The camp was named for Jean Baptiste Plauche, who commanded the Orleans Battalion of Volunteers in 1814–15 and became lieutenant governor of Louisiana in 1850. Camp Plauche was constructed on leased land as a staging area for troops moving through the New Orleans Port of Embarkation. With more than 300 buildings on a 425-acre tract, the camp was designed to accommodate about 30,000 men. Late in 1942 the post was converted into an organization and training center for battalions of port troops, railroad operating troops, and hospital service personnel. After the need of training lessened, the post was partially used as a prisoner of war camp. Camp Plauche was declared surplus on May 31, 1946.

POINTE COUPÉE FORTS. The French, Spanish, and Americans established posts, apparently on the same site, at old Pointe Coupée on the west side of the Mississippi River, in the present parish of the same name. Subsequent to the Indian massacre of the French at Fort Rosalie, Mississippi, in 1729, it is probable that Louisiana's Governor Perier dispatched a detachment to the settlements and that a small stockade was built at Pointe Coupée in late 1729 or 1730. French correspondence thereafter indicates its continuous operation into the period of Spanish occupation, when France in 1762 by the secret Treaty of Fontainebleau, ceded Louisiana to Spain.

British Captain Harry Gordon reported on October 9, 1766, that he found at Pointe Coupée 110 families and a stockaded fort garrisoned by 1 Spanish officer and 10 men. The Spanish called it Post Punta Cortada. Captain Philip Pittman, a British engineer in British West Florida in 1768, described the fort at Pointe Coupée as "a quadrangle with four bastions, built with stockades, and contains a very handsome house for the commanding officer, good barracks for the soldiers, store-houses, and a prison. . . . There are seldom more than twelve soldiers at this place, who are for no other purpose than to preserve good order" (Philip Pittman, *The Present State of the European Settlements on the Mississippi* [1770; reprint ed., 1973], p. 34). The Spanish apparently abandoned the fort as no longer needed in 1779.

Although the United States acquired Louisiana Territory by purchase in 1803, no efforts were made to dispatch troops to Pointe Coupée until the fall of 1804 when plantation owners there requested the presence of troops in anticipation of a slave revolt. The settlement's first American garrison, established in early 1805, consisted of 30 soldiers who occupied public buildings until they were evacuated in 1806 in compliance with an order of General James Wilkinson. A letter written by a Pointe Coupée resident on September 1, 1807, described the American "fort" there as consisting of a guardhouse and magazine and five other structures. In 1808 the post property was described as consisting of an old wooden building, a garden, and about 40 acres of adjoining land. The American post was apparently maintained until at least 1808.

FORT POLK. This large U.S. Army post is located about five miles southeast of Leesville in Vernon Parish. The 198,552-acre reservation, which extends about 10 miles north and south and nearly 15 miles east and west, occupied the greater part of the Vernon Division of the Kisatchie National Forest. The post was known as Camp Polk until it was designated Fort Polk on November 1, 1955, in honor of Leonidas Polk, West Point graduate, Episcopal bishop of Louisiana, and C.S.A. lieutenant general, who was killed at Pine Mountain, Georgia, June 14, 1864.

Designed as a training center for the Army's armored divisions then being organized, construction on the camp began in January 1941. Activated about May 1, 1941, the post's first trainee occupants were elements of the new 3rd Armored Division commanded by Major General Alvan C. Gillem, Jr. During World War II, the post accommodated a number of armored divisions, the 11th Airborne Division, and the 95th Infantry. From March 15 to June 30, 1943, part of the camp was used as a training center for the 5th Women's Army Auxiliary Corps. Near the end of the war, Camp Polk housed more than 4,000 prisoners of war. The post was closed on December 31, 1946, and placed in the charge of a caretaker detachment.

The post was reactivated and closed several times as dictated by national emergencies and federal defense budgets. The post was reactivated during the Korean War, the Berlin crisis, and the Vietnam War, in the course of which more than 700,000 soldiers were trained for duty in the Southeast Asia theater of war. At present Fort Polk is occupied by about 13,000 soldiers, contributing more than $130 million in annual military and civilian pay to the area's economy. The post is now undergoing an enormous building program estimated to eventually cost nearly a quarter of a billion dollars.

FORT PONTCHARTRAIN. FORT ST. JOHN.

CAMP PORT ALLEN. A World War II prisoner of war tent encampment housing about 500 Germans, it was located on the Port Allen Fair Grounds in the rear of the town's courthouse in West Baton Rouge Parish.

POWDER MAGAZINE BARRACKS (*Algier's Barracks*). In response to the possibility of a British invasion up the Mississippi to seize New Orleans during the War of 1812, General James Wilkinson ordered the erection of troop housing units, eventually known as Powder Magazine Barracks, to accommodate reinforcements for the defense of the city. On January 1, 1813, a contract was made for the construction within eight days of 16 barracks, each 27 by 70 feet, for about 1,600 men. The barracks were built on leased land on the right side of the Mississippi River in the Algiers section in east New Orleans. After the Battle of New Orleans in January 1815, the barracks were converted into a hospital for the wounded and the ill. On May 9, 1817, after it was decided to erect barracks at Baton Rouge, the War Department ordered the disposition of Powder Magazine Barracks.

CAMP PRATT. A Confederate training encampment ordered established by Governor Moore in May or June 1862, Camp Pratt was named for Brigadier General John G. Pratt, commander of the 9th Brigade of the Louisiana Militia. The camp of instruction, intended to accommodate Louisiana conscripts residing south of the Red River and west of the Mississippi, was located on Spanish Lake about five miles north of New Iberia in Iberia Parish.

FORT PROCTOR. PROCTOR'S LANDING TOWER.

PROCTOR'S LANDING TOWER (*Fort Proctor; Fort Beauregard*). Now surrounded by water, this fortification, originally designed for three stories in the form of a medieval castle or keep, is situated on the south side of Lake Borgne, a few hundred yards west of the mouth of Bayou Yscloskey near Shell Beach, in St. Bernard Parish. Known unofficially during recent years as "Old Fort Beauregard" because Major P. G. T. Beauregard was then engineering superintendent of forts in that area when it was erected, it is officially named the Tower at Proctor's Landing. On occasion it was also called Fort Proctor. On February 28, 1855, Congress appropriated $125,000 to cover the cost of the site and construction, with an additional appropriation of $25,000 in 1857. The site was bought on March 15, 1856, and building was begun soon after.

Since the terminus of the Mexican Gulf Railway was at Proctor's Landing, the fort was intended to prevent an enemy from using the railroad route to New Orleans. The tower was never completed, principally because the appropriations had been expended during 1856–59. A storm on August 11, 1860, leveled the town of Proctorsville, partially destroyed the officer's quarters outside the fort and damaged its glacis and revetment. The outbreak of the Civil War obviated any idea of completing the work, though it was recommended by the chief engineer of the Federal forces in New Orleans.

FORT QUITMAN (*Fort Butler*). This small Confederate earthen fortification, named in honor of former Governor of Louisiana John A. Quitman, was located on Gran Caillou Bayou in Terrebonne Parish. Apparently established in September 1861, when it was occupied by companies A and G of the 22nd Louisiana Volunteers until December, the defense was first named Fort Butler, then renamed Fort Quitman in January 1862. The redoubt, mounting two 32-pounder smoothbore guns, was intended to prevent enemy incursion into Louisiana by way of the bayou. When New Orleans fell to the Federals in April 1862, the guns were spiked and the fort was abandoned by its garrison numbering approximately 5 officers and 137 men.

FORT RANDOLPH. The site of this Confederate fortification is incorporated within the grounds of the Central Louisiana Hospital on the north side of the Red River and south of U.S. 71 in Rapides Parish. Fort Randolph and Fort Buhlow, about 500 yards to the north, were twin earthen forts built in the summer of 1864 and designed to prevent a possible new invasion of the Red River Valley by Federal forces. Captain Christopher Meyer Randolph, an engineer attached to General Simon Bolivar Buckner's staff, superintended construction of the two forts, which were never engaged in any battle action. After the war had ended, Major General F. J. Herron, en route to Shreveport with Federal troops, took possession of the two forts. In October 1928 the Daughters of the Confederacy dedicated monuments, constructed of the stone remains of the old Louisiana Seminary nearby, at the sites of the twin forts.

REDAN OF THE BAYOUS BASTION. NEW ORLEANS (FRENCH) FORTIFICATIONS.

FORT RICHMOND. FORT BATON ROUGE.

FORT RIDLEY. A Confederate fortification located at Brashear City, St. Mary Parish, apparently built in 1863, it was garrisoned by the Crescent Regiment in June and July 1863.

FORT RIGOLETS. FORT PETITE COQUILLES.

FORT RIGOLETS. FORT PIKE.

CANTONMENT (ROBINSON) ROBERTSON. A summer camp located in the pine woods about nine miles from Baton Rouge, it was used by the troops of the 1st Infantry during 1824 and 1825 to escape the threat of yellow fever in the city, where in former years summer epidemics had caused the deaths of many men in the garrison there. The camp was most probably named for Governor Thomas B. Robertson, although the Baton Rouge report for 1825 misnomered it Cantonment "Robinson."

CAMP ROMAN (*Camp Carrollton*). This Confederate Civil War camp, situated near Carrollton in Jefferson Parish, was occupied in the late fall of 1861 by the 17th Louisiana Volunteers under the command of Colonel Alfred Mouton. Although the other officer of the 17th was Lieutenant Colonel Alfred Roman, the camp was named for V. Roman, the owner of the plantation on which the camp was located.

CAMP RUSTON. A World War II encampment was established in late 1942 near Ruston in Lincoln Parish for the purpose of housing prisoners of war from North Africa. While awaiting their arrival, the post was temporarily occupied as a training center for recruits of the Women's Army Auxiliary Corps from March 15 to June 30, 1943, at which time it was deactivated for that purpose upon the arrival of the expected prisoners of war. The camp from then until the end of the war incarcerated more than 4,000 prisoners of war.

CAMP SABINE. This Army post, located four miles (by road) from the Sabine River in Sabine Parish, was occupied from April 1836 through August 1838. With the Texas revolution against the Spanish then in progress, it was determined by General Edmund P. Gaines that a post was needed closer to the Sabine River than Fort Jesup. The camp was established when Major Alexander R. Thompson arrived at the site from Fort Jesup on April 17, 1836, with five companies of the 3rd Infantry and nine companies of the 6th Infantry, aggregating about 394 men. General Gaines on July 21, 1836, wrote from the camp that he intended constructing a blockhouse and eight storehouses there. It is possible that Camp Sabine occupied the site of General Wilkinson's camp of 1806 during his campaign against the Spanish commanded by General Herrera during the dispute over the boundary between American and Spanish territory. The blockhouse after the Mexican War was converted into the historic "Blockhouse Church" used by the Beulah Baptist Church located 13 miles west of the town of Many.

FORT ST. CHARLES. FORT BATON ROUGE.

FORT ST. CHARLES. NEW ORLEANS (SPANISH) FORTIFICATIONS.

FORT ST. FERDINAND. NEW ORLEANS (SPANISH) FORTIFICATIONS.

ST. FRANCISVILLE POST. The town of St. Francisville in West Feliciana Parish in November 1810 was the headquarters of the so-called Committee of Five formed by the West Florida Convention to govern the territory seized from the Spanish. Here was established the capital of the short-lived Republic of West Florida, which stored a sizable array of ordnance and ammunition, apparently collected when Fort San Carlos at Baton Rouge was captured in September 1810.

FORT ST. (SAN) GABRIEL (*Fort at Manchac; Fort at Iberville*). This stockaded fort, at times called the Fort at Iberville or Fort at Manchac, was erected by the Spanish on the left bank of the Mississippi River and on the south side of Bayou Manchac (Iberville River), in present-day Iberville Parish. In 1766, during an inspection of the area, Spanish Governor Antonio Ulloa observed that the British had built Fort Bute on the left bank on the north side of the bayou, the international demarcation line between Spanish territory and British West Florida. The governor thereupon ordered a counter fort built. Construction was begun after April 29, 1767, and completed in 1768, when it mounted two 6-pounders and two 8-pounders, although the fort was designed for 10 or 12 cannon. After the British evacuated Fort Bute in July 1768, the Spanish garrison at Fort St. Gabriel was reduced to 13 men. In December 1769, when the Spanish fort was considered indefensible, it was abandoned by the Spanish military and turned over to six German families for their use.

FORT ST. JEAN BAPTISTE (*Fort Natchitoches*). This fortification at old Natchitoches was initially established by the French on an island in the Red River and was moved in the mid-1730s because of flooding to the mainland on the west side of the river, where it was occupied by the French and later the Spanish until the United States acquired the Territory of Louisiana in 1803. After the clearing of obstructions in the Red River, changes occurred among the river's islands and channels. A number of local historians believe that the first fort was located in the area between Jefferson Street and the Cane River and between Sibley and College avenues. It is also thought that the second fort occupied the present site of the American Cemetery on the east side of New Second Street. During the fort's early days, it was variously called Post of Natchitoches, Fort Natchitoches, and Post on Cane River.

Louis Juchereau de St. Denis, while commanding a French trading expedition into Spanish Texas in 1714, encamped for a time on the present site of Natchitoches. He left a detachment of men there with orders to erect a fortification and a storehouse. In 1719 a small force of men arrived to complete the fort on the island. During the same year, war having been declared between Spain and France, Lieutenant Philippe Blondel, commandant of the French fort, accompanied by some of his men, went to the nearby Spanish mission at Los Adaes and compelled its evacuation. But the Spanish returned in 1721 and established Presidio Los Adaes to replace the abandoned mission despite French protests. During the same year, the French post was rebuilt on the island's higher ground because of flooding. On October 5, 1731, the remnants of the Natchez Indian Nation, having suffered retributive justice by French arms after the Fort Rosalie massacre in 1729, unsuccessfully besieged Fort St. Jean Baptiste.

Based on architect-engineer Ignace Broutin's plan of 1733, the new Fort St. Jean Baptiste was begun on the mainland in 1736 and completed in 1737. Descriptions of the fort delineate a square, palisade-enclosed work with two bastions and two demibastions, armed with swivel guns and larger cannon, at the angles, with a large barracks complex along its north side, the commandant's residence, the powder magazine, and a guardhouse. French troops continued to garrison the Natchitoches post despite the cession of Louisiana territory to Spain in 1762. After the Louisiana Purchase was finalized by the United States in December 1803, by prior arrangement between representatives of Spain, France, and the United States, the fort's Spanish flag was lowered on April 26, 1804, and a detachment of

the 2nd Infantry under Lieutenant Edward D. Turner raised the American standard. A new post, Fort Claiborne, was built nearby by the Americans. Fort St. Jean Baptiste was finally abandoned in June 1819, to be replaced the following year by Camp Salubrity and Fort Selden, respectively three and six miles above Natchitoches.

In 1973 the Louisiana State Parks and Recreation Commission initiated plans for the reconstruction of the historic French fort. Assiduous research was made in French and Spanish archival repositories on the construction methods employed in Louisiana during the first half of the eighteenth century. The fort was reconstructed between downtown Natchitoches and Northwestern State University. Construction of the 10-building complex, based on Broutin's 1733 plan, was begun in November 1979. Of the $888,500 contract, about $500,000 was spent on materials. The recreation of Fort St. Jean Baptiste, including the Louisiana Purchase Museum delineating three centuries of Southwest history, was opened to visitors in mid-May 1981, but the formal dedication was not held until April 1982, when Louisiana celebrated its tricentennial.

FORT ST. JOHN (San Juan). NEW ORLEANS (SPANISH) FORTIFICATIONS.

FORT ST. JOHN (*Fort Pontchartrain; Spanish Fort*). This fort or redoubt, and its predecessors, have been variously called Fort on Bayou St. John, Fort on Lake Pontchartrain, and more frequently, Fort Pontchartrain, but it is more popularly known as Spanish Fort. Its site is located in New Orleans on the south side of Lake Pontchartrain on the left bank of the bayou in the very near environs of Beauregard Avenue and Robert E. Lee Boulevard. Originally situated at the mouth of the bayou, the site is now about 600 yards farther inland because part of Lake Pontchartrain had been landfilled. The strategic value of Bayou St. John for both military and commercial uses made its situation on Lake Pontchartrain's south shore a primary consideration for a military post. Just when the first fortification was established there has not been determined. A number of citations in French and Spanish official reports and correspondence make references to a fort or blockhouse on the site.

Captain Philip Pittman's *European Settlements on the Mississippi* (1770) states that the mouth of Bayou St. John was defended by a battery of six guns. Thomas Hutchins in 1773 reported that the fort was built of logs on a bank of shells and had four cannon manned by 12 soldiers. During the 1790s the fort was described as an earthen work "dressed with wood" and mounted eight or nine cannon. Construction of a new fort on the site by Americans began in 1808. On November 16, 1808, a report stated, "It is being built of brick to be filled in with earth. Its front covers the old works." On October 18, 1809, Major William MacRea sent the secretary of war plans of the works. The plans delineate a crescent-shaped barbette battery facing Lake Pontchartrain, gun embrasures on the sides, officers' quarters, a barracks, a powder magazine, a guardhouse, and a kitchen. Fort St. John was abandoned sometime between 1821 and 1825, most probably soon after the earlier date. The site of the fort is now incorporated within the City Park of New Orleans.

FORT ST. LEON. The French during the late 1740s built a fort that they named St. Leon on the west side of the Mississippi River at strategically important English Turn. In 1808 the Americans planned to erect a new fortification at the location. Major William MacRea, the U.S. Army's engineer at New Orleans, selected the site adjacent to that formerly occupied by the old French fort. MacRea on November 16, 1808, reported that the materials had been congregated there and construction began on the works. On March 18, 1810, he reported that construction on Fort St. Leon was completed to the point that authorization had limited him. He described the work as having a 4-foot-thick brick wall, 30 feet wide, covered with earth. A levee, reinforced by strong posts and planks, faced the river and was intended to mount nine 24- and 18-pounders, which could focus on a vessel for three miles as it approached and for about two miles after it passed.

One of two plans by engineer Bartholemy Lafon in 1813 shows two rows of barracks with porches facing each other and the officers' quarters in the rear of each row, the complex positioned on the east side of the river "below Wood's Ville." The second plan shows the semicircular levee or embankment and a low embankment at the rear with a bastion at each corner. The plan for the fort's projected completion, accomplished in 1814–15, delineates an enclosed work, about 160 yards on each side, with barracks, officers' quarters, the commandant's residence, two magazines, a guardhouse, and a kitchen. A contemporary newspaper in December 1812 reported that the barracks on the east side of the river were designed to accommodate 3,000 troops. The exigencies of the War of 1812 had hastened Fort St. Leon's completion. The British during their invasion of Louisiana were

unsuccessful on January 9, 1815, in getting past Fort St. Philip, and Fort St. Leon, although fully prepared to meet the enemy, had no role in the battle for New Orleans.

A township survey map prepared in recent years shows that the ruins of Fort St. Leon are located in Plaquemines Parish, with its site now within the Mississippi River Levee. In February 1963 low water exposed the ruins, and photographs of them were published in the February 28, 1963, issue of the New Orleans *Daily States* newspaper. A state commemorative plaque marks the fort site. It has been recently reported that archaeological explorations are in progress.

FORT ST. LOUIS. New Orleans (Spanish) Fortifications.

ST. LOUIS BASTION. New Orleans (French) Fortifications.

FORT ST. MARIE. A French fortification was built about 1723 on the east side of the Mississippi River at English Turn in Plaquemines Parish. A 1765 map prepared by an English officer shows both Fort St. Marie and later-built Fort St. Leon.

FORT ST. PHILIP (*Fort San Felipe*). Francisco Luis Hector, baron de Carondelet, governor of Louisiana, built this fort, begun in 1792 and completed in 1795, as a part of his plan to extend Spain's dominion over the entire Mississippi Valley and to prevent American encroachment. His plan included the establishment of a series of forts along the Mississippi River and the borders of the territory, including Fort St. Philip on the east or left bank of the river at strategic Plaquemines Bend, diagonally upriver from later-built Fort Jackson, in Plaquemines Parish. The fort has been called Fuerte San Felipe (Phelipe) de Placaminas, Fort Plaquemines, and the Fort at Plaquemines Bend.

A general contemporary description of the Spanish fort reported that the section facing the river was originally a bastioned terrace but eventually enclosed. The parapets, 18 to 20 feet thick and faced with brick, rose 17 feet from the bottom of the 20-foot-wide and 12-foot-deep ditch that surrounded the works. Inside were the commandant's house, two barracks to accommodate 300 men, and a powder magazine. The armament consisted of some 24 pieces of various caliber ordnance.

In February 1808, after American troops occupied Louisiana Territory, work was begun to improve Fort St. Philip. The renovation and

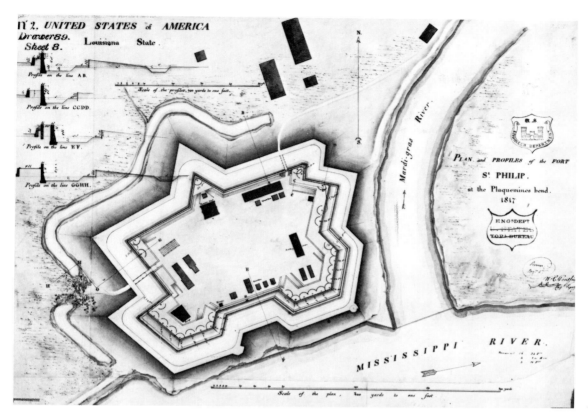

IV 2. UNITED STATES of AMERICA
Drawer 89.
Sheet 8.
Louisiana State.

Profile on the line A.B.

Profile on the line CC.DD.

Profile on the line EF.

Profile on the line GG.HH.

PLAN and PROFILES of the FORT
St PHILIP.
at the Plaquemines bend.
1817
ENGᴿ DEPT
TOPᴸ BUREAU

Mardi-gras River.

MISSISSIPPI   RIVER.

FORT ST. PHILIP. Plan drawn in 1817. (Courtesy of the National Archives.)

rebuilding program included the purchase of nearly two million bricks, more than 5,000 barrels of sand, and almost 9,000 barrels of lime. The new fort was constructed around and over the old Spanish works, with one of its original bastions repaired and eventually mounted with nine 24-pounders. By June 30, 1810, construction had been essentially completed.

Further construction in 1813 ceased, but when a British invasion of Louisiana was strongly suspected in the summer of 1814 work was renewed. Major General Andrew Jackson, having assumed responsibility for the Southwest's defense, ordered the replacement of the fort's aged Spanish barracks after they were reported completely rotted. On January 9, 1815, five British vessels, while attempting to pass the fort and reach New Orleans, began a nine-day but unsuccessful bombardment of Fort St. Philip. Its 366-man garrison valiantly withstood the more than 1,000 shells hurled at the fort. The Americans lost but two dead with seven more wounded. Fort Jackson, on the west side of the river and nearly opposite Fort St. Philip, was begun in 1814 and completed in 1815 to further defend the approaches to New Orleans. The repairs and significant enlargement of Fort St. Philip's works during the years 1840 and 1858 created a formidable fortress.

These two powerful fortifications, seized at the outbreak of the Civil War by Louisiana state forces, became the Confederacy's chief defenses, but for little more than a year. On the morning of April 18, 1862, Admiral David Farragut brought a Federal fleet of 17 wooden gunboats and 21 mortar schooners to Plaquemines Bend and bombarded the two forts with shells and bombs for six days and nights. On the seventh day Farragut successfully ran the gauntlet with 17 vessels and headed for New Orleans 60 miles upriver and ultimate victory. On April 28 the two forts were surrendered by the Confederates.

After the Civil War, and for the next 30 years, Fort St. Philip was hardly ever garrisoned, although major repairs and renovations were made on the works. Between the years 1895 and 1902, influenced by the incidence of the Spanish-American War, modern guns were emplaced at Fort St. Philip and Fort Jackson. During World War I, additions were made at Fort St. Philip, including a barracks, a hospital ward, mess halls, and officers' quarters. Both Fort St. Philip and Fort Jackson were abandoned in February 1922. Fort St. Philip was declared surplus and sold in October 1926 but not before its remaining guns were dismantled and removed. It is now privately owned.

CAMP SALUBRITY. This tent camp, less than three miles northwest of Natchitoches, was established in May 1844 by eight companies of the 4th Infantry, which had been ordered to Louisiana from Jefferson Barracks in Missouri to become a part of the American forces being congregated to march into Texas when it voted to be absorbed by the United States. The 4th Regiment, including Lieutenant Ulysses S. Grant, occupied the camp until July 2, 1845. The camp was reoccupied during the Civil War by Confederate infantry troops.

FORT SAN CARLOS. FORT BATON ROUGE.

FORT SAN CARLOS (ST. CHARLES). NEW ORLEANS (SPANISH) FORTIFICATIONS.

FORT SAN FELIPE. FORT ST. PHILIP.

FORT SAN GABRIEL. FORT ST. GABRIEL.

FORT SCURRY. YELLOW BAYOU REDOUBT.

SEDGWICK BARRACKS. GREENVILLE BARRACKS.

FORT SELDEN. This fort was established by elements of the 7th Infantry commanded by Lieutenant Colonel Zachary Taylor and named in honor of Joseph Selden, who served as a lieutenant in a Virginia regiment during the Revolution and as captain and major in the regular U.S. Army in the War of 1812. The post was located six miles above Natchitoches on Bayou Pierre near Grand Ecore. The post served as the headquarters of the Army's Western Department, and the troops there were intended to maintain order on the Red River. When the Treaty of Washington between the United States and Spain established the Sabine River as Louisiana's western boundary, Fort Jesup was established near the town of Many in May 1822, and Fort Selden's troops were used to garrison it.

FORT SMITH. FORT KIRBY SMITH.

SPANISH FORT. FORT ST. JOHN.

CAMP STAFFORD. A Louisiana National Guard encampment named in honor of Colonel Leroy H. Stafford killed in the Battle of the Wilderness on May 5, 1864, Camp Stafford was established in 1905 near Pineville in Rapides Parish on the former site of the Louisiana State Seminary, later renamed Louisiana State University. The camp was used for summer training by the National Guard. The site had been used as a camp during the Civil War and later by U.S. troops during the period of Reconstruction. In June 1916 Louisiana National Guard troops were congregated there to be mustered into the regular Army before being sent to police the Mexican border. In July 1917, after the declaration of war against Germany, elements of the 1st Louisiana Infantry assembled there before being moved to Camp Beauregard, then under construction two miles away. Later Camp Stafford's site was occupied by Camp Beauregard's post hospital.

STAR FORT. FORT BRASHEAR.

STAR FORT. CAMP PARAPET.

CAMP TALLULAH. One of a number of prisoner of war camps established in Louisiana during World War II, it was located near the town of Tallulah in Madison Parish.

CAMP TERRE AUX BOEUFS. In response to the tense international situation in the South, Secretary of War Henry Dearborn on December 2, 1808, directed General James Wilkinson to take command in New Orleans of the 3rd, 5th, and 7th Infantry regiments, four companies of the 6th Infantry, and several companies of the Light Dragoons, Light Artillery, and Riflemen, all being conscripted or raised in various states and to be congregated at New Orleans. General Wilkinson reported on May 29, 1809, that he selected a camp site on privately owned land about 12 miles below New Orleans near the French settlement of Terre aux Boeufs. Major Zebulon M. Pike arrived there on June 1, 1809, with 500 men to prepare the field for the camp, reportedly two lines of tents occupying ground about 800 yards long and 75 yards wide. During the summer months, the camp was gradually improved with rudimentary amenities. In the early fall, additional orders came through, and the troops were distributed to the city of New Orleans, establishing a garrison there, Fort Adams and Natchez. October 27, 1809, is the approximate date when Camp Terre aux Boeufs was abandoned.

FORT TIGOUYOU. A small earthen fortification built by the French about 1750, it was located on the south side of Lake Pontchartrain at the mouth of Bayou Tigouyou (probably today's Bayou Trepagnier in St. Charles Parish), west of Bayou St. John. The fort was still active when France ceded Louisiana to Spain in 1762. Captain Philip Pittman, in his *European Settlements on the Mississippi* (1770), noted that the entrance to Bayou Tigouyou into Lake Pontchartrain was defended by a small redoubt manned by a sergeant's guard detail. A citation in Charles Gayarre's

History of Louisiana reports that a hurricane on October 7–10, 1778 destroyed Tigouyou.

CAMP TIOGA. CAMP LIVINGSTON.

FORT TURNBULL (*Fort Humbug*). A fortification built in 1864 by the Confederates, it was a part of the complex of defensive forts, batteries, and entrenchments that encircled the city of Shreveport. The site, on the west bank of Bayou Pierre at the foot of East Stoner Street, is now occupied by the Confederate (Fort Humbug) Memorial Park, comprising some 70 acres along a bluff overlooking the Red River. Because few cannon were available, some of the defense's "guns" were charred logs fashioned to resemble cannon, and the fort acquired the nickname Fort "Humbug."

VIDALIA POST. FORT CONCORDIA.

VIDALIA REDOUBT. The Federals built this fort in January 1864 at Vidalia in Concordia Parish. It was a square redoubt with bastions that enclosed a courthouse and jail. The work mounted four 10-pounder rifles and two howitzers, and it was garrisoned by a battalion of the 8th Regiment of New Hampshire Volunteers, a squadron of the 2nd New Jersey Cavalry, and a section of artillery. All the territory in Federal possession was included in a picket line two miles in length, curving in a semicircle from the river to the river again. The huge ironclad *Benton* was in the river nearby.

CAMP VIENNA. The town of Vienna, now in Lincoln Parish about four miles north of Ruston, was occupied by the Confederates as an assembly point and training camp, probably beginning in May 1862 when the 28th Regiment was organized there. In October 1863 Brigadier General Paul O. Hebert established his headquarters at the camp. The town was also used as a camp for parolees in 1864.

FORT VIEUX. FORT DE LA BOULAYE.

CAMP VILLERE. This World War II post, established in 1942 and named for Jacques Philippe Villere, a Louisiana State Militia major general during the War of 1812 and later the state's second governor, is located less than three miles west of the town of Slidell in St. Tammany Parish on U.S. 190. The reservation comprises about 2,117 acres. The camp was established as a small arms range for the trainees at Camp Plauche at New Orleans. After the war it was used by both the Army and the Louisiana National Guard. In the 1960s it was converted into the tactical training center for Camp Leroy Johnson's troops. The 1,710-acre camp area containing barracks, mess hall, gun ranges, and an airfield was quit-claimed by the government to the state of Louisiana for the use of the Louisiana National Guard, with the provision of federal reoccupation should a war emergency occur.

VILLERE CANAL REDOUBT. During their invasion of Louisiana in 1814–15, British forces built a strong redoubt at the junction of the Villere Canal and Bayou Mazant (now Bayou Villere) in St. Bernard Parish.

CAMP WALKER. CAMP MOORE.

FORT WEITZEL. This fortification erected by Federal forces during the Civil War was located east of Brashear City (now Morgan City).

CAMP WILKINS. This camp, situated adjacent to Fort Jesup in Sabine Parish, was occupied 1844–45 by the 3rd Infantry. The post was named in honor of the then secretary of war, William Wilkins. The camp was established when eight companies of the 3rd Infantry, commanded by Lieutenant Colonel E. A. Hitchcock, arrived at the site from Jefferson Barracks, Missouri, on May 10, 1844. Two more companies of the same regiment arrived at the camp from Jefferson Barracks on April 23, 1845. The post was apparently abandoned when the entire command departed on July 7, 1845, for New Orleans and Texas.

FORT WILLIAMS. Begun in August 1862, this Federal fortification, actually a defensive line of heavily armed breastworks, embankments, entrenchments, and abatis, girdled the Baton Rouge Barracks and the greater part of the grounds of the Baton Rouge Arsenal. The works were named in honor of Brigadier General Thomas Williams, who was killed in the Battle of Baton Rouge on August 5, 1862. Shortly after Louisiana state troops seized the Arsenal and Barracks in January 1861, Confederate forces began fortifying Baton Rouge's riverfront to prevent any Federal naval transports from disembarking troops in an attempt to reoccupy the city. Although Union troops regained Baton Rouge in May 1862, they did not then take steps to improve the Confederate fortifications for their own defenses. The Confederate attack on August 5, 1862, however, compelled the necessity of

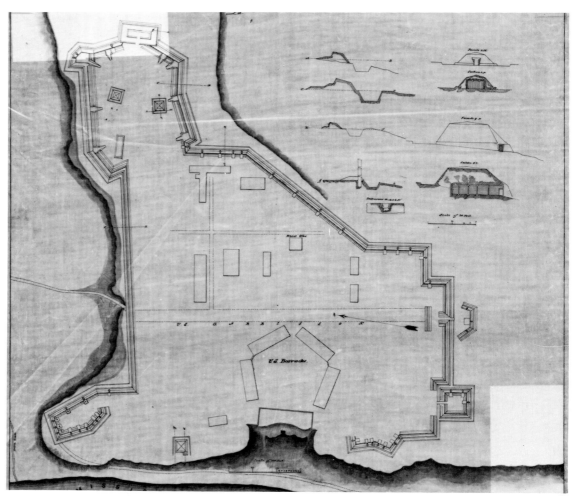

FORT WILLIAMS. (Courtesy of the National Archives.)

significantly enlarging and extending the Confederate defenses.

Lieutenant Geoffrey Weitzel, chief engineer, on August 8, 1862, three days after the battle, drew up a plan for the city's defense, recommending that all Federal forces be concentrated within the Arsenal grounds and quartered in the various buildings of the Barracks complex. Then the work of encircling the Barracks and most of the Arsenal grounds was begun under the supervision of Colonel Halbert E. Paine. In order to deprive Confederate forces of protective cover, all fences and trees were cut down and houses, including the post hospital, were burned, within a rifle shot distance of the Federal defense line. Most of the Federal troops left Baton Rouge on August 21 but returned on December 17, 1862, to continuously occupy Baton Rouge for the remainder of the war. The work of improving Fort Williams was renewed. In January 1865 the end of the defensive line was extended to the banks of the Mississippi River. The armament then along the line consisted of eleven 24-pounder siege guns, two 32-pounder pintle guns, four 8-inch howitzers and three batteries of field artillery. (See: BATON ROUGE ARSENAL and BATON ROUGE BARRACKS.)

FORT WOOD. FORT MACOMB.

YELLOW BAYOU REDOUBT (*Fort Scurry; Old Oak Fort; Fort Humbug; Norwood Plantation Fort*). An uncompleted Confederate fortification begun by forces under Brigadier General William R. Scurry, it was located about three miles northwest of Simmesport in Avoyelles Parish at the junction of Yellow Bayou and Bayou de Glaize. When superior numbers of Federals commanded by Brigadier General A. J. Mower approached the position on March 13, 1864, the Confederates abandoned the defenseless redoubt the very same day. Reports make no mention of armaments at the redoubt. Both Confederates and Federals have referred to the redoubt as Fort Scurry, Old Oaks Fort, Fort Humbug, and Norwood Plantation Fort. The grounds of the plantation, located in the near vicinity of the redoubt, were the scene where the last battle of the Red River campaign was fought.

CAMP ABRAHAM LINCOLN. CAMP BERRY.

ALGER GARRISON. The Alger brothers, Andrew and Arthur, residing in the Dunstan settlement, now Scarborough in Cumberland County, fortified their dwelling sometime in 1675, during King Philip's War. In October of that year, a party of Indians attacked the Alger Garrison, then defended by a small number of the settlement's men. Andrew Alger was killed and his brother Arthur was mortally wounded. The place shortly thereafter was abandoned by their surviving families.

FORT ALLEN (*Fort Ethan Allen*). During the fall of 1775, a strong battery was built to defend the town of Portland and named for Ethan Allen, who was responsible for capturing Fort Ticonderoga several months earlier. Initially a half-moon or crescent-shaped embrasured battery, mounting five guns and covering 100 yards of ground, it was later enlarged and enclosed, containing within a barracks and, no doubt, a magazine. The fort survived until the War of 1812 when one of its buildings was converted into a hospital to be used for the duration of the war. The site of the fort is now commemorated by the Fort Allen Park at Fore Street and Eastern Promenade.

FORT ANAWAGON. Built sometime before 1700 at the southern end of Southport Island (Cape Newagon) in present Lincoln County, it served as the major defense against Indian attack for the settlement.

FORT ANDREWS. Situated on Cushing's Island in Portland Harbor, Fort Andrews was a stone house erected by Christopher Leavett in 1623, subsequently owned by James Andrews. It is not known by whom, or when, the house was converted into a fort.

FORT ANDROS. FORT GEORGE (Brunswick).

FORT ANNE. Located in the village of Sheepscot, now Newcastle in Lincoln County, Fort Anne was cited by one historian as having been built about 1630, but it is more likely that it was erected much later. Destroyed in 1676 during King Philip's War, its remains are under a cemetery established in the 1730s.

ARROWSIC FORT. FORT MENASKOUX.

ASH'S POINT FORT. At Ash's Point in present-day Gouldsboro in Hancock County are the pur-

Maine

ported remains, actually traces of earthworks, of an old French fortification.

FORT AUGUSTA. The Penobscot proprietors established a fishing village at Small Point Harbor on the south side of present-day Phippsburg, Sagadahoc County, in 1716 and named it Augusta. Dr. Oliver Noyes, the colony's principal director, in 1718 erected a stone fort 100 feet square as an Indian defense. The Massachusetts government at first furnished a detachment of soldiers to garrison the fort, but after a while the men were withdrawn, probably to reinforce other places farther to the east. The settlement and the fort remained until about 1821, after which approximate date they were abandoned. Still in evidence are the remains of the fort's brick fireplace and chimney.

FORT BALDWIN. This modern-era fort was constructed on the military reservation occupying about 45 acres of ground, in Phippsburg at the entrance to the Kennebec River. About 38 acres are located on Sabino Hill, while the remaining acreage is on the shore below, covering part of the site of the Popham colony of 1607. The land was purchased in 1902, 1904, and 1905 from private owners by the government. The work of constructing Fort Baldwin, named for Colonel Jeduthan Baldwin, noted Revolutionary War engineer, began in 1905 and was essentially completed three years later. The fort was the last in the series of fortifications designed to defend the mouth of the river.

Initially there were two main components to the fort, with the batteries atop Sabino Hill and the administrative area established just to the north on the flat land of Sabino Head. The administrative center contained the post's headquarters, hospital, two barrack-blocks, a guardhouse, two mess halls, a bakery, and a storehouse. These frame-built structures were completely dismantled and removed shortly after 1924.

The armament of the fort consisted of three batteries, all of which survive intact. . . . The batteries were named and equipped as follows: Patrick Cogan (two 3-inch guns), John Hardman (one 6-inch disappearing gun), and Joseph Hawley (two 6-inch pedestal guns). Cogan and Hardman were officers in the Continental Army during the Revolution, while Hawley was an officer in the Union Army during the Civil War. . . . During World War I two companies of artillerists, about one hundred strong, were stationed at the fort. With the threat of naval attack receding in 1917, however, the gun from the Hardman Battery was sent to France. As the Great War drew to a close, Fort Baldwin was decommissioned; the remaining guns were removed by the Department of the Army in July, 1924; and a few weeks later the State of Maine acquired the fort as an historic site. [Robert L. Bradley, *The Forts of Maine, 1607–1945*, p. 37]

In 1942, during World War II, a number of concrete towers—fire control stations—were built on strategic headlands up and down the Maine coast. The towers enabled observers from various vantage points to report visual target locations, plotted by triangulation to allow coastal defense guns to find a target. One of these strange-looking towers was erected on the grounds of Fort Baldwin.

CAMP BERRY (*Camp Abraham Lincoln*). Late in 1861 the state of Maine established a training camp at Cape Elizabeth (Mackey's Island) in the area now known as Ligonia or Kerosene Corner, in South Portland. About 72 acres of level land of what was known as the Cape Trotting Park were enclosed for the camp. Originally named Camp Abraham Lincoln, the post's name was changed in 1863 to Camp Berry in honor of General Hiram G. Berry, 4th Maine Infantry, killed at Chancellorsville, Virginia. Ten large one-story wooden barracks were erected to house about 100 men each, in addition to 11 two-family dwellings for officers' quarters. The first regiment to rendezvous at Camp Berry was the 10th Maine Infantry, and the camp's first commandant was Colonel John Lynch, who took active command early in 1862. The post, which trained numerous Maine regiments, was most probably active until late in 1863.

FORT BLACK POINT. Erected in 1681, this defense has been cited as the "largest and strongest fortification ever built in the town," now Scarborough in Cumberland County. Joshua Scottow, influential landowner, gave 100 acres of his property to accommodate the fort. The defense was apparently erected after the settlement of Black Point was attacked on September 20, 1675, by a large band of Indians, at which time many houses were burned, and again on October 14, 1676. The fort was assaulted and destroyed by a large body of Indians on October 6, 1703, when it was being held by only eight men who finally abandoned it and found refuge aboard a vessel in the harbor.

CAMP BURDETTE. Most probably a Civil War encampment of short duration, it was located near old Fort Preble in Portland Harbor.

BURNHAM'S GARRISON. Early in King Philip's War (1675–76), the Burnham dwelling at Blue Point in present Scarborough was converted into a fortified garrison house.

FORT BURROWS. A War of 1812 fortification erected on Jordan's Point at Portland in 1813, it was named in honor of Captain William Burrows of the brig *Enterprise*. The site of the fort and the town's first meetinghouse, erected in 1670 and destroyed in the French and Indian War of 1690, is located at 58 Fore Street.

FORT BURTON. Benjamin Burton, who settled in Cushing, present-day Knox County, about 1750–51, converted his residence at the outbreak of the French and Indian War into a palisaded stone blockhouse, one of the largest defenses against Indians erected along the lower St. George's River.

FORT BUXTON. This Indian defense was erected in 1754 at Pleasant Point at today's Buxton in York County in response to a town meeting that voted funds to build a 40-foot-square palisaded fort "three and one-half feet in the ground and ten feet above." In addition to this fort, there were at least three garrison houses in Buxton.

FORT CASTINE. FORT UNITED STATES.

FORT CHARLES. FORT FREDERICK.

CLARK AND LAKE'S FORT. Erected by the Clark and Lake Company in 1654 at Squirrel Point on Arrowsic Island in present Sagadahoc County, this was a fortified industrial complex built by Major Thomas Clark and Captain Thomas Lake, two prominent Boston merchants. Considered remarkable for the period, it included a fort, a trading post, mills, a foundary, and a shipyard. In 1676, during the second year of King Philip's War, as with other English settlements, it was attacked and destroyed by the Indians. Since 1970 archaeological excavations have been conducted on the site, revealing foundations and numerous tangible remains of the buildings below ground.

FORT CLARK'S HILL. Actually a garrison house, this Indian defense was erected sometime after 1743 at Wiscasset in Lincoln County.

CAMP COBURN. Established in 1865, possibly post-Civil War, this camp's location has been tentatively identified as Coburn Gore in Franklin County.

CAMP CONEY (CONY). Established at or near Augusta, this post was active during 1865–66.

FORT COX'S HEAD. In 1812 a brick fort and a brick barracks for 100 men were erected at Cox's Head in Phippsburg, Sagadahoc County. In 1814 four cannon were moved from the fort at Hunniwell's Point and emplaced at the Cox's Head fort.

FORT DAMARISCOVE. In 1622 a stockade was built as an Indian defense for the earliest documented year-round settlement on Damariscove Island in Boothbay Harbor, Lincoln County. A half-century later, a palisaded fort was erected there in about 1676, the second year of King Philip's War against the settlements.

FORT DAYTON. Established as a trading post by the Massachusetts government in 1728–30, Fort Dayton was probably situated on the Saco River at Dayton in York County. It was garrisoned by a sergeant and 10 men with a few cannon.

(ROGER) DEARING'S GARRISON. In 1675 Roger Dearing converted his dwelling into a minimally fortified garrison house. It was located on the "Hasty Place or Nonsuch Farm" at Oak Hill in present-day Scarborough, Cumberland County.

FORT DUNNING. Established at Brunswick in Sagadahoc County, most probably shortly before or during King Philip's War (1675–76), this blockhouse or formidable timber garrison was erected by David Dunning on his property. It has been described as having been two-storied, with its upper story projecting about 4 feet on all sides beyond the lower, 40 feet long and 22 feet wide. Surmounted by a watchtower on top, the fort's walls were loopholed for musketry.

FORT EDGECOMB. An interesting rare example of an octagonal blockhouse, this still-standing square timbered, two-story structure of ash and pine was built on David Island at the entrance to Wiscasset Harbor in the town of Edgecomb, Lincoln County. Commanding the harbor, Fort Edgecomb fulfilled its purpose of protecting one of Maine's busiest shipping ports of the early nineteenth century. Across the river, on Jeremy Squam (Westport) Island, was Fort McDonough, earthworks thrown up in 1812.

On August 2, 1808, Secretary of War Henry Dearborn came to Davis Island, inspected the harbor, and issued building instructions for a defense there. Completed the following year, it consisted of the following components:

A massive stone revetment with twin bastions supported two 18-pounders, meant to provide fire across both the Sheepscot and Back Rivers. A brick magazine with vaulted roof was buried beneath the eastern bastion. . . . This magazine was completely buried in sand in 1961, since its state of deterioration posed a danger to the public. Above the lower batteries was a crescent-shaped earthwork which protected a single gun, a 50-pound Columbiad. Both of these levels were protected in the rear by a palisade. Scattered about the fort on this second level were a wooden barrack-block and two storehouses as well as a brick bakehouse, none of which survives above ground today. Above these buildings was a third level consisting of an earthwork with straight sides which covered two more 18-pounders. Behind these upper gun emplacements was a wooden blockhouse. . . .

The blockhouse is a remarkable post-and-beam structure of octagonal plan with an overhanging second story. Its diameter is twenty-seven feet at ground level and thirty feet at the upper level. In height it rises some thirty-four feet to the top of a watch-box which crowns the roof. In both the first and second stories there are horizontal musketry ports and embrasures. Today the blockhouse is shingled; this surface treatment, along with exterior trim and the sash in the watch-box, are late 19th-century modifications. The blockhouse was originally equipped with two carronades. . . .

The only times in which Fort Edgecomb's cannon were fired were on March 4, 1809, when they saluted President Madison's inauguration, and on February 14, 1815, when they signalled news of peace with Britain. [Robert L. Bradley, *The Forts of Maine, 1607–1945*, pp. 25–27]

During the last years of the nineteenth century, a group of concerned citizens launched a successful drive for funds to ensure the perpetuation of the blockhouse because Fort Edgecomb is the best-preserved installation of its period in Maine. The Fort Edgecomb State Memorial is maintained by the Maine State Department of Conservation.

FORT ETHAN ALLEN. FORT ALLEN.

FORT FAIRFIELD. The bitter boundary dispute between Great Britain and the United States, which resulted in the so-called Aroostook War, compelled Congress to issue a call for thousands of men to come to the aid of Maine and to order the construction of Fort Fairfield in 1839 in Aroostook County, 140 miles north of Bangor, to be used as a border defense. The fort, named for Governor John Fairfield, was situated on the south bank of the Aroostook River, six miles from its confluence with the St. John River. Fort Fairfield was abandoned on September 2, 1843. (See: FORT KENT.)

FORT FOSTER. Located near Machiasport, Washington County, on the east side of the Machias River near the "Rim," Fort Foster and the men who garrisoned it epitomized American patriotic resistance to the British during the early years of the Revolution. The "Rim" is a narrow neck of land between the lower reaches of the East Machias River on the north and the Machias River on the south. The confluence of these two rivers is at the upper end of Machias Bay. Recognizing its strategic value, the early settlers along each river united in erecting a system of earthen breastworks.

During the so-called "First Naval Battle of the Revolution" on June 12, 1775, the British ship *Margaretta* was fired upon from a wharf on Rim Point by Colonel Benjamin Foster and a small force of men he led. After dropping down to Machias Bay, the *Margaretta* was captured. Shortly afterward, a chosen Committee of Correspondence decided to build a fort at the "Rim." In July 1775 the British sent two vessels to retake the *Margaretta*. Entering Machias Bay they surrendered without resistance to Colonel Foster and Captain Jeremiah O'Brien. Three weeks later another expedition was dispatched from Halifax, the force consisting of 1,000 men on "a frigate, a twenty-gun ship, a brig of sixteen guns and several schooners." By this time, however, the townspeople had built a breastwork on Scott's Point, and when a party of 500 were landed they were driven back. The whole British task force returned to Halifax.

The inhabitants continued to fortify. In July 1776 they constructed a boom across the narrows at the "Rim," and a breastwork was completed south of the river in September. Sylvanus Scott, who lived on the "Rim," was ordered to build another breastwork near his home. This fortification, with a watchbox and barracks for the men, was Fort Foster. On August 13, 1777, the British sent two 44-gun frigates with two smaller warships under the command of Sir George Collier to deal with the recalcitrant Machias inhabitants. Benjamin Foster immediately took command of the fort. The British succeeded in landing superior forces the next morning, destroyed the defense's cannon, and left a deserted Fort Foster. On August 15 the people of Machias regained possession of the fort, and the British warships were harassed on their way to the sea.

FORT FOSTER. Situated on Gerrish Island near Kittery, York County, Fort Foster was located six miles northeast of Portsmouth. Established in 1900 as a subpost of Fort Constitution, on a

40-acre military reservation, it was named in honor of John G. Foster, a New Hampshire native and lieutenant colonel in the Corps of Engineers, who served with distinction in the War with Mexico and in the Civil War, attaining the rank of Major General, U.S. Volunteers. During World War II, Battery Bohlen mounted three 10-inch rifles on disappearing carriages while Battery Chapin mounted two 3-inch guns, besides two fixed and two mobile antiaircraft guns. At present, Fort Foster is maintained as a recreation and park area by the town of Kittery.

FOXWELL'S FORT. A fortified garrison house established about 1750, it was located at Blue Point in the village of Dunstan, now a part of modern Scarborough in Cumberland County.

FORT FRANKFORT. FORT SHIRLEY.

FORT FREDERICK (*Shurt's Fort; Pemaquid Fort; Fort Charles; Fort William Henry*). The Popham Colony and its protective screen, Fort St. George, established in 1607 near the mouth of the Kennebec River, proved to be a failure and was abandoned in less than a year. But a much more successful settlement prospered from about 1625 at Pemaquid, incorporated within present-day Lincoln County's town of Bristol, "which began its life as a small fishing village and ended as the burnt ruins of England's northeasternmost military outpost of the Thirteen Colonies." Pemaquid's first defense, Shurt's Fort or Pemaquid Fort, was erected in 1630 or 1631 as a stockade-enclosed warehouse and trading post fortified against piratical raids rather than Indian depredations. It was established by Abraham Shurt, who was the agent for partners Robert Aldworth and Gyles Elbridge, Bristol merchants. It was raided by pirates in 1632 and thoroughly pillaged, and destroyed in 1676 during King Philip's War.

Prompt steps were taken to refortify Pemaquid and Fort Charles, a true fort, was erected the following year. The only known description of the work was written by a contemporary who indicated it was "a wooden Redoutt with two gunns aloft and an outworke with two Bastions in each of which two greatt guns, and one att the Gate" (John Jonston, *A History of the Towns of Bristol and Bremen in the State of Maine, Including the Pemaquid Settlement*, p. 141). Fort Charles fell in 1689 to Penobscot Indians because the defense was garrisoned by a mere handful of men, all that remained after wholesale desertions instigated by the parsimony of New England politicians.

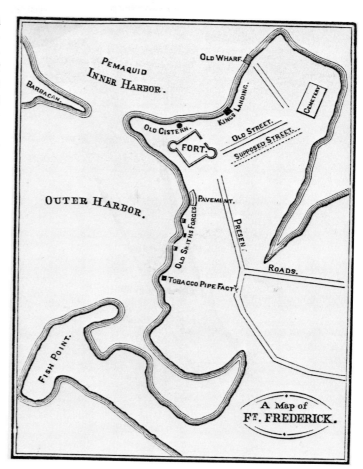

The refortification of Pemaquid consisted of what was probably the first stone fort built in New England. Fort William Henry was built at a cost to the Province of Massachusetts of 20,000 pounds:

In the summer of 1692 a large work force under the direction of Captains Wing, Bancroft, and March began the construction of Fort William Henry. Because the Indian assault on Fort Charles in 1689 had made effective use of a large bedrock outcrop as cover nearby, this prominent feature was incorporated within the new fortification. When finished in the early spring of 1693, Fort William Henry, as described by Cotton Mather, was indeed impressive, with a six-foot-thick curtain ranging in height from ten to twenty-two feet encompassing a quadrangle some 108 feet on each side internally. The outer wall was fitted with twenty-eight gun-ports and eighteen cannon, of which six were 18-pounders. Facing the entrance to the Inner Harbor, to the west, was a great corner tower twenty-nine feet high. The opposite corner was fitted with a fan-shaped bastion, while the north and south corners carried internal circular towers. The main entrance faced northeast and a secondary entrance, next to the large flanker, faced northwest. [Robert L. Bradley, *The Forts of Maine, 1607–1945*, p. 9]

The fort, despite its touted strength by Massachusetts Royal Governor Sir William Phips, had

FORT FREDERICK. Map showing the fort's location. (From A History of the Towns of Bristol and Bremen *by John Johnston, 1873.)*

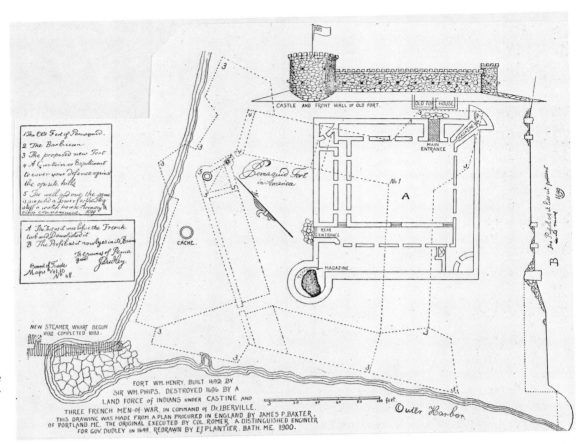

1 The Old Fort of Pemaquid.
2 The Barbican
3 The proposed new Fort
4 A Curtain or Expediment to cover your defence against the opposite hills
5 The well and over the same is proposed a Tower for the flag staff a watch house Armory & other conveniences. 1699

A The Text as it was before the French took and Demolished it
B The Profil as it now lyes in its Ruin
The ruins of Pema quid
Jno Gridley
Board of Trade
Maps Vol.10
No 48.

CASTLE AND FRONT WALL OF OLD FORT.

OLD FORT HOUSE

MAIN ENTRANCE

Pemaquid Fort in America

No 1

A

CACHE.

REAR ENTRANCE

MAGAZINE

Jno Profil as it now at present was the ruins 1699

NEW STEAMER WHARF BEGUN 1892 COMPLETED 1893.

FORT WM. HENRY, BUILT 1692 BY SIR WM. PHIPS. DESTROYED 1696 BY A LAND FORCE of INDIANS UNDER CASTINE AND THREE FRENCH MEN-OF-WAR, IN COMMAND OF Dr. IBERVILLE. THIS DRAWING WAS MADE FROM A PLAN PROCURED IN ENGLAND BY JAMES P. BAXTER, OF PORTLAND, ME. THE ORIGINAL EXECUTED BY COL. ROMER A DISTINGUISHED ENGINEER FOR GOV. DUDLEY IN 1699. REDRAWN BY EJ PLANTIER. BATH. ME. 1900.

Outer Harbor

FORT FREDERICK. Plan drawn by E. J. Plantier in 1900 based on a plan drawn by Colonel Romer in 1699. (Courtesy of the Maine Historical Society.)

serious construction defects. Engineer Colonel Wolfgang William Romer reported in 1699 that "the Fort of Pemaquid . . . seems to have been extremely ill-built and not defensible. There was no order observed in building it; its walls were made of clay mixed with sand brought from the sea-shore, instead of lime." In fact the mortar mixture was so bad that one of the fort's towers cracked when a pair of cannon were test-fired. In addition to this dereliction, the water well was outside the northwest wall, useless to a besieged garrison.

Early in August 1696, three French warships, with about 100 soldiers aboard and some 500 Indians under the command of Pierre LeMoyne d'Iberville, attacked Fort William Henry. Minus a water supply and handicapped by the collapse of a flanker after its gun was fired several times, the defenders under commandant Captain Pascho Chubb surrendered the next day. The men of the garrison were given safe passage to Boston and Fort William Henry, according to d'Iberville, "being completely demolished to the base of the foundations."

In 1729 a new defense was erected on the same site, using much of the ruins of the 1692 fort. Colonel David Dunbar, surveyor of His Majesty's Woods in America, arranged for the resettlement of six townships east of the Ken-

nebec River as a first line of defense against the French and Indians. He brought 200 Irish Protestants to Pemaquid, the central site. The rebuilding of Fort William Henry, renamed Fort Frederick was crucial to the resettlement, but the new construction turned out to be decidedly inferior to that of the former fort.

Dunbar's independent plan also included an improved design for Pemaquid's streets and house plots. Controversy and litigation, however, forced Dunbar to abandon the project in 1733. Eventually a number of the Scotch-Irish gained title to their lands and remained as the progenitors of many of today's Bristol residents. The fort gradually became utterly dilapidated. In 1759 its guns were shipped to Boston. On May 24, 1775, a Bristol town meeting "voted to pull down Pemaquid Foart [sic]. Voted that next Thursday May 30 be the day to pull down said Foart." This action, instigated by the first conflicts of the Revolution, was designed to deprive the British of the use of Fort Frederick, Pemaquid's last defense.

In 1902 the state of Maine was bequeathed the site of Fort William Henry. Six years later, aided by Colonel Romer's drawings of the 1699 ruins and evidence exposed by some archaeological excavations, a faithful replica of the fort's western tower was built. In 1923 a museum archaeologist performed minor excavations on the site in a vain effort to find suspected remains of Viking construction at Pemaquid. It was not until 1974, however, that the fort site was subjected to continuing controlled archaeological excavations, financed with funds from the National Park Service matched by state of Maine funds.

FORT FRIENDSHIP. A fortification erected about 1750 on Garrison Island at "Meduncook," present-day Friendship, Knox County, it housed all of the settlement's 22 families in 1755 during the French and Indian War.

FROST GARRISON. This garrison at Eliot, just north of Kittery in York County, "is the most military in nature of these early log buildings in Maine. This large, barn-like structure is of one and a half stories with an upper story overhang at the gabled ends of the building. Loopholes are cut into the first story log walls for musket fire. This was never a dwelling (there was no chimney for heat and cooking); rather, it functioned as a barn and was intended as a refuge in times of peril. Although it dates from the 1730s, it might as well have been built much earlier" (Robert L. Bradley, *Maine's First Buildings: The Architecture of Settlement, 1604–1700* [1978], p. 6).

CAMP (JAMES B.) FRY. This post, named for Union General James B. Fry, was a temporary Civil War encampment established at or near Augusta.

FORT GARRISON HILL. A square wooden blockhouse built about 1743 on Brimstone (Garrison) Hill, with its remains buried beneath the present-day Methodist Church, it was the earliest fortified Indian defense erected in the town of Wiscasset in Lincoln County.

GARRISON HOUSES. See: state of Massachusetts, GARRISON HOUSES.

FORT GEORGE. FORT ST. GEORGE'S (Knox County).

FORT GEORGE (*Fort Andros*). The first English fort erected on the bank of the Androscoggin River at present-day Brunswick in Sagadahoc County was that built by Governor Edmund Andros in 1688. The site of the stone fort, zigzag in form, is located just south of today's Bow Street. It was destroyed by Indians in 1694. In August 1715 a new fort named Fort George was begun on a ledge of rocks at the northern end of Maine Street and completed in the following December near the site of the former fort. "The walls of this fort were very thick and the stones were laid in mortar. It was finished with two bastions and two half-bastions, with flank[er]s on the top sufficient for cannon" (George Augustus Wheeler and Henry Warren Wheeler, *History of Brunswick, Topsham, and Harpswell, Maine* [1878], p. 627). Within its walls was a large two-story house, probably used by the fort's commandant and garrison. The fort's flagstaff was in the corner of the southwest bastion. After having effectively served as a defense against Indian attack and a refuge for the area's inhabitants, the General Court of Massachusetts, in the latter part of 1736 or early in 1737, decided to dismantle the fort despite vehement protestations by the inhabitants, who drew up an impassioned petition. The fortification, however, was razed, and the property reverted to its proprietors.

FORT GEORGE. The Penobscot Bay and River area for many years was the strategic site of French, English, and American fortifications, beginning with a trading post operated from 1626 to 1635 by the Plymouth Colony. The establishment in 1759 of Fort Pownall at Stockton Springs on the west side of the river above Castine on the bay proved to be an incentive for Anglo-American settlement of upper Penobscot Bay. In March 1775 the British attacked Fort Pownall and seized all its armaments and ammunition. Three months later, in July, American troops destroyed the blockhouse and ruined its system of ditches to deprive the British of its future use. By this time the village of Castine (then known as Majabigwaduce) had been established, and its inhabitants were engaged in the business of producing cut lumber. In 1779 the British finally became cognizant of the potential military value of Penobscot Bay:

On June 17th of that year an English force of 750 men and three sloops of war seized Castine and on July 2nd began the construction of Fort George on a commanding rise in the center of the small peninsula. Just over two weeks later the British learned of an American [naval] force assembling in Massachusetts which intended to retake the peninsula. . . . On July 24th the American force arrived, consisting of some forty-five ships mounting 328 guns and carrying up to 2,000 men.

Four days later the American infantry landed and the day after that they began shelling Fort George. . . . The British suffered sporadic bombardment over the next few days, but managed to further strengthen their fort. By the last day of July the fort was firing six cannon, and its ramparts had been made more defensible. . . . [The] American tactics were inept, and the enormous fire power of the Continental fleet was not used to batter the fort into submission. When six British ships sailed up Penobscot Bay on August 14th the American infantry and artillery were quickly embarked and the fleet fled northward. In the worst naval disaster in American history, not one vessel survived the action. [Robert L. Bradley, *The Forts of Maine, 1607–1945*, p. 23]

During the remaining years of the Revolution, the British continually made improvements to the fort, increasing its fire power to 18 guns, constructing brick magazines in two of the bastions and erecting officers' quarters and barracks lining the parade ground. When the British evacuated Fort George in January 1784, they did so after burning the fort's structures. When it was abandoned, Fort George was a square fortification with a timber-revetted curtain 200 feet to the side between four corner bastions, all surrounded by a deep ditch. Residents in the area speeded the deterioration of the fort by carrying off its bricks. In September 1814, during the last full year of the War of 1812, the British reappeared at the fort and frantically reconstructed its ramparts.

Abandoned in 1819, Fort George was left to the elements. In 1940 the state of Maine acquired the fort site, and twenty years later the Maine Legislature appropriated funds to conduct researches and reconstruct one of the magazines by the Bureau of Parks and Recreation. Today Fort George's earthworks constitute an impressive memorial to the presence of the British in Penobscot Bay in two wars.

GERRISH'S BLOCKHOUSE. This Indian defense, probably erected during 1675–76, was built by William Gerrish on the western side of Salmon Falls Brook, a mile above Quampeagan in the town of Salmon Falls on the Maine–New Hampshire border.

GIVEEN GARRISON. Erected by David Giveen, probably during King Philip's War (1675–76), it was located at or near present-day Brunswick, Sagadahoc County.

GOODWIN'S BLOCKHOUSE. Probably built in 1675, the Indian defense was located near Berwick, York County, above Gerrish's Blockhouse.

FORT GORGES. This massive, granite hexagonal fortress, named for Sir Ferdinando Gorges, Lord Palatinate of the Province of Maine, was begun in 1858 on what was known as Hog Island Ledge in Portland Harbor, about a mile north of Fort Preble, and completed in 1864 or 1865. The fort's double tier of casemates on five sides were intended to mount 95 guns. Fort Gorges was officially used only during World War I, when a wooden torpedo storehouse was added to house submarine mines. The coast defense property is owned by the city of Portland, which in 1983 refused a developer's offer of $480,000 for the remnants of Fort Gorges to convert the island landmark into a tourist attraction.

FORT GORHAM. This blockhouse was erected probably in 1733 or 1734 shortly after Gorham township in present Cumberland County was established. The defense, still in existence at least until 1750, stood on an eminence known for many years as Fort Hill.

FORT GRAY. The town of Gray, 16 miles north of Portland, was settled about 1750. A fort and a church built there in 1755 were nearly destroyed during the French and Indian War (1813), subsequent to which the town was largely rebuilt.

FORT HALIFAX. Erected on the point of land overlooking the confluence of the Kennebec and Sebasticook rivers in the town of Winslow in Kennebec County, the sole remaining structure of pre-Revolutionary Fort Halifax is the oldest surviving blockhouse in the United States. Constructed as an outpost in 1754–55 in compliance with an order of Governor William Shirley of Massachusetts, who reportedly had selected the site because of its strategic importance, the fort was named in honor of the Earl of Halifax, then secretary of state.

Major General John Winslow's original ambitious design, which would have required a permanent garrison of 400 men, a number the province could ill afford, was altered during the period of construction in favor of a fortification of more modest proportions. The fort's first commandant was General Winslow, for whom the town was named, who had come with 800 men in the spring of 1754. About 300 men remained to complete the complex of blockhouses, redoubts, barracks, and a large building that served as officers' quarters and storehouse. Although history records no attacks against the fort, there were a number of skirmishes in the area. In 1775 Colonel Benedict Arnold with 1,100 men stopped here en route to Quebec during his ill-fated invasion of Canada, although by this time the fort had become quite dilapidated. Most of the fort's works was demolished in 1797, sparing the blockhouse. In 1913 the Winslow Chapter of the Daughters of the American Revolution was organized, and in 1924 it acquired title to the fort site, maintaining it until 1965 when it was deeded to the state of Maine.

CAMP HALLECK. A Civil War point of assembly and training encampment at or near Augusta, it was in operation during 1862–63.

HAMILTON'S GARRISON. PINE HILL FORT.

HANCOCK BARRACKS. For years the dispute between the United States and Canada over the boundary between the two nations was focused on easternmost Aroostook County in northern Maine where it adjoined the Province of New Brunswick. In order to reinforce its claim, the United States government on May 5, 1828, established Hancock Barracks at Houlton on the Canadian frontier. After the final disposal of the boundary question, the dissolution of the post's garrison was begun. The imminent outbreak of the War with Mexico brought the final abandonment of Hancock Barracks on September 9, 1845.

HARNDEN'S (GARRISON) FORT. A minimally fortified defense located at Woolwich in Sagadahoc County, it was intermittently garrisoned during the mid-eighteenth century.

FORT HILL. FORT MARY.

FORT ISLAND. Situated at the entrance to the Damariscotta River in Boothbay's harbor, Lincoln County, Fort Island (sometimes called Webber's or Narrows Island) was fortified in 1812 after the outbreak of war with Great Britain.

JEWELL ISLAND POST. During World War II, several of the islands in Casco Bay near the entrance to Portland's harbor were fortified with gun batteries, including an installation on Jewell Island.

JORDAN'S FORT. A fortified blockhouse erected by Dominicus Jordan sometime between 1680 and 1690, it was located at old Spurwink, present-day Cape Elizabeth, in Cumberland County. In 1690 when Falmouth was devastated, Spurwink was deserted by its inhabitants, and remained unoccupied until peace was established in 1698. On August 10, 1703, Dominicus Jordan was treacherously killed during a trading session with a party of Indians.

KENNEBEC ARSENAL. This arsenal, which served as a manufactory for American armaments and equipment and as a storehouse for the ordnance, was established in 1828 during the border dispute with Canada's Province of New Brunswick. Located on the east bank of the Kennebec River at Augusta, the arsenal's commanders during its 75-year existence included such illustrious military men as Major Robert Anderson, who gained fame as the commandant of Fort Sumter in Charleston Harbor at the outbreak of the Civil War. Closed in 1903, many of the arsenal's granite-built structures of finely designed Greek Revival and Gothic Revival architecture are still being used by the state of Maine.

FORT KENNEBUNKPORT. Established in 1812 after the outbreak of war with Great Britain, this fortified battery stood on Kennebunk Point at the entrance to the river at Kennebunkport, York County.

FORT KENT. The northeastern boundary controversy between the United States and Great Britain, which eventually culminated in the six-week-long bloodless but bitter so-called Aroostook War (called the Madawaska War locally), began in 1783 at the end of the Revolution when the lines of demarcation between Maine and Canada were established. From the very first there were misunderstandings. A commission, after meeting for five years after the War of 1812, could not agree and disbanded.

During the 1820s agitation increased, and in 1827 the king of the Netherlands was selected as arbiter. To further confuse the issue, New Brunswick became a province, and in 1820 Maine became a state. About 12,000 square miles were claimed by both sides. The decision of the arbiter in 1831, who made no attempt to determine boundaries, recommended "a line of convenience," roughly dividing the disputed territory equally between the two nations, a decision that Maine refused to accept. In February 1839 a Maine land agent was captured by New Brunswick militiamen at the mouth of the Madawaska River just east of Houlton and imprisoned. Preparations for an armed confrontation were put in motion. The Maine and New Brunswick militias were mobilized; Congress authorized the raising of 50,000 troops; and Great Britain dispatched regulars to the area. Before blood could be spilled, however, President Van Buren sent Major General Winfield Scott to Maine to effect a compromise. He managed to keep the troops on both sides in check and by early spring had negotiated a mutual withdrawal of forces from the disputed area. Finally, the treaty negotiated by Daniel Webster and Lord Ashburton, signed in 1842, established today's borders between Maine and the Canadian provinces of Quebec and New Brunswick. The bloodless Aroostook War was over.

At the height of the crisis, Fort Kent was established in 1839 at the confluence of the St. John and Fish rivers at the northern tip of the state. Constructed by Maine militiamen, this blockhouse of squared cedar logs is just over 23 feet on each side at ground level and about 26 feet square at the level of the overhanging second story. In addition barracks, officers' quarters and other buildings were built. Completed in 1840, Fort Kent was named in honor of Maine's Governor Edward Kent. The post was abandoned on September 11, 1845.

In 1847 the state of Maine received the property from the government and sold it to one Mary Page for $250. The blockhouse again became state property in 1891 when it was conveyed to the governor and council for $300 with the stipulation that it would be protected and preserved as an historic site.

FORT KNOX. When the dispute over the northern boundary between Maine and Canada nearly culminated in armed conflict between the United States and Great Britain during the bloodless Aroostoock War of 1839, it was suddenly realized that the entire Penobscot Valley was completely defenseless in the event of a naval attack. Although the Webster-Ashburton Treaty of 1842 had finally resolved the border issue, the War Department and certain prominent Maine politicians decided to eliminate the Penobscot Valley's vulnerability. Between September 1843 and March 1844, about 125 acres of land in the town of Prospect were acquired, and the following summer an enormous fortress was begun, constructed of granite from Mt. Waldo, a few miles up the Penobscot River. Twenty years and nearly a million dollars later, Fort Knox was all but completed. A formidable defensive work, Fort Knox is definitely the state of Maine's most impressive fortification, one of the most remarkable still existing forts in America.

Fort Knox was named in honor of Major General Henry Knox, Washington's commander of the Continental Regiment of Artillery during the Revolution and America's first secretary of war. The fort was built to mount 137 guns, and its dimensions, including the glacis, dry moat and polygonal fort proper are 350 by 250 feet. North and south of the fort are additional batteries for thirty-nine guns. The main fort measures 252 by 146 feet with granite walls twenty feet high and forty feet thick. On the river side these walls contain eight massive vaulted casements for heavy guns which supported additional guns mounted above. In the center of Fort Knox is a large parade ground, under which are several bomb-proof storage areas. Around the parade ground are officers' quarters, barracks, and stables. In the northeast and southeast corners of the parade ground granite spiral staircases provide access to the various levels and the parapet. Garrisoned during the Civil War by fifty Maine volunteers and again in 1898 by a Connecticut regiment of some 350 men, this large fort was built to ensure that no enemy warships would ravage the Penobscot Valley communities. The state of Maine purchased Fort Knox from the U.S. Government on October 12, 1923, for $2,121 and assigned it to the State Park Commission on July 1, 1943.

FORT LARRABEE. This large timber-built fortification, occupying more than an acre of ground, was erected in 1735 on the bank of the Mousam River at Kennebunk in present York County (another citation reports that it was built "about 1720 or about the time of Lovewell's war"). In the form of a parallelogram, with a flanker or bastion in each of its angles, its 14-foot-high walls were fitted with three gates. All the structures within were one-story with "block windows," actually square holes to admit air and light, which could be blocked up or shuttered at a moment's notice. Fort Larrabee was demolished in 1762 at the end of the French and Indian War.

FORT LEVETT. A permanent post located about three and a half miles southeast of Portland on Cushing Island, this fort was named in honor of Christopher Levett who explored Portland's harbor in 1623 and erected the first fortified structure in the vicinity. The island during the 1600s and 1700s was intermittently fortified and occupied by refugees of the Indian wars or colonial military troops. The United States government in 1894 acquired a large tract of land at Spring Point on the island by purchase and during the Spanish-American War established Fort Levett with a garrison manning batteries of heavy artillery. The fort was in use during World Wars I and II, after which it was evacuated and abandoned. The 125-acre reservation and its buildings were sold in 1957 to a private investor.

Fort Levett during its active life was fortified by five batteries, four of them erected prior to

World War I: Battery Bowdoin (April 23, 1903), three 12-inch rifles, removed about 1944 or 1945; Battery Daniels (April 23, 1903), three 3-inch rifles, removed 1920; Battery Kendrick (April 23, 1903), two 10-inch rifles, removed about 1943; Battery Ferguson (June 22, 1906), two 6-inch Pedestal rifles, removed after World War II; and Battery Foote (post–World War I and casemated World War II), two 12-inch rifles, removed post–World War II.

FORT LEWIS. Erected prior to 1745 at Woolwich in Sagadahoc County, Fort Lewis was situated on the eastern shore of Merrymeeting Bay at the mouth of the Kennebec River.

FORT LOYAL. The first fortified defense of early Falmouth on Casco Bay, today's city of Portland, Fort Loyal or Loyall was a palisaded fort of logs mounting several light guns. It was erected about 1680 at the foot of India Street where its site is now commemorated by a tablet. The fort was a refuge for the area's settlers during the frequent Indian uprisings. In May 1690 the occupants of the fort commanded by Captain Sylvanus Davis were besieged for five days by a party of French soldiers under Sieur de Portneuf with an undetermined number of Indian allies. The terms of the truce finally agreed to were violated by the enemy after the fort's gate was opened, and most of the soldiers and refugees within were massacred, sparing only Captain Davis and four others who were taken to Canada. The fort was set afire and left a smoldering ruin.

FORT LUCIA. Established sometime between 1735 and 1745 by Samuel Waldo after the close of Lovewell's war, Fort Lucia was erected "at the mouth of the river St. George," in present Knox County.

FORT LYON. Named in honor of Brigadier General Nathaniel Lyon, U.S. Volunteers (Captain, 2nd Infantry), a Mexican War veteran, who was killed at Wilson's Creek, Missouri, August 10, 1861, Fort Lyon, a subpost of Fort McKinley, was erected after the Spanish-American War on Cow Island, four miles from Portland, on property acquired by purchase in 1873. The fort was armed by two batteries, Bayard and Abbot, the first mounting three six-inch rifles and the second mounting three three-inch rifles. Having served through World Wars I and II, Fort Lyon was declared surplus after World War II and turned over to the city of Portland.

FORT MCCLARY (*Fort William*). The site in Kittery on which the historical nucleus of Fort McClary stands was fortified as early as 1715 to protect the merchants of Massachusetts, which then included the present state of Maine, from "unreasonable duties" imposed by the colony of New Hampshire. Originally called Fort William for Sir William Pepperrell, who had a palisaded garrison house nearby, the name was changed after the American Revolution to Fort McClary in honor of Major Andrew McClary, killed at the Battle of Bunker Hill. The fortification had been hastily pressed into service during the war, when in 1776 powder and ammunition were provided for the battery of 9- and 12-pounders there. The battery served its purpose of preventing the British Royal Navy from attacking Portsmouth and Kittery's important shipyard.

Fort McClary was significantly strengthened during 1808–09 and completely rebuilt in the year or two subsequent to 1844 as a result of strained relations with Great Britain over the northeastern boundary, which had precipitated the Aroostook War, a bloodless six-week-long confrontation. The engineering drawings prepared in 1844 delineate the uniquely transitional blockhouse as the nucleus of the fort:

This blockhouse, the last to be built in Maine, is hexagonal in plan, each side measuring eighteen and a half feet in length. The ground floor is pierced with six vertical musket ports on each side, while in the second story there are a total of six embrasures and twenty-four horizontal musket ports. An attic in the half-story is fitted with three dormer windows for light and ventilation. . . .

The Fort McClary blockhouse is a curious mixture of building materials: the foundation is of mortared field-stone; the first story walls are of cut granite; and the second story is of log construction. . . . During the Civil War Fort McClary was further strengthened by a pentagonal granite curtain which was never completed. In addition, a brick barrack-block, a wooden cook-house with mess-hall, a chapel, hospital, guardhouse, and magazine (all of Brick) were constructed, but in 1869 work on the fort had ceased. This historic spot was to see one final episode of fortification in 1898 when the Spanish-American War prompted the installation of three 15-inch guns. In the First World War it was equipped as an observation post. [Robert L. Bradley, *The Forts of Maine, 1607–1945*, pp. 30–31]

FORT MCDONOUGH. Erected in September-October 1814 and named in honor of Lieutenant Thomas McDonough (Macdonough), naval hero of the recent Battle of Lake Champlain, Fort McDonough was a five-pointed-star earth-and-log defense mounting six 18-pounders, located at the northern extremity of Westport (Squam)

Island, opposite Fort Edgecomb, in Lincoln County. After the Treaty of Ghent, Fort McDonough gradually fell into disuse.

MCFARLAND'S GARRISON. About 1730 James McFarland built a two-story hewn-timbered 40-by-20-foot-long blockhouse on what is now the intersection of Maine and Mason streets in Brunswick, Sagadahoc County.

MCINTIRE GARRISON. The still-standing, well-preserved Micum McIntire Garrison in the town of York was built after 1707. The two-story, blockhouse-in-form structure was constructed of 8-inch-thick pine and oak square-hewn timbers, with a 14-inch overhang on all sides, and a large central chimney (rebuilt in 1909). Clapboard sheathing now hides the walls of sawn logs.

FORT MCKINLEY. A subpost of Fort Williams at Cape Cottage and located on a 192-acre site on the eastern half of Great Diamond (Hog) Island in Casco Bay, Fort McKinley was begun in 1893 and completed in 1900. Along with Fort Lyon on nearby Cow Island, it was the largest of the harbor defenses in the bay and intended to defend the Hussey Sound entrance to Portland Harbor. Its armament consisted of nine batteries of 21 guns, ranging from 3-inch guns to 12-inch rifles and mortars. Seven companies of men, housed in six large brick barracks, were required to man the defenses. The fort was fully garrisoned during both world wars. Declared surplus after World War II and turned over to the city of Portland by the government, the property was first sold to a Texas oil exploration company, which is now engaged in negotiations for its prospective resale to General Properties, Inc., a land development enterprise which has plans to convert the fort's buildings into single- and multi-family housing units.

FORT MACHIAS. FORT O'BRIEN.

FORT MADISON. FORT UNITED STATES.

FORT MARY (*Fort Hill*). Erected in 1708 on a rocky bluff overlooking Winter Harbor, now incorporated within the town of Biddeford Pool in York County, this defense (rebuilt in 1710) against Indian attack was commanded by John Hill, whose name was also used to designate it. In 1903 the Rebecca Emery Chapter of the Daughters of the American Revolution at Biddeford erected a commemorative stone monument at the fort site on a small peninsula below the mouth of the Saco River, about seven miles from the city of Biddeford.

FORT MENASKOUX (*Arrowsic Fort*). Erected in 1720 or earlier on Arrowsic Island in present Sagadahoc County, this defense was also known as Arrowsic Fort. In 1720 the fort, then commanded by Samuel Penhallow, was the scene of a council between 250 Indians representing the Abenakis and their allies, and the commandants of several Maine forts and 50 prominent English settlers. The island had been purchased from the Indians some 70 years earlier by two Boston merchants who established a trading enterprise there in 1654. (See: CLARK AND LAKE'S FORT.)

FORT NEW CASCO. The old settlement of Falmouth, now Portland, had been protected by Fort Loyal (Loyall) from 1680 until 1690 when it was attacked and destroyed by a large party of French and Indians who massacred most of its occupants. Reoccupation of the area, however, was not made until about 1700 when Fort New Casco was erected near the mouth of the Presumpscot River in what is now the town of Falmouth, just north of Portland. As designed by engineer Colonel Romer, the fort was a 70-foot-square palisade with bastions at its northwest and southeast corners and raised sentry boxes in the other two angles. The palisade enclosed a three-room commandant's residence, a guardhouse and a storehouse, with the fort's well protected by an extension of the palisade.

In 1703, two months after a council with the Indians had been held here, during which they expressed peaceful intentions, the fort nearly succumbed to furious attacks made by a large force of French and Indians. The defense was saved from certain capture by the opportune arrival of an armed vessel of the province. In 1705 engineer John Redknap designed and built a much larger fort incorporating much of the original fort designed by Romer. One of Redknap's drawings indicates that the much enlarged fort was an oblong square 250 feet long and 190 feet wide, with a perimeter of more than 1,000 feet, not including the bastions. The covered (covert) way, 230 feet long, ran from the fort proper to the shore, which was protected by a blockhouse. The fort's amenities included "convenience houses" (privies), doctor's offices, a blacksmith's shop, and a cistern. Never again assaulted by the enemy, Fort New Casco was dismantled in 1716 as part of the province's budget-cutting program to save maintenance costs.

FORT NEW GLOUCESTER. This blockhouse, which served for six years as a fort, church and refuge for New Gloucester's settlers, was erected in 1754 shortly after the outbreak of the French and Indian War. In 1788, its usefulness over, the blockhouse was reportedly "sold for seven bushels of corn." The present town seal commemorates the fortification.

FORT NOBLE. This fort was erected in Phippsburg, Sagadahoc County, by Colonel Arthur Noble in 1734 on his own initiative, a year after acquiring land there, as a refuge for the area's settlers. Noble later was an officer under Sir William Pepperrell during the successful expedition against Louisbourg in 1745 and served with distinction during the subsequent French and Indian War. A simplified sketch drawn in 1743 indicates Fort Noble was a square embrasured palisade enclosing a long one-story structure with end chimneys. Flanking the fort's central gate in the south side of the stockade were two-story corner blockhouses.

FORT O'BRIEN (*Fort Machias*). By the time the American Revolution erupted, the town of Machias had become a thriving center for Anglo-American lumber operations. In the first naval engagement of the war, which was precipitated by the fervently anti-British patriots of this frontier community, the British vessel *Margaretta* was captured on June 12, 1775. In anticipation of swift retaliation by naval forces from Halifax, the townspeople under the supervision of Jeremiah O'Brien and Benjamin Foster built a breastwork, named Fort Machias, on the bank of the Machias River. After two vain attempts to subdue the rebellious inhabitants and recapture the *Margaretta* later in the summer of 1775, the British sent two heavily armed frigates and two smaller warships under the command of Sir George Collier and finally dispersed the defenders. (See: FORT FOSTER.)

The Massachusetts government considered Fort Machias (or Fort O'Brien when the defense was renamed) important and appointed Colonel John Allan its commandant, who was ordered to recruit 100 men, a number increased to 300 after a damaging raid by the enemy. New muskets for the troops as well as two 9-pounders and one 6-pounder cannon were procured. The fort itself was repaired and strengthened, and barracks were constructed, but it saw no further action during the Revolution. A map drawn in 1864 indicates the "site of Old Battery" just to the north of a Civil War battery, showing a cres-

cent-shaped earthwork, some 90 feet long and 14 or 15 feet thick.

In September 1814, during a British naval offensive along the coast, five men-of-war carrying about 900 troops entered Machias Bay and took Fort O'Brien after its small garrison hastily abandoned the defense. Lingering there about two days or so, the British burned the barracks and carried off the fort's guns. Fort O'Brien was reactivated in late 1863, at which time an entirely new battery, a 150-foot-long, semisubterranean, timber-revetted earthwork, was constructed just south of its original site and armed with three 32-pounder smoothbores and two 24-pounder rifled cannon.

Fort O'Brien is to this day a prominent earthwork overlooking the Machias River in Machiasport.

PEMAQUID FORT. FORT FREDERICK.

FORT PENOBSCOT. FORT PENTAGOET.

FORT PENTAGOET (*Fort Penobscot*). On the site of today's town of Castine in Hancock County, on the east side of its peninsula on Penobscot Bay, Fort Pentagoet (Fort Penobscot, as it was alternately known), was for many years a French fortified stronghold, established to support their claim to all Maine territory north of the Kennebec River. During the long conflict between New France and New England, the place was frequently raided and pillaged, making it one of the most hotly contested on the North American continent.

The Plymouth Colony established a trading post here in 1629 but its occupants were driven out by an armed French expedition in 1635. The French then erected on the site a fort of stone and earth, with curtains 16 feet thick at the base and 6 feet wide at the top. Its 60-foot-square parade had been designed for a small garrison. In addition to its four angles occupied by 16-foot-square stone bastions, the fort's enclosure included a guardhouse, barracks, a two-story magazine with a well beneath it, a storehouse, and a small chapel to cater to the spiritual needs of the garrison.

In 1654 England, while at war with Holland, captured the French posts at Penobscot Bay, Port Royal, and St. John, retaining them until 1670, when they were returned to the French by the 1667 Treaty of Breda. Fort Pentagoet's armaments then consisted of 12 iron guns, the largest being 2 eight-pounders mounted on a platform and facing the bay. A Dutch privateer captured the fort and its 30-man garrison in 1674, and turned the fort's cannon on the works to knock the top of the walls inward over the enclosed buildings. The Dutch plundered the settlement and carried off the fort's guns.

In 1688 Sir Edmund Andros, governor of the Dominion of New England, raided Pentagoet and pillaged its surrounding French community. The French retaliated by demolishing Fort William Henry at Pemaquid. In 1722 the English returned to finally raze Fort Pentagoet and occupy the Penobscot peninsula.

The written record and local lore had long indicated that nothing was left of the fort beneath the rear lawn of Our Lady of Hope Catholic Church in Castine. In 1978, however, a fierce blizzard exposed a portion of the oldest stone fort in America, revealing the southwest corner of the wall. In 1980 archaeological studies were begun on the site, and since then properly supervised excavations have uncovered the walls of the officers' quarters and the barracks and a large number of artifacts.

PINE HILL FORT (*Hamilton's Garrison*). On Pine Hill near Berwick in York County stood a fort or blockhouse, surrounded by a 20-foot-high stockade of poles. Also known as Hamilton's Garrison, the defense was reportedly still in existence as late as 1750.

FORT POINT. FORT POWNALL.

FORT POPHAM. This half-moon granite fort, garrisoned several times, although never completed, is closely associated with England's first colonization attempt in New England. Until 1890 it was believed that here, on Hunniwell's Point at the mouth of the Kennebec River in Phippsburg, was the site of the 1607 Popham Colony and its short-lived Fort St. George. Documents found in Spanish archives, however, conclusively established that these first colonists had settled on Sabino Head, a half mile to the west (See: FORT ST. GEORGE.)

The 1809 battery at the river's mouth was irretrievably antiquated by 1857 when construction of a new fort was finally authorized for strategic Hunniwell's Point. Because of federal bureaucracy, no work was initiated on the new fort until 1862, well after the outbreak of the Civil War, when the planned work was named in honor of George Popham who founded the 1607 colony.

As designed and largely built, Fort Popham is of closed lunette form; that is, it is roughly crescent-shaped with defenses on all sides. In circumference the work measures 500 feet, while the sides facing the river rise to a height of over 30 feet. The walls, as in all of the major Civil War forts, were constructed of massive cut granite blocks which in this case were quarried on nearby Fox and Dix Islands. . . .

Internally Fort Popham was provided with a spacious parade ground containing two barrack-blocks (which do not survive); great subterranean cisterns to afford a besieged garrison an ample supply of water; and four magazines to provide powder to the fort's maximum of forty-two guns. As at Fort Knox, elaborate spiral staircases gave access to the casemates and parapet from the parade ground. [Robert L. Bradley, *The Forts of Maine, 1607–1945*, pp. 34–35]

Construction to complete Fort Popham, already outmoded by the technological advances of armaments made during the war, was halted in 1869. The fort was regarrisoned in 1898 in response to a threat by overrated Spanish naval power. The fort was deactivated shortly after the war, only to be reoccupied by troops, for the last time, during World War I. On January 28, 1924, the state of Maine purchased Fort Popham and its seven-and-a-half-acre reservation for $6,600. The Fort Popham State Memorial is now being maintained for the benefit of the public by the Bureau of Parks and Recreation.

FORT PORTER. FORT UNITED STATES.

CAMP POWERS. A temporary Civil War assembly and training post established at or near the city of Augusta.

FORT POWNALL (*Fort Point*). Sometimes known as Fort Point, this French and Indian War fort was erected on Wasaumkeag Point, now Fort Point, on the Penobscot River, a short distance above its mouth, at present Stockton Springs in Waldo County. It was built between May and July 1759 by 400 men under Massachusetts Governor Thomas Pownall, who had proposed to England's Prime Minister William Pitt to plug the mouths of the strategic rivers to prevent French and Indian passage to the seacoasts.

The only description of the fort was made by Joseph P. Martin in 1828 or 1829. A veteran of the Revolutionary War, Joseph Martin himself had never seen Fort Pownall but he recounted what had been related to him by a former resident there. Based on his recollections, "Fort Pownall's design was exceptional for its time and place. Instead of the familiar stockade with diagonally-opposed blockhouses, one giant blockhouse with its own bastions was built on substantial fieldstone footings. Surrounding this was a palisade, ditch, and glacis of four-pointed star form, all precisely laid out" (Robert L. Bradley, *The Forts of Maine, 1607–1945*, p. 20).

Two months after Fort Pownall was completed, the citadel of Quebec fell to General James Wolfe, spelling the certain doom of French dominion in North America. The presence of the fort, regularly garrisoned until the Revolution, precipitated the first significant settlement of the Penobscot River region. In March 1775 the British seized the fort and removed all of its guns and ammunition. Three months later, in July, troops under Colonel James Cargill of Newcastle destroyed the blockhouse to prevent its use by British troops during the course of the war.

FORT PREBLE. This coastal defense, located on Preble Point three miles southeast of Portland in the city's harbor, was built in accordance with authorization enacted by Congress on January 8, 1808. The first U.S. Army troops to arrive at the fort, while it was still under construction, were Captain Joseph Chandler's Company of U.S. Light Artillery, in compliance with written instructions of the secretary of war, dated October 31, 1808. Named in honor of Commodore Edward Preble, who commanded the American Naval forces in the War with Tripoli in 1804, the fort continued to be garrisoned with minor interruptions until the Civil War and continuously thereafter. The garrison was removed and the post was made a subpost of Fort Williams, in compliance with General Orders No. 11, Headquarters Department of the East, February 24, 1911. Thereafter, with the exceptions of the periods of World Wars I and II, when military personnel were temporarily assigned there, the fort was in charge of a caretaker detachment. The post was deactivated July 31, 1947. Pursuant to General Orders No. 22, Department of the Army, July 14, 1950, the fort was declared surplus to the needs of the Army.

PROUT'S NECK FORT. This frontier fortification erected at Prout's Neck in present Scarborough, Cumberland County, was built in 1703 about a year after the outbreak of Queen Anne's War between Great Britain and France in America (1702–11). Here a group of eight men successfully fought off an attack of French and Indians during the same year.

PROVINCE FORT (*Salmon Falls Fort*). The Province of Massachusetts in 1743 appropriated monies for the establishment of defenses in several populated settlements. On December 15 of the same year, military men met at Falmouth (Portland) and located the several forts or blockhouses to be built. The inhabitants of New Marblehead, now South Windham just north of Portland, began the erection of their fort as soon as they had obtained their part of the appropriation, knowing full well that should relations between Great Britain and France be again ruptured, the frontier settlements would become the victims of renewed savagery.

Province Fort, also known as Salmon Falls Fort, was completed and ready for occupancy in the summer of 1744. The palisaded fort, a blockhouse, was 50 feet square, two-storied, with walls 1 foot thick of hewn hemlock timber, the upper story jutting one foot on all sides over the lower, with a tier of portholes just beneath the overhang. Two 12-foot-square, two-storied flankers or "watch-boxes" were at diagonal corners, each armed with a swivel gun. Inside the stockade was a nine-pounder cannon facing the gate. The settlement successfully withstood the five Indian raids made against the township between 1747 and 1756, by which time five of the stronger log houses in the community were fortified with palisades and blockhouses or flankers.

FORT RICHMOND. This fort was erected in 1719 on the west side of the Kennebec River about 25 miles from the coast, opposite the upper end of Swan Island, at present Richmond, Sagadahoc County. Enlarged in 1723 and significantly renovated in 1740, Fort Richmond safeguarded the settlements of the lower Kennebec and Merrymeeting Bay until it was practically dismantled in 1755. A letter dated December 30, 1754, by John Winslow of Plymouth, Massachusetts, who had been appointed to the Kennebec River command by Governor William Shirley, reported, "This is a Wood Fortification Built with hewn Timber, Mounts Ten Guns, and is used as a place of Trade with the Indians carryed on by this Government, and is Twenty five Miles up the river from its Entrance into the Sea" (Stanley Pargellis, ed., *Military Affairs in North America, 1748–1765*).

FORT SACO. In 1693 a pentagonal fortification with a tower of stone was built at Saco Falls in what is now Biddeford, York County. Called Fort Saco, it was apparently continuously garrisoned until it was dismantled and replaced by Fort Mary at Biddeford Pool. Built by Major John Converse in accordance with the plan drawn by military engineer Wolfgang William Romer, Fort Saco was never attacked.

SACO BLOCKHOUSE. According to Henry E. Dunnack in his *Maine Forts* (1924), this blockhouse defense was erected by the Massachusetts government in 1728 at "Union Falls," 10 miles above Saco River's lower falls and that "the fort and its surrounding palisades were in existence as late as 1810."

FORT ST. CROIX. During the summer of 1604, a fortified settlement was founded by the Sieur de Monts, a French Huguenot, and Samuel de Champlain on St. Croix (Dochet) Island, off today's city of Calais in Washington County. The colonists suffered through a disastrous winter. Decimated by an epidemic of scurvy, starvation, and extreme exposure to the elements, the colony lasted barely a year, and its leaders moved the survivors across the Bay of Fundy to the site of Port Royal, Nova Scotia. Archaeological investigations on the island by the National Park Service have revealed burials and other traces of the original French settlement. An act of Congress, June 8, 1949, authorized establishment of the St. Croix Island National Monument. Extant to this day is the exaggerated sketch drawn by Champlain of the ill-fated colony.

FORT ST. GEORGE. The first English colony in New England was the so-called Popham or Sagadahoc settlement founded late in the summer of 1607 by the Northern Virginia Company, complementing a simultaneous colonial establishment at Jamestown in "Southern Virginia." The party of more than 100 all-male colonists, led by George Popham and Raleigh Gilbert, landed on Sabino Head at the mouth of the Kennebec (then the Sagadahoc) River, at today's city of Phippsburg. They first erected Fort St. George, then habitations and a small ship. There exists an illustrated plan of the Sagadahoc fort made by John Hunt, one of the colonists, which depicts the structures in enough detail to give an idea of their character. The primary source of information about the colony is the anonymous *Relation* written in 1608, which served as the basis for William Strachey's account in his *Histories of Travaile into Virginia Britannia* (1618):

[After the departure of Captain Edward Davis and Captain Edward Harlow with their ships the *Gift of God* and the *Mary and John*] they fully finished the fort, trencht and fortefied yt with twelve [nine?] pieces of ordinaunce, and built fifty [probably a printer's error for "fifteen"] howses therein, besides a church and a storehowse; and the carpenters framed a pretty Pynnace of some thirty tonne, which they called the *Virginia*.

Severe weather and ill luck, however, plagued them. A fire during the winter destroyed the storehouse holding most of their provisions, George Popham died, and Raleigh Gilbert had to return to England after learning from Captain Davis, who returned in the spring, that he had inherited the family's estates. This left the colony vulnerable and without effective leadership. Defeated, the survivors returned to England late in 1608.

The Popham Colony was located in the general area of Popham Beach on Sabino Head. The assumed site is on a 45-acre tract of land owned by the state of Maine. It is in the main unspoiled or desecrated by modern intrusions, except for the presence in its near environs of a small number of frame houses and the concrete remains of Fort Baldwin, a World War I coast defense installation.

FORT ST. GEORGE'S (*Fort George*). Two fortifications, built approximately a century apart, were so-named and located in the immediate and near environs of Thomaston in Knox County. The first was a pair of strong blockhouses, with a large area between them enclosed by palisades, erected in 1719–20 on the east side of the St. George's River about 16 miles above its mouth, at the river's bend directly in front of the site of the mansion later built by General Henry Knox. The main fortification, quadrangular in form with each side 100 feet in length, was built of hewn 20-inch-square timber, 16 feet in height. Within were barracks large enough to accommodate a large garrison and the all-important water well. From its southern wall there was a covered way, constructed of logs, leading to a large blockhouse on the bank of the river. From the time of its inception until it was dismantled in 1762, the fort had withstood a number of fierce assaults during the course of three wars that almost depopulated Maine.

The second Fort St. George's is located about four miles to the south in the town of St. George. The fort was begun in 1808 and completed in July 1809 under the supervision of Captain Thomas Vose of Thomaston, the town that the defense was intended to protect. Consisting of a rampart in the form of a crescent towards the river, with ordnance-mounted outworks, the fort proper included a small blockhouse, brick magazine, and barracks. The fort was not garrisoned until the outbreak of the War of 1812. "A year later, however, this garrison was transferred to another duty, and thereafter Fort St. George's was defended, incredibly, by just one elderly man. When a 74-gun English ship, *Bul-*

wark, sailed up the river in 1814, its crew had no difficulty in landing and spiking the American guns" (Robert L. Bradley, *The Forts of Maine, 1607–1945,* p. 27). At present Fort St. George's remains are more or less hidden in thick vegetation although its earthworks are quite tangible. The property is owned by the state of Maine.

SALMON FALLS FORT. PROVINCE FORT.

FORT SCAMMEL. Built in 1808 under the direction of H. A. S. Dearborn, son of the secretary of war, Fort Scammel was situated on the southwestern part of 12-acre House Island (known during the Revolution as Howe's Island) in Casco Bay near the entrance to Portland Harbor. An octagonal timbered blockhouse with a pointed roof surmounted by a carved wooden eagle with extended wings, it was named for Colonel Alexander Scammel, Revolutionary War adjutant general, who was killed at or near Yorktown in October 1781 while commanding the 1st New Hampshire Regiment. The blockhouse's upper story, projecting beyond the lower by about three feet, contained the gun battery. During the Civil War, the fort was significantly improved and enlarged to be fitted for 71 guns, including seven mortars and fieldpieces, but the Engineer Department report dated January 4, 1862, noted that "no portion of the armament is now in place." The fort has been used as the site for a lighthouse by the Department of Commerce since 1914.

FORT SHIRLEY (*Fort Frankfort*). Fort Richmond was obsoleted in 1752 when Fort Frankfort, later renamed Fort Shirley for the governor of Massachusetts, was erected in what is now the town of Dresden in Kennebec County. The fort, typical for that period in frontier history, had twin diagonally placed 24-foot-square, two-storied blockhouses in two angles of the palisaded 200-foot-square enclosure containing troop quarters and a 40-foot-long storehouse. Archaeological excavations conducted in 1975 unearthed the site of the fort's western blockhouse, just west of the Pownalborough Courthouse.

SHURT'S FORT. FORT FREDERICK.

FORT STAGE ISLAND. Built and garrisoned under the direction of Governor Edmund Andros in 1689, this small fort was situated on Stage Island at Cape Porpoise in Kennebunkport, York County. After Governor Andros returned to Massachusetts in 1690, the fort's garrison deserted.

FORT SULLIVAN. This post, the most eastern in the United States and the most northern on the Atlantic seaboard, was located on Moose Island, Passamaquoddy Bay, in the town of Eastport, Washington County. Troops were first stationed here in the spring of 1808 and the fort, actually a breastwork battery and a blockhouse named for General John Sullivan of Revolutionary War fame, was built under the supervision of Major Lemuel Trescott during the same year, most probably because of the protracted dispute over the nation's eastern boundary with the province of New Brunswick. In July 1814 an armada of 10 warships commanded by Sir Thomas Hardy entered the bay and seized the fort and town. They remained in British possession until formally surrendered to the United States on June 30, 1818. The post was upgraded and enlarged over the years and intermittently occupied until its last garrison was finally withdrawn in 1873.

FORT SUMNER. During the last decade of the eighteenth century, the United States, barely a score of years old, found itself pressured when England and France resumed armed conflict against each other in 1793. In 1794 Congress was persuaded by President Washington to authorize the fortification of key harbors. Fort Sumner, built in 1794 on Munjoy Hill in Portland, was the only fort established in Maine during this period, and the city's sole defense against an enemy attack by sea until Forts Preble and Scammel were erected in 1808–9. The site of the blockhouse fort named for Increase Sumner, governor of Massachusetts, is located at 60 North Street. During the War of 1812 its guns were remounted but never used. In 1827 one John Neal set up a gymnasium within the fort and was the first man to introduce parallel bars and leaping poles in New England. Fort Sumner Park is north of the Shailer School in the city of Portland.

FORT UNITED STATES (*Fort Madison; Fort Castine; Fort Porter*). The Americans in 1811 built Fort Madison, named for the president of the United States, the largest of the battery defenses at Castine in Hancock County. It was captured by the British late in the War of 1812 and renamed Fort Castine. When it was returned to the United States after the signing of the Treaty of Ghent formally ending the war, it was renamed Fort Porter for Major Moses Porter, Army engineer. After it was rebuilt and enlarged during the Civil War, it was designated Fort United States. The fort, still standing, is included within a public park maintained by the city of Castine since 1894.

VAUGHAN'S FORT. Erected by Colonel William Vaughan at Damariscotta in present Lincoln County, in about 1745, the settlers' refuge was a 100-foot-square stockade enclosing what was apparently a garrison house built of seven-inch-thick hewn timber.

FORT WESTERN. The site of the present Fort Western in the city of Augusta was used as a fur-trading post as early as 1625 by the settlers of Plymouth Plantation. The area was known as Cushnoc or Koussinoc and the fur trade carried on there helped to raise revenue to alleviate the Plymouth Colony's debts. John Alden, who was later immortalized by Longfellow, and John Howland were in charge of the post in 1634. By 1661 the fur trade had declined, and the colony sold the area to a group of wealthy businessmen who were known as the Proprietors of the Kennebec Purchase. The area was abandoned in 1669.

In 1749 the Proprietors returned. Fort Western, probably named for Governor Shirley's friend Thomas Western of Sussex, England, was built by the Plymouth Company in 1754 during the French and Indian War as a part of the defenses erected to protect the Kennebec River settlements. It held the supplies that were brought up the river in large ships and later taken by ox cart and small boats to Fort Halifax at Taconic Falls, now Winslow. Fort Western was garrisoned by 20 soldiers under the command of Captain James Howard, the first and only commander of the fort. The fort was never attacked. In 1769 the Proprietors of the Kennebec Purchase sold Captain Howard the fort and about 900 acres of surrounding land. The fort then became a trading post.

In the early days of the settlement, Fort Western played a major role in community life. Besides being a trading post, the first marriages and public meetings were held there. The first copy of the Declaration of Independence sent to the settlement arrived at Fort Western. The role of the fort in the American Revolution was incidental. General Benedict Arnold, controversial even in the early days of the war, launched his ill-timed march to Quebec from Fort Western in the fall of 1775. With 1,100 men, the no-torious Aaron Burr among them, he set out through the Maine forests to attack the British in Quebec, a project that ultimately ended in disaster. In 1779 the survivors of a Massachusetts expedition, defeated at Castine, stopped at Fort Western on their way home. Paul Revere was artillery commander of this party.

Eventually Fort Western became a tenement house and by the early 1900s was badly neglected, an unsightly fire hazard. In 1919 William Howard Gannett, a descendant of Captain Howard, restored Fort Western and presented it to the city of Augusta.

FORT WILLIAM. FORT MCCLARY.

FORT WILLIAM HENRY. FORT FREDERICK.

FORT WILLIAMS. In 1872 Congress appropriated funds for the establishment of a battery on Portland Head, site of the famous Portland Head Light, at Cape Cottage, about six miles south of Portland, and construction began on June 1, 1873. The battery was upgraded to an independent post in compliance with Special Orders No. 263, Headquarters Department of the East, November 11, 1898. On April 13, 1899 it was designated Fort Williams in honor of Brevet Major General Seth Williams, a distinguished veteran of the Mexican and Civil Wars.

Between June 1898 and October 1906, six gun batteries were emplaced at the fort: DeHart, Sullivan, Hobart, Blair, Keyes, and Garesché. In 1917 the 6-inch disappearing rifles were removed from Fort Williams and sent to France to be installed as field artillery, while the 12-inch D.C. guns remained as the main armament at Battery Blair. In December 1943, most of the old disappearing rifles at Fort Williams—brought there by oxen-drawn sledges almost 50 years before—were removed for scrap. After having served through World Wars I and II, Fort Williams was gradually phased out and placed in caretaker status until about 1961 or 1962, when the Department of the Army declared the fort surplus to its needs. Although the fort's gun batteries were demolished and the town of Cape Elizabeth converted the site into a park, the cracked concrete remains of the old batteries are still in evidence.

ABERDEEN PROVING GROUND (*Edgewood Arsenal*). Located approximately midway between Washington and Philadelphia, Aberdeen Proving Ground is a major test and evaluation installation of the U.S. Army. Established in 1917, it serves as a principal military center for research, development, and testing of arms, ammunition, track and wheeled vehicles, and general equipment. The strategic location and especially suitable topography dictated the selection of the site.

The Proving Ground incorporates approximately 80,000 acres of tidal water lands, the boundaries of which are defined on the north by the confluence of the Susquehanna River and Chesapeake Bay, and on the south by the Gunpowder River. Included is historic Spesutia Island, a name derived from the Latin for "Utie's Hope," a 2,300-acre manorial grant in 1661 to Colonel Nathaniel Utie, for whom this island was surveyed in 1658. A house built by Utie at one end of the island no longer stands.

Basically, the installation has two general areas separated by the Bush River. The southern part is commonly referred to as the Edgewood Area, while the northern segment is generally known as the Aberdeen Area. The growth of Aberdeen Proving Ground is essentially the story of today's Materiel Testing Directorate, whose roots stem from the winter of 1917–18, when the land was acquired by Presidential Proclamation for use as "an ordnance proving ground." To help feed APG's first contingent of troops in 1918, a lieutenant was placed in charge of 10 soldiers who spent the summer farming 100 acres near the Old Baltimore site. Formal confirmation did not come until January 9, 1919, when War Department General Orders No. 6 authorized the installation as "a permanent military post" named Aberdeen Proving Ground.

Staffing of initial operations began at the end of December 1917, when military and civilian personnel were transferred from Sandy Hook, N.J. During 1918, the former ordnance proving ground was completely displaced with all equipment moved to APG. The first gun fired on January 2, 1918, marked the official start of testing. In a formal ceremony, a woman pulled the lanyard on the three-inch gun of 1905 vintage.

Expansion during World War II resulted in reorganization and the development in 1943 of the Ordnance Research and Development Center (ORDC). Two years later, the ORDC was split into three major units under the titles of Development and Proof Services, Ballistic Research Laboratories, and the Aberdeen Ordnance Depot. The depot was later inactivated. More than 27,000

Maryland

soldiers were stationed at APG during the peak of the war. The world's first electronic computer, the ENIAC, the "Granddaddy of the Computer Age," was placed in operation at APG under a cloak of secrecy near the end of World War II.

In July 1971 the two areas of the Proving Ground were consolidated with the merger of Edgewood Arsenal, established in October 1917, with APG. The consolidation served to create one of the most diversified military installations in the nation and one of the foremost testing and research facilities in the world. The noted U.S. Army Ordnance Museum, which has the world's most complete weapons collection, is part of the U.S. Army Ordnance Center and School, APG's largest tenant organization.

CAMP ALBERT C. RITCHIE. FORT RITCHIE.

FORT ALEXANDER. FORT SUMNER.

CAMP ANDREW. CAMP WOOL.

FORT ARMISTEAD. Established in 1898 and designated the "Battery at Hawkin's Point," the defense on the Patapsco River in Anne Arundel County was renamed Fort Armistead during the same year in honor of Major George Armistead, Corps of Artillery, brevetted lieutenant colonel for gallant conduct while in command of Fort McHenry when it successfully withstood the bombardment of the British fleet on September 13–14, 1814. General Orders No. 78, War Department, May 25, 1903, announced the names of the

seacoast batteries on the reservation: Battery Irons in honor of 1st Lieutenant Joseph F. Irons; Battery McFarland in honor of Major Daniel McFarland; Battery Mudge in honor of 2nd Lieutenant Robert R. Mudge; and Battery Winchester in honor of Brigadier General James Winchester.

Near the end of 1917, during World War I, all of the fort's armament was removed and sent to more vulnerable positions because the new tactical defense methods adopted at Fort Armistead had eliminated the threat of enemy ships and submarines attacking Baltimore's harbor. An Act of Congress, approved March 4, 1923, authorized the secretary of war to sell the 45-acre reservation, as it was no longer required for military purposes. The city of Baltimore finally claimed the property preempting a land developer's plans and turned it into a public park.

The U.S. Navy took over the fort as an ammunition dump during World War II. It returned the site to the city in 1947, and for the next five years Fort Armistead gathered weeds. In 1952 the U.S. Army moved in again and set up an antiaircraft battery. Not long after this occupation, the fort was again obsoleted.

FORT BABCOCK. This small fortification, also known as Battery Babcock and City Battery, along with Fort Covington, was erected during the War of 1812 on the Ferry Branch of the Patapsco River to prevent the landing of enemy troops to attack Baltimore from the rear.

FORT ARMISTEAD. Artist's conception of the battery. (Courtesy of the National Archives.)

BATTERY BAILEY. An earthwork battery, one of the defenses of Washington during the Civil War, located about two miles north of Chain Bridge and four miles above Georgetown, D.C., it was erected during November–December 1862 and named in honor of Captain Guilford D. Bailey, 1st New York Artillery, who was killed at the Battle of Fair Oaks, Virginia, on May 31, 1862. One of the battery's parapets is now located in Westmoreland Park, northwest of Westmoreland Circle, in Montgomery County.

CAMP BATES. A Federal post established as a tent city to accommodate the 3rd New York Volunteer Cavalry, it was located near Poolesville, Montgomery County, which had as many as 20,000 Union troops encamped in its environs at various times during the Civil War.

BEAUMONT'S POINT FORT. One of the fortifications erected during the Revolution in the Annapolis area by the Council of Safety to repel any British attack, this defense stood atop a high cliff called Beaumont's Point on the north side of the Severn River.

CAMP BELGER. BELGER BARRACKS.

BELGER BARRACKS (*Camp Belger; Camp Birney*). Established at Baltimore and beginning as a tent encampment in 1862 named in honor of Colonel James Belger, quartermaster of the Middle Department of the Army, Camp Belger was occupied by a succession of Federal regiments. For a time in 1863, still a tent city, the post was called Camp Birney after Major General William Birney, who organized here the 7th Infantry, U.S. Colored Troops, Maryland Volunteers. Later in the same year, because of the post's continuous occupation, the city of tents was replaced by barracks and renamed Belger Barracks. It was located a short distance north of the intersection of North and Madison avenues south of Druid Hill Park.

BATTERY BENSON. One of the defenses of Washington during the Civil War, Battery Benson was located two miles west of Tennallytown, D.C., near Fort Sumner, between Forts Ripley and Mansfield, and west of Powder Mill Branch in Montgomery County. It was named in honor of Captain Henry Benson, 2nd U.S. Artillery, who died August 11, 1862, of wounds suffered at the second battle at Malvern Hill, Virginia, on July 1, 1862.

CAMP BENTON. A Federal troop encampment near Poolesville, Montgomery County, it was occupied by the 20th Massachusetts Infantry.

CAMP BERLIN. A Federal troop post established in the village of Berlin, Worcester County, located about seven miles from the seacoast, it was occupied by elements of the 8th Infantry in 1862 and 1863.

CAMP BIRNEY. BELGER BARRACKS.

CAMP BOONESBORO. A Federal post located at or near the town of Boonesboro, about 10 miles southeast of Hagerstown, in Washington County, it was occupied by elements of the 8th Infantry in 1862 and 1863.

CAMP BRADFORD (*Camp Cattlegrounds*). This processing center of Maryland volunteer draftees established in 1861 was located on the site of the former Maryland Agricultural Society's fairgrounds in a three-block area north of present 26th Street between Charles Street and Maryland Avenue. Named for Maryland's pro-Union war governor, Augustus W. Bradford, it was irreverently called "Camp Cattlegrounds" by the soldiers.

FORT BRADFORD. Located at Hagerstown, Fort Bradford was one of Baltimore's northern defenses during the Civil War.

CAMP BURNSIDE. This Civil War encampment on the outskirts of Annapolis was established in 1861 and occupied by the 8th Connecticut Volunteer Regiment.

CAMP CAMBRIDGE. This Civil War post was located at or near the town of Cambridge in Dorchester County and occupied by companies B and C of the 8th Infantry in 1864 and 1865.

CAMP CARROLL (*Camp Chesebrough*). Established in 1862 and named for its location on the former property of attorney Charles Carroll in southwest Baltimore, it provided temporary quarters for outfitting and training the 13th Pennsylvania Cavalry and light artillery regiments. The post was renamed Camp Chesebrough in 1863 when it was occupied by the 1st Connecticut Cavalry until March 1864, then replaced by the 1st Maryland Cavalry, who reinstated the former name of Camp Carroll.

FORT CARROLL. Located on artificially constructed Sollers Flats, a shoal converted into an island in the Patapsco River in the middle of

Baltimore's harbor, nine-sided Fort Carroll was begun in 1847. From 1849 to 1852 Robert E. Lee, then a major (brevetted colonel) of U.S. Engineers, supervised its construction. Short years later significant improvements were made in the efficiency of artillery and gunpowder that would have permitted attacking enemy ships to lob shells into Baltimore from a point out of sight of the fort. Because of this realized circumstance, the fort was never completed, although considerable importance was attached to the post during the Civil War. In 1850 it was officially designated Fort Carroll in honor of Charles Carroll, a signer of the Declaration of Independence.

Two batteries of artillerymen from Fort McHenry manned the island in 1898. General Orders No. 78, War Department, 1903, designated the fortifications at Fort Carroll as Battery Towson, Battery Heart and Battery Augustin. In 1917 the post was occupied by a detachment of the Coast Artillery. Its use ceased in 1920 when a permit was granted to the Department of Commerce to use the entire reservation for lighthouse purposes.

CAMP CASEY. In support of the many defensive fortifications encircling Washington, Union troops were encamped at strategic points around the city. One such post was Camp Casey, established in 1861 and occupied by the 5th New Hampshire Volunteers and the 4th Rhode Island Volunteers, located in Prince George's County in the area known at present as Cottage City, about a half-mile southwest of Bladensburg between the Bladensburg Road and the all-important Baltimore and Ohio Railroad.

CAMP CATTLEGROUNDS. CAMP BRADFORD.

CAMP CHAPIN. Established as a tent city in early September 1862 by the 116th New York Volunteers, Camp Chapin was located on a site near Druid Hill Park in Baltimore.

CAMP CHESEBROUGH. CAMP CARROLL.

FORT CONQUEST. Erected in 1637 under the direction of Governor Leonard Calvert and his Council, Fort Conquest was located on Palmer's Island (later known successively as Watson's, and then Garrett Island) at the strategic mouth of the Susquehanna River after dispossessing Captain William Claiborne and his trading establishment catering to the Susquehanna Indians.

The Marylanders, now in possession of the island . . . decided that one thousand pounds of tobacco should be spent toward the charge of settling a garrison' on the island. Many public spirited colonists agreed to contribute to the support of the garrison. When, however, it came to collect what had been guaranteed, the St. Mary's authorities found it a difficult matter. To avoid in the future the trouble caused by the collection of the contributions, the colonial lawmakers authorized "a levy towards the satisfaction of the charge of Fort Conquest." [Raphael Semmes, *Captains and Mariners of Early Maryland* (Johns Hopkins University Press, 1937), p. 312]

FORT COVINGTON. One of the forts that participated prominently in the defense of the city of Baltimore during the British naval attack against Fort McHenry on September 13–14, 1814, Fort Covington was built, along with Fort Babcock 500 yards downstream, earlier in the same year on the Ferry Branch of the Patapsco River to protect Fort McHenry's west and rear approaches. Major General Samuel Smith, U.S. Senator from Maryland, undertook the monumental task of strengthening and adding to the city's defenses. Fort Covington, one of his major defenses, was located in the Springs Garden section of the city and named in honor of Brigadier General Leonard Covington.

FORT CRAYFORD. This colonial defense, in reality a very substantially built structure, was erected in 1634–35 near Craney Creek, north of Fort Kent, in present Queen Anne's County. Both forts were built by trading entrepreneur Captain William Claiborne.

CRESAP'S FORT. In 1741 Colonel Thomas Cresap, who played a prominent part, often adventurous and dangerous, in the frontier development of Maryland, built a fortified dwelling at Oldtown, the first colonial settlement in what is now Allegany County, where the famous Indian trail from Virginia and Maryland to the West crossed the Potomac River. Colonel Cresap positioned his house, called Skipton after his birthplace in Yorkshire, England, on the Warrior Path to engage in the lucrative fur trade with the various tribes crossing the mountains. His house was used as a marker in the Treaty of Lancaster between the English and the Six Nations in 1744. Cresap, both as a trader and as a representative of the Maryland government, handed out food so generously that he was called "Big Spoon" by the Indians. Indian scouts, missionaries, traders, explorers, and surveyors depended on Cresap's hospitality and also stopped to buy supplies and horses and to hire scouts. Young George

Washington on his first surveying trip into the West was Cresap's guest in 1748. Cresap's Fort survived the frontier conflicts of the French and Indian War. His son Michael built a stone house a quarter of a mile away. The only remains of the fortification consist of the ruins of a stone chimney.

REDOUBT CROSS. FORT SUMNER.

FORT CUMBERLAND (*Will's Creek Fort; Fort Mount Pleasant*). Situated on the site of today's town of Cumberland, seat of Alleghany County, at the junction of Will's Creek and the North Fork of the Potomac River, Maryland's southern boundary, Fort Cumberland was ordered built by Governor Robert Dinwiddie of Virginia when the French and Indian War erupted in 1754.

Chartered in 1748, the Ohio Land Company of Virginia—of which Lawrence and Augustine Washington, older brothers of George Washington, were shareholders— was given a grant of 200,000 acres west of the Allegheny Mountains. During the winter of 1749–50, the company built a fortified storehouse and trading house on the south bank of the Potomac across from Will's Creek in what is now Ridgely, West Virginia. Trade with the Indians thrived, and larger facilities were added. In compliance with Governor Dinwiddie's directive in 1754, construction was begun on fortifications on the high ground across the Potomac on the Maryland side. First known as Fort Mount Pleasant, and often called Will's Creek Fort, it was renamed Fort Cumberland by Governor Dinwiddie in 1755 to honor the duke of Cumberland, third son of George II.

General Edward Braddock, with more than 1,400 trained British regulars, arrived in America

FORT CUMBERLAND. Plan drawn in 1755. (Courtesy of the Public Archives of Canada.)

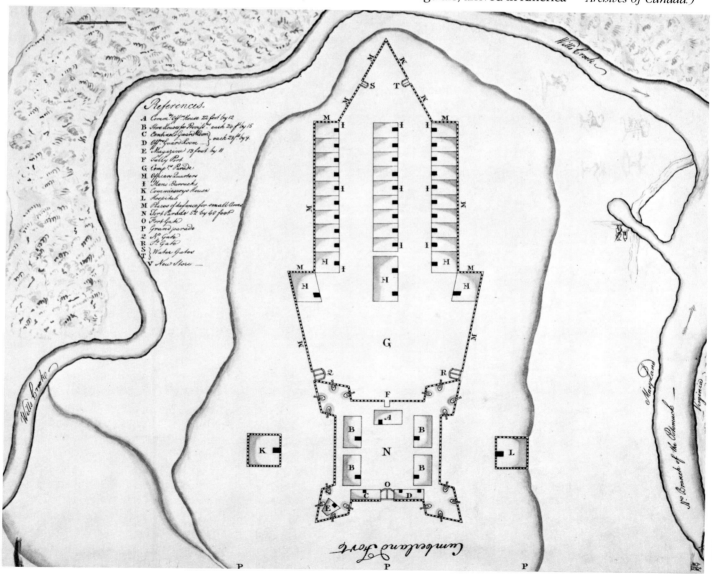

in 1755 to assume command of colonial forces. He ordered the combined force of his regulars and about 800 colonial troops to assemble at Fort Cumberland. From the outset, cocksure Braddock was handicapped by his abysmal ignorance of conditions in the wilderness. His army cut a new road across mountains and through nearly impenetrable forest toward the Forks of the Ohio and French-built Fort Duquesne at today's Pittsburgh, his target. On July 9, a month after leaving Fort Cumberland, Braddock's main force crossed the Monongahela to the site of present Braddock, east of Pittsburgh. His advance army was slaughtered, caught in a cleverly devised French and Indian ambuscade. It was a complete disaster in which Braddock was mortally wounded and 977 of his 1,459 men were officially reported killed or wounded.

The site of Fort Cumberland is located on the hill ascending from today's intersection of Washington and Greene streets and now occupied by the Emmanuel Episcopal Church. The log fort, its palisades reinforced by stone and mud, was a square with cannon-mounted bastions projecting from its angles. The fort proper contained large storehouses for provisions, headquarters, and the powder magazine. A log stockade, extending from the east wall of the fort almost down to Will's Creek, enclosed the barrack-blocks and a small parade ground. The grand parade ground west of the fort, now Prospect Square, was not enclosed. The last military use of the fort was made in 1794, when President George Washington as commander in chief reviewed troops congregated there to suppress the Whiskey Rebellion.

REDOUBT DAVIS. FORT SUMNER.

FORT DEFIANCE. A War of 1812 defense erected in the spring of 1813, Fort Defiance was situated on a bluff on the northwest side of the Elk River "at what is now called Fowler's Shore," in Cecil County. A work of considerable size, it stood about a mile down the river from Fort Hollingsworth.

FORT DETRICK. Located at Frederick, 44 miles northwest of Washington, D.C., and 45 miles west of Baltimore, and named for Major Frederick Louis Detrick, flight surgeon for the 29th Aviation Division, Fort Detrick is a multimission installation providing space for offices, laboratories, and advanced communications facilities, with its U.S. Army Garrison furnishing the logistics to facilitate the work accomplished by the many tenant units and activities. The Army

Medical Department considers Fort Detrick the free world's leading microbiological containment research campus. The current medical technology explosion is attributable in part to the laboratory safety equipment and procedures first developed at the installation after 1943, when the post first opened. Fort Detrick and its Army Health Services Command installation trace their roots to the small municipal airport that became known as Detrick Field in the 1930s. The first military presence at this 1,200-acre site was the 104th Observation Squadron of the Maryland National Guard, which set up its first summer camp here in 1931.

CAMP DRUID HILL PARK. In August 1861 the 21st Indiana Infantry established headquarters at Fort McHenry, and a regimental detachment camped for a while in Baltimore's then partially landscaped Druid Hill Park.

EDGEWOOD ARSENAL. ABERDEEN PROVING GROUND.

CAMP EMORY. Located in Baltimore on a site adjacent to Camp Millington, Camp Emory was occupied by the 38th Massachusetts Volunteers from October 13 to November 9, 1862.

FORT FEDERAL HILL. Located in south Baltimore, Federal Hill has a long history. It was so named by Commander Joshua Barney on May 1, 1788, who at the same time named his ship the *Federalist* on the occasion of Maryland's ratification of the Federal Constitution. Apart from the Civil War years, the principal use of Federal Hill from 1795 to after 1900 was for the observation of ships nearing Baltimore's inner harbor.

The eminence, originally a clay mine, was first fortified by Union soldiers under General Benjamin Butler in May 1861. After its completion late the same year, Fort Federal Hill mounted about 50 heavy cannon capable of not only raking every approach to the hill, but also bombarding the inner harbor and much of the southern part of the city. The fort was garrisoned by a succession of regiments from 1862 until the end of the war when it was abandoned. It is now a Baltimore city park.

FORT FOOTE. Situated on Rosier's Bluff on the east bank of the Potomac River in Prince George's County, about six miles below Washington, it was a part of that city's ring of defenses during the Civil War. Construction on the water battery was begun in the spring of 1863 under the supervision of William H. Seward, Jr., the

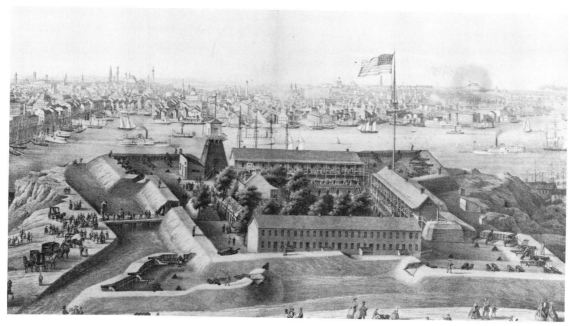

FORT FEDERAL HILL. A view of the fort as it looked in 1862, drawn by E. Sachse & Co. (Courtesy of The Peale Museum, Baltimore.)

24-year-old son of Lincoln's secretary of state. The post was officially designated Fort Foote on September 17 in the same year in honor of Rear Admiral A. H. Foote. The fort mounted eight 200-pounder Parrott guns and two 15-inch rifles. Discontinued on November 10, 1878, it is commemorated today by Fort Foote Park. In the woods to the left of the parking area are the concrete and stone gun emplacements and the remains of the reinforced earthworks, the best-preserved of all the Civil War defensive works surrounding Washington, the only one still retaining its original armament.

FORT FRANKLIN. FORT SUMNER.

FORT FREDERICK. Located southeast of Big Pool in Washington County, within the grounds of Fort Frederick State Park, this mid-eighteenth century British-built stone fort, featuring a massive arrangement of 17-foot-high walls, is today one of the nation's most perfectly preserved defenses dating from the French and Indian War. In 1754, when England and France went to war over their colonial possessions in North America, the British colony of Maryland became involved in the conflict.

Throughout the long years of the French and Indian War, Indian hostiles allied to the French raided frontier settlements, committing devastating depredations, killing and capturing English settlers. In 1756 Governor Horatio Sharpe prevailed upon the Maryland Assembly to appropriate funds to further English defensive measures. Part of the monies was devoted to erecting a strong fortification on North (now

called Fairview) Mountain. The governor named the fort for Frederick Calvert, Lord Baltimore.

Fort Frederick and a chain of smaller forts protected the Maryland frontier until 1758, when English forces captured French Fort Duquesne at the Forks of the Ohio (modern Pittsburgh) and terminated hostilities for the most part in the middle Atlantic colonies. In 1759 and 1760, English regulars and American provincial troops captured other important French strongholds, including Quebec and Montreal. By terms of the Treaty of Paris in 1763, France ceded her North American empire to Great Britain. A variety of troops served at Fort Frederick. Maryland provincial regulars, known as the Maryland Forces, constituted the primary garrison. They were augmented from time to time by militia units, troops

FORT FREDERICK. (Courtesy of the Maryland Forest and Park Services.)

from neighboring colonies, and by elements of the 60th Regiment of Foot, the "Royal Americans."

The ink was not yet dry on the Treaty of Paris when Ottawa Chief Pontiac forged a massive Indian confederation to oppose the English. About 700 settlers and a force of militiamen found protection within Fort Frederick's stone walls. Pontiac's Rebellion was shortly put down and peace returned to the frontier. A dozen years later, the Americans declared rebellion against their English cousins in the War for Independence. In 1777 the Continental Congress reactivated Fort Frederick as a prisoner of war camp, incarcerating British and Hessian soldiers and sailors. Colonel Moses Rawlings was its commander, and he had great difficulties providing adequate food, shelter, and security for the prisoners, even resorting to hiring out a number of them to local farmers as laborers.

In 1791 the state of Maryland sold the fort. From then until 1922, when the state bought it back, the area around the fort was farmed. During the Civil War, troops of the 1st Maryland Infantry (Federal) occupied the fort to protect the vital Baltimore and Ohio Railroad and the Chesapeake and Ohio Canal, and fought off a brief attack by Confederate raiders on Christmas Day, 1861. In the 1920s and 1930s, the State of Maryland initiated development of the present park. During the Great Depression of the 1930s, a company of men of the Civilian Conservation Corps (CCC) was assigned to reconstruct the fort's stone walls and locate the foundations of the original interior buildings.

FREDERICK BARRACKS (*Hessian Barracks*). Erected at Frederick in compliance with an enactment passed by the Maryland Assembly in 1777, these barracks were originally intended "to remove as soon as may be the Necessity of quartering Troops in private Houses." The law in part stipulated that a proper barracks be erected "in or near Frederick-Town . . . of plain and Strong Brick or Stone Work, with a Block house at each Corner, and ditched and palisaded in, sufficient for the Reception of two compleat Battalions with their Officers" (Lois B. McCauley, *Historical Prints*, p. 175). They were first used, however, to house the prisoners of war from General John Burgoyne's army, which had surrendered at Saratoga in 1777. They arrived in November 1780 and were imprisoned until July 1781. The second contingent of prisoners of war to arrive were soldiers of the German regiments that surrendered with Cornwallis's army at Yorktown. They were held from October 1781 until March 1783 when peace was officially

declared. Later the barracks were occupied by a regiment of the Potomac Home Brigade Infantry, Maryland Volunteers. Known locally as the Hessian Barracks, one of the limestone barracks buildings still stands on the grounds of the Maryland School for the Deaf in Frederick.

GARRISON FORT. This granite blockhouse-fort located near Pikeville in present Baltimore County was built by the Maryland authorities at the head of a branch of Jones Falls, now known as Slaughterhouse Run, which flows into the Patapsco River. The fortification, which is still standing near Garrison Forest, is about half a mile east of the present Garrison Road. Both were named after the garrison, or fort, which was probably erected in 1698.

CAMP GLENBURNIE. A temporary World War I tent camp, it was established on the Naval Rifle Range at Glenburnie, eight miles southeast of Baltimore, to accommodate the overflow of troops of the Corps of Engineers from Camp Laurel.

HESSIAN BARRACKS. FREDERICK BARRACKS.

CAMP (CANTONMENT) HICKS. A temporary Civil War post, it was located in or near the town of Frederick.

CAMP HEINTZELMAN. The principal Civil War encampment in the Poolesville area during the winter of 1862–63, it was occupied by General Samuel P. Heintzelman's 3rd Corps consisting of the 10th Vermont Infantry, 39th Massachusetts Infantry, 10th Massachusetts Artillery Battery, and part of the 11th New York Cavalry. Another regiment in this brigade, the 14th New Hampshire Infantry, was encamped southeast of Poolesville on the Gott Farm.

CAMP HOFFMAN. LAFAYETTE BARRACKS.

CAMP HOFFMAN. Located at the southern extremity of St. Mary's County on Point Lookout at the juncture of the Potomac River and Chesapeake Bay, it was the site of a developing summer resort just prior to the Civil War. In 1862 Federal authorities leased the property and built Hammond General Hospital with its 15 buildings arranged as spokes of a wheel connected at their inner ends by a circular corridor. On July 20, 1863, soon after the Battle of Gettysburg, a prisoner of war depot was begun on land adjoining the Army hospital. Officially named Camp Hoffman, probably for Colonel William A.

Hoffman, commissioner general of prisoners, it consisted in the main of two large rectangular compounds surrounded by heavily-guarded stockades, capable of holding 10,000 prisoners of war. Although much reduced by erosion, the hospital and prisoner compound area is now incorporated within a Maryland state park.

FORT HOLABIRD. Reportedly first opened in 1917 and officially established in March 1918 as a Quartermaster Department camp, it is located in the southeast corner of Baltimore, in the middle of an industrial neighborhood, and was named for Brigadier General Samuel Beckley Holabird, quartermaster general 1883–86. On August 1, 1942, the installation was transferred to the Ordnance Department and renamed the Holabird Ordnance Depot. Effective September 17, 1943, it was transferred to the Signal Corps and redesignated the Holabird Signal Depot. It was renamed Camp Holabird on July 31, 1947. Later upgraded to fort status, the post is now home of the U.S. Army Intelligence School and Counter Intelligence Records Facility.

FORT HOLLINGSWORTH. A small redoubt mounting a few small cannon, this fort was constructed during the War of 1812 in the spring of 1813 by the local residents in the area of Elk Landing, a village on the Elk River in Cecil County. After the British burned Frenchtown in late April 1813, they attempted to reach Elkton by water, but the guns at Fort Defiance about a mile further south on Elk Neck drove them back. The British then made an attempt to approach from the other side of the river, but Fort Hollingsworth's guns manned by militiamen forced them into retreat. The fort was named for the Hollingsworth family, several generations of which owned large tracts of land along the river and conducted a number of commercial enterprises.

FORT HORN. Located near Horn Point in the Eastport area of Annapolis and occupying the site on which the first civil war on American soil took place on March 25, 1655, Fort Horn was erected in June 1776 when the Council of Safety appropriated £5,900 to fortify the city. The plans for defense included the placing of obstructions in the river to prevent the threat of enemy men-of-war. Fort Horn was refortified during the War of 1812. No remains of the fort survive, and it is suspected that its site is now submerged.

FORT HOWARD. Located 17 miles below Baltimore, this post on the Patapsco River at North Point, so named by ship Captain Robert North in

1793, was established on June 6, 1899, when Battery E, 4th Artillery, arrived from Fort Monroe, Virginia, in compliance with Special Orders No. 127, Department of the East. On April 4, 1900, the reservation was designated Fort Howard in honor of Colonel John Eager Howard, Baltimore philantropist, distinguished soldier of the Maryland Continental Line during the Revolution, and a governor of Maryland for one term. In 1902 when six reinforced concrete coastal batteries were erected at Fort Howard, they were named in honor of famous Marylanders: Francis Scott Key, Colonel Davis Harris, Brigadier General John Stricker, Judge Joseph N. Nicholson, Lieutenant Levi Clagett, and Dr. Jesse W. Lazear. Called the "Bulldog at Baltimore's Gate," Fort Howard was the city's principal coast artillery defense. In 1917 the fort's garrison was doubled and its men were put on a wartime basis. To keep in practice, the gunners drilled by mock firing at steamers, the only craft sighted. On August 2, 1940, Fort Howard was transferred to the Veterans Administration, which constructed a hospital facility on the site.

FORT HOYLE. This post was established in October 1922 near Edgewood, about 32 miles northwest of Baltimore, in order to meet the need for an artillery range within what was then the Third Corps area. It was named in honor of Brigadier General Eli D. Hoyle, an artillerist, who had died a short time before the opening of the fort. Fort Hoyle was located on Gunpowder Neck between the estuaries of the Gunpowder and Back rivers. As the peninsula was divided in 1917 when the Neck was given to Edgewood Arsenal, which occupies its base and tip, Fort Hoyle used its middle and tip. The post was discontinued in 1940.

CAMP KELSEY. Early in November 1861, when the 10th Maine Infantry left their Patterson Park encampment in Baltimore for Relay House, Company F, commanded by Captain William Knowlton, was detailed to guard the trackage of the Baltimore and Ohio Railroad near Annapolis Junction where Camp Kelsey was established.

FORT KENT. Captain William Claiborne established a colony and trading post on the southern end of Kent Island in present Queen Anne's County in 1631 and soon put his men to work strengthening and fortifying it, to protect his colonists from the whites under Lord Baltimore as well as the Indians. About three years later, Claiborne began another settlement north of his fort near Craney Creek, which he called

"Craford" (Crayford), where he erected what became known as "Craford fort." Fort Kent and "Craford fort" seem to have existed until the residents of Kent Island submitted to Lord Baltimore's authority about 1647.

REDOUBT KIRBY. FORT SUMNER.

LAFAYETTE BARRACKS (*Camp Hoffman; Camp Lafayette Square*). Baltimore's Lafayette Square, dedicated as a public square in 1856 and surrounded by an iron fence, was bought by the city in 1857 for use as a park. Here, in September 1861, Colonel William L. Schley established Camp Hoffman (also known as Camp Lafayette Square), named for Genry W. Hoffman, prominent pro-Union Baltimore citizen, as a recruiting center for the Public Guard Regiment, a name he later changed to the 5th Regiment of Maryland Volunteers. In 1862 barracks were built to replace the tents, and the camp was renamed Lafayette Barracks. The upgraded Federal post served as headquarters for the 3rd Maryland Veteran Volunteers and was occupied by a succession of regimental units. After the war the site was restored to a park.

CAMP LAFAYETTE SQUARE. LAFAYETTE BARRACKS.

CAMP LAUREL. A temporary Corps of Engineers mobilization point and training encampment located on the Laurel Race Track, a half-mile from the town of Laurel in Prince George's County, it was established in 1918 to accept the overflow of troops from Camp Meade and house

FORT MCHENRY. (Courtesy of the Smithsonian Institution.)

them in State Fair buildings and tents. Camp Laurel was closed January 6, 1919.

FORT LEONARD WOOD. FORT (GEORGE G.) MEADE.

FORT LININGER. A temporary Union fortified position established in 1863, it was located at Oldtown, about 300 yards from the site of Cresap's Fort, in Allegany County, and occupied by elements of the Pennsylvania Volunteers.

CAMP LYON. A temporary encampment established in 1861 or 1862 near Poolesville, Montgomery County, it was occupied by elements of the 42nd New York Infantry, with Lieutenant Colonel James J. Mooney in command.

CAMP MCCLELLAND. McKIM BARRACKS.

FORT MCHENRY (*Fort Whetstone*). Fort McHenry at Baltimore, a National Monument and Historic Shrine, occupies a preeminent position in America's history. Here, where the flag flies day and night, the Stars and Stripes has a special significance for Americans. In the midst of bursting bombs and blazing rockets during the War of 1812, inspiration compelled Francis Scott Key to write "The Star-Spangled Banner."

The tip of a narrow peninsula, called Whetstone Point, was considered of great strategic value for the defense of Baltimore as early as the Revolutionary War. The peninsula separated the Northwest Branch and the Ferry Branch of the Patapsco River (now Northwest Branch is called Northwest Harbor, and Ferry Branch is part of the main estuary of the Patapsco River). During the Revolutionary War, the Provincial Convention of Maryland directed the Council of Safety Committee to provide for the defense of Baltimore. A group of local patriots agreed to undertake the project, and on March 16, 1776, they reported to the Council that "Our fort at Whetstone is ready to mount 8 guns and we shall use every exertion to expedite it." Although the fort never came under enemy fire, it deterred the British cruisers that operated in Chesapeake Bay from molesting Baltimore. In 1781 Fort Whetstone, as the defense works were then called, consisted of a battery, magazine, military hospital, and barracks. The scattered ordnance returns indicate that the types and numbers of cannon emplaced at the fort changed frequently.

The successful conclusion of the Revolutionary War and the adoption of the Federal Constitution did not bring the expected freedom from affairs in Europe. Relations with England

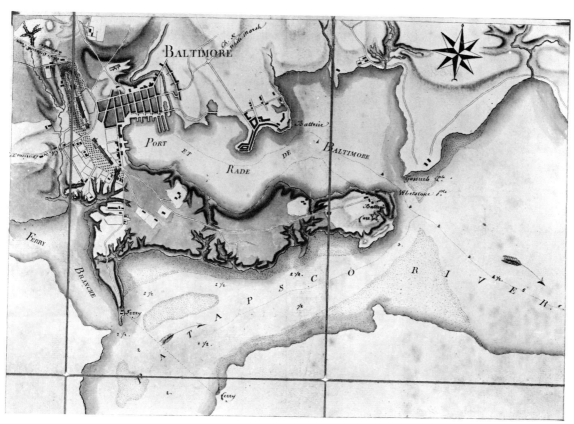

FORT MCHENRY. Map drawn by the French in 1781, showing Fort Whetstone and other Baltimore fortifications. (Courtesy of the Library of Congress.)

were strained, and both nations were frequently on the verge of armed conflict. Alarmed, the Maryland House of Delegates in 1793 passed a resolution authorizing the governor of the state, upon application of "the President, to grant permission to the Federal Government to erect a fort, arsenal or other military works" on Whetstone Point. Congress, in March of the following year, enacted legislation to fortify the principal seaports of the young republic, and included in the funds appropriated for this purpose was the sum of $4,225.44 for the erection of a 20-gun battery and small redoubt to defend Baltimore.

John Jacob Ulrich Rivardi, an experienced artilleryman and military engineer, was directed by the secretary of war to visit the city and draw up plans for a permanent harbor defense. The present star fort was located on and to the rear of the Revolutionary works. A report of the secretary of war, dated 1806, mentions that Fort McHenry was a "regular fortification of mason work, with batteries, magazines, and barracks, erected principally in years 1798, 1799, 1800." Shortly before the turn of the century, James McHenry, secretary of war and a resident of Baltimore, was honored by the bestowal of his name on the fort.

From its completion to the outbreak of the War of 1812, the history of the fort is routine and uneventful. It would be difficult to exagger-

ate the military unpreparedness of the United States at that time. The country was gravely deficient in arms and equipment. The Army was small, disorganized, badly trained, and lacking leadership. The Navy, consisting of a handful of ships, was asked to contest a rival that was the undisputed master of the seven seas. Since the bulk of its army was committed to Wellington's Peninsular Campaign in Europe, England in the beginning was compelled to rely principally upon its navy to vanquish the United States. In the summer of 1814, the enemy fleet in Chesapeake Bay was augmented and placed under the command of Vice Admiral Alexander Cochrane. In addition, Napoleon's capitulation permitted the transfer of four veteran regiments from the Continent to cooperate with the fleet.

At Bladensburg, the British met an American army of raw militia and put it to rout. The Battle of Bladensburg represents the nadir of American military effort during the War of 1812. That evening the British troops entered Washington. After a brief period of occupation, during which the federal buildings and a number of other structures were destroyed, the British troops boarded their transports, primed to take on their next target—Baltimore.

Unlike Washington, however, Baltimore was not defenseless. Under the leadership of Major General Samuel Smith, it had been preparing for the expected British attack. To defend the city, Smith had at his disposal a force of 12,000, consisting chiefly of Maryland, Pennsylvania, and Virginia militia, some regular Army units, and about 400 sailors. He managed to secure arms, ammunition, and equipment from the secretary of war and the governor of the state. He directed the repair of old batteries and the erection of new ones.

The British believed that the fortified eastern defenses of Baltimore could be taken without difficulty. According to their adopted plan, the city would be captured by a combined land and sea assault from the east. On September 12, about 4,000 British troops landed at North Point and marched toward Baltimore. But they found opposition so determined that they did not continue the attack, and decided to wait for the bombardment of Fort McHenry and the arrival of the fleet in the Northwest Branch where it could support the land forces. At dawn the next day, 16 British warships dropped anchor in the river about two miles below the fort. Although Fort McHenry's 36-pounder cannon could not hit the ships, they did prevent the fleet from coming nearer, and at two miles the British guns could not be aimed with accuracy. Two of the buildings within the fort were damaged during the bombardment, but there were few casualties and the heavy guns of the fort's outer battery were never silenced.

Shortly after midnight on the 14th, the enemy sent a landing force up the Ferry (now Middle) Branch of the Patapsco to attack the city from the south. Eleven of the 20 boats, however, mistakenly started up the Northwest Branch and were forced to turn about when they were shelled by a battery on the shore opposite Fort McHenry. The other 9 craft continued up the Ferry Branch but were forced to withdraw when shelled by the guns of Fort Covington, located about one and a half miles west of Fort McHenry. These failures combined with the fort's resistance decisively defeated the British and they withdrew.

Francis Scott Key witnessed the bombardment from the British fleet to which he and an American lieutenant had been sent to effect the release of a prisoner of war. The three men observed the action during the day of the 13th, but after darkness fell they felt that since the bombardment was continuing, it signified that the defenders were holding out. When dawn arrived, a heavy mist at first clouded the view, but eventually the sun broke through to reveal that the American flag over Fort McHenry was still flying. Later in the morning the three Americans were deposited on shore. Key went to an inn, probably the Indian Queen at Hanover and Baltimore streets, where he revised the notes he had penned during the night into a poem entitled "The Star-Spangled Banner."

On September 1, 1836, Fort McHenry was temporarily discontinued and turned over to the Corps of Engineers for repair and renovation. The post was reestablished by the 2nd Dragoons in May 1839. At the outbreak of the Civil War, the fort was judged obsolete as a defense, and the Federal government used it as a prisoner of war facility, especially for political dissidents. After the fort was garrisoned by infantryment from 1867 to 1900, it was apparently intermittently used by artillery units, probably for training exercises. Special Orders No. 160, Eastern Division, July 13, 1912, directed that Fort McHenry be finally abandoned by its last occupants, a company of the 141st Coast Artillery. In 1915 the city of Baltimore leased the reservation for use as a park, but during World War I the government reclaimed the fort and converted it into a hospital. In 1925 Congress designated old Fort McHenry and the acreage surrounding it a National Park, and in 1939 the site was named a National Monument and Historic Shrine.

MCKIM BARRACKS (*Camp McClelland*). The 6th Michigan Infantry established Camp McClelland, a post of tents, during the early summer of 1861 on the grounds of the McKim Mansion in Baltimore. The installation was located south of Greenmount Cemetery in the general area bounded by present Preston, Valley, Chase, and Homewood streets. In the early fall of the same year, probably in September, the camp of tents was replaced by barracks erected by the 6th Michigan and occupied by the 111th Pennsylvania Volunteers commanded by Colonel Matthew Schlaudecker. The post was then renamed McKim Barracks. In 1862 the barracks were converted into a 300-bed hospital. The McKim Mansion, situated on the right of the compound, was later used as a powder magazine. Directly in front of the post was a curved, sodded earthwork defended by three heavy artillery guns. The earthwork occupied the site of the post's former parade ground between John (now Preston) and Biddle streets. The hospital buildings were sold at auction in November 1865, and the earthwork was removed in 1869.

FORT MADISON (*[Old] Fort Nonsense*). Fort Madison was funded by Congress and built to government specifications in 1808–9. It was a masonry fort, mounting approximately 13 guns, with an elliptical face and several casemates built into the forward curtain wall. The fort was placed close to Severn River's shoreline and was intended to supplement the protection of Annapolis Harbor already offered by Fort Severn across the river. The fort was apparently abandoned shortly after the War of 1812. Government plans to refurbish Fort Madison in the early 1820s were never carried out. A notation on a hand-drawn map appearing in a locally printed book indicates that the fort was "dismantled" by 1832. The remains of the fort were sketched in 1850, showing that most of the masonry and brick had eroded away. The remains of the fort, according to an article in the *Naval Institute Proceedings* periodical, were still visible from the Naval Academy in 1932, but later removed during the upsurge of construction at the Naval Station during World War II. Still evident on higher ground behind Fort Madison, near the Commandant's Quarters of the North Severn Naval Station, is the site of a circular earthwork, approximately 80 feet in diameter, which is identified on a U.S. Coast and Geodetic Survey map of 1840 as "Old Fort Nonsense." This was probably an outwork of Fort Madison.

FORT MAIDSTONE. See: FORT MAIDSTONE in West Virginia chapter.

FORT MANSFIELD. A Civil War defense of Washington, Fort Mansfield was a connecting link between Forts Reno and Sumner and located near the Potomac River about two miles above the Chain Bridge in Montgomery County. The fort was named in honor of General Joseph K. F. Mansfield, who accomplished a great deal toward initiating and constructing Washington's defenses, only to be mortally wounded on September 17, 1862, at Antietam. The fort's location was centered in the area of Massachusetts Avenue and Worthington Drive.

FORT MARSHALL. Located on Murray's Hill (now occupied by the Sacred Heart Church), the center of today's Highlandtown, east of Baltimore's Patterson Park, Fort Marshall was built over a period of two months in 1861 by the 7th Maine Infantry. The large earthwork defense commanded the railroad to the south and the road to Philadelphia to the north. The fort, replacing the temporary tent camp formerly there, was garrisoned in 1862 by the 5th New York Artillery.

CAMP MEADE. FORT (GEORGE G.) MEADE.

FORT (GEORGE G.) MEADE (*Camp Meade; Fort Leonard Wood*). Named in honor of Major General George G. Meade, who commanded the Union forces at Gettysburg, Camp Meade was established on June 23, 1917, seven miles from the town of Laurel as a training center for World War I troops. General Orders No. 3, War Department, March 2, 1928, declared the post a permanent installation and renamed it Fort Leonard Wood because of the existence of Camp Meade in South Dakota. General Orders No. 6, War Department, March 5, 1929, redesignated it Fort George G. Meade. Since it was established, the fort has continued in military use and, greatly expanded, it was used as a training center for World War II troops. Fort Meade is still an active Army installation.

CAMP MILLINGTON. This Civil War tent encampment, probably established in 1861, was located east of Gwynns Falls in the area of Brunswick Street and Millington Avenue in Baltimore. It was occupied by the 128th New York Volunteers.

FORT MOUNT PLEASANT. FORT CUMBERLAND.

(OLD) FORT NONSENSE. FORT MADISON.

FORT NO. 1. The threats posed by the Confederacy's northern campaign in 1863 worried both the military and citizens in Baltimore. In response, Major General Robert C. Schenck ordered that the city's defenses be additionally strengthened by erecting fortifications, earthworks, and barricades at all the strategic approaches to the city. A numbered series of forts was erected, including Fort No. 1 located on the western edge of the city. Described as a six-sided earthwork surrounded by a ditch or moat, with 12 fieldpieces in its interior aimed toward the embrasures, the fort occupied an area on the north side of West Baltimore Street between the Jarvis Hospital and Smallwood Street. Fort No. 1 was removed on April 16, 1869, in compliance with a resolution of the City Council.

CAMP OBSERVATION. One of the Union army's points of defense near Poolesville on the western boundary of Montgomery County was Camp Observation, which overlooked White's Ferry at a bend in the Potomac River.

CAMP PAROLE. A large installation located about two miles west of Annapolis, Camp Parole was established in late 1862 or early 1863 as a holding facility for Union prisoners of war who had been released to Union authorities by the

Confederacy. It was designed to keep these men under military discipline until they were either reassigned to other Union units or allowed to return home. The camp also included a hospital complex of five buildings. About 70,000 soldiers passed through Camp Parole, but there were never more than about 8,000 at one time.

CAMP PATTERSON PARK. PATTERSON PARK BARRACKS.

PATTERSON PARK BARRACKS (*Camp Washburn; Camp Patterson Park*). In 1827 Baltimore resident William Patterson made a gift to the city of a plot of ground to be used as a public park. The tract included a portion of the earthworks that were constructed in 1814 to bolster Baltimore's defenses shortly before the British fleet's bombardment of Fort McHenry on September 13–14, 1814. In August 1861, the 7th Maine Infantry established the first Civil War encampment in the park and named it Camp Washburn. In October these first troops, ordered to the east to build Fort Marshall at today's Highlandtown, were replaced by those of the 10th Maine Infantry, who left Patterson Park a month later for Camp Relay House on the Baltimore and Ohio Railroad six miles away. The camp was then occupied in 1862 by the 110th New York Volunteers, who temporarily renamed the post Camp Patterson Park. The post's tent complex was dismantled to be replaced by a quadrangle of barracks, most probably erected by the New York troops, and designated Patterson Park Barracks. The post was located on what was then known as Hampstead Hill, on Patterson Park Avenue at the terminuses of Pratt and Lombard streets.

FORT PENDLETON. Erected during the Civil War to guard the bridge where the Northwestern Turnpike crossed over the Potomac River into Virginia (now West Virginia), this wooden fortification was located near Gorman on Route 50 in the extreme southwest corner of Garrett County. Fort Pendleton burned down in 1888.

CAMP RELAY HOUSE. A Civil War encampment surrounded by a fortified breastworks, called Camp Relay House, was established on the Baltimore and Ohio Railroad about six miles from Baltimore.

CAMP RICHMOND. Located three miles west of Annapolis near today's town of Parole, Camp Richmond was first used to house troops scheduled for embarkation to war fronts in the South. It was then later operated as a holding facility for paroled Union prisoners of war. Camp Richmond and Camp Parole, another such facility, adjoined each other, with only the railroad trackage separating them. During the war Annapolis was one of the Union's more important ports of embarkation and war matériels depot.

FORT RIPLEY (*Fort Sumner*).

FORT RITCHIE (*Camp Albert C. Ritchie*). Land for the installation was purchased in 1926 by the state of Maryland to be used as a training site for the Maryland National Guard, which constructed the original stone buildings on the post. The facility was named Camp Albert C. Ritchie in honor of Maryland's governor. In 1942 Camp Ritchie was taken over by the War Department and established as a Military Intelligence Training Center, which was deactivated in 1945. In 1951 the Army reactivated the post and changed its name to Fort Ritchie. Its primary mission was to provide support to the Alternate Joint Communications Center.

In 1964 the post was redesignated as a Class II installation under the U.S. Army Strategic Communications Command, and in 1971 the USASTRATCOM-CONUS headquarters was relocated from Alexandria, Virginia, to Fort Ritchie. In 1973 the command's name was changed to the U.S. Army Communications Command, and the USACC-CONUS mission was expanded to encompass the management of communications and electronics functions at approximately 120 agencies and activities throughout the continental United States, Alaska, Panama, and Puerto Rico. On July 1, 1975, USACC-CONUS was renamed the 7th Signal Command, which uses Fort Ritchie as its headquarters at present. The post is adjacent to the town of Cascade in the Catoctin Mountains, just south of the Pennsylvania border.

RODGERS BASTION. A formidable earthwork, it was constructed by a corps of volunteers on Hampstead Hill on the eastern edge of Baltimore prior to the unsuccessful British bombardment of Fort McHenry on September 13–14, 1814. Part of the bastion's site is now incorporated within historic Patterson Park. (See: PATTERSON PARK BARRACKS.)

CAMP RODMAN. A temporary World War II encampment near Aberdeen.

CAMP ROSE HILL. A Civil War encampment located at Cumberland in Allegany County, it was occupied by the 11th Indiana Infantry commanded by Colonel Lew Wallace. The site is located at 512 Dunbar Drive in Cumberland.

FORT ST. INIGOES. FORT ST. MARY'S.

FORT ST. MARY'S (*Fort St. Inigoes*). In 1632 Sir George Calvert, the first Lord Baltimore, a devout Catholic and a favorite of King James I, received a large royal grant making him the proprietor of a province that extended from the Potomac on the south to the 40th parallel on the north, encompassing the northern half of Chesapeake Bay. The king named the new province Maryland in honor of the queen, Henrietta Maria. George Calvert, however, died before the grant was consummated, and the charter was issued to his son, Cecilius Calvert, the second Lord Baltimore. Two small vessels, the *Ark* and the *Dove*, were fitted out to transport the two or three hundred prospective settlers, and two of Lord Baltimore's brothers accompanied them. One of the brothers, Leonard Calvert, was made governor of the province.

The first landing of the colonists on Maryland soil, after the *Ark* and the *Dove* entered the Potomac River, took place on St. Clement's (now Blakiston) Island. Here, on March 25, 1634, they celebrated mass, erected a cross, and "with devotion tooke solemn possession of the Country." The place finally selected for their first settlement was on the eastern bank of the St. George's (now the St. Mary's) River on the peninsula (today's St. Mary's County) jutting into Chesapeake Bay. Immediately after landing, they began the erection of a fort, which was completed in a month and mounted with ordnance. The fort was an elaborate defense, consisting of a palisade 120 yards square with four flanks (blockhouses or bastions). The fort's primary purpose was to serve as a protection against the Indians. At first probably some if not all of the colonists lived within its walls. The fort held the first meetings of the Maryland Assembly.

In 1644, after 10 years, there was little reason for Governor Calvert's colonists to maintain Fort St. Mary's, since the danger from the Indians had decreased as the colony grew in size. Another fortification, however, was required to satisfy a different need, that of collecting customs or duties from visiting trading vessels. The mouth of St. Inigoes Creek, about two and a half miles south of St. Mary's, was found to be ideal for the purpose. Fort St. Inigoes was erected on the extreme end of the right bank of the creek and garrisoned by six men who were provided with the necessary provisions and ammunition. An expert gunner was also posted at the fort and

had the primary duty of maintaining the guns there. Thomas Greene, the second governor of Maryland, continued the practice of adequately providing for the garrison. The fort also served as a refuge and was at times the place where some of the meetings of the Assembly and Provincial Court were held.

FORT SEVERN. Its site long incorporated within the grounds of the U.S. Naval Academy at Annapolis, Fort Severn was constructed on Windmill Point on the south side of the Severn River in 1808, some months after the search-and-seizure outrage committed against the American frigate *Chesapeake* by the British frigate *Leopard* just off the Virginia Capes. On the site of the fort was the former family residence of Walter Dulany, from whose son's heirs the ground was purchased by the government. Fort Severn was a cylindrical work enclosed by a 14-foot-high stone wall, its parapet sodded. Within the enclosure of about 100 feet in diameter was a platform about 3 feet lower than the parapet upon which eight guns were mounted *en barbette*, that is with their muzzles exposed above the top of the wall. In the center of the fort was a brick-built magazine and, shorewards outside the wall, stood the hot-shot furnace.

Although the British fleet sailed up the Chesapeake in 1814 and bombarded Fort McHenry, the presence of Fort Severn (then inadequately manned) seems to have deterred a British attack against Annapolis. The fort was still garrisoned by a company of the Corps of Artillery in 1845 when Secretary of the Navy George Bancroft secured the transfer, formally consummated on August 15, of Fort Severn from the War Department for the establishment of the U.S. Naval School, later the Naval Academy. The structures transferred with the reservation consisted of the fort, the commandant's residence, officers' quarters, enlisted men's barracks, a hospital, a blacksmith's shop, and a bakery. The original eight acres of the reservation roughly corresponds to the part of the Naval Academy grounds lying between the Chapel and the bay side of Bancroft Hall.

FORT SIMMONS. Located in Montgomery County, about three miles from the Chain Bridge, this Civil War defense of Washington was built during November–December 1861, mounting eight guns, and named in honor of Colonel Seneca G. Simmons of the 5th Pennsylvania Reserves, who aided in the fort's construction. Colonel Simmons was killed in action at the Battle of White Oak Swamp, Glendale, Virginia,

June 30, 1862. The site of Fort Simmons is at the intersection of Berkleley and Crescent streets, just east of Westmoreland Circle. Battery Simmons, an outwork of the fort, was located at the corner of Allen and Bayard streets.

FORT SMALLWOOD. Named in honor of General William Smallwood, the fort was built in 1900 on Rock Point, a promontory projecting into the Patapsco River in Anne Arundel County, on a 100-acre tract acquired by the government in 1896. Opposite and across the mouth of the river is Fort Howard. In 1926 the government sold the reservation property to Baltimore for use as a public park, which incorporates the still standing fortification.

CAMP SOMERSET. A temporary World War II encampment, Camp Somerset was established at or near Westover in Somerset County.

CAMP STANTON. A Civil War encampment established by Federal troops in 1863, serving through 1864, Camp Stanton was located at or near the town of Benedict on the Patuxent River in Charles County. The 7th Infantry Colored Troops, organized at Baltimore in September and October 1863, was mustered into service at Camp Stanton on November 12, 1863. The 9th Infantry Colored Troops was organized at the camp during the same month.

CAMP STONE. This temporary Civil War encampment located near Poolesville in Montgomery County was the 1861–62 winter quarters of the 1st Minnesota Infantry.

FORT SUMNER (*Fort Franklin; Redoubt Kirby; Fort Alexander; Redoubt Davis; Fort Ripley; Redoubt Cross*). This formidable military work, formed of a combination of three former independent forts, was located northwest of the Receiving Reservoir and overlooked the Potomac River at Little Falls, two or three miles above the Chain Bridge, in Montgomery County. In July 1861 three forts were erected in Montgomery County—Forts Ripley, Alexander, and Franklin. They were located northwest of the Maryland approach to the Chain Bridge and intended to protect both the bridge and the Receiving Reservoir of the Washington water system. Fort Ripley was named for Brigadier General James W. Ripley, then chief of ordnance; Fort Franklin was named for Brigadier General William B. Franklin; and Fort Alexander was named for Colonel Barton S. Alexander, who superintended the construction of the three forts.

In the spring of 1863, these forts were combined into a massive work known as Fort Sumner, named in honor of Major General Edwin Vose Sumner, leader of the 2nd Corps, who died on March 21, 1863. The perimeter of the fort was 843 yards and it mounted 25 guns. In addition, an outwork called Battery Alexander was constructed on a high bluff overlooking the Potomac to the left of Fort Sumner; this battery mounted four 24-pounder smoothbore guns. Later in the war, the forts were renamed: Fort Ripley became Redoubt Cross; Fort Franklin became Redoubt Kirby; and Fort Alexander became Redoubt Davis. These defenses were practically unchanged for the remainder of the war.

FORT TONOLOWAY. Located just west of the town of Hancock in Washington County, 25-acre Fort Tonoloway State Park commemorates the site of a short-lived French and Indian War frontier defense. Fort Tonoloway, a stockaded blockhouse, was built in 1755 on Evan Shelby's property in then Frederick County, shortly after General Braddock's defeat near Fort Duquesne. The fort was abandoned in 1756–57 after the substantial stone-built Fort Frederick had been completed.

CAMP WALLACE. A temporary Civil War encampment located at Cambridge in Dorchester County, it was occupied by the Eastern Shore Regiment, a Federal unit of Marylanders, which was organized there.

FORT WARBURTON. FORT WASHINGTON.

CAMP WASHBURN. PATTERSON PARK BARRACKS.

FORT WASHINGTON (*Fort Warburton*). The precursor of Fort Washington was Fort Warburton, built in 1808 and located on what was then known as Digges' Point (opposite Mount Vernon, Virginia) where Piscataway Creek joins the Potomac, in Prince George's County about 12 miles from the nation's Capitol. The defense was an enclosed, semielliptical work of stone and brick masonry, mounting 13 heavy guns. It was defended in the rear by an octagonal tower of masonry mounting 6 cannon, a brick magazine, and a one-company brick-built barracks.

In August 1814 the British fleet came up the Potomac. Fort Warburton alone guarded the water passage to Alexandria, Virginia and Washington. The fort's garrison consisted of 80 men commanded by Captain Samuel T. Dyson. The British squadron appeared before the fort on August 27, three days after Washington was captured by land forces. Dyson, instead of defending Fort Warburton from the waterfront, as was intended, blew up the fort's works and fled without firing a gun. Captain Dyson was later tried by court-martial and dismissed from the service. As a consequence of his dereliction, the British armada passed up the river unopposed and easily took Alexandria.

On August 31, 1815, after the close of the War of 1812, additional acreage was acquired from Thomas Digges, and a new fort, named for the nation's first president, was begun on the old fort site, now much enlarged. Fort Washington was designed by engineer Pierre Charles L'Enfant who drew up the plans for the nation's capital city. The new defense, constructed from 1815 to 1822–23, was described during the 1820s as an irregular-shaped work, its faces and flanks casemated, with a parapet length of 835 yards, planned for the mounting of 120 pieces of ordnance. The size of its garrison was projected during war for 800 men, for peace 100 men, and actual 55 men. On November 10, 1824, its garrison consisted of one company of the 3rd Artillery.

At the outbreak of the Civil War, Fort Washington was the only fort defending Washington. The fort was abandoned and reoccupied no less than four times between 1836 and 1872. It was regarrisoned on November 13, 1896, and became a part of the Coast Defenses of the Potomac. Between 1900 and 1904 the post was much improved and a number of new buildings were erected. In addition, eight batteries were constructed. From this period forward, the fort was continuously garrisoned and served during both world wars. Fort Washington was turned over to the Veterans Administration in August 1944, but that agency in 1946 relinquished the fort to the Department of the Interior.

FORT WHETSTONE. FORT MCHENRY.

WILL'S CREEK FORT. FORT CUMBERLAND.

CAMP WOOL (*Camp Andrew*). This Civil War site, including the confiscated property of Confederate Brigadier General George H. Steuart,

FORT WASHINGTON. (Courtesy of the National Park Service.)

was selected by Federal authorities at the beginning of the war because it commanded the city of Baltimore in all directions. It was first established and occupied by the 17th Massachusetts Regiment of Volunteers and named Camp Andrew for Massachusetts Governor John A. Andrew. It was bounded on the north by West Fayette Street and Fairmount (then Montrose) Avenue, on the east by Fulton Avenue, on the south by West Baltimore Street, and on the west by Smallwood Street. Later in 1861, the regiment's tents were replaced by a barracks quadrangle erected by the troops, with some of the buildings subsequently converted into hospital wards. In June 1862 Camp Andrew was renamed Camp Wool when it was occupied by the 7th Regiment, New York State Militia.

FORT WORTHINGTON. A Civil War defense of the city of Baltimore, Fort Worthington was erected by Federal troops and located on the heights northeast of the city for the purpose of guarding the Bel Air Road.

ACUSHNET FORT. There was a Revolutionary War fortification of some sort at Acushnet Harbor in Dartmouth, south of New Bedford, in 1776. The Massachusetts Legislature had provided for the 10 pieces of ordnance emplaced there.

CAMP ADAMS. A temporary Civil War mobilization center and training post at Quincy, it was established on July 5, 1861, by Cobb's Light Artillery after its organization. On August 8 they broke camp and, making stops en route, arrived at Baltimore, where the unit established Camp Andrew.

FORT ALLEN. FORT GLOUCESTER.

ALLERTON BATTERY. FORT REVERE.

ANDOVER GARRISONS. Under the Organization of 1644, there was one regiment of militia in each Massachusetts county, under the command of a sergeant-major. Essex County's chief officer was Daniel Denison of Ipswich. Twelve garrison houses were built in Andover in 1676 after the outbreak of King Philip's War. Four blockhouses were built on the Merrimack River about 1705, two of them in Andover. (See: GARRISON HOUSES.)

FORT ANDREW (*Gurnet Fort*). A resolution of the Massachusetts General Court, passed on June 3, 1776, provided that a fortification be erected by the towns of Plymouth, Duxbury, and Kingston at the Gurnet River at the entrance to Plymouth Harbor, with six guns (6- and 12-pounders) to be mounted. One of Massachusetts's two minor peninsulas, extending north and south into the sea between Scituate and Plymouth, extends far south along a great stretch of sand dunes that end at the Gurnet. The Pilgrims called the land "the gurnett's nose," apparently named after several similar headlands along the English Channel, so-called for the fish of that name caught along the Devonshire coast. The Plymouth (Gurnet) Lighthouse, 30 feet long, 20 feet high, and 15 feet wide with a "lanthorn" (lantern) at each end of the building, was first established there in 1768 by the Massachusetts Legislature.

During 1812–15 the fort was rebuilt and enlarged to accommodate 42-pounders. At the outbreak of the Civil War, the fort was once again renovated and heavily armed. It was then that it received the name Fort Andrew for the governor of Massachusetts. In 1869 Fort Andrew was ceded to the government, and in 1926 sold as surplus property.

Massachusetts

FORT ANDREWS. Located nine miles southeast of Boston at East Head on Peddock's Island, a mile south of Fort Warren, Fort Andrews was officially established in 1901 as a subpost of Fort Strong. Occupying an 88-acre tract acquired in 1898, the fort was named in honor of Brigadier General George Leonard Andrews, who was brevetted Major General of Volunteers in 1865 for meritorious service during the Federal campaign against Mobile and its defenses during the Civil War. During World War I, there were approximately 2,000 troops quartered at one time on Peddock's Island, most of them of the original 55th Regiment and its replacements. During World War II, Fort Andrews became headquarters for the 241st Regiment. In 1947 the installation was declared surplus to the needs of the Army. On November 22, 1957, Peddock's Island was sold for $35,000 to private investors for purposes of converting the property to recreational uses.

FORT ANN. FORT PICKERING.

FORT ANSON (*Fort at Pontoosack; Williams Garrison*). At the outbreak of the French and Indian War in 1754, the military district commander in western Massachusetts requested Colonel William Williams to erect a fort on or near the Housatonic River in the Pittsfield area, Berkshire County. Also referred to as the "Fort at Pontoosack" and Williams Garrison, it was apparently officially known as Fort Anson and built in September of that year. It was a 40-by-24-foot structure, with a gambrel roof and walls of 4-inch-thick white ash planking. An 8-foot-wide firing platform ran the perimeter of the building, with one of its angles or corners furnished with a flanker or blockhouse. Within was a 10-by-35-foot storehouse and a "soldiers' lodging-room."

APTUXET TRADING POST. The reproduction of this Plymouth Colony trading post is located near Shore Road in Bourne in present Barnstable County. The Pilgrims established three trading houses at a considerable distance from their home base at Plymouth: the first in 1627 at Aptuxet (Aptucxet) in today's town of Bourne, on the Cape Cod Canal; the second in 1628 on the Kennebec River at today's site of Augusta in Maine; and the third in 1635 on the Connecticut River, at present Windsor in Connecticut. The Bourne structure was described by contemporaries as "a house made of oak clapboards" with a boarded roof. Its site was excavated, the stone foundations uncovered, and all tangible evidence sifted by archaeologist Percival H. Lom-

bard, under whose direction the replica was constructed on its original site.

FORT ASHLEY. Fort Hill near Lake Onota in Pittsfield is the site of Fort Ashley, one of four colonial forts erected in the town. A blockhouse defense erected most probably during the summer of 1756, it soon attracted settlers, and a considerable community grew up around it.

FORT BAILEY. FORT WASHINGTON (Marblehead).

CAMP BANKS (*Camp Sutton; Camp Edmunds*). Winter Island at Salem was used for several years as a camping ground for the Massachusetts Volunteer Militia. The first occupation was in August 1853, when the 2nd Division established Camp Sutton (named for General William Sutton) and again in 1855. In September 1856 the 4th Brigade was encamped there in Camp Edmunds (named for Major General B. F. Edmunds). In August 1858 the 2nd Division occupied the field as Camp Banks (named for Major General Nathaniel Prentice Banks).

FORT BANKS. FORT GLOUCESTER.

FORT BANKS. This post was established in 1899 on land acquired during 1890–94 as the "Gun and Mortar Batteries," located one mile northeast of Winthrop at Grover's Cliff in Suffolk County. Known for a few months as Battery Winthrop, it was designated Fort Banks by General Orders No. 134, War Department, July 22, 1899, in honor of Major General Nathaniel Prentice Banks, U.S.V., who served with distinction during the Civil War. In 1902 the fort had an armament of sixteen 12-inch mortars manned by two companies of artillery, aggregating 218 men including 6 officers.

The last recorded instance of any big-gun firing at Fort Banks was in 1904, when in October of that year a gun squad of the 89th Coast Artillery ventured to fire a 12-inch mortar. The gun's lanyard was accidently pulled while the breech block was still partly open. The 800-pound projectile never left the muzzle but the breech block was completely blown off, causing 3 soldiers to suffer fatal injuries while 12 others were seriously hurt. It was most probably the worst practice firing disaster that ever occurred at any of the harbor's forts. Declared excess to Army needs on January 31, 1950, Fort Banks was placed in an inactive status on September 30, 1966.

CAMP BARTLETT. Located at Framingham, Camp Bartlett was a state encampment named in honor of Brigadier General William Francis Bartlett, U.S. Volunteers, distinguished veteran of the Civil War. Established in 1905, the camp was used by the Army from August to November 1917 as an infantry post for the organization of federal regiments from National Guard units.

BEARSKIN NECK FORT. The Sea Fensibles Barrack at Rockport was built by the inhabitants of Sandy Bay in 1814 during the war with Britain to house a company of local militia. About 12 men in all defended the fort at the end of Bearskin Neck. The Barrack, still standing, is two stories high, has two large chimneys, and four fireplaces. On September 14, 1814, the British frigate *Nymph* landed two groups of men during a dense fog. They surprised the fort's sentinel and spiked the fort's three guns.

BOSTON COMMON FORTIFICATIONS. Over a period of more than three centuries, the Common served as an outdoor stage for a series of dramas delineating Boston's long history, beginning with the excesses of rigid Puritanism. The relatively barren, open-land state of the Common contributed to its value for military purposes during the eighteenth century. Use of the ground was continuous as a training and drill field. As early as 1709 a young English officer, who commanded a company of artillery, threw up a small earthwork at the foot of the Common and drilled his men in artillery practice. But far greater uses of the Common were still to come.

In every account of Boston during the Revolution are described the disposition of the troops on the Common and the form of its fortifications. One of the best summaries marking their locations was written more than a century ago:

The positions of the British defences and encampments on the Common during the winter of 1775–76 were as follows: A small earthwork was thrown up at the northwest corner, a little higher up than the present entrance on Charles Street; this was designed for infantry, and held by a single company. The little elevation mentioned by the name of Fox Hill (near the Public Garden on Charles Street) was nearly or quite surrounded by water at times, and was hence called the "island," on this was a small redoubt. At the southwest corner—now intersected by the Boylston Street extension—was another breastwork for infantry.... On the westerly slope of the hill overlooking the parade, on which the flagstaff is now situated, was a square redoubt, behind which lay encamped a battalion of infantry. To the east, and on a line with the easternmost point of the hill, were two half-moons for

small arms, with a second battalion in its rear. About opposite Carver Street, resting on the southwest corner of the burial-ground, was a bastioned work, directly across Boylston Street. This was the second line. On the hill formerly known as Flagstaff Hill, but now dedicated to the soldiers' monument, the artillery was posted, protected by intrenchments. Immediately behind this hill, stretching from the burial-ground across to Beacon Street Mall, were the camps of three battalions of infantry.... None of the works were formidable except the most southern, which was connected with the line on the Neck. The Common was an intrenched camp, with a regular garrison of 1,750 men. [Samuel Adams Drakes, *Old Landmarks and Historic Personages of Boston* (1873)]

All this military occupation of a restricted territory left physical desecrations. The British soldiers in their need of firewood stripped private homes, including John Hancock's, in the neighborhood of their fences and steadily decimated the number of trees on the Common itself. When Washington's army occupied the city after it was evacuated by the British in mid-March 1776, they found the Common's landscape badly scarred by cooking holes, ditches, and fortification entrenchments, which remained as mementos of British military occupation until well after the turn of the century.

BOYLSTON FORT. The settlement of West Boylston, north of Worcester, was made as early as 1720. Its original settlers, who came from Marlborough, built a stockaded fort which stood until about 1790, exhibiting a number of bullet holes.

BREED'S HILL REDOUBT (*Bunker Hill Redoubt*). The Battle of Bunker Hill, June 17, 1775, on Charlestown's peninsula, has been misnamed in history books since the Revolution. The site of the battle was atop 62-foot-high Breed's Hill, about half a mile to the southeast. Breed's Hill was not selected by mistake by Patriot officers, as later reported by Boston's Committee of Safety, which had earlier decided to occupy Bunker Hill as a much more strategic commanding position; it was chosen deliberately by the officers under William Prescott and Israel Putnam. It was a critical error in judgment, because Bunker Hill could have been made almost impregnable, especially with the captured cannon from Fort Ticonderoga that Henry Knox brought back to Boston.

The Americans, during the night, had erected with much labor an eight-rods-square redoubt of bastions, flanking faces, breastworks, and entrenchments between two strong fences consisting of stone and rails, with two cannons at the front of the redoubt. It required three attacks by frontal assault by the British to finally overrun the defenders. No more than 1,500 Americans were in action at any one time. Their total casualties are estimated at 441, of whom 140 were killed and 301 wounded. British total forces numbered about 2,500, including the 400 men who participated alone in the third and final attack. Their losses in casualties numbered at least 1,150. Officially reported casualties were 19 officers and 207 men killed, and 70 officers and 758 men wounded—an incredible approximate percentage of 40 percent. It is little realized even today that the presence of American officers who had received military training in the French and Indian Wars was crucial to the defense of Breed's Hill. William Prescott, Israel Putnam, John Stark, Richard Gridley, and Thomas Knowlton were among these officers.

BRIDGEWATER FORT. A fort erected sometime before June 21, 1675, during King Philip's War, it was built by the settlers of Bridgewater in present Plymouth County on the south side of the Taunton River. The defense, also used for the storage of corn and "goods," had been constructed because the settlers refused to move to a safer seaside locality.

FORT BROOKLINE. This Revolutionary War defense erected in the spring of 1775 by the Patriots was located on Sewall's Point in Brookline just south of Boston. The fortification, erected under the direction of Colonel Rufus Putnam, mounted six guns and had quarters for a strong garrison (two companies of men were posted there on June 16, 1775). The Brookline fort was under fire only once during the war when it was attacked shortly after midnight on July 31, 1775, by a British floating battery.

BUNKER HILL REDOUBT. BREED'S HILL REDOUBT.

BURIAL HILL FORT. PLYMOUTH FORT.

FORT BURKE. A cordon of forts, erected in 1744 and 1745 from Fort Dummer in New Hampshire to the New York line to defend the northern frontier, included Fort Burke, built by Major John Burke in Bernardston (then Falltown) in present Franklin County. On November 11, 1743, the Massachusetts General Court had granted each town or township 100 pounds to pay for self-fortification. The Burke fort was described as having been 6 rods square, with palisades 10 to 12 feet high, enclosing a block-house armed with two swivel guns and eight houses used as barracks for a garrison of 20 men. At each corner there was an elevated watch tower. During an attack by Indians in 1747, Major Burke was wounded. For several years during the French and Indian War (1754–63), the fort was an almost continuously used refuge for dozens of the area's inhabitants.

CAMP CAMERON. CAMP DAY.

CHARLESTOWN POINT FORT. A battery was erected early in the history of Charlestown on the point of land formed by the junction of the Mystic and Charles rivers. Built of brick and sod on a stone foundation, it was intended to mount 10 "long" guns. No data has been found to indicate when it was constructed.

FORT AT CLARK'S POINT. FORT RODMAN.

COLE HILL BATTERY. PLYMOUTH FORT.

FORT CONANT. FORT GLOUCESTER.

CONNABLE'S FORT. In what is now North Bernardston in Franklin County, Samuel Connable in 1739 built his home in the form of a fortification. It was the second dwelling erected in the town, Major Burke's fort being the first as well as the largest. Connable's Fort served throughout King George's War (1744–48) and the French and Indian War (1754–63). The structure, enlarged before the Revolution, was still standing in a good state of preservation well into the present century.

COPP'S HILL REDOUBT. During the Americans' siege of Boston in the Revolution, the British built a redoubt on top of Copp's Hill, with its parapets constructed of earth-filled barrels. During the Battle of Bunker Hill on June 17, 1775, the British battery consisted of six heavy guns and howitzers, "three of which pieces, twenty-four pounders, were found on the reoccupation of the town after its evacuation by the British" on March 17, 1776, "spiked and clogged, so as to prevent their immediate use by the provincials" (Nathaniel B. Shurtleff, *A Topographical and Historical Description of Boston* [1871], p. 161).

CORN HILL FORT. FORT HILL.

COW FORT. FORT GLOVER.

FORT CROSS. FORT GLOUCESTER.

FORT DALTON. Land at Framingham was purchased by the state of Massachusetts in 1873 for the establishment of a permanent camp ground for the State Militia. In accordance with instructions, the 1st Brigade, consisting of infantry and artillery units, established the camp on August 5, 1873, and the 125-acre state campground was thus inaugurated. The building program was at once initiated, with its first structure being an arsenal. By 1895 more than 100 buildings for various purposes had been constructed on the reservation. The earthwork known as Fort Dalton, begun in 1883, and named in honor of the state's then adjutant general, Major General Samuel Dalton, was an earthen parapet 138 feet long with two flanks, 11 and 16 feet long. Its armament consisted of two 10-inch Rodman guns and four siege mortars. No data have been found to indicate when the battery was dismantled.

FORT DARBY (*Fort Miller*). Fears of pirate raids and foreign enemy invasion resulted in the erection of Fort Darby, Marblehead's first fortification, on Naugas Head on the northwest corner of the peninsula. At a later date, a breastwork was built at the entrance of Marblehead Harbor. Fort Darby, a name adopted from a similar headland at Derby in Dorsetshire, England, was probably erected sometime between 1629 and 1632 by settler-soldiers under the direction of Acting Governor John Endicott. The outbreak of the War of 1812 influenced the repair and renovation of the old fort, which was then used as a coastal lookout and as a drill area for Fort Sewall's troops. During the Civil War, the fort was reactivated as Fort Miller. The Spanish-American War brought the reactivation of Marblehead's fortifications. During the summer of 1898 two Spanish prize vessels, the *Sandoval* and the *Alvarado*, were sailed into the harbor in the custody of their captor, the cruiser *Marblehead*.

FORT DAWES. Named for William Dawes, compatriot of Paul Revere, and located on Boston Harbor's Deer Island (now connected to the mainland by a causeway), Fort Dawes was begun in late 1940 and commissioned on January 10, 1941. A month later it was designated a subpost of Fort Banks. Effective February 2, 1963, Fort Dawes was discontinued as a Department of the Army installation.

CAMP DAY (*Camp Cameron*). A Civil War mobilization encampment established by the 38th Massachusetts Volunteers in the summer of 1862, it was located on farm land in North Cambridge in the area of Massachusetts Avenue (then North Avenue). It was known as Camp Day because most of the land it occupied was owned by the Day family. Camp Cameron, however, was most probably its official name in honor of Simon Cameron, Lincoln's first secretary of war.

CAMP DEVENS. FORT DEVENS.

FORT DEVENS (*Camp Devens*). Construction of this post was begun on June 18, 1917. By authority of General Orders No. 95, War Department, July 18, 1917, the post was named Camp Devens in honor of Brevet Major General Charles Devens, U.S.V., a Civil War veteran and later attorney general under President Hayes. The post was a mobilization and training center for the 76th Division during World War I. After the close of the war, Camp Devens was used as a demobilization center and soon became an important training center for Reserve Officer Training Corps and Civilian Military Training Corps (CMTC) units. The name of Camp Devens was changed to Fort Devens by General Orders No. 10, War Department, November 5, 1931.

Following the outbreak of World War II in Europe (September 1939), plans were formu-

FORT DEVENS. Main entrance. (Courtesy of the U.S. Army.)

lated to increase the U.S. Army. In 1940 the first peacetime draft in United States history was instituted, and Fort Devens was designated a reception center for all New England men destined to serve for one year as "draftees." A gigantic, temporary-type building program was instituted in 1940 with the expansion of Fort Devens. More than 1,200 wooden buildings, including two new 1,200-bed hospitals, were constructed at a cost of $25,000,000. Three divisions trained at Fort Devens during World War II—the 1st, the 32nd, and the 45th—and the Fourth Women's Army Auxiliary Corps (WAAC) Training Center opened on post in April 1943. Three months later, the WAAC became the Women's Army Corps (WAC). In February 1944, a prisoner of war camp for 5,000 German soldiers opened at Fort Devens, remaining in operation until May 1946.

With the close of the war, Fort Devens once again was designated a demobilization center. On June 30, 1946, Fort Devens, for the second time in its history, was declared excess to the Army's need and was again put on caretaker status. With the outbreak of the Korean conflict, Fort Devens was again designated a reception center. In its long history of service, more than 400 units (including a U.S. Navy Air Squadron) have called Fort Devens home. Today it is the home of Headquarters USAG; 10th Special Forces Group (ABN); 39th Engineer Battalion (CBT); 36th Medical Battalion; Combat Support Battalion (PROV); Army Intelligence School; and 187th Infantry Brigade (USAR).

CAMP DEWEY (*Camp McGuinness*). The state's arsenal and campground in Framingham was used as a temporary mobilization center for volunteers during the short-lived Spanish-American War. Apparently officially named Camp McGuinness, the camp was also known as Camp Dewey, named for the admiral. (See also: FORT DALTON.)

FORT DORCHESTER HEIGHTS. The fortifying of Dorchester Heights, located in the southern suburbs of Boston, by the Americans during the night of March 4–5, 1776, under the cover of a diversionary bombardment, was the determining factor in forcing the evacuation of the city by the British less than two weeks later.

The plan to occupy Dorchester Heights evolved from the council of war held 16 Feb. '76. Agreeing with Washington that some offensive action should be taken before arrival of British reinforcements in the spring, but believing that they lacked the strength to attack Boston, Washington's generals proposed seizure of some position and forcing the enemy to attack. Unoc-cupied Dorchester Heights, the only ones in the Boston area not held by one side or the other was the obvious choice. As finally worked out, the plan was for this high ground to be fortified in the course of a single night, as had been done at Bunker Hill. . . . Heavy timber frames (chandeliers) were assembled, and gabions, fascines, and bales of hay were made up to fit into them. . . . The whole plan, needless to say, was made possible by Knox's "Noble Train of Artillery" from Ft. Ticonderoga, and by the assembly of sufficient gunpowder in the early months of 1776. [Mark M. Boatner III, *Encyclopedia of the American Revolution*, 1966, pp. 335–36]

The fortuitous occupation of the heights defeated British armament. Their guns could not be elevated sufficiently to target the American works. A plan to make a night attack by 2,200 troops against the American position was called off by General William Howe, and on March 7 he decided that Boston had become untenable and had to be evacuated.

FORT DUVALL. Construction of this post began in April 1920 and was officially established in 1921 on Little Hog Island, now Spinnaker Island, about a half-mile southeast of Hull, in Boston Harbor, the 15-acre site having been acquired for the erection of a modern seacoast battery. The reservation was named Fort Duvall in honor of Major General William P. Duvall, who died March 1, 1920. Battery Frank S. Long at the fort was armed with two giant 16-inch guns that had a range of 44,680 yards. It was named in honor of 1st Lieutenant Frank S. Long of the Infantry, who was killed in action in France, October 5, 1918.

The first of the World War II practice fires of only nine shots took place in 1942. Hull's residents had to be warned to evacuate their homes for the shoot. The houses, only 1,760 feet from the gun muzzles, sustained quite a bit of damage. After World War II the guns were dismantled and transported elsewhere, leaving the post under a caretaker. During subsequent years Fort Duvall and its near environs were used intermittently for other military needs. Its last use was as an annex for Hull public schools. The military reservation was recently purchased by a group of real estate developers who are building a condominium-townhouse complex of 105 units on top of the bunker system that was Battery Frank S. Long, with completion scheduled for March 1987.

FORT EASTERN POINT. FORT GLOUCESTER.

CAMP EDMUNDS. CAMP BANKS.

CAMP EDWARDS. A temporary sizable World War II and Korean War post near Falmouth, it was inactivated February 1, 1953.

ELLIS AND PHILLIPS FORT. The original settlers of Ashfield in present Franklin County returned about 1756, after having deserted it for nearly three years. They immediately proceeded to build a fort of 81 square rods enclosed by a 12-foot-high palisade, with a gate in its south wall, and a blockhouse-dwelling in the center surmounted by a small watchtower. Although it belonged to Chileab Smith, the fort was named apparently for two neighboring families. The defense was abandoned before the formal ending of the French and Indian War.

ELIZABETH ISLAND POST. Explorer Bartholomew Gosnold built a fort on one of the Elizabeth Islands in 1602. Passing Nantucket, Gosnold and his men entered Buzzards Bay, which they called Gosnold's Hope. On the westernmost of the islands they established a settlement and named it Elizabeth for their queen. They built a fort and a storehouse on a rocky islet in the center of a small lake of fresh water.

Almost three and a half centuries later, the U.S. government constructed a post on one of the islands.

After Pearl Harbor, the government was given permission to station some men on Nashawena, one of the Elizabeth Islands, because of its strategic location at the entrance to both Buzzards Bay and Vineyard Sound. They constructed one hundred and fifty buildings and a dock. Each day an Army boat from New Bedford brought supplies. The men remained on the island for nearly two years. Finally the unit was withdrawn and most of the contents removed, although the islanders themselves had to take down many of the buildings. [Alice Forbes Howland, *Three Islands: Pasque, Nashawena, and Penikese*].

CAMP ELLSWORTH. A temporary Civil War encampment, Camp Ellsworth was located at Fresh Pond in Cambridge.

FORT FEARING. FORT PHOENIX.

CAMP GARDNER. A temporary Civil War encampment, it occupied Winter Island at Salem.

GARRISON HOUSES. A much misused word, the term "garrison" house in New England during the seventeenth and early eighteenth centuries did not refer to a specific type of building, but rather to houses that were refuges for settlers or bases for militia. Although a number of these structures were built of hewn or sawn logs, most were of frame construction. In any case, New England's log structures must not be confused with the log cabin made famous on other American frontiers of the seventeenth, eighteenth, and nineteenth centuries, originally introduced into America by northern Europeans, particularly the Swedes and Finns in the mid-1600s.

The "garrison" houses or dwellings converted into minimally fortified havens were usually two-storied, with the upper story often projecting from eight inches to two feet beyond the lower. Loopholes or portholes for observation and musketry were excised in the walls in different parts of the house, especially in the upper story. Footsquare windows were usual, permitting air and light to enter the interior, with some of them fitted with thick substantial shutters, and others provided with only wooden blocks.

A number of the garrison houses had flankers, bastions, blockhouses or "mounts" (square bullet-proofed sentry boxes set at the corners of stockades atop strong posts from 14 to 40 feet in height), in opposite diagonal angles, with some so equipped at all four corners. Many of them were surrounded by palisades or stockades. During the seventeenth century, there was no practical need for roads to connect settlements or one garrison to a neighboring one, since there were no wagons and very few horses. Footpaths were the only links between any two garrison houses.

Virtually every established settlement or community in eastern New England had at least one originally designed "garrison" or a dwelling converted to the same use. Some Massachusetts towns—Andover, Deerfield, Greenfield, Haverhill, Northampton, and Swansea—had as many as a dozen. The aggregate number of these garrison houses was never determined. Nineteenth-century New England gazetteers delineate brief histories of the towns and are useful in determining which ones existed in 1775, often specifying the garrison houses by name and their approximate dates of service during the Indian outbreaks, beginning with King Philip's War in 1675, when many of the earliest garrisons were first established.

GILBERT HEIGHTS FORT. FORT GLOVER.

GILBERT'S FORT. The first garrisoned defense in the town of Brookfield in present Worcester County appears to have been Gilbert's Fort erected in 1688 and named for Deacon Henry Gilbert, who lived nearby. The fort stood at today's intersection of North Main and Maple streets. It has been described as having been quite large, as it housed both families and soldiers. Within the next half century, more than a dozen minimally fortified garrison houses were established in Brookfield and its environs. (See: GARRISON HOUSES.)

FORT GLOUCESTER (*Stage Fort; Fort Eastern Point; Fort Point; Fort Banks; Fort Cross; Fort Allen; Fort Conant*). Situated on Cape Ann and overlooking Gloucester Harbor, Fort Stage Park on the bluff, known as Stage Head, received its name from the fact that it was there that the Dorchester Adventurers Company, organized in England in 1623, erected its fishing "stages." The fortifications that existed there and in its immediate environs appear variously in the records as Stage Fort, Fort Eastern Point, Fort Point, Fort Gloucester, and Fort Conant. Fort Conant was also called, for unknown reasons, Fort Banks, Fort Cross, and Fort Allen. Apparently no official designation has ever been assigned.

The first defenses at Stage Head were rudimentary fortified breastworks erected in 1703 during Queen Anne's War. In 1743, just prior to the outbreak of King George's War, breastworks and a large platform were constructed to accommodate eight 12-pounder cannon. At approximately the same time, a fort was erected at what is now the end of Commercial Street in Gloucester and named Fort Libby. During the French and Indian War, the harbor's defenses were reactivated and renovated. At the outbreak of the American Revolution, public attention was focused on the relatively defenseless state of the town. A detachment of riflemen commanded by Major Robert Magaw was sent from the Continental camp at Cambridge for the town's protection. In October 1775 a company from Ipswich was ordered to Gloucester to assist the townspeople with the construction of new fortified breastworks at the town's strategic points, including Stage Head in the harbor.

In May 1794 the town ceded to the United States the land on Watch House Neck, where a fortified breastwork had been thrown up early in the Revolution, for the purpose of erecting a fort for the protection of the town. During the second year of the War of 1812, when British naval forces were raiding New England's seacoast, the government's fort on Watch House Neck was reinforced by more men and additional armament, and the old fort at Stage Head repaired and improved by the erection of barracks.

For nearly a score of years after the war with Britain, the Watch House Neck fort had been left in the charge of a caretaker. Sometime in 1833

vandalism was committed there, the fort was set afire, and all the timber works, including the barracks, were consumed. During the Civil War, the old Revolutionary War fort at Stage Head was reactivated as Fort Conant in honor of Roger Conant who was here during 1623–25. In addition, a seven-gun fort, known as the "Ramparts," was built and garrisoned by a company of artillery on the "high land of the farm of Thomas Niles" at Eastern Point.

FORT GLOVER (*Gilbert Heights Fort; Cow Fort*). Erected in 1863 on the site of Gilbert Heights Fort, the old War of 1812 battery, Fort Glover was located at Riverhead Beach on what is now Bubier Road in Marblehead. After the Civil War, the fort gradually became dilapidated and was nicknamed "Cow Fort" because herds of cows grazed at will within the ruined walls of the fort. Shortly after the outbreak of the short-lived Spanish-American War, Fort Glover was rescued from obscurity, completely renovated and upgraded as a coastal defense. Fort Glover was leveled in 1917.

CAMP (CURTIS) GUILD. Located 20 miles north of Boston at Boxford, Essex County, Camp Guild was named in honor of Major General Curtis Guild, Massachusetts Volunteer Militia, and governor of the state 1906–8. The post was initially used by the Massachusetts National Guard as a mobilization center in July 1917 and, thereafter, by the government for the mustering in of state troops.

GURNET FORT. FORT ANDREW.

HATFIELD FORT. Immediately after the outbreak of King Philip's War in 1675, the inhabitants of Hatfield in present Hampshire County erected an extensive 10-to-12-foot-high stockade, with a gate at either end, that enclosed about half of the houses in the settlement. The houses of four of the town's settlers were the four corners of the fort. On May 30, 1675 "from six to seven hundred Indians invaded Hatfield, their first work being to set on fire twelve buildings without the fortification. . . . A large number of the savages were busy in killing cattle or driving them off." The ensuing, protracted fight within the town and in the pasture resulted in heavy losses on both sides. On September 19, 1677, the town was again raided by Indians from Canada who inflicted "terrible slaughter upon men, women, and children, and captured and took away a large number" to Quebec. Some of the women captives were later redeemed by their husbands, who paid large ransoms for their release (Elias Nason, *A Gazetteer of the State of Massachusetts* [1874], pp. 251–252).

HAWK'S FORT. This defense, located at Charlemont in present Franklin County, was erected in 1745 during King George's War against the French.

FORT HEATH. Established as the "Gun Battery" in 1899 near Fort Banks, Fort Heath was situated on the mainland on Grover's Cliff near the town of Winthrop, about four miles northeast of Boston. The post was named in honor of Revolutionary War Major General William Heath, who also served as a delegate from Massachusetts to the Federal Constitutional Convention. In 1902 it was reported that Fort Heath's armament consisted of three 12-inch rifles mounted on disappearing carriages.

CAMP HILL. A stone marker at the eminence known as Camp Hill in Oxford, Worcester County, was erected by the General Ebenezer Learned Chapter of the D.A.R. in commemoration of the site of the camp of Colonel Nathan Rice's Regiment in Adam's Provisional Army in 1799 and 1800. The camp was visited by Alexander Hamilton in 1800.

FORT HILL (*Corn Hill Fort*). On May 24, 1632, Boston's first fort was begun on Corn Hill, then one of the city's three highest eminences, now known as Fort Hill, and completed in 1634. During the autumn of 1687, Governor Sir Edmund Andros replaced the original work with a four-bastioned palisaded fort with a barracks for its garrison. On April 18, 1689, one John Nelson led a large group of colonists to Fort Hill and demanded Andros surrender himself and the fort. This civil revolt led to the imprisonment of Andros at Castle William and his eventual shipment in chains to England for trial. Andros was vindicated by his peers. The fort was in use as late as the Revolution and leveled in 1797. In 1865 the hill was cut down and present Fort Hill Square was constructed.

HINGHAM FORTS. The outbreak of King Philip's War in 1675 compelled the inhabitants of Hingham in present Plymouth County to erect defenses and establish garrison houses at strategic points in and around the settlement. Hingham was then protected by three forts—one of which was on the top of Fort Hill, one at the cemetery, and the other "on the plain about a mile from the harbor."

FORT HOOSAC (*West Hoosac Blockhouse; Williamstown Blockhouse*). A stockaded blockhouse, erected in what was then known as West Hoosac, now Williamstown, in the spring of 1756, was later called Fort Hoosac. Ten soldiers, two swivel guns, and supplies of powder, shot, and food were provided. On June 11 two scouts were killed near the fort. Two weeks later, on June 26, a detachment of thirteen men from Fort Massachusetts, 5 miles to the east, were ambushed 15 miles down the Hoosic River. Eight were killed and five captured. On the evening of July 11, after three men from Fort Hoosac in search of stray cows were killed by Indians, the fort withstood repeated assaults. The Indians finally retreated, slaughtering all the cattle as they went but failing to set fire to the fort.

With the successful operations of General Jeffrey Amherst's forces in northern New York and the St. Lawrence Valley, incursions by the French and Indians ceased by 1760, and Fort Hoosac's garrison was withdrawn. It appears that the fort was subsequently used as the town's meetinghouse until it decayed and fell into ruins. Two commemorative monuments mark the site of the fort.

HUGUENOT FORT. The remains of the French fort built in 1687 at Oxford in present Worcester County are still in evidence off Fort Hill Road to the rear of the commemorative monument erected by the Huguenot Memorial Society in 1884. After the infamous 1685 revocation of the Edict of Nantes, issued by Henry IV of France in 1598 at the end of the wars of religion to define the rights of French Protestants (Huguenots), an estimated 50,000 refugees crossed the Atlantic to seek religious freedom in the New World, in the Carolinas, Virginia, New York (New Rochelle), Rhode Island and Massachusetts.

A party of Huguenot refugees, led by André Sigourney and Gabriel Bernon, from Rochelle, France, first settled an English-granted tract of land in present Oxford and erected a large, substantial stone-and-log palisaded complex of two blockhouses. It was a complete quadrangular fort with two bastions upon an eminence overlooking the village and the whole valley. The main two-story, 30-by-18-foot blockhouse was nearly centrally placed within the enclosure. The north and south sides of the fort measured 114 feet each and the east and west sides 108 feet, exclusive of the bastions. The destruction of the settlement and the fort by hundreds of Indians in 1694 dispersed the Huguenot settlers to Boston and New York. No authentic accounts of any attempt to resettle there are recorded until 1713, when the proprietors granted lands to others and the town was incorporated that year.

FORT INDEPENDENCE (HULL). FORT REVERE.

FORT INDEPENDENCE (*Castle William*).

Situated on Castle Island, now part of the mainland in Boston Harbor, Fort Independence is the oldest military installation in the United States. In the spring of 1634, four years after Boston was incorporated, Governor John Winthrop and members of his council visited the island and were so impressed with its strategic location that they each subscribed five pounds toward the erection of a fort there with two platforms. This first military defense of Boston has been described as a "castle with mud walls" with its masonry of lime concocted from oyster shells. In 1644 the arrival of a French warship in the harbor so alarmed the citizens that the fort, which had already decayed, was reconstructed of pine logs, stone, and earth, with 10-foot-thick walls enclosing a 50-foot-square compound. In 1665 the fort was repaired and enlarged, and "furnished with a small castle with brick walls three stories high," mounting nine pieces of ordnance. A year after the fort was accidently destroyed by fire on March 21, 1673, a new fort of stone was erected with four bastions and armed with 38 guns and 16 culverins, with the addition of a six-gun water battery.

In 1689 the people of Boston, in favor of the royal revolution in England, arrested Sir Edmund Andros, King James's royal governor, and confined him in the fort until he was sent to England

FORT INDEPENDENCE. Map of the Boston area and its fortifications in 1776 showing Castle William at the right. (From Pictorial Field-Book of the Revolution, by Benson Lossing. Courtesy of the Florida State Archives.)

to stand trial. During the administration of Sir William Phips, who was appointed governor by King William in 1692, the fort was named Castle or Fort William. The Crown at about this time contributed toward the construction of a new citadel with four bastions long known by the names of the Crown, the Rose, the Royal, and the Elizabeth. The new work's mounted ordnance consisted of 24 9-pounders, 12 24-pounders, and 18 32- and 48-pounders. This increase in defensive power proved to be fortuitous because of King William's War with France (1689–97) then being waged and accompanied by French invasions into the New England colonies.

From 1701 to 1703, military engineer Wolfgang William Romer was engaged to further fortify Boston Harbor. Under his direct supervision, Castle William was again upgraded and its armament augmented to 100 guns. Many years after the fort was largely destroyed by the British dur-

ing their evacuation of Boston in March 1776, a slate slab with a Latin inscription was found among the ruins, giving the dates when the work was begun and completed, and stating that it was constructed by Romer, "a military architect of the first rank." Beginning in 1740, Castle William again underwent renovation in anticipation of renewed war with the French. Bastion Shirley, named in honor of William Shirley, the new governor of Massachusetts, was built and mounted 20 42-pounders.

The Stamp Act, by which substantial revenue was to be raised in the Colonies, brought a storm of protest. The stamps arrived in Boston Harbor in September 1765 and were lodged for security at Castle William. The vigorous opposition in America prevented its enforcement. Although the Act was soon repealed and the stamps returned to England the following summer, its example of arbitrary royal authority precipitated the his-

FORT INDEPENDENCE. Aerial view of Boston Harbor showing the fort at the lower left corner. (Courtesy of the Massachusetts Department of Commerce and Development.)

toric struggle between Britain and America, with Boston the center of attack and Castle William the key to be possessed by the strongest hand.

Boston literally became a British military encampment as a significant number of troops arrived from England and Canada. The bloody incidents at Lexington and Concord in April 1775 provided the spark to ignite the American Revolution. Elements of Washington's formidable Continental Army were stationed in Boston's outlying suburbs and threatening the city. When Dorchester Heights overlooking the city was fortified by the Americans, armed with much of the ordnance that constituted Henry Knox's "Noble Train of Artillery" from Ticonderoga, British General Howe decided that Boston had become untenable and evacuated the city on March 17, 1776.

The British embarkation was a scene of general confusion, and it took 10 days before the transports were able to put to sea, bound for Nova Scotia. Before departing, however, British troops threw into the harbor the fort's stock of iron balls and shot, broke off ordnance trunnions, destroyed all the military stores they could not take with them, and finally blew up the citadel and the two powder magazines, to leave the island a mass of ruins. Castle Island thereafter remained unmolested for the remainder of the war. The Americans soon began the task of removing the ruins and restoring the fort into a state of defense. Epaulements were constructed on the remains of Shirley Bastion; the mutilated 42-pounders were given new trunnions, wrapped by strong iron hoops; and 21 32-pounders were emplaced after they were rescued from the American man-of-war *Somerset* wrecked off Cape Cod in 1778. The fort was then garrisoned by a newly raised company of artillery.

In August 1799 President John Adams visited Castle Island at the time that the government was contemplating the building of a new fortress there. It was during this visit by the president that the name of the fort was changed to Fort Independence. The first stone for the new fort was laid on May 7, 1801. On February 5, 1805, the five new bastions of the still-uncompleted fort were named Winthrop, Shirley, Hancock, Adams, and Dearborn. In 1833 Fort Independence's garrison was withdrawn, and the post given over to the Engineer Department for renewed construction, which was pursued intermittently until its completion in 1851. The pentagonal, five-bastioned fortification occupying the northern portion of the island was regarrisoned on January 4, 1851, and finally abandoned on November 25, 1879, in compliance with Special

Orders No. 206, Department of the East, November 18, 1879. An ordnance sergeant was put in charge of Fort Independence as caretaker.

In 1891 a bridge was constructed from Marine Park to the island, thus identifying it with the mainland and South Boston. When the Spanish-American War erupted in 1898, the government repossessed the fort and converted it into a mine and torpedo station. The causeway to Castle Island was built in 1925, and seven years later an automobile roadway to Fort Independence was opened to the public.

FORT JUNIPER (*Fort No. 1*). This Revolutionary War fortification was erected sometime in 1775 on Juniper Point at Salem. On June 19, 1776, the committee appointed by the Provincial Congress to review the seacoast defenses reported, "There are two forts erected on the Point of Land in Salem Harbour—No. 1 [Fort Juniper] and No. 2 or Old Fort [Fort Ann]. No. 1 contains 10 ambozeurs, has 2 twelve pounders with three small pieces" (Massachusetts Archives, cxxxvii, 93–95).

LAMB'S DAM REDOUBT. This American defense was located on the neck of land that then divided Boston and Roxbury. The battery was completed on September 10, 1775, and mounted four 18-pounder cannon. Lamb was a colonel in Washington's Continental forces then investing British-held Boston.

CAMP LANDER. This Civil War encampment was a permanent post from 1862 to 1865 for the accommodation of troops during the organization periods of a number of military units. Located on a 14-acre tract at Winham, just north of Danvers, in Essex County, the camp was named in honor of Brigadier General C. W. Lander of Salem, who died in action in March 1862. The camp had 20 well-built, one-company barracks, with each barrack fitted with two-tiered bunks furnished with straw instead of mattresses. Scattered over the campground were officers' quarters, a hospital, cook houses, a barber shop, and a storehouse. The site is now a playground called Pingree Park.

LANESBOROUGH FORT. Probably erected sometime in 1754, this log fort was established at Lanesborough, first known as New Framingham, in Berkshire County, and intended as a refuge for the settlement's inhabitants. In spite of their precautions, the settlers were driven by Indians to find a haven in the Pontoosack fort (Fort Anson) at Pittsfield. The site of the Lanesborough fort is located in the area between the cemetery in the center of the town and present Stormview Road.

LECHMERE'S POINT FORT (*Fort Putnam*). A strategically placed Revolutionary War "bomb battery," it was begun on November 29, 1775, at Lechmere's Point at Cambridge under the direction of Generals Israel Putnam and William Heath. Originally driven from the site by British floating water batteries, the soldiers returned to complete the fort by the following February. The defense was not called Fort Putnam until later.

FORT LEE. An earthwork fortification in the shape of a five-pointed star situated on a promontory overlooking Salem's harbor, Fort Lee was erected early in the Revolution and reportedly garrisoned by 3 officers and 100 artillerymen. The fort was renovated in 1862 for defense during the Civil War and last used as an active military post during the Spanish-American War. Its earthworks and stone powder magazine on an 11-acre site are still being maintained in a picnicking and park area after threats by the Army to level the works in 1957 were defeated by local residents.

FORT LIBBY. FORT GLOUCESTER.

CAMP LINCOLN. A temporary Civil War mobilization center established on or about July 19, 1861, Camp Lincoln was located at Worcester and occupied by the 21st and 25th Massachusetts Infantry Regiments.

LONG POINT BATTERIES. Two sand batteries were erected during the Civil War at Long Point in Provincetown on Cape Cod. A company of soldiers was stationed here, quartered in barracks constructed to accommodate them.

FORT LUCAS. A frontier defense erected about 1745 as a part of a line of forts extending from Fort Dummer in Vermont to the Hoosic River valley, Fort Lucas was located at Colrain in Franklin County.

MCDOWELL'S FORT. The cordon of forts erected during 1744–46 from Fort Dummer in Vermont to the New York line included McDowell's Fort at Colrain in Franklin County.

CAMP MCGUINNESS. CAMP DEWEY.

FORT MASSACHUSETTS. The English under Colonel Ephraim Williams built Fort Massachusetts, then the westernmost of a chain of forts, near the Hossac River in 1745 (during King George's War) within present North Adams, formerly called East Hossac, in Franklin County. The fort, erected on a stone foundation, was 60 feet square, with 12-foot-high walls of hewn pine logs. "The fort gate faced northward upon St. Francis Ledge, and the barracks were eleven feet wide, with sloping 'salt-box' roofs, located against the east and south walls. The mounts consisted of platforms twelve feet square on the northwest and southeast angles of the blockhouse walls, upon which were built watch-towers seven feet in height, pierced with loop-holes for the discharge of rifles" (Grace G. Niles, *The Hoosac Valley: Its Legends and Its History* [1912], p. 129).

The fort was subjected to numerous attacks by Indians led by French officers. Then, on August 26, 1746, it was besieged by a force of about 900 French and Indians led by Rigaud de Vaudreuil. After killing 45 of the enemy, the defenders had to surrender because of the lack of ammunition. The fort was burned. Rebuilt the following year, Fort Massachusetts was again assaulted on August 2, 1748, by some 300 French and Indians, but the defense led by Colonel Williams successfully withstood the series of attacks. A replica of the historic fort in North Adams commemorates the service rendered by Fort Massachusetts.

CAMP MEIGS. A temporary Civil War encampment located at Reading, north of Boston, it was occupied in 1862 by the 45th Massachusetts Volunteer Militia.

FORT MERRIMAC. FORT NICHOLS.

FORT MILLER. FORT DARBY.

MOON ISLAND REDOUBT. Chapter 16 of Acts of 1776 authorized a redoubt on Moon Island with four pieces of cannon, but it is not known whether this was constructed. Moon Island in Boston Harbor lies between Swuantum on the mainland and Long Island.

FORT MORRIS (*South Fort*). Erected about 1745, South or Morris Fort was located at Colrain in present Franklin County.

FORT MORRISON (*North Fort*). Colrain in present Franklin County was originally called Boston Township when it was first settled by emigrants from the north of Ireland. North or Morrison's Fort, one of three defenses erected in 1745 by Colrain's settlers, was commanded by Captain Hugh Morrison. The fort was again garrisoned from 1754 to about 1763 during the French and Indian War. An inscribed boulder commemorates the site of the frontier fort.

FORT NICHOLS (*Fort Merrimac*). In 1775 a battery, called Fort Merrimac or Fort Nichols, was erected by the Patriots at Salisbury Point opposite Newburyport at the mouth of the Merrimack River.

NOOK'S HILL FORT. On the night of March 9, 1776, in an effort to extend their commanding Dorchester Heights position by occupying and fortifying Nook's Hill a half mile away, the Americans sent a strong detachment to establish a battery there. Nook's Hill, officially known as Dorchester Hill, had a good view of Castle Island, Roxbury, and Boston's wharves. The British discovered the maneuver and bombarded the position, killing five men and forcing the detachment to retire. On the 16th, however, the Americans returned and succeeded in fortifying the hill, further convincing the British of the hopelessness of continuing their occupation of Boston. They evacuated the city the next day.

NORTH BATTERY. On January 8, 1644, it was agreed by the authorities that a fortification be erected at Walter Merry's Point on the shore of Boston Bay. Finally accomplished in March 1646 by the inhabitants, the defense was called North Battery, now Battery Wharf, just north of today's Sumner Tunnel. In 1706, in order to upgrade the city's fortifications for their better security, the inhabitants voted to extend the battery 120 feet. Repaired from time to time, and in use during the Revolution first by the British and then the Patriots, it was sold sometime between 1789 and 1796.

NORTH FORT. FORT MORRISON.

NORTHFIELD FORTIFICATIONS. Long a troubled frontier settlement, Northfield in present Franklin County suffered losses in human lives and property during the frequent Indian wars, beginning with King Philip's War in 1675. The settlers had built their dwellings close together and in 1673 ran a 10-foot-high stockade around the homes. The area covered about 30 by 40 rods. At least twice the settlement was abandoned after disastrous raids, the first time in September 1675 when Northfield's first fort and all the homes were destroyed. Resettled sometime after 1676, it was again broken up in 1690 and not reoccupied until 1713. Prior to 1724

Northfield was the northernmost frontier settlement in the Connecticut River Valley.

The series of forts erected at Northfield and in its immediate environs was spread over a period of about 75 years. Defenses were built in 1685, 1686, and 1688, followed by a hiatus until 1722 when two new forts were erected. In 1724 all the then existing forts were either rebuilt or renovated. In addition, at least several dwellings were converted into "garrison" houses for the intermittent occupation by militia. In 1751 the town voted to dispose of the forts, and they were dismantled in 1753. A year later the inhabitants, admitting they had been hasty, erected four new forts because of the outbreak of the French and Indian War.

FORT NO. 1. During their investment of British-held Boston, Washington's Continentals erected a battery, designated Fort No. 1, on the Charles River in Cambridge. The site of the fortification is believed to be on Putnam Avenue.

FORT NO. 1 (Salem). FORT JUNIPER.

FORT NO. 2. Another of the American batteries erected along the Charles River in Cambridge was Fort No. 2.

FORT NO. 2 (Salem). FORT PICKERING.

FORT NO. 3 (Cambridge). RED HOUSE FORT.

FORT NO. 3 (*Paterson's Fort; Prospect Hill Fort*). Immediately after the Battle of Bunker Hill, the Americans began to erect works on Prospect Hill in Somerville, a commanding eminence overlooking Charlestown and Cambridge. Here was built a citadel with outworks believed to have been the most formidable defense on the American line during the Continental siege of Boston, built by Colonel (later Major General) John Paterson and the regiment known then by his name (designated the 15th Continental Regiment on January 1, 1776). It was often referred to by soldiers of its garrison as "Mount Pisgar," but officially it was Fort No. 3 and popularly known as Paterson's Fort or the Prospect Hill Fort. For nine months, June 17, 1775–March 17, 1776, it withstood intermittent British bombardments. On December 31, 1775, General Nathanael Greene, who then commanded the troops on Prospect Hill, wrote that "We have suffered prodigiously for want of wood. Many regiments have been obliged to eat their provisions nearly raw for lack of fuel to cook them, and many more have suffered extremely from the terrible cold" (William R. Comer, *Landmarks in the Old Bay State* [1911], pp. 327–28).

On June 1, 1776, a flag symbolizing the United Colonies, bearing 13 stripes and the crosses of St. George and St. Andrew was first displayed atop the eminence, but in 1777 the crosses were removed and replaced by the stars. Many of the British soldiers of General Burgoyne's army that surrendered at Saratoga were held as prisoners of war and quartered on Prospect Hill from November 7, 1777, to October 15, 1778, guarded by American troops commanded by General William Heath.

In 1861 a temporary Civil War encampment was established on Prospect Hill for the mobilization of Somerville recruits. Company E of the 39th Massachusetts Infantry was mustered into service here on August 12, 1861, and then moved to Washington the following September. The site of Fort No. 3 is located at the present intersection of Munroe Street and Prospect Hill Avenue. A conspicuous pseudo-medieval memorial tower, surrounded by a small park, now crowns the hill. The observation tower and park were dedicated October 29, 1903.

PATERSON'S FORT. FORT NO. 3.

FORT PELHAM. Erected probably in 1745 at the town of Rowe in present Franklin County, Fort Pelham was a defensive link in the chain of forts extending from Fort Dummer in Vermont to the valley of the Hoosic River. The fort was described as having been a palisaded parallelogram enclosing approximately one and a half acres, surrounded by a ditch or trench, and furnished with mounts or watch-boxes 12 feet square and 7 feet high in all four angles. Its usual garrison consisted of 20 men.

FORT PHILIP. In May 1776 a fort was erected by the Americans near the northern end of Plum Island, at what is known as Light House Point, at Newburyport. The fort was reportedly armed by a few cannon and some mortars. In 1814 new fortifications were erected on the island. During the Spanish-American War, Plum Island was refortified by several fieldpieces manned by elements of the Massachusetts Volunteer Militia.

FORT PHOENIX (*Fort Fearing*). On May 14, 1775, the first naval engagement of the Revolutionary War took place off Fairhaven in New Bedford Harbor. The battle convinced the town's inhabitants that a fort was needed to protect the area. In response, the provincial government at Watertown finally authorized construction of a small fort on Nolscot Point in the village of Fairhaven. The defense was built of the material excavated for the foundation on which it stands. The project was completed in 1777. Some of the fort's 11 heavy cannon were obtained from Castle Island in Boston Harbor and others from a captured supply stored at New London. Captain Timothy Ingraham was then in command of the fort.

On September 5, 1778, New Bedford was attacked by elements of the British fleet under the command of General Sir Henry Clinton. Troops were landed in Bedford Village across the river. They marched through the town leaving a trail of destruction. An assault was then directed at the fort on Nolscot Point. Ingraham, unable to defend his fort, ordered it evacuated and the cannon spiked to render them useless to the British. Many of the garrison were wounded or captured, but a small number of the men escaped into the nearby woods. Major Israel Fearing arrived with his Wareham Militia and compelled the British to retire to their ships. The fort then became known as Fort Fearing, retaining that name until 1784 when it was officially designated Fort Phoenix.

During the War of 1812, the fort was garrisoned by about 100 soldiers. It was attacked but once, on June 13, 1814, by the H.M.S. *Nimrod*. The alert garrison quickly discouraged a landing party. The fort was abandoned after the war. Fort Phoenix was reactivated and renovated during the Civil War and rearmed with heavy artillery. The magazine that adjoins the fort's parapet was completed in 1865 and designed to hold 50,000 pounds of powder. Fort Phoenix, exhibiting Revolutionary War cannon, is now incorporated within a Fairhaven public park.

FORT PICKERING (*Fort William; Fort Ann; Fort No. 2*). As early as 1643 a defense named Fort William was begun on the present site of Fort Pickering on Winter Island in Salem's harbor and infrequently maintained by the town's inhabitants. During Queen Anne's War (1702–11), the fort was renamed Fort Ann, but an acrimonious debate ensued as to who should repair the old fort on Winter Island. In 1706 the governor ordered repairs on the fort, but the town meeting held on June 24 objected, stating that the maintenance of the fort was a provincial responsibility and expense. The matter was still being debated when the war ended. In late 1735 the General

Court stipulated that if Fort Ann should be renovated to mount 15 cannon, the sum of 600 pounds would be granted to accomplish the work.

During the Revolution the town of Salem voted on October 23, 1775, to block the harbor channel with the hulks of decrepit vessels and put the town's defenses in order, including the complete renovation of Fort Ann, designated Fort No. 2, and the construction of barracks on Winter Island. In 1794 the fort on the island was ceded to the government, which acquired additional ground for a military reservation. Four years later a new work was built on the site and designated Fort Pickering in honor of Salem-born Colonel Timothy Pickering, adjutant general, Continental Army, 1777–78, and secretary of war, 1795. An irregular work, occupying about an acre of ground, the brick fort had earth-and-stone embankments and a brick barracks for the garrison. Fort Pickering was renovated and upgraded during the War of 1812. The outbreak of the Civil War again influenced repairs on the fort. A portion of the reservation was occupied by the Treasury Department for lighthouse purposes since 1871. Fort Pickering is now the property of the town of Salem.

PLYMOUTH FORT (*Burial Hill Fort; Cole Hill Battery*). The founding of the Pilgrim settlement at Plymouth in 1620 was highly significant in the development of New England and the United States. Unfortunately, virtually all the historic sites relating to the settlement's earliest period have lost their original character and convey little impression of the colony. One exception is Cole's Hill, which is still the dominant landmark. The view from the hill of the surrounding land, Plymouth Harbor, and the sea conveys a vivid impression of the scene that greeted the *Mayflower's* 102 weary passengers, 50 men, 20 women, and 32 children (there were 3 births during the long voyage).

Cole's Hill rises from the bank of Plymouth Bay near the foot of Leyden Street, principal thoroughfare of the original settlement. It was the traditional burial place of the Plymouth colonists who died during the "starving time," the tragic first winter of 1620–21. The dead were reportedly buried at night, and their graves disguised to prevent the Indians from learning the dangerously weakened state of the survivors. In later years, the colonists from time to time, because of the exigencies of threatened war, mounted batteries of cannon on the hill to repel possible attack from the sea.

By the close of 1623, there were 180 persons in the colony. The settlement, now stretching down the slope of the hill to the bay, was surrounded by a half-mile-long stockade with four bastions. On the top of Burial Hill, commanding the settlement, was the fort-church, the colony's first defense built in 1622, which had an important role in both the civil and ecclesiastical life of the colony. The 24-foot-square fort was constructed of large sawn planks. On its roof, supported by massive oak beams that projected beyond the walls, were six cannon mounted behind a bulwark. The fort's walls were pierced by small porthole-windows to admit light into the interior. The fort was several times allowed to decay but then repaired and enlarged when attacks seemed imminent. It was finally pulled down at the end of King Philip's War in 1676. Burial Hill, filled with the graves and monuments of many generations, has been encroached upon by the expansion of the present town.

Cole's Hill is maintained by the Pilgrim Society as a public park. On its top stands the colossal memorial to the *Mayflower* Pilgrims, erected by the General Society of Mayflower Descendants. In a crypt beneath the monument are the skeletal remains uncovered during excavations in the eighteenth and nineteenth centuries (no burials were made on the hill after 1637). At the foot of Cole's Hill is Plymouth Rock, the legendary landing site of the Pilgrims.

FORT POINT. FORT GLOUCESTER.

FORT AT PONTOOSACK. FORT ANSON.

PROSPECT HILL FORT. FORT NO. 3 (Somerville).

FORT PUTNAM. LECHMERE'S POINT FORT.

RED HOUSE FORT (*Fort No. 3*). In 1775, at the strategic junction of two roads, one from Cambridge to Charlestown, and the other from Lechmere's Point, American troops under General Artemas Ward built a redoubt called Fort No. 3 or the Red House Fort because there was a red brick house on one corner of the intersection. These two roads were the only routes the British could take to attack Cambridge without crossing the Charles River. An entire regiment was permanently posted in this fort while General Israel Putnam's 1,000 Connecticut troops were encamped a half-mile away at Inman's Farm to support them.

FORT REVERE (*Allerton Battery; Fort Independence*). The earliest historical reference to the definite establishment of a fort at Nantasket Head, now Telegraph Hill, near the town of Hull situated at the tip of the peninsula, was during King Philip's War (1675–76) when the town's inhabitants erected some sort of fortification on the hill. In the spring of 1776, the Committee on Fortifications ordered fortifications erected at Allerton Point, adjoining Nantasket Beach, and plans were drawn for a pentagonal fort. The defense, first known as Allerton Battery then named Fort Independence, was reportedly completed sometime during 1777 but "was later destroyed in the evacuation of Boston." In 1778 General Washington sent French engineer Colonel Louis Duportail to rebuild the fort. Shortly after its restoration, Count d'Estaing landed a force of sailors and marines who erected a 30-gun battery there.

The next occupation of the general area for a defensive installation did not occur until more than a century later, when Fort Revere was built by the government at Nantasket Head in 1900 and named in honor of Paul Revere, lieutenant colonel of Artillery, Continental Army. The post was established as a subpost of Fort Warren on January 26, 1901, when a detachment of the 77th Company of the Coast Artillery took station there. Fort Revere was discontinued as an active post in compliance with orders dated July 31, 1947, and declared surplus on February 15, 1948.

During the nation's Bicentennial, a group of volunteer archaeologists initiated exploratory excavations on the site of old star-shaped Fort Independence built in 1777 and now located in the middle of the circle known as Farina Road, adjoining the walls and gun mounts of Fort Revere. The area encompassing the fortifications has been dedicated as Fort Revere Park.

RICE'S FORT. This frontier defense, located at Charlemont in Franklin County, was probably erected in 1745 during King George's War. Rice's Fort was apparently continuously garrisoned and served throughout the French and Indian War. In June 1755 Captain Moses Rice and Phineas Rice were killed by Indians while at work in a meadow near the fort.

FORT RODMAN (*Fort at Clark's Point; Fort Taber*). The outbreak of the Spanish-American War prompted the restoration of an obsolete fortification that dated back to the Civil War. From 1892 until 1898, the military reservation had been the temporary property of the city of New Bedford, which used it for recreation purposes, and was known as Marine Park. The War Department repossessed the reservation and the first modern

fortifications were established at New Bedford. The earliest fortification at Clark's Point during the Civil War was a sand battery known as the Fort at Clark's Point. It was later designated Fort Taber when actual construction was begun on a granite fort named in honor of Isaac C. Taber, who was then mayor of New Bedford. It was not until 1898 that it was renamed Fort Rodman in honor of Colonel William Logan Rodman, who was killed at Port Hudson, Louisiana, in 1863.

The original plans for the Civil War defense called for a three-tiered fort, but by the time two tiers had been completed in 1871, the idea was shelved. The granite blocks for the third tier lay unused until 1892, when the city utilized them to construct a seawall around the fort. Shortly after the turn of the century, four of the fort's batteries were completed. The first was Walcott Battery, followed by Barton Battery, Cross Battery, and Craig Battery. A still more modern battery, called Battery Milliken, was not installed until 1920. Fort Rodman was active throughout World War II. The post was declared surplus on June 5, 1947.

FORT RUCKMAN. Now an inactive post, Fort Ruckman is located in the summer colony of Nahant, located at the tip of a small peninsula jutting into Massachusetts Bay. It was established in 1921 as a subpost of Fort Banks on a 44-acre tract of land acquired by the government in 1899 and named for Brigadier General John W. Ruckman who died in 1921. A defense of Boston Harbor, the fort's electrically operated powerful 12-inch guns had a clean sweep of the sea almost as far as Newburyport.

CAMP SCHUYLER (*Camp Stanton*). A Civil War training encampment of tents, first called Camp Schuyler, was established in 1861 on the outskirts of Lynnfield in Essex County. In 1862 the post was renamed Camp Stanton in honor of Lincoln's then secretary of war, Edwin M. Stanton. Nine infantry regiments and four artillery batteries, represented by recruits from eastern Massachusetts, were trained at the camp, which was located on both sides of the old Turnpike, now Broadway.

CAMP SCOTT. A temporary Civil War encampment was established on June 28, 1861, by the 15th Massachusetts Infantry two miles south of Worcester's City Hall and named Camp Scott in honor of General Winfield Scott. The camp was terminated on August 7 when the men boarded trains for service in the South. The camp was located in the area adjoining the present intersection of Cambridge and Camp streets.

FORT SEWALL. Situated on the extreme point of land where the town of Marblehead is located, Fort Sewall was erected in 1742 after the General Court that year granted the town 690 pounds to erect a "good and sufficient breastwork and a platform for the accommodation of 12-pounders, or other guns equivalent." It was intended as a defense of the harbor against French warships. It was given the name of Fort Sewall, its only official designation, at a later period in honor of Samuel Sewall, chief justice of the Massachusetts Surpeme Court in 1814.

There has always been some kind of fortification on the site since 1634, when an earthwork was constructed there by the town of Salem. The settlement remained part of Salem until 1649, when the town of Marblehead was incorporated. The present fortification dates from the Revolutionary War, when it was garrisoned by Salem-native Colonel John Glover's famous Essex Regiment in 1775–76. On April 3, 1814, the man-of-war *Constitution*, popularly known as *Old Ironsides*, took refuge in Marblehead Harbor under the guns of the fort after being chased for three days by the British frigates *Tenedos* and *Endymion*. In 1861, when the Civil War erupted, the fort was in ruins, but the town raised $4,000, in addition to a government appropriation, to restore Fort Sewall to a state of defense. It was continuously garrisoned throughout the war by elements of Northern regiments. On May 22, 1892, Marblehead voted to accept the fort and its reservation for use as a public park after it was officially transferred to the custody of the town by the government. During the Spanish-American War, elements of the 5th and 8th Regiments of the Massachusetts Militia garrisoned the fort.

Another of Marblehead's historic landmarks is the old powder magazine built in 1755 during the French and Indian War and located on the old Ferry Road, now Green Street. It was used for the storage of munitions during the Revolution and the War of 1812. Marblehead was the first town in Massachusetts to form a regiment in 1775. During the War of 1812, one-fifth of its population of 6,000 people reportedly served in either the Army or Navy. In 1861 the Marblehead contingent of the 6th Massachusetts Infantry was the first to report to the State House in Boston, after President Lincoln's call for 75,000 volunteers.

FORT SHELDON. The chain of fortifications erected about 1745 from Fort Dummer in Vermont to the Hoosic River included the two fortified defenses built at Bernardston, Franklin County, by Ebenezer Sheldon and his brother, Elisha Sheldon.

CAMP SHEPPARD. A temporary Civil War encampment, Camp Sheppard was located in the vicinity of Spy Pond near Cambridge.

FORT SHIRLEY. In 1744, shortly after the outbreak of King George's War with the French, Fort Shirley was built in the present town of Heath (named for Revolutionary General William Heath) in Franklin County and named in honor of Governor William Shirley. Then located about two miles north of the village, the fort was 60 feet square, constructed of hewn pine, with its 12-foot-high walls enclosing barracks for the officers and men of the garrison. No data has been found to indicate when the fort was abandoned.

SOUTH BATTERY. Constructed in Boston in 1666, South Battery, or Sconce, stood at the foot of Fort Hill near today's Rowe's Wharf. It was destroyed by fire in 1760 but appears to have been rebuilt and was in use during and after the Revolution. The Barricado, which mounted batteries of guns, connected the North and South Batteries and commanded the city's Inner Harbor and Fort Point Channel.

SOUTH FORT. FORT MORRIS.

SPRINGFIELD ARMORY. The nation's oldest manufacturing arsenal, Springfield Armory's history goes back to 1777, when a "laboratory" and arms depot were established in government-leased buildings in what is now the downtown section of the city of Springfield. It was in January 1777 as he left the Princeton (New Jersey) Battlefield that General Washington commissioned his trusted aide, General Henry Knox, to find a suitable location for, and to establish, a major small-arms arsenal. Three months later, after an exhaustive survey, General Knox recommended Springfield as the site for the facility because of the town's location on the long, navigable Connecticut River and its ideal situation midway between New York and Boston. Before the next winter, ground was broken for the Springfield Armory.

On December 20, 1786, Daniel Shays, commanding 300 insurgents, took possession of Springfield's courthouse. Two weeks later, on January 5, with 1,100 men, he attempted to capture the arsenal to secure arms for his men.

State militia under General William Shepard fired into the insurgent ranks, killing 5 men and wounding several others. The rebels were dispersed, and the insurrection was terminated by the capture of its leaders.

Over the years, between the date of its establishment and its closing in April 1968, the Armory produced more than 9,000,000 weapons for the country's armed forces. In 1871 the Army had established an historic arms museum here, and Springfield's residents requested that it remain permanently. The Department of the Interior agreed and willingly consented to a permanent exhibit of more than 11,000 small arms and memorabilia. The museum is now contained within the main red-brick arsenal building erected in 1846. According to the Army, the contents of the museum are the most extensive of their kind in the United States and represent one of the largest collections in the world.

STAGE FORT. FORT GLOUCESTER.

CAMP (MYLES) STANDISH. A staging area and embarkation point during World War II and located in the city of Taunton, Camp Myles Standish (named for the famed Plymouth Colony's Pilgrim military leader) was deactivated in 1948 and conveyed to the Commonwealth of Massachusetts for use as a mental health facility. The use restriction having expired in 1973, the first phase (consisting of 117 acres) of the Myles Standish Industrial Park was initiated to encompass the former site of the Army post.

(OLD) FORT (MYLES) STANDISH. Established in 1863 and situated on Saquish Neck at the northern entrance to Plymouth Harbor, four miles from the city, Old Fort Standish occupied a seven-acre site later acquired by government purchase in 1870. In use during the Spanish-American War and World War I, the small fortification and its reservation land were purchased by a private enterprise in 1925.

FORT (MYLES) STANDISH. Established in 1900 on Lovell's Island in Boston Harbor, Fort Myles Standish served during World War II as a major troop staging area for the Boston Port of Embarkation. During the war, as its city of tents was rapidly replaced by many substantial barracks, the post processed 1,470,411 troops. Fort Standish was inactivated on January 7, 1946.

CAMP STANTON. CAMP SCHUYLER.

FORT STRONG. A fortification originally erected in 1776 on Noodle's Island in Boston Harbor to protect Charlestown and Chelsea, it was repaired and enlarged in 1814 and named in honor of antimilitant Caleb Strong, then governor of Massachusetts. The work was accomplished by the militia and hundreds of civilians in less than two months and garrisoned by the Winslow Blues. The fort served throughout the remainder of the War of 1812 and was abandoned when peace was declared.

In 1867 old Fort Strong was moved down the harbor to the east end of Long Island, five miles southeast of Boston. The fortification retained the same name, but it then honored Major General George C. Strong, U.S.V., who was mortally wounded during the assault against Fort Wagner, South Carolina, in 1863. In 1899 plans were made by the government for a new fortification on the island, and the work of construction was begun on September 13, 1900. In 1902 the fort mounted five 10-inch rifles, two 4.72-inch rapid-fire guns, and two 15-pounders. During World War I, about 1,500 men were in garrison at Fort Strong, mostly elements of the 55th Artillery. Sometime between World Wars I and II, Fort Strong became a subpost of Fort Banks. The post was declared surplus as of September 30, 1947.

CAMP SUTTON. CAMP BANKS.

FORT TABER. FORT RODMAN.

FORT TAYLOR. A frontier defense built in 1745, during King George's War (1744–48), Fort Taylor was located at Charlemont in Franklin County.

FORT WARREN. FORT WINTHROP.

FORT WARREN. A designation originally applied to the fortifications on Governor's Island, renamed Fort Winthrop, the name of Fort Warren was transferred in 1833 to the new works planned for Georges Island at the mouth of Boston Harbor, seven miles southeast of the city. The new Fort Warren was begun in 1837 and first occupied by troops in November 1861. Built of granite and occupying about 18 acres of ground, Fort Warren is the oldest of the harbor's island forts. The two-story, pentagonal-shaped fortress was named for Joseph Warren, Patriot leader killed at Bunker Hill in 1775. Casemated throughout and replete with tunnels leading from rampart to rampart, the fort was never directly involved in the Civil War and became a training

FORT WARREN. (Courtesy of the Massachusetts Department of Commerce.)

center for Union Army troops and a prison for about 5,000 captured Confederate soldiers and leaders, including Alexander H. Stevens, vice president of the Confederate States, and James M. Mason and John Slidell, Confederate commissioners to Great Britain. The Civil War hymn, "John Brown's Body," was composed at the fort and first sung by troops stationed there.

During the calm between the Civil War and the Spanish-American War, new and larger guns, including 12-inch cannon, were added to the fort's armament. But the fort's artillery never fired a shot at an enemy. In both World Wars it served as the control center for mine-laying operations in the harbor. On the island are 7 brick buildings and 15 frame buildings used as officers' quarters and auxiliary barracks. Deactivated after World War II, Fort Warren was declared surplus to the needs of the Army and put up for sale. In November 1957 the 28-acre military reservation was sold for $28,000 to real estate developers for planned conversion to recreational use.

FORT WASHINGTON. The only surviving fortification of the 10-mile-long chain of defenses erected in Cambridge and Charlestown to support the American siege of British-held Boston is the three-gun battery in what is now known as Fort Washington Park in Cambridge. The semi-circular earthwork with three embrasures, originally constructed by General Israel Putnam's troops, has been rebuilt and three post-Revolutionary War cannon emplaced. The one-acre park, surrounded by a commemorative metal fence with cannon- and halbert-designed posts and pickets, is located on Waverly Street just northeast of its intersection with Chestnut Street.

FORT WASHINGTON (*Fort Bailey*). The site of this fort in Marblehead is today occupied by Fountain Park on the lower end of Orne Street, just before it joins Beacon Street, opposite Gerry Island, in the section of town known as Barnegat, the town's first settled area. The site, long known as Bailey's Head, was occupied by Fort Bailey, a defense in use during the Revolution. During the War of 1812, the old fort was repaired, renamed Fort Washington, and manned by local citizens with aid as needed from the Lafayette Guards and Marblehead Light Infantry.

WATERTOWN ARSENAL. Established in 1816 in the town of Watertown, six miles east of Boston, the Arsenal was originally a depot for ordnance and the manufacture of small arms. By the year 1835, it was producing carriages and accessories for field, siege, and seacoast guns. During World War I, the Arsenal's laboratory produced finished steel components for armament and engaged in the design and manufacture of gun carriages. More recently, the Arsenal produced atomic cannon, antiaircraft guns, and most of the accessories needed for the use of Army missiles. A huge complex of 35 principal buildings, the Arsenal occupies a 119-acre tract on the north bank of the Charles River.

CAMP WELLFLEET. Located near South Wellfleet, midway between the towns of Orleans and Provincetown on Cape Cod, Camp Wellfleet was designated a Class I subinstallation of Camp Edwards. As of February 1, 1953, the post became a Class I subinstallation of Fort Devens. Effective June 30, 1961, Camp Wellfleet was inactivated and discontinued as a Department of the Army installation.

WEST HOOSAC BLOCKHOUSE. FORT HOOSAC.

WESTMINSTER FORTS. About the year 1743, the Massachusetts General Court made grants to enable settlers to erect fortifications for protection against Indians. The inhabitants of Westminster in present Worcester County accordingly erected 10 "forts," actually minimally fortified stockades around their dwellings. (See: GARRISON HOUSES.)

CAMP WIGHTMAN. A Civil War encampment located on Long Island in Boston Harbor, Camp Wightman was established on May 12, 1861. "The first regiment to be quartered at Long Island was the famous 'Fighting Ninth.' This regiment was . . . composed almost wholly of men of Irish birth, six of the companies were from Boston, and one each from Salem, Marlboro, Milford, and Stoughton. After a long tedious stay at Faneuil Hall in Boston, the soldiers were taken aboard the *Nellie Baker* . . . and soon arrived at Camp Wightman," named in honor of the Mayor of Boston (Edward Rowe Snow, *The Romance of Boston Bay* [Yankee, 1944], pp. 112–13). On June 26, 1861, the 9th Regiment sailed for Washington.

CASTLE WILLIAM. FORT INDEPENDENCE.

FORT WILLIAM. FORT PICKERING.

WILLIAMS GARRISON. FORT ANSON.

WILLIAMSTOWN BLOCKHOUSE. FORT HOOSAC.

FORT WINTHROP (*Fort Warren*). Roger Conant, Pilgrim member of the Dorchester Adventurers Company, which founded the first trading post at Salem, owned the 70 acres, later called Governor's Island, just off East Boston, while he was residing at Nantasket. In 1632 he leased the island, then known as Conant's Island, to Puritan leader John Winthrop, its first occupant who built his home there. In 1744 Ann Winthrop, heir to the family's estates, was informed that the government had decided to erect fortifications on the island, appropriating 500 pounds for a blockhouse and two batteries. Three acres of the Winthrop island property were purchased for the fort. On April 9, 1808, the government bought from descendant James Winthrop an acre on the island's southern point and three more acres on the summit, together with a 40-foot-wide road

between the two for $15,000, in preparation for the construction of Fort Warren, named in honor of Patriot activist Dr. Joseph Warren, killed during the Battle of Bunker Hill.

On May 23, 1808, Lieutenant Sylvanus Thayer, "the Father of West Point," began building the demilune battery on the island's southern point. He also erected the four-star-shaped fortress at the summit and its adjuncts, a brick guardhouse, and a small powder magazine. Another demilune was constructed on the island shore closer to Boston. In 1833 the Army announced that the defense's name of Fort Warren was to be applied to the new fortifications planned for Georges Island farther down the Harbor and that the Governor's Island fort was to be redesignated Fort Winthrop in honor of John Winthrop, the first governor of Massachusetts. Shortly before the outbreak of the Civil War, Fort Winthrop underwent a program of modernization, Sylvanus Thayer once again being the chief superintending engineer. The work was completed in 1872.

After the fort was regarrisoned for a short period during the Spanish-American War, Fort Winthrop was again placed in caretaking status. Four years later, in the late afternoon of September 7, 1902, disaster struck Governor's Island, which had become a Sunday tourist attraction. There were some 18,000 pounds of gunpowder stored in 100-pound barrels in the powder magazine. It has never been definitely established by investigators whether it was the carelessness of a pipe-smoking Boston tourist or the suspected vandalism by a group of 12 boys from East Boston that touched off the tremendous explosion. Providentially, most of the island's visitors had already left for the mainland. Two men were killed, one of them completely dismembered. The explosion did considerable damage. "The whole top of the island seemed to rise. Bricks, granite blocks weighing tons, earth and stones were scattered all over the island." The fort thereafter was permanently abandoned, but appreciable remnants of Fort Winthrop still remained to attract the curious. During the summer of 1941, the island was joined to the mainland at East Boston and cut down to enlarge Logan International Airport.

CAMP (JOHN E.) WOOL. A temporary Civil War encampment established on June 3, 1862, by the 34th Massachusetts Infantry after its organization, Camp Wool was located at the Agricultural Fairgrounds near Worcester and named in honor of General John E. Wool.

CAMP BACKUS. A temporary Civil War encampment established in 1861 for the organization of the 16th Michigan Infantry, originally known as (Colonel T. W. B.) Stockton's Independent Regiment, Camp Backus was located at Detroit. On September 16, 1861, the regiment, with an aggregate of 761 officers and men, left the camp for Virginia.

CANTONMENT BRADY. FORT BRADY.

FORT BRADY (*Fort Repentigny; Post at Sault Ste. Marie; Fort at Sault St. Marie; Post at St. Mary's; Cantonment Brady*). The first fortification located just east of Sault Ste. Marie, on an 18-mile-square seigniory fronting on the St. Mary's River, was granted on June 24, 1751, by New France's Governor La Jonquière to French Captain Louis le Gardeur de Repentigny, who erected the fort in the late summer of 1751 to protect France's Great Lakes fur trade. During the winter of 1751–52, his men cut 1,100 pickets, 15 feet long, for his fort, and timber for three more houses, about 30 by 20 feet each, which he erected in the spring. The fort enclosed four houses in a palisade measuring 110 square feet. In 1760, during the French and Indian War, the fort was captured by the English. It was destroyed by fire on December 22, 1762. Its site was reoccupied by Fort Brady 60 years later.

The first American military post at Sault Ste. Marie was established in June 1822 by Colonel (later Major General) Hugh Brady with companies A, B, D, I, and K of the 2nd Infantry, intended to guard the strategic strait. It was located on the former site of French Fort Repentigny on the south bank of the St. Mary's River, 15 miles from Lake Superior and 50 miles from Lake Huron. At first the post was known as the Post at Sault Ste. Marie, Michigan Territory. In 1823 and part of 1824 it was referred to as the Post at St. Mary's, Michigan Territory, and later in 1824 and part of 1825 it was called Cantonment Brady. In 1825 its name was changed to Fort Brady.

The post was garrisoned by regular troops until the Mexican War when they were temporarily withdrawn and their places taken by the 1st Michigan Volunteer Infantry. The Volunteers withdrew in the spring of 1848 and the post was unoccupied until June 1, 1849, when it was reoccupied by elements of the 2nd Infantry. In response to threatened Indian hostilities in Minnesota in 1857, the garrison was transferred to Fort Snelling and the public property of Fort Brady was left in the custody of an ordnance

Michigan

sergeant. The post remained unoccupied until May 8, 1866, when elements of the 4th Infantry were stationed there. An Act of Congress approved July 8, 1866, authorized the sale of the old post and establishment of a new Fort Brady in or near the town of Sault Ste. Marie, but it was not until November 25, 1892, that the new post was occupied. The new Fort Brady continued in use until it was inactivated November 25, 1944, and declared surplus on October 1, 1945.

BURNETT'S TRADING POST. The first permanent white settler of St. Joseph was William Burnett. Historical data indicate that he landed by canoe sometime between 1775 and 1782 and established his home and trading post on the west bank of the St. Joseph River, about one and a half miles upstream from its mouth. He also erected a warehouse near the mouth of the river close to the site of where La Salle's storehouse had been erected. In addition, Burnett owned a house on the Kankakee River where he spent his winters, and a warehouse in Chicago. He once sketched a map on which Chicago and its location appeared. It is among the first documents in which the site was rendered by that name.

His trading post was located on the west side of the river, north of Napier Bridge, below the bluff on the river bank a short distance north of the east end of Miller Drive in the city of St. Joseph. William Burnett, enterprising fur entrepreneur that he was, also owned several other trading posts in the region. After his death, about the year 1812, his oldest son James managed the trading post on the St. Joseph River until about 1833. In later years a ferry operated at the site of Burnett's Trading Post as there were no bridges in the locality across the river at that time. A state marker at Langley Avenue and Miller Drive in St. Joseph indicates the Burnett site.

CAMP BUTLER. Probably a temporary Civil War encampment, Camp Butler was reportedly located at or near Mt. Clemens in Macomb County.

CITADEL FORT. The first structure in Detroit's Citadel Fort was a barracks located on the southwest side of town, completed in September 1764 under the direction of Captain John Montresor, engineer. By 1767 the Citadel contained the barracks, a guardhouse, and a blockhouse. During the period from 1775 to 1778, in response to the pressures of the American Revolution, additional buildings were added: an officers' quarters barracks, a commissary store, and another structure of undetermined use. On June 11, 1805, the town and the fort burned to the ground.

COLDWATER TRADING POST. Indian chief Topinabee sold what is now Branch County to the whites in 1821. The next year, Joseph Godfrey established a trading post on the high bank of the Coldwater River at a point where the Oak Grove Cemetery is located in the town of Coldwater.

FORT COLLYER. FORT DRUMMOND.

CAMP CUSTER. FORT CUSTER.

FORT CUSTER (*Camp Custer*). One of the nation's 16 largest posts established to train World War I draftees and located five miles south of Battle Creek in Calhoun and Kalamazoo counties, it was named in honor of Lieutenant Colonel (Major General U.S. Volunteers) George A. Custer, famed leader of the 7th Cavalry, killed at Little Big Horn, Montana, in 1876. During World War I, some 40,000 troops were trained at the post, established primarily for the 85th Division, which occupied the cantonment of 1,282 buildings from August 1917 to July 1918. It was designated a demobilization center December 3, 1918. Following the war, most of the buildings were dismantled, but the site was continued in use as a summer training camp for the Reserve Officers Training Corps (ROTC) and the Citizens Military Training Corpos (CMTC). Designated a permanent post on August 15, 1940, it was renamed Fort Custer, and new construction was begun to accommodate World War II recruits. The first barracks were completed and occupied by troops on November 20, 1940. Fort Custer was inactivated on June 5, 1953.

FORT DE BUADE. By the year 1670, European influence, French and English, in the Upper Great Lakes extended southward to the Straits of Mackinac area. In 1671 a mission was established by Father Jacques Marquette at St. Ignace opposite modern Mackinaw City across the strategic straits. The mission served as a focal point for the Ottawa, the Chippewa, and the Huron in the region. By 1683, St. Ignace was also the site of a French military post, garrisoned by 30 soldiers commanded by Greysolon Dulhut. Fort de Buade, named for Louis de Buade, comte de Frontenac, the governor of New France, was established adjacent to the mission in 1689 by Louis de La Porte de Louvigny, who had arrived with 150 Canadian soldiers. The maintenance of a fortified post at the strategic location was a response to King William's War (1689–97) being waged by the English and to encroachments by British traders from Albany, New York, into the Mackinac Straits area after 1686.

Antoine de La Mothe Cadillac succeeded Louvigny as Fort De Buade's commandant in 1695. A year later, Louis XIV decreed the Upper Great Lakes closed to the fur trade. This edict was issued to control an oversupply of furs resulting from the increase in trading activity in the Upper Great Lakes. As a consequence, Cadillac sought and obtained permission to establish Fort Pontchartrain at Detroit and was able to convince many of the Straits area Indians to bring their furs there. The Jesuit missionaries were left with only a miniscule parish at St. Ignace and, by 1705, had abandoned the mission and returned to Quebec. By 1710 New France's government at Quebec had become cognizant of the importance of maintaining military sovereignty over the Straits of Mackinac area and made plans to reestablish a new post there (See: FORT MICHILIMACKINAC.)

FORT DETROIT (*Fort Pontchartrain; Fort Lernoult; Fort Shelby*). The highly strategic value of the 27-mile-long Detroit River strait between Lake Erie and Lake St. Clair, where the modern industrial city of Detroit now stands on its western bank, had been repeatedly noted by French explorers, missionaries, fur traders, and soldiers. Whenever the opportunity was presented, they reported as much to New France's military authorities. The narrow strait linking Detroit with Amherstburg and Windsor in Ontario is the gateway to the three western Great Lakes—Huron, Michigan, and Superior.

The last commandant of Fort de Buade on the Straits of Mackinac, Antoine de la Mothe Cadillac, whose name is memorialized in our modern society by a luxury automobile, was the acid-tongued Gascon who founded the fort and settlement. Granted a royal commission by Louis XIV to build a fortification there to circumvent English designs in the Old Northwest, Cadillac erected Fort Pontchartrain in 1701, naming it in honor of Louis Phelypeaux, Count Pontchartrain, minister of Marine and Colonies. The fort was a stockaded fortified settlement about 200 feet square situated on the first rise of ground from the river and located between present Griswold and Shelby streets, south of Jefferson Avenue. During the 1750s, the fort and village were enlarged three times. By the time Fort Pontchartrain was peacefully surrendered in 1760 to British

FORT DETROIT. Plan drawn in 1749. (Courtesy of the National Map Collection, Public Archives of Canada.)

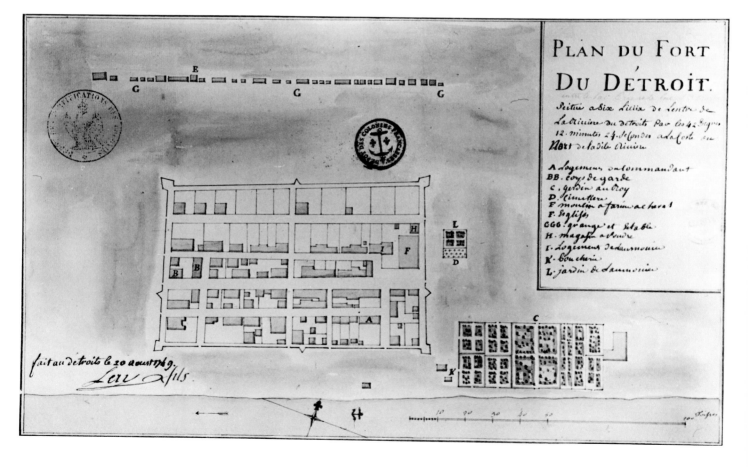

forces led by Robert Rogers, the French military town had assumed formidable proportions.

Changing its name to Fort Detroit, the British garrison successfully defended it for more than a year during Pontiac's War, one of the very few British posts to survive the Indian revolt. Henry ("Hair Buyer") Hamilton, commandant of Detroit 1775–79 and lieutenant governor of Canada simultaneously fomented Indian raids against American settlements in the Ohio Valley and strengthened Detroit's defenses. He supervised the addition of new blockhouses and batteries to the original defense, a 15-foot-high cedar stockade fortified with 11 blockhouses and batteries. On October 7, 1778, he left Detroit with a force of about 200 English and Indians and marched for 71 days through wilderness territory during the dead of winter to capture Vincennes in Indiana, where he was later surprised by George Rogers Clark and his small heterogeneous army, compelling Hamilton to surrender his garrison on February 25, 1779.

Clark began to make plans to assault Detroit. Anticipating such an attack, Captain Richard B. Lernoult in 1779 constructed a new defense, Fort Lernoult, just beyond the town's limits, in the immediate vicinity of today's Federal Building. The fort was a high earthen rampart with half-bastions, fronted by a ditch with a palisade in its middle. But Clark, unable to muster a sufficient force and congregate enough supplies, gave up the plan. Fort Lernoult was not surrendered to American authorities until January 11, 1796, when it was renamed Fort Shelby. Captain Moses Porter occupied Detroit when the British evacuated the town in compliance with the provisions of the Jay Treaty. Revolutionary War veteran Lieutenant Colonel John Francis Hamtramck, with elements of the First Legion, arrived on July 13, 1796, to take command of the garrison of about 400 officers and men. Some of the soldiers were barracked in Fort Lernoult, while the rest were quartered in the Citadel, the palisaded enclosure inside the town's stockade's west wall and just north of present St. Anne Street.

Catastrophic disasters spawn legends. The fiery holocaust that enveloped Detroit on the morning of June 11, 1805, was doubtless due to criminal negligence. It is known that the fire started in the stable in the rear of a bakery. By three o'clock in the afternoon, houses, stores, barns, St. Anne's Church, the Citadel, and the stockade all had been reduced to ashes. Only the old blockhouse near the river and the fort remained intact. Governor William Hull arrived on July 1, greatly shocked to find ashes where he had anticipated the capital would be situated.

Wasting no time, he administered the oaths of office to the men selected as secretary and judges on the following day. The fort's cannon fired a salute to proclaim the birth of Michigan Territory.

DETROIT ARSENAL. Located at Dearbornville (modern Dearborn), situated on the South Branch of the Rouge River, 10 miles from Detroit, this United States Arsenal was begun in 1833 and completed in 1837. It originally consisted of 11 brick buildings arranged around a square, 360 feet to a side. The principal structure, intended as a depot, was three stories, 120 feet long and 30 feet deep, and occupied the center of the eastern side of the square. The buildings were connected by a continuous 12-foot-high heavy masonry wall for protection. The fort was intended to be used for the mounting and equipping of artillery and for repairing small arms, rather than for housing troops. Despite this, troops were maintained at the Arsenal between 1851 and 1861 after Detroit Barracks was abandoned.

The old Detroit Arsenal served until it had outlived its usefulness and was put up for sale by the federal government at a public auction in 1877. The eleven buildings within the Arsenal walls gradually gave way to progress, and only one remains intact today. The Commandant's Quarters was used as a library, an American Legion Hall, city offices, the village hall, and a police station until it was turned into a museum in 1949. The building was completely restored to its original condition in 1959 and is primarily a military museum. The powder magazine, located outside of the Arsenal proper, was converted into a private residence in 1883. This building, now the McFadden-Ross House, was given to the City of Dearborn in 1950 for use as a museum.

DETROIT BARRACKS (*Post at Detroit*). In 1796 the old military post at Detroit was surrendered to the United States by the British. It served as headquarters for American troops in the Northwest after the conclusion of the War of 1812 and was known as Post at Detroit, occupying various sites. In 1839 it was designated Detroit Barracks. Although the post was abandoned in June 1851, a military establishment was maintained at the Detroit Arsenal until Fort Wayne was occupied in 1861.

POST AT DETROIT. DETROIT BARRACKS.

FORT DRUMMOND (*Fort Collyer*). British Fort Collyer, located at Michilimackinac during the War of 1812, was removed eastward to Drummond Island in Lake Huron after news of the Treaty of Ghent reached the British outposts. The new fort erected on the island in 1815 was named in honor of Lieutenant General Sir Gordon Drummond, commander of the Great Lakes district. In 1828 the fort was evacuated by the British when Drummond Island was declared to be American property.

CAMP EATON. Located near Island Lake in Livingston County, Camp Eaton was used for the mobilization of Michigan's National Guard regiments during the Spanish-American War. It was abandoned the same year when the soldiers were moved northward to the outskirts of Grayling in Crawford County.

FORT GEORGE. FORT HOLMES.

GRAND ISLAND POST. Les Grandes Isles was the name applied by early French explorers to the three islands extending across the entrance to Munising Bay on the south shore of Lake Superior in present Alger County. The designation Grand Island is still used for the largest of the group, but the other two islands have been renamed Wood Island and Williams Island. The fact that they were long inhabited by large bands of Chippewa Indians influenced the establishment of a trading post there by the North West Company. Later, because of American legal restrictions against British trading operations, the Canadian traders withdrew, and shortly thereafter the post was reestablished by the American Fur Company, which maintained it until about 1840.

FORT GRATIOT. A War of 1812 fort situated on the west bank of the St. Clair River, a half-mile from the outlet of Lake Huron, in the town of Port Huron, St. Clair County, Fort Gratiot was established on May 14, 1814, by elements of the 2nd Infantry commanded by Captain Charles Gratiot. When the Army reduced its forces in 1822, the post was abandoned, but then reestablished in 1828 because of unrest among the Indians in Wisconsin. Periodically evacuated and reoccupied, Fort Gratiot was finally abandoned about June 1, 1879.

CAMP GRAYLING. Located five miles southwest of the city of Grayling, this historic training ground of the Michigan National Guard since 1911 surrounds Lake Margretha and sprawls across some 130,000 acres, occupying parts of Crawford, Kalkaska and Otsego counties. Although Camp Grayling is primarily a tent camp, about 400 buildings exist in the main part of the reservation. The camp was used as a mobilization point and training ground for the infantry and as an Air National Guard base during World War II.

GROSSE ILE STOCKADE. Built in 1815 on land belonging to Alexander Macomb, who was then the commander of the Army's forces at Detroit, the stockade was located about three miles below the Macomb mansion on East River Road in Grosse Ile, to the east of the city of Detroit. Although it was intended to provide protection against marauding Indians, some historians maintain that the fort was erected by Americans to establish sovereignty over Grosse Ile, which was then a subject of border dispute between Great Britain and the United States. The stockade extended from the river several hundred feet west, then south about 200 feet, and back to the river, enclosing several acres. There were several log houses within the enclosure, the largest one facing the river used as officers' quarters. The two smaller buildings at the rear, with two more north and two south—six in all—formed the soldiers' barracks. The Grosse Ile Stockade was reportedly destroyed in 1819.

FORT HOGAN. A short-lived earthwork defense erected by 50 militiamen in 1832 on land belonging to Daniel Hogan in response to news of the Black Hawk uprising, it was located near the east end of Nottawa Prairie near Colon in St. Joseph County. Within three days, when it had become apparent that there was no Indian threat after all, the area's citizens and militia lost interest.

FORT HOLMES (*Fort George*). Situated on the highest point of Mackinac Island, 325 feet above the Straits and half a mile to the rear of Fort Mackinac is the site of Fort Holmes, which was built as Fort George by the British during their occupancy of the island 1812–14. The fort had been built soon after the British captured Fort Mackinac on July 17, 1812. During the unsuccessful American attack against Fort George on August 4, 1814, Major Andrew Hunter Holmes was killed. The fort, standing on the southwestern, heavily wooded bluff of the island and overlooking the harbor, was garrisoned by 57 men. The strategically placed British redoubt consisted of a two-story blockhouse with an underground powder magazine and was surrounded by cedar palisades and an earthen embankment.

After the war, when Mackinac Island was reclaimed by the United States, the fort was renamed Fort Holmes in honor of the major. The blockhouse, the central feature of the fort, was destroyed by the Americans, who made it a target for gunnery practice. In 1904 the Mackinac Island State Park Commission rebuilt the blockhouse, but not as a true representation. In 1933 a brush fire consumed the height. The fort was rebuilt in 1936 by Army engineers who erected an authentic two-storied reproduction surrounded by timbered earthworks.

LA FRAMBOISE TRADING POST. During the late summer of 1809, at his trading post at the junction of the Grand and Flat rivers, near present Grand Haven on Lake Michigan in Ottawa County, Joseph La Framboise, fur trader for John Jacob Astor's headquarters post on Mackinac Island, was shot and killed by a young Ottawa Indian who had been refused whiskey. His widow, at whose feet he fell dead, continued the operation of the Grand Haven post for 15 years. A striking, beautiful descendant of an Ottawa chief and a French father, Madame La Framboise was also licensed by Astor and made a snug fortune in the thriving trade.

During her frequent business trips to Astor's Mackinac headquarters, she became an influential arbitrator in Indian-white disputes and "Little Mother" to the Indian tribes in the Old Northwest. Her 17-year-old daughter Jossette wedded Captain Benjamin K. Pierce, commandant of Fort Mackinac and elder brother of Franklin K. Pierce, who later became president of the United States. Madame La Framboise sold out her fur-trading interests in 1824 and retired to Mackinac Island. She and her daughter, who died after only six years of marital bliss, were interred in a crypt beneath Mackinac Island's Ste. Anne's Catholic Church.

L'ANSE POST. After the Revolutionary War, the south shore of Lake Superior became dotted with fur trade posts of the North West Company, including L'Anse Post on Keweenah Bay in present Baroga County. Operated from about 1800 until the outbreak of the War of 1812, the post was inactive for the next few years until the founding of the American Fur Company by John Jacob Astor. A post was reestablished at L'Anse in 1817–18 under John Johnston, an educated half-breed from Sault Ste. Marie. In July of 1818, John Holiday of Mackinac Island was engaged to operate the L'Anse post and remained for the next 20 years, during which he established adjacent to the post's trading house a thriving agricultural complex where he raised Indian corn, peas, and garden vegetables. Beginning in the late 1830s, many individuals worked at the post. By the 1870s the fur trade was practically dead in the region. This was gradually brought about by the radical reduction by treaty of Indian-free land and the advance of mining and lumbering frontiers, and the ultimate establishment of a mostly non-Indian community at L'Anse.

FORT LERNOULT. FORT DETROIT.

CAMP LUCAS. Located about a mile from Sault Ste. Marie's business district, Camp Lucas was established by the Army during World War II to guard the locks at St. Mary's River Falls. Inactive since June 30, 1960, the camp was permanently discontinued in 1962.

CAMP LYON. This temporary Civil War encampment near Detroit was opened when the 1st Michigan Cavalry began recruiting on August 21, 1861. The camp served as a place of rendezvous and organization under the direction of Colonel Thornton F. Brodhead. The cavalry unit was mustered into service the following September 13.

FORT MACKINAC. FORT MICHILIMACKINAC.

FORT MIAMI. La Salle started out for the Illinois country with four canoes and fourteen men in September 1679, the day after the sailing of the *Griffon*, the vessel he had constructed at Niagara for a rendezvous in the upper Mississippi Valley. They paddled along the shore of Lake Michigan to the mouth of the St. Joseph River at present St. Joseph in Berrien County, where on November 4 he had a fort built, naming it Fort Miami for the Indian tribe inhabiting the area. It was about 40 by 80 feet, and faced the river on two sides. When six of his men deserted, he ordered his trusted aide, Henri Tonty, to go in search of them; after several days he returned with three of the men.

Father Louis Hennepin, a member of the party, briefly described the building of the fort: "There was an eminence with a kind of platform naturally fortified. It was pretty high and steep, of a triangular form, defended on two sides by the river and on the other by a deep ditch. . . . We began to build a redoubt of eighty feet long and forty feet broad with great square pieces of timber laid one upon another. . . . We employed the whole month of November about that work. . . . The approach of winter and the apprehension that M. La Salle had that his vessel was lost made him very melancholy." [Oscar J. Craig, "Ouiatanon: A Study in Indiana History" in *Indiana Historical Society Publications* 2, no. 8 (1893): 325–26]

Most of the early Old Northwest historians, including Francis Parkman himself, have mistakenly assumed that Fort St. Joseph was located at the mouth of the river and have confused it with Fort Miami, located farther up the river at Niles and maintained but a few years. La Salle's fort was apparently pillaged and burned by disloyal members of his expedition.

FORT MICHILIMACKINAC (*Fort Mackinac*).

Located on the Straits of Mackinac at present Mackinaw City, Cheboygan County, Fort Michilimackinac was an important bastion of French and English power and a vital fur-trade center. French hegemony in the American heartland was closely related to its control of the highly strategic straits, the crossroads of the upper Great Lakes connecting Lakes Michigan, Huron, and Superior. During the early interior explorations of North America, the Great Lakes and their related waterways were the principal routes into the continent for the French, the first Europeans to traverse them, and their importance did not escape them.

The earliest French activity on the straits centered on Mackinac Island and at St. Ignace, on their north side. In 1670–71, Père Claude Dablon founded a Jesuit mission on the island, which he named St. Ignace after the founder of his order, St. Ignatius. He was soon joined by Père Jacques Marquette, who brought his Huron Indians from the upper end of Lake Superior. In 1672 the mission was moved to the mainland on the north side of the straits, at which time Marquette took charge, and a fort was added to the mission. For some years after 1696, the French officially abandoned the straits, because of the overabundance of pelts which ruined the fur market in France and overflowed the storehouses in Montreal and Quebec. But illegal traders maintained contact with the Indians. The French finally returned in 1712 and during 1715–20 erected a new fort, Fort Michilimackinac, on the south shore of the straits.

The fortified trading post was built on the tongue of land known to the Indians as Pequotenong ("headland"), a site now occupied by the Michilimackinac State Tourist Park, one mile west of Mackinaw City. The interior log structures went up first. The perimeter of the compound was palisaded with pointed logs and blockhouses occupied the four angles, armed

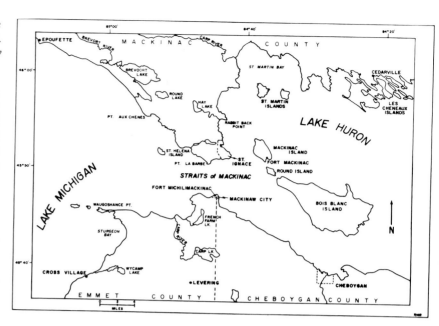

with six iron cannon. British forces under Captain Henry Balfour peacefully took over the fort in September 1761 during the last months of the French and Indian War. The British ensign replaced the French *fleur-de-lis* over Fort Michilimackinac, and the post gradually adopted a British atmosphere. Renovations included the extension of the stockade, the destruction of old French homes replaced by a new barracks, and a new house for the commandant. Salvageable materials, such as limestone foundations and chimneys, were used in the new construction, which led to interpretation difficulties for twentieth-century archaeologists.

In 1763, not quite two years after the British took possession of the straits, the most formidable Indian resistance that the British ever faced was initiated by an astute and purposeful Ottawa chief

FORT MICHILIMACK-INAC. The Straits of Mackinac. (Courtesy of the Mackinac Island State Park Commission, Mackinac Island, Michigan.)

FORT MICHILI-MACKINAC. Surrounded by the Great Lakes. (Courtesy of the Mackinac Island State Park Commission, Mackinac Island, Michigan.)

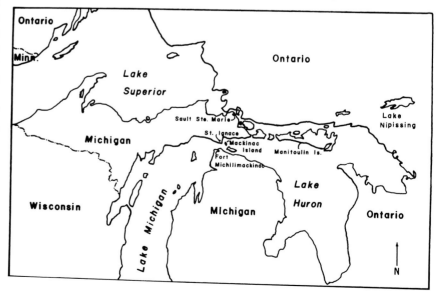

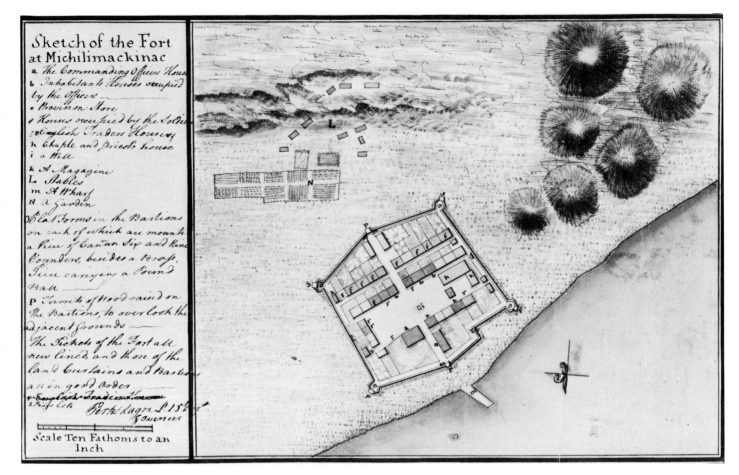

*FORT MICHILIMACK-
INAC. Plan of the origi-
nal fort. (Courtesy of the
Clements Library, Uni-
versity of Michigan.)*

on the Detroit River. The Indian conspiracy caught the complacent British military by surprise. Fort Detroit and Fort Pitt were the only exceptions. In rapid succession, Forts Sandusky, St. Joseph, Miami, and Ouiatanon fell. The largest of them all, Fort Michilimackinac, was the last to fall, and most of its 35-man garrison was massacred.

The British reoccupied Fort Michilimackinac, a near ruin, on September 22, 1764, and it was the only British-garrisoned outpost on the Great Lakes above Detroit until near the close of the War for Independence. Fort Michilimackinac's last commandant was Major Patrick Sinclair. He believed that Michilimackinac was much too vulnerable to attack by Colonel George Rogers Clark. Sinclair obtained official permission to move the fort to turtle-shaped Mackinac Island in 1780. The French, Indians, and the traders accompanied Sinclair's troops, and the mainland post was abandoned. The beach's wind-swept sands gradually obliterated the site and, "figuratively and literally, Fort Michilimackinac was buried in history." Today, a five-mile-long suspension bridge costing $100 million, completed in 1957, spans the straits between Mackinaw City and St. Ignace.

Mackinac Island evolved as the great fur-trad-

ing center of the northern Great Lakes. Sinclair built his fort, named Fort Mackinac, on the high, strategic stone bluff on the southeastern end of the three-mile-long island, overlooking the village and harbor. Today, the original stone ramparts, three blockhouses, sally ports, and officers' quarters are still there, completely renovated and faithfully maintained. On September 1, 1796, in compliance with the provisions of the Jay Treaty, Major Henry Burbeck, commanding 110 American soldiers, took over the occupation of Fort Mackinac, as Lieutenant Andrew Foster withdrew his British garrison, the last in the Old Northwest Territory.

In 1933–34, after intermittent considerations since the beginning of this century were given to the idea of constructing a replica of Fort Michilimackinac, the Fort Mackinac State Park Commission finally obtained funds to initiate archaeological explorations on the site. In 1959 concentrated procedures were undertaken for a $500,000 full-scale reconstruction of the fort on its original site. Within the perimeter of the 20-foot-high stockade are officers' quarters, barracks, the King's storehouse, a French church, British trader cabins, and the blockhouses mounting contemporary-period cannon. The 1763 massacre is reenacted annually on May 30. The three-acre, reoccupied fort site is almost within the shadow of the southern approach of the majestic Mackinac Bridge, linking Michigan's lower and upper peninsulas.

MOREAU'S TRADING POST. Reportedly established in a little-known Ottawa Indian village called So-wan-que-sake and located on present Irving Road, about six miles northwest of Hastings in Barry County, Moreau's post was erected in 1827 and abandoned in 1836. The original monument and plaque erected in 1914 to commemorate the site was replaced in 1966 by the local county historical society.

ONTONAGON TRADING POST. John Jacob Astor's American Fur Company operated a substantially built trading post at the mouth of the Iron River on Lake Superior, 13 miles west of the town of Ontonagon in the county of the same name. Established sometime after 1805 but before 1820, the Iron River trading post was active for many years, serving the Ontonagon Indians as well as those to the south as far as Lac Vieux Desert.

FORT PONTCHARTRAIN. FORT DETROIT.

FORT REPENTIGNY. FORT BRADY.

CAMP RIVER ROUGE PARK. The Army's 728th Military Police Battalion was established at Camp River Rouge Park at Detroit in 1942. The camp was a 22-acre security military police post established "in the interest of national health and safety." In a press release, dated November 19, 1945, the War Department declared the camp surplus property, as of November 15, 1945.

FORT SAGINAW. On July 25, 1822, a detachment of 3rd Infantry troops commanded by Major Daniel Baker from Fort Howard at Green Bay established a fortified post on the west bank of the Saginaw River, across from a large Chippewa village, 25 miles from the river's mouth, at the present city of Saginaw. Its establishment was intended to subdue the ill-tempered Chippewa. The troops erected a blockhouse and surrounded it with a strong stockade. Within the quadrangle were the officers' quarters on the north side while the three other sides were occupied by barracks accommodating soldiers and their families, aggregating about 150 persons, all under the subcommand of Captain John Garland of Company K, 3rd Infantry. All of the post returns are headed "Post of Saguina."

FORT MICHILIMACKINAC. Replica of the West Blockhouse as it looked in 1798. (Courtesy of the Michigan Tourist Council.)

In 1823 nearly the whole garrison was disabled by malaria. The post surgeon, Dr. Zina Pitcher, was so ill himself that he had to be carried on a litter to attend to his soldier patients. Despite his best efforts, many of the garrison died, forcing the abandonment of the fort and the removal in September 1823 of most of the remaining surviving troops and their families on two schooners to Detroit, leaving a token detachment until July 1824. Major Baker declared that "only Indians, muskrats, and bullfrogs can live in Michigan" (F. Clever Bald, *Michigan in Four Centuries* [1954]). The site of the fort many years later was occupied by the Hotel Fordney.

FORT ST. CLAIR. The name "St. Clair" was often used as an alternate spelling for Sinclair. Major Patrick Sinclair, later British lieutenant governor of the Mackinac Straits district, erected Fort St. Clair, 25 miles from Detroit, on the St. Clair River, in 1765 when he was in charge of transporting supplies from Detroit to Michilimackinac. The fort was reportedly abandoned 20 years later after the end of the American Revolution.

FORT ST. JOSEPH. In 1686, Daniel Greysolon Dulhut (for whom Duluth, Minnesota, is named), was ordered to build a fort between Lake Huron and Lake Erie to prevent English traders from operating in the upper Great Lakes. Dulhut, after leaving Michilimackinac with 50 *coureurs de bois*, selected a location at the head of the St. Clair River, on the present site of Port Huron, for a stockade that he named Fort St. Joseph. It shortly became the rendezvous for nearly 200 *coureurs de bois* and about 500 Indians representing various tribes in the region. Dulhut left sometime during the summer of 1687, and Governor Denonville sent Louis Armand de Lom d'Arce, baron de Lahontan, to take over the command of the fort. An ardent sportsman but in need of the convivial companionship provided in more populous places, Lahontan yearned for Montreal and Quebec. He decided the fort was not worth maintaining, and burned it and set out on August 27, 1688, for Michilimackinac.

FORT ST. JOSEPH. Once they had established a foothold on the St. Lawrence River, the French set out to expand the boundaries of New France in the final decades of the seventeenth century. One of the principal routes they used from the Great Lakes to the upper Mississippi Valley was the St. Joseph River, the Kankakee portage, and the Illinois River. This was La Salle's favored route. The military occupation of the region was effected very soon after his first trip up the St. Joseph River by the founding of a Jesuit mission in 1691 on the site of today's city of Niles in present Berrien County. The military fort and trading post, constructed there in 1697, was named for the river. This was the second French fort so named, the first built on the present site of Port Huron in 1686.

Situated one mile from the center of Niles, on a bluff above the river, Fort St. Joseph in the beginning was a rather crude palisaded enclosure, furnished with a few pieces of iron and stone ordnance. Considered highly strategic because it commanded the portage between the St. Joseph and Kankakee rivers, the fort in the subsequent decades was enlarged, improved, and renovated from time to time by the French. With the village of the Miamis on the right bank of the river and that of the Potawatomi on the left bank, almost immediately opposite, Fort St. Joseph became a favored rendezvous for many Indians and French traders.

Surrendered to the British at the end of the French and Indian War, captured on May 25, 1763, by Pontiac's Indians, who massacred most of the British garrison, reoccupied by the British the following year, captured but very briefly occupied by the Spanish, Fort St. Joseph ultimately passed into American possession after the Revolution, by which time much of the fort's settlement had ceased to exist. The remains of the fort's earthworks were still very much in evidence when the first American pioneers arrived to settle Michigan's fertile soil. Today, the site of the fort lies beneath an abandoned sanitary landfill, a rather ignominious epitaph for a historic frontier landmark. Fort St. Joseph was the only Michigan fort under four flags—French, British, Spanish, and American. The Fort St. Joseph Museum at Niles has an especially large and valuable collection of artifacts recovered from the old fort site and its vicinity. The official state marker, commemorating the fort, is on Bond Street, north of Fort Street.

POST AT ST. MARY'S. FORT BRADY.

FORT SAULT STE. MARIE. FORT BRADY.

POST AT SAULT STE. MARIE. FORT BRADY.

FORT SHELBY. FORT DETROIT.

CAMP SMITH. A temporary encampment situated on the shore of the lake near Battle Creek, Camp Smith was established on August 6, 1889, by Colonel Henry M. Black with elements of 10 companies of the 23rd Infantry, aggregating 286 men.

FORT WAYNE. The war scare of the 1840s, engendered by Canada's Patriot Rebellion that began in 1838 and the then ongoing bitter American-British dispute over the occupation of Oregon territory, resulted in the authorization in 1841 for the construction, actually begun in 1843, of Fort Wayne at Detroit. Named in honor of General Anthony Wayne and built on the right bank of the Detroit River at the foot of Livernois Avenue, then about two and one-half miles from the center of the city, it was completed in 1851 as a massive, square-bastioned fortress with stone barracks. Its 17-foot-thick walls were honeycombed with casemates embrasured for cannon and loopholed for rifle fire. The fort was first officially garrisoned by regular troops of the 3rd Cavalry on December 15, 1861.

The line of officers' quarters, then wooden structures, was laid out in 1879. New additional brick barracks were constructed during the period 1890–1910. Fort Wayne, which never fired a shot in anger, was used to train troops for service during the Civil War and was a major base during the Indian wars and the Spanish-American War. It served major support and training functions during both world wars. In May 1949 the government transferred title to the fort to the city of Detroit provided it would be maintained as a historical monument. The old stone barracks have been converted into a museum.

WAYNE STOCKADE. In 1793 the first American settlement was made on Michigan soil, accompanied by the raising of the American flag,

FORT WILKINS. (Courtesy of the Michigan Tourist Council.)

at Frenchtown, modern Monroe on Lake Erie, in 1796. The official raising of the American standard took place at the blockhouse, known as the Wayne Stockade, burned in August 1812 by the British.

FORT WILKINS. Named for Secretary of War William Wilkins, Fort Wilkins was established on May 28, 1844, on Keweenah Point between Lake Fanny Hooe (named for the commandant's sister-in-law) and Lake Superior, near Copper Harbor on Michigan's upper peninsula, to protect the area's copper miners from the Indians. General Hugh Brady left Detroit with Captain R. E. Cleary and companies A and B of the 5th Infantry to superintend the construction of a stockade and barracks. The fort did not see military action, for the Indians were friendly. The fort's commandant was Captain William Alburtus.

Fort Wilkins was evacuated on July 24, 1846, when the troops were withdrawn for service in the Mexican War. The fort was reoccupied in the fall of 1867 and finally discontinued August 30, 1870. Keweenah and Houghton counties later jointly purchased the site from the government and deeded it to the state. Today, the Fort Wilkins State Park incorporates the restored stockade and buildings of the fort.

CAMP WILLIAMS. A temporary Civil War encampment established in the spring of 1861 for the organization of the 4th Michigan Regiment, Camp Williams was located in the suburbs of the city of Adrian, Lenawee County. The regiment was mustered into service on June 20, 1861, and four days later entrained for Washington, D.C., and the war front.

FORT ADAMS. A fur-trading post operated by the Columbia Fur Company, Fort Adams was located at Lac Qui Parle in 1826.

AITKEN'S POST. William A. Aitken had a trading post at or near the present site of Gregory in Morrison County about 1850.

FORT ANTOINE. In 1685 fur trader Nicholas Perrot began the establishment of a series of log-built posts on and in the vicinity of Lake Pepin. He erected Fort Perrot at the southern end of the lake and Fort Antoine on its eastern shore two miles south of present Stockholm, Wisconsin.

BAKER'S POST. In 1832 Benjamin Baker operated a fur post two miles below the mouth of the Crow Wing River, on the east bank of the Mississippi, in present Anoka County.

FORT BEAUHARNOIS. Located on the west side of Lake Pepin, probably on Sandy Point, near present Frontenac in Goodhue County, Fort Beauharnois was established on September 18, 1727, by René Boucher, sieur de la Perrière. It was established to protect the French trade with the Sioux Indians. Occupying a site 100 feet square, with a 12-foot-high palisade enclosing log-built houses for the commandant and missionaries and the chapel, with other structures built by the men for themselves outside the stockade, the fort was named for Charles de la Boische, marquis de Beauharnois, the governor of New France.

Fort Beauharnois was abandoned in October 1728 because of Sioux hostility towards the French. It was reoccupied four years later and rebuilt on more elevated ground close to the original site. Once again rebuilt in 1750, the fort was finally abandoned sometime in 1756 when its garrison was withdrawn for military service against the British during the French and Indian War. Lake Pepin's shores were favored locations with a number of traders. There was still a post there in 1830, located on "Point des Sables," most probably operated by Astor's American Fur Company.

CAMP BEAVER CREEK. A temporary military post, Camp Beaver Creek was established on June 30, 1860, by Company F, 4th Artillery, about 16 miles north of Fort Ridgely.

FORT BIDDLE (*Crow Wing River Posts*). According to the notes compiled by Grace Lee Nute for her pioneering study of Minnesota's

Minnesota

fur-trading history (*Minnesota History Quarterly,* 11 [1930]),

James McGill wintered at Crow Wing River as early as 1771. Perrault wintered there in 1790. A house of the American Fur Company on Crow Island in the Mississippi was designated by Lawrence Taliaferro, the Indian agent at Fort Snelling, as Fort Biddle in 1826. In 1837 Clement H. Beaulieu established a trading post near the mouth of the river. Henry M. Rice also had an establishment in this locality. On a manuscript map of the Fort Ripley reservation drafted in 1848, a post is indicated opposite the mouth of Crow Wing River.

The area became the center of Indian trading for all the upper country.

BIG STONE LAKE POST. In 1823 Hazen Mooers had a trading post located on the west side of Big Stone Lake in present Big Stone County. During the years 1843–46, Martin McLeod also had a post on the lake.

FORT BOLIVAR. The Columbia Fur Company's post on Leaf Lake in present Otter Tail County was given the name of Fort Bolivar by Lawrence Taliaferro in 1826.

BOUYS POST (*Isle House*). This fur-trading post, also known as Isle House, was located at the outlet of Rainy Lake on American territory in present Koochiching County. It was probably established soon after 1816, when Astor's American Fur Company became the chief fur-trading concern in the region of the Great Lakes south of the international border.

CAMERON'S POST. John Cameron, one of Alexander Henry's men, built a fur post in 1803 "on the east side of the Red River at Rivière aux Marais, now the Snake River," in present Marshall County.

CANNON RIVER POSTS. Alexander Faribault, long a prominent American Fur Company factor, began trading at the Bois Plumé, frequently spelled Bois Plaine, on the Cannon River in 1826 or 1827. The posts he established in the vicinity of the river during the subsequent decade were on the present sites of Waterville and Morristown in today's Le Sueur County, at a large Sioux village on the northwest shore of Cannon Lake, and at Faribault in Rice County.

CASS LAKE POSTS. In 1794 Perrault erected a fort on Upper Red Cedar Lake (modern Cass Lake), at the entrance of the Red Cedar River in Beltrami County. Another North West Company post seems to have been close to the outlet of the Mississippi River. Between these two sites and west of the entrance of Tongue was a post of the American Fur Company, about 1820.

FORT CHARLOTTE. The Grand Portage National Monument on U.S. 61, about 38 miles northeast of Grand Marais and 49 miles southwest of the Canadian cities of Fort William and Port Arthur, commemorates the existence 200 years ago of the great fur-trading depot and rendezvous in the northeast corner of Minnesota on the north shore of Lake Superior. It was at this site—the Lake Superior terminus of the Grand Portage, the "great carrying place"—that a fur-

FORT CHARLOTTE. The reconstructed fort. (Courtesy of the Minnesota Department of Business Development.)

trading post was established in the late 1770s. Grand Portage, neither the longest nor the most difficult, was a vital link on the chain of 120 portages along the great artery of the Northwest fur trade.

The nine-mile portage route, connecting the Great Lakes with the interior network of waterways, was most probably used by the Indians long before the arrival of Europeans. The first recorded visit of a European was that of La Vérendrye, in 1731, who called it the Grand Portage and inferred that it was already well known by that name. From then until the French and Indian War, French traders pushed farther and farther into the Canadian Northwest, and practically all of the traffic passed over the Grand Portage. Voyageurs landed trade goods from large lake canoes at a post on the shore of Lake Superior and prepared them for portage to the Pigeon River and conveyance into the interior in smaller birchbark canoes. The North West Company of Montreal established Fort Charlotte in 1778 where the portage entered Pigeon River, as well as a stockaded lake post that served as a central depot at Lake Superior. The fort had been named for Queen Charlotte, King George III's consort.

The trade had grown to such proportions and competition between different interests was resulting in so many abuses that movements were under way for consolidation. After several preliminary "joint stocks," the famous, much-expanded North West Company was formally organized in 1783, some 20 years after the British had taken over Canada from the French. The next 20 years comprise the best-known period in the history of the Grand Portage, America's greatest fur depot. The great log stockade was especially busy every July and August, when the brigades bringing goods from Montreal met the trappers and traders coming in from their posts scattered throughout the region. Employees received—and largely spent—their annual wages, and the company held its annual meeting.

After 1803, when the North West Company established Fort William on the Kaministiquia, Grand Portage rapidly declined in importance. John Jacob Astor's American Fur Company built a post there after the War of 1812, which for a while was a central station in the Lake Superior fishing industry. Eventually proving unprofitable, it was abandoned, apparently in the 1840s.

In 1922 historians explored and mapped the portage route and discovered the remains of the principal posts. In 1936–37, the Minnesota Historical Society directed archaeological work at Grand Portage, and the following year the stock-

FORT CHARLOTTE. Stockade and gatehouse. (Courtesy of the Minnesota Department of Business Development.)

aded lake post was reconstructed under the auspices of the Bureau of Indian Affairs, U.S. Department of the Interior. The 770-acre National Monument was established on January 27, 1960, following conferences with the Minnesota Chippewa Tribal Council and the Grand Portage Band of the Chippewa Tribe, through whose reservation the route passes. A weathering stockade, with the Great Hall and gatehouse, has been reconstructed on the site of Fort Charlotte, the great North West Company depot and distribution center.

CAMP COLDWATER. FORT SNELLING.

COTTONWOOD RIVER POST. Records indicate a trading post as early as 1826 at the mouth of the Rivière aux Liards (Cottonwood River) in Nicollet County. Joseph Laframboise was the trader there in 1839.

CROW WING RIVER POSTS. FORT BIDDLE.

DICKSON'S POST. A trading post was established about 1800 at Lake Traverse in present Otter Tail County by Robert Dickson, an independent fur trader who later joined the "Michilimackinac Company," probably Astor's American Fur Company, the headquarters of which was located on Mackinac Island. Dickson, during the winter of 1805–6, operated a trading post just below Sauk Rapids, very probably on or close to the

Mississippi River. From 1824 to 1826, Henry Fisher, in the employ of Astor's Company, was operating a post along the lake, later replaced by François Frenière in 1844, possibly the same post established by Dickson. A Columbia Fur Company post, Fort Washington, was situated on the east shore of Lake Traverse in 1823. (See: FORT WASHINGTON.)

FORT DUQUESNE. The discovery of a 200-year-old French fort site about two miles north of Little Falls, Morrison County, was announced in 1983 by Douglas Birk of the Institute of Minnesota Archaeology. The find is being heralded as "a rare gem," possibly one of the earliest European settlements in Minnesota. The fort, believed to have been Fort Duquesne because of its location, was most probably established in 1752 by French trader-diplomat Joseph Marin and operated as a fur-trading post. Brief entries in Marin's journal and correspondence indicate that the post was abandoned in 1753–54. Archaeological investigations, indicating an 80-by-120-foot fort fronting on the Mississippi stood on the site, also unearthed a number of French-origin artifacts from beneath a surface unchanged by cultivation or urbanization.

ELK RIVER POST. David Faribault established a post on the Elk River in 1846, near the present town of the same name in Sherburne County.

FOND DU LAC POSTS. The North West Company in 1792 established Fond du Lac Post, ultimately becoming the chief agency of the department, on what was then the south or Wisconsin shore of the St. Louis River "where it comes to the still water level of Lake Superior, twelve miles distant in a straight line from the Minnesota Point." Later, in 1816, a post bearing the same name was established by Astor's American Fur Company on the opposite or Minnesota side of the river on a part of a village site, now incorporated within the city of Duluth.

FOREST CITY FORT. Being apprised of warring Sioux in the vicinity, the inhabitants of Forest City in Meeker County built a stockade within 24 hours, completing it just in time. Early the next morning, September 4, 1862, a large band of Sioux under Chief Little Crow split into two parties for attacks against Forest City and stockaded Hutchinson to the south. But the citizens in both towns were well entrenched in their defenses. The Indians had to be satisfied with killing a few people in the outlying areas and pillaging and burning houses. (See: SIOUX UPRISING FORTIFICATIONS.)

FORT GAINES. FORT RIPLEY.

GRANT'S FORT. Sometime between 1790 and 1796, Peter Grant, "a Nor'Wester," built a trading post opposite the mouth of the Pembina River, near the site of present St. Vincent on the Red River in Kittson County in the state's extreme northwest corner.

GREAT OASIS POST. According to Grace Lee Nute's notes, the American Fur Company operated a fur post for many years at the "Grande Lisière" or Great Oasis. Joseph La Framboise was in charge as late as 1834.

FORT GREENE. Grace Lee Nute places Fort Greene, a post of Astor's American Fur Company, "on the River Au Gris of the St. Peters below Big Stone Lake" in 1826.

GREY CLOUD ISLAND POSTS. About five miles long and one to two miles wide, Grey Cloud Island is situated in the south end of Washington County, bounded on the west and south by the Mississippi River and on the north and east by Grey Cloud Creek. Traders established posts on the island by 1836. Joseph R. Brown settled there in 1838, and Hazen Mooers and Andrew Robertson erected a post of log huts in 1839.

GROUNDMASTER'S POST. Alex Groundmaster established a post for the Hudson's Bay Company on Roseau Lake in Roseau County. It existed from 1825 to 1851.

HUTCHINSON FORT. Shortly after the eruption of the Sioux Uprising in early August 1862, the citizens of Hutchinson in McLeod County erected in the center of the town a timber stockade eight feet high, completed on August 27, which provided a safe refuge for more than 400 people during the Indian attack on the morning of September 4. Unable to penetrate the stockade, the Sioux burned the structures outside the walls, including Hutchinson Academy, "a frontier citadel of learning." Time having mellowed the bitterness of that harrowing time, the townspeople erected a statue of Chief Little Crow, who led the Sioux, which overlooks "the small waters of the Little Crow River." (See: FOREST CITY FORT and SIOUX UPRISING FORTIFICATIONS.)

ISLE HOUSE. BOUYS FORT.

CAMP J. M. BACON. Camp Bacon at Walker, on the west side of Leech Lake, in Cass County, was originally established on July 31, 1856, by companies A, E, H, and K of the 6th Infantry. The post was reestablished as Camp J. M. Bacon because of the Leech Lake affair, the last clash between Indians and United States troops. The post was presumably named in honor of Brigadier General John M. Bacon, then commanding the Department of Dakota. It was officially reactivated by Company G, 3rd Infantry, commanded by Captain W. E. P. French, on October 21, 1898. The post was occupied by a small garrison until the secretary of war approved its abandonment on April 27, 1900. Early in May, Company A, 7th Infantry, commanded by Captain G. W. MacIver, the camp's last garrison, was ordered to Seattle for Arctic service. (See: CAMP WILKINSON.)

LAKE TALCOT POST. The American Fur Company established a post about 1835 near Lake Talcot on the headwaters of the Des Moines River in Cottonwood County.

CAMP LAKE VIEW. This post near Lake City on Lake Pepin in Wabasha County was the encampment grounds of the Minnesota National Guard. During the years 1884 to 1890, it held encampments there and at other places. In 1891 Lake City residents donated the camp to the organization as a permanent encampment grounds. For the next 40 years the state's National Guard regularly used the campsite.

LAND'S END POST. A trading post called Land's End was situated about a mile above Fort Snelling on the Minnesota River. In 1831 it was operated by Joseph R. Brown.

CANTONMENT LEAVENWORTH. FORT SNELLING.

LEECH LAKE POSTS. The North West Company had at least two trading posts on the lake in Cass County, one on Otter Trail Point about 1785 and the other farther west as late as 1806, operated by Hugh McGillis. The Canadian lived comfortably with a small but choice library and a food supply that included butter and cheese. Lieutenant Zebulon Pike arrived at Leech Lake on February 1, 1806, after a harrowing march with his men through the frozen wilderness, his health at low ebb and his legs so badly swollen that he was unable to wear his own garments. McGillis hosted the lieutenant and provided him with larger clothing.

England's Union Jack flag was being properly displayed over the post. Pike had entered territory that was being disputed between the United States and England. Both nations claimed the region, which was in reality in the possession of the English through the presence of the Canadian fur companies. Pike's mission had been to reconnoiter the headwaters of the Mississippi as an official representative of the governor of upper Louisiana territory. He had mistakenly identified Leech Lake as the source of the river, which was some 80 miles to the west at Lake Itasca. On February 10, after having agreed to permit the display of the British standard, Pike violated the hospitality accorded him, overstepped his authority, and asserted American sovereignty by assembling a squad of his soldiers in the trading post's square and ordering them "to shoot down the offensive British flag." In its stead the American flag was displayed over the Canadian fur post, but not for long.

FORT LE SUEUR. In 1654 brothers-in-law Médard Chouart Groseilliers and Pierre Esprit Radisson, explorers and fur traders, first landed on an island identified as Isle Pelée or Bald Island in the Mississippi River, lying between present Hastings and Red Wing. In 1694 or 1695, Pierre Charles Le Sueur established a trading post on Isle Pelée, now Prairie Island, called Fort Le ueur.

FORT L'HUILLIER. Pierre Charles Le Sueur established Fort L'Huillier in 1700, near the junction of the Minnesota and Blue Earth rivers, as a headquarters for trading and mining. The fort consisted of three or four log cabins surrounded by a palisade. Le Sueur returned to France the following year, leaving a detachment of men at the fort until forced to evacuate by Indian hostility in 1702. Le Sueur brought with him much geographical data, later incorporated in various maps and travel accounts. He also reportedly had two tons of the local blue earth transported to Paris at great expense, only to learn that it was merely clay instead of the valuable copper ore he believed it to be. Fort L'Huillier's site is on a large natural mound, about 60 to 75 feet high, now occupied by farmland. All evidence of the fort's structures has been destroyed by cultivation.

FORT LEWIS. Located at Little Rapids on the Minnesota (St. Peter's) River, near the towns of Carver and Chaska in Carver County, Fort Lewis was a trading post established and operated by Jean B. Faribault in 1826.

CAMP LINCOLN. On November 9, 1862, General Sibley and his troops moved the 303 Indians, who had been condemned to death for their participation in the Sioux Uprising, to Camp Lincoln at South Bend in Blue Earth County. On December 4, however, the prisoners were removed to Mankato into safer custody, away from threatening whites who intended lynching the Indians.

LYND'S POST. From 1855 to 1857, James W. Lynd operated a fur post in Lyons Township, Lyon County. He later removed farther down the Redwood River to Lynd Township in the same county.

MCLEOD'S FORT. In 1840 Martin McLeod erected his fur-trading post on the right bank of the Minnesota River in Le Sueur County, just across from Traverse des Sioux in Nicollet County.

MAINE PRAIRIE FORT. Maine Prairie Township, organized in 1858 in Stearns County, was so named by its many pioneers from Maine, who came as its first settlers in 1856. The town of Maine Prairie Corners in 1862 was the site of one of the many "forts" erected in defense of the Sioux during their uprising. Maine Prairie's fort was a 100-foot-square palisade with a double row of timbers, 10 to 12 feet high, surrounding a substantially built two-story blockhouse. (See: SIOUX UPRISING FORTIFICATIONS.)

MILLE LACS LAKE POST. Astor's American Fur Company had a fur post on the northeast side of this lake in present Aitkin County about the year 1820. Diagonally opposite, on the lake's southwest shore, is today's Mille Lacs Lake Indian Reservation.

MOOERS' POST. Hazen Mooers, a trader long associated with the American Fur Company, became a free trader in the 1830s. He operated a trading post on the west bank of the Minnesota River opposite present Royalton and Little Rock in Morrison County for several years before 1835, at which time he removed across the river. As early as 1832 there was a post at Little Rock, established about 1834 by Joseph La Framboise, a trader of the American Fur Company. In 1835 Hazen Mooers was in charge of this post.

MOOSE LAKE POSTS. Evidence was found indicating that a Cleveland fur company operated a trading post on the American side of the lake, located in the extreme north central part of Lake County, in 1844. Later, the Hudson's Bay Company had a post there, presumably on the Canadian side.

CAMP MUELLER. In the middle of September 1899, the 12th Minnesota Volunteer Infantry Regiment returned to their homes in and around New Ulm in Nicollet County after having served in the Spanish-American War. A new camp was laid out to accommodate the regiment and formally named Camp Mueller in honor of 1st Lieutenant Louis Mueller, Company F, of New Ulm, who died on September 1 of typhoid fever.

CANTONMENT NEW HOPE. FORT SNELLING.

OLIVER'S GROVE POST. Joseph R. Brown erected a trading post in 1832 at Oliver's Grove, the present town of Hastings on the Mississippi River in Dakota County. Lawrence Taliaferro, the local Indian agent at Fort Snelling, ordered the post abandoned in September 1834. The site of the post is at the southwest corner of 2nd and Vermillion streets.

OTTER TAIL LAKE POSTS. Today's city of Ottertail in Otter Tail County was the site of an important fur-trading post on the main shore of the northeastern end of Otter Tail Lake, on the route from then flourishing Crow Wing to Pembina and the Selkirk Settlements. The post was in operation about the years 1850 to 1860. The remains of several trading houses have been found at the locality. One of them was probably the ruin of American Fur Company's post, which was discontinued in 1836.

PATCHATCHANBAN POST. Jean Baptiste Perrault in his *Narrative* refers to a trading house known as the Patchatchanban Post, which apparently was situated on Bowstring Lake, in present Itasca County, about 1785.

FORT PERROT. In 1683 pioneer fur trader Nicholas Perrot began the establishment of a series of rough log forts. He erected Fort Perrot at the southern end of Lake Pepin near Wabasha and Fort Antoine on the lake's eastern shore, two miles south of present Stockholm on the Wisconsin side of the lake.

PIKE'S FORT. A small military bivouac near the mouth of the Swan River, Pike's Fort was located about eight miles south of Little Falls in present Morrison County and occupied during the winter of 1805–6 by Lieutenant Zebulon Pike and the 21 soldiers of his expedition. Their small stockaded 36-foot-square complex of log houses reportedly took a month to erect after first establishing camp on October 16. Pike had been commissioned to explore the northern reaches of newly acquired Louisiana Territory. His orders were to find the source of the Mississippi River, select strategic locations for military outposts, and negotiate treaties with Indian tribes in the region. Winter having enveloped the northern wilderness very suddenly, combined with injuries and fatigue, forced Pike to halt some 100 miles above what is now Minneapolis.

Pike never found the Mississippi's source at Lake Itasca, having wandered off course some 80 miles to the east to Leech Lake through the snow-encrusted wilderness. (See: LEECH LAKE POSTS.) In March 1806 he and his men returned to their fort, where he had left nine injured or sick men. They bundled up all their gear and supplies and paddled downstream. The fort burned down 10 years later. The site of Pike's Fort was marked by a bronze memorial tablet on a cairn of stones by the Daughters of the American Revolution and unveiled on September 27, 1919. Completion of the Blanchard Dam in 1925, however, inundated the site. Early in 1984 Minnesota Power officials lowered the water level to permit work on the dam. Archaeologists of the Institute of Minnesota Archaeology seized the opportunity to search for the fort's remains. They found the fort's outline and various artifacts that were once possessions of the men on the expedition.

POKEGAMA LAKE POSTS. The North West Company's trading post, erected by Thomas Connor in the fall of 1804, on Pokegama Lake in present Pine County was an important trade center for several years. Later, apparently after Connor's post was discontinued, Astor's American Fur Company had traders stationed there.

CAMP POPE. Named in honor of General John Pope, this camp was located about a mile northwest of present Redwood Falls, near the confluence of the Minnesota and Redwood rivers, in Redwood County. Here General Henry Hastings Sibley and his troops encamped from April 19 to June 16, 1863, in preparation for his expedition against the Sioux in present North Dakota. The site has been commemorated by a tablet erected by the Minnesota Valley Historical Society.

During the third week of June, while the Civil War was raging elsewhere in the nation, General Sibley evacuated Camp Pope and started his army to the vicinity of Devil's Lake in North Dakota. His force

consisted of about 2,000 infantry, 800 cavalry, 150 artillerymen and a handful of scouts. . . . There were 225 mule-drawn wagons, filled with enough supplies for three months, and 100 wagons of ammunition, medical supplies, engineering equipment, and quartermaster stores. A large herd of cattle, intended to keep the men supplied with fresh beef, milled along with the train. Never before had so large a body of troops moved against the Sioux of the upper Missouri River country. [Robert G. Athearn, *Forts of the Upper Missouri*, p. 107]

CAMP RAMSEY. In response to the first call for volunteers for service in the Spanish-American War, the 2nd Regiment of the Minnesota National Guard, together with other state militia infantry units, was assembled at Camp Ramsey on the State Fair Grounds on the northwest edge of St. Paul, on April 29, 1898. The camp was named in honor of Alexander Ramsey, first governor of the territory of Minnesota, who was then still living. The infantrymen were mustered into the U.S. Army on May 6 and 7 as the 12th Minnesota Volunteer Infantry. Civil War veteran Colonel Joseph Bobleter of New Ulm commanded the regiment. On May 16 the regiment entrained for the South under orders to report at Camp George H. Thomas, Chickamauga National Park, Georgia.

READ'S LANDING POSTS. A village adjoining the city of Wabasha on Lake Pepin, Read's Landing is on the site occupied as a Sioux trading post by Augustin Rocque from about 1810 to 1825 or 1830; by his son, bearing the same name, from 1835 until his death about 1860; by an Englishman named Edward Hudson, who had served in the Army at Fort Snelling, from 1840 until he died in 1845; and by Charles R. Read, also English-born, who arrived in the Wabasha area in 1847. Read had come to the United States when he was 10 years old. He served in the U.S. Army during the Canadian Patriot Rebellion in 1837–38 and was captured by the British and condemned to be hung. He was pardoned and returned in 1847 to take charge of the trading post. Several other posts were operated in the area by smaller independent competitors from about 1840 to 1860.

RED LAKE HOUSE. About 1790 the North West Company established a trading fort somewhere on the east side of Red Lake in the Fond du Lac district, territory then claimed by the British. By 1826 the American Fur Company had established a post there.

RED LAKE RIVER POST. A trading post of the North West Company was located on the site of the present town of Red Lake Falls in Red Lake County. Jean Baptiste Cadotte was in charge of the post in 1798.

CAMP RELEASE. The site of short-lived but historic Camp Release is on U.S. 212, very close to the Minnesota River shore, in Lac Qui Parle County. A 50-foot-high granite monument commemorates the camp where the warring Sioux, before retreating into the Dakotas, released 269 captives to General Henry Hastings Sibley on September 26, 1862. (See: SIOUX UPRISING FORTIFICATIONS.)

RENVILLE'S FORT. Joseph Renville established a large stockaded trading fort in 1835 about a half mile from the southeastern shore of Lac Qui Parle in Chippewa County. After Renville's death in 1846, Martin McLeod operated the post until 1851.

FORT RIDGELY. Established on April 29, 1853, and constructed during 1853–54, Fort Ridgely was located less than a mile north of the Minnesota River at the mouth of the Rock River, about 20 miles above New Ulm, in Nicollet County. Probably initially established by Captain Samuel Woods, 6th Infantry, the post's first garrison was commanded by Captain James Monroe, 6th Infantry. Primarily intended to safeguard the frontier against the Sioux, Fort Ridgely was named by Jefferson Davis, then secretary of war, for three Army officers from Maryland, all of whom died or were killed during the War with Mexico: 1st Lieutenant Henderson Ridgely, 4th Infantry; 1st Lieutenant Randolph Ridgely, 3rd Artillery; and Captain Thomas P. Ridgely, 2nd Artillery.

The fort's principal buildings, including a two-story stone barracks and an adjacent single-story quartermaster's building, lined the sides of the 90-square-yard parade; the officers' quarters were comfortable frame buildings to the right and left of the parade. The major military post associated with the bloody Sioux Uprising of 1862, its successful defense on August 20 and 22, with the aid of many refugee volunteers, proved to be the turning point in the war. The fort was abandoned on May 22, 1867. Three years later on July 1, 1870, the reservation was transferred to the Interior Department. Today, the Fort Ridgely State Park, seven miles south of Fairfax, features the fort's original commissary building, restored as a museum, and the marked foundations of the fort buildings.

CAMP RIPLEY. FORT RIPLEY.

FORT RIPLEY (*Fort Gaines; Camp Ripley*). Established on April 13, 1849, Fort Ripley was situated on the west bank of the Mississippi, seven miles below the mouth of the Crow Wing River and nearly opposite the mouth of the Nokay River, in present Crow Wing County. Declared a military reservation on September 15, 1849 by President Zachary Taylor, the site is now included within the 20,000-acre National Guard reservation consituting Camp Ripley. The fort was intended to both control and protect the Winnebago Indians after they were resettled on a reservation west of the Mississippi, as stipulated by treaty, and to safeguard the area's settlements from Indian marauding.

Captain John B. S. Todd, with elements of the 6th Infantry, arrived on April 13, 1849, to form the fort's first garrison. Initially designated Fort Gaines in honor of Brigadier General Edmund P. Gaines, the name was changed to Fort Ripley on November 4, 1850, because the name Fort Gaines had been assigned by the War Department to another fortification on Mobile Bay. The new designation honored Brigadier General Eleazar W. Ripley, noted War of 1812 officer. Fort Ripley was evacuated on July 8, 1857, but reoccupied two months later on September 12 because of the threat of an Indian outbreak. During the bloody Sioux Uprising in August 1862, the fort was used as a shelter for many refugees. After a fire on January 14, 1877, had destroyed several buildings, including the officers' quarters, the fort was finally abandoned on July 11, 1877.

ROUSSAIN TRADING POST. A North West Company fur post established in 1793 on "Vermilion Lake," now Crane Lake in the northwest corner of the Superior National Forest, in St. Louis County, the trading post reportedly existed until 1866.

SACRED HEART TRADING POST. The township of Sacred Heart in Renville County was derived from the name given by the Sioux to Charles Patterson, an early trader who about 1783 established a post at the rapids of the Minnesota River, since called Patterson's Rapids. Patterson wore a bearskin hat, and "the bear being a sacred animal to the Indians, they called him the 'Sacred Hat' man, which gradually became Sacred Heart" (*History of the Minnesota Valley*, p. 817). The name was afterward used by the Sioux for his trading post.

FORT ST. ANTHONY. FORT SNELLING.

FORT ST. CHARLES. Located on Magnussen Island on the south shore of the Northwest Angle Inlet in Lake of the Woods, Fort St. Charles was established in 1732 by Pierre Gaultier de Varennes, sieur de la Vérendrye, as his westernmost headquarters. It became the focal point for French fur trade and exploration in a vast region for nearly two decades. The fort, when built, was the northwesternmost white settlement in what is now the continental United States.

The soldiers and voyageurs built a palisade fort of a double row of cedar posts, an enclosure 100 feet by 60 feet, holding a chapel, houses for the commandant and the missionary, quarters for the men, a warehouse, and a powder magazine. There were two gates opposite each other protected by bastions. "Trade was the name of the game at Fort St. Charles, the French bartering metal pots, bolts of cloth, musket balls and powder (La Vérendrye did not traffic in whiskey) with the Indians for furs, particularly the prime beaver skins that would command premium prices in the European hat trade" (*Minnesotan* 4, no. 4 [1978]:9).

In 1736 La Vérendrye sent a relief party from the fort to Michilimackinac, far to the east, for supplies. The party of 19 voyageurs in three canoes, led by La Vérendrye's son, Jean Baptiste, and Jesuit Father Aulneau, camped on a small island in the Lake of the Woods (now called Massacre Island), where Indians massacred them. The elder La Vérendrye brought the bodies back to the fort and buried them beneath the chapel. In the early 1750s, the fort was abandoned.

In 1908 an archaeological expedition under

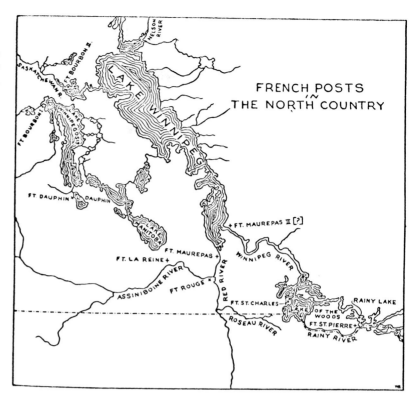

FRENCH POSTS IN THE NORTH COUNTRY

FORT ST. CHARLES. Map showing fort's location. (From "Fort St. Charles and the Northwest Angle," by Theodore C. Blegen. Courtesy of the Minnesota Historical Society.)

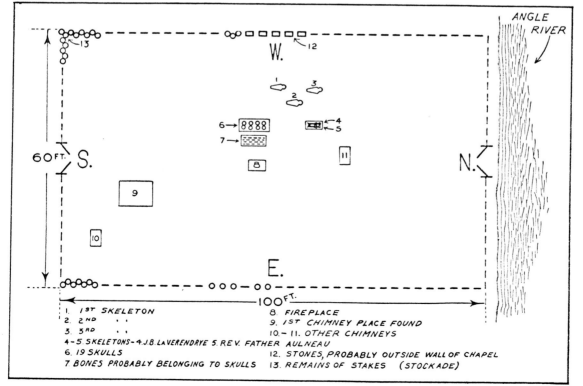

1. 1ST SKELETON
2. 2ND " "
3. 3RD " "
4-5. SKELETONS - 4 J.B. LAVERENDRYE 5. REV. FATHER AULNEAU
6. 19 SKULLS
7. BONES PROBABLY BELONGING TO SKULLS
8. FIREPLACE
9. 1ST CHIMNEY PLACE FOUND
10.-11. OTHER CHIMNEYS
12. STONES, PROBABLY OUTSIDE WALL OF CHAPEL
13. REMAINS OF STAKES   (STOCKADE)

FORT ST. CHARLES. Plan based on a sketch by Father J. Blain, made following excavations in 1908. (From "Fort St. Charles and the Northwest Angle," by Theodore C. Blegen. Courtesy of the Minnesota Historical Society.)

the auspices of the Historical Society of St. Boniface discovered the site. Excavations revealed the ruins of a large fireplace; the locations of the chapel, the priest's house, and the commandant's quarters; remnants of the palisade; and a number of skeletal remains of the Jean Baptiste de la Vérendrye party. In 1951 the Knights of Columbus erected a granite altar on the spot where the original chapel stood. Restored in 1960, Fort St. Charles is commemorated by a conjecturally reconstructed stockade of cedar poles. The foundations of the original huts have been marked and the chapel reconstructed of concrete "logs." The site is owned by the Minnesota Fourth Degree Knights of Columbus.

ST. CLOUD FORTS. The citizens of the town of St. Cloud in Stearns County erected "Fort Holes," one of three fortifications that were among the most formidable on the frontier. (See: SIOUX UPRISING FORTIFICATIONS.)

ST. JOSEPH FORTS. Directly west of St. Cloud, the inhabitants of St. Joseph ably defended themselves by erecting three pentagonal blockhouses built of one-foot-thick green timber. (See: SIOUX UPRISING FORTIFICATIONS.)

FORT ST. LOUIS. In 1793 Jean Baptiste Perrault, veteran trader, erected Fort St. Louis for the North West Company at Fond du Lac, which reportedly was maintained until about 1816, serving as the depot for the entire Fond du Lac department. According to Perrault's own account, Fort St. Louis was a stockaded complex of two 40-foot-long houses and a 60-foot-long warehouse or shed, construction of which apparently began in late August 1793, continued through the fall and winter and was completed in the spring of 1794. Grace Lee Nute reported:

Duluth lies at the junction of Lake Superior's north and south shores. One of its suburbs is Fond du Lac, which was the mother community for all the settlements at the head of the lake. The Fond du Lac, or St. Louis River, is found on the earliest French maps. It was part of the canoe route leading from Lake Superior to that part of the Mississippi Valley which lies above Little Falls.... The St. Louis River was scenically beautiful with deep gorges, dashing rapids and great pine trees before white men began to cut the timber in the nineteenth century. [Grace Lee Nute, *Lake Superior* (1944), p. 278]

FORT ST. PETER. FORT SNELLING.

FORT SANBORN. Established in 1862 by the 4th Minnesota Infantry to safeguard the settlements in the area from the Sioux, Fort Sanborn was located on the east side of the Red River, about 50 miles below Fort Abercrombie in North Dakota, at the town of Georgetown in Clay County. Named in honor of Colonel John B. Sanborn, 4th Minnesota Infantry, the small post consisted of palisaded barracks erected by the Minnesota Stage Company. The post was abandoned on March 21, 1863, because of the significant increase in Indian hostilities.

SANDY LAKE HOUSE. The North West Company in 1794 established a trading post on the west shore of Sandy Lake in present Aitkin County. The post was later moved to a new site at the mouth of the lake's outlet on a narrow point between the outlet and the Mississippi River. Sandy Lake House, with other North West posts on American territory, was surrendered to the United States in 1796.

SANDY LAKE HOUSE. Southwest view of the post as it looked in 1794, drawn by Evan Hart. (Courtesy of the Minnesota Historical Society.)

SAUK CENTRE FORT. The inhabitants of Sauk Centre and its near environs in Stearns County in 1862 erected a stockade built of tamarack logs, significantly enlarged in 1863 by the military into a substantial three-acre fortification armed with a number of howitzers. Army troops then garrisoned the major frontier post on the critical line of communications and supply from St. Cloud to Fort Abercrombie in North Dakota until 1865.

CAMP SAVAGE. A temporary World War II post used by the U.S. Army's Military Intelligence Service School for the training of soldiers in the Japanese language, Camp Savage was located adjacent to the Village of Savage, Glendale Township, in northern Scott County. The military chose Minnesota because its mixture of peoples from many European nations ensured a tolerant setting for the school. Nisei professional men and the best military authorities on Japan in the 1940s were recruited to instruct select Nisei candidates, beginning in the summer of 1942. The school, later moved from Camp Savage to Fort Snelling, closed in 1946. More than 6,000 Americans of Japanese, Korean, and Chinese descent had been graduated in the program, with at least 5,000 of them sent to strategic areas in the Pacific and later to Japan after that nation's capitulation.

SEMAT'S POST. Jerome Semat, an employee of noted trader Norman W. Kittson of the American Fur Company, established a trading house in 1821 in present Roseau County. According to Semat's own description, it was located on the Roseau River two miles above Roseau Lake. Semat's Post was discontinued about 1840. A Hudson's Bay Company trading facility, Groundmaster's Post, established in 1825 and closed in 1851, was also situated on the lake.

SIOUX UPRISING FORTIFICATIONS. Immediately following the outbreak in mid-August 1862 of the notorious Sioux Uprising, defenses were erected in many places in southern Minnesota. Most of the fortified positions were situated in or near towns and established by either their inhabitants or by Minnesota or Wisconsin civilian volunteers or militarized militia units. Many of the mostly temporary defenses were referred to as "forts" in the more than 50 towns or communities where they were established.

The war was precipitated by the marauding transgressions of a few young Sioux warriors who had killed three men and two women at a farmhouse. Mdewakaton Sioux Chief Taoyateduta,

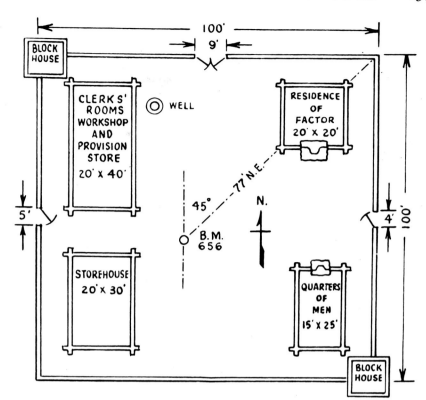

SANDY LAKE HOUSE. Plan of the post drawn by Evan Hart. (Courtesy of the Minnesota Historical Society.)

known as Little Crow to the whites, lived with his numerous tribesmen on the Lower Sioux Reserve on the Minnesota River. Knowing full well that his people would suffer swift retribution, the chief decided on August 17 to strike the whites first. He led his congregated Sioux warriors to first attack at dawn the Sioux Reservation agency where they killed 20 men, captured 10 women and children, looted the warehouses, and set other buildings on fire. That afternoon the Sioux ambushed 46 men of the Minnesota Volunteer Infantry from Fort Ridgely and killed 23 of the soldiers.

On August 19 the Indians unsuccessfully attacked the town of New Ulm, whose citizens had hastily erected barricades. On August 20 about 400 Sioux attacked Fort Ridgely itself, but the one-day delay enabled more than 200 reinforcements and about the same number of fleeing civilians from the surrounding countryside to reach the fort and defend it. The Indians were repeatedly driven back by cannon fire. The fort lost 3 men and 13 wounded, but the Sioux suffered many more casualties, possibly 100, among their wounded being Little Crow. On the morning of August 23, about 350 Sioux warriors again attacked New Ulm. The town suffered 34 dead and 60 wounded during that day and following night, with 140 structures burned to the ground.

On August 28 the governor authorized the militarization of the state's southern and southwestern frontiers. Defense lines, extending from

New Ulm to the Iowa border, were surmounted by forts at close intervals. The principal works garrisoned by soldiers were at New Ulm, Garden City, Winnebago, Blue Earth, Martin Lake, Madelia, and Marysburg. At villages where women and children still remained, the fortifications were generally constructed of earth or logs, with houses inside to shelter the noncombatants in case of attack. The other structures were usually square with bastions at the corners. At other points rifle pits were dug and temporary earthworks thrown up. These crude defenses effectively defended against Indian attack, though settlers outside the forts remained vulnerable.

Colonel Henry H. Sibley and 1,400 of the 6th Minnesota Infantry sped upriver from St. Paul to Fort Ridgely. One of the final battles of the war, fought between his troops and the Sioux at Wood Lake near the Upper Sioux Reserve, spelled the end of the uprising. Of the 303 Sioux originally condemned to die by hanging, 38 of them were actually hung at Mankato. It was Abraham Lincoln's intercession that saved the lives of the others. America's greatest mass hanging terminated one of the bloodiest episodes in frontier history, which had caused the deaths of some 750 people.

FORT SNELLING (*Cantonment Leavenworth; Cantonment New Hope; Camp Coldwater; Fort St. Anthony; Fort St. Peter*). Although the United States had gained jurisdiction over the Upper Mississippi Valley by the early nineteenth century as a result of the American Revolution and the later Louisiana Purchase in 1803, the vast territory of the Old Northwest lay beyond American settlement and was inhabited by fur traders and Indians still loyal to the British. After the War of 1812, the government sought to take physical possession of the wild frontier by establishing a chain of forts and Indian agencies from Lake Michigan to the Missouri River. These outposts were to be instruments of foreign policy, Indian pacification, police power, and ultimately of American expansion.

Established on August 24, 1819, Fort Snelling is located at the confluence of the Minnesota and Mississippi rivers, situated on a tract of land purchased from the Sioux by 1st Lieutenant Zebulon M. Pike, 1st Infantry, during the winter of 1805–6, but apparently not paid for until 1819. The original post, established by Lieutenant Colonel Henry Leavenworth, 5th Infantry, on the south side of the Minnesota River, was called both Cantonment Leavenworth and Cantonment New Hope. Flooding during the following spring

compelled the removal of the camp on May 5, 1820, to a new site, called Camp Coldwater, on the right bank of the Mississippi, about a mile and a half above the site where the fort was to stand. Colonel Joshua Snelling, 5th Infantry, arrived in August and selected the site for the permanent fort, construction of which began on September 10, 1820.

The fort was first known as Fort St. Anthony for the St. Anthony Falls in the near environs or Fort St. Peter for St. Peter's Indian agency established on the site. On January 7, 1825, the post was designated Fort Snelling as suggested by Brigadier General Winfield Scott who had inspected the post in early 1824. On June 6, 1857, the reservation and post were sold to land developers and platted as a townsite. The plan was abandoned, however, with the outbreak of the Civil War, during which the state used the fort as a training center, building additional barracks to house the thousands of Minnesota volunteers who joined the Union army.

In 1866, after the Civil War had ended, the regular army returned to make the fort the headquarters and supply base for the military Department of Dakota, which extended from the Mississippi to the Rocky Mountains. Regulars from Fort Snelling fought in the Indian campaigns and in the Spanish-American War. Between 1870 and the early 1900s, many new barracks, officers' quarters, and storehouses were built, while the decayed buildings of the old stone fort were demolished. In 1946, after serving as a recruiting and training center in both World Wars, Fort Snelling was decommissioned and turned over to the Veterans Administration and Army Reserve.

In 1956 the threat of a freeway through the heart of the old fort stimulated public efforts to save the remnants of the oldest buildings in Minnesota. Fort Snelling was designated Minnesota's first National Historic Landmark in 1960, and the following year the state Legislature established Fort Snelling State Historical Park. Since 1963 Minnesota has contributed public and private funds to develop the 2,500-acre park and rebuild the old fort.

SUNRISE RIVER POST. Maurice M. Samuel's trading post established about 1846 "was in front of Sunrise Island" on the west bank of the St. Croix River, a short distance below the mouth of the Sunrise River.

FORT UNION. Jonathan Carver's 1766–77 winter quarters may have been located in the vicinity of later historic Traverse des Sioux on the Minnesota River, near today's town of Traverse in

Nicollet County. About 50 years later, the Columbia Fur Company established Fort Union there, followed by a trading post erected by Astor's American Fur Company. Here, in 1841, a treaty was made with the Sioux by Governor James D. Doty of Wisconsin which, however, failed to be ratified by the United States Senate. Ten years later, on July 23, 1851, another treaty with the Wahpeton and Sisseton Sioux was concluded here by Governor Ramsey of Minnesota and Colonel Luke Lea, whereby the Indians ceded to the United States for purposes of white settlement the greater part of their lands in southern Minnesota. A year later this treaty, with several changes later accepted by the Sioux, received Senate ratification and was proclaimed by President Millard Fillmore on February 25, 1853. The site of the Treaty of Traverse des Sioux was commemorated on June 17, 1914, by a bronze tablet on a granite boulder erected by the local chapter of the D.A.R.

CAMP VAN DUZEE. A temporary Spanish-American War encampment at St. Paul, the camp was established on farm property on September 23, 1898, by the 14th Minnesota Volunteer Infantry and named for Colonel Charles Van Duzee, who was then seriously ill with typhoid at his home in the city. The site of the camp is at the present intersection of University and Hamline avenues.

VINCENT ROY'S POST. Jean Baptiste Perrault in his *Narrative* cites Vincent Roy's trading post at the junction of the Thief and Red Lake rivers, in present Red Lake County, in 1794.

WADENA TRADING POST. The county of Wadena, established on June 11, 1858, and organized February 21, 1873, derived its name from the Wadena Trading Post situated on the west bank of the Crow Wing River. The former post and ferry were between the mouths of the Leaf and Partridge rivers. It was reported that during its most populous period, about 1855 to 1860, more than a hundred people lived at the trading post.

WARROAD TRADING POST. This post in present Roseau County was probably established in 1820 by the American Fur Company.

FORT WASHINGTON. The Columbia Fur Company, founded by Joseph Renville and originally established in 1822 as Tilton and Company, conducted a thriving fur-trade enterprise from Lake Michigan to the Missouri River. In 1823 it established a post known as Fort Washington on the east shore of Lake Traverse in Le Sueur County. In 1827 John Jacob Astor's American Fur Company took it over.

WATAB POST. Reportedly an important fur-trading post from 1844 to 1855, it was located about two and a half miles north of the mouth of the Watab River, on the east side of the Mississippi River, in present Benton County.

CAMP WILKINSON. A temporary encampment situated at Sugar Point on Leech Lake, about four miles northeast of Walker in Cass County, it was established in early October 1898 to deal with the rebellious, armed Pillager Indians, a band of the Chippewa residing on the Chippewa Reservation, which occupied a good part of the lake's shore line. The Indians had bitterly complained of being defrauded by white speculators and of the frequent indiscriminate arrests of Indians by United States marshals. The fighting was precipitated by the attempt of a marshal to arrest certain Indians for selling whisky on the reservation. Troops of the 3rd Infantry, commanded by Captain (Brevet Major) Melville Cary Wilkinson, arrived from Fort Snelling. In the sharp skirmish known as the Sugar Point Battle on October 5, 1898, Captain Wilkinson was killed. The troop encampment was then named in Wilkinson's honor. This armed confrontation between Chippewa Indians and United States troops was called "the last Indian War in the United States."

WINNIBIGOSHISH HOUSE. Reportedly established in 1834, this trading post was located on the upper side of Lake Winnibigoshish, where Little Cut Foot Sioux Lake empties into "Lake Winni," in Itasca County. Several other trading posts were established in the area. The American Fur Company operated a post during the 1820s and 1830s near the mouth of the Pigeon (or "Second") River. Another early post is believed to have been located on the west side of the lake above the Mississippi River and below Sugar Lake. The Itasca County Historical Society has placed a marker indicating the site of an eighteenth-century Hudson's Bay Company trading post on Bowen's Point between Little Cut Foot Sioux and "Winni" lakes, although at no time did the company operate and maintain posts in the "Winni" Lake region. A much later post was established by William Fairbanks in 1890 near the mouth of the "First River."

ABERDEEN POST. A temporary post, first occupied March 30, 1871, by Company C, 16th Infantry, with Captain Thomas E. Rose in command, it was established at or near Aberdeen in Monroe County for the purpose of preserving the peace in the area during political difficulties. Evacuated on April 30, 1873, the post was temporarily reoccupied in October 1876 by Company A, 16th Infantry, under the command of Captain Charles E. Morse.

FORT ADAMS (*Cantonment Columbian Spring*). In 1698 a French mission was established by Fathers Davion and Montigny on Loftus Heights, then known as Davion's Bluff, on the left bank of the Mississippi River in what is now Wilkinson County. The site is of considerable historic interest in relation to the changing fortunes of the European powers in the lower Mississippi Valley in the eighteenth century, and in the later growth and development of the United States. Davion's Bluff became known as Loftus Heights following the ambush there in 1764 of an English force under Major Arthur Loftus.

The fort established there on October 5, 1798, by General James Wilkinson and constructed 1798–99, after the Spanish withdrew from the Natchez area, helped to mark and defend the boundary between Spanish and American lands east of the river. Consisting of a strong earthwork, barracks, and a magazine, named in honor of President John Adams, the fort located six miles above the Spanish border was considered by Wilkinson as "the most southerly tenable position within our limits," in accordance with the lines of demarcation defined in the Pinckney Treaty. Cantonment Columbian Spring, four miles to the east, was established in 1807 to accommodate the overflow of troops assigned to the fort. Both Fort Adams and the cantonment were abandoned in 1810. The town of Fort Adams, a small farming center, occupies the site of the mission. Its historic environment has been changed by the altered course of the Mississippi, now about a mile away.

FORT ANN. One of the secondary works erected by Confederate forces during the last week of March 1863 to support Fort Pemberton a mile to the west, Fort Ann was located on the Tallahatchie River near Greenwood in Leflore County.

FORT BEAUREGARD (*Railroad Redoubt*). The Union troops commanded by General Grant besieging Vicksburg referred to this Confederate

Mississippi

strongpoint known as the Railroad Redoubt, laid out in the fall of 1862 east of the city, as Fort Beauregard. The work was located immediately south of the Southern Railroad of Mississippi. The redoubt's few pieces of armament varied during the 47 days of the siege. Its site is on Clay street, adjacent to the statute of Jefferson Davis, in the Vicksburg National Military Park.

FORT BILOXI. FORT MAUREPAS.

CAMP BLYTHE. This temporary Confederate encampment was established after the Battle of Shiloh, April 6–7, 1862, when General P. G. T. Beauregard's army returned to Corinth (Alcorn County). The camp was occupied until its abandonment on May 29, 1862, by the brigade formerly commanded by Colonel A. K. Blythe (designated the 44th Mississippi Infantry at Corinth), the 2nd, 15th, and 154th (senior) Tennessee Infantry regiments, and Polk's Tennessee Battery. Colonel Blythe was killed at Shiloh while leading his troops in a charge against a Federal battery. The location of the camp is believed to have been on the Monterey-Corinth Road.

FORT BOGUE. Little is known of this War of 1812 defense. It was erected on the east side of Biloxi Bay at Ocean Springs on the Gulf of Mexico, which has eroded its site into oblivion.

BROOKHAVEN POST. This post in Lincoln County was established May 8, 1867, by Company B, 24th Infantry, under the command of 1st Lieutenant E. C. Gilbreth. Brookhaven Post was abandoned November 17, 1868.

CAMP CASS. Located at Bay St. Louis in present Hancock County, Camp Cass was established on May 23, 1834, by Company C, 2nd Artillery, from Fort Jackson. The post was evacuated November 22, 1834.

FORT (BATTERY) CASTLE. Considered one of the more strategic defenses of Vicksburg, Fort or Battery Castle on Castle Hill, just south of the present downtown section of the city and overlooking the Mississippi River, was the mansion constructed in the early 1840s by Thomas E. Robins, a nephew of Jefferson Davis by marriage. The turreted Castle was built of hexagonal bricks brought from England. The 17 acres of land were surrounded by a moat and bordered by a hedge of osage orange trees and included an artificial lake, extensive terraces, exotic trees, and flowers. The property was sold and resold, the last title change taking place in 1859. Used as a fortification by the Confederates during Grant's siege of the city, its armament mounted on the Castle's ramparts included the "Whistling Dick," one of the South's most powerful guns. The Castle was destroyed, probably by Union forces, in 1863.

CAT ISLAND RESERVATION. Cat Island, directly south of Gulfport in the Gulf of Mexico, was occupied by a French garrison during the mid-1700s. One hundred years later, the island was reserved by Executive Order dated August 30, 1847, for use as a military reservation. It was intermittently occupied by troops until 1878 when the secretary of war decided it was no longer needed for military purposes. Cat Island was subsequently transferred to the secretary of the interior.

FORT (BATTERY) CHAPMAN. This fortification was a position in the Confederate line of defenses for Corinth and located on the east side of the Mobile and Ohio Railroad. The Federal "Siege Trench" north of the town is considered the best-preserved earthwork remaining from the siege that pitted 110,000 Union troops against 66,000 Confederates in May 1862. The remaining trench runs about a half mile.

FORT (BATTERY) CLARK. Fort Clark was one of the 13 batteries laid off by Captain Cyrus B. Comstock to protect Fort Grant, so-named by the Federals to designate the fortifications erected to protect Vicksburg following the Confederate surrender of the city in 1863. The site of Battery Clark is bounded on the south by Grove Street, on the north by Jackson Street, and on the east by Farmer Street.

FORT COBUN. The Confederate fortification erected on Point of Rock, the highest elevation in the Port Gibson area, 40 feet above water level, Fort Cobun's strategic position was one of the reasons why Union Admiral David Dixon Porter was led to say that "Grand Gulf is the strongest place on the Mississippi." Grand Gulf was shelled and partially destroyed by Union naval forces in the spring of 1862 and again in April 1863. Grand Gulf Military Park, opened in 1962, contains two well-preserved forts and a number of the best-preserved Civil War gun emplacements and trenches.

CANTONMENT COLUMBIAN SPRING. FORT ADAMS.

COLUMBUS POST. The Post of Columbus was established by Company F, 34th Infantry, on April 30, 1867, and reinforced three days later by Company A of the same regiment. It was discontinued on March 26, 1869, but reoccupied October 8, 1876, by Company E, 13th Infantry, then finally abandoned on November 11, 1876.

CORINTH BATTERIES. BATTERY LOTHROP.

CORINTH POST. The Post of Corinth was established April 29, 1867, by Company E, 34th Infantry, followed immediately by Company I, 34th Infantry and Company F, 25th Infantry. The post was discontinued by Special Orders No. 154, Department of the South, July 19, 1870, and Company E, 16th Infantry, was directed to proceed to Taylor Barracks, Louisville, Kentucky.

FORT DEARBORN (*Fort Washington; Cantonment Washington*). Located about a mile from Washington, the first capital of Mississippi Territory (1809–11), in present Adams County, Fort Dearborn was constructed under the supervision of Territorial Governor W. C. C. Claiborne in 1802–3 and named for Henry Dearborn, secretary of war. The post was also known as Fort Washington. After Fort Dearborn was abandoned in 1809, a cantonment was garrisoned at Washington, at times used as headquarters by General James Wilkinson. Washington Cantonment was intermittently occupied by both U.S. Army regulars and Jackson's Tennessee troops during the early part of the War of 1812.

FORT DE LA POINT (*Old Spanish Fort; Krebs Fort*). Located on Krebs Lake, formerly Lake Chatahoula, one mile outside of Pascagoula in Jackson County, this structure known as the Old Spanish Fort is probably the oldest in Mississippi. It was built about 1718 by Joseph Simon de la Pointe on a land grant given his aunt by marriage, the Duchess of Chaumont, by Louis XIV. Fortified by its French occupants for defense against the Indians and Spanish, it was strongly built of hewn timbers, shell lime, and shells.

Baron Franz von Krebs of Germany emigrated to America in 1730, eventually settling in Mobile but also maintaining a home at Pascagoula. He married a daughter of Joseph de la Pointe and had a son, Hugo, and one daughter, Marie Josephine Krebs. Hugo Krebs came into possession of the property surrounding the lake and eventually both the fort and lake were renamed for Krebs. The Spanish, who took over the area by treaty in 1783, used the structure both as a

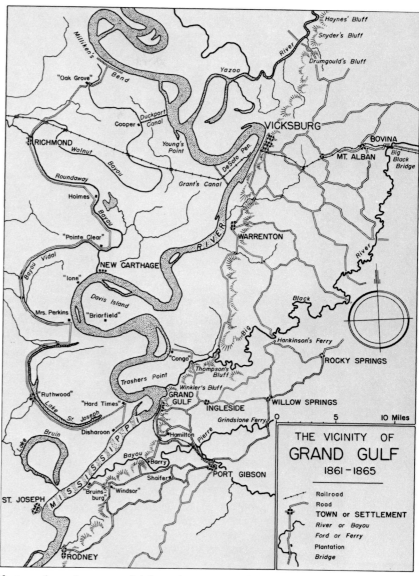

THE GRAND GULF VICINITY, 1861–1865 (Courtesy of the National Park Service.)

fort and a chateau, which today is popularly known as the Old Spanish Fort.

CAMP FARMINGTON. A temporary Civil War encampment occupied by Illinois troops, the post was established near the town of Farmington in Alcorn County in May 1862 during the Federal siege of Corinth.

CAMP FISK. Shortly after the close of the Civil War, Camp Fisk was established near Vicksburg for the general exchange of prisoners captured during the operations of both the Union and Confederate armies in the West.

FORT GARROTT (*Square Fort*). One of the nine major Confederate strongpoints guarding the approaches to Vicksburg, Fort Garrott was located about two-thirds of a mile south of the

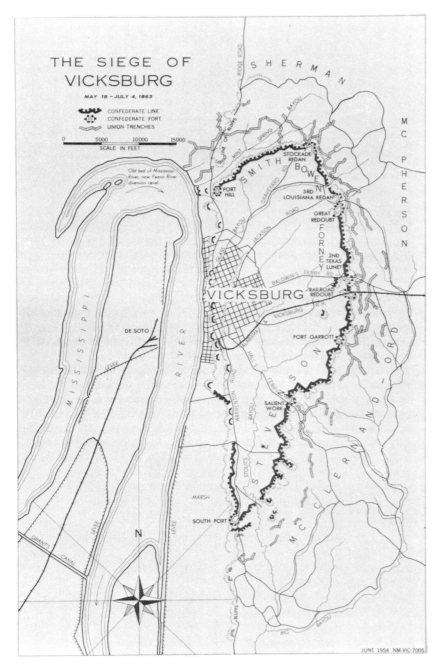

THE SIEGE OF VICKSBURG

MAY 18 – JULY 4, 1863

CONFEDERATE LINE
CONFEDERATE FORT
UNION TRENCHES

0   5000   10000   15000
SCALE IN FEET

FORT GARROTT. Map showing some Vicksburg defenses in 1863, with Fort Garrott to the east of the city. (Courtesy of the National Park Service.)

Southern Railroad of Mississippi. The fort guarded the sector of the Confederate line between the Salient Work on the south and the Railroad Redoubt (known as Fort Beauregard to Union troops) on the north. The defense was originally known as Square Fort but was renamed in honor of Brigadier General Isham W. Garrott, who was killed in this work on June 17, 1863. There were three guns mounted in Fort Garrott, one 6-pounder gun and two 12-pounder howitzers. Fort Garrott, laid out in the fall of 1862, was abandoned on the surrender of Vicksburg to Grant's Union forces on July 4, 1863, after a 47-day siege.

FORT GAYOSO. Fort McHenry.

FORT GRANT. The following enumerated and named batteries, known in aggregate by the Federal designation of Fort Grant, constituted a part of the fortifications Union forces constructed in the latter part of 1863 and early 1864 for the defense of Vicksburg, surrendered by the Confederates on July 4, 1863. The Fort Grant perimeter was roughly one-fifth the circumference of the Confederate line ringing "Fortress" Vicksburg.

No. 1: Battery Moore; No. 2: Battery Rawlins; No. 3: Battery Dollins; No. 4: Castle Battery; No. 5: Battery Comstock; No. 6: Battery Clark; No. 7: Battery Wilson; No. 8: Battery Boomer; No. 9: Battery Sherman; No. 10: Battery Crocker; No. 11: Battery Ransom; No. 12: Battery Melanchton Smith; No. 13: Battery Hickenlooper. In addition, to the north of the city along the Yazoo River was the Federal cantonment area on Haynes' Bluff.

GREAT REDOUBT. One of the Confederate line of defenses ringing Vicksburg, the Great Redoubt occupied a position northeast of the city.

FORT GREENWOOD. Fort Pembertton.

GRENADA FORT. The marker on U.S. 51 at the Grenada Dam (Grenada County) commemorates the location of the Confederates' main defensive position on the Yalobusha River occupied by troops under Lieutenant General John C. Pemberton against General Grant's advancing forces in the fall of 1862.

FORT HILL. Anchoring the left flank of the Confederates' line of Vicksburg defenses on the Mississippi River, Fort Hill's guns commanded the Union's right entrenchments as well as the river. The flags of England, France, Spain, the United States, and the Confederate States have flown over this historic site, where the bluffs meet the river, during the centuries-old struggle for control of the Mississippi. The Spanish erected Fort Nogales here in 1791, and Fort McHenry (1798) was the first American settlement at Vicksburg. The water today below the fort is not the Mississippi River—it changed its course in 1876—but the Yazoo Diversion Canal, bringing the waters of the Yazoo River into the old bed of the Mississippi.

FORT IGNATIUS. Fort McHenry.

CAMP JEFFERSON DAVIS (*Camp Lawson*). During the War with Mexico, the government purchased Greenwood Island and an adjacent tract of land on the mainland at East Pascagoula in Jackson County as suitable sites for a hospital and a military post. Camp Jefferson Davis, named for the later secretary of war under President Pierce, was established on the mainland in July 1848 by Brigadier General (Brevet Major General) David E. Twiggs, with elements of six regiments and the 2nd Dragoons, aggregating 1,949 men. Simultaneously, Camp Lawson was established on Greenwood Island. The chief feature of this large installation was its hospital, which was destroyed by a hurricane in 1859. Camp Jefferson Davis was abandoned sometime in October 1848, and Greenwood Island was turned over to the Interior Department in 1890.

KREBS FORT. FORT DE LA POINT.

CAMP LAWSON. CAMP JEFFERSON DAVIS.

FORT LEFLORE. One of the secondary works erected during the last week of March 1863 by Confederate forces to support their main strongpoint of Fort Pemberton, Fort Leflore was located on the left bank of the Yazoo River immediately below the confluence of the Yalobusha and Tallahatchie rivers. One of several small earthen fortifications in the Greenwood area, it was built to contest the Federal advance of the 1863 Yazoo Pass expedition. In April 1863 it exchanged cannon fire with Union forces. Remnants of the earthwork are still evident.

FORT LORING. Located near Itla Bena in Leflore County, Fort Loring is the estate formerly known as "Cureton," purchased by Colonel John Dabney McLemore from a New Orleans commission merchant before the Civil War. During the war, in the fall of 1862, Fort Loring was established there by General William Wing Loring and his army should Fort Pemberton, a few miles to the north near Greenwood, fail to halt the advance of Federal troops. Colonel McLemore provided from his plantation all the meat and corn the Confederate troops needed. After the war, the plantation was renamed Fort Loring in honor of the general.

FORT LOS NOGALES. FORT MCHENRY.

BATTERY LOTHROP. In late September and October 1862, Federal forces erected six batteries in and around Corinth in Alcorn County. Batteries Lothrop, Robinett, Williams, Phillips, and Tannrath were established by Captain Frederick Prime on the College Hill line. Battery Lothrop, an open work, was on the left of this line, on the high ground west of the Mobile and Ohio Railroad. Battery Madison, also an open defense, was thrown up one-half mile southeast of Corinth, about 100 yards south of the Memphis and Charleston Railroad.

LOWER FORT. A Confederate secondary strongpoint located on the right bank of the Tallahatchie, about a quarter of a mile above the confluence of that river and the Yalobusha River, near Greenwood in Leflore County, Lower Fort was erected during the last week of March 1863 in support of Fort Pemberton, the main work, several miles to the north.

CAMP MCCAIN. A World War II infantry division training center established in 1942, occupying a 42,243-acre reservation, Camp McCain was located near the town of Grenada in the county of the same name. The post was named in the memory of Major General Henry P. McCain. In a press release, dated September 19, 1945, the War Department listed the camp as surplus property, as of January 1, 1946.

FORT MCHENRY (*Fort Nogales; Fort Los Nogales; Fort Gayoso; Fort Ignatius; Fort Sugarloaf; Fort Mt. Vigie*). Spanish-built Fort Nogales or Los Nogales was situated on the later-occupied site of Fort Hill, one of the Confederacy's defenses of Vicksburg. By the terms of the Natchez Treaty of 1790, the Choctaw ceded a site to the Spanish for a new defense on what was called the "Walnut Hills," about a mile and a half below the mouth of the Yazoo River. By May 1791 two blockhouses and a large barracks had been completed. The main work, Fort (Los) Nogales, was

an enclosure made on the river side by a wall of masonry 12 feet high and 4 feet thick, and on the land side a ditch 4 feet wide and 3 deep, and palisades 12 feet high. Twelve cannon were mounted in the river battery, and a blockhouse with four howitzers, placed on an eminence in the rear, was included in the quadrangle, within which were also a powder magazine, the commander's house and barracks for 200 men. [Fortier, *Louisiana* 1: 445]

On a hill across a creek was a blockhouse called Fort Sugarloaf. About 1,000 yards to the rear of these works was Fort Mt. Vigie, a square palisaded-and-ditched earthwork, and 400 yards to the right and left were two small blockhouses called Fort Gayoso and Fort Ignatius.

Under the terms of the Treaty of San Lorenzo, popularly known as Pinckney's Treaty, signed at Madrid on October 27, 1795, Spain recognized the boundary claims of the United States as stipulated in the Treaty of 1783 (the Mississippi at the west and the 31st parallel at the south) and permitted free navigation of the Mississippi. After the Spaniards had gradually evacuated Natchez and abandoned their military posts on the east side of the river, the Americans renamed Fort Nogales, designating it Fort McHenry in honor of the then secretary of war, and garrisoned the fort. But after only two years of occupancy, American military protection was withdrawn and Fort McHenry was abandoned. Some sixty years later, Confederate troops occupied the strategic site and erected Fort Hill, one of nine defenses surrounding three sides of Vicksburg, which surrendered on July 4, 1863, after a 47-day siege by Union forces.

FORT MCPHERSON. Shortly after Federal troops occupied Natchez on July 13, 1863, they established a strongly fortified encampment there similar to Fort Grant at Vicksburg, and designated it Fort McPherson. The fort was abandoned in the summer of 1865. There is an excellent map titled, "Map of the Defenses of Natchez and Vicinity" by Captain John M. Wilson, in the National Archives. In addition, a detailed inspection report describing Fort McPherson and its garrison is found in the *War of the Rebellion: A Compilation of the Offical Records of the Union and Confederate Armies*, vol. 39, part 2, pp. 185–97.

BATTERY MADISON. Battery Lothrop.

FORT MASSACHUSETTS (*Fort Twiggs*). Lying 12 miles south of Gulfport on the mainland, historic Ship Island is the most important of the chain of small islands that defines the boundary between Mississippi Sound and the Gulf of Mexico. Since its discovery by Pierre Le Moyne, sieur d'Iberville, during his expedition to colonize Louisiana (claimed by La Salle for France in 1682), nearly three centuries ago, this strip of barren, sandy land, barely seven miles long and half a mile wide, was intermittently occupied, militarized and garrisoned by army and naval forces of France, Spain, Great Britain, the Republic of West Florida, the Confederate States of America, and the United States.

Originally known to the French as Surgeres in honor of the comte de Surgeres for many years, it eventually was named *Isle aux Vesseaux* or Ship Island, as we know it today. Using the island as a port and supply base, Iberville and his brother Bienville explored the mainland coast, ultimately establishing several forts and settlements. A fort and warehouse were constructed on Ship Island in 1717, and what was probably the first cargo of Mississippi pine lumber was exported from there in 1724. With the development of colonies along the Mississippi River, the importance of Ship Island as a depot decreased, but the French did not abandon its harbor.

Ship Island had no role in the American Revolution, but during the War of 1812 the British fleet commanded by Admiral Sir Edward Pakenham sailed up from Jamaica in December of 1814 to occupy the harbor as a base from which to attack Gulf of Mexico and Mississippi River ports. Pakenham died in action on the last day of the Battle of New Orleans. Twenty British warships and transports remained in Ship Island's harbor. On February 13, 1815, news arrived of the peace treaty that had been signed seven weeks earlier on December 25, 1814. The vessels sailed the following month, having occupied Mississippi Sound for nearly three months. Subsequently, the island was little used except as a port for the shipment of lumber until 1847, when the government declared it a military reservation. The first Army troops to occupy it arrived on June 14, 1849, commanded by Captain John H. Miller.

Construction of a brick fort was begun on the west end of the island in 1856 while President Franklin L. Pierce's secretary of war was Jefferson Davis. Work on the fort, however, had to be suspended for a time in 1860, when a hurricane wrecked vessels carrying building materials. The fort was still incomplete when the Civil War erupted in early 1861. Confederate forces seized the island 11 days after Mississippi seceded from the Union and made efforts to put the fort in a state of defense, naming it Fort Twiggs in honor of Major General David E. Twiggs. The Confederates occupied it until September 17, when they were threatened by the Federal naval forces blockading the mouth of the Mississippi. No actual engagement took place on Ship Island during the war. However, when the Federal warship *Massachusetts* sailed into its harbor shortly after its evacuation, it heavily shelled the fort, unaware that it had been abandoned. The Federals converted the island into a coaling and supply base, and troops arrived to complete the fort, renaming it Fort Massachusetts.

Ship Island served as a prison for Confederate soldiers. Records indicate that more than 5,000 prisoners of war were confined there and that

153 of them died during their imprisonment and were buried in the bleached sands. The island ceased to be a military reservation in 1870, and the troops of its last garrison were transferred to Forts Pike and Macomb in Louisiana. The last troops to occupy Fort Massachusetts were Japanese Americans who had volunteered during World War II to assist in the training of war dogs for Asian duty. The fort remains in an excellent state of preservation under the guardianship of the Gulf Islands National Seashore, a unit of the National Park Service. It is open for guided tours so that tourists and military history bluffs may view the remarkable engineering of its vaulted ceilings, key-arched entrances to the inner courtyard, and the casemates within thick walls.

FORT MAUREPAS (*Fort Biloxi*). The first European settlement in the lower Mississippi River Valley was established in 1699 at present Ocean Springs in Jackson County, on the site of Old Biloxi, when Paul Pierre Le Moyne, sieur d'Iberville, built Fort Maurepas, also known as Fort Biloxi, on the east side of the Bay of Biloxi. Although no traces of the fort remain, its site has been definitely determined to be on the headland extending into the bay, on what is now private property. Cannon balls have been unearthed and pieces of artillery salvaged from the depths of the bay in 1893 in front of the headland. The ordnance, known as the Iberville Cannon, have been mounted in Biloxi Community Park.

France delayed capitalizing on La Salle's explorations until 1698, when Louis XIV, influenced by England's colonizing efforts in the New World, ordered d'Iberville to rediscover the mouth of the Mississippi and to choose a defensible spot from which the French could defend their territory from other European nations. Carpenters, masons and cabinetmakers, and a man named Remy skilled in military engineering were among the 200 soldiers and colonists on the *Badine* and *Marin*. D'Iberville was accompanied by his equally talented brother, Jean Baptiste, sieur de Bienville. Although the expedition was organized in France, most of its members were Canadian, with the Le Moyne brothers having been born at the family home on the St. Lawrence River.

On February 10, 1699, d'Iberville anchored off Ship Island, 12 miles south of today's Gulfport on the mainland. (See: FORT MASSACHUSETTS.) Depositing most of the expedition on the island, he sailed with a small group to explore the area of the Mississippi's mouth. He finally decided on the Bay of Biloxi as the site for the settlement. He recorded in his *Journal*:

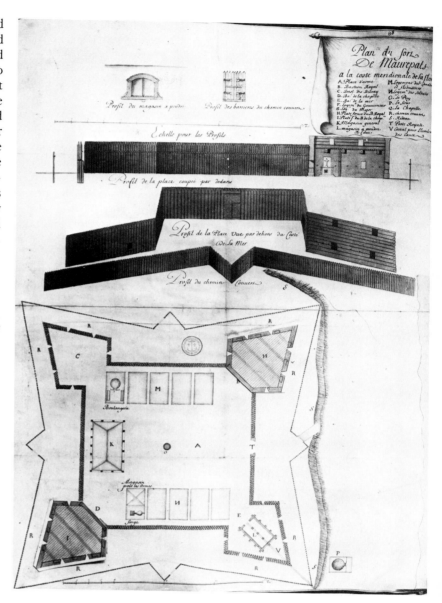

I put ten men to squaring logs for the bastions made of *pièce sur pièce*, a foot and a half thick. . . . I have no men who know how to hew; most of them are a day in felling a tree, which are in truth quite large—hard walnut and oak. I had a forge set up to repair the axes which are always breaking. . . . The 24th [of February] I had the cannons mounted on the bastions and entirely finished the fort. The 25th I set up the magazines and completed the lodgings for the garrison. [John Francis McDermott, ed., *The French in the Mississippi Valley*, pp. 107–109]

Another narrative reports that the fort included four embrasured bastions mounting 12 guns and surrounded by a ditch or moat.

The bastions of squared logs (the Royal Bastion and the Bastion of the Chapel) were diagonally opposite and were provided with wooden decks above which rose log parapets. The other two bastions (the Bas-

FORT MAUREPAS. Plan of the fort as it was in 1699. (Courtesy of the Archives of Canada.)

tion of Biloxi and the Bastion of the Sea [enclosing the powder magazine]), along with the four curtains, were formed by double rows of timbers planted vertically in the ground. . . . Outside the main body of the fort was a stockade with redans for additional defensive strength. [Robinson, *American Forts*, p. 24]

D'Iberville sailed for France to obtain additional supplies, and his brother Bienville engaged in exploring the Gulf coast and the banks along the Mississippi, visiting Indian villages to dispense presents and cement alliances. On January 7, 1700, d'Iberville returned to the Gulf with two men-of-war, the *La Renommée*, 50 guns, and the *La Gironde*, 46 guns, carrying provisions and supplies and 60 more colonists. Shortly after his return, he learned that the English were making plans to seize the strategic mouth of the Mississippi. On February 1, he set out from Fort Maurepas to seek a site on the river for a new fort. He selected a forested bluff about 50 miles upstream, one mile from today's Phoenix in Plaquemines Parish, and immediately began the construction of Fort de la Boulaye, the first French settlement in present Louisiana.

Food and supplies at Fort Maurepas were running out and the garrison's men daily searched the Gulf's horizon for the long-delayed additional supplies from San Domingo, then a French colony. Every ship destined for Biloxi touched at San Domingo and brought its fevers. In a later period, direct intercourse with Africa brought new fevers, equally pernicious. In December Bienville received news that two ships, commanded by his brothers Serigny and Chauteague, had anchored off Dauphine Island in the Gulf, bearing orders to abandon fever-ridden Fort Maurepas and remove to the Mobile River. Bienville laid the foundations for a new fort, St. Louis de la Mobile, which served as the official center of the colony for nine years, until removed to the present site of the city of Mobile.

The strategic value of Biloxi Bay, however, still interested the French. Less than 20 years earlier, Le Blond de La Tour, engineer-in-chief for the fortification of newly founded New Orleans, was assigned the task of refortifying Biloxi Bay. He arrived at Old Biloxi, near the site of abandoned Fort Maurepas, on December 17, 1720, and drew plans for a new fortification to be established as the new capital across the bay at New Biloxi. His beautifully drawn, watercolored cartographs were accepted, and construction began on a new Fort Louis. But work progressed at a snail's pace. Food and supplies were scarce, and because of the summer heat, it was impossible to work except before 9:00 A.M. and after 3:00 P.M. At night they were plagued by gnats and mosquitoes. In 1722 orders were finally received from France to abandon the long-

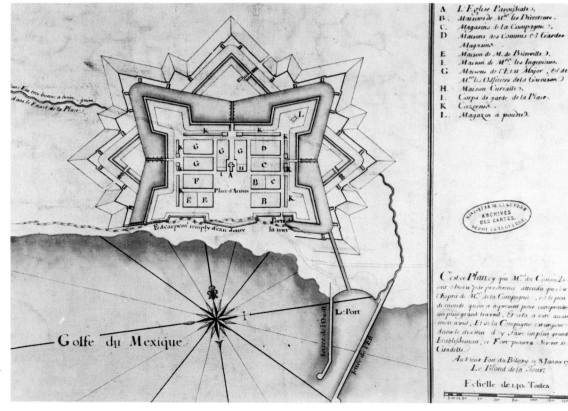

FORT MAUREPAS. *Plan for a "New Fort Biloxi" submitted January 8, 1721. (Courtesy of Archives du Ministère des Armées, Vincennes, France.)*

protracted, useless project, and to transfer the site of the colony's capital to New Orleans.

In 1910 a small, rough-surfaced stone slab was excavated on the site of Fort Maurepas. The crudely carved inscription reads: "COLONIE FRANCOISES 1699. PR LE MOYNE SR DE IBVLE L.P., P.L." This marker is presently in the collections of the Louisiana State Museum.

MIDDLE FORT. Laid out at the same time as Lower Fort and Fort Leflore, Middle Fort was located on the right bank of the Tallahatchie about a half-mile above Lower Fort.

CAMP MOORE. This camp, along with Camp Blythe, was established after the Battle of Shiloh, April 6–7, 1862, when General P. G. T. Beauregard and his troops returned to Corinth. It was in use until abandoned on May 29, 1862. Camp Moore seems to have been only referred to as such by the "5th Company of Captain W. T. Hodgson's Washington Artillery." The camp, named for Thomas O. Moore, governor of Louisiana, was located along the ridge of the old Monterey-Corinth Road on what is known today as North Parkway.

FORT MOORE. Named for Brigadier General John C. Moore, Fort Moore was a secondary work erected to support the fortifications at Fort Pemberton. It was located on the Tallahatchie River about one-half mile east of Fort Ann. These two fortifications, Forts Ann and Moore, were thrown up during the fourth week of March 1863.

FORT MORGAN. When the Confederate cavalry of Major General Earl Van Dorn, fresh from an easy victory at Holly Springs, attacked the small Federal garrison at Davis' Mills on December 21, 1862, the settlement in northern Benton County consisted of a few houses, and a sawmill and a flour mill located on the north bank of the Wolf River, 6 miles south of Grand Junction, Tennessee, and 20 miles north of Holly Springs, Mississippi. The Mississippi Central Railroad crossed the river over a 300-yard-long wooden trestle, which was destined to be the center of action that day. Today, the community is known as Michigan City, named by the people of that state who had settled on the site after the mills became extinct.

The Federal garrison of 250 men, commanded by Colonel William H. Morgan, had been entrusted with guarding the vital railroad trestle. Morgan had the sawmill converted into a blockhouse—named Fort Morgan by his troops—with an abatis of bales of cotton, and erected for-

tifications at the base of a nearby Indian mound. Morgan's men also removed the plank flooring at the south end of the trestle to prevent its use as a bridge. Shortly after noon on December 21, when the Confederate cavalrymen neared the river, they dismounted and advanced as infantry, charging precariously across the trestle. A hail of bullets checked their advance, leaving many casualties on the trestle and in the water below. Despite their superiority in numbers, estimated to have been about ten to one, the three Confederate attempts to force a crossing were defeated.

FORT MT. VIGIE. FORT McHENRY.

NATCHEZ POST. FORT SARGENT.

FORT NOGALES. FORT McHENRY.

OLD SPANISH FORT. FORT DE LA POINT.

FORT PANMURE (*Fort Rosalie*). In 1716 Jean Baptiste Le Moyne de Bienville, governor of Louisiana, built a fort and trading post on a high bluff overlooking the Mississippi River and adjacent to the Natchez Indian villages, and named it Fort Rosalie for the duchess of Pontchartrain, wife of the French minister of marine. A French outpost of empire established two years before New Orleans was founded about 175 miles to the south, Fort Rosalie became the thriving center of a growing settlement that evolved into today's gracious city of Natchez.

The post's palisaded wooden structures—officers' quarters, barracks, guardhouse, chapel, and powder magazine—were rotting in 1729. The French were entertaining ideas of rebuilding it of permanent brick, but their plans came to naught that year when the Natchez Indians, in league with other tribes in the area, staged an uprising, massacred most of the European inhabitants—both military and civilian—took many women and children as prisoners, and burned the fort. The following year the French rebuilt their fort.

When the British took over the vast territory at the end of the French and Indian War, they found the fort a near ruin. They rebuilt it in 1764 and renamed it Fort Panmure. Seized by an American force during the War for Independence, the post was recaptured by the British, occupied by the Spanish during the period 1783–98, and then reoccupied by the Americans. It was finally abandoned when Fort Adams was constructed in 1799, closer to the crucial line of demarcation between American and Spanish territory. Peter

Little in 1820 built the present square, red-brick Rosalie Mansion on part of the fort site, at the foot of South Broadway. In 1930 the mansion was acquired by the Mississippi State Society of the Daughters of the American Revolution which maintains it.

The famous term "Natchez Trace" is derived from the network of Indian paths and animal trails that were discovered by the early inland explorers and settlers who found them to constitute a wilderness road between today's Natchez and Nashville. The early French called it a *trace* and its English equivalent is "trail." The English, who used the trace principally for trading with the Chickasaw and Choctaw tribes, called it the "Path to the Choctaw Nation."

PASS CHRISTIAN POST. American troops were first stationed at Pass Christian, just east of St. Louis Bay, in 1812. The strategic site, at the entrance of Lake Borgne in the Gulf of Mexico, was intermittently occupied by the military during and after the War of 1812 until 1817 or 1818.

CAMP PATRICK HENRY. A Camp of Instruction for Confederate soldiers, Camp Patrick Henry was located a short distance north of the 1863 limits of Jackson. Today its site is well within the city limits and near where Millsaps College is now located. The camp was established in 1861 and abandoned in May 1863.

FORT PATTON. Located at Winchester in Wayne County, Fort Patton was built in 1813 during the Creek Indian War. Erected as a protection by the town's inhabitants, the fort served no real need as the Creeks did not venture to cross the Tombigbee River into Choctaw territory.

FORT PEMBERTON (*Fort Greenwood*). Historically and more popularly known as Fort Pemberton, Fort Greenwood was built in the latter part of February and early March 1863. The fort was located about four miles west of the present-day city of Greenwood in Leflore County and situated on the narrow neck of land separating the Tallahatchie and Yazoo rivers. Named for Lieutenant General John C. Pemberton, Confederate commander of the Mississippi and East Louisiana, the fort was armed with one 32-pounder rifle, three 12-pounder rifles, one 3-inch Whitworth rifle, one 10-pounder Parrott rifle, one 20-pounder Parrott rifle, and one 8-inch naval gun.

Union Admiral David Dixon Porter's gunboats, en route to Vicksburg early in 1863, were halted by Fort Pemberton's batteries and by the sunken hulk of the U.S. *Star of the West* (captured in Texas waters in April 1861) in the river channel, thus considerably delaying the fall of Confederate-held Vicksburg. The fort was finally abandoned in late May and early June 1863.

CAMP PETTUS. A Confederate encampment of assembly and organization located near Enterprise in Clarke County, it was ordered established on January 11, 1861, by Governor of Mississippi John Pettus and first occupied by eight companies of the state Militia. According to Confederate muster rolls, a number of regimental units were mustered into Confederate service there. No definite data have been found to indicate when Camp Pettus was closed.

BATTERY PHILLIPS. BATTERY LOTHROP.

BATTERY POWELL. A strongpoint in the defense line the Federals established to cover Corinth during the summer of 1862, Battery Powell was located several hundred yards northeast of where the Mobile and Ohio and the Memphis and Charleston Railroads crossed. Named for Major Albert M. Powell, 1st Missouri Light Artillery, chief of Artillery in the Army of the Mississippi, Battery Powell (which mounted four guns manned by Company K, 1st Missouri) was the scene of heavy fighting on October 4, 1862. Captured and temporarily occupied by the Confederates, it was retaken by Union troops. (See: BATTERY LOTHROP.)

RAILROAD REDOUBT. FORT BEAUREGARD.

BATTERY (FORT) RICHARDSON. A strongpoint in the line of defenses erected by Federal troops during the summer of 1862 to cover the approaches to Corinth, Battery Richardson was located about three-quarters of a mile west of the town and guarded the road to Kossuth. Named for Captain Henry Richardson, Company D, 1st Missouri Light Artillery, the battery emplaced four 20-pounder Parrotts. The defense was not assaulted by the Confederates during the Battle of Corinth on October 4, 1862. (See: BATTERY LOTHROP.)

BATTERY (FORT) ROBINETT. BATTERY LOTHROP.

ROGER'S FORT. A defense erected during the Creek War, Roger's Fort was probably erected in 1813 and located about six miles above Fort Patton at Winchester in Wayne County.

FORT ROSALIE. FORT PANMURE.

FORT ST. CLAUDE. FORT ST. PETER.

FORT ST. LOUIS. In 1721 proposals for a new Fort St. Louis and the establishment of New Biloxi were delineated in several elaborate watercolor drawings by Le Blond de la Tour, engineer-in-chief of Louisiana. Although considered important, the new fortification was never realized. (See: FORT MAUREPAS.)

FORT ST. PETER (*Fort San Pierre; Fort St. Pierre des Yazous; Fort St. Claude; Fort Snyder*). Variously known by several different names in old journals and on contemporary maps, Fort St. Peter was built as a typical palisaded, four-bastion fort on the right bank of the Yazoo River, about 12 miles northeast of Vicksburg, and designed for trade with the Chickasaw. Governor Bienville had authorized its construction in either 1718 or 1719, more probably in the latter year. A number of French concessions, sponsored by speculator John Law, were established in the fort's environs. After the collapse of his extravagant "Mississippi Bubble" enterprise in 1720, most of the inhabitants moved down to Fort Rosalie at Natchez. In 1729 local tribes of the Yazoo and Koroa Indians rebelled against the French, massacring all but a few of the area's European inhabitants and burning the fort. The bloody aggression was an extension of the more well-known Natchez Massacre in the same year. Fort St. Peter was not rebuilt by the French.

Fort St. Peter's site was known during the Civil War as Snyder's Bluff. In the late spring and early summer of 1862, Confederate forces laid out the fortifications centering on Drumgould's and Snyder's bluffs. Fort Snyder, extraordinarily armed, mounted 20 varied calibered guns, including rifles, smoothbores, and howitzers. The fortifications were abandoned by the Confederates on May 17, 1863, with Union forces occupying them two days later.

FORT ST. PIERRE DES YAZOUS. FORT ST. PETER.

FORT SAN PIERRE. FORT ST. PETER.

FORT SARGENT (*Natchez Post*). The Post of Natchez was first occupied by troops in 1798 and used briefly as headquarters by General James Wilkinson. He designated the post as Fort Sargent, a name that does not seem to have been in regular use officially. The post was intermittently occupied until about 1808.

SECOND TEXAS LUNETTE. A Confederate defense of Vicksburg, it occupied a position just north of the Railroad Redoubt (Fort Beauregard).

CAMP SHELBY. Named in honor of Colonel Isaac Shelby of the Virginia Militia who distinguished himself during the Revolution and later served as governor of Kentucky, Camp Shelby was established as a World War I encampment on July 18, 1917, to serve as a training post for the 38th Division (National Guard), which occupied the camp, August 1917–September 1918. Located 12 miles from Hattiesburg, Forrest County, in the southeastern part of the state, Camp Shelby was essentially a tent city, supplemented by 1,206 buildings, with a troop capacity of 36,000. Designated as a demobilization center on December 3, 1918, it was ordered salvaged March 13, 1919, and closed October 15, 1919.

Camp Shelby was re-created as an infantry division training facility during World War II, occupying an 86,000-acre reservation, almost seven times the size of the World War I training post. The post is now used for the training of National Guard and Army Reserve troops.

FORT SNYDER. FORT ST. PETER.

SOUTH FORT. One of the Confederate line of defenses guarding the approaches to Vicksburg, South Fort was located on the Mississippi below the city.

SQUARE FORT. FORT GARROTT.

STOCKADE REDAN. A fortified position in the Confederate line of defenses for Vicksburg, the Stockade Redan stood northeast of the city.

FORT SUGARLOAF. FORT MCHENRY.

BATTERY TANNRATH. BATTERY LOTHROP.

FORT TEXAS. Situated on the right bank of the Tallahatchie River, Fort Texas was an earthwork thrown up by Confederate troops in late February and early March 1863, designed to support Fort Pemberton one mile to the west. There is no record of the armament of Fort Texas, but it is unlikely that ordnance larger than 6- and 12-pounder field guns were emplaced in this work.

THIRD LOUISIANA REDAN. Another fortified position in the Confederate line of nine defenses protecting Vicksburg, this V-shaped work was situated just north of the Great Redoubt northeast of the city.

FORT TWIGGS. FORT MASSACHUSETTS.

CAMP VAN DORN. A World War II infantry division training post established on September 20, 1942, first known as Centreville Cantonment, it was located near Centreville, Wilkinson County, and soon designated Camp Van Dorn in honor of Confederate General Earl Van Dorn, who was killed at Spring Hill on May 8, 1863. A War Department release, dated September 19, 1945, listed the post as surplus property as of October 1, 1945. Parcels of the 41,000-acre reservation, plus improvements, were resold to prior owners during the summer of 1947.

FORT WADE. A Confederate defense located about half a mile from the Mississippi River, Fort Wade was erected in March 1863 and played a role in resisting the Federal bombardment of Grand Gulf on April 29, 1863. The fort's works, in a good state of preservation, are within the Grand Gulf Military Park at Port Gibson. Opened in 1962, the park has two well-preserved and maintained Civil War forts, a number of trenches, gun emplacements, and a museum. (See: FORT COBUN.)

CANTONMENT WASHINGTON. FORT DEARBORN.

FORT WASHINGTON. FORT DEARBORN.

BATTERY WILLIAMS. Considered the best-preserved of Corinth's Federal fortifications, Battery Williams was built in the fall of 1862 and mounted at least five 30-pounder Parrott rifles and an 8-inch siege gun. Much of the earthwork remains today, basically earthen walls thrown up against gabions. The battery's approaches were protected by an abatis fashioned of felled trees. A brick-manufacturing company now occupies part of the site. (See: BATTERY LOTHROP.)

FORT A. FORT GIRARDEAU.

CAMP ADAMS. JEFFERSON BARRACKS.

CANTONMENT ADAMS. JEFFERSON BARRACKS.

ALEXANDER BARRACKS. SCHOFIELD BARRACKS.

ARROW ROCK FORT. George C. Sibley, factor and Indian agent at Fort Osage, established a trading post for the government at Arrow Rock on the Missouri River in Saline County in the fall of 1813 after Fort Osage was temporarily abandoned during the War of 1812. A two-story, 30-by-20-foot blockhouse constructed of cottonwood logs, Fort Arrow Rock was armed with a swivel gun and three blunderbusses.

FORT B. FORT GIRARDEAU.

FORT BANKHEAD. A Confederate earthwork fortification, mounting seven guns, Fort Bankhead was erected some time in March 1862 above the town of New Madrid, about the same time Island No. 10 was fortified.

BATES TRADING POST. Moses D. Bates, originally a St. Louis businessman, established a trading post, probably in 1818, on the west side of the Mississippi at the present site of Hannibal in Marion County. He brought a boatland of dry goods and staples for his post located in the area later known as "Indian Mound" because of the five large mounds there. The actual site of the post was most probably eradicated when the overpass for U.S. 36 in Hannibal was built in 1958–59. Except for the personal weapons of the men who ran the post, it was not fortified.

BEAVER STATION FORT. FORT LAWRENCE.

FORT BELLEFONTAINE. Established in July 1805 and located on the right or south bank of the Missouri River, about four miles above its mouth, Fort Bellefontaine was the first U.S. military installation erected west of the Mississippi River. Its approximate site had been occupied by Fort San Carlos (St. Charles), erected by the Spanish in 1768. Both a military post and a government Indian factory, it was established by General James Wilkinson, as authorized by the War Department, on a site selected by the general on July 23, 1805, and constructed under the supervision of Lieutenant Colonel Jacob Kingsbury, 1st Infantry.

Missouri

The fort's name was chosen to represent the large spring of pure water in its near environs. Originally situated directly on the river bank, where it was subjected to flooding and erosion of the land it occupied, the post was moved to higher ground atop Belle Mont in 1810. The fort's Indian factory was discontinued in the fall of 1808 after Fort Osage was established, but maintenance of the military post was continued until Jefferson Barracks was established south of St. Louis. Fort Bellefontaine was abandoned on July 10, 1826. The post's buildings, however, were retained as warehouses for the storage of U.S. Army supplies until 1834.

FORT BENTON. A strong Union-built earthwork erected in March 1861 on Fort Hill in the town of Patterson, Wayne County, it was garrisoned by the 3rd Cavalry, Missouri State Militia, commanded by Colonel Edwin Smart. Forewarned in April of a large-scale Confederate cavalry raid, commanded by General John S. Marmaduke, Colonel Smart quickly loaded wagons with weapons, equipment, and provisions, setting afire what could not be hauled away, and escaped to Pilot Knob, but not unscathed, losing 23 killed, 44 wounded, and 53 missing (prisoners). The Confederate cavalrymen put out the fires and saved some of the remaining stores which they desperately needed. On September 22, 1864, a strong Confederate force again attacked Federal-held Patterson and destroyed much of the town, including Fort Benton on Fort Hill.

BENTON BARRACKS. A Civil War installation established by the Federal government that included a "Camp of Instruction" for Union recruits, Benton Barracks was constructed during September 1861 on 150 acres of ground west of the St. Louis Fair Grounds. It was discontinued on December 1, 1865.

BEST'S FORT. A War of 1812 defense erected by settler Isaac Best, the fort was situated close to the western end of Best's Bottom on the Missouri River near Loutre Island, at the mouth of the Loutre River, near the boundary between Montgomery and Warren counties.

BIRD'S POINT FORT. A Civil War earthwork erected by Union troops in 1862 and manned by Missouri Volunteers, the defense was located at Bird's Point on the Mississippi River, almost opposite Cairo in Illinois.

BOONE'S FORT (*Fort Daniel M. Boone*). A War of 1812 defense erected by Daniel Morgan Boone, son of celebrated Kentucky pioneer Daniel Boone, it was located in what was called Darst's Bottom on Femme Osage Creek, about six miles above its mouth, near the town of Matson. Boone's Fort was considered to have been the largest and strongest defense in what is now St. Charles County.

BUFFALO FORT. A War of 1812 defense built in 1812 by Missouri Rangers, it was located on Buffalo Creek, about two miles south of the town of Louisiana in Pike County. Intermittently suffering murderous raids by British-allied Indians, the town's settlers sought military assistance. In March 1813, after being refused a military garrison by the governor, the townspeople burned their fort and, taking with them as much of their movable property as possible, by both land and flatboat down the Mississippi, removed to St. Louis County.

FORT C. FORT GIRARDEAU.

CALLAWAY'S FORT. A War of 1812 defense, probably erected by 2nd Lieutenant James Callaway with a party of Missouri Rangers, the fort was located near the old French village of La Charette (Charlette), a site now occupied by the town of Marthasville, near the Missouri River in Warren County.

FORT CAP AU GRIS. A War of 1812 defense erected in the summer of 1813 by Missouri Rangers, this fort was located on Old Ferry Road on the Mississippi River, two miles east of Winfield and about eight miles above the mouth of the Cuivre River, in Lincoln County. It took its name from Cap au Gris, a high bluff on the east side of the river in Illinois, almost directly opposite. The State Historical Society of Missouri reports that the fort was burned to the ground on June 1, 1813. Another source maintains that the post was irregularly occupied until 1815.

CAMP CAREY GRATZ. A Civil War post located near the town of Rolla, the terminus of the Southwest Branch of the Pacific Railroad, Camp Carey Gratz was established on June 23, 1861, by Captain T. W. Sweeny, 2nd Infantry. On August 20, 1861, the post became the Headquarters, Army of the West.

CARLOS TERCERO BLOCKHOUSE. FORT DON CARLOS EL SEÑOR PRÍNCIPE DE ASTURIAS.

FORT CARONDELET. On May 18, 1794, Colonel Auguste Chouteau, fur entrepreneur and founder of St. Louis, wrote to Spanish Governor Baron de Carondelet at New Orleans, offering a practical plan for controlling the marauding Osages. He stipulated that if granted a monopoly of the Osage trade until 1800, he with his half-brother Pierre would construct and maintain a fort at the Osage villages and attempt to pacify them. Since the idea called for no Spanish monetary outlay, the governor accepted at once. Chouteau built his fortified post, named for the governor in appreciation, on Halley's Bluff (named for Colonel Anselm Halley) on the Osage River. Auguste Chouteau appointed Pierre Chouteau commandant of the post. For eight years, until 1802, the Chouteaus profited from the monopoly. At the end of that period, the post was transferred, most probably for a financial consideration, to trader Manuel Lisa and three of his associates.

CASTLIO'S FORT. An Indian defense, Castlio's Fort was erected in 1811 and located southwest of St. Charles, a few miles from Howell's Fort on Howell's Prairie.

CAMP CAVENDER. A Federal encampment established in 1861 and located near St. Louis, the post was probably named for Captain (later Major) John Smith Cavender, 1st Missouri Artillery.

FORT CELESTE. Established in 1789 by the Spanish and located at New Madrid, on the west bank of the Mississippi 10 miles below the mouth of the Ohio, Fort Celeste was erected in compliance with a directive issued by Governor Estevan Miró and named in compliment to his wife. Situated too close to the river when first built, the fort was partially destroyed when the bank eroded away and rebuilt farther down on more elevated land, before 1796. The new edition was an irregularly shaped, palisaded square, with blockhouses in all the four angles, and surrounded by a moat. It mounted eight cannon. With a garrison in 1796 consisting of 24 army regulars, the fort also served as the residence of the commandant of the Illinois or Upper Louisiana military district. New Madrid's first census, taken on December 31 of the same year, showed "159 head of families." Fort Celeste was turned over to Captain Daniel Bissell, 1st Infantry, on March 18, 1804. According to one source, the fort was regarrisoned by U.S. troops for a time. The *Encyclopedia of the History of Missouri*, however, reports the fort was burned down in 1800–1801.

FORT CHARLES. FORT DON CARLOS EL SEÑOR PRÍNCIPE DE ASTURIAS.

CAMP CLARK. A World War I encampment located just south of the town of Nevada in Vernon County, Camp Clark was the mobilization center for the Missouri National Guard, which had 14,756 officers and men mustered into service there on August 5, 1917.

FORT CLARK. FORT OSAGE.

FORT CLARK. Built in the summer of 1832 as a defense during the Black Hawk War, Fort Clark was located on the Collett family farm near Sublette, Adair County, by General John B. Clark and a large force of troops. A triangular-shaped palisade of split oak logs, it had a blockhouse in each of its three angles. According to local county histories, the fort stood for many years, used as a stable by the Colletts.

CLARK'S FORT. FORT OSAGE.

CLARK'S FORT. A War of 1812 defense, this fort was located about three and a half miles southeast of the town of Troy, Lincoln County, on the property of Major Christopher Clark's residence.

FORT CLEMSON. An Indian defense located on Loutre ("otter") Island, bridging the boundary between Warren and Montgomery counties, at the junction of the Loutre and Missouri rivers, Fort Clemson was erected in February 1812 by a company of troops of the 1st Infantry commanded by Captain Eli B. Clemson. Situated on the upper part of the island near the north bank of the Missouri River, the fort occupied a half-acre area in the form of a parallelogram. General William Clark named the fort after its builder and commander, Captain Clemson, who helped construct Fort Osage.

FORT COONTZ (*Kountz Fort*). Probably erected in 1812 and located on Boone's Lick Road, about eight miles west of St. Charles, the Indian defense was a log structure built by Colonel John and Nicholas Coontz. Many historians have misspelled the name of the two brothers, consequently misnaming the fort. On the commemorative boulder marking its site, it is spelled "Kountz" Fort. In 1924, Admiral R. E. Coontz of the U.S. Navy, a descendant, appealed to historians to correct the spelling. After the close of the War of 1812, the fort became a tavern.

COOPER'S FORT. Settlers in the region of Boone's Lick had been harassed by Indian raids even before the outbreak of the War of 1812 and constructed log forts for protection. A large stockade flanked by log-built structures adequate to accommodate 20 families, Cooper's Fort was erected in early 1812, probably by Missouri Rangers, on Captain Benjamin A. Cooper's property near the Missouri River opposite Arrow Rock, about two miles from Boone's Lick Salt Works and about four miles from Boonesboro in Howard County. The fort was reportedly the largest and most important of the Boone's Lick defenses.

FORT CÔTE SANS DESSIN. An Indian defense erected some time during the War of 1812 by settlers at the old French village of Côte sans Dessin ("hill without design"), it was situated on the Missouri at the mouth of the Osage River. In April 1815 three men and two women successfully defended the fort against a large force of Sauk and Fox Indians.

COX'S FORT. Located about three miles above Arrow Rock on the south bank of the Missouri River in Saline County, Cox's Fort was probably erected some time during the War of 1812 by Jesse Cox at the settlement known as Cox's Bottom.

CAMP CROWDER. A World War II Signal Corps post occupying 43,000 acres, located about 2 miles south of Neosho on U.S. 71 and 22 miles south of Joplin in Newton County, it was named Camp Crowder on September 17, 1941, while still under construction, in honor of Major General Enoch Herbert Crowder, author of the Selective Service Act of World War I. Closed temporarily after World War II, the post was reactivated during the Korean War. Branch U.S. Disciplinary Barracks was established at Camp Crowder in 1953 and closed in January 1958, during which time the only regular activity at the post was support of the prison.

FORT CURTIS. FORT HOVEY.

FORT D. FORT GIRARDEAU.

FORT DANIEL M. BOONE. BOONE'S FORT.

FORT DAVIDSON. An important Federal-built Civil War earthwork fortification erected in 1863 on a 300-acre open plain, close to the northern base of Shepherd Mountain and just west of the base of Pilot Knob, near Ironton, it was named in honor of General John Wynn Davidson and intended to protect the Pilot Knob and Iron Mountain mineral deposits. The fort was described as a hexagonal work, mounting four 32-pounder siege guns and three 24-pounder howitzers *en barbette*. On September 27, 1864, the Confederate army commanded by Major General Sterling Price suffered a bloody defeat at Fort Davidson, where General Tom Ewing and a relatively small number of defenders held off two-thirds of the Confederate force for 24 hours, inflicting 1,200 casualties, and then managed to escape to Rolla after spiking the guns and blowing up the works.

CANTONMENT DAVIS. Established in late September 1815 at the mouth of the Des Moines River in the northeast corner of Missouri, opposite the town of Warsaw across the Mississippi in Illinois, Cantonment Davis was the winter quarters of infantry troops en route to the Rock Island Arsenal (Fort Edwards).

FORT DETTE (DETTY). A temporary Civil War defense erected by Federal troops at Rolla in Phelps County, Fort Dette (Detty) was garrisoned by Company I, 49th Wisconsin Infantry, from April 15 to August 18, 1865.

FORT DON CARLOS EL SEÑOR PRÍNCIPE DE ASTURIAS (*Fort Charles; Fort Prince Charles; Carlos Tercero Blockhouse; Fort San Carlos del Misuri*). A Spanish force commanded by Captain Francisco Rui y Morales in 1767 established fortifications on both sides of the mouth of the Missouri River at its junction with the Mississippi. The major fort, originally intended for the north swampy side, was instead built on the south side and consisted of an 80-foot-square palisade including bastions in all the four angles. It was grandiosely designated Don Carlos el Señor Príncipe de Asturias, variously known as Fort Charles and Fort Prince Charles. A log-built blockhouse, 18 feet square and 7 feet high, was erected on the north side of the river and named San Carlos el Rey, Don Carlos Tercero, sometimes referred to as Fort San Carlos del Misuri. In April 1779 Spain became a participant in the American Revolution as an ally of France, aiding the cause of the Americans. In April 1780 when a British-led Indian force was dispatched to attempt a takeover of St. Louis, the fortifications at the mouth of the Missouri were destroyed by its Spanish garrison in compliance with orders, which was transferred to St. Louis to reinforce its military defense.

FEMME OSAGE FORT. Most probably an Indian defense erected by local settlers some time between 1812 and 1815, this fort was located between Marthasville and the Boone's Lick Road, near present Mechanicsville in St. Charles County.

FIERY PRAIRIE FORT. FORT OSAGE.

CAMP FRÉMONT. A temporary Union encampment established in 1861 and named in honor of General John C. Frémont, it was located in or near Cape Girardeau.

CAMP FRÉMONT. Located on the south side of Springfield in Greene County, this temporary Civil War encampment was named for General John C. Frémont and occupied August 5–11, 1861, by General Franz Sigel's Union command of two companies of cavalry, 17 companies of the 3rd and 5th Missouri Infantry regiments, and a battery with six pieces of artillery. The force was congregated for participation in the historic, fiercely contested Battle of Wilson's Creek southwest of Springfield.

CAMP GAILLARD. A temporary World War I encampment located on the public utility grounds at the Chain of Rocks Water Works in St. Louis, the post was named in honor of Lieutenant Colonel David DeB. Gaillard, 3rd Engineers, U.S.V. Established June 25, 1917, for the mobilization of engineer units, Camp Gaillard was discontinued on July 26, 1917.

CAMP GAMBLE. A temporary encampment located near St. Louis, Camp Gamble was established on April 13, 1849 by Captain John B. S. Todd, 6th Infantry, with detachments of infantry and dragoons, aggregating 80 rank and file.

FORT GIRARDEAU (*Forts A, B, C, D.*). The four Civil War defenses at Cape Girardeau built by Union troops in compliance with directives issued by General Grant during September 1861 were designated A, B, C, and D, and in aggregate known as Fort Girardeau. Fort A, a secondary defense on the river, was probably little more than an artillery emplacement, an ammunition depot, and a few tents for its men. On the site was a wind-driven gristmill that the troops used as a lookout tower. In photographs and sketches of this fort, the mill is often mistaken for a blockhouse. On June 9, 1862, the fort's artillerists fired a 32-gun salvo to mark the opening of the entire length of the Mississippi to the passage by Union gunboats.

Fort B occupied an elevation northwest of the town where the present Southeast Missouri State Teachers College now stands. The defense covered the approaches to the town via the Perryville and Jackson roads.

Fort C, a clay-built earthwork erected on a slope, was located southwest of the town on the eastern part of the grounds of the St. Francis Hospital. It commanded the Commerce, Bloomfield, and Gordonville roads. The clay in the defense, which remained whole at the end of the war, was used as a good source by a local brickmaker.

Fort D occupied a strategic elevation above the river south of the town. It was described as consisting of a triangular-shaped earthwork with rectangular projections at each corner for artillery emplacements. A trench or moat incorporating rifle pits surrounded its parade ground. Between periods of duty, the soldiers of Fort D's garrison bowled with 32-pound cannonballs on an alley constructed in the center of the parade. In the context of today's geography, the fort site is located on the northeast corner of Locust and Fort streets. Its central area was dedicated as a city park on October 17, 1937. A small stone museum stands on the spot formerly occupied by the fort's powder magazine.

On the morning of April 26, 1863, Confederate forces under Brigadier General John S. Marmaduke attacked Cape Girardeau, where General John McNeil was in command. Although superior in numbers, but poorly armed, the Confederates were defeated after four hours and retreated southward.

HALF MOON FORTS. Francisco Cruzat, who had the distinctive honor of having been the only lieutenant-governor of Upper Louisiana to serve a second term under Spanish rule, left New Orleans late in July 1780 and arrived in St. Louis two months later. On September 24 he took over the duties of his predecessor, Fernando de Leyba. Informed of British activities among the Indians and their preparations for again attacking St. Louis, Cruzat almost at once drew up plans to improve the town's defenses. He built an 18-foot-high stockade around St. Louis, "leaving open the part [facing] the river which is naturally fortified." He mounted many small cannon at all the strategic points, although he had available only small numbers of regular troops and militia to man them.

A map of Cruzat's fortifications is preserved in the Spanish archives at Seville. The area enclosed by the defenses lies approximately between what are now Lombard Street and Delmar Boulevard, and extended westward from the river to a line between 3rd and 4th streets. Four semicircular bastions, or "demilunes," and two larger angular bastions at the western corner were erected. The Spanish intended to replace these with stone structures. The first section of the line, being the north half moon or demilune on the river bank, was actually built of stone, surviving until some time between 1813 and 1820. It stood on a cliff about 20 feet above the water and commanded the river. Roofed and enclosed at its rear, it was provided with a guardroom and four cannon. Its site is now near the foot of Franklin Avenue, formerly Cherry Street. With the exception of the round tower on the hill, called Fort San Carlos, no other stone forts were erected during Cruzat's term of office.

HANNAH COLE'S FORT. An Indian defense erected in late 1814 on a river bluff in what is now Boonville, Cooper County, the fort stood on property owned by Hannah Cole, a widow with nine children. She was Boonville's first settler. The fort, said to have been the largest in the area, supplanted others nearby, and settlers fled there for safety.

HARTVILLE FORT. A Union-built fortification located at or near the town of Hartville in central Wright County, it was attacked and burned by Confederate troops in 1863.

HEAD'S FORT. Erected prior to the outbreak of the War of 1812, this Indian defense was named for Moses Head and located on Big Moniteau Creek, a few miles above the present town of Rocheport in Howard County.

FORT HEMPSTEAD (*McLain's Fort*). Probably built during the War of 1812 and situated on a bluff one mile north of the present town of New Franklin, near the Missouri River, in Howard County, the defense was first known as McLain's Fort. It was renamed in honor of Edward Hempstead, the first delegate from the Territory of Missouri to Congress.

FORT HOVEY (*Fort Curtis*). A Civil War defense erected by Union forces in 1863, Fort Hovey (also known as Fort Curtis) was located on Fort Hill between Ironton and Arcadia, Iron County. It was named for Colonel (later General) Charles Edward Hovey of the 33rd Illinois Infantry.

FORT HOWARD. Constructed in 1812 after the outbreak of the War of 1812, Fort Howard was located on the left bank of the Cuivre (Copper) River, two miles north of Old Monroe and two miles south of today's town of Winfield, Lincoln County. Built to consolidate the area's forces, the fort was one of the largest and most important defenses erected in Missouri during the war. It was named in honor of Benjamin Howard, first governor of the Territory of Missouri. It required 60 to 70 men, including Captain Nathan Boone's Mounted Rangers, nearly three weeks to build. Oblong in shape and running north-south, the fort covered an acre and a half of ground, with blockhouses in all the angles except the southeast corner, and could accommodate up to 30 families. The Battle of the Sinkhole was fought near the fort on May 24, 1815, when men of the garrison under Captain Peter Craig, reinforced by David Musick's Rangers from Fort Cap au Gris, pursued a large band of Sauk Indians, reportedly commanded by Chief Black Hawk, into a 60-foot-long sinkhole about a quarter of a mile north of Fort Howard. Ten whites, including Captain Craig, and an undetermined number of Indians, were killed during the day-long battle, which terminated when darkness fell.

HOWELL'S FORT. Located on Howell's Prairie between Dardenne Creek and Marthasville, southwest of St. Charles, the Indian defense was erected in 1811 by Francis Howell who settled in the area about 1797.

CAMP HUNT. A temporary Civil War encampment, Camp Hunt was established on February 5, 1862, by Captain William H. Higdon with two troops of "Merrill's Horse" (named for Union Colonel Lewis Merrill's 2nd Missouri Cavalry), aggregating 164 men. The camp was abandoned in July 1862.

CAMP JACKSON. Named for prosecessionist Governor Claiborne F. Jackson of Missouri, Camp Jackson was established on May 6, 1861, by Confederate Brigadier General Daniel M. Frost and a brigade of volunteer militia at Lindell Grove in the western outskirts of St. Louis, after failing to seize the Federal arsenal in the city. Colonel F. P. Blair, Jr., and Captain Nathaniel Lyon decided to attack Camp Jackson and eradicate the Confederate threat. In command of four volunteer regiments and a battalion of Army regulars, the Union officers on May 10, 1861, lined up their guns along the height, which is now Grand Avenue and Olive Street, and compelled Frost to surrender. The Union force took Frost captive and captured between 650 and 1,000 prisoners. Lindell Grove is now part of St. Louis University.

FORT JEFFERSON. A Federal-built Civil War fortification located at Jefferson City in Cole County, Fort Jefferson was established during the early part of 1861 and served in the Union cause until some time in 1863. The protection of the city was under the immediate command of Colonel Jefferson C. Davis.

JEFFERSON BARRACKS (*Camp Adams; Cantonment Adams; Cantonment Miller; Camp Stephens*). On March 4, 1826, Brevet Brigadier General Henry Atkinson and Major General Edmund P. Gaines were directed by the War Department to select a site near St. Louis for a large central garrison from which troops could conveniently be distributed to outlying posts throughout the Mississippi Valley. Four companies of the 1st Infantry, commanded by Major Stephen W. Kearny, occupied the site of the new cantonment to replace Fort Bellefontaine on the common of Vide Pouche ("empty pocket") on the west bank of the Mississippi below St. Louis. This cantonment was called Camp or Cantonment Adams in compliment to President Adams. On September 19, 1826, Brevet Brigadier General Henry Leavenworth, commanding a battalion of the 3rd Infantry, arrived and established a post, Cantonment Miller, adjoining Camp Adams.

General Orders No. 66, War Department, October 23, 1826, provided that the site of Camp Adams would be designated "The Jefferson Barracks," in honor of Thomas Jefferson who died the previous July 4. All the troops at Fort Bellefontaine were withdrawn soon thereafter. Black Hawk, captured in the last battle of the Black Hawk War, was escorted by Lieutenant Jefferson Davis to Jefferson Barracks where the Indian chief was imprisoned. As secretary of war, Davis organized the famous Second Cavalry, from which emerged Confederate Generals Albert Sidney Johnston and Robert E. Lee and Union Generals George H. Thomas and George Stoneman. Other Civil War generals from the Barracks included Ulysses S. Grant (sent to the post in 1843 as a lieutenant), W. T. Sherman, Don Carlos Buell, W. S. Hancock, John C. Frémont, James Longstreet, Joseph E. Johnston, G. B. Crittenden, D. M. Frost, A. A. Pope, and J. B. Hood.

With the exception of the period between April 24, 1871, and October 1, 1894, when the post was operated by the Ordnance Department and used as a recruiting station and for cavalry training, Jefferson Barracks was a regularly garrisoned post for most of the nineteenth century. In compliance with orders of the War Department, the post was thereafter garrisoned by troops of the line and served as a military post of the Department of Missouri. The orders also provided that a recruiting rendezvous be continued at Jefferson Barracks.

A battery of Missouri volunteer troops arrived at the Barracks on May 4, 1898, soon followed by the 1st Missouri Volunteer Infantry Regiment, which derisively named its leaky tent encampment Camp Stephens after the governor of Missouri. After the Spanish-American War, the troops at Jefferson Barracks settled into the monotony of garrison routine until the outbreak of World War I. The Barracks was immediately designated a clearing house for recruits from 12 states of the Middle West, and ordered to send 15,000 recruits to the Mexican border for training. After the war, the Barracks served as a demobilization center for overseas troops until March 19, 1919, when regular troops began to arrive. The history of Jefferson Barracks for the next 18 years is almost that of the 6th Infantry, which arrived November 3, 1920, after a march from Camp Jackson, South Carolina.

On September 3, 1940, Lieutenant Colonel Frank H. Pritchard arrived with the 11th Air Corps School squad to take charge of the post and convert it into an air corps replacement and training base. Jefferson Barracks became officially the first and most important Air Replacement Center in the United States on February 21, 1941. The War Department retained jurisdiction over Jefferson Barracks until June 30, 1946, when the post was declared surplus. A portion of what was Jefferson Barracks, at one time 1,125 acres, is now a historic park, dedicated in 1960, and administered as a museum property by a county agency.

CAMP JENNISON. Named for Dr. Charles Jennison, who helped organize the "Jayhawkers," antislavery Kansans on the Missouri-Kansas border during the Civil War, Camp Jennison was located at Kansas City and probably established in 1861.

KENNEDY'S FORT. Located one mile east of today's Wright City on U.S. 40 in Warren County, Kennedy's Fort was built by Thomas Kennedy with the help of neighbors in 1811. A veteran of the American Revolution, Kennedy settled in Missouri territory in 1808. The fort stood for four years and was probably dismantled when the War of 1812 ended in 1815. The site of the fort is on a 200-acre farm. During the Civil War, a number of forays and skirmishes took place in and about Wright City.

KOUNTZ FORT. FORT COONTZ.

LA PETITE PRAIRIE POST. This early trading post was established in 1794 by François Le Sieur at present-day Caruthersville in Pemiscot County.

FORT LAWRENCE (*Beaver Station Fort; Lawrenceville Mill Fort*). Known originally as Beaver Station Fort and Lawrenceville Mill Fort, this Civil War defense was erected by Union forces in 1861 on Beaver Creek in Taney County. On January 6, 1863, it was attacked and destroyed by Confederate troops.

LAWRENCEVILLE MILL FORT. FORT LAWRENCE.

FORT LEONARD WOOD. Nestled in the Ozark Hill country of south central Missouri, Fort Leonard Wood is two miles south of I-44, adjacent to the cities of St. Robert and Waynesville in Pulaski County. St. Louis, "the Gateway to the West," is located about 135 miles to the northeast. The military installation occupies about 70,000 acres, approximately 110 square miles, of hilly, wooded terrain in the Big Piney River area of the Clark National Forest. Ground-breaking on December 3, 1940, for the post, temporarily designated the VII Corps Area Training Center, presaged a five-month-long construction program that resulted in the erection of 1,600 buildings. On January 3, 1941, a War Department directive designated the post as Fort Leonard Wood, in honor of Major General Leonard Wood, Army chief of staff 1910–14.

During World War II, the 6th, 8th, 70th, 75th, and 97th Infantry Divisions trained at the fort, claimed to be the world's largest engineer training center. From January 1941 until it closed in 1946, the post trained some 300,000 troops. The post was reactivated in 1950, shortly after the outbreak of the Korean War in Asia. In 1955 recruits for the Army from 11 Midwest states received their basic training here. Fort Leonard Wood became a permanent installation on March 21, 1956.

FORT LE SIEUR (*Fort Portage des Sioux*). The reputed first settler of Portage des Sioux in St. Charles County was François Le Sieur, who established a trading post there before 1799, the year when the Spanish erected a fort on the site to counteract American and British encroachments. The only important event that took place at Portage des Sioux was the signing of three treaties in the summer of 1815 by the chiefs of Indian tribes in Illinois, Indiana, and Missouri and U.S. commissioners Governor Ninian Edwards of Illinois, Governor William Clark of Missouri, and trader Auguste Chouteau of St. Louis. The actual signings took place in a council house especially built for the occasion. The pacts marked the end of British-incited Indian hostilities in the area.

CAMP LILLIE. A temporary Civil War encampment located one mile south of Jefferson City, Cole County, Camp Lillie was occupied for a time in 1861 by Major General John C. Frémont and his Union forces.

FORT LOOKOUT. Established during the War of 1812 by Captain David Musick of the Missouri Rangers on April 11, 1813, on a site selected three days earlier by Colonel Daniel Bissell, 5th Infantry, Fort Lookout was located just below the village of Portage des Sioux, St. Charles County, on the bank of the Mississippi River. In addition, a gun battery was planted on an island in the river a mile below the blockhouse-fort, strategically placed to observe the junctions of the Mississippi, Missouri, and Illinois rivers.

CAMP LYON. A temporary Civil War encampment probably established in late 1861 by Union troops, Camp Lyon was located at Bird's Point, east of Charleston and opposite Cairo across the Mississippi in Illinois. The post was named in honor of General Nathaniel Lyon, killed August 10, 1861, in the Battle of Wilson's Creek.

FORT LYON. A temporary Union-built fortification named in honor of General Nathaniel Lyon, killed in action at Wilson's Creek, August 10, 1861, Fort Lyon was probably established in late 1861 or 1862 just south of Windsor in Benton County.

CAMP (BEN) MCCULLOCH. A temporary Civil War encampment established by Confederate troops, Camp McCulloch was located near Springfield in Greene County and named in honor of General Ben McCulloch, who was killed at Pea Ridge on March 7, 1862.

MCLAIN'S FORT. FORT HEMPSTEAD.

MCMAHAN'S FORT. A "family" fort probably erected in 1811 or 1812, this Indian defense was located on the south side of the Missouri River, about five miles from Cooper's Fort and near the town of Glasgow, Howard County.

FORT MADISON. FORT MATSON.

FORT MASON. Named for Lieutenant John Mason and located on the left bank of the Mississippi River in Ralls County, nine miles below Hannibal, Fort Mason was established in March 1812 by Army troops in response to an urgent request of Governor Benjamin Howard. Colonel Daniel Bissell dispatched a detachment of 2 officers and 30 soldiers from Fort Bellefontaine to the settlement at the site, which had been subjected to Indian raids. Garrisoned by Army regulars, probably intermittently, Fort Mason was abandoned May 1, 1814.

FORT MATSON (*Fort Madison*). Adair County histories make interchangeable use of both names for the same fortification erected in 1832 after the outbreak of the Black Hawk War. A military force commanded by Captain Richard Madison of Ralls County was sent to what is now Adair County and built a palisaded blockhouse in the eastern part of the present town of Sublette. A detached log building served as a powder magazine and a storehouse for supplies. The war having been relatively short-lived and with no further danger threatened, the fort was abandoned and the troops departed for home.

CANTONMENT MILLER. JEFFERSON BARRACKS.

FORT MULLIGAN. Masonic College at Lexington in Lafayette County was the site of Fort Mulligan, probably established in September 1861 by Union troops. It was named in honor of Colonel (later Brevet Brigadier General) James Adelbert Mulligan, who was captured at Lexington on September 20, 1861, and released in a prisoner exchange the following November.

NEW MADRID POST. U.S. troops established a post in 1804 at New Madrid, the old Spanish settlement on the north bank of the Mississippi, a short distance above the common boundary of Missouri, Kentucky, and Tennessee, as part of the American military occupation of Louisiana Purchase consummated the prior year. The post was maintained until some time in 1808.

FORT ORLEANS. The first European post in the Missouri Valley, Fort Orleans was established on November 15, 1723, on the left bank of the Missouri River, some miles above the mouth of the Grand River, in present Carroll County. Built by Étienne Véniard, sieur de Bourgmond, and named in honor of the Duke of Orleans, it was intended to prevent Spanish encroachments, protect the area's mines, and hopefully effect peace among the region's Indian tribes. The post was abandoned five years later in compliance with orders of Governor Périer issued at New Orleans in October 1727 because it was found to be unprofitable as a trade center and because an inordinate number of French soldiers were losing their lives in the fort's vicinity. The French apparently evacuated Fort Orleans in late 1728 or early 1729.

FORT OSAGE (*Clark's Fort; Fort Clark; Fiery Prairie Fort; Fort Sibley*). Three hundred miles and 26 days by keel boat from St. Louis, Fort Osage was the first United States government outpost in Louisiana Territory. Meriwether Lewis and William Clark selected the site in 1804 during their first exploratory trip into the uncharted wilderness, marking its place on their map as "Fort Point." Four years later, General William Clark superintended construction of the fort, originally called Clark's Fort or Fort Clark, and frequently referred to as Fiery Prairie Fort. Established in September 1808 on the south bank of the Missouri River, 20 miles east of present Kansas city, in Jackson County, it was officially designated Fort Osage on November 10, 1808.

Fort Osage had a two-fold purpose: to inform the Spanish, British, and the Indians that the American government would protect its newly acquired territory by military means, and to establish a friendly rapport with the region's Indians by providing them with a government-operated trading post. For almost two decades, Fort Osage was a place of congregation on the migration westward and a deterrent to foreign encroachments.

The fort was built of hewn white-oak logs on a high promontory overlooking the river. It was roughly pentagonal with five blockhouses. The building party consisted of an 81-man company of the 1st Infantry, for garrison duty under Captain Eli B. Clemson, and a company of 80 St. Charles Dragoons, mounted militia, who volunteered their services to General Clark for 30 days. The regulars, accompanied by U.S. factor George C. Sibley with his trade goods, came by keel boats from Fort Bellefontaine near St. Louis. Sibley's official status as factor there prompted the occasional use of the name "Fort Sibley" for the fort.

Because of the exigencies of the War of 1812, Fort Osage was evacuated in June 1813, but a factory was maintained for the Osage Indians at Arrow Rock and one for the Sauk (Sac) and Fox on Little Moniteau Creek. Sibley returned to the post late in the fall of 1815 to put it in order, and in July 1816 it was regarrisoned. The trading

FORT OSAGE. The fort reconstructed to look as it did in 1808. (Courtesy of the Missouri Division of Commerce and Industrial Development.)

house or factory at Fort Osage continued in operation until November 5, 1822, when the United States factory system was abandoned because of opposition of the fur companies. The fort thereafter was intermittently garrisoned and apparently entirely abandoned in 1827 when Fort Leavenworth in Kansas was established. The Fort Osage Restoration at Old Sibley, 14 miles northeast of Independence, was dedicated September 11, 1948, and contains the original blockhouse cannon.

CAMP OZARK. The Union-fortified town of Ozark in Christian County was captured by Confederate troops in 1863.

FORT PERUQUE. A fortified blockhouse defense erected by Union troops in 1861 and commanded by Captain Henry B. Denker, this fort was located at the foot of Peruque Bridge near the town of O'Fallon, St. Charles County. Constructed at the end of the trestle of the present Wabash Railroad over Peruque Creek, it was intended to protect the bridge from destruction by the Confederates, who wished to disrupt the transportation of Union troops.

FORT PIKE. During the Black Hawk War, a fort called Fort Pike was erected at the site of old St. Francisville, the first settlement in present Clark County, on the Des Moines River, 10 miles above its mouth. It was occupied for about three months by a company of troops from Pike County.

FORT POND. Located on the Dardenne Prairie, southwest of the present town of Wentzville in St. Charles County, Fort Pond was probably erected in 1812 by the Missouri Rangers. It consisted of a group of temporary, log-built, minimally fortified houses in the form of a hollow square. The defensive complex, reportedly still standing, continued to be occupied for some time after the end of the War of 1812.

FORT PORTAGE DES SIOUX. Fort Le Sieur.

FORT PRINCE CHARLES. Fort Don Carlos el Señor Príncipe de Asturias.

ROI'S FORT. Thibault's Fort.

ROUND STONE FORT. Claimed by some historians to have been built as early as 1690, the site of Round Stone Fort is at the present intersection of 3rd and Adams streets in the city of St. Charles. The actual date of the tower's construction is unknown. A circular structure about 30 feet high and approximately 30 feet in diameter, built of notched Burlington stone (mortar then being unknown), it was torn down after the Civil War for its building materials.

FORT ST. CHARLES. FORT SAN CARLOS.

ST. CHARLES FORT. Erected in 1804 at St. Charles, this defense was surrounded by a stockade which was later extended to the river at what is today the foot of Clay Street. Reportedly the strongest fort then existing north of the Missouri River, the structure in later years was a fur-trading post, and still later an apartment house. The post was destroyed in May 1960 for the use of the site as a parking space.

FORT ST. JOACHIM. The French in 1785 or 1786 built a fort at the old settlement of St. Joachim, now incorporated within the city of Sainte Genevieve on the Mississippi River. It seems the post was still standing in 1796. It was surrounded with planks to support the earth, which served at the same time as palisades. Two two-pounder cannon and a corporal and two soldiers were all that defended the fort. The fort, rebuilt or remodeled twice, survived until about 1804, when the United States exercised jurisdiction over the Louisiana Territory.

ST. JOSEPH POST. A Civil War post at St. Joseph in Buchanan County was established in August 1863 by Union Major S. A. Garth, 9th Cavalry, with four companies, aggregating 322 men. The post was discontinued in November 1864.

ST. LOUIS ARSENAL. Situated on the west bank of the Mississippi, in the southern part of St. Louis, within sight of Jefferson Barracks, the United States Arsenal was established in the autumn of 1827, and construction of its buildings of stone with slate roofs, except for the laboratories and sheds, was continued from time to time until about 1840, when they were completed and ready for use. The Arsenal proper was a three-story structure 120 feet long and 40 feet wide, besides a cellar and attic. During the troubled months of the first year of the Civil War, the largest supply of ammunition in the West was stored here. The Arsenal was closed in 1904. Standing on the southeast corner of 2nd and Arsenal streets, the main structure is still in use by the Air Force Charter Center.

ST. LOUIS POST. In 1762 Governor Kerlérec of Louisiana granted the Maxtent, Laclède and Company of New Orleans (the Louisiana Fur Company) a charter that awarded the privilege of trading with Indian tribes in the region for a period of eight years, a term later renewed. The grant led Pierre Laclède to the founding of St. Louis by his establishment of a trading post on the site. Laclède, accompanied by his clerk, Auguste Chouteau, then only 13 years of age, selected the site of the proposed trading post in the late fall of 1763, located just below the junction of the Mississippi and Missouri rivers.

The initial foundation of the settlement was made on February 15, 1764, when young Chouteau arrived from Fort de Chartres with 30 men, most of them "mechanics." They erected a palisaded complex of log cabins on the site where Barnum's Hotel later stood. The site ultimately became the greatest city in the Mississippi Valley. Early in April, Laclède himself joined them and named the settlement St. Louis in honor of Louis IX, whom Pope Boniface VIII had canonized in 1297 and who was the patron saint of Louis XV, the reigning monarch of France.

FORT SAN CARLOS (*Fort St. Charles*). Established April 17, 1780, by the Spanish on an elevation at the west end of the town of St. Louis, Fort San Carlos (known to the British and Americans as Fort St. Charles) was built to defend St. Louis from an anticipated attack by British and allied Indians during the American Revolution. In official Spanish correspondence, the defense was usually referred to as the Tower of San Carlos. Spain in the previous year had joined France to furnish aid to the American cause. Preparing for the assault, Lieutenant Governor Fernando de Leyba, military commandant of St. Louis, built a stone tower mounting five cannon and named it Fort San Carlos, ordered entrenchments and had them defended by 29 regulars and 281 townspeople, and posted cavalrymen at strategic points about the town. On May 26, 1780, the British attacked and, despite their superior numbers, were defeated.

Governor Leyba had originally planned to erect four towers, one on each side of the town, but funds to complete this project were insufficient. In 1792 Governor Baron de Carondelet issued a directive to incorporate the tower in a fort, which he referred to as the Fort of San Luis de Ylinoa. The new construction consisting of a stockade and a banquette mounted eight cannon. Later, when additional funds became available, a barracks was built within the fort. On March 9, 1804, fortified St. Louis was surrendered to American jurisdiction and turned over to Captain Amos Stoddard, Corps of Artillery. Fort San

Carlos was garrisoned by American troops until Fort Bellefontaine was completed and occupied in 1805.

FORT SAN CARLOS DEL MISURI. FORT SAN CARLOS EL SEÑOR PRÍNCIPE DE ASTURIAS.

CAMP SAND SPRINGS. A temporary Civil War encampment located at San Springs, Webster County, it was established on August 3, 1862, by Captain George T. Snelling with detachments of companies F and I, 10th Illinois Cavalry, aggregating 78 men, a number increased in September by additional detachments of the same companies and militia to 245 men. The post was captured and burned by Confederate forces in 1863.

FORT SAN FERNANDO. Several regional histories have referred to a fort of this name reportedly established during the Spanish period. It was apparently located in the area later known as Little Prairie in what is today's Pemiscot County in the so-called "Boot Heel" of the state. Erosion by the Mississippi River has since washed away the site of the fort.

FORT SAN JUAN DEL MISURI. Established about 1796 by the Spanish, it was located on the north side of the Missouri River at old La Charette ("the cart") between today's Marthasville and Dutzow in Warren County. A small fortification built of logs, it was probably erected by a small party of militia commanded by Lieutenant Antoine Gaultier and intended to safeguard new settlers in the area. The sites of both the town and the fort had disappeared entirely by 1804, washed away by flood waters.

SCHOFIELD BARRACKS (*Alexander Barracks*). Known originally as Alexander Barracks from 1863–65, this Army installation at St. Louis was redesignated in June 1865 as Schofield Barracks in honor of General John McAllister Schofield, Brigadier General, Missouri Volunteers, in 1861, and in command of the Department of Missouri, May 24, 1863, to January 30, 1864. In 1869 he was awarded the rank of major general and appointed superintendent of West Point. He later served as commander in chief of the Army, 1888–95.

FORT SIBLEY. FORT OSAGE.

SOUTH RIVER FORT. A reconstruction of this Union-built fortification is located at 4805 McMasters Avenue in Hannibal.

SPRINGFIELD FORTS. Union-built "Forts No. 1 to 5" near Springfield in Greene County, they were captured by Confederate troops in 1863.

STEPHEN COLE'S FORT. During the period just preceding the outbreak of the War of 1812, there were two forts in the Boone's Lick region of Cooper County that bore the name of Cole's Fort. The first was Stephen Cole's fort, built in early 1812 about two miles east of Boonville. After several disastrous Indian raids, the settlers decided they needed a stronger defense, and a new and much stronger fortification was erected in 1814 at Hannah Cole's in what is now East Boonville. Hannah Cole was Stephen Cole's sister-in-law. (See: HANNAH COLE'S FORT.)

CAMP STEPHENS. JEFFERSON BARRACKS.

STOUT'S FORT. An Indian defense erected in 1812 by the Missouri Rangers, Stout's Fort was located about a mile south of the town of Auburn in Lincoln County.

TALBOT'S FORT. An Indian defense erected in early 1812, Talbot's Fort was located on Loutre Island in the Missouri River. (See: FORT CLEMSON.)

THIBAULT'S FORT (*Roi's Fort*). The old French village of Côte sans Dessin ("hill without design") was once located on the left side of the Missouri River near today's town of Tebbets in Callaway County. On the hill that lent its name to the settlement were two defenses known as Roi's Fort and Thibault's Fort, with a powder magazine to serve both located between them. Jean Baptiste Roi founded the village, which has long since been abandoned. (See: FORT CÔTE SANS DESSIN.)

FORT THOMPSON. An earthen redoubt erected by Confederate forces near New Madrid, Fort Thompson was manned by troops under General John Porter McCown. Union General John Pope, upon reaching a position in the rear of New Madrid on March 3, 1862, and realizing the strength of the Confederate defense, sent to Cairo for siege guns, with which he fiercely shelled Fort Thompson's works. The defending Confederates, taking advantage of a furious storm, evacuated their fort at midnight and moved to Island No. 10, eight miles above New Madrid, leaving their guns and practically everything else behind. The loss of New Madrid, with the loss of Island No. 10 a month later, was a serious blow to the Confederacy.

CAMP TOTTEN. A temporary Civil War encampment located at or near the town of Franklin, Howard County, Camp Totten was named in honor of Union Brigadier General James Totten, commander of the Central District. While serving as Inspector General of the Military Division of the South, he was dismissed from the Army in 1870 for "disobedience of orders," "neglect of duty," and "conduct to the prejudice of good order and military discipline."

CAMP UNION. A temporary Civil War encampment established by Union forces in 1861, Camp Union was located one mile east of Brumley in Miller County.

CAMP UNION. A large Union army encampment established by Major Samuel D. Sturgis at Kansas City in the spring of 1861, Camp Union was occupied by a number of companies of the 1st Infantry, 1st Cavalry, 2nd Dragoons, and artillery batteries, aggregating at least 550 men, commanded by Captain William E. Prince, a strict New England disciplinarian. The site of the camp is at 10th and Central streets, near the Coates House, in Kansas City.

CAMP VEST. A Confederate encampment located near Boonville, Howard County, Camp Vest was named for George Graham Vest, a lawyer, who first represented his congressional district in the Provisional Confederate Congress, then later served as senator from Missouri to the Confederate States Congress.

WAYNESVILLE POST. The town of Waynesville in Pulaski County was overwhelmingly prosecessionist, and its citizens demonstrated their sentiment by flying the Stars and Bars of the Confederacy until Federal troops marched in on June 7, 1862, and took it over. A small fort was erected there as a Federal supply base on the route between Rolla and Lebanon.

WHITE'S FORT. Located two miles south of the Cuivre River, about 25 miles west of St. Charles, White's Fort was probably erected some time in 1811 or 1812 by troops led by a Captain White. The fort was the scene of an Indian massacre in which 12 soldiers were killed. The soldiers were buried near Old Monroe in Lincoln County, and their graves are still maintained by the government.

WOOD'S FORT. Government archival records indicate that this fort at present Troy in Lincoln County was built in 1812 and abandoned in 1815. Zachary Taylor, then a 7th Infantry captain, was supposedly stationed at the fort.

FORT WYMAN. The town of Rolla during the first winter of the Civil War quartered 20,000 Union troops in all sorts of buildings, private and governmental. It was fortified by a series of trenches and earthworks almost surrounding the city and covering a radius of about a mile. One of the two massive defenses that protected Rolla was Fort Wyman on a hill about a mile to the south. More than 400 feet square, with its outer works (outside the moat) of slanting timbers to cause cannonballs to glance off and upward, Fort Wyman was constructed in the form of a Greek cross, with its two pairs of arms measuring over 300 feet. In the center of the cross was a circular elevation, on which the heavy cannon were mounted.

FORT ZUMWALT. The 45-acre Fort Zumwalt State Park, located about two miles southwest of the town of O'Fallon in St. Charles County, contains the remains of the old fort, which originally was the residence of Jacob Zumwalt erected in 1798. Constructed of hewn oak logs, the four-room house was enlarged before the War of 1812 by the addition of two one-story wings, one to the east and the other to the south, with gun-ports cut into their walls. Shortly after the beginning of the war, a large stockade was constructed around the fort. In 1817 Jacob Zumwalt sold his property to Major Nathan Heald, former heroic commander of Fort Dearborn at Chicago, who with his wife was wounded and captured during the evacuation of the post that culminated in the infamous Indian massacre there.

FORT ALEXANDER. A trading post built in 1842 on the north bank of the Yellowstone River, nearly opposite the mouth of the Rosebud River, in the vicinity of present Cartersville in Rosebud County, Fort Alexander was established by fur entrepreneurs Charles Larpenteur and Alexander McKenzie and named for the latter. The post was discontinued in 1850.

FORT ANDREW. A trading post built in November 1862 by George Steell and 14 carpenters from Fort Benton on the north bank of the Missouri River, 15 miles above the mouth of the Musselshell River, Fort Andrew was a 125-foot-square, palisaded enclosure constructed of logs and named for Andrew Dawson of the American Fur Company. The post was probably abandoned in 1863.

FORT ASSINIBOINE. A temporary 100-foot-square trading post and depot built on the bank of the Yellowstone River, it was apparently located at the spot where the steamboat *Assiniboine* went aground in the summer of 1834. On a site still undetermined, it marked the first ascent of steamboats beyond the mouth of the river.

FORT ASSINIBOINE. The largest military post in Montana, established on May 9, 1879, by Colonel Thomas H. Ruger and troops of the 18th Infantry, and named for the Indian tribe, Fort Assiniboine was situated on the left bank of Beaver Creek about 4 miles above its confluence with the Milk River, approximately 10 miles southwest of Havre in Hill County. Occupied by principally cavalry troops, it was primarily intended to prevent the return of Chief Sitting Bull and his Sioux from Canada and to control the bands of Blackfeet in the area. The War Department closed the post on July 25, 1911, and turned it over to the Department of the Interior for disposition. Some of the post's original buildings are now occupied as a U.S. Agricultural Experiment Station.

CAMP BAKER. FORT LOGAN.

FORT BELKNAP. Named for Secretary of War William W. Belknap, this trading post was located on the south side of the Milk River, approximately opposite the town of Chinook in Blaine County. It was built by Abe Farwell in 1871 for Durfee and Peck of the Northwest Fur Company. The name of the post was adopted by the government's Fort Belknap Indian Agency, established 30 miles to the east. Fort Belknap was discontinued in 1886.

Montana

FORT BENTON. The first fort of this name was a trading post built during the winter of 1821–22 on the Yellowstone River near the mouth of the Big Horn River. Located near earlier Fort Manuel, it was established by Joshua Pilcher of the Missouri Fur Company. Fort Benton was abandoned in 1823.

FORT BENTON (*Fort Lewis*). First established in 1846 as Fort Lewis by the American Fur Company on the west or left bank of the Missouri River near the mouth of the Marias River, the fort was rebuilt by Alexander Culbertson for the same company in 1850 and formally renamed Fort Benton on December 25 of the same year in honor of Senator Thomas Hart Benton of Missouri. Situated at the head of steamboat navigation, its site is now occupied by the town of Fort Benton in Chouteau County. Purchased by the government, the fort was first garrisoned by U.S. troops on October 11, 1869.

In 1874, when it was found that adobe buildings of the post were inadequate to house the soldiers, quarters were rented in the town. As an Army post, Fort Benton was used to transfer freight from and to Forts Ellis and Shaw. It was abandoned on May 31, 1881, and its garrison transferred to Fort Shaw. On January 5, 1883, the military reservation was turned over to the Department of the Interior. The ruins of the fort, originally 250 feet square with a pair of bastions or blockhouses at diagonal corners, have been stabilized and are contained within a five-acre park, fronting the river on Main Street.

BIG HORN BARRACKS. FORT CUSTER.

BIG HORN POST. FORT CUSTER.

BIG HORN POST. FORT MANUEL.

CAMP BIG SPRING CREEK. CAMP LEWIS.

FORT BROWNING. Its site located two miles southwest of the present town of Dodson, Glacier County, Fort Browning was a trading post built in 1868 on the south side of the Milk River and named for then Secretary of the Interior C. H. Browning. The post was abandoned in 1872.

FORT BRULE. FORT MCKENZIE.

FORT C. F. SMITH (*Fort Ransom*). Established on August 12, 1866, and originally designated Fort Ransom in honor of Brigadier General Thomas E. G. Ransom, who died on October 29, 1864, this 300-foot-square fort was situated on a high bluff on the right side of the Big Horn River in present Big Horn County, on a site now incorporated within the Crow Indian Reservation. Established by Captain Nathaniel C. Kinney with troops of the 18th Infantry in compliance with an order by Colonel Henry B. Carrington, the name of the post was soon changed to Fort C. F. Smith in honor of Major General Charles Ferguson Smith, who died on April 25, 1862.

The post, along with Forts Reno and Kearny, was intended to safeguard the Bozeman Trail, the "old Montana Road," from marauding Sioux. The building of these posts precipitated the Red Cloud War, 1866 to 1868. The dramatic so-called Hayfield Fight, in which 31 U.S. troops held off attacks by an estimated 800 Cheyennes, took place about eight miles from the fort, besieged for six months in 1866–67. In recognition of the agreement made with the Sioux in the Fort

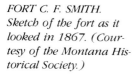

FORT C. F. SMITH. Sketch of the fort as it looked in 1867. (Courtesy of the Montana Historical Society.)

Laramie Treaty signed on April 29, 1868, the fort was abandoned three months later.

FORT CAMPBELL. A trading post built during the winter of 1845–46 by Harvey, Primeau & Company and named for Robert Campbell, it was originally a log-built stockade located on the south bank of the Missouri. In 1847 it was moved across the river about a mile west of Fort Benton and rebuilt of adobe, the first of its type in Montana. Sold to the American Fur Company about 1857, it was abandoned in 1860.

FORT CARROLL (*Carroll Landing Post*). During the height of steamboat trade on the Missouri River, Fort Benton found itself challenged by the new town of Carroll in present Chouteau County, located 25 miles west of the mouth of the Musselshell River in 1874. Designed to serve as both a trading post and a freight landing for steamboats, it was established by the Diamond R Transportation Company. The post's business gradually dwindled, and by 1882 the town had disappeared. The town, also known as Carroll Landing Post, near present Judith Landing, had military protection provided by 7th Infantry troops during the summers of 1874 and 1875.

CARROLL LANDING POST. FORT CARROLL.

FORT CASS (*Tulloch's Fort*). A trading post named Fort Cass in honor of Lewis Cass of Michigan was built by Samuel Tulloch for the American Fur Company in 1832. Often referred to as Tulloch's Fort, it was situated on the south bank of the Yellowstone River at the mouth of the Big Horn River very close to the boundary between present Yellowstone and Treasure counties. It has been described as a 130-foot-square fort built of cottonwood sapling pickets with two bastions or blockhouses at "the extreme corners." The post was abandoned in 1835.

FORT CHARDON. After Fort McKenzie was deliberately abandoned and later burned in 1844 by François Chardon and Alexander Harvey, who acted for the American Fur Company, they built a new trading post on the south bank of the Missouri River near the mouth of the Judith River and named it for Chardon. The stigma of Chardon's inhumane treatment of the Blackfeet at Fort McKenzie was transferred to the new post, and practically all the Indian trade in the area was lost. Alexander Culbertson, with a record of more than a decade of fair-dealing trade with the Indians, was sent by the Company to replace

Chardon in an attempt to recover their lost Blackfoot trade. But Fort Chardon was no longer useful. Culbertson abandoned it in 1845 and built a new post, Fort Lewis, three miles upriver from Fort Benton.

FORT CLAGETT (*Fort Cooke*). A trading post built in 1870 by T. C. Power and Bro. and originally known as Fort Cooke, it was first situated on the south side of the Missouri above the mouth of the Judith River, then later moved below the Judith, probably about 1872. The company's ledger shows use of the name Cooke until June 1872, when it was changed to Clagett in honor of William H. Clagett, representative to Congress from Montana. The post was apparently discontinued in November 1878.

FORT CONNAH. A trading post built on Post Creek, between present Ronan and St. Ignatius in Sanders County, it was established by Neil McLean McArthur of the Hudson's Bay Company. Begun in the fall of 1846 and completed by the summer of 1847, Fort Connah was the last HBC post established on American soil. The post was abandoned in either 1871 or 1872. The post's old storehouse is still standing.

FORT CONRAD. A post specifically established for trading with the Blackfeet, Fort Conrad was built in 1875 by Charles Conrad, a member of a St. Louis-Fort Benton firm, and stood on the south bank of the Marias River, 85 miles northwest of Fort Benton, in Glacier County, on a site now within the Blackfoot Indian Reservation. The connecting log cabins of the well-patronized fort formed three sides of a square 150 by 150 feet. Joseph Kipp, son of James Kipp of the American Fur Company, bought Fort Conrad in 1878. After the buffalo herds in the region were exterminated, Fort Conrad was sold to a James McDevitt. Not long after this transfer of proprietorship, the changing current of the river eroded the bank on which the fort stood, "and its logs rotted upon the sand bars of the Marias, the Missouri, and Mississippi rivers, perhaps all the way down to the Gulf of Mexico" (James Willard Schultz, *Blackfeet and Buffalo: Memories of Life Among the Indians*, ed. Keith C. Seele [1962], pp. 3–4).

CAMP COOKE. Established on July 11, 1866, on the south bank of the Missouri River just west of the mouth of the Judith River, as the first permanent military post in Montana, it was named for Brigadier General Philip St. George Cooke and garrisoned by elements of the 13th Infantry. Camp Cooke was occupied until March 31, 1870,

CAMP COOKE. View of the post drawn in 1868. (Courtesy of the Montana Historical Society, Helena.)

when the troops were withdrawn and the post was abandoned.

FORT COOKE. FORT CLAGETT.

FORT COTTON. FORT LEWIS.

FORT COTTON BOTTOMS. FORT LEWIS.

CAMP CROOK. Established on April 14, 1890, on a site near the old Tongue River Indian Agency by Major Henry Carroll with companies B, D, and M of the 1st Cavalry, Camp Crook was intended to protect the agent and the public property there. The post was abandoned in November of the same year.

FORT CUSTER (*Big Horn Post; Big Horn Barracks*). Established on July 4, 1877, by Lieutenant Colonel George P. Buell, 11th Infantry, on the bluff above the confluence of the Big Horn and Little Big Horn rivers, about two miles from the present town of Hardin in Bighorn County, Fort Custer was built a year after the Custer Massacre and intended to control the Sioux in the area. Originally known as Big Horn Post or Big Horn Barracks, it was officially designated Fort Custer on November 8, 1877, in honor of Lieutenant Colonel George A. Custer, 7th Cavalry, killed with all his troops in the Battle of the Little Big Horn on June 25, 1876. Fort Custer was abandoned on April 17, 1898, when elements of the 10th Cavalry and 25th Infantry were withdrawn. The D.A.R. erected a marker on the site of the post.

FORT ELIZABETH MEAGHER. Established in May 1867 by Brigadier General Thomas Thoroughman and Colonel Walter W. DeLacy of the Montana Volunteer Militia, and located about eight miles east of the town of Bozeman in present Gallatin County at the mouth of Rock Creek, the short-lived post was named for the wife of Thomas F. Meagher, former acting governor of the Territory. Fort Meagher was established in response to requests by the settlers in the valley who were anticipating attacks by hostile Crows and Sioux following the murder of John Bozeman a month earlier.

FORT ELLIS. Located on the left or south bank of the East Gallatin River, three miles west of Bozeman in Gallatin County, Fort Ellis was established on August 27, 1867, by Captain Robert S. La Motte with three companies of the 13th Infantry to safeguard the settlers and miners of the area from hostile Cheyenne and Sioux. The site of the fort had been particularly selected for its strategic location to control Bozeman, Bridger and Flathead Passes. The post was named in honor of Colonel Augustus Van Horn Ellis, 124th New York Infantry, killed on July 2, 1863, at Gettysburg. Considered surplus to its needs, the War Department abandoned the post and transferred the military reservation to the Department of the Interior on July 26, 1886.

FORT FIZZLE. Located about five miles west of the town of Lolo where the Lolo Trail enters the Bitterroot Valley in Missoula County, Fort Fizzle was a 200-foot-long, log-and-earth breastwork, 4 feet high, erected in July 1877 by elements of two companies of the 7th Infantry and local volunteers under the command of Captain Charles C. Rawn from Fort Missoula then under construction. The barricade was intended to halt the heroic march of Chief Joseph and his Nez Percé to the Canadian border. When the Indians, however, reached the position on July 28, 1877, they merely went around it and continued their trek. Subsequently, the makeshift fortification became popularly known by its uncomplimentary name of Fort Fizzle.

FLATHEAD POST NO. 1. A trading post established by Alexander Ross and Ross Cox in 1812 for Astor's American Fur Company, it was located on the north bank of the Clark's Fork River, near today's town of Noxon in Sanders County.

FLATHEAD POST NO. 2 (*Saleesh House No. 2*). At times referred to as the "2nd Saleesh House," this trading post was established in 1823 by Alexander Ross of the American Fur Company on the north bank of the Clark's Fork River in the immediate vicinity of the town of Eddy in Sanders County. The post apparently prospered and continued operations until 1847. According to *The Journals of David Thompson*, page cli., "Saleesh House had been replaced by Flathead Post or Fort, built farther up the Clark Fork, near the present railway siding of Eddy, Montana."

FORT GALPIN. A trading post established by Charles Larpenteur on September 23, 1862, it was named for Charles E. Galpin of La Barge, Harkness & Company and located on the north bank of the Missouri River about a dozen miles above the Milk River in the vicinity of modern Fort Peck.

FORT GILBERT. A trading post established in 1864 on the north bank of the Yellowstone River, it was located about five miles north of today's town of Sidney in Richland County. Fort Gilbert, according to a state historical marker near the site, operated until some time in 1867.

CAMP (FORT) GREEN CLAY SMITH. A temporary Army post established in 1867 during the Indian wars of 1866–68, it was located in Yellowstone Canyon four miles north of Fort Thomas F. Meagher.

FORT HARRISON. FORT WILLIAM HENRY HARRISON.

HELENA BARRACKS. This post was established on November 7, 1877, by five companies of the 3rd Infantry, commanded by Colonel DeL. Floyd Jones, on the Helena Fair Grounds about three miles outside the city. Helena Barracks was abandoned May 22, 1878.

FORT HENRY. FORT LEWIS.

FORT HENRY. THREE FORKS POST.

FORT HONORE. FORT LEWIS.

FORT HOWES. A 12-by-18-foot rock fortification built in 1897 by community cooperation during a threatened Cheyenne uprising, Fort Howes was located on a hillside about five miles northeast of present Otter in the southwest corner of Powder River County. Since no Indian outbreak occurred, the "fort" was neither occupied nor maintained.

FORT HOWIE. A temporary stockade erected by militia troops in 1867 during the Indian troubles, Fort Howie was located on the bank of the Yellowstone River, near the mouth of Shield's River, about seven miles east of Bozeman in Gallatin County.

HOWSE FORT. Established in 1810 by Joseph Howse for the Hudson's Bay company, this short-lived trading post was located either north of Lake Pend d'Oreille (formerly called Flathead Lake) on Clark's Fork River or near present Kalispell.

FORT JACKSON. Located on the Missouri River at the mouth of the Poplar River (Rivière aux Trembles), Fort Jackson was built by C. A. Chardon in December 1833 and named for President Andrew Jackson. Chardon with 20 men erected a palisaded post 50 feet square as a winter camp. Its approximate location is in the vicinity of the town of Poplar in Roosevelt County.

JANNEAU'S POST (*Fort Turnay*). A trading post established in 1879 by Francis A. Janneau (variously spelled by different sources), it was a stockaded fort about 100 by 150 feet with two bastions at diagonal corners. At times it was referred to as Fort Turnay, the derivation of which is unknown. Its site is within the city limits of Lewistown, Fergus County.

CANTONMENT JORDAN. During 1855–62, Captain John Mullan, 2nd Artillery, located and built what was known as the Mullan Road. Congress authorized its construction under the supervision of the War Department to connect Fort Benton, the head of navigation on the Missouri, with Fort Walla Walla, the head of navigation on the Columbia. The 624-mile-long wagon road was completed in 1862. In the winter of 1859–60, Captain Mullan established a winter camp which he called Cantonment Jordan, 2 miles east of present-day DeBorgia, Mineral County.

FORT KEOGH (*New Post on the Yellowstone; Cantonment on Tongue River; Tongue River Barracks*). Fort Keogh was first occupied on August 28, 1876, by companies C and I, 5th Infantry, and officially established on September 11, 1876, by Colonel Nelson A. Miles. It was located on the south or right bank of the Yellowstone, just to the west of today's Miles City, and less than two miles above the mouth of the Tongue River. The post was intended to serve as a base for operations against the Sioux Indians. In 1877 construction was begun on a site a mile to the west to establish a complex of permanent buildings.

Originally called New Post on the Yellowstone and Cantonment on Tongue River, and later Tongue River Barracks, the post was officially designated Fort Keogh on November 8, 1878, in honor of Captain Miles W. Keogh, 7th Cavalry, killed with the rest of Custer's command in the Battle of the Little Big Horn on June 25, 1876.

Fort Keogh served as an Army infantry and cavalry post until 1900, when it was used as an Army remount station where horses were trained for Army use. In 1908, the post was converted into a livestock experiment station. During World War I, the post was used as a quartermaster's depot. In 1924 the military reservation was transferred to the Department of the Interior. Today the Range and Livestock Experiment Station of the Department of Agriculture occupies Fort Keogh. Two of the original officers' quarters buildings are still standing and are occupied by employees.

KERCHIVAL CITY POST. FORT SHERIDAN.

FORT KIPP. Established in the spring of 1859 by James Kipp, chief American Fur Company agent at Fort Union, in opposition to Fort Stewart 600 feet away, for the Assiniboine Indian trade, Fort Kipp was located on the Missouri a few miles above the mouth of the Big Muddy River, in present Roosevelt County. The post, abandoned in 1860 by the Company, was burned almost at once by the Indians.

KOOTENAI HOUSE. A trading post established in 1807 by English-born David Thompson for the North West Company, Kootenai House was located a short distance from Lake Windemere in the northwest corner of today's Lincoln County. No data has been found to indicate when the post was abandoned.

KOOTENAI POST NO. 1. A trading post established in November 1808 by Finan McDonald for the North West Company, it was located on the north or right bank of the Kootenai River, nearly opposite the present town of Libby in Lincoln County. This was the first commercial enterprise south of the 49th parallel in "Oregon Country."

KOOTENAI POST NO. 2. A North West Company trading post established during the winter of 1811–12, it was located on the north side of the Kootenai River nearly opposite today's town of Jennings in Lincoln County.

KOOTENAI POST NO. 3. A North West Company trading post established in 1821, it was located on the Kootenai River above Kootenai Falls, near the mouth of Rainy (Rainey) Creek, in Lincoln County. The post was abandoned in 1824. William Kittson built a post on the same site in 1829 for the Hudson's Bay Company.

KOOTENAI POST NO. 4. (*Linklater Post*). Also known as Fort Kootenai (for the river) and Linklater Post (for the man who operated the post for many years), this trading post was established by Edward Berland in 1846 at the direction of Sir George Simpson, governor of the Hudson's Bay Company. It was located on the left bank of the Kootenai River below the mouth of Young Creek, about five miles below the 49th parallel. Another location is sometimes cited, reporting that it was on the right side of the Kootenai at the mouth of the Tobacco River. Berland died in 1852 and John Linklater came from Fort Colville each winter to take charge of the trade. Following the survey of the 49th parallel, the fort was moved about 1860 just north of the line. Following the discovery of gold in Wild Horse Creek, Linklater moved the post to Joseph's Prairie, where it was succeeded a few years later by Fort Steele. The fort was long an important fur post and center of hospitality.

FORT LA BARGE. This fort was established on June 28, 1862, one and a half miles above Fort Benton, by La Barge, Harkness & Company of St. Louis, and named for Joseph La Barge. It was found after one year of operation that the 300-by-200-foot fort was not competitive. It was sold by auction to the American Fur Company, which operated Fort Benton.

CAMP LEWIS (*Camp Big Spring Creek*). A temporary summer post established on May 10, 1874, on the Big Spring Creek Fork of the Judith River, Camp Lewis was located about two miles south of the present city of Lewistown, Fergus County, and intended to protect the trading interests in the area from Indian incursions. A detachment of the 7th Infantry from Fort Shaw on the Sun River established the post, first known as Camp Big Spring Creek, then named in honor of Major William H. Lewis. The camp was discontinued on November 1, 1874.

FORT LEWIS. FORT BENTON.

FORT LEWIS. A short-lived trading post on the right side of the Missouri River opposite Pablois Island, it was established in 1845 and located about 18 miles above Fort Benton. The fort was dismantled in 1846 and moved to the site of Fort Benton.

FORT LEWIS (*Fort Cotton; Fort Cotton Bottoms; Fort Honore; Fort Henry*). In 1842 the Union Fur Company established a small, short-lived trading post, known as Fort Cotton or Cotton Bottoms, on the right bank of the Missouri in Blackfoot country just above the future site of Fort Benton. After abandoning and burning Fort Chardon, Alexander Culbertson of the American Fur Company built a new post, the "Fort of the Blackfeet," also known as Fort Henry, Fort Honore (for Honoré Picotte), and Fort Lewis (for Meriwether Lewis), probably on the site of old Fort Cotton on the south bank of the Missouri, just above the mouth of the Marias River and three miles upriver from present Fort Benton. Culbertson's diplomacy was so successful among the Blackfeet chiefs that the Indians in 1846 brought to the fort some 21,000 buffalo robes, in addition to beaver, wolf, and fox skins. At the request of the Indians, Culbertson in the spring of 1847 moved Fort Lewis to a site three miles downriver on the north bank, six miles above the mouth of the Teton.

LINKLATER POST. KOOTENAI POST NO. 4.

FORT LISA. FORT MANUEL.

LISA'S POST. FORT MANUEL.

CAMP LODER. A temporary post located on Lodge Pole Creek near Fort Musselshell, Camp Loder was established in July 1879 by Major Guido Ilges, 7th Infantry, with companies A, D, G, and I, aggregating 193 men. The post was abandoned some time in September.

FORT LOGAN (*Camp Baker*). Located in the Smith River Valley on the west bank of the river, about 17 miles northwest of present White Sulphur Springs in Meagher County, this post was established on November 30, 1869, for the purpose of protecting the mining camps in the area in addition to the Fort Benton supply route from Indian hostiles, in particular the Blackfeet. In response to urgent requests from the settlers there, a company of the 2nd Cavalry from Fort Ellis was sent in compliance with an order of Major General Winfield Scott Hancock. In August 1870 the Army relocated the post some 10 miles to the southeast at the present site of Fort Logan, 40 miles east of Helena. First called Camp Baker for Major Eugene Mortimer Baker, 2nd Cavalry, commanding Fort Ellis, the post was officially designated Fort Logan on December 30, 1878, in honor of Captain William Logan, 7th Infantry, killed in the Battle of the Big Hole on August 9, 1877. Abandoned on October 27, 1880, the military reservation was sold at auction. In 1962 the fort's still remaining blockhouse was moved to the center of the parade ground.

FORT MCKENZIE (*Fort Piegan No. 2; Fort Brule*). In October 1831 James Kipp, acting for the American Fur Company, built a trading post, Fort Piegan, deep in the Blackfoot country, on the north bank of the Missouri, above the mouth of the Marias River. During the following spring, after the trappers left the post to take their winter catch of furs to Fort Union, the Indians burned it. Undiscouraged, Kenneth McKenzie sent David Dawson Mitchell to build a new post on the Missouri about six miles above the mouth of the Marias River, not far from the old site.

Mitchell's men erected a 1,420-square-foot quadrangular fort and defended it by two blockhouses at diagonal corners and several pieces of cannon. Mitchell named the post Fort McKenzie in honor of his superior. The fort was abandoned in the spring of 1844 after the trader François Chardon and his men ruthlessly murdered a number of Blackfeet. Since this massacre made Fort McKenzie untenable, Chardon burned Fort McKenzie and built a small new post downstream at the mouth of the Judith. Fort McKenzie's site thereafter became known as Fort Brule ("burned fort").

FORT MAGINNIS. Located about 25 miles northeast of Lewistown, Fergus County, on Ford's Creek, a tributary of the Musselshell River, Fort Maginnis was established by Captain Dangerfield Park with Company K of the 3rd Infantry on August 22, 1880. The fort was intended to safeguard ranchers, settlers, and travel routes from hostile Indians. The post was named for Major Martin Maginnis, 11th Minnesota Infantry, who was Montana Territory's delegate to Congress. The post was abandoned on July 20, 1890, except for a caretaking unit of two men to protect the public property on there. The reservation was transferred to the Department of the Interior on August 14, 1890. Ranchers in the area and Lewistown citizens later carried off the fort's buildings, piece by piece. Four miles from the fort site is the ghost town of Giltedge.

FORT MANUEL (*Fort Lisa; Fort Remon (Raymond); Fort Manuel Lisa; Lisa's Post; Big Horn Post*). Captain William Clark, of the Lewis and Clark Expedition, and his party camped at the junction of the Yellowstone and Big Horn rivers on July 26, 1806. He later reported that the Big Horn River was swarming with beaver. Manuel Lisa, one of the most detested men on the frontier, was the first of the large-scale traders to penetrate the upper Missouri. He left St. Louis in the spring of 1807 with 42 men and a keel boat loaded with trade goods. His financial backing was provided by William Morrison and Pierre Menard of Kaskaskia, Illinois.

At the mouth of the Platte River, Lisa met John Colter, who had been with Lewis and Clark, and who persuaded him to join the party. They arrived at the mouth of the Big Horn River, after several encounters with hostile Sioux and Assiniboine, and built a post which Lisa named for his son Remon. Dr. Merrill Burlingame in *The Montana Frontier*, p. 48, reported that

in the spring of 1809, accompanied by two partners of the [Missouri Fur Company], Andrew Henry and Pierre Menard, Lisa went to the Yellowstone again in charge of a large expedition, containing perhaps as many as 350 men, and near the original post, larger and more permanent quarters were built. Lisa had called his first little post Fort Remon for his son. Fort Remon was usually anglicized to Fort Raymond, but this and the second post were often referred to as Fort Manuel, Fort Manuel Lisa, Lisa's Post, or Big Horn Post.

Lisa's first two posts were located in what is now Treasure County.

FORT MANUEL LISA. FORT MANUEL.

FORT (THOMAS F.) MEAGHER. A temporary post established on August 27, 1867, Fort Meagher was located about four miles south of Camp Green Clay Smith, in Yellowstone (McAdow) Canyon.

CAMP MERRITT. Established in April 1890 on Lame Deer Creek, near the present town of Lame Deer in Rosebud County, near the Tongue River Indian Agency, by companies B, D, and M, 1st Cavalry, the post was intended to provide protection for the agency during protracted Indian difficulties. The agency site is now the Northern Cheyenne Indian Reservation. Special Orders No. 91, Department of Dakota, June 27, 1898, directed Company K, 8th Cavalry, to leave the post and that Camp Merritt was to be a subpost of Fort Keogh.

FORT MISSOULA (*Post at Missoula*). Located on the right side of the Bitterroot River at

FORT MISSOULA. (Courtesy of the Montana Historical Society.)

the mouth of Grant Creek, about four miles southwest of the town of Missoula, the post was established in response to the urgent requests of Missoula Valley's settlers, who feared an Indian uprising as a result of forcibly moving the Salish Indians to a reservation. Following the recommendation of Lieutenant Colonel Wesley Merritt, 9th Cavalry, on February 8, 1876, the post was established by Captain Charles C. Rawn, 7th Infantry. First called Post at Missoula, it was officially designated Fort Missoula on November 8, 1877. Troops from this post participated in the nearby Battle of the Big Hole in 1877 against Chief Joseph and his Nez Percé. The fort was garrisoned continuously until 1898, and thereafter intermittently until World War I, when it served as an Army mechanics school. Several of the original buildings stand amidst modern structures used by Army Reserve units and government agencies. The post's former quartermaster building is a State Historical Society museum, and an officers' quarters has been refurbished.

POST AT MISSOULA. FORT MISSOULA.

CAMP MORRIS. A temporary Army post established in 1883 and officially reported as having been situated on the "west side of Cottonwood Creek near the Sunset Grass Hills," Camp Morris was located on the approximate site of present Whitlash, in the northwest corner of Liberty County, just below the Alberta border.

FORT MUSSELSHELL. FORT SHERIDAN.

NEW POST ON THE YELLOWSTONE. FORT KEOGH.

OPHIR POST. A short-lived "trading" post established by Captain Jim Moore and a number of men when their steamboat *Cutter* was disabled as an emergency measure during the winter of 1864–65, it was located on the south bank of the Marias River, close to its junction with the Missouri, about 12 miles by land from Fort Benton. After an attack on May 25 by a band of Blood Indians, in which 10 white men of the post were killed in retaliation for the murder of a young warrior, the post was abandoned.

FORT OWEN. Located in the Bitterroot Valley about one mile north of Stevensville, Ravalli County, this influential trading post occupied a part of the building complex formerly known as St. Mary's Mission, established by Jesuit Father De Smet in 1841 and operated by Father Anthony Ravalli until 1850, when John Owen came

there after serving as post sutler at Camp Loring in Utah and purchased some of the mission buildings. He opened his trading post, grist mill, and farm which he called Fort Owen. The acquisition of title to the property is reported as having been the first formal land transfer in present Montana. Owen developed the post into the most important travel and trade center in that part of the territory. Father Ravalli, however, continued his mission work there on an intermittent basis until 1884. Ill health in 1871 caused "Major" Owen to close his post. A restored building on the site of Fort Owen (St. Mary's Mission) is now a State Historical Monument.

FORT PARKER. Located one mile south of the Yellowstone River, about four miles east of present Livingston in Park County, Fort Parker was built in the fall of 1869 as a result of the Fort Laramie Treaty of 1868. The treaty promised to construct an agency on the Yellowstone from which annuity goods would be distributed to the Crow Indians. The 200-foot-square, stockaded frontier fort that guarded and provisioned the Indians consisted of single-story log structures with bastions or blockhouses on the northeast and southeast corners. Outside the stockade were 25 adobe houses for the Indians, along with the cattle corral and stable. After the fort burned in 1872, Fort Parker II was constructed of adobe rather than logs, also 200 feet square, with the buildings facing inward. The post was abandoned in 1875 because of pressure to open the region for settlement.

FORT PEASE. A temporary trading post built in 1875 on the north bank of the Yellowstone River, about seven miles below the mouth of the Big Horn, Fort Pease was established by "Major" F. D. Pease (the first agent to the Crow Indians) and two partners, "having conceived the idea that a trading post" there would prove profitable. The three partners, aided by 25 men in the party, built a stockaded post about 100 feet square. The area's Crow Indians were friendly, but the Sioux were overtly hostile and threatening. In March of the following year, a number of soldiers and civilians arrived from Fort Ellis, and although none of those at the stockade but the traders wished to leave, all were forced to go, abandoning the post.

FORT PECK. Formerly located on the west bank of the Missouri River about one mile above the present site of Fort Peck Dam in Valley County, this prestigious stockaded fort was established in 1867 by Abel Farwell, member of the firm of Durfee and Peck who operated several trading posts along the river. The fort was 300 feet square, with 12-foot-high walls of cotton-wood logs set vertically, and three bastions and four gateways on the front, and two bastions on the rear. Within were various log-built structures occupied as barracks, storehouses, a blacksmith shop, stables, a corral, and even a slaughterhouse.

Although Fort Peck was not an Army post, it often served as temporary headquarters for military men and commissioners sent there by the government to negotiate with the Indians during the period preceding the historic Custer Massacre. Sitting Bull refused to attend any of these conferences but is said to have visited the fort privately on numerous occasions. In 1871 the Milk River Indian Agency was moved to Fort Peck from its former location at the mouth of People's Creek on the Milk River. The stockade thus remained a combination trading post and Indian agency until July 14, 1879, when the agency was moved to Poplar Creek and the trading post was abandoned. It was not until 1886, three years before Montana was admitted to the Union, that the Fort Peck Indian Reservation was established, having been named in honor of Colonel Campbell Kennedy Peck of the trading firm.

The principal reason for the abandonment of old Fort Peck was the erosion of the ledge on which it stood by the river. It is believed that the site crumbled into the Missouri just before the turn of the century. Since the name of Fort Peck had been so closely associated with the region, it was only natural that the great earthen dam project there should be so designated. The actual site of the fort has been inundated by the Fort Peck Reservoir.

FORT PIEGAN NO. 1. The Lewis and Clark Expedition on June 3, 1805, camped at the mouth of the Marias River on the north bank of the Missouri, just east of the present town of Loma in Chouteau County. In the fall of 1831, James Kipp of the American Fur Company built Fort Piegan on approximately the same site as a trading post for the Blackfoot Indians. Within 75 days, the traders completed their fort, consisting of three large log buildings for quarters, storerooms, and a trading room, surrounded by a 25-foot-high stockade loopholed for cannon and small arms.

Kipp named his post Fort Piegan in recognition of the first Blackfoot tribe to make peace with the Americans. In order to win these Indians away from the Hudson's Bay Company, he gave them 200 gallons of Blackfoot rum made from a barrel of whiskey. His liberality had the effect he hoped for, and in a few days he obtained 6,450 pounds of beaver from which his company realized $46,000 the next spring. As soon as the traders left in the spring with their haul of beaver for Fort Union, the Indians burned the fort. Undiscouraged, the Company returned shortly afterward and established a new post, Fort McKenzie, a few miles above the site of the other.

FORT PIEGAN NO. 2. FORT MCKENZIE.

CAMP POPLAR RIVER. Situated on the south bank of the Poplar River, two miles north of the Missouri, a site now occupied by the town of Poplar in Roosevelt County, this post was established on October 12, 1880, by companies B and F of the 11th Infantry. Camp Poplar River was abandoned on October 2, 1893, and its garrison transferred to Fort Assiniboine.

POPLAR RIVER POST. In November 1860, after finding both Forts Stewart and Kipp in ruins, Charles Larpenteur and his partner, Robert Lemon, established a new trading post 25 miles up the Missouri at the mouth of the Poplar River in present Roosevelt County, and settled in for the winter. To compete with them, the American Fur Company built a "wintering" post adjoining, called Malcolm Clark's Fort.

CAMP PORTER. In compliance with Special Orders No. 159, Headquarters Department of Dakota, dated November 2, 1880, Camp Porter was established on the Yellowstone River near Glendive Creek, by Company A, 11th Infantry, and Company B, 17th Infantry, under the command of 1st Lieutenant James Brennan, to protect the working parties constructing the Northern Pacific Railroad. In accordance with Special Orders No. 215, Headquarters Department of Dakota, dated November 19, 1881, the post was abandoned 10 days later, having served its purpose. The town of Glendive on I-94 in Dawson County now occupies the site.

FORT RANSOM. FORT C. F. SMITH.

FORT RAYMOND. FORT MANUEL.

REED'S FORT. Named for "Major" Alonzo S. Reed who, with a partner named Bowles, purchased the Story and Hoffman trading post in 1874 at the present site of Lewistown in Fergus County, it was moved about a mile and a half down Spring Creek and reestablished as a very active trading center during the latter part of the 1870s.

CAMP REEVE. FORT SHERIDAN.

FORT REMON. FORT MANUEL.

CAMP REYNOLDS. FORT SHAW.

RIVET'S POST. Louis Rivet built Fort Hawley in 1866 for the trading firm of Hubbell and Hawley and was in charge of it for one year. He then built a trading post for himself at the Big Bend of the Milk River in present Valley County in 1867 and traded for one season there. Rivet was engaged in the fur trade in Montana and Canada for many years.

CANTONMENT ROCKY POINT. Established on May 15, 1881, as a summer camp for the purpose of guarding stores and supplies while nearby Fort Maginnis was being built on Ford's Creek, a tributary of the Musselshell River, in Fergus County, the cantonment was garrisoned by Company G, 18th Infantry, commanded by 1st Lieutenant Daniel H. Floyd. It was abandoned November 8, 1881, when the fort was completed.

ROCKY POINT POST. Built probably in 1881 as a trading post by C. A. Broadwater & Company on the Missouri River, about 11 miles above the town of Carroll in Fergus County, it served as a government landing for Fort Maginnis. The Broadwater firm established a large mercantile house and warehouse there for the receipt and shipment of hides and wool.

ROULETTE'S POST. This short-lived trading post was established on the site of old Forts Stewart and Kipp in late 1862 by one of the Roulette brothers, who was financed by the American Fur Company. It was attacked and burned by resentful Assiniboine, who had been cheated by Roulette. The Indians killed seven traders who had remained within the stockade after the Company's steamboat *Nellie Rogers* had hurriedly taken on a cargo of furs and buffalo robes and smuggled Roulette aboard.

SALEESH HOUSE. A trading post established in November 1809 by David Thompson, it was situated on the north side of Clark's Fork nearly opposite the mouth of Prospect (Ashley) Creek, near the present town of Thompson Falls in Sanders County. Thompson was the greatest geographer of his time in British America and an explorer-trader for the North West Company.

SALEESH HOUSE NO. 2. FLATHEAD POST NO. 2.

FORT SARPY NO. 1. Built in 1850 on the north bank of the Yellowstone River, just below the mouth of the Rosebud, in present Rosebud County, this trading post catering to the Crow Indians was established by Alexander Culbertson of the American Fur Company and named for John B. Sarpy, one of the Company partners. Experienced trader Robert Meldrum was placed in charge of the new trading fort. In May 1855 the Company abandoned and burned "badly forted" Fort Sarpy, ultimately replaced by Fort Sarpy No. 2, south of the Yellowstone.

FORT SARPY NO. 2. Located on the south bank of the Yellowstone, near the mouth of the Big Horn River, in present Treasure County, this new Fort Sarpy was established about 1859 by the American Fur Company to renew trading with the Crow Indians. Robert Meldrum was again placed in charge. It was a 100-foot-square stockade with 15-foot-high, cottonwood-log walls, loopholed at the top for defense. The post, however, lasted but one season and was abandoned in 1860, signaling the end of the Company's "year-round, on-the-spot trade in the dangerous Crow country."

FORT SHAW (*Camp Reynolds*). Established on June 30, 1867, and located on the right bank of the Sun River, about 25 miles above its junction with the Missouri, the post was intended to protect the travel route between Fort Benton and the town of Helena. Major William Clinton, 13th Infantry, with companies A, C, D, F, and I, established the post, first called Camp Reynolds. It was designated Fort Shaw on August 1, 1867, in honor of Colonel Robert G. Shaw, 54th Massachusetts Volunteer Infantry, killed in action before Fort Wagner on July 18, 1863. Fort Shaw was abandoned on July 21, 1891. The military reservation was turned over to the Department of the Interior on April 30, 1892, which operated the former Army post as an Indian school from then until 1910.

FORT SHERIDAN (*Kerchival City Post; Camp Reeve; Fort Musselshell*). The various attempts made by the early settlers to establish a town at the confluence of the Musselshell and the Missouri rivers were failures. In 1866 a town called Kerchival City was established, but within two years it and its trading post disappeared. In March 1868 agents of the Montana Hide & Fur

Company of Helena arrived and laid out a town on the south bank of the Missouri, called it Musselshell, and built a warehouse. They were soon joined by Colonel George Clendennin, with his brother Richard, and James McGinnis, from Grand Island. The colonel at once constructed buildings for the purpose of establishing a trading post.

A company of troops of the 13th Infantry, commanded by Captain Nugent, came from Camp Cooke and took post for the summer there, building a stockade with bastions just below the town and naming it Camp Reeve. The post was abandoned after the town appeared to be firmly established. The friendly Gros Ventres and Crows flocked to the town in large numbers to trade. But the year 1868 appears to have been the zenith of its history. The buffalo had migrated to other ranges and the Sioux were raiding more frequently, killing a number of men in March 1869. A force of about 30 townspeople were raised and, commanded by Colonel Clendennin, had a pitched battle with a war party of about 200 Sioux. They routed the Indians, inflicting many casualties among them. Captured wounded Indians were killed in cold blood and horribly mutilated.

As a freighting town and trading post, the town of Musselshell also proved a failure because of Fort Benton's continued popularity. In August 1870 the Montana Hide & Fur Company closed its affairs there and abandoned its warehouse and trading post. But Colonel Clendennin resolved to carry on and continued the Indian trade. He razed the abandoned buildings, made considerable additions to his own buildings, and connected them with a stockade, establishing a compact, strong, and attractive fort to which he gave the name of Fort Sheridan. When the town of Carroll was founded about 60 miles above the mouth of the Musselshell in the spring of 1874, Colonel Clendennin broke up his establishment and in May of that year removed to the new town. Fort Sheridan was dismantled and the salvageable materials transferred to Carroll.

FORT SHERMAN. A trading post built by Peter Koch for Nelson Story and C. W. Hoffman of Bozeman in November 1873, Fort Sherman was established on a site just below the mouth of Casino Creek, on the south bank of Big Spring Creek, at present Lewistown in Fergus County. When trade proved unprofitable, the post and its improvements were sold in 1874 to "Major" Alonzo S. Reed. The old post is still preserved in a city park in Lewistown. (See: REED'S FORT.)

STANLEY'S STOCKADE. Located six miles south of the present town of Glendive in Dawson County, this fortified Army stockade was erected toward the end of July 1873 as an advanced supply depot for steamboat-hauled supplies for the Northern Pacific Railroad survey. Named for Colonel D. S. Stanley, who was in charge of the survey's military escort, the depot was also used as a base for General Alfred H. Terry's 1876 Indian campaign.

CANTONMENT STEVENS. Located on the present site of Stevensville in the Bitterroot Valley, Ravalli County, this cantonment was established in 1853 and named for Territorial Governor Isaac I. Stevens of Washington, who with Lieutenant (later Captain) John Mullan, 2nd Artillery, stayed at nearby Fort Owen during the railroad survey. The encampment included four log structures, tents, and a corral. Beginning in 1855 and continuing until 1862, Mullan supervised the construction of the 624-mile-long so-called Mullan Road connecting Fort Benton and Walla Walla. (See: CANTONMENT JORDAN and FORT OWEN.)

FORT STEWART. Apparently named for former Army Deputy Paymaster Lieutenant Colonel Adam D. Steuart and located in present Roosevelt County on the Missouri several miles above the mouth of the Big Muddy River, 35 miles above Fort Union, Fort Stewart was reconstructed or reestablished in November 1861 for the Assiniboine and Gros Ventre Indian trade by Charles Larpenteur and his partner, Robert Lemon. This second Fort Stewart actually occupied the same adjacent sites of Fort Kipp (American Fur Company) and the first Fort Stewart (Frost, Todd & Company), both of which were abandoned and then burned by the Indians in 1860. In 1862 Larpenteur and Lemon sold out to La Barge, Harkness & Company, formed in opposition to the American Fur Company. (See: FORT KIPP.)

CAMP TERRY. A military post located on the Yellowstone River at the mouth of the Powder River, near the town of Terry, Prairie County, Camp Terry was established as a depot of supplies for the 1876 Custer Indian campaign. Major Orlando Moore and infantry troops garrisoned the post during the summer and fall of 1876. It was thereafter intermittently garrisoned until 1882, when the North Pacific Railroad reached this point.

CAMP (IDA) THOROUGHMAN. Established on June 13, 1867, in compliance with an order of General Alfred H. Terry, Camp Ida Thoroughman was garrisoned by Colonel H. N. Blake and his troops. Blake named the post in honor of the wife of Brigadier General Thoroughman. The camp, four miles northeast of Livingston in present Park County, was occupied until September 28, 1867.

THREE FORKS POST (*Fort Henry*). In early April 1810, Pierre Menard and Andrew Henry with 32 trappers established a Missouri Fur Company trading post on the tongue of land between the Jefferson and Madison rivers, near the present-day town of Three Forks in Gallatin County. Their 300-foot-square double stockade, also known as Fort Henry or Henry's Post, had to be abandoned after a single summer of operation because of continuous troubles with the Indians. Attempts to establish posts at the site in 1832 by Henry Vanderburgh of the American Fur Company and by Jim Bridger of the rival Rocky Mountain Fur Company also failed. The arrival of the railroad in 1908 spawned the establishment of the town of Three Forks near the site.

CANTONMENT ON TONGUE RIVER. FORT KEOGH.

TONGUE RIVER BARRACKS. FORT KEOGH.

TULLOCH'S FORT. FORT CASS.

FORT TURNAY. JANNEAU'S POST.

FORT UNION. Often confused with the more famous Fort Union established in 1826 just across the Montana line in North Dakota, the second Fort Union was located on the north bank of the Missouri, on the site of the present-day town of Fraser in Valley County. The trading post was established by Kenneth McKenzie for the American Fur Company, with construction beginning in 1829. A year after the steamboat *Yellowstone* reached the post in 1832, Fort Union was in full operation catering to the Blackfoot trade. The fort was bought by the government and dismantled in 1866.

FORT VAN BUREN. Located on the right bank of the Yellowstone River at the mouth of the Rosebud River in present Custer County, near Miles City on I-94, Fort Van Buren (named for the President) was established in 1835 by the American Fur Company, the Company's second trading post on the river. Charles Larpenteur abandoned and burned the fort in 1842.

FORT WILLIAM HENRY HARRISON (*Fort Harrison*). Although this post in the city of Helena was authorized and named by Congress on December 13, 1892, it was not established until September 23, 1895. Its first garrison came from Fort Assiniboine and consisted of Field and Staff and companies B and E, 22nd Infantry, under the command of Captain Mott Hooten. Originally known as Fort Harrison, it was officially designated Fort William Henry Harrison on February 26, 1906. The post was abandoned on January 15, 1913, leaving a caretaking detachment of quartermaster troops there until April 1913. The post is now a Veterans Administration Hospital.

CANTONMENT WRIGHT. This post was one of Captain John Mullan's last camps established during the building of the long wagon road from Fort Benton to Walla Walla. The cantonment was established for the 1861–62 winter and located a quarter of a mile west of present Milltown in Missoula County. (See: CANTONMENT JORDAN.)

ALKALI STATION. Located just south of the North Platte River, about one mile south and three miles east of Paxton, Keith County, this former Pony Express station was converted into an Army post in 1864 for the purpose of safeguarding the Oregon Trail. First occupied by one company of the 7th Iowa Cavalry, the post was a quadrangular stockade, mounting blockhouses on the southeast and northwest corners and enclosing barracks, officers' quarters, storehouses, stables, and a corral. The post was abandoned in 1866.

CAMP ALVIN SAUNDERS. Located on the State Fair Grounds in Lincoln, this short-lived post was established in April 1898 to receive the 1st and 2nd Nebraska Regiments, formed from the National Guard, who were mustered into the Army for service in the Spanish-American War. Camp Alvin Saunders was closed about a month later.

FORT ATKINSON (*Camp Missouri; Cantonment Missouri; Cantonment Council Bluffs*). Located at Council Bluffs on the west bank of the Missouri River less than 10 miles above the later-founded city of Omaha, near the present town of Fort Calhoun (formerly Fort Atkinson), this post was first established on September 29, 1819, on the riverbank by Colonel Henry Atkinson with five companies of the 6th Infantry and a rifle regiment. The fort was a result of the so-called "Yellowstone Expedition," which aimed to establish a chain of outposts to exert American influence over the vast area acquired in the Louisiana Purchase. When established, it was the Army's most advanced western outpost.

Originally called Camp Missouri, then Cantonment Missouri, the post was moved on June 12, 1820, because of river flooding, to the height of Council Bluffs, about two miles south of its original site, and renamed Cantonment Council Bluffs. It was officially designated Fort Atkinson in compliance with the order of Secretary of War John C. Calhoun, dated January 5, 1821. The fort was abandoned on June 6, 1827, as recommended by Colonel George Croghan, inspector general of the Army. Its last garrison was transferred to Jefferson Barracks near St. Louis, with the post itself replaced as military guardian of the region by Fort Leavenworth in Kansas.

CAMP AUGUR. Probably named for Union General Christopher Colon Augur, who commanded the Department of the Platte with headquarters at Fort Omaha, the post may have been an adjunct of the fort for the purpose of using

Nebraska

the rifle ranges and engaging in other training programs. No information has been found to indicate when it was established.

BEAUVAIS STATION POST. Located just south of the bridge over the South Platte River below the town of Brule in Keith County, this Army post was established in 1864 by a company of the 1st Nebraska Cavalry. The troops built a 325-by-125-foot stockade enclosing barracks, officers' quarters, storehouse, stables, and a corral, with two gates in the south palisade facing the Overland Road. The post was abandoned in late 1865 or early 1866.

FORT BEAVER VALLEY. Located in Beaver Valley, 15 miles northwest of the town of Chadron in northern Dawes County, this temporary defense was built in early 1891 by local settlers who feared a Sioux attack in reprisal for the Wounded Knee Massacre on December 29, 1890, a short distance above the South Dakota line.

CABANNÉ'S POST. Located about nine miles (by land) above today's city of Omaha and some six miles below the town of Fort Calhoun, this fur-trading post was established by J. P. Cabanné between 1822 and 1826 for the American Fur Company. In the mid-1830s, Joshua Pilcher moved the post down the river to Bellevue, the oldest existing town in Nebraska, and placed Peter A. Sarpy in charge. "This trading post [in 1834] consists of a row of [white] buildings of various sizes, stores, and the houses of the *engagés*, married to Indian women, among which was that of Mr. Cabanné, which is two stories high" (Davis Thomas and Karin Ronnefeldt, *People of the First Man: Life Among the Plains Indians in Their Final Days of Glory* [1976], p. 25).

FORT CHARLES. In November 1795 an expedition of the Spanish-operated "Company of Explorers of the Upper Missouri" reached a large Omaha Indian village located about six miles below the present town of Omadi in Dakota County. After forming an alliance with Chief Black Bird and dispensing gifts, the leader of the expedition, Jacques Mackay, erected Fort Charles there and passed the winter. Mackay was a Scot who had traded for the British but had changed his allegiance to Spain.

FORT CHILDS. FORT KEARNY NO. 2.

FORT CLARKE. Located near the town of Bridgeport in Morrill County, Fort Clarke was a blockhouse erected in 1876 by U.S. Army troops to protect the property of Henry T. Clarke, who built the important bridge over the North Platte River to serve the Black Hills traffic. In 1910 a prairie fire destroyed the blockhouse and other structures in its immediate vicinity.

COLUMBUS POST. A large stockade erected in 1863 by the settlers and occupied by troops of the 7th Iowa Cavalry in 1864, this post was located in the center of the town of Columbus in Platte County. At the end of the Civil War, a detachment of "Galvanized Yankees" was stationed here to safeguard the bridge over the Loup River.

FORT COTTONWOOD. FORT MCPHERSON.

FORT COTTONWOOD SPRINGS. FORT MCPHERSON.

CANTONMENT COUNCIL BLUFFS. FORT ATKINSON.

FORT CROOK. When Fort Omaha proved to be too small for the assigned detachments, land was purchased in 1878 by the government for a new post, Fort Crook (named for General George Crook), to be located 10 miles south of Omaha at Bellevue in Sarpy County. Fort Omaha, however, remained in use. General Orders No. 41, War Department, dated July 1, 1895, designated Fort Crook as a place of confinement of general prisoners. Upon creation of the 7th Corps Area in compliance with General Orders No. 71, War Department, dated December 1, 1920, its headquarters were established at Fort Crook.

On May 3, 1924, the flying field at the post was designated Offutt Field. Fort Crook was apparently occupied continuously by the Army until April 1, 1948, when it was transferred to the Department of the Air Force. The post was significantly modernized into Offutt Air Force Base, the headquarters of the Strategic Air Command. Officers' quarters, barracks, and other historic buildings of the old Army post still remain.

CROOKS AND McCLELLAN POST. Ramsay Crooks and Robert McClellan in their earlier operations as partners were independent traders. There is considerable variation in the dates given for the building of this post, and its location is debatable. One historian reports it was located at Council Bluffs on the Missouri River and dates it 1808–9. H. M. Chittenden, however, states that the "wintering" post was built in 1810 on the west bank of the river a little above the mouth of Papillion Creek, and therefore near the later site of Bellevue in present Sarpy County. The post was abandoned in the spring of 1811, when Crooks and McClellan joined the Pacific Fur Company. Later they joined Astor's American Fur Company.

FORT FONTENELLE. FORT MITCHELL.

FORT GILLETTE. FORT KEARNY NO. 2.

GILMAN'S STATION POST. Located just north of the Platte River near the border of Lincoln and Dawson counties, southeast of Brady, Gilman's Ranch was a military station of some importance during 1864–66. A stockade about 150 feet square, with a detached seven-room barracks, was erected and garrisoned by detachments of the Nebraska Cavalry.

FORT GRATTAN. A short-lived Army defense located on the Oregon Trail, south of the North Platte River at the mouth of Ash Hollow Canyon and three miles from the present town of Lewellen in Garden County, Fort Grattan was established on September 8, 1855, by Colonel William S. Harney, 2nd Dragoons, immediately after his fight with the Sioux in the Battle of Ash Hollow, sometimes called the Battle of Blue Water. Named in honor of 2nd Lieutenant John L. Grattan, 6th Infantry, killed by Oglala Sioux near Fort Laramie, Wyoming, August 19, 1854, the fort was a two-bastioned sod earthwork intended to safeguard emigrant trains and the military mail route between Forts Kearny and Laramie. The post, lasting but three weeks, was abandoned on October 1, 1855. The sites of the fort and the battle area are now on privately owned ranchland.

FORT HARTSUFF (*Post on the North Fork of the Loup River*). Located on the left side of the North Loup River south of the present town of Burwell (Garfield County) in Valley County, this Army post was established on September 5, 1874, as "Post on the North Fork of the Loup River" to protect the settlers of the valley from marauding bands of Sioux. It was established by Captain Samuel Munson, 9th Infantry, on a site chosen by Brigadier General Edward O. C. Ord. The post was officially designated Fort Hartsuff on December 9, 1874, in honor of Major General George Lucas Hartsuff, who died on May 16, 1874.

Unneeded after Fort Niobrara was established in 1880 on the Niobrara River, Fort Hartsuff was abandoned on May 1, 1881. The post buildings were sold on July 20, 1881, and the military reservation was transferred to the Department of the Interior on July 22, 1884. The state restored the Army post and incorporated it within the Fort Hartsuff State Historical Park.

FORT INDEPENDENCE. A 24-foot-square, loopholed, log-built stockade, strongly banked with sod against flaming arrows, Fort Independence was erected by farmer William Stolley during the 1864 Indian War. Beneath the defense was an ingenious 88-foot-long stable for his livestock. The site of the fort is today incorporated within the 43-acre Stolley State Park just south of Grand Island in Hall County.

JUNCTION STATION POST. An Army post established adjacent to or near the Junction stage station during the 1864 Indian War, it was located approximately southeast of today's Grand Island exit on I-80 at the point where it intersects with U.S. 30. The stockaded complex of officers' quarters, barracks, and stables was located about a quarter of a mile from its corral and additional stables. The post was abandoned some time in 1866.

CAMP KEARNY. FORT KEARNY.

FORT KEARNY (*Camp Kearny*). Located on the west bank of the Missouri River, at the mouth of Table Creek, in present-day Nebraska City, Otoe County, the post was established as Camp Kearny on May 21, 1846, by Major Clifton Wharton, 1st Dragoons, and named for Colonel Stephen Watts Kearny, 1st Dragoons. The only substantial building erected was a blockhouse constructed under the supervision of 1st Lieutenant William E. Prince, 1st Infantry, who succeeded Wharton as post commander.

Designed to safeguard the Oregon Trail, the post was temporarily abandoned in June 1846, then reoccupied on September 15, 1847. Finally considered to be too distant from the travel route, it was permanently abandoned in May 1848, to be replaced by Fort Kearny No. 2. A reconstruction of the blockhouse stands today on its original site in Nebraska City.

FORT KEARNY NO. 2 (*Fort Childs; Fort Gillette; Fort Mitchell*). Located on the south bank of the Platte River, about eight miles southeast of the present city of Kearney, the post was established in May 1848 by two companies of Mounted Riflemen and constructed under the supervision of Lieutenant Colonel Ludwell E. Powell, Missouri Mounted Volunteers (Oregon Battalion). It was first called Fort Childs in honor of Major Thomas Childs, 1st Artillery. Officially designated Fort Kearny on December 30, 1848, the post was popularly known as New Fort Kearny. Considered one of the more important Army posts on the Oregon Trail, protecting the emigrant trains along its route, Fort Kearny also served as a frontier depot for vital military supplies between Forts Leavenworth and Laramie. The 10-mile-square reservation, declared by the President on January 18, 1849, included two supporting earthwork fortifications known as Fort Gillette and Fort Mitchell. Obsoleted by the arrival of the Union Pacific Railroad, Fort Kearny was abandoned on May 17, 1871, and the military reservation turned over to the Department of the Interior on December 2, 1876, for disposition. The site of the fort, now contained within the Fort Kearny State Park, is marked by only a few earthwork remains.

CAMP KEYA PAHA. A temporary Army post established to oversee the activities of the Indians in the area, Camp Keya Paha was an outpost of Fort Randall some 28 miles to the east and located on the north bank of the Keya Paha River south of the town of Naper in Boyd County. The post was active for a short time during 1879.

FORT LISA. Located on the west bank of the Missouri River and about 10 miles below Omaha and Council Bluffs, Bellevue in present Sarpy County is the oldest town in Nebraska. Tradition says that the noted trapper and fur trader Manuel Lisa so named the locality and built a trading post on the site in 1805, the first white habitation on present Nebraska territory. History, however, indicates that Lisa was in the town's vicinity only in 1807 and 1809. Hummel Park on River Drive in north suburban Omaha was at one time thought to be the site of both Lisa's and Cabanné's trading posts, but more recent research reports that this location is too far south.

LITTLE BLUE STATION POST. Located on the north side of the Little Blue River, about three miles northwest of the present town of Oak in Nuckolls County, this stockaded guard post was established in October 1864 during the Indian war by a company of the Nebraska Militia. Apparently intermittently garrisoned, the post was abandoned some time in 1866.

CAMP MCKEAN. OMAHA POST.

CANTONMENT MCKEAN. FORT MCPHERSON.

FORT MCPHERSON (*Cantonment McKean; Fort (Post) Cottonwood Springs; Fort Cot-* *tonwood*). Located on the south bank of the Platte River, 2 miles west of Cottonwood Springs and about 13 miles east of the present-day town of North Platte in Lincoln County, this post was first established as Cantonment McKean (named for Major Thomas McKean, 38th Pennsylvania Militia) on September 18, 1863, by Major George M. O'Brien with Company G of the 7th Iowa Cavalry. A five-company post, it was successively renamed Post or Fort Cottonwood Springs in February 1864 and Fort Cottonwood on May 18, 1864. On January 20, 1866, it was officially designated Fort McPherson in honor of Brigadier General James B. McPherson, killed near Atlanta on July 22, 1864.

The post's grave ground, declared a National Cemetery in 1873, became the site for the reinterment of the military dead of many of the fort cemeteries in the West, and is maintained to this day. Fort McPherson was abandoned on March 29, 1880, and its buildings were sold on May 23, 1881. The military reservation was turned over to the Department of the Interior on January 5, 1887, for disposition.

CAMP AT THE MILITARY BRIDGE, N.T. OMAHA POST.

FORT MIRAGE FLATS. A sod-built "blockhouse" defense, it was erected in early 1891 by settlers southeast of the town of Hay Springs, about 25 miles below the South Dakota line, in northwestern Sheridan County. The refuge was established in anticipation of Sioux reprisal after the Wounded Knee Massacre on December 29, 1890.

CAMP MISSOURI. FORT ATKINSON.

CANTONMENT MISSOURI. FORT ATKINSON.

CAMP MITCHELL. OMAHA POST.

FORT MITCHELL (*Fort Fontenelle*). A fur-trading post located at the junction of the Missouri and Niobrara rivers in present Knox County, it was established in 1833 by Narcisse Le Clerc of the American Fur Company and first named Fort Fontenelle for Lucien Fontenelle, one of his partners. Later, when Fontenelle was in charge of the post, he renamed it Fort Mitchell for his friend David D. Mitchell. The post was abandoned some time in 1837.

FORT MITCHELL. FORT KEARNY NO. 2.

FORT (CAMP) MITCHELL (*Camp Shuman*). An outpost of Fort Laramie located on the left or south bank of the North Platte River above Scott's Bluff, about a dozen miles east of the Wyoming line, it was established in August 1864 during the Indian war by Captain Jacob S. Shuman, 11th Ohio Cavalry, in compliance with an order of Brigadier General Robert B. Mitchell, commander of the Nebraska District. First called Camp Shuman, the post was very soon renamed Camp Mitchell (popularly known as Fort Mitchell) for the brigadier general who later became Governor of the Territory of New Mexico. The post was described as a 100-by-180-foot, loopholed adobe building, with a sentry tower at one corner, an adjoining log corral, and an enclosed parade ground measuring 66 by 164 feet. The post was abandoned some time in 1867.

FORT MONTROSE. An emergency defense established in early 1891 by the settlers of this farming community, located about 20 miles above Crawford in extreme northwestern Dawes County, about 2 miles below the South Dakota line, it consisted of a circular trench strengthened by a breastwork, with an underground 20-by-30-foot, 7-foot high chamber to shelter the families. The defense was built in expectation of a Sioux reprisal after the notorious Wounded Knee Massacre on December 29, 1890.

MULLALY'S RANCH POST. Located just south of the Platte River, about three miles south of the town of Gothenburg in western Dawson County, this Army post was established by Nebraska Cavalry troops early in the 1864 Indian War. It occupied a former Pony Express station known as Midway Station situated on the ranch then owned by Patrick Mullaly (variously spelled). The post consisted of a small stockaded enclosure incorporating officers' quarters, barracks, and stables. The original station is today included within the modernized main building of privately owned Lower 96 Ranch.

FORT NIOBRARA. Located on the south bank of the Niobrara River a few miles below the town of Valentine in Cherry County, Fort Niobrara was established by Major John J. Upham, 5th Cavalry, on April 22, 1880, to protect the area's ranchers and settlers from marauding Sioux and to oversee Indian activities at the Spotted Tail Agency. The site of the post, abandoned on October 22, 1906, is now within a National Wildlife Refuge maintained by the Department of the Interior.

POST ON THE NORTH FORK OF THE LOUP RIVER. FORT HARTSUFF.

NORTH PLATTE STATION (*Camp Sergeant*). Located at North Platte in central Lincoln County, situated between the North and South Platte rivers and seven miles west of their confluence, this post, also called Camp Sergeant (Sargent), was established on January 30, 1867, by Company I, 36th Infantry. The one-company post was intended to protect the Union Pacific Railroad and to serve as a base of supplies for infantry and cavalry detachments in the region. Temporarily abandoned on May 7, 1867, it was reestablished by Company B, 4th Infantry, and named in honor of Captain William Sergeant, 12th Infantry, mortally wounded in action at Gravely Run, Virginia, on March 31, 1865. In October 1867 Major Richard I. Dodge, 30th Infantry, moved the post from the north side to the south side of the railroad. The post was abandoned on May 31, 1881. The fort site is located on West Front Street in North Platte.

O'FALLON'S BLUFFS POST. Located between the south bank of the South Platte River and today's Sutherland Reservoir in western Lincoln County, the post was situated on the elevation known as O'Fallon Bluffs overlooking both the river and the Platte Valley Road. The one-company, 125-foot-square post was established by the 7th Iowa Cavalry in 1864 during the Indian war. It was abandoned some time in 1866.

FORT OMAHA (*Camp Sherman; Sherman Barracks; Omaha Barracks*). A temporary post was established at Omaha on August 19, 1863, for the training of volunteer troops for service in the Civil War. In 1866 the town of Omaha became headquarters of the Department of the Platte, apparently replacing the Post of Omaha. A new post, located near the Missouri River above the town (now within the city limits), was established on December 5, 1868, by Captain William Sinclair, 3rd Artillery, and named Camp Sherman or Sherman Barracks in honor of Lieutenant General William Tecumseh Sherman. In 1869 the name was changed to Omaha Barracks. On December 30, 1878, the post was officially designated Fort Omaha.

When the post was replaced by Fort Crook 10 miles to the south, its garrison was withdrawn in 1895, except for a detachment that remained until September 1896 to dispose of movable public property. When the government was unable to obtain a fair price for the reservation property, the post was reestablished and discontinued several times until 1947, during which time it served as an Army Balloon School during World War I and the major station for units of the 7th Service Command Headquarters. Seven buildings of the old post remain and are located on 30th Street between Fort Street and Laurel Avenue.

OMAHA BARRACKS. FORT OMAHA.

OMAHA POST (*Camp Mitchell; Camp McKean; Camp at the Military Bridge, N.T.*). Established in 1862, the Post of Omaha represented the headquarters of the Military District of Nebraska and used both the territorial capitol building and rented quarters in the town. The old Herndon House, located at the intersection of 9th and Farnam streets, accommodated headquarters while the troops were quartered in the capitol, which at a later date also housed headquarters. The 7th Iowa and other troops who were encamped on the west edge of Omaha informally named their tent clusters Camp McKean and Camp Mitchell after District commanders. A company-sized post was set up at North Omaha Creek after an 1864 Indian raid; this was designated Camp at the Military Bridge, N.T. The Post of Omaha was discontinued some time in 1866.

PAWNEE RANCH POST. Located at the point where Pawnee Creek and the Little Blue River meet, about seven miles southwest of Fairfield in Clay County, this was a palisaded Army post with a bastion in each of its four angles. Erected in 1864 during the crisis of the Indian war then raging on the Plains, the post was apparently regularly garrisoned during October and November of that year but only intermittently thereafter until 1866.

PILCHER'S POST. The Missouri Fur Company in the early 1820s, probably 1823, built a trading post and storehouse at Bellevue on the Missouri River in present Sarpy County and abandoned Fort Lisa up the river. Joshua Pilcher, after Lisa's death in 1820, headed the company until it was dissolved about 1829. The post at Bellevue was apparently put in charge of Lucien Fontenelle and Andrew Drips, who operated it for a number of years. It is not clear whether this post was the same as Pilcher's Post or Fort, sold in 1831 to the government for the establishment of the Indian agency officially known as "Council Bluffs at Bellevue."

PLUM CREEK POST. Located south of the Platte River at Plum Creek in the extreme northwest corner of present Phelps County, this post was established at the strategic location in 1864 as an intermediate station between Fort Kearny No. 2 and Fort McPherson. Situated between Plum Creek Ranch and the Oregon Trail stage station, the post was a 325-foot-square stockade enclosing six buildings, garrisoned by three companies of the 1st Nebraska Cavalry, commanded by Captain Thomas J. Majors, during the 1864 Indian War and by two companies of "Galvanized Yankees" after the war. Plum Creek Post was abandoned some time in 1866.

CAMP RECOVERY. Located three miles south of Cantonment Missouri (Fort Atkinson), this temporary camp was established in the spring of 1820 to treat soldiers of the post afflicted by debilitating diseases caused by the rampant unsanitary conditions during the winter of 1819–20.

POST AT RED CLOUD AGENCY. FORT ROBINSON.

CAMP RED WILLOW. Located a short distance east of present-day McCook in Red Willow County, this temporary post was established one mile from Red Willow Creek, a tributary of the Republican River, on May 18, 1872, in compliance with Special Orders No. 68, Headquarters Department of the Platte, dated April 30, 1872. It was garrisoned by Company B, 9th Infantry, and Company C, 2nd Cavalry, under the command of Captain J. D. Devin, 9th Infantry. The post was abandoned on November 4, 1872, in accordance with Special Orders No. 187, Headquarters Department of the Platte, dated October 24, 1872.

CAMP ROBINSON. FORT ROBINSON.

FORT ROBINSON (*Post at Red Cloud Agency; Camp Robinson*). Located north of the White River, near its confluence with Soldier Creek, and two miles west of today's town of Crawford, at the headquarters of the Red Cloud Indian Agency, the post was established on March 8, 1874, in compliance with an order of Lieutenant General Philip H. Sheridan. Its need was dictated by the armed revolt of the Sioux in reaction to the contravention of treaties by white settlers and miners and over difficulties associated with white occupation of the Black Hills region. Constructed under the supervision of Colonel John A. Smith, 14th Infantry, the post was first called Camp or Post at Red Cloud Agency, then renamed Camp Robinson on March 29, 1874, and finally officially designated Fort Robinson in January 1878, in honor of 1st Lieutenant Levi H.

Robinson, 14th Infantry, killed by Indians in Wyoming on February 9, 1874.

Nestled in a deep valley of the Pine Ridge and rimmed by high ridges and plateaus, the Fort Robinson Military Reservation covered some 36,000 acres, spanning both sides of the line between Sioux and Dawes counties. Many dramatic events took place at the post. In 1877 Chief Crazy Horse was bayoneted and killed there while resisting arrest. In 1879 about 64 Northern Cheyennes were killed at the post during an escape attempt. During World War I, the post became a remount station, reputedly the largest in the world, where many thousands of horses and mules were bred, trained, and distributed for Army use. During World War II, Fort Robinson became a training ground for K-9 dogs and a P.O.W. camp for German prisoners.

The post was declared surplus to the needs of the Army in 1948. Most of the post's buildings are still maintained and occupied by various state and federal agencies, and former officers' quarters provide hotel-style accommodations for visitors. The Fort Robinson State Historical Park and Museum stands on U.S. 20, one mile west of Crawford.

CAMP SERGEANT. NORTH PLATTE STATION.

CAMP SHERIDAN. This camp was first established on March 12, 1874, near the original site of the Spotted Tail Agency for the protection of the Brulé Sioux. When the Agency was moved to a new location, the post was reestablished adjacent to it on September 9, 1874, on the east or right bank of the west fork of Beaver Creek, about 12 miles above its confluence with the White River, in northern Sheridan County. Camp Sheridan was abandoned in May 1881. The site is on privately owned farmland about 14 miles north of the town of Hay Springs.

CAMP SHERMAN. FORT OMAHA.

SHERMAN BARRACKS. FORT OMAHA.

CAMP SHUMAN. FORT MITCHELL.

FORT SIDNEY (*Sidney Barracks*). Located at the present town of Sidney in the Lodgepole Creek Valley, Cheyenne County, this post was established on November 19 (December 13?), 1867 as Sidney Barracks, named for Sidney Dillon, New York attorney for the Union Pacific Railroad, for the protection of the railroad construction crews during the Indian wars. First a subpost of Fort Sedgwick in Colorado, Sidney Barracks became a separate or independent post in 1870. It was officially designated Fort Sidney on December 30, 1878. Ordered abandoned on May 23, 1894, its troops were withdrawn a week later. The military reservation was turned over to the Department of the Interior on November 14, 1894, for disposition of its buildings.

SIDNEY BARRACKS. FORT SIDNEY.

ANTELOPE STATION POST. Located in White Pine County, 25 miles southeast of Schell Creek Station (Fort Schellbourne), Antelope Station was a stop on the critical overland route for Pony Express riders and freighters operating between Hamilton and Elko in the 1860s and 1870s. California Infantry Volunteers very often garrisoned this station, beginning in 1864. Five years earlier Antelope Station had been burned by Indians.

CAMP (NEAR) AURORA. A temporary post located at Adobe Meadows 1 mile from old Aurora and 20 miles southwest of Hawthorne in Mineral County, placing it close to the California line, it was established by Captain Edward A. Rowe and Company A, 2nd California Volunteer Cavalry, from Fort Churchill on or about May 14, 1862. The post was designed to reestablish peace between the settlers and Indians in the region. The post was discontinued in August 1862, with the troops returning to Fort Churchill.

CAMP AUSTIN. The county seat of Lander County, the town of Austin was established in a mining area in 1862 after discoveries by William M. Talcott. It was previously called Pony Canyon because it was a shortcut on the route of the Pony Express. The origin of the name "Austin" is debatable. In 1865, when the mining town was experiencing a boom, it was occupied for a short period by a military detachment.

FORT BAKER (*Detachment at Las Vegas; Stockade at Las Vegas; Las Vegas Fort; Mormon Fort*). This post at Las Vegas was established early in 1862 in compliance with an order of Colonel James H. Carleton, 1st California Infantry, dated December 23, 1861. The three companies of infantry and one of cavalry, dispatched to Las Vegas, were initially known as "Detachment at Las Vegas." Reoccupying the abandoned Mormon Fort there, variously called "Stockade at Las Vegas" and "Las Vegas Fort," the post was officially designated Fort Baker, named in honor of Colonel Edward D. Baker, 71st Pennsylvania Infantry, killed on October 21, 1861, during the Battle of Ball's Bluff, Virginia.

The fort when erected by Mormon settlers in 1855 had served to found the town of Las Vegas. The 190-square-foot Mormon Fort was surrounded by a 10-foot-high adobe wall, 2 feet thick at the bottom and tapered to 1 foot at the top. On one side of the square were two-story houses. The fort was abandoned when the pioneering settlers were recalled to Salt Lake City in 1857 and 1858. Shortly after it was vacated, the fort served

Nevada

as a stage station and intermittently used patrol base. Fort Baker was never occupied by U.S. troops during the Civil War. Apparently Union Army officers and General Carleton applied the name "Fort Baker" to the Mormon Fort to mislead the Confederates while Carleton's "California Column" was secretly making preparations for their march from Fort Yuma, California, to New Mexico and Texas. No definite data has been found to indicate when the California troops abandoned the Las Vegas post. Part of the Mormon Fort, an adobe building, is located at 908 Las Vegas Boulevard.

CAMP BIG ANTELOPE CREEK. This Civil War post, located about 15 miles west of the present town of Imlay, Pershing County, was a field camp intermittently occupied during the war by Union troops out of Fort Churchill.

CAMP BLACK. Apparently there were at least two posts of this name in Nevada during 1865. All temporary, one was located at Massacre Lake in northern Washoe County, and the another in Paradise Valley, which was occupied in July and August 1865 by Captain Albert Hahn commanding Company I of the 6th California Volunteer Infantry.

FORT CALL (*Detachment at Callville; Fort Callville*). The old, now nonexistent town of Callville, located about 40 miles east of Las Vegas, was established by the Mormons as a port on the Colorado River. At times known as Fort Call

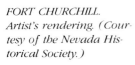

FORT CHURCHILL. Artist's rendering. (Courtesy of the Nevada Historical Society.)

or Fort Callville, it was intermittently occupied by troops from Camp Eldorado farther down the river. The site is now inundated by Lake Mead.

DETACHMENT AT CALLVILLE. FORT CALL.

FORT CALLVILLE. FORT CALL.

FORT CHURCHILL (*Churchill Barracks*). The first and most important military post in Nevada, Fort Churchill was established July 20, 1860, on the north side of the Carson River, about 30 miles below Carson City, near the present town of Weeks in Lyon County. Paiute on the warpath in May 1860 and subsequent interrupted Pony Express mail service led to the fort's establishment by Captain Joseph Stewart, 3rd Artillery, with troops from California. Named for Colonel Sylvester Churchill, inspector general of the Army, the post was frequently referred to as Churchill Barracks.

The post was built as a permanent installation consisting of adobe buildings erected on stone foundations in the form of a square, facing a central parade ground. Its average troop strength was 200. The Pony Express mail routes as far east as Ruby Valley were patrolled from the fort, also serving as a station. The Civil War made the fort an important facility as a major supply depot for the Nevada Military District as well as a base for troops patrolling the overland routes in the region. Although ordered abandoned on September 29, 1869, in compliance with an order of Major General George H.

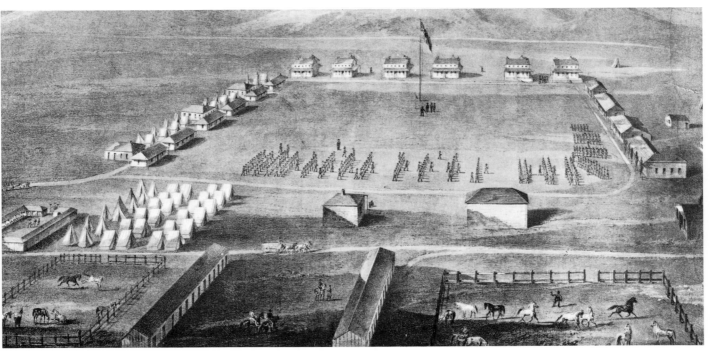

Thomas, because the post was no longer considered necessary for control of the Indians, it was not until June 15, 1871, that Fort Churchill was finally vacated and turned over to the Interior Department. The fort's adobe remains were deeded to the State Park System by the Nevada Sagebrush Chapter of the D.A.R. in 1956 and proclaimed a state park in 1957.

CHURCHILL BARRACKS. FORT CHURCHILL.

CAMP CLARK. Located at Carson City, Camp Clark was a temporary assembly and mustering-into-service post established in 1898 during the Spanish-American War.

COLD SPRINGS FORT. Active during the early 1860s and located in present Churchill County, some miles east of Sand Springs, this intermittently troop-occupied post was a Pony Express station, later serving as a stop on the Butterfield Overland Stage Line.

DETACHMENT AT DEEP CREEK STATION. Located about three miles northeast of Fort Trinity in present White Pine County, Deep Creek Station on the stage route was continuously garrisoned for a period of time during 1864.

CAMP DEEP HOLE. A former settlement in the gold-mining district in northwest Washoe County, north of the Smoke Creek Desert, its abandoned stage station became a Nevada Cavalry outpost in 1865.

CAMP DESERT ROCK. Now a ghost town within the 1,350-square-mile Atomic Energy Commission's Nevada Test Site, Camp Desert Rock was opened in September 1951 as a tent city 60 miles northwest of Las Vegas and about 5 miles southwest of the town of Mercury in Nye County. Troops and observers taking part in AEC's test series were quartered at the Sixth U.S. Army Class I installation, with its population fluctuating from a peak of well over 5,000 during test and maneuver periods to about 1,500 support troops between tests.

Participation of the Desert Rock troops in the various test series gave increased knowledge of the effect of atomic detonations on military equipment, materiel, and personnel. The men who came there from the Army, Navy, Air Force, and Marine Corps were carefully selected for clearance and for their ability to digest the special training. When the camp was discontinued in October 1957, its buildings were moved for use in other areas in the desert.

CAMP DUN GLEN. Situated in Dun Glen Canyon in the eastern range of the Humboldt Mountains, this post was located about six miles from present Mill City in Pershing County. A military post was first established there for a period in 1863 to safeguard settlers from Indian attack. In June 1865, after the area's inhabitants again requested military protection, Company B, 2nd California Cavalry Volunteers, commanded by 1st Lieutenant R. A. Osmer (shortly relieved by Captain George D. Conrad), reoccupied the campsite. During its occupancy, the post served as a depot for other troops operating in the field against Indian hostiles. In addition, the camp's cavalry scouted from time to time through the region, particularly along the overland travel routes. The camp was abandoned in August 1866.

EIGHT MILE STATION. FORT TRINITY.

CAMP ELDORADO (*Camp in El Dorado Canyon*). Situated on the west bank of the Colorado River near the mouth of El Dorado Canyon, temporary Camp Eldorado was established on or about January 15, 1867, by troops from Fort Mojave, Arizona, 50 miles to the south. Located 7 miles east of the present town of Nelson, Clark County, the post was intended to protect the important El Dorado mining region against Indian depredations. The camp was abandoned on August 24, 1867.

CAMP IN EL DORADO CANYON. CAMP ELDORADO.

CAMP FISH LAKE. A temporary, intermittently occupied military post was established some time between December 1866 and July 1867 at Fish Lake in southwestern Esmeralda County, by troops from Camp Independence in Owens Valley, California. The post was intended to protect the mining settlements in the area from Indian attack.

GENOA FORT (*Mormon Station*). The oldest settlement in Nevada at what is today the town of Genoa (a site then a part of western Utah) in Douglas County was founded in 1849 by Mormons when they built a log stockade known as the Mormon Station. A small group of the Church's followers, led by H. S. Beattie, built the station as a supply depot for trade with California-bound emigrants. Two years later, Mormon Station was transformed into a more formal trading post, with a new stockade enclosing more than an acre of ground on which a large log building was erected. Orson Hyde, one of the

Mormon Church's Twelve Apostles who arrived in 1855, made Mormon Station the seat of recently created Carson County, and changed its name to Genoa, with its fortification becoming variously known as the Stockade at Genoa or Fort Genoa. In 1857 the Mormons apparently sold out their interests there and returned to Salt Lake City. The original stockade burned down in 1910, but it has been reconstructed as a museum and is now included within a park.

DETACHMENT AT GRANITE CREEK. CAMP MCKEE.

GRANITE CREEK STATION. CAMP MCKEE.

CAMP HALLECK. FORT HALLECK.

FORT HALLECK (*Camp Halleck*). Located on the right bank of Cottonwood Creek at the foot of the northwestern slope of the Humboldt Mountains in Elko County, about a dozen miles south of today's town of Halleck on the Humboldt River, this post was established as Camp Halleck on July 26, 1867, to protect the settlers in the area and to safeguard the trackage of the Central Pacific Railroad. Established by Captain Samuel P. Smith, 8th Cavalry, the post was named for Major General Henry Wager Halleck. On April 5, 1879, the camp, a two-company post, was officially designated a fort. Abandoned on December 1, 1886, after Major General O. O. Howard, commander of the department, determined the fort to be unusable by the army, the military reservation was turned over to the Department of the Interior for disposition.

FORT HAVEN. Located on the Truckee River, a mile from Pyramid Lake and about four miles above the present town of Nixon in southern Washoe County, Fort Haven was a temporary earthwork thrown up on or about June 6, 1860, during the Paiute War by troops of the "Carson River Expedition," commanded by Captain Joseph Stewart, 3rd Artillery, and named in honor of Major General J. P. Haven of the California Militia. The earthwork-fort was abandoned in mid-July when Fort Churchill was established on the Carson River.

CAMP HAYS. Occupying Reed's Station, a stop on the Pony Express route, 20 miles east of Carson City in Lyon County, Camp Hays was a temporary post established by Nevada militiamen on May 1860 during the Pyramid Lake War against the Indians and named for Colonel John C. Hays, commander of the Washoe Regiment. The camp was abandoned on May 26, 1860, having lasted less than a month.

DETACHMENT AT LAS VEGAS. FORT BAKER.

LAS VEGAS FORT. FORT BAKER.

CAMP MCDERMIT. FORT MCDERMIT.

FORT MCDERMIT (*Quinn River Camp No. 33; Camp McDermit*). This post was located in the Santa Rosa Mountains on the right or north bank of the east fork of the Quinn River, just below the Oregon state line, at the present town of McDermitt, Humboldt County. Established on August 14, 1865, by elements of the 2nd California Cavalry and first called Quinn River Camp No. 33, it was shortly renamed Camp McDermit in honor of Lieutenant Colonel Charles McDermit, 2nd California Cavalry, killed in the immediate area on August 8, 1865, in an Indian ambush. The post was primarily intended to control the activities of the area's hostile Paiute and safeguard the region's travel routes. On April 15, 1879, the post, built around a parade ground 660 by 225 feet, was officially designated a fort. The post was abandoned on December 1, 1888. The reservation was turned over to the Interior Department on July 24, 1889. A number of the original buildings now serve as the headquarters of the Fort McDermit Indian Agency, which supports an Indian school.

CAMP MCGARRY (*Camp Summit Lake*). Located near the shore of Summit Lake in the isolated High Rock Canyon region of western Humboldt County, this post was probably established on November 23, 1865 (dates vary depending on source), to safeguard the emigrant route from Indian hostiles. Established first as a field camp by Major Albert G. Brackett, 1st Cavalry, it was called Camp Summit Lake, soon renamed for Edward McGarry, then Colonel of the 2nd California Cavalry. A very active post at its height, it served for a short time as headquarters of the two-fort District of Summit Lake, the other post being Fort Bidwell just across the California line. The post was finally abandoned on December 18, 1868, in compliance with an order of Brigadier General Edward O. C. Ord, and its last garrison transferred to Camp Winfield Scott. The reservation was turned over to the Interior Department on March 25, 1871. Remains of several of the post's stone buildings are still very much in evidence around a weed-covered, rectangular parade ground.

CAMP MCKEE (*Granite Creek Station; Detachment at Granite Creek*). Located on Granite Creek, near the present town of Gerlach in east central Washoe County, this post was first established in December 1865 by government troops occupying the Granite Creek stage station, which had been burned by Indians after they killed its three employees on April 1, 1865. Apparently temporarily abandoned, the post was reestablished on June 20, 1866, as Camp McKee. It was finally abandoned and "all of the Government stores were moved up to Fort McGarry in October, 1866."

MORMON FORT. FORT BAKER.

MORMON STATION. GENOA FORT.

CAMP NYE. Located in the Washoe Valley five miles north of Carson City, this Civil War field post was established in June 1862 and named in honor of James W. Nye, governor of Nevada from 1861 to 1864. The camp operated during the war as a base and depot for California and Nevada Volunteers. It was abandoned some time during the summer of 1865 after the Nevada troops were separated from service.

CAMP ORMSBY. Located on the Truckee River, about 10 miles from Pyramid Lake in Washoe County, this temporary post was established on June 2, 1860, immediately after the second Pyramid Lake battle fought the same day, by Captain Joseph Stewart, 3rd Artillery, commanding troops of the "Carson Valley Expedition." The camp was named in honor of Major William M. Ormsby, killed during the first Battle of Pyramid Lake on May 12, 1860.

CAMP OVEREND. A temporary post existing for only a few days, it was located at a place known as Summit Springs south of the town of Golconda, in the southeast corner of Humboldt County. The camp was established some time in June 1865 by 1st Lieutenant R. A. Osmer with Company B, 2nd California Cavalry, and named for 2nd Lieutenant W. G. Overend of the same unit.

PENROD HOTEL FORT. After the outbreak of the Pyramid Lake Indian War in May 1860, the Penrod Hotel in Carson City was hastily converted into a fortification by surrounding it with strong barricades manned by armed volunteers. Other communities in the region also took similar precautions.

CAMP POLLOCK. The site of this post is split between Washoe County, Nevada, and Lassen County, California. (See: CAMP POLLOCK in California chapter.)

QUINN RIVER CAMP NO. 33. FORT MCDERMIT.

FORT RUBY. CAMP RUBY.

CAMP RUBY (*Fort Ruby*). Located on the western side of Ruby Valley near the south shore of Ruby Lake, White Pine County, this post was established on September 1, 1862, as Fort Ruby by Colonel Patrick E. Connor, 3rd California Infantry, in compliance with an order of Brigadier General George Wright, for the purpose of protecting the emigrant travel and mail routes in the area. The post's first garrison, consisting of companies C and F, 3rd California Infantry, was commanded by Major Patrick A. Gallagher, who superintended the post's construction. On January 1, 1867, it was designated a camp. The completion of the Central Pacific Railroad obviated the further need of the post and an official order dated March 10, 1869, directed that it be evacuated. Camp Ruby was abandoned on September 20, 1869, by its last garrison, which consisted of Company I, 9th Infantry. Three of the post's original buildings still remain and are used for private ranching purposes.

CAMP SADLER. There were two camps of this name at and near Carson City. The first, a temporary Civil War training post, was established near the city at the mouth of Kings Canyon. The other was a temporary camp for the assembly and mustering-in of troops for service in the Spanish-American War.

FORT SAGE. Little data has been found on this apparently temporary post located in Washoe County, west of Pyramid Lake, 46 miles north of Reno, and established in the early 1870s to protect the emigrant travel route into California.

CAMP SCHELL. FORT SCHELLBOURNE.

FORT SCHELLBOURNE (*Schell Creek Station; Camp Schell*). A station on the Pony Express and Overland Stage route located on Schell Creek, about 45 miles north of Ely in White Pine County, it was in operation from 1859 to 1869. After its first building was burned by Indians in 1860, it was frequently occupied by troops to protect the mail and travel route. Originally known as Schell Creek Station, then very soon

Camp Schell, it was later named Fort Schellbourne. With the completion of the Union Pacific Railroad, which eliminated the need for stagecoaches, the fort was abandoned in 1869. The remains of the stage station are still evident on private ranchland near Schellbourne Pass.

SCHELL CREEK STATION. FORT SCHELLBOURNE.

CAMP SIBERT. CAMP WILLISTON.

CAMP SMOKE CREEK. This was a temporary post located on Smoke Creek, near the Smoke Creek Depot on the Honey Lake Stage route, in Washoe County, five miles east of the California line. The erection of quarters and stables was accomplished on December 15, 1862, by Lieutenant Henry W. Williams and elements of Company C, 2nd California Cavalry from Fort Crook, California. In October 1863 the California cavalrymen were relieved by a similar-sized detachment of cavalry troops from Fort Churchill. The camp was abandoned, reoccupied, and finally abandoned again. Responding to repeated pleas for protection from area settlers, troops from Fort Churchill replaced Camp Smoke Creek with nearby Camp Pollock in June 1864.

CAMP SOLDIERS MEADOW. A temporary military outpost established in 1862, this camp was located on what is now ranch property some 20 miles southwest of Camp McGarry on Summit Lake in western Humboldt County.

STOCKADE AT LAS VEGAS. FORT BAKER.

FORT STOREY. Located on the Truckee River about eight miles south of Pyramid Lake, Washoe County, Fort Storey was a temporary breastwork thrown up on June 3, 1860, by the Washoe Volunteer Regiment during the Paiute War. It was named in honor of Captain Edward Faris Storey of the Washoe Regiment's Virginia Rifles, who reportedly died on June 7 of wounds suffered in the fight with the Indians on June 2.

CAMP SUMMIT LAKE. CAMP MCGARRY.

FORT TRINITY (*Eight Mile Station*). A frequently occupied field camp during 1863–64, originally known as Eight Mile Station and later named Fort Trinity, it was located seven miles southwest of Ibapah, Utah, in White Pine County.

Troop detachments from Fort Ruby were often posted here to watch over emigrant trains.

WILLIAMS STATION. A trading post located on the Big Bend of the Carson River, northeast of Carson City, a site now inundated by the waters of Lahontan Dam, it was operated by two men named Williams, probably brothers. The post was raided by Indians on May 7, 1860. The proprietors were killed and the station was burned. The cause of the raid was said to have been the "misuse" of two squaws who were held by the Williams men against their will. The destruction of the trading post precipitated the Pyramid Lake War.

CAMP WILLISTON (*Camp Sibert*). Located at Boulder City, on the west side of Lake Mead, this post was originally known as Camp Sibert. The name was changed because of a conflict with a similarly named camp in Alabama. The new designation, Camp Williston, was made some time between July 10, 1941, and March 3, 1944. Records of the U.S. Bureau of Reclamation indicate that on September 24, 1940, officials approved a War Department request for land and utility service for the establishment of a "M.P. Battalion Camp" at Boulder Dam. Permission was also granted to use and occupy outpost camps of approximately one acre each at strategic positions near the dam and along the transmission lines. A Military Police Battalion of approximately 800 men, principally black troops, was posted about March 15, 1941, at points around the dam to prevent sabotage. The 751st Military Police Battalion was ordered to leave Camp Williston on March 9, 1944, and proceed to Fort Custer, Michigan, for final training before being sent overseas.

CAMP WILLOW POINT. A temporary post located in Paradise Valley at Willow Point on the Little Humboldt River, Humboldt County, it was established some time in August 1865 by Major Michael O'Brien, 6th California Volunteer Infantry. The post was abandoned in October of the same year.

CAMP WINFIELD SCOTT. Located at the head of Paradise Valley, Humboldt County, a few miles below the southern end of the Humboldt National Forest Reserve and about 45 miles north of Winnemucca, Camp Winfield Scott was established on December 12, 1866, by Captain Murray Davis with Company A, 8th Cavalry, intended to control the Indians in the area. Named in honor of Major General Winfield Scott, the post consisted of two adobe, four-room buildings occupied as officers' quarters, an adobe shingle-roofed, 120-by-30-foot barracks for 100 men, a stone hut for the commanding officer, storehouses, and a guardhouse. Camp Winfield Scott was abandoned on February 19, 1871, as it was no longer needed by the Army.

ALSTEAD'S FORTS. Cheshire County's northernmost town, Alstead had been designated as Number Four in the curved line of nine towns established by Massachusetts in 1735 to protect New Hampshire's southwestern quadrant from Indian attacks. The town's sole blockhouse-fort, constructed of heavy unpeeled logs, was built early in the Revolution and stood on Prentice Hill and served as a nightly haven for the women and children, while the men in their families were Patriot participants in the war against the British. Atop Cobb Hill, two families cooperated and built a circular stone fort, "eight feet across, squared off with a series of stone walls ringed about it upon which palisades could be raised." The two defenses were never attacked.

FORT ATKINSON. During King George's War (1744–48) against the French, a fort was built in the late fall of 1746 by Colonel Theodore Atkinson and his provincial army on the north side of what is called "Little Bay," near Union (now Sanbornton) Bridge in the town of Sanbornton, Merrimack County. The colonel's regiment, ordered to Lake Winnipesaukee to guard the frontier, passed the winter of 1746–47 there and continuously garrisoned their fort until October of the latter year, when Atkinson's force was disbanded.

FORT BELLOWS. In February 1752 Benjamin Bellows obtained a charter to the town of Walpole in present Cheshire County from Benning Wentworth, governor of the province of New Hampshire, and took possession after bringing his family from his native Lunenberg in Massachusetts. He erected a large, L-shaped residence about 100 feet in the arms and 20 feet broad, strongly built of logs and earth, and surrounded by a palisade. From the top of the fort he constructed a lookout or sentry box into the fork of a large elm tree, commanding an extensive view in all directions. Archival evidence indicates that Colonel Bellows "drew at public expense men and supplies for the fort, including a heavy iron cannon."

CANTERBURY FORT. On March 15, 1744, New Hampshire's Proprietors voted to build a fort at Canterbury, just east of the Merrimack River, in present Merrimack County. The fort, constructed of hewn, white oak timber, was situated on an elevation on the outskirts of the village, and became a frequent rendezvous for various provincial detachments, principally the force commanded by Captain Jeremiah Clough, throughout King George's War (1744–48). A let-

New Hampshire

ter written in 1758 indicates that there was more than one garrison in the town. Those outside of the main fort may have been only stockades, but there were several fortified enclosures called "forts."

THE CASTLE. FORT CONSTITUTION.

CASTLE FORT. FORT CONSTITUTION.

CAMP CONSTITUTION. CAMP FRY.

FORT CONSTITUTION (*The Castle; Fort William and Mary; Fort Hancock; Castle Fort; Walbach Tower*). For more than 300 years, Fort Point on Great Island (New Castle) was an active military site strategically guarding the entrance to Portsmouth Harbor. The remains of the fort reflect its service to the country in all of its wars. Part of the site is retained by the federal government as an active Coast Guard Station; the rest was returned to the state in 1961. It was placed on the National Register of Historic Places on July 2, 1973.

The first military installation on the site was a redoubt with four "great guns" erected in 1631. A timber blockhouse was built in 1666. With the ascension of William and Mary to the throne of England and the developing rivalry with France for dominance over North America, stronger fortifications were required. Cannon and military stores were sent over from England in 1692, and a breastwork was constructed to protect them. Their Majesties' fort, commonly called "The Castle" for 60 years, became Fort William and Mary and took its place as one of a line of so-called "castles" located along the coastal areas of the colonies. Although additional guns were sent and repairs and improvements made to the fort from time to time during the French and Indian wars, the breastworks remained essentially the same to the time of the Revolution: a rampart of turf about three feet high on which a barbette battery of guns was clamped to wooden platforms, protected by a stone wall about seven feet high with embrasures through which the guns were directed.

It was on the eve of the Revolution that the fort played its most dramatic role in history. On December 13, 1774, Paul Revere rode express from Boston with a message that the fort at Rhode Island had been dismantled and troops were coming to take over Fort William and Mary. The following day, drums were beat to assemble the Sons of Liberty, and 400 men from Portsmouth, Rye, and New Castle assaulted the fort and removed 100 barrels of gunpowder. The next

night a small party led by John Sullivan carried off 16 pieces of small cannon and military stores. This raid took place four months before the bloody incidents at Lexington and Concord and was an important link in the chain of events leading to the Revolution.

Governor John Wentworth immediately sent to Boston for military help. The sloop *Canceaux* arrived on December 17, followed two days later by the frigate *Scarborough* mounting 40 guns and carrying 100 marines. This prevented further raids by the Patriots but produced a dangerous state of tension. By the summer of 1775, Governor Wentworth and his family took refuge in the fort and lived there in discomfort for two months. A transport accompanied by the *Falcon* arrived with men to dismantle the fort and carry off the remaining cannon to Boston. Then, finally, on August 23, 1775, the governor and his family sailed to Boston on the *Scarborough*. Wentworth made a brief return a month later, when from the Isles of Shoals he issued a proclamation proroguing the Assembly—the last act of royal authority in New Hampshire. Fort William and Mary was never again occupied by a British garrison. During the war years, it was known to the Patriots as Fort Hancock. Very soon after peace was declared, it became Castle Fort or Fort Castle.

In 1791 the state of New Hampshire ceded to the United States the neck of land on which were situated the fort and a lighthouse. Castle Fort was repaired, renamed Fort Constitution, and garrisoned with a company of artillery. Renovations, which included a wall twice as high as that of the colonial fort, and new brick buildings, were completed in 1808. It is the ruins of this fort, its gateway and walls, that are to be seen today. It was an up-to-date installation at the time of the War of 1812 and was still serviceable during the Civil War when various units were trained there.

Improvements in artillery during the nineteenth century made it clear that the old fort would have to be replaced, and a new one was begun during the Civil War. It was to be a massive, three-tiered granite structure, a "casemated castle" but, like others begun at this time, it was never completed. The actual armament at the fort during the first year of the war consisted of 25 pieces of ordnance. The new Fort Constitution planned to occupy the site was calculated for 149 guns. Armored, steam-powered warships with heavy rifled guns made masonry forts obsolete.

Outside the fort, in the area now occupied by the Coast Guard, a completely new system of fortifications was built between 1897 and 1903.

FORT CONSTITUTION
Artist's conception of the
fort as it looked in 1808.
(Courtesy of Joseph P.
Copley, New Castle, N.H.)

This included a battery of two eight-inch guns on disappearing carriages, a mines casemate, a cable tank and a storehouse for mines. Portsmouth Harbor was mined during the Spanish-American War and during World Wars I and II.

The remains of the fort include the ruins of a Martello tower erected in haste during the War of 1812 when British ships hovered off the coast. It was officially named "Castle Walbach" or Walbach Tower on October 2, 1814, in honor of the commander of Fort Constitution since 1806. Surrounding the old fort are meticulously cut, unmortared granite walls which were begun in 1862. The casemates or vaulted embrasures were designed for the then new Parrott 100-pound rifled cannon. Robert Parrott, member of a prominent Portsmouth family, was stationed at the fort for two years after graduating from West Point. The lighthouse beyond the fort is the successor to the hexagonal one built in 1771 by Governor Wentworth. The house there is that of the lighthouse keeper and was moved from a site near Walbach Tower in 1897 to make room for Battery Farnsworth.

FORT CONTOOCOOK. The town of Boscawen, originally granted in 1732 as Contoocook, in present Merrimack County, on the west side of the river, was named for a British admiral who served under General Jeffrey Amherst during his 1758 campaign against the French. In 1739 the townspeople voted to erect a fort at the expense of the Proprietors. The defense, one of the first of the many protective log enclosures

in New Hampshire, was 100 feet square, built of 8-inch hewn logs, 7 feet high, and "above the logs such stuff," probably a *chevaux-de-frise* of pointed timbers to prevent scaling the walls. When it was found that this enclosure was not large enough to accommodate the entire community, another fortification, smaller, was erected nearby the following winter. In 1752 another fort, 110 feet square, was built, most probably replacing the smaller fort.

FORT DEARBORN. A World War II coastal defense, Fort Dearborn was built in 1941 at Rye just below Portsmouth Harbor and named for General Henry Dearborn. It last mounted two casemated 16-inch naval guns. In 1959 Fort Dearborn was declared surplus by the government and in March 1961 transferred to the state for park development.

CAMP FRY (*Camp Constitution*). Originally named Camp Constitution when established in 1861 with barracks for the 2nd New Hampshire Regiment, this Civil War assembly and training camp at Portsmouth was renamed Camp Fry, probably in honor of Union General James B. Fry, and served throughout the war, accommodating other military units as well.

GARRISON HOUSES. Actually fortified dwellings, "garrison houses" during the French and Indian wars were built in almost all organized New England towns and were particularly common in the frontier communities of Maine and

New Hampshire. The town of Durham, northeast of Portsmouth, had fourteen such defenses. Gilmanton in Belknap County had four garrisons, one at each corner of the town. Other "fortified" towns included Alstead, Amherst, Ashuelot, Canterbury, Concord, Dover, Exeter, Londonderry, Newmarket, Seabrook, Stratham, and Westmoreland. (See: GARRISON HOUSES in Massachusetts chapter.)

GREAT MEADOWS FORT. Originally known as Great Meadows, the town of Westmoreland on the Partridge River Branch of the Connecticut River in present Cheshire County was established in 1725 by Governor Jonathan Belcher of Massachusetts, designated by him as Number Two in the planned chain of Connecticut River "fort-towns" first intended as trading posts. Differences with the Indians, however, compelled the construction there of a square, horizontally laid log blockhouse. In addition, some time between 1741 and 1744, when King George's War broke out, a small fort was erected by settler Daniel How on his farm in the Westmoreland village area.

FORT HANCOCK. FORT CONSTITUTION.

FORT HINSDALE. Located at Hinsdale in the extreme southwest corner of the state in Cheshire County, near the east banks of the Connecticut River, Fort Hinsdale was built by Colonel Ebenezer Hinsdale in 1742 as a trading post. One of New Hampshire's most noted pioneers, he was a descendant of a prominent family of Deerfield, Massachusetts, where his mother, Mrs. Mary Hinsdale, in February 1704 had been captured by Indians and taken to Canada. Colonel Hinsdale was born after her return from captivity. Although educated at Harvard and ordained as a minister in Boston, he never actually entered the ministry but instead enlisted as an officer in the provincial army, and later established himself as a successful trader, gaining considerable prosperity.

IRISH FORT. In 1725 the "Scotch Irish" from Londonderry had a fort at what was then known as Penacook, later called Rumford, and finally Concord. A combined fort and meetinghouse was built and then forcibly taken over by a company of the Massachusetts Proprietors the following year. The land was cleared and settlers began to arrive permanently in 1727.

FORT KEENE. Originally known as Upper Ashuelot, the city of Keene under a new Massachusetts grant was named in honor of Sir Benjamin Keene of England, who was associated with Governor Benning Wentworth in the Spanish West Indies trade. A double-stockaded fort, begun there in 1736 or 1737 and completed in 1738, was burned by Indians in 1747. The site of the defense is near today's 300 Main Street in the city of Keene, the county seat of Cheshire County.

CAMP KEYES. A World War mobilization and training center, Camp Keyes was named for Governor Henry Wilder Keyes (1917–19) and located one mile east of the city of Concord.

CAMP LANGDON. A temporary World War II recruiting and training post, Camp Langdon was established in 1941 at or near the city of Portsmouth. It was named in honor of John Langdon of Portsmouth, who was one of the leading participants in the assault against Fort William and Mary on September 14, 1774.

NOTTINGHAM BLOCKHOUSE. On October 18, 1726, the Proprietors, meeting at the town of Hampton in present Rockingham County, voted to build a blockhouse with a roof, 60 feet long, 30 wide, and 10 high at recently established Nottingham on the North River. The blockhouse was completed in the spring of 1727. On Route 152 there are two stone markers, one on the site of the 1747 Indian raid and the other on the site of the blockhouse.

FORT NO. 4. Playing a very important role in the settling of central New England, old Fort No. 4, Charlestown, dates back two and a half centuries. The historic town is in the southern part of the state, but in 1744 it was the northernmost outpost on the edge of a vast wilderness inhabited only by Indians, most of them allied to the French. In 1735 Massachusetts laid out four townships along the Connecticut River's east bank, numbering them 1, 2, 3, and 4, respectively Chesterfield, Westmoreland, Walpole, and Charlestown. Remote from civilized enclaves, the settlement of Number 4 was very slow: in 1743 there were only nine or ten families, grouped close together for mutual protection and laboriously farming the land.

In November 1743 the settlement's men held a "council of war" and voted to build a fortification. The Proprietors of Number 4, however, found themselves in a perplexing situation. Their lands were originally grants from the Massachusetts Bay Colony, but after George II's authorized boundary survey in 1741, they learned that they were occupying New Hampshire territory. Realigning the boundary led to such a confusion of titles that a number of the Proprietors sold their original grants. Ineligible for funds from Massachusetts and denied assistance from New Hampshire because of the settlement's remoteness from the seacoast towns, the families remaining determined to erect a defense themselves, with Captain Phineas Stevens in command.

Collectively contributing 300 pounds toward construction expenses, they began by building new homes on plotted positions serving as cornerstones of an 180-by-156-foot rectangle, occupying three-quarters of an acre of ground. It was located near the bank of the Connecticut River, close to its junction with the Black River. The Connecticut was a principal route used by the French and Indians to ravage the New England settlements. The fort's crude cabins were erected on the inside of the perimeter against the palisades and built of 8-inch squared logs, laid horizontally and interlocked at the corners. A 30-foot-square watchtower was erected at the southwest corner of the stockade. Along the south curtain they built of giant logs 8 inches square the two-story Great Hall, 75 feet long and 30 feet wide, the front of which rose to a gable 26 feet over the fort's main gate. On July 4, 1746, John Maynard, a provincial soldier from Sudbury, Massachusetts, made a map of the fort. He had spent his leisure hours measuring logs, counting the posts in the stockade and drawing detailed sketches of the structures, including the names of their occupants.

An "up and down" sawmill had been set up by farmer-soldier John Spafford at Number 4 the year before the fort was built, thus making it possible to produce the sawn logs used to construct the Great Hall's walls, assembled with wooden pegs. The roof rafters were sawn logs 8 by 14 inches, each more than 30 feet long and weighing about 1,200 pounds. The stockade, 10 feet high with an overall length of 760 feet, was constructed of 8-inch-diameter logs set vertically, 4 inches apart to allow a sweeping action for defending muskets. There were 13 buildings, including the Great Hall that was used alternately as a barracks and a meeting hall as the need warranted, and three indispensable water wells.

With the outbreak of King George's War in 1744, the French wasted little time propagandizing their Indian allies, who began their widespread incursions in 1746. On April 19 of that year, a party of 40 French and Indians destroyed the sawmill and burned the gristmill at the head of Devil's Gully, adjacent to what is now Charlestown's Main Street, and took captive the miller and three other men. During the summer, there were numerous raids culminating in August,

when the Indians instituted a siege, burning the mills that were being rebuilt and all but one of the houses outside the fort, and slaughtering the cattle, horses, and most of the hogs.

The meager spring plantings were ruined and the fort's supplies shrunk. Another attempt was made to rebuild the gristmill but again it was destroyed. In consideration of the fort's few soldiers and sparse provisions, it became apparent to Captain Stevens that they must evacuate for the winter. When the French and their Indians retreated north to their winter quarters, the settlers buried their most prized possessions, abandoned the remainder, and made their way south to the safety of Sudbury, Groton, and Lunenberg in Massachusetts, their former homes.

During the winter Captain Stevens sought to influence a number of influential people in Massachusetts, stressing the need to maintain the fort so strategically situated at the crossroads of two invasion routes from Canada. The Great Indian Trail, which crossed the Vermont wilderness from New France, joined the Connecticut River just above the fort. Early in 1747 the Massachusetts Legislature, with a last-minute grant, sent a detachment of 30 farmer-soldiers under Captain Stevens to reoccupy Fort Number 4, arriving there on March 27.

Less than two weeks later, the fort was attacked by a force of 700 French and Indians. The battle raged for three days, with the enemy attempting all conceivable ways to burn the fort. Finally, defeated in their enterprise, with provisions almost exhausted, the destructives retreated and melted into the dense woods. The fort proved so impregnable that not one of its defenders was killed, and only two men were wounded. The assault was the last expedition by a major enemy force to penetrate southward along the Connecticut River. In 1753 Governor Benning Wentworth of New Hampshire named the fortified settlement Charlestown in honor of his friend, Admiral Sir Charles Knowles, then the governor of Jamaica. The admiral had been so impressed by Captain Stevens's three-day defense that he presented him with an expensive sword.

During the long years of the French and Indian War, great numbers of regular and provincial troops with ordnance and other military equipment and stores, accompanied by droves of cattle to feed the moving armies and defenders of the frontier posts, passed through Charlestown. During the summer of 1760, the town, now a settlement of about 200 inhabitants, was the assembly point from which 800 New Hampshire militiamen under Colonel John Goffe cut a road through the Vermont wilderness to

Crown Point on Lake Champlain, just in time to be participants in the capture of Montreal.

Fort Number 4 never capitulated to the enemy, and when the bloody hostilities finally came to an end it was dismantled to make way for the prosperous town that was growing up around it. Plans for its reconstruction were begun shortly after World War II by a group of local residents who organized themselves as the Old Fort Number Four Associates. In 1965 a modest appropriation was obtained from the state Legislature to spark the drive for additional funds. A local foundation and a chapter of the Daughters of the American Revolution contributed respectable sums of money.

Because of Maynard's dedication to detail in 1746, all of the features of the original fort are known with an exactitude not usually possible in most projects of historical reconstruction. The precise setting of the fort could not be duplicated because Charlestown's thriving community occupies the site where the military post stood. Slightly upstream on the river and near the bridge connecting Charlestown with Springfield, Vermont, a 20-acre tract of meadowland was acquired in 1960, affording a magnificent view of the valley and Mt. Ascutney across the river in Vermont. Construction of Captain Stevens's home was begun and completed the following year. Not until 1965 was construction again possible. By midsummer of that year, accumulated funds permitted the requisition of additional materials, and in the fall actual reconstruction began. By May 1, 1966, the massive Great Hall was well on its way toward completion, with the surrounding stockade ready for erection, faithfully duplicated with 700 logs, all New Hampshire pine. Today the re-creation of Fort Number 4, with about a half-million board feet of lumber in its construction, is a monument to the men who gallantly defended it.

CAMP ROCKINGHAM. A temporary World War I encampment near Salem in Rockingham County, it was used from June 25 to July 26, 1917, for the mobilization of the 14th Regiment's unit of engineers.

SALISBURY FORT. Intermittently active throughout the French and Indian War, this fort originally built as a defense against the Indians was located in Stevenstown, subsequently Salisbury, next to the Merrimack River, which is now a part of Franklin, in Merrimack County.

FORT SHATTUCK. Originally built as a dwelling in 1736–37 by Daniel Shattuck at Hinsdale, several years before Fort Hinsdale was erected nearby by Ebenezer Hinsdale, it was converted to a fort during King George's War (1744–48) by erecting an identical building on the other side of Ash Swamp Brook. The two structures "were connected by a plank palisade which was surrounded by pickets."

STAR FORT. The fishing "Shoalers" on Star Island, one of the Isles of Shoals chain lying off New Castle outside Portsmouth Harbor, petitioned the government for protection in 1653. They were granted "two great guns" to be mounted at their own expense within a crude stone fort on an elevation on the west side of the island, commanding the harbor's mouth. But it was not maintained, and the guns became buried in rubble. By the year 1670, the Isles of Shoals "were studded with fishermen's huts built of sod, rocks, or boards and shingles brought over from the mainland" (Charles E. Clark, *The Eastern Frontier: The Settlement of Northern New England 1610–1673* [1970], pp. 27–28).

In 1692, in response to a new petition, a detachment of 40 soldiers arrived, erected a new 50-foot-square stone fort on the site of the old one, and reconditioned the two guns. Either at the time of this reconstruction or shortly thereafter, nine 4-pounders were added to the fort's armament. In 1715 the New Hampshire Provincial Assembly elevated Star Island to the status of township and named it Gosport. In 1774 Fort Star was dismantled and its guns taken to Newburyport. Early in the Revolution, all the Shoalers on the islands were ordered to the mainland for their own protection, and the population was reduced from 284 to 44 or perhaps less.

FORT STARK. Jerry's (Jaffrey) Point, with the Piscataqua River on the left and Little Harbor on the right, on New Castle Island in Portsmouth Harbor, was first fortified, however crudely, soon after 1623, and held six brass guns. The point of land was originally named for Captain Neal Jaffrey. The defense on the point was more or less maintained until the Revolutionary era. Portsmouth's Committee of Safety had the cannons removed soon after the British arrived on December 17, 1774, to resume command of Fort William and Mary, blockading the harbor until August 22, 1775, when they evacuated the fort, surrendering it to the Patriots. In May 1776 the Committee directed that a battery be reestablished at Jerry's Point.

In 1873 a new battery was constructed there on a 10-acre reservation by the government and ultimately designated Fort Stark on April 4, 1900, in honor of John Stark, who commanded the New Hampshire forces at the Battle of Bennington. Named a subpost of Fort Constitution in 1905, Fort Stark was declared surplus as of December 31, 1949.

FORT SULLIVAN. Two earthwork forts were built in the latter part of 1775 at the Narrows, a channel on the Piscataqua River about a mile below Portsmouth by the men of the town and its vicinity. The star-shaped fort on the west side of the channel, on Pierce's (originally Washington) Island, was named Fort Washington, and the other on the east side on Seavey's (Jenkins's or Trefethen's) Island (the site of the present U.S. Navy Yard) was designated Fort Sullivan for General John Sullivan. A company of 40 men, commanded by Captain Robert Parker, was ordered to man these forts, with all of the fortifications in the harbor put in charge of Captain Titus Salten. Remains of these earthworks are still in evidence.

WALBACH TOWER. FORT CONSTITUTION.

FORT WASHINGTON. FORT SULLIVAN.

FORT WENTWORTH. Near the town of Groveton in Coos County stands a stone marker identifying the site of Fort Wentworth at or near the junction of the Ammonoosuc River with the Connecticut, on the south side of the former. It was supposedly built by Major Robert Rogers in 1759 while returning after his famous attack against the principal village of the French-allied St. Francis Indians. Exhaustive modern research fails to substantiate its existence. The monument perpetuates the errors or misinterpretations of an early New Hampshire historian. No such fort stood there in 1759.

FORT WILLIAM AND MARY. FORT CONSTITUTION.

CAMP ALFRED VAIL. FORT MONMOUTH.

AMATOL ARSENAL. Originally a subsidized loading plant for Army munitions, first operated by the Atlantic Loading Company, it was located in southern New Jersey at Amatol near the town of Hammonton, Atlantic County. Apparently first called Camp Amatol when plant construction began in March 1918, it was taken over by the Army's Ordnance Department and designated Amatol Arsenal on February 20, 1919. The Arsenal's principal postwar activity was the storage of ordnance material. It was probably discontinued in the mid-1920s.

CAMP BAYARD. A temporary Civil War recruiting center, Camp Bayard was located in the city of Trenton on a site west of South Broad Street and south of Cass Street.

BERGEN NECK FORT. FORT DELANCEY.

BILLINGSPORT FORT. During 1775, in compliance with an order of the Pennsylvania Council of Safety, a single row of *chevaux-de-frise* was placed in the Delaware River between Billingsport and Billings Island about 12 miles below Philadelphia. In June 1776 Robert Smith, who had devised the barrier, was ordered by the Council to begin the construction of a fort or redoubt at Billingsport. The original plan specified an earthen fort measuring 700 feet from bastion tip to bastion tip, with a 7½-foot-high parapet, fronted by a ditch 9 feet deep and 18 feet across. Shortages of material and workmen slowed construction. The plan of the works, however, was overambitious, and insufficient forces were available to garrison a defense that large. To accommodate the number of militiamen on hand, the fort's northwest salient was converted into a redoubt. Smith also added another row of *chevaux-de-frise* in the river. But Billingsport Fort proved indefensible from the land side.

In order to open their line of communications by water with General William Howe in Philadelphia, British military forces had to first eliminate the river barriers and then reduce Forts Mercer and Mifflin. A force consisting of elements of two British regiments landed below Billingsport on October 1, 1777, to attack the fort there from the rear or land side. Faced by an overwhelming number of the enemy, the fort's commander, left with only 100 men after desertions, ordered his garrison to spike the guns, burn their barracks, and evacuate the fort. The British took possession on October 2, systematically dismantled the fort, and cut through the

New Jersey

chevaux-de-frise, but refrained from immediately proceeding against the other two Patriot fortifications, a short distance upstream.

BLUE HILLS POST. Located at present Plainfield in Union County, this Revolutionary War encampment in 1776–77 occupied a 95-acre tract on the plantation owned by brothers Frederick and Cornelius Vermeule who had come from Bergen in 1736 and acquired some 1,200 acres of land. The post guarded the main road leading from Quibbletown (New Market) through Scotch Plains and Springfield and the mountain passes to the north. The camp's garrison, consisting of between one and two thousand men, included a company of the 1st Essex Regiment under Colonel Frederick Frelinghusen and most of the militia of Morris and Essex counties.

BRINK'S FORT. Located in Montague Township, Sussex County, Samuel Brink's Fort seems to have been a wood structure 50 by 24 feet, surrounded by a 59-square-foot palisade. It also functioned as a single-family dwelling. The fort's general location is shown on maps dated 1757 and 1777. Other than this limited data, nothing is known about this defense.

BULL'S FERRY FORT. Situated on the New Jersey shore, about four miles north of Hoboken, almost opposite New York City, Bull's Ferry Fort was a strong, palisaded and abatised blockhouse built in April 1780 and garrisoned by 80 Loyalist "Associated Refugees," ostensibly covering woodcutters for the British army but who were actually "wretched banditti" causing depredations against the inhabitants for many miles around. Here a Patriot force was ignominiously defeated although it outnumbered its defenders twenty to one.

On July 20 General Washington dispatched Brigadier General Anthony Wayne with his 1st and 2nd Pennsylvania Brigades and Colonel Stephen Moylan's Dragoons, aggregating some 1,700 men, with four small pieces of artillery to destroy the blockhouse. On the morning of July 21, they bombarded the blockhouse with their fieldpieces with no appreciable results. In his report of July 26, 1780, to the Congress, Washington wrote that although

the fire was kept up for an hour, *they were found too light to penetrate the logs* of which it was constructed. The troops during this time being galled by a constant fire from the loopholes of the house, and seeing no chance of making a breach with cannon, those of the First and Second Regiments, notwithstanding the utmost efforts of the officers to restrain them, rushed

through the abatis to the foot of the stockade with a view of forcing an entrance, which was found impracticable. This act of intemperate valor was the cause of the loss we sustained, and which amounted in the whole to three officers wounded, fifteen noncommissioned officers and privates killed, and forty-six noncommissioned officers and privates wounded. I have been thus particular lest the account of this affair should have reached Philadelphia much exaggerated. [Fitzpatrick, ed., *Writings of Washington* 19: 260–62]

The blockhouse was reportedly abandoned and burned by the "Associated Refugees" on August 9, 1780, less than three weeks after the attack which, in the end, turned out to be a futile exercise.

BURLINGTON BARRACKS. During the French and Indian War, barracks were built in Burlington, Trenton, New Brunswick, Amboy, and Elizabeth, by order of the Provincial Assembly. Each barracks accommodated 300 men. The Burlington Barracks, similar in construction to the Trenton Barracks, stood at the junction of East Broad Street and Assiscunk Creek, on the site of old St. Paul's Roman Catholic Church. From 1758 to 1776, the British continuously garrisoned troops there. When the redcoats were forced out of New Jersey by Washington's strategies at Trenton, Princeton, and Monmouth, Burlington Barracks was confiscated as Crown property and used as quarters for Patriot troops and for warehousing war munitions.

BURLINGTON CANTONMENT. This name appears in the outline index of Record Group 94 in the National Archives without any subsequent information about the camp.

BURLINGTON ISLAND FORT (*Matinicunk Island Fort*). The site of the first European settlement in what today constitutes New Jersey, Matinicunk, or Burlington Island as it is presently known, lies in the Delaware River opposite the eastern portion of the city of Burlington and separated from the mainland by a narrow channel. Burlington was founded in 1677 by English Quakers. It was the Dutch, not the English, who first discovered and explored the North and South rivers, as the Hudson and Delaware were known in early colonial history.

In March 1624 the West Indies Company directed Captain Cornelis Jacobsen May (Mey), for whom Cape May was named, to transport about thirty French-speaking Walloon families and a number of single men to establish a colony on either the North or South river. Eight single men were first landed on Manhattan Island, and most of the remaining colonists were taken to Fort Orange upriver on the Hudson at present Albany. Captain May then sailed up the Delaware to Matinicunk (Indian for "island of pines") Island, soon called by the Dutch Verhulsten Island—"high island" or "beautiful island." The primitive colony there was established by three or four Walloon families and eight single men. A palisaded fort was built on the downriver extremity of the island and enclosed the first "hutts of Bark," about 26 by 40 feet with arched roofs, copies of dwellings used by the Indians.

In the late fall of 1626, Governor-General Peter Minuit determined to consolidate New Netherland and had the island's settlers brought to New Amsterdam on the southern tip of Manhattan Island. At approximately the same time, the Dutch built Fort Nassau, their trading house, on the river's east bank opposite today's Philadelphia, to replace the Matinicunk Island fort. In 1659 Alexander d'Hinoyossia, vice-governor and agent for the Burgomasters of the City of Amsterdam, who then controlled part of the New Netherland's colony on the Delaware, appropriated or acquired the island as his own personal property and made many improvements. There, in the midst of cultivated fields, livestock, and servants, including a number of slaves, he resided in comparative luxury with his wife and seven children. He did not long enjoy his island retreat, for in 1664 the English took possession of all New Netherland.

CARMER'S FORT. Located in present Sandyston Township in Sussex County, the site of Carmer's Fort can be found in the area of the junction of the Dingmans Ferry-Bevans Road and Old Mine Road, about a half-mile southeast of the bridge and situated on a high hill overlooking the Delaware River. A contemporary map drawn by Jonathan Hampton dates the fort as early as 1758. The present site of Carmer's Fort is occupied by an abandoned T-shaped, partly two-storied farmhouse. The one-story stone section of the structure dates back to the colonial period and may have been the original fortified farm dwelling which quartered eight soldiers.

CAVEN POINT ARMY BASE. A port of embarkation during World War II, the Army installation occupied a 340-acre tract bordering on Upper New York Bay, almost due west of the Statue of Liberty, in Hudson County. It was purchased from Jersey City at the outbreak of the war. It was subsequently discontinued to be developed into a major training facility for northern New Jersey Army Reservists.

CAMP CHARLES WOOD. FORT MONMOUTH.

CHESTNUT NECK FORT. FORT FOX BURROWS.

CAMP COLES. FORT MONMOUTH.

FORT CONSTITUTION. FORT LEE.

FORT DELANCEY (*Bergen Neck Fort; Refugee Post on Bergen Neck*). Also known as Bergen Neck Fort and the "Refugee Post on Bergen Neck," Fort Delancey was located in Bayonne, most probably on a site now bounded by Avenue B, 52nd Street, and Avenue C, and 51st Street. It was situated on a ridge just west of the main stage and post road which ran from Bergentown to Bergen Point. Its strategic location made it a valuable prize during all the years of the war. The site for the fort was selected by the Patriots in July 1776. Across Kill van Kull on Staten Island, more than 30,000 British troops had been assembled in preparation for the attack on New York City. Anticipating that the British assault might be directed through Bergen Neck, General Washington ordered the fortifications be erected. In preparation, Washington also ordered the formation of a "Flying Camp" which was set up near Perth Amboy. This was a mobile force held ready to meet and oppose the British wherever they might land. From his headquarters at Perth Amboy, General Hugh Mercer sent a detachment of 300 militia to Bergen Neck.

The fort at Bergen Neck proved to be of little value since the British launched their attack on New York City from Long Island. Following the capture of the city, the British crossed the Hudson and seized Paulus Hook Fort, making the area untenable for the Continental troops. Bergen Neck was abandoned on October 5, 1776, as part of the Patriots' general evacuation of the area. Following the retreat, and for some time, it is doubtful if either side made any permanent use of the fort, although in April 1777 it was reported that Bergen Neck was in command of British Colonel Abraham Van Buskirk. Just when the fort was named Fort Delancey is not known, but it is probable that it occurred some time between 1777 and 1782. It was named in honor of Oliver DeLancey, notorious Tory of Westchester.

Fort Delancey, under the British, was used as headquarters for the Tory raiders and woodcutters. Under the command of Captain Thomas Ward, the "Refugees," as they called themselves, plundered the farms and homes in the Newark

Bay and Hackensack Valley areas. The Tories' influence in the area, however, did not go unchallenged. Several times during the years 1780–82 the Americans launched attacks on Fort Delancey, but the garrison there was strong enough to resist capture. During September 1782 the "Refugees" evacuated and destroyed Fort Delancey and, on October 5, 1782, they sailed for Nova Scotia.

DINGMAN'S FORT. This structure, located on the Old Mine Road in Walpack Township, Sussex County, not far from Carmer's Fort, was built by Adam Dingman in 1735 and modified several times since. Probably palisaded and minimally fortified in 1756 by the Frontier Guard, it quartered a small number of soldiers during the years of the French and Indian War. No remains are known to exist.

CAMP DIX. FORT DIX.

FORT DIX (*Camp Dix*). Occupying today a 49-square-mile tract in Burlington and Ocean counties, just south of Wrightstown, this post was officially established on July 18, 1917, as Camp Dix, and designated a cantonment area and training center for troops intended for service in World War I. It rapidly evolved as the nation's largest military reservation and trained three divisions and numerous other units during the war. It was named for Major General John Adams Dix, who during the nineteenth century served as a U.S. senator, governor of New York, ambassador to France, and secretary of the treasury.

The camp became a demobilization center following the armistice. From 1922 to 1926, it was a training ground for active Army, Army Reserve, and National Guard units and then remained in a caretaker status until 1933. From 1933 to 1939, the post served as a reception, discharge, and replacement center for the Civilian Conservation Corps (CCC). In 1939 the camp became a permanent Army installation and its name was changed to Fort Dix. It served as a reception center for men inducted under the Selective Service Act of 1939. Ten divisions and many smaller units either trained or staged here prior to assignment on the global battlefields of World War II.

After World War II, the reception center became the separation center, returning almost 1,200,000 soldiers to civilian life. In 1947 Fort Dix was designated a basic training center and later that year became the home of the 9th Infantry Division. In 1954 the 9th was transferred overseas, and the 69th Division reactivated at Fort Dix. In March 1956 the 69th was inactivated, and Fort Dix was officially named the United States Army Training Center, Infantry. During the 1950s Fort Dix experienced a tremendous growth and expansion. The overall renovation of the post continued as the World War II temporary wooden buildings disappeared to make way for barracks of brick and cement. Under the master construction plan, Fort Dix was converted from a wooden cantonment station to a modern Army post with buildings of permanent construction. During the Vietnam War, Fort Dix again expanded.

During the 70s, Fort Dix continued to experience significant improvements and reorganization in its installation and training missions. In October of 1978, the post implemented a significant change in training by integrating women into its Basic Training Program beside their male counterparts. In October 1979 the Pentagon reversed the decision made by a deputy Department of Defense secretary to close the post. The turnabout was made after a vigorous campaign by a coalition of members of Congress from New Jersey, Pennsylvania, Delaware, and New York.

CAMP EDGE. CAMP EDISON.

CAMP EDISON (*Camp Edge*). The town of Sea Girt in Monmouth County was the site of a State National Guard encampment as early as 1898, when troops were mobilized there for service in the Spanish-American War. The post was then simply called "State Camp." Camp Edge, presumably located on the same site as the original encampment, was established in 1917 for the mobilization and training of National Guard troops for overseas service and named in honor of Walter Evans Edge, Governor of New Jersey during World War I. The 104th Field Signal Battalion of the 29th Division was trained there. The camp was renamed Camp Edison when Charles Edison served as governor of the state from 1941 to 1944 and used as a troop training center for service during World War II. After the war, the post became a summer encampment for the New Jersey National Guard until 1954, at which time the unit transferred its training maneuvers to Camp Drum at Otis, New York.

FORT ELFSBORG (*Fort Elsinburgh; Fort Myggenborgh*). Once located on a point of land below the mouth of Varkens Kill (Salem Creek) on the east bank of the Delaware River, at the present site of the town of Salem, the remains of Fort Elfsborg, also known as Fort Elsinburgh, now lie beneath the waters of the river. Built in 1643 by New Sweden's Governor Johan Printz, the fort was a three-cornered earthen redoubt mounting eight 12-pounder iron and brass guns and one mortar, designed to control all traffic above Delaware Bay and render valueless the Dutch's Fort Nassau trading post.

Then considered the strongest and best-garrisoned fort on the river, it was manned by 14 soldiers and 5 officers. Printz's Swedish and Finnish colonists and "freemen" settled along the river from Fort Christina to Tinicum were then able to work their farms in relative security. The New Jersey marches, however, bred unbearable clouds of mosquitoes and gnats. "From the continued stinging and sucking of the mosquitos the people were so swollen, that they appeared as if they had been effected [infected] with some horrible disease. Therefore they called this Fort Myggenborgh" (Peter Lindstrom, *Geographia Americae*, trans. Amandus Johnson [1925], pp. 86–87). No doubt this contributed to the abandonment of the fort in 1651, when the Dutch built Fort Casimir across the Delaware and rendered Fort Elfsborg impotent. By 1655 the fort was in ruins.

ELIZABETHTOWN BARRACKS. In 1758 measures were taken by the British to station regular troops at various points in New Jersey. The precise date when the barracks were erected at Elizabethtown, presently the city of Elizabeth in Union County, has not been determined. It is known, however, that the barracks were erected on Cherry Street between Rahway Avenue and West Jersey Street, and occupied by British troops until 1775–76.

Conforming largely to the style of architecture of the still-existing Trenton Barracks, it was described as

three stories in height, extending from the crossroad toward the river, and stood facing the south, where the ground directly adjacent was the usual place of parade and exercise. This building was provided with outside stairs leading to the second and third stories. The basement and second stories were assigned to the private soldiery, while the upper apartments were reserved as officers' quarters. [*Daily Journal* (Elizabeth, NJ), 17 September 1932]

The troops usually assigned there varied from 400 to 600 men. In the early fall of 1775, the 47th Regiment, the last regular command to occupy the barracks, sailed to join the British forces occupying Boston. The British reportedly burned the barracks on February 25, 1779.

ELIZABETHTOWN CANTONMENT. In the index of Record Group 94 at the National Archives, the following statement appears: "Cantonment established at [Elizabethtown] and the Headquarters of the Eastern Division of the Army established there 1837." Beyond this, nothing else is known.

ELLISON'S FORT. Still in existence in the present-day village of Delaware in Warren County, about 200 yards from the river, the structure known as Ellison's (Allison's) Fort is a two-story, 35-by-24-foot dwelling of native fieldstone constructed probably around 1750. It was fortified by the Frontier Guard in 1756 during the French and Indian War and quartered 13 soldiers.

FORT ELSINBURGH. Fort Elfsborg.

FORT ERIWONICK. Fort Nassau.

CAMP EVANS. A World War II post established in March 1942 at Belmar in Monmouth County, it was named in honor of Colonel Paul Wesley Evans. Camp Evans was redesignated Evans Signal Laboratory on April 6, 1945.

FORT FOX BURROWS (*Chestnut Neck Fort*). During the Revolution, the poorly organized U.S. Navy avoided battle with British warships, relying instead on privateers, many of whom operated out of South Jersey coastal harbors which were protected by sandbars. Chestnut Neck, with a large settlement and storehouses, was such a haven. Situated on the south side of Little Egg Harbor River, or Mullica River as it is known today, the old village of Chestnut Neck is located about five miles inland from Great Bay in Atlantic County.

The privateers, armed with letters of marque from Congress, roamed both the coastal waters and high seas in search of British shipping. Once captured, the prize vessels were brought to Chestnut Neck and placed in the custody of a United States marshal, who was authorized to advertise and sell both ships and cargoes at auction to the highest bidders. In order to protect both the privateering base and the Batsto Ironworks, an earthwork named Fort Fox Burrows, also known as Chestnut Neck Fort, was erected in September 1776 overlooking the river. For some unknown reason, however, it was apparently never armed with cannon.

During the four months immediately preceding October 1778, some 19 British vessels were captured and sailed to Chestnut Neck. Sir Henry Clinton, commander of British forces in America, issued the order to "seize, pillage and destroy" this "nest of rebel pirates." A large British force consisting of 13 warships mounting 152 guns and carrying 1,690 men, appeared off Little Egg Harbor just before noon on October 5, 1778. At daybreak the next day, they began the assault by first bombarding Fort Fox Burrows, which the British believed was armed. Troops landed to take possession of the village. The town's militiamen, outnumbered, low on ammunition, and without artillery support, were forced to retreat. Chestnut Neck and its storerooms, homes, town tavern, and remaining prize ships were set afire and destroyed. The village was never rebuilt.

FORT GATES. SANDY HOOK DEFENSES.

CAMP HALSTEAD. A temporary Civil War calvalry encampment on the outskirts of Trenton, Camp Halstead was located near Moses Woods, now the junction of West Hanover and Passaic streets.

FORT HANCOCK. SANDY HOOK DEFENSES.

FORT HUDSON. SANDY HOOK DEFENSES.

CAMP JOCKEY HOLLOW. MORRISTOWN NATIONAL HISTORICAL PARK.

FORT JOHNS (*Fort Shapanack*). Situated on Old Mine Road in Walpack Township, Sussex County, on an elevation overlooking the Delaware River, and occupied by a private dwelling until 1974 when it was destroyed for the Tocks Island Reservoir Project, Fort Johns was a fairly large frontier post constructed in 1756. Designed to accommodate at least 100 soldiers, its palisade measured 120 feet square, with 15-foot-square bastions in three of its angles. The fourth corner was occupied by a 15-by-20-foot log cabin. Centered in the north curtain of the palisade and built on a stone foundation was a 50-by-25-foot wooden blockhouse. The extant plan of the fort also indicates a stone dwelling within the stockade measuring about 52 by 26 feet.

Sussex County histories refer to this defense as Fort Shapanack, named for the old village in which it stood. The name "Fort Johns" has been variously ascribed to one of three men: its owner, John Rosenkrans, in 1756; John Stevens, responsible for its construction; or John Johnston who designed the forts on the Delaware River. The fort was apparently the major refuge in the area

where settlers along the river could find protection during Indian incursions. Adjacent old Van Campen Inn, still in existence, was able to accommodate up to 150 people if necessary. Fort Johns existed as a military post for 27 years, or until the end of the Revolution.

CAMP KEARNY. A temporary World War I Motor Transport Corps base and camp, Camp Kearny was located on the Passaic River in South Kearny.

CAMP KENDRICK. A temporary World War I facility located adjacent to the U.S. Naval Air Station and Proving Ground at Lakehurst, Ocean County, this post was named in honor of Henry T. Kendrick, professor of chemistry, mineralogy, and geology, U.S. Military Academy, 1857–80. Occupying about 733 acres, the camp was established as a training center for the Chemical Warfare Service in September 1918 when the first troops arrived. The post was discontinued in March 1919 with the transfer of the property to the U.S. Navy for use as a lighter-than-air craft (balloon and dirigible) experimental station.

CAMP (JOYCE) KILMER. Nationally known as a World War II overseas embarkation and processing center for more than a million servicemen and located two miles east of New Brunswick, Camp Kilmer was first opened in June 1942 and named for noted World War I soldier-poet Joyce Kilmer who was killed in France. The Department of Defense decided to close the 1,573-acre installation of 1,230 buildings in the summer of 1962. In 1963 its last large military unit, the 2nd Army Corps Headquarters, pulled out and moved to Fort Wadsworth on Staten Island. Most of the vast property was either sold or allotted to various state and federal educational and job-training agencies. Remaining smaller parcels were sold to the highest bidders in early 1966.

KNOX'S ARTILLERY PARK. The site of the 1778–79 winter encampment of General Henry Knox and the Continental Artillery is located on the slope of the Second Watchung Mountain near the town of Pluckemin, in present Somerset County. After the general and his artillery departed in June 1779, the camp became a military hospital, which it remained for several years. Recent archaeological explorations on the site have uncovered numerous artifacts among the 13 mounds of stone, equidistant from each other, which appeared to be the remains of collapsed chimneys.

FORT LEE (*Fort Constitution*). After the Continental Army's siege of Boston, which the British were forced to evacuate on March 17, 1776, King George III and the War Office in London determined to end the "rebellion" as quickly as possible. The largest armada of British ships and troops that ever left England's shores sailed westward to America. By mid-August General Sir William Howe, the British commander in chief, had assembled an army of over 31,000 British, Hessian, and Loyalist troops on Staten Island. On August 22 the British landed on Long Island (Brooklyn) and five days later forced the Americans to retreat across the East River to Manhattan Island.

During that summer of 1776, the strategic importance of the Hudson River led General Washington to order the construction of fortifications on both banks of the river. Joseph Phillips, a battalion commander of a battery of New Jersey militia, initiated defenses by superintending the construction of an artillery battery on the Palisades, at present Fort Lee, Bergen County, with Colonel Rufus Putnam laying out the fortifications overlooking the river, opposite today's Washington Heights on the east bank where Fort Washington was being simultaneously built. Established on a promontory inaccessible on three sides, with heavy gun emplacements and supported on the west by a square-bastioned earthwork, Putnam's fort commanded the river below.

Early in September, Washington determined that 8,000 soldiers were to man the defensive positions on both sides of the river. On September 30 Major General Nathanael Greene was appointed commander of the New Jersey post. The post was called Fort Constitution until October 19, when it was renamed for General Charles Lee, who aided in the Continental defense of New York City. On November 14 Washington moved a large part of his army across the river in expectation of a British move. Two days later, the Battle for Manhattan was ended when much-touted Fort Washington fell to the overwhelming assault by the enemy, who captured more than 2,000 Continentals, one of the worst American defeats of the Revolution.

General Washington ordered Greene to move all excess military stores from Fort Lee, defended by less than 3,000 men in the face of 20,000 British and Hessians. Lord Cornwallis with his army crossed the Hudson from Dobbs Ferry to Closter's Landing on November 20 and marched five miles to Fort Lee, which was ordered abandoned by Washington. The British took 90 prisoners and killed about 20 men of the Continentals' rear guard. Washington later reported losing almost all the cannon at the fort, as well as baggage, several hundred tents, 1,000 barrels of flour, and other valuable stores. When the Continentals retreated to White Plains, the British took possession of the abandoned guns and stores.

The Palisades Interstate Park Commission reconstructed the historic site in time for the nation's observance of the Bicentennial. Walkways and overlooks in the park area command panoramic views of the lower Hudson River and the Manhattan skyline, as well as replicas of the Continental Army's 1776 fortifications. Architects reconstructed the three gun batteries and the rifle parapet, equipped with fraises using materials of the original stone bases made from indigenous rocks and topped by hand-hewn wood.

LIGHT HOUSE FORT. SANDY HOOK DEFENSES.

FORT LINCOLN. SANDY HOOK DEFENSES.

CAMP LITTLE SILVER. FORT MONMOUTH.

FORT MCMURTIE. Three McMurtie brothers—Thomas, Joseph, and Robert—built adjoining dwellings along the bank of the Delaware River, within present-day Belvidere Borough in Warren County. It is not known which of the three dwellings was fortified by the Morris County Militia under Captain Lemuel Bowers in January 1756. Neither have their exact locations been determined.

MATINICUNK ISLAND FORT. BURLINGTON ISLAND FORT.

FORT MERCER. In September 1777 General Sir William Howe's army seemed on the verge of victory after defeating General Washington at Brandywine, forcing Congress to seek a new address. Howe's army marched into Philadelphia to the plaudits of crowds of Loyalists. To securely occupy the city as winter quarters for the British forces, there was the need to implement safe supply routes which depended on the free navigation of the Delaware River. Not long after seizing the rebel capital, Howe made plans to capture the American posts south of the city that commanded the river's passage.

Reinforced Fort Mifflin on Mud Island, Pennsylvania, and Fort Mercer at Red Bank, New Jersey, guarded a line of underwater *chevaux-de-frise*. Further south, a Patriot post at Billingsport protected another line of *chevaux-de-frise*. The first British attack was made on October 1, when two regiments crossed to the New Jersey side of the river and took Billingsport. British naval craft began clearing a path through the undefended line of underwater obstructions. Less than a week after the October 4th Battle of German-town, instigated by the Continentals, General Howe ordered naval bombardment of both Forts Mifflin and Mercer, and dispatched about 2,000 Hessians to attack Red Bank.

The Red Bank assault group, under Colonel Count Carl von Donop, landed near present-day Camden and arrived at Fort Mercer [named for General Hugh Mercer killed in the Battle of Princeton] on October 22. The fort's garrison, mostly Rhode Islanders under Colonel Christopher Greene, had worked feverishly during the preceding days to improve the fortifica-tions; now they could only wait. Late in the after-noon, Donop attacked from three sides. Greene's men held their fire until the last minute, and then opened up with all they had. The Continentals, aided by gal-ley fire from the river, tore the enemy to pieces. Donop himself fell with over a dozen wounds, and some 400 other Hessians went down as well. Greene's losses were under 40. [Mark E. Lender, "Action on the Delaware, 1777," in New Jersey Historical Commis-sion *Newsletter* 8, no. 2, (October 1977)]

For five days, beginning on November 10, a British barrage reduced Fort Mifflin to splinters and made the fort untenable, forcing the Patriots to evacuate and set it on fire. A strong British force was landed at Billingsport and marched up the shore toward Fort Mercer. The British breached the fort's walls with heavy artillery, and the Americans blew up their own post as they retreated. Losing Fort Mercer spelled the end of the Patriots' control of the river. In the end, however, the British efforts came to naught. "Al-though the rebel capital had fallen, Washington's army remained intact [and] Congress functioned well enough in exile." In the following June, the British evacuated Philadelphia, and the Delaware was once again an American-controlled river.

CAMP MERRITT. One of the nation's largest U.S. troop embarkation posts of World War I, Camp Merritt was opened in September 1917 as a facility for the Port of Embarkation at Hoboken and was named in honor of Major General Wes-ley Merritt, cavalry leader during the Civil War. The post was first occupied on October 1, 1917, by the 49th Infantry Division. Before being offi-cially discontinued on January 31, 1920, Camp Merritt covered some 770 acres with 1,302 build-ings on a tract about one mile long and a half-mile wide, with the greater portion of the post's facilities located in neighboring Bergenfield, Cresskill, Dumont, and Tenafly. It was reported that 578,566 men passed through the camp on their way to Europe between November 1917 and November 1918. After its official closing, a guard of one company of infantry, Company K, 13th Infantry, remained there until June 11, 1920.

CAMP MIDDLEBROOK. Part of Washington's Continental Army encamped at Camp Mid-dlebrook, just north of the Bound Brook-Somer-ville area in Somerset County, from the fall of 1778 to the summer of 1779.

MIDDLETOWN BLOCKHOUSE. A block-house was erected probably in 1675, during King Philip's War, at Middletown (founded 1664) in Monmouth County. Built when hostile Indians congregated in the hills south of the village, the defense was constantly manned by six armed men. The fort was later used as a jail and court-house. The site of the blockhouse is now oc-cupied by the Christ Episcopal Church.

FORT MONMOUTH (*Signal Corps Camp; Camp Monmouth Park; Camp Little Silver; Camp Alfred Vail; Camp Coles; Camp Charles Wood*). Located in the seashore area of Mon-mouth County, nationally prestigious Fort Mon-mouth is an Army installation that has con-tinuously progressed in military electronics research, development, and training, since its in-ception on June 17, 1917, on the old abandoned Monmouth Park Race Track, between the towns of Little Silver and Oceanport. At its inception it was the only Signal Corps post in the country. Originally known as the Signal Corps Camp, it was also known as Camp Monmouth Park and Camp Little Silver before being officially desig-nated Camp Alfred Vail in honor of the New Jersey inventor, the partner and a financial backer of Samuel F. B. Morse.

In 1925 it became a permanent post and was renamed Fort Monmouth in honor of the Con-tinental soldiers who fought the British and Hes-sians in its environs during the indecisive Battle of Monmouth on June 28, 1778. On October 1, 1942, Camp Coles was established as an adjunct of Fort Monmouth at Lincroft, a short distance west of the Garden State Parkway and Red Hook, and named in honor of Colonel Roy Howard Coles, distinguished executive officer for the Chief Signal Corps Officer, AEF, World War I. On April 6, 1945, the camp was redesignated Coles Signal Laboratory. Camp Charles Wood, also es-tablished during World War II, was located on the grounds of Fort Monmouth. Still active, Fort

Monmouth is the home for various Signal Corps units engaged in electronics research, development, and training.

CAMP MONMOUTH PARK. FORT MONMOUTH.

CAMP MORGAN. Apparently a temporary encampment of the New Jersey National Guard occupied 1918–19, it was located at or near the town of Morgan in Middlesex County.

MORRISTOWN NATIONAL HISTORICAL PARK (*Fort Nonsense; Camp Jockey Hollow*). During two winters of the Revolutionary War, 1777 and 1779–80, the rugged hill country around Morristown in Morris County, about 30 miles east of New York City, sheltered the main encampments of the Continental Army, and was the headquarters of Commander in Chief George Washington. Here he systematically reorganized his forces almost within sight of the British lines at New York. Lafayette came here with the welcome news of the second French expedition in aid of the American cause; and here, despite cold, hunger, and disease, a new nation's will to independence was maintained. Thus for a time, this small New Jersey village became the military capital of an infant nation.

Before the war, Morristown had been a small, rustic frontier community, settled largely by people of New England origin. A short distance from the British lines on Manhattan and Staten Islands, Morristown was protected by the Watchung Mountains, a huge, natural earthwork. By keeping his lines of communication safely behind the hill barriers, Washington was able to hover about New York City and hold himself in readiness to move troops with relative rapidity to any threatened sector. Because it was located near the center of this defensive arc, Morristown became the scene of almost continuous military activity.

Soon after American troops took up winter quarters near Morristown in January 1777, General Washington began the tremendous task of congregating wagons, grain, and other military stores for the coming spring campaign. Most of these supplies were concentrated in Morristown at the "Continental Store," and their protection became essential. On May 28 Washington issued orders for one detachment to remain in Morristown "to strengthen the works already begun upon the Hill" on the outskirts of the village. The original design of the fort soon became obscured, and during the nineteenth century an erroneous legend originated that Washington ordered his

soldiers to build the redoubt merely to keep them busy, hence the name Fort Nonsense. Reconstruction of this fort, based upon documentary data and archaeological evidence, was accomplished by the National Park Service in 1937.

During the winter of 1779–80, General Washington used as his official headquarters a mansion built by Colonel Jacob Ford, an affluent iron manufacturer and landowner of Morristown. The main Continental Army, numbering up to as many as 10,000 men, was encamped in Jockey Hollow during that winter, five miles to the southwest. About 1,000 acres of this land, including all but three units of the military campsite, are within the present park boundaries. Most of the cantonment sites have remained relatively undisturbed, and small heaps of stones from the fireplaces of huts once used as barracks for officers and men still can be seen on the grounds.

Morristown National Historical Park was established by an act of Congress in 1933. About 1,051 acres in extent, it has three separate areas: Washington's Headquarters and the Historical Museum, Fort Nonsense, and the Continental Army encampment sites in Jockey Hollow.

FORT MOTT. One of the three forts erected to guard the approach to Philadelphia and surrounding territory, Fort Mott was located on the Delaware River about seven miles from the town of Salem in Salem County. The other two fortifications were Fort duPont on the Delaware shore and Fort Delaware on Pea Patch Island in the middle of the river.

In 1837 the U.S. Government purchased 104 acres of land from one Samuel Dunn, but apparently the tract was not developed for a defense until 1872, when work was begun on six gun emplacements, mounted on a high bank, beneath which were the powder magazines. Fire control towers were constructed at either end of the bank, behind which was a wide moat. The fort was not garrisoned until December 1897, when a detachment of Battery I, 4th Artillery, was sent from Washington, D.C. At this time, the fort was officially designated Fort Mott in honor of Major General Gershom Mott, veteran of the Mexican and Civil Wars. In 1902 it was reported that the fort, garrisoned by one artillery company, emplaced three 12-inch guns on disappearing carriages; three 10-inch guns, disappearing carriages; one 5-inch rapid-fire gun; and mounts for three more 5-inch guns, ordered but apparently not emplaced until a later date.

The fort remained garrisoned during the Spanish-American War and World War I. In 1943 Fort Mott was declared surplus property, the guns

FORT MOTT. Remains of the fort. (Courtesy of the New Jersey Department of Conservation and Economic Development.)

were dismantled, the troops withdrawn, and the officers' quarters moved across the river on barges. In 1947 the state of New Jersey purchased the fort site and converted it into a State Park. The remainder of the military reservation is maintained by the government as a wildlife refuge and bird sanctuary, called Killcohook.

FORT MYGGENBORGH. FORT ELFSBORG.

FORT NASSAU (*Fort Eriwonick*). The exact site of this fortified Dutch trading post built in 1626 on the east bank of the Delaware River, opposite today's South Philadelphia, has not been precisely determined. The latest historical research, however, indicates that it is located within an area roughly 100 yards of the intersection of Charles and Water streets in the city of Gloucester, north of the mouth of Timber Creek (Verkeerde Kil), in Camden County. After Fort Nassau was built, provided with palisades and battlements, the Dutch learned that it was needed only at certain times of the year—particularly in the winter season when the best animal pelts were to be obtained from the Indians. Intermittently garrisoned and staffed, Fort Nassau, apparently alternately known as Fort Eriwonick, was abandoned by the Dutch soon after New Sweden's Governor Johan Printz built Fort Elfsborg at present Salem in 1643 to control all river traffic above Delaware Bay, effectively rendering the trading post valueless.

NEW FORT. The actual location of this frontier fort has not been determined. It is probable, however, that it stood in or near the present town of Columbia on the Delaware River in Warren County.

Francis Bernard, newly appointed Royal Governor of New Jersey, arrived from England at Perth Amboy on June 14th, 1758. He arrived at a critical time. . . . The Indians were attacking all along the Delaware from No[r]manock Fort to above Port Jervis. Governor Bernard took immediate action. He ordered the construction of New Fort August 12, 1758. [*The North Jersey Highlander*, Winter 1976, pp. 20–21]

Other than that the fort was probably under-garrisoned because of the depletion of the Frontier Guard to a mere 50 men for the entire area, no further data have been found relevant to its history.

FORT NONSENSE. MORRISTOWN NATIONAL HISTORICAL PARK.

FORT NORMANOCK. One of seven frontier defenses built along the Delaware River during the French and Indian War, Fort Normanock ("fishing place") was erected during December 1755–January 1756 and was located on property belonging to Cornelius and Ameji Roosa Westbrook, near the present town of Newton in Sussex County. Judging by the number of men involved in its construction, the fort was apparently one of the larger defenses in the area. It stood on an elevation about a quarter of a mile west of the Delaware River, commanding an excellent view of the river's opposite bank. A great deal of conflict took place in its immediate environs. On November 17, 1763, Captain Benjamin Westbrook and 11 soldiers from the fort crossed the river into Pennsylvania to recover abandoned cattle and supplies. About three miles from the river, they were ambushed by Indians, and Captain Westbrook and five of his men were killed.

An empty shell is all that remains of the fort today.

CAMP OLDEN.

CAMP OLDEN. The first Civil War encampment in Trenton was located just outside of the Arsenal walls and called Camp Olden in honor of the governor. Later this name was given to the large camp on the Sandtown Road near Pond Run, where many of the New Jersey regiments were mobilized and mustered into Federal service.

OLD TAPPAN CANTONMENT. Tappan in New York and Old Tappan, Bergen County, in New Jersey, about two miles from the Hudson River, are separate but adjoining communities today, but during the Revolution it was one area and known as Tappan.

The arrival of the French fleet and a French army at Newport [Virginia] on July 10, 1780, greatly improved Washington's military prospects, and he set to work at once upon plans for a grand assault on New York City, with thirty to forty thousand men, aided by the French fleet. On August 8, 1780, Washington took up headquarters at Tappan, in the De Windt house, a low brick and stone cottage built by the Huguenot Daniel de Clerck in 1700 [the house was then owned by Major Frederick Blauvelt of the New York Militia]. [Adrian C. Leiby, *The Revolutionary War in the Hackensack Valley* (Rutgers University Press, 1962), p. 264]

With Washington were his chief officers, military aides, and the main body of his Continental Army, most of them long, professional campaigners, "ready to move at once to defend the Highlands or attack New York if an opportunity arose," but the assault never took place. Washington's army was originally encamped for several miles on either side of the town, but after two weeks, Washington shifted his forces a few miles to the south, since the forage at Old Tappan was exhausted.

FORT PAULUS HOOK. This Revolutionary War fort on the sandy spit of land or peninsula known as Paulus (Powle's) Hook on the west bank of the Hudson River, opposite the lower end of Manhattan Island, occupied a 15-block area centered at present Washington and Sussex streets in Jersey City (Lossing placed its main works at the intersection of Grand and Greene streets). The ground was first occupied by the Americans on April 5, 1776. Construction of the fort was begun at the end of May and guns were emplaced there before June 10, intended to block enemy shipping along the river. Additional construction was performed through the month of June, and other works were laid out on Bergen Neck, to the rear of Paulus Hook, on July 10.

On September 23, 1776, the British frigates *Roebuck* and *Tartar*, along with bomb vessel *Carcass*, came up the river and threatened bombardment of the Patriot position. The Americans precipitately abandoned their fort without a fight. Paulus Hook subsequently became the principal western outpost in the British defenses of New York. On July 14, 1778, the British cut a fosse through the neck connecting Paulus Hook to the mainland.

On the night of August 18, 1779, Major Henry "Light Horse Harry" Lee with a mixed force of Americans, in imitation of Anthony Wayne's recent surprise attack at Stony Point, seized heavily fortified Paulus Hook from the British but held it for only a few hours. During the battle Lee's forces killed 11 men and captured 108.

The fort's commandant was court-martialed but acquitted, and a sergeant who had abandoned his post was court-martialed and sentenced to be hung but was later pardoned. The post was abandoned by the British and reoccupied by the Americans on November 23, 1783.

CAMP PERRINE. A temporary Civil War installation, Camp Perrine was located on the east bank of the Delaware River opposite the old State Prison at Trenton.

PERTH AMBOY BARRACKS. Intermittently occupied quarters of the 3rd Waldeck Regiment of Hessian troops in late 1776 and 1777, the barracks was located "in the back of the city" of Perth Amboy, in a building "only large enough to house three hundred men."

PICATINNY ARSENAL. A major Department of the Army ordnance installation in the northwestern part of the state, Picatinny Arsenal five miles from Dover traces its origin to the events and personalities of the American Revolution. Rich in iron ore and water resources, from early colonial days this region flourished with mines, forges, furnaces, and ironworks. General Washington found the products of the iron industry of such priority to his logistics that he made it a point to survey the ironworks in Morris County in 1777, which he numbered at "between 80 and 100."

On September 6, 1880, the U.S. War Department established a powder depot in Rockaway Township, Morris County, on a 1,866-acre site in a 10-mile-long valley between mountain ridges which served as natural barricades. The new installation was called the Dover Powder Depot, after the closest large town, but Major F. H. Parker, its first commander, insisted on "Piccatinny," an Indian name for the most prominent peak in the area. The name was soon changed to "Piccatinny Powder Depot." In 1893 it became the "United States Powder Depot," name retained until 1907, when it was designated "Picatinny Arsenal."

At the outbreak of World War II, no other plant existed in this country capable of making anything larger than small arms ammunition. Picatinny began training more than 8,000 persons in the specialized techniques of the mass production of munitions. Civilian employment rose to 18,000, of whom 10,000 were women. By the end of the war, the Arsenal had a skilled pool of scientific and technical personnel. In subsequent years, its primary mission was to develop and improve conventional and nuclear weapons of large-caliber munitions. In 1975 the secretary of the Army announced the formation of a new command to be established at Picatinny Arsenal. The U.S. Army Armament Research and Development Command was established in 1977.

Although Picatinny Arsenal as an organizational entity no longer exists, it serves as the center from which the new Command directs some 5,400 employees at four large sites in three states. It is also the host installation to an array of "tenants," including foreign liaison offices, Army and Marine Reserve units, a new heliport facility for the Army National Guard, and a shooting range for State Troopers.

CAMP RARITAN. RARITAN ARSENAL.

RARITAN ARSENAL (*Camp Raritan*). The town of Edison, site of the former Raritan Arsenal, is located in northeast Middlesex County, about 14 miles south of Newark. Established on January 17, 1918, as the Raritan Ordnance Training Camp, also known as Camp Raritan, the Arsenal was constructed on the north bank of the Raritan River and served as a major storage, warehouse, and shipping terminal. In 1962 the Department of Defense announced that the Arsenal would be closed in 1964. Middlesex County since then has redeveloped the 3,200-acre tract into an educational, industrial, and recreational complex.

"FORT" RAWNSLEY. After hostilities with Mexico broke out on April 25, 1846, and General Zachary Taylor had crossed the Rio Grande three weeks later to occupy Matamoros, the governor of New Jersey was informed by secretary of war William Marcy that the government was seeking the service of volunteers. "Fort" Rawnsley was established as a recruiting station for militiamen and others on January 1, 1847, by Lieutenant Robert P. Maclay, 8th Infantry, in the city of Trenton, at a hotel at the intersection of Warren and Lamberton streets. From there, squads of recruits were forwarded to Governors Island for muster into Federal service. The recruiting station was closed March 15, 1847, and removed to Newark.

FORT READING. Located in the present town of Belvidere in today's Warren County, Fort Reading was one of the four forts authorized on December 28, 1755, by the New Jersey Provincial Legislature. A strong blockhouse 36 feet square and a 16-foot-square stone house enclosed within a 60-foot-square palisade, Fort Reading was erected in 1756 and formed the southern anchor of the New Jersey chain of forts on the Delaware River frontier. The fort was not involved in any military action during its existence.

REFUGEE POST ON BERGEN NECK. FORT DELANCEY.

REFUGEES' TOWER. SANDY HOOK DEFENSES.

CAMP RUFF. Most probably a temporary Civil War installation, Camp Ruff was reportedly located at Camden.

FORT AT SANDY HOOK. SANDY HOOK DEFENSES.

SANDY HOOK DEFENSES (*Light House Fort; Refugees' Tower, Fort Gates; Fort at Sandy Hook; Fort Lincoln; Fort Hudson; Sandy Hook Proving Ground; Fort Hancock*). Now discontinued, the Fort Hancock Military Reservation is situated on a sandy peninsula about a half-mile in width and extending five miles north from the mainland. West of the peninsula lie Sandy Hook Bay and the Navesink River, while to the east is the Atlantic Ocean. Title to Sandy Hook, discovered by Henry Hudson on September 4, 1609, is derived from Charles II, who granted to his brother James, duke of York, the region extending from the Connecticut River to the Delaware. Later, by a patent or deed, Richard Nicholls (the duke's representative in America) granted much of what is now Monmouth County, including Sandy Hook, to a group of proprietors, one of whom was Richard Hartshorne, progenitor of the Hartshorne family in America.

One of the most interesting structures on the peninsula, surrounded by Fort Hancock's

more modern buildings, is Sandy Hook Light, the oldest lighthouse in the United States. A white stone tower, 90 feet high, it was erected by New York merchants to protect shipping in the harbor and was first lighted on June 18, 1764. During the Revolution, the lighthouse and the old dwelling of its keeper were known as the Light House Fort or Refugees' Tower. The British fortified it as a base from which Tory refugees conducted their bloody raids. Some remnants of the log fortifications are still in evidence.

Sandy Hook remained in the possession of the Hartshorne family until 1807, when the United States government made its first purchase of land there for future military purposes. On Navesink Heights, to the rear of Sandy Hook, an eventually heavily armed defense named Fort Gates was begun after the outbreak of the War of 1812. One of its initial purposes was communication by signals with Fort Richmond on Staten Island, which in turn would relay signals to other forts in New York's harbor. Completed in March 1813, Fort Gates reportedly mounted 32 cannon, manned by five companies of Artillery and three companies of Riflemen. The total garrison amounted to 800 men in 1812 and 1813.

Plans were first drawn in 1847 to strengthen the nation's coastal defenses. Construction was begun on a large, star-shaped, granite fortification on Sandy Hook in 1859. At the outbreak of the Civil War in 1861, however, construction was suspended, and additional large appropriations were not made until after the war ended. But the fort at Sandy Hook was never completed, although a number of cannon had been already emplaced. Technical advances in weaponry and munitions during the war obsoleted what had

been built. The most visible portion of the unfinished fort, erroneously referred to as Fort Lincoln, and as Fort Hudson (a name suggested by the New Jersey Historical Society in 1864), for years supported Fort Hancock's water tower.

The only official name ever designated for the planned granite defense was "Fort at Sandy Hook." Governmental letterheads and maps used during the period of construction attest to that fact. The whereabouts of the thousands of tons of granite blocks that once formed part of the unfinished structure remained a mystery until the great coastal storm of March 1962 that ravaged the Jersey shore. Less than a half-mile from the tip of Sandy Hook, the shore line had been cut back some 250 feet by the storm. "What was uncovered for the first time in 60 years was a more than 300-foot-long, low massive seawall built by the Corps of Engineers at the turn of the century . . . . This monolithic graveyard represented the final remains of the dismantled portion of the "Fort at Sandy Hook" (George H. Moss, Jr., *Nauvoo to the Hook: The Iconography of a Barrier Beach* [1964] p. 59).

The Sandy Hook peninsula was turned into a proving ground for heavy weapons in 1874 when Secretary of War William Belknap authorized monies to build gun emplacements and bombproofs, accompanied by long-range targets placed at 500-yard intervals along the beach. Smokeless gunpowder was introduced there in 1891. In 1918 Sandy Hook Proving Ground was moved to Aberdeen, Maryland, because of the availability of more extensive ranges to test new weapons.

In 1892 and 1893, the government purchased all the remaining property held by private in-

SANDY HOOK DEFENSES. Remains of Fort Hancock, adjoining Sandy Hook State Park. (Courtesy of the New Jersey Department of Conservation and Economic Development.)

dividuals on Sandy Hook proper. A new primary coast defense on the northern end of Sandy Hook was begun in 1892 and officially designated Fort Hancock on October 30, 1895, in honor of General Winfield Scott Hancock. The first garrison to occupy the new works was established on March 14, 1898. During World War I, the post served as a training center; in World War II, it was occupied by antiaircraft units. Deactivated in 1950, Fort Hancock was reopened a year later as an antiaircraft base. Deactivated again in 1953, it reopened in 1956 as an important radar and missile installation. On January 8, 1962, the state of New Jersey took title to a 460-acre tract on Sandy Hook. On July 14 of the same year, it was opened to the public as the Sandy Hook State Park. Fort Hancock was declared surplus to the needs of the Department of Defense in 1972.

SANDY HOOK PROVING GROUND. SANDY HOOK DEFENSES.

FORT SEA GIRT. According to National Archives Record Group 393 records, Fort Sea Girt was reportedly active from 1897 to 1917. A somewhat abbreviated citation reads:

As early as 1892, it was proposed that the garrison of Fort Myer, Virginia, be sent to Sea Girt for target practice. It was not until 1897, however, that this was done when the garrison at Fort Hamilton, New York, was sent instead. Pursuant to War Department General Orders No. 84, June 7, 1905, Sea Girt became the site for the National Match in small arms competition. This annual competition was held at Sea Girt for several years. It is not known when this post ceased to be used for this purpose.

FORT SHAPANACK. FORT JOHNS.

SIGNAL CORPS CAMP. FORT MONMOUTH.

TOMS RIVER BLOCKHOUSE. During the American Revolution, a blockhouse was erected on a hill at Toms River, today the county seat of Ocean County. The American fort, garrisoned by 25 militiamen, was attacked by a well-armed party of 80 Loyalists on the morning of March 24, 1782. The defenders put up a gallant defense but were overcome by superior numbers, losing 9 men killed and 12 captured. The Loyalists admitted to 7 killed and wounded. The town of about a dozen dwellings and the blockhouse were burned to the ground, leaving as many as 100 women and children homeless, after their husbands and fathers were carried off as captives.

TRENTON BARRACKS. Standing on the grounds of the State House and fronting on South Willow Street in Trenton, the Old Barracks is the only survivor of the five eighteenth-century New Jersey barracks, the others being located in Burlington, New Brunswick, Elizabethtown, and Perth Amboy. The barracks is an E-shaped structure with a formal shrub-landscaped lawn occupying what was the barracks' yard. It was built in 1758 with money appropriated by the Provincial Assembly to relieve residents of having to billet British soldiers.

At the close of the French and Indian War, the building fell into disuse until the return of troops after the outbreak of the Revolution. Since the barracks accommodated only 300 men, others bivouacked on the surrounding meadow or were billeted in private homes, since an estimated 1,400 men had been posted at this pivotal location in the colonies. There were a number of British Light Dragoons, and certainly as many Hessians, stationed in the town, which offered pleasant winter quarters in December 1776.

Colonel Johann Gottlieb Rall, in command, had set up headquarters nearby on King (now Warren) Street. On the morning of December 26, when the Americans took the barracked men by surprise and routed them, Colonel Rall was mortally wounded. General Washington promptly withdrew with his army and about 900 prisoners to Newton, across the Delaware.

After the British surrender at Yorktown in 1781, the barracks functioned as a hospital for 600 Continentals wounded in the Virginia campaign. For more than a century after the Revolution, sections of the building were used variously as private apartments, a home for old ladies, and a private school. The structure was partitioned, altered, even cut in two when its central section was demolished for a street extension. In 1889 a group of Trenton women organized to raise funds to purchase the south wing. For many years the group, "The Old Barracks Association," maintained a small museum in this section.

In 1899 the Legislature acquired the northern section of the barracks for the state, and the city agreed to close the Front Street extension, making reconstruction of the lost segment of the structure possible. The Association deeded its property to the state, stipulating that on completion of restoration, control and management of the building remain forever with the Association. The present museum there opened in 1917.

VAN CAMPEN'S FORT. Known also as Van Camp's Fort, this French and Indian War defense was built by militiamen on the property of Colonel Abraham Van Campen located in Pahaquarry Township, Warren County, near Van Campen's Creek. Regional histories cite three different locations for the fort, depending on the author. The fort was contemporaneously described as a 20-foot-square blockhouse, a dwelling stone house 60 by 22 feet, and a small log house, palisaded about 65 feet square, for one family.

CAMP VOORHEES. Established on August 15, 1881, by the state as an annual National Guard "Camp of Instruction," Camp Voorhees was located at Sea Girt in Monmouth County. It is not known when the camp was discontinued.

FORT WALPACK. One of the four forts ordered built by Governor Belcher in 1755, this French and Indian War defense overlooking the Delaware River was located in Walpack Township, Sussex County. Its exact site has been lost in the mists of history. A contemporary described the fort as a wooden church and small blockhouse, palisaded about 50 feet square. The only church in the present township in 1757 was the Dutch Reformed Church erected on four acres of ground between 1737 and 1740. Four editions of the church stood on the original site, east of the Walpack Cemetery.

CAMP WASHINGTON. A temporary encampment established for the recruitment and mobilization of New Jersey volunteers in 1846, after war with Mexico broke out, Camp Washington was located at Jackson's Woods, situated to the south of Hamilton Avenue and east of what is now Chestnut Avenue, in Trenton.

WESTBROOK'S FORT. Although not shown on John Hampton's map of 1757, Westbrook's Fort was a minimally fortified, loopholed family dwelling built of local stone with a wood-shingled roof, originally erected in 1735 by Anthony Westbrook on his property located in present Montague Township, Sussex County. Archaeological researches at the site found no evidence to indicate the fort had been palisaded.

ABIQUIU POST. This temporary military post occupied rented adobe buildings at Abiquiu on the Rio Chama River, Rio Arriba County, at the mouth of Frijola Creek, about 45 miles northwest of Santa Fe. It was first established in April 1849 by the "Santa Fe Guards," a volunteer company of 3 officers and 75 men, under the command of Captain John Chapman, for the purpose of controlling the area's Navajo, Ute, and Jicarilla Apache Indians. In October 1849 the company was mustered out of service and the post abandoned. Abiquiu Post was reoccupied on January 29, 1850, by Company D, 2nd Dragoons, commanded by 1st Lieutenant Charles Griffin, 2nd Artillery. This unit was relieved on August 10, 1851, by elements of Company H, 3rd Infantry, which remained until November 5, 1851. Pursuant to orders, the garrison was withdrawn and the post wholly abandoned in October 1851.

ABÓ PASS POST (*Abó Station*). A temporary tent camp, also known as Abó Station, was established sometime in 1861 near the present town of Scholle, about 15 miles east of Bernardo, Socorro County, to protect Abó Pass. The short-term camp was garrisoned by 150 volunteer cavalrymen.

ABÓ STATION. ABÓ PASS POST.

POST OF ALBUQUERQUE. An important presidio founded in 1706 and military post during both the Spanish and Mexican regimes, Albuquerque became a U.S. Army outpost after the town was occupied by General Stephen Watts Kearny in 1846. The Post of Albuquerque was established on November 17, 1846, by Captain J. H. Burgwin, commanding companies G and I of the 1st Dragoons. Without troops for about a year, 1851–52, it was regarrisoned and became department headquarters on August 31, 1852, and supported a quartermaster depot, occupying rented quarters in adobe buildings. The post was discontinued on August 23, 1867.

ALGODONES QUARTERMASTER DEPOT. A small, temporary Army supply depot was established in 1851 in rented buildings in the town of Algodones, Sandoval County, about 45 miles south of Santa Fe. The post was discontinued the same year by the Army because of the incurred expense.

CAMP ANTON CHICO. The town of Anton Chico, Guadalupe County, was posted during 1863–64 by Company E, 2nd California Cavalry

New Mexico

Volunteers, in response to Confederate activities in the region.

CAMP BAIRD. Apparently a temporary Army post established some time prior to 1900, Camp Baird was reportedly located a short distance north of Deming in Luna County.

BARCLAY'S FORT. Located adjacent to the Mora River, near the present town of Watrous, Mora County, Barclay's Fort was established in 1849 by Alexander Barclay as a trading post catering to fur trappers and Indians. A two-story adobe-built structure with two circular bastions at opposite corners, surrounded by a 64-foot-square palisade, it enclosed living quarters, storehouses, and workshops. Outside the fort's walls were private dwellings, corrals, an ice house, an orchard of fruit trees, a garden, and about 200 acres of cultivated land. The post frequently served as a resting stop for military detachments in the region. The U.S. Army considered buying Barclay's Fort but balked at the asking price of $20,000 and, instead, established Fort Union. Barclay and his partner, Joseph Doyle, sold the trading post at auction to Samuel B. Watrous on February 21, 1853. About the turn of the century, the Mora River flooded and carried away most of the fort's remains.

FORT BASCOM (*Camp Easton*). A military post on the south bank of the Canadian River in San Miguel County, eight miles north of Tucumcari, was established on August 15, 1863, by companies F, 7th Infantry, and I, 1st New Mexico Volunteers, with Captain Peter W. L. Plympton commanding. The post was designed to protect central New Mexico's travel routes, prevent illegal trading with the Comanche and Kiowa, and to encourage settlement of the Canadian River Valley. Consisting of stone-built officers' quarters, and barracks and other buildings of adobe, the post was first named Camp Easton for Major Langdon C. Easton, Quartermaster's Department. In January 1864 it was officially designated Fort Bascom in honor of Captain George N. Bascom, 16th Infantry, killed on February 21, 1862, during the Battle of Valverde. The post was occupied until December 1870, when it was abandoned and the garrison and stores were transferred to Fort Union.

FORT BAYARD. Established on August 21, 1866, in compliance with an order of Brigadier General James H. Carleton, Fort Bayard was located 10 miles northeast of present Silver City, at the base of the Santa Rita Mountains, in Grant County. Established for the purpose of protecting the Pinos Altos mining district against the incursions of the Warm Spring Apaches, the post was named in honor of Brigadier General George D. Bayard, who died on December 14, 1862, of mortal wounds suffered at Fredericksburg, Virginia. On January 2, 1900, by direction of Secretary of War Elihu Root, Fort Bayard was discontinued as a garrisoned post, and 10 days later all buildings on the military reservation were turned over to the surgeon general of the Army for use as a sanitarium for the treatment of officers and enlisted men afflicted with pulmonary tuberculosis. Today it is operated as a Veterans Administration Hospital.

CAMP BEAR SPRING. A temporary post established in 1858 west of Pinos Altos, about 25 miles northwest of Socorro, it was garrisoned by companies B and E, 8th Infantry, and served as a base of operations to collect Navajo for the "Long Walk" to Fort Sumner.

BECK'S RANCH POST. An intermittently occupied Army outpost during 1859–60, it was located two miles northeast of Santa Rosa, Guadalupe County.

CAMP BLAKE. According to records of the Adjutant General's Office, Camp Blake was a grazing camp on the Rio Bravo, about three miles north of Fort Thorn, Doña Ana County, and first occupied on August 19, 1856, by Headquarters, 1st Dragoons. On August 27 Company F of that regiment arrived and was joined by companies H and I on September 8. These units, commanded by Major George A. H. Blake, were en route to Fort Tejon, California.

CAMP BOYD (*Camp Hillsboro*). Camp Boyd was located near Hillsboro, Sierra County. Although the site was occupied from June 1885 to September 1886, it was not referred to as Camp Boyd until March 1886; before then, it was apparently known as Camp Hillsboro. It was garrisoned by Company G, 8th Cavalry, and Company I, 10th Infantry, and served as a base for scouting expeditions and forwarding supplies to other posts.

CANTONMENT BURGWIN (*Fort Fernando de Taos*). Located about 10 miles south of Taos, on the Rio Grande del Rancho, a tributary of the Rio Grande, near the mouth of the Rio de las Ollas, and established August 14, 1852, the post was built under the supervision of 2nd Lieutenant Robert Ransom, 1st Dragoons. Intended to safeguard the Taos Valley against Indian depredations, it was named Cantonment Burgwin in honor of Captain John Henry Burgwin, who was mortally wounded during the battle with the Taos rebels on February 7, 1847. One citation reports that the post was also known as Fort Fernando de Taos. Abandoned May 18, 1860, it has since been reconstructed and occupied by the Fort Burgwin Research Center.

CAMP IN CANON LARGO. Located in San Miguel County, about 20 miles southeast of Fort Union, this temporary post was a base of operations for a 25-man detail of New Mexico Volunteers during the 30-day campaign against Comancheros in 1863.

CAMP CARSON. Located between Fort Craig and the Rio Grande River, probably in Socorro County, Camp Carson was a temporary tent post established in 1862 and garrisoned by militia assisting in the defense of the fort during Confederate activities in the area.

CEBOLETTA POST. A post was established sometime in September 1850 by elements of the 2nd Dragoons at the old village of Ceboletta (Sebolleta or Seboyeta), about 40 miles west of Albuquerque. It was intended to curb the illegal trading of guns and whisky to Indians. Apparently ineffectual, the post was discontinued in October 1851, with its last garrison transferred to Laguna.

CAMP CHUSCO VALLEY. This temporary field camp was established by Lieutenant Colonel Dixon Miles during the 1858 campaign against the Navajo. It was located 25 miles north of Gallup in McKinley County. A tenuous peace with the Navajo was effected on Christmas Day of the same year.

CLOVERDALE CAMP. Located at the village of Cloverdale in the extreme southwest corner of Hidalgo County, close to the Arizona line and less than 10 miles from the Mexican border, this post was established in 1882 to serve as an important depot and base of operations during the last campaign against the Apache. The camp was abandoned sometime in 1886.

CAMP CODY. A World War I training post established in 1917 and located two miles west of Deming, Luna County, Camp Cody was named in honor of William F. ("Buffalo Bill") Cody, celebrated plainsman, Army scout (1868–72), and later circus manager. A training center for the 34th ("Sandstorm") Division, the post's first contingent was the Minnesota National Guard, which formed the 135th Infantry Regiment. During its existence the camp trained some 30,000 troops. Camp Cody, discontinued in May 1920, was used as a Public Health Service sanitarium for veterans until 1922, when the facilities were transferred to the Deming Chamber of Commerce and operated by the Sisters of Holy Cross of Notre Dame until 1938.

POST AT COLUMBUS. CAMP FURLONG.

CAMP COMFORT. A temporary post established in 1858 and garrisoned by Company I, 8th Infantry, to observe the activities of the Mescalero Apache, Camp Comfort was located 25 miles southwest of Alamogordo in Otero County. The camp was abandoned sometime in 1859.

CAMP CONNELLY. A temporary Civil War encampment established in April 1862 on Governor Connelly's ranch property, "Los Pinos," at Polvadera, 12 miles north of Socorro, it was garrisoned by New Mexico Volunteers under General E. R. S. Canby.

FORT CONRAD (*Hay Camp*). Established by Major Marshall S. Howe, 2nd Dragoons, on September 8, 1851, and located on the west bank of the Rio Grande near Valverde, Socorro County, Fort Conrad was named in honor of Secretary of War Charles M. Conrad and served to curb the activities of hostile Indians and safeguard the travel route through the area. The post was abandoned on March 31, 1854, and replaced by Fort Craig 10 miles to the south. The fort's last garrison, consisting of Company K of the 2nd Dragoons and Company I of the 3rd Infantry, was then transferred to Fort Craig. For several years thereafter, Fort Conrad's site was used to raise forage for the new post and called Hay Camp.

CAMP COTTONWOOD. CAMP JOHNSON.

DETACHMENT AT COTTONWOODS. CAMP JOHNSON.

FORT CRAIG. Established by Captain Daniel T. Chandler, 3rd Infantry, on March 31, 1854, immediately after Fort Conrad was abandoned by one company each of the 2nd Dragoons and 3rd Infantry, which occupied the already built new quarters, Fort Craig was located on the right or west bank of the Rio Grande near the northern entrance of the Jornada del Muerte ("journey of death"). Intended to safeguard the area from bands of hostile Apache, the post was named for Captain Louis S. Craig, 3rd Infantry, murdered in California by Army deserters on June 6, 1852.

During the early months of the Civil War, the fort and its environs were protected by some 3,800 Federal regular, militia, and volunteer troops under Colonel E. R. S. Canby to contest an estimated 2,600 Confederates led by Brigadier General H. H. Sibley. The bloody major engagement on February 21, 1862, known as the Battle of Valverde, resulted from efforts to prevent the Confederates from using a river crossing by which they intended to cut off Fort Craig. After the sharp fighting was over, the Federals withdrew to the fort, and the victorious rebel column proceeded north toward Santa Fe, bypassing Fort Craig. The Union force lost 68 killed, 160 wounded, and 35 missing, while the Confederates lost 31 killed, 154 wounded, and 1 missing.

Abandoned early in 1885, the Fort Craig Military Reservation was transferred to the Interior Department on March 3, 1885. The ruins of the fort's 18 adobe buildings, located on the Armendaris Ranch, were donated in 1981 by its owners to the Archaeological Conservancy of Santa Fe for permanent preservation.

CUBERO POST. Located at the village of Cubero on the western edge of today's Laguna Indian Reservation in Valencia County, this temporary post was occupied by a small garrison of New Mexico Volunteers which guarded a store of ordnance supplies. On March 3, 1862, Confederate troops captured Cubero and seized 60 rifles and 3,000 rounds of ammunition.

FORT CUMMINGS. Located at the eastern entrance of Cook's Canyon, 53 miles west of the Rio Grande on the Mesilla-Tucson road in Luna County, Fort Cummings was established on October 2, 1863, in compliance with an order of Brigadier General James H. Carleton to curb the hostile Apache. The general reported "that except for Apache Pass, Arizona, the post guarded the most dangerous point on the southern route to California." Consisting of adobe-built, single-story buildings and surrounded by 10-foot-high adobe walls, the fort was named for Major Joseph Cummings, 1st New Mexico Cavalry, killed by Navajo Indians near Cañon Bonito on August 18, 1863. Evacuated and reoccupied twice between August 1873 and 1886, it was finally abandoned on October 3, 1886. The military reservation was turned over to the Interior Department on October 20, 1891. Numerous adobe ruins of the fort are in evidence on private ranch property.

CAMP DATIL. Located one and a half miles north of the town of Datil on Datil Creek, Catron County, this post was occupied from October 1885 to September 1886 by various garrisons, cavalry in 1885 and infantry in 1886. Camp Datil was intended to prevent raids by Gila Apache returning from incursions into Mexico.

CANTONMENT DAWSON. FORT WEBSTER.

DOÑA ANA POST. Located at Doña Ana in the Rio Grande Valley, about five miles northwest of Las Cruces, Doña Ana County, this post was first garrisoned on August 1, 1849, by elements of the 1st Dragoons and 3rd Infantry, to observe a Rio Grande crossing frequently used by Apache and to protect new settlements in the valley. Troops stationed there from August 1855 to February 1856 acted as escorts for the government's Pacific Railroad survey. Confederate troops commanded by General H. H. Sibley established a hospital here at the beginning of their New Mexico campaign in 1861.

CAMP EASTON. FORT BASCOM.

FORT EL GALLO. FORT WINGATE NO. 1.

FORT FAUNTLEROY. FORT WINGATE NO. 2.

CAMP AT FERNANDO DE TAOS. POST OF TAOS.

FORT FERNANDO DE TAOS. CANTONMENT BURGWIN.

FORT FILLMORE. Its site now located on the east bank of the Rio Grande, about six miles south of Mesilla, Doña Ana County, Fort Fillmore was established on September 23, 1851, by Lieutenant Colonel Dixon S. Miles, 3rd Infantry, with troops from the Post of El Paso (Fort Bliss), Texas. In 1851 the river flowed between Fort Fillmore and the town of Mesilla, but since then its course has changed.

Named for President Millard Fillmore, the post was designed to curb the activities of marauding bands of hostile Indians. A station on the Butterfield Overland Mail route and the El Paso–Fort Yuma stage line, the town of Mesilla was captured on July 25, 1861, by Confederate troops under Lieutenant Colonel John R. Baylor. Fort Fillmore was then commanded by Major Isaac Lynde, who more or less politely demanded that the Confederates surrender. When refused, he sent cavalry in a frontal attack that was both short-lived and eminently unsuccessful. The Federal troops precipitately withdrew to their fort, evacuating it the next day and retreating to Fort Stanton. Fort Fillmore was the only Western fort surrendered to an opponent without a defense. The fort was abandoned by the Confederates on July 8, 1862, in the face of the approach of a strong force of California Volunteers under General James H. Carleton. Mesilla and the fort were reoccupied by Lieutenant Colonel Edward E. Eyre with troops of the 1st California Cavalry. But on October 10, 1862, the soldiers were withdrawn and the post was abandoned.

FORT FLOYD. FORT MCLANE.

CAMP FURLONG (*Post at Columbus*). Established as Post at Columbus in early 1916 during General John J. Pershing's campaign against Pancho Villa, Camp Furlong was an encampment of tents and frame buildings important to the protection of the Mexican border three miles to the south. It was attacked by Pancho Villa and his army of raiders on March 13, 1916. Discontinued as a border post in 1918, the post was thereafter intermittently used by the Army until 1924. Remains of the camp, including the adobe-built headquarters building, are located adjacent to Pancho Villa State Park in the center of Columbus.

GALISTEO POST. A historic pueblo site located 22 miles south of Santa Fe, Galisteo first served as primarily a grazing camp for Army horses and mules, garrisoned by Companies F and I, 1st Dragoons, from November 1851 to January 1852. After the latter date, it was intermittently outposted by troopers until 1858.

CAMP GALLINA. CAMP SIERRA.

CAMP GARLAND. FORT STANTON.

CANTONMENT GARLAND. FORT THORN.

GILA DEPOT (*Camp on the Rio Gila; Depot on the Rio Gila; Rio Gila Depot*). This variously named temporary depot, located three miles south of the present town of Cliff in Grant County, served from May to July 1857 as the base camp for Colonel Benjamin L. E. Bonneville's expedition against the Apache in the upper Gila River region. Its approximate site was occupied temporarily in 1863 by elements of the 1st California Cavalry before they established Fort West about five miles to the northwest.

CAMP HACHITA. The town of Hachita, Grant County, was occupied sometime in 1886 by elements of the 6th Cavalry and 13th Infantry as a heliograph station during the final campaigns against the hostile Apaches.

HATCH'S RANCH POST. Located about 12 miles northeast of Anton Chico, on the west bank of the Gallinas River, in San Miguel County, Hatch's Ranch was a frequent stop for U.S. troops from Fort Union, 65 miles distant, engaged in campaigns against hostile Indians. The ranch, leased to the Army by Alexander Hatch, was mentioned as early as 1856 when its main building was described as a long, low adobe-built house with a 10-foot-high adobe wall around it. The ranch was intermittently garrisoned from 1859 to 1864 by elements of the 8th Infantry, Mounted Rifles, and New Mexico Volunteers. The site, on private property, contains remains of the ranch, including its large main building, 115 by 288 feet.

HAY CAMP. FORT CONRAD.

CAMP HENLEY. Located at Soldiers Farewell, 20 miles east of Lordsburg, Hidalgo County, Camp Henley was occupied by units of the 6th Cavalry and 13th Infantry during April–August 1886 as a base camp and heliograph station during the final campaigns against the Apaches.

CAMP HILLSBORO. CAMP BOYD.

JEMEZ POST. The historic Pueblo of Jemez in Sandoval County was the site of a temporary military post in the summer of 1849 for the campaign against the Navajo. In October it was reoccupied as a temporary headquarters. Colonel Thomas Fauntleroy later recommended that a fort be located there, but his suggestion was not carried out.

CAMP JOHNSON (*Detachment at Cottonwoods; Camp Cottonwood*). The site of this temporary post on the Rio Grande, first known as Detachment at Cottonwoods or Camp Cottonwood, is now located on New Mexico territory. In 1862, when it was a tent camp occupied by a company of California Cavalry Volunteers and Company A of the 3rd Artillery Volunteers under Captain William McCleave to observe Confederate activities along the Rio Grande, the site was officially considered to be on the Arizona side of the river, about 17 miles south of Fort Fillmore. However, because of the change in the course of the river and the political location of the eastern part of Arizona Territory into present New Mexico, the site is within today's Doña Ana County.

POST AT LA MESILLA. MESILLA POST.

LAGUNA POST. This temporary post, near the Laguna Pueblo on the Laguna Indian Reservation, Cibola County, was established by elements of the 2nd Dragoons after they had abandoned Cebolleta Post. It was established in October 1851 primarily to control illegal trading in the area, but like Cebolleta it was unsuccessful. In January 1852 the troops were withdrawn and transferred to Fort Defiance in Arizona.

CAMP LA HOYA. Located on the outskirts of the village of La Hoya, Socorro County, on the route of the scorching, sand-swept wastelands of the Jornada del Muerte east of the Rio Grande, this post was first established by dragoon troops as early as 1846 to guard the river crossing at this point. California Infantry Volunteers later intermittently garrisoned it until 1864 in opposition to Confederate troops in the area.

LAS CRUCES POST. This was a Civil War Quartermaster Corps supply depot and troop distribution center, occupying rented structures on the site of present-day modern Las Cruces in Doña Ana County.

LAS VEGAS POST. First garrisoned by Illinois and Missouri Volunteers during 1846–48, shortly after the government exercised jurisdiction in New Mexico, the town of Las Vegas in present San Miguel County became headquarters, February 1848–June 1851, for all military operations in the northern part of the territory. Its garrisons, housed in rented quarters, guarded the town and protected travel along the Santa Fe Trail.

CAMP LEWIS. Located about six miles south of Pecos, San Miguel County, Camp Lewis was a temporary post established in March 1862, prior to the Battle of Glorietta Pass (March 26–28), by units of the 1st Colorado Volunteers under Colonel John M. Chivington. The Federal command of 400 men left Camp Lewis on March 26 for Glorietta Pass, where it attacked and burned the Confederates' train of 80 supply wagons, forcing the rebel force to retreat down the Rio Grande and back into Texas.

CAMP LORING. An aggregate of various citations indicates that Camp Loring was the northernmost of military posts along the Rio Grande, located on the Red River, most probably in Taos County. It was apparently first mentioned in Army reports for 1858, when 75 men were there under the command of Lieutenant Laurence S. Baker. Colonel William Wing Loring, for whom this camp was named, became commander of the Department of New Mexico on March 22, 1861, but left that command when he defected to the Confederacy, turning it over to Colonel E. R. S. Canby on June 23, 1861.

CAMP LOS LUNAS. Located at Los Lunas, Valencia County, 22 miles south of Albuquerque, this camp was established on January 3, 1852, by Company G, 1st Dragoons, intended to curb the marauding and depredations by bands of Apaches and Navajo. Abandoned and reoccupied several times, Camp Los Lunas was finally wholly abandoned in October 1862.

LOS PINOS DEPOT (*Camp at Peralta; U.S. Depot*). Located on the east side of the Rio Grande at Peralta, Valencia County, this depot active during 1862–66 was known as Camp Peralta or U.S. Depot when first established. Los Pinos Depot was primarily a quartermaster storehouse and remount station, occupying rented quarters.

FORT LOWELL (*Camp Plummer*). Located on the Chama River southwest of the town of Tierra Amarilla, Rio Arriba County, the post was established on November 6, 1866, in compliance with an order of Brigadier General John Pope, and intended to protect the area's settlers against Ute and Jicarilla Apache raids. First called Camp Plummer for Captain Augustus H. Plummer, 37th Infantry, the post was designated Fort Lowell on July 13, 1868, in honor of Brigadier General Charles R. Lowell, who died on October 20, 1864, of wounds suffered at Cedar Creek, Virginia. Abandoned on July 27, 1869, as a military post, its buildings were taken over in 1872 as an agency for Ute and Apache tribes, transferred from Abiquiu, and consolidated with the Pueblo Agency in 1878.

CAMP LUNA. Located near Las Vegas and first established in 1904 as a National Guard encampment, its name was changed several times until 1929 when it was designated Camp Luna in honor of Maximiliano Luna, a well-known New Mexican who drowned in the Philippines during the Spanish-American War. In 1942 the War Department took it over as a training camp.

FORT LYON. FORT WINGATE NO. 2.

FORT MCLANE (*Camp Wheeler; Fort Webster; Fort Floyd; Fort McLean*). Located on the west side of the Rio Santa Rita, four miles south of the present town of Hurley, Grant County, this post was established as Camp Wheeler on September 16, 1860, by Major Isaac Lynde and two companies of the 7th Infantry, for the purpose of protecting the area's Santa Rita copper mines. The post was renamed Fort Floyd on December 1, 1860, for Secretary of War John B. Floyd. When Floyd, however, defected to the Confederacy, the post was redesignated Fort McLane on January 18, 1861, in honor of Captain George McLane, killed in a fight with Navajo on October 13, 1860. The post was occasionally referred to as Fort McLean or Fort Webster. It was abandoned on July 3, 1861, because of the exigencies of the Civil War and the garrison transferred to reinforce Fort Fillmore. In 1862 Fort McLane was reoccupied by elements of the 1st California Volunteers and garrisoned, probably intermittently, until the end of the war, when it was finally abandoned.

FORT MCLEAN. FORT MCLANE.

FORT MCRAE. Located about five miles west of the Jornada del Muerte and three miles east of the Rio Grande, the site of Fort McRae is on a mesa overlooking present-day Elephant Butte Reservoir, Sierra County. The post was established on April 13, 1863, by Captain Henry A. Greene, 1st California Infantry, to protect travel along the barren "journey of death" route and curb Indian marauding in the area. The post was named in honor of Captain Alexander McRae, 3rd Cavalry, killed on February 21, 1862, during the Battle of Valverde. Fort McRae was abandoned on October 30, 1876. The military reservation was finally turned over to the Interior Department on July 22, 1884. Stone foundations of the post's adobe-built structures remain in evidence on private ranch property.

CAMP MADDOX. This post, consisting of a ranch building and tents, was located about seven miles north of Glenwood in Catron County. It was established in 1885 by cavalry troops in response to the Apache uprising led by Chief Geronimo. Camp Maddox was abandoned sometime in 1886.

CAMP MAGOFFIN. Two chronologically contradictory citations appear for this post. According to National Archives records, Camp Magoffin was "occupied by Companies I and K, 8th Infantry and Company C, 3rd Infantry, in April 1854," without specifying location. The second citation reports the post was located in the present White Mountain Wilderness Reserve, near the town of Alto in southern Lincoln County, and occupied 1863–65.

FORT MARCY (*Post at Santa Fe*). Located adjacent to the Palace of the Governors in Santa Fe, the oldest government building still in use in the United States, Fort Marcy was established on August 23, 1846, by Brigadier General Stephen Watts Kearny. Named for Secretary of War William Marcy, it was the first U.S. Army fort in New Mexico. The site was selected by 1st Lieutenant William H. Emory, Corps of Topographical Engineers, and 1st Lieutenant Jeremy F. Gilmer, Corps of Engineers, who superintended construction of an irregularly shaped earthwork and a magazine-equipped blockhouse on a 60-to-100-foot-high elevation, about 1,000 yards to the northeast of the central plaza, commanding all of Santa Fe.

Fort Marcy was deactivated and its garrison withdrawn on August 23, 1867. From then until 1875, Santa Fe's military establishment was officially known as Post at Santa Fe, with officers' quarters, enlisted men's barracks, and buildings for the storing of military supplies. For a time during this period, it served as headquarters for the Military District of New Mexico. Reactivated in 1875, Fort Marcy was again abandoned in the spring of 1891 and turned over to the Interior Department on October 7, 1891, to be disposed of at public auction. On November 21, 1891, however, the directive was rescinded and Fort Marcy was once more reoccupied. Finally, on October 10, 1894, the post was permanently abandoned, with the military reservation transferred to the Interior Department on June 28, 1895.

MESILLA POST (*Post at La Mesilla*). The historic town of Mesilla on the Rio Grande, three miles southwest of Las Cruces, Doña Ana County, was occupied on August 1, 1861, by Lieutenant Colonel John R. Baylor after capturing nearby Union-held Fort Fillmore. He made Mesilla his headquarters and proclaimed possession of the territory in the name of the Confederacy. A year later, Carleton's California Column recaptured Mesilla. During 1863–64, troops of the 5th California Infantry Volunteers and New Mexico Infantry Volunteers garrisoned Mesilla Post, occupying rented quarters.

MEXICAN BORDER PATROL POSTS. The Mexican Revolution that erupted in 1910 and raged until late in 1916 involved the United States in the politico-military struggle. Overt Mexican actions that threatened American territory resulted in the assignment of U.S. troops all along the border from California to Texas. A number of New Mexico towns in areas near the border served as temporary posts for the patrols. With very few exceptions, particularly Columbus and El Paso, most of these posts were transitory, with troops shifting from one place to another in response to incidents along the international border.

CAMP MIMBRES (*Camp on the Rio Mimbres*). Located 20 miles northwest of Deming and less than 2 miles southwest of Dwyer, Luna County, the town of Mimbres served as a supply depot for 1st California Cavalry Volunteers from August 10, 1863, to September 16, 1864, and as a base of operations against the Apache in the Florida Mountains.

CAMP MISCHLER. This was a temporary post established in 1862 and occupied by an overflow of Union troops reinforcing Fort Craig, a few miles to the north on the Rio Grande in Socorro County.

CAMP OJO CALIENTE. Located on the right bank of the Alamosa River, 15 miles northwest of Monticello, in the extreme southwest corner of Socorro County, Camp Ojo Caliente was established in 1859 as an outpost of Fort Craig. Nine adobe buildings, a few of them substantially large, were erected and garrisoned by troops from the fort. The post was abandoned after the outbreak of the Civil War.

During the latter part of the 1860s, the post's buildings were occupied as the agency headquarters for the Warm Spring Apache Reservation, accommodating between 1,500 and 2,000 Indians. But by 1877 most of the Apache left the reservation and returned to their traditional homes. Those who remained, about 450, were transferred to the San Carlos Reservation in Arizona. Because of renewed problems with the Apache during 1877–82, troops were again posted at Ojo Caliente. In the late autumn of 1879, mostly Chiricahua Apache led by Victorio attacked the Ojo Caliente garrison, killed eight 9th Cavalry soldiers and made off with 46 horses. The post was abandoned in the spring of 1882.

CAMP AT PERALTA. LOS PINOS DEPOT.

CAMP PINOS ALTOS. Located seven miles north of Silver City, the town of Pinos Altos in

Grant County was a prosperous mining center in 1863. Because of threats posed by Indian marauders and white banditti, the town was posted from time to time by elements of the California Cavalry to protect the mining area.

CAMP PLUMMER. FORT LOWELL.

RAYADO POST. A post was established by elements of companies G and I, 1st Dragoons, at Rayado, Colfax County, on May 3, 1850, to safeguard the immigrant travel routes in the area. The post occupied rented quarters in a large mansion belonging to affluent landowner Lucien B. Maxwell. The troops were withdrawn on August 7, 1851. It was reoccupied between July 16 and September 18, 1854, in apparently rent-free quarters.

CAMP (WILLIAM C.) REID. A World War II post located at Clovis, Curry County, Camp Reid was established on April 25, 1942, to house and train railroaders from across the nation for service during the war. The camp was named for Captain William Clifford Reid, attorney for the Santa Fe Railroad, who organized Company F, 1st Territorial Infantry, in 1898 for service during the Spanish-American War. Camp Reid was occupied by the 713th Railway Operating Battalion, or "Santa Fe Battalion," sponsored by the railroad. This unit later served in North Africa, Italy, France, and Germany.

RICHMOND POST. Located on the Gila River at Richmond (renamed Virden in 1916), Hidalgo County, this post was established on May 3, 1882, by Captain George K. Brady, 23rd Infantry, with companies A, B, E, and G, for the purpose of scouting for Indian hostiles. The post was abandoned in September 1883.

CAMP ON THE RIO GILA. GILA DEPOT.

DEPOT ON THE RIO GILA. GILA DEPOT.

RIO GILA DEPOT. GILA DEPOT.

CAMP ON THE RIO MIMBRES. CAMP MIMBRES.

CAMP ROBLEDO. Located north of Las Cruces near Mt. Robledo and Fort Thorn, in Doña Ana County, this intermittently used camp was occupied 1861–63 by both Union and Confederate troops during campaigns against the hostile Apache.

CAMP ROSWELL. Located at Roswell, Chaves County, this was a temporary post established in November 1878, during the turbulent Lincoln County War, by Captain Henry Carroll with Company F, 10th Cavalry, for the purpose of curbing cattle rustling and preventing murderous incursions during the feud. The post was discontinued in February 1879.

SAN ISIDORO POST. Located at San Isidoro (Isidro), a small village two miles north of Las Cruces, Doña Ana County, the post was established on November 17, 1849, by Captain W. H. Gordon, 3rd Infantry, with Company H, aggregating 49 men. The post was abandoned in June 1850.

CAMP SAN PEDRO. A temporary post located at the village of San Pedro on the Jornada del Muerte emigrant travel route, 14 miles southeast of Socorro, it was occupied by California Infantry troops for a period during 1863–64.

POST AT SANTA FE. FORT MARCY.

PRESIDIO OF SANTA FE. Founded as La Villa Real de la Santa Fe de San Francisco in the spring of 1610 by Pedro de Peralta, governor and captain-general of New Mexico, the pueblo evolved as the Presidio of Santa Fe, the oldest capital within the boundaries of the present United States. The flags of four governments—Spain, Mexico, Confederate States of America, and the United States—have flown over its old Palace of Governors.

Excepting the period of the Pueblo Revolt, 1680–93, Santa Fe was a permanently garrisoned town during the regimes of both Spain and Mexico. Some 3,000 Pueblo Indians, after a five-day siege, forced the Spanish government there to surrender. The Spaniards fled south, with most of them resettling near El Paso. For 12 years the Indians commanded Santa Fe, razing churches and burning much that remained of the Spanish culture. In 1692, after several fruitless attempts to regain the presidio, Diego de Vargas took an expedition up the Santa Fe River and reoccupied the capital. Vargas at that time described Santa Fe as a pueblo-fortification with neither windows nor doors facing outward, with but one entrance, its entirety protected by embrasured towers and trenches.

Following the reconquest, the pueblo outgrew its walls. The government palace was a defensible fortress with walls five feet thick and flanked by two towers, the one on the east or right housing a chapel, the one on the west an arsenal with an attached dungeon. To the north, surrounded by walls, the grounds of the Palace of Governors extended for two blocks and included a patio, soldiers' barracks (reportedly fortified at one time), woodsheds, and outbuildings. The central plaza in front of the palace served as a *plaza de armas*. This complex later became a part of the U.S. military establishment, beginning on August 18, 1846, after occupation of the town by Brigadier General Stephen Watts Kearny and his troops. (See: FORT MARCY.)

FORT SANTA RITA. The "old post at the copper mines" was the private defense erected, probably in 1804, by Francisco Manuel Elguea to protect the Santa Rita copper mines in present Grant County, discovered in 1800. Both the fort and the mines were abandoned in the fall of 1838 because of repeated Apache incursions. The post was garrisoned by U.S. troops from April 1851 to September 1852, when it was replaced by Fort Webster. The old fort at the mines was built of adobe in the shape of an equilateral triangle with round towers at the three corners, surrounded by walls four feet thick. (See: FORT WEBSTER.)

SANTA TOMAS POST. Located six miles south of Mesilla at the town of Santa Tomas, Doña Ana County, this temporary post was established on December 2, 1854, by Captain W. Bowman with Company A, 3rd Infantry, aggregating 64 men, and abandoned on February 8, 1855.

FORT SELDEN. Located about a mile and a half from the east bank of the Rio Grande, 17 miles north of Las Cruces, at the southern end of the Jornada del Muerte travel route, in Doña Ana County, Fort Selden was established on May 8, 1865, in compliance with orders of General James H. Carleton. Intended to protect settlers in the Mesilla Valley and emigrant travel through the area, the post was named for Colonel Henry R. Selden, veteran of the Mexican and Civil Wars.

It took two and a half years of construction before the adobe-built post was considered completed. The complex included officers' quarters, barracks for two companies of troops, a 10-bed hospital, powder magazine, offices, storehouses, a bakery, workshops, and four corrals. Evacuated on March 11, 1877, when the railroad came through, the post was reoccupied on December 25, 1880, for Mexican border patrol duties. Captain Arthur MacArthur commanded the post from 1884 to 1886. His son, later General Douglas

MacArthur, spent part of his boyhood there. On August 23, 1890, Fort Selden was designated a subpost of Fort Bayard. The fort was permanently abandoned in 1891. Now the property of the state of New Mexico, the old fort has been completely restored as a state monument.

CAMP SHANNON. A World War I encampment, Camp Shannon was established at Hachita, Grant County, on March 11, 1917, by Colonel J. C. Waterman and companies F and H, 24th Infantry. The camp became a subpost of Camp Furlong on August 15, 1920, and was abandoned on June 30, 1922.

CAMP SHERMAN. This temporary post, located about 30 miles west of Winston, near Taylor Creek, in Catron County, was established in 1879 for the purpose of distributing supplies to Indians living in the Gila Mountains.

CAMP SIERRA (*Camp Gallina*). Located at the town of Gallina, Rio Arriba County, Camp Sierra was a temporary encampment established by Company K, 8th Infantry, in 1858, originally called Camp Gallina. The site was reportedly occupied for a brief time by Confederate forces in 1861.

SOCORRO POST. A post was established in rented quarters by Company E, 2nd Dragoons, in November 1849 at Socorro on the west bank of the Rio Grande for the purpose of protecting settlements in the area from Indian attack. The post was abandoned in 1851. The post was reactivated for a short period in 1863 and again during 1877–81. Between 1867 and 1890, the town was the center of one of the richest mining areas in the country.

FORT STANTON (*Camp Garland*). Originally situated on the Rio Bonito, about 10 miles west of Lincoln, on a site selected in mid-March 1855 by Colonel John Garland, 8th Infantry, the post was established on May 4, 1855, for the purpose of controlling the hostile Mescalero and White Mountain Apache. Lieutenant Colonel Dixon S. Miles established a camp named for Colonel Garland near the post's first site and built two blockhouses while the permanent post was under construction. When it was completed, it was designated Fort Stanton in honor of Captain Henry W. Stanton, 1st Dragoons, killed by Apache on January 19, 1855, in the near environs of the fort. The first commander of the post was Captain Jefferson Van Horne, 2nd Infantry.

Fort Stanton was evacuated and partially destroyed by the Federal garrison on August 2, 1861, in response to the invasion of New Mexico by Confederate troops from Texas. Held temporarily by the Confederates, it was reoccupied by Colonel Kit Carson, 1st New Mexico Infantry, in the fall of 1862, in compliance with orders of Brigadier General James H. Carleton. Fort Stanton was partially rebuilt in 1868, but reconstruction ceased in June 1869, when it was decided to build a new post two miles to the north, its present location, where substantial structures of stone were erected.

On August 17, 1896, Fort Stanton was abandoned as a military reservation and turned over to the Interior Department. On April 27, 1899, its buildings were transferred to the Public Health Service for use as a U.S. Marine Hospital. In June 1953 the Federal government discontinued the hospital for reasons of economy. The state of New Mexico obtained title to the property and now operates it as the Fort Stanton State Tuberculosis Hospital.

STAR FORT. FORT UNION.

FORT SUMNER. Located in the Bosque Redondo ("round grove") on the east bank of the Pecos River, south of the present town of Fort Sumner, De Baca County, this post was established on November 30, 1862, on the site of a trading post operated since 1851, in compliance with orders of Brigadier General James H. Carleton. He planned use of the post as a compound or reservation for the confinement of the Navajo Indians. Construction was performed by the troops of Carleton's California Column. It was named for Major General Edwin Vose Sumner.

In 1863 Colonel Kit Carson, 1st New Mexico Infantry, marched some 7,000 Navajo hundreds of miles ("the Long Walk") from Canyon de Chelly to Fort Sumner where several hundred Mescalero Apache were confined at the same time. Small bands of them, from time to time, attempted to escape, but they were tracked down and returned. By 1868 they had become pacified and faithfully promised to be amenable. Public sympathy influenced General William T. Sherman to allow them to return to their ancestral homes.

The post was then put up for auction. It was sold to affluent Lucien B. Maxwell, who transformed the officers' quarters into a 20-room mansion. In 1881 Billy the Kid was killed by Pat Garrett in one of its bedrooms. The Army transferred the military reservation, with the exception of its cemetery, to the Interior Department on March 25, 1871.

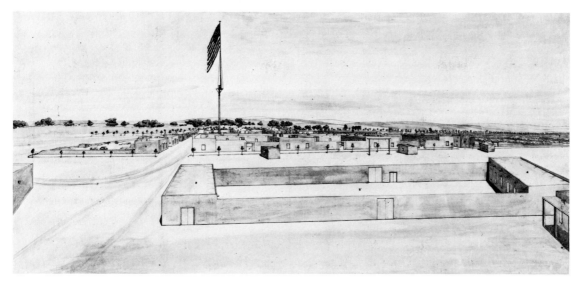

FORT SUMNER. View from the east side. (Courtesy of the National Archives.)

POST OF TAOS (*Camp at Fernando de Taos*). Known to explorers, missionaries, and colonizers from the time of Coronado (1540–42), and first settled in 1617, the old picturesque town of Taos is located about 55 miles northeast of Santa Fe. After Governor William Bent and five other Americans were murdered during the Taos Uprising of 1847, Missouri Volunteer troops were posted there, occupying rented adobe buildings, also known as "Camp at Fernando de Taos." From 1848 to 1852, Taos Post was garrisoned by U.S. Dragoons. Abandoned on June 14, 1852, the post was reportedly regarrisoned 1860–61.

CAMP TECOLATE. Located 10 miles south of Las Vegas, Camp Tecolate was a forage camp established for Fort Union. According to *New Mexico Place Names*, the village of Tecolate, from 1850 to 1860, was "one of a chain of posts established by the U.S. Army for forage and corn during the campaign against the Indians."

FORT THORN (*Cantonment Garland*). Located at the upper end of the Mesilla Valley, on the west bank of the Rio Grande, just north of the present town of Hatch, Doña Ana County, this post was established as Cantonment Garland on December 24, 1853, by Captain Israel B. Richardson, 3rd Infantry, and garrisoned by troops from abandoned Fort Webster. It was intended to guard the travel routes through the area from Apache and outlaws. When construction of a 600-by-520-foot defense was completed, the post was designated Fort Thorn in honor of 1st Lieutenant Herman Thorn, 2nd Infantry, who drowned in the Colorado River on October 16, 1849.

Occupying a site that proved to be unhealthful because of its proximity to a large reeking marsh, the post was abandoned in March 1859. Temporarily reoccupied by Confederate troops during 1861–62, Fort Thorn was recaptured on July 5, 1862, by troops of the California Column under Lieutenant Colonel Edward E. Eyre, which garrisoned it until sometime in 1863.

CAMP TOME. A temporary Army tent encampment, occupied by 20 troops from the Post of Albuquerque, Camp Tome was established in November 1848 very near the old Spanish village of Tome east of the Rio Grande, five miles northeast of Belen in Valencia County. The post was intended to protect local settlers from Indian incursions.

TORREON FORT. This stone tower is one of Lincoln's earliest structures. Built in the 1850s, its thick high walls protected the area's Spanish-Americans against bands of hostile Apache. The tower has recently been reconstructed as a tourist attraction.

FORT TULAROSA. Located on the left bank of Tularosa Creek, a half-mile from the center of the town of Aragon, Catran County, Fort Tularosa was established on April 30, 1872, by Captain Frederick W. Coleman, 15th Infantry, to provide protection for the new Apache reservation's agency headquarters. Elements of the 8th Cavalry and 15th Infantry garrisoned the fort. Plans were made to move the post to Old Horse Springs, 18 miles distant, but the idea was dropped when the reservation Indians, unhappy at Tularosa, returned to Ojo Caliente. Fort Tularosa was abandoned on November 26, 1874.

CAMP TUNI-CHA. A temporary outpost located near Newcomb, San Juan County, it was established sometime in 1858 and posted by

Company K, 8th Infantry, to maintain peace in the Tuni-Cha Valley occupied by the Navajo.

FORT UNION (*Star Fort*). The largest U.S. Army post guarding the nineteenth-century southwestern frontier, Fort Union was established on July 26, 1851, on a site already occupied by troops in camp. Strategically located near the junction of the Mountain and Cimarron branches of the Santa Fe Trail, about 25 miles northeast of Las Vegas, Fort Union was established by Lieutenant Colonel Edwin Vose Sumner, 1st Dragoons, commander of the Ninth Military Department (New Mexico Territory) as part of a general revision of defenses in the territory. It was aimed at removing the soldiers from the temptations of the towns and relocating them nearer the ranges of the Indians. The colonel moved his own headquarters to the eastern frontier and on the west bank of Coyote Creek, where wood, water, and forage were available.

The first of three forts that ultimately occupied the site consisted of a shabby collection of log buildings, but it served for a decade as the base for military activities in the area and as a key way station on the Santa Fe Trail. Fort Union also became the principal quartermaster depot of the Southwest, receiving supplies from the States and forwarding them to far-flung posts throughout the territory. When the Civil War broke out in 1861, Fort Union took on a new importance since a Confederate invasion of New Mexico was anticipated. Colonel Edward R. S. Canby, commanding Federal troops in the territory, in August ordered the immediate construction of a second fort across Coyote Creek from the first site. It was an earthwork fortification in the form of an eight-pointed star, with quarters in the demilunes, ditches, parapets, and bombproofs, all completed the same year. The new defense was known as Star Fort.

The need for additional facilities and services, combined with the steady deterioration of the earthwork, determined Brigadier General James H. Carleton in 1863 to order construction of a new post. The third and present site of Fort Union was located just north of Star Fort. Construction, begun almost at once, lasted until 1869. Most of the buildings' brick and adobe ruins are now in evidence at the fort. The new complex included ample quarters for officers and enlisted men, commodious warehouses, offices, workshops, and corrals. The ordnance arsenal occupied the site of the first post. Throughout its life, Fort Union was the principal supply depot for the Department of New Mexico.

The arrival of the Santa Fe Railroad in 1879 lessened Fort Union's importance, with its arsenal discontinued in 1882 and its supply activities largely ended. The fort was abandoned

FORT UNION. Ruins of the warehouse walls at the quartermaster depot. (Photograph by G. S. Cattanach, Jr. Courtesy of the National Park Service.)

FORT UNION. Ruins of the fireplaces and chimneys of the officers' quarters. (Photograph by Jack Boucher. Courtesy of the National Park Service.)

on February 21, 1891, and left in charge of a small caretaking detachment. On April 1, 1894, the reservation, with its grounds and buildings, reverted to the proprietors of the original land grant. Fort Union's preserved ruins and the site they occupy are now a national monument.

U.S. DEPOT. LOS PINOS DEPOT.

CAMP VALVERDE. A temporary encampment located in Socorro County, near Fort Craig and the site where the Battle of Valverde was fought in 1862, Camp Valverde was established sometime in 1864 and occupied by Company K, 1st California Cavalry Volunteers.

CAMP VIGILANCE. A temporary troop encampment located near Albuquerque, it was established in May 1852 by Major George A. M. Blake, 1st Dragoons, with companies F, G, and I, 1st Dragoons, and companies B and C, 3rd Infantry, aggregating 430 men. According to National Archives records, the post was discontinued in July 1852 but reoccupied for a time in 1853.

CAMP VINCENT. Located about 100 yards southwest of the junction of Taylor and Beaver Creeks in the Gila Wilderness, in Catron or Grant County, this temporary post was established some-

time in 1879 to defend the area against raids perpetrated by Victorio's Apache.

FORT WEBSTER. FORT MCLANE.

FORT WEBSTER (*Cantonment Dawson*). A confusing set of at least three sites was occupied by different editions of Fort Webster. Fort McLane was even considered as a possible fourth site. The main party of the United States-Mexican Boundary Commission in April 1851 occupied the old private Mexican defense, known as Fort Santa Rita, erected in 1804 by Francisco Manuel Elguea to protect the mines. An escort of one company of infantry, commanded by Captain Louis S. Craig, 3rd Infantry, accompanied the commission. The post was called Cantonment Dawson. After the party of commissioners left in October to continue the survey, the post was occupied by one company each of the 3rd Infantry and the 2nd Dragoons, and renamed Fort Webster for Secretary of State Daniel Webster.

On September 9, 1852, the post was shifted to the Rio Mimbres, about 14 miles northeast of the Santa Rita mines, where a new fort was erected under the command of Major Gouverneur Morris, 3rd Infantry, keeping the original designation of Fort Webster. Colonel Joseph K. F. Mansfield of the Inspector General's Department visited the post in October 1853 and recommended that it be moved to the Gila River where it could protect the emigrant travel route. Fort Webster was then abandoned on December 20, 1853, and its garrison transferred to Fort Thorn.

Still another Fort Webster is said to have existed briefly at the village of Mowry (Mimbres Station of the Butterfield mail route) [in Grant County]. It is reported that when the Overland mail route was abandoned at the outset of the Civil War, the station was converted into a fort called Fort Webster under the command of a Major Mowry, who resigned to join the Confederacy. If such a post existed, it was not an army post. [Robert W. Frazer, *Forts of the West* (1965), p. 107]

Brigadier General John Pope, apparently in 1866 established a temporary post, retaining the old name of Fort Webster, near the headwaters of the Rio Mimbres as a defense against hostile Apache. Its location is shown on Colton's 1877 map of the Arizona and New Mexico territories, placing it on the west bank of the river, some 15 miles north of Santa Rita. A replica of the first Fort Webster, originally at the Santa Rita copper mines, has been built three-quarter size at Pinos Altos, 18 miles away. (See: FORT MCLANE and FORT SANTA RITA.)

FORT WEST. Located on the east side of the Gila River, near its headwaters in the Pinos Altos Mountains north of Silver City, Grant County, Fort West was established by Major William McCleave, 1st California Cavalry, on January 24, 1863, in compliance with an order of Brigadier General James H. Carleton. Intended to safeguard the area's mining interests, the post was named in honor of Brigadier General Joseph Rodman West. The fort was abandoned on January 8, 1864, with its purpose assumed by Fort Cummings. Much of the building materials on the post were salvaged at the turn of the century and used in the construction of a nearby ranch headquarters.

CAMP WHEELER. FORT MCLANE.

FORT WINGATE NO. 1 (*Fort El Gallo*). Located at El Gallo, "the great spring," at the present-day town of San Rafael, three miles south of modern Grants, Cibola County, Fort Wingate was established on October 22, 1862, by Lieutenant Colonel J. Francisco Chávez, 1st New Mexico Infantry, pursuant to an order of Brigadier General James H. Carleton, as a forward post in the plan for Colonel Kit Carson's campaign against the Navajo the next year. The post was named in honor of Captain Benjamin Wingate, 5th Infantry, who was mortally wounded in the Battle of Valverde. Paul Horgan, in his *Lamy of Santa Fe* (1975), identifies the post as Fort El Gallo. The fort was abandoned in July 1868 and its last garrison transferred to Fort Wingate No. 2.

FORT WINGATE NO. 2 (*Fort Fauntleroy; Fort Lyon*). Located at Ojo del Oso (Bear Springs) on the road from Albuquerque to Fort Defiance, Arizona, in McKinley County, this post was established on August 31, 1860, by Captain William Chapman, 5th Infantry, and named for Colonel Thomas T. Fauntleroy, 1st Dragoons. When the colonel resigned his commission to join the Confederacy, the post was renamed Fort Lyon on September 25, 1861, in honor of General Nathaniel Lyon, killed in action on August 10, 1861, during the Battle of Wilson's Creek, Missouri. Although its garrison was withdrawn on September 10, 1861, because of the invasion of New Mexico territory by Confederate troops from Texas, a U.S. Army mail station was maintained there. Despite its new designation as Fort Lyon, it was referred to as Fort Fauntleroy in official correspondence throughout the Civil War.

When the fort was reoccupied in 1868 by the troops that had formerly garrisoned Fort Win-

FORT WINGATE NO. 2. (Photograph by Ben Wittick. Courtesy of the State Museum, Palace of Governors, Santa Fe, New Mexico.)

gate No. 1, it was redesignated similarly. Its garrison was withdrawn in 1911, leaving a small detachment there until March 19, 1912, at which time it was put in charge of a caretaking detail. In 1918, during World War I, the military reservation was taken over by the Ordnance Department for the storage of munitions and the Army designated it the Wingate Ordnance Depot. In 1925 a part of the reservation's buildings were turned over to the Bureau of Indian Affairs for use as a school for Navajo. In August 1960 the post was designated Fort Wingate Ordnance Depot, then redesignated Fort Wingate Army Depot when the Army was reorganized in 1962.

FORT ALBANY. FORT FREDERICK.

FORT ALDEN. Convincing solicitations made to the Marquis de Lafayette during the spring of 1778 by Cherry Valley's inhabitants brought about the construction of a strong fort, a stockade enclosing two blockhouses, to protect one of the most exposed situations in the Schoharie Valley. The fort was named for Colonel Ichabod Alden, who arrived in July of the same year with Continental troops to garrison the new post. Several months later, on November 11, the long-feared enemy attack came. A force of 200 Tories and more than 500 Indians under the dual command of Captain Walter Butler and Mohawk chieftain Joseph Brant caught the settlement by surprise. The fort barely withstood three hours of repeated assaults and sniping, during which numbers of Tories and Indians roamed through the village killing, pillaging, and burning. Colonel Alden's inefficiency and stupid obstinacy led to his own death and the killing of 15 soldiers. Twenty-two noncombatants, among them women and children, were killed, and 71 prisoners were taken, most of them released the next day.

Fort Alden was garrisoned until the summer of 1779, when its troops were withdrawn to join the Sullivan-Clinton campaign against the Iroquois troops. On April 24, 1780, Cherry Valley was again invaded by a party of about 80 Indians led by 2 Tories. Eight people were killed and 14 were taken captive. What structures remained after the 1778 raid—the fort, church, and a few houses—were put to the torch, leaving the settlement a complete desolation. Fort Alden's site is within the Cherry Valley Cemetery, close by its gates.

AMERSFORT BLOCKHOUSE. A blockhouse erected by the Dutch sometime during the 1630s, it was located in the Flatlands section of Brooklyn. Intermittently garrisoned, it probably survived until the early 1660s.

FORT AMHERST. FORT CROWN POINT.

FORT AMHERST (*Fort Miller*). This fort was erected in 1759 during the French and Indian War on the south bank of Halfway Brook in present Glens Falls, Warren County, to support a stockaded blockhouse built in 1755 on the north bank of the stream. The fort was surrounded on

New York

Note: Entries for New York City Revolutionary War defenses are listed by borough on pages 596–605, immediately following New York State listings.

three sides by a ditch, with its rear protected by an impassable swamp. Originally called Fort Miller, it was renamed Fort Amherst to honor General Jeffrey Amherst. The site, known as the Garrison Grounds, was the location of a fortified camp during 1757–58. Fort Amherst was rebuilt in 1775 and occupied by Baron Riedesel's Hessian troops in 1777. It was destroyed in October 1780 by Major Christopher Carleton and his raiders. The fort site is located at Halfway Brook and Glenwood Avenue in Glens Falls.

FORT ANNE (*Queen's Fort; Fort Schuyler; Mud Fort*). A veteran of several wars, Fort Anne was strategically located on the Champlain-Hudson route, at present Fort Ann, a summer resort village in Washington County, about halfway between Whitehall and Fort Edward. There is an unfortunate lack of credible historical data regarding the number of forts that occupied the site, but reason suggests that most of the fortifications were rebuilds.

The site, at the confluence of Wood Creek and Halfway Brook (formerly Cheshire's Brook), was first occupied as a fortified camp in 1690 by a motley army commanded by Governor Fitz-John Winthrop of Connecticut, but the planned land attack against Montreal was aborted because of contagions of smallpox and dysentery. Two years later Winthrop, leading another invasion attempt that was also aborted, again camped on Fort Anne's site. In 1709, during Queen Anne's War, the governors of four provinces agreed to pool their armed forces under General Francis Nicholson and invade Canada. The route of march was lined with forts. Fort Anne, the northernmost, was originally called the Queen's Fort or Fort Schuyler (for Colonel Peter Schuyler), but was renamed for the queen two years later.

Fort Anne was built by General Nicholson. A palisaded 140-foot square, it enclosed two large log buildings for the garrison. At each angle was a 20-foot-square bastion or blockhouse. The fort's water supply was obtained from Kane's Falls, one mile to the northwest, ingeniously piped through cedar pump logs. Before he withdrew with his decimated army, Nicholson burned the fort, but in 1711 he returned and rebuilt it, but the fort was allowed to deteriorate. Shortly after the outbreak of the French and Indian War, a new fort was erected on the site. In 1769 another fort, known as the Mud Fort, an earthwork, was constructed at Needhamville, a suburb of Fort Ann village. In 1777 Fort Anne served as a fortified refuge for Patriot soldiers retreating from Fort Ticonderoga. After the Battle of Saratoga, a final fort, probably a fifth edition, was erected on Fort Anne's site. The fort was surrendered to and burned by Major Christopher Carleton in October 1780 during his series of raids toward Albany.

FORT ARNOLD. WEST POINT'S FORTS.

ARNOT BARRACKS. A Civil War facility at Elmira, Arnot Barracks also served as a prison for Confederate prisoners of war. On August 26, 1984, ground was broken for a monument to commemorate the camp where nearly 3,000 Confederate soldiers died.

CAMP ARTHUR. A Civil War training post located on Staten Island, Camp Arthur was active during 1862.

FORT AU FER. Strategic Point au Fer, a tongue of land on the New York shore of Lake Champlain, about a mile south of Rouses Point, Clinton County, was a fortified military post garrisoned first by Americans and then by the British. William Gilliland, Irish land entrepreneur in the Champlain Valley, persuaded British authorities during the early 1770s to allow him to erect on the point a large stone building that came to be known as the White House. During the early days of the Continental Army's disastrous invasion of Canada in 1775, General John Sullivan ordered the "White House" fortified and provided with a strong brick barracks surrounded by a continually manned stockade. Throughout the years of the war, Point au Fer was a rendezvous for transient armies. The White House was destroyed by fire probably in 1805. Archaeological explorations, carried on intermittently for years in this century revealed that not far from the White House was a cemetery in which more than 160 Revolutionary War smallpox victims were buried.

AURANIA STOCKADE. Located in the present city of Rensselaer, this was a stockade erected in June 1624 by 30 Walloons (French Protestants) who had joined 18 Dutch families to colonize the area. The site of Aurania Stockade is located on Riverside Avenue in the city of Rensselaer near restored Fort Crailo.

BALCARRES REDOUBT. SARATOGA BATTLEFIELD FORTS.

FORT BALLSTON. Located at present Ballston Spa in Saratoga County, Fort Ballston was a fortified stockade enclosing the village's log meetinghouse. Probably erected in 1772 and surviving until about 1783, its site is on Front Street.

BATH BEACH BLOCKHOUSE. Located near the shore of Gravesend Bay in the Bath Beach section of Brooklyn, this blockhouse was erected in 1813 under the direction of Brigadier General Joseph G. Swift to prevent an enemy landing during the War of 1812.

BEEMIS HEIGHTS. FORT NEILSON, under SARATOGA BATTLEFIELD FORTS.

FORT BENDER. This War of 1812 defense was built on May 14, 1814, at Deep Hollow on present Lake Avenue, near Ravine Avenue, in Rochester. It was designed to repel an invasion inland by Sir James Yeo's fleet anchored at the mouth of the Genesee River.

BENSON'S POINT REDOUBT. A War of 1812 defense erected in 1814, it was located in the area between present 2nd and 3rd avenues, north of 106th Street, in New York City.

CAMP BLACK. MITCHEL FIELD.

BLOCKHOUSE NO. 1. A War of 1812 defense built in 1814, it was located within present New York City's Central Park, near its 7th Avenue entrance at 110th Street. Known as the Old Stone Tower, the blockhouse surmounted a high rock to command the surrounding terrain.

BLOCKHOUSE NO. 2. This War of 1812 defense, built in 1814, was located on the south side of present 114th Street, west of Morningside Avenue, in New York City.

BLOCKHOUSE NO. 3. A War of 1812 defense built in 1814, it was located on the south side of present 121st Street, west of Morningside Avenue, in New York City.

BLOCKHOUSE NO. 4. A War of 1812 defense erected in 1814, it was located on the south side of present 123rd Street, near 10th Avenue, in Morningside Park, New York City.

CAMP BLUEFIELDS. Located near the town of Blauvelt ("blue field") in Rockland County, Camp Bluefields was a World War I prisoner of war camp occupying the grounds of a former National Guard target range, now a county park.

FORT BLUNDER. FORT MONTGOMERY.

CASTLE BOGARDUS. A War of 1812 defense erected in 1813 or 1814, it stood on Lawrence Hill, near Hallet's Point, in the present borough of Queens, New York City. Occupying a site southeast of Fort Stevens, it was a strong, six-sided stone tower, with two of its stories loopholed and its top surmounted by several heavy cannon *en barbette*. The fort was named Castle Bogardus in honor of General Robert Bogardus. General Joseph C. Swift called it a "devil tower" in his report.

FORT BRADSTREET. THE OSWEGO FORTS.

FORT BREWERTON. One of the forts built in 1759 by British and provincial forces under Sir William Johnson to protect the Mohawk River route between Albany and Fort Ontario, Fort Brewerton was located at the west end of Oneida Lake at present Brewerton, Oswego County, and named for Captain George Brewerton, its builder. The fort was laid out as an 8-pointed star with 16 faces, each measuring about 30 feet. With a 480-foot-long parapet, it was defended by four 3-pound swivel guns and garrisoned by 20 to 100 men, depending on the exigencies of the war. An earthen embankment with a 20-foot-high, loopholed palisade and a ditch outlined the fort, which enclosed two water wells. An underground powder magazine was connected by a 100-foot-long tunnel. Fort Brewerton was dismantled in 1767 in accordance with a provision in a treaty made with the Indians. The site of the fort was used during the Revolution by both British and American forces while in transit. Today the one-acre Fort Brewerton State Reservation, located on U.S. 11, State and Lansing streets in Brewerton, commemorates the French and Indian War defense.

BREYMANN REDOUBT. SARATOGA BATTLEFIELD FORTS.

BROOKLYN, REVOLUTIONARY WAR DEFENSES. See New York City Revolutionary War Defenses section.

FORT BROWN. A War of 1812 defense located on the west side of United States Avenue, on the bank of the Saranac River at the bend southeast of Plattsburgh, Fort Brown was begun by Brigadier General George Izard in the spring of 1814 and completed in August by Brigadier General Alexander Macomb. It stood about 50 rods west of Fort Moreau, Plattsburgh's main defensive work.

CAMP BUCKNER (*Camp Popolopen*). West Point's Cadet Summer Camp was established in 1821 and located from that time to 1942 at Fort Clinton at the northeast corner of the athletic field east of the Plain. Summer Camp was transferred to Camp Popolopen on April 21, 1942. The name was changed to Camp Buckner on November 14, 1945, in honor of General Simon Bolivar Buckner, Jr., former commandant of cadets during 1933–36 at the United States Military Academy, who was killed in action on January 18, 1945, while leading his forces to victory in the conquest of Okinawa in the Pacific. The summer training area occupies some 80 acres of ground.

BUFFALO BARRACKS (*Poinsett Barracks*). Apparently originally called Buffalo Barracks but later designated Poinsett Barracks, it was established on May 6, 1839, and abandoned on September 30, 1845. It was located in the northern section of the city of Buffalo.

FORT BULL (*Fort Wood Creek*). Located on the right bank of Wood Creek, west of the present city of Rome, Fort Bull was at times referred to as Fort Wood Creek, but more often by the name of its commander, a Lieutenant Bull. Located at the western end of the Oneida Carrying Place, the fort was built in 1755 by Captain Marcus Petri in compliance with orders of General William Shirley. The star-shaped defense was surrounded by a ditch and a double row of palisades, the outer one 15 to 18 feet high and the interior one about 6 feet. The fort served as a depot, and its garrison guarded the portage to Fort Oswego.

Fort Bull was captured by a force of French and Indians under the command of Lieutenant Gaspard Joseph Chaussegros de Lery on March 27, 1756. Just after the fort was looted following the carnage, the fort's powder magazine accidently exploded and the bodies of the dead were blown to bits. De Lery's records show 105 English casualties, 70 killed and 35 captives taken to Canada. However, when Sir William Johnson inspected the ruins of the fort, he said he found the mangled bodies of 23 soldiers and 2 women, one of whom was the wife of Lieutenant Bull. Johnson figured the total casualties at 62 killed and missing.

Within a month after the disaster, Major General Charles Craven, ordered by General Shirley, took a detachment of men to the Oneida Carry to reinforce the hundred men already there, including engineers Patrick Mackellar and Thomas Sowers, busily laying out a new fort on or near Fort Bull's ruins. Again called Wood Creek Fort,

it had four bastions, a moat on three sides, and three buildings enclosed within the palisade.

FORT BURNET. THE OSWEGO FORTS.

BURNET'S FIELD BLOCKHOUSES. Five blockhouses, located on the Mohawk River, and Canada and Bellinger creeks, to protect the German Flatts settlements in Herkimer County, were built in April 1757 by Albany militiamen in accordance with orders of Sir William Johnson. On November 12, 1757, about 300 Indians, Canadian militiamen, and French marines attacked German Flatts, burned the blockhouses, 60 dwellings, and additional outbuildings.

BUSHWICK (BOSWYCK) BLOCKHOUSES. Two blockhouses were erected in 1662 or 1663 by French Huguenot settlers at the village of Boswyck (Bushwick), in the present borough of Brooklyn, Kings County. Forty men took turns garrisoning the defenses, one at each end of the village. The blockhouses may have survived as late as 1690.

CANADASAGA (KANADESAGA) FORT. Located one and a half miles northwest of present Geneva, Ontario County, this fort was built at the direction of Sir William Johnson in May 1756 for the Seneca Indians to earn their support in the war against the French. Johnson ordered the fort be built 150 feet square, with a palisade of 17-foot-long logs of either pine or oak, with two 24-foot-square blockhouses in diagonal corners. The Canadasaga village fort was destroyed on September 17, 1779, by troops of the Sullivan-Clinton expedition against the Six Nations.

FORT CANAJOHARIE (*Fort Cannatcho-eari*). Located at Canajoharie on the south side of the Mohawk River, opposite the mouth of East Canada Creek, Montgomery County, this fort was built in 1756 under orders of Sir William Johnson to serve as a depot and barracks, in addition to protecting the Upper Castle of the Mohawks. A square four-bastioned, 15-foot-high stockade, it was armed with swivel guns. The fort probably survived until about 1764 when it was abandoned.

FORT CANASERAGA. This fort for the Oneida and Tuscarora was located at the present town of Sullivan, a short distance northeast of Chittenango, Madison County. Captain Marcus Petri and 30 provincial soldiers were ordered by Sir William Johnson to build a fort at the Indian village on April 21, 1756. A 120-foot-square, 16-

foot-high defense, it was abandoned after the French and Indian War.

FORT CANASTAGONE. Built to protect the pioneer farmers on the north side of the Mohawk River, this fort was built in 1680 and located southeast of the present town of Rexford in Albany County. The fort survived Queen Anne's War and was abandoned about 1712.

FORT CANNATCHOEARI. FORT CANAJOHARIE.

FORT CARILLON. FORT TICONDEROGA.

FORT CARLETON. FORT HALDIMAND.

FORT CAUGHNAWAGA. A small blockhouse built in 1779, it was located at Sand Flats, just west of today's Fonda and torn down shortly after the Revolution. The white pioneer settlement in what is now eastern Fonda was destroyed by Sir John Johnson's raiders in the spring of 1780. The home of Douw Fonda, founder of the settlement, was burned down and its owner murdered. His three sons, Adam, Major Jelles, and John, served heroically during the years of the Revolution.

FORT CHAUNCEY. A minor defense for the naval base at Sackett's Harbor on Lake Ontario during the War of 1812, Fort Chauncey was probably erected in 1812 and named for naval Captain Isaac Chauncey. The fort consisted of a small loopholed, plank-covered circular tower, intended for small arms defense only. It was abandoned soon after the war ended.

FORT CHOUAGUEN. THE OSWEGO FORTS.

CITY BATTERY. CASTLE CLINTON.

CASTLE CLINTON (*West Battery; City Battery*). Castle Clinton National Monument on the New York City Battery was the last of the series of forts that, from 1626, successively guarded the lower end of Manhattan Island. As Castle Garden, theater, and immigrant depot, it symbolizes phases of the development of a nation. Castle Clinton was born of the tensions of the Napoleonic era. About two years after the renewal of war between France and Great Britain in 1803, a sharp reversal of English policy caused the seizure of more American shipping and the impressment of more American seamen into the British navy. The troubled months that followed

were climaxed, on June 22, 1807, by the firing upon the American frigate *Chesapeake.*

In New York mass meetings denounced the outrageous attack. At the same time, a great "fortification fever" swept the city, for New York, except for Fort Columbus on Governors Island, was virtually defenseless. It had been without protection since the destruction in 1790 of old Fort Amsterdam on the site of today's Custom House. Four new fortifications resulted. One of these was three-tiered Castle Williams on Governors Island. Opposite, some 200 feet off the southwest point of Manhattan Island, the West Battery was built, the fort that in 1815 would be named for DeWitt Clinton. It was the lineal descendant of a waterside battery that had protected New York as early as 1689. The other forts were Fort Wood on Bedloe's Island and Fort Gibson on Ellis Island.

Generally circular in shape, the West Battery was designed for 28 guns in one tier of casemates. Its eight-foot-thick walls of red sandstone stood upon a massive foundation of rough stone originally designed to support a multitier "tower" fort similar to Castle Williams. That foundation had been built up within an encompassing polygon of stone blocks in some 35 feet of water. A timber causeway with drawbridge connected the new fort to the New York City Battery of that day. Fronting upon the causeway was a magnificent sally port of the West Battery at the center of the gorge, or rear wall. Inside the rounded ends of that wall were the fort magazines. Quarters for the officers were at each side of the sally port passageway. There were no barracks for the enlisted garrison. Completed in the fall of 1811,

CASTLE CLINTON. (Courtesy of the National Park Service.)

the West Battery fired its 32-pounders in salute for the first time on Evacuation Day, November 25, the 28th anniversary of the departure of the British from New York at the close of the American Revolution.

During the War of 1812, the West Battery was an important part of New York City's defenses. For part of the war period, the West Battery may have served as headquarters for the defenses of New York City and vicinity. The war over, it became—as Castle Clinton—headquarters for the Third Military District (New York below the Highlands and part of New Jersey). The first general to command from the fort was Alexander Macomb. In 1816 he was succeeded by Major General Winfield Scott. He soon decided that Castle Clinton had outlived its military usefulness and, in 1821, he moved the district headquarters to Governors Island. Two years later, the Castle was ceded to the city of New York.

In June 1824 Castle Clinton was leased by the city as a place of public entertainment. Opened as Castle Garden on July 3, it soon

FORTS CLINTON AND MONTGOMERY. Map of the forts and their environs 1776–1777. (From Twin Forts of the Popolopen: Forts Clinton and Montgomery, New York, 1775–1777, *by William H. Carr and Richard J. Koke, July 1937. Courtesy of the Palisades Interstate Park Commission.)*

became one of the favored "places of resort" in the city. The interior of the fort became an ornamental garden; in time, a fountain was installed. It became the setting for band concerts, recitals, and demonstrations of the latest "scientific marvels," among them the telegraph in 1842. The gun rooms became a promenade and the officers' quarters a "saloon" where choice liquors and confections could be had.

On August 3, 1855, Castle Garden, under lease to the New York State Commissioners of Emigration, opened as an Emigrant Landing Depot. Made a part of the mainland within the prior months, the Castle was now enclosed on its landward side with some thousand feet of board fence. It was the floodtide of the great midcentury migration from Europe, the Irish and the Germans in the van. More than seven million immigrants passed through the Garden. On April 18, 1890, Castle Garden received its last immigrants. With control shifted to the U.S. Superintendent of Immigration, the Barge Office became a temporary landing depot, pending the opening of the newer, more commodious center on Ellis Island, on January 1, 1892.

Castle Garden, once again altered, became the entrancing New York City Aquarium. Some 30,000 people visited it on opening day, December 10, 1896. In the years that followed there were millions of visitors, until 1941 when the Aquarium was closed. Presumably, the building was to be torn down to make way for the Brooklyn–Battery Tunnel approaches. Because of the efforts of determined New Yorkers, the historic structure was not destroyed and, on August 12, 1946, the establishment of Castle Clinton as a national monument was authorized by act of Congress. Destruction of the Aquarium was stopped short of the original fort walls. In October 1950 the work of restoration began.

FORT CLINTON. FORT HARDY.

FORT CLINTON. WEST POINT'S FORTS.

FORTS CLINTON AND MONTGOMERY (*Fort Vaughan*). Known as the "Twin Forts of the Popolopen" of the Revolution, Forts Clinton and Montgomery surmounted the heights on the west shore of the Hudson River, 5 miles below West Point and about 45 miles north of New York City. They were separated by the little river, known today as Popolopen Creek, which joins the Hudson at a point directly between them. Planned in 1775 and built during 1776, Fort Montgomery was constructed first on the north side of the creek and named for Brigadier General

LANDMARK MAP
FORTS CLINTON AND MONTGOMERY
1776 - 1777

Revolutionary Roads
Modern Roads
Revolutionary Ramparts in Existence
Revolutionary Ramparts Destroyed
BUILDING SITES INDICATED IN BLACK.

Richard Montgomery, who was killed during a blinding snowstorm while unsuccessfully assaulting the Citadel of Quebec on December 31, 1775. During the course of its construction, engineers discovered that the rock formations on the south side of Popolopen Creek overlooked Fort Montgomery's partially built works. Consequently a second fort was laid out and constructed on the crags on that side of the creek. The new work was called Fort Clinton, in honor of Brigadier General George Clinton, New York Militia, who commanded the fort. A bridge was built across the creek to establish communication between the two forts.

On October 6, 1777, the still uncompleted forts were assaulted by both British and Hessian land and naval forces, under the dual command of Major General John Vaughan and Sir Henry Clinton, the latter a distant cousin of George Clinton. By five o'clock that afternoon, it was all over. The forts, inadequately garrisoned, were overrun by the enemy's forces. The day after the battle, Fort Clinton was renamed Fort Vaughan, in tribute to the British officer who led in its reduction, and temporarily occupied as a British base. Both Clinton brothers evaded the clutches of the enemy during the final minutes of the fighting and escaped. An undetermined number of Americans suffered death or wounds, with 263 of them captured, including 26 commissioned officers. The British and Hessian casualties, according to their own estimate, amounted to 41 dead and 142 wounded. On October 26, after learning of General Burgoyne's ignominious surrender at Saratoga to the north nine days earlier, orders to destroy Fort Clinton (Vaughan) and the bridge across Popolopen Creek were issued. Sir Henry's mission up the Hudson, which included the forced evacuations of Forts Constitution and Independence, the depopulation of Continental Village, and the burning of Kingston, dealt a severe blow to American morale.

Incorporated within Bear Mountain State Park, the remnants of the "Twin Forts" are located on either side of Popolopen Creek at the western terminus of today's Bear Mountain Bridge opposite Anthony's Nose. The remains of Fort Clinton, on the south side of the creek, can be seen close by the traffic circle at the entrance to the bridge. The few remains of Fort Montgomery are located at the water's edge on the north side of the creek.

FORT CLYDE. Probably built in the spring of 1777, Fort Clyde was located on the property of General George H. Nellis, about two miles southwest of Fort Plain, Montgomery County. Its construction owed to the energies of Colonel Samuel Clyde, an officer in the Tryon County militia. The fortification, intended to safeguard the inhabitants of Frey's Bush in the present township of Minden, consisted of a blockhouse in the center of a strong rectangle of palisades. The fort's only armament was a six-pounder signal gun.

COCHECTON POST. There were two forts in the Cushetunk Settlement. One was known as the Lower Fort, Fort Delaware, on the Pennsylvania side of the Delaware River, just north of present Milanville. The Upper Fort was located on the "Jersey side" of the river where the village of Cochecton in Sullivan County, New York, now stands. Cochecton, until 1769, was a part of Sussex County in New Jersey. The Cochecton Fort, built prior to 1760, consisted of a stockaded blockhouse. It was considered secondary in importance to Fort Delaware in Pennsylvania.

COLE'S FORT. This French and Indian War defense was located at present Port Jervis, Orange County, at the intersection of Jersey Avenue and East Main Street, its site now occupied by an elementary school. Cole's Fort was strategically important since it constituted the northern anchor of the chain of defenses and commanded the confluence of the Delaware and Neversink rivers. The fortified home of Wilhelmus Cole, a wooden structure 60 by 23 feet, was enclosed within a square stockade measuring about 120 feet to a side, in addition to two blockhouses and three other buildings. The fort was built by New Jersey militia because the Minisink region was then claimed by New Jersey. A great deal of war action took place in the area surrounding Cole's Fort during the Revolution. Count Casimir Pulaski's Legion arrived in the Port Jervis area in the late fall of 1778 and some of his troops were quartered in the fort. No data has been found to indicate when the fort was abandoned.

FORT COLUMBUS. Governors Island Forts.

FORT CONSTITUTION. Fort Independence (Peekskill).

FORT CONSTITUTION. The first American defense of the Revolution in the Hudson Highlands, Fort Constitution was erected on an island, roughly triangular in shape and consisting of less than 200 acres, opposite the United States Military Academy at West Point. Now a part of the USMA complex, the island is detached from the mainland by a marsh approximately half a mile wide.

The civilian responsibility for erecting defenses on Constitution Island, known at the beginning of the war as Martelaer's Rock, began with the New York Provincial Convention's assignment of Colonel James Clinton and Christopher Teappen to inspect the Highlands and render their report on proper sites for the establishment of fortifications. Their recommendation of two sites, the island and West Point, was followed by pressure by the Continental Congress to begin construction at once. The Convention, however, procrastinated until August 18, some two months later, when it appointed five commissioners (augmented to seven the next month) to oversee construction.

On September 7 the Committee of Safety received a letter from the commissioners requesting instructions regarding the plan of the defenses and construction costs. They were informed that it would be advisable to hold off until the arrival of Bernard Romans, who was then in Philadelphia obtaining a colonel's commission as a Continental Army engineer. In 1775 engineers in the American colonies were rarities, particularly those conversant with military science. General Washington had been fortunate in his search for just such a man, Lieutenant Colonel Rufus Putnam, a cousin of General Israel Putnam, whose touch of engineering genius at Dorchester Heights contributed to the Americans' ouster of the British from Boston.

But the commissioners had to be satisfied with Romans, a rather good Dutch botanist and cartographer, trained in England as an engineer. The pressures and temper of the times dictated the unfortunate selection of "a Dutchman turned English and a botanist turned engineer" to plan and construct the ill-designed fortress on Constitution Island. Romans inspected Martelaer's Rock and wrote a long report. His grand plan, transferred to paper with cartographic excellence, captivated the Convention, which approved his scheme for transforming Constitution Island. His delineation, which included a small battery at West Point where a farm was then situated, provided for a "Grand Bastion," five blockhouses, batteries, barracks, and storehouses, with the whole complex to be defended by 61 guns and 20 swivels. The "Grand Bastion" never materialized, and has been aptly described as The Fort That Never Was. Work began before the end of September despite bitter contention between Romans and the commissioners regarding what defenses were to go where and who was to supervise construction.

The history of Fort Constitution bridged all the years of the war. The eight-year span can be better comprehended if contemplated as consisting of two periods:

The first, when the responsibility of the construction of the fortifications in the Highlands was primarily left in the hands of civilians. This came to a fiery end with the destruction of the fortifications of Forts Constitution, Montgomery and Clinton in October of 1777. This period was followed by the erection of a new set of fortifications at West Point under military control and relying heavily on experienced foreign engineers. The fortifications eventually evolved into a vast complex of forts, redoubts and batteries on both sides of the River. Fort Constitution was refortified and this entire complex then became the main bastion in guarding the Hudson Highlands and the all-important Hudson River during the rest of the war. [John H. Mead, "History Beneath Our Feet," address made September 29, 1969]

West Point became the grand citadel and the key position in the Highlands. Constitution Island, on the east shore, became the supporting defense, offering the island's fire power against enemy naval forces. (See: WEST POINT'S FORTS.)

FORT CONTI. FORT NIAGARA.

CONTINENTAL VILLAGE. Late in 1776 the Patriots turned the Hudson River village of Peekskill, with more than 50 dwellings, into a vast storehouse, guarded by Fort Independence built in August. Three miles to the north was Continental Village, an army community designed to accommodate 2,000 troops. During the winter of 1776–77, British General William Howe in New York made plans to capture and destroy the rebel arsenal. Late on March 21, Howe embarked a force of 500 troops. At noon on March 23, the British landed at Peekskill. General Alexander McDougall, commandant of both the town and Continental Village, with only a small garrison, felt he could not make an adequate defense and evacuated. What munitions and supplies could not be at once transported were set afire.

On October 9, three days after Sir Henry Clinton's capture of Forts Clinton and Montgomery, he sent a force of regulars and Hessians to Peekskill to destroy the "rebel settlement" of Continental Village. They found the Patriot depot deserted, hurriedly evacuated when the Highland forts fell, with a train of wagons loaded with valuable military stores, warehouses crammed to the rafters, and newly built barracks intended to house 1,500 men. Despite a heavy rain that slowed demolition, the British and Hessians put the torch to what stores they could not take with them. These two disastrous British raids in 1777, "The Year of the Hangman," significantly magnified General Washington's tribulations.

CORLAER'S FORT. FORT SCHENECTADY.

CORLAER'S HOOK FORT. On May 25, 1812, New York City's Common Council provided the land required to construct a fort or battery on Corlaer's Hook for the defense of the city's harbor. An "open excavated" battery was constructed in the summer under the supervision of Colonel Jonathan Williams.

FORT COSBY. FORT SCHENECTADY.

FORT COVINGTON. In the autumn of 1812, General Wade Hampton built a palisaded fortification enclosing four blockhouses at the village of French Mills, just below the Canadian border, in present Franklin County. The town and fort were later named Fort Covington in honor of Brigadier General Leonard Covington who was mortally wounded in the Battle of Chrysler's Field fought across the border, on November 11, 1813. An outpost in the American defense of the St. Lawrence River, Fort Covington also served for a time as a hospital for the war wounded. In early February 1814, the fort was evacuated and its last garrison transferred to strategic Sackett's Harbor near Plattsburgh. On February 19 the British marched into the post and seized its military stores. Years later, it was claimed by some that Fort Covington's blockhouses stood for many more years. Others, contemporary regional historians, however, believe the fort was destroyed by the British in 1814.

FORT CRAILO. Located on Riverside Avenue in the city of Rensselaer (colonial Greenbush), across the river from Albany, Fort Crailo is the restored brick manor house built in 1642 by wealthy Killiaen van Rensselaer, the first patroon of Rensselaerwyck, a vast empire of about 700,000 acres. He named his dwelling Crailo ("row's woods") for his home in Holland. Originally a simple but strongly built structure, it later became a loopholed fort, surrounded by palisades, and was one of the New Netherland colony's first strongholds. Additions or improvements were made to the house in 1644, with the most significant ones made in 1762, 1790 and 1800. After the building was presented to the state in 1933, it was at once remodeled to conform with its condition in a pre-Revolutionary period. Many traditions are associated with Fort Crailo. It was here that the song "Yankee Doodle" was written

in 1758 by Dr. Richard Shuckburgh, a British army surgeon, while watching provincial militia being drilled in preparation for General Abercromby's later ill-fated attack against French-held Fort Ticonderoga.

FORT CRAVEN (*Fort Pentagon*). A French and Indian War defense, also known as Fort Pentagon because of its configuration, Fort Craven was begun by Major Charles Craven in 1756 to replace Fort Bull destroyed by the French and located on the southwest bank of the Mohawk within the modern city limits of Rome. Its site is on Whitesboro Street between Bouck and Mill streets. Before the fort could be completed, it was destroyed on August 31, 1756, in compliance with orders of Brigadier General Daniel Webb, after the fall of Oswego's forts to the French under Montcalm earlier in the same month.

CAMP CREEDMORE. CAMP FISHERS ISLAND.

FORT CROWN POINT (*Fort St. Frederic; Fort Amherst*). Long before the white man came, the water corridor formed by Lake Champlain and the Hudson River was a strategic passage connecting the northern wilderness of Canada with the domain of the Iroquois to the south. Its importance became more significant with the arrival of the French and the English to the New World. Claimed by the French on the basis of Champlain's discoveries in 1609, and the English by virtue of their alliances with the Iroquois tribes, Crown Point stood out as a natural bottleneck controlling the flow of traffic along the key north-south route. The point was destined to become one of the most hotly contested areas in North America during the middle 1700s.

On the most prominent point on the lake, where Lake Champlain narrows to less than one-third of a mile wide, the French as early as 1731 began the construction of fortifications that threatened the English colonies in the region. While construction was progressing, there was a revision in French military thinking. A request was made for a royal commission for a much stronger work on the lake's western shore. The design recommended called for a four-storied, stone machicolated tower, embrasured for cannon, with additions of a drawbridge and a portcullis. The 300-foot-square fort was armed with batteries aggregating 62 guns. Ultimately, adjoining the tower, a stone barracks and a church were built. The fortification, named Fort St. Frederic for Frederic Maurepas, secretary of state, became a base from which the French launched raids against the English settlements.

FORT CROWN POINT. Ruins of Fort St. Frederick, north end (left) and west side. (Courtesy of the National Park Service.)

FORT CROWN POINT. British plan of the new Fort Crown Point. (Courtesy of the National Map Collection, Public Archives of Canada.)

Not only was the fort planned as a permanent military establishment, it also served to guard the founding and rapid development of a French village in its environs. As French activity at Crown Point grew, the northern English colonies became increasingly concerned and began to strengthen their military positions. The French responded, nearly 25 years after Fort St. Frederic was built, by constructing another fort a day's march, about 16 miles, closer to the English, to be known as Fort Carillon, later renamed Fort Ticonderoga.

With the outbreak of the French and Indian War in 1754, the British began a series of attacks against the French positions. William Johnson's expedition against Crown Point fell short to culminate in the Battle of Lake George in 1755. The English were victorious four years later, however, when an 11,000-man army under General Jeffrey Amherst advanced northward to lay claim to Fort Carillon, the French stronghold at Ticonderoga, and then proceeded to Fort St. Frederic. Both were found in ruins, blown up by the French as they retreated northward to Isle-aux-Noix.

Amherst ordered that the remains of Fort St. Frederic be leveled. Then the construction of an English fortress was begun on a hill overlooking the ruins of the French fort. At the time of its conception, the fort was called Fort Amherst, but later it was renamed Fort Crown Point. Three years of work resulted in the largest fort in the colonies, three times the size of Fort Ticonderoga, at the stupendous cost of some $10 million to the home and colonial governments. It was a pentagon with five bastions, enclosing a six-and-a-half-acre parade ground, and a considerable complex of barracks. The truly impressive ramparts of solid masonry were 25 feet thick and nearly the same in height. The whole circuit along its ramparts, including the bastions, was 853 yards, just under half a mile. Outside the fort's walls were three supporting redoubts. A settlement of considerable size grew up beyond the fort's walls. Here lived retired British officers, soldiers garrisoned at the fort and their families, and merchants necessary to the survival of the fort.

In 1773 an accidental fire started in the main fort and quickly spread to adjacent sheds. When flames reached the powder magazine, the explosion blasted a hole in the south wall, causing the fire to spread further. The perimeter walls

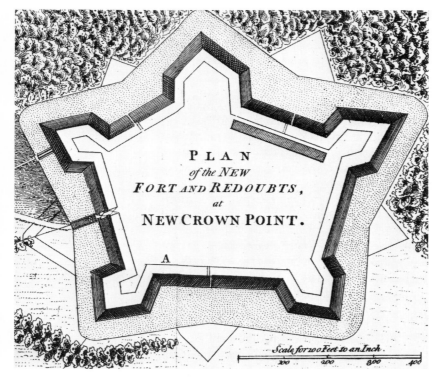

PLAN *of the* NEW FORT AND REDOUBTS, *at* NEW CROWN POINT.

A

Scale for 100 Feet to an Inch.

100   200   300   400

FORT CROWN POINT. Parade ground and ruins of the northeast barracks (left) and the southeast barracks (center). (Courtesy of the National Park Service.)

and bastions were ruined, and the great fort was virtually destroyed. The outbreak of the American Revolution halted plans for reconstruction of the Crown Point fort. The site, however, figured importantly as an observation post and a staging area.

The British retained their position at Crown Point until 1775, when Seth Warner and a force of Green Mountain Boys seized the fort two days after Ethan Allen's capture of Ticonderoga. In 1776 Benedict Arnold assembled a fleet, America's first inland navy, to repulse a British invasion from Canada. After meeting defeat at Valcour Island on Lake Champlain, but significantly retarding the British campaign timetable, the Americans retreated to Ticonderoga. Crown Point was reclaimed by the British and used in General Burgoyne's campaign of 1777. Following his defeat at Saratoga, Crown Point lessened in military importance and again became an observation post.

The Americans regained possession of Crown Point at the end of the war. The British town, destroyed during the war, and the fort were never rebuilt. A few years after the 1783 Treaty of Paris, the lands and the remains of Forts Crown Point and Ticonderoga were turned over to Union and Columbia colleges and eventually sold as farms. About the turn of this century, the state of New York acquired Crown Point from private ownership and since then has acquired the surrounding acreage, which contains the sites of the early French and English settlements. The remains of Fort Crown Point have been stabilized and are maintained by the Crown Point Foundation.

FORT CUMMINGS. Established on September 11, 1779, at present Honeoye, Ontario County, this temporary fort incorporated an Indian blockhouse often used by Tory Rangers. Named for Captain John N. Cummings, who was in command of 50 in charge of artillery, stores, and baggage, Fort Cummings was the fortified supply base from which the troops on the Sullivan-Clinton expedition advanced to Genesee Castle and leveled by fire the large Seneca town there. Honeoye, an Indian village in 1779, was not settled by whites until 1789, when it was called Pittstown; in 1808, the pioneer village was renamed Honeoye.

FORT CUMMINGS. A War of 1812 redoubt, one of a line of defensive fortifications planned by General Joseph G. Swift, Fort Cummings was built in 1814 and located between today's Putnam and Greene avenues in Brooklyn.

FORT DAYTON. The most important military post in the Herkimer County Settlements during the Revolution, Fort Dayton, at today's Herkimer on the north side of the Mohawk River, was strategically located to protect the inhabitants of German Flatts (the name given the 10-mile stretch of Palatine villages on both sides of the river). The fort occupied the site of the first Fort Herkimer, a wooden blockhouse of the French and Indian War (the site of the second Fort Herkimer, of Revolutionary fame, is located on the south side of the river). German Flatts being exposed to the threat of Indian incursions from all directions, the settlers petitioned Major General Philip Schuyler to provide them with a defensive work.

In the early fall of 1776, Schuyler sent Colonel Elias Dayton to German Flatts, where a fort was erected and named for him. Fort Dayton was a true fort, in that it possessed a stockade, blockhouse, bastions, curtains, barracks, an artillery park, and the rest of the appurtenances necessary for a complete fortification. It was constructed on ground now bounded by Main, Court, Washington, and German streets. It was from this fort, on August 4, 1777, that General Nicholas Herkimer marched with about 800 undisciplined, sharpshooting men to the relief of Fort Stanwix at today's Rome. Herkimer's column never reached Fort Stanwix; it was ambushed at Oriskany six miles from the fort. After the destruction of Fort Stanwix early in May 1781, Fort Dayton was more strongly garrisoned than ever before as it became the extreme western military outpost in New York State. The mid-Victorian mansion erected in 1884 by Dr. A. Walter Suiter and now owned by the Herkimer County Historical Society now occupies the Fort Dayton site.

FORT (MARTINUS) DECKER. The rebuilt edition of the original Decker house is located on West Main Street and Park Avenue in Port Jervis, Orange County. The fortified structure, built by Isaac Decker, had its lower story constructed of stone and the upper half-story of logs. One of the strongest defenses in the exposed Minisink settlements along the Delaware River, it served as a trading post and guardhouse. Sometime early in the Revolution, Major Martinus Decker erected a strong stockade around the dwelling for added protection. The fort and the stockade were burned during Joseph Brant's raid on July 20, 1779. The pursuit by 150 militiamen, most of them from the Goshen area, culminated two days later in the disastrous Battle of Minisink, in which at least 45 men were killed. The Decker house, rebuilt in 1793, is listed in the *National Register of Historic Places.*

FORT DENONVILLE. FORT NIAGARA.

FORT DESOLATION. FORT SCHUYLER (Utica).

FORT DES SABLES. A stockaded French fur-trading post established for the Seneca Indians in 1717 by Louis Thomas Joncaire, an influential interpreter and negotiator for the Iroquois, it was located in present Monroe County at the northwest corner of Irondequoit Bay, on a bluff now cut down for the Sea Breeze Expressway. A reproduction of the post stands in Ellison Park near today's town of Sea Breeze, a few miles north of the city of Rochester.

FORT DEVENS. One of the chain of small blockhouses erected in 1757, during the French and Indian War, under the supervision of Captain James Clinton, Fort Devens was located about a mile and a half north of the present town of Wurtsboro in southeastern Sullivan County.

FORT DEWITT. Located on Denansink Creek, Town of Deerpark, Orange County, this blockhouse was one of five built in 1757 by Captain James Clinton to house the Orange and Ulster "Guards of the Frontier" during the French and Indian War. The blockhouse may have survived until about 1787.

FORT DEYO'S HILL. One of the series of blockhouses built in 1757 under the supervision of Captain James Clinton for the protection of settlers, it was located near present U.S. 209, north of Kerhonkson, town of Rochester, in Ulster County. The blockhouse was apparently torn down in 1764.

FORT DIAMOND. FORT LAFAYETTE.

DOBBS FERRY FORTS. Dobbs Ferry was the Westchester County site of an important Hudson River crossing opposite present-day Tallman Mountain State Park on the west bank. It was first fortified by the Americans very early in 1776. The remains of the principal fortification and at least two redoubts built in the vicinity were still very much in evidence in 1850. Commanding a fine view of the river in both directions, the main fort was situated on the horseshoe-shaped eminence overlooking the ferry landing (today the site looms over the railroad right-of-way). In control of the ferry to old Paramus on the Jersey side (now included in Palisades State Park), these forts often harassed British shipping on the river.

To further protect the ferry, it was determined to construct on the heights of the Palisades a large wood-and-stone blockhouse about 1,500 feet north of the road going down to the ferry at Sneden's Landing (today just south of Tallman Mountain State Park). With construction taking nearly all summer, the fortification, with an additional battery of three guns nearby, was generally called the Dobbs Ferry Blockhouse. In early October 1776, General William Heath had a strong garrison posted at Dobbs Ferry: 500 infantry, 40 light horses, and an artillery company with two 12-pounders and a howitzer.

DOLSON BLOCKHOUSE. In 1735 Isaac Dolson built a log house, loopholed for musketry, in Middletown, Orange County. During the French and Indian Wars, Dolson erected a block-house and a stone house that area residents used for protection during raids.

CAMP DRUM. FORT DRUM.

FORT DRUM (*Pine Camp; Camp Drum*). Located nine miles from Watertown near Lake Ontario and the Canadian border, Fort Drum is reputed to be the largest Army installation in the Northeast, covering some 107,000 acres, and a major training center for all branches of the service. First used as a training center in 1908 for soldiers of the National Guard from New England states, the post was known as Pine Camp. It was renamed Pine Plains Military Reservation in 1938, Camp Drum on December 6, 1951, in honor of Lieutenant General Hugh A. Drum, former commander of the 1st Army and the New York National Guard, and finally designated Fort Drum in 1974. During World War II, three divisions trained there: the 4th Armored Division; the 5th Armored Division; and the 45th Infantry Division.

Today, the post supports many military missions. It is a base for training soldiers from the Army Reserve and Army National Guard each summer, boasting the largest concentration of Reserve component equipment in the United States. The Reserve component soldiers train for their two weeks of annual training at the post from April to September. Approximately 50,000 soldiers train at Fort Drum each summer, with as many as 15,000 on post during a two-week period. The post is also a winter warfare training center from January to March for about 10,000 soldiers.

FORT DUBOIS. New Paltz in Ulster County was first settled in 1678 by 12 Huguenot families who built log cabins on the east bank of the Wallkill River, which were replaced by stone dwellings about 1705. They named their palisaded colony New Paltz in honor of the town of Pfalz on the Rhine River in Germany, where they had found refuge from religious persecution. The Dubois stone dwelling built by Daniel Dubois, still standing on Huguenot Street as a National Historic Landmark, was minimally fortified by two gunports facing the street and a lookout window high in the attic's west wall.

FORT DUBOIS. Located at Cobleskill, Schoharie County, Fort Dubois was erected some time in April 1779 under the direction of Colonel Lewis Dubois. A large palisaded and ditched defense, occupying about three acres of ground, it was situated on an elevation on present-day Main Street about a mile east of Cobleskill's center. The fort was burned during the early summer by 300 warriors of the originally neutral Onondaga Nation who devastated the town in retaliation for the unwarranted attack against their towns by Colonel Gose Van Schaick's expedition in early April.

CAMP DUTCHESS. A temporary Civil War rendezvous encampment established in the late summer of 1862, Camp Dutchess was located about a mile northeast of the courthouse in Poughkeepsie. On October 11, 1862, the Dutchess County regiment was mustered into service as a component of the 150th New York Volunteer Infantry.

EAST FORT. THE OSWEGO FORTS.

FORT EDWARD (*Fort Nicholson; Fort Lydius; Fort Lyman*). During the eighteenth century wars, Fort Edward was one of the most important military posts between Albany and Canada. The general area of the fort was called the First, Long, or Great Carrying Place. It was the first and nearest point on the Hudson River where troops and military stores were landed for portage to and from the southern end of Lake Champlain (today's Whitehall).

British fortifications were constructed on the site in 1709, 1731, 1755, and 1757. The first, a stockaded affair erected by General Francis Nicholson during his aborted expedition against Canada, was named for its builder. The second fort was built to protect the trading post settlement established by John Henry Lydius, an Albany Dutchman, the first white man to settle in what is now the town of Fort Edward; this defense, called Fort Lydius, was destroyed by the French and Indians in 1745. The third fort, a preliminary to William Johnson's expedition against Crown Point, was initiated by General Phineas Lyman with 600 men and completed by engineer Captain William Eyre, and named Fort Lyman; after the Battle of Lake George, Johnson renamed it Fort Edward "in Honour to Our Young Prince," the Duke of York and Albany, eldest son of George II and brother of the future George III. The fourth and last, in 1757, came as a result of an accidental fire that destroyed the barracks in 1756.

During the French and Indian War, Fort Edward was a base for Robert Rogers's Rangers and

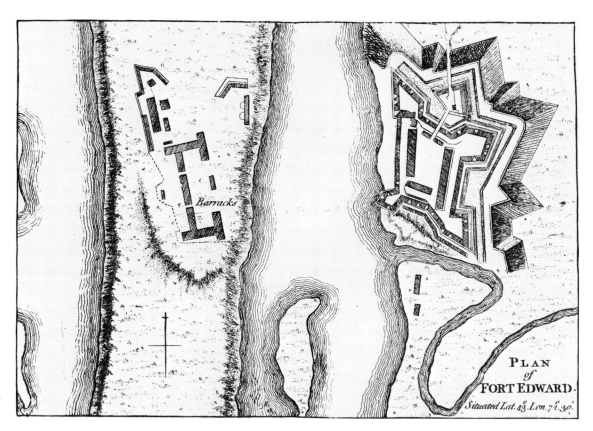

FORT EDWARD. Plan from a 1756 survey. (Courtesy of the Public Archives of Canada.)

British troops marching to Canada. The fort was also intended to guard nearly adjacent Rogers Island in the river that contained barracks, at least one redoubt, and other military structures. Constructed of timber and earth, the fort's walls were 16 feet high and 22 inches thick, with a 1,569-foot perimeter. It was defended by 8 brass and iron cannon emplaced on its ramparts, in addition to about 20 mortars. Its barracks, both on the mainland and the island, could garrison 500 troops.

Fort Edward was evacuated in 1766 and ordered razed on July 15, 1775, by the Albany Committee of Safety to prevent its use by the British. It was the site of Major General Philip Schuyler's headquarters in 1777 during the attempt to block General John Burgoyne's advance southward from Ticonderoga. Today, due to changes in the Hudson's course, most of the camp and fort sites are located on Rogers Island, linked to the mainland by S.R. 197. The actual site of 40-acre Fort Edward, privately owned, is located approximately in the center of the island.

FORT EHLE. The first home of Rev. John Ehle, a Palatine German, at Canajoharie, in present Montgomery County, was a log dwelling built in 1723, replaced in 1729, the year son Peter was born, with a single-story stone structure. In 1752

Peter erected a two-story addition to his parents' dwelling. In 1777 or 1778, it was loopholed and palisaded. There is no record of any enemy attacks.

FORT ESOPUS. Its site located in the immediate area of today's North Front Street, John Street, and Clinton Avenue in the present city of Kingston, this fort was originally built in 1658 in compliance with an order of Peter Stuyvesant, New Netherland's Director-General, as a defense against the region's Esopus Indians. It served as a base of operations for two Dutch military expeditions against these Indians in 1659 and 1663. During the two and one-half-week siege of the settlement by 400 to 600 warriors in September, 1659, they slaughtered most of the settlers' livestock and made many efforts to burn barns and grain reserves with fire arrows, while maintaining a continuous series of attacks. Finally, reinforcements arrived from New Amsterdam. The first stockade measured about 2,600 feet in circumference; the final palisaded area had a perimeter of just under a mile, surrounded by a moat and enclosing a guardhouse. Three enlargements of the original stockade were made in 1661, 1669, or 1670, and 1676–77.

A village called Esopus was founded nearby and chartered as Wiltwyck in 1661. The name of the town was changed to Kingston in 1669 by

Governor Francis Lovelace, in honor of his family home in Berkshire, England. The first popularly elected Senate of New York State first convened at the Senate House at Kingston (a stone structure originally built in 1676 by Colonel Wessel Ten Broeck) on September 10, 1777. The British fleet under Sir Henry Clinton broke through the cordon of American fortifications in the Hudson Highlands and sailed up the river. Troops landed at Kingston on October 16, 1777, set fire to virtually every building in the town, including the Senate House (rebuilt and still standing).

FORT FAILING. A fortified stone dwelling, originally built by Nicholas Failing and occupied by his son, Henry N. Failing, during the Revolution, Fort Failing was located about one mile west of Canajoharie, Montgomery County. During the latter part of the war, the structure became the property of Colonel Henry (Hendrick) Frey of the Albany militia and was occasionally used as a garrison house.

FORT FISH. A War of 1812 defense for New York City, Fort Fish was erected in 1814 in present Central Park near East 107th Street.

CAMP AT FISHER'S ISLAND. CAMP FISHERS ISLAND.

CAMP FISHERS ISLAND (*Camp at Fisher's Island; Camp Creedmore; Camp R. N. Scott; Camp Stephen B. Luce*). A temporary encampment, which was renamed by each garrison that used it, was established about 1879 on eight-mile-long Fishers Island off the northeast tip of Long Island and southwest of New London, Connecticut. It was used to provide rifle instruction for various Army units. The exact date of its discontinuance by the Army is not known, but records in the National Archives indicate that it was not occupied after 1888. During this century, the island became the headquarters of the Long Island Coast Guard.

FISHKILL BARRACKS. The largest of the Continental Army depots, Fishkill Barracks (Fishkill Supply Depot) in Dutchess County operated from 1776 until some time in 1882. It was more or less officially opened in the autumn of 1776, with magazines and provision storehouses initiated in August. In November 1776 General Washington requested the New York Provincial Convention to provide for the construction of sufficient barracks at Fishkill to accommodate 2,000 troops through the coming winter. Mud huts came first. When lumber became more plen-

tiful through a larger labor force, making use of conscientious objectors for the first time in American history, wooden barracks were constructed.

Facilities were erected on both sides of today's Route 9, one mile below the village of Fishkill. When the depot was first initiated, Fishkill Clove or Wiccopee Pass, just south of the village, was fortified with three gun batteries that remained there for the duration of the war. It is believed that the camp for the Corps of Invalids was situated near the top of the pass. Benedict Arnold, during his treasonable plan to weaken and surrender the citadel of West Point to the enemy, very often sent soldiers to Fishkill to cut wood or mount excessive guard duty. Fishkill was deactivated as a supply depot late in 1782, when the Quartermaster Commissary Department removed the remainder of the munitions and general stores.

FLATTS STOCKADE. The loopholed, brick-built dwelling belonging to Colonel Peter Schuyler, located on a bluff south of Fish Creek and Schuylerville, Saratoga County, was surrounded in 1715 by a stockade for the added protection of his superintendent and laborers from French and Indian attacks. The fortified structure could garrison about 100 troops. Flatts Stockade and the houses it enclosed were burned by the French on November 28, 1745.

FORT FOUR MILE POST. Located south of Fort Edward in present Washington County, this defense was one of the series of forts built in 1755 by Sir William Johnson along the "Old Military Road" between Albany and Montreal. The post was a stockaded enclosure, surrounded by a moat, and garrisoned 30 soldiers.

FORT FOX. The fortified and loopholed stone house of Philip Fox was located at the western end of Palatine Township, about a mile and a half north of Nelliston, Montgomery County. Fox's Mills was the name of this locality when General Robert Van Rensselaer and his troops made camp there on the night of October 19, 1780, during their pursuit of Sir John Johnson's raiders. Johnson's Tories and Indians burned the mill during the 1780 raid.

FORT FRANKLIN. LONG ISLAND FORTS.

FORT FREDERICK (*Fort Nassau; Fort Orange; Fort Albany*). In early 1614 Dutch traders under Captain Hendrick Christiaensen established Fort Nassau on Castle (later Van

Rensselaer) Island in the Hudson River, off the west bank and about a half-mile downriver from today's city of Albany. Now a part of the mainland, the site is under a bridge complex. The fort, measuring 36 by 26 feet and enclosed by a 50-foot-square stockade and a 180-foot-long moat, mounted 2 Breteuil cannon and 11 stone swivel guns. It was named in honor of William the Silent's son, Maurice, prince of the House of Nassau, then Stadtholder of Holland. Although strategically situated for defense, the island was subject to spring flooding when winter ice melted upstream. Threatened by destruction, Fort Nassau was abandoned in the spring of 1618 and the traders moved their business to the mainland on the bank of Norman's Kill or Creek.

In 1624 Captain Cornelis Jacobsen May (Mey) decided that the situation of the second Fort Nassau was too vulnerable. The post was moved upstream to the flatlands on the west bank of the river, where downtown Albany now stands, named Beverwyck in 1652 by Peter Stuyvesant. Captain May traced the lines for a quadrangular fort with proper salient angles and named it Fort Orange. Its exterior dimensions, including the bastions, measured 150 by 175 feet. The major portion of the region's Dutch trade with the Indians was carried on here. It was peacefully surrendered to the English when New Netherland fell in 1664 and occupied by 60 English soldiers, and renamed Fort Albany. Beverwyck was renamed Albany and New Amsterdam at the southern end of Manhattan Island became New York.

In 1673 a Dutch expeditionary force recaptured New York and reoccupied the fort, renaming it Fort Nassau. The military victory, however, was short-lived. The Treaty of Westminster the following year returned New York to England and the fort again was called Fort Albany. In 1675 Governor Sir Edmund Andros ordered the abandonment of the old fort and early the following year began a new fortification—The Fort at Albany or Fort Frederick—on the hill overlooking the city. The new defense was a ditched, quadrangular, bastioned work on the west side of the town. The site of the new wooden fort was halfway up the hill on what is now State Street, with its northeast bastion situated on present Lodge Street.

In 1702 Lord Cornbury, corrupt royal governor of New York (1702–8), decided that the fort was in a ruinous state and determined to have it replaced with a larger fort constructed of stone. Construction took two years. Except for minor repairs and periodic additions, this walled masonry fort, mounting 21 heavy cannon and enclosing the residence of the city's chief officer, officers' quarters, and barracks, remained essentially the same until its demolition in 1787–89. Governor Cornbury had called it Fort Anne for the then queen, but records indicate

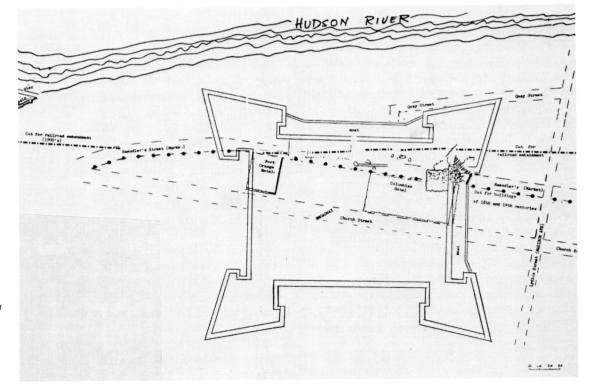

FORT FREDERICK. Site of Fort Orange. (From "Fort Orange 'Dig'" in a special reprint of the Commercial Courier, National Commercial Bank and Trust Co., November, 1971.)

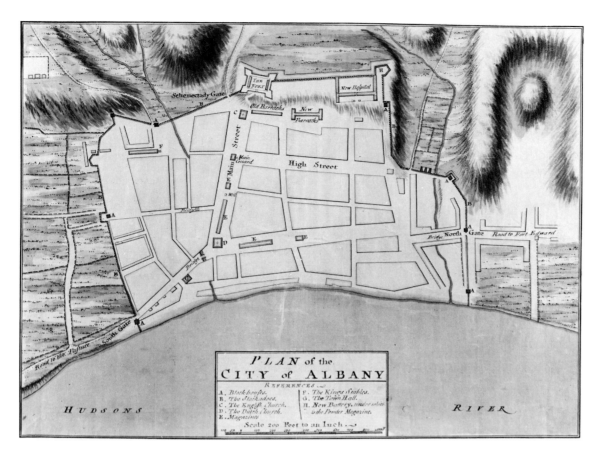

FORT FREDERICK. Plan drawn circa 1759. (Courtesy of the Albany Institute of History and Art.)

that this name was never used officially. In most documents and correspondence, the fort was usually called The Fort at Albany.

On June 27, 1782, General George Washington, Governor George Clinton, General Henry Knox, and General Von Steuben left the sloop that had brought them upriver from Newburgh, and were rowed to the Albany wharf. At six o'clock all the city's church bells began to ring, and Fort Frederick thundered a salute of 13 guns. Albany's Common Council decided two years after the war was over that the fort at the head of State Street had served its usefulness and should be torn down. Much of the stone was carried off by officers of the different churches to be used for building purposes. Two years later, the remains of old Fort Frederick were used by city workmen for the widening of State Street.

FREEMAN FARM. BALCARRES REDOUBT, under SARATOGA BATTLEFIELD FORTS.

FORT FRENCH. In 1696 the French built this temporary fort near Syracuse as a base for a raid on an Onandaga village. The raid, led by Count Ribert de Frontenac, governor general of Canada, involved 400 Indians and 1,600 French soldiers.

The site is now occupied by the Onandaga Sewage Treatment Plant.

FORT FREY. Famous in the annals of the Mohawk Valley, Fort Frey still stands well preserved at Palatine Bridge, on the north side of the Mohawk, almost opposite the city of Canajoharie. Heinrich Frey, a native of Zurich, Switzerland, settled there in 1689 to become the first white inhabitant in what was then Indian country, 40 miles west of Schenectady. The British palisaded Frey's cabin at the beginning of Queen Anne's War (1702–13) and used it as a military post until the end of the conflict. In 1739 his son Hendrick replaced the log dwelling with a quadrangle, loopholed stone building. There is no record that this structure was ever palisaded. The building served as a military post as well as a trading post. During all the years of the French and Indian War, a British garrison was again posted here to guard the strategic Mohawk River route. Hendrick Frey's three sons, John, Henry, and Bernard—took opposing views of the colonial upheavals at the outbreak of the Revolution.

FORT GAGE. A briefly occupied colonial earthwork, named for Brigadier General Thomas

Gage, was erected at Lake George in 1759, during the advance of General Amherst's army against Ticonderoga. The site is on a hill behind a modern motel complex, just west of U.S. 9, about a mile south of the recreation of Fort William Henry.

FORT GAINES. A War of 1812 redoubt at Plattsburgh, erected under orders of General Alexander Macomb, it was located a short distance south of Fort Moreau, on the east side of today's United States Avenue. Named for then Major General Edmund P. Gaines, it was never used.

GANAGHSARAGA FORT. This fort, located at present Syracuse, was built in April 1756 for the protection of the Onondaga by order of Sir William Johnson. The site is today occupied by the southwest corner of Route 173 and Route 11.

FORT GANSEVOORT (*White Fort*). A War of 1812 defense for the city of New York, Fort Gansevoort, also known as White Fort, was erected between present West 12th and Gansevoort streets on the Hudson River, in the summer and fall of 1812, and named for Colonel Peter Gansevoort, a distinguished Revolutionary War officer. The fort was strategically situated to command the river in both directions. Built of red sandstone, the fort contained magazines, arsenal, barracks, and hot-shot furnaces, and was portholed for 22 cannon. One citation reports it was demolished prior to 1849; another says it was removed in 1854.

FORT GARDINER. Located in the now unmarked village of Gardinersville, township of Wawayanda, Orange County, Fort Gardiner was probably erected in 1756 by Captain Richard Gardiner. Inhabited by one family, it apparently contained a wooden dwelling house, 5 log houses, a palisaded 100-foot square, and 2 swivel guns. In 1758 Captain Gardiner was appointed commander of the Frontier Guard and continued to serve in that capacity for the remainder of the French and Indian War. The actual site of this defense post has not been determined as yet.

FORT GEORGE. THE OSWEGO FORTS.

FORT GEORGE. Located a half-mile southeast of Fort William Henry (now reconstructed), Fort George's site at the head of Lake George served as a base for three colonial armies and as a large hospital for the smallpox-stricken remnants of the disastrous 1775–76 Canadian invasion forces commanded by Benedict Arnold and Richard Montgomery. In June 1759 General Jeffrey Amherst, with 10,000 troops en route to victory at Ticonderoga, occupied the former fortified encampment there used by both General William Johnson in 1755 and General James Abercromby in 1758. Prior to his defeat at Ticonderoga, Abercromby directed the construction there of more than 300 buildings—barracks, hospitals and storehouses—to later accommodate the many wounded and sick of his defeated army.

General Amherst had the complex or buildings renovated and began a new fort, which he called Fort George for George II. At the same time, he ordered buried the nearby remains of Fort William Henry. He also directed Brigadier General Thomas Gage to build Fort Gage, merely an earthen redoubt, on high ground a half mile to the south. Shortly after the outbreak of the Revolution, Fort George was seized by the Patriots under Seth Warner. The Americans evacuated it in 1777 in the face of General Burgoyne's advance southward from Ticonderoga. After the Battle of Saratoga, the fort was reoccupied by a small American garrison, which held it until the surprise arrival of Major Christopher Carleton's army of raiders in July 1780. A citation reports that the fort was destroyed at that time, but there are indications that Fort George was occupied by an American militia garrison for the remainder of the war. It is believed that it was finally abandoned in 1787 and allowed to deteriorate into a ruination.

FORT GIBSON. Though part of New York politically, Ellis Island in Upper New York Bay is much closer to the Jersey shore than to Manhattan's Battery. Together with Liberty (formerly Bedloe's) Island and a now-submerged mud reef, the three were known during the colonial period as the Oyster Islands. The smaller island was then little more than three acres of mud, sand, and oyster shells. During the next century and a half, it bore such names as Dyre's Island, Bucking Island, and Gibbet Island, before Samuel Ellis acquired the property sometime before 1785.

The Federal government obtained title to the island in 1808, after much litigation, as a part of its plans to fortify New York's harbor. During the early spring of 1812, about three months before war was declared in late June between Great Britain and the United States, the Ellis Island complex was apparently completed. Throughout the war one company of artillery manned the island's battery of 14 heavy guns and a bomb battery. Occasional British prisoners of war kept the artillerists company.

Late in 1814 Governor Daniel D. Tompkins, while in charge of New York City's defenses, bestowed names on two of the harbor's defenses: Bedloe's Island's star-shaped fort became Fort Wood in honor of Brevet Lieutenant Colonel Eleazar D. Wood, Corps of Engineers; Ellis Island's works became Fort Gibson in tribute to Colonel James Gibson, 4th Regiment of Riflemen. Both distinguished officers were killed during the Battle of Fort Erie, Canada, in September of the same year. After the Army had modernized Ellis Island's fortifications in the early 1840s, Fort Gibson became known merely as Battery Gibson (Cantonment Gibson in Oklahoma had been upgraded to Fort Gibson in 1832). During the Civil War, at the same time that the Army was outfitting Battery Gibson with new heavy armament, the Navy was constructing on the island sizable additional powder magazines.

It was the need in 1890 for a Federal immigration station in New York's harbor, to replace Castle Clinton that decided the future of Ellis Island. The Navy's stockpile of munitions there was removed to Fort Wadsworth on Staten Island on May 24, 1890. Ellis Island went into operation as the nation's most famous port of immigration on January 1, 1892.

FORT GOLGOTHA. LONG ISLAND FORTS.

GOVERNORS ISLAND FORTS (*Fort Jay; Fort Columbus; Castle Williams*). The site of Fort Jay on historic Governors Island in Upper New York Bay lies approximately a half-mile off the tip of Manhattan. Troops were stationed on the island for the first time in 1755. This first garrison of trained soldiers was the 51st British Colonial Militia Regiment under the command of American-born Major General Sir William Pepperrell. Governors Island was first fortified during the Revolution when General Charles Lee ordered armament-mounted breastworks established there. At the close of the war, the island became the property of the state of New York.

Star-shaped Fort Jay was constructed during the period 1794–1800 in anticipation of war with France. In 1800, by an enactment of the New York Legislature, Governors Island and the submerged land contiguous to it were ceded to the United States. Fort Jay was extensively rebuilt in 1806. At that time, all of the works except the walled counterscarp, the gate, the sally port, the magazine, and two barracks were torn down and rebuilt with stronger materials. The new fortification consisted of an enclosed pentagonal work with four bastions of masonry to hold 100 guns. On the north wall, a ravelin of two casemated flanks was added. The new fortification was completed in 1808 and renamed Fort Columbus. The change in the fort's name was probably caused by the unpopularity of the treaty with England that John Jay had negotiated in 1795.

A round, stone gun-battery emplacement known as Castle Williams, designed and built by Colonel Jonathan Williams, Engineer Corps, was

GOVERNORS ISLAND FORTS. Governors Island, with the Statue of Liberty and New York City in the background. (Courtesy of the U.S. Army.)

begun while Fort Jay was being rebuilt and completed in 1811. It was located at the northwestern end of the island. The twin forts, Castle Williams and Castle Clinton in Battery Park, were erected to guard the channel between the island and New York City.

Repairs were made on the fort under the appropriations of 1833 and 1836. These were the last major changes on the island's fortifications. The original name, Fort Jay, was restored in 1904 through the efforts of Elihu Root, secretary of war. This country's first overt action of World War I was made by troops from Governors Island. On April 6, 1917, at 3:12 A.M., Congress declared war against Germany. Eighteen minutes later, a battalion of the 22nd Infantry, then garrisoning the island, set out in Revenue Service boats to seize the German ships and their crews then in the harbor. By noon all of the German ships had been taken and the seamen interned on Ellis Island. On December 21, 1941, the Eastern Theater of Operations was established with Headquarters on Governors Island. It was placed under the command of Lieutenant General Hugh A. Drum, who also commanded the First Army. It was redesignated Eastern Defense Command on March 20, 1942. Since World War II Governors Island continued to be an important military center. Much of the island's activity was associated with the operations of Headquarters, First Army. The Army left Governors Island in 1966. Since that time, the island has been the headquarters of the Coast Guard in the New York district, which also maintains a training center there.

GREAT REDOUBT. SARATOGA BATTLEFIELD FORTS.

CAMP GREENBURGH. The temporary Revolutionary War headquarters for the French army commanded by General Jean Baptiste Rochambeau, Camp Greenburgh was located on Ridge Road in Hartsdale, Westchester County. The house that was occupied by Rochambeau is still standing.

CANTONMENT GREENBUSH. In 1663 the Dutch built a small stockaded fort at or near present East Greenbush, Rensselaer County, to protect the area's farms from Indian incursions. Manned by local militia units on a rotating basis, the fort reportedly stood until about 1690. The town was again militarily occupied in 1812 when the government bought a 400-acre tract located about three miles east of the village of Greenbush. On this site was established what came to be known as Cantonment Greenbush. It was the

headquarters and training center for the Northern Division of the Army during the War of 1812. Four barracks were located around a central square parade ground, with an arsenal, hospital, and guardhouse, as well as several smaller structures. About 4,000 men were stationed here from time to time during the hostilities. The government sold the land and buildings in 1831 to Hathorn McCulloch of Albany, whose family owned the site until the 1920s. The sole remaining building has been remodeled into several apartments.

CAMP (F. L.) GUENTHER. The Pan-American Exposition Grounds at Buffalo were posted by the military from May 13 to November 13, 1901, by troops commanded by Captain John P. Wisser, 73rd Coast Artillery, from Fort Monroe, Virginia.

FORT GUMAER. Located on Pioneer Hill near Hugenot in Orange County, this 40-by-45-foot stone house had a cellar and a high roomy chamber above the upper floor. Below the eaves of the house on two sides were portholes. The house provided shelter for 113 people after the Brandt Raid on October 13, 1778. An average of eight militiamen stayed nine months each year during the Revolutionary War.

FORT HALDIMAND (*Fort Carleton*). Long recognized during the colonial years for its strategic military importance, three-mile-long Carleton Island, then known as Buck or Deer Island, is situated in the south (American) channel of the St. Lawrence River, one mile off present Burnham Point State Park in Cape Vincent Township, Jefferson County, and at the river's entrance into Lake Ontario. The peak of its occupation came during the Revolution, when it was a major supply base and a springboard for Tory expeditions into the Mohawk and Schoharie valleys. It was from Carleton Island that brevetted Brigadier General Barry St. Leger left on July 19, 1777, with a large force to initiate his offensive against the Mohawk Valley in conjunction with Burgoyne's campaign, only to be defeated before the ramparts of Fort Stanwix.

In the late spring of 1778, Sir Guy Carleton, governor general of Canada and commander in chief of the British forces therein, resigned his dual position, because of the personal animosity between himself and Lord Germain, the British secretary of state. On June 27, 1778, he was replaced by Sir Frederick Haldimand. A month later, the new governor appointed an engineer, a naval lieutenant, and an army captain to proceed to the upper St. Lawrence River and there select a place best suited for a fort and shipyard. The three men were impressed by Buck Island's potential and in compliment to the ex-governor of Canada named the island Carleton and the proposed fort for Haldimand.

Captain Thomas Aubrey was commandant of the island while the fort was being built in accordance with the plan designed by engineer William Twiss. The head of Carleton Island is a low peninsula, connected to the mainland by an isthmus, on either side of which are two bays—North Bay and South Bay. To the rear the island rises swiftly to a steep bluff to a height of nearly 60 feet above the water. Upon this elevation stood Fort Haldimand, a work that occupied three-eighths of an octagon, extending from edge to edge of the cliff on which it was built. A formidable fortification, with a bastion in the center of each face of the ramparts, bomb-proofed magazines and barracks, Fort Haldimand was defended by 30 guns of various calibers. At least one nineteenth-century historian erroneously labeled the British post Fort Carleton. From the many hundreds of reports and pieces of correspondence, it has been learned that during the Revolution and for many years thereafter, Carleton Island was one of the principal British naval bases on Lake Ontario.

FORT HALF MOON. Camp Van Schaick.

HALF-MOON FORT. A stockaded fort or redoubt at the strategic ferry across the Mohawk River at present Waterford, in Saratoga County, about 14 miles above Albany, Half-Moon was built some time before 1692 during the administration of Governor Benjamin Fletcher. It was usually unoccupied except in time of a war crisis and always in need of repair. Colonel Wolfgang William Romer, chief British engineer, recommended in his August 26, 1698, report that the Half-Moon be reconstructed as a palisaded stone redoubt adequate to accommodate 30 or 40 men. The fort was finally completely rebuilt in 1703. During the French and Indian War, engineer Colonel Montresor again rebuilt the fort. Its site is located one mile south of Broad Street on Peebles (formerly Haver) Island.

HALF WAY BROOK FORT. This strategic palisaded blockhouse, located on Half Way Brook at the northern end of present Glens Falls, was built by the British as a midway station between Fort Edward and Fort William Henry on Lake George to serve as a rendezvous and depot for troops in transit and supply trains. One citation reports it was erected in 1755 and was the scene of many bloody skirmishes, including two French and Indian ambushes resulting in massacres in the summers of 1756 and 1758. The translated 1756–60 journals of Louis Antoine de Bougainville, however, indicate that in 1758 the "English built this year [a fort] halfway from Fort Edward to Lake St. Sacrement [Lake George] to serve as a depot and for safety to their convoys." The blockhouse possibly survived until about 1780.

FORT HAMILTON (*Fort Lewis*). The first known European explorer to enter the Narrows, the entrance to Upper New York Bay, adjacent to the present location of Fort Hamilton in Brooklyn, was Giovanni de Verrazano in 1524, an Italian commissioned by Francis I of France. Henry Hudson on his *Halve Maen* sailed through the Narrows in 1609 and introduced the Dutch standard to America. In 1657 Jacques Cortelyou had the Fort Hamilton area granted to him for the purpose of establishing the town of New Utrecht by first constructing a blockhouse on or near the later site of the fort.

On both the first and the last day of the Revolutionary War, the Narrows had seen action. On the day that the Declaration of Independence was signed in Philadelphia, a tiny American battery at what is now Fort Hamilton was attacked by the British warship *Asia*, inflicting both damage and casualties before being silenced. The British used its environs as a landing site on the morning of August 22, 1776, to begin their assault on George Washington's forces in New York City. During the War of 1812, a blockhouse and earthworks, defended by a battery of 30 guns and known as Fort Lewis, were constructed during 1812 and 1813 on Denyse Heights near the site of Fort Hamilton.

In 1819 the U.S. Army began to plan for a fort on the Brooklyn side of the Narrows. Construction of the present fort, named in honor of Alexander Hamilton, began on June 11, 1825, when its cornerstone was laid under the supervision of French engineer Simon Bernard. Leisurely and carefully constructed, the granite-built fort was completed in 1831. Finally, on November 1, 1831, Battery F of the 4th Artillery marched in as its first garrison. The original fort area was a "walled enceinte," today the Fort Hamilton Officers' Open Mess. Another defense, Fort Lafayette (originally Fort Diamond) had been built during 1813 and 1814 on Hendricks Reef, 200 yards offshore from Fort Hamilton. It was the first stone fort on the east side of the Narrows.

Today's Building Number 117, at the corner of Lee and Schum avenues, within the post's limits, was home for General (then Captain) Robert E. Lee of the Corps of Topographical Engineers and his family during his tour of duty there from 1841 to 1846, while Lee was selecting sites for future coastal fortifications in the New York area. The years preceding the Civil War were quiet ones for Fort Hamilton. Although its guns would never be fired during the conflict, the fort did its part in the war effort.

At the turn of the century, the fort lost its seaward wall to make way for the installation of disappearing guns. It was then garrisoned by four companies of infantry, aggregating 437 men, and one artillery battery of 147 men and three officers. Its armament consisted of 25 guns of various calibers. After World War I, Fort Hamilton became an infantry post. Before 1941 many of its heavy guns were removed. By the 1940s Fort Hamilton held a garrison of about 1,000 officers and enlisted men, becoming the home of the Headquarters of the 1st Division. During World War II, it was one of the Posts of Embarkation in the New York area for men being sent overseas.

The base area covers 155 acres, with an assortment of 100 stone, brick, and wooden buildings. In 1974 Fort Hamilton's Officers' Open Mess was declared a National Historic Landmark. Today the post is a subinstallation of Fort Dix, New Jersey, and the last remaining major U.S. Army installation in the New York metropolitan area. Fort Hamilton now serves as headquarters for the New York Area Command.

CAMP HARDIN. Located at Sand Lake, southeast of Troy, in Rensselaer County, Camp Hardin was a Civil War training encampment for Troy area recruits. It was abandoned about 1866 or 1867.

FORT HARDY (*Fort Vrooman; Fort Saratoga; Fort Clinton*). This fort replaced a series of earlier posts on the same site. The first was Fort Vrooman on Fish Creek, south of Schuylerville, Saratoga County. The stockaded defense was built in 1689 around the house of Bartel (Bartolomeus) Vrooman and intermittently garrisoned by militiamen. The French destroyed the fort in 1695. It was rebuilt as the first Fort Saratoga in 1709; the second was erected in October 1721 under the supervision of Captain Philip Livingston as a square, palisaded work, with a blockhouse in each angle, armed with 12 cannon, and manned by militiamen; and the third so-named was erected in 1739. It was rebuilt in 1745 as Fort Clinton (for Governor Charles Clinton) and in 1757 as Fort Hardy (for Governor Charles Hardy) by engineer Colonel James Montresor. Fort Hardy

covered 15 acres and included two 120-foot-long barracks and 3 storehouses. It was abandoned some time after the end of the French and Indian War. Its site is located on Coveville County Road near Schuylerville.

FORT HARRISON. Located on the north side of the Mohawk River, west of Caroga Creek, in present St. Johnsville, Montgomery County, Fort Harrison was erected in either 1736 or 1750, more likely at the latter date, depending on the authority cited. It was apparently a wooden blockhouse built as a temporary defense.

FORT HENDRICK. Sir William Johnson ordered the construction of this fort in 1756 for the protection of the Mohawk Indians at their village of Canajoharie. It was located at old Indian Castle on Conowadaga Creek in the town of Danube, just off N.Y. 5S, in Herkimer County. The defense was named in honor of Johnson's friend, Mohawk chieftain Hendrick, who was killed in the Battle of Lake George in September 1755. The 150-foot-square fort of squared, 16-foot-long pine or oak logs had two 24-foot-square blockhouses in diagonal corners. Fort Hendrick survived the French and Indian War and was apparently torn down in 1764.

FORT HERKIMER (*Fort Kouari; Herkimer Church Fort*). The history of the Mohawk Valley was enriched by the legacy left by Johann Yost Herscheimer and his eldest son, General Nicholas Herkimer. Johann's original home, a log house erected about 1723, stood less than a half-mile east of later-built Herkimer Church Fort. "Jan Jost" built a large stone house in 1740 just to the east of his old log home. He ran a store and trading post and furnished the English at Oswego with provisions and supplies. Located on the south bank of the Mohawk River across from present Herkimer, the dwelling became known as Fort Herkimer after it was extensively fortified by William Johnson. The Indians called it Fort Kouari ("bear") in tribute to "Jan Jost's" great strength. The target of many attacks during the French and Indian War, it proved to be a welcome sanctuary for the area's settlers.

The great house was truly a fort—40 feet wide and 70 feet long, two-storied, with its outer walls more than 2 feet thick. Each story was loopholed, as was the basement. The structure was surrounded by a ditch 6 feet deep and 7 feet wide, at a distance of perhaps 30 feet. The ditch was planted with well-jointed palisades, set obliquely, behind which was an earthen parapet to facilitate firing over the pickets. The angles of the parapet were occupied by four small bastions that reciprocally flanked each other. On the west side, backed up against the parapet, was a house apart that served as a barracks and guardhouse. The remains of Fort Herkimer were destroyed during the construction of the Erie Canal (completed 1825).

The fort was rebuilt in 1756 around the stone Herkimer Dutch Reformed Church, a quarter of a mile or so west of the original site and two miles east of the village of Mohawk. Palatine German settlers began construction of the church in 1740 to replace their small log church built in 1723, but because of the French and Indian Wars the church was not completed until 1767. The original one-story stone structure measured 48 by 58 feet, with square buttresses at the corners and a swivel gun in its open tower.

During the early days of the Revolution, the church was refortified and surrounded by a strong palisade and earthworks. The fort, then known as Herkimer Church Fort, was one of the more important Mohawk Valley defenses. It was used as a secondary headquarters by Marinus Willett; Benedict Arnold stopped here in 1777; and General Washington paid a visit in 1783. In 1812 the church, one of the oldest in New York State, was renovated, altered, and enlarged with the addition of a second story, a pitched roof, and a cupola. It is located on the bank of the Barge Canal, which replaced the old Erie Canal and was completed in 1918. The ramparts of the second Fort Herkimer were destroyed at that time.

General Herkimer's home, five miles east of the original Fort Herkimer site, overlooks the river in a 135-acre park maintained by New York State. The colonial brick house was built by Nicholas Herkimer in 1763, and it is here that the hero of Oriskany died after amputation of a shattered leg suffered 10 days earlier in the battle.

HERKIMER CHURCH FORT. FORT HERKIMER.

CAMP HERO. A World War II seacoast defense located at the eastern tip of Long Island, Camp Hero opened in 1941 to eventually comprise 278 acres of numerous buildings. A subinstallation of Fort Totten, its armaments included two 16-inch and one 6-inch batteries. The Army in November 1957 transferred the post to the Air Force for air defense; it was then renamed Montauk Air Force Station. The Air Force shut down its radar operation there on July 1, 1980, leaving the post in charge of a caretaking detail. On February 8, 1984, the General Services Administration auctioned off the property, with the exception of two parcels located within Montauk Point State Park.

FORT HESS. Another refuge for beleaguered Mohawk Valley inhabitants was Fort Hess, a small fortified stone dwelling occupied by John Hess. It stood between Palatine Church and St. Johnsville, a mile west of Fort Fox and about three-quarters of a mile south of Fort Klock, in Montgomery County.

FORT H. G. WRIGHT. In 1898 the War Department purchased a tract of land on the western end of Fishers Island in Long Island Sound, eight miles southeast of New London, Connecticut, and initiated construction of a post there. It was named in honor of Connecticut-born Brigadier General Horatio Gates Wright, who commanded the VI Corps, Army of the Potomac, 1863–64, and was chief of engineers, 1879–84. It was first garrisoned as a subpost of Fort Trumbull on February 9, 1901, by a detachment of Coast Artillery under the command of Major Constantine Chase.

At the turn of the century, the 333-acre post was armed with two 12-inch and two 10-inch rifles on disappearing carriages, with other emplacements under construction. In 1913 Fort H. G. Wright was made headquarters of the coast defenses of Long Island Sound. The post saw service in both world wars. In 1958 the Army abandoned the military base, and the major portion of the property was auctioned off for $350,000 to a corporation owned by the island's affluent summer residents.

FORT HILL. Most Mohawk Valley histories do not mention Fort Hill. Most probably a fortified dwelling, it was apparently built during the French and Indian War and located on a hill in the western part of St. Johnsville, near or on East Canada Creek, Montgomery County. Tradition says the fort was subsequently repaired and served as a refuge during the Revolution. Fort Hill may be the same as Fort House, also located in St. Johnsville.

FORT HORN. A War of 1812 defense of New York City, Fort Horn was built in the summer and fall of 1814 under the direction of Brigadier General Joseph G. Swift, Engineer Corps. Located in Morningside Park at 123rd Street and Amsterdam Avenue, it was named for Major Joseph Horn, who supervised its construction.

FORT HOUSE. Confusion reigned regarding the location of Fort House, due to an error in reporting by Jeptha Simms, Mohawk Valley historian, who placed it at the eastern edge of St. Johnsville. Fort House stood at the *western* end of the village. It was the home of George Klock, who fortified and stockaded it. Since there were other dwellings in the eastern part of the village owned by other members of the Klock family, including Fort Klock, George Klock called his fortified dwelling Fort House in honor of its builder, Christian House (Haus). The structure, since somewhat remodeled, stands one mile west of the town's center and six miles northwest of Nelliston. Fort House may be the same as Fort Hill.

FORT HUDSON. FORT WADSWORTH.

FORT HUNTER. The major incentive for the settling of the fertile Mohawk Valley by Germans and Dutch was the establishment of Fort Hunter in 1711–12 at the strategic confluence of the Mohawk River and Schoharie Creek in present Montgomery County. Significant in New York's colonial history, the fort was constructed on the site of an old Mohawk village to become the first English fortification among the Iroquois.

In 1709 a delegation that included Albany's mayor, Peter Schuyler, and several Mohawk chiefs made the long journey to London and the court of Queen Anne to obtain the authority to construct fortifications in the Mohawk Valley. At the time there were living in London numerous Palatine Germans (Protestants), refugees from French wars and religious persecution. The Indian chiefs offered the queen a tract of land called Schoorie (Schoharie) as a haven for the displaced people. Queen Anne gratefully accepted the offer. Successful in his mission, Schuyler returned with commissions to erect two forts—one at the mouth of Schoharie Creek, with the other, never constructed, in Onondaga Indian country.

Fort Hunter was named for Governor Robert Hunter, who brought 3,000 Palatines to America in 1709, the year he assumed the province's governorship. The fort was a square, 150 feet on each side, with a 12-foot-high palisade. At each of the four angles was a two-story, 24-foot-square, double-loopholed blockhouse or bastion, armed with seven- and nine-pounder cannon. On the inner sides of the palisade were five-foot-wide parapets. In the center of the fort was the famous Queen Anne's Chapel, ordered by Her Majesty for "my Mohawk Indians," a one-story, 24-foot-square limestone building with an attic. The chapel was well floored, with a 15-foot-square cellar lined with logs, apparently used as a powder magazine. Queen Anne furnished the communion set, the altar cloth, and other church appurtenances. She also periodically sent ministers to officiate at the services for the Indians.

A two-story, substantial stone parsonage 25 by 35 feet was built in 1734. During the Revolution it was fortified, palisaded, and garrisoned. New York City's Trinity Church supervised the chapel's affairs. In 1769 Sir William Johnson established one of his free schools at Fort Hunter with a class of 30 Indian pupils. The fort was kept under constant repair through the years but, as with all similarly built fortifications, the ravages of time caught up. Decaying old Fort Hunter was torn down at the beginning of the Revolution, and a new fort rose in its place, with Queen Anne's Chapel enclosed by strong palisades and cannon-mounted blockhouses at the four angles. During the war the fort was frequently garrisoned, with many Oneida and Stockbridge Indians using the chapel as a barracks.

The fort and the chapel were demolished in 1820 to make way for "Clinton's Ditch," the Erie Canal, but the old stone parsonage still remains and is one of the oldest structures in the Mohawk Valley. A good deal of the stone from Queen Anne's Chapel was used for the Schoharie Creek lock.

HURLEY BLOCKHOUSE. Erected by the Dutch during the early 1660s, this palisaded blockhouse protected the village of Hurley in present Ulster County against Esopus Indian incursions. The blockhouse possibly survived until about 1686.

FORT INDEPENDENCE (*Fort Constitution*). Of minor significance and relatively short-lived, Fort Independence was constructed at Peekskill in Westchester County during August 1776 under the direction of General George Clinton. In September a barracks was begun to accommodate the defense's garrison. The fort, initially called Fort Constitution for a short time, was situated on Tethard's Hill on Roa (Rahway) Hook on the east bank of the Hudson, opposite Dunderberg Mountain. Designed to guard the approaches to Peekskill Bay and ultimately Continental Village's munitions depot, this Patriot work was commanded by Major Israel Thompson. On March 23, 1777, a British force of about 500 men raided Peekskill, forcing the evacuation of the supply depot. (See: CONTINENTAL VILLAGE.)

At midnight, October 6, the day Forts Clinton and Montgomery in the Highlands fell to Sir Henry Clinton's British regulars and Hessians, Governor George Clinton arrived at Continental

Village, three miles north of Peekskill. In a council of war with General Israel Putnam and other staff officers, it was decided to evacuate the American defenses in and around Peekskill. Fort Independence shared the same fate with other American forts in the Highlands—ruthless destruction by Sir Henry's forces. Fort Independence was never rebuilt, and its blackened ruins have served as a reminder of the war for decades to Peekskill's people.

FORT INGOLDSBY (*Fort Winslow; Montresor's Blockhouse; Schuyler's Supply Depot*). The first of four forts at Stillwater, Saratoga County, all approximately on the same site on the west bank of the Hudson River, was erected by Colonel Peter Schuyler in 1709 and named Fort Ingoldsby in honor of Major Richard Ingoldsby, acting governor of the province of New York at the time. The second was built in 1756 by General John Winslow and named for himself. The third was constructed under the supervision of engineer Colonel James Montresor. These fortifications were stockaded and loopholed blockhouses, designed for Indian defense. Continental General Philip Schuyler, a descendant by marriage of Peter Schuyler, in an effort to check the advance of General Burgoyne's invasion army, built a fortified supply depot there during the first week of August 1777. With no evidences remaining of any of these fortifications, a New York State Historical Marker was placed at the approximate site.

FORT JAY. Governors Island Forts.

FORT JERSEY. A Revolutionary War blockhouse defense, Fort Jersey was located on the Mohochamack Fork of the Delaware River, two miles from the site of the Battle of Minisink, July 22, 1779, which culminated in the destruction of Port Jervis and other area settlements. Fort Jersey was abandoned after the war, probably about the year 1790.

FORT JOHNSON. Located on the Mohawk River in the town of Fort Johnson, three miles west of Amsterdam, Fort Johnson was erected in 1749 by Sir William Johnson as his residence. Two-story, surmounted by an attic, and substantially built of gray fieldstone, with portholes and a lead roof, it was known as Mount Johnson until 1755, when it became Fort Johnson with the construction of a strong palisade around it. Two blockhouses, large enough to garrison 40 men, were built in 1758 at either end of the property. During the French and Indian War, between 1754 and 1760, important Indian councils were held at the fort. Sir William lived here until 1763 when he moved to his new home, Johnson Hall, at Johnstown, leaving Fort Johnson to his son, Sir John Johnson. The Patriots stripped the building of its lead roof and molded the metal into bullets after confiscating the estate at the outbreak of the Revolution. Its site is listed in the *National Register of Historic Places*. In 1976 the Montgomery County Historical Society undertook its restoration as a Bicentennial project.

FORT JOHNSTOWN. Located at the present intersection of Perry and Montgomery streets in Johnstown, Fulton County, stone-built Fort Johnstown was erected in 1772 at the direction of Sir William Johnson, who then resided at nearby Johnson Hall. The palisaded defense was further fortified by a pair of blockhouses at diagonal corners. It served as an important frontier jail and military prison during the American Revolution. The structure today is maintained as the Fulton County Jail.

FORT KANADESAGA. This fort, erected in 1756 by order of Sir William Johnson, was located in the Indian village of Kanadesaga, the capital of the Seneca Nation, at the foot of Seneca Lake, now within the city limits of Geneva. The 100-foot-square fort was palisaded 15 feet high, with two 20-foot-square blockhouses at diagonal corners. The fort was destroyed in 1779 during the Sullivan-Clinton Expedition. In September 1975 archaeologists of the Rochester Museum discovered the first remains of the fort after digging for a month.

FORT KENTUCKY (*Fort Mud*). A small earthen redoubt also known as Fort Mud, this War of 1812 defense was located near the naval base at Sackett's Harbor on Lake Ontario and built sometime after the British attack in May 1813. Fort Kentucky was abandoned soon after the end of the war in 1815.

FORT KEYSER. Located one mile south of the old village of Stone Arabia, north of Palatine Bridge, Montgomery County, Fort Keyser was originally built during the decade preceding 1750 by Johannes Keyser (Kayser, Keisar) and his Palatine German family. The structure was all stone, approximately 20 by 40 feet. Because of its exposed situation during the French and Indian War, it was loopholed and minimally fortified. Sometime during the first two years of the Revolution, Fort Keyser was strongly fortified and served as a refuge for the area's inhabitants.

It was abandoned when Fort Paris was built a half-mile north in the spring of 1777 and was torn down in the 1840s. Fort Keyser's site is about a quarter of a mile east of the junction of S.R. 10 and C.R. 43 (Dillenbeck Road).

FORT KIMBER. George Kimber, a miller, built Fort Kimber in 1759 during the French and Indian War, at present Unionville, Orange County. It was apparently abandoned at the end of the war.

KING'S FERRY FORTS (*Fort Stony Point; Fort Lafayette*). In late 1779 Sir Henry Clinton made his last important effort to lure General Washington out of his West Point fortifications. The British general's targets were Stony Point (Rockland County) and Fort Lafayette at Verplanck's Point (Westchester County), respectively the western and eastern landings of King's Ferry, about 25 miles above New York City and half that distance below West Point. The two Points are commanding promontories, with 150-foot-high, rugged Stony Point jutting a half-mile into the Hudson River. King's Ferry, the gateway to the Highlands, was important to the Patriots because it was the closest safe crossing of the river to British-held New York City.

On May 30 Sir Henry personally led the expedition, embarking 6,000 British regulars and Hessians on more than 120 frigates, galleys, gunboats, and flatboats at King's Bridge (Spuyten Duyvil Creek). The next day, Major General John Vaughan landed with a force below Verplanck's Point, to come up behind Fort Lafayette; Sir Henry landed the rest of the troops three miles below the incomplete defenses of Stony Point on the west shore and with little trouble occupied the heights. After the bombardment of Fort Lafayette's works, garrisoned by only 75 Carolinians, the fort surrendered.

After the British had enlarged and strengthened the two forts, added 15 heavy guns at Stony Point and stores, and had them strongly garrisoned, Sir Henry dropped down the river and took up temporary headquarters at Phillipsburgh (now Yonkers) to await developments from West Point. Subsequent to reconnoitering Stony Point and Verplanck's Point for six weeks, General Washington ordered General Anthony Wayne to immediately make plans for a surprise night assault against Stony Point.

Wayne had under his command 1,200 infantry and a reserve force of 300 men under General John Muhlenberg, and Henry ("Light-Horse Harry") Lee and his cavalry for scouting and securing the environs of Stony Point. On the night of July 15–16, the Americans launched their attack. The swiftness and expertise of the assault overwhelmed the British and Hessians. The captured stores, supplies, and armaments were valued at approximately $180,655, prize money divided among Wayne (slightly wounded), his officers, and men according to rank. Stony Point's guns were then turned against Fort Lafayette across the river. Washington had ordered Major General Robert Howe to immediately march against Verplanck's Point, but Howe did not have the foresight to coordinate troops and supplies, and the main chance to take Fort Lafayette was gone. The successful Stony Point venture proved to be a tremendous psychological boost to Continental morale. After their victory, they withdrew with their spoils.

On July 19 Sir Henry reoccupied Stony Point with a force twice as large as the garrison he had lost there. He had the works rebuilt, even to completely enclosing the fort on the height. Fort Lafayette had its garrison augmented to more than 700 men. But later he could not see how he could possibly hold on to King's Ferry throughout the coming winter season. During the early fall, he suddenly abandoned both Points, much to Washington's gratification. The Continentals then reoccupied the strategic King's Ferry forts and remained there during the last years of the war.

FORT KLOCK. A massive, L-shaped story-and-a-half stone building with two-foot-thick limestone walls, thoroughly loopholed and resting on an elevation of solid rock, Fort Klock at St. Johnsville was built by Palatine German pioneer Johannes Klock in 1750 on the site of his former smaller home. On October 19, 1780, on the battleground known as Klock's Field just to the east of Fort Klock, militia under General Robert Van Rensselaer attacked Sir John Johnson's mixed force of raiders. During the dramatic action, many of the town's inhabitants found refuge within the fort. During the war John Klock resided at the fort and conducted a thriving business of fur trading. Still standing, as one of the few remaining Mohawk Valley trading posts, on today's S.R. 10, on the north bank of the Mohawk, less than one mile east of St. Johnsville's center, Fort Klock was restored by Tryon County Muzzle Loaders, Inc., and is now managed by Fort Klock Historic Restoration, Inc.

FORT KOUARI. FORT HERKIMER.

FORT LA PRÉSENTATION (*Fort Oswegatchie*). In 1749 Abbé François Picquet, a

40-year-old Sulpician Jesuit, founded the first white settlement where now stands the city of Ogdensburg, to lay claim to the land for his native France and to instruct and convert the region's Iroquois Indians. The site he selected for his mission and garrisoned military post (now occupied by the Notre Dame Church) had been first visited in the spring of 1626 by Father Gabriel Lalemant who, enamored of its sylvan splendor, named it La Galette ("the cake").

Located at the confluence of the St. Lawrence and Oswegatchie rivers, Fort La Présentation was a combined church, mission and school, trading post, and military citadel. It was named for the day Father Picquet was first here, November 21, 1748, Feast of the Présentation of the Blessed Virgin in the Temple. He returned with an expedition on May 30, 1749, to begin construction. The first mass at the site—the first in northern New York—was celebrated by Abbé Picquet, glorified in history as the "Apostle to the Iroquois," on June 1, 1749.

Fort La Présentation had been described as a square, with tower-shaped bastions in the four angles, surrounded by a wide moat and an entrenchment. Its soldiers and Indians were participants in the annihilation of General Burgoyne's army near Fort Duquesne in 1755. The fort was the center from which the French dispatched scalping parties that raided Mohawk Valley settlements during the crucial years 1758–59. When Quebec fell to the English in 1759, Father Picquet fled to New Orleans for safety, and Fort La Présentation was abandoned to the British who took over the post, renamed Fort Oswegatchie.

The English occupied it from 1760 until their evacuation in 1796 in compliance with the Jay Treaty. What was once a highly touted French military post had become an English settlement important only to British fur and lumber interests. In the course of establishing townships and protracted legal sales of unappropriated lands, practically all of what is now Ogdensburg ultimately became the property of Samuel Ogden.

FORT LAFAYETTE. KING'S FERRY FORTS.

FORT LAFAYETTE (*Fort Diamond*). In 1812 after the outbreak of war with Great Britain, the Federal government began the construction of Fort Diamond, so-called at first because of its shape, on two-and-a-half-acre Hendricks Reef about 200 yards off the Brooklyn shore of the Narrows, opposite later-built Fort Hamilton on the mainland. Completed in 1822 as the first

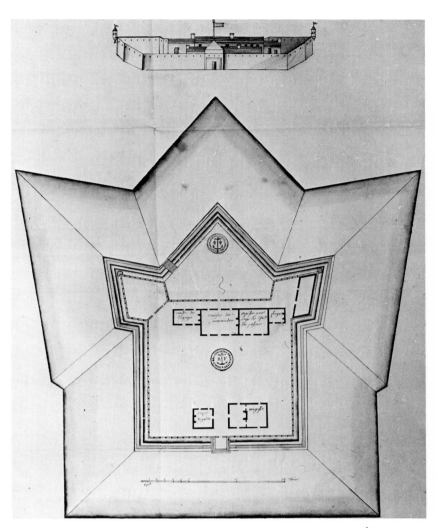

FORT LA PRÉSENTA-TION. Plan drawn in 1752. (Courtesy of the National Archives of Canada.)

stone fort on the east side of the Narrows (Fort Hamilton was the second), it more or less presaged the introduction of what became known as the Third System (from 1817 to just after the Civil War) of U.S. coast defense. With 8-foot-thick walls rising 30 feet, the fort mounted 73 guns in three tiers.

The fort was renamed Fort Lafayette on March 26, 1823, in honor of the Marquis de Lafayette after the general's last visit to America. Both Fort Lafayette, known as "the Brooklyn Bastille," and Castle Williams on Governors Island served as Civil War prisons. On December 1, 1868, the whole of the fort's interior was gutted by fire, necessitating complete rebuilding. During both world wars, Fort Lafayette served as a naval munitions magazine. It was not used since it was leased to New York City by the Navy in 1948, thwarting a move to convert the fort into a nightclub. In January 1960, after 148 years of intermittent military service, Fort Lafayette and the reef it stood on were obliterated by the beginning of construction on the Verrazano-Narrows Bridge, a massive suspension span linking Fort Hamilton

FORT LAFAYETTE. Painting by Seth Eastman. (Courtesy of the Architect of the Capitol, Washington, D.C.)

on the Brooklyn shore with Fort Wadsworth on Staten Island.

FORT LAIGHT. A War of 1812 defense of New York City, Fort Laight was built during the summer and fall of 1814 and named in honor of Lieutenant Colonel Edward W. Laight of the city's militia. The defense was located on the south side of present West 125th Street, 120 feet east of 11th Avenue.

FORT LAWRENCE. A War of 1812 defense of New York City, Fort Lawrence was constructed in 1814 by order of General Joseph G. Swift on the west side of Gowanus Creek, at the present junction of DeGraw and Bond streets in Brooklyn. It was defended by a battery of artillery.

FORT (DE) LÉVIS (*Fort William Augustus*). Located in the St. Lawrence River, downstream from the city of Ogdensburg, Fort Lévis was built in 1759 on Isle Royale to replace Fort La Présentation by French Captain François Pouchot, former commandant of Fort Niagara, and named in honor of Major General François Gaston de Lévis. The site of one of the last battles of the French and Indian War, it was captured by General Jeffrey Amherst's forces on August 25, 1769, after a severe bombardment of its works, occupied by the British, and renamed Fort William Augustus in honor of the Duke of Cumberland. The island, known today as Chimney Island, was reduced to six acres in 1957 for the construction of the St. Lawrence Seaway. It is situated east of the Seaway Skyway Bridge between Ogdensburg and Johnstown in Ontario.

FORT LEWIS. FORT HAMILTON.

FORT L'OBSERVATION. A French military outpost erected in 1757 and located about a mile and a half from Six Town Point on Henderson Bay, south of present Sackets Harbor, Jefferson County, Fort L'Observation was a square, log-built stockade with armament-mounted bastions in all its four angles. Commanded by Captain Coulon de Villiers, who captured Fort Necessity and received the surrender of Colonel George Washington, the post was intended to spy on English activities at Oswego.

LONG ISLAND FORTS (*Sag Harbor Fort; Fort Setauket; Oyster Bay Encampment; Fort Franklin; Fort St. George; Fort Slongo; Fort Golgotha*). The British occupation of Long Island during the American Revolution was reinforced by seven forts or cantonments, all targeted for destruction by American guerrilla forces. The only post within the limits of today's Nassau County was the reigning British fortified cantonment, Oyster Bay Encampment, headquarters of the Queen's Rangers. To the east, in Suffolk County, along the north shore of the Island, were Fort Franklin on Lloyd Neck, Fort Golgotha at Huntington, Fort Slongo on Treadwell Neck at present Fort Salonga, and Fort Setauket. The south shore was protected by Fort St. George at Mastic, established by Americans loyal to George III. The easternmost post was Sag Harbor Fort on Shelter Island Sound, 105 miles from British-held New York City. The only British fortifications to escape rebel wrath were the Oyster Bay Encampment, nerve center of British operations on the Island, and Fort Golgotha.

Within the cordon of British posts was the famous Patriot spy network known as the Culper Ring, the first American organization of espionage agents, which performed with distinction under the supervision of Major Benjamin Tallmadge, General Washington's chief of intelligence. It was Tallmadge's perception and enterprise after the capture of John Anderson (John Andre) that led to the startling disclosure of Benedict Arnold's treason.

FORT LOOK OUT. On a hill to the east of Fort Independence at Peekskill and north of Peekskill Creek was located a small American work called Fort Look Out. An adjoining elevation, Gallows Hill, was the site of the hanging of Edmund Palmer, a British spy, in the summer of 1780. A fine view of the Hudson River was commanded by these two hills. Fort Look Out was also destroyed when British and Hessian troops pillaged and burned the depot at Continental Village, three miles north of Fort Independence, the village of Peekskill, and most of the homes and farms in the environs of the town.

LOWER FORT (*Old Stone Fort*). The Lower Fort (as differentiated from Middle Fort and Upper Fort), also known historically as the Old Stone Fort, was St. John's Church, located one mile north of the town of Schoharie on present N.Y. 30. A refuge during Indian raids for Schoharie Valley's inhabitants before the Revolution, in 1778 the church was fortified by a strong stockade with two blockhouses. On October 17, 1780, it was assaulted by Sir John Johnson with a force of 800 Tories and Indians. The fort's 200 defenders successfully rebuffed the raiders during the hour-and-a-half battle.

FORT LYDIUS. FORT EDWARD.

FORT LYMAN. FORT EDWARD.

CAMP MCCLELLAN. CAMP TOMPKINSVILLE.

MADISON BARRACKS (*Fort Pike*). Located at the present town of Sackets Harbor on the south shore of Black River Bay on Lake Ontario, 11 miles west of Watertown, Madison Barracks was established in 1815 as Fort Pike, a name soon changed to honor President James Madison. In 1816 five companies of the 2nd Infantry occupied as yet unfinished barracks and officers' quarters, completed along with other structures in October 1819. The post was intermittently garrisoned until after the Civil War. From 1849–52, its quartermaster was Ulysses S. Grant, then a lieutenant. During 1893–99, additional construction significantly enlarged the size of the post. Occupying 108 acres, Madison Barracks in World War I was principally known as a hospital post. During World War II, it was used by both the Army and Navy. Madison Barracks was declared surplus on July 30, 1945.

FORT MARCY. Established during the War with Mexico, this post was named in honor of William L. Marcy, secretary of war under President Polk and former governor of New York

LOWER FORT. (Courtesy of the New York State Department of Commerce.)

State. It was reportedly located in New York City but its precise site is not known. Probably an encampment, Fort Marcy was presumably used as a staging area for New York troops recruited for the war.

FORT MASONIC. A War of 1812 defense of New York City, Fort Masonic was constructed on August 31, 1814, by the Grand Lodge of Free Masons, who numbered 750 and were headed by their Grand Master, De Witt Clinton. The fort was located on the block between Nevins and Bond streets in Brooklyn.

MAYFIELD FORT. SACANDAGA BLOCKHOUSE.

FORT MEIGS. WEST POINT'S FORTS.

FORT MICHIE. Established in 1900 on Gull Island in Long Island Sound, 12 miles from New London, Connecticut, Fort Michie was named in honor of 1st Lieutenant Dennis M. Michie, 17th Infantry, killed in action at San Juan, Cuba, on July 1, 1898. Occupying about 17 acres, Fort Michie, a subpost of Fort Terry, mounted two 12-inch and two 10-inch rifles on disappearing carriages, manned by a company of Coast Artillery occupying temporary officers' quarters and barracks. The defense was apparently dismantled soon after the end of World War I.

MIDDLE FORT. Located at Middleburg in Schoharie County, Middle Fort was the strongest of the three Schoharie Valley defenses. Its palisades enclosed an area of ground rather larger than that of Lower Fort at Schoharie, with armament-mounted blockhouses in the northeast and southwest angles. Within, on each side of the fort's gate, were the barracks. The village and its surrounding environs, known locally as Vrooman's Land, were first raided on August 9, 1780, by Joseph Brant, Mohawk war chief, with about 80 Indians and 6 Tories who set fires throughout the area. Eleven members of the prominent Vrooman family were carried off, with three others, the mother, father, and an eight-year-old son killed. After this bloody foray, the garrisons of all the Schoharie forts were strengthened.

During the three days, October 16–19, 1780, Schoharie Valley was devastated by a much larger force of destructives, 800 Tories and Indians led by Sir John Johnson. Bypassing Upper Fort during the night, the raiders arrived at Middleburg shortly after dawn on October 17 and soon invested the fort, garrisoned by 150 short-term Continentals and 50 militiamen under the command of Major Melancthon Woolsey, who was willing to participate in a parley leading to capitulation. But Timothy Murphy, a bold militiaman, differed with the commander's intent and fired at the enemy's white-flag team, driving it back in haste. Vociferous support by other militiamen and some Continental officers forced the weak-kneed major to relinquish command of the fort to Colonel Peter Vrooman, who directed a spirited resistance. Toward the middle of the afternoon, Johnson lifted the siege and withdrew with his forces to march five miles up the valley to Schoharie and the Lower Fort, continuing to lay waste to everything in their path. Soon after this display of resistance, the fort was locally dubbed Fort Defiance.

FORT MILLER. FORT AMHERST.

FORT MILLER. Colonel Samuel Miller's palisaded blockhouse was built in July 1755 at the "Little Carrying Place" on the left bank of the Hudson River, opposite the later established village of Fort Miller, in the town of Northumberland in Saratoga County. Its site is north of Bacon Hill on Fort Edward Road.

MILL ROCK BLOCKHOUSE. A War of 1812 defense of New York City, the blockhouse was erected on Mill Rock in the middle of the East River, opposite the mouth of the Harlem River. The defense burned down in 1821.

CAMP MILLS. MITCHEL FIELD.

FORT MISERY. A small French and Indian War palisaded blockhouse erected in 1755 by the English, Fort Misery stood atop an elevation on Moses Kill east of the Hudson River and south of Fort Edward in Washington County. Abandoned in 1764, it was briefly occupied by Patriots in July 1777 to guard the road between Schuylerville and Fort Edward.

MITCHEL FIELD (*Camp Winfield Scott; Camp Black; Camp Mills*). When the Air Force in 1961 closed 1,168-acre Mitchel Field near Hempstead on Long Island, Nassau County lost one of its oldest residents. The 185-year-old military installation first served as an enlistment center for Continental Army recruits shortly after the outbreak of the American Revolution. During the War of 1812 and the Mexican War, U.S. infantry detachments occupied Hempstead Plains as a training center. It was known as Camp Winfield Scott in the Civil War and Camp Black during the Spanish-American War.

In World War I, Camp Albert L. Mills was established there in August 1917. It became famous as the site for the mobilization and training of 42nd (Rainbow) Division and the Fighting 69th Regiment. In 1918 Camp Mills was transformed by the advance of technology in the skies, from a training center for ground troops to a base for aviators. Its name was changed to Mitchel Field in honor of Major John Purroy Mitchel, a former New York City mayor who was killed in a plane crash. During World War II, the base served as an important participant in the air defense of the eastern seaboard. Prior to its closing, Mitchel Field was the headquarters for several Air Force units, including the Continental Air Defense Command.

FORT MONTGOMERY. FORTS CLINTON and MONTGOMERY.

FORT MONTGOMERY (*Fort Blunder*). Initial construction of Fort Montgomery, situated at the north narrow end of Lake Champlain just above Rouse's Point, was begun in 1817 and designed to protect the American side of the border. In 1819 British and American surveyors found that the site was actually on Canadian territory. The almost immediate suspension of work on the fort, on which a great deal of money had already been spent, led to it being derisively named "Fort Blunder." The problem was not resolved until 1842 when the Webster-Ashburton Treaty slightly realigned the boundary to locate Fort Montgomery on American soil. Work on the fortification resumed and was carried forward into the Civil War. By 1865 it was ready for the mounting of armaments. The guns were installed but never used against an enemy, and the fort thereafter remained under garrison strength. In 1910 the guns were removed, and the fort and the land on which it stood fell into the hands of private owners. According to local historians, Fort Montgomery stood relatively intact until 1936, when the first Rouse's Point Bridge was built, making use of a good part of the fort's granite walls for construction of the span's approaches. Recently, when a new bridge was planned to replace the old bridge, efforts were initiated to retrieve the original stone and restore the fort as a historical monument.

MONTRESOR'S BLOCKHOUSE. FORT INGOLDSBY.

FORT OSWEGO. THE OSWEGO FORTS.

FORT MOREAU. A War of 1812 defense of Plattsburgh, Fort Moreau was a large redoubt constructed in September 1814 in compliance with orders of Brigadier General Alexander Macomb in order to check the advance of 14,000 British troops. It stood on the already fortified ridge between the mouth of the Saranac River and Lake Champlain and was flanked by two smaller works—Fort Brown, close to the river, and Fort Scott, on the lake shore. In addition, where the ridge projected into the lake, two blockhouses stood.

FORT MORTON. FORT WADSWORTH.

FORT MOUNT HOPE. This fort was constructed in 1755 during the French and Indian War as an outpost of Fort Ticonderoga. It stood on a hill a half-mile east of the present Fort Ticonderoga restoration, overlooking the outlet of Lake George into Lake Champlain. It was alternately captured by the French under Montcalm, and the British led by General Abercromby in 1758 and General Amherst in 1759. In 1776 it was rebuilt by American troops commanded by Colonel Jeduthan Baldwin and occupied by both British and American forces. Fort Mount Hope was purchased in 1946 from private owners and restored the following year.

FORT MUD. FORT KENTUCKY.

MUD FORT. FORT ANNE.

FORT NASSAU. FORT FREDERICK.

FORT NECK. This British fort, established in 1653, was located on Long Island. Originally an Indian fortified position, the site was captured during an assault led by Captain John Underhill. The fort was 30 yards square and had a 6-foot palisaded ditch.

FORT NEILSON. SARATOGA BATTLEFIELD FORTS.

FORT NELLIS. A short distance from better-known Fort Klock, Fort Nellis was the fortified dwelling of Christian Nellis located near St. Johnsville, Montgomery County. The affluent farmer had six sons—Henry, Christian, Robert, Adam, George, and Theobald, with only the first-named living with his father. The family was one of the most prominent in the Palatine settlements; the town of Nelliston to the southeast was named for the tribe. The Nellis property is one of the most remarkable illustrations of perpetuity in the Mohawk Valley. It has been occupied and operated by the male descendants of the family through a continuous chain of 10 generations, dating from William Nellis, who first obtained title to the property on October 19, 1723. Although Fort Nellis faced on Klock's Field, where Van Rensselaer's militia fought Tory and Indian raiders on October 19, 1780, it was not involved in the action. Most of the area's inhabitants took refuge in Fort Klock. Sometime after the war, the elder Christian Nellis was dragged to his death when his horses became frightened.

FORT NEVERSINK. FORT NEW JERSEY.

NEW FORT OSWEGO. THE OSWEGO FORTS.

FORT NEW JERSEY (*Fort Neversink*). Erected in 1756 during the French and Indian War by the New Jersey Frontier Guards, this fort, at times referred to as Fort Minisink, was located at present Port Jervis in Orange County, near the Delaware and Neversink rivers, an area then claimed by both the New York and New Jersey colonial governments. The site of the fort is at the present intersection of East Main Street and New Jersey Avenue.

FORT NEW PETERSBURG. Located in East Schuyler, Herkimer County, this fort consisting of three palisaded log houses was established in 1764 by Peter Hansclever's German settlers. It was raided by Tories during the Revolution.

FORT NEWPORT. Named for the fort's commander, a Captain Newport, this French and Indian War defense was erected in 1756 to guard the upper Wood Creek Landing. Situated on an elevation about a half-mile from Fort Bull, its site is on present Calvert Street between Arsenal Street and Brewer Alley in the city of Rome.

NEW WINDSOR CANTONMENT. After the British surrender at Yorktown, peace negotiations opened in Paris early in 1782. Although most Americans considered the Revolution practically at an end, with victory inevitable, the British still occupied New York City, Charleston, and Savannah, and America's French allies had withdrawn to deal with their problems in the West Indies and elsewhere. General Washington knew that vigilance could not be relaxed until a final peace treaty was signed. In October 1782 he ordered the troops of the Continental Army to move north to the Hudson Highlands and had a winter cantonment laid out in the precinct of New Windsor at Vails Gate, adjoining the southern edge of today's city of Newburgh.

This final encampment became the army's most substantial quarters of the Revolution. Log houses were laid out in precise rows to house the 7,000 officers and men. Continental troops constructed about 700 huts, each accommodating two squads. The entire camp was sectioned off into regular streets, an ultra-modern urban design for that era, with each regiment occupying and policing its own district. When the housing and other structures required for army life were completed, a chaplain suggested that a spacious hall be erected for religious services and other large congregations. Called the Temple of Virtue, the new structure measured 30 by 110 feet, with a cupola and flagstaff atop its shingled roof.

The eight months of occupation was a period of uncertainty and tribulation for the soldiers. Peace negotiations were protracted. While the Continental Congress debated policy, back pay was piling up, inflation was rampant, and discontent was growing, particularly among the officers. The tension was brought to a head by the circulation of the so-called Newburgh Letters, two documents urging the officers to rebel and force Congress to meet their demands for back pay and pensions. Appalled by the machinations among his officers, General Washington summoned them to a meeting in the Temple on March 15, 1783, and in a dramatic speech appealed to their patriotism. The strength of the general's character and statesmanship broke the conspiracy. Many historians believe that his prudent action saved representative government in America.

At New Windsor Cantonment, General Washington named the first soldiers to receive the Badge of Military Merit, a decoration he created to honor acts of heroism by enlisted men. The Purple Heart, awarded today for wounds received in battle, takes its design from this badge. On April 19, 1783, eight years to the day of the first bloodshed at Lexington and Concord, Washington announced the signing of a preliminary peace treaty. Anxious to return to their homes and families, the soldiers were granted temporary furloughs by Congress.

No longer in use, the cantonment's buildings were auctioned off for their lumber, with the exception of two officers' huts, which were moved a few miles away and used as private dwellings. One hut managed to survive 151 years of private ownership, to be finally rescued and returned in 1934 to the site of the cantonment, where it now stands on exhibit among a number of replicas. On May 8, 1965, New Windsor Cantonment was opened to the American people as a museum. The other hut was recently discovered as part of a barn, and restoration is in progress.

FORT NIAGARA (*Fort Conti; Fort Denonville*). Old Fort Niagara and its predescessors on the triangular point of land at the mouth of the Niagara River on Lake Ontario, at present Youngstown, had great importance during the early colonial conflicts to determine what European nation was to dominate North America. The first fort here was Fort Conti (1679) built by the great French explorer, René Robert Cavelier de La Salle and named in honor of his friend, the Prince of Conti. This was destroyed by Indians, probably in 1682, to be replaced by short-lived Fort Denonville (1687), built in compliance with orders of the then governor of New France, Jacques René de Brisay, the marquis de Nonville, and destroyed the following year. The first fort to be named Fort Niagara, built in 1725–27, was the so-called House of Peace, which remains to this day and is known as the French Castle, the oldest masonry structure west of the Hudson and east of the Mississippi.

The French and Indian War, precipitated in 1754 by dominion differences between England and France, influenced New France to draft plans to implement the strengthening of Niagara, the gateway to the Upper Mississippi Valley. In early October 1755, three vessels carrying Captain Francois Pouchot and five regiments left Fort Frontenac (today's Kingston, Ontario) for the Niagara frontier. In the next four years, military engineer Pouchot converted Fort Niagara from a crumbling House of Peace and a few semipermanent structures into an elaborate fortress of barracks, an ingenious system of earthworks, entrenchments and moats, a powder magazine, and complements of heavy artillery.

Fort Niagara was occupied by the French until 1759, when the bloody Battle of La Belle Famille forced its capitulation. During the Revolution, the British used the fort as a staging area for attacks against Patriot settlements in the Mohawk, Schoharie, and Wyoming valleys. By the terms of the 1783 Treaty of Paris, Fort Niagara became the property of the United States, but the British continued to occupy it until 1796, claiming that the Americans had not conformed with all of the stipulations of the pact. During the War of 1812, the fort was recaptured and temporarily occupied by the British.

In 1841 new building construction was begun adjacent to old Fort Niagara. During the Civil War, work was significantly increased when the government feared British entry into the war on the side of the Confederacy. After the war, the fortifications and the French Castle gradually became dilapidated through neglect brought on by its decrease in importance as a strategically located fortification. Restoration of the fort as a

FORT NIAGARA. Artist's rendition. (Courtesy of the National Archives.)

FORT NIAGARA. The "House of Peace." (Courtesy of the New York State Department of Commerce.)

King George II brought to Niagara by Sir William Johnson; and the Stars and Stripes of 1796, first raised at Niagara by a detachment of American artillerymen.

FORT NICHOLSON. FORT EDWARD.

NORTH BATTERY. RED FORT.

OLD FORT SCHUYLER. Connecticut troops under the command of Governor of Massachusetts Fitz-John Winthrop built this rough earthwork in 1692, when they were on their way to invade Canada. The fort is located on U.S. 4 on Wood and Halfway creeks in Washington County.

OLD STONE FORT. LOWER FORT.

FORT ONTARIO. THE OSWEGO FORTS.

FORT OQUAGA. During the Revolution, the Iroquois towns of Unadilla on the Susquehanna River and Oquaga (today's Ouaquaga) in Broome County, about 20 miles below Unadilla, were Joseph Brant's staging areas for Indian assaults against the settlements. In 1757, during the French and Indian War, a fort was erected at Oquaga for the Indians, after they had requested protection for their families, in compliance with orders of Sir William Johnson.

FORT ORANGE. FORT FREDERICK.

FORT OSWEGATCHIE. FORT LA PRÉSENTATION.

THE OSWEGO FORTS (*Fort Oswego; Fort George; Fort Ontario*). From the first English toehold in the Great Lakes region to a training base for United States overseas troops, a succession of military installations commanded the strategic mouth of the Oswego River on Lake Ontario. The importance of the location is reflected in the five battles fought in the immediate environs.

The designs of the various fortifications, both projected and actually constructed from 1727 through 1900, span the evolution of defensive works from the medieval concept in height, as seen in castlelike construction, to the modern concept in depth, as seen in underground coastal batteries. Included in these plans are two pentagonal five-bastioned forts, a square three-bastioned fort, an eight-pointed star-shaped fort, a rectangular four-bastioned fort, a temporary field fortification, a number of different redoubts,

historical monument was initiated in 1927 under the auspices of the Old Fort Niagara Association, a nonprofit organization. The old House of Peace or French Castle has been fully restored, replete with complements of cannon and a rebuilt drawbridge.

During World War II, Fort Niagara was in succession a reception center for Army draftees, replacement center, a prisoner of war facility, and a separation center. In 1945 the War Department declared the fort surplus to its needs and turned it over to the Niagara Frontier State Parks Commission. In 1953 because of mounting tensions of the cold war, the Army reacquired Fort Niagara on a lease basis from New York State. The army converted it into a headquarters for the anti-aircraft artillery network being established to defend the vital Niagara-Buffalo area and used it as a base for the logistical support of the area's Army units. On June 30, 1962, Fort Niagara was returned to the Parks Commission. Today three flags fly over the fort: the golden *fleurs-de-lis* of France brought by La Salle in 1679; the flag of blockhouses, retrenched batteries, and other minor works.

Oswego was considered crucial to the fate of the Empire. Without Oswego, there possibly would have been a long delay in the captures of Fort Niagara, Fort Frontenac, Montreal, and Quebec. The story of Oswego is one of the epic dramas of North America. Occupied by the Iroquois as early as the fourteenth century, its first history was recorded in the travels of New France's Jesuit fathers in 1654. Strategically located near the eastern end of the Great Lakes chain, it was the gateway to central New York and the Hudson Valley.

The sites of two of the forts, and the location of the third, are placed in present-day Oswego geography: Fort Oswego's site, on the west side of the river, is marked by a plaque at West First and Lake streets; Fort George's site is in Montcalm Park, at the junction of Montcalm and West Sixth streets; Fort Ontario is at the foot of East Seventh Street, overlooking the juncture of the Oswego River and Lake Ontario.

New York's Governor William Burnet, making efforts to encourage provincials to engage more actively in the Indian trade, established a trading post at Oswego in 1722, for the first time planting England's flag on the Great Lakes. The French, more or less in opposition, began erecting Fort Niagara at the mouth of the Niagara River in 1715 and secretly armed its "House of Peace" in the spring of 1727, a direct violation of the terms of the Treaty of Utrecht. In response, the English during the latter year rebuilt their trading house of stone, known to the French as Fort Chouaguen. It was enlarged with a great wall and armored bastions during 1741–43. Competing successfully with Niagara for the Indian trade, Indians came from as far north as Hudson Bay to Oswego to barter. For a short time, the fort was known as Fort Pepperrell for the conqueror of Fortress Louisbourg, but officially it

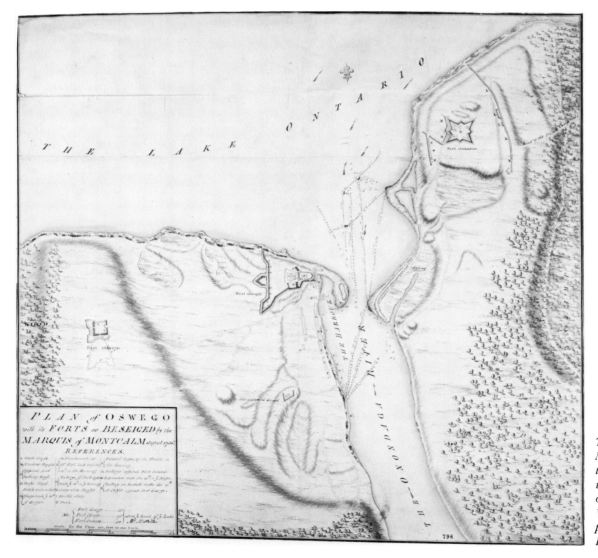

THE OSWEGO FORTS. Map of the forts and their environs as they were in 1756. (Courtesy of the Royal Archives, Windsor Castle. By permission of Her Royal Highness Elizabeth II.)

was Fort Oswego. By 1751 Colonel William Johnson, who in 1747 had become contractor for supplying the Oswego garrison, was Oswego's most important trader.

During the French and Indian War, in late 1755, Major General William Shirley decided to strengthen Fort Oswego's position before dealing with Fort Niagara the following spring. The first Fort Ontario, built on the bluff on the east side of the river's mouth, was on occasion referred to as the Fort of the Six Nations and East Fort. Fort George, begun on a ridge about a half-mile southwest of Fort Oswego, was at times known as New Fort Oswego, Fort Rascal, and West Fort, and never quite completed. The French under General Montcalm in early 1756 attacked Oswego and captured and destroyed all three fortifications. In 1759 British engineers designed and built a new pentagonal fort with corner bastions on the site of the original Fort Ontario. British troops garrisoned the new fort and trade at Oswego resumed.

By June 1774 only a few British soldiers were garrisoned at the fort, more or less engaged as caretakers. During the Revolution, British troops evacuated Fort Ontario in 1777 after the failure of the siege of Fort Stanwix at present Rome. In 1778 American forces burned Fort Ontario, but a small British force returned in 1782 and began to repair the damaged fort. It was surrendered in 1796 to United States troops under the terms of the Jay Treaty. In May 1814 a British expedition attacked and demolished Fort Ontario. Americans returned and repaired the fort and occupied it for the remainder of the war. Between 1839 and 1842, however, the United States rebuilt the fort with heavy masonry and continued to use it as a military station until after World War II. Archaeological investigations at Fort Ontario in 1975 represent the first known discovery and recording of material evidence from the eighteenth-century colonial period at this complex, intensely occupied, and repeatedly altered site. Fort Ontario's remains have been restored to its appearance during the 1860s, the last period of the post's importance in possible tactical operations. It is now a New York State Historical Site and Museum.

OSWEGO FALLS PALISADE. Little is known about this octagonal-shaped fortification located a short distance below Oswego Falls, at the present town of Fulton in Oswego County. Although there is a dearth of archival evidence, it is known that it was constructed by the British in 1758 or 1759 and intended to guard the important Oswego River route to Lake Ontario. Its site is on the east bank of the river, adjacent to South First Street.

FORT OX. This temporary French and Indian War defense was presumably built by Colonel John Bradstreet in 1756 at the junction of Ox Creek and the Oswego River, in present Oswego County. Bradstreet and his troops in July of the same year fought battles with the French under Captain Coulon de Villiers near the fort and on the island, known as Battle Island, in the Oswego River.

OYSTER BAY ENCAMPMENT. LONG ISLAND FORTS.

FORT PARIS. The site of Fort Paris is located about three-quarters of a mile east of S.R. 10, about midway between Hickory Hill Road (C.R. 33) and Stone Arabia Road (C.R. 34), in the town of Stone Arabia, Montgomery County. The fort was erected in early 1777 on land then owned by Isaac Paris (or his son of the same name), a native of the Alsatian city of Strasbourg. The fort consisted of the Paris farm and all outbuildings, the trading post, and a barracks for at least 100 men, all surrounded by a strong palisade with a blockhouse on its western side. The fort survived the Battle of Stone Arabia, October 19, 1780, although it was subjected to repeated attacks by Sir John Johnson's destructives. About 30 dead, including Colonel John Brown, commander of the fort, were found after the battle. Records in the National Archives indicate that Fort Paris, during the years 1780 and 1781, was intermittently garrisoned by detachments of the 4th New York Continentals.

PENTAGON FORT. FORT CRAVEN.

FORT PEPPERRELL. THE OSWEGO FORTS.

FORT PIKE. MADISON BARRACKS.

PINE CAMP. FORT DRUM.

FORT PLAIN (*Fort Rensselaer*). The strongest defense in the central region of the Mohawk Valley, situated near the confluence of Otsquaga Creek and the Mohawk River, at the present town of Fort Plain, Montgomery County, it was never officially called Fort Plain, a name adopted by the area's inhabitants when the fort was erected in 1776. During the summer of 1780, General Robert Van Rensselaer, commander of the region's militia, renamed the fort, out of apparent vanity,

Fort Rensselaer. The alchemy involved in retaining the original name was simple: the inhabitants heartily disliked the general and downgraded his debatable military talents, as evidenced by his inability to command the valley's strong 1,500-man militia force. He was later court-martialed for dereliction of duty but was acquitted. There is little doubt but that his family's wealth and social prominence influenced the military court.

During 1781-82, while Colonel Marinus Willett was in command of the Mohawk Valley's resistance efforts, a new defense was erected about 500 feet to the northwest of the 1776 fort. It was not an octagonal blockhouse, as many nineteenth-century regional historians believed. Sometime during the late summer of 1781, engineer Major Jean de Villefranche was requested by Colonel Willett to furnish a plan for a redoubt and a blockhouse to hold 200 men and a large powder magazine. Willett approved the plan sketched by Villefranche and sent a letter to General Washington with a copy. The blockhouse was square, not octagonal, and three-storied, built of hewn timbers about 15 inches square. "There were numerous port-holes for musketry, and in the lower story three or four cannons were placed. The first story was thirty feet in diameter, the second forty, and the third fifty. . . . The powder magazine of the fort was placed directly under the block-house for protection" (B. J. Lossing, *Pictorial Field Book of the Revolution*, p. 262).

On July 31, 1783, during his tour of the Mohawk Valley, General Washington inspected both the original fort and the exterior blockhouse complex. According to documentary evidence, the fortifications at Fort Plain were still in use for military purposes as late as 1786. The works were dismantled and the timbers used in the reconstruction of the many dwellings and barns that had been burned by the enemy. A number of these rebuilt structures still exist, some of them in the village of Fort Plain.

FORT PLANK. Erected in 1777, about two and a half miles southwest of Fort Plain, Fort Plank was one of its four supporting defenses in the area, the other three being Fort Clyde, Fort Willett, and Fort Windecker. The fort consisted of Frederick Plank's dwelling enclosed within a square palisade with its angles occupied by blockhouses.

PLATTSBURGH ARSENAL. Also known locally as the Champlain Arsenal, this U.S. Army munitions and ordnance storehouse was begun on May 1, 1809, and completed in August 1810. It was located at what was then Fredenburgh Falls, two miles up the river. The site is now located on Broad Street in the city of Plattsburgh. During the War of 1812, on July 30, 1813, Colonel John Murray with more than 1,400 British troops and marines crossed the border, and on the following day destroyed the arsenal, blockhouse, armory, hospital, and a military cantonment near the falls. After its destruction, the arsenal's site was used for public executions.

PLATTSBURGH BARRACKS. Established in September 1812 on the west shore of Lake Champlain, about a mile from the village of Plattsburgh, it was first occupied by a detachment of the 6th Infantry. U.S. troops were stationed at this 679-acre post from 1812 to 1825, again from 1838 to 1846, from 1848 to 1852, 1859 to 1861, and finally from 1865 to January 25, 1946, when the post was declared surplus. The facility was later occupied by the 820th Strategic Aerospace Division of the U.S. Air Force.

FORT PLUM POINT. Located about three miles north of West Point, just northeast of New Windsor, Plum Point is the site of a Patriot battery called Fort Plum Point or Machin's Battery, begun in early 1777 and named for Captain Thomas Machin, the engineer who constructed it. In the Hudson River opposite was Pollepel's (now Bannerman's) Island, the eastern anchor of Captain Machin's *chevaux-de-frise* line, which later proved useless when Sir Henry Clinton's armada easily maneuvered over and through the river barrier to attack Kingston. Machin's Battery mounted 14 guns at one time or another, 5 of which engaged in a harmless duel with the British warships.

POINSETT BARRACKS. Buffalo Barracks.

CAMP POPOLOPEN. Camp Buckner.

FORT PORTER. Situated on a 60-foot-high bluff at the northeast end of Lake Erie, a location now within the city of Buffalo, Fort Porter was established apparently on January 13, 1849, but not actually occupied until 1863 when it was used as a center for assembling and organizing volunteers for service during the Civil War. On the night of November 24–25, 1863, its blockhouse or "keep" was burned, supposedly by an arsonist. The fort was regularly garrisoned beginning in 1866. It was officially closed on June 28, 1926, to allow use of the reservation as an approach to the Peace Bridge then being constructed between Buffalo and Fort Erie.

POST BARRACKS. Located at the city of Elmira, Post Barracks was a temporary Civil War facility used for the training of recruits.

FORT PUTNAM. WEST POINT'S FORTS.

QUEEN'S FORT. FORT ANNE.

QUEEN'S FORT. FORT GEORGE AT THE BATTERY (See section on New York City Revolutionary War Defenses).

QUEEN'S FORT. FORT SCHENECTADY.

FORT RASCAL. THE OSWEGO FORTS.

CAMP RATHBUN. A temporary Civil War encampment, Camp Rathbun was located in or near the city of Elmira.

RED FORT (*North Battery*). A New York City defense located at the foot of Hubert Street on the Hudson River, 200 feet offshore, Red Fort was so-named for its construction of red sandstone. Also known as the North Battery, the fort was constructed so that its 16 guns could crossfire with the South West Battery (Castle Clinton) against enemy naval craft entering the river from the harbor. Begun in 1807 and completed in 1811, the fort was ceded by the government to the city in 1831.

RED HOOK BARRACKS. Located five miles north of Rhinebeck on the east side of the Hudson River in Dutchess County, Red Hook was the site of an important American post during the Revolution. The Patriot-built facility, continuously garrisoned, served several purposes. The New York troops posted there guarded the area against Tory activists, protected the river crossing, and maintained a protective guard around the Livingston family's powder mill located at Rhinebeck. The mill was the largest producer of gunpowder in New York during the war. The post was often used as a rest area for Continental Army units in transit from New England to the middle Atlantic colonies.

FORT REID. One of the forts erected by General John Sullivan during his expedition against the Iroquois villages in the summer of 1779 was Fort Reid (also Reed), located at present Elmira, Chemung County, and named for its commander, Lieutenant Colonel George Reid. It was situated at the junction of the Chemung (formerly Tioga) River and Newtown Creek.

FORT RENSSELAER. FORT PLAIN.

FORT RENSSELAER (*Fort Van Alstyne*). Situated on the east bank of Canajoharie Creek about a half-mile from its junction with the Mohawk River, within present Canajoharie in Montgomery County, the long, one-and-a-half-story stone-and-log Van Alstyne dwelling was fortified during the early days of the Revolution. Because of its central location, it became the rendezvous on many occasions for the Tryon County Committee of Safety, which directed the military and civil affairs in most of the Mohawk Valley. Originally called Fort Van Alstyne, it became known as Fort Rensselaer, named for the general, although his association with it was very tenuous, if it existed at all. Many distinguished people visited the Van Alstyne home during the colonial and Revolutionary days. General Washington was a guest there on August 1, 1783. Today the historic building, still structurally sound, is a private social club, owned and operated by the Fort Rensselaer Club, which restored and refurnished it. It is located on present-day Moyer Street, named for John H. Moyer, who came into possession of the property sometime after the war.

RHEIMENSNYDER'S FORT. Henry Rheimensnyder, one of the original settlers on what was known as Glen's Purchase, several miles north of Little Falls, in present Herkimer County, built a possibly palisaded blockhouse on his property soon after the outbreak of the Revolution. Occupying a site in or very near today's town of Dolgeville, called Snyder's Bush during the war, the blockhouse burned down a few years after the war's end, apparently through accident.

FORT RICHMOND. FORT WADSWORTH.

FORT RICKEY. Erected in 1759 during the French and Indian War on the Oneida Carry, Fort Rickey was a minor work erected by engineer William Eyre on the elevation directly opposite the entrance of West Canada Creek into Wood Creek, about two miles west of today's city of Rome. The plan of the timber fort shows it to have been in the form of a large T, with its leg a rectangle 80 feet long and 30 feet wide. By the time the fort was constructed, Fort Stanwix had become capable of providing adequate protection for the important portage. Fort Rickey was abandoned after the end of the war and left to rot.

CAMP R. N. SCOTT. CAMP FISHERS ISLAND.

CAMP ROBINSON BARRACKS. A temporary Civil War installation, this post was located in or near the city of Elmira.

CAMP ROCKAWAY BEACH. FORT TILDEN.

ROME ARSENAL. A United States arsenal erected in 1813 at the city of Rome for the duration of the War of 1812, it included a munitions and ordnance storehouse, workshops, officers' quarters, and barracks.

CAMP ROSE. A World War I encampment established in 1917 and garrisoned by the 1st Provisional Regiment to protect New York City's water supply, Camp Rose was located "near Pines Bridge" in the immediate vicinity of the Croton Reservoir in Westchester County. The camp was discontinued in 1919.

ROYAL BLOCKHOUSE. Its site located at today's approach to the bridge at Fort Edward, town of Moreau, Saratoga County, this blockhouse was probably erected in 1754 or 1755 during the French and Indian War to protect the Albany-Montreal route.

ROYAL BLOCKHOUSE. Located at today's town of Sylvan Beach, near the point where Wood Creek enters the eastern end of Oneida Lake, about 20 miles west of the city of Rome, the Royal Blockhouse was a large earthwork-surrounded two-story structure, with a watchtower as its third level. It was erected in 1759 by the British to guard their supply line from Albany and Schenectady to Fort Ontario at Oswego. The blockhouse was abandoned sometime in 1764.

ROYAL FORT. FORT SCHENECTADY.

SACANDAGA BLOCKHOUSE (*Mayfield Fort*). Occasionally referred to as the Mayfield Fort by nineteenth-century Mohawk Valley historians, the Sacandaga Blockhouse was probably erected in the spring of 1777 as an outpost against Tory and Indian incursions. It was located about 20 miles north of the Mohawk on the old Mayfield Patent, just off Van Den Burgh Road close to the southwestern shore of Sacandaga Lake in Fulton County. The defense was destroyed in June 1778 by a large band of Indians.

SAG HARBOR FORT. LONG ISLAND FORTS.

SAG HARBOR POST. A temporary War of 1812 encampment located at Sag Harbor in Suffolk County, Long Island, it was occupied during January and February 1814 by Captain James R. Hanham with 97 men.

FORT ST. CROIX. Located just west of the present town of North Hosoic, on the northeast bank of the Hoosic River, in Rensselaer County, the first Fort St. Croix was a Dutch cannon-protected stockade by Garret Cornelius Van Ness during the 1620s to protect his residence, gristmill, and sawmill. The defense was burned by Indians some years later. The second fort of this name was built sometime during the French and Indian War by 150 soldiers from Fort Half-Moon at present Waterford to protect the Dutch settlement and guard the trail to the Housatonic Valley.

FORT ST. FREDERIC. FORT CROWN POINT.

FORT ST. GEORGE. LONG ISLAND FORTS.

FORT ST. REGIS. The French in 1755, a year after the outbreak of war with England, established a fortification at the large Indian village at St. Regis on the St. Lawrence River in Franklin County, nearly opposite Cornwall, Ontario. The Jesuits had a mission there from about the same time. During the War of 1812, the British for a time occupied a fortified blockhouse at St. Regis.

FORT SAINTE MARIE DE GANNENTAHA. Located on the east shore of Onondaga (Gannentaha) Lake, one and a half miles north of present Syracuse and about a mile south of the town of Liverpool on N.Y. 57, this fort was erected in July 1656 by 50 French colonists who attempted to found the first permanent settlement and combined mission and military post among the Iroquois. Although invited by the Onondaga Indians, the colony was abandoned less than two years later because of their hostility. The reproduction of the French fortified stockade, enclosing a blockhouse and barracks, constructed in 1933 as a Public Works Administration project, stands on Onondaga Lake Parkway near Liverpool.

SALEM FORT. FORT WILLIAMS.

SALT POINT BLOCKHOUSE. Because of war in the Ohio region during 1794, western and northern New York settlements were being threatened by Indians, incited by British agents on the frontier. General Baron von Steuben was one of four men deputized and authorized by the governor to select sites and erect fortifications necessary for the state's frontiers. One of the sites chosen was on a bluff, later known as Salt Point, near the bridge over the Oswego Canal on the north side of today's city of Syracuse, close to the present intersection of Route 81 and Hiawatha Boulevard. The structure erected was a 20-foot-high, loophole-pierced blockhouse built of oak timbers, hewn square, and surrounded by 20-foot-high cedar palisades. The blockhouse, mounting a six-pounder cannon, was first occupied by troops in 1795. The war scare having abated, it was used for some time as a state storehouse for salt. The blockhouse was demolished in 1816.

FORT SARAGHTOGA. Located at the present town of Easton in Washington County, Fort Saraghtoga was erected in 1709, during Queen Anne's War, by General Francis Nicholson to protect the military road to Fort Nicholson (Fort Edward) at the Great Carrying Place. Large enough to garrison 450 men, the fort was 150 feet long and 140 feet wide and reportedly mounted six 12-pounder and six 18-pounder cannon. The fort, demolished in 1713, has been often confused with Saratoga (Schuylerville) across the Hudson.

FORT SARATOGA. FORT HARDY.

SARATOGA BATTLEFIELD FORTS. Old Saratoga was the place where the most decisive Continental victory of the Revolution marked the startling turning point of the war. The Jane McCrea atrocity, heavily propagandized throughout the region by the Patriots, aided in the outpouring of militiamen and volunteers to swell the ranks of the American army. Commanded by General Horatio Gates, the American army was determined to halt General John Burgoyne's British forces above Albany. The British campaign for 1777, the "Year of the Hangman," called for Burgoyne's army to come down the Champlain-Hudson route; Barry St. Leger's troops were to march east from Oswego along the Mohawk; and General Sir William Howe's forces to proceed up the Hudson from New York. The grandiose plan was to unite all three armies at Albany, split the colonies, and end the American rebellion.

To succeed, Burgoyne's campaign depended on mutually supporting armies. But St. Leger was defeated before the ramparts of defiant Fort Stanwix, and Howe was already at sea and deeply committed to the Philadelphia campaign when he received Lord Germain's conditional approval. Thus, except for an ineffective sally up the Hudson by Sir Henry Clinton, Burgoyne would have to shift for himself. Without support from New York City, Burgoyne's army became an isolated column in a vast and hostile wilderness, destined to fail to attain its goal, although it had captured Fort Ticonderoga, Fort Anne, and Fort Edward.

The two major engagements at Saratoga, September 19 and October 7, resulted in Burgoyne's defeat and ultimate formal surrender 10 days later. The American success encouraged hesitant France to openly intervene on the side of the colonists. Without the aid of the French, it is problematical whether the Revolution could have been fought to a successful conclusion, although four more years of fighting were necessary to bring final victory at Yorktown. Burgoyne's army retreated northward to the old settlement of Saratoga, now Schuylerville. Convinced that his position had become utterly hopeless, the general surrendered the 6,300 men remaining under his command, who laid down their weapons on the Field of Grounded Arms on October 17.

There were four principal fortifications, one American and three British, on the field of battle:

- FORT NEILSON (*Bemis Heights*). Both before and after the Saratoga battles, John Neilson farmed these heights. His restored home stands today as it did when American staff officers used it for quarters. The high ground here takes its name from Jotham Bemis who kept a tavern at the foot of the hill. Thaddeus Kosciuszko, lieutenant colonel in the Continental Army, chose and fortified the site. On the highest elevation of Bemis Heights was Neilson's barn, which was strengthened by a double tier of logs on three sides. A circular form of strong batteries extended southward to the river. In addition, the position was encircled by a deep trench and a row of strong palisades. In the rear, near the center of the American camp, was the bombproofed magazine. When it was completed, the defense was called Fort Neilson.

  The Americans' river fortifications constituted the key to the entire defense. Infantrymen and cannon here, together with batteries along the near riverbank, commanded the road, the flood plain, and the river, closing off the Hudson Valley route to Albany. This powerful American position forced Burgoyne to move through rough, wooded terrain west of the valley to attack the main defense on

Bemis Heights. The result was the battle on September 19, 1777, during which British columns were sent reeling into full retreat, suffering many casualties.

- BALCARRES REDOUBT (*Freeman Farm*). After the battle on September 19, 1777, Burgoyne hastily constructed a fortified line from the river to Breymann Redoubt. Here British troops built a redoubt 500 yards long and 12 to 14 feet high, manned by 1,500 men and mounting eight cannon. It was named for Lord Balcarres, one of Bourgoyne's officers. Benedict Arnold led troops in a series of costly and unsuccessful attacks against this work, the strongpoint of the British line of defenses.

- BREYMANN REDOUBT. This work was the right anchor of the British defense line. The redoubt was a single line of log breastworks about 200 yards long and from 7 to 8 feet high, covering the British right flank. Canadian troops posted in two log buildings defended the ground between the Breymann and Balcarres Redoubts. While Benedict Arnold led the assaults against the Balcarres Redoubt, troops prepared to attack this British position. Driving out the Canadians, they launched an assault against Breymann. At the height of the attack, Arnold rode over and joined the riflemen moving the flank and rear of the work. As Daniel Morgan and other commanders led their men over the front of the breastwork, Arnold entered from the rear. He fell wounded in the leg as the British position was overpowered.

- GREAT REDOUBT. On the hill behind Burgoyne's headquarters and two others to the north, the British constructed a system of fortifications known as the Great Redoubt, to guard the hospital, artillery park, and supply depot on the river flat and their boat bridge crossing the Hudson. Burgoyne withdrew his forces to this vicinity during the night of October 7, 1777. Dying General Simon Fraser, mortally wounded in the action during that day, was brought here to a house where he died the next day. After Fraser's burial on the night of October 8, Burgoyne began his retreat through the rain-soaked country, with the Americans following on his army's heels. Establishing a camp at Saratoga on October 10, the British were surrounded by an overwhelming force of American troops. A week later, Burgoyne surrendered to General Gates.

FORT SCHAGHTICOKE. An outpost of Albany's Fort Frederick, Fort Schaghticoke was built in the spring of 1703 near the junction of Tamhannock Creek with the Hoosic River, in the present town of Schaghticoke in northwestern Rensselaer County, just east of the Hudson River. The palisaded fort enclosed watchtowers and barracks furnished with cellars. It was rebuilt sometime between 1742 and the spring of 1746 (depending on the authority cited) and was garrisoned by two companies of regulars during King George's War. The fort underwent repair in 1756 and was abandoned at the end of the French and Indian War. It is known that early in the Revolution, probably in 1775, New Hampshire troops reoccupied the fort for a short time and were replaced by British Loyalists. Since the post is unknown after 1776, British troops or Loyalists may have burned the fort when they abandoned it.

SCHELL'S BLOCKHOUSE. Early in the Revolution, John Christian Schell, with the help of his eight sons, built a two-story blockhouse on his farm property at the isolated German settlement of Schell's Bush, about five miles north of Herkimer. On the afternoon of August 6, 1781, Donald McDonald, a Scotch Loyalist from Johnstown, at the head of about 60 Tories and Indians, raided the community. Schell, in the fields with his wife and sons, two of whom were captured (later released), escaped to their blockhouse, where the family put up a heroic defense until nightfall without suffering a single casualty. About a week later, the settlement was again raided. The elder Schell and one of his sons were caught in the fields and killed.

FORT SCHENECTADY (*Corlaer's Fort; Royal Fort; Queen's Fort; Fort Cosby*). Known in early colonial years by such names as Corlaer's Fort (for Arendt Van Curler), the Royal or Queen's Fort (for Queen Anne), and Fort Cosby (for royal Governor William Cosby), this historic fort on the Mohawk River was all these things: fur-trading center and northernmost fortified outpost; major assembly point for the English-Provincial and Revolutionary armies; Continental depot for armaments and supplies; and, in 1780, sanctuary for the persecuted Oneida and Tuscarora Indians.

"Schenectida" was founded in 1661 by Van Curler and immediately surrounded by a palisade. The first Dutch settlers banded their homes together for common protection, with their farms located outside the palisade. In today's geography, the original plat started at State Street, with the line running along the east side of Ferry Street to about the old Episcopal Church, then straight to the north side of Front Street, just a little beyond Washington Street, then southerly and parallel to the same back to State Street.

There was a blockhouse in one of the angles of the double row of high palisades, with barracks, gun-mounted platforms, and lookouts. Many years later, during the Revolution, when the town became an important depot, barracks were constructed outside the walls, which from time to time were further extended to encompass a greater area.

Schenectady in 1690 was a village of 80 houses and about 400 Dutch inhabitants. Despite repeated warnings by Albany's Committee of Safety, the people neglected to post guards at the town's gates and, according to local legend, obstinately built snowmen in the center of the open gateways. The night of Saturday, February 8, 1690, is inscribed in the annals of Schenectady as the town's worst disaster. On that fateful night, the Dutch were sound asleep in their houses while a blizzard raged. Just before midnight a force of 114 French and 96 Indians arrived at the village and silently filed through the open gates. When all the houses were surrounded, the Indian war whoop was sounded. The night air was rent with hideous screams as the invaders battered down doors and attacked half-awakened people with knife, club, and tomahawk. Within an hour, 60 inhabitants were dead. The village was set afire and 78 houses were burned.

The town was a ruination, remaining almost completely depopulated until the 1697 Treaty of Ryswick (Rijswijk), near The Hague, Netherlands. A new Fort Schenectady was built in 1705. It covered an extensive area surrounded by a triple stockade, with cannon-mounted blockhouses or bastions in all the angles. In 1735 the fort was rebuilt more substantially of hewn timbers on stone foundations. By the beginning of the Revolution, however, the fort's stockade was almost a ruination, as no repairs had been made since the end of the French and Indian War. It was partially dismantled, with its salvageable materials used for the construction of Continental Army barracks. The town during the war boasted a large amount of ordnance, the largest of which were the "Lady Washington" and the "Long Nine-Pounder" placed in the streets to command the gates.

Today the Schenectady Stockade Historic District, established in 1962, encompasses the general area that was surrounded by the palisade erected by the settlement's founders. Within the district are about 400 structures, some 50 of them with markers giving the names of the early owners and their dates of construction before 1825. The Stockade Association stressed that "the Stockade is not a museum or a reconstructed area, but a community which had endured since 1661, despite time and tragedies."

FORT SCHLOSSER. The French destroyed Little Fort Niagara (Fort du Portage) in 1759 to deprive its use by the British then besieging Fort Niagara. The following year the British, in need of a strong defense at the upper end of the important portage, ordered Captain Joseph Schlosser, a German officer in the Crown's service, to build a new fort there. A much larger defense, an earthwork with four bastions, was constructed on the site of the former French fort and named Fort Schlosser for its builder. During the Revolution the fort was garrisoned by a small British detachment that served as a guard over the portage. It was surrendered to the United States in 1796 in accordance with provisions of the Jay Treaty. In December 1813, during the War of 1812, the British captured Fort Schlosser and burned it.

FORT SCHUYLER. FORT ANNE.

FORT SCHUYLER. FORT STANWIX.

FORT SCHUYLER. Captain Peter Schuyler of Albany and nine other men volunteered their services, in response to a request of Governor William Burnet, to erect a fort on the site of "Indian Landing" on Irondequoit Creek close to where it empties into Irondequoit Bay on the eastern boundary of the present city of Rochester. Its purpose was to divert the Seneca Indian trade from the French at Fort des Sables. Schuyler and his men arrived in 1721 and erected the fort on a plateau close to the bank of the creek.

Strategically situated, oblong in form and quite large, Schuyler's fort commanded the creek and the trails leading to it. He and his men occupied the post for a year and then returned to Albany, at which time the command of the fort was given to Schuyler's cousin, Major Abraham Schuyler. The fort stood abandoned for many years until the day it caught fire and burned. The site of Fort Schuyler is occupied by a reproduction of the post erected about 1940 in Rochester's Ellison Park.

FORT SCHUYLER (*Fort Desolation*). Erected in 1758 and probably named for Colonel Peter Schuyler of New Jersey, nephew of Colonel Peter Schuyler of Albany, this small timber and earthen fort, surrounded by a moat, was located in the area between present Genesee Street and the

Mohawk River. It was one of the chain of similar defenses along the Mohawk-Oneida-Oswego route guarding the line of communication and supply to Fort Ontario. Abandoned after the French and Indian War, it was intermittently garrisoned during the Revolution by American troops who called it "Fort Desolation."

FORT SCHUYLER. Begun in 1833 on Throgs Neck in New York City's borough of the Bronx, this was situated on Long Island Sound opposite later-built Fort Totten. Fort Schuyler was named for Major General Philip Schuyler of Revolutionary War fame and established in 1856 when it was ready for the mounting of armaments. It was first garrisoned on January 17, 1861. During the Civil War, it was used as a prisoner of war compound. Between 1870 and 1877 the post was unoccupied. The fort's last garrison was withdrawn in 1934. In 1937 the old fort's 17 acres were leased to the state for the New York Maritime College.

SCHUYLER'S SUPPLY DEPOT. FORT INGOLDSBY.

CAMP SCOTT. This post was a temporary Civil War assembly and training encampment located at "Old Town" on Staten Island.

FORT SCOTT. A War of 1812 defense of Plattsburgh, Fort Scott was a hastily erected redoubt, smaller than nearby Fort Moreau, on the shore of Lake Champlain, constructed in September 1814 on orders of Brigadier General Alexander Macomb. The fortification was named for Lieutenant Colonel (later Brigadier General) Winfield Scott.

FORT SETAUKET. LONG ISLAND FORTS.

SEVEN-MILE POST BLOCKHOUSE. Located near present Glens Falls, north of Halfway Brook and seven miles south of Lake George, this important French and Indian War stockade-enclosed blockhouse was erected in 1755 by the British. The complex included storehouses and barracks for 800 troops, redoubts and earthworks, with the palisades pierced for cannon. The defense, however dilapidated, apparently survived through the Revolution.

CAMP SHANKS. One of the largest military troop concentration and embarkation bases during World War II, Camp Shanks was located at Orangeburg in Rockland County and named for General David Cary Shanks, commander of the New York Port of Embarkation during World War I. Its site as a military base dates to the Revolutionary War, when large elements of General Washington's Continental Army camped there twice. Opened on January 4, 1943, and closed July 21, 1946, Camp Shanks processed a total of 1,362,630 troops for overseas duty.

FORT OF THE SIX NATIONS. THE OSWEGO FORTS.

FORT SKENESBOROUGH. Fortifications involved in three wars were constructed at present-day Whitehall, in what was once Major Philip

FORT SCHUYLER. Reservation beneath Throgs Neck Bridge, with Maritime College beyond it. (Courtesy of Maritime College, Bronx, New York.)

Skene's baronial empire of 60,000 acres, with part of his domain spilling over into the disputed Hampshire Grants (now Vermont). The initial royal grant of 34,000 acres (a tract later augmented by land purchases) in 1759 led the English-born Scotsman to established Skenesborough (Whitehall after the Revolution) at the southern tip of Lake Champlain, the birthplace of the United States Navy.

The first defenses in Skenesborough were the British blockhouse and barracks on a hill to the west of Wood Creek, erected during the French and Indian War. The hill has since been bisected by S.R. 22. The site is between today's Presbyterian Church and the Masonic Temple. Archival sources do not reveal the name, if any, given the fort. Military tradition suggests that the fort was most likely named for Colonel John Wilkins of the 59th Regiment of Foot, which built the post and occupied it.

With the labor of black slaves, settlers, and a number of discharged soldiers whom he employed, Skene carved out a civilization, remarkable for that time, that included his mansion (Skenesborough House), settlers' dwellings, farms, gristmills, sawmills, iron foundries, and shipyards. He had a sloop constructed for lake transportation and he cut a road through the wilderness to Salem, nearly 30 miles to the south. In order to accommodate his enterprise of raising blooded horses, he had completed by 1770 an immense barn and stables. The barn, 134 by 35 feet and built of native bluestone, was taken over by the British in 1775 and converted into a loopholed fort.

Because of its strategic location at the head of Lake Champlain and its value as a shipyard, General Philip Schuyler was ordered to occupy and fortify Skenesborough. While shipwrights and blacksmiths were building Benedict Arnold's Lake Champlain fleet, the first ships of the new United States Navy, a gang of Dutch carpenters erected a barracks, 45 by 20 feet, and surrounded by a fortified stockade, built on or very close to the French and Indian War fort site. On October 11, 1776, Benedict Arnold's inland-sea navy, outgunned by General Sir Guy Carleton's invasion armada, fought the Battle of Valcour Island in Lake Champlain, but wrecked the British army's timetable.

During the War of 1812, the American military decided to reestablish fortifications at Whitehall (Skenesborough) because of its shipyards. A new blockhouse was constructed within the ruins of the old Revolutionary War fort. The barracks was erected on the site located between a point just south of the Masonic Temple and the north end of the present-day railroad tunnel.

The Skenesborough Museum at Whitehall has an interesting model of the harbor as it appeared in 1776. Under a long shed outside the Museum are the well-preserved remains of the War of 1812 schooner U.S. *Ticonderoga* (1814), which was a participant in a naval victory over the British on Lake Champlain.

FORT SLOCUM. This fort in Long Island Sound on 80-acre David's Island, geographically a part of New Rochelle, Westchester County, was established in 1861 for the defense of New York City and later named in honor of Major General Henry W. Slocum, distinguished Civil War veteran. During its century-long history, the fort served as a military hospital, a port for troop transports, an Air Force headquarters, a prisoner-of-war camp, a school for Army cooks, a Nike-Atlas missile base, and a school for U.S. Army chaplains. Its last occupant was the all-service Defense Information School, relocated at Fort Benjamin Harrison in Indiana when Fort Slocum was closed on November 30, 1965. Several months later, after the Departments of Defense and Agriculture were pressured by Congressmen, the demilitarized fort was pressed into emergency service as a quarantine station for animals brought from Africa. In July 1968 David's Island was purchased by the Consolidated Edison Company for the purpose of constructing there a nuclear-fueled electric generating plant.

FORT SLONGO. LONG ISLAND FORTS.

CAMP SMITH (*Camp Townsend; State Camp of Instruction*). Major General Frederick Townsend of Albany, adjutant general of the state, established this camp in 1882 for the training of New York National Guard units. The location, one mile north of Peekskill on a promontory known as Roman's Nose, was convenient to both steamboat and rail transportation to and from New York City. The 23rd Regiment of Brooklyn was the first to train here. Later trained at the camp was the famous 7th Regiment of Manhattan, known as the "silk stocking regiment" because so many wealthy New Yorkers were in it.

Called Camp Townsend only briefly, the camp was known as State Camp of Instruction until 1926, when it was renamed Camp Smith in honor of the then governor of New York, Alfred E. Smith. Today the camp is used by all federal and state military organizations for training, including the FBI and police forces from New York and several New England states. The Empire State Military Academy for the training of National Guard units is also located at Camp Smith.

SMITH CANTONMENT.

This post, located to the south of Fort Tompkins, was the major Army encampment for Sackets Harbor throughout the War of 1812. In its final form in 1814, the cantonment was a large, palisaded square enclosing barracks with blockhouses at the corners. It was abandoned and dismantled sometime in 1816.

SMITH'S CANTONMENT.

A Civil War encampment on Staten Island, the site of the cantonment is within the Fort Wadsworth reservation.

CAMP SPRAGUE.

Established in September 1861, Camp Sprague was a temporary Civil War encampment located at New Dorp on Staten Island.

FORT STANWIX (*Fort Schuyler*).

The defiant defense of the American garrison at Fort Stanwix during the critical month of August 1777 was substantially responsible for the turning back of Barry St. Leger's army, the western wing of the ambitious Burgoyne offensive from Canada to split the rebellious colonies. St. Leger's failure contributed to Burgoyne's defeat at Saratoga in October.

Fort Stanwix was located at the Oneida Carrying Place, the one-mile portage between the Mohawk River and Wood Creek, in the modern city of Rome. It was a highly strategic place on the water route between Lake Ontario and the upper Hudson River Valley. In 1758 General James Abercromby ordered General John Stanwix to take a force of men to the portage and there erect a strong fortification. The cost of construction was estimated to have been approximately $266,000, a stupendous sum of money in those days of the French and Indian War. The fort, however, played a minor role during the remainder of the conflict, and was allowed to fall into disrepair after 1760.

The Fort Stanwix Treaty of 1768, otherwise known as the Boundary Line Treaty, was negotiated by Sir William Johnson with more than 2,000 members of the Six Nations of the Iroquois Confederacy. Millions of acres were bought from the Indians for the paltry sum of 10,000 pounds. In 1784 a new treaty, also effected at the fort, between the United States and the Iroquois (minus the Mohawks, who accepted the British offer of land in Canada) provided a new western boundary. Four years later, in 1788, still another treaty was made at the same place, this time between New York State and the Iroquois, which threw open to settlement the major portion of western New York.

In 1776, with Forts Ticonderoga and Crown Point in the possession of the Americans, General Philip Schuyler was ordered to repair and strengthen Fort Stanwix, by then much dilapidated. The work took much longer than expected and the reconstruction was finally completed in the summer of 1777. The Patriots renamed it Fort Schuyler in honor of the general, which caused much historical confusion, for there was a Fort Schuyler at Utica, built at the same time as the original Fort Stanwix. Official American dispatches during the Revolution often referred to it as Fort Schuyler. Historians resolved the issue: they disregarded the change in name and retained its original name.

The fort had a perimeter of 1,450 feet, and in

FORT STANWIX. Plan of the reconstruction. (Courtesy of the National Park Service.)

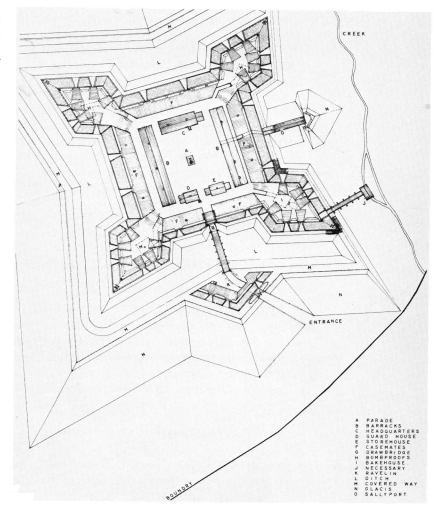

A   PARADE
B   BARRACKS
C   HEADQUARTERS
D   GUARD HOUSE
E   STOREHOUSE
F   CASEMATES
G   DRAWBRIDGE
H   BOMBPROOFS
I   BAKEHOUSE
J   NECESSARY
K   RAVELIN
L   DITCH
M   COVERED WAY
N   GLACIS
O   SALLYPORT

modern Rome's geography was bounded by Liberty, Spring, and Dominick streets, with Fort Stanwix's parade spanning Willett Street. The walls of the fort, with a bastion in each of its angles, soared 17 feet above the parade and consisted of 2-foot-square logs, flattened top and bottom, forming the rear walls of the barracks and storehouses. The dry moat was immense, 40 feet wide at the top, 16 at the bottom, and 14 deep. The parapets were embrasured for the fort's armament.

In 1781 Fort Stanwix was destroyed by fire and flood. Although substantially rebuilt, it never again engaged in any military action. During the War of 1812, an emergency fortified blockhouse was erected on its parade ground because the works had fallen into ruin through neglect and had become utterly useless as a defense. The fury of the war, however, left the place unmolested. Beginning in 1828, the blockhouse and its surrounding ruinous defenses were dismantled bit by bit as settlers and traders moved into the area. Fort Stanwix's site in the course of years was buried beneath the homes and businesses that eventually formed the city of Rome.

The National Park Service undertook the reconstruction of the fort in three phases, at an estimated cost of $9 million, part of a $50 million combined urban renewal and Department of the Interior project. Archaeological excavations were begun in 1970 to unearth the foundations of the fortification. The reconstruction was the focal point in the 18-acre National Park completed in August 1977, the bicentennial of St. Leger's unsuccessful siege of Fort Stanwix.

STATE CAMP OF INSTRUCTION. CAMP SMITH.

CAMP STEPHEN B. LUCE. CAMP FISHERS ISLAND.

FORT STEVENS. A War of 1812 defense of New York City, Fort Stevens was built in June and July 1814 at Hell Gate on Hallett's Point on the Queens County or east side of the East River. It mounted 12 pieces of heavy artillery. In the middle of the river, on Mill Rock, stood a blockhouse erected at the same time.

FORT STONY POINT. KING'S FERRY FORTS.

CAMP STRONG. One of the several names for the military encampment for troops of the Troy area during the Civil War, Camp Stevens was used particularly by a military unit known as the Black Horse Cavalry and located on the grounds of the Rensselaer County Agricultural Society on the outskirts of the city.

SYRACUSE RECRUIT CAMP. A temporary World War I encampment, located on the State Fair Grounds, four miles west of Syracuse, the 500-acre camp was established in 1917 for the organization of new military units. In 1918 it was designated a recruit center for limited-service men. The camp closed in 1919.

FORT TERRY. A permanent post established by the U.S. Coast Artillery in 1898, Fort Terry was located on 840-acre Plum Island off the tip of Long Island between Long Island Sound and Gardiners Bay, a short distance from Orient Point on the Island and 12 miles southwest of New London, Connecticut. Garrisoned by six companies of the Coast Artillery and mounting eight 12-inch mortars and two 10-inch rifles, it was named for Major General Alfred H. Terry, who served with distinction during the Civil War and on the western frontier, 1875–90. The post was closed after World War II. The Federal government, however, retained Plum Island and the U.S. Department of Agriculture maintains a laboratory there for research on hoof-and-mouth and other animal diseases.

THREE RIVERS BLOCKHOUSE. Located where the Oneida and Seneca rivers join to form the Oswego River, near the present town of Phoenix in Oswego County, this palisaded blockhouse (never properly named) was erected by New York provincial troops in 1759 in compliance with British orders. About 60 feet square and enclosing three storehouses, it was designed to protect the Mohawk-Oneida-Oswego route to Lake Ontario. The blockhouse probably was in ruins by the time of the Revolutionary War.

FORT TICONDEROGA (*Fort Vaudreuil; Fort Carillon*). Located just east of the village of Ticonderoga in Essex County, Fort Ticonderoga was the key to the defense of Canada, first for the French and then the British, and the Hudson River Valley for the Americans. Originally named Fort Vaudreuil for the governor-general of Canada when the French began erecting the fort in 1755, but soon renamed Fort Carillon ("a chime of bells") for the sound of the falls where Lake George (Lac St. Sacrement) flows into Lake Champlain, the fort was strategically situated to provide control of both the two-mile portage

FORT TICONDEROGA.
Reconstruction. (Courtesy of the New York
State Department of
Commerce.)

FORT TICONDEROGA.
Reconstruction overlooking Lake Champlain.
(Courtesy of the New
York State Department
of Commerce.)

ATTAQUES DES RETRANCHEMENS DEVANT LE FORT CARILLON
en Amérique
par les anglais commandés par le général Abercrombie contre les français
aux ordres du Marquis de Montcalm le 8 Juillet 1758.

RENVOIS.

A *Le fort Carillon.* B *Retranchemens, que les français ont commencé à faire le 7 Juillet,*
au matin. C *camp de l'armée française, où elle se rendit le 6 & resta sous les armes pendant*
la nuit du 7 au 8. Le 8 à la pointe du jour elle prit la position D *en ordre de bataille derrière les*
retranchemens. E *Les grenadiers & les piquets pour reserve derrière chaque bataillon.* F *Colonnes des*
anglais, qui attaquent les retranchemens à midi & demie. G *Pelotons de troupes legéres & provincia-*
les fusillant entre ces colonnes. H *Les canadiens sortent du retranchement, & attaquent une colonne*
anglaise en flanc. I *Chaloupes des anglais, qui parurent pendant l'attaque, & furent repoussées par*
l'artillerie du fort. K *Retraite des colonnes anglaises dans leur premier camp près des moulins à scier*
vers sept heures du soir ; leur troupes legéres couvrirent cette retraite par leur feu prolongé jusques
dans la nuit. L *Position des français après la retraite des anglais.* M *Batteries redoutes &*
retranchemens, que les français établirent après le combat.

C.P.S.C.M.

PLAN
DU FORT
CARILLON
Echelle

FORT TICONDEROGA.
French plan of Fort
Carillon. (Courtesy of
the Public Archives of
Canada.)

between the lakes and navigation northward on Lake Champlain.

After General Jeffrey Amherst and a 11,000-man army took possession of French Fort Carillon in July 1759, its name was changed to Fort Ticonderoga, and extensive reconstruction was begun on the works partially destroyed by the French upon evacuation. The rebuilt fort included barracks, officers' quarters, powder magazine, four batteries, a redoubt, storerooms, prison cells, a wharf, ovens, a lime kiln, gardens, and advanced works. After the French and Indian War, Ticonderoga was used as a military depot for the storage of British armaments.

On May 10, 1775, Ethan Allen and Benedict Arnold captured Ticonderoga from a skeleton garrison and two days later took possession of Fort Crown Point. The Continental Army, approximately 17,000 men, were besieging British-held Boston (April 1775–March 17, 1776), but without heavy siege artillery it was considered almost impossible to oust the British. The Americans' shortage of armament had prompted the seizures of Ticonderoga and Crown Point. On November 16, 1775, General Washington commissioned Colonel Henry Knox to remove the guns at Ticonderoga and transport them to the environs of Boston. Knox reached Ticonderoga on December 5, and within 24 hours, with the assistance of the garrison, was busy dismantling more than 50 heavy cannon, mortars, and howitzers. Knox's "Noble Train of Artillery" enabled the Patriots to ultimately force the British out of Boston.

Fort Ticonderoga was used as the headquarters for Major General Philip Schuyler's Northern Department during most of 1775 and 1776 while American forces under Benedict Arnold and Richard Montgomery made an unsuccessful attempt to capture Canada. In July 1777 General John Burgoyne's invasion army from Canada recaptured Fort Ticonderoga but was compelled to abandon it after the general's surrender at Saratoga in October. The fort's buildings were burned by the British garrison commanded by Brigadier General H. Watson Powell. In 1781, while General Barry St. Leger was holding fruitless meetings with Vermont commissioners to absorb that territory into Canada, his men made extensive repairs on the fort; the commissioners, however, decided that Vermont should become a part of the future United States.

Shortly after the 1783 Treaty of Paris was signed, the whole region began to be rapidly settled. There was no caretaking establishment at Ticonderoga, and the fort provided a convenient treasure trove for the early settlers. In 1796 the garrison grounds were granted to Columbia and Union Colleges as a source of income. William Ferris Pell, wealthy New York marble and mahogany importer, leased part of the grounds and erected a summer home. In 1820 he bought the entire property. The existence today of the faithfully restored colonial fort is entirely due to the remarkable dedication and work of the Pell family over a century and a half. The Fort Ticonderoga Museum of the French and Indian War and the Revolution maintains a magnificent exhibit of materials relating to the military occupation of the fort. Fort Ticonderoga is being operated as a private nonprofit historical and educational monument.

FORT TICONDEROGA. Reconstruction. (Courtesy of the New York State Department of Commerce.)

FORT TILDEN (*Camp Rockaway Beach*). The peninsular site of Fort Tilden at Rockaway Beach, adjacent to today's Riis Park in Queens County, was purchased from New York State on May 1, 1917. Prior to final negotiations, a garrison of 4 officers and 130 men established Camp Rockaway Beach on February 19, 1917. During construction of the Coast Artillery defense for New York Harbor, it was designated Fort Tilden in honor of Samuel J. Tilden, one-time Governor of New York and Democratic nominee for president in 1876.

By the mid-1920s Fort Tilden controlled a 30-mile fan of ocean with two of the most powerful U.S. coastal guns ever made, 16-inch rifles firing 2,100-pound projectiles a distance of 50,000 yards. Later, interlocking fire came from a similar battery completed during World War II on the Navesink Highlands near Fort Hancock. In addition to seacoast defense, Fort Tilden's garrison manned three three-inch anti-aircraft guns on fixed mounts. The fort's great guns were removed as obsolete a few years after World War II because air power and new amphibious techniques that allowed landings practically anywhere along the coastline had changed all the rules of defense. Its site now a part of the National Park Service's Gateway National Recreation Area, Fort Tilden still retains the concrete casemates of its 16-inch guns and a Nike missile launch site.

FORT TIMMERMAN. FORT ZIMMERMAN.

FORT TOMPKINS. This War of 1812 fortification located at Sackets Harbor on Lake Ontario served throughout the years of the conflict with Great Britain. Named for Governor Daniel D. Tompkins, it was the primary defensive work in the fortification system built around the village. It overlooked the harbor itself and commanded the approaches from Lake Ontario. Begun by the Navy as a small earthwork in 1812, by 1815 it became a fort with a strong palisaded two-story blockhouse. With its armament changing throughout the war, the greatest number of guns it mounted at any one time was 20 pieces besides two or three mortars. Fort Tompkins was abandoned about 1825 and completely razed about the year 1847.

FORT TOMPKINS. A War of 1812 defense of the city of Buffalo, located on what is now Niagara Street, Fort Tompkins was built shortly after the outbreak of war and burned in 1813. Its armament consisted of six or seven pieces of artillery.

FORT TOMPKINS. FORT WADSWORTH.

CAMP TOMPKINSVILLE (*Camp McClellan*). A temporary Civil War encampment on Staten Island, first called Camp McClellan for General George McClellan, it was renamed Camp Tompkinsville when the general fell out of respect.

FORT TOTTEN (*Fort at Willets Point*). This seacoast defense was located at the northeastern tip of Queens County alongside the Cross Island Parkway on Willets Point jutting out into Little Neck Bay, a cove off the East River. Directly opposite on the north bank of the East River, where it narrows to about three-quarters of a mile, was Fort Schuyler. The site for the military reservation later known as Fort Totten was purchased in two parts, the first in 1857 and the second in 1863. The reservation was not used for military purposes until 1862, when fortifications, based on preliminary plans drawn up by then Captain Robert E. Lee in 1857, were begun (never actually completed) and known as Fort at Willets Point. During the Civil War, a portion of the post was used as a recruit depot and temporary encampment for troops en route to the front.

In the early 1880s, the first seacoast mortar battery was designed and constructed at Willets Point. In 1898 the fort was named in honor of Brigadier General Joseph G. Totten, chief of engineers, 1838–64. Three years later the Engineer School was moved to Washington Barracks, after which time Fort Totten became a Coast Artillery post. During World War I, it was used as a training camp for troops designated for service overseas. In 1922, because warplanes added a new dimension to New York Harbor's forts, the 62nd Coast Artillery at the fort set up the prototype U.S. anti-aircraft installation.

During World War II, Fort Totten served as anti-aircraft artillery headquarters for the Eastern Defense Command, coordinating guns throughout New York and New Jersey for the city's defense. In 1954 it received Nike anti-aircraft missiles, which remained there for the next twenty years. The uncompleted granite works and later-constructed concrete batteries at 147-acre Fort Totten in 1983 were in the process of being transferred from the Army to New York City to eventually become a public park. Although the guns have been removed, the gateposts at the fort's entrance are surmounted by disarmed harbor mines, symbolic of the fort's service as the

Army's School of Submarine Defense in the nineteenth and early twentieth centuries.

CAMP TOWNSEND. CAMP SMITH.

FORT TYLER. Occupying about 14 acres on the two-mile-long sandspit at the tip of seven-mile long Gardiner's Island lying between the jaws of the easterly ends of Long Island, namely Orient Point and Montauk Point, Fort Tyler stood on land first acquired for use as a lighthouse reservation in 1851. In 1898 the reservation was transferred to the War Department, which erected a fortification to guard New York City from a largely nonexistent Spanish navy. The fort was named in honor of Brigadier General Daniel Tyler, who served with distinction during the Civil War. The fort was garrisoned in 1917 for service during World War I. Until about 1975 the ruins of Fort Tyler made an excellent target for United States Navy aircraft bombing practice.

UPPER FORT. One of the three principal fortifications guarding Schoharie Valley's settlements during the Revolution, Upper Fort was located on the west side of Schoharie Creek at Fultonham. It stood about 5 miles southeast of Middleburgh (Middle Fort) and about 10 miles south of the town of Schoharie, which was defended by Lower Fort. The 10-foot-high palisade walls of the fort enclosed barracks and a number of log huts for refugees, with blockhouses in the northwest and southeast angles. Schoharie Valley was devastated by Sir John Johnson's army of destructives in October 1780. Although Lower Fort and Middle Fort were attacked during the raid, Upper Fort was left unmolested.

CAMP UPTON. Serving throughout both World Wars I and II, Camp Upton was located about five miles northeast of the town of Yaphank in Suffolk County on Long Island. It was named in honor of Major General Emery Upton, distinguished veteran of the Civil War. The post was established on July 18, 1917, to first serve as a training camp for the 77th Infantry Division. Construction started June 21, 1917, and continued through 1918, during the course of which 1,486 buildings were erected for a capacity of some 43,000 troops. After World War I, the camp was discontinued, but the War Department retained the 15,000-acre reservation. Camp Upton was reactivated in early 1941 for service during World War II. It was retired as a reception center on August 31, 1944, after receiving some 500,000 recruits. The post provided rehearsal space for the very successful musical show *This is the Army* written by Irving Berlin. On September 26, 1944, the Army converted Camp Upton into a temporary convalescent hospital to accommodate 3,500 men with the addition of eight new masonry buildings.

FORT VAN ALSTYNE. FORT RENSSELAER.

FORT VAN AUKEN. The vulnerable Minisink settlements on and near the Delaware River were raided by Mohawk war chief Joseph Brant and a large force of Indians and a detachment of Tories on the night of July 19–20, 1779. Part of the army of destructives attacked old Minisink, today's Port Jervis in Orange County. One of the stockaded and fortified farmhouses here was that of Daniel Van Auken, who had erected a strong blockhouse in the rear of his home and barn. Van Auken, his family, and a number of refugees, holed up in the fort, withstood repeated attacks for about an hour without sustaining any casualties, except for family member Jeremiah Van Auken, who was captured outside the blockhouse and carried off as a prisoner.

CAMP VAN SCHAICK (*Fort Half Moon*). Also known as Fort Half Moon, Camp Van Schaick was established in August 1777 by General Philip Schuyler when he fortified Van Schaick Island in the Mohawk River very close to its mouth on the Hudson River, in the present town of Cohoes, Rensselaer County. Its site is occupied by the present intersection of Park and Van Schaick avenues. The fortifications erected consisted most probably of a blockhouse, barracks, and entrenchments. The Van Schaick Mansion built in 1735 by Anthony Van Schaick on the island served as headquarters during the French and Indian War for Sir William Johnson, General James Abercromby, and General Lord Jeffrey Amherst. In 1777 it was headquarters for Generals Philip Schuyler and Horatio Gates. It was here that plans were drafted to stop General Burgoyne's army at Saratoga, ultimately leading to the momentous American victory on October 17, 1777.

FORT VAN TUYLE. This fort was built by John Van Tuyle in 1771 near Greenville, Orange County. Constructed of stone, it had no roof until 1791 because Van Tuyle hoped to prevent Indians from burning him out with flaming arrows shot into the roof.

FORT VAUDREUIL. FORT TICONDEROGA.

FORT VAUGHAN. FORTS CLINTON AND MONTGOMERY.

FORT VIRGINIA. A War of 1812 defense of Sackets Harbor, Fort Virginia was built in the fall of 1814 and located to the east of Fort Kentucky. The fort was a square palisaded work with bastions in all its angles, a blockhouse in the center, and armed with 15 guns. Fort Virginia was dismantled about 1816 with the exception of the blockhouse, which stood until about 1865.

FORT VOLUNTEER. A War of 1812 defense of Sackets Harbor, Fort Volunteer was probably a minimally fortified work built sometime in 1814 by a number of Revolutionary War veterans who volunteered their services for 30 days. It consisted in the main of a long row of log huts extending along the shore of Black River Bay from the village to Fort Pike.

FORT VROOMAN. FORT HARDY.

FORT WADSWORTH (*Fort Richmond; Battery Weed; Fort Morton; Fort Hudson; Fort Tompkins*). Fort Wadsworth on Staten Island is most probably the oldest continuously garrisoned military position in the United States. Henry Hudson, an English mariner in the service of the Dutch East India Company, brought the Dutch flag to what is today's New York on September 11, 1609. Sailing past Fort Wadsworth's present site en route up the Hudson River, he named the island "Staten Eylandt" in honor of the Netherlands' governing tribunal, the States General. In 1626, after the founding of New Amsterdam on Manhattan Island, the Dutch bought Staten Eylandt from the Indian inhabitants there, and 10 years later the first defense was constructed, a blockhouse located on the heights overlooking the Narrows. In 1655 during the Indian massacre in retaliation for the murder of an Indian woman, the fort was destroyed. In 1663 a second blockhouse was built, marking the beginning of the uninterrupted garrisoning of the site that continues to this day. Staten Eylandt became Staten Island, and New Amsterdam was renamed New York for the Duke of York when the English took possession of New Netherland in 1664.

Fort Wadsworth's present flagstaff very likely stands on the approximate site of a signal pole, fitted with painted black and white kegs, which was used as a lookout to warn General Washington of the arrival of the British fleet of warships and transports, beginning on July 2, 1776. All of Staten Island was occupied, and a number of fortifications were built by the British at strategic points to ensure their position. Staten Island on August 22, 1776, was the springboard for the British invasion of Brooklyn across the Narrows. Their

FORT WADSWORTH. Painting of Fort Wadsworth and Fort Tompkins by Seth Eastman. (Courtesy of the Architect of the Capitol, Washington, D.C.)

occupation ended on Evacuation Day, November 25, 1783, when they boarded their transports and sailed eastward to England and home.

Shortly after the war, the area became known as Fort Richmond. The old blockhouse built of huge logs was sheathed by a red sandstone exterior. A small cottage served as officers' quarters, and the enlisted men's barracks were two-story structures. By 1808 four garrisons protected the Signal Hill area. Fort Richmond was at the edge of the Narrows, while Forts Morton and Hudson occupied the slopes of the hill, and Fort Tompkins was at its peak. The four forts had an aggregate of 164 guns.

With the advent of the War of 1812, it was determined that additional fortifications were needed to protect New York Harbor. Governor Daniel D. Tompkins of New York appropriated $25,000 for the purpose. Several artillery companies manned batteries on the island, and Fort Richmond was reinforced in August 1812 by 500 militiamen. By October an additional 12 companies of volunteers were stationed there. Forts Richmond and Hudson received 89 additional cannon in June 1813. The year 1814 was a period of more construction. Monies were appropriated to complete Forts Richmond and Tompkins in April, and the blockhouse and earthworks at Prince's Bay were strengthened. By 1815 the forts had a collective ordnance of 900 guns.

After war's end, the usefulness of the forts was over, and they gradually deteriorated into disrepair. For nearly 20 years, the posts would remain inactive until 1835, when Forts Richmond and Tompkins were formally declared unfit for

use. But a year later the Federal government repurchased the sites and the decaying defenses. Reconstruction of present Fort Tompkins and the battery later known as Battery Weed began in 1847, first garrisoned on August 8, 1861. On November 7, 1865, the War Department's General Orders No. 161 declared that "the military post on Staten Island, New York Harbor, now known as Fort Richmond, will hereafter be called Fort Wadsworth, in memory of the gallant and patriotic services of Brigadier General James S. Wadsworth who was killed at the head of his command in the Battle of the Wilderness, Virginia, on May 6, 1864."

A number of batteries had been installed during the war. The one in the best condition today is Battery Weed, which dated back to the War of 1812 and mounted 30 cannon. It was built at the water's edge in the form of a trapezoid with tiers of guns set in open-arched galleries facing the water. Each salient corner had an octagonal tower of stairs that led from one gallery to another. About 284 guns made Battery Weed one of the strongest fortifications on the East coast. On February 14, 1902, General Orders No. 16 designated the name of Fort Wadsworth to all fortifications on the west side of the Narrows. This included "Battery Weed, in honor of Captain Stephen H. Weed, 5th U.S. Artillery and Brigadier General in the United States Volunteers, who was killed in the Battle of Gettysburg, Pennsylvania, on July 2, 1863."

Fort Wadsworth entered the 20th century as a coast artillery post and remained as such until the end of World War I. Most of its present bar-

FORT WADSWORTH.
Aerial view looking
north. (Courtesy of the
U.S. Navy.)

racks, training areas and administrative buildings were erected during the 1920s and 1930s. Infantry units of the 1st Division comprised the bulk of the military personnel during this period. All infantry units were removed from Fort Wadsworth at the outbreak of World War II. Shortly thereafter, the fort came under the command of the Coast Artillery for the first time since 1919. After the war, the fort settled into daily peacetime routines. During the early 1970s, discussions were held concerning the closing of Fort Wadsworth and other Army bases in the New York area, but they ended with the Staten Island fort complex continuing its mission.

Fort Wadsworth is presently a subinstallation of Fort Hamilton across the Narrows in Brooklyn. One of the fort's major missions is its service as the home of the United States Army Chaplain Center and School. In addition, the 26th Army Band is stationed there, providing regular appearances at parades, sporting events, and other public functions in the New York area. A group of concerned citizens, calling themselves the Fort Wadsworth Committee, has urged state and federal legislation to establish Fort Wadsworth as a "Living National Park Memorial." The New York State Legislature unanimously passed such a resolution in 1976.

FORT WAGNER. Originally a two-story all-stone farmhouse and fort, later lengthened by an unattractive frame extension, Fort Wagner still stands a short distance from S.R. 5, less than two miles north of Nelliston in Montgomery County. Johan Peter Wagner II, son of Palatine German settlers, built the stone house in 1750. Soon after the outbreak of the Revolution, he fortified and palisaded his dwelling, with a blockhouse within the enclosure to billet troops and provide a refuge. Indians and Tories under Sir John Johnson attacked the fort in the fall of 1780 but were successfully repulsed by its garrison.

WALL STREET PALISADE. New York City's Wall Street, famous as the world's financial center, was originally a line of palisades running from the East River to the Hudson River across lower Manhattan Island. The Dutch under Peter Stuyvesant and later the English defended what then constituted the town with a wall along its northern boundary, principally to prevent Indian incursions.

The first palisade, a rather ineffective, rudimentary barrier, was erected by the town's inhabitants during the 1640s. A new substantially built palisade of 7-inch-thick logs with sharpened tops, 12 feet high, was erected between March 17 and

May 1, 1653. At that time only two gates were constructed in the wall: one was the Land Gate on Broadway and the other the Water Gate on Pearl Street near the East River. Sometime before 1660, the Dutch added two large stone bastions or blockhouses near William Street and Broadway. The stones from these defenses were later used to construct the new City Hall on Wall Street. In 1692 the English reconstructed the wall with the inclusion of several blockhouses. By 1699, however, the wall's usefulness was considered at an end because the threat of Indian invasion had become a remote possibility. Since both the wall and the blockhouses were already quite decayed by then and the town's limits were expanding, the barrier was torn down and the blockhouses left to deteriorate into ruinations.

FORT WALRATH. An unmanned blockhouse erected on Henry Walrath's property, a short distance from his farmhouse dwelling at St. Johnsville in Montgomery County, Fort Walrath was burned to the ground by Sir John Johnson's Indian and Tory destructives during their October 1780 invasion of the Mohawk Valley.

WATERVLIET ARSENAL. Located in the present town of Watervliet (formerly West Troy) in Albany County, this arsenal was established to manufacture arms for the War of 1812. It has continued to produce munitions for every subsequent war in American history. In the summer of 1967, the arsenal was designated a National

Historical Monument by the National Park Service. The present grounds of Watervliet Arsenal extend over 136 acres incorporating 81 buildings.

BATTERY WEED. FORT WADSWORTH.

WEST BATTERY. CASTLE CLINTON.

WEST FORT. THE OSWEGO FORTS.

WEST POINT'S FORTS. More than two years of intermittent frenetic efforts, accompanied by inept, indecisive engineering and bitter recriminations, first engendered by Bernard Romans, a cartographer turned self-styled engineer with very limited experience, availed Constitution Island's fortifications nothing but destruction. On October 7, 1777, the day after Popolopen Creek's twin Forts Clinton and Montgomery were overrun by Sir Henry Clinton's forces, Fort Constitution's works were found deserted, their small garrisons hastily evacuating to the north. The British wasted little time demolishing the island's ineffective bastions.

Competent military men, cognizant of the absolute need to refortify the Highlands, had profited by earlier lapses in judgment and inept engineering and resurveyed the region, settling on West Point as the nucleus of a new system of defenses on both sides of the river. Inefficiency delayed construction for several months following Henry Clinton's withdrawal. What finally

WEST POINT'S FORTS. The "S-curve" of West Point and Constitution Island. (Courtesy of the New York State Department of Conservation.)

WEST POINT'S FORTS. Fort Putnam, overlooking the Hudson River. (Courtesy of the U.S. Army.)

evolved, however, was variously and grandiosely called the Gibraltar of America and the Key to the Continent.

The man of the hour at West Point was Thomas Machin, whose genius put new heart into the project. Again he was given the task of spanning the river with a giant chain, the massive links of which were fashioned at the Sterling Ironworks. On the last day of April, 1778, relying on his experience at Fort Montgomery, he succeeded in floating the Great Chain across the Hudson on log rafts and anchoring it securely on the West Point and Constitution Island. Several of the links are memorialized on Trophy Point at the United States Military Academy.

On July 16, 1778, the new defensive works were examined for the first time by General Washington, who had made West Point his personal responsibility. He was greeted by an unprofessionally timed thirteen-gun salute by Fort Arnold's artillerymen. Colonel (later Brigadier General) Thaddeus Kosciuszko had the honor of escorting the commander-in-chief on the tour of inspection (French engineer Louis Duportail, Washington's chief engineer, was absent). Washington was much pleased with what he saw and complimented the Polish engineer.

West Point became the grand citadel and the key position in the Hudson Highlands. Constitution Island, on the east shore, became the supporting defense, protecting the Great Chain and boom (installed below the chain in late June) and offering the island's fire power against enemy naval forces. All of West Point's works were initially constructed of a hodgepodge of materials since there was not enough time to have them built of masonry. Eventually, through the years, some of the defenses were reconstructed of masonry.

The river's barriers consisted of the Water Battery and Battery Knox. Around the Point and lining the shore were Chain, Lanthorn, Green, and South batteries. Above, on the Point's plain (still called the Plain) stood Fort Arnold (renamed Fort Clinton in 1780) and Sherburne's Redoubt. To the southwest, high amid the rocky crags, was Fort Putnam (named for engineer Rufus Putnam) on Crown Hill, with 14 pieces of artillery, looming over Forts Webb, Wyllys, and Meigs, from north to south in that order, and protecting Fort Arnold from enemy assault from the south and west. West Point's artillery complement then consisted of nearly 60 cannon, with about 15 guns not yet mounted, most of them taken at Saratoga in 1777.

The construction of Redoubts One, Two, Three, and Four was initiated during the week following Anthony Wayne's brilliant *coup de main* at Stony Point on July 16, 1779. They were erected on a long ridge to the west and southwest of and higher than Fort Putnam. Washington moved his headquarters from New Windsor to West Point. The citadel was to be protected by his entire army.

Thus within a week of Washington's arrival at West Point, the fortress reached the greatest limit of its expansion. Every defensive position had been planned. From then until war's end those several works would be improved and maintained, but no new ones would be erected. Sixteen enclosed positions and ten major battery sites formed three roughly concentric defensive rings around the great chain. Each fort was capable both of defending itself and providing support by fire to its neighbors. No more formidable a position had ever been seen in the New World. . . . [In comparison with the European tradition of constructing single massive fortresses], West Point, the Gibraltar of America, was a prototype, a forerunner of things to come. [Dave Richard Palmer, *The River and the Rock: The History of Fortress West Point, 1775–1783*, p. 206]

The concentration devoted to West Point's defenses for a time precluded any attention to the refortification of Constitution Island. On May 31, 1778, a month after Captain Machin and his men successfully laid the Great Chain across the river, Colonel John Greaton's Massachusetts regiment built Greaton's Battery on the site of the old Gravel Hill Battery. Engineer Louis Duportail in the autumn built three small redoubts and another battery on the island, one of them on the site of Romans' two-story blockhouse to defend the eastern anchor of the Great Chain. In addition, North and South Redoubts, approximately two miles southeast of the island, were constructed on two sides of a hill near today's town of Garrison.

Inside the old Cadet Chapel at the Academy are black marble shields inscribed in gold letters with the name, rank, and dates of birth and death of the senior American generals in the Revolution. One shield has all of the inscription chiseled out except "Major General" and "1741." Major General Benedict Arnold, great-grandson of a Benedict Arnold who had been a royal governor of Rhode Island, was born in Norwich, Connecticut on January 14, 1741.

There was no doubt about Arnold's ability: he was one of the best field commanders in the history of this nation's military forces. Though General Washington went out of his way to see his "whirlwind hero" obtain the recognition he deserved, the Continental Congress continually kept him off promotion lists. For 15 months Arnold had been dealing through go-betweens with Major John André, General Sir Henry Clinton's talented adjutant. The time had come for a face-to-face meeting to settle final details and for Arnold to hand over the plans of West Point.

On September 22, 1780, just north of Tarrytown, André, using the alias of "John Anderson," was captured by volunteer militiamen who searched him and found the incriminating evidence of the West Point plot. Arnold learned what had happened the next morning over breakfast. He at once made excuses to his meal companions, went to his Tory wife in her bedroom, related to her the disastrous news, ran to his barge, and headed downstream to the British sloop *Vulture*. General Washington, en route to West Point, arrived half an hour later. Not until

about six hours after Arnold's escape did Washington and his officers learn the essential facts of the conspiracy. Arnold's treason, by all odds, was the general's greatest disillusionment.

Despite Sir Henry Clinton's entreaties, André was tried, convicted, and hanged as a spy at Tappan, New York. In 1821 his remains were taken to Westminster Abbey, where George III had had a monument erected to his memory. Benedict Arnold, after serving for a brief period in the field against his fellow Americans, took his family to England in 1781. He died in 1801 and was interred in a crypt in St. Mary's Church located on the Thames River waterfront in south London. In an effort to vindicate his memory, his four sons entered the British army, one of them attaining the rank of lieutenant general.

West Point remained inviolate. The Revolution's major battlegrounds shifted to Virginia and the Carolinas. The joint American-French victory over Cornwallis at Yorktown was the beginning of the end of Britain's efforts to subjugate her rebellious colonial cousins in America. The evolution of the prestigious United States Military Academy from the Revolutionary fortress of West Point did not come overnight. General Washington in 1778 clearly saw the need for an American military academy, learning a lesson from Revolutionary America's abject solicitation of foreign military expertise. Finally, after about a quarter century of protracted verbal sparring between old military stalwarts and Congress, Federal authorization on March 16, 1802, provided for a Corps of Engineers. The act specified that the Corps "shall be stationed at West Point, in the State of New York, and shall constitute a military academy." Operations began, appropriately, on July 4, 1802. Three months later its first class of two men graduated. This slight beginning evolved into what is now the most honored military academy in the world (See: Robert B. Roberts, *New York's Forts in the Revolution* [1980], pp. 120–48; *Notes*, pp. 444–46.)

WHITE FORT. FORT GANSEVOORT.

CAMP WIKOFF. A temporary encampment located at Montauk Point on Long Island, Camp Wikoff was occupied from August to October 1898, during the Spanish-American War emergency.

FORT WILLETT. The devastation of the Mohawk Valley's German Palatine settlements by Sir John Johnson's Indian and Tory raiders in the fall of 1780 dictated the need for additional defenses. A new fortification, named for Marinus

Willett, military commander of the Valley, was begun on high ground south of the Mohawk River, about one mile below St. Johnsville and four miles northwest of Fort Plain. It probably was not completed until the spring of 1781. The fort's palisades, mostly of oak and contributed by farmers in the area, were 15 feet high, with blockhouses at the northeast and southwest angles. It was reported that the enclosure could accommodate a thousand people. The fort was provided with a huge oven, the debris of which remained on the site for many years. Outside the walls were log stables to shelter the inhabitants' livestock in the event of a raid. After the war, each farming family that had contributed toward the stockade took home its share of the pickets and the fort was torn down, just as many other frontier posts were demolished when their usefulness was at an end.

FORT AT WILLETS POINT. FORT TOTTEN.

FORT WILLIAM AUGUSTUS. FORT LÉVIS.

FORT WILLIAM HENRY. FORT GEORGE AT THE BATTERY (See section on New York City Revolutionary War Defenses).

FORT WILLIAM HENRY. After Sir William Johnson's colonial troops defeated Baron Dieskau's French, Canadian, and Indian forces in the Battle of Lake George on September 7, 1755, he ordered a fort built on the site of his fortified encampment located at the southern end of the lake. The defense was intended to serve as a staging point for future English campaigns against the French. Johnson (later knighted for his victory by George II) changed the lake's name from Lac St. Sacrement to Lake George in honor of his king. On November 8 he named the new defense Fort William Henry in honor of two grandsons of George II, William, duke of Gloucester, and Henry, duke of Cumberland. At the same time, he renamed Fort Lyman at the Great Carrying Place to Fort Edward for another grandson.

Fort William Henry, begun three days after the battle, was a palisaded irregular square work with bastions in all its angles, measuring about 400 feet from point to point, and enclosing log barracks on the north and south sides. Casement rooms in the east and west barracks, with walls of brick and stone set against the logs of the curtain wall, were used as storehouses for provisions, hospitals for the sick and wounded, and bomb shelters in times of battle. Captain

FORT WILLIAM HENRY. Reconstruction. (Courtesy of the New York State Department of Commerce.)

(later Major) William Eyre directed its construction.

In March 1757 the fort's defenders easily rebuffed an attack by a small French force. Five months later, however, the fort was surrendered by Lieutenant Colonel George Monro (Munro) after being besieged for almost a week by a much larger, well-organized French force under General Montcalm. The massacre of the prisoners by Montcalm's Indians was the most infamous atrocity of the French and Indian War. The burning of Fort William Henry by the French served as a funeral pyre for the many defenseless victims slaughtered by Montcalm's frenzied Indians. Near the village of Lake George on U.S. 9 stands a privately built re-creation of the fort as it appeared in 1757 on its approximate site.

CASTLE WILLIAMS. GOVERNORS ISLAND FORTS.

FORT WILLIAMS (*Salem Fort*). Originally the first Presbyterian Church at Salem in Washington County, begun in 1774, the structure was never wholly completed. When it was taken over by the Patriot military at the beginning of the Revolution, it was first occupied as a

FORT WOOD. The fort's masonry serving as the base for the Statue of Liberty. (Courtesy of the National Park Service.)

barracks, then it was fortified as the settlement's only defense, commanded by Colonel Joseph McCracken. For a short time, the transformed church was called Salem Fort; then, in deference to General (Doctor) John Williams, it was renamed Fort Williams. The church-fort had a short life. The inhabitants of the settlement were forced to flee before the advance of Burgoyne's invasion army, and the fort was burned by the enemy, sometime during the last days of August 1777.

FORT WINDECKER. The stockaded and fortified farm dwelling of Johannes Windecker on the river road, south of the Mohawk in the village of Minden, it was located one and a half miles south of St. Johnsville, across the river, in Montgomery County. Fort Windecker was one of the better-fortified Mohawk Valley dwellings, with a blockhouse in one of its palisade's angles.

CAMP WINFIELD SCOTT. MITCHEL FIELD.

FORT WINSLOW. FORT INGOLDSBY.

FORT WOOD. The most celebrated piece of sculpture in America is Bartholdi's immense female figure of "Liberty Enlightening the World," the beacon of hope for more than 16 million immigrants. It commands the entrance to New York's Upper Bay from the east end of 12-acre oval-shaped Liberty Island, formerly known as Bedloe's Island. The magnificent 151-foot-high copper-sheathed figure, atop a granite and concrete pedestal, was a gift of the French people to commemorate the alliance of the two nations. It is not generally known that the base for the Statue of Liberty, an 11-pointed star, was a fort constructed during the War of 1812 and named Fort Wood in honor of Lieutenant Colonel Eleazer D. Wood, who was killed during the conflict with Great Britain.

During the three centuries of varying ownership, the island was used as a farm, a summer residence, a pesthouse, a gallows, a military prison, a dump, a military hospital, a quarantine station, a fort, and finally, the home for the eternal symbol of freedom. The island lies 2,950 yards from New York's Battery Park, 1½ miles from Jersey City, and about 20 miles from Sandy Hook. It was called Minissais ("lesser island") by the Indians and Great Oyster Island by the early colonists. Isaac Bedloe (or Bedlow), New Amsterdam-born, was the first white owner of the property, receiving it from the colony's first English governor, Richard Nicholls. On Bedloe's death in 1672, his widow inherited the island but sold it four years later to James Carteret of New Jersey for £81 of Boston money. It afterwards came into the possession of Captain Archibald Kennedy, who commanded the British naval station in New York's harbor. He occupied the island as a summer residence, and for a number of years it was called Kennedy's Island.

In 1738 a rudimentary quarantine station was established there. A smallpox epidemic was ravaging South Carolina just as the scourge had raged in New York about eight years earlier. New York's alarmed inhabitants insisted that all suspected vessels should anchor at Bedloe's Island and their passengers be examined by physicians. In 1758 the Corporation of the City of New York bought the island for 1,000 pounds. During the Revolution the island held a hospital for British wounded, with a number of wooden barracks erected to house the overflow of redcoats.

Ownership of the island was transferred to the state of New York for fortification purposes in 1796, with the stipulation that the city be permitted to use it as a quarantine station whenever the need arose. By an act of the state Legislature in 1800, the island was ceded to the federal government, which occupied it as a military station. Fort Wood was built in 1814 and defended by a mortar battery of 24 guns. During the next twenty years, it was abandoned and reoccupied eight times. The fort's latest design was intended to mount 77 guns and hold a garrison of 350 men. In 1849 it was taken over temporarily as an examining hospital for immigrants. Two years later a separate hospital was begun there and completed in 1853. This post medical facility was a three-story brick building situated at the northwestern extremity of the island. Within the fort's quadrangle was a two-story brick barracks. With the outbreak of Civil War hostilities, Fort Wood was reoccupied on January 18, 1861. At war's end, the fort was left in the charge of a caretaking detachment.

Bedloe's Island, at the traditional gateway to America, was chosen by Liberty's sculptor, Frédéric-Auguste Bartholdi. The great project was the ruling passion of his life, and he labored long and hard to raise the necessary funds on both sides of the Atlantic to bring the plan to completion. The supporting framework for the female colossus was built by the famous French engineer, Alexandre-Gustave Eiffel. The statue was formally presented to the United States by the Franco-American Union in Paris on July 4, 1884. The statue, in 214 cases, was shipped to New York in May, 1885.

October 28, 1886, marked a new era for Fort Wood. That day, amid great fanfare, the Statue of Liberty standing in the center of the granite structure was dedicated. President Grover Cleveland accepted the work on behalf of the people of the United States. The island and Fort Wood, however, continued to play a role for the Army. The fort was reestablished during November 1886, and in October 1894 it became a subpost of Fort Columbus, originally named Fort Jay. In 1887 an acre at the north end of the island had been set aside for a lighthouse reservation and placed under the authority of the Lighthouse Board, which at the time operated the light in the statue's torch.

In April 1899 Fort Wood became a military recruiting center. During November 1901 an Army board studying locations of military posts for use as training garrisons recommended that Fort Wood be made a permanent Army installation, and it continued to serve as a recruiting station. Based on the Board's findings, a Signal Corps subdepot was established there in 1904. In July 1916 a fire on Black Tom Wharf at Jersey City, situated 750 yards west of the island, caused a series of explosions that rained shrapnel and large pieces of iron. The Army's structures on the island suffered a great deal of damage, but the Statue of Liberty and the fort's ramparts were almost unscathed.

During World War I, Fort Wood became a part of New York City's coastal defense. After the war, the coastal defenses and depots on the island were closed, and Fort Wood was garrisoned by a khaki-uniformed company of the 16th Infantry and the Military Police of the 1st Division, which patroled the harbor. By presidential proclamation on October 14, 1924, the Statue of Liberty was declared a National Monument, with its boundaries at the outer edge of old Fort Wood, but the War Department continued to administer the entire island. In August 1933 the Statue was transferred to the National Park Service. After the Japanese attack on Pearl Harbor on December 7, 1941, Naval Intelligence placed restrictions on visitors to the island, and a Coast Guard observation platform was installed on the old fort.

The National Park Service renewed its prewar redevelopment of the island after the end of World War II, and during the 1950s the last of the Army structures were torn down and the island converted into a park with a tree-lined esplanade extending its entire length. Time and the elements took their toll on the Statue of Liberty, prompting a multi-million-dollar fund drive across the country to restore the statue and the Great Hall of nearby Ellis Island. The restoration of the statue was completed in time for its centennial in 1986, and there are plans to renovate Ellis Island's immigrant station for its 100th anniversary in 1992.

FORT WOOD CREEK. FORT BULL.

FORT WYLLYS. WEST POINT'S FORTS.

FORT ZIMMERMAN (*Fort Timmerman*). From extracts of various records in the Montgomery County Department of History and Archives, it is evident that the Mohawk Valley's prolific Zimmermans and Timmermans are genealogically branches of the same family tree. More than two centuries ago, local German and Dutch chroniclers, careless and inefficient in their chores, mistakenly and frequently substituted a T for the Z in the family's surname, thereby causing endless confusion for posterity's historians and genealogists. Nineteenth-century scribes carried forward the deception. Geographers, ap-

parently in an effort at impartiality, named two parallel streams, less than a mile apart in St. Johnsville's environs, Zimmerman Creek and Timmerman Creek.

During the early years of the Revolution, the brothers Conrad and David Zimmerman, descendants of Jacob Zimmerman, immigrant from the German Palatinate, fortified and palisaded their dwelling, standing near their gristmill on Zimmerman Creek, about a mile above Fort Nellis. The fort was assaulted without success a number of times by bands of Indians and Tories. The numerous family served conspicuously in the Revolutionary cause. Conrad Zimmerman was wounded at Oriskany but was able to return home under his own power. A Revolutionary roster, by no means definitive or complete, of the Zimmermans and Timmermans, shows that at least 15 members of the clan served in the Tryon County Militia; 2 of them were killed in action, while another was wounded and taken prisoner to Canada.

NEW YORK CITY
Revolutionary War Defenses
Including Brooklyn, Manhattan, and Staten Island

Brooklyn

Beginning with General Charles Lee, a succession of New York City commanders during the winter and spring of 1776 had come to the same inescapable conclusion. In order to guard the city from enemy assault through Long Island (Brooklyn), a continuous line of entrenchments, strengthened by forts and redoubts in strategic places, would have to be erected from Red Hook to Wallabout Bay. Most of the defense line was ready and manned by May 30. Improvements on the works continued right up to the moment when the British and the Hessians swarmed out of Staten Island and launched attacks by way of Denyse Point and Gravesend Bay.

General Washington and his staff determined

to pull back the Patriot troops from Gowanus Bay through Prospect Park to Jamaica, with the purpose of resorting to their forts should enemy pressures become critical. General Washington sent reinforcements across the river from New York during the night of August 26–27, and he himself arrived in Brooklyn at 8 A.M. General Howe's clever feints at the American west flank drew Washington's reserves to that sector, leaving the opposite flank exposed. Howe and Sir Henry Clinton with 10,000 men made a nine-mile, five-hour, forced night march without being detected by the Patriots, outflanking the entire rebel line by coming through the unfortified and unguarded Jamaica Pass while British troops feinted before the other hill passes.

At Flatbush Pass, the Americans realized they were in a very precarious situation. They fled to their forts, covered by the brave, almost suicidal counterattacks of the Maryland and Delaware regiments against a horde of Hessians, with General Cornwallis and his Fraser Highlanders as yet undiscovered behind the Americans. Soon it was all over, with all the fighting terminating at about two o'clock on the afternoon of August 27.

As is common with casualty reports released by opposing armies, Patriot figures varied greatly from those of the British. Reasonable estimates by historians report the Patriots suffered a loss of about 1,400 men, with 312 killed and the remainder wounded, captured, and missing (Washington's figure was 800; Sir Henry Clinton's estimate was 6,000!). The British officially reported 89 American officers, including Generals John Sullivan and Lord Stirling, and 1,097 others as prisoners. The British and Hessians had a combined loss of a bit less than 400 killed and wounded.

Apprehensive that General Howe might launch an assault against New York with fresh troops from Staten Island, a council of war on the afternoon of August 29 determined to evacuate Brooklyn Heights and reassemble the beaten army on Manhattan Island. That morning General Washington in anticipation had ordered General William Heath to congregate all available watercraft and move them to the East River by nightfall.

The secret extrication of nearly 12,000 men from the Brooklyn forts was accomplished by the rare combination of extraordinary skill and courage aided by a dense fog. It was a feat that was destined to become one of the most memorable events of the war. With the loss of only three soldiers who remained behind to pillage and fire heavy cannon mired in deep mud, General Washington had the remainder of his troops, guns, supplies, and horses across the river and safe on Manhattan Island by seven o'clock on the morning of August 30. The entire evacuation took, almost unbelievably, only six hours.

FORT BOX. A small redoubt mounting four guns, Fort Box was built by the Patriots in early 1776 and was probably named for Major Daniel Box, a "brigade-major" under General Nathanael Greene. It was located on Bergen's (Boerum's) Hill, on or very close to Pacific Street, a short distance above Bond Street. During the War of 1812 the site, or ground very close to it, was occupied by Fort Fireman.

FORT BROOKLYN. Otherwise known by the British as The Citadel, Fort Brooklyn was located at the intersection of Pierrepont and Henry streets, the highest point on Brooklyn Heights, about four blocks southwest of Fort Stirling. Begun in 1780 and reportedly covering five acres of ground, it was by far the most complete fortification erected by the British during their occupation of Brooklyn. The fort was 450 feet square, with ramparts 40 to 50 feet above the bottom of the encircling ditch, itself 20 feet deep. The angles were occupied by bastions, and within the enclosure were substantial barracks and two bombproofed powder magazines. Construction of the fort was still continuing in July 1781, at which time it was garrisoned by 200 Hessians and mounted 18 cannon. The fort was torn down during the 1820s to be replaced by residential housing.

FORT CORKSCREW. Erected in early 1776, this Patriot defense stood on a high conical hill (since drastically reduced) on a site now bounded by Atlantic Avenue, Court, Pacific, and Clinton streets. The soldiers first named it Fort Cobble Hill, then the Spiral Fort, and finally Fort Corkscrew. The British maintained the post until July 3, 1781, when they leveled off the hill somewhat so that the guns of captured Fort Stirling on Brooklyn Heights could adequately cover it. Shortly after the outbreak of the War of 1812, the site was refortified and renamed Fort Swift for General Joseph G. Swift, engineer, who erected a new fort there.

FORT DEFIANCE. A Patriot redoubt, built in April 1776 and mounting four 18-pounders and one 3-pounder, it was named Fort Defiance by Colonel Henry Knox's artillerymen, who were posted there. Henry R. Stiles, nineteenth-century historian, locates the fort's site near the intersection of today's Conover and Van Dyke streets in the Erie Basin area of Red Hook. It has since been determined that the actual site is at Dwight and Beard streets, several blocks to the southeast. On September 27 the British destroyed the works of Fort Defiance because it had fired on British naval craft during the Battle of Brooklyn a month earlier.

FORT GREENE. Occupying the center of the Americans' Brooklyn line of defenses, Fort Greene stood about 300 yards to the left of Fort Box and a short distance above Bond Street, between State and Schermerhorn streets. Completed by May 30, 1776, the star-shaped fort was provided with an interior well and two powder magazines, and mounted six guns. The fort was described by Colonel Moses Little, its commander, as the largest of the Brooklyn defenses, corroborated by the fact that its garrison consisted of a whole regiment, the 12th Massachusetts Continentals. There is some documentation that the British renamed it Fort Sutherland in November 1778. During the War of 1812, it was reoccupied by American troops and renamed Fort Masonic. The fort should not be confused with the Fort Greene of the War of 1812 (Fort Putnam during the Revolution), the site of which is in today's Fort Greene Park.

NARROWS FORT. Constructed in the spring of 1776, this Patriot redoubt—with its companion defense, Flagstaff Fort, opposite on the Staten Island shore—was intended to prevent the entry of enemy shipping into New York's harbor. It was located close to strategic Denyse Point on the Narrows. Its-site is included within present Fort Hamilton.

OBLONG REDOUBT. Built by the Americans in the spring of 1776 and destroyed by the British on September 27 of the same year, the defense stood to the left of Fort Greene, on the opposite side of the Flatbush-Jamaica road. It was located at the present intersection of De Kalb and Hudson avenues. During the War of 1812, Oblong Redoubt's site was occupied by Fort Cummings.

FORT PUTNAM. From the Oblong Redoubt, the American defense line extended northeastward to the crest of the hill in what is now Fort Greene Park, where the fourth in the chain of works was erected in the spring of 1776. Star-shaped like Fort Greene, Fort Putnam was somewhat smaller and mounted at least five guns. It was one of the main objectives of the British attack during and after the Battle of Brooklyn, August 27–29, 1776. The fort was named for Colonel Rufus Putnam rather than General Israel Putnam. Archival evidence indicates that the British in 1782 erected a "new" square-shaped fort on Fort Putnam's site. It would be reasonable to assume, however, that Fort Putnam was *converted* into an equilateral work. During the War of 1812, Fort Putnam was renamed Fort Greene for General Nathanael Greene.

FORT STIRLING. Begun on March 1, 1776, as the first American fort to be constructed in Brooklyn, Fort Stirling—named for General Lord Stirling (William Alexander)—was located on the bluff at the very edge of Brooklyn (Columbia) Heights on today's Columbia Street, spanning the two-block distance between Clark and Orange streets. Also known as Fort Half-Moon because of its

open rear, Fort Stirling was intended to command the mouth of the East River. After the Americans were forced out of Brooklyn, the British posted a strong Hessian garrison at the fort because of its eminently strategic position.

Manhattan

Early in January 1776, about two months before the British were forced to evacuate besieged Boston, General Washington at Cambridge received the disturbing news that the British had outfitted a new expedition, with Sir Henry Clinton as its commander. Believing that it was destined for New York, General Charles Lee and a column of Connecticut troops were ordered to march to that city and take preliminary possession. His entry into New York on February 4 coincided with the arrival of Clinton, en route to North Carolina, off Sandy Hook.

The Patriots camped on the Fields, the site of today's City Hall. General Lee assigned his engineer the task of surveying the salients to be fortified. In company with Lord Stirling, Lee roamed the city and its environs. The more they inspected, the more they became convinced that a complete defense of the city was impractible. Surrounded by water on all sides, the island of Manhattan offered almost unlimited opportunities for enemy attack.

Lee bequeathed to Stirling the monumental problem of fortifying an island city with open approaches on every hand. Promoted to brigadier general a month earlier by Congress, Stirling spent every waking moment in planning and initiating defenses, driving troops to ever greater efforts. In the days that followed, more regiments departed from Boston by land and sea to garrison New York and work on the city's defenses. By the time Washington arrived on April 13, some defensive beginnings had been made in Manhattan, Brooklyn, and on Nutten (Governors) Island. The city then constituted only the southern end of today's borough of Manhattan; Brooklyn and Staten Island were suburbs of the "metropolis."

"New York . . . was transformed by the emergency into a fortified military base. . . . Forts, redoubts, batteries, and intrenchments encircled the town. The streets were barricaded, the roads blocked, and efforts made to obstruct the navigation of both rivers. . . . It was here around New York and Brooklyn that the War of the Revolution began in earnest." The following listings locate the defenses in the context of today's geography. A number of the American fortifications were taken over by the British during their occupation of the city and modified, strengthened or enlarged, with additions of their own. (See: Robert B. Roberts, *New York's Forts in the Revolution* [1980], pp. 264–326, for complete delineations.)

BADLAM'S REDOUBT. CITIZEN'S REDOUBT.

BAYARD'S HILL REDOUBT. FORT BUNKER HILL.

FORT BUNKER HILL (*Independent Battery; Bayard's Hill Redoubt*). This extensive, sod-banked earthwork, completed by April 16, 1776, by the Americans, covered the area now bounded by Centre, Broome, Mott, and Grand streets.

CITIZENS REDOUBT (*Badlam's Redoubt*). This Patriot defense, mounting eight guns, was built in the early spring of 1776. It stood on Rutgers Hill at Market and Madison streets, just east of the old Jewish cemetery.

FORT COCK HILL. This American earthwork defense was constructed in 1776 and located on the summit of Inwood Hill, approximately in line with today's 207th Street, just south of Spuyten Duyvil Creek, which defines Manhattan Island's northern boundary.

FOREST HILL REDOUBT. FORT TRYON.

FORT GEORGE AT THE BATTERY. In the year 1630, Johannes de Laet published *Beschryvinghe van West-Indien*. The book included a new map on which were shown, for the first time, the names "Manhattes" and "N. Amsterdam." Four years earlier the settlement of New Amsterdam had been created on the southern tip of Manhattan Island, establishing the colony of New Netherland in the New World, under the aegis of the Dutch West Indies Company, chartered by Holland in 1621 and organized in 1623. From 1626 until the outbreak of the Revolution, Fort George, originally Fort Amsterdam, along with its subordinate batteries, was the principal defensive work on Manhattan Island. During the subsequent century and a half, the fort underwent several physical transformations and royal name changes. On the site now occupied by the United States Custom House, bounded by Whitehall, State, and Bridge streets and Bowling Green, the fortification was renamed Fort James in 1664, Fort Willem Hendrick in 1673, Fort James again in 1674, Fort William

Fig. 2. S
The Fort in New York.

THE EXPLANATION OF FIG. 2.

1. The chappell.
2. The governor's house.
3. The officers' lodgings.
4. The soldiers' lodgings.
5. The necessary house.
6. The flag-staff and mount.
7. 7. The centry boxes.
8. 8. Ladders to mount the walls.
9. The well in the fort.
10. The magazine.
11. The sallyport.
12. The secretary's office.
13. The fort gate.
14. A horn-work before it.
15. The fort well and pump.
16. Stone mount.
17. The iron mount.
18. The Town mount.
19. 19. Two mortar pieces.
20. A turn-stile.
21. Ground for additional building to the governor's house
22. The armory over the governor's kitchen.

Henry in 1691, Fort Anne, or Queen's Fort, in 1703, and Fort George in 1714. Partially destroyed by fire in 1741, it was finally demolished in 1790.

When General Charles Lee arrived in New York on February 4, 1776, he was met by deputations from the Committee of One Hundred, which opposed any military occupation of the city, fearing a destructive bombardment from Sir Henry Clinton's armada of British warships anchored offshore. But Lee disregarded all objections. He and Lord Stirling, who was assigned the task of fortifying the city, kept Continental troops working feverishly to border the island with redoubts and earthworks on which were mounted more than a hundred guns, many of them from Boston where the British had abandoned them after their evacuation of that city.

Ruthlessly determined, General Lee ordered the two bastions and ramparts on the north side of Fort George, facing Bowling Green, torn down. In a report to Congress, he gave his reasons for the seemingly reckless destruction:

This fort cannot be defended, but as it is not possible in our hands to render it a fortification of offence

FORT GEORGE AT THE BATTERY. Plan of the fort as it was in 1695. (From A Description of the Province and City of New York, With Plans of the City and Several Forts as They Existed in the Year 1695, *by Rev. John Miller.)*

FORT GEORGE AT THE BATTERY. View of the fort and New York City from the southwest as they looked in 1731–1736. (Courtesy of the Museum of the City of New York.)

against the enemy, it might in their possession be converted into a citadel to keep the town in subjection. These considerations have induced me to throw down the northeast and northwest bastions, with the communicating curtain, so that being entirely open behind, and a commanding traverse thrown across the Broad Way [200 yards north of the fort] with three guns mounted, it is impossible for the enemy to lodge themselves in and repair the fort.

Most of the heavy artillery at Fort George and the Grand Battery was transported up Broadway to the Commons and, shortly thereafter, to King's Bridge. The Continentals left a minimum of ordnance on Manhattan's southern tip: Fort George, two 12-pounders and four 32-pounders, though it could mount 60 guns; the Grand Battery, thirteen 32-pounders, one 24-pounder, two 2-pounders, and four mortars, though the battery could emplace 90 guns.

Old Fort George, kept in costly repair for 160 years, was condemned by an act of the State Legislature on March 16, 1790, specifying that the land beneath the fort should forever be reserved for the erection of public buildings. A marble slab marking the site of the fort's southwest bastion was originally set in place in 1818. In 1904 subway construction workers removed the marker and reset it on the lawn of Battery Park in 1907.

FORT GEORGE ON LAUREL HILL.

There are still remains of Revolutionary fortifications on the west bank of the Harlem River, on an eminence known today as Fort George Hill. The site, east of Broadway at 192nd Street and Audubon Avenue, is marked by a D.A.R. tablet that reads: "In grateful remembrance of the Patriot Volunteers of the Pennsylvania Flying Camp led by Colonel William Baxter of Bucks County, Pennsylvania, who, with many of his men, fell while defending this height, 16 November 1776, and was buried near this spot."

The fortifications were overrun by superior numbers of troops of the famed Black Watch (Scotch Royal Highlanders) and Hessians during the British attack on Fort Washington a half mile to the west. During the winter of 1779, Laurel Hill was connected to Fort Tryon. The following winter, the British circumvallated Laurel Hill's redoubts. The defenses were named Fort Clinton for a short period, then renamed Fort George. The site of the fort is now occupied by George Washington High School.

GRENADIER'S BATTERY.

The circular battery, on the bank of the Hudson River at the present intersection of Washington and Harrison streets in lower Manhattan, was constructed by Captain Abraham Van Dyck's Grenadier Company of New York Independents. Armed with three 12-pounders and two mortars, with a line of breastworks extending along the river to Hubert Street, the defense was initiated while General Charles Lee was still in command of the city.

HORN'S HOOK FORT.

Horn's (Hoorn's) Hook, a projection of land now partly hidden by the East River Drive and incorporated within Carl Schurz Park, was the immediate area of a strong Patriot work. It consisted of a battery of nine guns, six of them mortars, with breastworks and entrenchments. The site of the fort itself is now occupied by the Gracie Mansion (1799), the official home of New York City's mayors, on the south side of 89th Street and East End Avenue.

The East River, at this point only 700 yards wide, is at the entrance to all-important Hell Gate, the gateway for British penetration into upper Manhattan by way of the Harlem River.

HOSPITAL REDOUBT. By April 1, 1776, the hospital then situated at West Broadway and Worth Street in downtown Manhattan was fortified by a strong breastwork, described as "composed solely of dirt and sod," about 10 feet thick and 7 feet high, with a 12-foot-wide ditch surrounding the whole.

FORT INDEPENDENCE. The strongest Revolutionary War defense in what is now Bronx County, until the British rebuilt captured Fort Number Four, Fort Independence was located on the heights between the old Boston and Albany Post Roads, on the west side of Giles Place, about 1,000 feet north of where it intersects Sedgwick Avenue. Fort Independence Park, at the south end of the Jerome Park Reservoir, now incorporates the site of the Patriot defense. The earthen fort was a rough parallelogram with bastions in the northwest and southwest corners, enclosing a stone-based barracks, officers' quarters, stone powder magazine, and a number of tents. In 1958 five amateur archaeologists unearthed sections of the fort, along with numerous artifacts of the Revolutionary period.

INDEPENDENT BATTERY. FORT BUNKER HILL.

JERSEY BATTERY. Located in downtown Manhattan on present Reade Street west of Greenwich Street, to the left of Grenadier's Battery, Jersey Battery stood close to the Hudson River shore to effectively enfilade any enemy attempt to land troops in its environs. The Patriot work was a five-sided fort, mounting two 12- and three 32-pounders, with line entrenchments connecting it to the Grenadier's Battery.

JONES HILL FORT. A circular battery, embrasured for eight guns, this Patriot defense stood a little north of the present intersection of Broome and Pitt streets. A differing citation locates the site at Grand and Columbia steets. It was built on the property of Thomas Jones, Loyalist historian, who authored a history of the war from his point of view. After the Continentals evacuated the city, the defense was taken over by the British on October 2 and significantly strengthened with fraises and pickets.

KING'S BRIDGE REDOUBT. Considered highly strategic by both the Americans and the British, King's Bridge was located at the point where the old Post Road crossed Spuyten Duyvil Creek, separating Manhattan Island from the Bronx. The name Kingsbridge is still attached to its environs. There is no documentation available to describe the American defense at King's Bridge, but it may be reasonably assumed that at least a small redoubt was constructed there to guard the bridge. After the Americans were forced off Manhattan Island in the fall of 1776, the British on November 22 occupied King's Bridge and erected a semicircular earthwork on the south side of the Creek on Broadway.

FORT KNYPHAUSEN. FORT WASHINGTON.

LISPENARD'S REDOUBT. Standing on Lispenard's Hill, named for Leonard Lispenard, wealthy brewer and delegate to the Provincial Convention, these works were the western anchor of the line defending New York City. A double post with a redoubt covering the approach from the country to the north and a battery guarding the Hudson River side, Lispenard's Redoubt was located at today's intersection of Varick and Laight streets in downtown Manhattan. The defensive complex had a change in names, instigated by enemy reconstructions after the Americans evacuated the city.

MCGOWN'S PASS REDOUBT. A redoubt was constructed on one of two small, steep hills within the northeast corner of today's Central Park, at about the intersection of Fifth Avenue and East 107th Street, just above the home of Andrew McGown (McGowan). The hill is now commemorated by the Fort Clinton Monument, a cannon surmounting a huge flat boulder, to which is attached a tablet: "This Eminence Commanding McGowan's Pass Was Occupied by British Troops Sept. 15, 1776 and evacuated Nov. 21, 1783. Here Beginning Aug. 18, 1814, the Citizens of New York Built Fort Clinton to Protect the City in the Second War with Great Britain." The old Post Road ran between the two hills of McGown's Pass. Considered highly critical terrain, the pass was prominently involved in the Revolutionary battle for Manhattan.

MONTRESOR'S ISLAND. Strategically situated at the mouth of the Harlem River, Montresor's (now Randall's) Island was owned by Captain John Montresor, the British army's chief of engineers in the Colonies. He bought the island in 1772 and resided there with his family until 1783, except for a period of several months, when the Americans had control of the island and used it as an isolation area for Continental troops stricken with smallpox. British forces occupied it on September 10, 1776, fortified it, and used it as a stepping stone in Sir William Howe's campaign to oust Washington's troops from Manhattan Island. On September 23 a Continental attack against the island turned into an embarrassing fiasco.

FORT NUMBER ONE. Colonel James Swartwout and Dutchess County minutemen constructed this small square fort during the late summer of 1776 on the southwest slope of Spuyten Duyvil Hill, just north of the Henry Hudson Monument, at today's West 230th Street and Sycamore Avenue.

FORT NUMBER TWO. During August–September 1776, Colonel Swartwout and his minutemen built this small, probably circular, abatised fort on the crest of Spuyten Duyvil Hill. Its site is located near the intersection of West 230th Street and Arlington Avenue.

FORT NUMBER THREE. Colonel Swartwout's minutemen also built this fort during the late summer of 1776. It was a square, abatised earthwork located on the eastern side of Spuyten Duyvil Hill on a line with present Netherland Avenue, between West 227th and 231st streets.

FORT NUMBER FOUR. A square, palisaded earthen redoubt, about 70 feet to a side and surrounded by a ditch, Fort Number Four was one of the supporting defenses for Fort Washington and King's Bridge. It was located at the south end of today's Jerome Park Reservoir, 700 feet east of Sedgwick Avenue. British and Hessian forces twice assaulted the fort and finally captured it. Fort Number Four was one of the defenses ordered demolished by Sir Henry Clinton in the fall of 1779 in order to obtain the required manpower for his campaign in the South.

FORT NUMBER FIVE. The British built this square abatised earthwork, probably during the late summer of 1777. Located on Kingsbridge Road, the fort was designed to cover the approach to the Dyckman Bridge spanning the Harlem River. The site of the fort is on the grounds of the U.S. Veterans Hospital, formerly a Catholic orphan asylum.

FORT NUMBER SIX. Construction of this earthwork was initiated by the British on May 19, 1777. Also located on the present grounds of the U.S. Veterans Hospital, the site of Fort Number Six is at Kingsbridge Road and Sedgwick Avenue.

FORT NUMBER SEVEN. Earthworks were constructed by the British on November 15, 1776, at the present-day intersection of Fordham Road and Sedgwick Avenue. Reconstruction of the work into a square abatised fort was begun by them on July 19, 1777.

FORT NUMBER EIGHT. Unlike the other forts and redoubts of the Americans' so-called Exterior Defense Line, Fort Number Eight was built by the British. It stood on the east side of the Harlem River, on today's New York University's campus, on University Heights in the Fordham section of the Bronx. A boulder inscribed "The Site of Fort Number Eight, 1776–1783" stands on Battery Hill 80 yards south of N.Y.U.'s Hall of Chemistry. The massive Schwab Mansion (1857), just beyond the marker, was erected within the site. The fort covered the advance of Lord Percy's troops and Hessians during their attack on Fort Washington, actively participating in the bombardment of the Patriot defense. On October 20, 1782, Fort Number Eight underwent demolition by the British, twelve days after they had abandoned it. Excavations in 1965 for a new N.Y.U. campus building unearthed numerous Revolutionary artifacts, most of them preserved in the Valentine-Varian House Museum, headquarters for the Bronx County Historical Society.

OYSTER BATTERY. Citations are at odds on whether Oyster Battery and McDougall's Battery were interchangeable names for the same Patriot defense, armed with two 32-pounders and three 12-pounders. One report claims the two were one and the same, and located behind Trinity Church. Nineteenth-century historian Benjamin Lossing says Oyster Battery stood in the rear of No. 1 Broadway (Washington's brief headquarters on the west side of the street), and that McDougall's Battery, with a complement of four guns, was located southwest of Trinity Church. Double identities for fortifications in American history are common.

FORT PRINCE CHARLES. According to historian I. N. Phelps Stokes, this earthen redoubt was erected by the Americans as Fort Number Nine in 1776, taken over by the enemy after the battle for Fort Washington on November 16, and renamed Fort Prince Charles or the Charles Redoubt. He locates its site on Marble Hill, at Fort Charles (Corlear) Place and Kingsbridge Avenue.

FORT TRYON (*Forest Hill Redoubt*). The site where Patriot troops demonstrated their most stubborn resistance to vastly superior numbers of the enemy before the downfall of Fort Washington is now commemorated high on the wooded elevations at the northern end of Manhattan Island. A small redan appropriately named Forest Hill Redoubt by the Americans, it was the northern outpost of Fort Washington and located where the main observation platform, flagpole, and memorial plaques are situated in Fort Tryon Park.

On November 16, 1776, the fortification on the 250-foot-high hill overlooking Inwood Village, between Fort Washington and Fort Cock Hill, was being held by Colonel Moses Rawlings and 250 Maryland and Virginia riflemen, supported by two six-pounders manned by gunners of the Pennsylvania Artillery. Outnumbering the defenders more than ten to one, 3,000 Hessians commanded by Lieutenant General Wilhelm Knyphausen crossed King's Bridge and attacked the American position in two columns. Two and a half hours after the assault began, the Hessians finally clambered over the redan's ramparts and bayoneted those Americans who refused to lay down their arms. Fort Washington fell the same day. The Patriots were forced off Manhattan Island, not to return for nearly seven years. The British in 1778–79 erected sizable Fort Tryon and a barracks on the site of the redoubt, naming the new fort for the last royal governor of New York.

In 1933 the historical site was presented as a gift to New York City by John D. Rockefeller, Jr., who purchased the property that shortly became Fort Tryon Park. A private residence was dismantled and an observation platform replaced it, providing panoramic views of the Hudson River, the East River, and the upper reaches of Manhattan Island.

TURTLE BAY DEPOT. The small rock-rimmed cove called Turtle Bay in the East River at the foot of 47th Street has been since filled in to become the plaza one block north of the United Nations Assembly Building. It was the site of a British storehouse and magazine captured in a bold raid late on the night of July 20, 1775. The daring amphibious foray was conducted by the Liberty Boys, led by Marinus Wil-

lett, John Lamb, Isaac Sears, and Alexander McDougall, Sons of Liberty activists who later attained additional fame. A part of the captured stores was shipped to Washington's army besieging British-held Boston and the remainder forwarded to Fort Ticonderoga where General Richard Montgomery's troops were congregating for their role in the invasion of Canada. In 1776 the Patriots built a redoubt at Turtle Bay, on a site between today's 44th and 46th Streets, just south of the former British depot.

FORT WASHINGTON (*Fort Knyphausen*). Intended to protect all of upper Manhattan, Fort Washington was situated on the island's highest elevation, on a 230-foot-high, mile-long hill, covering the ground between present 181st and 186th streets along Fort Washington Avenue. The fort commanded the Hudson to the west, the valley of Broadway and Laurel Hill to the east, and the country down to about today's 120th Street to the south.

Laid out by Rufus Putnam, General Washington's engineer, the fort's construction was begun on June 20, 1776. Originally planned as a five-bastioned fortress, Fort Washington eventuated as an extensive, crude, pentagonal earthwork, without the improvements dictated by military science to withstand attack or siege. Haste had precluded the building of what could have been an eminently strong fortress. The fort had neither ditch nor palisade, no barracks, casemates, or source of water supply, and suffered from weak outworks.

The treachery of English-born William Demont, adjutant to Continental Colonel Robert Magaw, probably influenced General William Howe's decision to postpone pursuit of Washington's army beyond White Plains, turn about, and take care of bypassed Fort Washington. Less than a week after the Battle of White Plains, Demont deserted on the night of November 2 and went directly to General Lord Percy's camp at McGown's Pass, bringing with him the plans of Fort Washington. The *chevaux-de-frise* in the Hudson proved to be an abysmal failure: the British frigates *Phoenix* and *Rose* without any trouble sailed over the barrier, unscathed by Patriot artillery fire from both riverbanks. During the night of November 14–15, enemy naval craft convoyed a large flotilla of troop-laden flatboats up the river into Spuyten Duyvil Creek and down the Harlem River to an assembly point that became the springboard for British assaults westward.

Early on the morning of the 16th, General Howe launched vicious assaults up the steep, rocky hill from the three sides of Fort Washington. Outnumbering the defenders three to one, Hessian troops pushed up the hillside in the face of concentrated rifle fire and scaled the ramparts of Fort Washington's earthworks. American soldiers ran frantically for the fort's central redoubt, where they finally surrendered, but not before a number of them had been mercilessly bayoneted.

General Washington across the river at Fort Lee, with spyglass in hand, watched with consternation and sorrowful regret the loss of some of his best troops. The capture of Fort Washington gave the British what they sought—New York and its great natural harbor. On November 21 the American defense was renamed Fort Knyphausen for Hessian General Baron von Knyphausen, who had captured Forest Hill Redoubt. Under British control, it was occupied by Hessian troops for most of the remaining years of the war. They used it as a headquarters, with the addition of barracks, a hospital, and bakehouses.

A monument with a Revolutionary War cannon mounted on it was erected on Fort Washington Avenue to mark the site of the fort. Years later the landmark was demolished. Today the site is commemorated by a towering flagpole on Fort Washington Avenue in Gordon Bennett Park between 183rd and 185th Streets, the highest natural point on Manhattan Island.

WATERBURY'S BATTERY. Built by the Americans in the spring of 1776, this battery of seven guns was located at the foot of Catherine Street at its intersection with Cherry Street. Close by was another artillery position, the Shipyard Battery, armed with two guns.

WHITEHALL BATTERY. Located behind General Washington's short-lived headquarters at No. 1 Broadway, on what was once known as the Whitehall Dock (now South Ferry), Whitehall Battery stood a little to the east of the Grand Battery and was armed with two 32-pounders.

Staten Island

This 57-square-mile island, bordered on the south and west by Upper and Lower New York bays, and separated from New Jersey by Kill van Kull and Arthur Kill, became the springboard for the massive invasion of Brooklyn by the British and their Hessian mercenaries in the last week of August 1776. It also served as an advanced base for British forays against American posts in New Jersey. The island is approximately one mile across the Narrows from Brooklyn and seven miles across Upper Bay from Manhattan's Battery.

On July 2, 1776, General William Howe began an unopposed takeover of Staten Island, landing troops by the thousands; on the 13th his older brother, Admiral Lord Richard Howe, arrived with more troops from England, including thousands of Hessians. On August 12 Sir Henry Clinton returned from his Charleston campaign with more troops and joined the Howe brothers on the island, which supported a normal population of only 2,000 farming and seafaring people. It was the greatest overseas expeditionary force ever congregated by the British, with the number of soldiers and seamen, rank and file, aggregating about 42,000 men.

The British completely occupied Staten Island, erecting forts and redoubts on all the strategically important heights and shore points, and converting almost every dwelling and tavern from Kill van Kull to Raritan Bay into billets. And there they stayed until the end of the Revolution. At present there are no conclusive documentations to identify all the British fortification sites on the island. A Revolutionary War period map in the Richmondtown Museum shows various tentative sites, but little actual work has been done to develop them.

DECKER'S FERRY FORT. This British strongpoint was located opposite Bayonne Neck, facing today's Bayonne–Staten Island ferry landing in the town of Port Richmond on Kill van Kull. The ferry to Bergen Neck was also covered by the fort's guns. When the Americans fled the island in the face of the British landing, they burned the stone house belonging to a Tory named Decker. One week after the British arrived, they took over the dwelling and converted it into a fort. It was involved in the unsuccessful large-scale Patriot raid commanded by General John Sullivan on the first anniversary of the invasion of Brooklyn, August 22, 1777.

FLAGSTAFF FORT. The Americans had a redoubt called Flagstaff Fort, garrisoned by several hundred men in June 1776 on Signal Hill at the Narrows. This site has been continuously fortified for more than 300 years, ever since 1663 when David Pietersen de Vries built a blockhouse there. Near today's town of Rosebank, this location and much more of the surrounding ground is now occupied by Fort Wadsworth.

The British wasted little time strengthening and rebuilding the Patriot defense. By July 1779 a redoubt and a line of gun platforms had been constructed to mount about 26 cannon; two months later, there were six 24-pounders and four 18-pounders. In 1782 the fortification had five bastions and several barbette batteries. The British occupied this post and others on the island until they evacuated New York in late 1783.

FORT RICHMOND. This British post was situated on the top of the hill overlooking the present-day restored village of Richmondtown, located on the grounds of the La Tourette Country Club. The fort, consisting in the beginning of three earthen redoubts, was laid out by General James Robertson on July 9, 1776, just one week after General Howe landed with his troops. On October 3, 1779, there were three great redoubts covering both sides of the crest of the hill, with the garrison encamped between the works. In 1777, when Fort Richmond was the headquarters of Hessian Major General von Lossberg, two American raids, one in January and the other in August, were repulsed by the fort's garrison.

WATERING PLACE REDOUBTS. These fortifications at today's Tompkinsville were constructed at the spring on what was later called Pavillion Hill. The area had been occupied by the Patriots prior to the arrival of the British, who added three redoubts during the last two weeks of July 1776. The two most important redoubts had been described as circular, double abatised, and palisaded, with 200 men in each. A 1782 British military map not only delineates the forts but also notes that 2,000 men could parade in order of battle in front of them, evidencing the great extent of ground the works covered.

* * *

The following British posts on Staten Island have not been sufficiently documented to allow adequate descriptions of them:

- AMBOY FERRY POST. Located on the southwestern shore of the island, this post was garrisoned in 1777 by three companies.

- DUTCH CHURCH FORT. This fortified stone church at Port Richmond was destroyed by General Stirling and his troops during their raid on January 14–15, 1780.

- ELIZABETH FERRY REDOUBTS. Three redoubts, armed with one 18-pounder and four 24-pounders, were garrisoned by three Hessian companies in 1777.

- FORT GEORGE. Located at St. George, this was considered "only an encampment."

- FORT KNYPHAUSEN. Located at St. George, this earthen redoubt commanded the harbor from its position on an eminence known during the Revolution as the Watering Place and today as Fort Hill. Named for Hessian General Wilhelm Baron von Knyphausen, the redoubt's troops repulsed the assault by General Stirling during his 24-hour raid in January 1780.

- OLD BLAZING STAR POST. This fortified inn, garrisoned by Hessians, stood on the north bank of the mouth of Fresh Kills, west of Richmondtown.

North Carolina

CAMP ADVANCE. A Confederate Civil War encampment located near Garysburg, Northampton County, Camp Advance was named for Governor Zebulon B. Vance and was established in the fall of 1862. The camp continued in service throughout the war.

CAMP ALAMANCE. Located on the Alamance Battlefield near modern Burlington, it was established in May 1861 and continued for the duration of the war.

FORT ALLEN. An unfinished Confederate two-gun defense, Fort Allen was located near the town of Lane, a short distance south of Fort Ellis, in Craven County.

CAMP AMORY (*Fort Amory*). A Federal encampment located on the south side of the Trent River from New Bern, Camp Amory was established in 1862 and occupied by the 45th Massachusetts Volunteer Militia Regiment. The camp consisted of two large barracks capable of accommodating five companies of men each. Between the barracks buildings were the hospital tents. The rectangle was enclosed by a line of officers' tents on the opposite side of the encampment from the river. Fort Amory, located a half-mile away, was part of a mile-long defensive line between the Trent and Neuse rivers. Both were named for the brigade commander, Colonel Thomas Jonathan Amory, who died of yellow fever at New Bern on October 8, 1864.

FORT AMORY. CAMP AMORY.

CAMP ANDERSON. A Confederate encampment located at or near Garysburg in Northampton County.

CAMP ANDERSON. A Confederate post located within present-day Wilmington's city limits, Camp Anderson opened in June 1861 when the 4th North Carolina Regiment established the camp.

FORT ANDERSON. Located about 12 miles south of Wilmington on a hillside overlooking the Cape Fear River are the remains of old Brunswick Town, the first settlement on the river and the home of two royal governors, that has lain buried since the Revolution. At the outbreak of war in 1775, the people, fearing that British warships would sail into the harbor and bombard the town, moved to either Wilmington or other less exposed settlements. By 1776 the town was abandoned, and during that year it was

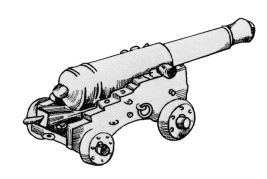

burned by either the British or Tories. After the war, several families moved back to Brunswick and rebuilt homes, but the town never recovered. By 1830 it was completely abandoned. In 1842 the townsite was sold for $4.25 and added to the lands of Orton Plantation.

During the Civil War, a Confederate fort was built diagonally across the ruins of the town. Known as Fort Anderson, it was constructed of sand and extended from the river to Orton Pond, a distance of more than a mile. The fort consisted of massive earthworks and two batteries with five gun emplacements in each, in addition to many other emplacements for 32-pounder rifles. After the fall of Fort Fisher across the river, Fort Anderson withstood a month-long siege by Federal forces and was abandoned by the Confederates after it was severely bombarded for three days, February 17–19, 1865. With its fall, it became possible for the Union army to march freely on Wilmington, and three days later it was occupied by Federal troops. The earthworks of Fort Anderson, complete with gun emplacements intact, stand today as a great monument of the War Between the States and a vantage point from which to view the preserved ruins of old Brunswick Town.

FORT ANDERSON. A defense erected by Federal troops after their capture of New Bern on March 14, 1863, Fort Anderson, garrisoned by the 92nd New York Infantry with Lieutenant Colonel Hiram Anderson, Jr., in command, was an earthwork on the north bank of the Neuse River directly opposite New Bern. It was flanked on both sides by swamps and approachable only in front along a narrow causeway. A year to the day after the fall of New Bern, Confederate troops attacked and briefly besieged Fort Anderson, but the arrival of Union gunboats relieved the defenders pinned down in the fort.

CAMP ARGYLE. A temporary Confederate encampment, Camp Argyle was located in the Beaufort–Morehead City area.

CAMP ASHE. A temporary Confederate encampment, occupied by 8th North Carolina Infantry troops, Camp Ashe was located at Topsail Sound, 12 miles from Wilmington.

FORT ASTOR. Located on the north bank of the Trent River, just south of New Bern, Fort Astor was erected by Confederate troops early in the war to protect the city.

CAMP BADGER. Named for George E. Badger, North Carolinian and former secretary of the Navy under Presidents Harrison and Tyler, Camp Badger was established near the city of Raleigh by the Confederates and used for the duration of the war.

CAMP BADGER. A temporary Confederate encampment located near Fort Fisher and Camp Wyatt on Confederate Point on the north side of the Cape Fear River, Camp Badger was named for former Secretary of the Navy George E. Badger.

CAMP BAKER. A temporary Confederate encampment, possibly fortified, it was located on the Roanoke River near the town of Hamilton in Martin County.

CAMP BAKER. A temporary Confederate encampment, Camp Baker was located at or near the town of Greenville in Pitt County.

FORT BARNWELL. Located at the junction of Cotechney Creek and the Neuse River, two miles north of present-day Barnwell in Craven County, Fort Barnwell was erected in April 1712 by South Carolinian Colonel John Barnwell to protect the German Palatine settlements during the campaign against the warring Tuscarora Indians.

FORT BARTOW (*Fort Foster*). Fort Bartow, an earthwork mounting nine 32-pounder guns commanded by Lieutenant B. P. Loyall, was located on Pork Point on Roanoke Island. It was erected by Confederate troops for the defense of the island and Roanoke Sound. Bombarded by the Federal fleet on February 7, 1862, the fort was taken the following day by Union forces. Renamed Fort Foster for Brigadier General John G. Foster, it remained in their possession until the end of the war.

CAMP BATTLE. A temporary World War II encampment located on the site of a former C.C.C. camp just northwest of the city of New Bern, Camp Battle was established during the early days of the war. It was occupied by coastal artillery units primarily intended to guard the bridges over the Neuse and Trent rivers. Camp Battle was named in honor of Confederate Major General Cullen A. Battle.

CAMP BEAUFORT. A temporary, probably fortified Confederate encampment, Camp Beaufort is believed to have been located at Topsail Inlet near Bogue Island, south of Fort Macon and the Morehead City area.

FORT BEAUFORT. Located at Topsail Inlet leading to the city of Beaufort, Fort Beaufort was a Federal-built granite defense mounting 40 guns of various caliber.

CAMP BEAUREGARD. A temporary Confederate encampment, this camp was located near the town of Ridgeway in Warren County.

CAMP BEECH GROVE. Its site now occupied by the Beech Grove Church on present-day N.C. Rural Road 1401, nine miles west of New Bern, Camp Beech Grove was established in 1864 and occupied by elements of the 3rd and 12th New York Cavalry.

CAMP BELVIDERE. A temporary, possibly fortified Confederate encampment, Camp Belvidere was located near Belvidere Plantation on the west side of the Cape Fear River, about 10 miles southwest of the city of Wilmington.

CAMP BENBOW. Probably a temporary Confederate encampment, Camp Benbow was reportedly located 14 miles below Wilmington.

FORT BENJAMIN. A Union defense located at Shepherdsville, opposite Newport, in Carteret County, Fort Benjamin was garrisoned by elements of the 9th Vermont Volunteer Regiment.

FORT BETHABARA. During the French and Indian War, the Cherokee in western North Carolina rose against the white settlers. Following several massacres along the Catawba and Yadkin rivers in 1759, settlers fled in panic to the Moravian settlement at Bethabara established in 1753, now called Old Town in present central Forsyth County. Anticipating a possible attack by the Indians, the Moravians erected a palisade around their town and posted sentries. "Fort" Bethabara, fortunately, never had to test the strength of its defenses. With the defeat of the Cherokee in 1761, the palisade was removed and life in the settlement returned to normal.

CAMP BLACKJACK. After the fall of New Bern to Federal forces in March 1862, General Lawrence O'Bryan Branch concentrated his troops at a fortified encampment, designated Camp Blackjack, five miles east of Kinston in Lenoir County.

FORT BLANCHARD. FORT PARKE.

BATTERY BOLLES. FORT FISHER.

CAMP BOYLAN. A temporary Confederate organization encampment established June–August 1861, this camp was located near the city of Raleigh. Company E of the 10th N.C.T. (1st North Carolina Artillery), known as the Wilmington Light Artillery, was mustered into state service here in August 1861.

FORT BRAGG. Known today as the "Home of the Airborne," Fort Bragg is located 50 miles south of Raleigh and 10 miles northwest of Fayetteville. Encompassing about 200 square miles, the post serves some 158,000 persons, including 40,000 assigned active duty soldiers. The present post is far from its modest genesis in 1918, when 127,000 acres of desolate sandhills and pine trees were designated as a U.S. Army installation. Camp Bragg emerged as a field artillery site on August 21, 1918. It was named in honor of Confederate General Braxton Bragg, a former North Carolinian artillery officer.

Congress decided in February 1922 that all artillery units east of the Mississippi River would be consolidated here. The installation became a permanent Army post and was redesignated as Fort Bragg on September 30, 1922. Artillery observation balloons were used as platforms for the first military parachute jump here in 1923. But two decades passed before Fort Bragg became an airborne training site. The fort grew slowly, reaching a total of 5,400 men by the summer of 1940. With the threat of World War II and the passage of the Selective Service Act, a reception center was built here and Fort Bragg exploded to a population of 67,000 men within a year.

In 1942 the first airborne units trained here in preparation for combat. All five World War II airborne divisions—the 82nd, 101st, 11th, 13th, and 17th—trained in the Fort Bragg–Camp Mackall area. (Camp Mackall, 40 miles west, established in 1943, was a major training facility until 1948. See: CAMP MACKALL.) The 82nd Airborne Division was assigned here in 1946 upon its return from Europe. In 1951 XVIII Airborne Corps was reactivated here and Fort Bragg became widely known as Home of the Airborne. The Psychological Warfare Center (now the 1st Special Operations Command) was established here in 1952, and Fort Bragg became headquarters for Special Forces (Green Beret) soldiers.

More than 200,000 young men underwent basic combat training here during 1966–70. At the peak of the Vietnam War in 1968, Fort Bragg's military population rose to 57,840. On July 1, 1973, Fort Bragg came under the U.S. Army Forces Command headquartered at Fort McPherson, Georgia. Fort Bragg and neighboring Pope AFB form one of the largest military complexes in the world.

CAMP BRANCH. Named for Confederate Brigadier General Lawrence O'B. Branch, Camp Branch was located four miles below New Bern, near the Neuse River, and was active until the fall of the city to Federal troops on March 14, 1862. Another Camp Branch was a fortified encampment outside the town of Winton, near Murfreesboro, in Hertford County. Troops of the 9th New York Infantry stormed the town in March 1862, pillaged and burned it, and destroyed the Confederate encampment.

CAMP BRANCH. A World War II training facility named in honor of Confederate Brigadier General Lawrence O'B. Branch, Camp Branch was located west of the town of Beaufort in Carteret County.

FORT BRANCH. A Confederate earthen work, Fort Branch was constructed late in 1862 on the site of a prior battery to block the passage of Federal ships and troops up the Roanoke River into agriculturally rich eastern North Carolina and, as the war progressed, to protect the Confederate shipyards at Edward's Ferry, about six miles north of Scotland Neck, and the navy yard at Halifax. Completed in two months and ready to have the big guns emplaced by February 4, 1863, the fort was located on present S.R. 125, three miles southeast of the town of Hamilton, at Rainbow Banks in Martin County. Fort Branch was evacuated on April 10, 1865, after the Confederate occupants threw much of the ammunition into the fort's well and dumped the artillery into the river.

FORT BROWN. According to a National Archives citation, Fort Brown was a temporary Confederate fortification near New Bern, mounting eight guns, two of which were powerful Columbiads. The fort was evacuated when the Federals seized New Bern and its environs on March 14, 1862.

CAMP BRYAN GRIMES. A Spanish-American War recruiting and training encampment established in 1898 near the city of Raleigh, it was named for the Confederate general.

FORT (BATTERY) BUCHANAN. FORT FISHER.

CAMP BURGWIN (BURGWYN). A fortified Confederate encampment located on Bogue Is-

land at or near the present community of Atlantic Beach, just west of Beaufort, in Carteret County, Camp Burgwin (Burgwyn) was established in 1861 for several regiments, including the 7th and 26th Regiments N.C.T. (Infantry), assigned to assist in the defense of nearby Fort Macon. Named for Lieutenant Colonel Henry K. Burgwyn, the camp was abandoned in early March 1862 when its troops were withdrawn to defend New Bern from Federal forces.

CAMP BURGWYN. A prominent Confederate encampment, active throughout the war, located northeast of Wilmington, Camp Burgwyn was occupied from time to time by numerous military units, including the 50th North Carolina Infantry in March 1864.

FORT BURNSIDE. After the Battle of Roanoke Island on February 8, 1862, Union forces occupied the island and began building a new defense, known as Fort Burnside (probably named for General Ambrose Everett Burnside) on the north end of the island. The fort was constructed with the help of a number of freed able-bodied Negro men who had escaped up the Chowan River from their owners and fled to the protection of the Union banner.

BURNT CANE-BRAKE BLOCKHOUSE. During 1792–93, because of raids perpetrated by hostile Cherokee and Creek, guards were stationed for the protection of the frontier along the French Broad River in present Madison County. They also occupied or garrisoned three other blockhouses—Hough's, at Painted Rock, and at Warm Springs.

FORT BUTLER. Located across the Hiwassee River from the present-day town of Murphy in Cherokee County, just above the Georgia border in the southwestern corner of the state, Fort Butler was erected in early 1838 by General Winfield Scott and named for then Secretary of War Benjamin F. Butler. Fort Butler was one of the temporary fortifications built to accommodate congregated Cherokee pending their tragic "Trail of Tears" march to barren Indian Territory in the West.

CAMP BUTNER. Located at present Butner in southwest Greenville County, Camp Butner was a World War II Army post occupying a reservation encompassing parts of three counties. It was established in 1942 as an infantry and reassignment center and named in honor of World War

I veteran, Major General Henry Wolfe Butner. The camp was closed in 1948.

CAMP CAMERON. Reportedly located near present-day Jacksonville in Onslow County, Camp Cameron was a small temporary Confederate encampment occupied September–October 1862 by Company H of the 41st N.C.T. Regiment (3rd North Carolina Cavalry).

CAMP CAMPBELL. A temporary Confederate training encampment located near Kinston in Lenoir County, Camp Campbell was probably named for Colonel Reuben Campbell, who retreated to Kinston with his troops from New Bern in March 1862.

FORT (BATTERY) CAMPBELL. A well-proportioned earthwork, Fort Campbell was an outlying work of Fort Caswell located one mile to the east on Oak (now Smith) Island near present-day Southport. It was built by Confederate forces sometime between 1862 and 1864. The fort was last garrisoned by elements of the 3rd North Carolina Artillery, when it was abandoned and destroyed on January 16, 1865, after the fall of Fort Fisher.

FORT (BATTERY) CAMPBELL. A Confederate defense located on the north side of the Cape Fear River between Forts Lee and Meares near Wilmington, Fort Campbell's ordnance consisted of one 30-pounder Parrott, one 8-inch seacoast howitzer, one 32-pounder smoothbore, and two 9-inch Dahlgrens mounted on navy carriages.

CAMP CANAL. A temporary Confederate training camp, probably established in 1861, Camp Canal was located at or near Morehead City, Carteret County.

CAMP CAROLINA. A large Confederate encampment established in 1861 near Morehead City, Camp Carolina was captured by Union forces on March 23, 1862, during their campaign against Fort Macon. Elements of the Union army occupied the site for the remaining years of the war. The State National Guard later trained here for a time. The site of the camp is now the Morehead City Park.

FORT CASWELL (*Fort Lane; Fort Spinola*). Originally known as Fort Caswell when built on the south bank of the Neuse River south of New Bern by North Carolina troops during 1775–76 to protect New Bern from British warships, it was named in honor of North Carolina's first governor. Seized by state troops prior to the actual outbreak of Civil War hostilities, it was strengthened as a three-gun battery and renamed Fort Lane by the Confederacy. After the capture of New Bern on March 14, 1862, by Union forces, it was renamed Fort Spinola when occupied by Federal troops. Remains of the old fort are still visible today.

FORT CASWELL. One of the better-preserved examples of the Endicott Era coastal defense fortifications is Fort Caswell, on Oak Island at the strategic mouth of the Cape Fear River, just offshore of the town of Southport on the mainland. Oak Island was first fortified in 1825–26, when the original Fort Caswell was begun as a brick work surrounded by earthen ramparts and named in honor of Major General Richard Caswell, Revolutionary War veteran and first governor of North Carolina. Prior to the actual outbreak of the Civil War, the fort was seized by state troops on January 8, 1861, and held by the Confederates, who heavily reinforced it, until the fall of Fort Fisher January 16–17, 1865, when its garrison blew up the fort and abandoned it.

Following the war, Fort Caswell suffered the fate of many such fortifications and was more or less abandoned by the Federal government until a wave of interest was generated in the nation's coastal defenses. The almost-forgotten fort was reactivated and received modern coast defense armament in accordance with recommendations of the Endicott Board of Fortifications (1885), with seven batteries, each named for a military hero, constructed of masonry between 1895 and 1902.

After World War I, Fort Caswell was placed in caretaker status, then declared surplus by the War Department, and sold to private interests. With the outbreak of World War II, however, the government reacquired the old fort for use as a Navy depot. Subsequent to the war, it again was declared as surplus property. In 1949 the Baptist State Convention of North Carolina purchased the military reservation and established the North Carolina Baptist Assembly there.

FORT CHASE. This fort was one of several fortified positions on a line west of New Bern, between the Neuse and Trent rivers, established after March 14, 1862, by the occupying Union forces and named for Union officers.

CAMP CHRONICLE. A World War I training camp located on the west side of present South Linwood Street in Castonia in central Gaston

County, Camp Chronicle was operated in connection with an artillery range at the foot of Crowders Mountain. The camp was named in honor of Major William Chronicle, killed at the Battle of Kings Mountain, South Carolina, on October 7, 1780.

CAMP CLARENDON. A temporary Confederate encampment located at or near Garysburg, Northampton County.

CAMP CLARK. Located on Kittrell's Springs in Granville County, Camp Clark was a temporary fortified cavalry encampment occupied by elements of the 2nd North Carolina Cavalry in 1861.

FORT CLARK. Located about three-fourths of a mile east of Fort Hatteras on Hatteras Inlet and nearer the sea, Fort Clark was an irregular-shaped redoubt mounting five 32-pounders and two smaller guns. The Confederate defense was named in honor of then governor of North Carolina, Henry Toole Clark. The fort, along with Fort Hatteras, was surrendered about noon on August 29, 1861, to a joint Army-Navy task force from Fortress Monroe under General Benjamin F. Butler and Flag-Officer Silas Stringham. In the afternoon, after leaving part of the land forces and three vessels to hold the forts and guard the Inlet, the fleet sailed with 670 Confederate prisoners. (See: FORT HATTERAS.)

CAMP CLINGMAN. This Confederate encampment was established during the summer of 1861 on a site now located on French Broad Avenue near Philip Street within the present city limits of Asheville. It was named for Brigadier General Thomas L. Clingman, former U.S. Senator.

CAMP CLINGMAN. A temporary Confederate encampment, apparently established in 1862, and located near Goldsboro in Wayne County, it was probably named for Brigadier General Thomas L. Clingman.

FORT COBB. A Confederate battery mounting four guns rescued from a sunken ship, Fort Cobb was located at Cobb's Point four miles below Elizabeth City in Pasquotank County. It was destroyed on February 10, 1862, by bombardment by ships of a Union task force.

CAMP COLLIER. Probably a temporary Confederate encampment, Camp Collier was located near Goldsboro in Wayne County.

COLSON'S SUPPLY DEPOT. A fortified Revolutionary War depot built in 1781 to store and protect supply and arms for General Nathanael Greene's forces, it was located near Mt. Gilead in Montgomery County.

FORT COMFORT (*Fort Conpher; Fort Jones*). A Federal-built three-gun defense, also known as Fort Conpher, the fort was located on the east side of the town of Plymouth, between Columbia Road and the Roanoke River, in Washington County. It fell into Confederate hands when forces under General Robert Frederick Hoke took Plymouth on April 20, 1864. The defense was renamed Fort Jones in honor of Colonel J. G. Jones, 35th Regiment N.C.T. (Infantry) who was killed leading the charge against the fort.

FORT CONPHER. FORT COMFORT.

COOWEECHEE BLOCKHOUSE. This short-lived Spanish defense was erected in the autumn of 1566 by Captain Juan Pardo and his 14-man expedition, which had been ordered to explore the country's interior by Pedro Menéndez de Avilés, founder of St. Augustine. The blockhouse is believed to have been located at an Indian village known as Cooweechee in western North Carolina near the Tennessee border.

CAMP CRABTREE. The 26th North Carolina Regiment was organized at this camp of instruction on the Crabtree Plantation, three miles west of Raleigh, on August 27, 1861. Its first commanding officer was Zebulon B. Vance.

CAMP DANIEL. A temporary Confederate encampment located near Kinston in Lenoir County.

DAVIDSON'S FORT (*Fort Rutherford; Upper Fort*). Also known as Fort Rutherford and Upper Fort, Davidson's Fort was originally a fortified dwelling and refuge on Davidson's Plantation located near the present-day town of Old Fort in Burke County. The structure was converted into a fort by North Carolina militia under Brigadier General Griffith Rutherford during his expedition against the Cherokee in the late summer and fall of 1776.

CAMP DAVIS. Established originally in 1861 as a Confederate infantry training camp, Camp Davis was located on Middle Sound, known today as Topsail Sound, in Pender County. The post was thereafter intermittently occupied by various Confederate units until at least June 1864.

CAMP DAVIS. A World War II Coast Artillery anti-aircraft and infantry training base located at Holly Ridge, 31 miles northeast of Wilmington, in Onslow County, Camp Davis opened in April 1941 and attained a maximum of 60,000 men and women. The Air Corps had developed a large and relatively high-altitude-type balloon, and most barrage balloon activity was transferred to the Coast Artillery Corps. Plans evolved quickly to expand the barrage balloon force. By November 1, 1941, five battalions of three batteries each were being organized and trained at the Barrage Balloon Training Center at Camp Davis, North Carolina.

Closed in October 1944, Camp Davis was reactivated for a brief period in the summer of 1945 as an Air Force convalescent hospital and redistribution center. The post was named in honor of Major General Richmond Pearson Davis (1866–1937), a North Carolinian and World War I veteran.

FORT DAVIS (*Fort Strong*). A Confederate complex of fortifications comprising several batteries, Fort Davis was located three miles south of Wilmington opposite Big Island Shallows. It was evacuated on February 22, 1865, after an engagement with Union gunboats commanded by Rear Admiral David Porter. At the end of the war, the defense became known as Fort Strong.

FORT DEFIANCE. Located close to the Yadkin River near the present city of Lenoir in Caldwell County, Fort Defiance was erected in 1776 during the campaign against the hostile Cherokee. Militia and volunteers under Captain Jacob Ferree constructed the defense and garrisoned it for a short time until the warring Indians returned to their villages in the Cherokee Nation. During 1788–92 General William Lenoir, a leading participant in the Battle of Kings Mountain, South Carolina, October 7, 1780, constructed a strong, heavy-timbered farmhouse on the site of the frontier defense and named his new home Fort Defiance.

FORT DEFIANCE (*Fort Russell*). A Confederate defense also known as Fort Russell, it was a three-gun emplacement located near the center of Roanoke Island on the main north-south causeway or road. The island and forts were captured by Union forces on February 8, 1862, during General Burnside's expedition by sea against the Confederacy's coastal defenses in North Carolina. Fort Defiance's guns were the only ones on the island that were not spiked.

The Confederates lost 2,500 men captured by Union forces in addition to suffering 143 killed, wounded, and missing among their land forces; the Federal losses were 14 in the naval force and 264 in Burnside's land division. After leaving a garrison on Roanoke Island, Burnside proceeded to New Bern, capturing that place on March 14 after a siege.

FORT DILLARD (*Fort Wingfield*). A Union-built defense, also known as Fort Wingfield, located on the Chowan River in Chowan County on the plantation-farm owned by Dr. Richard Dillard, it consisted of a blockhouse and earthworks erected by "Buffalo Soldiers" (North Carolinian Union sympathizers) in September 1862. Union warships provided protection on the river. The fort and Dr. Dillard's plantation home were destroyed on March 23, 1863, by a detachment of Confederate troops commanded by Lieutenant Colonel J. E. Brown, 42nd Regiment N.C.T. (Infantry) dispatched there by Lieutenant General D. H. Hill.

FORT DIXIE. A Confederate work mounting four 24-pounders, Fort Dixie was the left flank of a line of entrenchments known as the Croatan Line, about 10 miles below New Bern, on the west bank of the Neuse River. The fort was abandoned by the Confederates on March 13, 1862, shortly before the final battle for New Bern.

FORT DOBBS. A western outpost of the Province of North Carolina during the French and Indian War, Fort Dobbs was home base for a company of some 50 Rangers who patrolled the frontier from 1755 or 1756 until it was abandoned in 1764. Standing on an eminence about two miles north of the present-day town of Statesville in Iredell County, the fort was begun in the autumn of 1755 by Captain Hugh Waddell of the Rangers and completed the following year. It was named for Governor Arthur Dobbs, who had persuaded the Provincial Assembly to make an appropriation for its construction. A 1756 description reports it was an oblong square, 53 by 40 feet with blockhouses in opposite angles that measured 24 and 22 square feet and were 24½ feet high, with three stories. Troops appear to have garrisoned Fort Dobbs almost continuously from the time of its completion until 1762. After its abandonment, the structure is said to have stood there until well after the Revolution, during which it served as a rendezvous for militia troops. According to tradition, the logs of the fort were later removed for use in the construction of a schoolhouse nearby.

FORT DOBBS. Governor Arthur Dobbs in May 1755 visited the town of Beaufort and selected a site on the southwest point of Beaufort Inlet for the building of a fortification. When he inspected the fort named for himself in June 1756, he found it almost finished, but because of its poor construction considered "in no condition of defence" to accommodate a garrison. The governor's judgment in selecting the site on Bogue Banks has been sustained by future military engineers. A fort was located there almost continually from his day until the twentieth century, within a few hundred feet of the original site selected in 1755. Fort Dobbs was replaced in 1808 by Fort Hampton, which was in turn replaced in 1834 by Fort Macon, which remains today as a state park.

FORT DUTTON (*Fort Union*). A fortification built by Union troops after their capture of New Bern on March 14, 1862, Fort Dutton was located on the south bank of the Neuse River. Also known as Fort Union, it was a component of the Federal complex of defenses established to ensure the occupation.

CAMP ELLIS. One of the state's first recruiting and organization camps established after Governor Ellis arbitrarily put North Carolina into the Confederacy, Camp Ellis was set up in May 1861 on the 16-acre grounds of the State Fair Grounds in Raleigh's eastern suburbs. In a short time, more than 5,000 recruits assembled there and formed into companies.

FORT ELLIS. A Confederate eight-gun battery, Fort Ellis was located four miles south of New Bern on the bank of the Neuse River. It was named for North Carolina Governor John Willis Ellis, who died in Monroe County, Virginia, on July 6, 1861, after he took his state out of the Union. The fort was garrisoned by the Pamlico Artillery Guards, a company only two months old. Its commander, Captain J. M. Mayo (later major of the 59th Regiment), was seriously wounded in the blowing up of its magazine when the fort appeared in danger of falling into Federal hands during the Battle of New Bern on March 14, 1862, subsequent to which the Confederates were finally driven further inland. A short distance south of Fort Ellis was an unfinished two-gun fort known as Fort Allen.

FORT ELLIS (*Fort Shallowbag Bay*). Located at Ballast Point on Shallowbag Bay opposite Nags Head on Roanoke Island, this three-gun fort was referred to as "Fort Ellis" in Union reports but was called Fort Shallowbag Bay or Ballast Point Battery in Confederate correspondence.

FORT EMBREE. In 1838, during the period of the removal of the Cherokee to the West, Fort Embree was one of the collecting stockades. It stood on a hill one mile southwest of Hayesville, just above the Georgia border, in Clay County.

FAYETTEVILLE ARSENAL. The U.S. Arsenal at Fayetteville, Cumberland County, was authorized by Congress in 1836. Very soon after the outbreak of war in 1861, it was taken over by North Carolina troops. The site of the arsenal, destroyed by General Sherman in 1865, is located on present-day U.S. 15A.

CAMP FEREBEE. A temporary Confederate encampment located four miles from the town of Snow Hill in Greene County, Camp Ferebee was occupied from December 1862 to March 27, 1863, by elements of the 59th Regiment (4th North Carolina Cavalry), commanded by Colonel Dennis Ferebee.

CAMP FEREBEE. A temporary Confederate encampment named for cavalry Colonel Dennis Ferebee, it was located near Garysburg in Northampton County.

CAMP FISHER (*Camp Hill*). The 6th Regiment N.C.T. (Infantry) commanded by a Colonel Fisher trained at Camp Hill at or near the town of Salisbury, Rowan County, in 1862. The name of the camp was later changed to Camp Fisher to reflect the replacement of the ranking commander in the Confederate military district.

FORT FISHER (*Battery Bolles*). Prior to the outbreak of the Civil War, there were no fortifications on what was then known as Federal Point, on the peninsula between the Atlantic Ocean and the Cape Fear River. In April 1861 however, the state of North Carolina placed a battery there and sent the Wilmington Light Infantry to man the guns. This fortification, known as Battery Bolles (named for Captain Charles P. Bolles) was the beginning of Fort Fisher, named in honor of Captain Charles F. Fisher, who was killed at the first Battle of Manassas in 1861.

Fort Fisher, the enormous earthwork defense at the tip of Confederate Point (renamed from Federal Point), was the key to the Cape Fear defenses. In July 1863 Major (later Colonel) William Lamb assumed command at Fort Fisher, which included Battery Bolles, and began construction on what was to evolve into the strongest earthwork installation of the Confederacy. The fort was L-shaped, with the angle pointing northeast, out to sea. The northern front, which extended some 682 yards across the peninsula, was the horizontal arm of the L. The eastern face, running approximately 1,898 yards down the beach, was the vertical arm. At its southern tip was the famous Mound Battery, whose two long-range guns protected many a blockade-runner. About a mile from the "Mound" and near the tip of Confederate Point on the river side was Battery Buchanan, which was considered a part of the main works. A line of rifle pits protected the rear of the fort in case of an attack from the river.

For three years the Confederates in Fort Fisher kept the mouth of the Cape Fear River open to blockade-runners, protected the city of Wilmington, and fended off the Federal blockading squadron hovering offshore. By the end of 1864, however, Union leaders determined that the fort must be taken and the Cape Fear closed to Confederate commerce. Accordingly, a land-sea expedition of 56 warships, plus troop transports and landing barges, was prepared at Hampton Roads, Virginia, under General Benjamin F. Butler and Admiral David Porter. Their first assault against the fort, on Christmas Day of that year, was a failure. On January 12, 1865, Admiral Porter's fleet again appeared off Fort Fisher. This time the Federal troops, commanded by General Alfred H. Terry, were successful, and Fort Fisher was taken after a desperate battle. The fleet alone fired more than two million pounds of projectiles in the two attacks, which constituted the heaviest land-sea battle of the war. Within a month Wilmington, 18 miles to the north, was in Federal hands.

In 1960 portions of Fort Fisher were dug out of the sand, and a state park was established. A museum along with a well-preserved line of exposed earthworks are today a popular tourist attraction. Also present on the site is the preserved original Fort Fisher monument in "Battle Acre." The nearest town to the remains of Fort Fisher is the community of Kure Beach, one mile to the north.

CAMP FLORIDA. A temporary Confederate encampment located on Topsail Island on the Outer Banks in Pender County.

CAMP FLOYD. A temporary Confederate post located at Weldon in Halifax County, Camp Floyd was occupied by the 38th Regiment N.C.T. (Infantry) in February 1864.

FORT FORREST. An unfinished Confederate redoubt mounting seven guns, Fort Forrest was situated on the mainland opposite Roanoke Island and protected the west side of Croatan Sound, which was obstructed by a double line of 16 sunken vessels and a system of pilings. It did not play an effective part in the battle for Roanoke Island and was burned by the Confederates on February 7, 1862.

FORT FOSTER. FORT BARTOW.

CAMP FRENCH. A temporary French encampment located about two miles below Wilmington on the Cape Fear River and in operation as early as March 1862, Camp French was situated in the rear of a long line of batteries and occupied by a company of marines in 1862.

FORT FRENCH. A Confederate fortification located just south of Wilmington on the northeast fork of the Cape Fear River, Fort French was a redoubt consisting of three guns and a bombproof. Usually manned by one company of artillerymen, it was occupied by Company K of the 1st North Carolina Artillery from January 1862 to June 1863.

CAMP GASTON. A temporary Confederate encampment located near New Bern, Camp Gaston was intermittently occupied between October 1861 and February 1862.

FORT GASTON. A Union two-gun earthwork defense built in 1862 and located about six miles from New Bern, Fort Gaston was maintained for the remaining years of the war by Federal forces to defend the Atlantic and North Carolina Railroad crossing over the Trent River. The fort was named for Judge William Gaston, who owned large parcels of land in the area.

CAMP GATLIN. A temporary Confederate encampment located behind Fort Lane on the Neuse River east of New Bern, it was occupied by the 27th Regiment, North Carolina Troops, during January–March 1862. It was evacuated by the Confederates when New Bern fell to the Federals on March 14, 1862.

CAMP GEORGIA. A Confederate encampment located on Roanoke Island, it was established by more than 1,400 Georgia troops in September 1861. It is believed that shortly before the battle for Roanoke Island on February 8, 1862, these troops were transferred to Virginia.

CAMP GORDON. Located on the Tar River six miles below Greenville in Pitt County, Camp Gordon was a Confederate cavalry outpost, established probably in late September 1862.

CAMP GRAHAM. A Confederate encampment active during 1861–62, Camp Graham was located on the Newport River opposite Shepherdsville, Carteret County, near later established Fort Benjamin.

FORT GRANVILLE. Located on the northern tip of Core Banks at the present-day town of Portsmouth at Ocracoke Inlet in Carteret County, Fort Granville was actually established by newly appointed Governor Arthur Dobbs in 1755 although it existed in name only since 1753, when it had been funded by a £2,000 appropriation by the North Carolina Assembly. Governor Dobbs, on a tour of the coast, reached Ocracoke Inlet on May 9, 1755. "Within twenty-four hours he had not only fixed a site for Fort Granville on Core Banks but had designed the structure, describing it later as 'a fascine Battery, secured by piles, with 2 faces'" (David Stick, *The Outer Banks of North Carolina* [1958]). By late 1757 the fort was sufficiently built to be put in active use when it was garrisoned by Captain Charles McNair and a company of men. From then on, the strength of Fort Granville's garrison varied according to the exigencies of the French and Indian War and the state of the province's finances. With the signing of the Treaty of Paris in 1763, its last garrison was withdrawn and the fort abandoned.

CAMP GREENE. A temporary World War I training post named in honor of General Nathanael Greene of the Continental Army, Camp Greene was established on July 18, 1917, about two miles west of the city of Charlotte. Construction of the installation, designed for a capacity of 48,500 men, began on July 20, 1917, and continued through 1918. The 2,100-acre post was primarily a tent camp, supplemented by 1,125 temporary buildings. It was designated a demobilization center on December 3, 1918, and ordered salvaged on January 20, 1919. Camp Greene was abandoned June 30, 1919.

FORT GREY. A fortification erected in 1863 by Union troops, Fort Grey was located at the southern terminus of Warren's Neck, facing Tabor Island, on the Roanoke River at Plymouth,

Washington County. The earthwork defense was named in honor of Colonel Charles Grey, 96th New York Infantry, who was killed leading a charge across the Neuse River Bridge at Kinston on December 14, 1862. On Williams Street in Plymouth is a marker: "Union Earthworks. The main line of Union defenses during the Battle of Plymouth, April 17–20, 1864, was built across the road at this point." The town's Confederate garrison, commanded by General Henry Wessells, consisting of four infantry regiments with artillery and cavalry, surrendered to Brigadier General (later Major General) Robert F. Hoke's numerically superior land and sea forces on April 20th after three days of intense fighting.

GROVE CAMP. CAMP PALMER.

GUATARI BLOCKHOUSE. In 1566, during explorations through the interior of the Southeast in compliance with orders of Pedro Menéndez de Avilés, founder of St. Augustine, Captain Juan Pardo with an 18-man expedition erected a blockhouse at Guatari on the headwaters of the Wateree [Catawba] River. No more definite location has ever been determined for the site of the Spanish fortification.

GUM SWAMP FORT. A Confederate defense about one mile west of Dover in Craven County, the location (sometimes referred to as Green Swamp) of Gum Swamp Fort was a strong position in opposition to Federal troops. The engagement here on May 22, 1863, resulted in the routing of the 25th and 56th North Carolina Infantry Regiments defending the fort. Sergeant Andrew S. Bryant of Company A, 46th Massachusetts Infantry, received the Medal of Honor for his gallantry in the action. Present-day U.S. 70 crosses the railroad about 100 yards from the site.

FORT HALL. This Confederate fortification was erected in October 1861 on the Pungo River in Hyde County.

CAMP HAMILTON. A temporary Confederate encampment located near Kinston in Lenoir County.

FORT HAMPTON. FORT MACON.

FORT HANCOCK. In 1778 Captain de Cottineau of the French frigate *Ferdinand* and Captain Le Chevalier de Chambray, an artillerist, teamed up to lead a group of French volunteers interested in aiding the American cause during the Revolution. With a small measure of assistance from the government of North Carolina, they erected a fort on Cape Lookout, about four miles south of Harkers Island in Carteret County. It was later named Fort Hancock, apparently for Enoch Hancock, the owner of the island property. It is believed that the fort was garrisoned for two years and dismantled in 1780. As late as 1899, remains of brickwork and breastworks were still in evidence at the site, today commemorated by a state marker on S.R. 1335 at Shell Point of Harkers Island.

FORT HATTERAS. The Confederates began construction of Fort Hatteras and its supporting redoubt, Fort Clark, about three-quarters of a mile to the east, in the early summer of 1861 at Hatteras Inlet on the Outer Banks. Fort Hatteras, the principal defense, was located one-eighth of a mile from the Inlet and commanded the strategic channel. Roughly a square work, about 250 feet wide, it was built of sand with its exterior sheathed by two-inch-thick planks planted into the ground and covered with marsh turf. The fort's armament consisted of twelve comparatively short-range 32-pounder smoothbore guns, four more of which were not mounted. A new, 10-inch rifled gun arrived at the fort from Richmond in late August and was mounted, but no ammunition had been provided for it.

When the French fleet of seven warships, with an aggregate of 143 guns, under the joint command of General Benjamin F. Butler and Commodore Silas H. Stringham, leaving from Hampton Roads, appeared in the late afternoon of August 27, there were about 580 men, including eight companies of the 17th North Carolina Infantry and elements of the 10th North Carolina Artillery, stationed at Hatteras Inlet under the command of Colonel W. F. Martin. Federal amphibious landings after heavy bombardments led to the surrender of both Forts Hatteras and Clark on August 29 and gave Union forces an effective entrance into the interior of the state. After the victory Union troops occupied the two forts. Ocean tides during the subsequent decades gradually eroded the point of land to wash away the sites of Forts Hatteras and Clark.

CAMP HEATH. This Confederate encampment was located on Scott's Hill near Wilmington in New Hanover County.

CAMP HILL. CAMP FISHER.

CAMP HILL. A Confederate recruiting encampment, Camp Hill was located near Garysburg in Northampton County and named for Major General Daniel Harvey Hill. The 4th North Carolina Infantry was organized here in May 1861.

FORT HILL. The site of Confederate batteries, named Fort Hill for General Daniel H. Hill, at the mouth of the Pamlico River in Beaufort County, enabled the general's forces to besiege Washington in the spring of 1863. There is a commemorative marker on N.C. 33 south of the town of Chocowinity, indicating the site of the fort five miles to the east.

CAMP HILTON. A temporary Confederate encampment located near Kinston in Lenoir County.

CAMP HOFFMAN. A Union encampment located on the north side of the Atlantic and North Carolina Railroad, near the town of Tuscarora northwest of New Bern, Camp Hoffman was a post of regimental size established after the occupation of New Bern on March 14, 1862.

CAMP HOKE. A Confederate encampment named in honor of General Robert F. Hoke, it was located near Kinston in Lenoir County.

CAMP HOLMES. Probably established in 1861, Camp Holmes was a Confederate encampment located near Weldon in Halifax County.

CAMP HOLMES. One of several Confederate "Camps of Instruction" located at and near Raleigh, Camp Holmes opened in 1861 and was active until April 1865. Colonel Peter Mallett (Mallet) served as commandant here and led a battalion known as the Camp Holmes Guard or Mallett's Battalion. In 1862 he was in charge of conscription in the state.

FORT (BATTERY) HOLMES. Situated on Smith's Island in the mouth of the Cape Fear River, Fort Holmes was a substantial Confederate fortification with four auxiliary batteries and entrenchments circumscribing the entire island. It was evacuated by the Confederates on January 16, 1865, and taken possession of by Federal land and naval forces on the following day.

FORT HOLMES. A Confederate defense of New Bern, Fort Holmes was evacuated on or just prior to March 14, 1862, when Federal forces took possession of the town.

HOUGH'S BLOCKHOUSE. BURNT CANEBRAKE BLOCKHOUSE.

FORT HUGER. FORT RENO.

HUGGINS' ISLAND FORT. A Confederate defense mounting six guns and guarding the entrance to Bogue Inlet, it was located near present-day Swansboro in Onslow County. The fort was attacked and burned by Union troops on August 19, 1862.

FORT HUNTINGTON. A temporary Army post located in the Cherokee Nation in western North Carolina, Fort Huntington was established in February 1836 by Brevet 2nd Lieutenant John S. Hooper, with Company E of the 4th Infantry, aggregating 34 men. The post was abandoned in May 1836.

FORT HYDE. Constructed in late 1711 or early in 1712 at Core Point on the Pamlico River, near the town of Bath, the state's oldest community, in present-day Beaufort County, Fort Hyde served as a defense and refuge during the Tuscarora War, which began in September 1711 with widespread massacres and did not end until 1715. The fort was named for Governor Edward Hyde.

CAMP IRWIN. A temporary Confederate encampment located at or near Rutherfordton in Rutherford County.

CAMP JACKSON. A Confederate post of considerable size located at Wilmington and used 1863–65, Camp Jackson consisted of wood barracks and rows of tents. Evacuated by the Confederates early in 1865, the post's barracks were occupied February 24–26, 1865, by Union troops consisting of the 3rd Brigade, 2nd Division.

CAMP JETER. This Confederate post was located in the present vicinity of Cherry and Flint streets in the city of Asheville.

FORT JOHNSON. A Confederate defense located near the city of Wilmington.

CAMP JOHNSTON. This Confederate encampment, named for General Joseph E. Johnston, was located at Falling Creek on the north side of the Neuse River, about six miles west of Kinston and four miles east of La Grange, in Lenoir County.

FORT JOHNSTON (*Fort Pender*). Fort Johnston was located on the west bank of the Cape Fear River, about four miles from its mouth, atop a six-acre bluff, a site now surrounded by the town of Southport (formerly Smithville) in Brunswick County. Begun in 1745 and completed in 1764, it was first known as Johnston's Fort, named in honor of Governor Gabriel Johnston. On the night of July 19, 1775, a band of Patriots seized the fort and burned it. No efforts were made during the Revolution to rebuild the fort.

After the strategic site was ceded by the state in 1794 to the federal government provided a new fort was built there, it was occupied by U.S. troops. In 1804 a new fortification constructed of masonry and brick, designated Fort Johnston, was begun under the supervision of Lieutenant Joseph Gardiner Swift, West Point's first graduate, and completed in 1809. The post during the next half-century was repeatedly abandoned and reoccupied. From April 17, 1861, to January 17, 1865, Fort Johnston was in the possession of the Confederacy to protect its blockade-runners, during which time it was occasionally referred to as Fort Pender. The alternate name was applied probably in honor of Confederate General William Dorsey Pender, who was severely wounded at Gettysburg and died at Staunton, Virginia, on July 18, 1863, following leg amputation. Fort Johnston was finally abandoned in February 1881.

FORT JONES. FORT COMFORT.

CAMP JOURDAN. A Union encampment established on or about February 9, 1862, on Roanoke Island, it was named in honor of Lieutenant Colonel James Jourdan, 56th New York Infantry.

CAMP LAMB. A large Confederate encampment established in 1862, it was located near the city of Wilmington. The 61st N.C.T. Regiment (Infantry) was organized here in August 1862. The camp was occupied by General Robert F. Hoke's division, Army of Northern Virginia, in January 1865.

FORT (BATTERY) LAMB. A Confederate fortification named for Colonel William Lamb, commander of Fort Fisher, and located on the west side of the Cape Fear River at Reeve's Point, below Price Creek, Fort (or Battery) Lamb served as a reserve magazine for Fort Fisher on the opposite side of the river. On January 18, 1865, the USS *Tacony* anchored off the fort and sent troops ashore to destroy its gun carriages and essential works. The ensuing explosion within the fort caused the deaths of more than 200 men. A Union court of enquiry later determined that the explosion of Fort Lamb's magazine was caused by drunken troops and sailors plundering the fort. A sailor was seen entering the magazine with a lit candle just before the explosion.

FORT LANE. FORT CASWELL.

FORT (BATTERY) LEE. A Confederate two-gun battery on the northeast side of the Cape Fear River, covering both the upper and lower obstructions and the mouth of the Brunswick River directly opposite, Fort Lee was situated between Fort Stokes and Fort Campbell.

CAMP LEVENTHORPE. A temporary Confederate encampment located at or near Garysburg, Northampton County, it was named for Colonel (later Brigadier General) Collett Leventhorpe, 11th North Carolina Infantry.

CAMP LEVENTHORPE. A temporary Confederate post located at Fowler's Point near Wilmington, it was occupied by the 11th North Carolina Infantry commanded by Colonel Collett Leventhorpe in June 1862.

CAMP LONG. A Confederate camp located at or near Garysburg, Northampton County, Camp Long was established in 1862. The 63rd Regiment N.C.T. (5th North Carolina Cavalry) was organized here in October 1862.

FORT MCFADDEN. Meager information indicates that this defense was erected in the 1760s for protection from the Cherokee and Catawba Indians. It was located on Mountain Creek near the present city of Rutherfordton in Rutherford County. An additional citation reports that Fort McFadden was still in existence in 1776 and used during that year's expedition against the Cherokee.

FORT MCGAUGHEY. Erected about the year 1765 and used throughout the Revolution, Fort McGaughey was located within the present-day town of Westminster in central Rutherford County.

CAMP MCINTOSH. A temporary Confederate encampment located near Goldsboro in Wayne County.

CAMP MACKALL. A subinstallation of Fort Bragg about 40 miles to the east, Camp Mackall is located 3 miles east of Hoffman in Richmond County. It was named in honor of Private John Thomas Mackall, the first paratrooper killed in North Africa. During World War II, Camp Mackall, first activated in 1940 and dedicated in 1943, was the second largest Airborne training center in the nation. Probably deactivated in 1948, the post is now used as a recreation retreat for Army personnel. (See: FORT BRAGG.)

CAMP MCLEAN. A temporary Confederate encampment located near Goldsboro in Wayne County.

CAMP MACON. A Confederate recruiting and organizing encampment located at or near the city of Macon, Warren County, Camp Macon was established in 1861.

FORT MACON (*Fort Hampton*). Located on Bogue Island at Topsail (now Beaufort) Inlet in Carteret County, two miles from Beaufort and Morehead City, today's well-preserved remains of Fort Macon occupy a site that reaches back in history to early colonial times when Beaufort and its environs were subjected to intermittent pirate raids and temporary Spanish occupation in 1747. One year after the Spanish invasion, the North Carolina Legislature appropriated £4,000 to erect four forts, one of them to be near old Topsail Inlet. But despite continuing raids and an impending French menace, the money remained unspent.

Beaufort was protected during the War of 1812 by a small stone fort probably built in 1809 and named Fort Hampton in honor of Colonel Andrew Hampton, North Carolina Militia, who was a participant in the Battle of King's Mountain, South Carolina, in 1790. This fort was destroyed by a severe hurricane soon after the 1815 treaty of peace ending the war. The present structure, a Third System fortification, was begun in 1826 and named in honor of Nathaniel Macon, Speaker of the House of Representatives and United States senator from North Carolina. It is a pentagonal masonry work with casemated quarters in all faces and surrounded by a dry ditch. Designed to mount 56 guns *en barbette* and six flank howitzers in counterscarp casemates, the fort was garrisoned initially in December 1834.

Seized by North Carolina forces in April 1861, Fort Macon was held by the Confederates until April 26, 1862, when, after a 10-hour bombardment by Federal forces, Colonel Moses J. White surrendered it and his 500-man garrison to Brigadier General John Grubb Parke, who was promoted to Major General very soon thereafter. Fort Macon was the final objective in the North Carolina coast campaign launched the previous summer by the combined Federal land-and-sea forces under Major General Benjamin F. Butler and Rear Admiral Silas H. Stringham. With the fall of Fort Macon, the North Carolina coast from Beaufort to the Virginia line was occupied by Federal forces. After dispossessing the Confederates, the fort was occupied by troops of the 5th Rhode Island Brigade. For the remainder of the war, the fort served as a military and civil prison and an important coaling station for Union ships. On April 28, 1877, Fort Macon was closed as a garrisoned station and placed in a caretaker status.

Fort Macon was regarrisoned during the Spanish-American War to man the two 100-pounder Parrott rifles, two 10-inch mortars, and two bronze 12-pounder Napoleons, the only guns mounted at that time in the fort. In 1924 the fort and the reservation of some 400 acres were transferred to the state of North Carolina for park purposes, but at the outbreak of World War II, the fort was reoccupied by the Federal government. Because of the strategic importance of Beaufort Inlet, a detachment of the 224th Coast Artillery remained in some numbers until October 1946, when once again the fort was returned to North Carolina. The Division of State Parks of the Department of Conservation and Development of the state now maintains Fort Macon as a historical monument.

CAMP MANGUM. One of the Confederate "Camps of Instruction," Camp Mangum was established in November 1861 and located three miles west of the 1862 city limits of Raleigh on the North Carolina Central Railroad. In the spring of 1862, spears or lances were issued to new recruits at the camp because of the shortage of weapons.

CAMP MARTIN. A temporary Confederate encampment located near Kinston, Lenoir County.

CAMP MASON. Probably a temporary Confederate encampment, Camp Mason was located near the town of Graham in central Alamance County.

CAMP MASON. A temporary Confederate encampment located at or near Goldsboro, Wayne County.

CAMP MASSACHUSETTS. A fortified Union encampment located one and a half miles across the Trent River from New Bern, Camp Massachusetts was almost adjacent to the Atlantic & North Carolina Railroad, and in the rear or next to Fort Spinola. The post was probably established not long after Federal troops took possession of New Bern on March 14, 1862. On May 1, 1863, the camp was the headquarters of the 45th Massachusetts Volunteer Militia.

FORT (BATTERY) MEARES. Located south of Fort Campbell on the Cape Fear River near Wilmington, Fort Meares was a Confederate five-gun battery consisting of one 8-inch seacoast howitzer, one 32-pounder long smoothbore, one 9-inch Dahlgren on a navy carriage, one 32-pounder rifled cannon, and one dismantled 24-pounder rifled gun meant to be replaced by a 37-pounder rifled gun.

FORT MERCER. A Union-built fortification located a little more than a mile outside of what was then Plymouth's town limits, Fort Mercer was one of the defenses captured (April 18) when Confederate General R. F. Hoke's land and naval forces attacked and took the town during April 17–20, 1864. The Federals lost 2,834 men, including prisoners of war, and a considerable quantity of supplies. Jefferson Davis promoted Hoke to major general for the victory.

FORT MONTEIL. A Union fortification on the south side of Shallowbag Bay, on the east side of Roanoke Island, Fort Monteil's location was the same as that of Confederate Fort Ellis ("Ballast Point Battery"). The fort was named in honor of Lieutenant Colonel Viguer de Monteil, 53rd New York Infantry, who was killed on February 8, 1862, during the attack against Fort Defiance (Fort Russell) in the center of the island.

FORT MORGAN. FORT OCRACOKE.

MOUND BATTERY. FORT FISHER.

CAMP NETHERCUTT. A temporary Confederate encampment located near Kinston, Lenoir County.

NEWPORT BARRACKS. Located at Newport in Carteret County, these wooden Confederate barracks used during the winter of 1861–62 were captured by Union forces on March 22, 1862.

FORT OCRACOKE (*Fort Morgan*). Situated on Beacon Island in Pamlico Sound, Fort Ocracoke, or Fort Morgan as it was called by the Union during the Civil War, was abandoned by the Confederates when Federal forces on August 28–29, 1861, captured Hatteras Inlet. On August 23, 1861, the fort was described as "a square redoubt with epaulments, constructed of moist sods twenty-four feet thick, and capable of resisting any bombardment directed against it." The fort's armament then consisted of two 8-inch Columbiads and seven 32-pounder cannon, with "the supply of powder, shell, shot, friction primers, fuses" wholly inadequate (D. H. Hill, Jr., *Bethel to Sharpsburg*, p. 172).

FORT OREGON. Soon after the outbreak of the Civil War, it became obvious to military officials of North Carolina and the Confederacy that the small vessels of their miniscule navy were incapable of preventing Federal forces from taking control of the inlets in the Outer Banks. Since the inlets were crucial to the basic supply route to much of the state, plans were made for defending them with shore fortifications. Among the four constructed during the early summer of 1861 was Fort Oregon, a small work on the south side of Oregon Inlet. It was abandoned by its Confederate defenders when Federal naval forces on August 28–29, 1861, bombarded the forts, forced their capitulation, and took possession of the inlets. Since then, Oregon Inlet has moved to the south, and the site of Fort Oregon has long since eroded.

PAINTED ROCK BLOCKHOUSE. The site of this defense erected in 1793 now lies within or near the present community of Paint Rock on the French Broad River in western Madison County. (See: BURNT CANE-BRAKE BLOCKHOUSE.)

CAMP PALMER (*Grove Camp*). Camp Palmer, sometimes referred to as Grove Camp, was a fortified Union encampment located near New Bern and occupied in early 1864 by elements of the 3rd and 12th New York Cavalry. The camp's actual location was on the highway between New Bern and Fort Barnwell.

FORT PARKE (*Fort Blanchard*). The smallest Confederate defense on Roanoke Island, Fort Blanchard was an earthen four-gun battery about half a mile south of Fort Huger on the eastern end of the island. After its capitulation on February 8, 1862, it was occupied and renamed Fort Parke by Union forces.

CAMP PATTON. A Confederate training camp established in 1861, Camp Patton was located on present-day Chestnut Street, east of Charlotte Street, in the city of Asheville in central Buncombe County. It was probably named for Captain Thomas W. Patton, who served in the Confederate forces. The camp occupied land that he owned since his home was nearby.

FORT PEARSON. A Union-built defense near New Bern, Fort Pearson was occupied by the 5th Massachusetts Infantry in April 1864.

FORT PENDER. FORT JOHNSTON.

CAMP PENDERS. A Confederate encampment, probably minimally fortified, Camp Penders was located near the town of Hamilton on the Roanoke River, in Martin County. The camp was probably situated adjacent to Fort Branch.

CAMP PENDLETON. A Union encampment across the Trent River from New Bern, Camp Pendleton was located about a mile across the "drill plain" behind Camp Amory.

CAMP PETTIGREW. A Confederate encampment established in 1862, Camp Pettigrew was located near Wilmington.

CAMP PETTIGREW. A Confederate encampment established in 1861 near Weldon in Halifax County.

CAMP PETTIGREW. A Confederate encampment located on Topsail Island in the Outer Banks, Pender County, Camp Pettigrew was a one-company post occupied during November–December 1863 by Company D, 13th Battalion of the North Carolina Light Artillery.

CAMP PIERCE. A Union camp located on the south side of the Trent River near New Bern, Camp Pierce occupied an abandoned Confederate post.

FORT POINT. FORT RENO.

CAMP POLK. A temporary World War I post, located on the State Fair Grounds at Raleigh, Camp Polk was named in honor of Colonel William Polk, Continental Army, who served throughout the Revolution. Construction was authorized on September 14, 1918, for the establishment of a training camp for the Tank Corps. Additional construction for a permanent tank school was authorized on September 30, 1918. The post's maximum strength of 234 officers and 4,586 enlisted men was reached in November 1918. Construction was abandoned December 9, 1918, and the post ordered salvaged on April 20, 1919.

FORT POLLOCK. In 1712 the province of North Carolina ordered the construction of a fort on the shore of Core Sound, principally to overawe the Indians. The fort was named Fort Pollock in honor of the governor.

CAMP POOL. A fortified Confederate encampment located at present-day Seymour Farm on Tower Hill Road, adjacent to the Neuse River, east of Kinston in Lenoir County, Camp Pool was named for Lieutenant Colonel Stephen Decatur Pool who commanded an artillery battalion here in 1862. Earthworks, gun emplacements and other remains are still visible along the river.

CAMP RALEIGH. The 8th North Carolina Regiment, commanded by Colonel H. M. Shaw, occupied Camp Raleigh on the north end of Roanoke Island from December 1861 to February 1862. Most of the Confederate forts and camps on the island were occupied and renamed during Union occupation.

FORT RALEIGH. Fort Raleigh National Historic Site on Roanoke Island, situated between the Outer Banks and North Carolina's easternmost mainland, is the location of the earliest English colonizing attempts within the limits of the present United States and the birthplace of the first English child born in the New World, Virginia Dare, on August 18, 1587. Sir Walter Raleigh, granted a charter by Queen Elizabeth, made two attempts at permanent settlement in 1585–86 and 1587, but they failed principally because of supply problems and overt Indian hostility.

Roanoke Island was first visited by two white men in 1584. On April 27, 1584, Captains Philip Amadas and Arthur Barlowe left the west of

FORT RALEIGH. Map drawn for a survey in 1896. (From The Conquest of Virginia: The First Attempt, *by Conway Whittle Sams, p. 490.)*

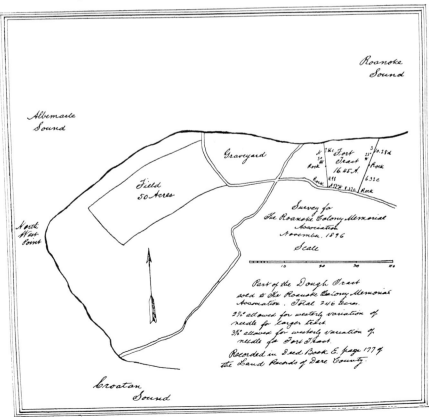

England in two barks to explore the North American coast for Sir Walter Raleigh. They surveyed the length of North Carolina's coastline and decided that Roanoke Island was an ideal place for England's first colony in the New World. Originally consisting of 108 persons, it was founded by Raleigh's cousin, Sir Richard Grenville. Settling on the north end of Roanoke Island during the last days of July 1585, the colonists constructed dwellings, erected a fort, and began to plant crops while Grenville, after appointing Ralph Lane as governor, returned to England for additional supplies. But the colony fared badly. Sir Francis Drake visited the island in 1586 and took the surviving colonists back to England. Soon after Drake's visit, Grenville returned but found the colony deserted. After hopelessly searching along the coast, he left 15 men to occupy the island for Queen Elizabeth and returned to England.

The second colonizing expedition, consisting of 150 settlers, arrived at Roanoke Island in 1587 under the leadership of John White. Finding only desolation and the bones of one of Grenville's men, they set about rebuilding the settlement. When John White returned to England for supplies, he found it in danger of invasion by Spain. In 1588 Queen Elizabeth, refusing to spare a large ship for a return voyage to Roanoke Island because of the emergency, reluctantly dispatched two small pinnaces but they never arrived. The colonists at Fort Raleigh were, in a sense, sacrificed that England might employ all her fighting strength against the naval power of Spain in the battle against her Armada. When White finally returned to the colony in August 1590, he found that the colonists had disappeared.

The hardships of the first colony under Governor Lane, 1585–86 and the disappearance of the "Lost Colony" of 1587 taught the English to grow in colonial wisdom, culminating in the successful settlement of Jamestown, Virginia, in 1607.

Fort Raleigh was designated a National Historic Site in 1941. The fort built by Governor Ralph Lane was investigated by archaeologists in 1947–48 and restored in 1950. In the spring of 1982, archaeologists initiated a $275,000 effort to find the remains of the lost "Cittie of Raleigh" in preparation for the 400th anniversary of the first English colony in the New World, with the festivities beginning on July 13, 1984.

CAMP RANSOM. Located at Wise's Forks, east of Kinston on today's U.S. 70, Camp Ransom was established in 1863 and occupied by Confederate

Brigadier General Matthew W. Ransom's 35th North Carolina Infantry.

CAMP RANSOM. Probably established in 1861, Camp Ransom was a Confederate encampment located near Weldon in Halifax County.

FORT READING. This colonial defense was constructed late in 1711 or early 1712 as a place of refuge during the Tuscarora War, which erupted in September 1711 with a series of massacres and did not end until 1715. The final defeat of the Tuscarora Indians forced them northward, where they ultimately joined the Iroquois Confederacy. Fort Reading was named for Lionel Reading, a locally prominent planter, and located on his plantation on the south side of the Pamlico River opposite the Beaufort County town of Washington.

CAMP RENO. A temporary camp established in the environs of New Bern by Union forces after their capture of the town on March 14, 1862.

FORT RENO (*Fort Huger; Fort Point*). Formerly Confederate Fort Huger (named for General Benjamin Huger), mounting 12 32-pounder guns, and also known as Fort Point because of its location at Weir's Point on Roanoke Island, the fort was renamed Fort Reno, after its capture by Union forces, in honor of General Jesse Lee Reno, killed at South Mountain in September 1862 during the Antietam campaign.

ROANOKE ISLAND FORTIFICATIONS. The island's Confederate fortifications consisted of Forts Bartow, Blanchard, Burnside, Defiance, Ellis, Forrest, Huger, Lane, Russell, and Sullivan. Forts Bartow, Blanchard, and Huger were renamed Forts Foster, Parke, and Reno respectively after their capture by Union forces. Union-built Fort Monteil occupied the former site of Confederate Fort Ellis.

ROANOKE ISLAND POST. The island was occupied from January 1865 to March 1866 by Captain F. F. Lehmann, 103rd Pennsylvania Volunteers, with detachments of various state volunteer units plus two companies of the Rhode Island Artillery.

CAMP ROBERTSON. Located four miles from Snow Hill, probably on the Kinston-Snow Hill Road, in Greene County, this camp was occupied by Brigadier General Beverly H. Robertson's

North Carolina Cavalry Brigade during December–January 1862–63.

CAMP ROBINSON. A Confederate encampment probably established in 1861, Camp Robinson was located near Weldon in Halifax County.

FORT ROLLINS. A palisaded and ditched Confederate defense occupying about an acre of ground, Fort Rollins was erected in early April 1865 at Blowing Rock, Watauga County. It was named for Major W. W. Rollins, who garrisoned the fort with 200 men of the 3rd North Carolina Infantry.

FORT ROWAN. A Union-built four-pointed fort located on the Atlantic & North Carolina Railroad within today's city limits of New Bern, Fort Rowan mounted one 100-pounder Parrott gun, four 32-pounders, and one 8-inch mortar. In early 1864 the fort was garrisoned by Company F of the Rhode Island Artillery.

CAMP (DAN) RUSSELL. Camp Russell at Raleigh was General Hospital No. 13 (Pettigrew Hospital) during the Civil War. Its facilities included a dispensary, guardhouse, stables, bathhouse, and laundry. The surgeon then in charge was Edmund B. Haywood. After the war, it became the Confederate Soldiers Home.

FORT RUSSELL. FORT DEFIANCE.

FORT RUTHERFORD. DAVIDSON'S FORT.

RUTHERFORDTON POST. The town of Rutherfordton was occupied by Army troops June 1871 to October 1872. Captain V. K. Hart, 7th Cavalry, with Company C, and Battery A of the 4th Artillery, aggregating 135 men, established the post on June 27, 1871, in compliance with Special Orders No. 28, Headquarters Post of Chester, North Carolina, dated June 25, 1871.

SALISBURY MILITARY PRISON. A large Confederate military prison located at Salisbury in Rowan County, it was first constructed around an old cotton mill in the fall of 1861. It was considered a good camp for guards as well as prisoners until October 1864, when it was suddenly inundated with 10,000 fresh Union army prisoners transferred from overcrowded camps in Virginia. The lack of barracks space and tents and shortages of food and medical supplies, in addition to a serious outbreak of typhoid fever because the prison well had gone bad, created chaos, and prisoners began dying at an alarming rate. During the early afternoon of November 24, 1864, thousands of prisoners attempted a preconceived, concerted escape. During the short furious battle with the Confederate guards, somewhat less than 200 inmates were shot down. At least 16 prisoners were dead and more than 60 wounded; 2 guards were dead with 10 others wounded. Before the camp finally closed down in March 1865, more than 500 prisoners succeeded in escaping by one means or another. Another 3,500 died of typhoid. Their bodies were interred in mass graves just outside the camp perimeter.

SANDY RIDGE CAMP. This fortified Confederate encampment was located in Craven County east of Dover on what is known as the Old Dover Road. A substantial engagement was fought here on April 20, 1863, involving several regiments from each side.

FORT SAN JUAN DE XUALLA. "In compliance with the orders of [Pedro Menéndez de] Avilés, [Captain] Juan Pardo left Santa Elena [South Carolina] November 1, 1566, with a party of twenty-five soldiers 'to discover and conquer the interior country from there to Mexico.' . . . The season was far advanced, and there was so much snow on the mountains that he could not proceed. He remained fifteen days at Juada," an Indian village at the foot of the Alleghenies. (Woodbury Lowry, *The Spanish Settlements within the Present Limits of the United States: Florida 1562–1574* [1959], p. 275). Here he built a blockhouse which he named Fort San Juan de Xualla and left Sergeant Boyano in command of a small garrison. The site is believed to be the modern Qualla Cherokee Reservation in Swain County.

FORT SCOTT. One of the stockades established in late 1837 and 1838 for the congregation of Cherokee Indians before removal to Oklahoma's Indian Territory, Fort Scott was located at Aquone, a community in western Macon County, on the Bantahala River.

FORT SHALLOWBAG BAY. FORT ELLIS.

FORT SHAW. A Confederate fortification on Oak Island, on the west side of the Cape Fear River, just south of present-day Southport in Brunswick County, Fort Shaw was located between Fort Caswell and Fort Campbell and protected Confederate blockade-runners.

CAMP SLOAN. A Confederate post located adjacent to the North Carolina Military Institute (1858) in Charlotte, Camp Sloan's site is at today's intersection of Morehead Street and Independence Boulevard.

FORT SPINOLA. FORT CASWELL.

FORT STEVENSON. Also spelled Stephens, Stephenson, and Stevens, Fort Stevenson was a Union defense located on the west bank of the Neuse River just west of New Bern. Its armament consisted of five 32-pounder guns manned in February 1864 by Company H, 5th Rhode Island Artillery, aggregating 43 men.

CAMP STOKES. A Confederate encampment, probably temporary, Camp Stokes was located at or near the town of Greensboro in Guilford County.

CAMP STOKES. A Confederate post located adjacent to the North Carolina Military Institute (1858) in Charlotte, Camp Stokes occupied ground near the present-day intersection of Morehead Street and Independence Boulevard.

FORT STRONG. FORT DAVIS.

FORT SULLIVAN. A Confederate defense located on Roanoke Island.

CAMP SUTTON. A temporary World War II engineer training center established on March 7, 1942, Camp Sutton was located near Monroe in Union County. The post was named in honor of Frank Howie Sutton, who enlisted in the Royal Canadian Air Force and was killed in Libya on December 7, 1941. A press release, dated September 19, 1945, and issued by the War Department, listed this 2,473-acre post as surplus property, effective October 1, 1945.

FORT THOMPSON. A Confederate 13-gun sod installation—10 guns bearing on the river and only 3 on the land approaches—Fort Thompson was located on the Neuse River about six miles below New Bern. It was directly involved in the furious battle for possession of the town on March 14, 1862.

FORT TOTTEN. A strong fortification erected by Union forces after the capture of New Bern on March 14, 1862, Fort Totten stood on the western edge of the city, between today's U.S. 17 and 70. Originally its entrenchments extended all the way across New Bern, from the Trent to the Neuse. The main fort, in the center of the defense line, was a four-bastioned pentagonal work mounting 26 guns. It was reported that after the fort was built, negro church groups met there for services.

FORT UNION. FORT DUTTON.

UPPER FORT. DAVIDSON'S FORT.

CAMP VANCE. A Confederate training camp, probably established in 1861 and located near Sulphur Springs in central Buncombe County, Camp Vance was named for Colonel (later General) Robert B. Vance of the 29th North Carolina Infantry which trained here.

CAMP VANCE. A Confederate post located at or near Drexel, Burke County, Camp Vance was probably named for North Carolina's war governor, Colonel Zebulon B. Vance.

CAMP VANCE. Located in the Beaufort–Morehead City area, Camp Vance was most probably named for North Carolina Governor Zebulon B. Vance.

CAMP VANCE. Adjacent to Fort Branch, on the Roanoke River, near Hamilton in Martin County, Camp Vance was named in honor of Governor Zebulon B. Vance.

CAMP VANCE. Probably named for North Carolina's war governor, Camp Vance was located at or near Goldsboro, Wayne County.

CAMP VANCE. Established in 1862 near Kittrell in Vance County, this Confederate post was named for Governor Zebulon B. Vance.

CAMP VANCE. Probably established in 1863, Camp Vance was located near the city of Raleigh and named for the state's war governor.

CAMP VANCE. A temporary Confederate encampment established in 1861 near a community then known as Carolina City, about one mile west of Morehead City opposite Bogue Island, Camp Vance in January 1862 was garrisoned by 42 officers and 766 enlisted men.

CAMP VANCE. Established in 1861 or 1862, Camp Vance was located near Garysburg.

FORT VANCE. A permanent Confederate training post established in 1861 at the town of Drexel about four miles east of Morganton, Burke County, Fort Vance was named in honor of North

Carolina's war Governor Zebulon B. Vance. On June 28, 1864, the post was raided and captured by about 250 to 300 Federal troops led by Colonel George W. Kirk, who had brought his command all the way from Morristown in Tennessee. The main purpose of the raid, however, was not to pillage and destroy Fort Vance, but to capture a train on the Western North Carolina Railroad, make a swift dash to Salisbury to release Federal prisoners, and possibly to burn the important railroad bridge over the Yadkin River just north of the town. (See: SALISBURY MILITARY PRISON.) But the Confederate military prison at Salisbury was warned before Kirk could cut the telegraph wires. After burning Morganton's depot and destroying the Fort Vance installation, the colonel and his men returned to Tennessee with 130 prisoners.

WARM SPRINGS BLOCKHOUSE. BURNT CANE-BRAKE BLOCKHOUSE.

FORT WARREN. A Civil War fortification at Plymouth, Washington County, Fort Warren was in operation 1861–65.

CAMP WASHINGTON. A temporary Confederate encampment established in 1861, Camp Washington was located near Portsmouth on the Pamlico Sound side of the Outer Banks at Ocracoke Inlet.

CAMP WASHINGTON. A temporary Confederate encampment located near the town of Edenton in Chowan County.

CAMP WASHINGTON. A temporary Confederate post located at or near Hertford in Perquimans County.

FORT WASHINGTON. Actually a complex of batteries, Fort Washington was erected by Union forces at the present-day intersection of Market and 10th streets in the town of Washington on the Pamlico River in Beaufort County. The fortification mounted four 32-pounders, two 12-pounders, and two 6-pounders.

FORT WESSELLS. Also known as the 85th Redoubt because it was built by the 85th New York Infantry, Fort Wessells was one of the Union-built defenses of Plymouth on the south bank of the Roanoke River and named for Brigadier General W. H. Wessells. Its present-day site is at the intersection of Campbell and Wilson streets in Plymouth. Very soon after Confederate General Robert F. Hoke took over command of the army from General George E. Pickett in early 1864, he made plans to attack Plymouth. The strategic town, an important supply depot for the Federal land forces in eastern North Carolina, was then garrisoned by 2,834 troops, consisting of four infantry regiments, two companies of the 2nd North Carolina Union Volunteers, a detachment of cavalry, six guns of the 24th New York Independent Battery, and two companies from the 2nd Massachusetts Heavy Artillery, all units under command of General Wessells. The Confederates launched their massive attack on April 17, bombarded the forts, and surrounded the town. General Wessells was finally compelled to run up the white flag at 10 A.M. on the 20th.

CAMP WHITING. A Confederate encampment established in January 1864 at Lockwood Ferry Inlet in Brunswick County, near the South Carolina line, Camp Whiting was garrisoned from January to May 1864 by Company D of the 13th North Carolina Light Artillery.

CAMP WHITING. A temporary Confederate encampment located two miles east of Wilmington, Camp Whiting was established on January 2, 1863, as the winter quarters for 8th North Carolina Infantry troops under the command of Colonel H. M. Shaw. The camp was probably named in honor of General William H. C. Whiting, who was later mortally wounded on January 15, 1865, in the defense of Fort Fisher under attack by Union forces. He died on March 10, 1865 on Governors Island in New York Harbor.

CAMP WILKES. A temporary Confederate encampment, established in October 1861, Camp Wilkes was located two miles from Fort Macon.

CAMP WILLIAMS. A temporary Confederate post located at or near Snow Hill in Greene County.

FORT WILLIAMS. The principal Union fort at Plymouth on the Roanoke River, Fort Williams stood at the present-day intersection of Jefferson and Fort William streets and was named for General Thomas Williams. The fort was the last defense to fall to Confederate forces on April 20, 1864.

WILMINGTON POST. This post was established in the city of Wilmington on May 23, 1866, by Company D, 8th Infantry, under the command of Captain Royal T. Frank. The post was abandoned on July 24, 1868.

CAMP WINFIELD. Probably a temporary Confederate encampment located adjacent to the Hatteras Lighthouse near the inlet.

FORT WINGFIELD. FORT DILLARD.

CAMP WINSLOW. Probably a temporary Confederate encampment located at or near the city of Asheville.

CAMP WINSLOW. A Confederate training camp established in early 1861 in eastern Halifax County, near the town of Halifax, Camp Winslow was later moved across the river to the environs of Garysburg by Lieutenant Colonel William Dorsey Pender, who began the construction of barracks there.

CAMP (FORT) WOOL. A large Union encampment, also known as Fort Wool, was established just east of the village of Hatteras. After Federal forces captured nearby Forts Hatteras and Clark, the community was overrun by Union soldiers.

FORT (BATTERY) WORTH. Also known as Fort Hal, Fort Worth was a Union-built entrenched earthwork facing the Roanoke River at Plymouth's western city limits. The battery mounted one 200-pounder gun. On the last day of the Confederate siege of the town (April 17–20, 1864), it was attacked by Brigadier General Matthew W. Ransom's brigade.

CAMP WYATT. A Confederate encampment, Camp Wyatt was located two miles north of Fort Fisher in New Hanover County and named in honor of Henry Lawson Wyatt, the first North Carolina soldier killed in action in the Civil War, at Bethel Church, Virginia, on June 10, 1861.

CAMP WYATT. A Confederate post used for the duration of the war, Camp Wyatt was located near the city of Raleigh and named in honor of Henry Lawson Wyatt, the first North Carolina soldier killed in action, at Bethel Church, Virginia, June 10, 1861.

YOUNG'S FORT. During the Revolution, in 1778, Thomas Young constructed his new home about two miles north of Houstonville, Iredell County, with the idea of defense against bands of armed Tories in the area. Two two-storied, portholed structures of logs were erected and connected on the second floor by a walkway or bridge. Young's family lived in one and the other served as a distribution point for supplies and information for Patriot troops in the region.

North Dakota

FORT ABERCROMBIE. The first U.S. Army post in North Dakota, Fort Abercrombie was established August 28, 1857, on the left or west bank of the Red River of the North at Graham's Point, about 12 miles north of the present city of Wahpeton, Richland County. It was intended to protect Red River Valley's settlers from Indian hostiles. Established by Lieutenant Colonel John J. Abercrombie, 2nd Infantry, the post—originally consisting of a drab group of scattered buildings without a stockade—later became important in the control of the region's Sioux Indians. Evacuated on July 25, 1859, it was regarrisoned in July 1860 and later rebuilt.

The most dramatic role Fort Abercrombie played was during the Sioux Uprising in Minnesota in 1862, when it was besieged for more than six weeks by the Sioux while the post was garrisoned by only 78 regulars and Company D of the 5th Minnesota Volunteer Infantry, most of its troops having been withdrawn to the Southwest because of the exigencies of the Civil War. Following the siege, the fort was rebuilt with the construction of blockhouses and palisades, completed in 1863, although there was no stockade wall on the river or east side.

Fort Abercrombie's last garrison was withdrawn on October 23, 1877. The post was finally abandoned on October 23, 1878, and its buildings sold to new settlers in the area. The Army transferred the military reservation to the Interior Department on July 14, 1880. Fort Abercrombie is now a state park, administered by the National Park Service, with a restored stockade, blockhouses, and a guardhouse located at the eastern end of the town of Abercrombie.

FORT ABRAHAM LINCOLN (*Fort McKeen; Fort Lincoln*). Established on June 14, 1872, by Lieutenant Colonel Daniel Huston, 6th Infantry, for the protection of the engineers and labor crews engaged in the construction of the North Pacific Railroad, the post was located on the right bank of the Missouri River at the mouth of the Heart River, about three miles south of the town of Bismarck. The temporary post was first named Fort McKeen in honor of Colonel Henry Boyd McKeen, 81st Pennsylvania Infantry, killed in the Battle of Cold Harbor, Virginia, on June 3, 1864.

On August 15, 1872, the post was moved to a permanent site a few miles farther south of Bismarck. On November 19, 1872, it was officially designated Fort Abraham Lincoln in honor of the martyred President. A year later, it was upgraded to a nine-company infantry and cavalry post. Three years later, in 1876, this was the post from which General Custer departed for the ill-

*FORT ABRAHAM LIN-
COLN. (Courtesy of the
North Dakota State
Highway Department.)*

fated Battle of the Little Big Horn. In 1878, by order of the secretary of War, the Ordnance Depot for the Department of Dakota was established on the reservation.

The War Department abandoned Fort Abraham Lincoln on July 22, 1891, as no longer needed and turned the reservation over to the Department of the Interior for disposition. The original reservation is now a State Park with a partially restored fort. On March 2, 1895, Congress authorized the establishment of Fort Lincoln on the east side of the river as a replacement for Fort Yates largely because it was then nearly 50 miles from the nearest railroad. Construction, however, did not begin until about 1899, and it was not sufficiently completed to be garrisoned until 1903. The post was garrisoned intermittently through the years until just before World War II. During the war it served as an alien internment camp. Later it provided accommodations for a number of small state and federal agencies. About 1963 Fort Lincoln became the Lewis and Clark Job Corps Center. When that facility was discontinued, the post was turned over to the United Tribes of North Dakota as a job training center for Indians, a function it is still filling.

ARIKARA POST. FORT MANUEL LISA.

CAMP ATCHESON. Established on July 18, 1863, Camp Atcheson on the northeast shore of Lake Sibley (Devils Lake) in Griggs County, was General H. H. Sibley's base camp during his expedition's campaign against the Sioux. The camp was named for Captain Charles Atcheson of Sibley's staff. When the general was told by friendly Chippewa Indians that the Sioux he was pursuing were fleeing from the Devils Lake region toward the Missouri River, he at once ordered trenches dug and breastworks thrown up. Inside the fortification, he placed all his sick men, tired horses, baggage train, the cattle, and surplus supply wagons, and left two companies of infantry to protect them. Traveling light, Sibley succeeded in driving the Sioux across the Missouri near Bismarck and returned to the base camp a month later. Camp Atcheson was occupied longer by his troops than any of the other camps established along the route of the expedition, most of them one- or two-night layovers.

FORT ATKINSON. FORT BERTHOLD.

CANTONMENT BAD LANDS. This post, also known as "Cantonment at Little Missouri Crossing," was established on November 10, 1879, by Captain Stephen Baker with Company B, 6th Infantry, on the west bank of the Little Missouri River, near the present town of Medora in Billings County. Stationed there to protect the construction crews on the Northern Pacific Railroad, the troops erected quarters for one company and other necessary structures of logs, and a frame hospital. The post was abandoned March 4, 1883.

CAMP BARBOUR. General Henry Atkinson's 1825 expedition, consisting of 435 infantrymen and 40 cavalrymen, was sent out by the government to the Upper Missouri to provide some protection for the traders in the region while evidencing a show of strength to the hostile Indian tribes there. The troops established a temporary camp on the south bank of the Missouri, a short distance from the mouth of the Yellowstone, on the site of an abandoned and partially burned trading post. Occupying the only standing building surrounded by three remaining sides of the stockade, the post was called Camp Barbour in honor of the new secretary of war, James Barbour.

FORT BERTHOLD (*Fort Atkinson*). A 120-foot-square trading post built in 1858–59 by Charles Larpenteur and associates, Fort Atkinson was located about 200 feet from the left bank of the Missouri River below the mouth of the Little Missouri in McLean County. The site has since been covered by the impounded waters of the Garrison Reservoir. The post was purchased by the American Fur Company in 1862 and renamed Fort Berthold, replacing the company's first Fort Berthold established in 1845. It was most probably named for Bartholomew Berthold, brother-in-law of Pierre Chouteau.

Brigadier General Alfred Sully on August 29, 1864, left Captain Abraham B. Moreland in command of a company of the 6th Iowa Cavalry in an encampment outside the fort's stockade to protect the trading post from bands of marauding Sioux Indians. A week later, Moreland's troops occupied the fort. Because of a disagreement with the American Fur Company agent there, the troops erected log structures outside the stockade and occupied them in April 1865. The post was evacuated June 14, 1867, when Fort Stevenson (originally known as New Fort Berthold) was established about 12 miles below Fort Berthold. In 1868 Fort Berthold became agency headquarters on the reservation established for the Arikara, Gros Ventre, and Mandan Indians, and operated as such until 1874, during which period it was still active as a trading post.

CAMP BRIGGS. Established and occupied May 2–26, 1898, in the city of Fargo, Camp Briggs was a temporary encampment for the State National Guard.

FORT BUFORD. Located on a site selected by Major General Alfred H. Terry on the left or north bank of the Missouri River, just below the entrance of the Yellowstone and about three miles below Fort Union, Fort Buford was established on June 15, 1866, by Captain William G. Rankin, 31st Infantry, and named in honor of Major General John Buford, who died at the age of 37 on December 16, 1863, of exposure and exhaustion brought on during the Battle of Gettysburg. The Army post was intended to safeguard the emigrant travel route to Montana as well as navigation on the river.

In 1867 Fort Union was dismantled and its salvageable materials were used to appreciably enlarge Fort Buford. The fort, with the exception of Fort Abraham Lincoln, had a history more varied than any other post in North Dakota. Chief Nez Percé leader Chief Joseph, after his surrender in 1877, was brought through Fort Buford. Chief Sitting Bull and his followers came there to surrender in the latter part of June 1881. The subduction of the Sioux and the arrival of the railroads in the region combined to influence the War Department to close the fort as no longer useful. Abandoned on October 1, 1895, with its last garrison transferred to Fort Assiniboine in Montana, the post's buildings were disposed of at public auction. The military reservation was turned over to the Interior Department on October 31, 1895. Fort Buford Historic Site, one mile south of the town of Buford, McKenzie County, encloses the restored officers' quarters, magazine ruins, and the post's cemetery.

CHABOILLEZ POST. FORT PAMBIAN.

FORT CLARK. Established in 1831 for the American Fur Company by trader James Kipp among the Mandan Indian villages on the Missouri River, about eight miles below the mouth of the Knife River, the site of Fort Clark, named in honor of William Clark, is two miles north of the present-day town of Fort Clark, Oliver County. The trading post stood less than a mile below and on the opposite side of the river from former Fort Mandan, Lewis and Clark's 1804–5 winter quarters.

During the summer of 1837, a devastating smallpox epidemic invaded the Mandan villages. The pestilence was carried up the Missouri aboard the steamboat *St. Peter's*, which stopped at Fort Clark on June 19. On July 14 the first Mandan died, and by August 11 they were dying so fast that an accurate count could not be made. By September 19, at least 800 Indians had succumbed. By the end of the year, their population, an estimated 1,600 in June, had dropped to about 100. The epidemic continued up the Missouri to other tribes, with an estimated 15,000 Indians dying in the path of the scourge.

Under the aegis of the American Fur Company, Fort Clark became one of the leading trading centers of the Upper Missouri, ranking after Fort Union and Fort Pierre. Fort Clark was abandoned following the amalgamation of the fur-trading companies in 1860. The site is now a State Historic Park.

FORT CROSS. FORT SEWARD.

FORT DAER. This Hudson's Bay Company trading post was built in September 1812 by Captain Miles Macdonell, Lord Selkirk's agent for the establishment of the Red River Colony on his land grant, which extended into what is now American territory. The site of Fort Daer, on the west bank of the Red River at the mouth of the Pembina River, is now occupied by the town of Pembina, just below the Manitoba line. The fort was named in honor of Lord Selkirk, who was also Baron Daer. A competing Northwest Company post stood nearby and bitter friction developed between the two. In 1816 the Nor'-Westers seized Fort Daer and occupied it for a few months. The fort was finally abandoned in 1822 after the merger of the Hudson's Bay and Northwest companies.

FORT DILTS. Fort Dilts State Park now occupies the site where Captain James L. Fisk's immigrant train of 80 wagons, bound for Montana's gold mines, was corraled in defense formation for 14 days in September 1864 and withstood Sioux Indian attacks. During the siege, cavalry troops from Fort Rice aided in the defense of the makeshift six-foot-high sod breastwork. The "fort" was named in honor of Jefferson Dilts, a scout for the expedition, who was killed while on a reconnoitering mission. Fort Dilts State Park, a few miles west of present-day Rhame in Bowman County, memorializes the site.

FORT FLOYD. FORT UNION.

FORT GEORGE H. THOMAS. FORT PEMBINA.

GRAND FORKS HOUSE. A Northwest Company trading post, known to the traders as Grandes Fourches, located on the Red River in the vicinity of the present-day city of Grand Forks, it was built in 1807 by Alexander Henry, Jr.'s men from Pembina. After demarcation of the international boundary, the Canadian trading posts on American territory were abandoned.

CAMP GREELEY. CAMP HANCOCK.

HAIR HILLS POST. PEMBINA RIVER HOUSE.

CAMP HANCOCK (*Camp Greeley*). When originally established as Camp Greeley by the Army on August 9, 1872, on the east bank of the Missouri, at Bismarck, this post's purpose was to protect the Northern Pacific Railroad's construction crews. After the railroad was completed through Bismarck, the post was enlarged to become a supply depot for other Dakota posts, particularly Fort Abraham Lincoln, and was renamed Camp Hancock. The post consisted of a log barracks, 100 by 20 feet, and six other buildings. Camp Hancock was discontinued in 1877. Its location is now occupied by the Camp Hancock State Historic Site, with the post's sole remaining building a museum featuring a transportation exhibit.

HEART RIVER CORRAL. SULLY BASE CAMP.

HENRY HOUSE. Also referred to as Fort Henry, this was the fur-trading post established by Alexander Henry, Jr., of the Northwest Company in 1801 on a site just north of the mouth of the Pembina River in the present-day city of Pembina. The post consisted of a high stockade, enclosing a storehouse, stable, blacksmith shop, and some whitewashed buildings.

CAMP HOUSTON. This temporary post was established on the upper Heart River by Company I, 7th Cavalry, on June 21, 1880, for the purpose of protecting railroad construction crews at present-day Dickinson in Stark County. Camp Houston was abandoned on November 25, 1880, by Company B of the 7th Cavalry.

CAMP JOHNSON. Occupying the site of General John Frémont's camp of 1839, Camp Johnson was a temporary post established in 1863. Its location is now known as the Birch Creek Historic Site, two miles east of Hastings in Barnes County.

FORT KIPP. Also known as Kipp's Post, this 96-foot-square stockaded trading post was established for the Columbia Fur Company by James Kipp on the north or left bank of the Missouri River near the mouth of the White Earth River in present-day Mountrail County during the winter of 1825–26 for trade among the Assiniboines. In 1827 the Columbia Fur Company merged with the American Fur Company. In 1830 the new company, which took the name of the latter, ordered Kipp to begin the construction of Fort Clark and abandon the post he had built four years earlier.

FORT LEWIS. FORT MANUEL LISA.

FORT LINCOLN. FORT ABRAHAM LINCOLN.

FORT LISA. FORT MANUEL LISA.

FORT MCKEEN. FORT ABRAHAM LINCOLN.

FORT MANDAN. FORT MANUEL LISA.

FORT MANDAN. This was the camp of the Lewis and Clark Expedition established during the winter of 1804–5. It is believed that the site of the old fort built on the north bank of the Missouri River is about three miles southeast of the marked Fort Mandan State Historic Site, possibly in the middle of the present riverbed because of changes in the course of the river. The triangular-shaped stockade was described by Sergeant Patrick Gass, who played an important part in the expedition:

The following is the manner in which our huts and fort were built. The huts were in two rows, containing four rooms each, and joined at one end forming an angle. When raised about 7 feet high a floor of puncheons or split plank were laid, and covered with grass and clay; which made a warm loft. The upper part projected a foot over and the roofs were made shed-fasion, rising from the inner side, and making the outer wall about 18 feet high. The part not enclosed by the huts we intend to picket. In the angle formed by the two rows we built two rooms, for holding our provisions and stores. [*North Dakota History* 22, nos. 1 and 2 (1955): 18–20]

The fort was strong enough to discourage an Indian attack. Other than an attack on a hunting party by the Sioux, the explorers had no serious problems with the Indians. During the winter the thermometer dropped to forty degrees below zero. It was during this period that the explorers employed Charbonneau as interpreter. His captive wife, the celebrated Sacajawea, the "Bird Woman," who was to accompany them, was to play an important role in the success of the expedition. On April 7, 1805, the party again set out on its explorations which were to ultimately find them at the end of the year on the Pacific Coast. When the explorers returned in August of 1806, they found that only one house in the rear bastion and several pickets next to the river were all that remained of the old fort on the Missouri River. According to the original journals of the expedition, the buildings had been burned by accident. The site of the Lewis and Clark camp is located approximately 14 miles west of Washburn in McLean County.

FORT MANUEL. FORT MANUEL LISA.

FORT MANUEL LISA (*Fort Lewis; Fort Lisa; Fort Mandan; Arikara Post; Fort Manuel; Fort Vanderburgh*). A confusing array of names designated the four trading posts along the Missouri River erected by Manuel Lisa and his associates under the aegis of the Missouri Fur Company of St. Louis, founded in 1808–9. Fort Lisa, variously known also as Fort Manuel Lisa, Fort Lewis, and Fort Mandan, was erected in 1809 in the vicinity of Emanuel Creek under the supervision of Manuel Lisa and Reuben Lewis, brother of explorer Meriwether Lewis, and was managed by Lewis until 1812, when it was abandoned. It was reoccupied as Fort Vanderburgh for a short time during 1822–23. The site, since inundated by the impounded waters of the Garrison Dam, is near present-day Pick City in Mercer County.

Ray H. Mattison's "Report on Historic Sites of the Garrison Reservoir Area" (*North Dakota History*, January 1955) locates the sites of the four posts:

One known as Fort Lisa was built in 1812 five or six miles below old Council Bluffs near the present city of Omaha; another known as the "Arikara post" also known as "Fort Manuel Lisa" just below the present North Dakota-South Dakota boundary line; Fort Manuel at the mouth of the Bighorn River; and one built among the Mandans and Gros Ventres, either in the vicinity of Mannhaven or Emanuel Creek or Emanuel Rock.

FORT MORTIMER. This fur-trading post on the Missouri River, just below the mouth of the Yellowstone, was erected in 1842 by Fox, Livingstone and Company of New York, also known as the Union Fur Company, as competition for the American Fur Company's Fort Union, three miles to the west. Fort Mortimer was built near the remains of old Fort William, with some of its still remaining buildings used as storehouses. Four years later, the fort sold out to the competition. In 1858 an adobe-built trading post, a resurrected Fort William, occupied the same site. In 1866 the salvageable remnants of this post were used in the building of Fort Buford.

NEW FORT BERTHOLD. FORT STEVENSON.

FORT PAMBIAN (*Chaboillez Post*). Reputedly the first fur-trading post in North Dakota, Fort Pambian, also referred to as Chaboillez Post, was erected by Charles Chaboillez of the Northwest Company in 1797 on the south side of the mouth of the Pembina River, about three miles south of the Canadian line. The post's buildings burned down in 1815. The site is now included within Selkirk Park on Stutsman Street in the city of Pembina.

PARK RIVER POST. A trading post was erected by Alexander Henry in 1800 on the west side of the Red River, about a quarter of a mile from the mouth of the Park River, in present Walsh County.

FORT PEMBINA. PEMBINA HOUSE.

FORT PEMBINA (*Fort George H. Thomas*). Established on July 8, 1870, on the left bank of the Red River of the North, just above the mouth of the Pembina River, about a mile and a half south of the city of Pembina, this U.S. Army post was first named Fort George H. Thomas in honor of the Civil War general who earned the sobriquet of The Rock of Chickamauga. It was established by Captain Loyd Wheaton, 20th Infantry, in response to the petition of the Minnesota Legislature to Congress for the posting of troops at Pembina because of Indian unrest in the Red River Valley and anticipated depredations by the Sioux who found a refuge across the border in Canada.

The fort was officially designated Fort Pembina on September 6, 1870. It was abandoned on September 26, 1895, after a fire on March 27, 1895, largely destroyed the post. The military reservation was turned over on December 2, 1895, to the Interior Department, which auctioned off its remaining buildings in 1902. The site of the post is adjacent to the Pembina Airport off I-29.

PEMBINA HOUSE (*Fort Pembina*). This Hudson's Bay Company trading post, also referred to as Fort Pembina, was erected in 1803 on the north side of the mouth of the Pembina River. It was operated until 1823, when boundary litigation determined that it stood on American territory. In 1863 a detachment of Minnesota Volunteers established a temporary cantonment on the site of Pembina House to protect the region's settlers during the late days of the so-called Sioux Uprising, which ravaged Minnesota's settlements. The site is on Rolette Street in the city of Pembina.

PEMBINA MOUNTAIN POST. PEMBINA RIVER HOUSE.

PEMBINA RIVER HOUSE (*Hair Hills Post; Pembina Mountain Post*). Established in 1800 in the environs of the present-day city of Pembina, this post, also known as Hair Hills Post and Pembina Mountain Post, was one of Alexander Henry, Jr.'s substations erected in the interests of the Northwest Company. Designed primarily for trade in furs with the Indians, Henry gradually cultivated the post's surrounding rich, fertile ground into a veritable vegetable factory, growing giant-sized cabbages, potatoes, melons, beets, parsnips, onions, turnips, and carrots. No archival evidence was found to indicate when the post was closed.

FORT RANSOM. Located on the right side of the Sheyenne River, approximately 75 miles above its junction with the Red River of the North, Fort Ransom was established on June 18, 1867, on a site selected by Brigadier General Alfred H. Terry and built under the supervision of Captain George H. Crosman, 10th Infantry. The post was intended to keep the hostile Sioux in check and protect the emigrant route from Minnesota to Montana's gold fields. Named in honor of Brevet Major General Thomas E. G. Ransom, U.S. Volunteers, who died of wounds on October 29, 1864, the fort was protected by 12-foot-high breastworks made of sod and logs, surrounded by an eight-foot-deep ditch. Fort Ransom was abandoned July 31, 1872, when Fort Seward was established near Jamestown. The military reservation, located near the town of Fort Ransom, was turned over to the Interior Department on July 22, 1884, for disposition.

FORT RICE. Located on the right bank of the Missouri River, about 10 miles north of the Cannonball River's mouth, and just below the present-day town of Fort Rice in Morton County, Fort Rice was established by Brigadier General Alfred Sully on July 11, 1864, during his campaign against the hostile Sioux. Built under the supervision of Colonel Daniel J. Dill, 30th Wisconsin Infantry, the post originally consisted of rudimentary huts of cottonwood logs with earth-covered roofs. It was rebuilt in more substantial form in 1868. The post was officially designated Fort Rice on May 12, 1864, by Secretary of War Edwin Stanton in honor of Brigadier General James Clay Rice, killed in the Battle of Laurel Hill, Virginia, on May 10, 1864. After Fort Yates was established to the south on the same side of the river, Fort Rice was considered no longer required. It was abandoned on November 25, 1878, but temporarily garrisoned by a small caretaking detachment until February 6, 1879, to dispose of the post's improvements. The military reservation was turned over to the Interior Department on July 22, 1884. Part of Fort Rice's site is now a state park, enclosing several reconstructed block-houses.

FORT SEWARD (*Camp Sykes; Fort Cross*). Located on the right bank of the James River near present Jamestown in Stutsman County, at the point where the Northern Pacific Railroad crossed the river, the post was established on May 27, 1872, by Captain John C. Bates, 20th Infantry, to protect the railroad's construction crews. First called Camp Sykes for Colonel George Sykes, 20th Infantry, it was renamed Fort Cross on September 7, 1872, in honor of Colonel Edward E. Cross, 5th New Hampshire Infantry Volunteers, who was killed at Gettysburg, July 2, 1863. The post was officially redesignated Fort Seward on November 9, 1872, in honor of former Secretary of State William H. Seward, who died on October 10, 1872. The post was abandoned on September 30, 1877. The military reservation was transferred to the Interior Department on July 14, 1880, for disposition. In 1925 the site of Fort Seward, on a bluff about two miles northwest of Jamestown, was donated by the Northern Pacific Railroad as a state park.

SHEYENNE RIVER POST. In 1825 the American Fur Company had a trading post on the Sheyenne River, about 50 miles from its junction with the Red River, probably in present Ransom County.

STANDING ROCK AGENCY POST. FORT YATES.

FORT STEVENSON (*New Fort Berthold*). Established on June 14, 1867, by Major Joseph N. G. Whistler, 31st Infantry, and located on the left bank of the Missouri River above the Knife River's mouth, Fort Stevenson was first occupied by troops from Fort Berthold, about 12 miles to the north, which it replaced. The post, originally known as New Fort Berthold, was officially designated Fort Stevenson at the direction of Secretary of War Edwin M. Stanton on April 12, 1864, in honor of Brigadier General Thomas G. Stevenson, who was killed a month later in the Battle of Spotsylvania, Virginia.

The arrival of the railroads and the pacification of the Sioux dictated the abandonment of the fort on July 22, 1883, with its last garrison transferred to Fort Buford. The post was transferred to the Fort Berthold Indian Agency on August 7, 1883, and used as an Indian school until 1894. The military reservation was then turned over to the Interior Department on February 13, 1895, for disposition. The site has since

been inundated by the impounded waters of the Garrison Dam.

SULLY BASE CAMP (*Heart River Corral*). This temporary post, also known as the Heart River Corral, was the most advanced base of Brigadier General Alfred Sully's 4,000-man expedition in 1864 against the hostile Sioux. Occupied for 10 days by a 125-man military guard and 250 emigrants, it was located on the Heart River in the southeast corner of Stark County. A stone marker on the site commemorates its occupation by U.S. troops.

CAMP SYKES. FORT SEWARD.

TILTON'S POST. James Kipp, agent for the Columbia Fur Company, in May 1823 began erecting a trading fort on the prairie between the winter village of the Mandan Indians and the future site of Fort Clark a mile away, about three miles from the present town of Fort Clark in Oliver County. The trading establishment was named for J. P. Tilton, one of Kipp's associates, who with five other men operated the post. Because of continued overt Arikara Indian hostility, the post was abandoned sometime in May 1824. Kipp then erected a trading house in the Mandan village across the Missouri, and the old fort was abandoned. The logs from the old palisades were floated down to the village, where several more structures were added to Kipp's establishment, active until about 1826.

FORT TOTTEN. One of the most attractively located U.S. Army posts on the Plains during the Indian wars, Fort Totten was established July 17, 1867, by Captain Samuel A. Wainwright, 31st Infantry, on the south side of Devils (Minnewaukan) Lake on a site selected by Brigadier General Alfred H. Terry, adjacent to the present-day town of Fort Totten in Benson County. Serving also as one of the Army's chain of posts to safeguard the emigrant travel route from Minnesota to Montana's gold fields, Fort Totten was primarily intended to initiate the placing of the region's Indians on reservations. The post's first, hastily built structures were replaced by permanent brick-constructed buildings in 1869–70. Named in honor of Brigadier General Joseph Gilbert Totten, the Army's chief engineer, who died on April 22, 1864, the post is situated within the boundaries of the Fort Totten (Devils Lake) Indian Reservation, established on January 11, 1870.

Fort Totten was abandoned when its last garrison was withdrawn on November 18 (December 31?), 1890. Transferred to the Interior Department on October 4, 1890, the reservation and the post became the headquarters for the Fort Totten Indian Agency and its industrial school. One of the West's best preserved Army posts, practically all of its brick buildings are still standing around its parade ground, converted by the state into a park.

TURTLE RIVER POST. A Hudson's Bay Company trading post, established in November 1812, it was located on the Red River at the mouth of the Turtle River, about 18 miles north of the present city of Grand Forks.

FORT UNION (*Fort Floyd*). Originally established as Fort Floyd in 1828 by Kenneth McKenzie of John Jacob Astor's American Fur Company on the left bank of the Missouri River, three miles above the mouth of the Yellowstone, the trading post soon became known as Fort Union, eventually the greatest concentration point of the western fur trade. Brigadier General Alfred Sully on August 18, 1864, occupied the post, garrisoning it with one company of the 30th Wisconsin Infantry to protect the post's traders and the U.S. military property stored there temporarily for the new post to be established nearby. The military's evacuation of the trading post was completed on August 31, 1865. Two years later, Fort Union was purchased by the Federal government, entirely dismantled, and its salvageable materials used in the substantial enlargement of Fort Buford.

FORT VANDERBURGH. FORT MANUEL LISA.

FORT WILLIAM. Occupying the site of the Army's later-built Fort Buford in McKenzie County, Fort William was a two-bastioned, 150-by-130-foot trading post built by William Sublette and Robert Campbell, fur traders of St. Louis, in opposition to Fort Union, and named for Sublette. Construction was begun on August 29, 1833, and completed by Christmas of the same year. During the summer of 1834, Sublette's firm sold out to the American Fur Company and the property was moved to Fort Union.

FORT YATES (*Standing Rock Agency Post*). Established as the headquarters for the Standing Rock Sioux Indian Agency on December 23, 1874, on the right bank of the Missouri River at the present town of Fort Yates, about 10 miles above the South Dakota line, in Sioux County, the post was originally called Post at Standing Rock Agency. Its first garrison consisted of Company E, 17th Infantry, under the command of Captain Edward Collins. On December 30, 1878, it was officially designated Fort Yates in honor of Captain George W. Yates, 7th Cavalry, killed on June 25, 1876, in the Battle of the Little Big Horn, the massacre of Custer's command. Although Fort Yates was abandoned on September 11, 1903, as a military post, the post remains the headquarters for the Standing Rock Reservation.

FORT ADAMS. One of the chain of forts on the critical supply line established by General Anthony Wayne during his northward march with the troops of his Legion in 1794 to subjugate the Indians in the Northwest Territory, Fort Adams was begun August 2 on the south bank of the St. Marys River, 25 miles north of Fort Recovery and 10 miles north of the present town of Celina, Mercer County. Named by Wayne in honor of the then vice president, John Adams, the fort was a comparatively small square fort when finally completed. Roughly diamond in shape, with 18-foot-square blockhouses occupying the two most external angles, the fort's interior consisted of two hipped-roof buildings, the commandant's quarters and a guardhouse. With little room for the storage of supplies, the fort was principally intended to be a strongpoint along the route of march and a control over the river traffic. Lieutenant James Underhill and 40 invalids were left to hold the fort. After the victory at Fallen Timbers and the Treaty of Greene Ville, Fort Adams was abandoned.

ALUM CREEK BLOCKHOUSE. Located on Alum Creek, seven miles east of the present town of Delaware, this blockhouse was erected in 1812. The defense survived until at least 1849.

FORT AMANDA. A War of 1812 stockade situated on the west bank of the Auglaize River, nine miles northwest of present Wapakoneta in Auglaize County, Fort Amanda was built over a period of about six months, from the summer to the later fall of 1812. Erected by Kentucky troops under Colonel John Poague, in compliance with orders of General William Henry Harrison, and named probably for the colonel's wife, the intermittently garrisoned post was used as a supply depot and a rest stop for troops in transit. The fort was abandoned after the Treaty of Ghent. In 1915 a 50-foot-high, granite obelisk was erected on the site to commemorate the fort.

CAMP AMMEN. A Civil War encampment at or near Ripley, Brown County, Camp Ammen was probably named for Captain (later Colonel) Jacob Ammen, who served with the 12th Ohio Volunteer Infantry and later as commander of the 24th Ohio Volunteers. No record has been found to indicate when the camp was established or discontinued.

CAMP ANDREWS. A Civil War encampment located at or near Mt. Vernon, Knox County, the post was named in honor of Colonel Lorin Andrews, who before the war was president of

Ohio

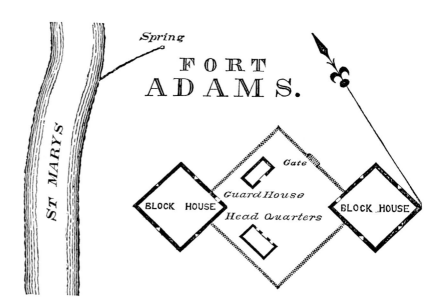

FORT ADAMS. Plan drawn by B. Van Cleve in 1794.

Kenyon College. He volunteered for service and served as colonel of the 4th Ohio Infantry. He became ill in West Virginia and was taken home to Gambier, Ohio, where he died on September 18, 1861. No archival data have been found to indicate when the camp was established or discontinued.

CAMP ARTHUR. A Civil War encampment, probably temporary, Camp Arthur was located at or near Urbana in Champaign County.

FORT AVERY. A War of 1812 defense probably situated on the east side of the Huron River, Fort Avery was located in the vicinity of the present-day town of Avery, a few miles north of Milan, in Erie County. The site of the blockhouse was selected by General Simon Perkins. For more than a century, there was much confusion regarding its name since it had been referred to as Camp Huron, Camp Avery, Fort Huron, Fort Avery, and Captain Parker's Fort.

FORT BALL. Situated on the left or west bank of the Sandusky River on the site of the present-day city of Tiffin, Seneca County, Fort Ball was a War of 1812 fortification erected in 1813 by Colonel James V. Ball, in compliance with orders of General William Henry Harrison. A strong stockade, reportedly capable of accommodating 500 men, Fort Ball was established as a temporary strongpoint and depot for supplies.

FORT BARBEE (*Fort St. Marys*). Built by General Anthony Wayne in 1794 as a supply depot, Fort St. Marys stood on the west bank of the St. Marys River, at the present city of the same name, in Auglaize County. Commanded by Captain John Whistler before he built Fort Dearborn at Chicago, the post was maintained until 1796. In 1813, during the War of 1812, the fort was rebuilt and reoccupied by troops under the command of Colonel Barbee, in compliance with orders of General William Henry Harrison. The fort served as a depot for a large quantity of provisions and munitions for distribution to the forts and Harrison's troops to the north. On September 18, 1818, a treaty was signed here between the government and the Ottawa, Shawnee, and Wyandot tribes, opening large tracts of land for white settlement.

BIG BOTTOM FORT. In the autumn of 1790, a company of 36 men came from Marietta to a place of pioneer settlement on the Muskingum River known as the Big Bottom. Here they built a blockhouse on the east bank of the river, four miles above the mouth of Meigs Creek, near present Stockport in Morgan County. In the "winter of 1790," 1789–90 or 1790–91, it was the site of a bloody Indian massacre. The site is now occupied by the Big Bottom Park, which encloses an inscribed four-sided granite marker erected in 1905 to memorialize the settlers killed there.

FORT BLACK. A strong War of 1812 outpost built of logs was erected at present-day New Madison in Darke County in the fall of 1813 under the direction of Lieutenant James Black, commanding a detachment of Preble County troops to protect the area's pioneer settlers against marauding bands of Indians allied to the British. The town of Madison, renamed New Madison in 1831, was platted on the site of the fort in December 1817.

BLOOMINGVILLE BLOCKHOUSES. During the fall of the first year of the War of 1812, two palisaded blockhouses were erected in the Bloomingville settlement in Erie County. Irregularly garrisoned by American troops, the blockhouses served mainly as places of refuge throughout the war.

CAMP BROUGH. A temporary Civil War encampment, probably an assembly point for recruits, Camp Brough was located near Gallipolis, Gallia County, and named for Governor John Brough of Ohio.

CAMP BROWN. Established August 19, 1861, Camp Brown occupied a tract at Park Street and Euclid Avenue, today the intersection of Euclid Avenue and East 46th Street, in the city of Cleveland. One citation claims that the Civil War encampment consisted of 10 acres of land; another account reports the camp was barely large enough for pitching tents, so a drill and parade ground was established on the corner of Kinsman Street and Case Avenue on 14 acres of flat land, corresponding today with Woodland Avenue and East 40th Street. Camp Brown was the home of the 37th Ohio Volunteer Infantry, one of Ohio's "German" units, the majority of its men speaking German. At the end of September, the unit left for Camp Dennison, where it was mustered into service on October 2, 1861.

FORT BROWN. Located 16 miles south of Fort Defiance, at the junction of the Auglaize and Little Auglaize rivers, near present-day Oakwood in Pauling County, Fort Brown was a War of 1812 fortification ordered built by General William Henry Harrison to facilitate the transportation of supplies for his army.

CAMP BUCKINGHAM. A Civil War camp named for Brigadier General C. P. Buckingham, adjutant general of Ohio, Camp Buckingham was established in September 1861 at Mansfield in Richland County by the Sherman Brigade, organized by U.S. Senator John Sherman (brother of General William T. Sherman) with General R. Brinkerhoff.

CAMP BULL. Located near Chillicothe, Camp Bull was a substantial double-hewed log building, part of which was used as quarters for British prisoners taken during the War of 1812. No archival data were found to indicate when the camp was established or discontinued. Camp Logan, a Civil War post, was located on the site.

CAMP BUSHNELL. A temporary training encampment established during the Spanish-American War located on the outskirts of Columbus, Camp Bushnell was named for Asa Bushnell, governor of Ohio at the time. The area of the campsite, formerly known as Bullett Park, is now a part of Bexley, a Columbus suburb.

FORT CAMPUS MARTIUS. On April 7, 1788, a large crudely built wooden flatboat moved along the shore of the Ohio River, maneuvered through the mouth of the Muskingum River, and anchored a short distance upstream. General Rufus Putnam, noted Revolutionary War veteran, and 47 followers, all New Englanders, came ashore and initiated the founding of the first permanent city in the Northwest Territory, representing a minute parcel of the 1.8-million-acre tract of land they had acquired from Congress a year earlier. They built a fortification at Picketed Point at the confluence of the two rivers, surveyed the environs, platted lots and streets, and planned locations for the office of the Ohio Company, homes, and public buildings.

An extensive fortification, a regular parallelogram with an exterior line of 720 feet and the sides of its interior courtyard 144 feet long each way, Campus Martius ("field of Mars") was completed with blockhouses, surmounted by watch towers, and interior structures for homes and businesses. By August a number of families joined the pioneer community. Since many of the newcomers were veterans of the Patriot cause, they elected to recognize French armed assistance during the Revolution by naming the town Marietta after Queen Marie Antoinette. The fort, never attacked by Indians, who were overawed by its obvious strength, was largely dismantled following the Treaty of Greene Ville, with the salvageable materials used to erect new dwellings. Today the Campus Martius Museum, enclosing the two-story Rufus Putnam residence, stands at 2nd and Washington streets in Marietta.

CAMP CARLISLE. A temporary Civil War encampment established in 1862 for the organization of and mustering in of recruits for the Union army, Camp Carlisle was located opposite Wheeling, West Virginia, in Belmont County, Ohio.

CAMP CHARLOTTE. A temporary encampment located at Pickaway Plains on the Scioto River in Rose County, Camp Charlotte was established in 1774 by Lord Dunmore and his army for the purpose of compelling the Indians to sign a treaty that marked the Ohio River as the southern boundary of their domain. Lord Dunmore then returned to Virginia via Fort Gower.

CAMP CHASE. Located in what was then the outskirts of the city of Columbus and first used as a training camp for Civil War recruits, Camp Chase later became more important as a prison camp. In 1863 there were about 8,000 Confederate soldiers imprisoned there. Today the sites of the camp and the Confederate cemetery are on Sullivan Avenue west of Powell Avenue.

CHILLICOTHE BARRACKS. During the War of 1812, U.S. troops were quartered in a very large double-hewed building standing on the site of the present-day corner of 2nd and Walnut streets in Chillicothe.

CAMP CIRCLEVILLE. A temporary Civil War encampment, probably a rendezvous point for recruits, this camp was located near the town of Circleville in Pickaway County. Most of them were mustered in at Camp Chase at Columbus.

CAMP CLARK. Also known as Camp Fairgrounds, Camp Clark was a Civil War assembly point and mustering-in center established in 1861 on the Clark County Fair Grounds at Springfield. The 44th Ohio Volunteer Regiment was organized and trained here and mustered into service on October 14, 1861.

CAMP CLAY. A Civil War encampment established between April and July 1861, Camp Clay was located at what was then known as Pendleton, approximately three miles east on the Ohio from downtown Cincinnati, opposite Newport, Kentucky. The area is now within Cincinnati's city limits. Two full regiments of infantry, the 1st and 2nd Kentucky (Union) were mustered into service there, although most of the men were from Ohio.

CAMP CLEVELAND. A large Civil War camp located on the outskirts of Cleveland, it served as a rendezvous and center for preliminary instruction for more than 15,000 officers and men who served enlistments lasting from 90 days to 3 years on battlefields and in camps and garrisons throughout the country between 1862 and 1865. Five Union army camps had been established in 1861 and disbanded prior to the establishment of Camp Cleveland, four of them located east of the Cuyahoga River, and the fifth, Camp Wade, on University Heights, west of the river, and south of Cleveland.

President Lincoln called for more troops on July 2 and 4, 1862. Out of a national quota of 300,000 men, Ohio Governor David Tod had to fill a quota of 36,858. Camp Cleveland was therefore established on the former site of Camp Wade. The new camp was larger, covering more than 35 acres, its boundaries stretching from present Railway Avenue on the north to Marquardt Avenue on the south. As volunteers and draftees arrived, rough but serviceable barracks buildings were quickly constructed by civilian carpenters. The headquarters area contained buildings for the camp staff—two for the commandant, three for quartermaster's stores, and a stable. An arsenal was located in the center of the camp. Other structures included a guardhouse and a chapel. A camp of discharge for more than 11,000 troops at the end of the war, Camp Cleveland was closed during the month of September 1865.

CAMP COLERAIN. Originally a Methodist camp meeting ground located on the Colerain Pike 11 miles from Cincinnati, Camp Colerain was a temporary Civil War encampment where Hamilton County men enlisted in Kentucky (Union) regiments.

COLUMBUS ARSENAL. FORT HAYES.

COLUMBUS BARRACKS. FORT HAYES.

CAMP CORWIN. Probably named in honor of Thomas Corwin, governor of Ohio in 1840–42 and Minister to Mexico under President Lincoln, Camp Corwin was established in August 1861 on a hill two and one-half miles east of Dayton, Montgomery County. Here several companies of men drilled during the early days of the Civil War. The camp was discontinued after a short period of use.

CAMP (DICK) CORWINE. A Civil War encampment named for Major Richard M. Corwine who was in charge of river defense during the "siege of Cincinnati" in 1862, Camp Corwine was apparently a garrisoned fortification overlooking the Ohio River along Fort View Place on Cincinnati's waterfront.

FORT DEFIANCE. When General Anthony Wayne and his army arrived at the junction of the Maumee and Auglaize rivers, the site of today's city of Defiance, in mid-August 1794, he laid out the lines for a new fort to be situated on a height overlooking the confluence of the two rivers. Fort Defiance was so named by Wayne apparently as a gesture of defiance against the

Indians of the Northwest Territory and their friends the British. The defense was a parallelogram in outline, with a 22-foot-square blockhouse, also serving as barracks, at each of its four angles. The blockhouses had an embrasure in each of the three outside walls for a howitzer and a fireplace and chimney inside. The 60-foot curtains were composed of 15-foot-long pickets that were 1 foot thick. A picket ravelin projected onto the point formed by the converging rivers. This was the limit of construction when Wayne and his army left the site and advanced to the Miami towns and the Battle of Fallen Timbers near the present-day city of Toledo.

When Wayne and his men returned to Fort Defiance after their victory, he ordered the fort strengthened against artillery fire. The improvements included a dry ditch 14 to 16 feet wide and 8 feet deep on all sides excepting the riverfront, and large gabions were emplaced around the curtains of the fort. A pulley-operated drawbridge was constructed to allow passage over the ditch for one entrance and a 4-foot-wide earthen bank was thrown up for the opposite gate. During this period, the officers' quarters and two storehouses were completed. The fort was apparently abandoned at the end of 1797. When General William Henry Harrison arrived there in 1813, he found Fort Defiance in ruins and built a new fort, Fort Winchester, 80 yards from Wayne's fort.

CAMP DELAWARE. A Civil War encampment, Camp Delaware was established in the summer of 1862 for the organization of companies F and G, 96th Infantry, on a farm one and a half miles south of the city of Delaware, the ground occupied lying between the Columbus Road and the river. On September 1, 1862, the 96th units left camp for Cincinnati. The 5th Colored Infantry was organized here in 1863. In June of the same year, another camp for colored soldiers was opened on farmland about a mile south of the city and nearly opposite the first encampment. Camp Delaware was in operation until at least the summer of 1864.

CAMP DENNISON. The largest Civil War encampment in Ohio, Camp Dennison was established as an induction and training center about 18 miles northeast of Cincinnati near the town of Milford (known also as New Germany) and named for Ohio Governor William Dennison. The stone house of Christian Waldschmidt (1804) on Milford Road served as the camp's headquarters.

During the summer of 1863, the state was shaken by the most serious threat of invasion by the Confederates. On the night of July 13, Kentucky cavalry leader General John H. Morgan's raiders slipped through the northern suburbs of Cincinnati without opposition, despite some 40,000 Union troops deployed at various points across Ohio to search for him. The Confederates halted to feed their horses within sight of Camp Dennison. A running fight day and night followed, with Federal troops pursuing the raiders across more than a dozen counties, finally to the environs of the town of West Point, where Morgan surrendered. At Buffington Island near Portland on the Ohio River, there was a pitched battle where today stands the battlefield monument. Another monument marks the site of Morgan's final surrender.

CAMP DENNISON. A temporary Civil War encampment named for Ohio Governor William Dennison, it was established in 1861 for the 16th Infantry near the town of Wooster in Wayne County.

FORT DEPOSIT. Located on the left or north bank of the Maumee River, near present-day Waterville, Lucas County, Fort Deposit was a temporary establishment erected by General Anthony Wayne to store the excess baggage the troops of his Legion carried. The fort consisted of three rectangular enclosures with corner bastions in various combinations. The works averaged 7 feet in height, and the largest of the three enclosures was approximately 650 by 360 yards. Small breastworks outside the enclosed structures functioned as guard posts. Fort Deposit was abandoned shortly after the Battle of Fallen Timbers.

FORT DILLIE. This was a strong blockhouse erected sometime between 1790 and 1793 during the Ohio Indian wars on the west side of the Ohio River, opposite the mouth of Grave Creek in what is now Belmont County. Built by the area's early settlers, it was the scene of a desperate struggle fought about 250 yards below the fort. Fort Dillie was abandoned soon after the signing of the Greene Ville Treaty in 1795.

CAMP FAIRGROUNDS. A temporary Civil War encampment established on Fairfield County's fairgrounds near Lancaster.

FARMERS CASTLE. Located opposite Backus Island at the settlement of Belpre on the Ohio River in what is now Washington County, and about 10 miles downstream from Marietta, Farmers Castle was built about 1791 or 1792 with the cost of its construction paid for by the Ohio Company. The settlement had a total population of 220 people, of which 70 were able-bodied men. The fortification consisted of 13 houses in two rows parallel with the riverfront. A palisaded complex with two-story blockhouses in the angles, Farmers Castle's only piece of armament was a small swivel gun, which was fired occasionally to impress any hostile Indians who might be watching the settlement. The Treaty of Greene Ville of 1795 ended the Indian war. The usefulness of Farmers Castle as a fort ended shortly thereafter.

FORT FERREE. This War of 1812 fortification was built by the right wing of General William Henry Harrison's army in the fall of 1812. General Robert Crooks, who commanded a Pennsylvania detachment here, erected a stockade of split and round timbers enclosing a spring, with blockhouses at all four corners as well as a barracks and other defenses. The town of Upper Sandusky, which ultimately became the county seat of Wyandot County, was established on the fort site, today located in the yard of the Wyandot County Courthouse.

FORT FINDLAY. A temporary War of 1812 fortification, it was erected in June 1812 on the south bank of Blanchard's Fork by Colonel James Findlay of Cincinnati. It was a stockade about 50 yards square, with blockhouses in all its angles and a ditch in front. Fort Findlay served as a depot for military supplies for General William Hull's army en route to Detroit. The fort was abandoned in 1815 after the end of the war. The city of Findlay, county seat of Hancock County, occupies the site.

FORT FINNEY. In late September 1785, a company of Pennsylvania troops commanded by Captain Walter Finney was dispatched along the Ohio River to the mouth of the Miami River near which, in November, he built a temporary fort named for himself on the north bank of the Ohio. It was located close to the Indiana state line, six miles from the present town of Cleves in Hamilton County. On January 31, 1786, a treaty was finally consummated with the Delaware, Wyandot, and the reluctant Shawnee, by which the Indians ceded two-thirds of Ohio to the government. In August 1786 the post was evacuated, and Finney and his troops moved down the river to the Falls of the Ohio, at present-day Louisville, Kentucky, where a second Fort Finney was established and garrisoned until about 1793.

FORT FRYE. After the Big Bottom massacre on the Muskingum River, 30 miles north of Marietta, in early January 1791, a detachment of men under Lieutenant Joseph Frye (who had served as drummer boy during the Battle of Bunker Hill) arrived and erected a triangular stockade with a two-story blockhouse in each of the three angles. The fort was located on the east bank of the Muskingum near Beverly in Washington County. Subsequent attacks by the Delaware and the Wyandot were successfully repulsed by the fort's defenders with the loss only of a few cattle. Across the river stood Fort Tyler, a blockhouse erected in 1789. Fort Frye, abandoned in 1796 or soon thereafter when a peace had been assured with the warring tribes, was gradually dismantled and its salvageable materials used in the construction of new homes up and down the river.

CAMP GARRINGTON. Its site located on present U.S. 35 and S.R. 7 at Gallipolis, Gallia County, Camp Garrington was an early Civil War camp established for the first mustering of Ohio troops for service in the early western Virginia campaigns. A hospital was later built here, at one time housing as many as 4,000 wounded soldiers.

CAMP GIDDINGS. A temporary Civil War encampment located on the grounds of the County Agricultural Society at Jefferson in Ashtabula County, Camp Giddings was established in August 1861 and named in honor of Joshua R. Giddings, U.S. senator and consul to Canada, who procured an order from the War Department for the enlistment and organization of a regiment from northeast Ohio. The 29th Ohio Infantry was organized on August 11 and went into camp on August 19. By December 1, the regiment was fully organized, and on Christmas Day morning the regiment left Camp Giddings, via Ashtabula, for Camp Chase near Columbus.

CAMP GODDARD. A temporary Civil War encampment located near the city of Columbus, it was named for Colonel (later General) C. B. Goddard of the Ohio Militia, who commanded a regiment here.

CAMP GODDARD. Janesville in Muskingum County had two military camps during the Civil War for the mobilizing of state troops. Camp Goddard was established on the grounds of the Muskingum County Agricultural Society and named for Colonel (later General) C. B. Goddard of the Ohio Militia. The 62nd, 116th, and

159th Ohio Volunteer Infantry Regiments assembled here. The site of the camp is now the Muskingum County Fair Grounds.

FORT GOWER. Located at the confluence of the Ohio and Hocking rivers at present-day Hockingport in Athens County, Fort Gower, named for Earl Gower, was a short-lived log blockhouse erected in the fall of 1774 by Lord John Murray Dunmore as a depot for supplies while he and his small militia army were en route to pacify the Shawnee and Mingoes of the upper Ohio Valley. On October 31, after a month of harassment activity, Dunmore forced a treaty upon the Shawnee leaders. What Dunmore lacked in military skill and scruples was provided from the ranks by such men as Daniel Boone, Daniel Morgan, George Rogers Clark, and others who played major roles in later frontier history.

FORT GREENE VILLE. By the far the largest and most imposing fortification in the Northwest Territory, Fort Greene Ville was erected in the fall and winter of 1793–94 by General Anthony Wayne and the troops of his Legion on the present site of the city of Greenville in Darke County. Wayne "created, in effect, a town within walls that he named after his compatriot of the Revolutionary War, Nathanael Greene" (David A. Simmons, *The Forts of Anthony Wayne* [1977], pp. 12–13). Laid out in the configuration of a small modern city, bordered on the north by Greenville and Mud Creeks, the fort was roughly a 50-acre rectangle, about 1,800 feet long and 900 feet wide. The 10-foot-high palisades, a mile and a quarter long, were loopholed with a 2-foot-high banquette. The fort's four bastions, with sentry boxes at their salient angles, occupied the corners of the rectangle while single-story blockhouses were built near the center of each wall.

The huts for the enlisted men were arranged in two rows around the exterior walls. They were log structures measuring approximately fourteen by seventeen feet with clapboard roofs and chimneys that were "raised considerable above the tops of the roofs" to prevent a potentially disastrous fire in an all wooden fort. One log hut held about ten men. Bakehouses, stables, guardhouses, and officers' huts were also erected for each of the four Sub Legions.

Carrying the urban analogy further, the interior was divided into eight sections that from an overhead perspective had the appearance of city blocks. The sections held buildings for General Wayne, the brigadier generals, the lieutenant colonels commanding the Sub Legions, the laboratory (for ammunition manufacturing) and powder magazine, the hospital stores, the contractors, Quarter Master General and other staff officers of the Legion. Both Generals Wayne and Wilkinson were known to have had "a house" constructed for their use. Wayne's house was used as a council house during the treaty negotiations. "Parades" or drill grounds were cleared in several of these sections by cutting the tree stumps "lower than the surface of the ground." It was Wayne's practice to erect small outposts or "redoubts" around his encampment for protection while the main fortifications were being built. At Greene Ville, eight redoubts were built consisting of picket walls with a banquette and loopholes that surrounded a one-story blockhouse. [David A. Simmons, *The Forts of Anthony Wayne* (1977), p. 13]

Eighteen months later, in August 1795, at this fort, the chiefs of the various Old Northwest tribes assembled to surrender 20 million acres of their tribal lands to the government. Eight months after the historic signing of the Treaty of Greene Ville, the fort was abandoned, its garrison withdrawn in the spring of 1796. In the fall of the same year, avid settlers swarmed into the valley, dismantled the fort, and burned the remainder to salvage the nails and iron hinges for their new homesteads, leaving but a few barracks to gradually disintegrate within the blackened palisades.

CAMP GURLEY. A temporary Civil War encampment named in honor of John A. Gurley, congressman from Cincinnati, Camp Gurley was located near the city. The 4th Ohio Cavalry, recruited in Cincinnati and Hamilton County, was stationed at the camp before transferring to Camp Dennison.

FORT HAMILTON. After General Harmar's ignominious defeat in the autumn of 1790, the campaign against the hostile Indian tribes in the Northwest Territory was renewed the following year by General Arthur St. Clair. He established Fort Hamilton in September 1791 on the east bank of the Miami River, 35 miles north of Cincinnati, at the present-day city of Hamilton in Butler County. A strongly fortified stockade, the fort was one of the chain of defenses planned by St. Clair along the line of communications identical to that established two years later by Anthony Wayne.

Fort Hamilton was a rectangular, 15-to-20-foot-high double-palisaded, ditched work with a banquette or firing step built around the interior of the curtains. Two of the four-sided bastions in each angle had artillery platforms with embrasures fitted with shutters. Blockhouses, probably two-storied, were later erected within the other two bastions and used as storehouses. Log-built barracks with lean-to type roofs lined three sides of the interior curtains; a single-story frame officers' quarters stood in the northern part of the fort. Fort Hamilton, having outlived its usefulness, was abandoned late in 1796 or early 1797.

FORT HARMAR. In September 1785, in response to authorization by Congress, a pentagonal, star-shaped, log-built stockade was built on the north side of the Ohio River near the mouth of the Muskingum River at present-day Marietta. Fort Harmar, named for General Josiah Harmar, was erected by U.S. troops, artillery and infantry, under Captains John Doughty and Jonathan Heart. It was not intended as an Indian defense but to keep squatters off Indian lands and hold back white settlement until the vast territory could be surveyed and offered for sale.

Enclosing about three-fourths of an acre, the 120-foot-long walls of Fort Harmar were constructed of large timbers laid horizontally to a height of 12 or 14 feet. At each of the five corners, instead of the usual blockhouses, were pentagonal bastions mounted with cannon. The enlisted men's barracks, divided into 30-foot-long rooms and furnished with fireplaces, extended along the main walls. The officers' quarters were within the bastions. The fort was occupied by U.S. troops until September 1790, when they were ordered to Fort Washington at Cincinnati.

CAMP HARRISON. A Civil War encampment, probably temporary, Camp Harrison was established at the Cincinnati Trotting Park, six miles north of the city, as a camp of instruction.

FORT HAYES (*Columbus Arsenal; Columbus Barracks*). Columbus Arsenal, established in 1861, with the addition of a shot tower erected in 1864, and used as a munitions depot, was renamed Columbus Barracks in 1875 when the arsenal was transferred to the General Recruiting Service. The barracks were substantially expanded and became important as an induction center in the two world wars and the Korean War. In 1922 Columbus Barracks was redesignated Fort Hayes in honor of President Rutherford B. Hayes. The post was discontinued sometime in the late 1960s.

CAMP HOBSON'S CHOICE. This was a temporary camp established by General Anthony Wayne on the east side of Mill Creek where it joins the Ohio River at Cincinnati to accommodate the overflow of his troops at Fort Washington.

FORT HUNTINGTON. A small, temporary War of 1812 fortification was erected at Cleveland in May 1813 by troops under Captain Stanton Sholes. Situated about 50 yards from the shore of Lake Erie, near today's Seneca Street, the post was named Fort Huntington in honor of Ohio's ex-governor.

HURON BLOCKHOUSE. When the first rumblings of war with Great Britain became prevalent in 1811 in the town of Huron in Erie County, 30 men were congregated, enlisted as the Huron Rangers, and built a blockhouse near the shore of the lake. Captain Joshua Cotton commanded Huron Blockhouse's garrison throughout the War of 1812.

CAMP HUTCHINS. A temporary Civil War encampment, Camp Hutchins was established in October 1861 near the town of Warren in Trumbull County, for the organization and training of the 6th Ohio Cavalry, originally recruited by the Hon. John Hutchins. After receiving three months of training, the cavalry troop was ordered to move to Camp Chase near Columbus in January 1862, thus discontinuing Camp Hutchins.

FORT INDUSTRY. A small, short-lived fortification, Fort Industry was erected in 1794 by a detachment of General Anthony Wayne's army after its victory in the Battle of Fallen Timbers, fought several miles southwest of present-day Toledo. It stood on a bluff on the left bank of the Maumee River, a few miles from its mouth, in what is now the city of Toledo. The site of the fort is located at the corner of Monroe and Summit streets. The origin of the fort's name is not known. No mention is made of Fort Industry, either in official reports or General Wayne's diary of the Northwest Territory campaign.

CAMP JACKSON. A briefly occupied Civil War rendezvous for recruits established in April 1861, it was "a hastily improvised camp in the woods beyond the railroad depot" at Columbus and named Camp Jackson by Governor William Dennison. During the last week of May, Camp Jackson's barracks were dismantled so that they could be moved to a new camp four miles west of the city. The new 160-acre encampment, under national control, began to be occupied about June 1. It was named Camp Jackson until June 20, after which date it was known as Camp Chase. Later a prisoner of war camp, it was located on present Sullivant Avenue west of Powell, within today's city limits of Columbus. (See: CAMP CHASE.)

FORT JEFFERSON. Now occupied by Fort Jefferson State Park in the present town of Fort Jefferson on S.R. 121 in Darke County, several miles directly south of historic Greenville, the site is where General Arthur St. Clair built Fort Jefferson in October 1791 after his disastrous battle with Chief Little Turtle's large Indian force. St. Clair's army suffered some 900 casualties, which was more than General Washington lost in any of his Revolutionary War battles. A square palisaded work, with 114-foot-long sides, and a bastion in each of its angles, Fort Jefferson was strengthened in the summer of 1792 by the addition of a pair of two-storied blockhouses outside the walls. The fort was abandoned in the fall of 1796. "In the 1930s, an archaeological exploration revealed an underground powder magazine measuring eight feet square and twenty-five feet deep. . . . Two tunnels were discovered: an eighty-foot shaft connected the magazine to the interior of the fort and another led to a spring on the southwestern slope" (David A. Simmons, *The Forts of Anthony Wayne* [1977], pp. 10–11).

FORT JENNINGS. This fort was erected in September 1812 by Colonel William Jennings, by order of General William Henry Harrison, on the site of the present town of Fort Jennings on the Auglaize River in the southwestern corner of Putnam County.

CAMP JEWETT. CAMP WOOL.

CAMP JOHN MCLEAN. A temporary Civil War encampment located at or near Cincinnati, this training camp was named for Judge John McLean and occupied by the 75th Ohio Infantry commanded by Colonel N. C. McLean, a son of the justice.

JOHNSON'S ISLAND PRISON CAMP. The largest Confederate cemetery in Ohio is located on Johnson's Island in Sandusky Bay. In 1861 the U.S. government leased this 300-acre island for a prison camp for Confederate officers captured by Union forces. Throughout the Civil War, a total of some 15,000 Confederate prisoners of war were confined on the island. In the fall of 1864, a conspiracy was concocted to release the prisoners, numbering about 2,500 at the time. The plan was to arm them, burn Sandusky, Cleveland, and other Lake Erie cities. The captain of the only U.S. warship in the Great Lakes, the *Michigan*, captured the conspirators at Sandusky who were to relay the signal to the raiders on boats in the bay. The capture foiled the raid, and the Confederate raiders escaped to Canada.

FORT JUNANDOT. FORT SANDUSKY.

KIRKWOOD'S BLOCKHOUSE. Its site in the present-day town of Bridgeport in Belmont County, across the Ohio River from Wheeling, West Virginia, Kirkwood's Blockhouse was a strong frontier post erected in 1779–81 by a Captain Robert Kirkwood, a Delaware officer in the Continental Army. It is not known when the defense was abandoned.

FORT LA DEMOISELLE. FORT PICKAWILLANY.

CAMP LATTY. A temporary Civil War recruitment and training center at Napoleon in Henry County, Camp Latty was established in 1861, occupying probably both public buildings and adjoining property owned by the Latty family, for the purpose of organizing the 68th Ohio Volunteer Infantry consisting of volunteers and conscripts from several northwestern Ohio counties. The camp was named for Judge Alexander Latty, who was instrumental in establishing the camp. When the 68th Infantry was moved to Camp Chase at Columbus on January 21, 1862, Camp Latty was apparently discontinued.

FORT LAURENS. The only Revolutionary War fort built in Ohio, its site now incorporated within 82-acre Fort Laurens State Park, short-lived Fort Laurens was erected in the fall of 1778 by General Lachlan McIntosh, commandant of Fort Pitt, on the west bank of the Tuscarawas River, a half-mile south of present-day Bolivar in Tuscarawas County. The general named the defense in honor of his friend Henry Laurens, president of the Continental Congress. When the fort was completed on December 9, it was garrisoned by 150 men under Colonel John Gibson. Continuously under siege and attack by Indians throughout the winter, with a number of its defenders killed, the beleaguered fort, near starvation, was finally relieved by a force of 500 men under General McIntosh. The octagonal-shaped, log-built fort, occupying about an acre of ground, was abandoned on August 2, 1779, after it was considered to be totally untenable. In 1972 after 194 years, the burial ground of at least 23 Revolutionary War soldiers was discovered 200 feet west of the original gate of Fort Laurens by archaeologists in the employ of the Ohio Historical Society.

CAMP LEWIS. Located in Pickaway County, southeast of the present site of Circleville, Camp

Lewis was established during Lord Dunmore's campaign of 1774 to attack Indian villages in the Northwest Territory. The temporary post was named for General Andrew Lewis, who fought under Lord Dunmore.

CAMP LEW WALLACE. A temporary Civil War encampment named for Lewis Wallace, Union general and author of the classic *Ben Hur*, it was established in early 1862 northwest of Columbus and discontinued by the end of the same year.

CAMP LIMA. A temporary Civil War encampment, Camp Lima was located at or near the town of Lima in Allen County.

CAMP LOGAN. A temporary Civil War encampment established near Chillicothe, Ross County, Camp Logan was located on the site of the War of 1812 Camp Bull.

CAMP LUCAS. A temporary Civil War encampment occupied July and August 1861, Camp Lucas was located on the old Olive Branch fairground in Batavia Township, Clermont County. Organized at Camp Lucas, the 34th Ohio Volunteer Infantry (the 1st Zouave Regiment) by September 1 was moved to Camp Dennison near Cincinnati.

CAMP MCARTHUR. A temporary Civil War rendezvous and recruiting encampment, Camp McArthur was located at or near Urbana in Champaign County.

FORT MCARTHUR. A War of 1812 fortification erected in midJune 1812, during General William Hull's campaign to take Detroit and ultimate disgraceful defeat there, Fort McArthur was established on the Scioto River about three miles west of present-day Kenton in Hardin County and named for Colonel Duncan McArthur, who had it built under his direction. Occupying about a half-acre of ground, the palisaded fort, commanded by Captain Robert McClelland, enclosed log-built huts for the soldiers and was reinforced by blockhouses in the northwest and southeast angles. The fort was abandoned after the end of the war.

CAMP MCCLELLAN. A temporary Civil War encampment located at or near Marietta in Washington County.

CAMP MANSFIELD. Established in July 1862 at Mansfield, Richland County, for the recruitment and training of soldiers for the 102nd Ohio Volunteer Infantry, Camp Mansfield was discontinued by December of the same year when the regiment left.

MANSFIELD BLOCKHOUSE. This frontier War of 1812 fortification in South Park in downtown Mansfield, Richland County, was built in the fall of 1812. A military garrison occupied it after the Battle of the Thames in Canada, where the great Shawnee chief Tecumseh was killed.

MASSIE'S STATION. In early 1791 Nathaniel Massie founded a settlement along the Ohio River, some 12 miles above the present town of Maysville, Kentucky, then called Limestone. By the middle of March, it was enclosed with pickets, with blockhouses at each angle. The town was laid out into lots and the name changed from "Massie's Station" to Manchester in later-established Adams County. This was the first settlement in what was known as the Virginia Military District and the fourth in Ohio, with Marietta, Cincinnati, and Gallipolis being older.

CAMP MASSILLON. A temporary Civil War encampment, Camp Massillon probably occupied a tract along the Tuscarawas River, at or near the city of Massillon in Stark County.

CAMP MEIGS. A temporary Civil War encampment established for the organization of the 51st Ohio Infantry from September 17 to October 26, 1861, Camp Meigs was located near the city of Dover in Tuscarawas County.

FORT MEIGS. Two victories on land and one on an inland sea assured the future of Ohio during the second year of the War of 1812. The three-year-long conflict had its major action in Ohio between May and September 1813. Here, in May and again in July 1813, the large strongly built fort and its garrison of regulars and militiamen withstood sieges by a force of British regulars, Canadian militiamen, and Indians. Very soon after the second siege was lifted, the Americans defended themselves admirably against the same enemy force at Fort Stephenson at present-day Fremont, and in September an American armada captured the British fleet in the Battle of Lake Erie.

The strategic location for Fort Meigs was chosen by General William Henry Harrison as a supply depot and base of operations because its site on the bluff on the right bank of the Maumee River, opposite the rapids, commanded the principal land route to Canada. The fort, built during the winter of 1812–13 and named in honor of then Governor Return J. Meigs, was large enough to accommodate 2,500 men and immense quantities of supplies. After the signing of the peace treaty in 1815, Fort Meigs was abandoned. An interpretation of the entire period and Ohio's significant participation during the war constitutes the main emphasis of the re-creation of nine-acre Fort Meigs at Perrysburg near Toledo by the Ohio Historical Society, completed in the mid-1970s.

FORT MIAMIS. The old abandoned French trading post of Fort Miamis, located on the left bank of the Maumee River, 15 miles from its mouth, at the present-day city of Maumee in Lucas County, was completely rebuilt in 1785 by the British as an outpost for their strongly entrenched position at Detroit. In 1794, at the time of General Anthony Wayne's victory at the Battle of Fallen Timbers near Toledo, the fort was commanded by Major William Campbell. After the British evacuated the fort following the Treaty of Greene Ville, American troops took possession on July 11, 1796, but abandoned it in 1797. During the War of 1812, the British reoccupied the fort for a time. After the war, Fort Miamis reverted to a trading post while the Maumee Valley was being rapidly settled by American homesteaders.

CAMP MILLARD. A World War II railroad battalion training center for the Transportation Corps, Camp Millard was located near Bucyrus in Crawford County. In a press release, dated September 19, 1945, the War Department declared the leased 249-acre camp surplus property as of October 1, 1945.

CAMP MONROE. Reportedly a temporary Civil War encampment located near the city of Cincinnati.

CAMP MONROEVILLE. A temporary Civil War encampment, Camp Monroeville in Huron County was established in 1861 for the organization of the 123rd Ohio Volunteer Infantry.

CAMP MORDECAI BARTLEY. A temporary Civil War encampment located at or near the city of Mansfield, Richland County.

CAMP MORROW. A temporary Civil War encampment established in 1861 for the organization of the 33rd and 56th Ohio Volunteer Infantry Regiments, Camp Morrow was located near Portsmouth in Scioto County. Originally established on ground soon considered too low for drainage and health reasons, the camp was relocated on January 20, 1862, to the Renshaw Place, a short distance north, just outside Portsmouth's city limits.

FORT MORROW. A War of 1812 outpost on the Greenville (Greene Ville) Treaty Line, Fort Morrow was located in the Delaware Reservoir area of northern Delaware and southern Marion counties. Nothing remains of the half-acre fort within sight of the old Military Road by which more than 10,000 troops and supplies moved northward to forts and battle areas. A single marker on S.R. 229 east simply states: "Fort Morrow. A stockade fort built by Capt. Taylor about 1812, and a place of common refuge for the pioneers during many Indian attacks." At the site are the graves of 13 unknown and several known veterans of the war. When Nathaniel Wyatt, Sr., and his family settled in the area in 1806, they were the first white residents of present Marion County. On 200 acres in present Waldo Township (then part of Franklin County), Wyatt built a two-story brick tavern, 20 by 36 feet, before the war. Sometime during 1812 or 1813, Fort Morrow was erected. A palisaded enclosure, it contained two two-story blockhouses and the tavern, defended by one cannon.

FORT NECESSITY. En route during its campaign to take Detroit from its British occupants, General William Hull's army, between June 11 and June 19, 1812, advanced from Urbana to the banks of the Scioto River where Fort McArthur was hastily erected. From here a detachment was sent ahead to continue the road building, "but heavy rains having rendered the morasses along the Blanchard River almost impassable, another encampment was made, with stockade and blockhouses, named Fort Necessity, near the south line of Hancock County," in present Hardin County (*Echoes* 12, no. 7 [1973], p. 2).

FORT NESBIT(T). Built in 1813 by troops commanded by Captain Nesbit(t), this blockhouse, reportedly used as a military supply station during the War of 1812, was erected at about the same time as Fort Black, about four miles to the northeast. The fort stood in the extreme southwest corner of Darke County.

CAMP NOBLE. A temporary Civil War encampment located at or near the town of Tiffin in Seneca County.

FORT PICKAWILLANY (*Fort La Demoiselle*). This was the palisaded trading post of Pickawillany, or Picktown, established in 1748 by the English among the Miami. Situated at the junction of the Great Miami River and Loramie's Creek, three miles north of Piqua, Tecumseh's birthplace (1768), in Miami County, it was raided on June 21, 1752, by Charles Langlade with 200 French and Indians from Detroit. After several hours of fighting, the fort surrendered and was burned. One English trader and five Indians were killed, including Miami chieftain La Demoiselle, for whom the fort was alternately named by the English because of his fidelity.

CAMP PIQUA. A temporary Civil War encampment located on the east side of present-day S.R. 66, just northwest of Piqua, Miami County, Camp Piqua was used as a drill ground for newly mustered-in recruits.

FORT PIQUA. A small stockade built as a depot by General Anthony Wayne's army in 1794, Fort Piqua was located about three miles north of Piqua and garrisoned by troops commanded by Captain J. N. Vischer. The post may have been built on the site of Fort Piqua, erected by the French in 1752 after their destruction of Fort Pickawillany, the English trading post. Fort Piqua was abandoned in 1795 after the signing of the Treaty of Greene Ville.

FORT PORTAGE. General William Hull, during his campaign to take British-occupied Detroit in 1812, built this temporary stockade for the sick and disabled soldiers of his command. It was located on the right or south bank of the North Branch of the Portage River, about 250 yards west of the Dixie Highway (U.S. 25), near the city of Portage in Wood County. Since it was not built for defense, the stockade was minimally fortified.

CAMP PORTSMOUTH. A temporary Civil War encampment, known as Camp Portsmouth, was reportedly located on the outskirts of the city of Portsmouth, Scioto County.

CAMP PUTNAM. The first Civil War encampment located at Marietta was Camp Putnam, established during the last week of April 1861 on the old fairgrounds in the outskirts of the city. It was named for General Rufus Putnam of Revolutionary War fame. The 1st Light Artillery Regiment, consisting of six companies, with six guns, arrived from Cleveland in compliance with orders of the governor and occupied the camp on April 23. These were the first troops to arrive in Washington County. The next was the 14th Volunteer Militia Regiment, followed by the 18th Regiment on its way to Virginia. Camp Putnam operated until at least October 1862.

RAVENNA ARSENAL. This arsenal located at Ravenna in Portage County was inactivated in June 1962. The arsenal's munitions storage capability was placed in "mothball" status.

FORT RECOVERY. While his army was spending the winter of 1793–94 at Fort Greene Ville, General Anthony Wayne dispatched Major Henry Burbeck 23 miles to the north with a detachment of troops to construct a fort on the site of General Arthur St. Clair's disastrous defeat in 1791, at the present town of Fort Recovery in Mercer County. Wayne finally called the post Fort Recovery after considering other designations. Major Burbeck in late December 1793 constructed a rectangular palisaded fortification with blockhouses in the form of bastions in all four angles. The 20-foot-square blockhouses were originally single-storied. The fort's commandant, Captain Alexander Gibson, later added a projecting second story on each blockhouse, and cupolas were apparently built on the roofs for lookout posts. Fort Recovery was abandoned in 1796. The state of Ohio, under the auspices of the Ohio Historical Society, reconstructed Fort Recovery one-third its original size on a nine-acre site on S.R. 49. It consists of two blockhouses (one a museum) enclosed within a palisade.

FORT ST. CLAIR. The forts and battle sites of the Indian Wars serve as evidence of the military efforts that were necessary before the Old Northwest could be opened to American settlement. Indian resistance to American occupation of the land north and west of the Ohio River centered at the Miami Indian villages at the head of the Maumee River. Located here was Kekionga, the present site of Fort Wayne, Indiana, and it was this Indian village that was the objective of three major expeditions, all of which started from Fort Washington at Cincinnati.

Two of the expeditions moved through Preble County. In 1791 General Arthur St. Clair took a more direct route than General Josiah Harmar had taken. Moving along the tributaries of the Great Miami River, he arrived at the Wabash, at the present site of Fort Recovery. Here, on November 4, he was decisively defeated by the Indians under Little Turtle. Two years later, General Anthony Wayne followed St. Clair's route through Preble County, but continued to the Auglaize

River and then marched down that stream to the Maumee and to victory at Fallen Timbers.

Fort St. Clair, one in a line of small supply forts, was constructed in 1791–92 by order of General James Wilkinson and named in honor of General St. Clair, who was still governor of the territory. The fort, about a mile north of the present-day town of Eaton, was built primarily as a protection for the army supply line between Fort Hamilton to the south and Fort Jefferson to the north. A small garrison was stationed there. The only major action at the fort involved one of militia convoys on November 6, 1792. At dawn Chief Little Turtle and a band of warriors swept in upon the camp in a surprise attack. A fierce battle took place with first one side and then the other gaining the advantage. The militia finally found refuge in the fort when the ammunition gave out. When they returned to the fray, they found the Indians gone, along with most of the pack horses—a major loss for the Americans. Fort St. Clair State Memorial, established in 1923, occupies an 89-acre tract and is located immediately west of Eaton on S.R. 122 and 355.

FORT ST. MARYS. FORT BARBEE.

FORT SANDUSKY (*Fort Junandot; Fort Wyandot*). A fortified English fur-trading post erected in 1745 on the north side of Sandusky Bay, on the south shore of Lake Erie, several miles west of present-day Sandusky in Erie County, it was captured by the French in 1751, who then built Fort Sandusky on the site. It was evacuated in 1754 when the French moved to a new fort, Junandot (Fort Wyandot) on the east side of the Sandusky River at present-day Bay View. This fort was in turn abandoned after the fall of Fort Duquesne at Pittsburgh. In 1761 the British constructed a blockhouse on the site of the original Fort Sanduski. It was captured and destroyed on May 16, 1763, during Pontiac's rebellion, and its garrison was massacred.

FORT SENECA. A temporary War of 1812 post, Fort Seneca was erected in 1813 by a detachment of General William Henry Harrison's army as a supply depot. A large stockade occupying several acres, it stood on the right bank of the Sandusky River, on the site of the present village of Old Fort, nine miles from the city of Tiffin in Seneca County.

CAMP SHERMAN. A World War I post, Camp Sherman was located near Chillicothe and garrisoned in the spring of 1917 by the 83rd Division. It was named in honor of General William Tecumseh Sherman of Civil War fame, in compliance with General Orders No. 95, War Department, July 18, 1917. Camp Sherman was abandoned in 1921.

FORT STEPHENSON. An American War of 1812 fortification on the west side of the Sandusky River, on the site of the present city of Fremont, Fort Stephenson was a strongly constructed rectangular blockhouse complex, occupying about an acre of ground and surrounded by high palisades and a deep ditch. Here 21-year-old Major George Croghan, nephew of George Rogers Clark, in command of a 160-man garrison, on August 2, 1813, successfully defended the fort against attacks by a British force of about 500 regulars and 800 Indians under General Henry Proctor.

On August 1 the enemy came up the river and appeared before the fort. After Croghan's indignant refusal to surrender the post, British gunboats in the river, armed with five 6-pounders, bombarded Fort Stephenson all night but inflicted only superficial damage. The next day they attempted to take it by frontal assaults. Croghan's only piece of ordnance was a six-pounder, which he moved from port to port, firing in different directions. The gun was repeatedly loaded with grapeshot and fired point-blank into the massed enemy. Finally, Proctor's troops and Indians broke and retreated in disgrace to Malden. This was the British general's last invasion of American territory. Major Croghan became a national celebrity, Congress presented him with a gold medal, and promoted him to lieutenant colonel. The site of Fort Stephenson is in Fremont's Birchard Liberty Park. In the northwest corner of the park is Colonel Croghan's grave and nearby is "Old Betsy," his famous cannon.

FORT STEUBEN. Four stone posts are reminders today of a fort that once stood along the Ohio River, which was named in honor of the Revolutionary War drillmaster, Major General Friedrich Wilhelm August Baron von Steuben. The site of Fort Steuben is just north of Adams Street along the west side of S.R. 7 in Steubenville. The four stone markers indicate where the blockhouses had stood from 1787–94. The story of Fort Steuben began in May 1785, when the Continental Congress enacted the Northwest Land Ordinance of 1785, a law that provided for a survey of federal lands west of the Ohio River. When the survey was initiated in September 1785, Thomas Hutchins, the chief surveyor, was immediately confronted by rumors of Indian unrest. After surveying only four miles of the base line, he suspended operations and returned to New York.

When Hutchins returned to Ohio in 1786, Congress assigned about 150 soldiers under the command of a Major Hamtramck to protect the surveying parties. Sometime between July 21 and mid-September, he selected a site for a fort to house his troops and to serve as a base camp for the surveying party. The only detailed description of the fort is contained in a drawing and notes made by Major Erkuries Beatty in the spring of 1787 when he visited the fort on an inspection trip. His notes indicate that it was a log structure located some 300 feet from the Ohio River. The fort was basically square with blockhouses set diagonally at each of the corners. Within the confines of the fort, eight structures are shown, excluding blockhouses that served as the enlisted men's barracks. Hamtramck, who had served as an aide to Von Steuben during the Revolution, probably selected the name for the post.

Although the garrison at Fort Steuben was withdrawn in late 1787 when the first phase of the survey ended, the fort stood until 1794, when it was dismantled after having been partially destroyed by fire. In its short history, the fort provided a nucleus for the settlement that later became Steubenville.

CAMP STEUBENVILLE. A temporary Civil War encampment located at or near the town of Steubenville in Jefferson County.

CAMP TAYLOR. A large temporary Civil War encampment situated east of the Cuyahoga River on the outskirts of the city of Cleveland, Camp Taylor was located on the fairgrounds of the Cuyahoga County Agricultural Society on Kinsman Street and established on April 22, 1861. The site today corresponds with East 30th Street and Woodland Avenue, the present location of Cuyahoga County College, Metropolitan Campus. Here four regiments—the 7th, 8th, 14th, and 21st Ohio Volunteer Infantry—of about 4,000 officers and men, were organized and given preliminary training. After these regiments were ordered south, Camp Taylor was closed in time for the Cuyahoga County Fair to be held in early October.

CAMP THOMAS. Probably a temporary Civil War encampment, Camp Thomas was located about five miles north of Columbus, in what is now the Oletangy Village section of the city. Named for U.S. Adjutant General Lorenzo Thomas, the camp was established prior to October 1861. It is not known when the camp was discontinued.

CAMP TIFFIN. A Civil War encampment established on September 2, 1861, Camp Tiffin was located northwest of the town of Wooster, in what was then known as Quinby's Grove, in Wayne County. Essentially a recruitment camp, its first occupants were men of the 16th Ohio Volunteer Infantry, followed by the 41st, 120th, 102nd, and the 107th (German Regiment). The camp was last used by the 169th Ohio National Guard in 1864.

CAMP TOD. Cleveland's fourth Civil War encampment established in 1861 and named for Ohio Governor David Tod, Camp Tod was located somewhere along Woodland Avenue, although its exact site remains a mystery to this day. The 45th Ohio Volunteer Infantry was organized here and ordered to Camp Chase at Columbus in December, where its 300 recruits were consolidated with the 67th Ohio Volunteer Infantry. It is not known when the camp was officially closed.

CAMP TOD. A temporary Civil War encampment, Camp Tod was named in honor of Governor David Tod and located on the site of Old State Quarry, three miles west of Columbia.

FORT TYLER. Late in the spring of 1789, a blockhouse was erected on the west side of the Muskingum River, near the present site of the Baltimore and Ohio Railroad station at Waterford in Washington County. The defense, garrisoned under the command of Major Dean Tyler, was known as Fort Tyler.

CAMP VANCE. A temporary Civil War encampment located near the town of Findlay in Hancock County.

CAMP WADE. During the summer of 1861, U.S. Senator Benjamin Wade and Congressman John Hutchins received permission from the War Office to organize the 2nd Ohio Volunteer Cavalry. The recruits rendezvoused at Camp Wade, situated on University Heights, west of the Cuyahoga River and south of Cleveland, in the area known today as East Tremont. By August 26 about 100 men were at the camp located on a plateau in front of Cleveland Institute, a private preparatory school formerly known as Cleveland University. The camp was bordered by Hershal Street, now West 5th Street; Franklin Street, now

Jefferson Avenue; Literary Street, now Literary Road; and University Street, now West 7th Street. The cavalry unit was mustered in at Camp Wade on October 10 and left the heights to occupy the former site of Camp Taylor at the fairgrounds on October 21. The regiment left Cleveland on December 2 for a more "regular camp of instruction" at Camp Dennison. The former site of Camp Wade was later occupied by Camp Cleveland.

FORT WASHINGTON. The strongest and most important of the posts established during the campaign against the Indians of the Northwest Territory, Fort Washington was built by Major John Doughy who had been sent with troops from Fort Harmar in September 1789 to erect a fort overlooking the mouth of the Licking River for the protection of the settlers on the Symmes Purchase, today's downtown Cincinnati. Completed during the following winter, Fort Washington was a perfect 200-foot square constructed of hewn timber, with two-story frame buildings with gable roofs and central chimneys, and five-sided, two-story blockhouses with hipped roofs in all four angles. Two triangular ravelins were added on the fort's north and west sides, palisaded, with the apex of each occupied by a small two-story blockhouse. During the early 1950s, excavations for a new building in downtown Cincinnati uncovered what proved to be Fort Washington's powder magazine, an irregular four-sided structure about 10 or 12 feet across. Fort Washington was headquarters for all military operations in the Northwest Territory during the period 1790–95. The fort was abandoned in 1804.

WESTLAWN BARRACKS. A U.S. Army installation known as Westlawn Barracks was established near the city of Canton and occupied by troops from 1901–9.

CAMP WILLIS. A barracks complex located in Upper Arlington, a Columbus suburb, Camp Willis was established in 1916 to house Ohio National Guard units later sent to patrol the border during the Mexico punitive expedition. It was named for Frank Willis, then governor of Ohio.

FORT WINCHESTER. A War of 1812 defense located on the Auglaize River about 80 yards above old Fort Defiance on the Maumee River, on the site of the present town of Defiance, Fort Winchester was erected in 1813 by troops under General William Henry Harrison. The fort was named in honor of Tennessee pioneer General James Winchester, whose Kentucky troops were annihilated in a surprise dawn attack on January 22, 1813, by British and Indians under General Henry Proctor on the Americans' sprawling, unguarded encampment at Frenchtown on the Raisin River, just south of Detroit. Only 33 men were known to have escaped. Out of an army of 800 men, one-third were killed, either in the attack or during the succeeding Indian massacre of the American wounded and prisoners.

CAMP WOOD. The second Civil War encampment in Cleveland was Camp Wood, consisting mostly of tents, established on August 17, 1861, on the east side of Forest Street on a twenty-acre plateau, one-half mile from Kinsman Street, corresponding today with the East 37th Street and Woodland Avenue area, site of a vast housing project. The 41st Ohio Volunteer Infantry was the only regiment to occupy the camp, remaining there until November 6, when it was ordered to report to Camp Dennison near Cincinnati.

CAMP WOOL (*Camp Jewett*). Camp Wool, located near the city of Athens, was a mustering-in center for recruits in the area. Its name was originally Camp Jewett, but was changed a few weeks after it opened in April 1861.

FORT WYANDOT. FORT SANDUSKY.

CAMP ZANESVILLE. A temporary Civil War encampment located at or near the town of Zanesville in Muskingum County.

CAMP (OLD FORT) ARBUCKLE. The first military installation bearing the name of Arbuckle was a temporary post established on June 24, 1834, on the Arkansas River near the mouth of the Cimarron by Captain George Birch, 7th Infantry, with two companies of troops from Fort Gibson. Named for then Colonel Matthew Arbuckle, this early Army post located just west of present-day Sand Springs near the city of Tulsa was intended to impress the area's Osage Indians. Consisting of a substantially built palisaded blockhouse and a number of cabins, it was often referred to as Old Fort Arbuckle. It was abandoned November 11, 1834. In 1983 the Tulsa County Historical Society abandoned plans to recreate the post on an eight-acre tract and deeded the property back to its proprietors.

CAMP ARBUCKLE. Established in May 1850 by Captain Randolph B. Marcy and Company D, 5th Infantry, and named for Brigadier General Matthew Arbuckle, the post was located one mile south of the Canadian River and a mile west of the present town of Byars in McClain County. Situated on the road from Fort Smith to Santa Fe, Camp Arbuckle was intended to protect emigrants from Indian attack. Abandoned on April 17, 1851, the troops were moved to a permanent site farther south near the Washita River to erect Fort Arbuckle.

FORT ARBUCKLE (*Fort Near the Crossing of the Washita River; Cedar Camp*). Located on the right side of Wild Horse Creek, about four miles south of the Washita River and seven miles west of the present town of Davis in southern Garvin County, the last and permanent post named for Brigadier General Matthew Arbuckle was established on April 19, 1851, by Captain Randolph B. Marcy, with troops of the 5th Infantry, two days after they had abandoned Camp Arbuckle. First called Fort Near the Crossing of the Washita River, or Cedar Camp, it was officially designated Fort Arbuckle on June 25, 1851, for the general who died 10 days earlier. All but five of the garrison, who remained to guard the post property, were sent to Utah on February 13, 1858, in connection with the Mormon campaign, or Utah War. The fort was reoccupied in June of that year by volunteers fearing a Comanche uprising. Regular troops arrived to garrison the post June 29, 1858.

Fort Arbuckle was evacuated on May 3, 1861, and occupied the next day by Texas troops for the Confederacy. After the war, on November 18, 1866, the post was reoccupied by two companies of U.S. Army troops from Fort Gibson.

Oklahoma

Fort Arbuckle was permanently abandoned on June 24, 1870, and its reservation land was turned over to the Chickasaw Nation two weeks later in compliance with the stipulations of the treaty signed on April 28, 1866.

ARMSTRONG ACADEMY CAMP. During the Civil War, from 1862–65, Confederate troops occupied Armstrong Academy (1844), an educational facility, located about two and a half miles north of the town of Bokchita, Bryan County, as a camp and hospital. The Academy burned down in 1921.

CAMP AUGUR. Named for Brigadier General Christopher C. Augur and located in southern Tillman County, about nine miles southwest of Grandfield, Camp Augur was a post–Civil War encampment that operated during 1873–74 as a field subpost of Fort Sill.

FORT BEACH (*Fort Otter*). Established on August 13, 1874, by Captain Warren C. Beach, 11th Infantry, and located on Otter Creek near the present town of Tipton in western Tillman County, Camp Augur was a temporary depot, fortified by a redoubt, used to supply Fort Sill's troops in the field. Sometimes referred to as Fort or Camp Otter, the post occupied the site of the first Camp Radziminski.

FORT BLUNT. FORT GIBSON.

BOGGY DEPOT CAMP. The Choctaw Indian center of Old Boggy Depot, 15 miles southwest of Atoka, was occupied by Confederate troops, white and Indian, during 1862–65.

CAMP CANADIAN. FORT HOLMES.

CANTONMENT (*Cantonment on the North Fork of the Canadian River*). Located on the North Canadian River, near the present town of Canton in Blaine County, Cantonment—never really known as a fort—was established on March 6, 1879, by Colonel Richard I. Dodge with six companies of the 23rd Infantry. The post was referred to as simply Cantonment, or officially, as Cantonment on the North Fork of the Canadian River. The outpost was established after the outbreak of the Northern Cheyenne, known as the Dull Knife Raid, brought demands from white settlers in Kansas for another military post to guard against further trouble with the Indians on the Cheyenne-Arapaho Reservation in Indian Territory.

When the subdued Cheyenne were finally allowed to return to their former homes, there was no further need for the post, and orders by the War Department to abandon it were issued on June 14, 1882, with its last garrison transferred to Fort Sully. On September 7, 1882, the post was turned over to the Interior Department, which contracted with a group of Mennonite missionaries to operate a boarding school there for Cheyenne-Arapaho children. About three years after the school opened, an infantry company was temporarily posted at Cantonment because of trouble arising over the fencing of the Indian lands. In 1898 the government took over the school from the Mennonites and maintained it until 1949.

CEDAR CAMP. FORT ARBUCKLE.

CAMP NEAR CHEYENNE AGENCY. FORT RENO.

FORT CHICKAMAUGA. Originally an early cavalry cantonment consisting of about five buildings, Fort Chickamauga is believed to have been established sometime between 1830 and 1840, a half-mile north of present-day Cookson in Cherokee County. It stood on one of three military roads running from Fort Smith to Fort Gibson. By an 1881 Act of Congress, reaffirmed in 1954, a military commitment was made that ultimately enabled Fort Chickamauga and the 4th Cavalry to be commissioned as the only cavalry training center still in existence in the nation. Fort Chickamauga, reactivated on November 1, 1973, as Headquarters of the 4th Cavalry, has been in the process of having its original buildings rebuilt and enlarged with the addition of 50 new buildings. The Fort Chickamauga National Historical Society came into being on November 12, 1975.

CAMP ON CHICKASKIA RIVER. This post, located on the Chickaskia River in north central Oklahoma, in the area known as the Cherokee Strip, was established on July 12, 1884, by Captain Frank Bennett, 9th Cavalry, with six companies of troops, aggregating 389 men, from Fort Reno. More troops arrived from other military posts soon after. Occupied until October of the same year, the post was intended to keep intruders out of Cherokee Indian territory.

CHOUTEAU'S GRAND RIVER POST. Although this trading post was established during the late 1790s by the Chouteau family of St. Louis, it did not become fully active until 1817 at present Salina on the Grand River in Mayes County. At the site of the post, on which the Salina High School now stands, a spring once used by the post is enclosed by a blockhouse built in post-Chouteau days by Cherokee chief John Ross. The post was later moved to the Three Forks area opposite Fort Gibson.

CHOUTEAU'S THREE FORKS POST. In 1822 Auguste Pierre Chouteau moved the Salina trading post southward to Three Forks, a half-mile south of the present town of Okay, at the junction of the Arkansas, Verdigris, and Grand rivers, in Muskogee County. Six years later, the government purchased the property from the Chouteau interests for use as a Creek Indian Agency.

FORT COBB. Located on the Washita River at the present town of Fort Cobb, Caddo County, and named in honor of Secretary of the Treasury Howell Cobb, Fort Cobb was established on October 1, 1859, by Major William H. Emory, 1st Cavalry, with two companies of cavalry and one company of the 1st Infantry. The post was intended to safeguard the agency for the new reservation established for the Comanche, Waco, Caddo, and Tonkawa, after they were moved from Texas. The post was evacuated by its Army garrison on May 3, 1861, after the outbreak of the Civil War. Two days later, it was occupied by Confederate militiamen from Texas, who were later attacked by Indians who killed most of the Confederate garrison and partially burned the post. In November 1868 Fort Cobb was reoccupied when Comanche and Kiowa Indians were moved there with Colonel William B. Hazen, 38th Infantry, as agent. In December 1868 Major General Philip Sheridan occupied the fort when he initiated his campaign against the Plains Indians. Three months later, however, on March 12, 1869, Fort Cobb was permanently abandoned when it was replaced by Fort Sill.

FORT COFFEE. This post was established on June 17, 1834, at Swallow Rock on the right or south bank of the Arkansas River, near the town of Spiro in LeFlore County, and named for Brigadier General John Coffee of Tennessee. Fort Coffee was intended to halt the shipment of whisky up the river into Indian Territory and to protect relocated Chickasaw and Choctaw Indians. After Fort Coffee was abandoned on October 19, 1838, its buildings were used as a Choctaw school for boys by Methodist missionaries. The Fort Coffee Academy was closed after the outbreak of the Civil War when it was occupied by Confederate troops. During the first week of

October 1863, Fort Coffee was captured and burned by Union troops.

CAMP COMANCHE. This was a temporary post established on July 16, 1834, by Colonel Henry Dodge with elements of the 1st Dragoons, for the purpose of conferring with Comanche chiefs. This meeting culminated in a treaty with the Plains Indians a year later. Camp Comanche was located on the east bank of Cache Creek on the Fort Sill reservation. The Dragoons camped there July 16–18 while 75 of them, along with noted artist George Catlin, who were too ill to proceed farther with the expedition, remained in a nearby field infirmary for another 20 days.

FORT NEAR THE CROSSING OF THE WASHITA RIVER. FORT ARBUCKLE.

CAMP DAVIDSON. Located on Otter Creek, about four miles east of the town of Humphreys, Jackson County, Camp Davidson was an intermittently occupied post established in 1878 by troops from Fort Sill to protect the area's cattle trails. The camp served until about 1882.

FORT DAVIS. Located near present-day Bacone College, one mile east of the town of Bacone, Muskogee County, Fort Davis was established by Confederate General Albert Pike in November 1861 and named for Jefferson Davis, who had been stationed in the region when he was a lieutenant in the U.S. Army. It was reported that the sum of nearly one million dollars was spent by the Confederates for the construction of this log and plank headquarters base that served as a springboard for the Battle of Pea Ridge. The fort was captured and burned on December 27, 1862, by Union troops, including the 3rd Indian Home Guard, under Colonel W. A. Phillips.

CAMP DONIPHAN. A World War I cantonment located on the Fort Sill reservation, in the area between Medicine Bluffs and Grierson Hill, Camp Doniphan was established in August 1917. The cantonment, constructed to accommodate 30,000 men, housed successively the 36th and 35th Infantry Divisions. After the war the post was occupied by the Oklahoma National Guard for training purposes.

FORT EDWARDS. FORT HOLMES.

FORT EDWARDS. Located on the south bank of the Canadian River, near the mouth of the Little River and approximately opposite abandoned Fort Holmes, this historic trading post near present-day Holdenville in Hughes County, and its proprietor, James Edwards, long prospered doing a flourishing business with Indian traders and Texas emigrants.

CAMP FILLMORE. Known officially as Camp near Fort Washita, Camp Fillmore was established on June 14, 1851, by Captain Isaac Lynde, 5th Infantry with companies C and F, aggregating 103 men. On July 11, 1851, companies B, E, and K arrived, and Major (Brevet Lieutenant Colonel) John Abercrombie, 5th Infantry, took command. The post was abandoned in August of the same year.

CAMP FRANK. A temporary post established in September 1898 by 2nd Lieutenant T. E. Morrill, 1st Artillery, with Battery G, aggregating 193 rank and file from Fort Point at Galveston, Texas, Camp Frank was located one mile southeast of Ardmore in Carter County.

FORT GAINES. The only post return for Fort Gaines is for April 1849, and states that it was located in Indian Territory and commanded by Captain John B. S. Todd, 6th Infantry, with troops consisting of Company A of the 6th Infantry and a detachment of Company D, 1st Dragoons.

CANTONMENT GIBSON. FORT GIBSON.

FORT GIBSON (*Cantonment Gibson; Fort Blunt*). Fort Gibson is located on the left bank of the Grand River, three miles above Three Forks—where the Grand, Verdigris, and Arkansas rivers join—at present-day Fort Gibson in Muskogee County. Intermittently occupied and evacuated, Fort Gibson was established on April 21, 1824, by Colonel (later General) Matthew Arbuckle, 7th Infantry, with troops from Fort Smith, Arkansas. "Founded originally to check the Osages, the post had an important civilizing influence on the entire Southwest and was a frequent conference site, outfitting point for military and exploratory expeditions, and rendezvous for Army officers, government commissioners, writers, artists, missionaries, traders, and adventurers" (Kent Ruth, *Great Day in the West* [1963], p. 190).

Initially designated Cantonment Gibson for Colonel George Gibson, commissary general of the Army, the post was redesignated Fort Gibson in 1832. Temporarily evacuated in May 1836 and reoccupied in January 1837, Fort Gibson was ordered abandoned on June 8, 1857, with its last troops leaving in September 1857, when the military reservation was turned over to the

Cherokee Nation. Occupied by Confederate troops early in the Civil War, Fort Gibson was recaptured by Union troops and Cherokee volunteers under Colonel William A. Phillips on April 5, 1863. They repaired the old buildings and erected a mile-long earthen fortification, defended by 18 cannon and manned by 6,000 troops, on the hill above the fort. The new defensive work was named Fort Blunt for Major General James G. Blunt. Fort Gibson was reoccupied by regular Army troops on February 17, 1866.

Finally abandoned on September 22, 1890, the military reservation, except for its National Cemetery, was turned over to the Interior Department on February 7, 1891. It was temporarily reoccupied as Camp at Fort Gibson from April 6, 1897, to November 1897, and again from April 7, 1901 to November 19, 1901. Subsequently, over the years, many of the post's numerous buildings were either demolished or converted into private dwellings. Beginning in 1936, a number of Fort Gibson's old buildings were restored, including the log stockade, as an historical landmark.

CAMP GRUBER. A 66,114-acre World War II infantry training center located 18 miles southeast of Muskogee, near the town of Braggs, Camp Gruber was dedicated on July 19, 1942, when it was named in honor of Brigadier General E. L. Gruber, author of "The Caisson Song," who died May 30, 1941. The post was deactivated in 1947.

CAMP GUTHRIE. Its site located in the city of Guthrie, Logan County, north of Oklahoma City, Camp Guthrie was established in 1889 in the early days of the capital of Oklahoma, 1890–1910. The post was abandoned in 1891.

CAMP HOLMES. FORT HOLMES.

FORT HOLMES (*Camp Canadian; Camp Holmes; Fort Edwards*). A short-lived two-company post located on the east bank of the Little River, a short distance above its confluence with the Canadian River, near the present-day town of Bilby in Hughes County, it was established on June 21, 1834, by 2nd Lieutenant Theophilus H. Holmes, 7th Infantry, in compliance with an order of Colonel Henry Leavenworth, 3rd Infantry. Strategically situated near the crossing of the Canadian on the Old Osage Trail at the terminus of the military road, the post was originally called Camp Canadian, then renamed Camp Holmes for the lieutenant. Although it was never officially designated a fort, the post was historically known as such. The site, however, was afterward considered unhealthful, and the post, about a year later, was abandoned. The post had been occasionally misnamed Fort Edwards because it was located nearly opposite the site of the Edwards Trading Post.

CAMP ILLINOIS. FORT WAYNE.

CAMP JACKSON. A temporary post established on February 24, 1833, by Brevet Major N. Young, 7th Infantry, with companies A and D, Camp Jackson was located on the Fort Gibson reservation.

CAMP LEAVENWORTH. This temporary camp was named for General Henry Leavenworth, who died of injuries suffered on a buffalo hunt on July 21, 1834, near the town of Kingston in Marshall County, while en route from Fort Gibson to Wichita Village in western Oklahoma for a peace conference with Plains Indians at Camp Comanche. Consisting of 500 Dragoons, with notable officers and civilians including Lieutenant Jefferson Davis and famous artist George Catlin, the historic expedition continued under Colonel Henry Dodge. The site of Camp Leavenworth is probably beneath the waters of Lake Texoma, about two miles south of Kingston.

FORT MCCULLOCH. A Confederate fortification located on the south bank of the Blue River, north of Durant in Bryant County, Fort McCulloch was constructed early in 1862 by General Albert Pike and named in honor of Brigadier General Ben McCulloch of Texas, who was killed by sharpshooters on March 7, 1862, during the Battle of Pea Ridge, Arkansas. The extensive earthworks, a five-pointed star in design, mounted 18 cannon manned by 3,000 Confederates. It was during his command of the fort that General Pike resigned from the Confederacy when he refused orders to move to Fort Smith. Fort McCulloch, never attacked by Union forces, was abandoned after the war.

CAMP MCINTOSH. A temporary Confederate post established in early 1862, Camp McIntosh was located five miles east of Anadarko in Caddo County.

CAMP MASON. This short-lived post was established in June 1835 by Major R. B. Mason, 1st Dragoons, and a force of 250 troops, on the north bank of the Canadian River near the town of Lexington in Cleveland County. The purpose of the post was to serve as a place for a conference with the western Indians as had been

arranged by Colonel Henry Dodge during his expedition the preceding year. More than 5,000 Indians, including representatives of all the Civilized Tribes, are said to have attended the meeting in late August 1835. After the peace conference and the abandonment of Camp Mason, its site was taken over by Auguste Chouteau, son of Pierre Chouteau of the Missouri Fur Company, as a fur-trading center, retaining the name Fort Mason between then and 1837 when it closed.

CAMP NAPOLEON. A temporary encampment established in 1865 near present-day Verden in Grady County, Camp Napoleon was the site of a large Indian conclave held on May 26 intended to establish closer relations between the Civilized Tribes of Indian Territory, which had sympathized with the Confederacy during the Civil War, and the Plains Indians. The camp was so named because of the supposed attendance of an emissary of Mexican Emperor Maximilian, a puppet of Napoleon III.

FORT NICHOLS. Misnamed as a fort, this temporary military post was established on June 1, 1865, by Colonel Kit Carson, 1st New Mexico Infantry, two miles north of the town of Wheeless in Cimarron County. Probably named for Captain Charles P. Nichols, 1st California Cavalry, the post was intended to protect the Santa Fe Trail. Fort Nichols was abandoned on or about September 22, 1865.

CAMP OKLAHOMA. In General Orders No. 14, dated August 13, 1889, establishing the post, Oklahoma City is referred to as "Oklahoma Station, I.T. (Indian Territory)." The temporary post, occupied by elements of the 5th Cavalry, was abandoned in October in compliance with General Orders No. 22, October 8, 1889, breaking up the camp.

CANTONMENT ON THE NORTH FORK OF THE CANADIAN RIVER. CANTONMENT.

FORT OTTER. FORT BEACH.

CAMP OTTER CREEK. CAMP RADZIMINSKI.

OTTER CREEK STATION. CAMP RADZIMINSKI.

PERRYVILLE DEPOT. Perryville was a village on the Texas Road not far from the present town of Savanna in Pittsburg County. Here in 1862 Confederate forces established a military post and a supply depot. A battle fought here on

August 27, 1863, between Federal forces commanded by General James G. Blunt and the Confederates under General William Steele ended with the defenders beaten, many of the stores captured, and all the buildings of the depot and town burned.

CAMP PHOENIX. FORT TOWSON.

CAMP RADZIMINSKI (*Camp Otter Creek; Otter Creek Station*). First established on September 23, 1858, by Captain Earl Van Dorn, 2nd Cavalry, this post was originally located on the left bank of Otter Creek near present-day Tipton. In November the camp was moved some miles upstream, and in March 1859 it was moved to the right bank of the creek, about three miles west of present Mountain Park in Kiowa County. Intended as a base of operations against the Kiowa and Comanche, the post, originally known as Camp Otter Creek or Otter Creek Station, was renamed in honor of 1st Lieutenant Charles Radziminski, 2nd Cavalry, who died of tuberculosis on August 18, 1858. The post was abandoned on December 6, 1859. It was immediately occupied by Texas Rangers, who remained there for about a year, patrolling the border and skirmishing with Indians.

FORT RENO (*Camp near Cheyenne Agency*). Located on the north or right bank of the North Canadian River, four miles west of the present town of El Reno in Canadian County, and first known as Camp near Cheyenne Agency, the post was established in July 1874 after the Cheyenne Uprising by Lieutenant Colonel Thomas H. Neill, 6th Cavalry, to protect the Darlington (Cheyenne-Arapaho) Indian Agency located directly across the river. Although declared a military reservation on July 17, 1874, its first buildings were not erected until the following year, when the post was named in honor of Major General Jesse L. Reno, killed on September 14, 1862, in the Battle of South Mountain, South Carolina. After it was abandoned as a military post on February 24, 1908, the post became an Army remount station, and in 1938 the Reno Quartermaster's Depot. In 1949 the reservation became the Fort Reno Livestock Research Station.

CAMP ROBINSON. A short-lived subpost of Fort Sill, Camp Robinson was established in 1871 on Otter Creek in the near environs of the first site of Camp Radziminski, near the town of Tipton, Tillman County.

CAMP RUSSELL. Located near the south bank of the Cimarron River, seven miles north of Guthrie in Logan County, Camp Russell was established in April 1884 by companies E, F, and G of the 9th Cavalry under the command of Captain Henry Carroll. A subpost of Fort Reno, the camp was intended to enforce the laws against encroachments of the "Sooners" or "Boomers" before the Oklahoma Land Rush officially started at noon on April 22. Within a few hours, 1,920,000 acres were claimed or settled under bedlam conditions. By nightfall Oklahoma City had a population of 10,000. Camp Russell was maintained until 1886 to establish law and order in the territory.

CAMP SCHOFIELD. A temporary four-day encampment established on September 16, 1889, three miles east of Chilocco in Kay County, for extensive Army field maneuvers, Camp Schofield was occupied by two battalions of the 5th and 7th Cavalry from Fort Reno and probably named for former Secretary of War John M. Schofield.

FORT SILL (*Camp Wichita*). The site of Fort Sill, three miles north of Lawton, on U.S. 277, Comanche County, was staked out in 1869 by General Philip Sheridan and was originally called Camp Wichita. The fort was intended to be a base for pacifying the Indian tribes of the southern Great Plains. The general later named the frontier site for a West Point classmate and friend, Brigadier General Joshua W. Sill, who was killed on December 31, 1862, in the Battle of Stones River, Tennessee. Sheridan personally laid out the plan for the post and drove the first stake into the ground January 8, 1869.

The first garrison at Fort Sill consisted of the 10th Cavalry and the 6th Infantry. Known as the Buffalo Soldiers, black troopers of the 10th Cavalry won fame as an elite unit of the Indian Wars and for assisting in the construction of the stone buildings that comprise Fort Sill's Old Post. This work was begun in 1870 and completed in 1875. Most of the original buildings stand today. The original officers' quarters are still in use. Many of the other buildings now house the Fort Sill Museum complex. On January 9, 1902, the arrival of the 29th Battery of Field Artillery began the process of changing the fort from a cavalry to a field artillery post. This was completed with the arrival of the first Field Artillery Regiment in 1907 and the departure of the 13th Cavalry, the last cavalry unit at Fort Sill.

In 1909 construction of the new post began to accommodate an increasing garrison. With the post offering excellent training opportunities in

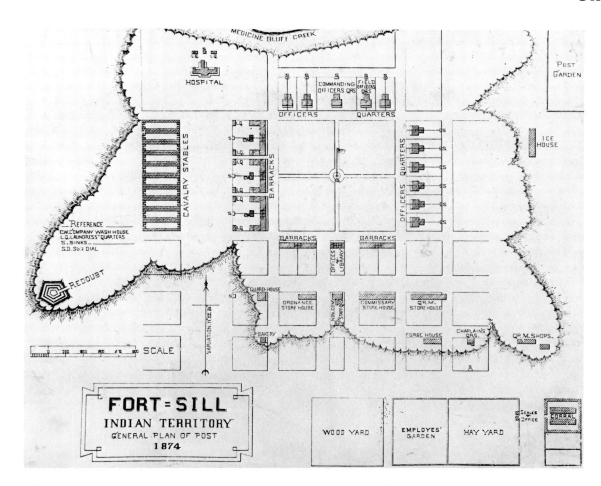

both firing and handling the field artillery, a School of Fire for Field Artillery, the forerunner of the U.S. Army Field Artillery School, was established in 1911. The years between the world wars saw the mechanization of artillery, and the development of advanced fire control and fire direction techniques had, by 1939, made Fort Sill world renowned.

On May 25, 1953, the Artillery entered the atomic age when Fort Sill soldiers fired the first atomic artillery round at Frenchman's Flat, Nevada. In 1954 the Artillery entered the missile era when Fort Sill cannoneers fired the Honest John rocket on post. Fort Sill became the Artillery and Missile Center in 1957, home of the Artillery and Missile School. On December 1, 1968, Fort Sill again became the United States Army Field Artillery Center (USAFACFS) with the separation of the Field Artillery and Air Defense branches.

Consisting of 94,268 acres or 147 square miles, Fort Sill today is the home of the U.S. Army Field Artillery School, the primary teaching institution for field artillerymen in the Army, the U.S. Marine Corps, and dozens of allied nations. The school trains more than 14,000 officer and enlisted students annually and is involved in the future development of field artillery equipment, tactics, and doctrine. Also located on post is the Field Artillery Board, the oldest test agency in the Army. It plans, conducts, and reports on the service testing of new field artillery items. During Fort Sill's long and colorful history, this board has tested everything from mules to missiles.

FORT SMITH. Usually considered as being located in Arkansas, the first Fort Smith, named for General Thomas A. Smith and initially occupied during the periods 1817–24 and 1833, was a stockade across the border in Indian Territory, the home of the Five Civilized Tribes, today's state of Oklahoma after minor adjustments along the state line were made. It was located at the mouth of the Poteau River at Moffett in Sequoyah County. Excavations are in progress at this site. Reconstructed or stabilized buildings are at the 1838–71 site of the second Fort Smith, which includes Judge "Hanging" Parker's courtroom—all under National Park Service jurisdiction. The second Fort Smith site is at the intersection of 2nd Street and Roger Avenue.

CAMP STEELE. A temporary Confederate post situated in Choctaw country, Camp Steele was located about 20 miles west of Fort Smith in Indian Territory.

CAMP SUPPLY. FORT SUPPLY.

FORT SUPPLY (*Camp Supply*). Located near the junction of the North Canadian River and Wolf Creek, one mile east of the present town of Fort Supply in Woodward County, Fort Supply was established in November 1868 by Captain John H. Page, 3rd Infantry, in association with Major General Philip Sheridan's winter campaign against the Plains Indians. Originally called Depot on the North Canadian and Camp Supply, the post was officially designated a fort on December 30, 1878. The military reservation, officially abandoned on October 6, 1894, was turned over to the Interior Department the following year. The site of Fort Supply is now occupied by the Western State Hospital, authorized by the territory of Oklahoma in 1903.

CANTONMENT TOWSON. FORT TOWSON.

FORT TOWSON (*Camp Phoenix; Cantonment Towson*). Originally located on the east bank of Gates Creek, about six miles north of the Red River, this post was established in May 1824 by Major Alexander Cummings, 7th Infantry, and intended to put an end to outlawry perpetrated by both whites and Indians along the Red River, then the international boundary between the United States and Mexico. The post was abandoned in June 1829, with most of its structures burned not long thereafter. The post was reestablished on April 26, 1831, by Major Stephen Watts Kearny, 3rd Infantry, just south of the creek, about two miles northeast of the present town of Fort Towson in Choctaw County. Designed to safeguard the Choctaw Nation and renew a guard over the Red River frontier, the new post was initially called Camp Phoenix, then Cantonment Towson on November 20, 1831, and then finally Fort Towson on February 8, 1832, so-named in honor of Colonel Nathan Towson, paymaster general of the Army.

Fort Towson, abandoned by the Army on June 8, 1854, was then taken over by the Choctaw to serve as their nation's capital. During the Civil War, the post was occupied by Confederate troops as the headquarters of their Indian Territory Department. Noted Confederate Cherokee general, Stand Watie, surrendered his Indian forces there on June 23, 1865. Fort Towson is now a ruin, with massive stone and masonry walls scattered over some 12 acres of the 77-acre site, today owned by the Oklahoma Historical Society, which stabilized the post's remnants and is preserving them as a state historical landmark.

CAMP WADE. A temporary Army post, probably located on the Cimarron River just north of Red Rock Creek, Camp Wade was established in 1889 near the present city of Kingfisher (formerly Lisbon) in Kingfisher County.

CAMP WASHITA. A temporary Army post, Camp Washita was established in 1834 by Captain Dean with companies A and C of the 3rd Infantry from Fort Towson, in connection with General Leavenworth's expedition and located near the mouth of the Washita River in present Bryan County. Consisting of a blockhouse and barracks, this post had no relationship with later established Fort Washita. Camp Washita was probably 3 miles north of the Red River and a short distance from the Washita, under Lake Texoma.

FORT WASHITA. Established in April 1842 by Captain George A. H. Blake, 2nd Dragoons, on a site selected by Colonel Zachary Taylor, 1st Infantry, in 1841, to protect the Chickasaw and Choctaw from hostile Indian tribes, particularly those based in Texas, Fort Washita was located on the left bank of the Washita River, about 30 miles from its confluence with the Red River, in present Bryan County. It was abandoned by four troops of cavalry on May 1, 1861, shortly after the outbreak of the Civil War, and occupied by Confederate troops throughout the war years, never to be reoccupied by Federal soldiers. In 1962 the Oklahoma Historical Society purchased the 117-acre site and has since restored it.

FORT WAYNE (*Camp Illinois*). Originally located south of the Illinois River, just west of the Arkansas line, on the site of the present town of Watts in Adair County, this post was established by Captain John Stewart, 7th Infantry, with troops from abandoned Fort Coffee on October 29, 1838, and called Camp Illinois. The site, however, proved to be extremely unhealthful, causing the deaths of a number of men, including Captain Stewart. Construction was halted in June 1840 and a new site was selected on the north side of Spavinaw (Flag) Creek, near the Arkansas boundary, in present Delaware County. The new post was established on July 20, 1840, by Lieutenant Colonel Richard B. Mason, 1st Dragoons, and designated Fort Wayne in honor of General Anthony Wayne of Revolutionary War fame. Originally intended as a link in a line of forts extending north and south and as protection for a planned military road from Fort Snelling, in Minnesota, to Fort Towson, the post was abandoned on May 26, 1842, by the War Department, believing it served no useful purpose. Its last garrison was transferred north to establish Fort Scott in Kansas. Fort Wayne was taken over by the Confederacy shortly after the outbreak of the Civil War and used as a recruiting center during 1861 by Cherokee General Stand Watie. On March 26, 1871, the post's land and property were turned over to the Interior Department for disposition.

WIGWAM NEOSHO. A trading post, 1829–33, established, named, and operated by ex-Governor Sam Houston of Tennessee, it was located on high ground about two miles east of the present town of Okay in Wagoner County. After Houston resigned as governor, he came West and located adjacent to Fort Gibson, then a remote cantonment in the wilderness. Nothing remains today to mark the site of Wigwam Neosho, the Oklahoma residence of one of the great figures in Western American history.

CAMP WICHITA. FORT SILL.

CAMP ABBOT. On December 4, 1942, the War Department announced that an Army engineer replacement and training center would be named Camp Abbot in honor of Brigadier General Henry Larcom Abbott and located in Deschutes County. The camp was dedicated on September 2, 1943, and was active for about a year. Its site had been occupied temporarily by Abbot on September 2, 1855, when he was in command of a party engaged on one of the Pacific Railroad Survey projects.

CAMP ADAIR. Situated on the west side of the Willamette Valley north of Corvallis, Camp Adair was a World War II training center of some 50,000 acres spanning parts of Benton and Polk counties. Named in honor of West Point graduate cavalryman Lieutenant Henry Rodney Adair, who was killed on June 21, 1916, at Carrizal, Mexico, Camp Adair was constructed in 1942–43 and dedicated on September 4, 1943, although it had been occupied by troops for some time prior to that date. The post was discontinued May 23, 1946.

ADOBE CAMP. A small temporary post located on the Silvies River in Harney Valley, Harney County, Adobe Camp was established on September 18, 1865, by Captain L. L. Williams with Company H, 1st Oregon Volunteer Infantry. Occupying a piece of land approximately 25 yards square, the post was protected by a 30-inch-high sod wall with an inside 30-inch-deep ditch. The post was abandoned when nearby Camp Wright was established by the same troops on October 3, 1865. (See: CAMP WRIGHT.)

CAMP ALDEN. Subsequent to the Battle of Evans Creek on August 24, 1853, a crucial event in the Rogue River Indian uprising, General Joseph Lane had his troops temporarily encamped at Hailey's Ferry near Upper Table Rock in present Jackson County. The post was named in honor of Captain Bradford Ripley Alden, 4th Infantry, who had been severely wounded in the battle. The post was replaced by Fort Lane a few weeks later. (See: FORT LANE.)

CAMP ALVORD. Established in June 1864 by Captain George B. Currey, 1st Oregon Volunteer Cavalry, with cavalry and infantry elements, during the campaign against southeastern Oregon's Indians, Camp Alvord was located in what is now known as the Alvord Valley, near the town of Andrews, in Malheur County and named for Brigadier General Benjamin Alvord. The camp was used until June 1866, when it was aban-

Oregon

doned in favor of a new post, Camp C. F. Smith, on Whitehorse Creek in Harney County.

CAMP ASTORIA. A temporary post located on the south bank of the Columbia River, 10 miles from its mouth, near the city of Astoria, it was established on May 31, 1850, by Company L, 1st Artillery, commanded by Lieutenant Talbot, who was relieved on June 18 of the same year by Captain Hatheway. The same garrison occupied Camp Astoria until October 11, 1851, when the post was abandoned, the troops being transferred to Columbia Barracks.

FORT ASTORIA (*Fort George*). Today's port of Astoria near the mouth of the Columbia River claims the distinction of being the oldest American city west of the Rockies. On May 11, 1792, Americans first came ashore at the site of Astoria and laid claim to the vast, uncharted Oregon country for the United States. Captain Robert Gray, in command of the three-masted ship *Columbia*, on a trading expedition organized by a group of Boston merchants, maneuvered through the treacherous reefs and breakers that guarded the mouth of the river, an accomplishment never attempted by earlier Spanish and British navigators, thus affording the opportunity of establishing the claim.

Thirteen years later, in December 1805, the Lewis and Clark Expedition, consisting of 31 men and Indian woman-guide Sacajawea, reached the Pacific coast, raised the American flag for the second time, and established Fort Clatsop, four and a half miles southeast of Astoria's site. The third raising of the American standard and the first modest settlement of Astoria occurred in 1811, when a party of fur traders landed from the ship *Tonquin* and built Fort Astoria. This was an expedition of the Pacific Fur Company, founded by John Jacob Astor of New York, who ultimately became America's premier trader. Fort Astoria lasted only two years under the American flag. Because of the War of 1812 and reports of British warships cruising offshore in the Pacific, Astor wisely sold his holdings to the Northwest Company, a British company operating in Canada. The transfer of Fort Astoria ownership was made on October 23, 1813. When the American flag was hauled down to be replaced by the British standard on December 12 or 13 by Captain William Black, commander of the British sloop-of-war *Raccoon*, the fort was renamed Fort George.

The British maintained formal command of the post until 1818, when a treaty of joint occupation gave British and Americans equal rights to trade in the region. But the enterprising agent at the post, Dr. John McLoughlin, although effectively preventing Indian mayhem against both the British and the Americans, succeeded in ruining the Americans' business by controlling Indian customers, bidding higher for furs, and underselling them. In 1824 Dr. McLoughlin moved his trading headquarters 100 miles up the Columbia, where he built Fort Vancouver. Fort Astoria was temporarily abandoned the following year, but was reoccupied by the Hudson's Bay Company in 1830 after its merger with the Northwest Company. By the 1840s, Astoria had become a thriving American settlement, and on March 7, 1847, the Astoria post office was established, the first west of the Rockies. A replica of one of the fort's blockhouses stands on the site of the original fort on Exchange Street between 14th and 15th avenues.

AUBURN BLOCKHOUSE. Today a ghost town, Auburn was located about 10 miles southwest of the present city of Baker and near the east end of Phillips Reservoir. Auburn, with a Civil War population of more than 5,000 people, was protected by a blockhouse erected in 1862. But by 1868 the town had declined so much that there was no need for the blockhouse. Various Army expeditions of the Civil War camped nearby and used Auburn as a supply and recreational center.

BACHE FORT. Wyeth's *Journals* refer to the Bache Post established in 1829 near The Dalles on the Columbia River in present Wasco County. Here, in 1830, Bache and 11 others were massacred by the Indians. The post was probably named for a descendant of Richard Bache (1737–1811), Philadelphia merchant, who married Benjamin Franklin's daughter Sarah.

FORT BAILEY. A temporary post established in 1855 during the campaign against the Rogue River Indians, Fort Bailey was a fortified tavern located five miles south of Cow Creek, near the present town of Wolf Creek in Josephine County, and occupied by Oregon Volunteer troops under the command of Captain Joseph Bailey, Company A, 1st Battalion, Mounted Volunteers.

CAMP BAKER. Established in 1862 and garrisoned by elements of the 1st Oregon Volunteer Cavalry, Camp Baker was located about a half-mile west of the town of Phoenix in Jackson County and intended to observe the activities of Confederate partisans in nearby Jacksonville. Used during the remaining years of the war, the post was named in honor of Major General Edward D. Baker who was killed at Balls Bluff, Virginia, on October 21, 1861.

CAMP BARLOW. A temporary Civil War encampment established in 1862 and occupied by four companies of Oregon Volunteers, Camp Barlow was located about two miles north of Oregon City, Clackamas County.

BIG BEND CAMP. Established on May 30, 1856, by detachments of the 1st Dragoons, 3rd Artillery, and the 4th Infantry, and occupied until late in 1857, it was a strongly fortified post originally erected by a company of 33 Oregon Volunteers under Captain John Porter and located at the "big bend" of the Rogue River in Willamette County. The post's garrison on September 30, 1857, consisted of companies F and I of the 1st Dragoons, three companies of the Mounted Rifles, and four companies of the 3rd and 8th Infantry.

FORT BIRDSEYE. The square, strongly built hewn-timbered house built by David Birdseye was palisaded in 1855 during the Rogue River Indian uprising and used as a refuge by the area's settlers. It was located on the south bank of the Rogue River near the mouth of Birdseye Creek, in the present village of Rogue River, Jackson County.

CAMP C. F. SMITH. Located on Whitehorse Creek, a half-mile north of Whitehorse Ranch, cattle center, in Harney County, Camp Smith was established on August 12, 1866, by a battalion of the 18th Infantry, under the command of Captain Nathaniel C. Kinney, and named for Major General Charles Ferguson Smith. Most of the post's troops were withdrawn on July 23, 1869. Finally, Camp C. F. Smith was abandoned on November 9, 1869.

FORT CHAMPOEG (*Willamette Post; Fort Wallace*). In 1811 William Wallace and J. C. Halsey, agents for John Jacob Astor's Pacific Fur Company, came down from Astoria and established Willamette Post (also known as Fort Wallace) on the Willamette River, about 25 miles north of the present city of Salem, near today's Yamhill-Clackamas county line. After the fur-trading company was purchased by the Hudson's Bay Company, the post was renamed Champooick, later somewhat anglicized to Champoeg. Two damaging fires and a major flood in December 1861 took their toll. The original or lower part of the town was finally destroyed by the flood of 1892. The area is now the 492-acre Champoeg Memorial State Park.

CAMP CLACKAMAS. A temporary post active less than a month during June–July 1862, the camp was located at the mouth of the Clackamas River about a mile north of Oregon City. Camp Clackamas replaced nearby Camp Barlow and was garrisoned by the four companies of Oregon Volunteers from the latter post, who were relieved in mid-July by a single company.

CAMP CLATSOP. CAMP RILEA.

FORT CLATSOP. The oldest of all American settlements on the Pacific Coast, near the mouth of the Columbia River and four and a half miles southeast of later-established Fort Astoria, Fort Clatsop has an eminent rank in history. This was where Meriwether Lewis and William Clark spent

FORT CLATSOP. Reconstruction. (Courtesy of the Oregon State Highway Travel Division.)

the bleak winter of 1805–6, after they had carried the flag of the United States from St. Louis to the shores of the Western Sea. The first American military post anywhere west of St. Louis, it was the first habitation by Americans along the Pacific seaboard. In 1955, as part of the sesquicentennial observance of the arrival of Lewis and Clark, Fort Clatsop was totally reconstructed on the exact site of the original post. Lieutenant Clark's drawings and sketches, found in the expedition's journals, were followed faithfully. The celebrated fort was 50 feet square, with three rooms along one wall and four along the other, and with a military parade ground occupying the center square. The re-creation of Fort Clatsop was later established as a National Monument by the National Park Service.

CAMP COLFAX. A temporary post located on South Willow Creek, about six miles east of Ironside Mountain, and one mile west of the town of Ironside, Malheur County, Camp Colfax was established about August 24, 1865, by Company F of the 1st Oregon Volunteers. Again occupied during the summer of 1867, the post was probably named for Schuyler Colfax, Speaker of the House of Representatives, who visited Oregon in the summer of 1865.

CAMP CROOK. FORT HARNEY.

CAMP (CURREY) CURRY. Located at Indian Springs on Silver Creek, near Canyon City, Harney County, Camp Curry or Currey was established in 1865 and occupied by detachments of California, Oregon, and Washington Volunteer Infantry regiments. The camp, named for Colonel George B. Curry (Currey) of the 1st Oregon Volunteer Cavalry, consisted of about 40 10-by-12-foot cabins constructed of stone and hewn logs, with a cellar or storehouse excavated in the adjacent hillside. More substantial than others in the Oregon country, the post was intended to provide military protection for emigrants traveling through Harney Basin. The post was abandoned in 1866 because of the proximity of Fort Harney.

CAMP DAHLGREN. A temporary post occupied for one month, August 22–September 20, 1864, Camp Dahlgren was established by Captain John M. Drake, 1st Oregon Volunteer Cavalry, and located in the vicinity of the present-day town of Paulina in Crook County. Captain Drake had already occupied Camps Maury and Gibbs but had to move his camp because of poor forage.

FORT DALLES (*Camp Drum*). This fort was located on the site of a former Northwest Company trading post (1820) on the left or south bank of the Columbia River at The Dalles in Wasco County and established on May 21, 1850, by two companies of Mounted Riflemen, commanded by Captain Stephen S. Tucker, in compliance with an order of Lieutenant Colonel William W. Loring, Mounted Riflemen. In 1847 Dr. Marcus Whitman bought the Methodist Mission at The Dalles and established the Presbyterian Mission. It was here in the same year that he, his wife, and 12 others were massacred by the Cayuse Indians. The establishment of the military post was the response to the Indian uprising, with the added responsibility of protecting emigrant travel on the Oregon Trail.

The military post, encompassing the old mission site, was first called Camp Drum, most probably in honor of Captain Simon H. Drum, who was killed in the attack against Mexico City on September 13, 1847. In July 1853 it was officially designated Fort Dalles. The elaborate post, a semicircular complex of frame buildings, was substantially rebuilt in 1856. French *voyageurs* gave the name Dalles ("flagstones") to the stretch of the Columbia River where the post and town were located. The post was not regularly garrisoned after 1861 but was used as a quartermaster's depot. Apparently, the last time it was garrisoned was from March 27 to May 22, 1867. The War Department, on March 28, 1877, transferred the military reservation to the Interior Department for disposition. The old surgeon's quarters, built in 1858, is all that remains of Fort Dalles. It serves as a museum.

CAMP DAY. Company L, 3rd Artillery, commanded by Lieutenant Lorenzo Lorain, established temporary Camp Day in late June 1860 at a point southwest of Klamath Lake, near the present town of Kino, Klamath County, for the purpose of safeguarding the Klamath Road during the Piute War to the southeast in Nevada. Named in honor of Lieutenant Edward Henry Day, 3rd Artillery, who died on January 2, 1860, apparently at Fort Umpqua, Camp Day was abandoned on October 6, 1860.

CAMP DRUM. FORT DALLES.

CAMP GALICE. This post was reportedly an arsenal and powder magazine built in 1854 during the Rogue River Indian rebellion. It was located at the town of Galice, 12 miles west of Merlin, in Josephine County.

FORT GEORGE. FORT ASTORIA.

CAMP GIBBS. This supply and grazing encampment at the north base of the Maury Mountains in Crook County was in use for a short period in the summer of 1864 during the Snake Indian War. The short-lived post was probably named for Governor Addison C. Gibbs.

POST AT GRAND RONDE AGENCY. FORT LAFAYETTE.

CAMP HARNEY. FORT HARNEY.

FORT HARNEY (*Camp on Rattlesnake Creek; Camp Steele; Camp Crook; Camp Harney*). Located on the right side of Rattlesnake Creek, about 12 miles east of the present town of Burns, Harney County, the post was established on August 16, 1867, as a base of operations against Indian hostiles, particularly the Piute and Bannock, in southeastern Oregon. Built subsequent to the establishment of a depot on Harney Lake by Lieutenant Colonel George Crook, 23rd Infantry, the post was first known as Camp on Rattlesnake Creek; then named Camp Steele for Colonel Frederick Steele, 20th Infantry; again renamed Camp Crook for Colonel Crook; and then, on September 14, 1867, Camp Harney for Brigadier General William S. Harney. On April 5, 1879, the post was officially designated a fort. The installation was abandoned on June 13, 1880.

FORT HENRIETTA. Located near the west bank of the Umatilla River at present-day Echo in western Umatilla County, Fort Henrietta was established on November 18, 1855, by elements of the 1st Oregon Mounted Rifles, commanded by Major Mark A. Chinn, in connection with the campaign to suppress the general Indian uprising in eastern Oregon and Washington. Consisting of a 100-foot-square stockade with two bastions constructed of round logs, the fort was erected on the Umatilla Indian Reservation, after the agency buildings had been destroyed by the Indians. The post was named in compliment to the wife of Major Granville O. Haller, 4th Infantry. Fort Henrietta was abandoned in 1856.

FORT HILL. Located just northeast of present Valley Junction in Polk County, Fort Hill was so-named when settlers in the Willamette Valley erected a blockhouse on its summit in 1855–56. The Federal government sent troops there and established Fort Yamhill on August 30, 1856. The blockhouse was later moved to the Grand Ronde Indian Agency, and then moved again to the town of Dayton where it was established in a public park. (See: FORT YAMHILL.)

FORT HOSKINS. First located on the Luckiamute River, a tributary of the Willamette River, near the mouth of Bonner Creek, and about 12 miles northwest of Corvallis in Benton County, Fort Hoskins was established on July 26, 1856, by Captain Christopher C. Augur, 4th Infantry, and named in honor of 1st Lieutenant Charles Hoskins, 4th Infantry, who was killed on September 21, 1846, in the Battle of Monterrey, Mexico. Settlement of the controversy over its site, which had been refused approval by Brigadier General John E. Wool, dictated the moving of the post in September to the eastern entrance of the Siletz Indian Reservation, established after the Rogue River Indian War, about 40 miles northwest of Corvallis, where it was intended to control the Indians and protect the area's settlers. The troops were withdrawn on April 10, 1865. The military reservation was turned over to the Interior Department on February 16, 1881, for disposition.

CAMP HUMBUG. CAMP MCDOWELL.

FORT KLAMATH. Located about eight miles from the north end of Klamath Lake, about 40 miles above the California line, Fort Klamath was established on September 5, 1863, by Major Charles C. Drew, 1st Oregon Cavalry, in compliance with orders of Brigadier General George Wright. Designed as a two-company post, its construction was superintended by Captain William Kelly, 1st Oregon Cavalry. Strategically situated near the travel routes leading to both California and Idaho, Fort Klamath was intended to oversee the activities of the area's Indians.

The fort became an important center during the Modoc War in northern California's Lava Beds, December 1872–April 1873, furnishing both troops and supplies. Finally, on June 4, the warring Modoc leader, Captain Jack, was captured. Six of the Modoc leaders, tried before a military tribunal at Fort Klamath, were found guilty of murder and condemned to die. On October 3, 1873, Captain Jack and three of his followers were hanged. Two of the condemned Indians were rescued from this extreme penalty by order of the president. The 157 Modoc captives remaining at Fort Klamath were sent to the Quapaw Reservation in Indian Territory, while the Modocs under old Chief Schonchin, who had abided peacefully on the Klamath Reservation throughout the hostilities, remained there. The military reservation was turned over to the Interior Department on May 4, 1886, but plans to open the land to public sale were suspended. The post's last garrison was withdrawn in July 1889, except for a small caretaking detachment that remained until June 23, 1890.

FORT LAFAYETTE (*Post at Grand Ronde Agency*). In 1863 a small detachment of Oregon Volunteers established a temporary outpost of Fort Yamhill at the headquarters of the Grand Ronde Agency in northwest Polk County. The troops unofficially named the post Fort Lafayette.

FORT LAMERICK. A short-lived post located at Big Meadows, about two miles north of the Rogue River, in the extreme northeast part of Curry County, Fort Lamerick was established on May 1, 1856, by Oregon Volunteer troops during the last months of the Rogue River War, and named in compliment to Brigadier General John K. Lamerick. The post, reportedly nothing more than a minimally fortified low breastwork of logs, was abandoned during the summer.

FORT LANE. Located on the south bank of the Rogue River, near the mouth of Bear Creek, in the vicinity of the present town of Central Point in Jackson County, Fort Lane was established on September 28, 1853, by Captain Andrew J. Smith, 1st Dragoons, and named in honor of Brigadier General Joseph Lane, first territorial governor of Oregon. The purpose of the post was to protect the agency headquarters of the Rogue River Indian Reservation on the north side of the river, opposite Fort Lane. The post was abandoned on September 17, 1856.

FORT LEE (*Fort Wascopam*). The first white settlement at The Dalles on the Columbia River was a Methodist mission established in 1838 by Daniel Lee and H. K. W. Perkins. In 1847 the mission was sold to Dr. Marcus Whitman, Presbyterian missionary, for $600. The Whitman Massacre in November of the same year led to the abandonment of the mission and the establishment of Fort Lee by volunteer troops in January 1848, named for Major Henry A. G. Lee of the Oregon Rifles. The post was also known as Fort Wascopam, from the Indian name for a nearby spring.

FORT LELAND. Established in the fall of 1855 by Oregon Mounted Volunteers on Grave Creek, Josephine County, as a base of operations during the Rogue River War of 1855–56, the post was actually a palisaded tavern called Grave Creek House, belonging to McDonough Harkness and Jesse H. Twogood. The name of Leland applied to the fort was in memory of Martha Leland Crowley, an emigrant who died in 1846 and was buried on Grave Creek.

CAMP LINCOLN (*Camp on the South Fork of John Day's River*). A temporary post originally called Camp on the South Fork of John Day's River, then renamed Camp Lincoln for the president, Camp Lincoln was established on March 15, 1864, by Lieutenant James A. Waymire, 1st Oregon Cavalry, in the vicinity of present-day Dayville in western Frant County. The post, intended to protect the military road and the area's settlers, was abandoned on May 1, 1864.

CAMP LOGAN. Located on Strawberry Creek, about six miles south of Prairie City in Grant County, Camp Logan was a temporary post established during the summer of 1865 by a detachment of the 1st Oregon Volunteer Infantry, commanded by Lieutenant A. B. Ingram, to protect the military road during the widespread Indian troubles in the region. The post was apparently abandoned sometime during the late summer of 1866. Another citation reports that it was evacuated on November 28, 1868.

CAMP MCDOWELL (*Camp Humbug*). A temporary field camp alternately located on both sides of Camas Creek, about four miles east of present-day Ukiah in Umatilla County, Camp McDowell was established during the early summer of 1865 by Company F, 1st Oregon Infantry, for the purpose of observing the activities of the area's Indians. Since the troops only spent a week there, and then crossed the river to another site a half-mile away, the company named the post Camp Humbug.

MCKAY'S FORT. FORT UMPQUA.

CAMP MCKINLEY. A temporary Spanish-American War encampment officially established by the Oregon National Guard on April 29, 1898, one week after the war broke out, on the racetrack grounds at Irvington Park in the city of Portland, Camp McKinley was named in honor of the president. It was here that the 2nd Oregon Infantry was mustered into service. The camp was located just east of what is now Northeast 7th Avenue, between Northeast Brazee and Northeast Fremont streets. Between May 11 and May 16, 1898, the regiment was moved to the Presidio of San Francisco, from which post it embarked for

Manila on May 25. Camp McKinley apparently closed on May 19, 1898.

CAMP MAURY. The first of three temporary foraging field camps established during the Snake War of 1864, Camp Maury was located on the south side of Maury Creek, near the base of the Maury Mountains, in Crook County, and established on May 1, 1864, by Captain John M. Drake in command of a company of the Oregon Cavalry. The camp was occupied until July 21, 1864, when it was moved five miles to the west to a new site called Camp Gibbs for the purpose of obtaining better forage for the cavalry's horses.

CAMP MEDILL. A temporary field camp established in 1858, Camp Medill was located on Grave Creek in Josephine County.

FORT MINER. A citizen-built blockhouse fortification erected in early 1856 at the mouth of the Rogue River, just north of present-day Gold Beach on U.S. 101 in Curry County, it was a refuge for more than 100 men, women, and children during a month-long Indian siege, which was not lifted until Army regulars and volunteer troops under the command of Lieutenant Colonel Buchanan came to the rescue.

FORT ORFORD. Located on Trichenor Bay at Port Orford in Curry County, Fort Orford was established on September 14, 1851, by 2nd Lieutenant Powell T. Wyman, 1st Artillery. The post was constructed by troops under the command of Lieutenant Colonel Silas Casey from Astoria in October. The village of Port Orford had been founded by Captain William Trichenor of the *Seagull* in June 1851. In July 1851, the settlers erected two blockhouses, also called Fort Orford, on Fort Point. These defenses were entirely separate from the military post, which was abandoned on July 10, 1856. The civilian fortifications were destroyed by the Port Orford fire of October 10, 1868.

CAMP OWYHEE (RIVER). A temporary post established probably sometime during the early 1860s, Camp Owyhee was located on the Oregon side of the border with Idaho, almost opposite the old fur-trading post of Fort Boise at the confluence of the Snake and Boise rivers. The Owyhee River flows into the Snake about a mile south of this point. The camp was located at or near the present town of Owyhee in Malheur County.

CAMP POLK. A temporary encampment established in 1865 by Captain Charles LaFollette with Company A of the 1st Oregon Volunteer Infantry, Camp Polk was located on the west bank of Squaw Creek, about three miles northeast of the present town of Sisters in Deschutes County. The post was apparently abandoned in early 1866. Another citation locates the post on the Crooked River, about five miles west of Prineville, at the present junction of U.S. 26 and 126, about 35 miles to the east.

CAMP RANDOLPH. A short-lived post on Three Mile Creek, near Fort Dalles, Camp Randolph was established on May 26, 1859 by companies E and H, 1st Dragoons, Company H of the 4th Infantry, and a detachment of Engineers. The command left camp on June 4, 1859, to join the Wagon Road Expedition to Salt Lake City.

CAMP ON RATTLESNAKE CREEK. FORT HARNEY.

CAMP RILEA (*Camp Clatsop*). Located near Astoria and Warrenton, Camp Rilea was originally established in 1927 as Camp Clatsop, a summer training area for the Oregon National Guard. Additional land was purchased during the 1930s and at the outbreak of World War II the camp was operated as a Federal post for infantry training. The military reservation, now owned by the state of Oregon, was renamed Camp Rilea in 1959 in honor of Major General Thomas E. Rilea, former adjutant general of Oregon, who died in Portland on February 4, 1959.

CAMP RUSSELL. A Civil War recruiting, rendezvous, and training center established on December 15, 1864, on the State Fair Grounds a mile and a half east of the city of Salem, Camp Russell was named in honor of Major General David Allen Russell, who was killed at the Battle of Opequan, Virginia, on September 19, 1864. The 1st Oregon Volunteer Infantry, with at least four companies, was organized and mustered into service here in 1864–65. The State Fair pavilion was converted into a barracks, kitchen, and drill hall. The State Fair Grounds are located at the intersection of present 17th Street and Silverton Road in northeast Salem.

SILETZ BLOCKHOUSE. An Army protection for the Siletz Indian Agency, the two-story blockhouse stood on a site within the present town of Siletz in Lincoln County. The same blockhouse erected in 1856 by Lieutenant Philip H. Sheridan at Yaquina Bay, it had been dismantled in 1858 and floated in sections up the Siletz River to the agency. The Army post was garrisoned until 1866. (See also: YAQUINA BAY BLOCKHOUSE.)

FORT SMITH. A temporary Oregon Volunteers post garrisoned 1855–56 during the Rogue River War, it was actually the stockaded house of William Henry Smith located on Cow Creek, about four miles above the present town of Glendale in Douglas County.

CAMP ON THE SOUTH FORK OF JOHN DAY'S RIVER. CAMP LINCOLN.

CAMP STEELE. FORT HARNEY.

FORT STEVENS. A Coast Artillery installation located on Point Adams, on the south side of the Columbia River at its mouth, about nine miles west of Astoria, Fort Stevens was first an earthwork completed in 1865 under the supervision of Captain George H. Elliot, Corps of Engineers, and furnished with muzzle-loading cannon of 8- and 15-inch caliber. It was named in honor of Isaac I. Stevens, first territorial governor of Washington, who as a major general of Volunteers, was killed at Chantilly, Virginia, on September 1, 1862. Later, long after deterioration of the original work, it was equipped with concrete-emplaced artillery batteries of 10- and 12-inch rifles. During its final years, continuing through World War II, emphasis on its primary artillery function—the denial of the mouth of the river to an enemy—was principally on submarine mines, including the protection of the mine fields by small- and medium-caliber rifles.

Fort Stevens was first garrisoned by Company B, 8th California Volunteer Infantry, and

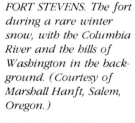

FORT STEVENS. The fort during a rare winter snow, with the Columbia River and the hills of Washington in the background. (Courtesy of Marshall Hanft, Salem, Oregon.)

later, until 1884, by companies and detachments of the Army. From November 1884 to March 1898, the post and surrounding military reservation of nearly 800 acres were under the control of the U.S. Engineers. The post was not garrisoned, but its artillery was under the care of an ordnance sergeant. On March 10, 1898, the post was regarrisoned. During the next few years, new buildings were constructed to accommodate and service at least three batteries of artillerymen which took post there. Occupation by military units was continuous thereafter until the post was abandoned by the Department of Defense in 1947. Once, during World War II, on the night of June 21, 1942, the fort was shelled by a Japanese submarine. The enemy's vessel being out of range of any gun at Fort Stevens or within the entire harbor defense area, the fort's commanding officer chose not to return the brief barrage. The ineffectual shelling is significant as the first foreign attack on a continental military installation since the War of 1812.

CAMP STUART. A temporary post located near the site of where Fort Lane was later erected, Camp Stuart was established by Captain (Brevet Major) Phil Kearny, 1st Dragoons, in June 1851. Named in honor of 2nd Lieutenant (Brevet Captain) James Stuart, Mounted Riflemen, who died on June 18, 1851, of wounds suffered during an action against the Rogue River Indians, the camp was located southeast of Medford in Jackson County.

FORT UMPQUA (*McKay's Fort*). A fur-trading post established in 1832 on the Umpqua River, either by Desportes McKay or Thomas McKay, and alternately known as McKay's Fort, Fort Umpqua was later acquired by the Hud-

son's Bay Company and operated at five different locations in the same area until 1850. The final fort, consisting of four log buildings enclosed within a 12-foot-high palisade with bastions at two of its corners, was located on the left or west side of the river, opposite the mouth of Elk Creek. The site is about 35 miles east of present-day Reedsport, near the town of Elkton, in Douglas County.

FORT UMPQUA. Located on the west or north bank of the Umpqua River, about two miles above its mouth on Winchester Bay, Douglas County, Fort Umpqua was established on July 28, 1856, by Captain Joseph Stewart, 3rd Artillery, and intended to observe the activities of the Indians on the Grand Ronde and Siletz Reservations. The first buildings of the post consisted of structures dismantled and moved from abandoned Fort Orford about 75 miles down the coast. Fort Umpqua was abandoned on July 16, 1862.

CAMP UNION. A temporary encampment established on July 4, 1860, by Major Enoch Steen with detachments of dragoons and infantrymen, Camp Union was located on Silver Creek, about 30 miles north of Harney Lake, in Harney County.

FORT VANNOY. Located on the right or north bank of the Rogue River, about four miles west of Grants Pass, Josephine County, Fort Vannoy was established in late October or November 1855. Important during the Rogue River War of 1855–56, serving as the headquarters post for the Oregon Volunteers, it consisted of a complex of log buildings within a low stockade or breastwork. The post was located on the Margaret Vannoy donation land claim, which adjoined the James N. Vannoy claim.

FORT WALLACE. FORT CHAMPOEG.

CAMP WARNER. Occupying two different sites in the Warner Valley, Camp Warner was established on August 10, 1866, and originally located 20 miles east of Warner Lakes in southeast Oregon. Because it was later considered impractical to cross the chain of lakes and swamps, in September 1867 the post was relocated as a permanent-type post 15 miles west of the lakes on Honey Creek, at what is now known as the Fort Warner Ranch, near Lakeview in Lake County. The post was named for Captain William Horace Warner, who was killed by Indians in September 1849, probably in Surprise Valley, just across the California line. Camp Warner was abandoned on September 3, 1874.

FORT WASCOPAM. FORT LEE.

CAMP WATSON. One of Oregon's longest occupied so-called temporary and most active posts set up during the Civil War years, Camp Watson was established on July 12, 1864, by Oregon Volunteer troops near the John Day River, south of U.S. 26, near the town of Mitchell. It was intended to protect the Dalles–Canyon City travel route from bands of marauding Snake Indians who were opposed to the influx of miners into the region. The post was named in honor of 2nd Lieutenant Stephen Watson, 1st Oregon Volunteer Cavalry, who was killed in action against the Snake Indians near the Crooked River on May 18, 1864. Eventuating as a rather elaborate post for the time, Camp Watson was a 15-foot-high palisaded complex of a dozen log-built huts for the enlisted men's barracks, four for the officers' quarters, a hospital, guardhouse, a commissary and quartermaster storehouse, and three corrals and stables. Camp Watson was abandoned on May 24, 1869.

CAMP WHITE. Located near the Rogue River in southern Oregon, north of Medford in Jackson County, Camp White was a World War II training post authorized in January 1942 and was dedicated on September 15 in honor of Major General George Ared White, a veteran of the Spanish-American War and World War I and former adjutant general of Oregon who died on November 23, 1941. The post was divided into two sections—one part trained principally division infantry troops, and the other trained special services forces. The post was declared on permanent inactive status in April 1946. The camp's large general hospital was taken over by the Veterans Administration as a Domiciliary Service. The area is now designated as White City. The reservation's surplus land was transferred to Jackson County.

WILLAMETTE POST. FORT CHAMPOEG.

FORT WILLIAM. A trading post established by Nathaniel J. Wyeth in the autumn of 1834 on Sauvie Island in the Columbia River, two miles northwest of Portland, Fort William occupied two sites. The first site was near Warrior Point on the north end of the island, but it was moved to the center of the island on higher ground after spring flooding engulfed the first location. In 1837 the Hudson's Bay Company leased the property for use as a farm.

WILLIAM HENRY FORT. A short-lived fur-trading post established by the Northwest Company in 1813, it was located near Newberg in Yamhill County.

CAMP WITHYCOMBE. Located just east of Clackamas, Camp Withycombe was named for James Withycombe, governor of Oregon, 1915–19. The reservation was established in 1909 under a lease arrangement with option to purchase. The government was the leasee and the purchase option was exercised in 1910. Originally known as the Clackamas Rifle Range, it was designated Camp Withycombe during World War I. The 257-acre camp is now operated by the Oregon National Guard. In 1979 preliminary plans were drawn up for a building on the reservation designed for use as the National Guard Military Museum and Research Center.

CAMP WRIGHT. A temporary encampment located on the Silvies River northwest of Malheur Lake, in the vicinity of present Buchanan in Harney County, Camp Wright was established on October 3, 1865, by Captain Loren L. Williams, 1st Oregon Infantry, and named in honor of Brigadier General George Wright, who drowned in the wreck of the *Brother Jonathan*, which foundered off Crescent City, California, on July 30, 1865, with the loss of about 300 lives. Camp Wright was abandoned sometime after the middle of April 1866.

FORT YAMHILL. Located in the Grand Ronde Valley, on what is now known as Fort Hill, near the Yamhill River, about 25 miles southwest of Dayton in Yamhill County, Fort Yamhill was originally a blockhouse erected in late 1855 by the area's settlers, who feared that the contagion of widespread Indian rebellions would spread to the Grand Ronde Reservation. The citizen defense became part of a palisaded U.S. Army fort on August 30, 1856. It was first garrisoned by a detachment of the 4th Infantry under the command of 2nd Lieutenant William B. Hazen. Abandoned on June 30, 1866, the blockhouse was moved from the top of Fort Hill to the Grand Ronde Agency, three miles away, where it was used as a jail. In 1911 it was moved to Dayton, where it is now preserved in a city park.

YAQUINA BAY BLOCKHOUSE. Erected by Lieutenant Philip Sheridan in 1856, this blockhouse at the mouth of the Yaquina River on Yaquina Bay, across from Toledo in Lincoln County, was intended to protect the headquarters of the Indian agent there. In 1858 the blockhouse was dismantled and floated upriver to the Siletz Indian Agency, where it became known as the Siletz Blockhouse.

ALLEGHENY ARSENAL. The Allegheny Arsenal at Pittsburgh was built in 1814–16 on a 31-acre tract of land near the Allegheny River at a cost of $300,000. It was designed by Benjamin Henry Latrobe, President Jefferson's engineer for the national Capitol, and constructed under the direction of Colonel Abraham R. Wooley. The arsenal played an important role in the manufacture of war munitions and the storing of supplies during the Civil War, Indian wars, and the Spanish-American War. As early as July 1861, there were 400 men employed at the arsenal, which also served as a military garrison. An explosion in the "laboratory" building on September 17, 1862, caused the death of 75 boys and girls who were working there at the time. In 1909 the government turned the arsenal over to the city, which sold the installations at auction in 1926. A small number of historic relics are within Arsenal Park in Pittsburgh. The site of the arsenal is at Butler and 40th streets.

FORT ALLEN. Located at the present town of Weissport in Carbon County, Fort Allen was erected in 1756 under the immediate supervision of Benjamin Franklin at what was then the Moravian community of New Gnaden Huetten on the Lehigh River. The fort was considered one of the three most important posts east of the Susquehanna during the French and Indian War. The original Moravian mission among the Indians was founded across the river at the site of today's city of Lehighton in 1742 by Count Louis von Zinzendorf. Named in honor of Chief Justice William Allen of Pennsylvania, the fort was a 12-foot-high stockaded structure 125 feet long and 50 feet wide, with a bastion in each of the long sides and a half-bastion at two opposite corners, defended by two swivel guns, and situated about 70 yards from the river. In one corner of the fort was a 19-foot-deep well, known to this day as the Franklin Well. The three buildings within the palisade were two barracks and one officers' quarters.

It is believed that the defense was regularly garrisoned until about 1761, and that thereafter it was intermittently occupied by provincial troops. It is known that the fort was still standing in 1780. A visitor to the community in 1787 found that the defense had disappeared and that part of its site was occupied by the home of Colonel Jacob Weiss of Philadelphia, who had purchased the land where Weissport stands today in 1784. The site of the fort was many years later occupied by the Fort Allen Hotel on the present-day corner of Bridge and Franklin streets.

Pennsylvania

ALLENTOWN CAMP. CAMP CRANE.

FORT ANTES. Built by Colonel John Henry Antes in 1776, Fort Antes stood on a high bluff at the mouth of Antes Creek, on the south side of the West Branch of the Susquehanna River, opposite the town of Jersey Shore in Lycoming County. The palisaded defense, which also served as a refuge for the area's settlers, covered at least a quarter of an acre. It was probably defended by at least one cannon and intermittently garrisoned by Pennsylvania militia. Abandoned during the Great Runaway—the general exodus of the region's settlers in compliance with Governor Hunter's orders—it was partially burned by the Indians. Colonel Antes later returned and rebuilt his fort. After the signing of the 1783 Treaty of Paris, which restored peace to the Susquehanna Valley, the fort was allowed to fall into decay.

CAMP ANTHONY WAYNE. A temporary camp established on May 18, 1926, on the grounds of the Sesquicentennial International Exposition at Philadelphia, Camp Anthony Wayne was garrisoned by troops selected from various military organizations and designated the "Sesquicentennial Exposition Force" to do all in their power to make the event a success and to present to the public a favorable impression of the Regular Army. The camp was abandoned December 10, 1926, following the close of the exhibition.

FORT ARMSTRONG. A Revolutionary War frontier fort, Fort Armstrong was located on the east bank of the Allegheny River, about 40 miles above Pittsburgh, just south of present Kittan-ning in Armstrong County, on the site of an old Delaware Indian town. In the spring of 1779, in compliance with orders of General Washington, who was then planning the campaign against the towns of the Six Nations subsequently carried out by General John Sullivan, Colonel Daniel Brodhead ascended the Allegheny with a strong force as far as Venango, fortifying several points along his route as bases for Sullivan's operations. He began the construction of a strong palisaded fort in June under the supervision of Lieutenant Colonel Stephen Bayard, who completed it at the end of July. It was named in honor of Colonel John Armstrong, who in 1756 commanded the Susquehanna forts. The fort was probably abandoned not long after the completion of Sullivan's operations.

FORT ARMSTRONG. A War of 1812 two-story blockhouse defense, armed with one 12-pounder and four brass 4-pounders, Fort Armstrong was erected on the south shore of Lake Erie in April 1814 by Major Ralph Marlin, 22nd Infantry, to assist in the defense of the town of Erie while the British fleet was hovering offshore. The blockhouse was probably dismantled sometime in 1816 or 1817.

FORT AUGUSTA. Located at the present city of Sunbury, on the east bank of the Susquehanna River in Northumberland County, Fort Augusta stood well in advance of the line of frontier defenses and was the most impressive of the forts built by Pennsylvania during the French and Indian War, the one longest garrisoned by Provincial troops, and the last one used for military purposes. Begun in July 1756 by troops

FORT AUGUSTA. Model. (Courtesy of the Pennsylvania Department of Commerce.)

under the command of Colonel William Clapham, its construction was continued under the supervision of Major James Burd, and until June 13, 1765, the fort was continuously garrisoned by Pennsylvania troops. Its name was selected by Governor Robert Morris, most probably in honor of the Princess Augusta, then the widow of the late Prince of Wales and mother of the future George III.

Surviving fort plans, journals, and correspondence describe Fort Augusta in considerable detail. Its general design was square, with bastions at the four corners; including the bastions, it measured 204 feet on a side, and resembled the smaller French Fort Duquesne. From the two bastions nearer the river, palisades strengthened with blockhouses extended laterally to guard the extent of riverfront against attack from the landward side. Over the fort in 1756 the British flag, red with the crosses of Saint George and Saint Andrew on a blue corner field, flew on a 70-foot-high flagpole. When the fort was completed, it mounted at least 12 cannon and two swivels.

After the close of the war, despite Fort Augusta's importance as a strategic defense for the province, a vehement outcry was raised by the region's "peace at any price" party of that day, and the fort was partially dismantled, probably in 1766. After the outbreak of the Revolution, Fort Augusta became the headquarters of Pennsylvania's military department of the Upper Susquehanna. In the spring of 1778, when large bands of British-allied Indians were demoralizing Pennsylvania's frontiers, the fort's garrison had no rest. The Wyoming Massacre later the same year deluged Fort Augusta with destitute refugees. Most of the garrisons were withdrawn, the Indians soon followed, and burned everything that was left undefended.

The only part of Fort Augusta still remaining at Sunbury is the powder magazine, a brick-walled, tomb-like structure. A 60-foot-square model of the fort occupies the lawn of the museum that houses relics of the fort and other artifacts relating to the history of the Susquehanna.

CAMP BALLIER. A temporary Civil War encampment, Camp Ballier was located west of Ridge Road in Philadelphia.

CAMP BANKS. A temporary Civil War encampment, Camp Banks was located on the east side of Germantown Road in Philadelphia.

FORT BEDFORD (*Fort Raystown*). Constructed in 1758 on a strategic bluff overlooking what is now known as the Raystown Branch of the Juniata River, Fort Bedford was the rallying point for the entire pre-Revolutionary western frontier and the springboard for General John Forbes's famous expedition against French Fort Duquesne at modern Pittsburgh. The village that grew up around the post became, for a brief period, the county seat of western Pennsylvania. A stone building, still standing on the fort's grounds as the fort's last remaining structure, served in 1794 as General Washington's headquarters during his march against the Pennsylvania insurrectionists during the Whiskey Rebellion.

The town, originally known as Raystown, founded in 1751 by a man named Ray, is indebted for its existence and history to geography: the location here of a gap through the Allegheny Mountains through which passed most of the great migrations that opened up the West during the eighteenth and nineteenth centuries. Called Fort Raystown when built by the troops under Colonel Henry Bouquet, it was officially renamed on December 1 of the same year in honor of the Duke of Bedford. Standing for about a decade, the fort served as the supply depot for the vanguard of men who, over a period of four months, hacked out of 100 miles of trackless mountains and forests the Forbes Trail as a military highway for the capture of Fort Duquesne. So accurate was General Forbes's direction that today's U.S. 30 virtually parallels the right of way carved out by the axes and spades of an army of British regulars and provincial soldiers.

Colonel Bouquet and his engineer, Captain Harry Gordon, constructed one of the strongest of the frontier forts at Bedford. In the configuration of today's geography, the fort occupied 7,000 square yards of ground bounded on the north by the river, on the east by Richard, on the south by Pitt, and on the west by Juliana streets. In addition to its five bastions, loopholed for swivel guns, it had a "Galley with loop-holes" extending from the central bastion on its north front to the river bank, in order to secure the water approaches. The fort's main gate was in the south curtain on Pitt Street, originally known as Forbes Road. Other entrances were a smaller gate in the west palisade and a postern gate opening to the north. Ample quarters for the officers and the garrison were arranged within the compound. The hospital and an additional large storehouse were located outside to the south while the traders' houses stood about 100 yards to the southwest. In addition to its 18-foot-high palisades, Fort Bedford was also protected to the south and west by an 8-foot-deep moat, 10 feet wide at the bottom and 15 feet wide at the top.

The first instance of a British military post being captured by American colonials occurred in 1769 when Fort Bedford was seized by the so-called "Black Boys" under Captain James Smith to effect the release of 18 fellow colonials held prisoner there for burning a trade goods train sent by Philadelphia merchants. Despite a proclamation by the Crown to the contrary, enterprising merchants persisted in trading with the Indians. The "Black Boys," so-called because they daubed their faces with soot to disguise themselves, fought against all trade with the Indians who, they claimed, bartered for such trade goods as guns and powder, knives and tomahawks, to wage war against the frontier's settlers. The fort, then lightly garrisoned, was swiftly overpowered, the soldiers' arms seized, and the prisoners released. Within hours, the fort was evacuated by the "Black Boys."

By the time this event took place, Fort Bedford was in a state of disrepair, and no efforts were made to renovate the post. It was practically a ruination by the outbreak of the Revolution, and much of its salvageable timber was used by new settlers in the area to build their homes. A number of dwellings in Bedford County were stockaded and minimally fortified during the Revolution to take the place of the fort and served as havens for refugees from British-allied Indian raids. Fort Bedford Park and Museum of today were developed by the people of the city in 1958 and dedicated at the time of Fort Bedford Bicentennial Celebration. The Museum's central display is an accurately reproduced large-scale model of the old fort.

BEESON'S BLOCKHOUSE. A strong log blockhouse defense, it was erected in 1774 within today's city limits of Uniontown, Fayette County, by Henry Beeson, who founded the community several years earlier. The blockhouse stood on the site of the present county jail.

FORT BEVERSREDE. In order to restrain the enterprising Swedes who were encroaching on Dutch-claimed territory on both sides of the Delaware River, the Dutch in April and May 1648 erected a fortified outpost of the Dutch West Indian Company on the east bank of the Schuylkill River (site still undetermined), in the old Indian district of Passyunk (still so named), now a part of Philadelphia. The primary interest of both competing colonizing nations was to monopolize the area's lucrative Indian trade.

Fort Beversrede consisted of a large log house enclosed by a palisade. Its construction elicited vociferous opposition from New Sweden's Governor Johan Printz. While the fort was nearing completion, a Swedish subaltern visited the place and, failing to intimidate its occupants, cut down all the newly planted fruit trees there. The Swedes then resorted to vandalism by twice tearing down the palisades. In September Printz adopted the ingenious device of making Fort Beversrede virtually impotent by constructing a stockaded 30-by-20-foot fort directly in front of the Dutch establishment, "the back gable of their house being only twelve feet from the gate of our fort."

The Dutch at the time had only six "able-bodied" men on the Delaware to protect their interests. The failure of the Dutch West Indian Company to take steps to vindicate Dutch honor and reassert their claims to the territory rested in their reluctance to antagonize Sweden, then a military power and an ally of the Dutch in Europe. The building in 1651 of Fort Casimir at today's New Castle, Delaware, by Peter Stuyvesant severely crippled Swedish colonization. Fort Beversrede was then apparently abandoned after it appeared to have diminished significantly in military importance. In 1655, by order of the Dutch West India Company's directors, Stuyvesant fitted out a large expedition, sailed into the Delaware, and compelled the capitulation of the Swedish forts. Although Fort Beversrede was abandoned as a military post, it was no doubt used for some years by the Dutch as a trading house.

CAMP BIDDLE. A Civil War receiving station for draftees and other recruits during 1864–65, Camp Biddle was located on the grounds of Carlisle Barracks.

BIG BEAVER BLOCKHOUSE. Located in the present town of New Brighton, at the intersection of Main and 3rd streets, in Beaver County, this blockhouse defense was built in 1788 by order of the War Department. It was in existence as late as 1793, when it was garrisoned by a sergeant and a few soldiers. William Wilson of Pittsburgh operated a trading store there from 1791 to 1793.

FORT BIGHAM (BINGHAM). Variously dated by differing historical authorities as having been built in 1749 or 1754 by Samuel Bigham (Bingham), this strongly built stockaded blockhouse was located a few miles west of the present town of Mexico in the Tuscarora Valley, Juniata County, on what was then known as the Traders' Path. Constructed to protect settlers and traders in the region, Fort Bigham was attacked on June 11, 1756, by a party of French and Indians. The raiders killed 5 of its occupants, carried off 18 others as prisoners, and burned the fort. It was reportedly rebuilt four years later by traders but abandoned and again burned by Indians in the spring of 1763.

FORT BOSLEY. Situated in the forks of the Chillisquaque on the east bank of its north branch at Washingtonville, Montour County, Fort Bosley was a grist mill that was strongly stockaded, fortified, and garrisoned by a small force of soldiers (20 men at most) in 1777 as a protection against British-allied Indian marauders. There is no account on record of the defense ever having been attacked. It was apparently dismantled after the Revolution.

CAMP BRISBIN (*Camp Couch*). A temporary Civil War encampment established on June 28, 1861, east of Harrisburg, by Captain Brisbin, it was first called Camp Couch for Major General D. N. Couch, but later became known as Camp Brisbin.

BROWN'S FORT. FORT MANADA.

BROWN'S FORT. A Revolutionary War palisaded fort erected in 1778 on the Susquehanna River at Pittston in the Wyoming Valley, Brown's Fort was captured and apparently destroyed by British and Indians in 1778.

FORT BURD. REDSTONE FORT.

CAMP CADWALADER. The need for a permanent installation for the congregating and organization of Civil War draftees and volunteer recruits within the city of Philadelphia led to the establishment of Camp Cadwalader in 1861. The camp was the most important military rendezvous in the city. It consisted of an extensive complex of barracks and auxiliary structures enclosed by a high fence and was located on Islington Lane, east of Ridge Road. At times the camp was over capacity, and during the latter period of the war it was vehemently criticized by both soldiers and the area's public. Many regiments were organized and mustered into service here, and a large proportion of returning regiments were sent to the camp for discharge.

CAMP CAMAC WOODS. The area of Camac Woods, as it was then known during the Civil War, is now in the neighborhood of 11th Street and Montgomery Avenue in Philadelphia. The area was used from time to time by military units as a rendezvous and training ground.

CAMP CAMERON. A temporary Civil War cavalry encampment located east of Harrisburg, it may have been named in honor of Secretary of War Simon Cameron. The camp was reportedly located three miles south of Camp Curtin.

CAPTAIN SMITH'S FORT. FORT SWATARA.

CAMP NEAR CARLISLE. CARLISLE BARRACKS.

CARLISLE BARRACKS (*Fort Lowther; Camp near Carlisle; Washingtonburg Post*). The first real military camp at Carlisle was established with the arrival of a mixed force of British and Provincial troops, commanded by Colonel John Stanwix, on May 30, 1757, about two years after the decisive defeat of General Edward Braddock's army near Fort Duquesne. At first it was simply known as the Camp near Carlisle, then as Washingtonburg, and later received its present name—Carlisle Barracks.

An examination of conditions on the Pennsylvania frontier in the 1750s explains Colonel Stanwix's construction of entrenchments at Carlisle, located at the juncture of the north-south, east-west routes of Indian trade. Beginning in 1730, a flood of settlers had crossed into the rich Cumberland Valley. These rapidly expanding settlements encroached on the lands set aside by treaty for the Indians. As a result, the once-friendly relations between the Indians and the government began to fray, and by 1753 were ripped apart by alliances formed between the French and the Indians. The Valley became the scene of many raids by the Indians. An old stockade that had been erected in Carlisle at an early date had fallen into decay, so it was rebuilt and garrisoned to protect the inhabitants. As the frequency of the raids increased, a new stockade, Fort Lowther, was constructed west of the present Public Square in the borough, with today's High Street running through its center.

Colonel Stanwix and his forces had intended to march on to Ohio Valley positions. However, while in Carlisle, he received word that a French-Indian force was preparing to hit the area. He decided to establish a strong defense here, rather than move on, and so constructed the camp which was referred to earlier. In his command was a battalion of the Royal Americans (British 62nd Regiment) and 1,000 Pennsylvania, 300 Maryland, and 600 Virginia Provincials. The Royal American Regiment (later redesignated the 60th and renamed the King's Royal Rifle Corps) exists today.

In May 1758 a large depot was ordered built at Carlisle. With the erection of storehouses and barracks, the first actual buildings appeared in Stanwix's camp, the forerunner of present-day Carlisle Barracks. The post was the most secure English position in the West, and served throughout the French and Indian War as a supply base and springboard for expeditions to the West. With the Indian wars over, an uneasy peace existed until the beginning of the Revolutionary War. The post became an armory for the manufacture of muskets and ammunition in 1769, and it continued to function as supply headquarters for the forces to the west.

By the time the Revolutionary War got under way, Carlisle Barracks had taken its shape as a permanent military reservation. Remote from the actual theater of operations, garrisoned by troops of Washington's Continental Army, on the direct supply route to the western frontier, and in the center of a rich agricultural area, Carlisle Barracks was designated as the Quartermaster Supply Headquarters for the Western Department. The necessities of war led to further expansion of activities at Carlisle. The availability of many skilled armorers in the area and supplies of iron nearby, plus its strategic location, made Carlisle the logical site for an arsenal.

The arsenal's main magazine, erected in 1777, still stands. It is the second oldest building on the post and is now known as the Hessian Powder Magazine Museum. The magazine was reputedly built by Hessian prisoners captured at the Battle of Trenton and sent by Washington to the Barracks for any labor that might be necessary. The oldest building on post is the Mill Apartments, believed to have been built between 1761 and 1768. It is fitting that Carlisle Barracks is now the home of the Army's senior education institution, since the post, the second oldest United States military post, was also the home of what is believed to have been the service's first education institution, a school for artillerists established in 1777, the first of 10 different Army schools located at the installation. The post was named Washingtonburg for General George Washington during the war. However, it was not until 1801 that the old post actually became federal property when it was purchased from the heirs of William Penn. The post gained its current name about 1807.

With the outbreak of trouble in western Pennsylvania over the new whiskey taxes, General Washington personally assembled at Carlisle the largest force ever under his command, about 14,000 men, to quell the so-called Whiskey Rebellion of 1794. The forerunner of the Armor School, the School of Cavalry Practice, was established here in 1838 and remained at this location until 1861. On the afternoon of July 1, 1863, Confederate cavalry commanded by Generals J. E. B. Stuart and Fitzhugh Lee approached the community of Carlisle attempting to join forces with General Richard S. Ewell, who had briefly occupied the town and barracks June 27–29. Upon arriving at Carlisle, the two cavalry forces found

CARLISLE BARRACKS. The Hessian Guardhouse. (Courtesy of the U.S. Army.)

the town held by members of the 21st and 22nd New York Militia Regiments. Stuart sent Lee's forces to demand an unconditional surrender or to suffer a bombardment. With the surrender refused, the Confederate forces opened fire with small-caliber artillery. After bombarding the area for a short time, another request was issued for the unconditional surrender, which was again refused. A second barrage began, and torches were applied to a lumberyard near the military installation. About 10:00 P.M. on this date, the Confederates applied torches simultaneously to the barracks and buildings of Carlisle Barracks attempting to force the surrender of the militia forces. Sometime after midnight, Stuart ordered Lee's barrage stopped, and the units moved toward Gettysburg to join the main forces of the Confederate Army.

The Carlisle Indian Industrial School was located here from its founding in 1879 until its closing in 1918. From 1920 to 1946, Carlisle Barracks was the home of the Medical Field Service School. The School for Government of Occupied Areas, the Adjutant's General School, the Chaplain School, the Military Police School, the Army Security Agency School, and the Armed Forces Information School were located here during the period 1946–1951.

Since 1951 Carlisle Barracks has been the home of the U.S. Army War College. The U.S. Army Combat Development Command Institute of Advanced Studies was established here in 1962. In February 1973 the Institute was made an integral part of the War College and renamed the Strategic Studies Institute. Its mission of performing comprehensive and in-depth studies of strategic interest for the College and for the Department of the Army continues. In 1967 the U.S. Army Military History Institute was established here, and on May 8, 1970, the General Omar N. Bradley Museum was dedicated as an integral part of the Institute.

The U.S. Army Military History Institute has the primary mission of preserving historical books, papers, and artifacts relating to the military history of the United States, and making these sources of information available for research by both civilian and military scholars. In addition to historical materials collected throughout the Army, many personal papers of distinguished military leaders have been added to the Institute. The Institute now contains approximately 300,000 books, over 20,000 periodicals, and thousands of collections of documents, photographs, and personal papers. It is regarded as an outstanding source of research in the field of military history.

FORT CHAMBERS. This frontier defense at present Chambersburg, Franklin County, was one of five forts local settlers agreed to build at the meeting of October 30, 1755. Erected in the winter and spring of 1756 by Colonel Benjamin Chambers, the fortification stood on the bank of Conococheague Creek, just west of today's North Main Street, midway between Market and King streets. The largest and strongest defense in the area, it consisted of a high stockade enclosing the colonel's dwelling, his flour and saw mills, and a large, two-story stone building with its roof covered with sheet lead to protect it from fire arrows. The fort was armed with at least two 4-pounder swivel guns that Colonel Chambers obtained from the provincial government. Often garrisoned by the militia, organized by the colonel, the fort was attacked by Indians from time to time. It was probably partially dismantled after the end of the French and Indian War.

CAMP CHASE. A Civil War encampment probably established in 1861, Camp Chase was located on present 51st Street, east of Darby Road, in Philadelphia.

CAMP CHESTNUT HILL. A Civil War military hospital, known as Camp Chestnut Hill, was located between Abington and Springfield avenues, near the Reading Railroad, in Philadelphia.

CLAYPOOLE'S BLOCKHOUSE. A frontier defense erected about 1791, Claypoole's Blockhouse stood on the east bank of the Allegheny River, just above the present town of Ford City, Armstrong County.

CAMP COLT. This temporary World War I training post was first known as Camp U.S. Troops, Gettysburg prior to March 19, 1918, when it was renamed in honor of Samuel Colt, who patented the first revolver in 1835. Camp Colt was established in June 1917 on Gettysburg's battlefield for the purpose of mobilizing, concentrating, and training troops of the Tank Service. The post's commanding officer was Captain (later General) Dwight Eisenhower who ultimately became president of the United States. Discontinuing tank training on November 18, 1918, Camp Colt was abandoned on August 15, 1919.

CAMP COPELAND (*Camp Reynolds*). A Civil War encampment located at or near Pittsburgh, Camp Reynolds was called Camp Copeland for Brigadier General Joseph Copeland, who was ordered by the War Department to take command of the post on July 4, 1863. The camp was renamed Reynolds, but when it was closed April 29, 1865, its name was again Camp Copeland.

CAMP COUCH. CAMP BRISBIN.

CAMP COUCH. A Civil War encampment named for General Darius Nash Couch, Camp Couch was located across the Susquehanna River from Harrisburg, between the towns of West Fairview and Wormleysburg.

FORT COUCH. A Civil War defense built in 1863 at Lemoyne, Cumberland County, and named for General Darius Nash Couch, it was constructed before the Battle of Gettysburg to oppose the expected Confederate drive against Harrisburg. The site, then known as Hummel's Heights, consists of breastwork remains at 8th and Ohio streets.

COUCH'S FORT. A Revolutionary War defense and refuge haven, Couch's Fort, also mentioned in the annals of the Whiskey Insurrection of 1794, was located near Pittsburgh, about a quarter of a mile south of the Bethel Presbyterian Church, in Bethel Township, Allegheny County. The spring, which was within the fort, is still flowing.

CAMP CRANE (*Allentown Camp*). Located on the grounds of the Lehigh County Agricultural Society almost in the heart of the city of Allentown, Lehigh County, contrary to the Army's practice of situating its camps away from populated areas, Camp Crane's unit was a corps—the U.S. Army Ambulance Service—the only detached one to serve during World War I. Commonly known during its early days as Allentown Camp, after it was established in late May 1917, it was officially designated Camp Crane on March 1, 1918, in honor of Brigadier General Charles H. Crane, surgeon general, 1882–83. The post was closed on April 10, 1919.

FORT CRAWFORD. Located at Logan's Ferry, about 16 miles north of Pittsburgh, on the southeastern bank of the Allegheny River, Fort Crawford was a stockaded defense built in May 1778 by Colonel William Crawford, who intermittently commanded the post until 1780. From the time of its inception until the close of the Revolution, it was continuously garrisoned, first by Continental Army troops, then by elements of the Rangers and militia, and it served primarily as a depot and distribution point for supplies and war munitions. After the war, apparently few efforts were made to maintain the fort. The last notice of Fort Crawford related to the Indian

troubles of 1791–95, by which time the fort was practically a ruination.

CAMP CURTIN. The first mobilization camp in Harrisburg for Union recruits during the Civil War, Camp Curtin was established soon after Governor Andrew Curtin in April 1861 issued orders for the establishment of an encampment near the city. Then located two miles north of Harrisburg, on the county's extensive fairgrounds, the site of Camp Curtin is today within the city limits on Maclay Street, between 4th and 5th streets, and extending to the Pennsylvania Railroad. Because of its location on the railroad line to Washington, Camp Curtin became Pennsylvania's largest mobilization and training center and served throughout the war.

FORT DANA. In response to the threatened advance by Confederate forces on Philadelphia, a "Committee of Defence" was authorized by Philadelphia's City Council in June 1863 to establish a number of redoubts commanding the approaches to the city. The largest of the works was Fort Dana, probably named for General Napoleon J. T. Dana, located at the Falls of the Schuylkill. As far as is known, no guns were mounted, as the threat ended with the Battle of Gettysburg. Several of the fortifications, including Fort Dana, remained for several years after the war.

FORT DELAWARE. There were, during the French and Indian War, two forts in the Cushetunk Settlement, established by Connecticut Yankees, one on the Pennsylvania side of the Delaware River, known as the Lower Fort, and the other on the Jersey side, called the Upper Fort. The one that has been reconstructed and used as a museum, now called Fort Delaware, is the one originally erected on the Pennsylvania side, near the present village of Milanville in Wayne County, five miles above Narrowsburg, New York. The site of the other defense, a stockaded blockhouse, originally located "about forty rods below the fording place," is at Cochecton, New York (this location was, until 1769, a part of Sussex County, New Jersey). Sometime prior to 1763, the Lower Fort was enlarged to a palisaded fort with a blockhouse at each corner. Standing on a bluff overlooking the bend of the Delaware, it was rectangular in shape. Its long side, facing the river, measured 116 feet, and its width measured 80 feet. Within the palisade, protected by several swivel guns, were three log houses and a well. By the time of the outbreak of the Revolution, the fort had fallen into disrepair.

FORT DEPUY. FORT DUPUI.

DESHLER'S FORT. This stone fort built in 1760 by Adam Deshler, Switzerland native, was located on Coplay Creek, just below the present town of Egypt in Lehigh County. Adjoining his house on the north was a large frame building, large enough to accommodate 20 soldiers and store military supplies. Deshler was employed by the Provincial government to furnish supplies to the soldiers. The stone house stood until about 1940.

FORT DEWART. "The fort on the top of Allegheny Hill," located half a mile northeast of U.S. 30 in present Somerset County, was erected in 1758 as a way station along Forbes Road from Carlisle to Pittsburgh during General Forbes's campaign against French Fort Duquesne. Never regularly garrisoned, Fort Dewart however was of some use to British and Provincial troops during the war.

FORT DICKINSON. A 25-mile stretch of the Susquehanna River below the mouth of the Lackawanna River (including the present city of Wilkes-Barre) was known in Colonial times as the Wyoming Valley, scene of the famous massacre in July 1758 perpetrated by John Butler's Tories and Indians. Long claimed by both Connecticut and Pennsylvania, the valley became over the years the battleground of bloody clashes known as the Pennamite Wars, with Connecticut Yankees pitted against Pennsylvania partisans known as Pennamites. The incidence of the Revolution temporarily suspended the war between the two factions, but it resumed as soon as the 1783 Treaty of Paris was signed. The Pennamites at Wilkes-Barre built themselves a strong fortification called Fort Dickinson with four small blockhouses occupied as outposts. The defense was fortified with two 4-pounder cannon, two swivels, and one "wall-piece" and garrisoned by 100 men. On the morning of July 23, 1784, a large force of Connecticut Yankees marched into the village of Wilkes-Barre and laid siege to Fort Dickinson. After several days of bloody forays on both sides, the fort capitulated.

FORT DUDGEON (*Tomahawk Camp*). A temporary way station established in 1758 on Forbes Road, the military road cut through the mountains and forests between Carlisle and Pittsburgh during General John Forbes's campaign against Fort Duquesne, Fort Dudgeon (also called Tomahawk Camp) was located a short distance north of today's U.S. 30, near the present town of Jennerstown in Somerset County.

FORT DUPUI (*Fort Depuy*). The first known settler in the area of present Monroe County was the Huguenot Frenchman, Samuel Dupui (Depuy), who settled there in 1727. His spacious stone house, replacing an original log-built one, was considered by British military authorities during the French and Indian War as an admirable place for defense. It was further strengthened, stockaded, and garrisoned by British and Provincial troops between December 1755 and May 1758. The fort stood near the town of Shawnee, five miles east of Stroudsburg.

FORT DUQUESNE (*Trent's Fort; Fort Prince George*). Originally planned to be established at Logstown or Chiningué (today's town of Ambridge on the Ohio River), Fort Duquesne was erected in the spring of 1754 at the strategic Forks of the Ohio, within present Point State Park in Pittsburgh, where the Monongahela and the Allegheny merge to form the Ohio. Named in honor of Ange de Menneville, Marquis Duquesne, governor general of Canada, 1752–55, it served until its destruction in November 1758 as headquarters of the commander on the Ohio and was by far the largest of the four French forts in the region. A regular military structure, although constructed mostly of timber, it was in the form of a square about 80 feet on a side, but inclusive of its projecting bastions covered an area about 155 feet square. Some original outlying works facing the Allegheny were developed in early 1758 into a so-called second fort. French-allied Indians occupied huts east of the fort.

Considering the bitter struggle between the English and the French for the Forks of the Ohio, it seemed remarkable that neither party intended originally to erect a fort here. The British-chartered Virginia Company had first selected the site of present McKees Rocks just above Pittsburgh, while the French planned a fort at present Ambridge, then an Indian settlement known to the English as Logstown and to the French as Chiningué.

In order to preempt French designs to occupy the environs of the Forks, men under Captain William Trent hurriedly set about building a storehouse in March 1754, completed in April by Ensign Edward Ward. Captain Claude-Pierre Pecaudy, sieur de Contrecoeur, had in the meantime prepared to complete French occupation of the Ohio and came down from Niagara. On April 16 the French force of 600 men camped a short distance above the Forks where, on the same day, Ensign Ward had completed the storehouse's stockade. On the next day, Contrecoeur forced Ward, with only a 41-man detachment, to surrender Trent's Fort, also known as Fort Prince George. On the morning of April 18, the English and their Indians left, leaving the French in possession of the Forks. By the middle of June, the French had largely completed the main works of Fort Duquesne, using much of the English-prepared squared timbers stored for the future at Trent's Fort. Seizure of the Forks completed the successful French occupation of the region but precipitated the beginning of a long, bitter struggle to hold the country against British counterattack, though Britain and France were officially at peace.

The decisive, crushing defeat of the British army under General Edward Braddock on the Monongahela, not far from Fort Duquesne's ramparts, on July 9, 1755, provided the French with a windfall of valuable stores left almost at their threshold. It was three years before the English could launch another attack on this place, a setback that led to the formal declaration of war, issued in London on May 17, 1756, and published in America between two and three months later, initiating the Seven Years' War in Europe.

The period from 1755 to 1758 was one of frontier forays. In response to frequent French and Indian murderous raids, Pennsylvania raised troops for its own defense and erected its first and most remarkable series of frontier forts. During the summer and fall of 1758, an army of considerable forces under General John Forbes carved out of the wilderness a new 100-mile-long military road from Carlisle to the Forks of the Ohio. It then became increasingly apparent to the French that Fort Duquesne, with a garrison of less than 300 men, was doomed. At a council of war on November 19, French officers concurred that the fort must be evacuated. The defenders began the task of demolition while Forbes's army was only "five or six leagues away," finally mining 50 to 60 barrels of spoiled powder in the fort's powder magazine. The tremendous explosion that reduced the fort to rubble was heard by the British and Provincials some miles distant. The French retreated to Fort Machault at the present site of Franklin, their last headquarters on the Ohio, precariously maintained from November 1758 to August 1759.

Fort Duquesne had been crucial to the defense of the Ohio country. The loss of the fort laid the country open to English traders, soldiers, and settlers. In 1759 the strategic position at the Forks of the Ohio was reoccupied by a new British defense—Fort Pitt— a work of uncommonly large size and extensive outworks.

FORT DURKEE. Located at present Wilkes-Barre, Fort Durkee was the first fort erected by Connecticut settlers in the Wyoming Valley, built during the spring and summer of 1769. The fort stood 1,000 feet from Fort Wyoming, erected in opposition in 1771 by Pennsylvania authorities, and was named for their leader, John Durkee, a French and Indian War veteran. The establishment of Fort Durkee precipitated the Pennamite War. In 1771 the fort was captured and destroyed by Pennamites. In the configuration of today's Wilkes-Barre geography, Fort Durkee was situated on a site between Ross and South streets.

EIGHTY-NINTH REGIMENT CAMP. A temporary Civil War encampment, it was located in the Nicetown section of Philadelphia.

FORT EVERETT. A French and Indian War defense and citizen refuge erected about 1756, Fort Everett was garrisoned by troops guarding the area south of the Blue Mountains, between the Schuylkill and Lehigh rivers. The fort was located east of Lynnport, Lehigh County, on or near present S.R. 143.

FORT FAYETTE (*Fort Franklin; Fort La Fayette*). Located on a site across Penn Avenue at Hand (10th) Street, east of present Point State Park at the Forks of the Ohio in Pittsburgh, Fort Fayette was erected in 1791–92 to replace dismantled Fort Pitt in response to the vociferous demands of the town's inhabitants for protection against Indian attacks. Originally named Fort Franklin during its construction period, then designated Fort La Fayette after its completion, the defense became popularly known as Fort Fayette. The post served as a chief supply base for General Anthony Wayne's army during 1792–94. The fort stood about 100 yards from the bank of the Allegheny River, about a quarter of a mile from Fort Pitt's former garrison. It was composed of pickets 12 feet high with bastions in the corners, three of which enclosed pentagonal two-story log blockhouses. The fourth, southeastern bastion was a brick powder magazine. Two log buildings, the commandant's and staff quarters on the northern side and the barracks for 200 soldiers on the western side, were two stories high. From 1794 until 1812, the fort was garrisoned by only a detachment of troops. During the War of 1812, Fort Fayette served as Commodore Perry's headquarters for supplies and the training of troops. In 1815 its garrison was withdrawn, the fort was abandoned, and the property parceled as lots for public sale. The site is today occupied by the Edison Hotel.

FIFTEENTH REGIMENT CAMP. A temporary Civil War encampment located north of Ridge Road in Philadelphia.

FIFTY-EIGHTH REGIMENT CAMP. A temporary Civil War encampment situated between Wissahickon Creek and Norristown Road in Philadelphia.

FORTY FORT. Located at the present town of Forty Fort, a few miles southwest of Wyoming, in Luzerne County, Forty Fort was named for the first forty settlers from Connecticut who erected the defense in 1772. When Colonel John Butler's notorious Tory raiders and British-allied Indians invaded the Wyoming Valley in the summer of 1778 and captured Fort Wintermute at Exeter and Jenkins Fort at West Pittston, refugee settlers flocked to the safety of Forty Fort. Garrisoned by less than 400 men, consisting mostly of six companies of militia, commanded by Colonel Zebulon Butler, a Continental officer home on furlough, the besieged fort was finally forced to capitulate. Despite assurances by Tory Colonel Butler, his Iroquois Indian allies massacred about 300 men, women, and children in the valley.

FOURTH UNION LEAGUE REGIMENT CAMP. A temporary Civil War encampment located west of Broad Street in Philadelphia.

FRANKFORD ARSENAL. Established on May 27, 1816, Frankford Arsenal was the second oldest arsenal in the United States, named for the town of Frankford, now a part of the city of Philadelphia. Originally consisting of two stone buildings on a 20-acre tract, it was expanded by the acquisition of additional acreage in 1837, 1849, 1917, 1943, and 1951, until it encompassed 110 acres occupied by 234 buildings, located between Route I-95 and the Delaware River.

The arsenal was essentially an ordnance research and engineering center, engaged on projects dealing with fire control, instrument and guidance systems, armaments, pilot ejection catapults, direct fire weapons, and chronometers. On November 22, 1974, the secretary of the Army publicly announced the decision to close Frankford Arsenal by the end of 1977. On July 14, 1983, the 167-year-old arsenal was put up for auction by the General Services Administration. About 170 buildings and 80 acres of ground were sold to a Salem, Massachusetts, developer.

FORT FRANKLIN. FORT FAYETTE.

FORT FRANKLIN (*Old Garrison*). Constructed by Captain Jonathan Heart at the junction of the Allegheny River and French Creek in the present city of Franklin, under instructions of Congress to General Josiah Harmar, Fort Franklin was completed in April 1787 and ultimately accomplished a reconciliation between the government and the Seneca Indians. The fort was a 16-foot-high palisaded parallelogram about 100 feet square, including its outworks. The fort was apparently abandoned in 1794. In 1796 what was known as the Old Garrison was constructed to replace Fort Franklin and occupied until 1799 by U.S. troops. The structure later became the first jail in Venango County. Its site at the foot of 10th Street in Franklin is now under water.

FRONTIER FORTS. Pennsylvania's settlements were spared the horrors of attack, pillage, and massacre well into the eighteenth century principally because of William Penn's record of scrupulously fair treatment of the Indians, although he left America's shores for the last time in 1701. But the French and Indian War (1754–63), precipitated by the establishment of French fortifications along the Ohio and George Washington's ignominious surrender of Fort Necessity at Uniontown, embroiled the colony in a long, costly and brutally fought war on its frontiers, which at the outset were entirely defenseless. During the course of the conflict, some 200 defenses, running the gamut from full-scale Provincial fortifications to minimally fortified stone-and-log structures, were built along the colony's frontiers.

English, Irish, Scotch, and Welsh émigrés preceded the much later arrival of waves of emigrants from continental Europe, with thousands of them penetrating the Cumberland Valley to establish farming homesteads and new settlements in what was then a wilderness. It is not difficult to analyze the reasons that induced the Indians to commit their depredations throughout the province, though the policy of the government had always been of a peaceful character and was based on the principle of fair dealing with the natives. But as the Indians almost daily saw themselves pushed back by the inexorable advance of the whites, eventuating in the loss of their hunting and fishing grounds, either by fair purchase or, more often, by fraudulent actions by the settlers, they felt they had no recourse but vengeful destruction and cold-blooded massacre. The annihilation of Braddock's army on the Monongahela near Fort Duquesne in 1755 provided the spark to set the frontiers aflame.

Literally hundreds of settler-built defenses were erected, ranging from loopholed dwellings and planked stockades to large palisaded enclosures mounting from one to four blockhouses, which intermittently served to accommodate refugees and Provincial military garrisons. It is not within the scope of this compilation to list, locate, and describe most of these rudimentary defenses. The most definitive work relating to Pennsylvania's colonial defenses is the two-volume *Report of the Commission to Locate the Site of the Frontier Forts of Pennsylvania* (1916).

CAMP GAINES. FORT SNYDER.

CAMP GALLAGHER. A temporary Civil War encampment located south of Ridge Road in Philadelphia.

FORT GEORGE. PATTERSON'S FORT.

FORT GRANVILLE. An important link in the chain of early frontier defenses, Fort Granville was erected in 1755–56 on the north bank of the Juniata River, on the west side of the Susquehanna, about a mile and a half southwest of present Lewistown, Mifflin County. While most of the garrison were in the Tuscarora Valley protecting settlers engaged in harvesting, a small force of French and Indians under Captain Coulon de Villiers, who had defeated Colonel George Washington at Fort Necessity, attacked and destroyed the fort on August 3, 1756.

FORT GREENE. A temporary defensive fortification erected at Valley Forge, General Washington's 1777–78 winter headquarters, Fort Greene was named for General Nathanael Greene.

GULPH MILLS ENCAMPMENT. The Continental Army marched from Whitemarsh to the present town of Gulph Mills, Montgomery County, northwest of Philadelphia, and encamped on nearby hills, December 13–19, 1777, while en route to General Washington's winter quarters at Valley Forge.

FORT HALIFAX. Erected about half a mile north of the present Halifax, Dauphin County, Fort Halifax was the first of the two permanent posts established by Colonel William Clapham's battalion (the later Augusta Battalion). It was named by Governor Morris, presumably for George Montagu Dunk, earl of Halifax. Begun in June 1756, it was garrisoned by various detachments from Fort Augusta until its evacuation in October 1757. It was square in design with bastions at the four angles. Including these bastions, it measured about 160 feet on a side, with 65-foot curtains between the bastions. The gate apparently was in the west side toward the river. Two of the bastions were furnished with platforms, and there was a storehouse at the south side of the enclosure. During the 16 months of occupancy, it served as the chief post on the line of communications between Fort Augusta and the settlements.

FORT HAMILTON. Begun in December 1755 and completed the following month, Fort Hamilton, which stood at the present city of Stroudsburg, Monroe County, was garrisoned by Provincial troops until the fall of 1757. It presumably was named for James Hamilton, who was then a member of the Governor's Council, and had served as Lieutenant Governor from 1748 to 1754 and was to serve as such again from 1759 to 1763. The fort consisted of a large house surrounded by a poorly built square stockade with four half-bastions. The stockade probably was about 80 feet square, and may have enclosed more than the one reported building. The fort was the first of the Provincial chain undertaken by the Provincial Commissioners. After its evacuation, the fort seems to have fallen rapidly into ruins. When Pontiac's War broke out, Robert Levers, writing on August 21, 1763, to urge that troops be stationed here, spoke of Fort Hamilton having been built "where the Remains of it now stands." However, when troops were posted here two or three months later, new quarters (Fort Penn) had to be provided.

HAND'S BLOCKHOUSES. A Revolutionary War isolation hospital located on today's S.R. 60 in present Crafton, Allegheny County, it was erected in 1777 by General Edward Hand to care for Fort Pitt's troops. The original two-story log structure was protected by blockhouses.

FORT HARRIS. A small Revolutionary War defensive work, Fort Harris was situated at the mouth of Lycoming Creek, near present Montoursville, in Lycoming County.

CAMP HASTINGS. A temporary Civil War encampment, Camp Hastings was established in

September 1861 on what was then known as the Fair Grounds, on the left side of 8th Street, in Mt. Gretna, Lebanon County, for the purpose of mobilizing, organizing, and mustering in recruits for the 93rd Infantry Regiment.

FORT HENRY. Located two miles north of the present site of Bethel in the western corner of Berks County, Fort Henry was built in February 1756 under the directions of Captain Christian Busse and garrisoned by Provincial troops until about the end of 1758. Consisting of one or more buildings within a palisaded enclosure, the fort was more substantially constructed, commodious, and well maintained. The origin of its designation is uncertain. It presumably honored some member of the British royal family, possibly William Henry, duke of Gloucester and Edinburgh, a younger brother of the later George III. According to a post return dated December 17, 1758, Fort Henry was then garrisoned by 17 men, a number somewhat reduced from an earlier roster. How much longer the fort remained garrisoned is not known. Captain Busse resigned from the service on May 11, 1759, shortly before the start of the campaign of that year. Fort Henry may have been totally evacuated at that time. The fort served as a patrol station in 1763–64 during Pontiac's War, but it is indefinite whether the buildings of the original fort had survived and were used during this period.

HESSIAN (P.O.W.) CAMP. After General John Burgoyne's surrender at Saratoga in 1777, German mercenaries, mostly Hessian, were held prisoners at various places until the end of the war. Those brought to Reading, Berks County, in 1781, were encamped until 1783 in huts on the hillside a quarter of a mile to the north of the town.

CAMP HESTONVILLE. A temporary Civil War troop-training encampment, probably established in 1861, Camp Hestonville was located near the present intersection of Girard and Lancaster avenues in west Philadelphia.

CAMP HINKS. This post was established in December 1865 by Captain (Brevet Major) Henry C. Kerr, 2nd Independent Company, U.S. Volunteers, with Company F, 7th Regiment, aggregating 99 men. At the end of January 1866, the post was garrisoned by 168 men. The troops were engaged doing guard duty at the Quartermaster's Department. Camp Hinks was apparently evacuated at the end of March 1866.

FORT HUNTER. Standing on the east bank of the Susquehanna River, at the mouth of Fishing Creek, near present Rockville, Dauphin County, Fort Hunter was the grist mill belonging to Samuel Hunter, converted into a stockaded blockhouse in 1755–56. The site is now occupied by the Fort Hunter Museum, six miles north of Harrisburg. Provincial troops garrisoned the fort until late 1758, when it was evacuated and apparently partially dismantled. In 1763 however, at the outbreak of Pontiac's War, it was temporarily reoccupied by troops for use as a patrol station.

FORT HUNTINGTON. One of the temporary fortifications built in late 1777 by Continental Army troops for the defense of General Washington's winter headquarters at Valley Forge, Fort Huntington was named for Brigadier General Jedediah Huntington. It was abandoned by the army when Valley Forge was evacuated on June 19, 1778.

FORT HYNDSHAW. Located near the west bank of the Delaware River, south of present Bushkill, Monroe County, about 12 miles northeast of Stroudsburg, Fort Hyndshaw was, from January 1756 to July 1757, the farthest northeastern defense garrisoned by Provincial troops during the French and Indian War. It was apparently a rather poorly built stockade about 70 feet square, probably furnished with two bastions, enclosing the home of James Hyndshaw. On June 19, 1757, the fort was evacuated and its troops removed to Fort Hamilton at Stroudsburg.

FORT INDIANTOWN GAP. This post 14 miles north of Lebanon derives its name from the many Indian communities that flourished in its environs two and a half centuries ago. After General Braddock's defeat in 1755, French-allied Indians raided many of the frontier settlements in the region. The section between Manada Gap and Swatara Gap, now the site of Fort Indiantown Gap, was fiercely attacked. As a defense measure, a number of forts and blockhouses were erected in the area, one of which was Swatara Fort, located to the north of Indiantown.

In 1933 the Pennsylvania government started to acquire land for a training area for the National Guard. Construction between 1933 to 1940 provided the structures for the accommodations of the troops. In 1940 Indiantown was designated a National Guard campsite; the following year, the Federal government leased the property. During World War II, Fort Indiantown was one of the nation's most important military posts. It was a staging area for the New York Port of Embarkation. Among the units given final training here were the 3rd Armored Division, the 1st, 5th, 28th, 37th, 77th, and 95th Infantry Divisions, prior to going overseas. After World War II until the end of September 1946, the fort was a separation center primarily for troops returning from Europe. It was inactivated in September 1946. In February 1951 Fort Indiantown Gap returned to active status when it became the home of the 5th Infantry (Red Diamond) Division to the end of August 1953. The division's mission was to train 32,000 troops as replacements for assignment to Korea. The fort was deactivated on September 1, 1953.

JENKINS' FORT. The fortified home of Judge John Jenkins at present West Pittston, Luzerne County, about 10 rods northeast of the Pittston Ferry Bridge, Jenkins' Fort was stockaded in the late summer of 1776 as a refugee haven and military defense in support of neighboring Fort Wintermute. Jenkins' Fort was destroyed during Colonel John Butler's destructive and murderous Tory-and-Indian raid in early July 1778. During the many subsequent years, a large part of the bluff on which it stood was washed away by the river current, and a considerable portion of the site is now the river's bed.

JOHN HARRIS' FORT. About the year 1705, John Harris, Sr., erected his log dwelling on the bank of the Susquehanna River where now stands Harrisburg, the capital of Pennsylvania. In October 1755, after General Braddock's ignominious defeat, his son, John Harris, the actual founder of the city, built a substantial stockade around his loopholed home. During the remaining years of the war, it was intermittently garrisoned by Provincial troops. There are few historical references to Harris' Fort.

FORT LA FAYETTE. FORT FAYETTE.

LEAD MINE FORT. ROBERDEAU'S FORT.

FORT LEBANON (*Fort William*). A French and Indian War defense located east of present Auburn, Schuylkill County, Fort Lebanon was begun in November 1755. Sometime in 1757, the fort was renamed Fort William, most probably in honor of William Augustus, duke of Cumberland, George II's only living son. Constructed of timber, the fort consisted of a 14-foot-high, 100-foot-square stockade enclosing a barracks, a 30-by-20-foot storeroom, a 12-foot-square magazine, and two buildings occupied by refugee settlers

of the area. The fort was probably evacuated in May 1758 when British military successes assured the safety of this frontier. By the time of the outbreak of Pontiac's War in 1763, Fort Lebanon, or Fort William, was a near ruin and uninhabitable.

FORT LE BOEUF. More properly called Fort de la Rivière au Boeuf, it was the second French fort in Pennsylvania, standing on the stream known today as Leboeuf, at the site of present Waterford, Erie County. It was the first fort on the upper Ohio, and it and Fort de la Presqu'isle guarded the two ends of the portage. Begun in July 1753 and completed the following month, it was garrisoned until early August 1759, when it was evacuated and destroyed by the retreating French. Contemporary descriptions show it as a square palisaded fort with bastions in all four angles. Barracks and other structures lined the four sides of the square while the bastions were occupied as a guardhouse, chapel, infirmary, and the commandant's storehouse.

On December 11, 1753, Major George Washington appeared at the fort to deliver a message from the governor of Virginia demanding by what authority the French had established themselves on Virginia-claimed territory. The French commandant's reply was actually a rebuff, saying that any dispute over territory must be adjudicated by those who had the authority to do so, namely Governor Duquesne of Canada. During the French and Indian War that broke out six months later, a large force of British regulars and Provincials laid siege to the French stronghold of Fort Niagara, and the garrisons of Fort Le Boeuf and other minor posts were summoned as reinforcements. Fort Niagara fell, and in 1759 the French themselves destroyed Fort Le Boeuf.

The British army in 1760 used the site of Fort Le Boeuf for a depot, burned by the Indians in 1763, and in 1794 the Americans erected a blockhouse nearby to protect the area's settlers. The Pennsylvania Historical and Museum Commission operates a museum on the site, illustrating the history of the French fort. Across the street are the foundations of the 1794 blockhouse.

CAMP LEGIONVILLE. General Anthony Wayne's army camped near present Ambridge, Beaver County, about 22 miles above Pittsburgh, from November 1792 to April 1793, preparing for the campaign that led to the Battle of Fallen Timbers against the Northwest Indians.

FORT LEHIGH. Located near today's town of Petersville and about five miles northwest of present Bath, Northampton County, Fort Lehigh was a settlers' blockhouse defense probably erected in early 1756. It strategically commanded the entrance to Lehigh Gap and stood at the junction of the road to Fort Allen at Weissport to the north and the road to Fort Norris to the east. Described as a well-built, formal fortification with a stockade, it was garrisoned by Provincial troops for the first five months of 1758. The fort was presumably abandoned sometime near the end of that period.

CAMP LETTERMAN. Located about one mile east of Gettysburg on the York Pike, Camp Letterman was a general hospital established about a month after the Battle of Gettysburg for the care of the wounded of both the Union and Confederate armies. It was named for Jonathan Letterman, medical director of the Army of the Potomac. The site is now occupied by Natural Springs Park.

FORT LIGONIER. The first English fort west of the Alleghenies, erected on the site of the old Indian town of Loyalhanna, now modern Ligonier, Westmoreland County, Fort Ligonier was established by the vanguard of General John Forbes's army in September and October 1758 during his march against Fort Duquesne and named in honor of Sir John Ligonier, military adviser to William Pitt. During Pontiac's War, the fort was unsuccessfully attacked by Chief Guyasuta and a horde of Indians in June 1763. The fort was officially abandoned in 1765.

After World War II, citizen actions were undertaken to restore the historic fort. Today the recreation of the fort features a popular museum exhibiting many military artifacts and general Americana relating to colonial America more than two centuries ago.

FORT LOUDOUN. Located about a mile southeast of the present town of Fort Loudon, Franklin County, and a little more than a mile from fortified McDowell's Mill, considered indefensible, which it replaced as a Provincial defense, Fort Loudoun was erected in 1756 by Colonel John Armstrong and named in honor of John Campbell, earl of Loudoun, then in command of the British army in America. The post has been occasionally confused with another fort Loudoun built about the same time at Winchester, Virginia.

Fort Loudoun was first garrisoned by the Provincial troops previously posted at McDowell's Mill. It was occupied by troops until June 1758, when they joined General John Forbes's army

en route to take Fort Duquesne. Subsequently it served as a post on the line of communications to Fort Pitt, was a base for Colonel Henry Bouquet's two expeditions during Pontiac's War, and was garrisoned by a small British detachment until November 1765. It was the latest-used Provincial fort in what was then Cumberland County.

FORT LOWTHER. CARLISLE BARRACKS.

FORT LYTTLETON. This French and Indian War defense stood just northeast of the present town of Fort Littleton, a locality at one time known as Sugar Cabins, in Fulton County. The fort was begun by George Croghan in December 1755, and was named by Governor Morris a month later in honor of Sir George Lyttleton, chancellor of the exchequer, 1755–56, who in November of the latter year became Baron Lyttleton after his retirement. A 100-foot-square stockaded defense of the usual form with bastions at the four angles, the fort was garrisoned by Pennsylvania troops until General John Forbes's campaign in 1758 and by various detachments of British regulars and Provincial troops until 1760. When Pontiac's War erupted in 1763, Fort Lyttleton was occupied for a short time by local volunteers. A year later it was deserted and in ruins.

MCALEVY'S FORT. This Revolutionary War frontier blockhouse was erected in 1778 on a bluff overlooking Standing Stone Creek, at the present town of McAlevy's Fort, Huntingdon County, by Colonel William McAlevy, pioneer settler and Revolutionary officer. The blockhouse served as an Indian defense and a refuge for the area's settlers.

CAMP MCCLELLAN. A temporary Civil War training encampment, it was located in the Nicetown section of Philadelphia.

FORT MCDOWELL. Located at the present village of Markes, Franklin County, McDowell's Mill was originally a "private fort" built on the property of John McDowell, first appearing in military plans as a proposed supply depot for General Braddock's campaign in 1755. Garrisoned by Provincial troops March–December 1756, it was replaced by nearby Fort Loudoun. McDowell's Fort, however, was occupied during February–April 1757, by other military units.

FORT MACHAULT. The last of the four fortifications built by the French on the Ohio, Fort

Machault stood at the present site of the city of Franklin, Venango County, and was named in honor of Jean-Baptiste Machault d'Arnouville, French minister of marine, 1754–57. In the original French plans, Fort d'Anjou was to have been built at this site, but the project was dropped, and in 1755 new plans were made under a new name. Originally designed as a small redoubt constructed in July 1755, it developed into a small-sized fort the following year and was completed apparently in 1757.

Fort Machault generally resembled Fort de la Presqu'isle. It was a partially palisaded square with bastions at the four angles, with the rear of the enclosed buildings forming two sides of the square and part of another. The stockade's single gate was on the east side, facing the Allegheny River. After the French destroyed Fort Duquesne at the Forks of the Ohio, Fort Machault served from November 1758 to August 1759 as the last French headquarters on the Ohio. The victorious British in 1760 built Fort Venango near where the French fort had stood; it was destroyed by the Indians in 1763 during Pontiac's Rebellion. (See: FORT VENANGO.)

FORT MCINTOSH. Built in June 1778 by order of General Lachlan McIntosh on the north or right bank of the Ohio River, at the mouth of Big Beaver Creek, on the site of the present city of Beaver, about 30 miles northwest of Pittsburgh, Fort McIntosh was one of the few American forts remaining on the frontier at the end of the Revolution. Here, in 1785, the United States concluded a treaty with the Indians. Constructed under the direction of Chevalier de Cambray, a French engineer, the fort was a substantially built palisade furnished with bastions and armed with at least one 6-pounder. During the time between the end of the war and its abandonment during the winter of 1790–91, there were periods when Fort McIntosh was unoccupied. The site of the fort is located on River Road in the area bounded by Bank, Insurance, and Market streets.

CAMP MCREYNOLDS. A temporary Civil War encampment, Camp McReynolds was located near the junction of Ridge Road and Columbia Avenue in Philadelphia and existed at least from January through April, 1862.

FORT MANADA (*Brown's Fort*). When briefly garrisoned by Provincial troops from January 1756 to April 1757, Brown's Fort became Fort Manada, which stood north of present Manada Hill, Dauphin County. It derived its name from the mountain pass it guarded. Its garrison consisted of detachments of the company posted at Fort Swatara. No contemporary description of the fort survived. It was probably James Brown's fortified, loopholed log-built house surrounded by a palisade.

MARCUS HOOK FORT. FORT SNYDER.

FORT MATAMORAS. OLD STONE FORT.

CAMP MEADE. A temporary Spanish-American War training encampment established in 1898 and named for the famed Civil War general, Camp Meade covered three square miles, about half a mile northwest of Middletown, Dauphin County. The camp was visited by President William McKinley on August 27, 1898.

FORT MECOPONACKA. In 1641, three years after the founding of New Sweden on both sides of the Delaware River, the Swedes erected the minor defense known as Fort Mecoponacka at Upland, present Chester, Delaware County, 14 miles from Fort Christina at today's city of Wilmington in Delaware.

CAMP MEIGS. A temporary Civil War encampment, Camp Meigs was located north of Nicetown Lane and Old Second Street in Philadelphia.

MERCER'S FORT. FORT PITT.

CAMP MEREDITH. Probably a temporary Civil War encampment, Camp Meredith was located near Greencastle, Franklin County.

FORT MIFFLIN (*Mud Fort*). Built on Mud Island in the Delaware River, near the mouth of the Schuylkill River, a short distance below Philadelphia, Fort Mifflin occupied the site of a previous fort originally erected during the years 1771–77, begun by the British and completed by the Patriots. The older fort, locally designated the Mud Fort, was defended by 300 Americans, four blockhouses, and 20 cannon against the British forces commanded by General William Howe during the siege from September 27 until the night of November 15–16, 1777, when it was evacuated by its garrison, escaping to Fort Mercer across the river. The defense had been reduced to a shambles by bombardment from the British batteries on Province Island 400 yards away.

The site on Mud Island was renamed Fort Mifflin in 1795 in honor of Major General Thomas Mifflin, Continental Army, Pennsylvania's first governor. A new fort of masonry was begun there in 1798 and completed in 1800. Thereafter the

FORT MIFFLIN. (Courtesy of the U.S. Naval Institute, Annapolis, Maryland.)

post was abandoned and reoccupied several times. Additions were first made in 1814 and intermittently continued during subsequent decades until the end of the Civil War when it was abandoned. Fort Mifflin was designated a National Historic Landmark in 1915 and later restored. The present outer fortifications date from the Civil War period. During World War I, the post was used for the storage of munitions, and during World War II, it was occupied by an antiaircraft battery.

MILL CREEK FORT (*Ogden's Fort*). Constructed in 1772 after the cessation of hostilities between the Connecticut settlers and the Pennamites, and situated on the north bank of the creek, which at one time was the northern boundary of the city of Wilkes-Barre, Mill Creek Fort occupied the site of the Pennamite blockhouse known as Ogden's Fort, captured and burned in 1770. Probably used as a defense against Tory and Indian infiltration during the Revolution, no archival evidence has been found to indicate when the fort was abandoned.

FORT MOLNDAL. In 1646, Johan Printz, New Sweden's governor, built a water-powered grist mill defended by two blockhouses on Cobb's Creek in the present city of Philadelphia. The location has been determined definitely as just above the Woodland Avenue Bridge on the east side of the creek. The mill served Swedish and Dutch colonists for generations and was the first power plant in Pennsylvania and the industrialized Delaware River Valley.

FORT MORRIS. During the French and Indian War, the town of Shippensburg, Cumberland County, was the site of two military establishments. The first was a provision supply depot for General Braddock's army, consisting of existing structures belonging to Edward Shippen, the town's proprietor. The second establishment was a fort authorized by Governor Morris when he learned of Braddock's defeat on the Monongahela on July 9, 1755. Begun in the early fall of 1755 and named in honor of the governor, it was still not fully completed a year later, although Provincial troops were stationed there in May 1756. It was regularly garrisoned in September of that year and apparently had no garrison after 1759. Fort Morris was maintained by Shippen for some time. He unsuccessfully attempted to have troops assigned to it during Pontiac's War in 1763–64. How much longer the structure survived is not known.

MUD FORT. FORT MIFFLIN.

FORT MUHLENBERG. A temporary fortification erected during 1777–78 for the defense of General Washington's winter quarters at Valley Forge, Fort Muhlenberg was named for Brigadier General Peter Muhlenberg. (See: VALLEY FORGE.)

FORT MUNCY. Erected in 1778 by Colonel Thomas Hartley three and half miles north of the town of Muncy, Lycoming County, it was destroyed by British troops and Indians and rebuilt, all in the same year. It was again attacked and destroyed in 1779. Fort Muncy was once again rebuilt in 1782 by Lieutenant Moses Van Campen. After the close of the Revolution, the fort was allowed to decay.

FORT NECESSITY. The scene of the opening battle of the French and Indian War, short-lived Fort Necessity stood at the eastern end of Great Meadows Swamp near present U.S. 40, just west of the town of Farmington and 11 miles east of Uniontown, Fayette County. Begun by 22-year-old Lieutenant Colonel George Washington, in command of less than 300 men including reinforcements, on May 30, 1754, it was formally surrendered on the morning of July 4 to the force of 600 French and Indians from Fort Duquesne under the command of Captain Coulon de Villiers, which had attacked the fort the previous day. Historical records and archaeological evidence reveal the fort to have consisted of a single low structure in the center of a circular stockade, a little over 50 feet in diameter. The defense was the result of the failure to reinforce the Forks of the Ohio at present Pittsburgh in time to prevent French seizure of the strategic site in the spring of 1754. (See: FORT DUQUESNE and FORT LE BOEUF.)

On May 27 an Indian messenger from Seneca Chief Half King, a bitter enemy of the French, arrived at Washington's camp at Great Meadows with the news that the hiding place of a party of French had been discovered on Chestnut Ridge five miles to the west. Washington and a detachment of 40 or more men immediately set out from Great Meadows in darkness and at dawn reached Half King's camp. The united Virginians and Indians started for the French camp, situated two miles to the north. Washington's forces were discovered trying to surround the French party, and they immediately opened fire on the French.

FORT NECESSITY. Reconstruction on the Fort Necessity National Battlefield Site in Farmington. (Courtesy of the National Park Service.)

The French leader, Ensign Joseph Coulon de Villiers, Sieur de Jumonville, and nine of his men were killed, one was wounded, twenty-one were captured, and one escaped during the 15-minute battle. Washington lost one man. The French survivor reached Fort Duquesne and related to Captain Pierre de Contrecoeur, the fort's commandant, the fate of Jumonville and his men.

When Captain Coulon de Villiers forced the capitulation of Fort Necessity on July 4, he had his revenge for the death of his brother Joseph, sieur de Jumonville. George Washington and his dispirited men were permitted to withdraw with the honors of war to return home to Virginia. Villiers's men broke up the cannon and demolished Fort Necessity. Relating that his own losses were 30 killed and 70 wounded, Washington estimated that 300 of the French and Indian force were killed and many more wounded, figures no doubt greatly exaggerated.

The Fort Necessity National Battlefield Site containing the reconstructed stockade is administered by the National Park Service. Two acres in extent, it is entirely surrounded by Fort Necessity State Park, a 311-acre recreational area including the 234-acre tract purchased by George Washington in 1769 and owned by him until the time of his death.

FORT NEW (NYA) GOTTENBURG. Located on Tinicum Island in the Delaware River, below the mouth of the Schuylkill, near modern Essington, Fort New (Nya) Gottenburg was established by Johan Printz, governor of New Sweden, in August 1643, as the first white man's settlement in Pennsylvania. Designed to command the Delaware, it was built of stout hemlock logs laid one upon the other and defended by four brass cannon. The governor also erected Printzhof, a palatial two-story dwelling of hewn white cedar with interior paneling and chimney brick imported from the homeland, considered to have been the finest home in America between Virginia and Manhattan. The fort was destroyed by fire on November 25, 1645, but was almost immediately rebuilt. There is no record of when it passed out of existence. It was probably destroyed by the Dutch in 1655 when they captured New Sweden, several days before they took Fort Christina at Wilmington and destroyed it on September 25, 1655.

FORT NEW (NYA) KORSHOLM. Completed in early 1647 and situated on the site of a former Dutch West India Company trading post, Fort New (Nya) Korsholm was erected by Johan Printz, governor of New Sweden, to further secure the Delaware River from Dutch encroachments and to improve the Swedish beaver trade. The fort was situated on the south side of an island near the mouth of the Schuylkill, probably about 27 miles east of Fort Christina at present Wilmington, Delaware. The fort, built of logs filled up with sand and stone, was surrounded by palisades and mounted with large guns. Printz's fort was destroyed by Indians in 1653. Amandus Johnson, Swedish historian, maintains that the fort was located on Province Island, in the Passayunk district of Philadelphia. In the context of present-day geography, the site of the fort is on the bank of the Schuylkill near the Penrose Avenue Bridge.

FORT NORRIS. A short-lived French and Indian War defense planned for construction in December 1755, and erected a month or two later, Fort Norris stood between present Kresgeville and Gilbert, Monroe County. Garrisoned by Provincial troops until the early fall of 1757, it consisted of a group of structures surrounded by an 80-foot-square stockade furnished with four half-bastions. It was named in honor of Isaac Norris, Speaker of the Provincial Assembly. Some weeks after the Easton Indian conference held July 21–August 7, 1757, Fort Norris was evacuated. Thereafter neglected, the fort apparently succumbed to decay and ultimate demolition by the advance of settlement after the war.

FORT NORTHKILL. A relatively short-lived French and Indian War defense intended as an outpost of Fort Lebanon, Fort Northkill was erected in the spring of 1756 and abandoned about the end of September 1757. Garrisoned by detachments from Fort Lebanon, Fort Northkill stood northwest of present Shartlesville, Berks County, near the stream from which it took its name. It appears to have consisted, rather inadequately, of a log house surrounded by a stockade about 32 feet square with half-bastions at the four corners.

OGDEN'S FORT. MILL CREEK FORT.

OLD GARRISON. FORT FRANKLIN.

OLD STONE FORT (*Fort Matamoras*). A defense and refuge for Indians at present Matamoras, Pike County, a few miles south of Port Jervis, New York, this one-and-a-half-storied stone structure, sometimes referred to as Fort Matamoras, was built about 1740 by Simon Westfael, one of the earliest Dutch settlers in the region.

CAMP ONE HUNDRED TWENTY-FIRST REGIMENT. A temporary Civil War encampment, it was located east of Germantown Road in Philadelphia.

CAMP PATTERSON. A temporary Civil War encampment located at Point Breeze Park in Philadelphia.

PATTERSON'S FORT (*Fort George*). Originally established as a "private fort" erected probably in early December 1855, it took its name from James Patterson, who on February 4 of that year had obtained a warrant for land at present Mexico, Juniata County. It was garrisoned by Provincial troops from about the end of 1755 until the end of August 1756. First intended as a temporary post, it was accorded some permanent status and the apparently official name of Fort George, in honor no doubt of George II. However, it continued to be more popularly known as Patterson's Fort.

PATTON'S FORT. A French and Indian War post located near present Linglestown, Dauphin County, Fort Patton was a station for the Paxton Rangers who defended the mountain gaps and settlers' farmsteads along the Blue Mountains from the Susquehanna River to Swatara Creek near Indiantown, against Indian incursions from 1756 to 1763.

FORT PENN. A defense that served during two wars, located at Stroudsburg, and named for Governor John Penn, it replaced Fort Hamilton, which was abandoned in 1757. Fort Penn was built under the probable supervision of Colonel Jacob Stroud, an officer in the Provincial forces during the French and Indian War. It is uncertain exactly when the fort was erected, but in 1763 it was garrisoned by Provincial troops. Later, following the Battle of Wyoming, July 3, 1778, it served as a refuge from subsequent Tory and Indian attacks. Fort Penn was located in the block bounded by Centre, Main (Elizabeth), and Chestnut streets in the eastern part of the city of Stroudsburg.

CAMP PHILADELPHIA. Since Philadelphia had been designated as the rendezvous for Civil War draftees from the state's eastern counties, an 80-acre encampment known as Camp Philadelphia was established in the fall of 1862 near the western border of the city, a short distance north of Market Street. Within a few weeks, more than 7,000 men were assembled here and housed in a tent city.

PHILADELPHIA'S REVOLUTIONARY WAR REDOUBTS.

The following is excerpted from B. J. Lossing's *Pictorial Field-Book of the Revolution* (1851), vol. 2, page 309:

[In addition to the numerous military encampments spread from the Schuylkill to the Delaware], the line of intrenchments . . . extended from the mouth of Conoquonoque Creek, just above Willow Street, to the "Upper Ferry" on the Schuylkill by strong palisades. The first redoubt . . . was near the junction of Green and Oak Streets, and then near the forks of the roads leading to Frankford and Kensington. The second redoubt was a little west of North Second and Noble Streets; the third, between North Fifth and Sixth; and Noble and Buttonwood Streets; the fourth, on Eighth Street, between Noble and Buttonwood; the fifth, on Tenth, between Buttonwood and Pleasant; the sixth, on Buttonwood, between Thirteenth and North Broad; the seventh, on North Schuylkill Eighth, between Pennsylvania Avenue and Hamilton Street; the eighth, on North Schuylkill Fifth and Pennsylvania Avenue; the ninth, on North Schuylkill Second, near Callowhill Street; and the tenth, on the bank of the Schuylkill, at the "Upper Ferry."

In the context of today's Philadelphia geography, no doubt the names of some of the thoroughfares and locations have been changed in the course of the city's developmental expansion.

FORT PITT (*Mercer's Fort*).

On November 27, 1958, with the pealing of church bells, the skirling of bagpipes, and the thunder of artillery, Pittsburgh began a year-long celebration of its 200th birthday. Despite freezing cold and the threat of snow, more than 10,000 people congregated at the Forks of the Ohio, near the small brick redoubt (Bouquet's Blockhouse) that survives as the only remainder of Fort Pitt's outworks. June 27, 1959, was the opening night of *The Golden Crucible,* a bicentennial pageant about Pittsburgh's historic past. It was staged and performed in the 2,500-seat amphitheater at Point State Park on the "Golden Triangle" of land between the Monongahela and Allegheny rivers.

In the five forts built [there] . . . between 1754 and 1792, one may see almost all the types of construction utilized by military engineers in North America in the eighteenth century. Fort Prince George [Trent's Fort] provided a minimum defense, consisting merely of a squared-log house surrounded by a simple stockaded enclosure without ditch. Fort Duquesne was a timber and earth fort of common type with horizontal log front and palisaded rear face. Mercer's Fort presented a square arrangement of log houses which in themselves served as the curtain walls of the fort and which were joined by palisaded bastions. Fort Pitt, partly built of brick masonry, was a dirt fort with five bastions and distinguished by its uncommonly large size and extensive outworks. Fort Fayette was a bastioned stockade fort with double-storied blockhouses at the corners, a variation then becoming common on the frontier. Of the five forts once standing in the triangle of modern Pittsburgh, Fort Duquesne and Fort Pitt are the only ones generally known to have existed and these two forts are commonly confused in the public mind. [Charles Morse Stotz, "Defense in the Wilderness," *Drums in the Forest* (1958), p. 119]

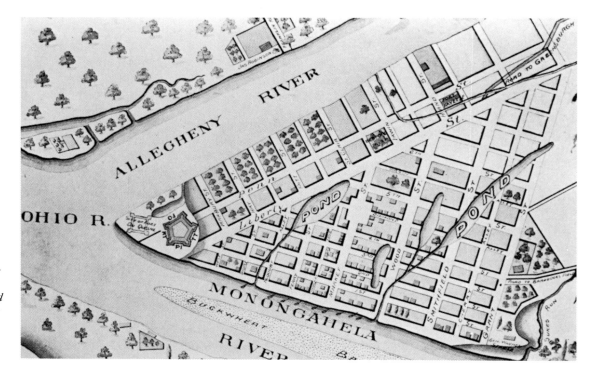

FORT PITT. Map of Pittsburgh in 1795 showing Forts Pitt and Duquesne at the left and Fort Fayette at the upper right. (Drawn by Jos. Eichbaum & Co. in 1892.)

Modern Pittsburgh commands the Forks of the Ohio, where more than two centuries ago in a contest for empire, Great Britain and France battled for control of the American frontier. To establish her claim to the country west of the Alleghenies, France began construction in 1753 of a chain of forts along the Ohio River in western Pennsylvania. In the same year, the governor of Virginia sent Lieutenant Colonel George Washington to Fort Le Boeuf at present Waterford to influence the French to leave the country, which was also claimed by Great Britain. In 1754 the French captured the outpost (Trent's Fort) at the Forks that had just been erected by a force of Virginians. Then, at Fort Necessity, they ousted a large detachment of other Virginians, commanded by Washington, who had arrived too late as a reinforcement. The French built a fort of their own at the Forks, Fort Duquesne, which assured their control of the Ohio Valley until 1758. French occupation would have been ended in 1755 had General Edward Braddock not been defeated in the still-controversial Battle of the Monongahela, only eight miles from the Forks.

The overthrow of the French began in 1758, when a 6,000-man army commanded by General John Forbes marched west from Carlisle to Fort Ligonier, the last outpost before the final thrust against Fort Duquesne. Realizing they were hopelessly outnumbered, the French evacuated their fort and mined 50 barrels of spoiled powder in its magazine, utterly destroying Fort Duquesne barely two days before the British arrived on November 25.

The triangle of land presented a stark scene of devastation. No effort was made to reconstruct the French fort—the damage was quite irreparable. Provisions were made to secure the area with a barracked garrison and a temporary defense under the supervision of Colonel Hugh Mercer while plans were formulated for the establishment of an elaborate fortification. Erected between December 1758 and late July 1759, the temporary work was never formally named, but in reports and correspondence the name Mercer's Fort was almost consistently used to designate it. Situated on the bank of the Monongahela, it stood slightly more than 1,000 feet from the ruins of Fort Duquesne. The plan of the fort was kept simple, its four sides lined with log structures serving as curtains between the unelevated palisaded bastions. The powder magazine was partially buried in the south bastion.

Preliminary plans for Fort Pitt was scrapped for the finalized pentagonal design developed by engineer Captain Harry Gordon because it

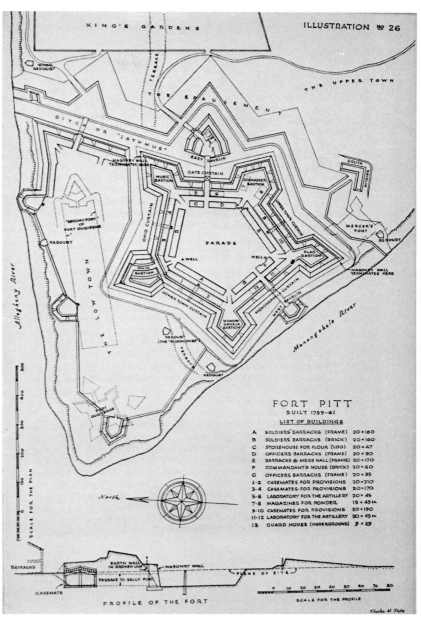

FORT PITT. Plan of the fort. (From "Defense in the Wilderness," by Charles Morse Stotz, in Drums in the Forest, by Alfred Procter James and Charles Morse Stotz, 1958, p. 163. Courtesy of the Historical Society of Western Pennsylvania.)

better suited the triangular shape of the site between the two rivers. The entire fort, including its five bastions and outworks, occupied 17.6 acres of the Point. It was by far the most elaborate frontier fortification built by the British in America. During Pontiac's War, 1763–64, Indians unsuccessfully besieged Fort Pitt from the end of May until August 1, 1763. Thereafter the fort was granted little attention by military headquarters. Only proven needs for repair and maintenance merited monetary appropriations.

Fort Pitt was dismantled over a period of years, most of it having disappeared by 1800. Historians have been unable to determine the total monies expended on its construction. The costs, of course, had to take into account the significant contributions of the many artisans and

FORT PITT. Artist's drawing of Point State Park at the "Forks of the Ohio." (Courtesy of the Pennsylvania Bureau of State Parks.)

the common labor of thousands of soldiers. It has been estimated that to construct a true replica of Fort Pitt and its outworks by today's modern building methods would cost a minimum of $10 million.

Bouquet's Redoubt or Blockhouse was purchased by private parties during Pittsburgh's early days. In 1894 the property was deeded by its owner to the Pennsylvania chapter of the D.A.R. and is maintained to this day by the organization. The sites of four of the five forts are now incorporated within the 36-acre Point State Park (Fort Fayette's site, a short distance to the east, is presently occupied by the Edison Hotel). The handsomely designed memorial, the result of 29 years of planning and construction, commemorates and preserves the significant historical role of the area during the French and Indian War. (See also: FORT DUQUESNE and FORT FAYETTE.)

FORT PRESQUE ISLE. More properly known as Fort de la Presqu'isle, this French fort stood on an elevation overlooking the lake at the present site of the city of Erie. Its name was derived from the adjoining peninsula (*presqu'ile*

in modern French). Surviving descriptions indicate the fort consisted of a 120-foot-square, 15-foot-high palisade of horizontally laid chestnut logs, enclosing log buildings lining the four interior sides of the square. It was the first and the last of the French forts in Pennsylvania, begun in 1753 and occupied until August 1759.

The capitulation of Fort Niagara to British and Provincial forces on July 25, 1759, spelled the end of the French posts in the Ohio country. Fort Presque Isle was evacuated and burned by its garrison sometime during the second week of August. English forces under Colonel Henry Bouquet in 1760 replaced it with British Fort Presque Isle on or near the same site. In 1763, during Pontiac's War, it was captured and burned by Indians. The Americans in 1795 erected a blockhouse near the site, at the foot of present Ash Street in Erie, where the Wayne Memorial stands. General Anthony Wayne died at the blockhouse in 1796, and his body was later removed to the city of Wayne near Philadelphia. The peninsula, now the Presque Isle State Park, reentered history in 1813, when timber cut from its forests was used to construct Commodore Oliver Perry's Lake Erie fleet.

FORT PRINCE GEORGE. FORT DUQUESNE.

FORT RAYSTOWN. FORT BEDFORD.

FORT REDSTONE (*Fort Burd*). The first fortification built by the English in western Pennsylvania was a strong, square loopholed log storehouse erected in February 1754 at the mouth of Redstone Creek on the Monongahela at present Brownsville, Fayette County. It had been intended as a supply base for the ill-fated Fort Prince George (Trent's Fort) at the Forks of the Ohio. It was reportedly later burned by the French. In late September or early October 1759, Colonel James Burd built a new defense on the same site. First known as Fort Burd, it was later designated Redstone Fort. It was abandoned by its garrison in 1763 during Pontiac's War.

CAMP REYNOLDS. CAMP COPELAND.

CAMP REYNOLDS. A temporary World War II mobilization and training post, Camp Reynolds was located at or near Greenville, Mercer County.

ROBERDEAU'S FORT (*Lead Mine Fort*). The American Revolution was already under way when the scarcity of lead for bullets threatened the fate of the colonies. Fort Roberdeau was built during late April and May 1778 at the present-day village of Union Furnace, Blair County, to protect lead mining operations in the Sinking Valley. Under the direction of Brigadier General Daniel Roberdeau, head of the mining enterprise, militia, Rangers, and local settlers aided in the construction of the fort, first known as Lead Mine Fort. A four-bastioned palisaded work with horizontally laid logs, it was defended by two cannon. It consisted of officers' quarters and barracks, an underground powder magazine, kitchen, blacksmith shop, and the lead smelter.

Although the lead mining operation continued for several years, the enterprise ended in disappointment. The probable yield from the mine was initially greatly exaggerated. While Roberdeau's Fort was abandoned as far as lead mining was concerned, it was too strongly constructed as a defense to be deserted. For many years thereafter, it served as a frontier fort for the protection for the area's settlers. As a Blair County Bicentennial project, it was reconstructed on its original site and includes a working lead smelter similar to the one used during the Revolution.

SCHUYLKILL ARSENAL. Originally a powder magazine established by the government on July 6, 1799, the Schuylkill Arsenal was located at 26th Street and Grays Ferry Avenue in downtown Philadelphia. From its Schuylkill River dock, U.S. Navy frigates were loaded with gunpowder as an annual tribute to the Barbary pirates, and in 1803, the Lewis and Clark Expedition was outfitted here. In 1814, during the War of 1812, the Army was in need of a "laboratory" for the supply of ordnance stores and established a headquarters depot at the Arsenal. It was kept busy distributing vital supplies through all the wars leading up to World War II, when it was used as a cooks and bakers school. Prior to its closing in March 1958, it was a training post for Army Reserve units in the Philadelphia area.

CAMP SCOTT. A Civil War camp established in 1861 on the York Fair Grounds, southeast of the town, Camp Scott was named in honor of General Winfield Scott. By May 1861 six full regiments were stationed here.

CAMP SECURITY. Established in 1781 to accommodate British and Hessian prisoners of war, Camp Security was a 20-acre compound surrounded by a 15-foot-high stockade guarded by York County militia and located four and a half miles southeast of the town of York. The camp was used continuously to the end of the Revolution.

SEVENTY-FOURTH REGIMENT CAMP. A temporary Civil War encampment, it was located east of Schuylkill Road in Philadelphia.

SEVENTY-THIRD REGIMENT CAMP. A temporary Civil War encampment, it was located east of Schuylkill Road, adjacent to the 74th Regiment encampment, in Philadelphia.

CAMP (GEORGE A.) SHARPE. A World War II prisoner of war encampment named for General George Gordon Meade's personal orderly, Camp Sharpe was established on the grounds of the Gettysburg Battlefield and operated from November 1943 to July 1944, and again during an undetermined period of time in 1945.

FORT SHIRLEY. A short-lived French and Indian War defense, Fort Shirley was erected on Aughwick Creek at the site of present Shirleysburg, Huntingdon County, at a location where George Croghan had resided. Fortified by Croghan in September 1755, his home became a Provincial post in December, and was garrisoned by Pennsylvania troops until abandoned in September 1756. Sometimes referred to as Croghan's

Fort, it was named by Governor Morris in January 1756 for General William Shirley, governor of Massachusetts since 1741, and recently designated commander in chief of the British forces in North America.

SIXTY-SEVENTH REGIMENT CAMP. A temporary Civil War encampment located in the Nicetown section of Philadelphia.

CAMP SLIFER. A short-lived Civil War encampment located probably south of Chambersburg, Franklin County, Camp Slifer was in use from April 19 to June 12, 1861, and named in honor of Eli Slifer, secretary of the Commonwealth of Pennsylvania. The camp was one of many in and around the city, where General Robert Patterson's army of approximately 18,000 men, mostly three-month enlistees, assembled to move into the Shenandoah Valley to contain the Confederate forces under General Joseph E. Johnston.

FORT SNYDER (*Marcus Hook Fort; Camp Gaines*). Because the city of Philadelphia was being considered by the British to be a vulnerable point for attack, a temporary War of 1812 encampment was established in late September 1814 for Pennsylvania Reserve troops and located at present Trainer, Delaware County. It was first called Camp Marcus Hook or Marcus Hook Fort for its locality. But on October 7, 1814, it received the name of Camp Gaines for General Edmund R. Gaines who was then in command of the military district. Then the commandant of the post, Major General Isaac Worrell, in November designated it Fort Snyder in honor of Brigadier General Thomas Snyder. In early December, when the threat of a British attack evaporated, the encampment was broken up and its troops returned to Philadelphia.

FORT STANDING STONE. In 1762, near present Huntingdon, settlers erected a stockade fort, later partially destroyed. When the Revolution broke out, the defense was rebuilt on a more extensive scale. In July 1778 Continental Army troops and militia were stationed here to defend the area against British and Indian attack. The fort stood at the confluence of Stone Creek and the Juniata River, a short distance east of the town.

CAMP STANTON. A temporary Civil War post, Camp Stanton was located near Girard College, west of Broad Street, in Philadelphia.

STAR REDOUBT. This was one of the temporary defenses established in 1777–78 at Valley Forge, to protect General Washington's winter headquarters. The Star Redoubt was so named because of its star-like configuration. (See: VALLEY FORGE.)

STIRLING REDOUBT. Another of the temporary defenses erected for the protection of General Washington's winter headquarters at Valley Forge, the redoubt was named for Major General William Alexander, Lord Stirling. (See: VALLEY FORGE.)

CAMP STOKLEY. A temporary Civil War encampment established probably in 1861, Camp Stokley was located near the Schuylkill River, just below Wissahickon Creek, in today's Fairmount Park, Philadelphia.

FORT SULLIVAN. This temporary Revolutionary War fortified depot was constructed in compliance with General John Sullivan's orders during his campaign against the towns and villages of the Six Nations. Built in August 1779, it was located on the site of present Athens, Bradford County. Early in October 1779, the fort, having served its purpose, was demolished in order to prevent its occupation by the enemy.

CAMP SUMMERALL. CAMP TOBYHANNA.

FORT SWATARA (*Captain Smith's Fort*). A French and Indian War defense, Fort Swatara was named for the gap where Swatara Creek flows through the Blue Mountains. The site of the fort is located near the present towns of Inwood and Lickdale, Lebanon County. Occasionally referred to as Captain Smith's Fort for Captain Friedrich Schmitt (Frederick Smith), commander of Fort Swatara, the fort was garrisoned by Provincial troops from the end of January 1756 until May 1758. The fort was located north of the present site of Fort Indiantown Gap. A large boulder and bronze tablet now mark the site of Fort Swatara on Range Road, one-half mile west of the town of Inwood.

CAMP TOBYHANNA (*Camp Summerall*). A World War I post located near Tobyhanna, Monroe County, and Lehigh, Wayne County, Camp Tobyhanna's reservation was acquired by purchase by the government in 1914–15, for use as an artillery range. It was sometimes called Camp Summerall without authorization. During the period July–October 1918, the post was a Tank Corps training center. On October 1, 1918, all training personnel were transferred to Camp Polk, discontinuing Camp Tobyhanna.

TOMAHAWK CAMP. FORT DUDGEON.

TRENT'S FORT. FORT DUQUESNE.

CAMP UNION. A temporary Civil War encampment probably established in 1861, Camp Union was located north of Ridge Road in Philadelphia.

VALLEY FORGE. Although no battle was fought at Valley Forge, located beside the Schuylkill River 22 miles west of Philadelphia, the area represents one of the most significant chapters in American history. Of the 11,000 men who began the bitter winter encampment here in December 1777, approximately 3,000 died before General Washington broke camp six months later. His Continental Army soldiers first staggered into Valley Forge on December 19, exhausted, half-frozen and near-starved.

Although General John Burgoyne's invasion army was decisively defeated and captured at Saratoga two months earlier, Philadelphia was occupied by the British. After the Americans suffered defeat at Brandywine and Germantown, Washington had one objective in mind—to keep the Continental Army together and weld it into a viable fighting force. Trained by Baron von Steuben, the 8,000 survivors of the winter encampment formed the nucleus of an American army that went on to win the War of Independence.

Approximately 900 clay-chinked, twig-thatched log huts, regularly placed in brigade and company streets, were quickly erected and fitted with wooden bunks. To defend the encampment, six or more temporary fortifications, named for officers of Washington's general staff, were constructed during the winter under the supervision of French engineer Brigadier General Louis L. Duportail. On June 19, 1778, six months later to the day, the encampment was evacuated and the forts abandoned.

Valley Forge received its name from an iron forge on Valley Creek, which flows through the park. The original forge was an important munitions plant for Colonial troops, but was destroyed by British mercenaries in September of 1777. Today, the 2,255-acre Valley Forge State Park exhibits replicas of the soldiers' huts, visited by hundreds of thousands of tourists each year.

FORT VASA. A mill protected by two blockhouses erected in late 1646 or early 1647 by Johan Printz, governor of New Sweden, Fort Vasa (Wasa) was located a short distance from Fort New Korsholm on the Schuylkill River, at a place known to the Indians as Kinsessing, in present Philadelphia. Fort Vasa was no doubt named for the royal dynasty of Sweden, the House of Vasa (1523–1654), founded by Gustavus I.

FORT VENANGO. After the French evacuated and destroyed Fort Machault, their last headquarters on the Ohio, in August 1759, its location at present Franklin, Venango County, was occupied by British troops. In the summer of 1760, they erected a strong fortification, called Fort Venango, on a new site, about 40 rods farther up the river and closer to the mouth of French Creek. The fort was garrisoned by a small number of troops under the command of Lieutenant Francis Gordon, who exercised control over the line of communications between Lake Erie and Fort Pitt. Nothing of an unusual nature occurred at Fort Venango until the late spring of 1763, when the post was surprised and captured by a large party of Seneca Indians acting in concert with Pontiac's Rebellion. With the exception of Lieutenant Gordon, who was subjected to slow torture until he died the next day, the rest of the garrison were immediately massacred. Fort Venango was then burned to the ground by the Indians.

FORT WASHINGTON. A small earthen redoubt, Fort Washington was one of the defenses built in 1777–78 for the protection of General Washington's winter headquarters at Valley Forge. The carefully preserved redoubt stands near the Memorial Arch within Valley Forge State Park. (See: VALLEY FORGE.)

FORT WASHINGTON. A Civil War defense of the city of Harrisburg, Fort Washington was constructed in early July, 1863, on Washington Heights on the west side of the Susquehanna, the natural line of defense for the city. The Confederate invasion into Pennsylvania, where it was defeated at Gettysburg, had created panic in the capital city, and entrenchments were hurriedly constructed to counter the threat.

WASHINGTONBURG POST. CARLISLE BARRACKS.

CAMP WAYNE. A temporary Civil War encampment, Camp Wayne was located near West Chester, Chester County.

FORT WHEELER. A revolutionary War stockade-type fort, Fort Wheeler was built in 1778 by

Lieutenant Moses Van Campen, noted Indian scout, and located on Fishing Creek about three miles from present Bloomsburg, Columbia County. It served for the remainder of the war as a refuge against British-allied Indians, by whom it was once attacked.

WICACO BLOCKHOUSE. After the Swedes established the first settlements along the banks of the Delaware River, a group of colonists at Wicaco, now South Philadelphia, in 1677 began to use a small loopholed log blockhouse, erected in 1669 as an Indian defense, for the purpose of religious services. In 1700 they built the present Gloria Dei, or Old Swedes' Church, on the same site, located on today's Delaware Avenue near Christian Street. The oldest church in Philadelphia, it separated from the mother church in Sweden in 1789, and in 1845 was admitted into the Convention of the Protestant Episcopal Church of the Diocese of Pennsylvania. Still an active religious center, Gloria Dei Church was declared a National Historic Site in 1942.

FORT WILKES-BARRE. A Revolutionary War defense begun in 1776 and completed in 1778, it was a ditched work in the form of a parallelogram, with flanking towers at the angles, and protected by one four-pounder cannon. Its only gate opened toward the Susquehanna River to the northwest. The fort, located in the public square of the city of Wilkes-Barre, was surrendered with Forty Fort to Colonel John Butler's Tories and Indians in early July 1778.

FORT WILLIAM. FORT LEBANON.

CAMP WILLIAM PENN. The village of La Mott, originally called Camptown, in Montgomery County, was platted at the close of the Civil War on the site of former Camp William Penn, a training encampment for Negro troops who enlisted for service in the Union forces from 1863 to 1865.

FORT WINTERMUTE. A Revolutionary War defense erected in 1776 by members of the Win-

termute (Wintermoot) family, it consisted of a stockade surrounding their minimally fortified dwelling and was located in the present town of Exeter, between Wyoming Avenue and the Susquehanna River, in Luzerne County. The Wintermutes were strongly suspected of being Tories by their neighbors. When Colonel John Butler and his notorious army of Tory raiders and British-allied Indians invaded the Wyoming Valley on July 1, 1778, the Wintermutes welcomed Butler the next day and made only a token resistance to the demand for surrender. Although the Tory leader personally guaranteed their safety, Fort Wintermute on the following day was set afire and burned down, either by accident or design, along with other defenses in the Valley.

FORT WYOMING. Erected in January 1771, during the bloody territorial dispute known as the Pennamite War, by Captain Amos Ogden and 100 men under his command as authorized by the Pennsylvania authorities, and located near the intersection of present Northampton and River streets in Wilkes-Barre, it was intended to reduce Fort Durkee, the stronghold of the Connecticut Yankees. It was later seized by the Connecticut faction and destroyed. It was rebuilt on the same site in 1778 as a Revolutionary War defense, served briefly as a mobilization camp for General John Sullivan's army in 1779, and was dismantled in 1784 after the withdrawal of the Continental and Pennsylvania garrisons from the Wyoming Valley.

FORT ZELLER. The state of Pennsylvania's oldest existing "fort," Fort Zeller is located a half-mile north of present Newmanstown, Lebanon County. Originally erected in 1723 by a Huguenot, Henri Sellaires, who changed his name to Heinrich Zeller, it was rebuilt in 1745 of solid masonry two stories high at one end and one at the other, originally fitted with portholes instead of windows. Although it was not fortified as its name implies, the Zeller dwelling served for many years as a strong refuge during the Indian wars.

Rhode Island

FORT ADAMS (*Brenton's Point Fort; Castle Hill Fort*). One of the largest seacoast fortifications constructed in the United States, Fort Adams at Newport was intended to protect the entrance to Narragansett Bay. The fort was successfully adapted to changing technology and ultimately became the command center for the most strategic complex of coastal batteries in the Northeast. It was briefly the site of the United States Naval Academy during the opening months of the Civil War.

William Brenton arrived in Newport in 1683 with a charter from Charles II for a tract of land that came to be known as Brenton's Point. He protected his farm property with two cannon he ordered from England. The site of today's Fort Adams stands on the location of Brenton's guns. In 1740, fearful of French invasion, the inhabitants erected an observation post on the site. Earthen fortifications were built there during the French and Indian and Revolutionary wars. It was unanimously voted at a Newport town meeting, held on April 29, 1776, "to enter at once into the defence of the town," and three days later a large body of men marched to Brenton's Point and began the erection of a fort, called Castle Hill Fort. Early in December, a British fleet carrying 6,000 troops appeared in the bay, forcing the abandonment of the incomplete fort, and occupied the town for three years. When they left in October 1779, they burned the barracks they had erected on the Point.

In 1793 Congress, anticipating war with France, took steps to again protect the entrance to Narragansett Bay. Major Louis Toussard was given the task of building a new fortification. On July 4, 1799, it was named Fort Adams for the second president of the United States. Over the entrance arch to the fort was an inscription that read "Fort Adams, the Rock on which the Storm will beat." The defense then consisted of an enclosed masonry work, indented for guns, with a brick magazine, and barracks to accommodate one company of soldiers. Additional guns were installed during the War of 1812. By the end of the war, the fort was in disrepair and neglected and was condemned by the Board of Engineers. Finally Congress made an initial appropriation of $50,000 to rebuild the fort. Lieutenant Colonel Joseph G. Totten, later engineer general of the Army, supervised the project. Begun in 1824, the new Fort Adams was essentially completed in 1857. A permanent garrison established in 1842 remained until 1853.

In 1861 Fort Adams was transferred to the Department of the Navy for the use of the Naval Academy. National Archives records indicate that

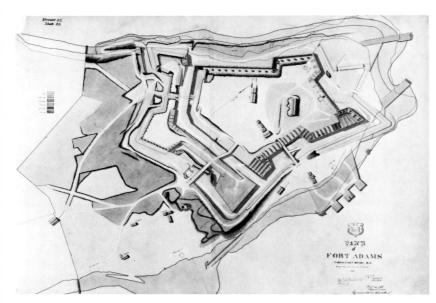

FORT ADAMS. Plan drawn in 1834. (Courtesy of the National Archives.)

of 200 and a war complement of 2,400 men with 468 mounted cannon, although at no time was it ever garrisoned or armed at full strength. During later wars, new weapons for active defense were emplaced in the vicinity of Fort Adams. Massive reinforced concrete bunkers containing disappearing guns, rifle mounts, and mortars were constructed. The fort was comprised of the now extinct Batteries Wright, Reilly, Talbot, Dalton, and Bankhead. Fort Adams was discontinued on November 30, 1953, to become an inactive subinstallation of the Boston Army Base. In 1958 it was used to house Navy personnel.

Today Fort Adams includes the 1824-era masonry fort, a hollow pentagon measuring 1,000 by 1,200 feet overall; the fort's outworks and two redoubts; six Endicott-period batteries; ten brick or frame officers' quarters; and two brick warehouses. The stabilized and restored fortress, on Fort Adams Drive off Harrison Avenue, is maintained by the Rhode Island Department of Natural Resources.

FORT ANNE. FORT WOLCOTT.

CAMP ARNOLD. A Civil War training encampment set up in Riding Park, Pawtucket, in December 1861, it was named in honor of Lieutenant Governor Samuel Arnold. It was used by the 1st Cavalry until it left Rhode Island in the spring of 1862. (See also: CAMP HALLETT.)

the fort was regarrisoned by the Army on October 14, 1862. Within five years the fort became obsolete. Powerful rifled cannon, developed during the war, could have reduced the once-impregnable granite walls into rubble. The fort's three tiers of cannon protected the East Passage into the bay, and extensive earthworks provided protection from land assault. The walls were of granite shipped by schooner from Maine, where it was quarried.

The fort, with a perimeter of 1,793 yards, was designed to accommodate a peacetime garrison

FORT ADAMS. Aerial view of the fort as it stands today. (Courtesy of the Rhode Island Development Council, Providence, Rhode Island.)

BARKER'S HILL FORT. A large British-built redoubt, it was located on the east side of Rhode Island near Middletown.

FORT BARTON (*Tiverton Heights Fort*). Commissioned in 1777 as Tiverton Heights Fort, the earthwork defense was a joint project of Rhode Island and Massachusetts. Built on a high hill, it commanded the crossing at Howland's Ferry. The fort was renamed Fort Barton for Lieutenant Colonel William Barton, who led a daring raid against British-held Portsmouth on July 9, 1777, capturing General Richard Prescott. The British takeover of Aquidneck (Rhode) Island threatened not only all of Rhode Island but also Massachusetts. The fort on Tiverton Heights was the Patriots' response to the threat.

From Fort Barton, Generals Nathanael Greene, John Sullivan, and Lafayette, in August 1778 witnessed the discouraging retreat of Continental forces from the Battle of Rhode Island, fought on the hills of Portsmouth. During the three days preceding the battle, Patriot armies converged at Fort Barton, which was hard put to accommodate more than 10,000 men. The soldiers were transported by 86 flatboats, each large enough to carry 100 men, from Howland's Ferry to Portsmouth. But the assault designed to drive the British from New England was repulsed. The failure was blamed on the lack of cooperation from the French fleet.

Today, along the serpentine, 550-foot-long path leading to the summit of Tiverton Heights are markers explaining the area's topography. From the observation tower built in the fort's center, one can view the length of Aquidneck Island, the Atlantic Ocean, Narragansett Bay, Fogland Point, Stone Bridge, Butts Hill, and the site of Howland's Ferry at the foot of Lawton Avenue.

BEAVER HEAD FORT (*Conanicut Battery*). At the end of Fox Hill Road in Jamestown on Conanicut Island, there still remain the distinct earthworks of Conanicut Battery or Beaver Head Fort. Constructed by Rhode Islanders in May 1776, the fort was captured by the British in December 1776 to keep the Continental Navy bottled up in Providence's harbor. The name of the fort is derived from the shape of Conanicut Island southwest of Mackeral Cove. In 1900 the federal government purchased the site of the Revolutionary War site and built thereon Fort Getty.

BEAVER TAIL FORT. In May 1776 the Patriots built on the southern tip of Conanicut Island an earthwork fort to complement Fort Beaver Head.

CAMP BEECKMAN. Established during World War I, Camp Beeckman occupied the former training site of the Rhode Island National Guard, 19 miles south of Providence.

BLISS HILL FORT. The eastern end of the Patriots' line of fortifications was at Bliss Hill, at what is now called Green End, in the town of Middletown on Aquidneck (Rhode) Island. The Americans on August 17, 1778, erected the fort located not far from the Newport city line.

BONNET POINT FORT. Across the West Passage of Narragansett Bay, on the mainland in South Kingstown (Kingston), opposite the southern half of Conanicut Island, was a Patriot earthwork called Bonnet Point Fort, built in 1777 and continuously occupied by the Americans. The elliptical defense was rebuilt twice, during the War of 1812, and in the Civil War when the Confederate cruiser *Alabama* threatened the mainland towns.

BRENTON'S POINT FORT. FORT ADAMS.

BRISTOL FERRY FORT. In February 1776 a committee was formed to order the construction of fortifications on Rhode Island at Bristol to protect Bristol Ferry. American troops posted at both Bristol and on the island were engaged in the work of construction. Located on the Portsmouth side, where today stands the community of Bristol Ferry, it was evacuated by the Patriots when the British seized Newport.

BRISTOL MUD BATTERY. Situated at the northern terminus of the Bristol Ferry, it consisted of an earthen breastwork occupied by a company of American troops. It stood a short distance west of the intersection of Hope and Church streets in Bristol.

FORT BROWN. FORT WETHERILL.

BULLOCK'S POINT FORT. A substantial Patriot defense at Bullock's Point in East Providence was erected before 1777.

BULL'S GARRISON. Jeriah (Jireh) Bull maintained a garrison house on Tower Hill at Pettaquamscut, located between present Wakefield and Narragansett Pier, during the seventeenth century's bloody Indian wars. The garrison house was burned by the Indians after ten men and five women and children were killed; only two people managed to escape. Samuel G. Drake, in his *History of the Indian Wars in New England,* commented that "a want of Watchfulness was probably the Cause of this sad Butchery. The House was of Stone, and might easily have been defended; but the People probably thought the Presence of the Army warranted Security."

CAMP BURNSIDE. Under an order from Governor William Sprague, the 2nd Rhode Island Volunteers Regiment was organized between April and June 1861 at Providence to serve for a minimum of three years or for the duration of the Civil War. The camp was named for General Ambrose Burnside, who invented a breechloading rifle in 1856. Major John S. Slocum, 1st Regiment, was in command. On June 22, 1861, the regiment proceeded to Washington.

According to Rhode Island State Records Commission, Camp Burnside was temporarily occupied by the 14th Rhode Island Heavy Artillery, a Negro regiment with white commissioned officers. The Naval War College at Newport reported that a Camp Burnside was established on Beaver Tail at the southern tip of Conanicut Island, Jamestown, where the Navy maintained a radar installation during World War II.

BURR'S HILL FORT. In May 1778 soon after the British attack on Warren, fortifications were built on Burr Hill in that town. A guard was maintained there day and night during the remainder of the Revolution.

BUTTS HILL FORT. Located behind the American Legion Post on Sprague Street in Portsmouth, Butts Hill Fort was built by the British in 1777 as part of their defense system for the control of Aquidneck (Rhode) Island. The fort was occupied by the Patriots in 1778 to become an island base for the Continental troops under General John Sullivan. The substantial defensive work played a major role in the Battle of Rhode Island. Butts Hill was still a key position, manned in part by French forces, when the Marquis de Chastellux visited it. The Rhode Island campaign of 1778 included an unsuccessful joint action between the Americans and French naval forces under Admiral Charles d'Estaing, the first such attempt after the alliance between the Continental Congress and France. Remains of the earthworks are still evident today on Sprague Street in Portsmouth, between S.R. 114 and 138. Commemorative markers in the immediate vicinity indicate the fort's significance during the Revolution. The fort offered an outstanding view of the Sakonnet River to the east and Narragansett Bay to the west, with Middletown in the distance.

CASTLE HILL FORT. FORT ADAMS.

FORT CHASTELLUX. FORT DENHAM.

FORT CHURCH. Constructed in 1940 at Little Compton in Newport County, the coast defense was named for Colonel Benjamin Church who killed and remorselessly dismembered King Philip at Mount Hope in 1676. There were three sections to the fort. The West Reservation was equipped with a pair of 16-inch guns in casemates that were so well equipped with amenities that they could have continued operation of the guns without being dependent on outside sources for either power or light. An unusually expert job of camouflage was accomplished on the works, with the buildings made to resemble a farm when observed from the air. The East Reservation was armed with two eight-inch guns and contained the theater, fire station, supply depot, and lodgings for the soldiers. The casemates were concealed by earth, and the other structures were camouflaged to give an appearance of a large summer residence. The South Reservation, some distance from the other two, was located on high ground with a commanding view of the ocean. The guns here were also of the eight-inch variety. After World War II, the fort was evacuated and put on the inactive list. In 1954 the property was resold to its former owners, or to others, by the federal government.

COASTER'S ISLAND FORT. Located off the coast at Newport, Coaster's Island was reinforced with additional defenses by the Americans after they regained Newport from the British in 1779.

CODDINGTON'S COVE FORT. The remains of an elliptical fort built by the British in 1778 are located on the corner of Coddington and Maple avenues in Newport.

CODDINGTON'S POINT FORT. During the Revolution, the British built a heavy gun battery at Coddington's Point in Newport.

COLLEGE HILL FORT. PROSPECT HILL FORT.

FORT CONANICUT. FORT WETHERILL.

CONANICUT BATTERY. BEAVER HEAD FORT.

FORT DANIEL. At East Greenwich was a formidable Revolutionary fort erected by the famous Kentish Guards to prevent the entrance of the British fleet into the harbor. Colonial records indicate that nine guns were mounted at this fort. It was located on a high bank, near the entrance to East Greenwich harbor. During the Revolution, East Greenwich thrived from a seafaring economy. Its inhabitants included a group of citizens who contributed substantially toward the prosecution of the war. Among the more illustrious were James Varnum, Continental Army general, William Greene, governor of Rhode Island during the war (and who used his residence as a capitol), and Dr. Peter Turner, a military surgeon in General Nathanael Greene's regiment. General Greene himself was born just south of East Greenwich. The Kentish Guards, one of the oldest military units in the country, was formed here.

FORT DENHAM (*Fort Chastellux; Fort Harrison*). Among the last fortifications built in Rhode Island during the Revolution was the battery on Hallidon Hill in Newport, commanding at short range the batteries at Brenton's Point and Goat Island. Built by the French, the fort was called Fort Chastellux in tribute to the marquis. After the war, its name was changed to Fort Harrison, the fort site being located on the Harrison farm. At a still later date, it was renamed Fort Denham, apparently from some local association. A part of the work was situated between Berkeley and King streets. The older name was transferred to present-day Chastellux Avenue, a Newport thoroughfare running back up the hill from the waterfront where the French army landed (now King Park). During 1798–1800, the work was repaired, rebuilt, and enlarged for the continued defense of the main entrance to Narragansett Bay and Newport's harbor.

FORT DUMPLINGS. FORT WETHERILL.

CAMP DYER (*Camp of Rhode Island Militia*). Located on Quonset Point, in Warwick, it was named Camp Dyer on May 7, 1898. Previously it had been known as Camp of Rhode Island Militia because of the state militia's summer maneuvers there. The camp area was later absorbed into the U.S. Naval Air Station which opened in July 1941.

ELDRED'S ONE-GUN BATTERY. Located on the east side of Conanicut Island, it was manned by bold John Eldred, who fired shots at British ships in the bay. When one day a shot passed through the mainsail of an enemy vessel, a landing party seized the gun and put it out of commission.

FERRY LANE REDOUBTS. During the Revolution, the Patriots built two circular redoubts to the south of Fox Hill Fort in Providence. They were located probably not far from Angell Street.

FOGLAND FERRY FORT. In December 1776 the British, having captured Portsmouth, began to strengthen American works seized by them by erecting a redoubt on the east side of the island at Fogland Ferry.

FOX HILL FORT. At a Providence town meeting convened on July 31, 1775, most of the business transacted concerned the defense of the town. Fortifications were ordered built on Fox Hill, to be armed with a battery of six 18-pounders and four fieldpieces. Because of the many changes made in Providence topography during the decades following the Revolution, the fort's site is somewhat uncertain, but the area bounded by Brook, Thompson, and Tockwotten streets more than likely covers the ground on which the important defensive work stood. Another citation states that the fort stood just north of India Point Park, on India Street, south of Wickenden Street and near Brook Street. Subsequent landfill has extended the shoreline.

FORT GEORGE. FORT WOLCOTT.

FORT GETTY. Located five miles west of Fort Adams, this coast defense on Conanicut Island in Narragansett Bay was established in 1900 on the site of old Fort Beaver Head. Named in honor of Colonel George Washington Getty, 4th Artillery, who served with distinction during the Mexican and Civil Wars, the fort was developed between 1900 and 1909 on about 31 acres of land purchased by the government in 1900. In addition to the main work, the fort included Batteries Toussard, House, and Whiting, with a total of seven guns, three of them 12-inch disappearing rifles. Battery Whiting's guns were later removed to another fort.

Fort Getty was temporarily garrisoned by artillery units during World War I when it was listed as a subpost of Fort Greble, and was reduced to caretaker status after the Armistice. Subsequent to its use during World War II for secretly training POWs for functions in local German government in preparation for the fall of Germany, it was declared surplus by the Army in 1948. At the outbreak of the Korean War in 1954, the Navy took over the defense, but it was again declared surplus within several months. The deteriorated work was purchased by the city of Jamestown in 1955 for recreational purposes.

FORT GREBLE. Located on Dutch Island, about five miles west of Newport, Fort Greble was named in honor of 1st Lieutenant John T. Greble, 2nd Artillery, the first officer of the regular Army killed in the Civil War. The fort's site, approximately 80 acres, was purchased by the government in 1864, but the fort was not established until 1900. In 1902 the fort was reported as being garrisoned by two companies of artillery, 229 men and 8 officers, manning the following ordnance: three 10-inch disappearing rifles; one 16-inch Armstrong gun; two 15-pounder rifles; and eight 12-inch mortars.

The post was deactivated in 1906 and placed in caretaker status. Maintained during the subsequent years, Fort Greble was reactivated in World War I, after which it was downgraded to become a rifle range during World War II.

FORT GREENE. The first attempt to fortify Easton Point near Newport was in 1776, when Patriot farmer-soldiers threw up a breastwork in a single night. Its guns so annoyed the British man-of-war *Scarborough* that she was obliged to slip her cables and withdraw as quickly as possible. Fort Greene was later built on the site. During 1798–1800, the fort's works were rebuilt and enlarged to continue the defense of Narragansett Bay and Newport's harbor. In addition, on North Point, an elliptical stone-scarped battery for 12 or 13 guns was erected. When all was completed, the works were named Fort Greene for Rhode Island's most distinguished general in the Revolution. The defense occupied an area of about 20,000 square feet on the military reservation acquired by the Federal government in 1799. By enactment on February 23, 1887, the reservation was given to the city of Newport to be used as a public park, and it was so utilized since 1891. Battery Park, at Washington and Battery streets, now occupies the site of the fort.

FORT GREENE. Situated at Point Judith on the Narragansett peninsula projecting into Rhode Island Sound, Fort Greene was completed in 1940 and named for Nathanael Greene, the State's Revolutionary War hero. When the site was acquired by the federal government in 1934, it was known as the Point Judith Military Reservation until 1940. The coastal defense was active throughout World War II. After the war, it was used for weekend coastal defense activities of the Rhode Island National Guard. Inactivated on July 31, 1947, it was declared excess to the Army's needs on December 31, 1949, and sold to the state for park development purposes. Currently it is being jointly used by the state, the city of Newport, and the Army Reserve.

GREEN END FORT. Located on the northern side of the Vernon Avenue Extension in Middletown, overlooking Green End Pond and Block Island Sound, the fort was constructed by the British in 1777 as the eastern anchor of their defense system on Aquidneck (Rhode) Island. It is believed that part of the fort's walls extended to Battery Park in Newport, the site of Fort Greene. When the British retreated back to Newport, General John Sullivan maneuvered his 10,000-man army onto the island on August 9, 1778. Six days later, American forces marched south to engage the British at Green End Fort, just north of Newport.

CAMP HALLETT. A Civil War rendezvous camp at Cranston, established on October 4, 1861, it was a temporary tent assembly point until more adequate quarters could be built. The camp was named for Colonel George W. Hallett of the Providence Horse Guards. During the first week of December 1861, some of the troops removed from Camp Hallett to new barracks being erected in the Riding Park near Pawtucket, then named Camp Arnold for the state's lieutenant governor, S. G. Arnold. When the barracks were completed, the remainder of Camp Hallett's soldiers removed to Camp Arnold.

FORT HAMILTON. On Rose Island in Narragansett Bay, a mile northwest of Fort Wolcott, extensive fortifications were begun at the turn of the nineteenth century. Quadrilateral in form, it was designed as a regular masonry work of stone, brick, and sod, with four bastions, two polygonal and two circular or tower-shaped, one converted to a lighthouse and the other roofed over in later years. During World War II, anti-aircraft guns were emplaced near the lighthouse. The fort was designed for 60 guns, with bombproofed barracks to accommodate 300 men. The fort was still uncompleted when the War of 1812 broke out, and was never finished, although the barracks, considered the finest in America at that time, were completed. The fort, named Fort Hamilton for the Patriot statesman Alexander Hamilton, has never been used except as a quarantine station for the city of Newport.

FORT HARRISON. FORT DENHAM.

FORT HILL (*Hog Pen Point Fort*).

There was yet another fort in the harbor. It was not, however, in Rhode Island, but was built on territory so near that it has since, by a change in the [Massachusetts–Rhode Island] line been brought within [Rhode Island's] borders. This is the work on Fort Hill, in East Providence. In the days of the Revolution this land was in the town of Rehoboth, and the point of land jutting out into the river, at the base of the hill, was called Hog Pen Point. . . . Rehoboth voted . . . on the sixth day of November, 1775, that a committee be chosen "to wait on a committee of the town of Providence to consult on fortifying Hog Pen Point." Whether any action was taken by the town of Providence in this matter is not known . . . but a week later, the town of Rehoboth "voted it expedient to fortify Hog Pen Point." [Edward Field, *Revolutionary Defences in Rhode Island,* pp. 75–77]

The fort was maintained until after the War of 1812. Today there are still some remains of the earthworks in evidence. In 1918 the fort site was used temporarily, by arrangements with the proprietors of the ground, as a station of the Coast Defenses of Narragansett Bay.

HOG PEN POINT FORT. FORT HILL.

HONEYMAN'S HILL FORT. The Americans, on August 17, 1778, erected a fort on Honeyman's Hill in Middletown, during their advance on British-held Newport.

FORT INDEPENDENCE. Subsequent to the judgment made at a Providence town meeting on October 26, 1775, a fort was built on Robin Hill at Field's Point, conspicuous from both the river and the bay. It is not known when the name, Fort Independence, was given the fort. The fort, existing to this day, is 110 feet long at its greatest extent, and varies in width from 53 to 60 feet inside the embankment. During the Revolution it was connected by earthworks with another defensive work on Sassafras Hill. During the War of 1812, these two forts were made more effective by the addition of a third, Fort William Henry, located at the southeast extremity of Field's Point. All are now gone, except Fort Independence, now restored, with its surrounding area converted into a park.

FORT (PHILIP) KEARNEY. A small coast artillery post was established in 1909 on South Ferry Road, on the east slopes of a hill overlooking Narragansett Bay and Conanicut Island. It was built on the site of the former village of South Ferry, one and a half miles south of Saunderstown and eight miles west of Fort Adams.

The fort was named in honor of Major General Philip Kearny, distinguished Mexican War veteran, who was killed in action, September 1, 1862, at Chantilly, Virginia. In 1905 the government bought 25 acres of the hill land. Coast artillery units were stationed here during World War I to assist Forts Getty and Greble prevent enemy vessels from passing up the bay to Providence. Mines were laid and a net was strung across the water to obstruct the entry of enemy submarines. A subpost of Fort Adams, the fort was reactivated in 1940, and during the last days of World War II was operated as an auxiliary clandestine school for selected prisoners of war, preparing them for administrative positions as civil servants in postwar Germany. When the last of the German prisoners of war left in 1946, Fort Kearney was discontinued.

KETTLE POINT WORKS. In October 1775 the Americans built earthwork batteries on Kettle Hill in East Providence.

LAWTON'S VALLEY FORT. This fort was built by the British in 1776 on the south side of Lawton's Valley near Middletown on the west side of Aquidneck (Rhode) Island.

FORT LIBERTY. FORT WOLCOTT.

FORT LOUIS. FORT WETHERILL.

FORT MANSFIELD. On about 70 acres of land purchased by the federal government in 1898, Fort Mansfield was built two years later on Napatree Point, eight miles south of Westerly. At the strategic end of a small peninsula, Napatree Point is located opposite Fishers Island at the eastern end of Fishers Island Sound. The fort was named in honor of Major General J. F. K. Mansfield, Mexican War veteran and inspector general, 1853–61, who was mortally wounded at the Battle of Antietam.

In 1902 the fort, a subpost of Fort Wright, was garrisoned by one company of artillery. The armament consisted of one 8-inch disappearing rifle, one 8-inch carriage mounted, with emplacements for two more rifles. Remains of the fort are still in evidence. Just to the east of Fort Mansfield is Watch Hill, a signal station during the French and Indian War when smoke was generally used for signaling. Later a watch tower was built there and manned during the Revolution and the War of 1812.

FORT NECK. This Revolutionary War fort was located on Pawtuxet (Cranston) Neck, just off

Fort Avenue, facing Providence across the Seekonk River and just north of the river's mouth in Narragansett Bay. An historic marker at 52 Fort Avenue, placed there by the Cranston Historic District Commission, commemorates the site of the fort, one of a number of Narragansett Bay defenses erected by the Patriots in the face of invading British forces. The granite walls of the fort were raised in the fall of 1775 and enclosed a battery of two 18-pound cannon manned by the Pawtuxet Rangers, a company of militiamen, in 1776, when the British occupied Newport. Some little time later, a watch house was built adjoining the fort to accommodate a day-and-night guard, The Rangers, who later became known as the Pawtuxet Artillery Company, again defended the fort during the War of 1812. The fort was abandoned in 1870, and its granite blocks were utilized as foundation stones in nearby Victorian residences.

FORT NECK LOT. FORT NINIGRET.

FORT NINIGRET (*Fort Neck Lot*). At Charlestown, south of U.S. 1, there is the site of one of the state's oldest forts, called Fort Neck Lot or Ninigret for the illustrious Niantic sachem. The remains of the earthwork fort, once believed to have been built by the region's Indians, have been uncovered, and because bastions and other evident signs of military engineering expertise were found, archaeologists and historians have concluded that it was constructed by early Dutch traders during the early seventeenth century and used as an outpost for trading with Rhode Island's Indians. The fort is historically reputed to have been the site of an early diplomatic alliance arranged by Captain John Mason with the Niantics to aid in the war against King Philip of the Wampanoag who was finally killed at Mount Hope. The three-quarter-acre fort site was dedicated in 1883 as a memorial to the Narragansett and Niantic tribes.

NORTH BATTERY FORT. A semicircular redoubt, calculated for about eight guns, the battery was located on a point of land near Newport, about three-quarters of a mile northeast of Fort Wolcott on Goat Island. The fort, begun by the Americans, was never completed because the British had taken Newport.

OWL'S NEST FORT. The British, while occupying Newport, built Owl's Nest Fort on Gould Island, a little wooded island lying in Narragansett Bay, nearly midway between Conanicut Island and Aquidneck (Rhode) Island. It is believed the island was fortified in 1778.

POPASQUASH FORT. Before the close of the year 1776, the whole shore of Narragansett Bay was well protected. The General Assembly had ordered that artillery companies be established in all the seaboard towns, and for the protection of these batteries, breastworks had been thrown up at Barrington, Nayatt Point, Quidnessett, Wickford, Boston Neck, Watch Hill, Noyes' Neck, and at Point Judith. There was also a battery at Popasquash Point, Bristol, with six 18-pounders.

PROSPECT HILL FORT (*College Hill Fort*). One of the most formidable defenses erected by the Americans in Rhode Island during the Revolution was Prospect Hill Fort, also known as College Hill Fort, in Providence. Begun on May 16, 1777, the works extended some distance around the signal beacon (giving the hill the prior name of Beacon Hill), already in place. "This fort was probably the only one in the town built from plans prepared before the work was commenced." (Edward Field, *Revolutionary Defenses in Rhode Island* [1896], p. 74). The fort was reported as having measured 300 by 150 feet within the parapet, with a bastion in each of the four angles, surrounded by a ditch, and capable of mounting 58 guns. Part of the fort stood on the present-day corner of Congdon and Bowen streets, today the site of the Roger Williams Memorial, also called Prospect Terrace.

QUAKER HILL FORT. This Revolutionary War defense was erected by the Patriots to the east of Butt's Hill Fort.

CAMP OF RHODE ISLAND MILITIA. CAMP DYER.

ROBIN HILL FORT. Built by the Americans in 1775, Robin Hill Fort was located in Providence on a bluff overlooking the Seekonk River.

ROGER WILLIAMS TRADING POST. Located in the town of Wickford, the trading post established by the founder of Rhode Island stood on the west side of the Post Road (U.S. 1), just south of Smith's Fort. It is believed the trading post was built in 1636 or 1637. Somewhere in the immediate vicinity, Williams had built his residence in 1644. In 1651 he sold out to Richard Smith of Cocumscussoc in order to finance a trip to England to resolve conflicts about colonial jurisdiction over Newport and Portsmouth. Historians generally believe that Williams's settlement did not survive King Philip's War (1675–76).

ROSE ISLAND FORT. When the British evacuated Newport in 1779, the Americans reoccupied it and built additional defenses on Rose Island, just south of today's Newport Bridge in the East Channel. The fort was armed with 40 pieces of heavy artillery. At the turn of the century, the island became the site of Fort Hamilton.

FORT ST. GEORGE. FORT WOLCOTT.

SEEKONK GARRISON. Probably a minimally fortified and palisaded dwelling located in Seekonk, now East Providence, it was nearly the only surviving structure in the town after King Philip's ravaging Indians, on March 26, 1676, had practically annihilated a sizable force of Englishmen and friendly Indians from Massachusetts, and burned the town, reducing 40 houses and 30 barns to ashes.

SMITH'S FORT. Located at Cocumscussoc on U.S. 1 (the Pequot Path), between East Greenwich and Wickford, Smith's Fort is the second edition of the fortified blockhouse built by Roger Smith in about the year 1640, not long after Roger Williams had established an alliance with the Narragansetts in the area and built a trading post nearby. Smith's blockhouse was burned by King Philip's Indians in 1676. His son rebuilt the blockhouse two years later, using some of the timbers from the charred garrison house. During subsequent years, the structure was enlarged from what was a story-and-a-half, three-room structure. On the north lawn of the property is the marked burial ground that holds the remains of 40 settlers killed during the Indian wars.

FORT SULLIVAN. Probably erected in 1778 when General John Sullivan was in command of Rhode Island's forces, the fort stood on the high ground on the west side of the Providence River in the city of Providence. The intersection of today's Chestnut and Friendship streets borders the square on which Fort Sullivan was built. It is generally believed the fort was the first to be obliterated after the Revolution.

TIVERTON HEIGHTS FORT. FORT BARTON.

TONOMY HILL FORT. "Tonomy" is an appellation corrupted from Wonumetonomy, the name of the last sachem of the Aquedneck, who were conquered by the Narragansett before the arrival of the English. On December 18, 1775, barracks were ordered built on Tonomy Hill. In March 1776 a General Assembly committee recommended that a fort be built there. In 1777 there was in place a strong line of entrenchments running northerly along the crest of the height from Easton's Pond to Coddington's Cove. Tonomy Hill itself was occupied by a strong redoubt.

TOWERING HILL FORT. According to Lossing's *War of 1812,* "Towering Hill near Newport . . . one mile east of the North Battery, and due north from the city . . . commanded the whole town. Remains of Revolutionary works [are still] there. A small block-house built in 1799 or 1800 [remains] entire." This described hill may be the same as Tonomy Hill.

TURKEY HILL FORT. To the west of Butts Hill Fort was Turkey Hill, which was also fortified by the Americans.

FORT VARNUM. On April 18, 1943, Fort Varnum in Narragansett was dedicated in ceremonies attended by a host of dignitaries and officers and men of the Narragansett Bay Command's defenses. The new fort, the fourth bay defense to honor a Revolutionary War hero of Rhode Island, was named for General James Mitchell Varnum. On July 1, 1958, the House Armed Services Committee at Washington approved a Senate-passed bill that directed the Army to transfer Fort Varnum, a decaying fortress virtually abandoned by the Army in 1948, to the state, which permitted its use by the National Guard for training purposes. The 23 buildings on the 34-acre military reservation were renovated, and all but a few have been converted to mess halls, barracks, supply rooms, classrooms, and storage.

WARWICK NECK FORT. Early in January 1776, the General Assembly ordered "that a number of men, not exceeding fifty, be stationed at Warwick Neck, including the Artillery Company in Warwick; the remainder to be minutemen; that Col. John Waterman have the command." When the British fleet appeared in Newport's harbor in early December 1776 and occupied the town, Rhode Island's governor was informed that "there ought to be a good redoubt at Warwick Point [now Rocky Point]. If they [the British] attack Providence it will be by land. They will pass up the bay to Warwick Neck perhaps, then land and march to the town." (Edward Field,

Revolutionary Defenses in Rhode Island [1896], pp. 84, 89). A substantial defense was therefore built on the Neck. A force of artillerymen and minutemen was stationed at the fort throughout the Revolution, as it was considered one of the most important posts on Narragansett Bay.

FORT WASHINGTON. FORT WOLCOTT.

FORT WETHERILL (*Fort Conanicut; Fort Brown; Fort Louis; Fort Dumplings*). The original fortification on the eastern side of Conanicut Island, two miles below Jamestown and directly opposite Fort Adams in Newport's harbor, was a battery built in 1776. It was constructed on the strategic peninsula where 100-foot-high granite cliffs overlooked the eastern channel of Narragansett Bay. First named Fort Conanicut, it was renamed Fort Brown for its first commander, "General" Abdiel Brown. The small but substantial post was equipped with heavy armament for the times, eight 18-pounder guns. During its occupation, Brown fired at the British men-of-war *Scarborough* and *Scimitar* in an attempt to drive the British fleet out of Newport's harbor in December 1776. Once the British had fully occupied Newport, they turned their attention to Brown's battery, capturing it without a shot being fired, and held it for two years. The British destroyed the post when they were forced to abandon all of Conanicut Island in the face of French landing forces in August 1778.

In 1798 the battery was rebuilt as Dumplings Fort, so named for the huge boulders that from a distance resembled dumplings. It was a round tower bastion of stone, about 80 feet above the water and 15 to 20 feet above the rock on which it was constructed. The reconstruction of this fort and others on the bay were superintended by Major Louis Toussard, a Frenchman who had served gallantly with the American forces during the Revolution, losing an arm in the Butts Hill action. His first name was very temporarily appended to the fort. Dumplings Fort was never completed, armed, or garrisoned, remaining abandoned until the Spanish-American War. In 1899 more property around the fort site was purchased to border on present-day Ocean Street, and the battery was enlarged in 1902, 1904, and 1907. In 1906 several 12-inch disappearing rifles were emplaced. On April 14, 1900, its name was changed to Fort Wetherill in honor of Captain Alexander M. Wetherill, 6th Infantry, who was killed in action at San Juan Hill, Santiago, Cuba, on July 1, 1898.

The fort was garrisoned during World War I by seven artillery companies of the Narragansett Bay Coast Defense. After the Armistice, the fort was reduced to caretaker status, with its heavy guns stored at Fort Adams. It was regarrisoned in World War II and, like Fort Getty, was used for German prisoners of war. In 1951 it was transferred to the Navy. During the 1960s Jamestown considered purchasing the property. Finally, in 1983, after years of bickering between the state and the federal government, the surplus military reservation was transferred to the state at no cost, with the provision that the property be converted to park or recreational use.

FORT WILLIAM HENRY. With the coming of peace after the Revolution, the old defenses in Providence became deserted and forgotten, and so they remained until the outbreak of the War of 1812. Soon after hostilities began, it was considered expedient to fortify Field's Point by erecting a battery there. The fortifications that had remained deserted for 30 years were resurrected and strengthened, and an additional fort was erected near the end of Field's Point, just above high water, and the name of Fort William Henry given to it. In addition, a fort of considerable size was built near Broad Street, between present-day Pearl and Somerset streets, and a line of breastworks constructed, extending across the Point to near Mashapaug Pond. (See: FORT INDEPENDENCE).

FORT WOLCOTT (*Fort Anne; Fort George [St. George]; Fort Liberty; Fort Washington*). Historic Goat Island, at the entrance to Newport's harbor from Narragansett Bay, had been fortified as early as 1700 when an "earthen battery" was built there. Since then various fortifications, and several editions thereof, undergoing name changes, were erected on the site of the battery. Goat Island (Indian, *Nante Sinunk*) was purchased from Chief Cochanaquoant by Benedict Arnold and John Greene, together with Coaster's Island and Dyer's Island for six pounds, ten shillings (probably in the equivalency of trade goods) on May 22, 1658. Benedict Arnold, who was associated with Roger Williams in the founding of Rhode Island, was the great-great-grandfather of Benedict Arnold, the "whirlwind hero" of the Revolution. On May 27, 1672, John Greene conveyed his title to the first two named islands to Benedict Arnold who, in turn, sold them to the town of Newport on May 1, 1673.

When the "earthen battery" was found inadequate for the defense of Newport's harbor, a new and stronger one was ordered built on May 6, 1702, "sufficient to mount twelve pieces of ordnance or cannon." (George W. Cullum, *His-

torical Sketch of the Fortification Defenses of Narragansett Bay [1884], p. 5). As soon as the new defense was completed, it took the name of Fort Anne, after England's queen who succeeded William III upon his death on March 8, 1702. Almost coincident with her accession, hostilities broke out in Europe and America. The fort was enlarged by appropriations from time to time by the Assembly. After peace was effected by the Treaty of Utrecht, the fort's garrison was disbanded.

When the accession of George II became known in 1727, the Rhode Island Assembly sent a memorial to His Majesty, stating that "a regular and beautiful fortification of stone with a battery" had been built at Newport, large enough to accommodate 50 cannon, which the monarch was asked to furnish. Not until three years later was its name changed to Fort George (sometimes referred to as Fort St. George), a designation retained until the outbreak of the Revolution, when, and until 1784, it was called Fort Liberty. The defense was completed in 1735 with its cost estimated to have been £10,000 in the depreciated currency of the colony.

The War of Jenkins's Ear in 1739 between England and Spain influenced the Assembly to order the full repair of Fort George, accompanied by arming it with sufficient guns. In 1740 watchtowers were ordered placed on Point Judith, Castle Hill, Brenton's Point, Sachuest Point, and on Conanicut Island. In 1741 in anticipation of war also with France, the Assembly ordered Fort George's battery enlarged to accommodate 10 or more additional cannon. In 1749 the fort was reportedly armed with 25 guns in the lower battery and 12 cannon on platforms.

At the outbreak of the Revolution, the Goat Island defense was the only fort in the colony. While Fort George was not permanently garrisoned, a guard was maintained there, since it was well equipped, mounting 50 guns and its magazine full of powder. In 1774 because of the mounting spirit of rebellion in the colonies, it was thought advisable to transfer the guns and ammunition to Providence. In 1776, however, the fort was rearmed with 25 guns, 18- and 24-pounders, with a garrison of 50 men commanded by Captain Samuel Sweet.

When the British captured and occupied Newport, they also took over the Goat Island defenses, renaming them Fort George. It was from Fort George that they bombarded Count d'Estaing's French fleet in 1778. As soon as the Patriots regained the fort, it was renamed Fort Washington. In 1794 the 18-acre military reservation was ceded to the United States government.

Lossing in his *War of 1812* reports on the fort's condition prior to the second war with Britain. It was built of stone cemented with lime, equipped with a brick and stone magazine, a sally-port, ditch, reverberatory furnace, and supported by two wings or bastions, both facing the harbor. Revetments of stone were laid in lime cement and parapets were supplied with sod. The batteries, though designed for ten cannon, had five pieces, 32-pounders each. There were bombproofed brick barracks two stories high and officers' quarters for one company.

The work on Goat Island in 1798 was rechristened Fort Wolcott to honor the Revolutionary War services of Connecticut Governor Oliver Wolcott who had very recently died (December 1, 1797), and also in compliment to his son, the Secretary of the Treasury under Presidents Washington and Adams. The fort's former name of Fort Washington was appropriately transferred to the defense on the Potomac River opposite Mount Vernon. The fort's garrison was withdrawn on May 22, 1836. Since 1869 the Navy Department has made use of it. It is now the home of the United States Torpedo Station.

FORT ANDERSON. THICKETTY FORT.

FORT ARBUTHNOT. FORT MOULTRIE.

CAMP ASYLUM. A Confederate military prison operated during 1864–65, Camp Asylum was located in the city of Columbia, in what was then the South Carolina State Hospital for the Insane.

FORT BALFOUR. A Revolutionary War defense erected by the British was established in either late 1780 or early 1781 and located at present Pocotaligo, Beaufort County. The fort, defended by one 6-pounder and garrisoned by about 25 regulars, 90 militiamen, and a well-equipped troop of cavalry, was attacked and captured by American forces under Colonel William Harden on April 18 (April 12?), 1781. After paroling their prisoners, the Americans left the fort in ruins.

FORT (BATTERY) BARNES. A Confederate defense in use 1861–63, it was located in St. Andrews Parish, just west of Charleston and north of the present intersection of U.S. 17 and S.R. 61. There is no record available of its armament.

BEACH BATTERIES. Built by Confederate forces in 1862 to protect the backside of Sullivan's Island, they were located in Mt. Pleasant, across the Wando River from Charleston. Its armament in 1865 consisted of one 32-pounder smoothbore and one 32-pounder rifled and banded.

BEAUFORT ARSENAL. The former headquarters of the Beaufort Artillery, one of the oldest militia companies in the country, organized in 1776 and disbanded in 1783, Beaufort Arsenal was established in 1795 on the site of the old brick-and-tabby courthouse in the town of Beaufort. In 1852 the Arsenal was rebuilt and expanded by the addition of a barracks adequate to accommodate 250 men and protected by a battery of six guns. In 1861 Federal forces occupied Beaufort and seized the Arsenal, destroying its store of guns and gun carriages. In 1934, as a WPA project, the building was enlarged with the addition of wings. One of the new wings was occupied by the Beaufort Museum while the main building continued to serve as headquarters for the militia.

BEAUFORT FORT (*Port Royal Fort*). In April 1715, shortly after the outbreak of the Yamassee War (1715–16), a small garrison of militia erected a fortification on Port Royal Island. Beaufort Fort, also known as Port Royal Fort, was probably

South Carolina

located south of Beaufort, either on Spanish Point or on the site of the present U.S. Navy Hospital a short distance farther south, in Beaufort County. "During 1721 and part of 1772 the Independent Company of Foot, a regular British infantry unit, was stationed there. In 1724 the fort was rebuilt. It probably consisted of earthen walls surrounded by a palisade. . . . In 1734 a new fortification, Fort Prince Frederick, was completed to replace dilapidated Beaufort Fort." (Larry E. Ivers, *Colonial Forts of South Carolina, 1670–1775* [1970], pp. 38–39).

BATTERY BEAUREGARD. Located about the middle of Sullivan's Island, east of Fort Moultrie, it was built by Confederate forces between 1862 and 1863. The battery was involved in the battle of April 17, 1863, between Union naval forces and the Confederate forts on the island. Its armament in 1865 was one 10-inch Columbiad smoothbore, one 8-inch Columbiad rifled and banded, three 8-inch seacoast howitzers, three 32-pounders rifled and banded, two 24-pounders rifled and banded, one 6-pounder smoothbore, and one 6-pounder rifled.

FORT BEAUREGARD. This Confederate fortification at Bay Point on Phillips Island, Port Royal, along with Fort Walker standing opposite across St. Helena's Sound, was captured on November 7, 1861, by Union forces consisting of Admiral Samuel Du Pont's fleet of 17 vessels and three brigades of land forces under General Thomas W. Sherman. During the next three days, the fleet and land forces moved up the rivers and inlets behind the harbor entrance, and took possession of Port Royal and Beaufort.

BATTERY BEE. Built by Confederate forces in 1862, it was located on the western end of Sullivan's Island. Its armament at the beginning of 1865 consisted of 11 cannon and mortars. The battery was blown up on February 18, 1865.

BELLE ISLE GARDENS FORT. This Confederate fortification, located four and a half miles south of Georgetown, off U.S. 17, was captured by a Union naval force in 1865.

FORT (BATTERY) BROUGHTON. Established in 1735, Broughton's Battery was part of colonial Charleston's fortifications. It was located on the present site of White Point Gardens (the South Battery), at East Bay Street and Murray Boulevard. Originally a detached battery, it was connected with the main city wall by an extension of the fortifications in the 1750s. The site today is contained within a park exhibiting monuments and relics.

BATTERY BROWN. Built by Union forces, Brown's Battery was located near the middle of Morris Island in Charleston Harbor. It contained two 8-inch Parrott rifles.

FORT BULL. A Charleston defense built by Confederate forces in 1863, it was located just south of Bee's Ferry on the Ashley River. Its armament is not known.

FORT (BATTERY) CAPRON. By General Orders No. 112, Adjutant General's Office, August 6, 1898, a mortar battery on Sullivan's Island in Charleston Harbor was designated Fort Capron in honor of Captain Allyn K. Capron, 1st Volunteer Cavalry, killed in action at La Quasina, Cuba, June 20, 1898. General Orders, AGO, July 22, 1899, changed the designation from Fort Capron to Battery Capron. This structure was designed to hold sixteen 12-inch mortars but was divided into two batteries (Capron and Butler) of eight 12-inch mortars on June 15, 1906.

CHARLESFORT. The area around Port Royal has been called by historians one of the most discovered parts of the globe, having been explored by the French, Spanish, and English. In May 1562 French Huguenots under Jean Ribaut (Ribault) entered the mouth of the St. Johns River near the point where St. Augustine was founded in 1565 by Pedro Menéndez de Avilés, calling the stream the River of May. From here Ribaut sailed northward, giving names to nine rivers and inlets. Finally the exploring colonists came to another stream, much larger than the others. They named this one Portus Regalis (Port Royal). It was here on an island or bordering mainland, between the Broad and Port Royal rivers, that Ribaut established his settlement and erected Charlesfort, a small earth-and-log fortification, named in honor of his sovereign, Charles IX of France, the first French habitation within the present United States.

During Ribaut's absence in France to obtain reinforcements, the small band of colonists faced by adversities soon abandoned the fort. After incredible hardships, they returned home. Although a monument was dedicated in March 1926 in the memory of Ribaut's Huguenots on Parris Island, where the Spanish erected Fort San Felipe in 1566, the debate as to where Charlesfort was located still continues. A number of archaeologists are of the opinion that the short-lived French post was on the Broad River in the area of Pigeon Point in Beaufort rather than Parris Island where the remains of the Spanish settlement were found during the late 1970s on the grounds of the U.S. Marine Corps base.

CHARLESTON HARBOR DEFENSES. The Civil War defenses at and in the near environs of Charleston Harbor consisted principally of many Confederate and Union gun batteries, a number of them intermittently manned. Those listed and located were of particular significance during the bloody four-year war.

CHARLESTON POST. The Post of Charleston was established on April 15 by elements of the 6th Infantry and 10 companies of the 128th U.S. Colored Troops. The post was abandoned by batteries E and I, 5th Artillery, on April 21, 1879.

CHARLES TOWNE'S FORTIFICATIONS. Charles Towne Landing at modern Charleston is a 200-acre exhibition park located on the site of the first permanent settlement in South Carolina, established during the period 1670–72. Today, no records have been found to show the dimensions or materials used for any of the buildings in Charles Towne. The evidence, however, seems to indicate that it was a scattered, irregularly laid out settlement. The opened ditches and parapets on the site today represent the fortified area during the settlement's earliest period. In 1672 the original bounds of the fortifications were expanded and a new palisade was erected. As settlers continued to pour into the new colony, the need for a better situation for the town became acute. Finally, in 1679, the decision was made to move the town proper to the Oyster Point peninsula at the confluence of the Ashley and Cooper rivers.

During 1670 and 1671 the first South Carolina colonists protected their settlement at Albemarle Point with a moat and a palisade fence. When Charles Town was moved to its present site in 1680 it was likewise fortified. The fortifications were soon expanded and improved until the town was surrounded by earthworks and palisades encompassing an area about a mile north and south, and a half mile east and west along the Cooper River in the southeastern part of present Charleston.

The Charles Town militia provided the fortifications' garrisons in time of emergency, but a full-time Captain of the Fort, or Commander of the Fortifications, was appointed by the government to care for the cannon, gunpowder, etc. The principal components of the fortification were six bastions, diamond or triangular shaped works, and two half moons, works in the shape of a half circle. The bastions and half moons, constructed of earth, wood, and bricks, protruded beyond the walls. Each was actually a separate fort containing its own cannons and assigned militia garrison. Blake's and Granville's Bastions were located on the southeast side of the fortification near the intersection of present Water and East Bay streets. Ashley's Bastion stood near the intersection of present Church and Water streets. Colleton's Bastion was located near the intersection of Meeting and Tradd streets. Johnson's Covered Half Moon (actually a demilune covering the gate) was near the intersection of Meeting and Broad streets. Carteret's Bastion was located near the intersection of Meeting and Cumberland streets. Craven's Bastion was near the east end of Market Street. And a half moon was located on the waterfront near the east end of Broad Street. In addition to the bastions and half moons, a watch house, later replaced by Broughton's Battery [1735], and entrenchments were located at White Point Gardens on the southern point of the peninsula.

Except for minor extensions and constant repair work this remained the composition of Charles Town's fortifications until 1745 and 1746, when a new wall with five bastions was constructed from Craven's Bastion, at the east end of Market Street, south-southwest almost to Ashley River near the west end of present Beaufain Street. In September 1752 a hurricane destroyed most of the town's fortifications, necessitating extensive repairs. After Britain defeated France and Spain in 1763 the fortifications were allowed to go to ruin. [Larry E. Ivers, *Colonial Forts of South Carolina, 1670–1775* (1970), pp. 40–42]

FORT CHARLOTTE. Erected in 1765–66 on the west bank of the Savannah River, nearly opposite the mouth of the Broad River, about 45 miles above Augusta, stone-constructed Fort Charlotte played an important role in South Carolina's history. The 50-by-40-foot, two-bastioned fortification, named in honor of Queen Charlotte, wife of George III, was intended to protect white settlements in the Long Cane region from Indian incursions. Located near present Mt. Carmel, McCormick County, Fort Charlotte was the last fort erected in the area during the Colonial era. It was the scene of the first overt act of the American Revolution in South Carolina, the seizure of the fort by Major James Mayson on July 12, 1775. Today the site of the fort lies beneath the impounded waters of the Clark Hill Reservoir.

CITADEL ARSENAL. The Citadel derived its name from the buildings in which it was first housed, located in Marion Square, Charleston. Erected apparently in 1842 with state funds as an arsenal, it was first garrisoned by federal troops, then by state troops, until they were replaced in March 1843 by the 20 students who comprised the first Corps of Cadets, the nucleus of what later evolved as The Citadel, a part of the South Carolina Military Academy. The arsenal burned in 1865 and was never reopened.

COLUMBIA POST. The Post of Columbia was established on April 24, 1866, in compliance with General Orders No. 26, Department of South Carolina. It was occupied continuously until December 20, 1877, when it was abandoned in accordance with Special Orders No. 184, Department of the South.

FORT CONGAREE NO. 1. In 1718 Captain Charles Russell and a dozen men built and garrisoned Congaree Fort near the site of a deserted Indian village, located in present Cayce, on the east bank of the Congaree River, a short distance above its mouth, in Lexington County. It was apparently a partially palisaded and ditched earthen structure with two bastions at the corners opposite the river and a ravelin protecting its gate. The fort served as a government trading post or factory until 1721. In 1722 the fort was abandoned.

FORT CONGAREE NO. 2. In 1748 a defense, also known as Fort Congaree, was erected on the west side of the Congaree River to protect the area from Iroquois marauders, normally living along the Ohio River, who penetrated South Carolina's frontier and committed widespread murder and depredation during the late 1740s. The fort's site is within the present city of Cayce, about two and a half miles north of the old fort, in Lexington County. A palisaded and ditched earthen fortification, it was garrisoned by British regulars assigned to South Carolina. In 1754 the fort's commander, Lieutenant Peter Mercier, led his garrison to Virginia, where they joined Lieutenant Colonel George Washington's expedition to the Ohio River. Mercier was killed by French besiegers during the battle at Fort Necessity at Great Meadows in Pennsylvania.

CAMP CROFT. A World War II infantry replacement training center occupying about 19,000 acres, activated and named for Major General Edward Croft on January 10, 1941, Camp Croft was located six miles from the city of Spartanburg. The post was declared surplus on November 12, 1945.

CAMP DAVID HUNTER. Captain Richard H. Jackson, 1st Artillery, with companies H and K of the 1st Artillery, and Company D of the 2nd Artillery, aggregating 177 men, established this camp at Summerville, Dorchester County, on

August 5, 1875. The post's last return is dated October 31, 1875.

FORT (BATTERY) DELAFIELD. Built by Union forces sometime during 1862–63, it was located on the south end of Folly Island in Charleston Harbor. Its armament is unknown.

FORT DORCHESTER. About 25 miles northwest of Charleston, near the head of navigation of the Ashley River, the state of South Carolina assisted in restoring the old Colonial town of Dorchester, settled in 1695 by a zealous band of Puritans from Massachusetts Bay. For almost two centuries, the community thrived as an important trading post and shipping port. During the French and Indian War, sometime between 1757 and 1760, the colonists built a fort there for protection. The defense, standing about 50 feet from and 15 feet above the Ashley River, was built of "tapia," more commonly known as "tabby," composed of oyster shells embedded in a matrix of burnt shell lime. Its plan was that of a squared redoubt with half-bastions at each of the four angles.

The fort was renovated and expanded after the Council of Safety in July 1775 ordered its occupation in defiance of the British. In November 1775 it was commanded by then Captain Francis Marion, "the Swamp Fox." During the war, both the town and the fort changed possession at least three times, the last time in December 1781 when they were recaptured by General Nathanael Greene and Colonel Wade Hampton. The Revolution and the end of seagoing commerce with Great Britain finished Dorchester. By 1811 it was totally abandoned. Today the Old Dorchester Historical State Park at Summerville contains the well-preserved hollow shell of Fort Dorchester.

FORT DREADNOUGHT (*Fort Galphin*). This fort was situated on an elevation, known as Silver Bluff, on the east bank of the Savannah River, about 15 miles below Augusta. It consisted of the palisaded brick residence of George Galphin, well-known Indian trader in the region. Known to the English as Fort Dreadnought, it was seized and garrisoned by British troops, particularly since Galphin was an ardent supporter of the Revolutionary cause. On May 21, 1781, American troops under Colonel Henry "Light-Horse Harry" Lee and Brigadier General Andrew Pickens took the fort after a short furious battle, capturing 126 prisoners and an abundance of military stores.

FORT EDISTO. A fort erected during the Yamassee War (1715–16), it was located on the plantation of James Rawlings, on the east bank of the Edisto River, near today's Givhan's Ferry State Park, Dorchester County. The defense guarded what was then known as the Savannah Path, at the strategic western entrance into the province's settlements. It was garrisoned by army units from May 1715 to December 1716.

ELLIOTT'S FORT. The residence of Thomas Elliott, located on his plantation on the west bank of Rantowles Creek, 12 miles west of Charles Towne, Charleston County, was fortified during the Yamassee War (1715–16). A local militia post from April to August 1715, it was thereafter garrisoned until March 1716 by army units.

FORT EUHANIE. In September 1716, William Waites, Sr., factor for the Indian trade, was ordered by the Board of Indian Commissioners to establish a trading post on the Little Pee Dee River near present Yauhannah, Georgetown County.

FENWICK'S FORT. Robert Fenwick's plantation home, located about eight miles southwest of Charles Towne, was fortified during the Yamassee War. It was garrisoned by militia during the period May–August 1715. From August 1715 to March 1716, it held an army garrison.

FORT FREDERICK. A tabby-built fortification built between 1731 and 1734 and located on Cat Island, Fort Frederick defended Port Royal. It survived until about 1743. Port Royal was left undefended until Fort Lyttleton was belatedly erected in 1758 near Beaufort.

FORT FREMONT. Established in 1899, after the end of the Spanish-American War, Fort Fremont is situated on the tip of St. Helena Island, the largest of Beaufort County's many barrier islands, four miles southeast of Port Royal. Named in honor of Major General John Charles Fremont, a native South Carolinian, and intended to protect the entrance to Port Royal Sound, the fort was a massive complex of concrete bastions and gun emplacements, garrisoned by one company of artillery manning three 10-inch disappearing guns and two 4.7-inch rapid-fire guns. It was apparently deactivated just prior to the outbreak of World War II. The preserved fortification is now privately owned.

FRONTIER DEFENSES. Most of the large number of South Carolina's colonial frontier defenses, established for the most part during the Yamassee War (1715–16) and the Cherokee War (1760–61), were stockaded private dwellings, some of them garrisoned by quasi-military units or British regulars for short periods. Those listed and located were of singular importance. (See: Larry E. Ivers, *Colonial Forts of South Carolina, 1670–1775,* 1970.)

FORT GALPHIN. FORT DREADNOUGHT.

BATTERY GARY. A Confederate defense located on the Mount Pleasant side of Charleston Harbor, it commanded the bridge to Sullivan's Island as well as the entrance to Hog Island Channel. The battery's armament consisted of two 8-inch rifles.

FORT GETTY. This post on Sullivan's Island, Charleston Harbor, was established in February 1902 by Lieutenant Colonel Charles Morris, with the 3rd, 10th, and 117th Companies of the Coast Artillery. It was named in honor of Colonel George Getty, 4th Artillery, and Brevet Major General U.S.V. The post's last return is dated May 1903.

FORT GILLMORE. A Union-built defense located near Fort Welles (renamed from Confederate Fort Walker after its capture) on Hilton Head Island near Beaufort, it was named for Brigadier General Quincy A. Gillmore, victor of the Fort Pulaski operation.

BATTERY GLOVER. A Confederate defense located on James Island, Charleston Harbor, and fronting on the Ashley River, it was an open battery with a wet ditch on the front and flanks, a magazine, and a large bombproof. The fort was armed with three 8-inch rifles.

GODFREY'S FORT. The fortified dwelling on Richard Godfrey's plantation, known today as Middleton Gardens, located on the west bank of the Ashley River, 14 miles northwest of Charles Towne (modern Charleston) in Dorchester County, it served as an army garrison from May to August 1715 during the Yamassee War.

FORT GRANBY. James Cayce's two-story dwelling and cotton storehouse was erected in 1770 and located on the Congaree River, near the old village of Granby, across the river from Columbia, Richland County. The structure was seized by the British during the Revolution and fortified as a ditched square redoubt with strong parapets, bastions, and an abatis. Its garrison in

1781 consisted of 350 men, mostly Loyalists, under the command of Major Andrew Maxwell. A force of American troops under Henry "Light-Horse Harry" Lee on May 15, 1781, captured Fort Granby after a short bombardment. The spoils of war included a considerable quantity of ammunition, salt, and liquor.

GRANVILLE BASTION. Constructed between 1700 and 1705, Granville Bastion was the fortification that formed the southeast corner of the original line of military works that completely surrounded the 1680 resettlement of Charles Towne (modern Charleston) on Oyster Point. Part of its remains were discovered in 1925 during excavations in preparation for the construction of the Masonic Order's new Omar Temple. The major part of Granville Bastion is still buried beneath the pavement of East Bay Street.

FORT GREGG. FORT PUTNAM.

BATTERY HARLESTON. A defense erected by Confederate forces in 1862–63 and located on James Island, Charleston Harbor, its armament in 1865 consisted of four 10-inch Columbiad smoothbores.

HEARN'S FORT. A Yamassee War fort erected in early 1716, it was located on John Hearn's plantation on the west bank of the Santee River, west of present Orangeburg. In May 1715 a large party of Catawba Indians raided the plantation and killed John Hearn.

Shortly afterward the same war party ambushed a company of horsemen who were enroute to Hearn's plantation where they intended to build a fort. One third of the horsemen were killed and the remainder were routed. It was probably the same war party which destroyed Schenckingh's Fort. A fort was built and an army garrison was established at Hearn's plantation in March 1716 to guard the strategic northern entrance into the South Carolina settlements. The Northern Rangers, . . . a score of horsemen, were probably stationed there from December 1716 to June 1718. [Larry E. Ivers, *Colonial Forts of South Carolina, 1670–1775* (1970)].

FORT HOLMES (*Fort Williamson*). A ditched and abatised (or palisaded) breastwork built by the British in 1781, it stood on the site of another breastwork, a temporary American defense, erected in 1775 by Colonel Andrew Williamson after he defeated a British garrison there in one of South Carolina's earliest Revolutionary War battles. Fort Holmes guarded the spring that was the sole water supply for nearby British-held Fort Ninety-Six, unsuccessfully besieged by General Nathanael Greene and his army of Continentals in May 1781. (See: FORT NINETY-SIX.)

FORT HOWELL. An earthwork defense, covering about three acres, erected by Union troops in early 1864 on Hilton Head Island, it was named in honor of Brigadier General Joshua Blackwood Howell who, as a colonel of the 85th Pennsylvania Volunteer Infantry, was later killed on September 14, 1864, at Petersburg, Virginia, and posthumously promoted to brigadier general. Fortified by four large gun turrets, Fort Howell apparently joined with Fort Sherman and Fort Mitchel to protect the north end of the island. A vital Federal outpost from November 1861 throughout the Civil War, Hilton Head served as a staging area for Union operations in the Beaufort area. Some speculation about the location of Fort Howell centers on its proximity to "Mitchelville," a community of barracks-type buildings housing black refugees, on the west side of Fish Haul Creek, with the fort on the opposite bank. After the war, the forts no longer served military purposes. Troops remained on the island, however, until the middle of the 1870s, evacuating gradually from 1874 to 1878. The site of the fort and its remains are now private property.

CAMP JACKSON. FORT JACKSON.

FORT JACKSON (*Camp Jackson*). Established as Camp Jackson on July 18, 1917, as a base training center during World War I, it was officially designated as Fort Jackson in 1940. Although named in honor of Major General Andrew Jackson, seventh president of the United States, the post is actually located on the former estate of General Wade Hampton, seven miles east of Columbia. About 45,000 men of the 30th and 80th Infantry Divisions trained here before departing for France to fight under General John Pershing. Between World War I and World War II, the post served as a training area for the South Carolina National Guard.

It is estimated that during World War II, with the installation once again under federal control, more than a half-million men received some form of training at Fort Jackson. Nine divisions, among them some of the Army's noted, trained here. After the war, it became a replacement center. The 31st "Dixie Division" trained here during the Korean War. Literally thousands of troops were trained by other units at Fort Jackson during the Korean and Vietnam conflicts. The first all-female brigade was established here in July 1974. Nearly 50,000 recruits are trained here annually. Similar to almost all other U.S. Army posts, Fort Jackson is a multimission installation. In addition to its primary mission of training initial entry soldiers, Fort Jackson hosts various military activities which are tenanted or satellited on the installation by common service support.

FORT JOHNSON. South Carolina's most important colonial defense and the oldest of Charleston Harbor's forts, Fort Johnson was built in 1704–8 on Windmill Point on the east end of James Island, south of Charleston, and named for General Sir Nathaniel Johnson. It was then a triangular-shaped defense with three bastions, a battery guarding the harbor entrance, and a ravelin in front of its gateway, the whole surrounded by a palisade-planted moat. A British garrisoned post in 1765, it was seized by a band of Charleston's citizens who trained the fort's guns on a cargo ship carrying despised tax-levying tea stamps, threatening to sink it unless the captain returned to England, which the ship's master did. It was here, on September 15, 1775, that Colonel William Moultrie, in command of the fort, raised the blue-and-white flag—three white crescents on a blue field—South Carolina's standard, for the first time. It was from Fort Johnson's gun battery that the first shell was fired over Fort Sumter at 4:30 A.M. on April 12, 1861, literally signaling the beginning of the Civil War.

Fort Johnson was then a quadrilateral work, constructed of bricks and palmetto logs. It was unsuccessfully assaulted twice by Union land and sea forces. Fort Johnson was finally evacuated, along with other Charleston Harbor defenses, on the night of February 17, 1865, when General Sherman threatened to cut off all communications with Charleston.

FORT KEOWEE. Fort Prince George.

FORT LAMAR. A Confederate defense at Secessionville on James Island, Charleston Harbor, it was named in honor of Colonel Thomas G. Lamar, who later died of a fever contracted in 1863 on the island. Fort Lamar's armament during the siege of 1862 consisted of two 8-inch howitzers, three 32-pounder cannon, and two 2 1/2-pounder rifled guns.

FORT LYTTLETON. Located on Spanish Point, nearly two miles south of Beaufort across the harbor, Fort Lyttleton was begun in 1758 as a replacement for abandoned Fort Frederick and was intended to protect Port Royal Sound from naval attack. Work performed on its construction

was slow, and it took four years to complete. Named for Governor William Henry Lyttleton, the tabby-built fort was built in the form of a triangle, 400 by 375 feet, with its base on the Port Royal River and its point on the inland side. The point was a bastion and the corners at the base were half-bastions. At the outbreak of the Revolution, it was seized by South Carolina forces. Attacked during the Battle of Port Royal Sound on February 3, 1779, the defense's garrison spiked the guns and blew up the fort. In 1978 archaeological excavations uncovered the entire front wall of the fort, which was about 7 feet in breadth and up to 10 feet in depth, in addition to the fort's barracks and other tabby structures.

BATTERY MARSHALL. This battery, built by Confederate forces in March 1863, was located on the eastern end of Sullivan's Island, overlooking Breach Inlet, in Charleston Harbor. General Quincy A. Gillmore in 1865 lists its armament as consisting of 14 various calibered smoothbores, rifles, and howitzers.

BATTERY MEADE. Construction of Battery Meade and Battery Rosecrans by Union forces on Morris Island, Charleston Harbor, was begun on the night of July 28, 1863, with the purpose of advancing parallels and ultimately taking the Confederates' Battery Wagner at the end of the Island, where Union artillerists could more effectively train their immense Parrott guns on Confederate-held Fort Sumter. Confederate sniping was not the only factor that slowed construction. On an old map Morris Island was called "Coffin Land"; it had been used as a quarantine burying-ground for Charleston, and during construction many corpses were discovered. By August 17 the parallels were completed and Battery Wagner was taken by assault. But the Federals advanced no farther.

FORT MIDDLETON. Fort Ninety-Six.

FORT MITCHELL. Fort Howell.

FORT MOORE. In the winter of 1715, during the Yamassee War, Fort Moore was built near the abandoned Shawnee Indian village of Savannah Town (later called New Windsor), across the Savannah River from present Augusta, Georgia, to protect the major northwestern entrance into South Carolina. The fort stood atop a 200-foot-high bluff on the east bank of the river. The defense was a large structure, about 150 feet square, surrounded by a four-and-a-half-foot-high planked wall. Cannon were emplaced in roofed bastions at each corner. Within were officers' quarters, barracks, a guardhouse, a powder magazine, traders' storehouses, and other buildings. Its garrison of Provincial troops varied from 10 to 40 men until 1746. British regulars were posted there intermittently from then until 1766 when Fort Moore, one of the province's most important frontier posts, was abandoned after 50 years of guarding a vital frontier.

FORT MORRIS. On December 31, 1860, Governor Francis W. Pickens ordered Major General John Schnierle to select a site on Morris Island where a battery could be established beyond the range of Fort Sumter's guns. The governor's directive was carried out and a battery known as Fort Morris was built, consisting of four 24-pound field howitzers. Its situation was such that it commanded the main ship channel.

FORT MOTTE. Its site located near the present town of Fort Motte in Calhoun County, Fort Motte was originally the two-story plantation mansion of Rebecca Motte, widow of wealthy Jacob Motte, who had been a fervent Patriot until his death. Because of its strategic location, overlooking the juncture of the Congaree and Wateree rivers, British forces seized the house, forced Mrs. Motte to move her living quarters to a farmhouse on the nearby hill, and fortified the mansion with a high palisade, earthworks, and an abatis, surrounding the whole with a deep ditch or fosse. The British stronghold was an important depot that sorted out and stored war supplies shipped from Charleston and then reshipped them via the Congaree and Wateree to British posts farther west. On May 8, 1781, Continental forces under General Francis Marion and Colonel Henry "Light-Horse Harry" Lee attacked the fort. Mrs. Motte readily agreed that her palatial home should be burned down rather than allow it to remain in British hands. She provided the Americans with the bow and fire arrows that were presents to her husband years earlier. The fortified house was set afire and its garrison hurriedly evacuated. The site is memorialized by an inscribed granite boulder erected by the Rebecca Motte Chapter of the D.A.R.

FORT MOULTRIE (*Fort Sullivan; Fort Arbuthnot*). There have been three Fort Moultries. The first of these was the palmetto and sand fort of the American Revolution, originally known as Fort Sullivan for a Captain O'Sullivan who was appointed in 1674 to maintain a signal cannon on the strategically placed island and to fire it when any vessel approached Charles Towne. It was renamed by the South Carolina Assembly in honor of Colonel William Moultrie, following the repulse of a formidable British fleet on June 28, 1776. When the British captured the post in 1780, they renamed it in honor of Vice Admiral Mariott Arbuthnot, General Sir Henry Clinton's naval counterpart in the siege, whose marines captured Fort Moultrie shortly before Charleston fell. The name, of course, lasted no longer than the British occupation of Charleston. Fort Moultrie No. 1 disappeared in the post-Revolutionary years, apparently swallowed by the sea.

In 1794, when war with Great Britain ap-

FORT MOULTRIE. (Courtesy of the National Park Service.)

peared imminent, Congress appropriated money for coastal defenses. Construction was begun on Fort Moultrie No. 2. With the easing of tensions following the Jay Treaty, work was suspended, then renewed. A typical First System work, the fort was an enclosed five-sided structure completed in early November 1798, during the quasi-war with France. Fort Moultrie No. 2 was battered by high tides in 1803 and wrecked by the hurricane of 1804. Four years later, in 1808, when war with Great Britain again threatened, the construction of Fort Moultrie No. 3 was commenced. A masonry work of the Second System, the fort was completed and garrisoned in December 1809. This is the Fort Moultrie of today, although it was greatly modified during the Civil War, the years 1872–76, and between 1897 and 1903. There are no surface remains of the first two Fort Moultries.

The present Fort Moultrie's low 15-foot-high walls, covering 1 1/2 acres, were built of sand faced with brick inside and out. Full armament was about 40 guns. Three brick barracks built within the courtyard housed up to 500 men, and a powder magazine held up to 500 barrels of gunpowder. A furnace used to heat solid shot was also built in the courtyard. The barracks and furnace were destroyed in the Civil War, but the fort's original walls and powder magazine stand intact.

In the mid-1830s, while the U.S. government was trying to relocate the Seminole Indians to open Florida to settlement, Osceola, a self-made leader of the Seminole, who opposed emigration to the west, fought a guerrilla war against settlers and the U.S. Army. Finally captured, he and 200 other Indians were confined at Fort Moultrie to isolate them from other Seminole still fighting the war. Osceola died in Moultrie from malarial complications after only one month of confinement.

In December 1860, Major Robert Anderson, when threatened by South Carolina secessionists, evacuated Fort Moultrie and transferred its garrison to Fort Sumter. Three and a half months later, South Carolina artillerists from Fort Moultrie, with their counterparts at Fort Johnson, participated in the bombardment of Fort Sumter, which sparked the Civil War.

New improvements in naval and coastal artillery came after the Civil War, among them the development of breech-loading, rapid-fire guns. Battery Jasper at Fort Moultrie was built in 1896 to hold these powerful new weapons. The huge concrete structure would also provide protection against increasingly powerful naval armament. Although never tested in battle, such coastal bat-

teries played a substantial role in safeguarding the shores of the United States from enemy attacks. After World War II, when new weapons had completely transformed tactical and strategical concepts, forts like Fort Moultrie became obsolete, and in 1947, after 171 years of service, it was officially deactivated. In January 1961 the National Park Service took over its administration. The fort is located on West Middle Street on Sullivan's Island.

NECK BATTERY. FORT WAGNER.

FORT NINETY-SIX (*Fort Middleton; Fort Williamson; Star Fort*). The historic town of Ninety-Six and its near environs, which began as a trading post in the 1730s, eventually comprised a complicated complex of fortifications, most of which were erected during the Revolution. Located about 10 miles southeast of present Greenwood, the original Fort Ninety-Six (two miles west of the Revolutionary fort) was built in November 1759 by Governor William Henry Lyttleton and a small army of militia in response to the beginnings of trouble with the Cherokee. The fort, a small, square stockade built around a barn, was so named because it was 96 trail miles from there to Keowee in the Cherokee Lower Towns, where Fort Prince George was constructed in 1753. The defense, also known as Fort Middleton, was unsuccessfully attacked twice by Cherokee war parties. Lyttleton's fort was garrisoned by militia forces until April 1761, when a new and stronger stockade was constructed around it.

When news of the Revolution's first armed conflicts at Lexington and Concord, Bunker Hill, and the Continental Army's siege of Boston arrived in the South, American rebels and British Loyalists in South Carolina drew up sides. When Major Andrew Williamson, in command of Fort Charlotte, learned that about 1,500 Tories intended to cross the Saluda River near Ninety-Six, he determined to intercept them. On November 19, 1775, Williamson and 500 men marched to Ninety-Six, erected a roughly square breastwork covering about 185 yards in a field near the town, and prepared to engage the Tories. The Tories arrived, took over the town, converted the jail into a fortification, and for two days unsuccessfully besieged Williamson's fort. This was the site of Fort Holmes, the palisaded, four-bastioned defense built by the British in 1781 to guard the spring that was the water supply for Fort Ninety-Six. (See also: FORT HOLMES.)

Ninety-Six, and the area around it, was returned to British control in the spring and summer of 1780 after

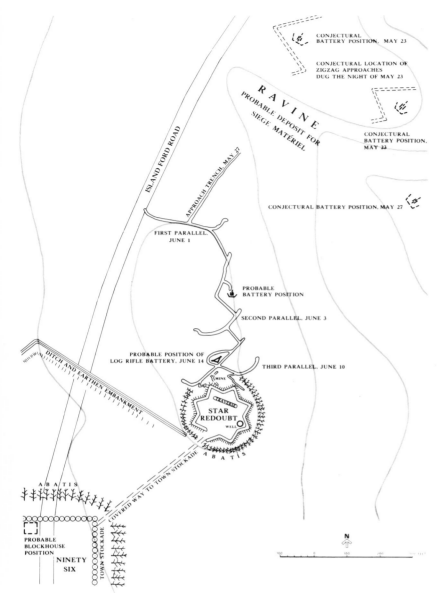

FORT NINETY-SIX. Map of the attack May–June 1781. (Courtesy of the National Park Service.)

the fall of Charleston. Under the command of Lieutenant Colonel John Harris Cruger, an extensive fortification system was built which included the Star Redoubt [the principal British position beyond the town's stockade area], the stockade, a number of blockhouses around the town, and Fort Holmes on the site of Fort Williamson. . . . The 1781 siege of Ninety-Six by General Nathanael Green and his Continental regulars and southern militia . . . began on Tuesday, May 22. Inside the forts were 550 Tories. Among them were Loyalist militia units from New York and New Jersey. Greene opened the siege with something less than 1,000 Continentals (eventually he was joined by Lee's legion) and only light artillery. Trenches were dug around the Star Fort under the direction of Kosciuszko who had built the West Point defenses.

A number of devices were tried by the Americans including a Maham tower and a mine in an attempt to blow it up. . . . On June 17, it was learned that a relief column of 2,000 men was on the way from Charles-

ton under the command of Lord Rawdon. A final assault was tried against Fort Holmes and the Star Redoubt. . . . The Americans were driven off with heavy losses. A cease-fire was arranged to exchange prisoners and bury the dead, and on the nineteenth, Greene lifted the siege and withdrew. The Americans lost fifty-eight killed, seventy-six wounded and twenty missing. The British lost twenty-seven killed and fifty-eight wounded. [Lord Rawdon reached Fort Ninety-Six on June 21. Realizing that he could not effectively hold the position, he ordered Lieutenant Colonel Cruger to destroy the fort]. [Sol Stember, *Bicentennial Guide to the American Revolution* 3:97–98]

PALACHACOLA FORT. FORT PRINCE GEORGE.

PASSAGE FORT. Located at Bloody Point on Daufuskie Island, surrounded on three sides by the present Intercoastal Waterway, Beaufort County, Passage Fort was a palisaded structure intermittently garrisoned by militia scouts from December 1717 until 1764. Early in 1728, a Yamassee Indian war party surprised the fort and killed or captured every one of its garrison.

FORT PEMBERTON. Erected by Confederate forces in 1862 and located at the junction of Elliott's Cut and the Stono River, in Charleston Harbor, Fort Pemberton was the anchor of the rebels' so-called Western Line of defenses and named for General John Clifford Pemberton. This fortification was described by Brigadier General P. G. T. Beauregard in his inspection report of September 1862 as "a strong work" with "an armament of 20 guns of various calibers." The remains of the powerful Confederate work are reportedly in excellent condition today.

FORT PICKENS. One of the earliest Confederate defenses erected in 1861 in the Charleston Harbor area was Fort Pickens, named in honor of Governor Francis W. Pickens. It was a small work situated on Battery Island in the Stono River, about two miles upstream from its mouth.

CASTLE PINCKNEY. Diminutive Castle Pinckney is situated on a three-and-a-half-acre island in Charleston Harbor, at the mouth of the Cooper River. It was once owned by a Quaker named Shute and called Shute's Folly before it was converted as a harbor defense and renamed for Charles Cotesworth Pinckney, American statesman and diplomat, and native Charlestonian. Originally constructed in 1798, it was ceded to the United States by the state of South Carolina in 1805. The fort was rebuilt in 1828–31. Seven days after the state's secession declaration, Confederate partisans surprised Union engineers who were refortifying the island, and took possession. It remained in Confederate hands until evacuated in February 1865. The first Union prisoners of war brought to Charleston during the summer of 1861 were held captive in Castle Pinckney, where casemates were fitted up with bunks for the prisoners. In 1924 Castle Pinckney was declared a National Monument.

FORT PLEASANT. Haddrel's Point, the site of Fort Pleasant during the Revolution, in Charleston Harbor, was fortified by the Americans prior to the unsuccessful British attack against Charleston in 1776. On April 25, 1780, it was occupied by British troops. The fort was later used as an encampment for Patriot prisoners of war. Haddrel's Point is the site of the modern town of Mt. Pleasant.

PORT ROYAL FORT. BEAUFORT FORT.

FORT PRINCE FREDERICK. Built during the years 1731 to 1734, this Provincial fort replaced Beaufort Fort and occupied the present site of the U.S. Navy Hospital, three miles south of the city of Beaufort. A small fortification, 125 by 75 feet, with 4-foot-high tabby-built walls on three sides, its open eastern side was a parapet on which was mounted a battery of guns commanding the Port Royal River. The confines of the fort were crowded with barracks and a powder magazine. The fort was intermittently garrisoned by varying numbers of Provincial troops and British regulars until 1758 when Fort Lyttleton was begun. Its still-existing tabby walls are being maintained by the staff of the hospital.

FORT PRINCE GEORGE (*Palachacola Fort*). In 1723 Palachacola Fort, or more properly Fort Prince George, was built by Captain William Bellinger on the east side of the Savannah River, in the northwest corner of Jasper County, about 35 miles northwest of Savannah, Georgia. It was garrisoned by South Carolina Rangers "until the new colony of Georgia assumed responsibility for the fort and its garrison in 1735." Georgia troops apparently occupied it until 1742.

FORT PRINCE GEORGE (*Fort Keowee*). As early as 1729, the South Carolina Provincial Assembly considered locating a fort among the Cherokee to guard the northern entrance into the province, to protect the Cherokee from French-allied Indians, and to safeguard the presence of traders in the area. Finally, in 1753, Gov-

ernor James Glen led an expedition into the Cherokee Nation's Lower Towns and built Fort Prince George, also known as Keowee Fort because of its location 90 yards from the east bank of the Keowee River, near the Cherokee village of Keowee, 11 miles southwest of present Pickens. A 200-foot-square ditched fortification, surrounded by palisade-topped earthen walls, with a bastion in each of its angles, it enclosed the commandant's quarters, a barracks, storehouse, powder magazine, kitchen, and a guardhouse. Completely rebuilt in 1756 and again in 1765, it was garrisoned by detachments of one of South Carolina's British Independent Companies until 1764, when they were replaced by elements of the Royal American Regiment, who remained until about 1766.

During the Cherokee War (1760–61) the fort, commanded by Lieutenant Richard Cotymore, was besieged by the Cherokee for five months, beginning in January 1760. Lieutenant Cotymore was ambushed and murdered in February. In retribution, the fort's garrison killed a number of Cherokee being held as hostages at the fort. During the long siege, it was reported that the garrison lost more men because of a contagion of smallpox than by Cherokee bullets. Finally, in June, a large relief force of British regulars and Provincials reached Fort Prince George from Charles Towne and raised the siege. The fort was abandoned in 1768.

State archaeologists during 1966–68 completed exploratory excavations in the area, with the town of Keowee, lying on both sides of the river, the focal point. There was a sense of urgency about the project, and about the continued excavation of old Fort Prince George, because in the summer of 1968, waters impounded by dams of the huge Keowee-Toxaway power complex would begin swallowing up the sites of the Indian towns and the fort. During August and September 1966, the archaeologists uncovered the fort's northeast bastion and a treasure of colonial artifacts. Today its site lies beneath the waters of Keowee Lake.

PRINCE'S FORT. A Revolutionary War fortification, located on an elevation near the head of one of the branches of the North Fork of the Tyger River, seven miles northwest of present Spartanburg, Prince's Fort was probably erected in late 1779 or 1780 and garrisoned by a British and South Carolina Royalist force under the command of Lieutenant Colonel Alexander Innes. Circular in shape, built of heavy timbers from 12 to 15 feet high, surrounded by a ditch, with its front abatissed, Prince's Fort derived its name from a William Prince who lived in its near environs.

BATTERY PRINGLE. A Confederate defense situated on the Stono River side of James Island in Charleston Harbor, Battery Pringle underwent intermittent Union naval bombardment from July 4–9, 1864. Today's condition of the battery's remains is considered excellent.

FORT PUTNAM (*Fort Gregg*). In early 1863, when it became apparent Union ironclads would attack Fort Sumter, Confederate forces erected a defense known as Battery Gregg at Cummings Point on Morris Island in Charleston Harbor. Forts Wagner and Gregg, captured successively by the advance of parallels, were evacuated by the Confederates on September 6, 1863. Fort Gregg was renamed Fort Putnam by General Quincy A. Gillmore whose forces occupied the defense. Fort Putnam's armament included two 100-pounder Parrott guns.

BATTERY REED. In order to secure the vulnerable eastern shore of James Island, Confederate forces in 1862 increased the size of a two-gun work near Secessionville, initially known as the Enfilade Battery, and renamed it Battery Reed in honor of one of the officers killed during the June 16, 1862, Union attack on Secessionville. To support Battery Reed, a series of fortifications were begun in mid-1863 by Confederate troops. Listed from Battery Reed, the major batteries were Rion, Tatum, Haskell, Cheves, and near Fort Johnson, Battery Simkins.

FORT RIPLEY. Constructed by Confederate forces in 1862 on a shoal between Castle Pinckney and Fort Sumter, Charleston Harbor, Fort Ripley was named for General Roswell Sabine Ripley. According to General Quincy A. Gillmore's 1863 report, it was a small work designed for two guns, "built on the 'Middle Ground,' upon a crib work of pine logs, faced on the outside with palmetto logs." Apparently never armed, it was used as a signal station.

BATTERY ROSECRANS. BATTERY MEADE.

FORT RUTLEDGE (*Fort Salvador*). Located at present Clemson, Oconee County, Fort Rutledge was built on the grounds of John C. Calhoun's plantation home in the spring of 1776 by Colonel (later General) Andrew Williamson in response to violent incursions by British-incited Cherokee. Named for Governor John Rutledge, the fort was also referred to as Fort Salvador in

tribute to Captain Salvador, the colonel's English-Jewish guide, who had been killed and scalped by the Cherokee. In September Williamson marched north with his troops to join the expedition from North Carolina against the Middle and Overhill Cherokee towns. The Indians were ultimately forced to sue for peace, and in a treaty signed on May 20, 1777, they ceded to South Carolina much of the present northwestern area of the state. The grounds of Clemson Agricultural College contain both the site of Fort Rutledge and John Calhoun's well-maintained original homestead.

ST. HELENA ISLAND POST. This post, located just east of Beaufort, was established in December 1863 by Colonel Joseph R. Hawley, 7th Connecticut Volunteers, with 10 companies of his Volunteer Regiment and 10 companies of New Hampshire Volunteers, aggregating 1,837 men. The post was occupied until June 1864.

SALTCATCHERS FORT. Situated on the west side of the Salkehatchie (Saltcatchers) River, a short distance east of present Yamassee, Beaufort County, this stockaded fort was constructed by Captain James McPherson and his company of Southern Rangers between the years 1728 and 1731. Its purpose was to scour the area between the Combahee and Savannah rivers to protect Beaufort's settlers from Yamassee Indian incursions. When Saltcatchers Fort was destroyed in 1734, its garrison was transferred to Fort Prince George.

FORT SALVADOR. FORT RUTLEDGE.

FORT SAN FELIPE (*Fort San Sebastian; Fort San Marcos*). The sites of the long-sought sixteenth-century settlement of Santa Elena—once considered the alternate capital of Spanish Florida—and one of its defenses, were discovered during the summer of 1979 under a part of the golf course on the Parris Island Marine Base on Port Royal Sound, Beaufort County. The once thriving settlement founded in 1566, just one year after St. Augustine, had 60 houses, three different forts, and a peak population of 400 before being abandoned in 1587.

Archaeologists believe the fort is the one known to history as San Felipe II, the oldest European military structure ever found in the United States. Almost as long as a football field and large enough to hold 500 people, it served to protect the people of Santa Elena from marauding Indians and Frenchmen from 1570 to 1576. A moated area near the Santa Elena site that long has been identified as Charlesfort, a structure erected by a French Huguenot expedition commanded by Jean Ribaut in 1562, has since been determined to have been the Spanish structure known as Fort San Marcos. It is now the prevailing opinion of archaeologists that the French post was located on either Port Royal Island or on the mainland along the Broad River in the area of Pigeon Point in Beaufort. The third fort in the Santa Elena area, San Felipe I, has not yet been found.

The earliest fort and settlement on the site were built in 1566 by an expedition under Pedro Menéndez de Avilés, then governor of Florida and also founder of St. Augustine. He had been sent to the New World by King Philip of Spain to obliterate the fledgling French settlement of Fort Caroline in Florida. The Spaniards complied with the royal directive and massacred the garrison there, renaming the French fort San Mateo. Sixteenth-century Spanish Florida was a rich temptation to the French. Every year millions in gold passed through what was then the Bahama Channel, now the Straits of Florida, en route to Spain. With a foothold on the coast, the French hoped to plunder the Spanish treasure fleets.

Menéndez built Fort San Felipe and established the settlement of Santa Elena to protect the coastal flank of the route of the treasure fleets and prevent further settlement attempts by the French. The settlement, however, struggled through a series of traumatic events, and its end came in 1587, hastened by the attack by Sir Francis Drake on St. Augustine. Called back to St. Augustine to reinforce the Spanish defense there, the settlers never returned to Santa Elena. It is known that unlike San Felipe I, which was triangular in form, San Felipe II was a rectangle surrounded by a moat and a wall constructed of mud and sticks. Guns were emplaced on top of the wall. Within were two strong houses, one of which contained the royal storeroom for the settlement's provisions.

The designations of Fort San Felipe I and Fort San Felipe II may be a little puzzling. A fort named San Felipe, built in 1566, was also known as Fort San Sebastian in some historical references. The powder magazine blew up in that fort, and it was rebuilt on slightly higher ground and continued to serve as the fort for Santa Elena, retaining the name of Fort San Felipe, logically leading to the designations. The Indians burned it down in 1570. When the Spanish returned shortly thereafter, they erected a new fort some 200 yards to the south and named it Fort San Marcos. The first Fort San Felipe, or Fort San Sebastian, has not been found, and there is reason to believe that it had been encroached upon by the river and now lies destroyed in the marsh.

Archaeological explorations, funded by grants, are continuing and the site has been declared off limits by the Marines. In addition, efforts are also continuing to locate the elusive Charlesfort, the oldest white habitation in what is now the United States.

FORT SAN MARCOS. FORT SAN FELIPE.

FORT SAN SEBASTIAN. FORT SAN FELIPE.

CAMP SAXTON. Named for Brigadier General Rufus Saxton, military governor of the Union's Department of the South and located near Beaufort, Camp Saxton was occupied by Union forces beginning in November 1861. There the 1st South Carolina Volunteers, first of the Federal negro regiments, did garrison duty under Colonel Thomas W. Higginson, former Unitarian minister, who commanded the regiment.

SCHENCKINGH'S FORT. Located on the south bank of the Santee River, 20 miles northwest of present Moncks Corner, Berkeley County, this fort was built during the Yamassee War in May 1715, on the cattle ranch owned by Benjamin Schenckingh. One month later, a Catawba Indian war party and allied tribesmen attacked the fort and its 30-man army garrison. The war party gained entrance by pretending to demand negotiations. They killed or captured all but a few of the defenders, and burned the fort. Today the site is covered by Lake Marion.

CAMP SEVIER. A temporary World War I training camp named in honor of Brigadier General John Sevier, U.S.A., who served with distinction as a Colonel of the North Carolina Militia at the Battle of King's Mountain, South Carolina, in 1780, and became Tennessee's first governor. Camp Sevier was located about five miles from Greenville. It was established on July 18, 1917, to serve as a training camp for the 30th (old 9th) Division of the National Guard, which occupied the post August 1917–May 1918. Camp Sevier was designated as a demobilization center on December 3, 1918, and ordered salvaged January 30, 1919. After the post was turned over to the Public Health Service on April 1, 1919, it was closed as an Army training facility.

FORT (BATTERY) SHAW. Constructed by Union forces in 1863, this battery was located on the southern edge of Morris Island in Charleston Harbor. Its armament is unknown.

FORT SHERMAN. The three-mile-long road, called Hilton Head Historic Parkway, leads from the island's main highway to an extensive group of fortifications constructed during the Civil War. The guns of a 73-ship Union armada on November 7, 1861, in the Battle of Port Royal silenced the Confederate forts on the island, and 13,000 Federal troops commanded by General T. W. Sherman staged one of the largest amphibious invasions attempted prior to World War II.

The name of Confederate Fort Walker was changed to Fort Welles, behind which a strong earthwork was constructed and named Fort Howell. Hilton Head was made the Headquarters of the Department of the South in April 1862. In September 1864 the two miles of earthworks on the island became known as Fort Sherman, an 800-acre military reservation and naval base. Structures included barracks, administrative buildings, warehouses, and a hospital. A town grew up in its near environs, and soon there were about 50,000 soldiers and civilians on the island. In April 1866 the Post of Hilton Head was established. It was abandoned on January 14, 1868.

BATTERY SIMKINS. A Confederate strongpoint on James Island in Charleston Harbor, Battery Simkins was located 1,100 yards in front of Fort Johnson. The battery was subjected to heavy bombardment on July 3 and 10, 1864, and February 11, 1865, from Union guns on Morris Island.

STAR FORT. FORT NINETY-SIX.

FORT SULLIVAN. FORT MOULTRIE.

FORT SUMTER. Old Fort Sumter, standing on a shoal at the entrance to Charleston Harbor, was partially restored in preparation for the Civil War Centennial. Casemates sealed for many years were reopened and other long-buried parts of the original fort uncovered. National Park Service archaeologists discovered a treasure of Civil War relics, including cannons sealed in casemates.

At 4:30 A.M., April 12, 1861, a mortar battery at Fort Johnson on the east end of James Island in the harbor fired a shell that burst directly over Fort Sumter. This was the signal for a general bombardment by other Confederate batteries in the harbor. For 34 hours, April 12 and 13, Fort Sumter was battered with shot and shell. Then the Federal commander, Major Robert Anderson, agreed to evacuate. On April 14, he and his small garrison left the fort with the full honors of war. On the following day, President Lincoln issued a call for 75,000 militia. The tragedy of the American Civil War had begun.

CHARLESTON HARBOR DEFENSES. (Courtesy of the National Park Service.)

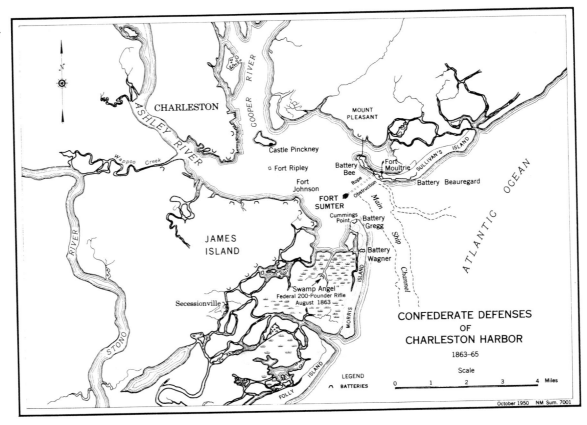

CONFEDERATE DEFENSES OF CHARLESTON HARBOR 1863–65

Two years later Fort Sumter, now a Confederate stronghold, became the scene of a stubborn defense. From April 1863 to February 1865, its garrison withstood a series of devastating bombardments and direct attacks by Union forces from land and sea. It has been estimated that between April 5, 1863, and September 4, 1864, some 3,500 tons of shells were hurled against its walls. Fort Sumter was evacuated only when Federal forces under General Sherman bypassed Charleston from the rear. At the end, buttressed with sand and bales of cotton as well as its own fallen brick and masonry, it was stronger than ever militarily. Only the least exposed wall remained standing, with the rest constituting jagged remnants amid piles of debris. No other fort in the United States has ever been so mercilessly battered, over so prolonged a period. The fort entered history as a symbol of resistance and courage for the entire South.

The war of 1812 had demonstrated the gross inadequacy of the coastal defenses of the United States. The crowning indignity had been the burning of Washington. One of the sites selected by the military Board of Engineers for a new fort was a shoal opposite Fort Moultrie. This was the genesis of Fort Sumter. With the guns of the projected fort crossing fire with those of Fort Moultrie, the commercial city of Charleston would be most effectively protected against attack. Plans for the new fort were drawn up in 1827 and adopted on December 5, 1828. Progress was slow, however, and as late as 1834, the fort was no more than a hollow pentagonal rock "mole," two feet above low water and open at one side to permit supply ships to pass to the interior. Meanwhile, it had been named Sumter in honor of Thomas Sumter, the "Carolina Gamecock" of the Revolution.

Fort Sumter in December 1860 was a five-sided brick masonry fort designed for three tiers of guns. Its 5-foot thick outer walls, towering nearly 50 feet above low water, enclosed a parade ground of roughly one acre. Along four walls extended two tiers of arched gunrooms. Officers' quarters lined the fifth side—the 316-foot gorge. Three-story brick barracks for the enlisted garrison paralleled the gunrooms on each flank. Owing to the sheer magnitude of the project and the lack of funds during 1858 and 1859, Fort Sumter was still unfinished when, late in December, gathering events prompted its occupation by artillery troops. Eight-foot-square openings yawned in place of gun embrasures on the second tier. Of the 135 guns planned for the gunrooms and the open terreplein above, only 15 had been mounted. Most of these were ap-

parently 32-pounders, none heavier. On December 20, 1860, South Carolina seceded from the Union. On the night of the 26th, fearing attack by Charleston's excited populace, Major Anderson removed his small garrison from Fort Moultrie out to Fort Sumter to be ultimately subjected to a two-day bombardment that resulted in his evacuation and occupation by Confederate forces.

In the 1870s, Fort Sumter was reconstructed. The new fort stood only half its original 50-foot height. The one remaining wall was lowered to fit the new configuration. During the Spanish-American War, a massive concrete gun emplacement called Battery Huger was constructed across the center of the fort. During World War II, its outmoded cannon were replaced with anti-aircraft guns. Modern offensive weapons obsoleted all of America's "impregnable" forts of yesteryear. In 1948 Fort Sumter was deservedly designated a National Monument.

SWAMP-ANGEL BATTERY. One of the most famous offensive guns employed during the Civil War was the so-called "Swamp-Angel," an eight-inch, 200-pounder Parrott rifle mounted by Union forces on August 17, 1863, behind a sandbag parapet on Morris Island in Charleston Harbor. In order to support the massive piece of armament, piles were driven into the marsh at a point

FORT SUMTER. Scale model. (Courtesy of the National Park Service.)

that commanded the city of Charleston. On the night of August 21, after a warning had been sent to the Confederate commander, General P. G. T. Beauregard, the gun fired its first projectile into the heart of the city. On August 23, during its 36th firing, the breech of the gun was blown out. Two weeks later it was replaced by two 10-inch mortars.

BATTERY TATUM. A Confederate battery built in mid-July 1863, it was located on the eastern side of James Island and intended to support Battery Reed.

THICKETTY FORT (*Fort Anderson*). A strongly fortified Revolutionary post occupied by Loyalist forces, originally built shortly after the beginning of the war as a defense against the Cherokee, Fort Anderson, or Thicketty Fort as it was more commonly known, was located 10 miles southeast of Cowpens, on the headwaters of the Pacolet River, Cherokee County. Prior to the Battle of King's Mountain, Colonel Isaac Shelby marched 600 men to Thicketty Fort on July 29, 1780, and on the next day, without firing a shot, forced the capitulation of the fort by his show of troop strength.

FORT TRENHOLM. A strong Confederate position on the Stono River in defense of Charleston, Fort Trenholm was named in honor of George Trenholm, secretary of the treasury of the C.S.A. The fort in 1863 mounted 14 varied pieces of ordnance, including Columbiads, howitzers, and field guns.

CAMP WADSWORTH. A World War I training camp established on July 18, 1917, and located about three miles west of Spartanburg, Camp Wadsworth was named in honor of Brigadier General James S. Wadsworth, who was killed on May 6, 1864, while commanding a corps during the Wilderness Campaign in Virginia. Established to serve as the training camp for the 27th Division of the National Guard, which occupied the post September 1917–May 1918, Camp Wadsworth then became a training center for other units, May 1918–January 1919. It was designated a demobilization center on December 3, 1918, ordered salvaged February 4, 1919, and officially closed March 25, 1919, although the post's headquarters was maintained until September 1919.

FORT (BATTERY) WAGNER (*Neck Battery*). A strong Confederate defense located on Morris Island, Neck Battery—later known as Fort or Battery Wagner—played an important role in the defense of Charleston. On April 7, 1863, it was engaged in an exchange of bombardments with Union naval forces. On July 9, 1863, its garrison of 700 Confederate troops was directly involved in opposing the landing of 2,000 Union soldiers. Fort Wagner was finally evacuated in the early morning of September 7, 1863, after 58 days and nights under difficult conditions, subjected to heavy artillery fire. Defiant until the very end, its garrison—usually consisting of less than 1,000 men—held off a force of 11,000 Federal troops armed with some of the heaviest artillery then in existence and assisted by a Union armada of heavily gunned and armored vessels.

FORT WALKER. FORT WELLES.

FORT WATSON. One of the line of British-built Revolutionary War defenses that stretched from Charleston to Fort Ninety-Six, Fort Watson was located on Wright's Bluff, atop a 50-foot-high Indian mound, where the Congaree and Wateree rivers join to form today's impounded waters of Lake Marion, near Summerville, Clarendon County. It was named for Colonel John Watson, who erected the triple-abatised fort. On April 15, 1781, General Francis Marion and Colonel Henry "Light-Horse Harry" Lee surrounded the fort with troops, besieging it until April 23, while Major Hezekiah Maham built an ingenious log tower surmounted by a platform. The fort's defenders, 80 British soldiers and 40 Tories, on the morning of the 23rd found themselves under direct fire from a detachment of American riflemen perched atop the tower. Before day's end, the fort's commander surrendered his fort. Fort Watson was the first post in South Carolina to be taken from the British.

FORT WELLES (*Fort Walker*). Located on Hilton Head Island on strategic Port Royal Sound, Confederate Fort Walker stood opposite Fort Beauregard at Bay Point on Phillip's Island. During the November 7, 1861, operations of the Union fleet of 50 ships under Commodore Samuel F. Du Pont, armed with 155 guns, Fort Beauregard was quickly put out of action. Fort Walker then was subjected to consistently heavy bombardment, finally forcing it to capitulate after about 13,000 Federal troops were landed to besiege the fort on all sides. The Confederate defense was renamed Fort Welles in honor of Secretary of the Navy Gideon Welles. It was redesigned to resist Confederate attack from land as well as sea, with an elaborate system of earthworks nearly two miles long. (See also: FORT SHERMAN.)

BATTERY WILKES. Built by Confederate forces in 1862, this battery was located in St. Andrews Parish just above the Stono River, on the Savannah and Charleston Railroad.

FORT WILLIAMSON. FORT HOLMES.

FORT WILLIAMSON. FORT NINETY-SIX.

WILLTOWN FORT. A defense erected during the Yamassee War (1715–16) to protect the village then called Willtown (New London), it was located on the east bank of the Edisto River about 28 miles southwest of Charles Towne (modern Charleston). Militia troops garrisoned the fort from April to August 1715. Attacked by an Apalachee war party and allied tribesmen in July 1715, the Indians were decisively repulsed by the militiamen. During August 1715–March 1716, the fort was used as a base for South Carolina's patrol boats.

FORT WINYAH. The first of two fortifications of this name was a defense erected in 1715 during the Yamassee War and garrisoned by a detach-

ment of militia troops. It was probably located on the south side of the Black River, northwest of the present city of Georgetown. The second was a War of 1812 fort situated on Blyth's Point, Georgetown Harbor, which was evacuated in 1814. A portion of the reservation was turned over to the Treasury Department in 1857 to be used as a site for a lighthouse.

FORT WELLES. Photograph taken in 1862. (Courtesy of the Massachusetts Commandery Military Order of the Loyal Legion and the U.S. Army Military History Institute.)

South Dakota

FORT AUX CEDRAS (*Loisel's Post; Cedar Fort*). This fur post located on Cedar (American) Island in the Missouri River, about one mile south of present Chamberlain, Brulé County, was originally established by Registre Loisel in 1809. The post was burned by Indians in 1822, but was rebuilt and operated later that year by the Missouri Fur Company. (See: FORT RECOVERY.) The island now lies beneath the impounded waters of the Fort Randall Reservoir.

FORT BARTLETT. FORT SULLY.

FORT BENNETT (*Post at Cheyenne Agency*). Located on the right bank of the Missouri River, below the mouth of the Cheyenne River, on the Cheyenne River Indian Reservation in Stanley County, it was established on May 17, 1870, as Post at Cheyenne Agency by Captain Edward P. Pearson, 17th Infantry, for the purpose of protecting the agency's Indians. On December 30, 1878, the post was officially designated Fort Bennett in honor of Captain Andrew S. Bennett, 5th Infantry, who was killed on September 4, 1878, during a fight with Bannock Indians at Clark's Fort in Montana. Ordinarily a one-company post, partially palisaded with its open side facing the river, it was occupied for a time by nine companies of troops following the Custer Massacre in 1876. Fort Bennett was abandoned on November 18, 1891. Part of the site has been inundated by the Oahe Reservoir.

FORT BOUIS. FORT DEFIANCE.

FORT BRASSEAUX. FORT RECOVERY.

BROWN'S POST. RONDELL'S POST.

BROWN'S POST. SIECHE HOLLOW POST.

BRULÉ POST. WHITE RIVER POST.

BUFFALO LAKE POST. Established in 1843 or 1844, this fur-trading post was located on the east side of Buffalo Lake in Marshall County and operated by Joseph R. Brown. In 1846 Brown sold the post to H. H. Sibley for the American Fur Company. It is not known when the post was discontinued.

CAMPBELL'S POST. A palisaded trading post established by Colin Campbell for the Hudson's Bay Company in 1822, it was located seven miles southwest of present Frederick, Brown County. It was apparently discontinued in 1828.

CEDAR FORT. Fort Aux Cedras.

CEDAR FORT. Fort Recovery.

CHANOPA POST (*Two Woods Lake Post*). Located on the east side of Two Woods Lake in the northwest corner of present Deuel County, this trading post may have been in existence before 1835 when Joseph La Framboise operated it. After he left, François La Bathe reportedly ran it for Pratte, Chouteau & Company for many years. It is not known when Chanopa Post was discontinued.

CHERRY CREEK POST. A satellite of the American Fur Company's Fort Tecumseh, this trading post, established in 1829, was located about five miles up the stream from the present town of Cherry Creek in Ziebach County. A local tradition maintains the post was burned about the year 1866 by Indians who were rivals for its trade.

CAMP CHEYENNE (*Camp of Observation*). An Army field post established as Camp of Observation in the summer of 1890 near the Forks of the Cheyenne River, east of present Elm Springs, Meade County, it was soon designated Camp Cheyenne, designed as a base of operations during the period of the feverish Sioux Ghost Dance or Messiah War. Garrisoned by five companies of troops, three cavalry and two infantry, and a detachment of Indian scouts armed with two Hotchkiss guns, the post was directly involved in the tragic Wounded Knee Massacre on December 29, 1890. Camp Cheyenne was abandoned early in 1891 after a semblance of peace was restored on the Sioux reservations.

POST AT CHEYENNE AGENCY. Fort Bennett.

CHEYENNE FORKS POST. First mention of this trading post appeared in 1828. Its exact site is undetermined, but it was located at or near the Forks of the Cheyenne River, east of present Elm Springs, in Meade County. The post was active until at least 1843.

FORT CHOUTEAU. Fort Pierre No. 1.

CAMP COLLIER (*Camp at the Mouth of Red Canyon*). This temporary palisaded, log-built 125-foot-square post, with blockhouses of bastions in diagonal corners, enclosing tents for the troops, was established in June 1876 as Camp at the Mouth of Red Canyon to safeguard the route of the Cheyenne–Black Hills stage line through Red Canyon. Located on a site, now private property, about five miles north of Edgemont, Fall River county, Camp Collier was abandoned on June 2, 1877. All of its surplus military stores were removed to Camp Hat Creek to the southwest in Wyoming.

CAMP CROOK. During the Army's efforts to eject mining prospectors from the Black Hills region, General George Crook established his cavalry headquarters at this post in 1876, located in Pennington County, in the area of the Pactola Reservoir. The site of the camp now lies beneath the impounded waters of the reservoir.

POST AT CROW CREEK AGENCY. Fort Thompson.

FORT DAKOTA. Located on the left bank of the Big Sioux River, at the present city of Sioux Falls, Minnehaha County, Fort Dakota was established on May 1, 1865, by Captain Daniel F. Eicher, 6th Iowa Cavalry, in compliance with an order of Brigadier General Alfred Sully. Garrisoned first by volunteer soldiers until June 8, 1866, when they were replaced by Army regulars, the post was one of several established to guard the frontier between the white settlements and the Sioux country. Fort Dakota was abandoned on June 18, 1869, a week after the reservation was officially transferred to the Interior Department. The site of the post is on Phillips Avenue, between 7th and 8th streets, in Sioux City.

FORT DEFIANCE (*Fort Bouis*). Located on the west bank of the Missouri River, near the mouth of Medicine Creek, in present Lyman County, Fort Defiance was established in 1845 by ex-employees, one of them named Bouis, of the American Fur Company in competition with their former employer. The date when the post was discontinued or abandoned depends on the historical authority cited, as early as 1846 and as late as 1851. According to one citation, Fort Defiance was still active during the winter of 1850–51, when a particularly virulent smallpox epidemic decimated Sioux populations in nearby villages and camps.

FORT DES ROCHE. Fort James.

CAMP DEWEY. This temporary Spanish-American War encampment was set up at Sioux Falls for the purpose of assembling and training militia units before being assigned to war areas.

DICKSON'S POST. FORT VERMILLION NO. 1.

DISAUL TRADING POST. This post was established in 1815 at the mouth of Emanuel Creek in present Bon Homme County by Emanuel Disaul, a French-Canadian trader. For many years, he was the only white inhabitant in the county.

FORT DOLE. In 1862, when the Upper Sioux were preparing to go on the warpath and threatening the Yankton Sioux for refusing to join them, Yankton Indian agent, Dr. Walter Burleigh, built an octagonal, loopholed two-storied blockhouse of 22-inch-thick timbers, 26 feet in diameter, and armed it with one six-pounder Dahlgren gun and two three-pounders. He named the defense in honor of the then Commissioner of Indian Affairs, William P. Dole. The blockhouse stood at present Greenwood, near the Fort Randall Dam, in Charles Mix County.

CAMP EDWARDS (*Camp near Preston Lake; Cantonment Oakwood*). Consisting of 5-foot-high earthen breastworks about 100 feet square and enclosing a log structure, this post was originally known as Camp near Lake Preston, or Cantonment Oakwood, for the Oakwood lakes in the area, near the present town of Lake Preston in Kingsbury County. Some little time after it was first occupied, it was apparently renamed Camp Edwards, as borne out in National Archives records. It was reportedly reoccupied after the Sioux Outbreak in 1862, and again during 1864–65 during the final months of the Civil War by Minnesota Volunteers.

FRENCH POST. FORT LOOKOUT NO. 2.

FROST-TODD TRADING POST. The partnership of D. M. Frost and Captain John B. S. Todd (Frost, Todd & Company), the latter a cousin of Mary Todd Lincoln and formerly of the 6th Infantry, established a profitable trading post on the Missouri River near the Yankton Sioux Indian Reservation. The post was active until 1861.

FORT GALPIN. In 1857 Charles Galpin replaced his temporary trading camp near Chantier Creek, 14 miles northwest of Pierre, with a 125-foot-square, partially stockaded post on the west bank of the Missouri River, about three miles above Fort Pierre. Within two years, however, Galpin closed his namesake post and a half-mile below it erected a new one, Fort Pierre II, perhaps in part with building materials taken from the old post.

FORT GEORGE. Established in August 1842 by Fox, Livingston & Company on the right bank of the Missouri River, 20 miles below Fort Pierre, in Stanley County, Fort George was a stockade approximately 155 by 165 feet, with projecting blockhouses at two opposing corners. Archaeological excavations by the Smithsonian Institution in recent years indicate that the configuration of the post was unusual since the buildings, several equipped with adobe brick fireplaces, were separated from the walls by a wide alley or yard rather than joined to the walls. The combination of bitter competition with the American Fur Company and liquor finished Fort George when it was burned in 1845 by Indians hired by rival traders.

GORDON STOCKADE. Located on French Creek in the Black Hills, about three miles east of Custer, the Gordon Stockade was built in December 1874 by the first group of prospectors, led by John Gordon, in search of the gold first discovered on August 2, 1874, by two civilians accompanying George Custer's cavalry expedition. In contravention of military prohibitions, in order to protect themselves from the hostile Sioux, 28 prospectors built an 80-foot-square, 10-foot-high stockade enclosing several cabins. Very little gold, however, was found, and in April 1875 the stockade was abandoned when cavalry troops arrived to oust the trespassers. A re-creation of the stockade has been erected on the site.

GRAND RIVER AGENCY POST. A two-company post established in May 1870 at the Grand River Agency and located on the west bank of the Missouri River, at the confluence of the Grand River, five miles north of Mobridge, Walworth County, it enclosed some 20 log buildings with plank-and-mud roofs. Periodic flooding of the Missouri finally compelled the transfer of the agency and garrison to Fort Yates. The site, abandoned on June 6, 1875, now lies beneath the impounded waters of the Oahe Dam.

FORT HALE (*Post at Lower Brulé Agency; Fort Lower Brulé*). Located originally on the right bank of the Missouri River near the present town of Fort Lookout on the Lower Brulé Indian Agency, and established as Post at Lower Brulé Agency by Captain George W. Hill, 22nd Infantry, on June 8, 1870, the post was moved on July 21, 1870, some 15 miles upstream (north) to a point opposite the mouth of Crow Creek, near present Chamberlain, Brulé County. On December 30, 1878, the post was officially designated Fort Hale in honor of Captain Owen Hale, 7th Cavalry, killed on September 30, 1877. The post was sometimes called Fort Lower Brulé. Fort Hale was abandoned on May 20, 1884, and its buildings were turned over to the Indian agent for reservation use on July 7, 1884. The site of the post is now submerged in the waters of the Big Bend Dam.

FORT JAMES (*Fort La Roche; Fort Des Roche*). Situated on the right side of the James River at its junction with Firesteel Creek, this post was first established in September 1865 as Fort La Roche or Des Roche by Captain Benjamin King, 6th Iowa Cavalry, in compliance with an order of Brigadier General Alfred Sully. The post was a quadrangle made of stone and hewn logs that was intended to garrison troops for stagecoach protection and serve as a guard along the frontier between the white settlements and the country occupied by the Sioux. Fort James was abandoned on October 6, 1866, and its salvageable materials were used by the area's settlers for private construction.

FORT KIOWA (*Fort Lookout No. 1*). The first of the four posts known as Fort Lookout was designated as Fort Kiowa after the Smithsonian Institution in 1950 completed researches and exploratory excavations at the site on the west side of the Missouri River, 12 miles above the present town of Chamberlain, Brulé County. A fur-trading post established in 1822 by the American Fur Company, it was a 140-foot-square palisaded complex of log buildings and a storehouse in the form of a right angle, with a blockhouse at its south corner and a wooden tower on the opposite corner. The post was abandoned in 1825. Its site most probably has been eroded by the Missouri River.

LA BARGE'S POST. FORT LOOKOUT NO. 2.

FORT LA FRAMBOISE NO. 1 (*Fort Teton No. 1*). In the fall of 1817, French trader Joseph La Framboise and a group of trappers traveled overland from Prairie du Chien in Wisconsin to the mouth of the Bad River, where they built a fortified trading post on the west side of the Missouri River, just below the present city of Fort Pierre in Stanley County, across the river from the capital of Pierre. The fort was also known as Fort Teton because the Bad River was then alternately called the Teton River. The post was abandoned in 1820. In 1822 the Columbia Fur Company rebuilt the post and renamed it Fort Tecumseh.

FORT LA FRAMBOISE NO. 2. A short-lived trading post established in 1862 by La Barge, Harkness & Company in competition with Fort Pierre, and located on the Missouri River three miles above its opposition, Fort La Framboise was abandoned within a year. Its approximate site lies on the western side of today's Oahe Dam.

FORT LA ROCHE. FORT JAMES.

LOISEL'S POST. FORT AUX CEDRAS.

FORT LOOKOUT NO. 1. FORT KIOWA.

FORT LOOKOUT NO. 2 (*French Post; La Barge's Post*). Located about 300 yards from the right bank of the Missouri River, about 10 miles above present Chamberlain, Brulé County, this trading post operated on the same site under three names at different periods of time during the second quarter of the nineteenth century. First established in 1831 and historically known as Fort Lookout No. 2, it was called French Post until about 1840. Between then and 1851, it was known as La Barge's Post, named for the famous La Barge family of river pilots and traders of St. Louis, associated with the La Barge, Harkness & Company enterprise. During 1950 and 1951, the Smithsonian Institution conducted archaeological researches and discovered the site of a rectangular trading post dating from its earliest period of occupation. It appeared to have become an utter ruin first, then it burned. Subsequently, a second post was constructed on the same site, only to suffer a similar fate. Both editions of the post appeared to consist of a single building, measuring about 70 by 20 feet, without any evidence of a palisade having been built around it.

FORT LOOKOUT NO. 3. It has not been determined when this trading post was established, although it is definitely known to have been in existence in 1833. Researches and archaeological explorations by the Smithsonian Institution in the early 1950s, however, led to conclusions that it was the same as Fort Kiowa (Fort Lookout No. 1). Its identity will never be fully established since the site now lies beneath the Missouri River to the east of Fort Hale's location near the town of Chamberlain.

FORT LOOKOUT NO. 4. Located on the right bank of the Missouri River, about 10 miles above present Chamberlain, Brulé County, very near the site of the former trading post known as Fort

Lookout No. 2, this Fort Lookout was a military post established on July 31, 1856, by Captain Nathaniel Lyon, 2nd Infantry, in accordance with orders of Colonel William S. Harney, 2nd Dragoons, who so named the post because of its proximity to the former trading post. Intended to oversee the activities of the Indians in the area, the post was designed to be a rather elaborate installation, with a quarter-of-a-mile-long parade ground, with barracks on either side, and three officers' quarters at one end, and the guardhouse and headquarters building at the other end. Despite the efforts put into its construction, the fort was abandoned on June 17, 1857. Most of the post was dismantled and its salvageable materials shipped downriver to Fort Randall.

FORT LOWER BRULÉ. FORT HALE.

POST AT LOWER BRULÉ AGENCY. FORT HALE.

MCCLELLAN'S TRADING POST. Reportedly the second trading post on the Upper Missouri, established by Robert McClellan in 1805, it was located a short distance below the mouth of the James River to the east of present Yankton. The post was still in operation when the Lewis and Clark Expedition came downriver in 1806. McClellan's Post was abandoned later the same year.

MCLEOD'S POST. This was an American Fur Company trading post established in 1843 and located just above the site of Mooers' Post (1818) at Hartford Beach on Big Stone Lake in present Roberts County. Martin McLeod was its first trader. Antoine Frenier was the last known trader there in 1857 when the post was apparently abandoned.

FORT MANUEL. Manuel Lisa was one of the more prominent fur traders on the Upper Missouri and the guiding spirit in the organization of the profitable Missouri Fur Company. His name was attached to such widely separated trading posts as Fort Lisa in Nebraska, Lisa's Fort in North Dakota, and Fort Manuel in Montana. On August 8, 1812, he and associates established Fort Manuel in Sioux country on the west bank of the Missouri River, eight miles below the North Dakota line, about 30 miles north of Mobridge and east of Kenel in present Corson County. It was abandoned by the traders on March 5, 1813, after 15 of them were killed by a large party of British-inspired Sioux.

Two still-controversial mysteries surround the fort. It is believed by a number of historians that, despite the short life of the post, Lisa's dealings with the Sioux somehow helped to weaken their alliance with the British and contributed to the final outcome of the War of 1812 and the continued American control of the area. The second mystery concerns Sacajawea ("Bird Woman"), the young Indian girl who guided the Lewis and Clark Expedition. Dakota and Wyoming historians still disagree on whether she died of a "putrid fever" and was buried here on December 20, 1812, or at Fort Washakie, Wyoming, in 1884. In any case, Fort Manuel was the "home" of Charbonneau, her husband, during its brief existence.

FORT MEADE (*Camp Sturgis; Camp Ruhlen*). Located in the Black Hills on the east side of Bear Butte Creek, 14 miles northeast of Deadwood and two miles from present Sturgis in Meade County, Fort Meade was established on August 28, 1878, by Major Henry M. Lazelle, 1st Infantry, on a site selected by Lieutenant General Phil Sheridan. Temporary Camp Sturgis, named for a lieutenant killed during the Custer Massacre, was established near the site to accommodate the troopers constructing the post. Originally called Camp Ruhlen, for Lieutenant George Ruhlen, quartermaster in charge of its construction, the post was intended to control the area's Sioux and to protect the Black Hills mining operations. On December 30, 1878, the post was officially designated Fort Meade in honor of Major General George Gordon Meade of Civil War fame. In 1944 the military reservation and its buildings, many of them original, were transferred to the Veterans Administration for use as a hospital.

MOOERS' POST. A fur-trading post established in 1818 or 1819 and operated by Hazen Mooers, it was located on the west side of Big Stone Lake, on a site now incorporated within the Hartford Beach State Park in Roberts County. Varying dates, from 1824 to 1830, have been given for its discontinuance.

MOREAU-ROBAR POST. This short-lived trading post was established in 1865 by Moses Moreau and Solomon Robar at Linden Beach, two miles south of the site of the old Mooers' Post on Big Stone Lake in Roberts County.

CAMP AT THE MOUTH OF RED CANYON. CAMP COLLIER.

FORT PIERRE NO. 1. The fort as it looked in 1857. (Painting by A. Sully. Courtesy of the South Dakota State Historical Society.)

CANTONMENT OAKWOOD. CAMP EDWARDS.

OAKWOOD POST. RONDELL'S POST.

CAMP OF OBSERVATION. CAMP CHEYENNE.

OGLALA POST. RAPID CREEK POST.

PAWNEE HOUSE. TRUDEAU'S HOUSE.

FORT PIERRE NO. 1 (*Fort Chouteau*). Located on the west side of the Missouri River, about three miles above the mouth of the Bad (Teton) River, and about three miles northwest of the capital city of Pierre across the river, Fort Pierre was an important trading post established in 1831 by Bernard Pratte & Company to replace Fort Tecumseh. First named in honor of Pierre Chouteau, the post was purchased for $45,000 by the government for military purposes on April 14, 1855, and first garrisoned by troops on June 7. Two years later, however, because of the lack of adequate forage and timber in the area, the fort was abandoned on May 16, 1857. Part of the post's salvageable building materials were used in the construction of Fort Randall (1856) to the south, just above the Nebraska line.

FORT PIERRE NO. 2. In 1859, when Charles Galpin of the American Fur Company decided that the location of his trading post (Fort Galpin), 14 miles northwest of Pierre, proved unsatisfactory, he and his associate traders moved a half-mile below it and established (New) Fort Pierre. About 1862 they moved to Farm Island, four miles east of Pierre, to be under the protection of Old Fort Sully. The post was reportedly occupied by a company of soldiers during the winter of 1862–63.

PILCHER'S POST. FORT RECOVERY.

CAMP NEAR PRESTON LAKE. CAMP EDWARDS.

FORT PRIMEAU. A temporary trading post established in the late 1850s or early 1860s by La Barge, Harkness & Company and named for Charles Primeau, an early trader on the Upper Missouri and one of the company's partners, it was located on an elevation overlooking the Missouri River in present Stanley County. The site now lies beneath the waters of the river, about one mile north of the Oahe Dam.

FORT RANDALL. Located on the south side of the Missouri River, a quarter of a mile from the bank of the river and just north of the Nebraska line, across the present Fort Randall Dam from Pickstown in Gregory County, Fort Randall was established by Captain Nelson H. Davis, 2nd Infantry, on August 4, 1856, to replace Fort Pierre and keep the peace among the area's tribes. During 1870–72, the post was rebuilt about a quarter of a mile farther from the river. The fort was apparently named for Lieutenant Colonel Daniel D. Randall, deputy paymaster general of the Army. On July 22, 1884, a good part of the military reservation was abandoned, a number of its buildings auctioned off, and its garrison reduced. Fort Randall was officially abandoned on December 7, 1892. The remains of the reservation's last structure, a yellow stone chapel originally built by infantry troops, were restored in 1950.

CAMP RAPID. A National Guard encampment established about 1925 by Brigadier General William A. Hazle, Camp Rapid was located on present U.S. 14, then about one mile north of Rapid City. The site was leased by the government during World War II for use as a mobilization and training center for National Guard troops and other recruits. In July 1942 the post was taken over by the Air Corps and maintained until November 1943, when the post was returned to the National Guard, together with all its installations. Camp Rapid's site is now located at 2328 West Main Street in Rapid City.

RAPID CITY BLOCKHOUSE. Despite U.S. Army prohibition against white settlement in the Black Hills, an area reserved by government order for the Sioux, about 200 settlers penetrated military lines and founded Rapid City. In 1876, after most of them deserted the frontier town because of ambushes by the Sioux, the remaining settlers erected a two-story, 30-foot-square blockhouse where they were besieged by the Indians for most of the month of September. Soon afterward, the government relented and permitted settlement of the region. The site of the blockhouse is located at the present intersection of Rapid and 5th streets in Rapid City.

RAPID CREEK POST (*Oglala Post*). An American Fur Company satellite fur-trading post, also known as Oglala Post, was established in 1830, with Thomas L. Sarpy as its operating trader, on the Cheyenne River at the mouth of Rapid Creek in present Pennington County. In February 1832 Sarpy was killed when a candle ignited a barrel of gunpowder and destroyed part of the post in the explosion. It is not known whether it was rebuilt, but it remained in operation until 1834, when the area's Indians moved their villages and camps to the environs of Fort Laramie. The site of Rapid Creek Post was reportedly occupied as a headquarters encampment by the 6th Cavalry in 1890 during the Sioux Ghost Dance uprising.

FORT RECOVERY (*Fort Brasseaux; Pilcher's Post*). The multiplicity of names and dates for this trading post and its predecessor, Fort Aux Cedras (Cedar Fort), are confusing and speculative. Most historical authorities are certain that Fort Recovery was built on the site of the former post established in 1809 on Cedar (American) Island (formerly in Lyman County but incorporated within Brulé County in 1889), almost opposite the city of Chamberlain, in the Missouri River. The former post was burned by Indians in 1822 and replaced with Fort Recovery in the same year by the Missouri Fur Company. It was also known as Pilcher's Post for Joshua Pilcher, who operated Fort Recovery for the company, and as Fort Brasseaux for Antoine Brasseaux of St. Louis, a company employee and possible operating trader at the post after Pilcher left. Fort Recovery

was abandoned in 1830. American Island was engulfed by the impounded waters of the Fort Randall Dam project. (See also: FORT AUX CEDRAS.)

RONDELL'S POST (*Brown's Post; Oakwood Post*). Established by Major James R. Brown in 1835 and located on the James River, 25 miles northeast of Aberdeen, Brown County, the trading post was named Oakwood because of a grove of large oak trees in its near environs. The post was discontinued in 1851. Its site, commemorated by a D.A.R. marker, lies within Rondell Park, named for François Rondell, a later operator of the post.

ROSEBUD AGENCY POST. In 1878, when the Red Cloud Agency was moved and became Pine Ridge, Spotted Tail Agency was also moved and renamed Rosebud. The new location of this Brulé Sioux Agency was on the South Fork of the White River, east of Pine Ridge Agency, at the present town of Rosebud in Todd County. Sixteen companies of troops were stationed at this post to both control and protect the Brulé Sioux. Chief Spotted Tail was killed here by another Indian in 1881. His grave, memorialized by a white shaft, is located within the reservation's cemetery. The post was discontinued in 1891 after peace was restored on the Sioux reservations after the Messiah Craze.

CAMP RUHLEN. FORT MEADE.

SIECHE HOLLOW POST (*Brown's Post*). In 1844, Joseph R. Brown, long affiliated with the American Fur Company, had a trading post, also known as Sieche (Indian, "bad") Hollow Post, on the headwaters of the Minnesota River in Roberts County.

FORT SISSETON (*Fort Wadsworth*). Located on the elevated tableland long known as Coteau des Prairies, 16 miles southwest of Lake City, Marshall County, and named for the Sisseton band of the Sioux, Fort Sisseton was established by Major John Clowney, 30th Wisconsin Infantry, on August 1, 1864, after the bloody Sioux Uprising of 1862, to control the activities of Indian hostiles along the northern frontier and to safeguard the travel route westward to the recently discovered gold mines in Idaho and Montana. Originally named Fort Wadsworth in honor of Brigadier General James S. Wadsworth, mortally wounded on May 8, 1864, in the Battle of the Wilderness, Virginia, the post was officially redesignated Fort Sisseton on August 29, 1876, because there was already an Army post named Fort Wadsworth on Staten Island, New York. Fort Sisseton was abandoned on June 9, 1889, after the reservation was transferred to the Interior Department for disposition on April 22, 1889. During the 1930s, restoration of the fort was initiated by the Works Progress Administration under the supervision of the National Park Service. The South Dakota Parks Department now maintains the reservation.

CAMP STURGIS. FORT MEADE.

FORT SULLY (*Fort Bartlett*). Originally located on the east side of the Missouri River, just north of Farm Island, about four miles below Pierre, it was established on September 14, 1863, by Brigadier General Alfred Sully during his campaign against the hostile Sioux. The post was first known as Fort Bartlett for Lieutenant Colonel E. M. Bartlett, 30th Wisconsin Infantry, its first commander. In 1864, at Bartlett's instigation, the post was officially designated Fort Sully. It was abandoned on July 25, 1866, because its site was considered unhealthful, and relocated about 25 miles above Pierre, near Oahe Lake in present Sully County. On October 30, 1894, its garrison was withdrawn except for a small detachment, which remained until November 30 to terminate the affairs of the post, shortly after the military reservation was officially transferred to the Interior Department for disposition.

TABEAU'S POST. An independent fur-trading post established and operated 1795–1804 by Pierre Antoine Tabeau, it was located on the east bank of the Missouri River, near an Arikara Indian village. Tabeau was paid a visit by Lewis and Clark in 1804 while they were en route westward. The site of the post, about 10 miles north of Mobridge, Campbell County, was periodically inundated and gradually eroded by the river.

FORT TECUMSEH. Established in 1822 on the west bank of the Missouri River north of Fort Pierre and named for the famous Shawnee chief killed in the War of 1812, it was the leading and most profitable post operated by the Columbia Fur Company. Fort Tecumseh was sold to the American Fur Company in 1827 and discontinued in 1832 when Fort Pierre took over its operations and moved its salvageable buildings.

FORT TETON NO. 1. FORT LA FRAMBOISE NO. 1.

FORT TETON NO. 2 (*Teton Post*). Established in 1828 by P. D. Papin & Company, near the mouth of the Bad (Teton) River, south of Fort Pierre, this trading post was taken over in 1830 by the American Fur Company, which removed its property to Fort Tecumseh.

TETON POST. FORT TETON NO. 2.

FORT THOMPSON (*Post at Crow Creek Agency*). Located on the east side of the Missouri River at the mouth of Soldier Creek, on land occupied by the Crow Creek Indian Reservation, about 20 miles above today's city of Chamberlain and 2 miles south of the present town of Fort Thompson, Buffalo County, Fort Thompson was established by Captain Nelson Minor of the Dakota Cavalry in September 1864 and named for Colonel Clark W. Thompson, superintendent of Indian Affairs at St. Paul, Minnesota. Originally a complex of some two dozen buildings surrounded by a 300-by-400-foot stockade, garrisoned by two companies of Iowa Volunteers, it had been enlarged to 450 by 650 feet by the time it was dismantled in 1878.

The post, serving as agency headquarters for the reservation, was also known as the Post at Crow Creek Agency. It was reportedly abandoned on June 9, 1867, as an independent post and the garrison, except for a detachment of troops, transferred to Fort Sully. It was turned over to the Crow Creek Agency in 1871 for reservation use. In 1880 the government established an industrial boarding school here and operated it until 1920 when it was closed and Indian education transferred to a newly organized school district.

TRUDEAU'S HOUSE. (*Pawnee House*). Reputedly the first dwelling built by a white man in what is now South Dakota, this log-built residence was erected by Jean Baptiste Trudeau, a schoolteacher, in 1794 and operated as a trading post until 1797. It was generally known as Trudeau's House, but sometimes called Pawnee House because it was the headquarters of the region's fur trade with the Pawnee Indians. The post was located on the north side of the Missouri River, probably about 10 miles above Greenwood in Charles Mix County.

TWO WOODS LAKE POST. CHANOPA POST.

FORT VERMILLION NO. 1 (*Dickson's Post*). Originally a Columbia Fur Company trading post established by half-breed William Dickson (Dixon) in 1822 and located on the north side of the Missouri River on Audubon Point, about halfway between the James and Vermillion rivers, about six miles below Gayville. The post was taken over by the American Fur Company in 1835 and operated until 1850.

FORT VERMILLION NO. 2. The first American Fur Company trading post on the Upper Missouri, Fort Vermillion was established in 1833 on the north bank of the Missouri River, in the near environs of the present town of Burbank, between Elk Point and Vermillion, in Clay County. It was abandoned sometime in 1851.

FORT WADSWORTH. FORT SISSETON.

WHETSTONE AGENCY POST. Located on the right bank of the Missouri River, about 30 miles above Fort Randall, on the Whetstone Indian Reservation (now incorporated within the Rosebud Indian Reservation), and established on May 10, 1870, the post was a cottonwood-built stockade enclosing buildings against its inside walls with blockhouses at two diagonal angles. Fort Randall troops, commanded by Captain DeWitt C. Poole, 25th Infantry, who also served as the Indian agent, garrisoned the post. After it was abandoned on April 30, 1872, the post was converted into a supply depot for other Indian reservation agencies. Frequently flooded by the river, the site was gradually eroded away and now lies underwater, about 18 miles northwest of the Fort Randall Dam.

WHITE RIVER POST (*Brulé Post*). This trading post was a satellite of the American Fur Company's Fort Tecumseh. Established in 1830 and located on the Missouri River at the mouth of the White River in present Mellette County, it was sometimes referred to as Brulé Post. No archival information has been found to indicate when the post was discontinued.

FORT YANKTON. During the bloody Sioux Uprising of 1862 that ravaged Minnesota, a 45-foot-square stockade was erected by Yankton's citizens to serve as a refuge and defense for themselves and the residents of Sioux Falls, a town practically depopulated by the threat of Indian attack. The center of the stockade site is located at present Broadway and 3rd Street in Yankton.

FORT ADAIR. Built in 1788 near Knoxville by John Adair, this blockhouse fort was used as a depot of supplies for the Cumberland Guard, which furnished armed protection for parties of emigrants to the Cumberland Settlements (Nashborough), now modern Nashville. John Adair financed the expedition led by Isaac Shelby and John Sevier that defeated the British in the Battle of King's Mountain, South Carolina, October 7, 1780.

FORT ADAMS. FORT PICKERING.

FORT AMMEN. A strategic Union fortification erected on the Tennessee (Holston) River for the defense of Loudon, and named in honor of Brigadier General Jacob Ammen, U.S. Volunteers, Fort Ammen was located 28 miles southwest of Knoxville.

CAMP ANDREW JACKSON. A World War I troop mobilization and training encampment established in 1917, it was located in Belle Meade, or Centennial Park, in or near Nashville.

CAMP ANDY JOHNSON. FORT JOHNSON.

CAMP ARMISTEAD. Located on the west bank of the Tellico River, about 50 miles south of Knoxville, in what is now Monroe County, and named in honor of Colonel Walker K. Armistead, 3rd Artillery, Camp Armistead was established on June 30, 1832, by elements of companies A and B, 2nd Artillery, under the command of Lieutenant F. S. Belton. The post was abandoned on March 3, 1835.

FORT ASSUMPTION. The first fort known to have been erected on the site of modern Memphis (Fourth Chickasaw Bluff), Fort Assumption was built on August 15, 1739 (Assumption Day on the church calendar) by 4,000 French and Choctaw allies under Jean Baptiste le Moyné, sieur de Bienville, governor of Louisiana, during his campaigns against the English-allied Chickasaw (1735–40). The French abandoned and destroyed it in 1740 after peace was made. The site was not refortified until the Spanish under Manuel Gayoso de Lemos crossed the Mississippi and, in defiance of the authority of the United States, constructed Fort San Fernando de Barrancas, completed in the spring of 1795. After Pinckney's Treaty was signed, the Spaniards surrendered their outpost, replaced by Fort Adams built by American forces under Zebulon Pike. (See: FORT PICKERING.)

Tennessee

CAMP BEAUREGARD. A Confederate encampment and staging area located at the present junction of U.S. 70 and S.R. 20 near Jackson, Madison County, Camp Beauregard was activated in May 1861 under the command of Colonel William H. Stephens. Normal procedure was for companies to assemble in their home communities, then congregate here for organization into regiments. At least five Confederate regiments were trained at the camp.

FORT BELL CANTON. This fort on the Holston (Tennessee) River was erected in 1797 on the approximate site of present Lenoir City, Loudon County, to protect the Cherokee lands from white encroachment. The post was abandoned in 1800.

FORT (BATTERY) BILLINGSLEY. A Union-built defense of Knoxville, located between Gay Street and First Creek, it was named in the memory of Lieutenant J. Billingsley, 17th Michigan Volunteers, who was killed in action in front of Fort Sanders on November 20, 1863.

CAMP BLOUNT. Located on present U.S. 231, just south of Fayetteville, Lincoln County, at the old stone bridge over the Elk River, Camp Blount was established in October 1813 for the mobilization of some 3,500 infantry, cavalry, and artillery troops under Major General Andrew Jackson for his punitive operations against the warring Creeks in present Alabama. The site was also used for military encampments during the Second Seminole War and the Civil War.

FORT BLOUNT. Located on the west bank of the Cumberland River, two and a half miles southwest of present Flynn's Lick, Jackson County, Fort Blount was erected sometime between 1784 and 1788 (depending on the authority cited) to safeguard the route of pioneering homesteaders between the East and the Cumberland Settlements, modern Nashville. The old structure still stands and is used as a county jail.

CAMP BOONE. Established by the Confederacy in 1861 as a staging and training camp for Kentucky recruits, Camp Boone was located just south of the Kentucky line, north of Clarksville, Montgomery County. A number of infantry and cavalry regiments were mobilized, organized, and trained here. One of its earliest commanders was Brigadier General Simon Bolivar Buckner.

CAMP BRADLEY. A Union encampment established after the Battle of Stone's River and during the Federal occupation of Murfreesboro in 1863, Camp Bradley was named for Colonel Luther Bradley, 31st Illinois Infantry, who was killed in the battle.

FORT (REDOUBT) BRANNAN. An earthwork fortification built by Union troops in 1863 to protect Murfreesboro against Confederate attack, Fort Brannan was named for General John Milton Brannan, chief of artillery for the Army of the Cumberland from October 1863 to June 1865. The earthworks have been preserved.

FORT BRUCE. A Union-built defense situated on a high bluff at the mouth of the Red River, at the bend of the Cumberland River, just below Clarksville, Montgomery County, Fort Bruce was named for Colonel Sanders D. Bruce, who commanded the Federal forces at Clarksville.

FORT BUCKNER. FORT SANDERS.

BURNT STATION. GILLESPIE'S FORT.

FORT (BATTERY) BUSHNELL. A Union-built defense of Chattanooga, this fortification was a line of earthworks located on a bluff overlooking the Tennessee River, east of Georgia Avenue and near Payne (now Battery) Place. Battery Bushnell was leveled after 1880.

FORT BYINGTON. A Union defense of Knoxville, built in 1863 during General Longstreet's siege of the city in November 1863, Fort Byington was located on "The Hill" on the campus of the University of Tennessee and consisted of a battery of cannon and a brigade of infantry. The fortification was named in honor of Major Cornelius Byington, 2nd Michigan Volunteers, who was mortally wounded on the morning of November 24, 1863, while leading an assault against the Confederate rifle trenches in front of Fort Sanders.

CAPITOL REDOUBT. FORT JOHNSON.

FORT (REDOUBT) CARPENTER. A short line of cannon-bristling entrenchments erected by Union forces in defense of Chattanooga, the redoubt stood on Cameron Hill.

FORT CASINO. Located on the hill now occupied by Nashville's main reservoir, on the west side of 8th Avenue South, Fort Casino was one of a chain of forts forming the Federal outer defense line of the city. Its guns along with those of Fort Negley to the northeast across the Franklin

Pike opened the Battle of Nashville, December 15–16, 1864.

FORT CASS. Erected about April 1835 during the Creek War, Fort Cass was located at Calhoun in Cass County. It was abandoned on December 12, 1838.

FORT CASWELL. A Revolutionary War defense erected probably in 1776, Fort Caswell was located at Sycamore Shoals on the Watauga River, near the town of Watauga, Sullivan County. It was named in honor of Governor-elect Richard Caswell of North Carolina. The fort was under the command of Colonel John Carter, Captain James Robertson, and Lieutenant (later Colonel) John Sevier, subsequently first governor of Tennessee.

CAMP CHEATHAM. A Confederate regimental training encampment established in April or the early part of May, 1861, Camp Cheatham was located three miles west of Springfield, near the town of Cedar Hill, in Robertson County. The post was named in honor of Benjamin Franklin Cheatham, its first commander, who was in 1861 appointed brigadier general in the Provisional Army, Independent State of Tennessee.

FORT CHEATHAM. An early Confederate defense of Chattanooga, Fort Cheatham was a 200-foot-long semicircle of earthworks, located in the area bounded by 4th Avenue, between 23rd and 28th streets. When a large housing project was begun in the area in 1939, efforts were made to preserve the earthwork remains.

COLUMBIA ARSENAL. Established at Columbia, Maury County, by the government in 1888 and built 1888–90, Columbia Arsenal was abandoned except for caretakers in 1901. The reservation was transferred to the Columbia Military Academy, founded in 1904. The Arsenal was used as a training center for Spanish-American War troops, then given up by the Army in 1902.

FORT COMSTOCK. One of the series of Knoxville defenses built by Union forces, Fort Comstock was located on Summit Hill, a site now occupied by the Lawson McGhee Library on West Church Avenue. The fort was named in honor of Lieutenant Colonel Comstock, 17th Michigan Volunteers, who was killed during the unsuccessful Confederate siege of Knoxville, November 17–December 5, 1863.

FORT CONFISCATION. A Union defense of Nashville, built probably in late 1863, Fort Confiscation was located in the eastern part of the city and reportedly covered some 14 acres of ground.

FORT (BATTERY) COOLIDGE. A Union-built defense of Chattanooga, Fort or Battery Coolidge was reported by the Office of the Chief Engineer on June 29, 1864, as having its magazine completed and in use, and available for infantry occupancy.

FORT CREIGHTON. FORT WOOD.

FORT CRUTCHFIELD. A Union defense of Chattanooga, Fort Crutchfield stood between Fort Lytle and Fort Mihalotzy. The report of the Chief Engineer, Headquarters Department of the Cumberland, dated June 29, 1864, stated that, although its outer works were not yet finished, its parapet was completed, platform finished, and guns mounted, with its magazine completed and in use.

FORT DEFIANCE. SEVIER'S STATION.

FORT DES ECORES. FORT PICKERING.

FORT DICKERSON. Situated on present Fort Dickerson Park Heights, this strong Union fortification was a major factor in the defense of Knoxville during the Confederate siege, November 17–December 4, 1863. It was occupied by Colonel Daniel Cameron's 2nd Brigade of the 3rd Division. Including all the works between Fort Stanley and Fort Higley, the fort was named in the memory of Captain Jonathan C. Dickerson, 112th Illinois Volunteers (mounted infantry), who was killed in action near Cleveland, Tennessee.

FORT DONELSON. A strong Confederate fortification, its remains encompassed within a National Military Park today, located on the Cumberland River just west of Dover, Stewart County, Fort Donelson was built shortly after the outbreak of the Civil War. Named for Brigadier General Daniel Donelson, who chose the site for the fort, it covered some 97 acres with earthworks, rifle trenches, and water batteries. General U. S. Grant's taking of the fort on February 16, 1862, after a four-day siege, was a critically decisive victory for the Union cause. Also, after almost a year of war in which Confederate forces had been uniformly successful, this triumph did much to uplift the flagging spirits of Union supporters.

The capture of Fort Donelson opened an avenue into the very heart of the Confederacy by way of the Tennessee and Cumberland rivers, forcing the immediate evacuation of Columbus and Bowling Green, and delivering western Tennessee and all of Kentucky into Federal hands. General Simon Bolivar Buckner, reluctantly accepting Grant's demand for "unconditional and immediate surrender," delivered to the victorious Union forces between 12,000 and 15,000 officers and men as prisoners of war. The Federal losses were about 5,000 killed and wounded, and 450 missing. Fort Donelson National Military Park, established by Congress in 1928, is administered by the National Park Service.

FORT ELSTNER. A Union-built defense of Knoxville, Fort Elstner was probably named for Brigadier General George Ruter Elstner.

BATTERY FEARNS. A Knoxville defense erected by Union forces, Battery Fearns was located on Flint Hill and named in honor of Lieutenant Adjutant Charles W. Fearns, 45th Ohio Volunteers (mounted infantry), who was killed in action on November 18, 1863, in front of Fort Sanders.

CAMP FORREST (*Camp Peay*). A World War II infantry training center, originally established in 1926 for the training of the Tennessee National Guard, Camp Forrest was a 43,662-acre installation established on January 10, 1941, and located near Tullahoma in Coffee County, 50 miles northwest of Chattanooga. First called Camp Peay during its construction, it was officially designated Camp Forrest in honor of Lieutenant General Nathan Bedford Forrest, noted Confederate officer. Near the end of the war, the post was used as a camp for prisoners of war. Camp Forrest was deactivated June 30, 1946.

FREELAND'S STATION. A Revolutionary War defense, one of the principal stations of the Cumberland Settlements (modern Nashville), Freeland's Station was a stockaded and bastioned complex of several houses erected by George, James, and Jacob Freeland. Felix Robertson, son of Colonel James Robertson, and the first white child born in the settlement, was born here on January 11, 1781. Four days later the fort, garrisoned by 11 men and several families, including Colonel Robertson, was attacked by a large party of Indians, who were successfully repulsed by the defenders.

CAMP GARESCHE. A Civil War encampment established by Union forces in the environs of Murfreesboro in early 1863, Camp Garesche was named in the memory of Lieutenant Colonel Julius Peter Garesche, chief of staff, Army of the Cumberland. He was beheaded by a cannonball on the morning of December 31, 1862, during the Battle of Stone's River, just west of the city limits. The officer was then on horseback in company with General William Starke Rosecrans and several aides just east of the present National Cemetery.

FORT GARESCHE. A defense of Nashville erected in 1863 at "Hyde's Ferry" by the 182nd Ohio Volunteers Regiment commanded by Brigadier General J. B. Tower and Colonel L. Butler, Fort Garesche was named in honor of Lieutenant Colonel Julius Peter Garesche, chief of staff, Army of the Cumberland, who was killed on December 31, 1862, in the Battle of Stone's River near Murfreesboro.

FORT GILLEM. FORT SILL.

GILLESPIE'S FORT (*Burnt Station*). Located about two miles northeast of present Rockford, south of Knoxville, in Blount County, James Gillespie's Fort was attacked on October 13, 1788, by about 300 Indians under half-breed John Watts. The fort's defenders held out until their ammunition was exhausted. Seventeen were massacred and their bodies burned in the holocaust of the fort burning; 28 men, women, and children were taken prisoner. The locality was thereafter known as Burnt Station.

FORT GRANGER. In the summer of 1794, blockhouses garrisoned by regular Army troops were established at Southwest Point (near present-day Kingston), Tellico Blockhouse (near Loudon), and Fort Granger (on the Holston River, near Lenoir City).

FORT GRANGER. An array of fortified breastworks was built by Union forces in 1862 to the east of Franklin, 20 miles south of Nashville, in Williamson County. The largest and strongest of them was Fort Granger, named for General Gordon Granger. Here, on November 30, 1864, on the hills overlooking the Harpeth River, was fought one of the bloodiest battles of the Civil War. Fort Granger and its associated works were garrisoned by 8,500 men and mounted 24 pieces of artillery. It is estimated that 6,000 Confederates and 2,500 Federals lost their lives during the 55-minute-long, savagely fought engagement between the Confederates under General John Bell Hood and Union forces under General John McAllister Schofield. Six Confederate generals were among the dead.

FORT HARKER. FORT NEGLEY.

CAMP HARRIS. One of the earliest training encampments established by the Confederates during the Civil War, Camp Harris was located just south of Estill Springs in Franklin County. The area was heavily fortified to protect the highway and railroad bridges over the Elk River. General Braxton Bragg, commanding the Army of Tennessee in 1863, established his command post here briefly.

FORT HARRIS. Confederate troops under General Leonidas Polk in 1861 built Fort Harris on the Third Chickasaw Bluff, 16 miles upstream from Memphis.

FORT HENRY. Located on the right or east bank of the Tennessee River, 12 miles from Dover, the county seat of Stewart County, Fort Henry was begun in May 1861 by Confederate forces. Fort Heiman faced it from the Kentucky side of the river. Fort Donelson on the Cumberland River, 12 miles away, was constructed at the same time. Both were established to protect navigation on both rivers. Fort Henry was a bastioned earthwork, mounting 17 guns, and garrisoned by a force under Brigadier General Lloyd Tilghman. On February 6, 1862, Fort Henry was assaulted by a small armada of Union gunboats under the command of Admiral A. H. Foote. The fort's defenders held out for about two hours, then most of the troops evacuated to escape to Fort Donelson. General Tilghman surrendered the fort and his 60 remaining men. From there, General U. S. Grant marched his army to besiege Fort Donelson.

FORT HIGLEY. All of the Federal fortifications on the hill west of the railroad embankment, on the south side of the Tennessee River at Knoxville, were called Fort Higley in the memory of Captain Joel P. Higley, 7th Ohio Cavalry, who fell in action at Blue Springs, October 10, 1863.

FORT HINDMAN. A Confederate fortification built during the 1863 Chattanooga campaign, Fort Hindman was named for Brigadier General Thomas C. Hindman of Arkansas, who then commanded a brigade of infantry.

HIWASSEE GARRISON. Located in the south suburbs of present Dayton, Rhea County, at the junction of the Tennessee and Hiwassee rivers, Hiwassee Fort was built in early 1807 to protect settlers and travelers along the Indian frontier. The troops at the Southwest Point post, abandoned during the same year, were transferred to Hiwassee Garrison. The Hiwassee fort was abandoned in 1815.

FORT (RUSSELL) HOUSTON. FORT (DAN) MCCOOK.

HOUSTON'S FORT. Located on Little Nine Mile Creek, about six miles from Maryville, Blount County, Houston's (Station) Fort was established by James Houston in 1785, close to the Indians' Great War Path. From here, in 1786, John Sevier led 160 horsemen against the Cherokee towns. In 1788, after 31 men from the fort were killed in a nearby apple orchard by Cherokee, about 100 Indians attacked the fort. They were repulsed by the garrison, which included some of the frontier's most noted riflemen. Archival records do not indicate when Houston's Fort was abandoned.

FORT HUNTINGTON SMITH. A large Federal earthwork on Temperance Hill in Knoxville, fronting 150 yards on Weicker Avenue and occupying the site of the Green School, the fort was named in the memory of Lieutenant Colonel W. Huntington Smith, who was killed in action at Campbell's Station.

ISLAND NO. 10 FORTIFICATIONS. So named because it was the tenth island in the Mississippi River south of its junction with the Ohio, Island No. 10 was situated in Madrid Bend, between Tennessee and Missouri, and it controlled the river in both directions. Confederate forces under General Leonidas Polk constructed two miles of fortified earthworks along the banks of the island. In the face of a large-scale assault by Union land and naval forces, after the fall of New Madrid on the Missouri shore, the Confederates initiated evacuation of the island on April 7, 1862. It was too late to retreat, however, and 7,000 Confederates, including 3 generals, were forced to surrender, caught between Union troops and the swamp. With Island No. 10 in Union possession, the only Confederate stronghold on the Mississippi above Memphis was Fort Pillow.

FORT JOHNSON (*Camp Andy Johnson; Capitol Redoubt*). In late February 1862, General

Don Carlos Buell ordered Captain James St. Clair Morton to consult with Andrew Johnson, military governor of Tennessee (appointed by President Lincoln), regarding the establishment of strong defenses throughout the capital city of Nashville. Actual construction was begun in August 1862 and continued intermittently until the Confederate campaign in late 1864 spurred intensive efforts. Captain Morton converted the Capitol into a strong fortification. A stockade of cedar logs surrounded the building, reinforced by barricades of bales of cotton and earthen parapets. Fifteen pieces of heavy artillery were emplaced at strategic points around the Capitol, which was used to accommodate a garrison of several companies of infantry and artillery.

FORT JONES (*Stone Fort*). This Union defense of Chattanooga stood on the rocky hill south of present 10th Street on Market Street, with 11th Street about in its center. Because excavation was difficult on the rocks, material was brought in for the construction of the fort. In 1880 the fortification was leveled for the building of the U.S. Custom House and post office on the site.

KILGORE'S STATION. Located about a mile west of Cross Plains, Robertson County, this important early stockaded fort was erected in 1779 by Thomas Kilgore, a close friend of Colonel James Robertson, noted Tennessee pioneer. It became a widely known center of the congregation and departure for the settlers in this part of Tennessee and southern Kentucky.

FORT LOUDOUN. Plan based on archaeological work and a plan drawn during the original fort's existence. (Courtesy of the Fort Loudoun Association.)

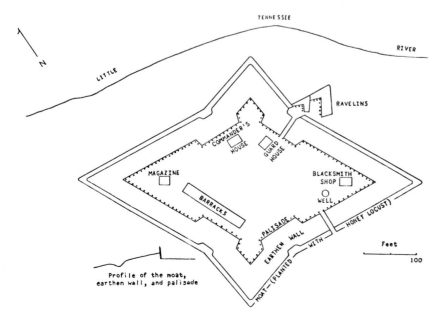

FORT KING. Constructed during the September–October 1863 Confederate siege of Chattanooga, Fort King was a Union defense named for Brigadier General John H. King who commanded an infantry brigade.

KING'S MILL FORT. The site of King's Mill is at the mouth of Reedy Creek on the south fork of the Holston River at Kingsport, Washington County. One of the first water-powered mills in Tennessee, the gristmill was constructed of heavy stone by Colonel James King in 1774. Converted into a fortified defense during the Revolution, it was intermittently garrisoned by troops during the long war.

FORT LEE. Located on Limestone Creek at present Watauga, Carter County, Fort Lee was constructed in 1776 under the direction of noted frontiersman Lieutenant (later Colonel) John Sevier, subsequently Tennessee's first governor, as a Cherokee and Revolutionary War defense. The fort was named in honor of General Charles Lee, who then commanded American forces in the South. On July 20, 1776, a large party of warring Cherokee attacked Fort Lee and began a two-week siege. Crowded with women and children, the fort had only 40 men to defend it. John Robertson was in command, with John Sevier as his subordinate commander. The Cherokee, however, found it impossible to take Fort Lee by assault or siege. They withdrew when they learned that a large relief force of Virginians were en route to Fort Lee.

FORT LOUDOUN. Located on the Little Tennessee River just north of the present town of Vonore, off U.S. 411, Monroe County, Fort Loudoun was built in 1756–57 and named for John Campbell, earl of Loudoun, who was then commander of British forces in America. The fort was the first structure built by the English in present Tennessee and their farthest southwestern outpost in Colonial America. Erected in response to a request by the Overhill Cherokee, then allied to the English, and serving as a barrier against French penetration into the Mississippi Valley, Fort Loudoun was a palisaded, diamond-shaped defense with a bastion projecting at each of its four angles, and surrounded by a dry moat.

Growing disaffection between the British and Cherokee broke out into open war, and the Indians laid siege to the fort in February 1760. When Captain Paul Demere, commander of the fort, finally surrendered in August, after seven months of intolerable hardships, he obtained a promise of safe conduct to Fort Prince George in present South Carolina for all the soldiers and their families. After the fort was evacuated, the Indians destroyed it. Less than 15 miles from Fort Loudoun, the Indians attacked the line of refugees, killed 27 soldiers and 3 women, and took all the survivors as prisoners, later ransomed and delivered to Fort Prince George.

Extensive archaeological excavations at the fort site in the 1930s yielded exact information on its size, shape, and construction. In 1937, the WPA began reconstructing portions of the fort. Completed in the 1960s, the re-creation of the fort and its immediate environs is administered by the Fort Loudoun Association.

FORT LYTLE (*Star Fort*). A Chattanooga defense constructed by Union forces in 1863, originally known as the Star Fort, Fort Lytle stood on College Street between Hooke (now 13th) Street and Frank (now 14th) Street, and extended down to Fannin Street. An immense earthwork in the shape of a five- or six-pointed star, its outside walls were fully 20 feet high, with surrounding dry ditches 10 to 15 feet deep and wide. A report of the Department of the Cumberland's Office of the Chief Engineer, dated June 29, 1864, stated that all its ordnance was mounted and the parade, parapets, platforms, and magazine all completed.

FORT (DAN) MCCOOK (*Fort (Russell) Houston*). A defense of Nashville built by Federal forces in 1862 and originally named for Russell Houston, a local Union sympathizer, it stood on high ground at 16th Avenue South and Division Street. Later it became Fort McCook in honor of General Dan McCook who was mortally wounded at Kenesaw Mountain, Georgia, in 1864.

MARR'S FORT. Originally located at present Old Fort, south of Benton, Polk County, Marr's Fort was a blockhouse built in 1814 on the bank of the Ocoee River in Cherokee country by East Tennessee militia on a road under construction to allow supply trains to follow them to the relief of Jackson's forces at New Orleans. The two-story blockhouse built of hewn 8-by-12-foot oak logs with 72 portholes was intended to protect the militia and the supply trains from the Cherokee Indians. Marr's Fort was reoccupied by troops in 1835 while negotiations were under way to deprive the Indians of their lands. The structure was dismantled and relocated three times since its construction, first in 1922 to the campus of the Polk County High School at Ben-

ton. It now stands on county property south of the courthouse.

FORT MIHALOTZY. A Chattanooga defense erected by Federal troops, Fort Mihalotzy covered a considerable part of Cameron Hill south of 6th Street. Its actual site is at present 221 Boynton Terrace on Cameron Hill. A similarly named defense was built by Union forces at Knoxville.

MILAN ARSENAL. Located three miles east of Milan, Gibson County, Milan Arsenal was begun in January 1941 and completed in January 1942. During World War II, its maximum employment reached 15,000. In November 1945 the 25,400-acre arsenal and field service depot reverted to standby status until the Korean War.

FORT MITCHEL. A Union-built defense located at or near Buck Lodge in Sumner County, it was named for General Ormsby Mitchel.

FORT MORTON. A Union defense of Nashville, Fort Morton was erected in 1862 west of the Franklin Pike by Captain James St. Clair Morton. It stood just south of South Street, which at that time marked the city limits.

FORT NASH. This fort located on Garrison Fork at Beech Grove, on the border of Bedford and Coffee counties, northeast of Shelbyville, was established about 1793 to protect the area's settlers and travelers to and from the southwest. Until its abandonment, about 1804, it was an important stopping place and administrative center.

FORT NASHBOROUGH. The history of old Fort Nashborough, the progenitor of modern Nashville, goes back to Christmas Day, 1779, when James Robertson, pioneering explorer, land speculator, and the "Father of Tennessee," led a small party of settlers across the ice-covered Cumberland River and began constructing a fortified settlement. During the following spring, a flotilla of about 30 flatboats carrying women, children, and household goods arrived at the infant settlement. The fort was named Fort Nashborough by its leaders in honor of Revolutionary War General Francis Nash who was mortally wounded on October 4, 1777, at the Battle of Germantown, Pennsylvania.

The palisaded, black locust-wood structure, built without a single nail, with hinges and latches fashioned from wood, consisted of two blockhouses and puncheon-floored cabins connected by breezeways. The re-creation of the fort in 1930 is located at 1st Avenue North and Church Street

FORT NEGLEY. Photograph of the Chattanooga fort, taken when the fort was in use. (Courtesy of the Tennessee State Library.)

in downtown Nashville and maintained by the city.

FORT NEGLEY. Union-built Chattanooga defense Forts Negley and Phelps, covering an extensive area, were located south of Montgomery Avenue (now Main Street) and on what is now Mitchell and Read avenues. The forts were not leveled until after 1885; about two years later, the site was divided into streets and residential lots.

FORT NEGLEY. Plan of the Chattanooga fort drawn in 1865. (Courtesy of the Tennessee State Library.)

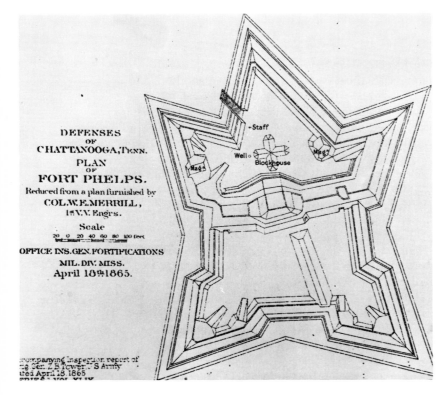

FORT NEGLEY (*Fort Harker*). A strong Union defense located on St. Cloud Hill at present Chestnut Street and Ridley Boulevard in South Nashville, Fort Negley was erected in 1862 by Captain James St. Clair Morton. A favorite picnic area, the hill was selected by the captain as the site for a key strongpoint in his line of defenses south and west of the city. The trees on the hill, including many old oaks, were felled to clear lines of fire for the cannon. The fort was built of stone, earth, logs, and railway rails in the European style, and was named for General James S. Negley, but the name was later changed to Fort Harker in honor of General Charles G. Harker, killed in the Battle of Kenesaw Mountain, Georgia. In Nashville, the fort is still known today, however, as Fort Negley. Its guns opened the Battle of Nashville, December 15–16, 1864, when Confederate General Thomas Hood's forces unsuccessfully attempted to oust the Federals from the city. During the Reconstruction period, the fort was used as a meeting place for the Ku Klux Klan.

FORT PALMER. A Chattanooga defense erected by Federal forces in 1863, Fort Palmer was located on 9th, 10th, and 11th streets, later known as Park Place. Before 1870, most of the works were leveled for a residence.

FORT PATRICK HENRY (*Fort Robinson*). In late 1760 Colonel William Byrd was ordered to proceed to Fort Loudon with about 600 Virginians to relieve the beleaguered garrison there. One of the blockhouses or forts he built during the long march was located, in the winter of 1760–61, on the north bank of the South Fork of the Holston River, nearly opposite the upper end of Long Island, at present Kingsport, Sullivan County. Colonel Byrd named the fort for John Robinson, one of his partners in the ownership of the lead mines near Fort Chiswell in Virginia. An extensive fortification, it was furnished with a bastion in each of its angles and gates spiked with large nails.

The site of this French and Indian War defense was reoccupied in September 1776 by forces under Lieutenant Colonel William Russell, who erected a new fortification in compliance with orders of Colonel William Christian to serve as a base during their successful campaign against the hostile Cherokee. The 100-yard-square, bastioned fort was named in honor of Revolutionary War patriot Patrick Henry. Following the subjugation of the Cherokee, the Avery Treaty was consummated on July 20, 1777, on Long Island, about a quarter of a mile west of the present Holston River Bridge. The Indians ceded to the whites a broad domain for settlement in accordance with the pact, which was soon violated by the settlers. Fort Patrick Henry was continually garrisoned throughout the Revolution.

CAMP PEAY. CAMP FORREST.

FORT PHELPS. FORT NEGLEY (*Chattanooga*).

FORT PICKERING (*Fort San Fernando de Barrancas; Fort Des Ecores; Fort Adams; Fort Pike*). In the spring of 1795, Don Manuel Gayoso de Lemos and Spanish troops crossed the Mississippi River to the Fourth Chickasaw Bluff at the mouth of the Wolf River (modern Memphis), declared himself governor, and raised the flag of Spain for the first time, taking possession of the territory in the name of his sovereign. Here, on the site of French Fort Assumption (1739), in what is now Auction Park, he erected Fort San Fernando de Barrancas, sometimes called Fort Des Ecores, named in honor of the Prince of Asturias. The United States government declared the fort an invasion by a foreign power.

In the spring of 1797, possibly April, the Spanish dismantled their fort, then burned it, removing its garrison to Fort Esperanza across the river. This was done in accordance with the Treaty of San Lorenzo, April 26, 1796, whereby Spain agreed to evacuate the east side of the Mississippi. On May 26, 1797, Captain Isaac Guion, 3rd Infantry, two companies of his regiment, and several artillerymen to man his guns, left Fort Washington at Cincinnati to take possession from the departing Spanish troops. Chickasaw Bluffs was occupied on July 20, but it was

not until October 22 that the fort was completed. It was christened Fort Adams in honor of President John Adams, but the name was soon dropped. The fort was left in the care of a garrison of a lieutenant and 30 soldiers, reinforced on February 9, 1798, by two companies of the 3rd Infantry.

In 1801 Captain Zebulon M. Pike, under orders of General James Wilkinson, arrived to relocate Fort Adams, which was found to be on low, unhealthful malarial ground. To replace Fort Adams, he selected a suitable location two miles down the bluff, in what is now Crump Park, and erected a new fort bearing the name of Fort Pike for a short time, then designated Fort Pickering for the secretary of state under President Washington. Fort Pickering was abandoned in 1806 (an alternate citation reports it abandoned about 1810).

FORT PIKE. FORT PICKERING.

FORT PILLOW. On June 4, 1862, Federal forces captured Fort Pillow (named for General Gideon J. Pillow), an important Confederate defense on the Mississippi River near the mouth of Coles Creek, 18 miles west of Henning, Lauderdale County, and about 40 miles north of Memphis. On April 12, 1864, in order to end the depredations committed by the fort's Federal garrison, Confederate Brigadier General Nathan Bedford Forrest with his cavalry troops attacked and retook the fort. Of the garrison of 551 white and black troops, 221 were killed; the remainder, many wounded, were taken prisoner. The House of Representatives Committee on the Conduct of the War concluded that the Confederates were guilty of atrocities after the fort had surrendered; the Confederacy maintained that the House report was Northern propaganda, that the Federal casualties were the result of the troops' refusing to surrender. To this day, the Fort Pillow "Massacre" remains a controversial issue.

CAMP POLAND (*Camp Wilder*). A Spanish-American War training encampment established probably in June 1898 on the outskirts of Knoxville, it was first named Camp Wilder for General John T. Wilder. In the middle of August, it was renamed Camp Poland in honor of Brigadier General J. S. Poland who died at Chickamauga, Georgia, on August 7, 1898.

FORT PRUDHOMME. Located on the Second Chickasaw Bluff, just below the mouth of the Hatchie River, in Tipton County, Fort Prudhomme was built by Robert de La Salle in 1682, on his first voyage down the Mississippi River. One of the first forts or habitations of any kind built in the Tennessee country by Europeans, it was named for Pierre Prudhomme, armorer of the expedition. When Prudhomme failed to return from a hunting trip, La Salle erected the small temporary fort for protection during the search. After lost Prudhomme was found, La Salle left him in charge of the fort and continued his exploration of the Mississippi. On April 6, La Salle and his party discovered the three outlets of the river into the Gulf of Mexico. On the explorer's return trip, he became ill and remained at Fort Prudhomme for 40 days before being able to continue upriver. The fort was then abandoned to fall into ruins.

FORT PUTNAM. A Union-built defense of Chattanooga, Fort Putnam was a large earthwork of walls and ditches occupying the area of 4th and Lindsay streets, in the rear of Brabson Square. It was leveled after 1886.

FORT RANDOLPH. A defense erected by Confederate forces under General Leonidas Polk, Fort Randolph was located west of Covington and just south of Randolph on the Second Chickasaw Bluff overlooking the river in Tipton County.

FORT ROBINSON. FORT PATRICK HENRY.

FORT ROSECRANS. The fortifications built by Union troops at Murfreesboro and in its immediate environs were designated as Fortress Rosecrans, named for General William S. Rosecrans. The works—four redoubts, nine lunettes, two demilunettes, a redan, and two curtains—were constructed as a unified line immediately after the Battle of Stone's River (December 31, 1862–January 2, 1863) just west of Murfreesboro's city limits. Much of the fortifications has been destroyed and leveled by the extension of the city limits. However, about one quarter of a mile of Fortress Rosecrans remains and is the property of the city.

CAMP ROSS. A supply base for Tennessee troops during the Creek War of 1812–13, Camp Ross was located on the Tennessee River, one mile west of Chattanooga's city limits, at the mouth of Chattanooga Creek.

RUCKER'S REDOUBT. Located near New Markham in Lake County, Rucker's Redoubt consisted of a 1,200-yard-long line of five batteries that constituted the mainland's Confederate headquarters for strategic Island No. 10 in the Madrid

Bend of the Mississippi River. At the west end, Battery No. 1 mounted three 8-inch Columbiads and three 32-pounders. Preventing passage of Federal gunboats downriver, it withstood continuous attack for two weeks, until floodwaters forced its virtual abandonment on April 2, 1862. Covered by the Federal gunboats, Major General John Pope landed part of his 25,000-man army on the west shore of Madrid Bend, outflanking Confederate defenses and causing the abandonment of the island on April 8, 1862. Brigadier General W. W. Mackall, during the retreat, was compelled to surrender the remnants of his Confederate force on the northern outskirts of Tiptonville.

FORT SANDERS (*Fort Buckner*). A Union-built, bastioned, deeply ditched earthwork, originally called Fort Buckner, occupying the ridge two blocks north of Strong Hall on the campus of the University of Tennessee in the city of Knoxville, was the scene of General James Longstreet's unsuccessful assault upon the city's Federal defenses at dawn on November 29, 1863. Brigadier General William P. Sanders, employing dismounted cavalry to stem the Confederate advance from the west, was fatally wounded November 18, 1863, on the ridge, presently occupied by the lawn of the Second Presbyterian Church on Kingston Pike. Immediately after General Sanders's death, the defense was renamed in his memory.

FORT SAN FERNANDO DE BARRANCAS. FORT PICKERING.

SEVIER'S STATION (*Fort Defiance*). Located at present New Providence, Montgomery County, approaching the city of Clarksville from the north, Sevier's Station was a stone blockhouse built in 1791 by Colonel Valentine Sevier. The frontier defense was attacked by a band of some 40 to 50 Indians, mostly Cherokee, on November 11, 1794. All the men of the fort, with the exception of Sevier and William Snyder, were out. The Indians killed six people, including Sevier's son Joseph. Sevier and Snyder successfully defended the blockhouse during a furious hour-long attack. The outpost was thereafter known as Fort Defiance.

CAMP SHAEFER. An encampment established after the Battle of Stone's River (December 31, 1862–January 2, 1863) and during the Federal occupation of Murfreesboro, it was named in the memory of Colonel Frederick Shaefer, who commanded the 2nd Brigade in General Philip

Sheridan's division. He was killed during the Stone River battle.

FORT SHERIDAN. A Chattanooga defense erected by Federal forces, Fort Sheridan was an elaborate work of embankments surrounded by immensely deep and wide ditches. It was located on the extreme south end of Cameron Hill and named for General Philip Sheridan. It was largely leveled about 1880 to be replaced by a private residence.

FORT SHERMAN. One of the defenses erected by Union forces at Chattanooga in 1863 after the Battle of Chickamauga, Georgia, was Fort Sherman, named in honor of either General Francis T. Sherman or General William T. Sherman. Occupying the top of the hill at Walnut and 5th streets, the fort was an immense enclosure of 20-foot-high earthen walls, with a wide and deep ditch surrounding the foot of the hill. It was leveled about 1880 and its lands developed for several residences.

CAMP SILL. This Federal encampment was established in the environs of Murfreesboro after the Battle of Stone's River to the west of the city and during its occupation by Union forces. The fortified camp was named in the memory of Brigadier General Joshua Woodrow Sill, who commanded the 1st Brigade in General Sheridan's division. He was killed during the first hours of the battle on December 31, 1862. All three of Sheridan's brigade commanders were killed during the furious engagement.

FORT SILL (*Fort Gillem*). This strong Nashville defense was mostly built by Federal forces under the command of Brigadier General Alvan C. Gillem in 1862 and named for him. It was renamed Fort Sill in 1863, probably in honor of Brigadier General Joshua W. Sill, who was killed on December 31, 1862, in the Battle of Stone's River near Murfreesboro. The fortification stood on ground now occupied by Fisk University's Jubilee Hall located at 17th and 18th Avenues North on Jefferson Street. The university's Drama Department still utilizes one of the fort's original barracks.

Fort Sill was just one of Nashville's 20 miles of forts, bristling with heavy guns supported by underground magazines, breastworks, trenches, and rifle pits. Nashville was crucial because it was the arsenal and supply depot for the major Union operations in the South. Enormous supplies coming daily by river and rail to Nashville were essential in sustaining Sherman's invasion force in the Georgia Campaign. After Sherman left Atlanta in his famous "March to the Sea," these backup stores and rail transport facilities were still maintained.

CAMP SMARTT. This Confederate staging and training area, located near McMinnville on present S.R. 108 in Warren County, was established in the summer of 1861 by Colonel Benjamin J. Hill who organized and commanded here the 35th Tennessee Infantry until his promotion to brigadier general. Discontinued for a time, the camp was reactivated in 1862 by Colonel Marcus J. Wright, who was promoted to brigadier general while commanding the post. The camp was then mainly used as a center for Confederate conscripts.

FORT (POST AT) SOUTHWEST POST. Constructed in 1791–92 by General John Sevier at Southwest Point, at the junction of the Clinch and Tennessee rivers, in the suburbs of present Kingston in Roane County, the fort housed at various times territorial militia and Army regulars who protected the settled area from Indian depredations. It was a favored place for emigrants and travelers to new settlements. The garrison was withdrawn in 1806 and moved to Hiwassee Garrison. In 1974 archaeologists of the University of Tennessee made exploratory excavations at the site and unearthed part of the fort's walls as well as Indian and Civil War artifacts.

FORT STANLEY. A Union defense and all its outworks built in 1863 and situated on the hill at the end of Gay Street, on the south side of the river, in Knoxville, Fort Stanley was named in the memory of Captain C. E. Stanley, 45th Ohio Volunteers (mounted infantry), who fell mortally wounded in the action near Philadelphia.

STAR FORT. Fort Lytle.

STONE FORT. Fort Jones.

CAMP (BOB) TAYLOR. A temporary Spanish-American War training encampment for recruits, established in the late spring of 1898, Camp Taylor was located at Fountain City, just north of Knoxville.

TELLICO BLOCKHOUSE. Territorial militia and Army regulars were stationed at various times at the Tellico Blockhouse, erected in 1794 on the border of the Cherokee Nation, on the Little Tennessee River, at the present town of Loudon in Monroe County. In 1806 its garrison was withdrawn and transferred to Hiwassee Garrison.

FORT THOMAS. A Union fortification at Gallatin, Sumner County, one of its principal purposes was to guard the vital railroad line from Bowling Green, Kentucky, to Gallatin. The fort was garrisoned by various units of Indiana and Wisconsin regiments, who engaged in frequent clashes with Confederates in the mountainous terrain of north-central Tennessee.

CAMP TYSON. The only World War II Barrage Balloon Training Center, a unit of the Coast Artillery corps, Camp Tyson was named for the late Brigadier General Lawrence Davis Tyson and located near Paris in Henry County.

FORT W. D. WHIPPLE. A Union defense erected in 1862 at Nashville, Fort Whipple was located between Fort Gillem (Sill) and Fort Garesche, and named for Brigadier General William Denison Whipple.

FORT WATAUGA. Located on the Watauga River near present Elizabethton, Carter County, Fort Watauga played an important part in Tennessee's early history. The fort was erected in 1772 by settlers from North Carolina and Virginia as a protection against the area's Indians. In the spring of the same year, the settlers formed the Watauga Association, the first such agreement west of the Alleghenies, to obtain from the Indians by lease a tract embracing the northeast corner of Tennessee. Later in the same year, the Transylvania Treaty was consummated at Fort Watauga, whereby the Cherokee agreed to sell to the Association the land between the Ohio River and the watershed of the Cumberland River. Increasing disaffection between the Indians and the settlers, however, resulted in war on the frontier. On July 21, 1776, the fort was attacked and besieged by a large body of Cherokee. The settlers under Captain James Robertson successfully repulsed the Indians, forcing them to finally lift the siege.

CAMP WILDER. CAMP POLAND.

FORT (BATTERY) WILTSIE. A large Federal earthwork was located in the rear of Vine Avenue between Gay and Walnut streets when General James Longstreet besieged Knoxville, November 17–December 4, 1863. The defense line ran along this ridge, from Fort Hill (Surrey Street and Saxton Avenue) 2,400 yards east to Fort Sanders (17th Street and Laurel Avenue) 1,400 yards west. Ten forts crowned these heights, five east and four west of this point. Fort Wiltsie was named in the memory of Captain Wiltsie, 20th Michigan Volunteers, who was mortally wounded during the siege.

FORT WOOD (*Fort Creighton*). Located in east Chattanooga, the Fort Wood Historic District is four-by-three blocks in area and includes 120 buildings in the neighborhood of the University of Tennessee campus. The site of an immense earthwork embracing more than a city block and consisting of high walls and an elaborate magazine, surrounded by deep and wide ditches, it was first called Fort Creighton, then later renamed Fort Wood. The fort was leveled by 1880. Three cannon were emplaced within the area by the National Park Service as part of its interpretive program of Civil War battles in the vicinity.

FORT WRIGHT. A Confederate fortification situated on the Chickasaw Bluffs on the Mississippi, Fort Wright was situated a short distance upstream from Fort Pillow, about 40 miles north of Memphis. The fort was erected in 1861 by forces under General Leonidas Polk.

FORT (BATTERY) ZOELLNER. This Federal defense of Knoxville was located between Fort Sanders and Second Creek. It was named in the memory of Lieutenant Frank Zoellner, 2nd Michigan Volunteers, who fell mortally wounded in the assault upon the Confederates' rifle trenches in front of Fort Sanders on the morning of November 24, 1863.

FORT ZOLLICOFFER. A Confederate defense probably built in 1861 and located seven miles south of Nashville, it was abandoned after the fall of Fort Donelson in 1862. The fort was named in the honor of Brigadier General Felix Kirk Zollicoffer who was killed in eastern Tennessee.

CAMP ADAMS. Located on Salado Creek about five miles from San Antonio, Camp Adams was first established by Captain William Prescott's company (Adams Rifles) of the Texas Volunteers. A popular campsite used by both sides during the Civil War, it was occupied early in the war by U.S. forces evacuating the state. The Union Department of Texas was headquartered at San Antonio and commanded by Brigadier General David E. Twiggs who, on January 18, 1861, surrendered all Federal posts and property to state authorities before resigning his Federal commission and joining the Confederacy.

FORT ADOBE (WALLS). Located on the Canadian River above the mouth of a stream later called Bent's Creek in present Huchinson County, in the Texas Panhandle, this trading post was established by William Bent, probably during the winter of 1845–46, first as a log-built house, then of adobe the following year. In the spring of 1848, unable to pacify the hostile Comanche and Kiowa, Bent blew up the post's interior, leaving its adobe walls standing. Later, in 1864, troops led by Kit Carson made use of the walls in a battle against marauding Indians. When the buffalo hunters arrived nearly 10 years later, the remnants of the walls still stood four or five feet high. On June 27, 1874, Comanche Chief Quanah Parker with about 700 Comanche, Cheyenne, and Kiowa warriors attacked and besieged the "fort" occupied by the buffalo hunters. It was the Indians' last attempt to put an end to the ruthless slaughtering of many thousands of buffalo. Twenty-eight sharpshooting white men and one woman for three days battled the Indians, finally defeating them.

THE ALAMO. A compound as large as a city block, never intended to be a fort, and located in the heart of San Antonio, the Alamo is a shrine visited by every Texan and many thousands from around the world. Here, in 1836, some 183 men fought to the death in the climax of a 13-day drama. The famous "fort" was originally a church, part of the San Antonio de Padua Mission, established by Franciscan fathers in 1716. Two years later it was renamed for the Spanish viceroy and called San Antonio de Valero. Begun in 1744, the church was completed in 1761. After San Antonio de Valero was secularized in 1793, the Franciscan fathers departed, and the mission joined with adjacent settlements to become San Antonio de Bexar. A few years later, it was occupied by Mexican soldiers from a town called Pueblo de San José y Santiago del Alamo, and soon it became known as the Alamo.

Texas

THE ALAMO. (Courtesy of the San Antonio Chamber of Commerce.)

The leader of the Alamo's defenders was adventurer and democrat William Barrett Travis; the besieging army of nearly 5,000 Mexicans was led by General Antonio López de Santa Anna, dictator and tyrant. Travis's men included such frontiersmen as James Bowie, David Crockett, and James B. Bonham. On February 23 Santa Anna's force first attacked, then besieged the Alamo. The Texans had been ordered three times by revolutionary authorities to abandon it and as many times they refused. Travis gathered supplies, measured his powder, and strengthened the defenses. The Mexican assault on March 6 began at 5 A.M., and shortly after 9 A.M. every Texan defender and 1,500 Mexicans lay dead. Santa Anna had the corpses of the Texans burned. Forty-six days later, on April 21, at San Jacinto, some 750 Texans battled 1,500 Mexicans, destroyed them, captured Santa Anna, and dictated independence. "Remember the Alamo" was their battle cry.

FORT ANÁHUAC. Located on a bluff on the east shore of Galveston Bay, near the mouth of the Trinity River, within the city limits of the town of Anahuac, Chambers County, Fort Anáhuac was a customshouse and a fort established in 1831 in compliance with an order of General Manuel de Mier y Terán and designed to stop American colonization and prevent the entry of goods from the United States into Texas. The 30-by-40-foot, adobe-brick fort was constructed in 1831–32 by the forced labor of prisoners under the direction of Colonel John Davis Bradburn. Evacuated on July 13, 1832, after a mutiny staged by its garrison, the fort was reoccupied in January 1835 by a small Mexican garrison. On July 30, 1835, it was captured by Texas Volunteers commanded by William B. Travis. In 1836 it was gradually dismantled by settlers for its bricks. A major portion of the fort was lost by erosion into the bay. Its remnants are now enclosed within Fort Anáhuac Park.

FORT ARANSAS. FORT SHELL BANK.

FORT ARANSAS (*Camp Semmes*). A Confederate fortification located on the northeastern end of Mustang Island in Aransas County, the fort consisted of sand embankments surrounding artillery-mounted wooden platforms. Also known as Camp Semmes, it was garrisoned by mostly elements of the 8th Texas Infantry commanded by Major William O. Yager.

CAMP AUSTIN (*Austin Arsenal; Post of Austin; Camp Sanders*). The first Austin Arsenal was established in 1845 in the capital of Austin and occupied a building then situated on West Avenue between 8th and 9th streets. During the Civil War, another arsenal was established and occupied a stone building erected sometime in the 1850s. The structure, still standing, is located on 19th Street near Congress Avenue.

The city of Austin first became a military post on November 20, 1848, when the Post of Austin was established by two companies of the 1st Infantry under the command of J. H. King. They erected and occupied temporary weatherboarded and shingled buildings located on a 236-foot square, enclosed by a fence or stockade. There were probably no troops at the post from 1852 until after the Civil War, when Austin was reoccupied in 1865 by 6th Cavalry troops under the command of Major General George Custer. The Post of Austin, moved in 1866 to a site on the left bank of the Colorado River, a mile west of the city, was then renamed Camp Sanders in the memory of Captain William Sanders, 6th Cavalry, who was killed at Campbell's Station, Tennessee, on November 16, 1863. Camp Sanders was abandoned in August 1875.

CAMP AUSTIN. A temporary Confederate post located on Lake Austin near the town of Matagorda, Camp Austin was occupied by troops during the yellow fever epidemic in the summer of 1863.

FORT AUSTIN. This was the state's fortified Capitol occupied for a time during 1840–41 by Texas 1st Infantry troops. Mounting several pieces of ordnance, Fort Austin was surrounded by a strong stockade and a ditch. In June of 1840, it was garrisoned by two companies of troops aggregating 118 officers and men who maintained a guard against vandalism for a couple of months. After this garrison was withdrawn, a small military guard was posted there until March 1841.

POST OF AUSTIN. CAMP AUSTIN.

AUSTIN ARSENAL. CAMP AUSTIN.

CAMP BANDERA. Located on the Medina River near the present town of Bandera, this Confederate outpost was first established by a company of 1st Texas Mounted Rifles commanded by Major Edward Burleson.

FORT BANKHEAD. A small Confederate sand battery armed with two 24-pounder siege guns, Fort Bankhead was located near the quarantine station on Galveston Island, west of Fort Point, and intended to protect the obstructions and torpedoes extending across the channel in the bay. The defense was named for Brigadier General S. P. Bankhead.

CAMP BARKELEY. A World War II infantry division training center located in the west central part of the state, nine miles southwest of Abilene, 77,436-acre Camp Barkeley was activated on February 15, 1941. Actual construction had begun on December 17, 1940. One of the state's largest military establishments during the war, it was named in the memory of Private David D. Barkeley, who was killed in the Meuse-Argonne in World War I. The camp was one of the only two in the nation named in honor of enlisted men. The first major military unit to occupy the camp was the 45th Infantry Division, a National Guard organization of troops from Oklahoma, Arizona, New Mexico, and Colorado, commanded

by Major General William S. Key. The post was later used as an armored division training camp. Camp Barkeley became surplus to the Army's needs on March 21, 1945.

CAMP BARNARD BEE. A Confederate encampment located near Columbia on the Brazos River in Brazoria County, this post was established in 1864. On April 30, 1865, it became the headquarters for the Central Sub-district of Texas. In May 1865, it was garrisoned by the 13th Texas Volunteer Infantry.

CAMP BEAUMONT (*Camp Spindletop*). Located in the present city of Beaumont, Jefferson County, on Spindletop Hill near the present intersection of Sulphur Drive and Highland Avenue, this Confederate encampment, also known as Camp Spindletop, was established in 1862 by Colonel A. W. Spaight's 2nd Texas Infantry. In addition to this post, a battery consisting of two 12-pounder howitzers was emplaced on the Neches River, three miles below the town. Camp Beaumont was abandoned sometime in 1864.

CAMP BELKNAP. A Confederate encampment located near Fort Belknap in Young County, Camp Belknap was established on March 17, 1862, by James M. Norris as a Ranger station for the Frontier Regiment. Garrisoned by Captain J. J. Cureton's company of troops, the post engaged in frontier patrol duty until March 1864, when the Frontier Regiment was consolidated at Fort Belknap.

FORT BELKNAP. Originally located on the left (north) bank of the Salt Fork (Red River) of the Brazos River, 10 miles above its junction with the Clear Fork of the Brazos, near the present city of Graham in Young County, Fort Belknap was established on June 24, 1851, by 5th Artillery troops commanded by Captain Carter L. Stevenson, on a site selected by Lieutenant Colonel William G. Belknap, 5th Infantry. The post was intended to guard the emigrant route from Fort Smith, Arkansas, to Santa Fe, and to protect the settlers in the Red River area from hostile Indians.

First named Camp Belknap, the post was officially designated a fort on November 1, 1851. During this same month, its site was moved two miles downriver. It was abandoned on February 23, 1859, because of the insufficiency of good water there, and its garrison transferred to Camp Cooper. During the Civil War, it was occupied by Confederate Texas troops for operations against the Kiowa and Comanche. Fort Belknap was temporarily reoccupied by Army regulars during the late spring and summer of 1867, to be withdrawn for the establishment of Fort Griffin on July 29, 1867. Thereafter, for a brief period, Fort Belknap was occupied as a base of operations against the Indians and to provide escorts for the mail line. It was finally abandoned in September 1867, again for reasons of insufficient good water, to be replaced by Fort Griffin and Fort Richardson.

CAMP BENAVIDES.

A Confederate encampment located on the Rio Grande River below Ringgold Barracks, this post served as a temporary headquarters for Colonel Santos Benavides and elements of the 33rd Texas Cavalry.

FORT BEND.

A pioneer blockhouse on the site of present Richmond, Fort Bend County, the defense was constructed in November 1821 by William Little and others in the big bend of the Brazos River. Its site was selected by Stephen F. Austin and became the nucleus of a settlement established by members of the Old Three Hundred, settlers who were awarded land grants in Austin's first colony. The name of the fort was given to the county when it was created in 1837. When the county was fully organized the following year, Richmond became the county seat and absorbed the Fort Bend settlement.

TEXAS DEFENSES ESTABLISHED 1846–1898.
(*From* Forts of the West: Military Forts and Presidios and Posts Commonly Called Forts West of the Mississippi River to 1898, *by Robert W. Frazer. Copyright 1965, 1972 by the University of Oklahoma Press.*)

CAMP BERLIN.

This Confederate post established in the spring of 1861 and located 10 miles from Brenham, Washington County, served as the principal recruiting and muster station for Germans residing in the area.

FORT (CAMP) BERNARD.

A Confederate defense situated on the east bank at the mouth of the San Bernard River in Brazoria County, it was established probably in late 1863 and mounted two 24-pounder iron smoothbores and two 12-pounder Parrott rifles. The fort, commanded by Major Henry Wilke, was frequently shelled by two Federal gunboats in January and February 1864.

BIRD'S FORT.

Located about three miles east of the present town of Birdsville, northwest of today's city of Dallas, on the main branch of the Trinity River, Bird's Fort was established during the winter of 1841–42 by Captain John (Jonathan) Bird and a 45-man company of Texas Rangers commanded by Captain Alexander W. Webb. Consisting of a stockade mounting a blockhouse and enclosing several cabins, it was designed to both promote settlement in the area and protect it against Indian marauders. Shortly after the post was established, the term of enlistment of the Rangers expired, and they disbanded to return to their homes, leaving the fort unoccupied. A number of families, however, settled there, thus establishing the first permanent settlement on the upper Trinity River.

FORT BLISS (*Post at El Paso; Camp Concordia*).

The various dates and locations of present Fort Bliss and its five predecessors began in 1848 with the establishment of a post at Franklin on Smith's (Coon's) Ranch, now a part of downtown El Paso, in the immediate vicinity of the intersection of Main and Santa Fe streets. On December 27, 1846, Colonel Alexander W. Doniphan and his 1st Missouri Mounted Volunteers rode into Paso del Norte (now Ciudad Juárez, opposite El Paso across the Rio Grande River in Mexico). Doniphan was treated royally by the Mexicans there, although he and his men two days earlier had battled and defeated the Mexican army's Vera Cruz Dragoons some 25 miles to the north. Doniphan stayed only a week, advancing to Chihuahua.

Meanwhile the Mexican War afforded marauding Apache opportunities to raid American and Mexican ranches alike. U.S. troops occupying conquered territory found themselves pursuing Indians throughout the countryside. One such column, a detachment of the 1st Dragoons headed by Major Benjamin Beall, crossed the Hueco Mountains in November of 1847 and camped on Ponce de Leon's Ranch, on what is now the site of El Paso, across the river form old Paso del Norte. No effort was made to set up a permanent garrison, but it could be said that this was the beginning of Fort Bliss. On November 7, 1848, the War Department issued General Orders No. 58, directing the establishment of a post at El Paso. But not until September 1849 did the troops arrive—six companies of the 3rd Regiment of Infantry under command of Brevet Major Jefferson Van Horne. Companies I and K and a howitzer battery were assigned to San Elizario, and companies A, B, C, E, and the Regimental Staff came on to what is now downtown El Paso.

The post was established on the Coon's Ranch, the current site of the Civic Center, and remained there until 1851, when it was abandoned. It was known as the Post of El Paso or, more properly, the Post opposite Paso del Norte, Mexico (renamed Ciudad Juárez in 1888) and it lasted until August 17, 1851. At that time a chain of forts was being established between Santa Fe, New Mexico, and San Antonio, Texas, and the El Paso garrison, except for a handful of men, was transferred to Fort Fillmore, about eight miles southeast of Las Cruces, New Mexico. However, renewed Apache raids prompted reestablishment of the El Paso post. The 8th Infantry moved into Magoffinsville (near present Magoffin and Willow streets) in December 1853, again establishing the Post of El Paso, a name by which the post was known until March 8, 1854, when it was renamed Fort Bliss in honor of William Wallace Smith Bliss, a veteran of the Florida Indian War and the Mexican War, later private secretary to President Zachary Taylor, who died in 1853 at the age of 38. Fort Bliss then became a well-established post, gaining a reputation as a highly desirable station.

On March 31, 1861, all Texas posts, including Fort Bliss, were surrendered to the Confederacy by order of Major General David E.

FORT BLISS. Replica of the old Fort Bliss. (Courtesy of the U.S. Army.)

Twiggs, who shortly thereafter joined the Confederate forces. The post served as headquarters for Confederate campaigns until the California Column—the 1st California (Union) Cavalry under Colonel J. H. Carleton—reached the area on August 20, 1862, and drove out the Confederates, but not until they burned the fort's buildings and emptied the storehouses. Federal forces made no attempt to regarrison the post until the war had ended, when Fort Bliss was reoccupied by the Army's 5th Infantry on October 16, 1865.

By February 1868 the Rio Grande had turned the fort's parade ground into a morass and was eroding the foundation of the barracks. A new site of 300 acres was selected about three miles east of the old post, on the Stephenson Ranch well back from the river, near the present Concordia Cemetery. The name Fort Bliss was

FORT BLISS. The 1917 Auxiliary Cavalry Remount Depot. (Courtesy of the U.S. Army.)

suspended for a time and the designation of Camp Concordia was adopted. Two barracks were built, holding 200 men each, and six adobe quarters for officers were constructed. On March 23, 1869, however, orders were received to restore the name Fort Bliss. The post was abandoned in 1877, by which time general peace reigned over the frontier and the garrison was redistributed in the North where the action was. But within several months, the region around El Paso was once again in turmoil, with renewed Indian raids, widespread cattle rustling by whites, and frequent gunfights.

A Congressional investigation resulted in the Army being ordered to reoccupy El Paso. Elements of the 9th Cavalry and 15th Infantry arrived on January 1, 1878, to find the Concordia post in ruins. Quarters were rented in town, south and east of the original site on Coon's Ranch, using the Public Square (now Jacinto Plaza) as a parade ground. With Concordia useless, a board of officers selected a site for a new Fort Bliss and settled on land at the west edge of town, on a bluff overlooking the Rio Grande, designed to be a permanent location. Fort Bliss was back in business, at the fifth site in its history. Congress and the railroads, however, ruined its promised permanency when Congress gave its approval for the Rio Grande and El Paso Railroad to lay a right of way across the parade grounds. It was time for Fort Bliss to move again.

In March of 1890, the secretary of war was authorized to sell the property on the river and purchase a new site within 10 miles of the city limits, occupying not less than 1,000 acres, and

to build there the necessary buildings and quarters. La Noria Mesa is a rise of land overlooking the valley leading northeast from El Paso, and it was here that the present Fort Bliss was established in a wasteland of sand and cactus.

In October 1893 the post was occupied by the 18th Infantry, and Captain William H. McLaughlin was its first commander. New construction included an administration building, mess hall, two barracks for enlisted men, and a power plant on the east side of the main parade ground, and 14 two-story quarters for officers, 3 two-story quarters for noncommissioned officers, supply buildings, a guardhouse, and a corral on the west side. Most of these buildings are still in use today.

Except for a period of several months during the Spanish-American War, when practically its entire garrison was distributed in the war zones of Cuba and the Philippines, Fort Bliss was continuously in use by the Army. It served throughout the Mexican border disturbances, both World Wars, the Korean War, and the controversial, long-protracted Vietnam conflict. Today one of the major installations in the nation, Fort Bliss serves under its parent headquarters, the U.S. Army Training and Doctrine Command at Fort Monroe, Virginia.

FORT BOGGY. Located on the north bank of Boggy Creek, about two and a half miles north of present Leona and five miles south of Centerville in Leon County, Fort Boggy was a two-story blockhouse erected in 1840 by a company of minutemen known as the Boggy and Trinity Rangers under Captain Thomas N. B. Greer. Serving as headquarters for the quasi-military force, the fort afforded protection for the first settlements on the Leon Prairie. The community that grew up around the fort retained the name long after the blockhouse was abandoned. In 1936 the Texas Centennial Commission erected a commemorative marker on the site.

CAMP BOSQUE. A Confederate encampment located seven miles from Waco in McLennan County, and established in the early summer of 1861 by Colonel William H. Parson, Camp Bosque served as a "Camp of Military Instruction" for recruits from surrounding counties.

CAMP BOVEDA. A Federal campsite located on Los Olmos Creek two miles east of Riviera in Kleberg County, Camp Boveda was first established by General Zachary Taylor during the Mexican War. In December 1863 it was the temporary headquarters for Major General N. J. T.

FORT BLISS. Signpost at today's fort. (Courtesy of the U.S. Army.)

Dana's 13th U.S. Army Corps. The Union troops engaged in intercepting Confederate cotton-laden wagon trains bound for the Mexican port at Bagdad across the Rio Grande River.

CAMP BOWIE. There were two U.S. Army camps named in honor of Texas patriot James Bowie, who was killed in the defense of the Alamo. The first was established in September 1917 three miles from Fort Worth during World War I and abandoned in December 1919. The second Camp Bowie, established at Brownwood in September 1940, was the first World War II major defense construction project in the state. Both posts were established as training centers for the Texas National Guard's 36th Division.

An infantry and artillery training center, the Brownwood camp was first occupied at the end of December 1940 by the 36th Division's 111th Quartermaster Regiment, commanded by Major General Claude V. Birkhead. As Camp Bowie expanded from an original 2,000 acres to a 120,000-acre reservation by October 1942, it was occupied, in addition to the 36th Division, by the Iowa National Guard's 113th Cavalry, the VIII Army Corps and Headquarters, troops of the Third Army under General Walter Krueger, and various units of the Medical Service, Field Artillery, Armored Division, and a WAC contingent. In August 1943 a prisoner of war camp large enough to accommodate 3,000 prisoners was established on the post. Camp Bowie was declared surplus by a War Department directive, effective August 31, 1946, and permanently abandoned September 30, 1946.

CAMP BRECKENRIDGE. Located on the site of the present city of Breckenridge, Stephens County, this Confederate post was a Frontier Regiment Ranger station established on March 21, 1862, by Colonel James M. Norris. It was abandoned probably in March 1864, when the Frontier Regiment was consolidated at Fort Belknap.

CAMP BRENHAM (*Camp Randle; Woodward's Spring Camp*). Located about three miles southeast of Brenham, Washington County, this Confederate encampment (also known as Camp Randle and Woodward's Spring Camp) was a rendezvous for troops designated for service at posts along the Texas coast.

FORT BROWN (*Fort Taylor; Brownsville Barracks*). Located at present Brownsville in Cameron County, on the left bank of the Rio Grande, opposite the Mexican city of Matamoras, Fort Brown was established on March 28, 1846,

by Colonel Zachary Taylor, 6th Infantry, just prior to the outbreak of war with Mexico, and built under the supervision of Captain Joseph K. F. Mansfield, Corps of Engineers. A strong bastioned work adequate to garrison 500 men was laid out and a battery of four 18-pounders, bearing directly on Matamoras, was immediately emplaced. Originally called Fort Taylor, its name was changed to Fort Brown in honor of Major Jacob Brown, 7th Infantry, commander of the fort, who died on May 9, 1846, after he was mortally wounded during the Mexican bombardment. In 1848 Brownsville Barracks was established adjacent to the fort.

Evacuation of Fort Brown started on March 9 and was completed on March 20, 1861, upon orders of Brigadier General David E. Twiggs, who surrendered all the posts in Texas to the Confederacy. It was occupied by Confederate troops until November 6, 1863, when it was evacuated before advancing Federal forces and burned. The town of Brownsville was occupied by Union troops the following day, but it was recaptured by the Confederates on July 30, 1864, and occupied by them until the end of the war. Following the Civil War, Brownsville was again occupied by U.S. troops in the summer of 1865, at which time temporary huts were erected within the city limits and occupied for the subsequent two years. In the spring of 1867, when plans had been approved for permanent quarters on the site of the old fort, construction was begun on new buildings. The town was soon struck by a severe hurricane, demolishing all the buildings occupied by the troops as well as those under construction. During the years 1868–69, while the troops were quartered in the town, new barracks were erected on the site of those destroyed.

On April 26, 1895, the site occupied by Fort Brown was purchased by the government. Because there had been some conflict between the garrison and the citizens of Brownsville, resulting in some bloodshed, the post was evacuated in 1906, and the military reservation was transferred to the Department of Agriculture. The fort was reoccupied on February 26, 1913, during the border troubles with Mexico. Thereafter, occupation of Fort Brown was continuous. It was declared surplus on March 5, 1946. On July 22, 1948, the front 162 acres of the post were deeded to the city of Brownsville.

BROWN'S FORT. Located on San Pedro Creek, near present Grapeland, Houston County, Brown's Fort was built in late 1834 by the Brown family, who migrated to Texas from Illinois earlier the same year. They were members of Rev. Daniel

Parker's Pilgrim Church party, some of whom trekked farther into Indian country to establish Parker's Fort in present Limestone County. In May 1836 a number of the survivors of the murderous attack by Comanche and Kiowa against Parker's Fort found a haven at Brown's Fort and built new homes in its environs.

BROWNSVILLE BARRACKS. FORT BROWN.

CAMP BUCHEL. CAMP CEDAR BAYOU.

CAMP BUCHEL (*Camp Wharton*). This Confederate encampment, also known as Camp Wharton, was established in 1862 near the town of Wharton by Captain Edmund P. Turner, Major General John M. Magruder's aide, and named for Colonel August Buchel.

CAMP BUGLE. CAMP DRUM.

CAMP BULLIS. Located northwest of San Antonio on the Leon Springs Military Reservation and named for John Lapham Bullis, this subpost of Fort Sam Houston was established in 1917 as a target range and maneuver ground for Fort Sam Houston and Camp Travis. Never a permanent installation, it was used as a training area for both regular Army and Texas National Guard troops. In 1922 Camp Bullis was consolidated with Fort Sam Houston. The 2nd, 88th, and 95th Infantry Divisions made extensive use of the post during World War II. Since the war Camp Bullis was used extensively by Reserve Component personnel from all the services as well as federal law enforcement personnel as well as civil law enforcement agencies. The Texas National Guard maintains an armory on the post.

CAMP BURLESON. An encampment for 1st Infantry Regiment troops occupied during the spring and summer of 1839, it was named for Colonel Edward Burleson, then commander of the 1st Infantry. The post was located near present Bastrop, west of the Colorado River, a few miles downstream from the town.

FORT BURLESON (*Fort Milam*). Established on August 26, 1838, at the falls of the Brazos River in Falls County, Fort Burleson (also known as Fort Milam) was a temporary Indian defense named for Colonel Edward Burleson, later a U.S. senator, who died at Austin in 1851.

CAMP CABELL. A temporary Spanish-American training facility located at Dallas and occupied for a time by the 2nd Texas Volunteer Infantry,

Camp Cabell was named in honor of Confederate General Ben E. Cabell.

FORT CANEY. Three fortified Confederate posts located on the east bank of the mouth of Caney Creek and a gun battery situated on its opposite bank in Matagorda County were completed by March 16, 1864. All four works were referred to as Fort Caney. In April they were renamed or designated for either prominent military men or residents in the area. Fort Ashbel Smith was named for the colonel commanding the west bank, batteries on the east flank were named Fort Hawkins, in honor of a prominent planter in the San Bernard River area, and Fort Rugely, for Captain E. S. Rugely of Matagorda. The sand battery near the Gulf was named Fort Sandcliffe in honor of the engineer that superintended the construction of the works at this site. The garrisons had been constructed under attack from Federal vessels, with much of the construction taking place under cover of night. Their ordnance consisted of one 30-pounder rifled Parrott and four 32-pounder smoothbores. The troops stationed at the posts consisted of elements of the 4th and 15th Texas State Regiments.

CAMP CARTER. CAMP HEBÉRT.

CAMP CASA BLANCA. CAMP MERRILL.

CASTOLON ARMY DEPOT (*Camp Santa [Elena] Helena*). Established in 1903 and discontinued in 1911, the Castolon Army Depot, also known as Camp Santa (Elena) Helena, was located on the Rio Grande River in the Big Bend National Park, Brewster County. Adobe buildings still remain to this day on the site of the pre-World War I border post.

CAMP CAZNEAU. A 1st Infantry Regiment encampment occupied on March 5, 1840, as well as for an undetermined period before and after that date, Camp Cazneau was named for William Leslie Cazneau, then commissary general of the Republic of Texas and located on Onion Creek near Austin, in the environs of the present Bergstrom Air Force Base.

CAMP CEDAR BAYOU (*Camp Buchel*). A Confederate encampment located on Cedar Bayou (Cedar Lake Creek), which spans the boundary of Brazoria and Matagorda counties, and established in December 1863, the post garrisoned by 1,273 troops was also known as Camp

Buchel for Colonel August Buchel, then the commanding officer in the area.

FORT CHADBOURNE. Located on the east side of Oak Creek, about 30 miles above its junction with the Colorado River, and four miles northeast of the present town of Fort Chadbourne in northeastern Coke County, Fort Chadbourne was established on October 28, 1852, by Captain John Beardsley, 8th Infantry. Intended to guard the emigrant travel route from Fort Smith, Arkansas, to Santa Fe, it was named in the memory of 2nd Lieutenant Theodore L. Chadbourne, 8th Infantry, killed on May 9, 1846, in the Battle of Resaca de la Palma during the Mexican War. The post was surrendered to the Confederacy on March 23, 1861, in compliance with an order of Brigadier General David E. Twiggs. Fort Chadbourne was reoccupied by U.S. troops on May 25, 1867, renovated and somewhat rebuilt. Although abandoned on December 18, 1867, because its water supply failed, it was used for about a year thereafter as a picket post intermittently garrisoned by Fort Concho troops. There are a number of the post's buildings remaining today, either in use or in ruins, on private ranch property.

CAMP CHAMBERS. A Republic of Texas troop encampment located on the west bank of Arenosa Creek, the eastern boundary of Victoria County, near the present-day town of Inez, Camp Chambers was occupied by the Texas Army, then commanded by Colonel Edwin Morehouse, from August to possibly early November 1837. It was named in tribute to Major General Thomas Jefferson Chambers, "who had recruited several hundred volunteers for the Army in the United States." The general was assassinated at Anahuac on March 15, 1865.

CAMP CHAMBERS. An intermittently occupied Texas Army encampment established in May or June 1840 and located on the east side of the Brazos River, west of present-day Marlin in Falls County, Camp Chambers was most probably named for Major General Thomas Jefferson Chambers. The post was abandoned sometime in late February or early March of 1841.

CAMP CHEMICAL. A World War II post established in December 1941, almost immediately after the attack on Pearl Harbor, Camp Chemical was located on the grounds of Dow Chemical's Plant A at Freeport on the Gulf of Mexico in order to protect the industrial facility from sabotage by land or submarine attack from the sea.

Within three days, a company of 150 men of the 36th Division of the Texas National Guard, which had already gone into the regular army, set up camp beside Plant A. Dow provided barracks. In rapid succession, a company of regular infantry joined them and a group of Coast Artillery installed two six-inch naval guns on the beach at Quintana and overlooking the harbor. Two look-out towers about fifty feet tall went up, one near the place where the Old Surfside Hotel once stood and the other near the Boilers toward San Luis Pass. A company of men with seven anti-aircraft guns were posted around Plant A and the construction work at Plant B. Also, a mounted beach patrol of the U.S. Coast Guard with police dogs were sent to the beaches. [James A. Creighton, *A Narrative History of Brazoria County*, p. 364]

On December 11th, at the War Department, Dow Chemical's Plant B was planned and the company was asked to have it in operation within six months. In 1942 Camp Chemical became a combined industrial-military complex, with row upon row of barracks constructed to house both hundreds of civilian workers and the Army and Navy personnel. After the war, Dow Chemical's officials feared that Camp Chemical would become a slum area and permission from the government was secured to raze it. The result was that "people came from all over the country, carrying the old community off piece by piece at a price."

FORT CIBOLO. Located on Cibolo Creek, a few miles northwest of Shafter, Presidio County, in the Big Bend country of the state, Fort Cibolo, built in 1857, was one of three quadrangular adobe forts erected during the late 1850s by affluent rancher Meliton Faver as defenses against the Apache Indians. Fort Cibolo's walls were three to four feet thick, spaced with gun emplacements, and mounted circular watchtowers at two of its angles. The defense was often garrisoned by troop detachments in transit between Fort Davis and Fort Leaton, the latter a trading post near Presidio on the Rio Grande. Fort Cibolo is presently in use as a ranch bunkhouse and storeroom. (See also: FORT CIENAGA and FORT MORITAS).

FORT CIENAGA. A quadrangular adobe fort located at Cienaga Springs, near Shafter in Presidio County, it was one of three such defenses built by cattle baron Meliton Faver, who became wealthy selling beef to the government for consumption by the Army and the Indians. The fort, like Fort Cibolo, was no doubt occasionally used by Army detachments. (See also: FORT CIBOLO and FORT MORITAS.)

CAMP CLARK. A Confederate encampment located on the south side of the San Marcos River, near the city of San Marcos in Guadalupe County, Camp Clark was one of the instruction camps established by Governor Edward Clark in 1861. The 4th Texas Infantry Regiment was mobilized there, and several companies were organized and trained at the camp for several months before being assigned to active duty. In 1862 Camp Clark served as a training facility for the 36th Texas Cavalry Regiment. This regiment, called the 32nd Texas Cavalry by its troops, served in the Red River campaign of 1864.

FORT CLARK (*Fort Riley*). Located at the head of Las Moras Creek opposite the town of Brackettville in Kinney County and established on June 20, 1852, Fort Clark was intended to safeguard the San Antonio–El Paso travel route. First named Fort Riley for the 1st Infantry's commanding officer, it was officially designated Fort Clark on July 16, 1852, in honor of Major John B. Clark, 1st Infantry, who died on August 23, 1847, during the War with Mexico. Surrendered, along with other Texas posts, to the Confederacy on March 19, 1861, in compliance with the order of Brigadier General David E. Twiggs, it was briefly occupied by Confederate troops. Fort Clark was regarrisoned by U.S. troops under Captain John A. Wilcox, 4th Cavalry, on December 10, 1866. It was thereafter continued as a permanent military post until inactivated in 1946.

POST ON THE CLEAR FORK OF THE BRAZOS. FORT PHANTOM HILL.

COFFEE'S FORT. An important fortified trading post built by Holland Coffee and Silas Colville in late 1836 or early 1837 on the Red River at present-day Preston in northern Grayson County, Coffee's Fort frequently supplied quartermaster officers at Texas Army posts and troop detachments operating in the area. The site now lies beneath Lake Texoma.

FORT COLEMAN. FORT COLORADO.

CAMP COLLIER. A Confederate encampment located at Vaughn's Springs on Clear Creek in Brown County, it was established by Colonel James M. Norris on March 23, 1862, as a ranger post for the Frontier Regiment (46th Texas Cavalry). It was garrisoned until the regiment's consolidation at Fort Belknap in March 1864.

CAMP COLORADO. Established on August 2, 1856, and first located on Mulewater Creek, six miles north of the Colorado River, on the travel route between Fort Belknap and Fort Mason, in Coleman County, Camp Colorado was intended to protect the frontier's settlers from Indian hostiles. In July 1857, because the site had become infested by mosquitoes and turned malarial, the post was moved to a new site on Jim Ned Creek, about 22 miles to the north. On February 26, 1865, the post was abandoned by Federal troops and taken over by Texas State troops, which occupied it until the end of the Civil War. Camp Colorado, however, was not regarrisoned by U.S. troops after its evacuation by its Confederate occupants.

FORT COLORADO (*Fort Coleman*). A Texas Ranger post, alternately known as both Fort Coleman and Fort Colorado, located on Walnut Creek, a confluence of the Colorado River, about seven miles east of Austin, and established in June 1836 by Colonel Robert M. Coleman who was a participant in the Battle of San Jacinto, it was intended as an Indian defense. Colonel Coleman died by drowning in the Brazos River at Velasco on July 1, 1837. The fort consisted of a complex of log-built cabins enclosed by a strong palisade mounting blockhouses at two diagonal angles. The fort was abandoned in November 1838.

CAMP COMSTOCK. One of a number of Mexican border patrol posts along the Rio Grande River to combat Mexican raids against the settlements in lower Texas, Camp Comstock was established in 1914 and located at the town of Comstock in Val Verde County. It was abandoned in 1917 at the beginning of United States participation in World War I.

FORT CONCHO (*Camp Hatch; Camp Kelly*). Located at the junction of the Concho and North Concho rivers at present San Angelo in Tom Green County, and established on December 4, 1867, by elements of the 4th Cavalry under Captain George P. Hunt from Fort Chadbourne, the post was designed to protect settlers in West Texas from the hostile Apaches. First called Camp Hatch in honor of Major John P. Hatch, it was renamed Camp Kelly in January 1868 in honor of Captain Michael J. Kelly. The name was again changed in March 1868 to Fort Concho. On June 20, 1889, it was abandoned, and the military reservation passed into private ownership. In 1929 the old administration building was acquired and renovated to house the West Texas Museum, now the fort Concho Museum.

CAMP CONCORDIA. FORT BLISS.

CAMP COOPER. Established on January 3, 1856, and located on the north bank of the Clear Fork of the Brazos, five miles east of the mouth of Otey's Creek on the newly established Comanche Indian Reservation, Camp Cooper was designed to both safeguard the El Paso–Red River travel route from hostile Comanche and to control the reservation Indians. Established by Colonel Albert Sidney Johnson, the post was first garrisoned by three companies of cavalry commanded by Major William J. Hardee, 2nd Cavalry. The post was surrendered to the Confederacy's Texas troops on February 21, 1861, in accordance with an order of Brigadier General David E. Twiggs. After the war, the post was not regarrisoned by Federal troops.

CAMP CORPUS CHRISTI. FORT MARCY.

CAMP CRAWFORD. FORT MCINTOSH.

FORT CROCKETT (*Camp Hawley*). A Confederate Galveston Island defense and Coast Artillery training base named in honor of David Crockett, the Alamo hero, Fort Crockett was located at the western end of the island's seawall. Fort San Jacinto guarded the eastern end of the island, while Fort Travis protected Galveston Bay. Constructed in 1897, Fort Crockett was first garrisoned by Battery G, 1st Artillery. According to records in the National Archives, a part of the reservation was occupied by the 1st Volunteer Infantry (Texas Immunes) at Camp Hawley in July 1898. On September 8, 1900, a vicious storm hit Galveston Island and largely destroyed most of the fort's buildings. The fort was not garrisoned again until 1911, when it became a mobilization center during the border troubles with Mexico.

During World War I, two U.S. Marine regiments were quartered at Fort Crockett and trained for heavy artillery. When the Coast Artillery was reorganized in 1926, the fort became the home of the 69th Coast Artillery (anti-aircraft) and was occupied by the 13th Coast Artillery. On April 10, 1942, the fort became headquarters for a part of the Gulf Sector, Southern Coastal Frontier. Engineers, Ordnance, and Signal Corps units operated at the fort during the remainder of World War II. Fort Crockett was declared surplus to the needs of the Army and transferred to the General Services Administration in September 1953. Four years later, part of the reservation was put up for auction, and the city of Galveston purchased a portion for recreation use. The site of the fort is located on Seawall Boulevard in Galveston.

CAMP CROGHAN. FORT CROGHAN.

FORT CROGHAN (*Post on Hamilton Creek; Camp Croghan; Camp Hamilton*). Located on the right (north) bank of Hamilton Creek, about 10 miles above its junction with the Colorado River, at the present-day town of Burnet, Fort Croghan was established as Post on Hamilton Creek on March 18, 1849, by Brevet 2nd Lieutenant Charles H. Tyler, 2nd Dragoons. After the post was moved on October 12 to a new location about three and a half miles above the first site, it was named Camp Croghan for Colonel George Croghan, inspector general of the Army. Shortly thereafter, it was renamed Camp Hamilton for the creek. Finally, in 1850, it was officially designated Fort Croghan. The post was abandoned in December 1853. Fort Croghan's parade ground and several of the post's log buildings are preserved in a Burnet city park.

CAMP CRUMP. A Confederate encampment located near Jefferson, Marion County, and named for Colonel Philip Crump, 3rd Texas Lancers (Cavalry), Camp Crump was occupied during the entire summer of 1862 by the cavalry regiment.

CAMP CURETON. A Confederate Frontier Regiment encampment located in Archer County at the Gainesville–Fort Belknap road crossing of the West Fork of the Trinity River, Camp Cureton was established on March 17, 1862, and garrisoned by elements of Captain J. J. Cureton's force. The post was active until about March 1864, when the Frontier Regiment was concentrated at Fort Belknap.

CAMP CUSHING. A World War II facility located adjacent to Fort Sam Houston at San Antonio, Camp Cushing was named for Colonel Edward B. Cushing, who served with the U.S. Engineers in World War I.

FORT D. A. RUSSELL (*Camp Marfa*). Located on a plateau overlooking the town of Marfa, Presidio County, and originally established in 1914 as Camp Marfa, headquarters for the Big Bend District which included eight border patrol outposts along the Rio Grande, the post's name was officially changed to Fort D. A. Russell in honor of David Ashley Russell, distinguished veteran of the Mexican War. During World War II, the post was significantly enlarged. In November 1943 a German prisoner of war camp was established on the post. Fort D. A. Russell was declared inactive in December 1945, and in 1949 the military reservation property passed into private ownership.

DALLAS ENCAMPMENT. Located on the Fair Grounds, about three miles southeast of Dallas, this substantial Confederate complex was established in late 1861 and consisted of several separate campsites, each named for the respective company commanders. The encampment was apparently active during the winter and spring of 1862.

POST AT DAVID'S LANDING. FORT RINGGOLD.

FORT DAVIS. By 1854 depredations by the Apache and Comanche had grown to such alarming proportions that the military authorities in San Antonio found it essential to build a fort in West Texas to protect the El Paso–San Antonio road and to control the Indians. In October 1854 the commander of the Department of Texas, Major General Persifor F. Smith, personally selected the site, a box canyon near Limpia Creek in the Limpia (Davis) Mountains, north of the present town of Fort Davis in Jeff Davis County. The new post was named Fort Davis by the general in honor of Jefferson Davis, then secretary of war and later president of the Southern Confederacy. Lieutenant Colonel Washington Seawall, 8th Infantry, occupied the site on October 7, 1854, and two weeks later began construction of what eventuated as a shabby collection

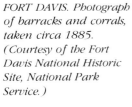

FORT DAVIS. Photograph of barracks and corrals, taken circa 1885. (Courtesy of the Fort Davis National Historic Site, National Park Service.)

of more than 60 pine-slab structures scattered irregularly up the canyon and not built to last. The post was evacuated on April 13, 1861, by order of Brigadier General David E. Twiggs. Garrisoned by Confederate troops for less than a year, the fort was then intermittently occupied by bands of Indians and Mexicans who more or less deliberately destroyed the post. Fort Davis was reoccupied on July 1, 1867, by Federal troops commanded by Lieutenant Colonel Wesley Merritt, 9th Cavalry, who completely rebuilt it on the plain outside the canyon. The first buildings were of stone, but economy caused a change to adobe. Not until the 1880s, after the Indians had been subdued, were all the buildings completed. By then it was a major installation, with quarters for 12 troops or companies, both cavalry and infantry. More than 50 structures finally composed Fort Davis. The post was abandoned on June 30, 1891, after military consideration decided it was no longer necessary. In 1961, by an act of Congress following acquisition of the military reservation from private ownership, Fort Davis became a National Historic Site, administered by the National Park Service.

FORT DEBRAY. FORT ESPERANZA.

FORT DEFIANCE. FORT GOLIAD.

CAMP DEL RIO (*Post of San Felipe; Camp San Felipe*). This site on san Felipe Creek near Del Rio in Val Verde County was first occupied in about 1857 for overnight camps and for years afterward because of its location and availability of water. Confederate troops intermittently used

the campsite throughout the Civil War. The first regular Army camp there was established on September 6, 1876, by Company E, 10th Cavalry, and called Post of San Felipe or Camp San Felipe, then an outpost of Fort Clark, for the protection of the Rio Grande frontier. The name of the post was changed to Camp Del Rio on or about March 31, 1881. It was garrisoned until May 8, 1891, when the troops were withdrawn and transferred to Fort Clark. The post was reoccupied in 1914 and again discontinued in 1922.

CAMP DIX. A Confederate outpost located at Black Waterhole, where the Sabinal-Uvalde Road crossed the Frio River in Uvalde County, Camp Dix was established on April 4, 1862, by James M. Norris of the Frontier Regiment, and Rangers under Captain J. J. Dix garrisoned the post. It was active until the consolidation of the regiment at Fort Belknap in March 1864.

CAMP DRUM (*Camp Bugle*). Located at Zapata on the Rio Grande, about 50 miles south of Laredo, this Army post was established in 1851 and abandoned in 1852. The most intriguing point in its short history concerned the post's designation. C. H. Tyler of the 2nd Dragoons arrived soon after its establishment with orders to establish a camp and call it Camp Bugle. He found another officer of the 4th Artillery already on the site, however, who had secured an order from another authority to use the name Camp Drum. The post's abandonment may have been prompted by the local friction.

FORT DUNCAN (*Rio Grande Station; Camp Eagle Pass*). Located on the left (east) bank of the Rio Grande at Eagle Pass in Maverick County, Fort Duncan was first established as Rio Grande Station on March 27, 1849, by Captain Sidney Burbank, 1st Infantry. When its first permanent buildings were erected in 1850 on leased property, the post was renamed for Colonel James Duncan of the Inspector General's Department. Evacuated by Federal troops on March 20, 1861, in compliance with an order of Brigadier General David E. Twiggs, it was garrisoned during part of the Civil War by Confederate cavalry troops. Fort Duncan was reoccupied by Federal troops on March 23, 1868, but mainly because of protracted disagreements between the government and the owners of the property regarding its purchase price, the post was abandoned on August 31, 1883.

Disturbances along the border, growing out of smuggling and horse and cattle rustling, became so frequent that Fort Clark's commanding officer was directed in March 1886 to send one company of infantry to establish a camp at Eagle Pass, on the site of old Fort Duncan. On April 7, 1886, Headquarters Department of Texas directed that the new post should be referred to as the Camp at Eagle Pass, or Camp Eagle Pass, and not as Fort Duncan. On February 10, 1893, it became an independent post, but these orders were revoked on June 9, 1894, and it again was made a subpost of Fort Clark. The post continued to be principally concerned with the maintenance of law and order along the border until after the outbreak of World War I when its importance was emphasized by the possibility of a

FORT DAVIS. A closer view of the barracks, taken circa 1885.

German attack in the vicinity. After the war, the need for border outposts diminished, and the post was discontinued about February 1927.

FORT EAGLE GROVE. FORT MOORE.

CAMP EAGLE PASS. FORT DUNCAN.

CAMP EDWARD CLARK. A temporary Confederate encampment established in May 1861 on San Antonio's Alamo Plaza, this post became Colonel Earl Van Dorn's headquarters.

EL FORTIN. FORT LEATON.

FORT EL MORITO. FORT MORITAS.

POST AT EL PASO. FORT BLISS.

FORT ELLIOTT (*Cantonment North Fork of the Red River; Cantonment on the Sweetwater*). This post in the Texas Panhandle was known as Cantonment North Fork of the Red River when it was established on February 3, 1875, in its original location. On June 5, 1875, however, it was relocated farther north near the headwaters of Sweetwater Creek, a confluent, near the present town of Mobeetie (formerly Hidetown) in Wheeler County, and established by Major Henry Cary Bankhead, 4th Cavalry, in compliance with General William Tecumseh Sherman's orders. The post was designed to contain the Indians on their respective reservations. First called Cantonment on the Sweetwater, it was officially designated Fort Elliott on February 21, 1876, in honor of Major Joel H. Elliott, 7th Cavalry, who was killed in action on the Washita River, Indian Territory, on November 27, 1868. For part of the time, the post was garrisoned by three companies of Negro troops and five companies of white cavalry, usually aggregating less than 500 men. Fort Elliott was abandoned on October 1, 1890, its last garrison evacuating the post three weeks later. The military reservation was transferred to the Interior Department on October 14, 1890. The post's buildings were sold at public auction on March 20, 1900.

FORT ESPERANZA (*Fort Debray*). Fort Esperanza was a Confederate defense located at Saluria on the northeastern tip of Matagorda Island in Calhoun County. It was built in early 1863 by slave labor under the direction of Caleb G. Forshey. Despite its official Confederate designation as Fort Esperanza, it was referred to as Fort Debray on several maps by Lieutenant Colonel Felix Blucher in honor of Colonel (later Brigadier General) Xavier Blanchard Debray, a French soldier and diplomat who emigrated to Texas in 1852. The fort was defended by a battalion of artillery until November 29, 1863, when its Confederate garrison retreated to the mainland before Federal forces moving up the island under General Nathaniel P. Banks.

FORT EWELL. Located on the right (south) bank of the Nueces River where the heavily traveled San Antonio–Laredo road crossed the river, in present southern La Salle County, about 25 miles southeast of Cotulla, adobe-built Fort Ewell was established on May 18, 1852, by Lieutenant Colonel William W. Loring, Mounted Riflemen, and named for Captain Richard S. Ewell, 1st Dragoons, a veteran of the Mexican War and later a lieutenant general in the Confederate forces. The post was abandoned on October 3, 1854. Its site was reportedly occupied as a Confederate headquarters during the Civil War for Colonel John S. Ford in February 1864, who used the encampment as depot for supplies and a staging area for troops.

CAMP FANNIN. A World War II infantry replacement and basic training center, Camp Fannin was located 10 miles northeast of Tyler in Smith County, and named for James Walker Fannin, Jr. Construction was begun on the 14,000-acre wooded, hilly site on December 1, 1943, with Colonel John A. Robenson assuming command on March 16, 1943. The first trainees arrived in June and the formal dedication of the camp was held on September 6, 1943. Troop capacity at the height of war operations was 18,680. All except the cantonment was declared surplus on January 19, 1946.

FORT FISHER. A temporary Republic of Texas Ranger defense was erected in the spring of 1837 at the Waco Indian village on the Brazos River, on the site of the present city of Waco. It was named for William S. Fisher, the Republic's secretary of war. The post was most probably abandoned in the early summer of the same year. Its site, near today's Baylor University in Waco, is occupied by a reconstruction of the fort on the banks of the river, completed in 1968, and houses the Colonel Homer Garrison Museum. The Texas Ranger Hall of Fame, located nearby, was dedicated on February 7, 1976.

FORT FITZHUGH. The first settlement in present Cooke County, Fort Fitzhugh was built about 1847 approximately three miles southeast of today's Gainesville. It has not been determined whether the troops who constructed and garrisoned the defense were United States militiamen or Texas Rangers. However, there is no doubt the garrison was commanded by William Fitzhugh, who later became a colonel in the Confederate Army. National Archives records do not indicate how long the fort operated. It was reportedly used as a Ranger post prior to the Civil War and served as a mustering center for troops from communities in the county soon after the war broke out.

CAMP FORD. A Confederate prison located near Tyler, Smith County, Camp Ford held both Union Army officers and enlisted men from 1863 until the end of the Civil War. Reportedly the largest prisoner of war compound west of the Mississippi, the stockade contained some 6,000 Union troops at its zenith in the spring of 1864.

CAMP FUNSTON. CAMP STANLEY.

POST OF GALVESTON (*Galveston Barracks*). The military history of the Post of Galveston, unofficially known as Galveston Barracks, began in 1861, when the state of Texas and the Confederates made the city of Galveston a center of mobilization and commenced the construction of extensive coastal fortifications. On October 8, 1862, the city was occupied by U.S. naval forces after it had been abandoned by the Confederates. On December 25, 1862, companies D, G, and I, 42nd Massachusetts Infantry, landed at Galveston. On January 1, 1863, Confederate troops recaptured the island of Galveston. On June 5, 1865, the 114th Ohio Infantry landed at Galveston and was followed on June 18, 1865, by the Headquarters of the 3rd Brigade, 2nd Division, 13th Army Corps. General Orders, dated April 19, 1870, ordered the abandonment of the Post of Galveston by Company G of the 11th Infantry.

GALVESTON BARRACKS (*Post of Galveston*).

FORT GATES. Located on the left (north) bank of the Leon River, about six miles southeast of the present town of Gatesville in Coryell County, Fort Gates was established on October 26, 1849, and named in honor of Captain (Brevet Major) Collinson Reed Gates, 8th Infantry, distinguished veteran of the Mexican War, who died on June 28, 1849. The post's barracks was an unorthodox octagonal-shaped, single-story structure that boasted a fireplace at each of its eight sides. Fort Gates was abandoned in March 1852.

FORT GOLIAD (*Presidio La Bahia; Fort Defiance*). In early February 1836, the old Spanish presidial town of Goliad (1749) on the west bank of the San Antonio River was occupied by Colonel James W. Fannin and a band of Texas recruits to renovate and strengthen Presidio La Bahia in preparation for the Mexican invasion. Naming it Fort Defiance, the colonel's improvements consisted in constructing blockhouses, palisades, ditching, and mounting artillery necessary for its defense.

On May 31, 1836, General Thomas J. Rusk's Texas Army of about 300 men, while in pursuit of Mexican forces, camped in the environs of the presidio, near which the infamous Goliad Massacre had taken place nine weeks earlier. They collected the remains of some 330 Texas prisoners after suffering defeat in the Battle of Persido, held a military funeral, and buried the bodies. Colonel Sidney Sherman and perhaps two companies of cavalry were left in the town to establish a headquarters post in the old presidio, which he called Fort Goliad rather than Fort Defiance, Colonel Fannin's name for it. After a short occupation at this time, the town was not used again by sizable military forces except as an assembly point for volunteers in the area and an overnight campsite for transient military detachments.

FORT GRAHAM. Located on the site of the old Anadarko Indian village of José María, about a mile from the east bank of the Brazos River, some 14 miles west of the present town of Hillsboro in Hill County, Fort Graham was established on March 27, 1849, by Captain Ripley A. Arnold, 2nd Dragoons, in compliance with an order of Colonel William S. Harney. The post was no doubt named in honor of Lieutenant William M. Graham, 11th Infantry, who was killed on September 8, 1847, in the Battle of Molino del Rey. Fort Graham was abandoned on October 6, 1853. The post's stone-and-log-built barracks, completely renovated, now serves as a recreation clubhouse for the Fort Graham Hunting and Fishing Club on the northeastern bank of Lake Whitney.

FORT GREEN. An important headquarters post for a number of Confederate Army units in 1864, Fort Green was located at the tip of Bolivar Peninsula in Chambers County, on the channel leading into Galveston's harbor.

CAMP GRIERSON. Located eight miles southwest of the town of Best, Reagan County, Camp Grierson (also known as Grierson's Springs) was established near an ever-flowing spring at the head of Live Oak Creek. Because of its water availability, the Chichester Stage Line from Fort Concho to Fort Stockton was routed through it. Colonel Benjamin Grierson established his fortified post here, consisting of a large stone building, a guardhouse, stables, and a corral, and it was occupied by Army details from 1878 to 1880.

FORT GRIFFIN. LITTLE RIVER FORT.

FORT GRIFFIN. FORT SABINE.

FORT GRIFFIN (*Camp Wilson*). Located about half a mile from the right bank of the Clear Fork of the Brazos River in present Shackelford County, about 25 miles north of Albany, Fort Griffin was established on July 29, 1867, by Lieutenant Colonel Samuel D. Sturgis, 6th Cavalry, to replace Fort Belknap. An important supply post for buffalo hunters, the substantially garrisoned post was designed to safeguard the cattle trails and protect the settlers in the area. First called Camp Wilson for 2nd Lieutenant Henry Hamilton Wilson, 6th Cavalry, who died on December 24, 1866, it was officially designated Fort Griffin on February 6, 1868, in honor of Colonel Charles Griffin, 35th Infantry, commanding the department, who died on September 15, 1867. Fort Griffin was abandoned on May 31, 1881. Its site is now contained within a 520-acre state park.

FORT GRIGSBY. A Confederate defense built in October 1862, Fort Grigsby was located on the Neches River seven miles above its mouth, not far from the present Port Neches Park, in Jefferson County. Situated on a ridge known as Grigsby's Bluff, it was constructed of oyster shell and mud, bulkheaded with heavy timbers, and defended by two 24-pounder smoothbores, supported by a magazine and bombproof.

CAMP GROCE (*Camp Liendo*). Probably established in 1862, about three miles east of Hempstead in Waller County, Camp Groce was a Confederate prisoner of war compound situated on the Liendo Plantation and named for its owner, Colonel Leonard W. Groce. A complex of four barracks guarded by 60 to 80 militia, it probably never held more than 200 to 300 Federal prisoners. By August 1, 1865, five companies of the 99th Illinois Regiment occupied Hempstead. The troops were quartered at Camp Groce, under the command of Major General George A. Custer.

CAMP HAMILTON. FORT CROGHAN.

POST ON HAMILTON CREEK. FORT CROGHAN.

FORT HANCOCK (*Camp Rice*). Occupying three different sites, this U.S. Army post was first established as Camp Rice on April 15, 1881, six miles northwest of abandoned Fort Quitman, by 1st Lieutenant S. L. Woodward and Company K, 10th Cavalry. Originally a subpost of Fort Davis, it was designed to prevent incursions by Indian hostiles from across the Rio Grande. This site was abandoned and the post moved on July 9, 1882, to a point on the Southern Pacific Railroad. Six weeks later, however, it was once again moved to higher ground on the left bank of the Rio Grande, about 52 miles southeast of El Paso, at the present town of Fort Hancock in Hudspeth County. On May 14, 1886, the post was officially designated Fort Hancock to honor the memory of Major General Winfield Scott Hancock who died on February 9, 1886. The post was abandoned on October 5, 1895, and transferred to the Interior Department for disposition on November 1, 1895.

CAMP HARLINGTON. This temporary World War I post, located at Harlington, Cameron County, 25 miles north of Brownsville, was an overseas mobilization point for the 26th Infantry, 1st Division, American Expeditionary Forces (AEF).

CAMP HATCH. FORT CONCHO.

FORT HAWKINS. FORT CANEY.

CAMP HAWLEY. FORT CROCKETT.

CAMP HEBÉRT. An important Confederate rendezvous and staging point for troops from several counties, Camp Hebért was established in 1861 and located on the railroad's right-of-way two miles below Hempstead in Austin (now Waller) County. By November 1, 1861, there were three camps at or near Hempstead—Camp Groce, Camp Hebért, and Camp Carter. The first two were said to have been east of Clear Creek opposite each other; Camp Carter's location has not been determined.

FORT HEBÉRT (*Fort Virginia Point*). A Confederate defense established in November 1861 and located on strategic Virginia Point on the mainland opposite Galveston Island, heavily fortified Fort Hebért, also known as Fort Virginia Point, was named for General Paul Octave Hebért who commanded Galveston's defenses.

CAMP HOOD. FORT HOOD.

FORT HOOD (*Camp Hood; South Camp Hood*). Located between Killeen and Gatesville in Bell County, this prestigious, still-active World War II post was opened as Camp Hood on September 18, 1942, and named for Confederate General John Bell Hood. It occupies the site of old Fort Gates erected in 1849 as an Indian defense. During the war, the post was principally a tank destroyer center, although many branches of the Army trained here. The troop capacity of the camp was more than 95,000 in late June 1943. North Camp Hood was established shortly after the main cantonment area was founded west of Killeen. Now called North Fort Hood, it is located 17 miles north of the main post. After the war, it was occupied by Texas and Oklahoma National Guard and Army Reserve units for summer training. On April 15, 1950, South Camp Hood was designated Fort Hood. In the late 1970s, the post was the largest concentration of armored power in the nation.

FORT HOUSTON. A Republic of Texas defense located about two miles west of present Palestine in Anderson County, Fort Houston was a stockaded blockhouse built immediately after the Battle of San Jacinto on April 21, 1836. It was named in honor of General Sam Houston, who had ordered its establishment. The first fortification named for the hero of the Texas Revolution, it was an important point of defense on the frontier from 1836 to 1839, and abandoned in 1841 or 1842.

FORT HOUSTON. A major Republic of Texas military center on the Indian frontier east of the Trinity River, Fort Houston was erected in the fall of 1836 at the village of Houston, which had been established the year prior on the site of the present Texas metropolis. The fort was considered a strongly built work, described 10 years after its completion as measuring 150 by 80 feet, with two rows of cabins inside. It probably had at least one two-story blockhouse within the stockade. Its use as a military defense apparently ended in 1841 or 1842.

HOUSTON POST. CAMP LUBBOCK.

CAMP HOWZE. A World War II infantry division training center covering some 59,000 acres located in northern Texas, six miles northeast of Gainesville in Cooke County, Camp Howze was located on the site selected by the War Department on December 28, 1941, and named for Robert Lee Howze. With construction starting in April 1942, the camp was a temporary cantonment designed for immediate use and was hurriedly built. In August the Station Complement Quartermaster Detachment arrived, and in September the 84th Infantry Division was activated. The camp's troop capacity was about 40,000, with hospital beds for 1,271. The post was declared surplus on February 18, 1946.

CAMP HUDSON (*Camp on the San Pedro*). Located on the right bank of the Devils (San Pedro) River, some 40 miles northwest of Del Rio, in Val Verde County, Camp Hudson (misnamed a fort in some official records) was established on June 7, 1857, by 1st Lieutenant Theodore Fink, 8th Infantry, and named in honor of 2nd Lieutenant Walter W. Hudson, 1st Infantry, who died on April 19, 1850, of wounds suffered in an action with Indians near Laredo. The post was designed to protect the road from San Antonio to El Paso from Indian hostiles. Evacuated by Federal troops on March 17, 1861, in compliance with an order of Brigadier General David E. Twiggs, Camp Hudson was intermittently garrisoned by Confederate troops. After the Civil War, the post was reoccupied by Federal troops in 1867 but then permanently abandoned on April 12, 1868.

CAMP HULEN. A World War II troop training center located at Palacios on Tres Palacios Bay in Matagorda County, Camp Hulen was a Texas National Guard summer encampment converted to Federal use during the war emergency and named for General John A. Hulen of the organization. Construction began on the 1,460-acre post on September 14, 1940, and the first troops arrived on September 23 and began immediate training while occupying a temporary tent city. By August 1942 permanent-type buildings largely replaced the tents. Troop capacity at the height of war operations was 14,560. Camp Hulen was declared surplus by the War Department on May 31, 1946, and returned to the Texas National Guard.

CAMP INDEPENDENCE. A Republic of Texas military post located on the east side of the Lavaca River, about five miles from old Texana and four miles southwest of present Edna in Jackson County, Camp Independence was occupied by part of the Texas Army from December 1836 until the troops were ordered furloughed in compliance with an order of President Sam Houston on May 18, 1837. The last troops left the post in November 1837.

FORT INGE (*Camp Leona*). Located on the left bank of the Leona River, two miles south of the present city of Uvalde, Fort Inge was established on March 13, 1849, by Captain Sidney Burbank with elements of the 1st Infantry and named in honor of Lieutenant Zebulon M. P. Inge, 2nd Dragoons, who was killed in the Battle of Resaca de la Palma. The post was intended to protect the southern frontier from Indian and Mexican bandit depredations. Intermittently garrisoned, it was evacuated by Federal troops on March 19, 1861, and occupied by Texas troops during the Civil War. Fort Inge was reoccupied in 1866 by Federal troops, then permanently abandoned on February 28, 1869.

CAMP IVES. Located on Turtle Creek in eastern Kerr County, a subpost of Camp Verde four miles to the south, Camp Ives was established on October 2, 1859, by Company I, 2nd Cavalry, under the command of Lieutenant Wesley Owens. The post was temporarily abandoned on March 13, 1860, when its garrison escorted Robert E. Lee to the Rio Grande. The troops returned on October 20, 1860, and remained until January 28, 1861, when Camp Ives was abandoned. Texas forces used the post in 1861 as a muster station for Confederate troops. The Frontier Battalion reportedly camped here periodically throughout the Civil War.

FORT JACKSBORO. FORT RICHARDSON.

CAMP JACKSON (*Camp King's Ranch*). Located on the far-flung King Ranch, about 35 miles southwest of Corpus Christi, in Kleberg County, this Confederate post known as Camp Jackson was established probably in 1861 by troops stationed in the lower Rio Grande Military District as General Hamilton P. Bee's headquarters. In 1863 several companies of Confederate troops were posted on the campsite.

FORT JACKSON. In 1859 the Federal government planned to fortify Pelican Spit just across the channel from the city of Galveston. By the time Texas seceded from the Union, three structures were built to accommodate a garrison, but no fortifications had been constructed. When the Confederacy took over, earthworks were thrown up and several guns emplaced. Known as Fort Jackson, the location was manned by Confederate troops under the command of Colonel W. M. Stafford. On October 5, 1862, a Federal fleet appeared off Galveston Island, bombarded the city, then moved into the harbor. The Confederate defenders were withdrawn to Virginia Point and Galveston was captured.

FORT JOHNSTON. Located on the right bank of the Red River opposite the mouth of the Washita, four miles north of Pottsboro in Grayson County, Fort Johnston was established by Colonel William G. Cooke and built by two companies of troops of the 1st Infantry under the command of Captain John Holliday during December 1840 and the first months of 1841. The defense was one of the series of forts planned along the Texas frontier from the Red River to the Nueces by Albert Sidney Johnston, secretary of war of the Republic of Texas, to put a stop to frequent Comanche raids. The post was abandoned in May 1841.

CAMP (JOSEPH E.) JOHNSTON. A temporary post located on the south side of the North Concho River in northwestern Tom Green County, it was named for Joseph E. Johnston, U.S. Army topographical engineer. Five companies of the 8th Infantry, aggregating 284 people including families and servants of their officers, garrisoned the post between March 15 and November 18, 1852, when the troops were transferred to Fort Chadbourne.

CAMP KELLY. FORT CONCHO.

CAMP KING'S RANCH. CAMP JACKSON.

KINNEY'S FORT. This fortified trading post established by Henry L. Kinney and William P. Aubrey in 1839 was the nucleus of the first American settlement on the site of modern Corpus Christi. One of the most impressive and strongly garrisoned private forts in the Texas republic, it allowed Aubrey and Kinney to trade with the Mexican towns along the Rio Grande. The fort was located in dangerous territory, where neither Texan nor Mexican authority held sway during the fort's early years. A visitor in 1844 reported that the fort was garrisoned by at least 30 men and mounted several cannon. The town of Corpus Christi had been settled around the post before U.S. Army troops arrived there in July 1845.

PRESIDIO LA BAHIA. FORT GOLIAD.

FORT LANCASTER. Located on Live Oak Creek, just above its junction with the Pecos River, near the present town of Sheffield in Crockett County, and established on August 20, 1855, by Captain Stephen D. Carpenter, 1st Infantry, the post was originally called Camp Lancaster for 1st Lieutenant Job R. H. Lancaster, 2nd Dragoons, and intended to safeguard the San Antonio–El Paso road and to protect the transit of supplies and immigrants from Indian hostiles. It was designated a fort on August 21, 1856. Texas seceded from the Union on January 28, 1861, and Brigadier General David E. Twiggs, commanding the Department of Texas, ordered abandonment of all Federal forts. On March 19, 1861, the Federal troops evacuated Fort Lancaster. During the Civil War, the post was intermittently occupied by Confederate Army units. After the war, U.S. troops used Fort Lancaster's site as a subpost in the fall of 1867 and briefly during 1868 and 1871. The ruins of the fort are now contained within a 130-acre park commemorated as the Fort Lancaster State Historic Site.

CAMP LANGTRY. Located at Langtry in Val Verde County, Camp Langtry was established in 1914 for the protection of American citizens on the Mexican border. It was abandoned in 1917 at the beginning of the United States' involvement in World War I.

FORT LAVACA. A Confederate defense situated on a bluff overlooking Lavaca Bay in the immediate environs of Port Lavaca in Calhoun County, Fort Lavaca consisted of two platformed batteries aggregating nine guns defended by Major D. D. Shea's 4th Battalion of the Texas Artillery in October 1862. The guns were removed to Fort Esperanza on Matagorda Island in 1863.

FORT LEATON (*El Fortin*). A trading center and intermittently used unofficial U.S. Army headquarters until almost the turn of the century, this fortified 200-foot-square, adobe-built trading post, also known as El Fortin, was built in 1848 by Mexican War veteran Ben Leaton, located four miles east of Presidio on the Rio Grande. One of the largest adobe structures ever built in Texas, Leaton's massive fortress covered almost an acre of ground and was comprised of some 40 rooms and a large corral. Renovation of the property was begun in the 1930s. The restored original structure is now the property of the state of Texas.

CAMP LEE (*Camp Powderhorn*). Located on Powderhorn Bayou near the town of Indianola on Matagorda Bay in Calhoun County, this post, alternately known as Camp Powderhorn, was first established in March 1861 by Major C. C. Sibley,

U.S. Army. During the Civil War, Confederate infantry and cavalry troops periodically occupied the site. In October 1863 Colonel W. R. Bradfute, then commanding that part of the coast, made the post his headquarters.

CAMP LEONA. FORT INGE.

CAMP LIENDO. CAMP GROCE.

FORT LINCOLN. Located on the west bank of the Río Seco, two miles northwest of the town of D'Hanis in Medina County, Fort Lincoln was established on July 7, 1849, by 1st Lieutenant James Longstreet, 8th Infantry. The post was named in the memory of Captain George Lincoln, 8th Infantry, killed on February 23, 1847, in the Battle of Buena Vista during the Mexican War. Fort Lincoln was abandoned on July 20, 1852, after the line of frontier settlements advanced westward. Its remains today consist of preserved ruins and a reconstructed building.

FORT LIPANTITLÁN. Located on the Nueces River near its mouth, three miles west of present San Patricio in Nueces County, this Mexican defense was established in 1831 by order of General Manuel de Mier y Terán. It was intended to prevent the illegal entry of Americans and goods from the United States and to promote Mexican colonization of Texas territory. On November 4, 1835, the fort was captured by Texas Volunteers, who may have destroyed the fort at that time. The fort or its ruin was successfully defended during the battle of Lipantitlán on July 7, 1842, by 192 men commanded by James Davis.

LITTLE RIVER FORT (*Fort Smith; Fort Griffin*). Located "near the Three Forks of the Little River," on the bank of the Leon River and about a mile above that river's junction with the Lampasas, in present Bell County, it was established in November 1836 by Lieutenant George B. Erath and a detachment of Texas Rangers. A blockhouse or log-built fort, probably palisaded, it was built for the protection of the Little River settlement. The fort was first named Fort Smith for Major William H. Smith, who took over from Captain Robert M. Coleman the command of the Rangers on the frontier in December. It was more commonly known as Little River Fort, however, and this was its official designation during the 1839–41 period. At a later date, it was called Fort Griffin for Moses Griffin, a local settler, who apparently maintained the defense for some years after it was abandoned by the Texas government.

CAMP LOGAN. A World War I training center, earlier a Texas National Guard encampment, Camp Logan was established in July 1917 just beyond the western limits of the city of Houston. Trouble between black soldiers quartered at the camp and local police resulted in a riot on August 23 and the declaration of martial law in the city. In 1918 the post was used for the hospitalization of war wounded. Camp Logan was discontinued in October 1919.

CAMP LUBBOCK (*Houston Post*). This Confederate encampment, formerly known as Houston Post, was located near Buffalo Bayou at Harrisburg in Harris County. It was later officially designated Camp Lubbock for Governor Francis Richard Lubbock. The most important campsite in the Houston area, it served as central headquarters for Major General John Magruder, who was in command of all Confederate troops in Texas, Arizona, and New Mexico. The post was periodically used by infantry regiments ultimately assigned to coastal fortifications.

CAMP MABRY. Located in northwestern Austin and named for W. H. Mabry, former adjutant general of Texas, Camp Mabry was established in 1890 as a summer encampment for the Texas Volunteer Guard. It became an Army post during World War I and was used for training various military units. The post was reactivated in World War II as a troop replacement and supply center. Parts of the original Camp Mabry reservation became the Army Reserve Armory. Officer candidates and members of the 27 Austin National Guard units participate in training demonstrations and testing of military equipment on the post's maneuver area.

CAMP MACARTHUR. A World War I training center, named in honor of General Arthur MacArthur, was established July 18, 1917, on the outskirts of the city of Waco. Troops mobilized from Mexican border service were transferred to the new camp and trained for overseas duty. First used for the training of Texas National Guard troops, the camp was designated in August 1918 by the War Department as a training center for infantry. Camp MacArthur was abandoned on May 15, 1919, and its site incorporated within the city of Waco.

FORT MCINTOSH (*Camp Crawford*). Located on a bluff on the left bank of the Rio Grande, just above Laredo in Webb County, on the site of a Spanish presidio, this long-enduring military post was established on March 3, 1849, by 2nd Lieutenant Egbert Viele, 1st Infantry. Originally named Camp Crawford for Secretary of War George W. Crawford, it was officially designated Fort McIntosh on January 7, 1850, in memory of Lieutenant Colonel James S. McIntosh, 5th Infantry, who died on September 26, 1847, of wounds suffered in the Battle of Molino del Rey. It was one of the line of military posts established along the Rio Grande after the Mexican War to prevent Indians from crossing the border into Mexico.

Fort McIntosh was abandoned in 1858, reoccupied, again abandoned, then reoccupied in December 1860. The post was evacuated by Federal troops on March 12, 1861, after Brigadier General David E. Twiggs surrendered the Department of Texas to the Confederacy to be garrisoned by Texas Confederate troops until the end of the Civil War. Reoccupied by Federal troops on October 23, 1865, the post was relocated about a half-mile below the original site and completely rebuilt with permanent structures during 1868–77. Fort McIntosh was thereafter continuously occupied until May 31, 1946, when it was permanently abandoned. The reservation was purchased by the city of Laredo in 1947. Laredo Junior College and Texas A & I University now occupy part of the grounds.

FORT MCKAVETT (*Camp San Saba*). Located on a high rocky bluff on the right bank of the San Saba River, at the present town of Fort McKavett in Menard County, the post was established on March 14, 1852, by Major Pitcairn Morrison, 8th Infantry. First known as Camp San Saba, it was later officially designated Fort McKavett in honor of Captain Henry McKavett, 8th Infantry, killed on September 21, 1846, in the Battle of Monterrey. In compliance with an order of Brigadier General David E. Twiggs, the post was abandoned on March 22, 1859, and its garrison transferred to Camp Cooper.

Fort McKavett was periodically occupied during the Civil War by Confederate troops. Reoccupied by U.S. troops on April 1868, by which time the post was in a state of almost complete disrepair, it was rebuilt under the direction of Colonel Ranald S. Mackenzie, 41st Infantry. By 1876 there were stone-built barracks for eight companies, a dozen officers' quarters, hospital, magazine, guardhouse, a large headquarters building, and other structures. Fort McKavett was permanently abandoned on June 30, 1883. Several of the original stone buildings are presently being occupied as residences.

FORT MAGRUDER. A Confederate defense of Galveston, Fort Magruder was a sand battery on the gulf side of Galveston Island, nearly opposite the foot of Church Street. It was armed with one 10-inch Columbiad and two 32-pounder smoothbores, and closed in the rear with a bombproofed traverse containing magazines and quarters. It protected Fort Point and South Battery, with a good command over the gulf and the bay.

FORT MANHASSET. A Federal defense located on the Galveston beach road, about six miles below Sabine in Jefferson County, Fort Manhasset was constructed by Union forces in September 1863. It was named for a U.S. coal tender that had sunk off the beach. Consisting of three redoubts, its principal one mounting two 32-pounder howitzers, and two lunettes, the fort was established to guard the land approach to Sabine Pass just above the town of Sabine.

FORT MARCY (*Camp Corpus Christi*). The first Federal fort on Texas soil and named in honor of William L. Marcy, secretary of war under President Buchanan, Fort Marcy was established at Corpus Christi during the Mexican War in early 1846 after General Zachary Taylor moved his troops there from St. Joseph's Island on August 15, 1845. The entire 8th Infantry Regiment was here in 1845–46. A supply post (probably abandoned along with Fort Marcy in 1857) was established at Corpus Christi in August 1849, and General Persifor Smith moved his headquarters there in 1852 or 1853, possibly using the designation of Fort Marcy for it. Camp Corpus Christi was established in rented quarters in November 1850 by Lieutenant Colonel J. J. Abercrombie with two companies of the 5th Infantry. During the Civil War, Confederate engineers repaired two of Fort Marcy's gun platforms and constructed three additional ones on the fort site. The defense mounted four pieces of ordnance consisting of one 18-pounder siege gun, one 12-pounder siege gun, and two 12-pounder howitzers.

CAMP MARFA. FORT D. A. RUSSELL.

FORT MARTIN SCOTT. Located on Baron's Creek, a tributary of the Pedernales River, about two miles south of Fredericksburg in Gillespie County, Fort Martin Scott was established on December 5, 1848, by Captain Seth Eastman, 1st Infantry, and named in the memory of Lieutenant Colonel Martin Scott, 5th Infantry, killed on September 8, 1847, in the Battle of Molino del Rey. Subsequent to April 1853, the post was intermittently but frequently occupied by small garrisons who used it more often as a forage depot than for actual defense. Evacuated by its Federal garrison at the beginning of the Civil War, the fort was held by the Confederates throughout the war. Briefly reoccupied by U.S. troops on October 18, 1866, Fort Martin Scott was permanently abandoned on December 28, 1866.

FORT MASON. Located on the right bank of Comanche Creek near the Llano River, a tributary of the Colorado, near the present town of Mason in the county of the same name, Fort Mason was established on July 6, 1851, by Captain Hamilton W. Merrill, 2nd Dragoons, and named in honor of 2nd Lieutenant George T. Mason, 2nd Dragoons, killed on April 25, 1846 at La Rosia near Fort Brown. The post was designed to protect the German settlements in the area. Although ordered abandoned by Brigadier General David E. Twiggs on February 5, 1859, the post was intermittently occupied until March 28, 1861, when it was evacuated by Federal troops and surrendered to the Confederacy. Reoccupied after the Civil War in 1866, it was permanently abandoned on March 23, 1869.

A reconstructed officers' quarters on the crest of Post Hill marks the location of the fort. A number of crumbling foundations still evidence the sites of some of the post's original 23 buildings which included barracks, officers' quarters, storehouses, a hospital, guardhouse and stables. Primarily a cavalry post, Fort Mason was duty station for such military figures as Albert Sidney Johnston, John Bell Hood, and Robert E. Lee. Fort Mason was Lee's last command in the U.S. Army.

FORT MAXEY. A World War II infantry training center located about 10 miles north of Paris in Lamar County, Camp Maxey was named in honor of Samuel Bell Maxey, Confederate Army officer and U.S. senator (1875–87). The post was activated on July 15, 1942, with a troop capacity of 45,000 men. Camp Maxey was put on inactive status on October 1, 1945.

CAMP MERRILL (*Camp Casa Blanca*). A temporary Army post on the south side of the Nueces River in northeastern Jim Wells County, about 25 miles northeast of Corpus Christi, it was established in 1852 on a site formerly known as Camp Casa Blanca (1849) and named for Captain Hamilton W. Merrill, 2nd Dragoons. The town of Casa Blanca later developed on or near the site, but the settlement soon vanished.

FORT MERRILL. Located on the right side of the Nueces River, near the town of George West in Live Oak County, Fort Merrill was established on March 1, 1850, by Captain Samuel M. Plummer, 1st Infantry, and named in honor of Captain Moses E. Merrill, 5th Infantry, killed on September 8, 1847, in the Battle of Molino del Rey. During one two-month period in 1854, everyone on the post was on the sick list, stricken with malaria contracted in the river's bottomlands. Fort Merrill was abandoned on December 1, 1855.

FORT MILAM. FORT BURLESON.

FORT MILAM (*Fort Sarahville de Viesca*). A Texas Ranger post of the Republic of Texas period located near the Falls of the Brazos River, four miles southwest of the present town of Marlin in Falls County, it was established in 1834 at the newly founded settlement of Sarahville de Viesca, the capital of Sterling C. Robertson's colony. The name of the village was given in honor of Robertson's mother, Sarah Robertson, and the governor of Texas, Auguste de Viesca. Originally named for the settlement, the fort was renamed Fort Milam on December 27, 1835, in honor of Colonel Benjamin Rush Milam, killed on December 7, 1835, in the attack on San Antonio. It is not definitely known when Fort Milam was abandoned.

CAMP MITCHIE. A Mexican border patrol post established in 1914 for the protection of American citizens from the Madero Revolution and Mexican raids, Camp Mitchie was located on the west side of San Felipe Springs near Del Rio in Val Verde County. The post was abandoned in 1922.

FORT MONTGOMERY. Located about a mile and a half upstream on the Rio Grande above Fort Brown, Fort Montgomery was constructed by troops of the U.S. 13th Army Corps in early 1864. The work was named in honor of a Captain Montgomery, 1st U.S. Texas Cavalry, who was killed in action early in the Civil War. The fort consisted of several redoubts connected by rifle pits which extended across the bend of the river. With a front about 600 yards across, it enclosed a 100-acre area in the rear. The fort's ordnance consisted of one 24-pounder smoothbore and two 20-pounder Parrotts.

FORT MOORE (*Fort Eagle Grove*). A Confederate defense, also known as Fort Eagle Grove, Fort Moore was located about five miles south-west of the city of Galveston. It mounted two 32-pounders and two 18 pounders.

FORT MORITAS (*Fort El Morito*). Built by wealthy Meliton Faver on his extensive ranch near the town of Shafter in Presidio County, Fort Moritas, also called Fort El Morito, was one of three quadrangular adobe-built fortresses built in the late 1850s as defenses against the Apache. (See also: FORT CIBOLO and FORT CIENAGA.)

FORT MUD ISLAND. FORT SAN LUIS PASS.

FORT NACOGDOCHES (*Old Stone Fort*). Known in Spanish records as La Casa Piedra ("the Stone House") or the Stone Fort, it was built in 1779 by Antonio Gil Ybarbo on the northeast corner of the block immediately north of Main Plaza in present Nacogdoches. Considered to be the birthplace of the Texas Republic, it was one of the most important buildings in East Texas but only occasionally utilized a fort. Ybarbo used the structure as a jail and a commissary for storing merchandise for the Indian trade. Also known in American history as Fort Nacogdoches, it had a long succession of occupants.

Although the house was built on public land, the Spanish government recognized it as Ybarbo's private property. On June 20, 1805, he sold it to José Luis de la Bega, who a year later resold it. Although both house and land passed into private hands by the Spanish grant of June 4, 1810, the building's significance in Texas history and its use as a governmental center was only just beginning. In 1813 the green flag of the Gutiérrez-Magee Expedition's Republic of Texas waved over the Old Stone Fort; Dr. James Long made it the headquarters of his short-lived Republic of Texas in 1819; and in 1826–27 during the Fredonian Rebellion, the structure was the capitol of Fredonia. Colonel José de las Piedras, the Mexican commandant, took refuge in the building during the Battle of Nacogdoches on August 2, 1832.

The Old Stone Fort continued to be important to the Republic of Texas. Persons who came from the United States in 1835 and 1836 to fight for Texas Independence were administered the oath of allegiance there. Nacogdoches became a military center of considerable importance as a troop staging area and base of planning for the various Indian campaigns in East Texas to the close of the Cherokee War in July 1839. After independence had been achieved, the first district court of the Republic was held in the Old Stone Fort on March 17, 1837. During the Civil

War, it was garrisoned for a time by Confederate troops.

On June 12, 1901, the old building was sold to other private Nacogdoches interests, and despite strenuous efforts to rescue it from oblivion, the building was torn down in 1902. The salvageable materials, particularly the stone, were bestowed to the Cum Consilio Club of Nacogdoches, which used them to erect a museum building in 1907 on the northwest corner of Washington Square. In 1936 the Texas Centennial Commission appropriated $20,000 for the purpose of rebuilding the Old Stone Fort. The stone from the old building was again used, and the house was reconstructed exactly as it originally stood, but this time on the campus of Stephen F. Austin College, where it is used as a museum of East Texas history.

FORT NELSON. This Galveston defense was erected on Virginia Point by Union troops after their capture of the island city.

CAMP NEWTON D BAKER. A World War I auxiliary camp of Fort Bliss, three miles northeast of El Paso, Camp Baker served as a Signal Corps center, an overseas mobilization point by elements of the 1st, 5th, and 7th Divisions of the AEF, and as a mobilization point for Mexican border duty by the 15th Cavalry Division. The post was discontinued in 1920.

CANTONMENT NORTH FORK OF THE RED RIVER. FORT ELLIOTT.

NORTH CAMP HOOD. FORT HOOD.

PRESIDIO NUESTRA SEÑORA DE LORETO LA BAHIA DE ESPÍRITU SANTOS. Popularly known today in its abbreviated form as Presidio La Bahia, this Spanish presidio with its companion Nuestra Señora de Espíritu de Zuñiga Mission, has occupied three different sites. Established on April 4, 1721, by Captain Domingo Ramón, under orders of the governor of Texas, the Marqués de Aguayo, its first location was in the vicinity of La Salle's old Fort St. Louis, on the right bank of Garcitas Creek, about two miles above its mouth, near present-day Port Lavaca in Victoria County. Its site was partially excavated in 1951 by the Texas Memorial Museum, and many Spanish artifacts from the presidio as well as French objects from La Salle's old fort were uncovered.

In 1726, because of continuous Indian harassment, the presidio and mission were moved 10 leagues to the northwest to a new location on the Guadalupe River at what is now known as Mission Valley. Here successful farming and cattle raising enabled the presidio to supply other Texas missions, in addition to amply providing for its Indian adherents. In 1749, however, the presidio was again relocated, this time for realigning it with the Spanish forts farther west between Mexico and Los Adaes. The third and final site was and is today on a limestone bluff on the south bank of the lower San Antonio River near present-day Goliad.

Presidio La Bahia's original structures on Garcitas Creek were constructed of wood and earth. The second edition boasted one or two buildings of stone. Then, on its final site, a number of stone buildings were erected. In 1772 work on stone walls and fortifications was undertaken. The fort's chapel was finished in the 1790s. The south barracks were not constructed until 1810. Post returns for 1780, during the peak of the Spanish period, indicate two companies of troops, aggregating 80 soldiers, were stationed at the presidio.

The restoration of Presidio La Bahia and the chapel was begun in 1963. Between 1963 and 1967, the Kathryn O'Connor Foundation obtained permission from the Catholic bishop of Corpus Christi for the continued restoration, and under the direction of an architect and an archaeologist, La Bahia was completely restored to its original condition. During the excavations made to shore up weakened walls, evidences were found of nine layers of previous occupation. Thousands of artifacts, including guns, were uncovered. They are now on display in the presidio's museum, located in the restored officers' quarters. On April 9, 1968, Mrs. Lyndon B. Johnson, wife of the late president of the United States, unveiled and dedicated the National Historic Landmark plaque at the entrance to the presidio, which is located a quarter of a mile south of the Goliad State Historic Park.

OLD STONE FORT. FORT NACOGDOCHES.

CAMP OWEN BIERNE. A World War I post located on the Fort Bliss military reservation, it was located eight miles southeast of El Paso. The camp was activated probably in late 1916 and discontinued in 1919.

PARKER'S FORT. A true reproduction of Fort Parker is contained within a state park located two miles south of the Navasota River and three miles north of Grosebeck on S.R. 14 in Limestone County. It was on this spot in 1834 that a small colony of pioneers from Illinois chose to settle. Led by their patriarch, Elder John Parker, they laid out fields, planted crops and, as protection against the Indians, built a sturdy stockaded fort. The colonists worked hard and prospered until the morning of May 19, 1836, when several hundred Comanche and Kiowa Indians attacked their fort. In the battle that followed, a number of the settlers were killed, among them Elder John Parker and his sons, Silas M. and Benjamin F. Parker. Some made their escape to Fort Houston in present Anderson County. Several, taken captive, were ransomed to nearby settlements during the next few years. But Cynthia Ann Parker, nine-year-old daughter of one of the settlement's leaders, grew up as a captive, wedded Comanche Chief Pete Nocona, and became the mother of noted Comanche leader Quanah Parker. Cynthia Ann was recaptured by General Sul Ross on the Pease River in 1860. Unreconciled to civilized society and yearning for the free Indian life, she pined away and died 10 years later near the town of Palestine in Anderson County. Parker's Fort was not reoccupied after families returned to the area.

CAMP (CANTONMENT) PEÑA COLORADO (*Camp Rainbow Cliffs*).

Originally a temporary encampment known as Camp Rainbow Cliffs, established in August 1879 about four miles southwest of present Marathon in Brewster County, it was designed to "occupy and scout the country and open a wagon-road from Fort Davis to Fort Clark." In March 1880 the post was formalized and permanent-type adobe and timber-built buildings were constructed. It was designated Camp or Cantonment Peña Colorado ("red bluff"). As the only Army post then in the vast Big Bend region, the post was intended to prevent Indian raids into Mexico and to keep the peace along the Rio Grande. Camp Peña Colorado was abandoned on February 11, 1893, after West Texas had been cleared of Indians.

FORT PHANTOM HILL (*Post on the Clear Fork of the Brazos*).

Located on the Clear Fork of the Brazos River, about 15 miles north of the present city of Abilene in Jones County, this post was one of a chain of forts designed to safeguard both the emigrant travel route from Fort Smith, Arkansas, to Santa Fe, and the trails to the California gold fields. It was established on November 14, 1851, by Major John Joseph Abercrombie, 5th Infantry. Officially designated as Post on the Clear Fork of the Brazos, it was also known as Fort Phantom Hill, a name that is open to conjecture. Abandoned on April 6, 1854, and burned, its site became a station on the Butterfield Over-land stage line from 1858 to the outbreak of the Civil War. Subsequent to the establishment of Fort Griffin in 1867, the site was again occupied until about 1880 as an intermittently used tented picket post.

FORT POINT (*Fort Sulakowski*).

A heavily armed Confederate defense established in 1861 on the northeastern end of Galveston Island, at the mouth of the harbor, Fort Point was the principal Galveston headquarters for Confederate troops stationed on the island. It was renamed Fort Sulakowski on March 11, 1864, in honor of Colonel Valery Sulakowski, General Magruder's chief of engineers. The fortification mounted at least eight assorted rifled guns, howitzers, and mortars.

FORT POLK.

Located at Point Isabel near the mouth of the Rio Grande River in Cameron County, Fort Polk was established on March 26, 1846, by Colonel (later General) Zachary Taylor, 6th Infantry, and named in honor of President James K. Polk. Consisting of troop barracks, officers' quarters, warehouses, and dock facilities, the post was designed as a depot to supply Taylor's forces along the lower Grande. Fort Polk was abandoned on February 19, 1850.

CAMP PORT ARTHUR.

A World War I post, Camp Port Arthur in Jefferson County was occupied by Company D of the 19th Battalion, U.S. Guards, during 1917–18.

POWDER HOUSE HILL FORT.

One of the strongest fortifications built by the Confederates in 1863 to defend San Antonio against attack by Union forces was an earthwork supported by flank defenses on Powder House Hill, constructed by the general's engineers around the arsenal.

CAMP POWDERHORN. CAMP LEE.

CAMP PRAIRIE LEA.

A Confederate post located on the San Marcos River about 17 miles southeast of San Marcos in Caldwell County, it was a major camp established in early 1861 for the military instruction of recruits from surrounding counties.

CAMP PRESIDIO.

A Mexican border patrol post established prior to World War I, Camp Presidio was located in the town of Presidio, about three blocks north of Main Street. It consisted of troop barracks, officers' quarters, headquarters, guardhouse, bathhouse, stables, and probably a few storage buildings.

CAMP PRISONTOWN. Situated on a bluff overlooking Verde Creek, two miles from Camp Verde, this stockaded Confederate complex of several well-built structures was a major prisoner of war camp housing Union troops captured along the Texas coast.

FORT QUINTANA. A Confederate defense situated on the south bank of the Brazos River, on the west side of the river's mouth, at the old town of Quintana, opposite Fort Velasco, in Brazoria County, Fort Quintana was established probably over the winter of 1863–64. Built of live oak and strengthened by earthworks, two guns were mounted on its sod parapets to support the Confederate defense of the vital channel.

FORT QUITMAN. Located on the left bank of the Rio Grande, approximately 70 miles below El Paso, in south central Hudspeth County, Fort Quitman was established on September 28, 1858 by companies C and H of the 8th Infantry. Intended to protect the stage line and the emigrant routes, it was named in honor of Major General John Anthony Quitman, who died on July 17, 1858. The post was evacuated on April 5, 1861, by order of Brigadier General David E. Twiggs and occupied by Confederate troops until its capture on August 22, 1862, by Federal troops under the command of Captain John C. Cremony, 2nd California Cavalry. The Union troops were withdrawn in 1863 and the post was not regarrisoned until January 1, 1868. Fort Quitman was abandoned on January 5, 1877. It was temporarily reactivated in 1881 for the campaigns against the Apache and permanently abandoned the following year. A full-scale reproduction of the fort is located on I-10, about 20 miles west of Sierra Blanca.

CAMP RABB. A Confederate camp located on the San Antonio–Eagle Pass road where it crossed Elm Creek in northeastern Maverick County, Camp Rabb was established on April 7, 1862, by James M. Norris as a Texas Ranger post for the Frontier Regiment. Intended to guard the frequently used road, it was commanded by Captain Thomas Rabb until the regiment's consolidation at Fort Belknap in March 1864.

CAMP RAINBOW CLIFFS. CAMP PEÑA COLORADO.

CAMP RANDLE. CAMP BRENHAM.

CAMP RICE (*Fort Hancock*).

FORT RICHARDSON (*Fort Jacksboro*). Located on the right (south) bank of Lost Creek, a tributary of the Trinity River, adjoining the town of Jacksboro, in Jack County, the post was first established as Fort Jacksboro by two companies of the 6th Cavalry, commanded by Major Samuel H. Stark, who arrived on July 4, 1866. Its garrison was withdrawn in the spring of 1867, with its troops distributed to Fort Belknap and to Camp Wichita at Buffalo Spring. On November 19, 1867, orders were issued for the establishment of a permanent post at Jacksboro. The new post, intended to control the hostile Comanche and Kiowa, was named in honor of Major General Israel B. Richardson, who died on November 3, 1862, of mortal wounds suffered in the Battle of Antietam. Fort Richardson was abandoned on May 22, 1878. For a brief period thereafter, its buildings were used for an Indian school. The present Fort Richardson State Historical Park, established in 1968, adjacent to the city of Jacksboro, preserves the fort's ruins.

FORT RILEY. FORT CLARK.

CAMP RINGGOLD. FORT RINGGOLD.

RINGGOLD BARRACKS. FORT RINGGOLD.

FORT RINGGOLD (*Post at David's Landing; Camp Ringgold; Ringgold Barracks*). Located on the left bank of the Rio Grande at David's Landing, just below Rio Grande City, in Starr County, it was established on October 26, 1848, after the close of the Mexican War, by Captain Joseph H. La Motte, 1st Infantry. The fort was first known as Post at David's Landing, then as Camp Ringgold, and finally as Ringgold Barracks on July 16, 1849. The post was officially designated Fort Ringgold on December 30, 1878, in honor of Captain Samuel Ringgold, 3rd Artillery, who died on May 11, 1846, of wounds received in the Battle of Palo Alto. Abandoned on March 3, 1859, in compliance with an order of Brigadier General David E. Twiggs, its garrison was transferred to Camp Hudson. The post was reoccupied, however, on December 9, 1859, because of Mexican border violations. It was again evacuated on March 7, 1861, by its Federal troops after the outbreak of the Civil War. Fort Ringgold was reoccupied by U.S. troops in June 1865. Construction of a new post was begun in 1869 on a location a short distance above its original site, and most of the work was completed in 1875. By 1886 frame and brick buildings had replaced the post's adobe structures. The post was officially abandoned in October 1906 and put in the charge of a caretaking detachment. It was intermittently occupied during the continuous border difficulties with Mexico between 1913 and 1917. On March 1, 1941, the post was garrisoned by 400 troops for World War II duties. In August 1944 Fort Ringgold was inactivated and declared surplus by the War Department.

RIO GRANDE STATION. FORT DUNCAN.

POST ON THE RIO LLANO. FORT TERRETT.

FORT RUGELY. FORT CANEY.

CAMP SABINAL. Located near the Sabinal River in eastern Uvalde County, Camp Sabinal was established on July 12, 1856 by Captain Albert G. Brackett, 2nd Cavalry, to protect the vital San Antonio–El Paso road. The post was occupied until November 1856. During the Civil War, the site was used as a Texas Ranger post.

FORT SABINE (*Fort Griffin*). A Confederate defense built in the spring of 1863 to guard the strategic entrance to Sabine Pass and located about a mile and a half east of the town of Sabine in Jefferson County, Fort Sabine stood on high ground, commanding both the Texas and Louisiana channels. At first mounting two 12-pounder Mexican field guns and a battery of four 18-pounder smoothbores, the defense was soon reinforced with additional armament and renamed Fort Griffin for Colonel W. H. Griffin. On September 8, 1863, in a 45-minute battle, its garrison of 46 Irish stevedores, recruited in Houston and Galveston, commanded by Lieutenant Richard Dowling, successfully repulsed a strong Union naval attack, sinking two gunboats, damaging a third, and driving off the remainder of the fleet. Fort Griffin was surrendered to Federal troops on May 25, 1865.

ST. JOSEPH'S ISLAND DEPOT. Located on St. Joseph's Island, in present Aransas County, this was an important U.S. Army depot established by an order of General Zachary Taylor and in operation from the summer of 1845 until the outbreak of the War with Mexico in 1846. During the month of August 1845, General Taylor briefly had his headquarters on the island. Garrisoned at different times by troops of the 7th Infantry and the 3rd Artillery, the depot stored large quantities of ordnance, quartermaster and subsistence supplies for transshipment to the general's main encampment at Corpus Christi. The depot was probably located at the southern

end of the island, on the north side of Aransas Pass.

FORT ST. LOUIS. Located on the west bank of Garcitas Creek at the head of Lavaca Bay, an inlet of Matagorda Bay, about ten miles east of Placedo in Victoria County, the site commemorates the first French attempt to colonize the Gulf coast, which created special Spanish interest in Texas. In 1685 René Robert Cavelier, sieur de La Salle, intending to plant a colony near the mouth of the Mississippi, errantly led 400 colonists and soldiers instead into present Texas, where he founded Fort St. Louis. A month later, he moved it to a new location five miles above the mouth of Garcitas Creek. A temporary wooden defensive structure, it served as a base for his explorations of the surrounding country.

Hunger and Indian attacks disheartened the colonists, and the venture was a failure from the beginning. La Salle, after reconnoitering to the south and west, started north, hoping to reach Fort St. Louis in Illinois country, but mutineers murdered him. Two years later, Indians attacked the fort and wiped out most of the remaining Frenchmen. Two survivors, however, blundered their way through the trackless wilderness in search of the Mississippi, found the river, and ultimately the mouth of the Arkansas where Arkansas Post stood, established by the French in 1686. A Spanish expedition under Captain Alonso de León, which had been sent to investigate reports of French encroachment in Texas, finally found the remains of the French fort and burned it.

The failure of La Salle's colony ended French attempts to colonize Texas. The French, however, later established themselves at the mouth of the Mississippi and continued to threaten Texas along the Louisiana frontier, but they never again seriously contested Spain's hold on Texas. The site of Fort St. Louis has been accepted by most historians after its discovery and has been substantially confirmed by archaeological investigation.

FORT ST. LOUIS DE CARLORETTE (*Fort Teodoro*). Known today as Old Spanish Fort, located 17 miles from present Nocona in Montague County, Fort St. Louis de Carlorette was built in 1719 by Bernard de la Harpe, a French trader, at the principal village of the Wichita Indians. The French traders abandoned the trading fort several years later. In 1762 the Spanish occupied it when the Louisiana Territory was ceded to Spain by France. The post had been described by the Spanish as an oval-shaped structure, surrounded by a stockade and a ditch. Ruins of the fort were discovered in 1859 and matched the description.

CAMP SALMON. A Confederate encampment located near Sloan's Ranch on an arm of Hubbard Creek at the Eastland-Callahan county line, Camp Salmon was established by Colonel James M. Norris in March 1862 as a Ranger station of the Frontier Regiment. Commanded by Captain John Salmon, the post served as headquarters for scouting expeditions until the regiment's consolidation in March 1864.

FORT SAM HOUSTON (*San Antonio Quartermaster Depot; Post of San Antonio*). Since the founding of San Antonio in 1718, an army has been closely associated with its history. First it was the Spanish who based troops in the area as protection for their missions and colonists. Next came Mexican troops that took over the garrison when Mexico secured its independence from Spain. In 1836 San Antonio was the site of the historic battle at the Alamo between the Texans and General Santa Anna's Mexican army. Following the admission of Texas into the Union in 1845, San Antonio again became a garrison city with the arrival of elements of the U.S. Army. After the Mexican War, a depot was established there, and most of the time San Antonio served as department headquarters, with troops quartered in barracks in the vicinity of Military Plaza—

Plaza de las Armas—and at the Alamo and its environs.

In May 1870, the city donated 40 acres to the government for the establishment of a permanent post in the northeast section of the city, known as Government Hill, with additional land donated in 1871 and 1875. Construction of the post began in 1876. The original post was the San Antonio Quartermaster Depot, followed in 1881 by permanent quarters for the headquarters staff. In 1885 construction was begun on barracks, officers' quarters, and other structures to accommodate 12 cavalry companies. The post, encompassing all the Army facilities, was then known as Post of San Antonio. It was officially designated Fort Sam Houston on September 10, 1890, in honor of the patriot who had played a leading role in the military and political history of Texas.

The birth of military aviation occurred on Fort Sam Houston's reservation on March 2, 1910, when Brigadier General Benjamin Foulois, then a lieutenant in the Signal Corps, was on duty there with a government-purchased Wright biplane. The pioneer experiment by Foulois and his associates is said to have led to the establishment of the Aviation Section of the Signal Corps in July 1914. In 1916 General John J. Pershing led the border expeditions against Pancho Villa in an operation based out of Fort Sam Houston. World War I brought the reservation's last sizable expansion. Nearly twice the land already occupied, 2,118 acres were purchased for Camp

FORT SAM HOUSTON. The Fourth U.S. Army Quadrangle. (Courtesy of the U.S. Army.)

Travis and 104 acres for the construction of a general supply depot. Shortly after the outbreak of World War II, Fort Sam Houston became the cradle of airborne infantry and conducted the first airborne maneuvers between the post and Fort Clark at Brackettville in 1942. The post is still in operation.

CAMP SAMUEL F. B. Morse. A temporary World War I post located at Leon Springs, Bexar County, the facility was used as a Signal Corps training center from May 1917 to August 1918.

PRESIDIO SAN AGUSTÍN DE AHUMADA. Located at the Indian town of El Orcoquisac, a short distance east of the left bank of the Trinity River, in the vicinity of present Wallisville, Chambers County, this fortified and garrisoned presidio was established in late May or early June 1756, by Jacinto de Barrios y Jáuregui, governor of Texas, and was intended to block French activities among the local Indians and to protect its companion mission. Named in honor of Agustín de Ahumada y Villalón, Marqués de los Amarillas, viceroy of New Spain, it has been also referred to as Presidio de Orcoquisac. A storm on September 4, 1766, damaged the presidio's buildings, which were later relocated on higher ground a short distance from their original site. The presidio was officially discontinued in 1772. In the fall of 1965, an archaeological excavation of the presidio's second location, just northeast of Wallisville, was conducted by the Texas Archeological Salvage Project. Several thousand Spanish colonial and Indian artifacts were recovered.

POST OF SAN ANTONIO. FORT SAM HOUSTON.

SAN ANTONIO ARSENAL. A unit of the San Antonio Ordnance Center, which included Camp Stanley, the San Antonio Arsenal was established in 1858 to furnish arms and ammunition to troop units guarding outlying settlements and has been in continuous operation until the late 1970s. In 1919 at the end of World War I, the 21-acre reservation contained 38 buildings. During World War II, the volume of operations was enormous, with about 220,000 tons of munitions received and 168,000 tons shipped from July 1, 1941, to December 31, 1945. The Arsenal is presently owned by a chain of retail stores.

PRESIDIO SAN ANTONIO DE BÉJAR (BEXAR). Originally located on the west side of the San Antonio River, two miles above the San Antonio de Valero Mission, within the present city limits of San Antonio, the garrisoned presidio was established on May 5, 1718, by the Marqués de Aguayo, governor of Texas. In 1722 the presidio was relocated almost directly across the river from the mission. After the abandonment of the mission, its buildings were occupied by soldiers from Alamo de Parras in the province of Coahuila. Because of this military association, the former mission came to be popularly known as the Alamo, for many years an important military post. In addition, the presidio was also garrisoned. Until the end of the Spanish and Mexican periods of colonial occupation, the Alamo remained the principal unit of walled defense. Presidio San Antonio de Bexar was captured by the Texans under Benjamin R. Milam in December 1835, the Alamo being the last of San Antonio's defenses to fall. When General Santa Anna recaptured the presidio in March 1836, the last stand of the Texans was made in the Alamo. The entire San Antonio area remained in nominal control of the Mexican military until after the Battle of San Jacinto.

SAN ANTONIO QUARTERMASTER DEPOT. FORT SAM HOUSTON.

FORT SAN BERNARD. A Confederate defense located on the east bank of the mouth of the San Bernard River in Brazoria County, it was built in 1862 and mounted four guns—two 12-pounder Parrott rifles and two 12-pounder smoothbores. The fort was continuously manned by Confederate troops until the end of the Civil War.

PRESIDIO OF SAN ELIZARIO. More properly designated by the Spanish as the Presidio of Nuestra Señora del Pilar y Gloriosa San José, but commonly known as the Presidio of San Elizario, it was established in 1773 and located about 25 miles below El Paso at San Elizario, then on an island which has since become a part of the mainland as a result of changes in the course of the Rio Grande. The presidio continued to be militarily occupied during the Mexican period until after Texas gained its independence. The presidio was garrisoned on September 15, 1849, by U.S. troops, companies I and K of the 3rd Infantry, under the command of Captain William S. Henry. The garrison was withdrawn in September 1851. During the civil War, the presidio was intermittently occupied by first Confederate troops in 1861, and later by the California column in 1862.

CAMP SAN FELIPE. CAMP DEL RIO.

POST OF SAN FELIPE. CAMP DEL RIO.

FORT SAN JACINTO. Located at the eastern end of Galveston Island and named for the historic Texan victory at the Battle of San Jacinto, the fort was begun in 1898 and completed in 1901. Its first garrison, consisting of Battery G, 1st Artillery, under the command of Captain Clermont L. Best, arrived on April 20, 1898. Fort San Jacinto preceded Fort Crockett on the western end of the island as the original headquarters post of the Galveston harbor defenses. The hurricane of 1900 caused considerable damage to the still-uncompleted fortification, and it was not completely restored until 1906 and not regarrisoned until 1911. The Endicott period coast defense included Batteries Mercer, Heilman, Hogan, and Croghan. The fort's reservation originally contained 419 acres, but it was significantly enlarged by additions swept in by the Gulf of Mexico, and in 1944 it contained over 1,000 acres. At the outbreak of World War II, the fort's guns, which commanded the approach to Galveston Bay, were manned by the 265th Coast Artillery. In 1950 Fort San Jacinto was principally used as a United States radio compass station.

FORT SAN LUIS PASS (*Fort Mud Island*). A Confederate defense located on Mud Island in Brazoria County, on San Luis Pass leading into Galveston Bay, the fort was an earthwork, also known as Fort Mud Island, mounting at least one 18-pounder smoothbore, manned by elements of the 13th Texas Infantry under the command of Captain S. L. S. Barlowe.

CAMP ON THE SAN PEDRO. CAMP HUDSON.

CAMP SAN SABA. FORT McKAVETT.

PRESIDIO DE SAN SABÁ. More popularly known as Presidio de San Sabá, the Presidio of San Luis de las Amarillas was established some little time before May 1757 by Colonel Diego Ortiz de Parilla and located on the left (north) bank of the San Sabá River, one mile northwest of the present town of Menard. The presidio, named for Agustín de Ahumada y Villalón, marqués de las Amarillas, was designed to protect the San Saba de la Santa Cruz Mission, simultaneously founded on the south side of the river. The mission failed in its purpose to convert the Lipan Apache Indians, whose only interest in it was the possibility of obtaining Spanish military aid against their Comanche enemies. In 1758 the Comanche and their allies attacked the mission and set fire to it; a disaster, only three survived of its hundreds of inhabitants. The presidio successfully defended itself although ten soldiers and two priests were lost. In 1761 the presidio's original wooden buildings were replaced by stone structures. Although the presidio was maintained until 1769, the mission was never rebuilt by the Spanish. No remains of the mission are extant, but the presidio has been partially restored on the original foundations in the present San Sabá Historic Park.

PRESIDIO DE SAN XAVIER DE GIGEDO. Also known as Presidio San Francisco Xavier, it was located south of the San Gabriel (San Xavier) River, near the present town of Rockdale in Milam County. It was established in 1751 by Captain Felipe de Rábago y Téran with an initial complement of 50 soldiers to protect the three missions founded in 1747 in its immediate environs. Late in 1755, its garrison was removed. On May 18, 1756, the viceroy decreed the abandonment of the presidio and the establishment on the San Sabá River of a new one to replace it.

FORT SANDCLIFFE. FORT CANEY.

CAMP SANDERS. CAMP AUSTIN.

CAMP SANTA (ELENA) HELENA. CASTOLON ARMY DEPOT.

FORT SARAHVILLE DE VIESCA. FORT MILAM.

FORT SCURRY. A Confederate defense probably built in 1863 and located near City Hospital, it stood at the end of an extensive line of entrenchments that surrounded Galveston. The fort was later named Fort Scurry in honor of Brigadier General William R. Scurry, who was mortally wounded on April 30, 1864, in action at Jenkins' Ferry in Arkansas.

CAMP SEMMES. FORT ARANSAS.

CAMP SHAFTER. Located at the town of Shafter, 19 miles north of Presidio, this was a Texas National Guard post established in 1916 to protect the surrounding mining district from border raids, seldom having its maximum garrison of 50 soldiers. Abandoned in 1920, its remains presently consist of two adobe-built structures and a few ruins.

FORT SHELL BANK (*Fort Aransas*). A Confederate defense situated at the junction of Aransas and Corpus Christi bays in Nueces County, near the present town of Port Aransas, it was built in 1862 and garrisoned by elements of the 8th Texas Infantry. The fort was alternately known as Fort Aransas.

CAMP SHERMAN. A temporary Confederate encampment located on the courthouse grounds in the town of Sherman, Grayson County, the post was a principal rendezvous point in early 1861 for five Texas cavalry regiments destined for service in Arkansas.

FORT SIDNEY SHERMAN (*South Battery*). A Confederate defense, originally known as the South Battery, located on Galveston Island at the foot of 21st and 22nd streets on the Gulf beach, the fort was a sod redoubt mounting two 14-inch Columbiads and one 32-pounder. Manned by elements of Colonel Joseph Cook's Heavy Artillery Regiment, the fort was renamed in 1864 to honor an officer in Cook's regiment who was killed in action.

CAMP SLAUGHTER. A large Confederate encampment located on the Brazos River near the town of Columbia in Brazoria County, the post was established in 1863 by elements of the 4th Texas Infantry and named for Brigadier General James E. Slaughter. The post had several barracks and a large hospital for Confederate wounded.

FORT SMITH. LITTLE RIVER FORT.

FORT (ASHBEL) SMITH. FORT CANEY.

SOPHIA'S FORT. ZINK'S FORT.

SOUTH BATTERY. FORT SIDNEY SHERMAN.

SOUTH CAMP HOOD. FORT HOOD.

SPANISH BLUFF FORT. The *Texas Handbook,* volume 2, reports that this defense on the Trinity River, 15 miles northeast of present Madisonville in Madison County, "was established by the Spanish as early as 1805. The Gutierrez-Magee Expedition expelled the Spaniards and occupied the fort in 1812. In 1813 the Spanish recaptured the fort, butchered the inhabitants, and destroyed the town."

CAMP SPINDLETOP. CAMP BEAUMONT.

CAMP STANLEY (*Camp Funston*). A World War I post originally established as Camp Funston, Camp Stanley was a subpost of the San Antonio Arsenal and operated as an ammunition storage depot, although it was first designated as an infantry cantonment. Named on October 2, 1917, for Brigadier General David Sloane Stanley, it is located on the Leon Springs Military Reservation about 20 miles northwest of San Antonio. In 1922 the post became a subpost of Camp Travis and was intended to be occupied as a temporary garrison at peace strength. On July 1, 1947, Camp Stanley was consolidated with the San Antonio General Distribution Depot, and on July 1, 1949, was designated as part of the Red River Arsenal, Texarkana, under the jurisdiction of the chief of ordnance.

FORT STOCKTON. Located on Comanche Creek at the present town of Fort Stockton in Pecos County, 250 miles east of El Paso, and established on March 23, 1859, by elements of the 1st Infantry, Fort Stockton was intended to safeguard the San Antonio–El Paso mail route. Originally called Camp Stockton, it was soon officially designated a fort and named for Commodore Robert Field Stockton, U.S. Navy, a distinguished veteran of the Mexican War. The post, consisting of mostly adobe buildings, was evacuated in April 1861 by order of Brigadier General David E. Twiggs. It was reportedly briefly occupied by Confederate troops who burned the fort after abandoning it. The ruined post was reoccupied on July 7, 1867, by Federal troops of the 9th Cavalry under the command of Colonel Edward Hatch, and completely rebuilt. Fort Stockton was permanently abandoned on June 30, 1886.

FORT SULAKOWSKI. FORT POINT.

FORT SULLIVAN. Located one and a half miles east of the present village of Port Sullivan on U.S. 190 in Milam County, Fort Sullivan was established by Augustus W. Sullivan in 1835 as a fortified trading post at the intersection of the Houston-Waco and Austin-East Texas roads.

CANTONMENT ON THE SWEETWATER. FORT ELLIOTT.

CAMP SWIFT. A World War II post, activated on May 4, 1942, as an infantry division training center, and named for Eben Swift, was located in Bastrop County, about 36 miles southeast of Austin. Planned originally for 30,000 troops, Camp Swift was later greatly expanded. Effective January 31, 1947, the post was declared surplus by the War Department.

FORT TAYLOR. FORT BROWN.

FORT TENOXTITLÁN. Located on the east bank of the Brazos River in present Burleson County, near the point where the San Antonio–Nacogdoches road crossed the river, it was established in the fall of 1830 by Lieutenant Colonel José Francisco Ruíz and garrisoned by 100 cavalrymen in compliance with an order of General Manuel de Mier y Terán. The fort was intended to prevent the illegal entry of emigrants and goods from the United States and to Mexicanize Texas. The fort's name was derived from the ancient capital of the Aztecs, today's Mexico City, before the Spanish conquest. Although the fort was abandoned in August 1832, the trading post and settlement of Tenoxtitlán survived until about 1860.

FORT TEODORO. FORT ST. LOUIS DE CARLORETTE.

FORT TERÁN. Located on the right bank of the Neches River, opposite the mouth of Shawnee Creek, about three miles west of the present town of Rockland in Tyler County, Fort Terán was established in October 1831 by order of General Manuel de Mier y Terán. The fort was designed to prevent the illegal entry of Americans into Mexico and to foster Mexican colonization of Texas. Fort Terán was abandoned soon after the Battle of Nacogdoches on August 2, 1832.

FORT TERRETT (*Post on the Rio Llano*). Located on the east bank of the North Fork of the Llano River, a tributary of the Colorado, 14 miles west of present Roosevelt in Sutton County, it was established as Post on the Rio Llano on February 5, 1852, by Lieutenant Colonel Henry Bainbridge, 1st Infantry, and designed to protect the settlements on the old San Antonio Road against Comanche depredations. The post was officially designated Fort Terrett on October 16, 1852, in honor of 1st Lieutenant John C. Terrett, 1st Infantry, killed on September 21, 1846, in the Battle of Monterrey. The fort was abandoned on February 26, 1854. Some of Fort Terrett's old buildings are reportedly still in use today as the headquarters and outbuildings of a private ranch.

CAMP TRAVIS. A World War I infantry mobilization and training center, Camp Travis was established at San Antonio in 1917 and named in honor of William B. Travis, martyred hero of the battle of the Alamo. Some 112,000 draftees from Texas, Arizona, New Mexico, and Oklahoma were trained at the camp. The units stationed there included the 90th Infantry Division. Camp Travis was consolidated with Fort Sam Houston in 1922.

FORT TRAVIS. A Republic of Texas defense built in 1836 on the east end of Galveston Island and named in the memory of William B. Travis, hero of the Alamo, Fort Travis was an octagonal earthwork mounting 6- and 12-pound guns from the *Cayuga*. Its garrison, commanded by James Morgan, was withdrawn in 1844.

FORT TRAVIS. In 1898–99, as a part of the federal government's military development of Galveston Island, a second Fort Travis was constructed on Bolivar Point where a Confederate defense called Fort Green was located during the Civil War. Its turn-of-the-century works, which with Fort San Jacinto guarded the entrance of Galveston Bay, included Batteries Davis and Ernst. Fort Travis was active through World War II, when two more batteries, Kimble and No. 236, were added. The Bolivar Point site is now a Galveston County park encompassing the preserved batteries.

CAMP VAN CAMP. An outpost of Fort Belknap established near Newcastle in Young County on April 30, 1859, the post was named in the memory of Lieutenant Cornelius Van Camp, a topographical officer in Earl Van Dorn's Expedition, who was killed in a battle at Wichita Village, Indian Territory, on October 1, 1858. Camp Van Camp was abandoned on August 28, 1859.

CAMP VAN DORN An early Confederate training post located on the banks of Buffalo Bayou near the town of Harrisburg, Harris County, Camp Van Dorn was a large instruction and drill encampment for about 20 companies of Confederate troops. The post was named for General Earl Van Dorn.

FORT VELASCO. Located on the left bank of the Brazos River near its mouth, at the old town of Velasco in Brazoria County, Fort Velasco was a short-lived fort established in 1832 by Colonel Dominic Ugartchea in compliance with an order of General Manuel de Mier y Terán. Established to prevent the illegal entry into Mexico of Americans and goods from the United States and to Mexicanize Texas, it was the last in the series of such posts designed for that purpose. It was evacuated on June 27, 1832, after an attack by forces under John Austin.

In May 1836 the Republic of Texas built a temporary defense on the site, which consisted of a few swiveling cannon in timber-backed sand emplacements that looked out to sea and over the mouth of the river. During the winter of 1863–64, Confederate troops cleared the ruins of the old Republic fort and constructed a new strong defense on the site. Situated opposite Fort Quintana, the fort was commanded by Colonel Joseph Bates and garrisoned by the 13th Texas Infantry, supported by a detachment of artillerymen. The fort's armament reportedly consisted of six 24-pounder smoothbores mounted on sand parapets.

CAMP VERDE. Located on the north bank of Verde Creek near Bandera Pass, in southern Kerr County, Camp Verde was established on July 8, 1856. In 1857 about 40 camels were corraled here as part of the U.S. Army's famous experiment to use them for overland transportation across water-scarce western Texas. The post was evacuated and surrendered to Confederate forces on March 7, 1861. A second Camp Verde, established on March 31, 1862, by Colonel James M. Norris for the Frontier Regiment, was located two miles below the first post. It was occupied in scouting duties until the regiment's consolidation at Fort Belknap in March 1864. The original Camp Verde was reoccupied by U.S. troops on November 30, 1866. Its last garrison was finally withdrawn on April 1, 1869. The post's restored barracks is located in the present town of Camp Verde.

FORT VIRGINIA POINT. FORT HEBÉRT.

CAMP WALLACE. A World War II training center for anti-aircraft units located 15 miles north of Galveston, Camp Wallace was formally opened on February 1, 1941, and was named in honor of Colonel Elmer J. Wallace, 59th Coast Artillery, who was mortally wounded during the Meuse-Argonne offensive in 1918. Anti-aircraft units from Camp Wallace periodically practiced at the west end of Galveston Island and on San Luis Peninsula, since both areas were then uninhabited. The men referred to Camp Wallace as "Swamp Wallace."

FORT WASHINGTON. The northeastern tip of Matagorda Island in present Calhoun County was first occupied during the Texas Revolution by General Albert Sidney Johnston, who apparently had a briefly occupied earthwork defense erected there. During the War with Mexico, General Zachary Taylor temporarily stationed troops there. Shortly after the Civil War erupted, two companies of the 4th Texas Artillery Bat-

talion garrisoned and significantly strengthened the defense. It is not definitely known when the post was designated Fort Washington. In October 1861 its armament included four 24-pounders, two 18-pounders, and one 6-pounder. The fort's commander later relocated the fort about two miles up the strategic Cavallo Pass to a site facing the channel leading into Matagorda Bay. The new defense was named Fort Esperanza.

CAMP WAUL. A Confederate training post located seven miles from Brenham, Washington County, Camp Waul was established in early 1862 and named for Colonel (later Brigadier General) Thomas N. Waul, who organized the unit later known as Waul's Texas Legion.

CAMP WHARTON. CAMP BUCHEL.

CAMP WICHITA. This post was established at Buffalo Spring in Clay County on April 20, 1867, by Captain (Brevet Major) Benjamin T. Hutchins in command of companies C and E of the 6th Cavalry. Camp Wichita was primarily intended to guard the route of courier communications between the region's frontier posts. The camp was abandoned on March 10, 1868, largely because of the area's shortage of water resources.

CAMP WILSON. FORT GRIFFIN.

CAMP WILSON. This post was a camp of instruction on the Fort Sam Houston reservation from July 1916 to December 1916. An attempt was made to change its name to Camp Cecil Lyon, but this was overruled by the secretary of war since the post already honored President Woodrow Wilson. In April 1917 Camp Wilson became the mobilization point for most Texas National Guard units. Camp Wilson was absorbed by Camp Travis in July 1917.

CAMP WITHERALL. A large U.S. Army encampment established during the spring of 1861, Camp Witherall was located on the beach near the mouth of the Rio Grande in Cameron County. It was established as a mobilization point for Federal troops destined for New York after the surrender of all U.S. property in Texas to the Confederacy during March and April by Brigadier General David E. Twiggs.

FORT (CAMP) WOLTERS. A World War II U.S. Army induction and infantry replacement training center located three miles east of Mineral

Wells in Palo Pinto County, it had its beginnings in 1925 when it was established through the efforts of Brigadier General Jacob F. Wolters as a field training camp for the 56th Brigade of the National Guard (the 112th Texas Regiment and the 113th New Mexico Regiment), which he commanded. The city of Mineral Wells donated 50 acres and leased 2,300 surrounding acres to be used three weeks of each year for National Guard maneuvers. Shortly after the outbreak of World War II, the citizens of the town leased and purchased additional land to increase the size of the post to 7,500 acres. Named Camp Wolters in honor of the general, the camp served primarily as an infantry training center with a troop capacity, at the height of operations, of about 25,000. A War Department directive, effective June 27, 1946, placed Camp Wolters in the category of surplus.

After the reservation was purchased by a group of local businessmen, who named it Camp Wolters Enterprises, many of the post's barracks were relocated and converted into homes, schools, and warehouses. The post was reactivated by the government in February 1951 and designated Wolters Air Force Base to accommodate the Aviation Engineer Force, established in April 1951, as a training base for the Korean War. On July 1, 1956, the base returned to Army control, became Camp Wolters again, and the post's principal mission was the Army Primary Helicopter School. On June 1, 1963, Camp Wolters was redesignated Fort Wolters, a permanent military installation, used for the training of troops for the Vietnam conflict. The closing of Fort Wolters was announced by the Army in April 1973. A committee of 30 community leaders requested the Army not to retain the post in caretaker status and to surrender Federal jurisdiction over the reservation property, to which the government agreed in February 1975.

CAMP (G. W. F.) WOOD. Located on the east bank of the Nueces River at the present town of Camp Wood in south central Real County, Camp Wood was established on May 20, 1857, by Lieutenant J. B. Wiod with one company of the 1st Cavalry. It was established on the site of the abandoned Spanish mission known as San Lorenzo de la Santa Cruz, founded by Franciscan missionaries in 1762. After the outbreak of the Civil War, the post was formally surrendered to Texas state troops on March 15, 1861, and was never reactivated by Federal troops. During the war, it was garrisoned intermittently by units of Colonel James M. Norris's Confederate Frontier Battalion and by Texas Rangers for a number of years following the war.

WOODWARD'S SPRING CAMP. CAMP BRENHAM.

FORT WORTH. Located on the West Fork of the Trinity River at the present city of Fort Worth, it was established on June 6, 1849, by Captain Ripley A. Arnold, 2nd Dragoons, and named in honor of colonel William Jenkins Worth, 8th Infantry, a distinguished Mexican War veteran who died on May 7, 1849. Two months later, the post was moved from the bank of the river because of flooding to a nearby site on the bluff. First called Camp Worth, it was officially designated a fort on November 14, 1849. The log-built post was intended to protect the then thinly populated area from Indian hostiles. Fort Worth was abandoned on September 17, 1853, and its last garrison transferred to Fort Belknap. After the Civil War, when the huge cattle drives trailed up through the then miniscule community, Fort Worth became an important trade and supply point. When the United States entered World War I, Fort Worth again became a busy military camp. Camp Bowie, where the 36th Division trained, was established on the western outskirts of the city. Within a radius of 15 miles of the city, three large aviation bases were established for the training of American and Canadian flyers.

ZINK'S FORT (*Sophia's Fort*). The town of New Braunfels on the Comal River in present Comal county was founded on March 21, 1845, by pioneering German homesteaders, among whom were Prince Carl of Solms-Braunfels and his fiancée, Princess Sophia Salm-Salm. They at once built a temporary defense on the bank of the river against Indian attack. It was named the Zinkenburg (Zink's Fort) for Nicolaus Zink, the surveyor who laid out the settlement. This first fort was strengthened by an embankment facing the open prairie and well-placed gabions, and defended by cannon. It was replaced by a second fort, begun on April 28, 1845, and named the Sophienburg (Sophia's Fort) for Princess Sophia. This defense, however, was never completed. The Prince resided in the blockhouse, the only finished part of the fort, for a brief period before he departed for Germany on May 5, 1845. The blockhouse stood until it was destroyed in a storm in August 1886. Both defenses stood within today's city limits of New Braunfels. Zink's Fort was on the south bank of the river near the intersection of Zink Street and Castell Avenue. Sophia's Fort stood on the site now occupied by the Sophienburg Museum, on the corner of Academy and Hill streets, five blocks from the first fort.

FORT ASHLEY. Located on the west shore of Lake Utah, where the city of Provo now stands, Fort Ashley was established in 1825 by William H. Ashley, fur entrepreneur. The first trading post in what is now Utah, it operated for approximately three years, amassing $180,000 worth of furs. It was to this point that Ashley is supposed to have hauled his wheeled cannon in 1826, the same year he sold the lucrative post to the Rocky Mountain Fur Company.

CAMP BATTLE CREEK. So named because it was the place where, on February 28, 1849, the first armed conflict occurred between whites and Indians in Utah. Brigham Young had sent a party of men to the area, 36 miles south of Salt Lake City, to locate sites for settlements. The site of the pitched battle, now known as Pleasant Grove, was selected because of a large grove of cottonwood trees bordering a clear stream. An armed camp was established here by the settlers.

FORT BEAR RIVER. Bear River City, just north of Brigham City in Box Elder county, was established and settled in 1866 by a group of mostly Scandinavian Mormons from Brigham City. Their first homes were dugouts, roofed with poles, willows, straw, and earth, built in the west bank of the Bear River, just north of the present bridge. They were advised by the Mormon Council to "fort in" to protect themselves from Indians. In the fall of 1867, the settlers began building homes within a fort on a hill enclosing 10 acres of ground. The dwellings were built close together in regular rows on all four sides of the square. The corrals and stockyards were located outside the enclosure. In 1868 there were about 40 families residing inside the fort, which lasted for a number of years.

CAMP BEAVER. FORT CAMERON.

POST OF BEAVER CANYON. FORT CAMERON.

POST NEAR BEAVER CITY. FORT CAMERON.

FORT BERRYVILLE. A Mormon settler fort, built in 1864, it consisted of log cabins inside a square enclosure with large doors at two opposite ends of the complex. Located in southwest Utah, 30 miles north of the Arizona border, the town was first named Berryville, later renamed Glendale.

CAMP BINGHAM CREEK. Surrounded by magnificent snow-capped mountains, the upper-

Utah

most peaks of which rise 10,000 feet, the town of Bingham lies in the upper fork of a narrow winding canyon located about 26 miles south of Salt Lake City. In its livelier days, Bingham Canyon boasted a population of 15,000 people, frequenting at least 30 saloons. Before ore was found, it was essentially a logging camp founded by Mormon pioneers who built a sawmill in the mouth of the canyon in 1864. Timber from here was used in the construction of the Mormon Tabernacle in Salt Lake City. The two Bingham brothers, Thomas and Sanford, had settled in the canyon with their cattle and horses to farm the area. In 1864 Company L, 2nd California Cavalry Volunteers, camped here during the month of July. The approximate site of the camp is on Bingham Creek south of Midvale.

BINGHAM'S FORT. The district in the city of Ogden first known as Lynne Ward, and today as Five Points, was settled in 1849 by a group of Mormon settlers. In 1859, when Erastus Bingham, his son Sanford, and others arrived, the settlement was organized as a branch of the Latter-day Saints Church, with the elder Bingham as bishop. From then on it was known as Bingham's Fort. In 1853 the settlers began building a fort as a protection from the numerous hostile Indians. The houses in the fort were built of logs, and all faced the inside square. It was located north of 2nd Street, west of Washington Boulevard, and extended northwest along Harrisville Road.

The fort's walls measured 120 by 60 rods, 6 feet thick and 12 feet high, built of rock and adobe. It had a gate or entrance in the west side, and had the walls been completed, there would have been a similar one on the east. In 1855 Brigham Young visited the fort and advised the settlers to abandon the fort to build a real city on a more advantageous site between the Ogden and Weber rivers. Work was halted and most of the settlers removed to Ogden. Bingham's Fort, however, continued to be occupied for some years. It was Brigham Young who proposed that the new settlement be named for the noted Hudson's Bay Company explorer and fur trader, Peter Skene Ogden.

BROWN'S FORT. Captain James Brown, the first Mormon settler in present Weber County, arrived in 1849 and took up residence in Miles Goodyear's Fort Buenaventura along the Weber River in present-day Ogden. In May 1850 the river flooded and inundated the fort. He moved the Goodyear cabins, along with a majority of the fort's residents, to a site about 40 rods

southeast from the original fort and renamed the new complex Brown's Fort. It was situated near 29th Street, east of the Union Pacific tracks. The dwellings were arranged in fort style, enclosing about a 100-yard square. The pioneer cabins of Goodyear's fort as well as those erected in Brown's Fort, were constructed of cottonwood logs, with roofs of poles, rushes, and earth. Only a few houses had puncheon floors, made by splitting logs in two and smoothing the split sides with axes or adzes; the other cabins had dirt floors.

Settlers, Mormons and others, continued to arrive in Weber County, many of them settling in the vicinity of Brown's Fort, located in Ogden's southwest section. The center of town then was at 24th or 25th streets and Washington Boulevard. A few years later, after Brown had erected a water wheel in the Weber River to generate power for a molasses mill, he was accidentally killed when he was caught and crushed in the mill's rollers.

FORT BUENAVENTURA (*Goodyear's Fort*). The half-acre square of stockaded cabins was the first settlement in what is today's state of Utah. It was established by Miles Goodyear in 1846 as a trading post and sold to the Mormons a year later for $1,950, turning over the land and improvements, 75 cattle, 75 goats, 12 sheep, 6 horses, and a cat; Goodyear retained his furs, skins, traps, and most of his horses, and set out for California. Goodyear's Fort, together with Brown's Fort, served as the foundation for the city of Ogden. Goodyear's original cabin, the oldest structure in the state, is now in the State Relief Society Building in Tabernacle Park, on Washington Boulevard between 21st and 22nd streets.

FORT BUTTERMILK. Mormon settlers built this fort in 1851 on a site that later became the town of Holden, 10 miles north of Fillmore, Millard County.

CALL'S FORT. Brigham Young in July 1853 ordered Brigham City's settlers to secure themselves once again in a fort because of increasing Indian unrest. A second fort (the first was Fort Davis) was built about three blocks north and two blocks west of today's center of Brigham City. The new fort extended north and south about 25 rods and was seven or eight rods wide, later extended an additional 20 rods southward. No walls were ever built around the fort, but the log structures were built close together and enclosed the fort on three sides, with only the south end open.

FORT CAMERON (*Camp Beaver; Post of Beaver Canyon; Post near Beaver City*). Established May 25, 1872, this military post was located on the right side of the Beaver River, two miles east of the town of Beaver. The post was established by Major John D. Wilkins, 8th Infantry. Originally named Camp Beaver or Post near Beaver City, and sometimes referred to as Post of Beaver Canyon, it was renamed Fort Cameron on June 30, 1874, in tribute to Colonel James Cameron, 79th New York Infantry, killed on July 21, 1861, at Bull Run. The fort was built of locally quarried basaltic lava stone and arranged around a rectangle 700 by 620 feet. When the railroad finally came through, the post was considered as no longer necessary. It was abandoned on May 1, 1883, and almost immediately sold to the Mormon Church for educational purposes. The fort's buildings, donated by the Church to the Brigham Young Academy at Beaver, were dedicated on September 26, 1898. Today there are just two of the original Army buildings remaining and the site itself is being used for recreational purposes by Beaver City's citizenry.

CANYON STATION POST. This lightly garrisoned and fortified post was one of the Pony Express stations in western Utah, northeast of the Goshute Indian Reservation. The station was located between Willow Springs Post (15 miles) and Deep Creek Post (12 miles), also on the mail route.

CEDAR FORT. Forty miles southwest of Salt Lake City and located in the 22-mile-long, 7-mile-wide Cedar Valley in Utah County, Cedar Valley was first settled by Mormons in 1852. Because of recurrent Indian troubles, the settlement was temporarily abandoned three times, but in 1855 a stone fort was built, 133 feet square, with walls 10 feet high and 4 feet thick. The settlement was raided by Camp Floyd soldiers in 1858, revenging the suspected killing of a sergeant by other Mormons.

CAMP CEDAR SWAMPS. This was a temporary camp on the northeast edge of the Great Salt Lake, in Box Elder County, occupied for about one month in 1863 by troops of the 2nd California Cavalry.

FORT CLARA (*Fort Santa Clara*). Located on the Santa Clara River, the town of Santa Clara

in Washington County was settled by mostly Swiss Mormons. During the winter of 1855–56, they were instructed to build a fort for their protection against Indian incursions. Constructed in less than 10 days, it was located approximately a half-mile from the center of the town. It measured 100 feet square, with walls 2 feet thick and 12 feet high.

CAMP CONNESS (*Camp Rush Valley; Government Reservation in Rush Valley*). This verdant valley, about 50 miles southwest of Salt Lake City, was first occupied in 1855 by Lieutenant Colonel Edward Steptoe and his California Volunteers. Camp Conness, named for John Conness, unsuccessful contender for California's governorship, was established by California Volunteers who guarded Rush Valley's grazing area during the Civil War. Horses from Camp Floyd and Fort Douglas were often pastured here. The valley was intermittently occupied by military units until 1869.

COVE FORT (*Willden's Fort*). This fort, a short distance north of the town of Cove Fort in Millard County, was built by Mormons in 1867 during the Ute Black Hawk War, to protect the Church's just completed Deseret Telegraph line. The site of the fort was originally occupied by Willden's Fort, a minimally fortified dugout with three rooms, built by Charles Willden in 1860, and sold to the Mormons in 1866. Cove Fort, preserved to this day, was constructed of black volcanic rock, with a dozen rooms or apartments built of the same material against the inner walls of the 100-foot-square enclosure. Its 18-foot-high walls are 4 feet thick at the bottom, tapering to 2 feet at the top. The fort's entrances are two thick wooden gates filled with sand to withstand Indian fire arrows. Walks on the parapet and loopholes in the walls provided defenders with good observation of attackers. A well in the fort's center square supplied ample water and a bell near the well served as a tocsin in case of Indian attack. Now privately owned, maintained by generations of the Kesler family since 1903, Cove Fort served for many years as a Church-operated Communications center, way place, supply station, and cattle ranch.

FORT CRITTENDEN (*Camp Floyd*). Fairfield, the site of this Army post established August 24, 1858, is in Cedar Valley, west of Utah Lake. It was settled by Mormons in 1855. A year later the settlers built a rock fort for protection against marauding Indians. Colonel Albert Sidney

COVE FORT. (Courtesy of the Utah Travel Council, Salt Lake City, Utah.)

Johnston, 2nd Cavalry, with 2,500 troops, arrived to take over the town during the Mormon (Utah) War. Originally named Camp Floyd for Secretary of War John B. Floyd, the post was designated Fort Crittenden on February 6, 1861, after Secretary Floyd "deserted" to the Confederacy. The post's new designation was in honor of Senator John J. Crittenden of Tennessee. Abandoned on July 27, 1861, the fort was briefly reoccupied in October 1862 by Colonel Patrick E. Connor, 3rd California Infantry, and elements of his command. But by the time Connor took over the post, some of its buildings had been sold to the Overland Mail Company, and many of the other structures had been demolished. Fort Crittenden was finally abandoned and replaced by Camp Douglas at Salt Lake City, 44 miles to the northeast. The Army transferred the military reservation to the Interior Department on July 22, 1884. The post has been completely obliterated except for a commemorative monument and its military cemetery.

FORT DAVIS. The first fort built at Brigham City in Box Elder County was Fort Davis, later known as the Old Fort, erected by William Davis, the settlement's presiding officer, whose house was the first inside the fort. Built in the fall of 1851, it was about 15 rods long and about 6 rods wide, with a clear stream running through the center of the defense. In the spring of 1852, however, the settlers abandoned the fort and moved out to their farms in the open country.

FORT DAVY CROCKETT (*Fort Misery*). Fort Davy Crockett was a fur-trading post situated on the left bank of the Green River in Brown's Hole Valley, Moffat County, near the present-day Colorado-Utah line, and established in 1837 by Philip Thompson and William Craig. Named in the honor of David Crockett, martyred in the Battle of the Alamo in 1836, it was a single-story, cottonwood-log building with three wings, but apparently without a stockade. The post, however, did not profit and was nicknamed Fort Misery in derision by other trappers who frequented it. The post was abandoned in 1840. Its site lies within today's Dinosaur National Park.

DEEP CREEK STATION CAMP. In 1864 a detachment of California Volunteers garrisoned this station for both the Pony Express and the Overland Stage. The station was located in the vicinity of present-day Ibapah in Tooele County.

FORT DESERET. Just outside today's town of Deseret in Millard County, Fort Deseret was erected in 1866 as a protection against Indians during the Ute Black Hawk War. Mormons of all ages, formed into competing teams, completed the bastioned defense in just 10 days. The fort's walls were 3 feet thick at the bottom and half that at the top. Remains of the walls of the 550-foot-square fort still exist in the Fort Deseret State Park. The name Deseret is derived from a word in the Book of Mormon, which means "honey bee." Brigham Young had decided to call the Mormon territory the State of Deseret, but Congress would not accept this designation and instead named the territory Utah for the Ute Indians.

DEWEY'S CAMP. This was a state militia encampment, commanded by Captain Dewey, in the Thistle Valley, Sanpete County. The camp was attacked and besieged in 1866 by a large number of well-armed Ute Indians. When word arrived at Fairview of the militiamen's plight, militia Colonel John L. Ivie, with 25 men from Mount Pleasant and Fairview, arrived to rescue the men there from annihilation.

CAMP DODGE. Major Noyes Baldwin, 1st Battalion Cavalry, Nevada Volunteers, with companies A, B, and F, aggregating 233 men, took post on December 1, 1865, one and a half miles south of Provo. The camp was discontinued on February 27, 1866.

FORT DOUGLAS. "Pursuant to orders from department Headquarters, a Military Post is hereby established at [Salt Lake City], to be called Camp Douglas." Thus, on October 26, 1862, Orders No. 14 officially founded Camp Douglas, named for recently deceased Senator Stephen Arnold Douglas as suggested by President Lincoln in tribute to his old political debating adversary.

The reentry of the Army into Utah Territory was a continuation of the struggle between the government and the Mormons. When President James Buchanan five years earlier declared that a "state of substantial rebellion" existed in the territory, and had determined to send a large military force to put an end to the "Mormon Menace," the wheels were set in motion for a prolonged period of strife between the Army and Brigham Young's Mormons, which lasted over a decade. After the Mormons had instituted a short scorched earth policy in the path of Colonel Albert Sidney Johnston's expedition, a truce was effected, stipulating that the Army would locate at least 40 miles south of Salt Lake City in Cedar Valley, near Provo. The post established was first known as Camp Floyd, later renamed Fort Crittenden.

In October 1862, while most of the bloody action of the Civil War was taking place in the East, Colonel Patrick E. Connor was ordered to Utah Territory to protect the mail routes from Indian attack. Connor had under his command a large detachment of California and Nevada Volunteers, consisting of 1,000 infantry, 500 cavalry, a battery of artillery, and some 200 wagons, but en route nearly half of the men were withdrawn or diverted, and only about 859 troops arrived at Salt Lake City. While it was generally understood that Connor's job was to control the Indians, he had far different instructions from Secretary of War Edwin Stanton. One historian believes that the expedition was sent "to overawe the Mormon people, the loyalty of whose leaders the Secretary of War had discovered some pretext for doubting." This was during the time when Utah, desiring admission into the Union, had been informed that the government would not permit or tolerate the practice of polygamy.

After a 100-day exhausting march from California to Salt Lake City (July 12–October 21, 1862), Colonel Connor and his troops entered the city. The Army continued on, stopping three miles east of the city at a site just north of Red Butte Creek and near the present military cemetery. Here Camp Douglas was established. But despite

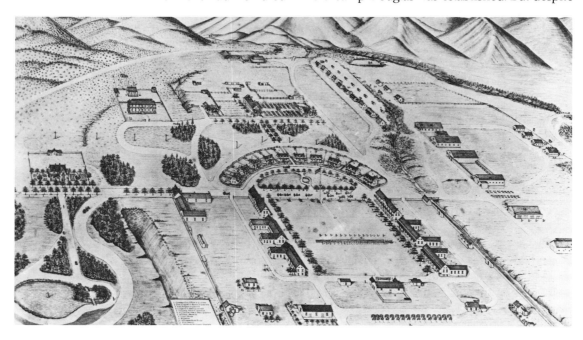

FORT DOUGLAS. (Courtesy of the National Archives.)

the government's warnings, all was peace and quiet in the Valley of the Jordan. The Mormons tolerated the soldiers and they in turn visited the city for recreation.

The troops set to work excavating some 32 pits, 13 feet square and 4 feet deep, over which tents were erected, accommodating 12 men each. The entire post was surrounded by a trench 10 feet wide and 10 feet deep to serve as a drain. A hospital, quartermaster building, guardhouse, and officers' quarters were constructed of wood and adobe for the first winter, and a bake house with a large oven was built to supply the camp with bread and pastry. Connor and his men participated in two major Indian battles after he established the post. The first was the Battle of Bear River in January 1863, and the second was the Battle of Tongue River on August 29, 1865.

The transition from Camp Douglas to Fort Douglas came in 1876, after the post had been almost completely rebuilt under the command of General John E. Smith. Wooden buildings were replaced by substantial structures of stone, which was quarried in Red Butte Canyon above the post. Many different units of the infantry, cavalry, and artillery have been stationed at the fort during its long history. During both World Wars, Fort Douglas housed numbers of P.O.W.s on its 9,000-acre reservation of 170 buildings.

In 1979 the Pentagon decided to close Fort Douglas and have it declared excess to the needs of the Army by the end of fiscal 1981, at a cost savings of about $792,000 annually. The Army dropped from its post inventory about 98 acres, 66 units of family housing, and 55 administrative storage buildings. Periodic attempts have been made to close the fort, and its acreage has been reduced by transfers of property to adjacent University of Utah. Its role as headquarters of Army Reserve activities has increased, and the fort is now the headquarters of the 96th Army Reserve Command. The central part of the fort and its cemetery were placed on the National Register of Historic Places in 1970, and the post became a National Historic Landmark in 1975. The Fort Douglas Military Museum displays exhibits, photos, and murals delineating the role of the military in the development of the Salt Lake City area.

FORT DUCHESNE. Established by Major Frederick W. Benteen, 9th Colored Cavalry, on August 20, 1886, it was located on the Uintah River on a site selected by Brigadier General George Crook, about 10 miles above the confluence of the Duchesne (Du Chesne) and Uintah rivers in Uintah County. The post was specifically established to control hostile Uncompahgre and White River Ute. The fort was ordered evacuated and abandoned in 1892, but the directive was rescinded before it was carried out. It was finally abandoned in 1910 when the post's buildings became the headquarters for the Uintah and Ouray Indian Reservation. The 9th Colored Cavalry was rushed to Cuba in 1898 at the outbreak of the Spanish-American War and never returned to Utah.

CAMP EASTMAN. This post on Chicken Creek, about 60 miles south of Camp Floyd and 14 miles south of the town of Nephi, was established for the purpose of observing the movements of restless Indians and to protect government herds grazing in the Chicken Creek Valley. The post's garrison, a detachment of the 2nd Dragoons and Company C of the 5th Infantry, with Captain Thomas H. Neill, 5th Infantry, in command, had marched from Camp Crossman on January 22, 1859, and took post on Chicken Creek the same day.

FORT EPHRAIM (*Little Fort*). In February 1854 a number of Mormon families, compelled to leave Spring City about two months earlier because of Indian depredations, made preparations to locate a new settlement on Pine (Cottonwood) Creek, now the city of Ephraim in Sanpete County, about a dozen miles south of their former homes. Their first project was the building of a fort, erected on a 1 1/2-acre site, surrounded by 7-foot-high walls, with just one gate in the west wall. A number of adobe and stone houses, with a meeting house in the fort's center, were erected within the enclosure. This fort was later known as "Little Fort" to distinguish it from the larger one built a year later because of the influx of new arrivals. The "Large Fort" enclosed an area of about 17 acres of land and embraced the block on which the "Little Fort" stood. The walls of the new defense were 14 feet high and 4 feet thick at the top, with two gates, one on the east, and one on the west sides. Early in 1868 Fort Ephraim was incorporated as a city by an act of the Utah Legislature.

FARMINGTON STOCKADE. In early 1854 many Mormon families at Farmington, Davis County, met together on March 12 and decided to build a wall around the town as a protection against Indians. The first town survey being too small, an addition was made to the original survey on the south, making the plat in the form of an L, rendered necessary to avoid locating a line of the wall through a swamp. Begun in late March and completed in the spring of 1855, the perimeter of the walled town measured 833 feet, enclosing 112 lots, 6 lots to a block. There were seven entrances or gates in the 12-foot-high walls. The Farmington settlers thereafter had no problem with Indian incursions, with many roving bands bent on depredations passing by without an act of aggression.

FARR'S FORT. Early in 1850 Lorin Farr, who had built the first sawmill and the first gristmill in Weber County, and other settlers who were located north of the Ogden River, erected a fort to protect themselves against Indian attack. It was located one and a half miles northwest of the mouth of Ogden Canyon, and about a block north of the river. Five acres of land were enclosed within the fort by their houses, which were joined end to end, facing the inner square. The rears of the houses formed the outside walls. The north wall of the fort, however, was never completed. It is believed that Farr's Fort was abandoned in 1853 when Lorin Farr, Weber County's leading pioneer, moved into a new dwelling on 21st Street and Washington Boulevard in Ogden. Eventually the expansion of the city absorbed Farr's Fort.

CAMP FLOYD. FORT CRITTENDEN.

CAMP FOUNTAIN GREEN. In May of 1866, Major John Clark of the Territorial Militia set up a temporary camp at Fountain Green in Sanpete County during the Ute Black Hawk War.

CAMP GEORGE. Captain John H. Dalton, with Company C, 1st Battalion of the Nevada Volunteer Cavalry, aggregating 91 men, established a post in January 1866 near Fort Ephraim in the Sanpete Valley.

GOODYEAR'S FORT. FORT BUENAVENTURA.

GOVERNMENT RESERVATION IN RUSH VALLEY. CAMP CONNESS.

FORT GROUSE CREEK. Situated in the northwest corner of Utah, in Box Elder County, close to the Nevada border, the little town of Grouse Creek in 1878 was guarded by a Mormon fort built of logs four rods square.

FORT GUNNISON. Located at today's Gunnison in Sanpete County, this fort was built by Jacob Hutchinson, who named the defense and refuge for Captain John W. Gunnison, topographical engineer, explorer, and author. Captain Gunnison, with R. W. Kern, artist and topographer, and Jacob Creutzfeldt, botanist, comprised the personnel of the scientific division of the expedition to survey railroad routes, escorted by Captain R. M. Morris with a detachment of Army troops. Captain Gunnison was killed by Indians on the Sevier River in 1853.

FORT HAMILTON (*Fort Walker*). Mormon settlers built this fort in 1852, located five miles south of Cedar City in Iron County. The fort was first named Walker, and in 1857 the little settlement was known as Sidon. In 1869 the fort was renamed Fort Hamilton in honor of John Hamilton, and the town was also renamed for him.

FORT HARMONY (*Fort New Harmony*). During the fall of 1852, pioneer John D. Lee and several other Mormons located on Ash Creek, about 25 miles south of Cedar City in Washington County, at a place they called Harmony, where they built a fortified post. The Harmony Settlers, however, found a more advantageous site a few miles farther upstream on Ash Creek and during the summer of 1854 moved to the new location. Late in the fall of the year, they erected a fort, designated Harmony, which became a noted rendezvous for friendly Indians. Lee was their agent, as well as the presiding elder of the settlement. In 1862 the fort was washed away by floodwaters caused by 28 days of continuous heavy rains. Two of Lee's children were killed when the walls of his home collapsed. The settlers moved to the head of Ash Creek, where New Harmony was established and endures to this day. John D. Lee was directly implicated in the infamous Mountain Meadows Massacre in 1857 when 121 non-Mormon emigrants, most of them from northern Arkansas, were murdered.

FORT HERRIMAN. The town of Herriman was first settled by Mormon Henry Herriman in 1851. Two years later others flocked to the settlement and preparations were made to fortify themselves because of threatened Indian violence. In 1854 a fort was built, a concrete structure enclosing about two and a half acres. In 1858, because of the arrival of Johnston's army, the town was temporarily abandoned. Herriman is about 14 miles southwest of Salt Lake City.

KANAB FORT. The town of Kanab in Kane County was involved in Indian hostilities as early as 1865, when a Paiute band stole a herd of horses. Jacob Hamlin was authorized to build a fort at Kanab, which was really little more than an outpost protecting St. George, Santa Clara, and Virgin. It was begun in 1865, mainly to re-settle new Mormon emigrants who occupied log cabins in the fort until farm sites could be assigned to them. The fort was a 112-foot-square cedar-log stockaded enclosure that also included a 20-by-30-foot stone building. A heating oil explosion in December 1870 destroyed part of the fort and killed six occupants.

KAYSVILLE FORT. It was probably in June 1854 that Kaysville's fort was laid out, surveyed, and walls planned to enclose a square consisting of what now constitutes three tiers of blocks north and south and three east and west, or about 108 rods square. But the work so ambitiously begun was never completed, nor was the part that was finished ever used for the purpose of defense against the Indians, for which it had been designed. The work continued, however, with some interruptions, for four years until the arrival of Colonel Johnston's army in 1858. Brigham Young ordered the evacuation of Kaysville, whose settlers, fearing depredations by the military, moved south. Some of the original settlers returned to Kaysville after the threat of war was alleviated by a truce between the Mormons and the Army.

FORT KINGDON. FORT KINGSTON.

FORT KINGSTON (*Fort Kingdon*). The so-called Morrisite affair at Fort Kingston (Kingdon), located in Weber County just south of Ogden, was the most significant western religious defection from the Mormon Church and, since it ended in violence, was widely reported outside Utah. Joseph Morris, an uneducated Welshman converted to Mormonism in 1849, emigrated to Utah in 1853, settling in Weber County where he established a farm. Six years later, he reported having visions that revealed him to be the seventh angel spoken of in the Revelation of St. John. Morris proclaimed himself the new Prophet and wrote Brigham Young, requesting a personal interview. When Young ignored the solicitation, Morris bombarded with letters other leaders of the Church in Salt Lake City, citing the need for reforms in the Church of the Latter-day Saints.

From the beginning Morris had a coterie of about 100 neighbors who believed him to be the new Prophet. Within a year he had enrolled 600 more former Mormons, a number of them armed to protect him. Morris was served with writs issued by the chief justice of the Court, but he ignored the summons. The Court then ordered the arrest of Morris and several of his leading

followers. Richard T. Burton, a prominent Mormon, with 250 troops of the Mormon Militia took up positions on the heights above Fort Kingston and informed the Morrisites that they had 30 minutes in which to surrender or the fort would be assaulted.

"Inside the fort Prophet Morris withdrew to his quarters for a revelation. It came, but a trifle late: the thirty minutes elapsed just as he returned to his people, who were assembled in the open yard of the fort. . . . Burton gave the order to fire. A cannon ball exploded into the fort, killing two women and blowing the jaw off a young girl. A second cannon ball killed two more women. The militia was then ordered to close in on the fort, whereupon the Morrisites began firing. They killed a militiaman. The siege lasted for three days," at the end of which the Morrisites capitulated.

Morris was reported to have screamed, "All who are for me and my God, in life and death, follow me!" The militiamen, in answer, fired point-blank. Morris and two of his main supporters were killed, as were two more women. The revolt was over. Seventeen years later Burton was arraigned for murder but was vindicated with honor by the Court. "Ninety-six Morrisites were indicted for resisting arrest, ten of them for the murder of the militiaman. Sixty Morrisites were tried, convicted and fined $100. Seven of the ten indicted were found guilty of second degree murder and given long prison sentences. (Irving Stone, *Men to Match My Mountains* (1956), pp. 266–68).

FORT KIT CARSON. FORT ROBIDOUX.

LITTLE FORT. FORT EPHRAIM.

LITTLE STONE FORT. On Monday, August 5, 1850, Brigham Young and Herbert C. Kimball selected the site for a new city, named Manti, in Sanpete County, and on May 27, 1852, construction of the town fort was begun. It covered a quarter of a block and was completed a month later. Its dedication took place on July 3, and 76 men were credited with the amount of time each contributed to the task. The number of days amounted to 696, and 85 days' labor was credited to boys. Recorded in the minutes of the City Council meeting of December 23, 1853, was a letter from Brigham Young, instructing the Saints to build a larger fort to more adequately protect themselves against Indian incursions. When plans were finalized, Manti's first defense was called the Little Stone Fort. (See: FORT MANTI.)

FORT LOGAN. About 80 miles north of Salt Lake City, in Cache County, a new Mormon settlement organized a volunteer militia in 1859 and constructed their first log dwellings in a double line, most probably enclosed by a wall. This defense was called Fort Logan.

FORT MALAD. The Malad Valley, spanning the Idaho-Utah state line, was used as a cattle-grazing region in early Utah days. The first attempt made to settle it was made in 1855, when about 15 families located a settlement on the east side of the Malad River, nearly opposite the present town of Washakie, in Box Elder County. During the subsequent three years, the settlers built an adobe fort enclosing about an acre of ground, inside of which they dug cellars and erected log houses. The little settlement, besides having its crops destroyed by grasshoppers, was broken up in 1858 because of continuous Indian troubles.

FORT MANTI. In compliance with a request of Brigham Young, a new fort of stone and adobe, enclosing an area of about 50 acres, was begun in 1854 at the Mormon settlement of Manti. The Temple Block was situated in the center of the fort, which absorbed the Little Stone Fort, built two years earlier. The walls of the new fort were 8 feet high, with its base 3 feet thick tapering off to 18 inches at the top. The rock used for its construction was mostly limestone. After the death of Walker, Ute chief, on January 29, 1855, an aura of peace settled over the Sanpete Valley. Manti began to expand and its borders went beyond the limiting bounds of "Stone Forts," "Log Forts," and "Little Stone Forts."

FORT MEEKS. The first settler on Paria Creek was Peter Shirts, who located a claim at a point about four miles below the present-day town of Old Paria, about 35 miles northeast of Kanab, in Kane County. Shirts apparently settled there just before the outbreak of the Ute Black Hawk War in 1865. He erected a substantial stone house and made a trench from the house to the creek to serve as an escape passage should he and his family be besieged by Indians. Paria, from a Paiute Indian term meaning "muddy water," was originally spelled Pahreah. Over the years, it had been corrupted to its present spelling.

In 1869 Navajo from Arizona, the boundary of which is just below Old Paria, were constantly raiding Mormon settlements in southwestern Utah, driving off herds of livestock and causing depredations in general. There were only two known places where hostile Indians could cross the Colorado River, the Ute Crossing, and 35 miles down the river, the crossing at the mouth of Paria Creek, later known as Lee's Ferry. The stealing of up to 1,500 animals north of Kanab demonstrated that permanent guards had to be established at both crossings. Church authorities and the Mormon Militia ordered the people in isolated settlements to seek safety elsewhere. A detachment of the militia arrived and ordered Peter Shirts's family to vacate. After they left, the militiamen built a stone fort adjoining the Shirts stone dwelling and a company of men was garrisoned there for some time afterward. The station on Paria Creek was named Fort Meeks for William Meeks, its first president. The Ute Crossing to the north, named Wah-wiep or Wahweap, was similarly fortified and garrisoned.

FORT MISERY. FORT DAVY CROCKETT.

FORT MOAB. In 1851 the Church sent 41 Mormons to the site of Moab, just below Arches National Park, in Grand County, to establish a mission. Their first obligation was the building of a stone fort. In September 1855 the fort was repeatedly attacked by Indians, killing three settlers. After this loss, they hastily abandoned the fort. It was 20 years before another effort was made to resettle Moab.

FORT MONTEZUMA. The San Juan Valley in the extreme southeastern corner of the state, in today's San Juan County, was first entered by enterprising Mormons in 1879. Prior to actual settlement, a stone fort was built at the mouth of Montezuma Creek. In December 1879 some 200 Mormons were directed to go to the fort and establish a permanent settlement. The march took four months because of unusually heavy snowfalls. The town of Bluff is 15 miles to the east; much closer is the hamlet of Montezuma Creek.

MORONI FORT. Moroni, one of the eight original settlements of Sanpete County, was settled in March 1859. Countless incidents, some of them bloody, led to the outbreak of the Ute Black Hawk War in April 1865. General Wells immediately ordered a stockade or fort built. A stone observation tower was erected with walls three feet wide and five feet high, with portholes affording observation of the entire valley. As Indian depredations increased, settlers from the outlying areas were ordered inside the defense. A dozen horsemen were hired to guard and care for the livestock at all times.

MOUND FORT (*Ogden Stockade*). The Mound Fort area as a settlement dates back to the fall of 1848, when Ezra Chase and his family and other Mormons located on the north side of the Ogden River, in the immediate vicinity of today's Washington Avenue and 12th Street in Ogden. Begun in the fall of 1853, Mound Fort stood to the east and adjoining the great clay mound extending from 9th to 12th Streets. The mud or adobe walls, 16 feet high and 3 feet thick, intended to enclose the fort, were never completed. The clay mound was the main feature of the fortification. Indian hostilities in 1854, while Ogden was being established, compelled its settlers to construct walls around the new settlement. Mound Fort, which also enclosed a school, was for about 70 years an educational center in the city of Ogden. In May 1919 the ruins of the old mud walls were located.

MOUNT PLEASANT FORT. In August 1858 an exploring committee was appointed to select a favorable site for a settlement on Pleasant Creek in Sanpete County. A petition sent to Brigham Young elicited a letter of advice: "You must build a good, substantial fort and live in it, use every precaution that is necessary against the Indians. Your fort must be twelve feet high and four feet thick, built of either stone or adobe and laid in lime mortar." (Kate B. Carter, *Our Pioneer Heritage* 9: 132–33). The colonizing Mormons followed Young's advice to the letter. Today's location of Mt. Pleasant was selected and a site was surveyed for the fort.

On May 13, 1859, four men were appointed captains to superintend its construction, one for each side of the fort. One hundred and ten men with teams of horses and wagons set to work, and by July 18 it was completed. It was considered the finest fort in Sanpete County, and it encompassed the block later known as the Tithing Yard, 26 rods square, enclosing about five and a half acres of ground between Main and First North, and State and First East streets. Built of native rock, the walls surrounding the compound were 12 feet high, 4 feet wide at the bottom, tapering to about 2 feet at the top. There were portholes every 16 feet, about 7 feet from the ground. A bastion or watchtower in one corner of the fort afforded a view of the surrounding country. Two large, heavy gates were built into the center of the north and south walls.

In 1865 or 1866 it became necessary to erect a second fort in order to protect the livestock from Indian thievery. The new defense, begun on June 4 and completed in two weeks, enclosed about five acres and was located directly north of the first fort. As soon as there were sufficient settlers to protect themselves from marauding Indians, they began to erect homes outside the two forts.

CAMP MURRAY. The town of Murray, five miles south of Salt Lake City, was occupied in September 1885 by elements of the 6th, 9th, and 21st Infantry, as a camp for the instruction of recruits.

NARROWS BREASTWORKS. Located about five miles beyond Echo in Summit County, these breastworks built of rock were manned by Mormon Volunteers in 1857–58 to oppose the entry into Utah Territory of U.S. troops. Diplomacy, however, effected a truce and the Mormon defenses allowed federal troops to march toward Salt Lake City.

FORT NEPHI. The Mormon settlement at Nephi in Juab County was protected by a moated wall, built in 1851. Near here Brigham Young and Chief Wakara negotiated a peace, ending the Walker War.

FORT NEW HARMONY. FORT HARMONY.

OGDEN STOCKADE. MOUND FORT.

CAMP PACE. In 1867 General William B. Pace and elements of the Mormon Militia arrived in Gunnison to further protect the settlers against Indian depredations and to drill his militiamen in military maneuvers. Sometime after his arrival, a rock bastion was begun on the northeast corner of the enlarged fort, the intention being to ultimately surround the principal part of the town with a rock wall, similar to other Sanpete County walled towns. Tons of rocks were hauled in preparation for the project but, the Indian war being over, further prosecution of the work was terminated.

FORT PROVO. FORT UTAH.

CAMP RAWLINS. Established on July 30, 1870, Camp Rawlins was located on the north bank of the Timpanogos River, two miles from Provo, near the base of the Wasatch Mountains. The post was named in the memory of Secretary of War John A. Rawlins, who died on September 6, 1869. Two companies of the 13th Infantry, under the command of Captain Nathan W. Osborne, garrisoned the temporary tent camp until July 9, 1871, when the post was no longer considered necessary.

CAMP RELIEF. Major John M. O'Neill, 2nd California Cavalry Volunteers, with 475 men, established this post in compliance with orders dated April 14, 1864. The men furnished protection to emigrant trains en route to Idaho. The camp was located in the immediate vicinity of today's village of Webster Junction in Cache County, about two miles below the Idaho border. The post was apparently abandoned in late May, 1864.

FORT RICHMOND. Mormon settlers erected a log fort at Richmond, Cache County, in 1859, to protect the dugouts and log cabins they had built earlier. Richmond is located 6 miles south of the Idaho line and 13 miles north of Logan.

FORT ROBIDOUX (*Fort Kit Carson*). The Fort Robidoux Monument, six miles from Roosevelt in Uintah County on U.S. 40, commemorates the Indian trading post established by Antoine Robidoux on the Old Spanish Trail in 1832. The post, surrounded by an adobe wall, was located near the confluence of the Uintah (Duchesne) River, the Green River, and the White River, and across the White River from Ouray. Kit Carson established his winter quarters here in 1833–34. The migratory habits of traders and trappers have led to some confusion. This trading post has for many years been mistaken for Robidoux's second trading post in Utah, Fort Wintey (anglicized from Uintah), often called Fort Robidoux, on the Whiterocks River, near the present town of the same name. Fort Robidoux was destroyed by Indians in 1844.

ROCK FORT. The Mormon village of Rockport on the Weber River was first settled in 1860 by Henry Reynolds. Because of impending Indian trouble, the settlers there were advised to move to Wanship four miles to the north. Pleading to remain, they were permitted to do so provided they would build a fort. A stone fort was erected, with walls eight feet high and two feet thick. The remains of the fort still exist in the Rockport Reservoir State Park on U.S. 189.

ROUND VALLEY POST. During August 1857 Captain William D. Smith, with four companies of the 2nd Dragoons, established a post at Round Valley in Rich County, about five miles south of Bear Lake.

CAMP RUSH VALLEY. CAMP CONNESS.

FORT SALT LAKE CITY. During the summer of 1847, after the Mormons arrived at the present site of Salt Lake City, 17 log-and-adobe dwellings and a fort were their very first construction tasks. This first fort was called North Fort. A little later a second was built immediately to the south, separated by a wall, and occupied by later arrivals. This was called South Fort. North Fort stood on the site now occupied by Pioneer Park, at 3rd South and 2nd West streets.

SALT LAKE CITY POST. The capital of Utah was garrisoned between December 1865 and March 1866 by Lieutenant Colonel William M. Johns, 3rd Battalion, California Infantry, with 177 men. They left Camp Douglas on December 7 and established the post the same day.

FORT SANTA CLARA. FORT CLARA.

SANTAQUIN FORT. The town of Santaquin is located in the extreme south end of Utah County, its boundaries extending to the north line of Juab County. The townsite, situated on Summit Creek, near the mouth of Summit Creek Canyon, occupies an elevation overlooking a great part of Utah Valley. It was first settled in the summer of 1851 by Benjamin F. Johnson and other Latter-day Saints. When the so-called Walker Indian War broke out in the summer of 1853, the settlers of Summit Creek (the town's first name) evacuated and moved to Payson, six miles to the northeast. The permanent settling of Summit Creek occurred in the spring of 1856, when Johnson and others reestablished themselves there. None of the dwellings built by the former settlers were then standing, the Indians having destroyed nearly everything combustible. The first task by the new settlers was the buildings of a fort. The houses within the defense, together with the surrounding wall, made quite a formidable fortification, providing ample protection against Indian attack. Later in the same year, the settlers erected an 18-by-32-foot schoolhouse within the fort.

SMITHFIELD FORT. On October 10, 1859, pioneering Mormons settled on what was then known as Summit Creek (later Smithfield) in Cache County. One of the foremost problems troubling the settlers was that posed by the native Indians, mostly Shoshoni. Despite Brigham Young's warnings, the settlers here built their homes on spacious acreage. On July 23, 1860, the chief of a band of Indians, camped close to the settlement, was arrested because one of his warriors had stolen a pony. What began as a heated argument ended in bloodletting. The settlers realized then they had to fortify themselves. They built a well-planned and organized enclosure or fort, covering an area 40 rods wide and 120 rods long, with the creek running through its center. About 70 families built new dwellings within the walled enclosure. For about two years they maintained the Smithfield Fort, and when it appeared that the strained relations between them and the Indians had improved, the settlers evacuated the fort and built new homes in the area which had been properly surveyed and designated as the townsite of Smithfield.

FORT SOWIETTE. FORT UTAH.

SPRING CITY FORT. This young Mormon settlement, about 20 miles north of Manti, in Sanpete County, was raided by a host of Indians on August 2, 1853, depriving the settlers of all their livestock. The rudimentary fort was constructed of log cabins joined to each other, with a hollow square in the center for the animals. That morning the livestock had been driven out by six or eight herdsmen to the grazing grounds when up to 200 Indians made a sudden appearance, some circling the fort, while others rounded up the stock. A messenger was sent to Manti to plead for help. Spring City's inhabitants evacuated their fort and homes and went to Manti where they were made as comfortable as possible in the center of Manti's fort. After peace was made with the Indians some time later, Spring City's former settlers returned to their first homes.

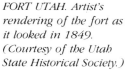

FORT UTAH. Artist's rendering of the fort as it looked in 1849. (Courtesy of the Utah State Historical Society.)

FORT THORNBURGH. Established on September 17, 1881, this fort, originally a tent camp, was first located at the junction of the Green and White rivers in northeastern Utah, during the aftermath of the bloody Ute war. At the request of the Interior Department, the post was moved 35 miles to the northeast to a site on Ashley Creek, a tributary of the Green River. Established by Captain Hamilton S. Hawkins, 6th Infantry, and named in honor of Major Thomas T. Thornburgh, 4th Infantry, killed by Ute on September 29, 1879, the post was designed to control the Ute and protect their agents.

After the troops moved to Ashley Creek, they still had to live in tents during the first winter. The second winter saw the men barracked at other posts because no money had been appropriated by the government for construction. Finally, eight adobe structures were built in 1883, but by this time it was too late. Squatters had moved into the area, making it too costly to obtain a clear title. The Army abandoned the fort after the winter of 1883–84. The military reservation was transferred to the Interior Department on July 22, 1884.

FORT UINTAH. FORT ROBIDOUX.

FORT UTAH (*Fort Provo; Fort Sowiette*). In March 1849 John S. Higbee, at the head of 30 Mormon families, left Salt Lake City to establish a new settlement on the Provo River, 45 miles to the south. The place chosen was a favorite Ute Indian fishing ground. The colonists established themselves on the river's south bank, near its mouth in Lake Utah. Construction and farming were begun at once and within several weeks

they had built a fort, plowed 225 acres of land, and planted rye, wheat, and corn. This first fort, originally called Fort Provo and later Fort Utah, began as a closely knit cluster of log cabins with a single cannon on a platform for protection.

"Historically, few groups of whites managed to establish and maintain as generally harmonious relations with their Indian neighbors as did the Latter-day Saints. Fort Utah was one of the first Mormon settlements to profit from Brigham Young's enlightened (for his day) views on Indian-white affairs" (Kent Ruth, *Great Day in the West* [1963], p. 254). Young wrote in 1857 that he had proved by experience that it was far cheaper to feed and clothe the Indians than to fight them.

In 1853 Provo's settlers built a second fort, nicknamed Fort Sowiette, near or on the same site occupied by the 1849 fort. Sowiette, the principal war chief of the Ute, had a fond regard for his Mormon neighbors. When Chief Walker (Walkara) planned to attack Fort Utah, Sowiette garrisoned his own warriors within the stockade and prepared to assist in its defense. Walker and his braves besieged the fort all night, howling and whooping, but in the morning finally withdrew without attacking. The site of the fort is now Sowiette Park at Fifth West and Fifth North streets.

FORT WAH-WIEP. FORT MEEKS.

FORT WALKER. FORT HAMILTON.

WILLDEN'S FORT. COVE FORT.

CAMP WILLIAMS. Situated on the Jordan Narrows, at present-day Camp Williams on S.R. 68, between Utah and Salt Lake counties, Camp Williams was first selected as a training camp for the Utah National Guard in 1914. As with some of the nation's older states, Utah has had a long tradition of militia service.

One of Utah's first laws created a territorial militia with the name "The Nauvoo Legion," recalling a similar organization which had been established by the Mormons in Illinois. All male adults between the ages of 18 and 45 were liable for this service. As early as 1854 the Legion had 1,744 in the infantry and 1,004 in the cavalry. . . . The Legion met in annual musters from 1849, and performed service in Indian campaigns and guarding the mail routes. In the Utah War of 1857–58, a force of about 3,000 men . . . [was] mobilized to defend Zion against the government's Utah Expedition. Under the command of Lieutenant General Daniel

H. Wells, some of these troops harassed the Army's supply train and built defensive works in Echo Canyon. . . . Throughout much of the territorial period, units of the gaily uniformed Legion had annual musters and encampments, and the Lehi units often bivouacked near Jordan Narrows—a site which was to become the training headquarters of the Legion's successor, the Utah National Guard. . . . In 1870 Governor J. Wilson Shaffer, a Civil War veteran and "northern reconstructionist," forbade the militia to muster, and the organization remained relatively inactive until 1887 when Congress abolished the Legion by a specific provision to the Edmunds-Tucker Act. At the time of its suspension, the Legion consisted of 13,000 efficiently armed and well-drilled men. . . . Upon the organization of the National Guard Association of the United States in 1878, the term "National Guard" had become a general designation for the organized militias of the various states and territories. The conflict between the Mormons and the federal government having been largely resolved, the territorial legislature, in March 1894, authorized the governor, Caleb W. West, to establish "The National Guard of Utah." By the end of the year, 14 companies of infantry, 3 troops of cavalry, and 2 batteries of light artillery—all told, about 400 men—were enlisted. [Thomas G. Alexander and Leonard J. Arrington, "Utah's First Line of Defense: The Utah National Guard and Camp W. G. Williams, 1926–1965," in *Utah Historical Quarterly* 33, no. 2 (1965)]

The Utah National Guard has served in all the wars from the Spanish-American War right through the Vietnam War, including Mexican border duty in 1916. In 1914 and 1915, President Woodrow Wilson set aside 18,700 acres of public domain near the Jordan Narrows for "permanent maneuver grounds." In 1922 the state purchased 153 acres, and another 199 acres in 1931. All the accumulated acreage made an excellent site for a training camp. World War I held up construction of facilities at the Jordan Narrows. After the war, it was used only one year (1922) before 1926, when the Guard units started using it as a permanent site. In 1928 the camp was named for Brigadier General W. G. Williams, adjutant general.

At first Camp Williams consisted of pup tents. In time new, more permanent, and modern facilities were constructed. In return for funds, which the Federal government had provided to construct facilities and to support the Guard, the state had agreed that it would make all National Guard facilities available in time of national emergency. Camp Williams became a subpost and training site for Fort Douglas during World War II. By June 1943 Army engineers had built more than 100 structures at the camp. When the Army had completed its training program, Camp Williams was declared surplus and was returned to the state of Utah in November 1944. The first postwar meeting of the Guard was held in November 1947 at the camp, and the first postwar training encampment was held there the following June. Almost all annual Guard encampments have been held at Camp Williams since that date.

FORT WINTEY. FORT ROBIDOUX.

BATTERY PARK REDOUBT. During the War of 1812, Battery Park at Burlington on Lake Champlain was the site of a military encampment for some 4,000 troops assembled from many Vermont towns. In June 1813 a battery of guns fronted by a long parapet was constructed here 100 feet above the waters of the lake. On August 3 a British gunboat and two armed sloops, one and a half miles offshore, began a bombardment of Burlington's lake shoreline. Aided by several armed scows of Captain (Commodore by courtesy) Thomas Macdonough's Lake Champlain navy, the attack was repulsed in 20 minutes.

CAMP BAXTER (BARRACKS). In April 1861 St. Johnsbury in Caledonia County was selected as the rendezvous for the 3rd Vermont Regiment which assembled on the town's Fair Grounds. Evolving as a large training post for recruits from all over the state, it was named Camp Baxter for the state's adjutant general. Instead of tents to shelter the trainees, the main building on the grounds was enlarged to a length of 300 feet, furnished with three tiers of bunks for 1,000 men. The dining hall ran through the center of the buildings. Two auxiliary buildings were erected for the kitchen and a hospital. The post was used, at least intermittently, throughout the Civil War and was known to the Army as Baxter Barracks.

BLOCKHOUSE POINT FORT (*Fort Loyal*). When the remnants of General John Burgoyne's defeated army retreated to Canada in 1777, the British retained possession of fortified Point Au Fer on Lake Champlain near Rouses Point. They also occupied Fort Loyal, a strong blockhouse built in July 1781 by Loyalist Captain Justus Sherwood on the west side of North Hero Island at a place then known as Dutchman's Point, later renamed Blockhouse Point. Both were held by the British for 13 years after the 1783 Treaty of Paris ending the Revolution.

BRATTLEBORO BARRACKS. A Civil War post located at Brattleboro, it was established on August 1, 1863, and commanded by Major William Austine. Garrisoned by two companies of drafted men, the post was officially designated U.S. Barracks. At the end of March 1864, the post was combined with "Draft Rendezvous," also at Brattleboro, under the command of the same officer.

FORT BRIDGMAN. Located at the present town of Vernon on the Connecticut River in

Vermont

Windham County, just north of the Massachusetts line, Fort Bridgman was a two-story blockhouse erected by Orlando Bridgman on his farm in 1738. It has been described as a 20-by-38-foot loopholed defense, built of large square timbers laid horizontally and locked together at its angles. Fort Bridgman was reportedly more pretentious than Fort Sartwell, which was built the same year at Vernon. Fort Bridgman stood until about the year 1824.

FORT CASSIN. A War of 1812 defense located at the mouth of Otter Creek on Lake Champlain, just above today's popular lake resort of Basin Harbor and eight miles northwest of the city of Vergennes, Fort Cassin was named in honor of naval Lieutenant Stephen Cassin, commander of the armed schooner *Ticonderoga*. The officer led the defense of this fort on May 14, 1814, when British gunboats attacked it in an effort to sail up Otter Creek and destroy Captain Thomas Macdonough's fleet, then being constructed at the Vergennes shipyards. The British were repulsed after a half-hour's sharp exchange of cannon fire. Thus Macdonough's armada was rescued from certain destruction to achieve a significant victory on the lake the following September. As a reward for his valorous service, Lieutenant Cassin was awarded a gold medal by Congress.

CHAMPLAIN ARSENAL. Established in 1828 at Vergennes, on the site of a former iron and steel mill, the Champlain Arsenal occupied 28 acres of ground and consisted of stone-built officers' quarters, barracks, magazine, and ordnance and munitions storehouses. During the War of 1812, the iron mill furnished over 177 tons of cannonshot for the Battle of Plattsburg on Lake Champlain in September 1814. The Arsenal was discontinued in 1872.

FORT COOKE'S HILL. A Revolutionary War defense located at present Corinth in Orange County, it was erected on October 16, 1781, by two companies of troops on Cooke's Hill near the center of town.

FORT DEFIANCE. Located at the town of Barnard, Windsor County, Fort Defiance was erected by militia troops during August–September 1780 and named on November 2, 1780. It was not active after 1781 and abandoned after the Revolutionary War.

FORT DE PIEUX (*De Warm Stockade; Fort Pointe à la Chevelure*). Pointe à la Chevelure was the name given by the French to the promontory on the eastern or Vermont shore of Lake Champlain opposite Crown Point. The origin of the name is open to conjecture. In 1690 a detachment of soldiers under Captain Jacob (Jacobus) De Warm from Albany built a small temporary fort or stockade at the site for the purpose of observing the activities of the French in the Champlain Valley. There is reason to believe that Dutch fur traders from Albany camped there from time to time.

After repeated solicitations from the Canadian military authorities, royal permission was granted for a new fort at Pointe à la Chevelure, where the first significant narrowing of the waterway offered the obvious location for a defense against attempted British encroachment on Canada. The stockaded French fort, completed in September of 1731 and named Fort De Pieux ("pious") was 100 feet square, with bastions at each angle and three buildings enclosed within the palisades. Its initial garrison consisted of 2 officers and 20 men. This small post was regarded as only a temporary establishment until royal consent could be obtained for the construction of a stronger defense, Fort St. Frederic, completed in 1737, at Crown Point.

A settlement grew up around the fort. In 1759 during the French and Indian War, its inhabitants abandoned their homes there because of an anticipated British and Indian invasion of Canada via the Lake Champlain route. In 1760 Mohawk raiders destroyed the village completely. After the defeat of the French, the small peninsula became known by the British as Chimney Point because of its stark picture of chimneys rising from the blackened ruins. The eastern terminus of today's Champlain Bridge, Chimney Point is located about eight miles southwest of the town of Addison.

DE WARM STOCKADE. FORT DE PIEUX.

FORT DUMMER. The first English settlement in what is now the state of Vermont, Fort Dummer was erected near present Brattleboro in the spring and summer of 1724 by the province of Massachusetts for the protection of the northern frontier and named for William Dummer, lieutenant-governor of the province. A strong defense nearly square in design, 180 feet to a side, the fort was constructed of horizontally laid hewn yellow pine timbers by Lieutenant Timothy Dwight under the supervision of Colonel John Stoddard, both men from the town of Northampton in Massachusetts. The fort, minus a stockade when completed, was defended by 12 pieces of ordnance, 8 of them mounted on swivels. In

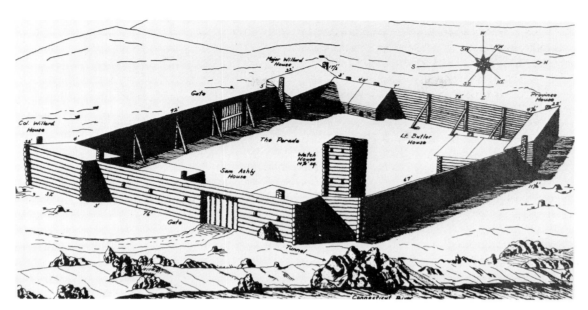

FORT DUMMER. Artist's rendering based on a 1747 drawing. (Courtesy of the Vermont Development Department.)

October of the same year, it was attacked by a party of 70 Indians, who killed or wounded 5 men of the garrison. Subsequently, a palisade of squared timbers 12 feet long was erected around the fort, to enclose an acre and a half of ground. Fort Dummer was one of the two northernmost military outposts until the British conquest of Canada. The fort was dismantled in 1763. Fort Dummer's actual site is now submerged by the impounded waters of the Vernon Dam.

FORT ETHAN ALLEN. One of the largest U.S. Cavalry and Field Artillery training posts in the nation, located about five miles from Burlington, Fort Ethan Allen was established on August 5, 1892, on purchased land once owned by the Revolutionary War patriot for whom it was named, and first occupied on September 28, 1894. Deactivated in 1943, Fort Ethan Allen was used primarily for military storage until it was taken over by the Air Force in 1952 and redesignated the Ethan Allen Air Force Base. Despite many petitions and Congressional resolutions to the contrary, the base was closed in May 1960. In 1962 the property and buildings were declared surplus by the General Services Administration, to be gradually transferred to primarily the University of Vermont and, to a lesser degree, St. Michael's College.

FORT FREDERICK. In 1773 Ira Allen and Remember Baker built a two-storied blockhouse at Winooski River's falls at the present town of Winooski, Chittenden County, to principally protect their lands from New York claimants. With Ethan Allen, famed leader of the Green Mountain Boys, and two other brothers, they had formed the Onion River Land Company to sell

parceled Winooski properties to homesteaders. Named Fort Frederick in honor of the Prince of Wales, father of George III, the site of the fort is at the bridge on Main Street in Winooski.

FORT HILL (*Fort Putney*). Prior to the outbreak of King George's War in 1744, the settlers of the town of Putney in present Windham County erected a defense against the French and their allied Indians. Called Fort Hill, or Fort Putney, it stood on an elevation in the center of what was then known as the Great Meadows. The fort apparently served throughout the war.

FORT DUMMER. Monument marking the site of the fort. (Courtesy of the Vermont Development Department.)

FORT LA MOTTE. FORT STE. ANNE.

FORT LOYAL. BLOCKHOUSE POINT FORT.

FORT MOTT. A Revolutionary War defense erected in 1777 at Pittsford, northwest of Rutland, in present Rutland County, it was named for John Mott, militia commander. It was described as a palisaded square occupying about three-quarters of an acre and enclosing a log-built structure which took the place of a blockhouse. (See also FORT VERGENNES.)

FORT NEW HAVEN. Revolutionary War patriot Ethan Allen reportedly erected a blockhouse about the year 1769 in the town of New Haven in present Addison County to protect the lands the Allen brothers owned from the encroachments of New York land speculators.

FORT POINTE À LA CHEVELURE. FORT DE PIEUX.

FORT PUTNEY. FORT HILL.

FORT RANGER. The second of two Revolutionary War defenses erected at the town of Rutland, Fort Ranger was established in 1778 on a high bluff at Mead's (now Rutland) Falls, just east of the center of town. A large substantially built fort of unhewn hemlock logs, it served until 1781 as headquarters for Vermont's troops.

FORT RUTLAND. The first of Rutland's two Revolutionary War defenses, it was erected in 1775 near the present junction of North and South Main streets and consisted of a maple stockade enclosing a small building used for the storing of ammunition and provisions.

FORT STE. ANNE (*Fort La Motte*). In the summer of 1666, the French established the first white settlement on Lake Champlain as both a defense and a springboard for continued military operations against the Mohawks to the south. King Louis XIV's viceroy in Canada, Lieutenant General Alexandre de Prouville, marquis de Tracy, had ordered Captain Pierre de St. Paul, sieur de la Motte (La Mothe) of the Carignan-Salieres Regiment to erect a fort on the south side of the oblong, rock-rimmed forested island that guards the lake's outlet, known today as Isle La Motte, one of the Hero Islands, in present Grand Isle County. The captain erected log-built bastions, surrounded by a 96-by-140-foot palisade, enclosing in addition a Jesuit chapel dedicated to Ste. Anne, where the first mass in Vermont was held. During the 1670s, probably in 1676, the French deliberately destroyed Fort Ste. Anne. A shrine maintained by the Order of St. Edmond commemorates the site of the French fort. During the War of 1812, the British in 1814 anchored their Lake Champlain fleet off Isle La Motte and emplaced on its shore a battery of three long 18-pounder guns to guard the landing of supplies at Chazy on the New York shore.

FORT SARTWELL. In 1737 Josiah Sartwell erected a fortified dwelling known as Sartwell's Fort, 2 miles south of Fort Dummer, and about 100 rods northwest of Fort Bridgman, built the same year, at present Vernon in Windham County. The fort, a two-story thoroughly loopholed blockhouse, was built of hewn timbers, 38 feet long and 20 feet wide, very similar to nearby Fort Bridgman. The blockhouse was owned by Josiah Sartwell and his descendants for about 100 years. In 1837, it was dismantled and replaced by a farmhouse, constructed with much of the fort's timbers.

FORT VENGEANCE. FORT VERGENNES.

FORT VERGENNES (*Fort Vengeance*). During the winter of 1779–80, a Revolutionary War fort was built about a mile from present Pittsford in Rutland County. When one of its garrison named Vergennes was killed by Indians, the soldiers named the defense for him. The fort was misnamed Fort Vengeance by a number of historians apparently because of the similarity in pronunciation. Fort Vergennes was the northernmost of three forts guarding the frontier against the British and their allied Indians who were raiding from Canada via Lake Champlain, still under British control despite General John Burgoyne's defeat at Saratoga in 1777.

FORT WARREN. A Revolutionary war defense, Fort Warren was erected in 1779 on an elevation at the foot of Lake Bomoseen, directly east of Castleton in present Rutland County, as a defense of the northern frontier. The road from the north was the route of American retreat before the southward advance of Burgoyne's army in 1777. The road had been protected by Colonel Seth Warner's rear guard troops who fought the Battle of Hubbardton, seven miles north, on July 7, 1777, in an effort to block the British advance. The town of Castleton later took over the fort's storehouse and used it for both religious and town business until 1790.

FORT ABBOT. A Federal battery during the War of the Rebellion, located on the south side of the Appomattox River, near its junction with the James, a short distance west from City Point, today's Hopewell, just above Petersburg, it was one of the fortifications constituting lines of entrenchments for the defense of the camps at City Point. It was laid out and constructed in October 1864, under the direction of Lieutenant Colonel H. W. Benham, U.S. Engineers. It is believed that the work was named in compliment to Captain (Brevet Brigadier General Volunteers), Henry L. Abbot, U.S. Engineers, in command of the siege train of the Army of the Potomac, whose depot and base of operations were at or near this point. After the evacuation of Petersburg and Richmond, followed by the surrender of the Army of Northern Virginia, these works were gradually dismantled and abandoned.

FORT ALBANY. Located immediately to the northwest of the present junction of South Arlington Ridge Road and South Nash Street, in Arlington, it was a Union bastioned earthwork built in May 1861 to guard the convergence of the two roads leading to Long Bridge, near today's Pentagon. It had a perimeter of 429 yards and emplacements for 12 guns. It was well provided with magazines, embrasures, and bombproofs. The ground on which Fort Albany stood was cut away for the construction of the Henry G. Shirley Memorial Highway in 1942.

CAMP ALEXANDER. This World War I post was originally established in August 1917, about three miles from Newport News, in connection with the Port of Embarkation and as part of Camp Hill, and was named in honor of Lieutenant John H. Alexander, 9th Cavalry, a black graduate of the U.S. Military Academy in 1887. Camp Alexander was used as a training and embarkation post for mostly black stevedore regiments and labor battalions until November 11, 1918, when it was abandoned and ordered sold.

FORT ALEXANDER. Part of the Confederate defense line around Richmond, its site now lies within the confines of Battlefield Park.

ALEXANDRIA DEFENSES. At the outbreak of the Civil War, it was determined to fortify Alexandria because of its proximity to Washington, its importance in commanding the navigation of the Potomac, and its connection with the railroad system of the South. After possession of Alexandria was established, a large bastioned work called Fort Ellsworth was soon under con-

Virginia

struction. About September 1, 1861, Fort Worth, on Seminary Heights, about one and a half miles west of Fort Ellsworth; Fort Reynolds, one and a half miles north of Fort Worth; and Fort Ward, between the two, were commenced. Somewhat later Fort Barnard, three-quarters of a mile north of Fort Reynolds, was begun. About the middle of September, Fort Lyon, located on the heights about one mile southwest of the city, was commenced. In 1862 Forts Wead, Farnsworth, and O'Rourke, south of Hunting Creek and near Fort Lyon, were constructed. Fort Willard, near the mouth of the creek, was built about the same time. A work of considerable strength called Fort Williams, located between Forts Worth and Ellsworth, was built in 1862. Between Forts Ward and Worth an almost continuous line of trenches, supported by powerful batteries, covered the line of defense; this was continued to Fort or Battery Garesché, near Fort Reynolds. Early in 1863 a barbette battery of six guns was built on Jones' Point, and called Battery Rodgers. The fortifications were held by Union troops until the cessation of hostilities, when they were gradually dismantled and abandoned.

CAMP (RUSSELL A.) ALGER. A Spanish-American War training post, consisting of a large encampment of tents, established in 1898, Camp Alger was located on the Washington, Ohio and Western railway line between Falls Church and the suburban development of Dunn-Loring. It was named for Russell Alexander Alger, secretary of war to President McKinley. By August 1898 more than 35,000 troops were stationed at the camp. The fighting would be over before many of these soldiers could see action.

FORT ALGERNOURNE. FORT MONROE.

REDOUBT (BATTERY) ANDERSON. This redoubt, also known as Battery Anderson, was a strong Union position on the Bermuda Hundred line near Petersburg in Prince George County.

ANDERSON BLOCKHOUSE. This Revolutionary War two-story, loopholed blockhouse was one of the best-known defenses on the Wilderness Road. It stood in Carter's Valley on the outer edge of the Holston River settlements, about four miles southeast of Moccasin Gap in Scott County. Erected sometime prior to 1782 by John Anderson, it played host to hundreds of emigrants en route to Kentucky.

CAMP ANDREW. Named for John Albion Andrew, governor of Massachusetts, who was responsible for training and "polishing" the Massachusetts State Militia, Camp Andrew was established at Alexandria shortly after the outbreak of the Civil War. The 6th Massachusetts Infantry stationed there was the first regiment dispatched to Washington after President Lincoln's call for troops.

CAMP ARLINGTON. A large Union encampment established on Arlington Heights in 1861, serving at least through 1862, its quartered troops included elements of the 8th Infantry.

ARLINGTON CANTONMENT. This post at Arlington, three miles southwest of Washington, was a subpost of Fort Myer and was in charge of all military funerals at the Arlington National Cemetery and guarded the Tomb of the Unknown Soldier.

CAMP ASHBY. A temporary World War II training post at Virginia Beach, Suffolk County, the camp was named in honor of Confederate Brigadier General Turner Ashby, 7th Virginia Cavalry.

AUDLEY PAUL'S FORT. A French and Indian War period defense erected in 1757 under the direction of Lieutenant Audley Paul of the Virginia Rangers, Paul's Fort was a strongly built stockaded post, possibly enclosing a blockhouse or bastion, located at Big Spring, today's Springfield, on the present Botetourt-Rockbridge county line. The fort apparently served throughout the remaining years of the war.

BACON'S FORT. A French and Indian War defense, date of its construction undetermined, Bacon's Fort was located on the Colchester Road, between what is now known as Philomont and Airmont in southwestern Loudoun County.

FORT BALDWIN. A Confederate defense built in 1864, approximately 500–600 yards north of Confederate Fort Gregg, Fort Baldwin was located on the west side of Petersburg. (See also: PETERSBURG SIEGE.)

CAMP BANKS. A Union encampment located near Alexandria, Camp Banks was established as a post for paroled and exchanged prisoners and operated during the period 1862–63.

FORT BANKS. A Union defense built in 1862 by Federal troops, Fort Banks was located near Strasburg, Shenandoah County.

FORT (CAMP) BARBOUR. A War of 1812 brick-built fortification erected probably over the winter of 1814–15 for the defense of Norfolk, the post was named in honor of James Barbour, governor of Virginia, 1812–14. At the close of the war, the fort was dismantled, and its bricks were sold on March 9, 1816, to private individuals.

FORT BARNARD. A redoubt built by Union forces in late 1861 at Alexandria, Fort Barnard was named for General John Gross Barnard, chief engineer of Washington's defenses. With a perimeter of 250 yards and emplacements for 20 guns, it was designed to command the approaches to the city of Alexandria via Glebe Road and Four Mile Run. It stood at the intersection of South Oxford and 22nd Street South, where a large percentage of its remains is still in evidence. (See also: ALEXANDRIA DEFENSES.)

FORT BEAUREGARD. A Confederate defense built in 1861 on high ground two miles southeast of Leesburg, on the road to Tuscarora, Loudoun County, Fort Beauregard was captured by Union forces in March 1862.

CAMP BECKWITH. A Union cavalry encampment probably established in late 1861 near Lewinsville, Fairfax County, it was named for Major (later Brevet Brigadier General) Edward G. Beckwith. During the early hours of October 2, 1863, Confederate troops under Lieutenant Colonel Elijah V. White with 150 men of the 35th Virginia Cavalry Battalion attacked the camp.

FORT BELVOIR (*Camp Humphreys; Fort Humphreys*). Located on the Potomac River near Accotink in Fairfax County, prestigious Fort Belvoir dates back to 1910, when its site was purchased by the government. Known as the White House Tract or Belvoir, it was the 2,500-acre colonial manor estate granted to Colonel William Fairfax in the late 1730s, on which he built his elegant home, completed in 1741. In 1912 the reservation was transferred to the War Department, and authorization for a camp there was issued on December 23, 1917, with construction beginning in January 1918 and continued into 1919. The post was named in honor of Brigadier General Andrew A. Humphreys, distinguished Civil War veteran. Designated as an engineer replacement and training post in May 1918 and demobilization center on December 3, 1918, but retained as a permanent reservation, its name was changed to Fort Humphreys in 1922. In 1935 the post was redesignated Fort Belvoir, now operating as the U.S. Army Engineer Center.

FORT BENNETT. A small Union-built outwork of Fort Corcoran to the south, it was constructed in May 1861 and located on the south side of the Potomac, about a half-mile above Aqueduct Bridge, at Arlington Heights. With a perimeter of 146 yards, the redoubt had emplacements for five guns. Its site is located at North Queen and 21st Road North.

FORT BERRY. A Union redoubt constructed in 1863 about three miles from the Long Bridge, on the north flank of Alexandria's defenses, Fort Berry had a perimeter of 215 yards and emplacements for 10 guns. Named in honor of Major General Hiram G. Berry, killed in the Battle of Chancellorsville on May 2, 1863, its site is located at present South Monroe and 17th Street.

BLACKMORE'S FORT. An important Virginia frontier defense of the Revolutionary War period, Blackmore's Fort was built in 1774 by the brothers Captain John and Joseph Blackmore. It served until after the last Indian raid of 1794 and was one of the great stopovers on the Wilderness Road during the settlement of Kentucky. The fort was located on the north side of the Clinch River at the present village of Fort Blackmore in Scott County.

BLACK'S FORT. A Revolutionary War period palisaded fort built in 1776 as a defense against

FORT BELVOIR. Abbot Hall and Post Headquarters. (Courtesy of the U.S. Army.)

the warring Cherokee, Black's Fort was located at present Abingdon in Washington County. On December 14, 1864, about 10,000 Federal troops under General George Stoneman attacked and burned Abingdon's Confederate supply depot and barracks.

FORT BLACKWATER (*Terry's Fort*). One of Colonel George Washington's chain of forts erected in 1756 during the French and Indian War, Fort Blackwater was built by Captain Nathaniel Terry and garrisoned by men under his command. The defense was located where the Carolina Road crossed the Blackwater River, just northwest of present U.S. 220, near today's city of Rocky Mount, Franklin County.

FORT BLENCKER. FORT REYNOLDS.

CAMP BOWERS. A Federal Civil War encampment named for Lieutenant Colonel George Bowers, the post was located about four miles from Portsmouth.

FORT BOYKIN. A War of 1812 earthwork fortification in the shape of a seven-pointed star, with gun emplacements and a bombproofed powder magazine, Fort Boykin was located on a bluff overlooking the James River near present Smithfield, Isle of Wight County. It was reportedly renovated and enlarged during the Civil War.

FORT BRADY. Built by Federal troops in the fall of 1864 after the Confederates were driven from Fort Harrison in September, Fort Brady was located north of the James River, near Richmond, in eastern Henrico County. The fort served the Union as a guardian over the river's traffic until abandoned after the evacuation of Richmond in April 1865.

FORT BRACKENRIDGE. One of the forts built or manned by command of Colonel George Washington, this French and Indian War defense was erected in 1756 on the Jackson River, 16 miles from Fort Dickinson, in Bath County.

CAMP BRIGGS. A Federal rendezvous for drafted men and volunteers at Alexandria, Camp Briggs operated during 1863–64.

FORT BROWN. This was a temporary defense erected by Confederate forces at the mouth of the York River on Gloucester Point.

FORT BUFFALO. A Union-built defense, Fort Buffalo stood at the intersection of modern U.S. 50 (Arlington Boulevard) and S.R. 7 (Leesburg Pike) in Fairfax County. The remains of the fort were demolished during the 1950s and the site is now occupied by office buildings.

FORT BURNHAM. FORT HARRISON.

CAMP BUTLER. In 1861 Federal forces established Camp Butler at Newport News and named the post in honor of General Benjamin F. Butler, commander of Fort Monroe. It extended from the bluff where Christopher Newport Park is now located to Newport News Point. The camp was discontinued at the end of the Civil War after serving briefly as a prisoner of war encampment.

BYRD'S FORT. FORT DINWIDDIE.

FORT C. F. SMITH. A Union defense built early in 1863 and located on Arlington Heights one mile west of the Aqueduct Bridge and on the road to Chain Bridge, in Arlington County, it was named in honor of Major General Charles F. Smith who died of disease at Savannah, Georgia, April 25, 1862. With a perimeter of 368 yards, the fort had emplacements for 22 guns.

FORT CALHOUN. FORT WOOL.

CAMP CALIFORNIA. An encampment established in 1861 by Union troops, Camp California was located on Fairfax Road near the Fairfax County Courthouse at Alexandria. The city and its environs were described during the winter of 1861–62 as a vast Federal campground and provision depot. "Many trains follow each other, daily and nightly, bringing men from eastern, middle, northern, and western states."

CAMPBELL'S FORT. FORT LEWIS (*Roanoke County*).

CAPTAIN HARRIS'S FORT. FORT MAYO.

CAMP CAPTAIN JOHN SMITH. General Orders No. 43, War Department, 1907, specified troops were directed to proceed to the Jamestown Tercentennial Exposition at Norfolk to arrive not later than April 24, 1907. Their camp at the Exposition was later named Camp Captain John Smith and Major General Frederick D. Grant was ordered to assume command of the camp. General Orders No. 236, War Department, 1907, directed that the camp be abandoned on or about December 1, 1907.

FORT CASS. A fortification built in August 1861 in the Arlington Line of Union defenses, Fort Cass was a lunette (a field work with two faces converging to form a salient angle, with two parallel flanks), with a perimeter of 288 yards and emplacements for 13 guns. Fort Cass was located in the Arlington-Rosslyn area, just south of 10th Street North and Wayne Street.

FORT CENTREVILLE. This almost circular substantial Confederate defense, with an extensive line of earthworks on either side of it, was constructed in the village of Centreville in Fairfax County, during the winter of 1861–62. When the Confederates evacuated this line, dummy guns of logs were placed along the earthworks so that the lines, as well as the fort, would look occupied. The fort itself was not abandoned until the Federals launched their Peninsula Campaign.

CHAFFIN'S BLUFF DEFENSES. These Confederate fortifications were an extensive grouping of forts, battery positions, and rifle trenches overlooking the James River south of Richmond. Their construction began in 1862 to deny the Federal navy access to the Confederate capital. Various fortified lines were strengthened and continued in use until the Confederates abandoned them in April 1865.

FORT CHARITY (*Fort Hope in Faith*). In the fall of 1611, Sir Thomas Dale and 350 men from Jamestown, of which Dale was later Governor, built the city of Henrico (Henricus or Henricopolis) on the site of the Indian village of Kecoughtan, about 10 miles below present Richmond at the great bend of the James River. Henrico was named in honor of Prince Henry, King James I's eldest son. Dale's orders were to move the inhabitants of Jamestown to the new city and establish it as the capital of the colony. Dale dispossessed the Indian inhabitants and secured the site and its near environs by erecting Fort Charity, Fort Elizabeth, Fort Coxendale, Fort Patience, and Fort Mount Malady, "a retreat or guest house for sick people."

The proposed city occupied ground on the neck of Farrar's Island, where it then joined the mainland. In 1618 Governor Sir George Yeardley was instructed to select a suitable site there for a "University of Henrico," already incorporated in the town's charter. Accordingly, 10,000 acres were set aside and monies were collected in England to finance the college. The Indians, however, destroyed the city in 1622 during their massacre forays, and the migration from Jamestown never

took place. Nevertheless, Henrico marked the first significant expansion of the colony upriver from Jamestown. A small tract of the original town is now owned by the Virginia Society of the Colonial Dames of America and commemorated by two stone monuments.

FORT CHARLES. In 1611 or 1612 Sir Thomas Gates, after the Kecoughtan Indians became hostile, erected two small forts or stockades, Fort Charles and Fort Henry, named for the sons of Charles I, astride the mouth of Hampton Creek, probably the site of the present town of Hampton. The sites of the two forts are unknown.

FORT CHARLES. After the Indian massacre in 1644, Fort Charles, named for Charles I, was built at the Falls of the James River, present Richmond, in 1645.

CHARLOTTESVILLE BARRACKS. The most significant event connecting Albermarle County with the American Revolution was the selection of a site within its borders for the establishment of a camp for the Convention Troops who were the British prisoners of war captured at Saratoga in October 1777 when General John Burgoyne surrendered. The prisoners were first sent to Boston. The following year Congress, failing to ratify the stipulations of the Convention, ordered them to be removed to Charlottesville via Lancaster, Pennsylvania, and Frederick, Maryland. They reached their new quarters on the north bank of Ivy Creek early in January 1779 and remained until October 1780. Originally occupied by the militia, Charlottesville Barracks has ever since been popularly known as the Barracks.

CAMP CHESSENESSIX. A fortified War of 1812 British encampment established by Rear Admiral George Cockburn in early 1814 on Tangier Island off the Potomac River in Chesapeake Bay, it was intended to harbor British warships and store quantities of supplies. Camp Chessenessix had only three of its sides completed, each side 259 yards long, mounting 8 24-pounders with emplacements for 12 more guns of the same caliber. The island's garden had vegetables of all kinds growing. There was a church, 20 houses built and laid out in streets, and a hospital to accommodate 100 sick and wounded men. At the end of May 1814, Commodore Joshua Barney with an armada of 16 vessels came down the bay and attacked Tangier Island.

FORT CHISWELL. A French and Indian War fortification erected in 1760–61 as winter quarters by Colonel William Byrd en route with troops to relieve Fort Loudoun on the Holston River besieged by Cherokee, Fort Chiswell was located about eight miles east of present Wytheville, Wythe County, and named for Colonel John Chiswell, proprietor of nearby lead mines. Fort Chiswell continued to serve until about 1790 as a military post, arsenal, and supply depot.

FORT CHRISTANNA. To ameliorate Indian unrest following the bloody Tuscarora War of 1711–13, Governor Alexander Spotswood established two forts at which he attempted to settle friendly Indians, augmented by small English garrisons. One of these was Fort Christanna. In Brunswick County, on an expanse of rising ground overlooking the Meherrin River, lie the archaeological remains of the fort, begun in August 1714 by Governor Spotswood as a defense against hostile Indians. The fort site, about two and a half miles south of modern Lawrenceville, is strategically located on the south side of the river where it makes a prominent bend in its course.

The fort was garrisoned from 1715 until about 1720, when it lost importance as the frontier swept past. Brunswick County was formed in 1720, by which time the actual frontier was already considerably west of Fort Christanna. With the consent of the colonial government, a local tribe of friendly Indians, the Saponi, occupied the fort and its environs until 1732 when they were given land elsewhere for use as a reservation. In 1978 archaeological excavations definitely discovered Fort Christanna's site and uncovered many artifacts.

FORT CHRISTIAN (*Daniel Smith's Fort; Glade Hollow Fort*). Fort Christian, also referred to as Daniel Smith's Fort, but better known as Glade Hollow Fort, stood between present Dickensonville and Lebanon on Cedar Creek in Russell County. It was erected in 1774 as an Indian defense by Daniel Smith, a surveyor and militia captain, and named in honor of Colonel William Christian, who then was in charge of erecting defenses on the Clinch River. Archival records do not indicate when the fort was abandoned.

CHRISTY'S FORT. One of the French and Indian War forts built or manned by command of Colonel George Washington, Christy's Fort was erected in 1756 on Jackson's River, 15 miles from Fort Dinwiddie, in Bath County, and initially garrisoned by 40 men.

FORT COLLIER. From this heavily fortified strongpoint, Confederate fortifications formed a semicircle west and north of the town of Winchester in Frederick County. Fort Collier was abandoned by its garrison during the third Battle of Winchester on September 19, 1864, during General Philip Sheridan's Shenandoah Valley Campaign.

FORT CONVERSE. A Civil War defense located at Hopewell (City Point), Fort Converse was established by Union forces and manned by Negro troops to guard General Benjamin Butler's pontoon bridges across the James River during the siege of Petersburg. The site of the fort is now occupied by the U.S. Reformatory.

FORT CORCORAN. A Union bastioned earthwork built in May 1861, Fort Corcoran was located in Arlington Heights on the Georgetown-Falls Church road and named for Colonel Michael Corcoran, 69th New York Infantry, who was subsequently captured on July 22, 1861, and tried for piracy. The fort had a perimeter of 576 yards and emplacements for 10 guns. The site of the fort is now occupied by the intersection of Key Boulevard and Ode Street.

FORT COXENDALE. FORT CHARITY.

FORT CRAFFORD (*Mulberry Island Point Battery*). Known from 1610 by Jamestown's colonists as Mulberry Island, it is now a peninsula of about ten square miles of land and reclaimed swamp, today occupied by Fort Eustis. Its first prominent settler was John Rolfe, who cultivated and cured tobacco that competed successfully in European markets and brought economic stability to Jamestown. On the west side of the Virginia Peninsula, Mulberry Island played no part in the Revolutionary War, although Lord Cornwallis surrendered at Yorktown, only six miles away. During the Civil War, the confederates built a string of fortifications from Yorktown to Mulberry Point, anchoring the western end of the line at Fort Crafford, still a prominent landmark here. The Confederates occupied the fortifications until they withdrew their troops to Richmond during the Peninsula Campaign.

Fort Crafford, a five-sided earthwork fortification originally called the Mulberry Island Point Battery, was constructed in 1861 and 1862 as an anchor of the Confederate defense line which stretched across the Virginia Peninsula, flanked by two broad navigable rivers, the York and the James. Although Fort Crafford is known primarily as a Civil War construction, some historians believe it was built on an earlier fortification dating from the colonial period. Its location on the shore of a comparatively narrow part of the James River made it a logical place for such an earthwork. In the center of the fort is the foundation of a colonial home, believed to have been erected by Carter Crafford, who operated a ferry between Mulberry Island Point and Isle of Wight in the eighteenth century. The residence was used as headquarters for the Civil War fort and occupied as late as World War I. In 1925 the house was sold to the College of William and Mary, which used its bricks to repair the Wren Building in Williamsburg.

The Confederates abandoned their island battery on May 2, 1862. Fort Crafford is mentioned no more in Civil War records, although it stayed in Federal control until the end of the war. The island once again became a farming community, but the earthworks remained and became known as Fort Crafford. In 1918 the government purchased all of Mulberry Island and established a balloon observation school and coast artillery training center. It was then officially designated for Virginia-born Brevet Brigadier General Abraham Eustis, the first acting commander of Fort Monroe and commandant of the Artillery School of Practice. Fort Crafford was placed on the Virginia Historic Landmark Commission's Register in 1973 and declared a National Historic Place in 1974.

FORT CRAIG. A lunette in the Federal Arlington Line of defenses, Fort Craig was constructed in August 1861 with a perimeter of 324 yards and emplacements for 11 guns. It was located at the present intersection of South Court House Road and 4th Street South.

CRANEY ISLAND FORTIFICATIONS. Located at the mouth of the Elizabeth River, commanding the entrance to Norfolk's harbor, Craney Island was fortified in 1812 by American regular troops and militiamen under the command of General Robert B. Taylor. On the west side of the island, then connected to the mainland by a narrow footbridge, the general built several redoubts and on the east side a fort, defended by two 24-pounders, one 18-pounder, and four 6-pounders, manned by 150 seamen from the *Constellation,* 400 militiamen, one company of riflemen, two companies of light artillery, and 30 men from Fort Norfolk. In the river channel were 20 armed gunboats.

On June 22, 1813, a strong British armada attacked the island. Landing forces assaulted the island's defenses from two sides but were decisively repulsed, losing more than 200 men killed and wounded. Norfolk and Portsmouth were thus rescued from certain destruction. Craney Island today is a part of the mainland and occupied by a U.S. Navy fuel depot.

CAMP CUSTIS. A Civil War encampment, Camp Custis was located on the grounds of the Arlington Plantation owned by G. W. P. Custis, father-in-law of General Robert E. Lee.

FORT CUSTIS. FORT JOHN CUSTIS.

DANIEL SMITH'S FORT. FORT CHRISTIAN.

FORT DARLING. A strong Confederate defense of Richmond, Fort Darling was built in 1862 by Captain A. H. Drewry on the 90-foot-high bluff, known since as Drewry's Bluff, on the west side of the James River, about 12 miles downriver from today's Richmond National Battlefield Headquarters in Chimborazo Park. On the morning of May 15, 1862, a flotilla of five Federal gunboats, including the famous *Monitor,* steamed up the James and began a four-hour bombardment against the strategically placed fortification. The accurate fire of the Confederate batteries proved too much, and the fleet was forced to retire down the river. In 1864 Union General Benjamin Butler's Army of the James failed in its attempt to capture Fort Darling from the land side. The fort continued to defend the water approach to Richmond until the downfall of the Confederate capital on April 3, 1865.

FORT DEKALB. FORT STRONG.

FORT DICKINSON. A French and Indian War defense located on the Cowpasture River, four miles below the present town of Millboro in Bath County, Fort Dickinson, erected in 1756 and garrisoned by 250 men, was one of the line of forts built or manned by command of Colonel George Washington.

FORT DINWIDDIE (*Warwick's Fort; Byrd's Fort*). A prominent French and Indian War defense located on Jackson's River, five miles west of the present town of Warm Springs, in Bath County, Fort Dinwiddie was erected in 1755 around the house of William Warwick and named for Governor Robert Dinwiddie. Its garrison in 1756 numbered from 60 to 100 men. Known locally as Warwick's Fort and Byrd's Fort, it served as a frontier defense until as late as 1789. It is believed that the original Warwick residence and its fortifications were torn down about 1805.

FORT DIX. A Union defense located near Suffolk in Nansemond County, Fort Dix was begun on September 25, 1862, with its construction under the supervision of General John J. Peck, Fourth Army Corps. The fort was named in honor of General John A. Dix, commanding the Department of Virginia.

FORT EARLY. A temporary Confederate square earthwork defense begun in mid-June 1864 by troops under General Jubal A. Early, Fort Early was located two miles west of Lynchburg in Campbell County and defended by his army of 8,000 men and 22 pieces of artillery, intended to oppose Union General David Hunter's campaign to take the vital rail center. General Hunter's staff included Colonel William McKinley and General Rutherford B. Hayes, both of whom later became presidents of the United States. General Jubal's forces decisively repulsed Hunter's furious two-day attacks (June 17–18) and compelled the suspension of the Union campaign. Now within the city limits of Lynchburg, Fort Early's restored earthworks are located at the intersection of Fort and Vernon avenues.

FORT EDWARD JOHNSON. A temporary Confederate defense located on the crest of 3,760-foot-high Shenandoah Mountain, near the town of Churchville in Augusta County, Fort Johnson was garrisoned by 3,000 men under the command of Brigadier General Edward Johnson.

FORT ELIZABETH. FORT CHARITY.

FORT ELLSWORTH. ALEXANDRIA DEFENSES.

FORT ETHAN ALLEN. A strong Union bastioned earthwork fortification built in September 1861 in the Cherrydale section of Arlington, it was designed to command all the Virginia approaches to the Chain Bridge. Fort Ethan Allen had a 736-yard perimeter with emplacements for 39 guns and was equipped with an interior bombproof shelter, a magazine, and a guardhouse. Some of its remains are located at present Glebe and Military Roads.

FORT (ABRAHAM) EUSTIS. Established on March 25, 1918, after the government purchased Mulberry Island on the west side of the Virginia Peninsula, about 11 miles southeast of Williamsburg, Camp Eustis was an important Coast Artillery Training Center and Balloon Observers School during World War I, named in honor of Brevet Brigadier General Abraham Eustis, War of 1812 veteran and first commander of the Coast Artillery School at Fort Monroe. In 1923 it became a permanent post and was redesignated Fort Eustis. In 1925 the Balloon Observers School and Camp Wallace, a subpost and artillery firing range, were consolidated with Fort Eustis. A Coast Artillery Replacement Center in 1941, the post became a prisoner of war camp during World War II. In 1962 Fort Eustis was officially designated the U.S. Army Transportation Center. (See: FORT CRAFFORD.)

FORT EVANS. One of three temporary Confederate fortifications on high ground on different sides of Leesburg, Loudoun County, Fort Evans was established in 1861 and named for Brigadier General Nathan G. Evans. It stood a mile east of the town, on the Edwards Ferry Road.

FORT FARNSWORTH. ALEXANDRIA DEFENSES.

FISHERMAN'S ISLAND CAMP. A World War I Coast Artillery defense of Chesapeake Bay, the post was located two miles south of Kiptopeke in Northampton County. First acquired in 1891 as a quarantine station, permission was granted on February 13, 1917, to mount guns on the island and use buildings and wharves as were necessary. By an act of November 19, 1919, the 225-acre reservation was transferred to the War Department for disposition.

FORT FREDERICK. One of the French and Indian War defenses built or manned by command of Colonel George Washington, Fort Frederick was erected in 1756 on the west bank of the New River, at Ingles Ferry, in Montgomery County.

GALLOWAY'S FORT. FORT TRIAL.

FORT GARESCHE. ALEXANDRIA DEFENSES.

FORT GEARY (*Fort Johnston*). One of three Confederate earthwork defenses in the near environs of Leesburg, Loudoun County, Fort Johnston was constructed in 1861 one and a half miles west of the town on the Alexandria Road and named in honor of General Joseph E. Johnston. On March 7, 1862, Colonel John W. Geary and his 28th Pennsylvania Infantry attacked Leesburg and captured Fort Johnston, immediately renaming it Fort Geary. During the next three years, control of Leesburg constantly changed as armies crossed and recrossed the county.

FORT GEORGE. FORT MONROE.

FORT GEORGE. A French and Indian War bastioned defense, Fort George was built in April 1757 by Captain William Preston in compliance with an order of Major Andrew Lewis. It was located on the Bullpasture River, about five miles from the present town of McDowell in Highland County and probably named in honor of George II.

FORT GERMANNA. To settle the general Indian unrest following the Tuscarora War of 1711–13, Governor Alexander Spotswood established two forts at which he planned to settle friendly Indians, reinforced by small English garrisons. One of these was Fort Germanna, built in 1714 on the south bank of the Rapidan River, where present S.R. 3 crosses the river, in Orange County. After Indians could not be induced to settle there, the fort was subsequently occupied by German immigrants who were to develop an iron industry in the area. Later, the governor himself erected a home in the near environs of the fort.

FORT GILMER. An important redoubt in Richmond's line of outer defenses, Fort Gilmer was successfully defended by Confederate troops, including the Union attack on September 29–30 during the Battle of New Market Heights, until just prior to the evacuation of the city. Fort Gilmer was abandoned during the very early hours of April 3, 1865.

GLADE HOLLOW FORT. FORT CHRISTIAN.

GLOUCESTER FORT. A French and Indian War period fort was established in 1756 at strategic Gloucester Point on the York River in compliance with orders of Governor Robert Dinwiddie. It was defended by 15 guns of various calibers, which were not in good working condition because of poor construction due to the scarcity of skillful engineers.

CAMP GRAHAM. A Union cavalry encampment established in 1861 and located on the outskirts of Arlington, it was probably named for Brigadier General Lawrence Pike Graham who commanded units of the Army of the Potomac.

FORT HAGGERTY. A small Union earthwork of Fort Corcoran, constructed in May 1861, Fort Haggerty had a perimeter of 128 yards and emplacements for four guns. It was located on North Arlington Road between 19th Street and Wilson Boulevard in Arlington.

FORT HALLECK. A temporary Union fortification located at or near Suffolk, it was probably named in honor of Major General Henry W. Halleck, who was occupied for most of the Civil War as President Lincoln's military adviser and General in Chief.

CAMP HAMILTON. When Fort Sumter was bombarded in April 1861, Fort Monroe was garrisoned by approximately 400 men. When Virginia passed the Ordinance of Secession in May 1861, its garrison was increased to about 6,000 Federal troops. However, only about 1,400 soldiers could be accommodated in the fort. Camp Hamilton was established in 1861 at Phoebus, just north of the fort, to accept the overflow.

HARPER'S FORT. One of the chain of French and Indian War forts built or manned by command of Colonel George Washington, Harper's Fort was erected in 1756 on the Bullpasture River in present Highland County and initially garrisoned by 50 men.

FORT HARRISON (*Fort Burnham*). This was a key defensive position in the line of earthwork fortifications that General Robert E. Lee had built encircling Richmond. It is generally believed that Fort Harrison, located to the southwest of the city, was named after a prominent family owning land in the vicinity. Lee's chain of forts was begun in 1862 and completed, for all practical purposes, by the summer of 1864. Fort Harrison was captured by Federal forces on September 29, 1864, when there were only some 40 Confederate artillerists defending it, and most of them were either killed or captured. The fort was renamed Fort Burnham in honor of General Hiram Burnham, who was killed in the surprise Union assault. After the war, the fort regained its former name. Now preserved as a part of the Richmond National Battlefield Park, Fort Harrison serves as a park headquarters and museum.

FORT HENRY. FORT CHARLES.

FORT HENRY. Following the Indian massacre of 1644, Governor Sir William Berkeley and the Assembly ordered forts built along six Virginia rivers. One of the defenses was Fort Henry, erected by Captain Abraham Wood in 1645–46, near the mouth of the Appomattox River, on the present site of Petersburg in Prince George County. Destined to become one of the most important posts in what was then the Virginia line of defenses, Fort Henry the following year was permitted to be converted into a military-trading center, together with 600 surrounding acres, provided Captain Wood maintained a garrison of 10 soldiers there for three years.

CAMP (PATRICK) HENRY. A subinstallation of Fort Eustis, north of Newport News, Camp Patrick Henry was established by the Transportation Corps in 1942 as the staging area for the Hampton Roads Port of Embarkation. On June 1, 1946, the camp was transferred to the control of the command, Fort Eustis, along with other elements of the Norfolk Army Base. At the present time, Camp Patrick Henry is used principally as a storage area. It has been used from time to time as a difficult-driving range for training heavy-truck drivers and in shock and vibration tests on military vehicles by the transportation Engineering Agency.

HICKEY'S FORT. One of the French and Indian War defenses built or manned in 1756 by command of Colonel George Washington, Hickey's Fort was located in present Patrick County, on a site not as yet determined.

CAMP (A. P.) HILL. A World War I post named in honor of Lieutenant General Ambrose Powell Hill, who commanded General Lee's Third Corps and was killed on April 2, 1865, during the Confederacy's final defense of Petersburg, Camp A. P. Hill was established in August 1917, in connection with Port of Embarkation, Newport News. Included in its northern area was a camp for stevedore regiments and labor battalions which, on August 15, 1918, was detached and constituted a separate entity designated Camp Alexander. Camp Hill served as an embarkation cantonment until November 11, 1918, thereafter for purposes of debarkation. With a capacity for 10,000 troops, the post was used by about 63,000 men en route overseas and approximately 35,000 returning. The camp's headquarters personnel was transferred to Camp Stuart on October 7, 1919, when the post was abandoned to be sold.

FORT (A. P.) HILL. Located in Caroline County, two miles from Bowling Green and 22 miles southeast of Fredericksburg, Fort A. P. Hill was established as an Army training facility on June 11, 1941, pursuant to War Department General Orders No. 5. In its first year, the installation was used as a maneuver area for the II Army Corps and for three activated National Guard divisions from Mid-Atlantic states. In the autumn of 1942, the post was the staging area for the headquarters and corps troops of Major General Patton's Task Force A, which invaded French Morocco in North Africa. During the early years of World War II, the post continued to be a training site for corps and division-sized units. Beginning in 1944, field training of enlisted replacements from nearby Forts Lee, Eustis, and Belvoir was conducted.

During the Korean War, Fort A. P. Hill was a major staging area for units deploying to Europe, including the VII Corps Headquarters and the Third Armored Cavalry Regiment. The fort was the major center for the training of Engineers (out of Fort Belvoir) during the Vietnam War. The post is a subinstallation of Fort Lee. It is used year round for military training with annual troop strength of over 70,000 active and reserve troops of the Army, Navy, Marines, and Air Force. The installation was named in honor of Lieutenant General Ambrose Powell Hill, a Virginia native who distinguished himself as a Confederate commander during the Civil War. Rising from the rank of colonel to major general in three months, General Hill took command of one of General Lee's three corps in 1863. Two years later, as Grant's forces laid siege to Petersburg, the general was killed while he was riding his stallion, Champ, to the front. He had not yet reached his 40th birthday.

HOG ISLAND FORT. A small fort or blockhouse was built in 1608 on Hog Island ("Isle of Hogges") by the Jamestown colonists on the south side of the James River, intended for both additional security from the Spanish and the raising of hogs.

FORT HOKE. An important Confederate link in Richmond's ring of outer defenses, Fort Hoke was probably named in honor of General Robert Frederick Hoke. The fort has been partially restored and is included within the Richmond National Battlefield Park.

FORT HOOD. FORT POWHATAN.

FORT HOPE IN FAITH. FORT CHARITY.

CAMP HUMPHREYS. FORT BELVOIR.

FORT HUMPHREYS. FORT BELVOIR.

FORT HUNT. Located at Sheridan's Point in Fairfax County, 7 miles from Alexandria and about 12 miles south of Washington, Fort Hunt was established in 1898 and named in honor of Colonel Henry J. Hunt, 5th Artillery (Mexican War) and Brevet Major General of Volunteers

(Civil War). During the World War I, Fort Hunt served as part of the Coast Defenses of the Potomac in the Mid-Atlantic Coast Artillery District. The fort was used through World War II as an adjunct of the Central Intelligence Agency. Abandoned after the war and converted into a park, the post's principal Army structures still remaining include one residence and several coast defense batteries and fire control stations, with no attempt at historic preservation.

FORT JACKSON. FORT MILROY.

FORT JACKSON. A Union defense located in Arlington, about 50 yards south of the intersection of the present 14th Street railroad bridge and the Virginia end of Long Bridge, Fort Jackson was constructed in 1861 by troops of the 7th New York Infantry and garrisoned by Massachusetts, New Hampshire, and New York infantry units.

JAMES FORT. The first permanent settlement in America by the English was proof of their determination to establish themselves in the New World. The defeat of the Spanish Armada in 1588 by the English during the reign of Queen Elizabeth had paved the way for English colonization of America. Sir Walter Raleigh had made several unsuccessful attempts a score of years earlier to establish an enduring settlement along the Carolina coast of Roanoke Island (now commemorated by Fort Raleigh National Historic Site). It remained for the Virginia Company of London, chartered April 10, 1606, to found the first permanent English settlement in America.

The story of Jamestown began on May 13, 1607, when the first Virginia colonists, after several months of voyaging out of England and a brief stay on Cape Henry, sailed up the James River and selected Jamestown Island, then a peninsula, as a place for a settlement, built around "James Citie Forte," a triangular bastioned defense, mounting several small brass cannon, designed for protection against Spanish assault and Indian attack. It is believed that almost the entire site of this fort was long ago eroded into the James River. The colonists disembarked from their three small ships—the "flagship" *Susan Constant,* commanded by Captain Christopher Newport, the *Godspeed,* commanded by Captain Bartholomew Gosnold, and the *Discovery,* commanded by Captain John Ratcliffe. The first years at Jamestown were trying ones—a continual struggle against sickness, hunger, and inexperience, in addition to the disadvantages of its unhealthful location.

Within a few months, Captain John Smith became the dominant personality at Jamestown. His vigorous leadership did much to keep the colony together during its first two and a half years. His departure for England in October 1609, seemingly under duress after he had been disabled by a gunpowder explosion, marked the beginning of the terrible "Starving Time," when nine-tenths of the colonists died. Discouragement was so great that the survivors planned to desert the colony. It was only the timely arrival of the newly appointed governor, Lord Delaware, with men and supplies, that actually prevented the abandonment of Virginia. Gradually, Jamestown took on a look of permanence, and plantations spread up and down the rivers. By 1614 the settlement could boast of houses and streets and could well be called a town.

The efficient, yet necessarily stern, government of Sir Thomas Dale did much to stabilize the colony, particularly through his assignment of private holdings and his rigid enforcement of a stringent disciplinary code of laws. About 1610–11, experimentation in tobacco culture, ably advanced by John Rolfe, proved successful. This established the economic basis on which the colony became prosperous. This is the same John Rolfe who married Pocahontas, daughter of the Indian Chief Powhatan, in 1614, in the church at Jamestown. This marriage helped to bring a period of peace with the Indians.

Settlements now spread outward along the James, but Jamestown was the political, social, and economic center of the colony. In 1619 it was the scene of the meeting of America's first representative legislative assembly. During this same year, steps were taken to export maidens from England to Virginia to become wives of the settlers, joining those of their sex already in the colony. The first of them arrived the following spring. The first Negroes, too, were brought to Virginia in 1619 and sold as servants, but slavery was not established until later. In 1622 there was a sudden uprising of the Indians that resulted in wholesale destruction of life and property. Warned by a friendly Indian, Jamestown escaped the massacre, though for a time the whole life of the colony was threatened. Partly as a result of these events, the Virginia Company of London, which had directed the affairs of the settlement since its founding, was dissolved, and Virginia became a royal colony in 1624.

During the 1955 archaeological excavation season, three exploratory projects were completed to find traces of the 1607 "James Citie Forte." The excavations encompassed the area of the Confederate fort built in 1861, which possibly occupied a small part of the 1607 site. Testing was done within the interior of the Confederate defense and beneath its south embankment, but no recognizable trace of the First Fort was found. It was already known that artifacts and burial traces were uncovered when Confederate troops built their fort and accumulated earth for the embankments from within the fort enclosure and from the moat which surrounded the embankments, no doubt destroying some remains of the First Fort. Historical records, however, state that the First Fort was built entirely of logs, timber, and earth. There was a ditch on the exterior and behind the ditch, on the inside, a log palisade. Each of the three corners had a raised bastion.

Jamestown Island—except Jamestown National Historic Site, which is administered and maintained by the Association for the Preservation of Virginia antiquities—is part of Colonial National Historical Park. The park, also including Yorktown Battlefield, 23-mile-long Colonial Parkway, which connect's Jamestown, Williamsburg, and Yorktown, and Cape Henry Memorial, is a part of the National Park System administered by the National Park Service.

FORT JAMES. After the second Indian uprising, which occurred in 1644, new forts were established on the major rivers in the Virginia colony, including Fort James, built in 1645 on the Chickahominy near present-day Lanexa in New Kent County, about 20 miles west of Williamsburg on U.S. 60. In 1646 Lieutenant Thomas Rolfe, the son of John Rolfe and Pocahontas, was granted Fort James, with 400 acres of adjoining land for a term of three years.

FORT JAMES. Another defense named Fort James was erected in the late 1660s on Tyndall's Point (present-day Gloucester Point), across from Yorktown, in Gloucester County.

FORT JOHN CUSTIS (*Fort Winslow; Fort Custis*). A World War II post established in 1942 at Kiptopeke in Northampton County, it was first designated Fort Winslow. The name received so much criticism from the local people that it was changed to Fort Custis. But mail for the post became so confused with that for Fort Eustis on the west shore of the Virginia Peninsula that the fort's final official designation became Fort John Custis.

JOHN MASON'S FORT. A French and Indian War defense built or manned by command of Colonel George Washington, John Mason's Fort

was erected and garrisoned by 30 men in 1756 near present Salem in Roanoke County.

JOHN MILLER'S FORT. One of the series of temporary French and Indian War defenses built or manned by orders of Colonel George Washington, this fort was erected and garrisoned by 60 men in 1756 on Jackson's River in present Bath County.

JOHN'S CREEK FORT. One of the chain of French and Indian War defenses built or manned by command of Colonel George Washington, John's Creek Fort was erected in 1756 near present Newcastle in Craig County.

FORT JOHNSON. One of the larger fortifications near the southern terminus of the Confederate line of defenses encircling Richmond, Fort Johnson survived the surprise assault by Union forces during the attack on Chaffin's Bluff in September 1864 when the Federals captured nearby Fort Harrison. Fort Johnson then became the anchor for a new recessed Confederate line that kept the Union army out of Richmond until April 1865.

FORT JOHNSTON. FORT GEARY.

KELLER'S FORT. One of the temporary French and Indian War defenses built or manned by command of Colonel George Washington, Keller's Fort was erected in 1756 about 10 miles from present-day Woodstock in Shenandoah County.

CAMP KEYES. A Union army encampment established in 1861 on Upton's Hill in Alexandria, the post was named for General Erasmus Darwin Keyes, whose infantry division participated in the March–July 1862 Peninsular Campaign in the area around Fair Oaks and Malvern Hill.

FORT LEE. For at least 300 years, the area of Virginia now called Fort Lee has been inhabited. The roads, and later the railroads, on which tobacco was transported to market became the avenues of mobilization and troop support during the American Revolution and the Civil War. These roads passing through Fort Lee linked Petersburg, three miles to the west, and City Point (today's Hopewell), both vital supply and communication centers on the Appomattox River. In the summer of 1864, General Grant decided the capture of Petersburg was essential to the Union cause in order to cut the important supply lines into Richmond. The struggle for Petersburg continued for 10 long months before General

FORT LEE. Aerial view of Mifflin Hall. (Courtesy of the U.S. Army.)

Lee evacuated the city. One week later, Lee surrendered at Appomattox Court House, 100 miles to the west.

Just 18 days after a state of war with Germany was declared, the first Camp Lee was selected as a state mobilization camp and later became a division training camp in June of 1917. Building began and within 60 days 14,000 men swarmed over the newly designed military installation. When construction ended, there were accommodations for 60,335 men. On July 15, 1917, the War Department announced that the camp would be named in honor of General Robert E. Lee, the most famous of the Confederate Civil War commanders. After World War I, Camp Lee was taken over by the Commonwealth of Virginia and designated a game preserve. Later, portions of the land were incorporated into the National Military Park of Petersburg.

In October 1940 the War Department ordered the construction of another Camp Lee on the site of the earlier installation. Built as rapidly as the first, construction was still ongoing when the Quartermaster Replacement Training Center started operation in February 1941. Camp Lee was also the home of a Medical Replacement Training Center (MRTC), but, as the Quartermaster training increased, it was decided to relocate the MRTC at Camp Pickett. Later the QMARTC was redesignated as an Army Service Forces Training Center, but it retained its basic mission of training Quartermaster personnel. By the end of 1941, Camp Lee was the center of both basic and advanced training of Quartermaster personnel and held this position throughout the war.

When World War II ended, the fate of Camp Lee was in question. In 1946 the War Department announced that Camp Lee would be retained as a center for Quartermaster training. Official recognition of its permanent status was obtained in 1950, and the post was redesignated as Fort Lee. Immediately, troops began Quartermaster training for the Korean War and continued for the next three years. After the Korean War, progress was made on an ambitious permanent building program. Under the 20-year program, Fort Lee changed from an installation of temporary wooden structures to a modern Army post of permanent brick and cinder block buildings.

Profound changes were evident at Fort Lee during 1962. The post became a Class I military installation under the Second United States Army. The Quartermaster School became a part of the Continental Army Command service school system and was also selected to serve as Home of the Quartermaster Corps and Corps Historian. In October 1963, Camp Pickett and Camp A. P. Hill were established as subinstallations of Fort Lee. In July 1973 Fort Lee came under the control of the U.S. Army Training and Doctrine Command.

FORT LEWIS (*Campbell's Fort*). A French and Indian War defense erected in 1756 by Major Andrew Lewis, probably by command of Colonel George Washington, Fort Lewis was located near present-day Salem in Roanoke County. Initially garrisoned by 30 men and standing on land owned by James Campbell, the fort was alternately known locally as Campbell's Fort. The Council of War at Augusta Court House on July 27, 1756, specified that Campbell's Fort should be 60 feet square with two bastions and garrisoned by 50 men. During the war, men of Colonel William Byrd's 1st Virginia Regiment assembled at Fort Lewis for an expedition against the Cherokee.

FORT LEWIS. Located on the Cowpasture River in northeast Bath County, south of Williamsville, Fort Lewis was erected sometime between 1750 and 1757 by Charles Lewis. In 1762 Charles Lewis married and built a manor house adjoining the fort. Remains of the defense were still in evidence as late as the early 1900s. In 1774 Charles Lewis, then 38 years old, was colonel and commander of the 13-company Augusta County Regiment, which participated in the Battle of Point Pleasant, West Virginia, on October 10. Colonel Lewis was killed during the action. His home is still standing, maintained by the George Washington Creek Chapter of the Sons of the American Revolution located at Warm Springs.

FORT LOUDOUN. This French and Indian War defense was erected near Winchester in 1756–57 in present Frederick County by Colonel George Washington as authorized by the Virginia Assembly after General Braddock's defeat in 1755 near Fort Duquesne. Named in honor of General Lord Loudoun, then commander in chief of British forces in America, the square bastioned fort had double-palisaded, earthen-core walls, barracks large enough to garrison 450 men, and mounted 24 guns. Part of its southwest bastion still stands on the site at the present intersection of Loudoun and Peyton streets in Winchester. George Washington began his career at Winchester (incorporated in 1752), the oldest city west of the Blue Ridge, as surveyor to Lord Fairfax in 1748. Winchester had an important role in the French and Indian War, the Revolution, and the War Between the States. During the Civil War, the town was captured and recaptured 73 times, 7 times during one day. The First, Second, and Third Battles of Winchester occurred in 1862, 1863, and 1864.

FORT LYON. One of the largest and strongest forts in the 37-mile-long chain of Federal defenses surrounding Washington, Fort Lyon was located at James Drive and Kings Highway in Alexandria. It mounted 30 various caliber guns and 6 mortars. It was additionally reinforced by a battery east of Kings Highway and a blockhouse to the northwest.

FORT MCCAUSLAND. A defense erected by Confederate troops under General Jubal Early and named for General John McCausland, it was located on Langhorne Road, west of Clifton Street, in Lynchburg, Campbell County.

FORT MCCLELLAN. A Civil War defense erected by Federal troops and named for General George McClellan, it was located at or near the town of Suffolk.

MCNEILL'S FORT. One of the series of French and Indian War defenses built or manned by command of Colonel George Washington, McNeill's Fort was erected in 1756 in Montgomery County and garrisoned by 30 men. Its exact location has not been determined as yet.

FORT MCPHERSON. A Federal-built defense, never completed, it was located in present Arlington Cemetery, west of present McPherson Avenue, opposite the Rough Riders Memorial. The fort was named in honor of General James Birdseye McPherson of Ohio, who was later killed near Atlanta, July 22, 1864.

FORT MAGRUDER. A Civil War defense erected by Federal troops, Fort Magruder was located near colonial Williamsburg. "As the war progressed many other buildings [in Williamsburg] suffered at the hands of Union soldiers, notably the brick advance buildings that had once flanked the approach to the Governor's Palace. These were pulled down to provide bricks to be made into chimneys for officers' huts at Fort Magruder, which lay a few miles outside the town" (Ivor Noël Hume, *Here Lies Virginia: An Archaeologist's View of Colonial Life and History* [1963], p. 92).

FORT MANASKIN (*Fort Matuxon*). After the Restoration in 1660, Governor Berkeley resumed control and initiated a program to reinforce the colony's defenses. He established a fort in New Kent County on the Pamunkey River to help defend the frontier against Indians. This fort was known as Fort Manaskin (and as Fort Matuxon) and may have been garrisoned by Indian allies.

FORT MARCY. One of the Union-built defenses guarding the Virginia approaches to the Chain Bridge over the Potomac was Fort Marcy on the Leesburg-Georgetown Turnpike, begun on September 24, 1861, quickly completed, and named in honor of Brigadier General R. B. Marcy, Chief of Staff for General George McClellan. Its armament consisted of 15 various calibered Parrotts, 2 howitzers, and 3 mortars.

MARTIN'S HUNDRED FORT. FORT WOLSTENHOLME.

FORT MATTAPONY. FORT ROYAL.

FORT MATTAPONY. In 1657, as Virginia settlements moved up the colony's rivers, the first Fort Mattapony was built near the site of present-day Walkerton in King and Queen County. Edward Digges, who later became governor, laid out the fort and Major (later Colonel) Thomas Walker commanded the defense, which was probably torn down in 1677. The Walker family still owns the land surrounding the fort site. The colonial defense's name was derived from the Mattaponi Indian tribe, which still has a reservation near Walkerton. Settlement continued westward and a second Fort Mattapony was erected in 1677 near present-day Milford in adjoining Caroline County. This defense apparently was either abandoned or destroyed in 1678.

FORT MATUXON. FORT MANASKIN.

FORT MAURY. Part of the Confederate line of defenses around Richmond, Fort Maury's site is now included within Battlefield Park. The fort was probably named for General Dabney Herndon Maury.

FORT MAYO (*Captain Harris's Fort*). Included in the March 1756 list of Colonel George Washington's French and Indian War defenses, Fort Mayo (also known as Captain Harris's Fort) was erected in 1756 on the Mayo River in Patrick County, just above the North Carolina line.

FORT MILROY (*Fort Jackson*). One of the Federal defenses around hotly contested Winchester, Fort Milroy was named in honor of General Robert Huston Milroy. The general's suppression of Confederate guerrilla activities in West Virginia was so vigorous that the Confederates put a price on his head. After Confederate troops took Winchester and captured Fort Milroy during the Third Battle for the city on September 19, 1864, the defense was renamed Fort Jackson. The fort was located in the northern section of Winchester, on what is now Fairmont Avenue, on ground now owned by the Shenandoah Valley Cooperative.

CAMP MISERY. A Union camp established after the Battle of Second Manassas or Second Bull Run on August 29–30, 1862, Camp Misery was a camp for convalescents, stragglers, and recruits, a part of the Alexandria command. Originally called Camp Convalescent, it soon became known as Camp Misery. At one time, in the fall of 1862, the camp held more than 10,000 men. Later it was designated "Camp Distribution" and used as a rendezvous for men fit for duty.

CAMP MITCHELL. A temporary War of 1812 encampment, Camp Mitchell was located one mile outside of Richmond.

FORT MONROE (*Fort Algernourne; Fort George*). More than 370 years ago, the third fort to be erected in the English-speaking colonies of America was constructed on the site now occupied by Fort Monroe and the United States Army Training and Doctrine command. Recognition of the military value of the site dates from its earliest exploration under the command of Captain Christopher Newport in 1607. Captain Newport's expedition reached the entrance of Chesapeake Bay on April 26, 1607, and landed at Cape Henry. Parties were immediately dispatched to explore the southern shores of the bay for a suitable anchorage. After several unsuccessful searches, they rowed to a point of land where they found a channel and "sounded twelve fathom." This put them in such "good comfort" that they named the point Cape Comfort and later Old Point Comfort to distinguish it from New Point Comfort, located at the mouth of Mobjack Bay, some 20 miles to the north. The three ships of Newport's expedition, *Godspeed, Susan Constant,* and *Discovery,* reached Point Comfort on April 30, 1607. From this point Newport's men made further expeditions that resulted in the establishment of the first permanent colony in America at Jamestown.

On October 3, 1609, Captain James Davis arrived from England with 16 men in the pinnace *Virginia.* Under the guidance of Captain James Ratcliffe, these men, aided by a detachment from Jamestown, constructed a fort at Point Comfort. When completed, the structure was named Algernourne Fort in honor of William de Percy, the first Lord Algernon, who had come to England with William the Conqueror in 1066. At first, the fort was a simple earthwork, but by 1611 it was a well-stockaded and sturdy fortification. Within its walls were a magazine, seven heavy guns, several smaller weapons, a storehouse, and the quarters for the 40-man garrison under the command of Captain Davis. (Captain Ratcliffe had been killed by Indians while on a trading expedition up the York River). In 1612 the fort was accidentally destroyed by fire. Captain Davis immediately attempted to rebuild the fort, but due to sickness and lack of provisions, little progress was made. During an inspection of Point Comfort in 1621, it was reported that there were "practically no fortifications capable of resisting a foreign enemy."

In 1630 a new fort was planned, and command of the project was given to Captain Samuel

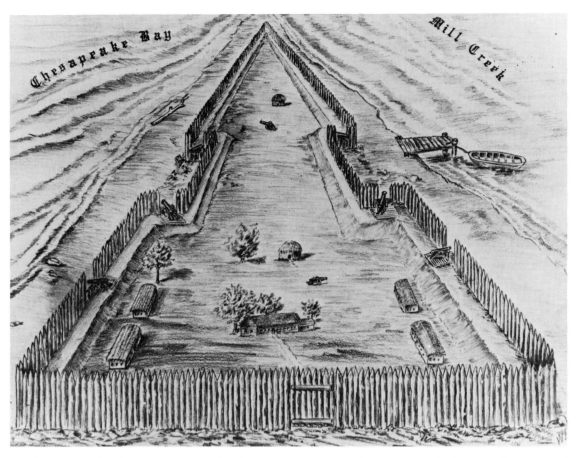

FORT MONROE. Artist's conception of Fort Algernourne as it looked in 1609. (Courtesy of the Fort Monroe Casemate Museum, Fort Monroe, Virginia.)

Matthews. In 1632 he reported that the fort was completed. Due to lack of maintenance, the fort soon fell into decay and was finally abandoned in 1665. Dutch raiders ventured up the James and burned or captured a number of vessels laden with tobacco. As a result, a force was returned to Point Comfort and the fortifications were reconstructed. In 1667 the fort was destroyed by a storm. Little was done in the way of refortifying Point Comfort between 1667 and 1728. It was not until Spain declared war on England in 1727 that work on the fortifications at Point Comfort was begun in earnest. The new fort was named in honor of the reigning king of England, George II. In 1749 Fort George was destroyed by a hurricane. Thereafter, the garrison consisted of one man who was charged with the care of what remained of the ruined fort at Old Point Comfort. To alleviate the boredom of his lonely occupation, the caretaker began exhibiting a light at night for the benefit of passing ships. In 1802 a lighthouse, which is still in operation, was built on the point.

During the Revolutionary War it was reported that there were only six guards at Old Point Comfort and a guard of twelve men at Newport News. The War of 1812 further demonstrated the need of an adequate coastal defense system

when British troops marched on Washington and set fire to the nation's capital. In 1816 a board was appointed by Acting Secretary of War George Graham to make recommendations for a coastal defense system for the United States. The board was headed by Brevet Brigadier General Simon Bernard, a former aide-de-camp of Napoleon. The board planned a series of forts which were to extend from Maine to Louisiana. General Bernard is reputed to have personally designed Fort Monroe.

Collection of materials for the fortifications at Point Comfort was begun in 1818, and actual construction began in March 1819. At this time construction was also begun at Fort Calhoun (later Fort Wool), which was to be built on an artificial island in the middle of Hampton Roads. Construction of the fortifications progressed steadily. The exterior wall was 10 feet thick and 12 feet high, and a wet ditch surrounded the work. A battery mounted 42 pieces of ordnance, and embrasures facing the sea were constructed for 84 guns.

Fort Monroe was designed following the general plan of the fortifications designed by Marshal Vauban at Toul, France. The fort consisted of seven fronts and covered approximately 63 acres of ground. The original armament was planned to be 380 guns, but this was later extended to 412 guns, which were, however, never all mounted. The fort housed a peacetime garrison of 600 men and a planned wartime garrison of 2,625 men. No other fort in the United States was of comparable size, and no fort in Europe not enclosing a town was any larger.

Fort Monroe received its first official U.S. Army garrison on July 25, 1823, when Company G, 3rd U.S. Artillery, was transferred from Fort Nelson near Norfolk to guard military convicts being used in the construction programs. In 1825 Fort Monroe's garrison was the largest in the United States, with one-third of the artillery troops and approximately one-tenth of the entire U.S. Army within its walls. The fort was officially designated as Fort Monroe in 1832 when the secretary of war directed "that work at Old Point Comfort be called Fort Monroe and not Fortress Monroe." Prior to that time, the fort had been unofficially designated Fortress Monroe in honor of James Monroe, fifth president of the United States, who held office when construction was begun in 1819.

The opening of hostilities between the North and South found Fort Monroe with a garrison strength of 400 men. Six weeks later the garrison numbered 6,000 men with approximately 1,400 at the fort and the balance going to Camp Hamilton, established at nearby Phoebus, today's city of Hampton to accommodate the overflow. Later a similar camp was established at Newport News and named Camp Butler (in honor of Major General Benjamin F. Butler, commander of Fort Monroe). On March 9, 1862, hundreds of soldiers and visitors lined the ramparts and beaches of Fort Monroe to witness naval history in the making. It was on this date that the first battle of ironclad vessels was fought in Hampton Roads, between the *Monitor* and the *Merrimack.* One of the few forts in the South not captured by the Confederates, Fort Monroe served as a springboard for many land and naval expeditions.

In 1824 Fort Monroe became the site of the "Artillery School of Practice," the Army's first artillery school. In 1907 the school was reorganized and designated the Coast Artillery School. During World Wars I and II, the mission of the post, and the Fort Monroe–based Coast Artillery, was to defend the Chesapeake Bay and Hampton Roads area. Though never attacked, the guns of the Coast Artillery, aided by antisubmarine nets and mine-planting service, stood as a significant deterrent to enemy invasion. However, by 1946, even the awesome weapons of the Coast Artillery had become obsolete. As part of an Army-wide reorganization, the school was transferred to Fort

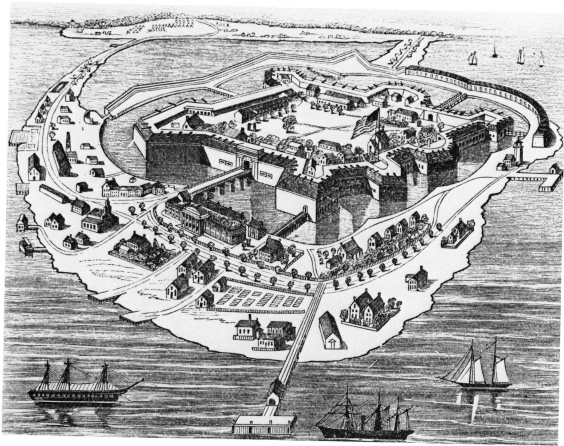

FORT MONROE. Artist's rendition of the fort in 1861. (Courtesy of the Virginia State Library.)

FORT MONROE. Aerial view of the fort as it looks today. The original fort is the area surrounded by the moat. (Courtesy of the U.S. Army.)

Winfield Scott, California, to make room for Headquarters, Army Ground Forces, which was relocated at that time at Fort Monroe from Washington, D.C.

Since then, there have been various reorganizations and redesignations. In 1948, Headquarters, Army Ground Forces, became Office, Chief of Army Field Forces. On February 1, 1955, Headquarters, Continental Army Command (CONARC) came into existence with its name redesignated as Headquarters, United States Continental Army Command, in 1957. In 1973 as part of a major Army reorganization, CONARC was disestablished and the U.S. Army Training and Doctrine command (TRADOC) was established.

MOORE'S FORT. A large Revolutionary War defense built on the Clinch River on land owned by William Moore, it was attacked numerous times by Indians, who killed many settlers and militiamen in and around the fort. Its site is now the town of St. Paul in Russell County.

CAMP MORRISON. Four large World War I camps were built in the vicinity of Newport News soon after the area was selected by the government as headquarters of the Hampton Roads Port of Embarkation. One of the camps was Camp Morrison, established in September 1917 and named after the nearby village of Morrison, about five miles north of Newport News and one mile east of the James River in Warwick County. It was used primarily as a concentration and embarkation post for air service troops until November 11, 1918. The camp's garrison was withdrawn in September 1919 and the depot absorbed by the Norfolk Quartermaster Intermediate Depot in 1923.

FORT MOUNT MALADY. FORT CHARITY.

MULBERRY ISLAND POINT BATTERY. FORT CRAFFORD.

FORT MYER (*Fort Whipple*). A Union defense of Washington, Fort Whipple was built in 1862 at Arlington, on property then known as the Arlington Estate overlooking the Potomac. It was named in honor of Major General Amiel W. Whipple who died on May 7, 1863, of wounds suffered at Chancellorsville. Situated on high ground northeast of Arlington Boulevard and Pershing Drive, it was a bastioned earthwork with a perimeter of 640 yards and emplacements for 47 guns. Fort Whipple was maintained as a military post after the war. Replaced by permanent type buildings beginning in 1872, it was renamed Fort Myer on February 4, 1881, in honor of Brigadier General Albert J. Myer, former commander of the post and first U.S. Army Chief Signal Officer, who died on August 24, 1880. Divided by the Arlington National Cemetery into two separate areas, Fort Myer today serves as headquarters for the famous 1st Battle Group, 3rd Infantry, whose duties include providing protection for the President and the Capitol, guarding the Tomb of the Unknown Soldier, and furnishing military units for ceremonies held within the Cemetery.

FORT NELSON. A Revolutionary War defense erected in 1776 on the left bank of the Elizabeth River, just below Portsmouth, Fort Nelson was named in honor of General Thomas Nelson, governor of Virginia. On May 9, 1779, the combined British Collier-Mathew sea and land expedition attacked Fort Nelson after its 150-man garrison under the command of Major Thomas

Matthews hastily abandoned the fort. The British landed forces, burned the fort with its American flag still flying, and seized Portsmouth and Norfolk. A U.S. Naval Hospital was constructed in 1823 on the site of Fort Nelson.

A second Fort Nelson was begun in 1794 on the west side of Norfolk's harbor, opposite Fort Norfolk. Originally a triangular-shaped, two-bastioned earthwork, occupying about two acres of ground, mounting two batteries of embrasured 24-pounder guns, and enclosing a two-story structure, Fort Nelson underwent extensive improvements during 1802–4. The fort was abandoned in 1824.

FORT NORFOLK. In 1794 President George Washington ordered the construction of Fort Norfolk on a four-and-a-half acre site on the east side of the Elizabeth River. Originally constructed of sod, Fort Norfolk stood on the opposite side of the river from Fort Nelson, which was built during the same period, so that both forts could work in conjunction to defend Norfolk, Portsmouth, the Navy Yard, and the area's commerce. During the very early 1800s the fort was not used to any extent, and it fell into disrepair. In June 1807, however, with the surrounding area facing the threat of another war, it was determined to completely repair and renovate Forts Norfolk and Nelson. During the War of 1812, the fort's Virginia militiamen, the crew of the frigate *Constellation,* and a small number of U.S. regulars defended Norfolk and Portsmouth from British attack. From 1824 to 1849, the fort was intermittently used for short periods. In 1849 the U.S. Navy obtained possession of the fort for the establishment of a large powder and munitions magazine with four-foot-thick walls, completed in 1856.

Abandoned upon Virginia's secession from the Union, Fort Nelson was held by the Confederates from April 19, 1861, until they evacuated Norfolk on May 10, 1862, when it was retaken by 6,000 Union troops under General John E. Wool. In March 1863 General Benjamin F. Butler removed the prisoners of war and stores and transferred Fort Norfolk to the U.S. Navy. In June 1923 Fort Norfolk was reoccupied by the Army when the offices of the Norfolk District were moved to the fort. Except for a brief period between 1935 and 1942, the Corps of Engineers occupied Fort Norfolk. Its original buildings faithfully maintained by the Norfolk District, old Fort Norfolk, standing at the west end of Front Street in Norfolk, in 1976 was added to the State and National Registers of Historic Landmarks.

FORT O'RORKE (O'ROURKE). Named in September 1863 for Colonel Patrick Henry O'Rorke, 140th New York Infantry, killed at Gettysburg on July 2, 1863, the Union defense was located at Fort Drive and Park Place. (See: ALEXANDRIA DEFENSES.)

FORT PATIENCE. FORT CHARITY.

CAMP PATRICK HENRY. In connection with the reestablishment of the Hampton Roads Port of Embarkation during World War II, Camp Patrick Henry was created near Newport News in Warwick County as a troop staging area to handle troops destined for Europe. The site of the camp is now occupied by the Newport News Airport.

CAMP PENDLETON (*State Military Reservation*). The Virginia State Military Reservation, consisting of approximately 920 acres and located at the south end of Virginia Beach, was taken over by the U.S. Army on September 21, 1940, for the duration of World War II. Renamed Camp Pendleton, it was first occupied, along with Fort Story at Cape Henry, by detachments from Fort Monroe and a detachment of the New York 244th Coast Artillery.

PETERSBURG SIEGE. In excess of 42 forts and 136 associated batteries were constructed by Confederate and Federal forces during 1862–65 on the south side of the Appomattox River, encircling the city of Petersburg. The fortified positions were named in honor of either active unit commanders or officers killed in battle (some batteries were designated by numerals). The great aggregation of fortifications served as a backdrop for the grim 10-month struggle, beginning in mid-June 1864, during which General U. S. Grant's Union army gradually but relentlessly surrounded Petersburg and cut General Robert E. Lee's railroad supply lines from the south.

For the Confederates it was 10 months of desperately hanging on, hoping the Northerners would tire of the war. For the soldiers of both armies it was 10 months of rifle bullets, artillery, and mortar shells, relieved by only rear-area tedium, drill and more drill, salt pork and corn meal, burned beans and bad coffee. To the individual soldier it added up to sloshing in mire and steaming trenches in summer; shivering in ice, snow, and mud in winter. Somehow most survived disease and desperately endured the coldest wartime winter they could remember.

Grant's troops suffered frightful losses attacking Lee's entrenched Confederate troops at Cold

Harbor, 16 miles northeast of Richmond (May 31–June 12, 1864). Moving south across the James River, Grant threw his forces against Petersburg on June 15. Except for a series of Union fumbles, the city might well have fallen in the initial attacks. Federal commanders, perhaps shaken by the Cold Harbor disaster, failed to press home their assaults, allowing the relatively few Confederate defenders to hold on until Lee transferred his army south from Richmond. General Grant was then compelled to settle down for a siege.

Hardly had the siege begun when coal miners of the 48th Pennsylvania Infantry began digging a 511-foot-long tunnel 20 feet beneath Elliott's Salient, an extensive Confederate chain of batteries east of the city. The plan, an idea originated by the Pennsylvania division's commander, Lieutenant Colonel Henry Pleasants, was to blast a mighty gap in the Confederate line by exploding four tons of black gunpowder in the tunnel and rush in before the Confederates could recover from the shock. The explosion, before dawn on July 30, blew up an entire battery, creating a crater 170 feet long, 60 to 80 feet wide, and 30 feet deep. More than 280 Confederates were killed or wounded in the blast. But the defenders quickly rallied and their artillery raked the attacking Federals. Then Confederate infantry waded in, and in an orgy of shooting, clubbing, and bayoneting, the Southerners virtually annihilated one Union division.

The Battle of the Crater proved there could be no shortcut to taking Petersburg. Grant's next target was the Weldon Railroad, running due south from Petersburg. After three days of heavy fighting (August 18–20) in brutal heat, the Federals remained astride the steel rails, permanently cutting another of Lee's major supply lines. By now little food or fodder remained in Petersburg or Richmond. All that Lee had left was one rickety railroad and his worn-out horses and wagons. In late September Confederate cavalry commander Wade Hampton led 4,000 horsemen around the Union rear to rustle Northern cattle for Petersburg's hungry defenders. The "Beefsteak Raid" netted 300 prisoners and, more important, 2,400 beeves.

Approaching cold weather in November ended large-scale efforts by both sides, but rifle, artillery, and mortar fire continued. During the winter of 1864–65, cold and miserable soldiers of both sides worked with pick and shovel to strengthen their lines and build rude shelters. There were signs of scurvy among the southerners. By January Lee's army had lost its fighting edge. Casualties and desertion left only 50,000

cold and hungry Confederate soldiers in the trenches. Grant's forces increased to 110,000 well-equipped, well-fed—but nonetheless homesick and weary—troops. At the same time Grant was exhausting Lee's men, Federal supplies rattled continuously over the newly completed U.S. military railroad from City Point (now Hopewell) to the front.

In March Lee desperately attacked the Union siege line, not quite sure what he might achieve. But he quickly captured Fort Stedman, a Union stronghold east of the city and about 1,400 yards north of the Crater. If he were to break Grant's line, he might lift the long-protracted siege. But Grant counterattacked and in four hours crushed Lee's "Last Grand Offensive." There now remained in April only one railroad to the south, the Southside. Once that was cut, Petersburg was lost and Richmond with it. Lee pulled his men together, and led them off down the road and eventually to Appomattox. The Confederacy's long dying was nearly over. Within weeks the last Confederate soldier laid down his arms.

Administered and maintained by the National Park Service, today's Petersburg National Battlefield Park is adjacent to the Fort Lee Military Reservation to the east. An auto battlefield tour has been carefully designed with stops to allow visitors to walk around the grounds of still-existing fortification remains and the sites of important batteries long since gone.

CAMP (FORT) PICKETT. Located near Blackstone in Dinwiddie County, this 46,000-acre post was established on July 3, 1942, and named in honor of Confederate Major General George Edward Pickett, celebrated for his famous charge at Gettysburg. A military reservation with more than 1,500 buildings, Camp Pickett trained as many as 75,000 men at one time for overseas battlefields. The camp's first fighting unit was the 79th Division, arriving the same day the post was formally established. The 3rd Division arrived in September 1942 and was the first unit to undergo the amphibious training course inaugurated here.

Camp Pickett was deactivated in the spring of 1947, reopened in August 1948, but deactivated again in the spring of 1949. It was reactivated in August 1950 to train men for the Korean War. It was once again deactivated on June 26, 1954. In the fall of 1960, a renovation of the post was initiated for the purpose of establishing a training area for all reservists of the Second Army. Continuously in service since then, the camp was determined a permanent military reservation by the Army and officially designated as

Fort Pickett, today a semiactive subinstallation of Fort Lee.

POINT OF FORT ARSENAL. Located on the south side of the Rivanna River, about two miles northwest of its confluence with the James, near the present-day town of Dixie in Fluvanna County, the Point of Fort Arsenal was one of Virginia's principal military installations during the Revolution. It was the only military center operated by the Commonwealth during the post-Revolutionary period of the eighteenth century. It stood on land then owned by David Ross, who was a quartermaster in the Virginia militia. The Arsenal was attacked by approximately 400 British troops under Lieutenant colonel (later Colonel) John Graves Simcoe, commander of the Queen's Rangers, while Baron von Steuben was there training recruits for General Nathanael Greene's army. Forewarned of Simcoe's approach some days earlier, von Steuben evacuated the post, taking what supplies he could across the James River but abandoning a large quantity of stores. The British entered the Arsenal, destroyed many of its buildings, and 2,500 "stand of arms," in addition to quantities of rum and brandy. During its 20-year active history as an arsenal, a supply and ammunition depot, and a basic training camp, the post played a vital role until about 1801 in the defense of Virginia's western frontier.

FORT POWHATAN (*Fort Hood*). Located on the James River in Prince George County, across the river from Jamestown Island, this fort stood on John Hood's 200-acre plantation where there were two large tobacco warehouses and a wharf. It was at this point that Fort Hood, later known as Fort Powhatan, was built in 1781, near the site where the local militia in 1779 had positioned two guns that became known as Hood's Battery.

To Virginians the Revolution had seemed far removed until the costly May 1779 invasion of Hampton Roads by British warships, prompting state officials to initiate defense measures. In November of that year, Governor Thomas Jefferson had recommended to the state Board of War that heavy cannon be mounted at several strategic spots along rivers in the Tidewater, including two at a place known as Hood's, 35 miles below Richmond, to protect both Petersburg and Richmond from British naval attack. On January 3, 1781, British warships commanded by turncoat Benedict Arnold, with land forces under Colonel John Simcoe aboard, sailed up the James and attacked Hood's Battery, and occupied Richmond two days later. A week later, the British fleet

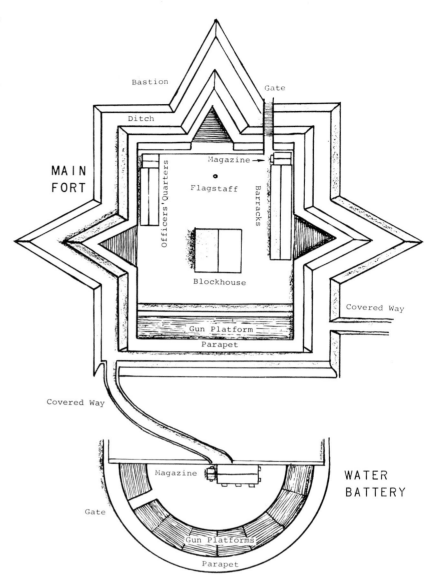

returned down river and halted long enough to completely dismantle Hood's Battery, carrying off its artillery.

At the end of January 1781, it was determined to build a substantial fortification at what was known as Wind Mill Hill, just below the old battery, with 8 heavy cannon, a barracks, powder magazines, and a variety of ditches and other outworks. A strong redoubt occupied by 60 men and at least 2 field pieces would defend against rear attacks. Construction of the new fortification, however, was sporadic due to shortages of brick and labor. Ironically, Fort Hood was finally completed after its need was no longer required.

In 1808, when another war between the United States and Great Britain seemed certain, the Federal government purchased the 10-acre tract that included Fort Hood for the construction of Fort Powhatan. A new masonry fort was built, and after war broke out in 1812, it was provided with

FORT POWHATAN. The hospital, storehouse, and workshop were outside the main fort complex, on the east side. (Courtesy of the Virginia State Library.)

artillery. In February 1814, the five-bastioned fort mounted 22 varied-caliber pieces of artillery, with a covered way leading to a water battery on its north side. During the war, the British made no efforts to attack Richmond or Petersburg, and as the conflict neared its end, the fort was used principally as a supply depot.

During the Civil War, Fort Powhatan was reactivated by the Confederates as a defense against Union attacks on Richmond. In 1862 Federal gunboats bombarded the fort. In 1863 Federal forces seized the fort and destroyed its magazines and gun platforms. A year later, several Union Colored Regiments occupied Fort Powhatan and successfully repulsed an assault by cavalry troops commanded by General Fitzhugh Lee, General Robert E. Lee's nephew. After the war, the fort was abandoned. Today, there are still evidences of Fort Powhatan's ruins, with only a shallow moat or ditch and a weed-choked parapet remaining.

FORT RAMSAY (*Fort Upton*). A Union defense constructed in 1861 at Upton's Hill in Arlington, it was originally known as Fort Upton. On November 16, 1861, it was renamed in honor of Lieutenant Colonel (later Brevet Major General) George Douglas Ramsay, chief ordnance officer of the Army. The fort occupied ground belonging to the old Upton Mansion (still standing), with the top of its upper story used as a signal station. The site of Fort Ramsay is located on the 1100-numbered block of John Marshall Drive.

FORT REYNOLDS (*Fort Blencker*). A Union redoubt built in September 1861 and located about three miles northwest of Alexandria, it stood on a height above the section now known as Shirlington. It had a 360-yard perimeter and emplacements for 12 guns. Originally called Fort Blencker, the defense was renamed Fort Reynolds on September 17, 1863, in honor of Major General J. F. Reynolds, killed July 2, 1863, at Gettysburg. The site of Fort Reynolds today is within Fort Reynolds Park on 31st Street South, east of South Woodrow Street. (See also: ALEXANDRIA DEFENSES.)

FORT RICHARDSON. A Union redoubt with a perimeter of 316 yards and emplacements for 15 guns, Fort Richardson was constructed in September 1861 to cover the left flank of the newly established Arlington defense line. It was named for Major General Israel Bush Richardson who, later mortally wounded at Antietam in September 1862, died near that battlefield on November 3, 1862. The site of Fort Richardson is located on the Army-Navy Country Club's golf course.

RICHMOND'S DEFENSES. The struggle for Richmond preoccupied Northerners and Southerners alike for four years. Situated at the head of navigation on the James River and only 110 miles from the Federal capital of Washington, Richmond was a symbol and a prime psychological objective. If the Confederacy lost its capital, Southerners might lose their will to fight. But there were more compelling reasons, for besides being the political center of the confederacy, it was a medical and manufacturing center, and the principal supply depot for troops operating on the Confederacy's northeastern frontier.

The Army of Northern Virginia was only one factor in the successful defense of the confederate capital from 1861 to 1865. Another was the fortifications built by the South that nearly encircled the city. The outer line of defenses, stretching for more than 65 miles, was approximately 10 miles from the capital. Within the ring was an intermediate line about 4 miles from the city. And just outside the city limits stood a series of star forts as inner defenses. These forts and breastworks, along with others such as the trenches built at Cold Harbor, 16 miles northeast of Richmond, served to help defeat the numerous attempts by Union armies to capture the coveted capital of the confederacy.

Of the seven major drives launched against Richmond, two brought Union Forces almost within sight of the city—McClellan's Peninsular Campaign of 1862, culminating in the Seven Days' Battles, and Grant's crushing campaign of 1864. For two years, while the armies fought indecisively in northern Virginia, Maryland, and Pennsylvania, Richmond entrenched and applauded General Lee's unbroken successes in keeping Northern armies impotent. In March 1864 General Ulysses S. Grant assumed command of all Union armies in the field. Attaching himself to the Army of the Potomac, Grant embarked on a relentless campaign against Richmond and the Army of Northern Virginia.

In a series of flanking movements designed to cut Lee off from the Confederate capital, Union forces slipped past the Southerners at the Wilderness and Spotssylvania Court House, although they suffered heavy casualties. At Cold Harbor, Grant's massive frontal assaults against the strongly entrenched Confederate line failed dismally with appalling losses. For 10 days the badly mauled Federals and starving Confederates broiled in the trenches; then Grant withdrew, crossed the James, and drove toward the important rail center of Petersburg. Richmond withstood all attacks until Grant's successful 10-month siege of Petersburg forced General Lee to retreat westward from that city on April 2, 1865. Richmond was abandoned the following day. His surrender at Appomattox Court House and the collapse of the Confederacy followed swiftly. Today's Richmond National Battlefield Park commemorates the Seven Days' Battles, Cold Harbor, and five lesser campaigns.

BATTERY RODGERS. Located at Alexandria, near Jones' Point overlooking the Potomac, Battery Rodgers was one of the largest of the Defenses of Washington. Constructed in 1863, the powerful battery was armed with one 15-inch Rodman gun, weighing a massive 25 tons, and five 200-pound Parrott rifles. The battery was named in honor of Captain George Washington Rodgers, a U.S. Naval Academy graduate, who was killed on August 17, 1863, during the attack on Fort Wagner in Charleston Harbor. (See: ALEXANDRIA DEFENSES.)

ROGER SMITH'S FORT. Following the devastating Indian massacre of 1622, several new forts were erected. One was erected in 1623 at "Warrasquoyacke" (variously spelled during the early years of Jamestown), near the mouth of Lawne's Creek, in the area of Burwell's Bay, Isle of Wight County. Based on colonial descriptions of the fort's situation, it was probably located opposite Mulberry Point, the site of today's Fort Eustis. Probably in the form of a blockhouse, it was built on the tobacco plantation owned by Captain Roger Smith who resided on James Island. Colonial records do not indicate the exact site of the fort or how long it existed.

FORT ROYAL (*Fort Mattapony*). Located on the Mattaponi River, one and a half miles south of the present town of West Point, King and Queen County, Fort Royal (also known as Fort Mattapony) was one of the new defenses erected in 1645 or 1646 following the Indian massacre of 1644, the second in Virginia's history. Intermittently occupied, the fort was garrisoned during Bacon's Rebellion in 1676.

FORT RUNYON. A Union bastioned earthwork, the largest of the Defenses of Washington, begun on May 24, 1861, by New York and New Jersey troops, Fort Runyon was located about a half-mile southwest of Jefferson Davis Highway and Boundary Drive in Arlington. Named in honor of Brigadier General Theodore Runyon, the fort had a perimeter of 1,484 yards, enclosing

12 acres, and was designed to protect the Long Bridge over the Potomac.

FORT SCOTT. Located on present Fort Scott Drive in the Aurora Hills section of Alexandria, Fort Scott was a detached lunette (an outwork with two faces and an open entrance) built in May 1861 and named for General Winfield Scott, then general in chief of the Army. It was one of the original forts constructed, but the later expansion of Alexandria's defenses, about two miles to the west, placed it in the rear of the line of defenses. Fort Scott had a perimeter of 313 yards and emplacements for eight guns. Small remains are in evidence just to the west of the Drive entrance to the Fort Scott Recreation Area.

SEWALL'S POINT FORT. A small fort was built in 1692 or 1693 on Sewall's Point to protect shipping in Norfolk's harbor. Its site is now occupied by part of the Norfolk Navy Yard.

SHELBY'S FORT. A Revolutionary War defense located in the present city of Bristol, on the Tennessee line, in Washington County, it was built in 1776 by Colonel Evan Shelby, noted Indian fighter and founder of the city, originally known as Sapling Grove. It was at this fort that the campaign was planned that culminated in the defeat of the British at the Battle of Kings Mountain, South Carolina, on October 7, 1780.

FORT SMITH. A Union-built Civil War defense of Washington, Fort Smith was located in Alexandria at the intersection of 24th Street North and 21st Road.

SMITH'S FORT. Named for Captain John Smith, vigorous leader of Jamestown during its earliest years, Smith's Fort was erected in 1609 on the south bank of the James River, about two miles from the mouth of Gray's Creek, in what is now Surry County, near the town of Surry. The defense is shown as the "New Fort" on Captain Smith's map of Virginia. It stood on the site of "Smith's Fort Plantation," on property owned by John Rolfe, founder of Virginia's tobacco industry, who wedded Pocahontas. Surry County's oldest brick dwelling was built in 1651–52 by Thomas Warren on land purchased by him from Thomas Rolfe, the son of Pocahontas and John Rolfe. Archaeological explorations have confirmed the location of Smith's Fort.

STAR FORT. A Civil War defense located on a hill near Winchester in Frederick County, it was built by Union forces in 1862. Abandoned by the Federals several months later, it was occupied in 1863 by Confederate troops until the Third battle of Winchester, September 19, 1864, when Union cavalry recaptured the works and took the town.

STATE MILITARY RESERVATION. CAMP PENDLETON.

FORT (BATTERY) STEPHENS. A Confederate-built fortification, part of Richmond's outer defenses, the preserved remains of Fort or Battery Stephens lie on a two-acre wooded tract at the intersection of Pams Avenue and Norcliff Road, between U.S. 1 and I-95, in eastern Chesterfield. The fort encloses about an acre at the south end of the lot, presently a matter of dispute between preservationists and a utility company which has plans to obliterate the Civil War fort and replace it with a water tower. Fort Stephens, as it appears today, has an open-ended rectangular wall six to ten feet high with a four-to-six-foot-deep moat around it. Inside, four earthen artillery ramps lead up to the parapet.

FORT STORY. Long known as the Army's amphibious training center for the Transportation Training Command, Fort Story was considered a "temporary" post for 44 years until it became a major subordinate post of the U.S. Army Transportation Training Command, a subpost of Fort Eustis, in 1961. Fort Story is situated at the tip of historic Cape Henry, 18 miles east of Norfolk and 6 miles north of Virginia Beach. It covers 1,394 acres, an area fronting on nearly 4 miles of beach that makes it ideal for amphibious training. The post was named for Major General John Patten Story, chief of the Artillery School at Fort Monroe for many years.

The reservation was acquired by the government in 1914 and was established in February 1917 as a Coast Artillery fort guarding the southern entrance to Chesapeake Bay. For this mission, Fort Story boasted the heaviest armament of any Atlantic coast fort. Its 16-inch rifles and howitzers, plus three batteries of 6-inch guns, all have been dismantled. Because of its strategic location, however, it continues to maintain its status as an important link in the nation's anti-aircraft defense network. Toward the close of World War II, Fort Story was the site of a convalescent hospital opened in September 1944. It accommodated over 13,000 patients up to the time of its closing in March 1946. The same year marked the arrival of the first DUKW (amphibious truck) company on the post. although Fort Story did not officially become a Transportation Corps installation until

July 1948. Since that time, it has trained amphibious truck units, terminal service battalions, terminal service companies, and platoons for service in Europe, the Far East, and the Arctic. Still a subinstallation of Fort Eustis, Fort Story is under the jurisdiction of the U.S. Army Training and Doctrine Command (TRADOC).

Historically, the reservation is the site of the first landing of the Jamestown settlers on April 26, 1607, after a storm-tossed voyage from England in three small ships. The Cape Henry Memorial, a handsome granite cross erected by the Daughters of the American Colonists in 1935, is one of Fort Story's landmarks.

FORT STRONG (*Fort DeKalb*). A Union lunette marking the north end of the Arlington Line of Defenses, Fort Strong was constructed in August 1861 and had a perimeter of 318 yards, with emplacements for 15 guns. It was located near the intersection of Lee Highway and Wayne Street. First known as Fort DeKalb, the fort was renamed Fort Strong in honor of Major General George Crockett Strong, who was mortally wounded while leading a charge against Fort Wagner on Morris Island, Charleston Harbor, in July 1863.

CAMP STUART. A World War I post named in honor of Major General J. E. B. Stuart, outstanding cavalry leader of the Confederacy's Army of Northern Virginia, Camp Stuart was established in August 1917 in connection with the Newport News Port of Embarkation. After serving as an embarkation cantonment until November 11, 1918, it was thereafter used for purposes of debarkation and demobilization until September 1919. Camp Stuart's Headquarters opened on August 21, 1917, and closed on November 29, 1919, when the post was abandoned to be sold.

FORT TAYLOR. A Union defense located near the southeast corner of Broad and Roosevelt streets, in the area of Seven Corners, in Falls Church, Fairfax County, it was constructed by Federal troops on property then belonging to L. William Taylor. The fort commanded a range of hills to the west of Arlington heights.

TERRY'S FORT. FORT BLACKWATER.

FORT TILLINGHAST. A lunette in the Union's Arlington Line, Fort Tillinghast was built by Federal troops in August 1861. Located at Arlington Boulevard and 2nd Street North, it had a perimeter of 298 yards and emplacements for 13 guns.

FORT TRIAL (*Galloway's Fort*). A French and Indian War defense built in 1756 by command of Lieutenant Colonel George Washington, Fort Trial, also known as Galloway's Fort, was located on the Smith River, near present Stanleytown, in western Henry County.

FORT UPTON. FORT RAMSAY.

FORT VAUSE. A French and Indian War frontier defense, originally a small minimally fortified dwelling, Fort Vause was located at the western edge of present Shawsville in Montgomery County. It was built in 1755, presumably under the direction of Colonel Ephraim Vause (variously spelled), an early settler on the Roanoke River. He surrounded his home with a 100-foot-square, 15-foot-high wall of strongly built palisades, enclosing barracks and cabins, garrisoned by 70 local troops. In June 1756 Fort Vause was attacked by a large body of French and Indians, who killed or captured most of the troops and settlers who had sought safety there. The Council of War at Augusta Court House later ordered the fortification rebuilt and regarrisoned.

CAMP WALLACE. A subinstallation of Fort Eustis, Camp Wallace was established in October 1918 as the Upper Firing Point for artillery units of Camp Eustis. In March 1919, it was renamed in honor of Colonel Elmer J. Wallace, who had been killed in action in France the previous October. Camp Wallace remained on inactive status during the 1930s but was used during World War II to house troops from Fort Eustis. Camp Wallace was placed under control of the Transportation Corps, along with Fort Eustis, in 1946, and at present is used for amphibious training, as a troop bivouac area, and as a test area for the Transportation Engineering Agency.

FORT WARD. A strong Union fortification constructed at Alexandria in 1861, Fort Ward was the fifth largest in the cordon of Washington's defenses. With five bastions and 35 guns, it was considered by Major General John G. Barnard, chief engineer of the Defenses of Washington, to be "one of the major works in the defense system." Fort Ward was named in honor of Commander James Harmon Ward, the first naval casualty in the Civil War, killed aboard ship at Mathias Point on the Potomac River, July 27, 1861. Fort Ward was occupied by elements of the New York and New Jersey Artillery, and detachments of the 13th New Jersey Infantry, who did much of the construction on the rifle pits as well as the fort itself.

In 1961 the city of Alexandria purchased 40 acres of woodland surrounding the fort and established the area as an Historic Park. The northwest bastion was then restored to appear as it did during the war. The guns in the bastion are exact replicas of those mounted in Fort Ward from 1861 to 1865. To complement the site, a Museum and Officers' Hut were constructed. The completed project was dedicated on May 30, 1964. The only Union fort in the Defenses of Washington to be developed into a major Civil War memorial, the Fort Ward Museum and Historic Site is located on West Braddock Road, between King Street (S.R. 7) and Seminary Road. Fort Ward is listed on the National Register of Historic Sites.

WARWICK'S FORT. FORT DINWIDDIE.

WASHINGTON'S CIVIL WAR DEFENSES. With the outbreak of the Civil War in the spring of 1861, the city of Washington, D.C., was virtually defenseless in the event of a Confederate attack. On May 24, 1861, the date that Virginia's vote of secession from the Union became effective, Union troops crossed the Potomac River, occupying Alexandria and Arlington Heights. Three forts were constructed to serve as supply bases for the occupation forces. After the Confederate victory at Manassas (the Battle of First Bull Run), on July 21, 1861, the North began erecting forts on both sides of the river for the defense of the Capital city. By the end of 1861, over 40 forts and batteries had been built. After the second Confederate victory at the Battle of Second Bull Run in August 1862, the system of fortifications, now known as the Defenses of Washington, was enlarged and strengthened. By late 1862, the city of Washington had become the most heavily fortified location in the Western Hemisphere. It was completely surrounded by 161 armed and unarmed forts and batteries connected by 37 miles of military roads and trenches, with 905 mounted guns.

FORT WEED. Initially called Redoubt A, this Union defense at Alexandria was named Fort Weed in honor of Brigadier General Stephen A. Weed, 5th Artillery, killed at Gettysburg, July 2, 1863. It was constructed by 34th Massachusetts Infantry troops, commanded by Captain Andrew Potter. The site of Fort Weed is located at Monticello Road and Fort Drive. (See also: ALEXANDRIA DEFENSES.)

FORT WEST. In 1609 two years after the founding of Jamestown, Captain John Smith sent Captain Francis West and a detachment of men up the James River. On an island by the Falls of the James, they established Fort West, in the vicinity of the foot of present 9th Street in Richmond. Confronted by "intolerable inconveniences," however, the men soon returned to Jamestown to escape the Indians. Archival records indicate that a trading post was established there in 1637.

FORT WHIPPLE. FORT MYER.

FORT WILLARD. ALEXANDRIA DEFENSES.

FORT WILLIAM. A French and Indian War frontier defense, probably erected in early 1756, Fort William was one of the forts built or manned by command of Colonel George Washington, who assigned 75 men to garrison it. Fort William was located on the Catawba Creek Branch of the James River, about three miles west of present Fincastle, Botetourt County.

FORT WILLIAMS. ALEXANDRIA DEFENSES.

FORT WINSLOW. FORT JOHN CUSTIS.

FORT WOLSTENHOLME (*Martin's Hundred Fort*). Located on the east side of the James River, a few miles southeast of Colonial Williamsburg, Wolstenholme Town was founded in 1619 on the 21,500-acre Martin's Hundred Plantation (later reestablished as Carter's Grove Plantation), chartered by the Virginia Company of London in 1617 or 1618. The name of Wolstenholme Towne, the headquarters of Martin's Hundred, was derived from John Wolstenholme, who was one of the more prominent shareholders in the Martin's Hundred Society. On the morning of Good Friday, March 22, 1622, Virginia Indians, led by warrior Chief Opechancanough, staged a well-planned and coordinated uprising against the colonists, massacring them in their dwellings and in the fields, from present-day Richmond through the Tidewater area. Jamestown, however, had been forewarned by a friendly Indian, and strengthened its defenses and escaped the slaughter.

Archaeologists, funded by the National Geographic Society and led by Ivor Noel Hume, in 1978 discovered the buried remains of the almost forgotten seventeenth century town, its fort, and evidence of the 1622 massacre. Fort Wolstenholme is the first all-timbered fortification found in Virginia from the earliest Colonial period. Measuring roughly 131 feet long and 86 wide, the irregular, four-sided palisaded fort was fitted in each of its angles by a raised watchtower or bastion. Historical records indicate that by the end of 1622, some 20 people had returned to Martin's Hundred. Archaeological evidence indicates that through the next 20 years or more, there was scattered reoccupation in the vicinity of the old site.

FORT WOODBURY. Located just to the rear of the present Arlington Court House, this Union lunette in the Arlington Line of Defenses was constructed in August 1861. With a 275-yard perimeter and emplacements for 13 guns, the defense was named for engineer Captain (later Major General) Daniel Phineas Woodbury, United States Military Academy graduate, who assisted in the building of Washington's defenses.

FORT WOOL (*Fort Calhoun*). Situated on an artificial island known as the "Rip Raps," on the south side of the channel from Chesapeake Bay into Hampton Roads, Fort Wool was constructed to furnish cross fire with Fort Monroe on the north side of the channel. Originally called Fort Calhoun in honor of Secretary of War John C. Calhoun, the fort was planned by engineer General Simon Bernard as a tower battery with three tiers of casemates. Designed to mount 216 guns, its interior crest measured 381 yards. Its peacetime garrison was fixed at 200 men and the wartime garrison at 1,130 men.

Although work on Fort Calhoun was begun at the same time as Fort Monroe in 1819, construction progressed slowly because its foundation took much longer to lay than originally planned. The Civil War found the fort still incomplete. A few guns were mounted in the fort, garrisoned by one or two companies of Union troops. On March 18, 1862, the name of the fort was changed to Fort Wool in honor of Major General John E. Wool, then in command of the Union's Department of Virginia with headquarters at Fort Monroe. Construction resumed after the war continued until about 1870. Then in 1902 it was partially modernized by emplacements for coast artillery guns. It was garrisoned during World Wars I and II. No longer required for national defense, Fort Wool, never completed, was turned over to the state of Virginia in 1967. The City of Hampton partially restored Fort Wool as a tourist attraction and in May 1985 began daily boat trips to the island.

FORT WORTH. ALEXANDRIA DEFENSES.

FORT YORK. About 1755–56, the province of Virginia established a fort at the "Town of York," today's Yorktown, on the south bank of the York

YORKTOWN BATTLE-FIELD. (Courtesy of the Virginia State Travel Service.)

River, and armed it with 11 18- and 9-pounders and 10 1-pounders.

YORKTOWN BATTLEFIELD. The surrender of British forces at Yorktown on October 19, 1781, marked the virtual close of the American Revolution, ending seven long years of war. While the Treaty of Peace was not signed until two years later, the victory at Yorktown was the decisive event in the struggle to establish the United States as an independent nation.

In 1781 the American War of Independence reached its seventh year. The British had practically abandoned efforts to reconquer the northern states, but still had hopes of regaining the southern part of the colonies. General Charles Cornwallis, in the spring of the year, marched into Virginia from North Carolina at the head of a British army. He believed that if Virginia could be subdued, the states to the south of it would readily return to British allegiance.

The Marquis de Lafayette, with a small American force, was operating in Virginia, but was unable to meet Cornwallis in open battle. British forces marched up and down Virginia almost at will, but failed to break the resistance of its people. In July, in response to orders from New York, Cornwallis moved down the James River to Portsmouth, in preparation for sending part of his army to New York, which General Washington was threatening. Countermanding orders soon reached Cornwallis, however, directing him to fortify a naval base in the lower Chesapeake.

Cornwallis, on advice of his engineers, chose Yorktown for the base and transferred his whole army there early in August. He began fortifying the town and Gloucester Point opposite. Meanwhile, a large French fleet, under the Comte de Grasse, was moving up from the West Indies for combined operations with the allied French and American armies. De Grasse proceeded to blockade the mouth of Chesapeake Bay, to cut off Cornwallis from help by sea. Washington moved his forces toward Virginia to attack by land. The general's forces included part of the main American army operating on the Hudson River, and the French army under Comte de Rochambeau.

While de Grasse maintained a strict blockade by sea, the combined armies, numbering over 16,000 men, gathered at Williamsburg during the middle of September. On the 28th they marched down the peninsula and laid siege to Yorktown, garrisoned by only 7,500 men. Cornwallis almost immediately abandoned his outer line of defenses and retired within the town. On the night of October 6, the allied armies opened entrenchments and a few days later, with their batteries in position, began a heavy bombardment of the British position. Their fire soon subdued that of Cornwallis's guns, and they were able to close in at shorter range. Two outlying British redoubts were stormed on the evening of October 14, and the British became desperate. Cornwallis made an attempt to escape by way of Gloucester, but his boats were scattered by a storm. On the morning of October 17 he sent out a flag of truce and asked General Washington for a discussion of terms of surrender.

On the following day, commissioners met at the Moore House, just behind the American lines, and drafted articles of capitulation. In accordance with these articles, the British army marched out of Yorktown at 2 P.M. of the 19th, between the American and French armies drawn up to receive them, and laid down their arms. The long war was practically over and American independence became a reality. Near the upper end of Main Street is the Yorktown Victory Monument, erected by the government to commemorate the French alliance and the victory over Cornwallis. Its cornerstone was laid in 1881 at the celebration of the centennial of the surrender.

FORT ALDEN. A temporary blockhouse located at present-day Snoqualmie, King County, and situated about 60 feet south of the Snoqualmie River, a short distance above its falls, it was erected in 1856 by the Northern Battalion of the 2nd Washington Volunteer Regiment. The defense was named for Captain James Alden.

ALEXANDER'S BLOCKHOUSE. A substantial two-storied log blockhouse erected in 1855 on Whidbey Island by settler John Alexander, the defense was later moved to today's city of Coupeville, the county seat of Island County, where it is still preserved.

AMERICAN CAMP. Camp San Juan Island.

FORT BELLINGHAM. Located about 25 miles south of the Canadian border, at the present town of Bellingham on Bellingham Bay, it was established to protect the Whatcom mining district on August 26, 1856, by 9th Infantry troops commanded by Captain George E. Pickett. Fort Bellingham was abandoned on April 28, 1860.

FORT BENNETT. A temporary stockade located on the north bank of the Walla Walla River, about six miles west of present Walla Walla and two miles east of the former Whitman Mission, Fort Bennett was built in December 1855 by Oregon Volunteers and named in honor of Captain Charles Bennett, killed on December 7 during the "Battle of Frenchtown." It was abandoned sometime in 1856.

CAMP BONNEVILLE. Located near the city of Vancouver in Clark County, Camp Bonneville is a major training site for Fort Lawton's ARCOM (Army Reserve Command) units, headquartered at Seattle.

BORST'S BLOCKHOUSE. Also known as Fort Borst, it was a temporary defense erected by settlers late in 1855 or early 1856 on Joseph Borst's land claim near Centralia, Lewis County, on the Chehalis River, just west of its juncture with the Skookumchuck. The fort was later occupied as a supply depot by the Territorial Militia. The blockhouse has been moved from its original site and is now in Fort Borst Park, immediately southwest of the intersection of I-99 and Harris Avenue in Centralia.

FORT CANBY (*Fort Cape Disappointment*). Located on the north bank of the entrance to the Columbia River, Fort Cape Disappointment was a U.S. military post established on April 5, 1864,

Washington

two years after the cape was first armed with smoothbore cannon to protect the river's mouth from enemies. On January 28, 1875, it was renamed Fort Canby in honor of General Edward Canby who was killed in the Modoc Indian War. Later periodically improved and enlarged, the post had a rather active history until after World War II. Abandoned by the Army in 1950, Fort Canby is now contained within the 1,700-acre Fort Canby State Park, located two miles southwest of Ilwaco off U.S. 101.

FORT CAPE DISAPPOINTMENT. FORT CANBY.

FORT CASCADES (*Fort Rains*). Located on the right bank of the Columbia River at the foot of the Cascades, the lower of the river's two rapids, near today's Bonneville Dam, Fort Cascades was established on September 30, 1855, by Captain Granville O. Haller, 4th Infantry. To support the fort, two garrisoned blockhouses were erected on the north bank of the Columbia, one approximately midway along the rapids and the other at its head, about five miles above the fort. The middle two-storied blockhouse, named for Major Gabriel Rains, was years later reconstructed from its original timbers by the Skamania County Historical Society and relocated a half-mile west of the Bonneville Dam. Temporarily evacuated on June 14, 1861, Fort Cascades was reoccupied two months later because of the threat of renewed Indian outbreaks. Finally abandoned on November 6, 1861, the reservation was surrendered to private claimants on February 2, 1867.

FORT CASEY. Presently located within Fort Casey State Park on Whidbey Island, three miles south of Coupeville, Fort Casey was one of the Coast Artillery posts established during the late 1890s for the defense of Puget Sound. It was named for Brigadier General Thomas Lincoln Casey, chief of engineers, 1888–95. Together with the heavy batteries of Fort Worden and Fort Flagler, its guns guarded the entrance to Admiralty Inlet, the only entrance to Puget Sound that could be navigated by warships at that time. The three forts formed a "triangle of fire," the key point in the fortification system designed to prevent a hostile fleet from reaching such prime targets as the Bremerton Navy Yard and the cities of Seattle, Tacoma, Olympia, and Everett.

A small detail of troops arrived at the fort shortly after the completion of the gun emplacements, living in tents until barracks were completed. Later, the first arrivals were joined by a larger garrison of 200 enlisted men and 6 officers. Mounting of the guns in 10 variously named batteries was completed by January 26, 1900. The first test firing was performed on September 11, 1901. During World War I, Fort Casey was used for training activities. After the war, the Army entered one of its periods of austerity, and the fort was placed in caretaker status. A salvage program was initiated and all armament was scrapped and melted down for other purposes between 1922 and 1945.

The onset of World War II brought new life to Fort Casey, and it was reactivated as a training center. Barracks were rebuilt and anti-aircraft guns were mounted in the old emplacements. In 1950 Fort Casey was once again placed in caretaker status when it was no longer required for military uses. In 1956, the General Services Administration put it up for sale. The Washington State Parks and Recreation Commission acquired Fort Casey at that time.

CAMP (FORT) CHEHALIS. A short-lived Army post located at Gray's harbor, near the mouth of the Chehalis River, Camp Chehalis (never officially designated a fort) was established on February 11, 1860, by Captain Maurice Maloney, 4th Infantry. Abandoned on June 19, 1861, it was temporarily reoccupied in August 1861 to protect the new Indian agency in its vicinity. It was permanently abandoned before the end of the year.

CAMP CHELAN. A temporary Army post located on the Columbia River at Lake Chelan, it was established and occupied by three companies of the 2nd Infantry on September 2, 1879. It was abandoned on October 13, 1880, and its troops transferred to Camp (later Fort) Spokane.

CHINOOK POINT POST. FORT COLUMBIA.

FORT COLUMBIA (*Chinook Point Post*). A coast artillery post originally established as Chinook Point Post in late 1896, Fort Columbia stands at Chinook Point on the north shore of the Columbia River opposite, and about six miles within the river's mouth, between the towns of Megler and Chinook. Together with the batteries of Fort Canby and Fort Stevens, Fort Columbia's guns guarded the river's mouth. It was declared obsolete after World War II. On March 28, 1947, the three forts of the Harbor Defenses of the Columbia were listed as surplus by the War Department. Fort Columbia was stripped of its armament, and on March 31, 1948, transferred to the jurisdiction of the War Assets Administration. The Washington State Parks and Recreation

Commission applied for the property for historical monument purposes on August 26, 1948. On May 12, 1950, a major portion of the reservation was officially transferred to the state of Washington. A dedication ceremony was held on June 17, 1951, and the old coast artillery post became Fort Columbia Historical State Park.

COLUMBIA BARRACKS. VANCOUVER BARRACKS.

FORT COLVILE. This long-enduring, profitable trading post was founded in 1826 by George Simpson, governor of the Hudson's Bay Company, on the east side of the Columbia River, about one mile west of the present town of Kettle Falls, Stevens County. It was named in honor of Andrew W. Colvile, the head of the company. A palisaded fort about 208 feet square, its trading operations were supported by several additional log buildings outside its walls. During its later years, the name of the fort was erroneously spelled "Colville." Abandoned in 1871, its original site is now beneath the waters of Lake Roosevelt, which was formed after the building of Grand Coulee Dam.

FORT COLVILLE (*Harney's Depot*). Located on a flat on the left side of Mill Creek, seven miles above its junction with the Colville River and about three miles east of present Colville, Stevens County, this Army post was established on June 15, 1859, to control the area's hostile Indians and to provide a base for the Northwest Boundary Commission. Established by Captain Pinkney Lugenbeel, 9th Infantry, in compliance with an order of Brigadier General William S. Harney, it was first called Harney Depot, later renamed Camp Colville, then officially designated Fort Colville. Its name was derived from the earlier established Hudson's Bay Company trading post, located 14 miles to the west, and named for the company's chief officer, Andrew W. Colvile. Abandoned on November 1, 1882, the military reservation was transferred to the Interior Department on February 26, 1887, for disposition.

CONNELL PRAIRIE BLOCKHOUSE. FORT HAYS.

COOK BLOCKHOUSE (*Davis Blockhouse*). One of the largest of the more than 11 blockhouses erected during the 1855–56 Indian War on Whidbey Island by James Davis, Davis Blockhouse was unique in its design for year-round use and included a fireplace. Restored in the early 1930s, it is now known as Cook Blockhouse, located adjacent to the present Sunnyside Cemetery just south of Coupeville.

FORT COWLITZ. A small trading post established by the Hudson's Bay Company in 1837, it stood on the left bank of the Cowlitz River, near the present town of Toledo, in Lewis County. It was one of the posts for which the company claimed indemnity by the United States in 1865.

CROCKETT BLOCKHOUSES. Two blockhouses, connected by a stockade, were erected in 1855 on John Crockett's farm on Whidbey Island. One of them, restored by the WPA in 1938, still stands on the old farmhouse property. The other, after being exhibited at the Alaska-Yukon Pacific Exposition at Seattle in 1909, was moved to Point Defiance Park in Tacoma.

CAMP DAVID S. STANLEY. On May 31, 1917, American Lake, near Cosgrove in Thurston County, was the tentative site for the present Fort Lewis. By June 16, however, a site two and a half miles southeast of the lake was selected.

DAVIS BLOCKHOUSE COOK BLOCKHOUSE.

FORT DECATUR (*Seattle Blockhouse; Fort Duwamish*). This two-storied, 14-foot-high, 25-by-40-foot blockhouse, named Fort Decatur, was garrisoned by U.S. Marines from the USS *Decatur*, who manned two 9-pounder cannon during the Indian siege of Seattle in 1855. Later, a stockade was erected across the base of the Seattle Peninsula and a second blockhouse near the Duwamish River was built by Seattle's settlers. The site of Fort Decatur lies at the present intersection of 1st Avenue and Cherry Street. The site of the second blockhouse, known as Fort Duwamish, is located just south of the Puget Sound Power and Light Plant.

FORT DUWAMISH. FORT DECATUR.

FORT EBEY. Located on Ebey island in the Snohomish River, about eight miles above its mouth and east of present Everett, Fort Ebey was named for Colonel Isaac N. Ebey, U.S. Customs Collector, who was later killed and dismembered by Haida Indians in 1857. Fort Ebey, a single-story blockhouse, was built in 1855 by Washington Territorial Volunteer troops who were later transferred to Fort Alden.

FORT EBEY. Fort Ebey State Park is located on Whidbey Island, eight miles south of Oak

Harbor off Highway 20 on Valley Drive. The fort was originally established as a Coast Artillery installation in 1942 to supplement Forts Casey, Flagler, and Worden, all of which are currently Washington State Parks. The War Department declared Fort Ebey surplus property soon after World War II and donated the reservation to the state in 1968. Fort Ebey was stabilized in 1980 and the 226-acre State Park that encloses it was opened to the public in February 1981.

EBEY BLOCKHOUSE. This was one of four blockhouses built in 1855 near Coupeville on Whidbey Island by Jacob Ebey, father of Colonel Isaac N. Ebey whose later death by Haida Indians was responsible for the construction of some of the island's defenses. A 12-foot-high palisade originally surrounded Ebey's dwelling and connected the four blockhouses, one at each corner. The present Ebey Blockhouse was restored by a later owner of the property.

ENGLISH CAMP. Located on Garrison Bay about a mile from Roche Harbor on San Juan Island, English Camp was a British post maintained from 1860–72 by Royal Marines to support the Queen's claim to the island. The establishment of the post was occasioned by the so-called Pig War in 1859, an international boundary dispute that lasted for a dozen years. The present boundary was finally fixed in 1873. San Juan Island was reputedly the last place in the United States where the British standard was officially displayed. English Camp's original blockhouse, several other structures, and the Royal Marine Cemetery still occupy the site, part of the San Juan Island Historical Park maintained by the National Park Service. (See also: CAMP SAN JUAN ISLAND.)

FORT FLAGLER. Fort Flagler Stage Park, encompassing 783 acres and surrounded on three sides by salt water, is located in Jefferson County on the north end of Marrowstone Island, across the bay from Port Townsend. Fort Flagler, along with the heavy batteries of Fort Worden and Fort Casey, guarded the entrance to Puget Sound. These Coast Artillery posts, established in the late 1890s, became the first line of a fortification system designed to prevent a hostile fleet from reaching such targets as the Bremerton Navy Yard and the cities of Seattle, Tacoma, Olympia, and Everett.

Construction began in 1897. By 1900 the initial installation of armament was completed along with barracks for units of the 3rd Artillery. Final construction was completed in 1907. Fort Flagler

was placed in caretaker status in 1937, and many of its original buildings were removed. In 1940 it was reactivated with new construction for World War II and the Korean War, training engineers and troops for amphibious warfare. Fort Flagler was closed on June 7, 1953, and purchased as a State Park in 1955.

FORT GILLIAM. An Army post of short duration located on the right bank of the Columbia River, close to today's Bonneville Dam and near the site of later-built Fort Cascades (1855), Fort Gilliam was established in January 1848 by Oregon Volunteer troops from Oregon City as a supply depot and base of operations during the Cayuse Indian War. Named for Colonel Cornelius Gilliam, who established the post, it was often referred to as the Cabins or as Camp at the Cabins.

CAMP HANFORD. Located a mile and a half north of Richland, on the Columbia River, in Benton County, the sprawling Hanford Reservation was established in 1943 by the Atomic Energy Commission (AEC) for the production of plutonium. It had been used by the Army on a permit basis as a support for air defense units assigned to the facility, administered by the AEC and operated by the General Electric Company. In March 1961 the Department of Defense decided to return the property to AEC authority since the air defense units there were inactivated, with no future Army use contemplated. An independent installation until July 1, 1959, it became a subpost of Fort Lewis.

HARNEY'S DEPOT. FORT COLVILLE.

CAMP HAYDEN. A World War II Coast Artillery defense of Puget Sound, equipped with camouflaged batteries of 16-inch guns, Camp Hayden was established in 1941 at the northwest tip of Clallam County, near Cape Flattery and Crescent Bay. It was named in honor of Brigadier General John L. Hayden, former commanding officer of the Harbor Defenses of Puget Sound. In 1948 the post's big 16-inch guns near Tongue Point, east of Crescent Beach, were scrapped because they were determined to be obsolete by the Army. In 1949 Camp Hayden was declared surplus by the Department of the Army. Now a county park, the original gun emplacements are being used as a civil defense headquarters in case of an emergency.

FORT HAYS (*Connell Prairie Blockhouse***).** Located on Connell's Prairie, 18 miles southeast of Tacoma, Fort Hays was one of two cedar log blockhouses built in 1856 by Washington Territorial Volunteer troops and named for Major Gilmore Hays, 2nd Regiment. Fort Hays has been preserved on its original site atop a hill overlooking Connell Prairie.

FORT HENDERSON (*Fort Patterson*). A temporary blockhouse outpost established during the general Indian uprising, Fort Henderson was located on the Snoqualmie River, near the mouth of Patterson Creek, below present Fall City in King County. It was built in 1856 by a detachment of Washington Territorial Volunteers from Fort Tilton.

FORT HENNESS. A large stockade with blockhouses at diagonal corners, and enclosing cabins and a school for children, Fort Henness was built by Grand Mound Prairie settlers during the 1855–56 Indian war. It was located near the town of Grand Mound in present Thurston County and named in honor of Captain Benjamin L. Henness of the Washington Territorial Volunteer Regiment, although the defense had no military connection. One citation, however, states that it was temporarily garrisoned by a company of volunteer militia. The fort was reportedly occupied by 224 people, representing 30 families, who lived there for 16 months during the emergency.

INDIAN WAR (1855-56) DEFENSES. The Yakima War and the Indian uprising in 1855 by large factions of the Spokane, Coeur d'Alene, and Palouse tribes led to the erection of numerous hastily built stockades and blockhouses. At least 11 of the defenses were located on the east side of Whidbey Island, Puget Sound's largest. Most of the forts were of short duration, intermittently occupied by settlers or Washington Territorial Volunteer troops. A very small number of them have been restored and are preserved as historical landmarks.

CAMP (GEORGE) JORDAN. This World War II Army post, located at 1st Avenue South and South Spokane Street in Seattle, was established for black troops, in connection with the Seattle Port of Embarkation, who served as stevedores. Named in honor of Sergeant George Jordan, who was awarded the Congressional Medal of Honor on May 7, 1890, for meritorious service in action during 1880–81, Camp Jordan opened on September 20, 1942, was formally dedicated in November 1943, and closed sometime in 1947.

FORT LANDER. The blockhouse for this temporary fortification was constructed in 1856 in Seattle by Washington Territorial Volunteer troops, then moved a short distance up the Duwamish River to a site off the river's south bank, where it was completed and enclosed by a 98-by-58-foot bastioned stockade. It was named for Captain Edward W. Lander, 2nd Regiment, who supervised its construction. Its site in modern Seattle is located a quarter of a mile south of the King County Airport's administration building.

FORT LAWTON. One of the major reasons for the establishment of Fort Lawton on Magnolia Bluff, three miles from downtown Seattle, was to provide military protection for the Bremerton Navy Yard, established in 1891. The War Department's plan was encouraged by the city's civic leaders for economic reasons. From 1866 to 1898, there was minimal military protection for Puget Sound. Seattle's citizens contributed the site for a permanent military post. By February 1898 title to the various parcels of land had been conveyed to the government and construction of numerous buildings and gun emplacements began in June of that year. The first units were completed in December 1899, and on February 9, 1900, the post was dedicated and named in honor of Major General Henry Ware Lawton, who had been killed at San Mateo in the Philippines on December 19, 1899.

First used as a Coast Artillery installation when the first troops arrived on July 26, 1901, Fort Lawton went through a series of service phases. In succession, it became an infantry post (1902–27), an engineer training facility (1927–41), and finally, a home for the Transportation Corps for use as an embarkation and demobilization center during World War II and the Korean War. Thereafter it became a support center for Puget Sound Air Defense activities. When this function was phased out in 1967, the fort was closed as a fully active post, although some support activities remain. In 1968 Fort Lawton was designated a subinstallation of Fort Lewis. The same year, the 124th U.S. Army Reserve Command (ARCOM) was activated with headquarters on the post. The major units at the fort now are the U.S. Army Garrison, Fort Lawton, and 124th U.S. Army Reserve Command. Major portions of the post were declared surplus, transferred to the city, and converted into Discovery Park, administered by the Seattle Department of Parks and Recreation.

FORT LEWIS. Located about 11 miles east of Olympia and 13 miles southwest of Tacoma, still-active Fort Lewis is one of the nation's largest Army installations. It was named in July 1917 in honor of Captain Meriwether Lewis, coleader of the famous Lewis and Clark Expedition. The first troops arrived in September of that year, and by December there were more than 48,000 men in training on the post's 70,000 acres, funded by a Pierce County bond issue to purchase the site. When completed, the complex included more than 1,700 buildings and 50 miles of roads, ranking it as the largest training camp constructed during World War I.

Since the first units of the 91st Division were prepared here for World War I service, more than a million men have been trained on the post. Known as Camp Lewis until 1927, it was declared a permanent Army post and officially designated Fort Lewis. Since then, the number of buildings on the post was increased nearly three times. World War II expansion increased its acreage to more than 86,000 with 832 miles of paved roads. An addition to Fort Lewis became necessary during the war, and its training facilities were expanded with barracks and auxiliary buildings, a complex known as North Fort Lewis. Since then, the North Fort was used for the training of troops for the Korean War, the 1961 Berlin crisis, and the Vietnam War. It now handles an average of 10,000 men for each eight-week training period. Fort Lewis is presently under the jurisdiction of the U.S. Army Forces Command (FORSCOM).

FORT MALONEY. One of the few regular Army posts erected during the 1855–56 Indian War, Fort Maloney was located on the north bank of the Puyallup River, on present Meridian Street in the town of Puyallup, southeast of Tacoma. A typical two-story blockhouse, with the exception that its lower story had only a six-and-a-half-foot-high overhead, it was built by 4th Infantry troops under the direction of Captain Maurice Maloney.

CAMP MUCKLESHOOT PRAIRIE. FORT SLAUGHTER.

CAMP MURRAY. The state of Washington in 1903 purchased about 220 acres at American Lake, 12 miles south of Tacoma, for use by the National Guard. Maneuvers and encampments were held there for several years until 1915, when a permanent installation was established and named Camp Murray for Isaiah G. Murray, a pioneer settler in the area. Engineers of companies E and F, 2nd Regiment, U.S. Army, arrived at Camp Murray on April 3, 1917, for training and ultimate duty in World War I. Improved and enlarged over the years and continued in use as the headquarters of the Washington National Guard, Camp Murray is presently one of the major training sites for ARCOM (Army Reserve Command) units of Fort Lawton at Seattle.

FORT NACHES. Located about nine miles above the mouth of the Naches River where it joins the Yakima River in the present city of Yakima, Fort Naches was a temporary regular Army post established in May 1856 as a base for operations against the hostile Indians. It was built by 9th Infantry troops commanded by Colonel George Wright. The area's settlers named it "Basket Fort" because its large rectangle was constructed of wickerworks of willow filled with earth, known as gabions. Called Fort Na-Chess by Colonel Wright, it was officially listed as Camp Nechess River. Fort Naches was abandoned at the end of the campaign.

FORT NEZ PERCÉS. FORT WALLA WALLA.

FORT NISQUALLY. An important Hudson's Bay Company (HBC) trading post, Fort Nisqually (spelled Nesqually until 1843 when it was reconstructed) was established in 1833 by Archibald McDonald on a bluff overlooking Puget Sound, in the vicinity of today's Du Pont, about 17 miles southwest of present-day Tacoma. In 1839 the Puget Sound Agricultural Company was formed as a subsidiary of the HBC and operated the post. In 1843 the post was destroyed and its profitable trading operations were moved to a new site about two miles to the northeast, where a larger bastioned fortified post was built, with its name changed to Nisqually. Three years later, however, the international boundary was established at the 49th parallel, placing the location of the new post on American territory. In 1867 the U.S. government purchased the company's extensive holdings for $650,000. By the year 1934, only portions of the post's granary and the factor's residence remained. These were moved to Point Defiance Park at Tacoma, where a careful reconstruction of the former Hudson's Bay Company trading post now stands.

FORT OKANOGAN. A trading post established in 1811 by John Jacob Astor's American Fur Company, Fort Okanogan was located on the Okanogan River, about a half-mile from its mouth, four miles east of present Brewster. It was originally a small but profitable 16-by-20-foot post constructed of driftwood. During the War of 1812, it was taken over by the Northwest Company and subsequently operated by the Hudson's Bay Company (HBC) following the merger of the two

trading companies in 1821. In the 1830s, its trading operations were moved less than a mile away to a site on the Columbia River, where a new much larger post with a 15-foot-high bastioned stockade was erected surrounding four buildings. The Hudson's Bay Company began to phase out Fort Okanogan's operations when the area became American territory in 1846. Final abandonment of the post was completed in 1860. Today's Fort Okanogan Historical Museum, established and maintained by the Washington State Parks and Recreation Commission, is located near the site of the trading post.

OLYMPIA BLOCKHOUSE. In April 1856, during the Indian war emergency, a large temporary log blockhouse was erected by Washington Territorial Volunteer troops in the town of Olympia in present Thurston County. It was located on the public square at the corner of Main and 6th streets, today's Capital Park.

FORT PATTERSON. FORT HENDERSON.

CAMP PICKETT. CAMP SAN JUAN ISLAND.

FORT RAINS. FORT CASCADES.

CAMP SAN JUAN ISLAND (*American Camp; Camp Pickett; Camp (Fred) Steele*). When it appeared in 1859 that actual hostilities might break out on San Juan Island, located in the straits between British Columbia and the United States, both Great Britain and the United States rushed troops to the scene. The crisis was precipitated by the killing of a pig owned by the Hudson's Bay Company post by an American farmer when the animal wandered into the lat-

ter's garden. Known in history as the Pig War, it was actually the renewal of the boundary dispute between the two nations. The 1846 treaty, while supposedly fixing the 49th parallel as the demarcation line between Canada and the United States, had not definitely established the international boundary. Both British subjects and American citizens occupied the island.

On July 27, 1859, a company of 9th Infantry troops established an Army post on the island near Griffin Bay. First known as American Camp, the post was named Camp Pickett two weeks later, apparently for Captain George E. Pickett (later a Confederate general who gained fame at Gettysburg), then stationed at Bellingham Bay with elements of the 9th Infantry. In June 1863 the name was changed to Post of San Juan for obvious reasons. In March 1867 it was again changed to Camp (Fred) Steele. When it was learned that this name conflicted with Fort Fred Steel in Wyoming, the post was officially designated Camp San Juan Island on November 23, 1868. No blood was shed and American and British troops became fast friends while the boundary dispute was being internationally debated by high-level officials. Finally, through arbitration by neutral Germany's Emperor Wilhelm I acting as intermediary, the present boundary was established in 1873. Camp San Juan Island was abandoned on July 1, 1874. (See also: ENGLISH CAMP.)

SEATTLE BLOCKHOUSE. FORT DECATUR.

FORT SIMCOE. Located in the Simcoe Valley, approximately midway between Simcoe and Toppenish creeks, 38 miles southwest of Yakima, Fort Simcoe was established as a base of opera-

FORT NISQUALLY. Restoration at Point Defiance Park, including the original factor's house and granary building. (Courtesy of the Tacoma Chamber of Commerce.)

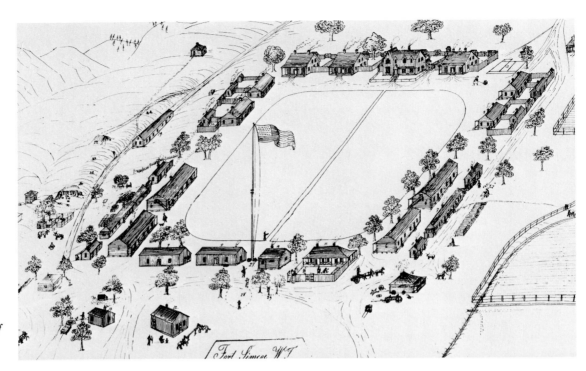

FORT SIMCOE. Artist's rendering. (Courtesy of the University of Washington.)

tions during the Yakima War. It was constructed on August 8, 1856, by Major Robert S. Garnett, 9th Infantry, in compliance with an order of Colonel George Wright. The name of the fort was derived from the valley and the creek, named in honor of John Simcoe, the first lieutenant governor of Upper Canada. The fort was abandoned on May 22, 1859, after Indian hostilities had ended and the region was opened for settlement. The fort's last garrison was transferred to Fort Colville and the post's buildings were turned over to the Interior Department's Bureau of Indian Affairs to serve as headquarters for the Yakima Agency and Indian School which occupied the site until 1923. In 1953 the Washington State Parks and Recreation Commission began restoration of five of the original military structures—the commanding officer's residence, three other officers' quarters, and a blockhouse. The complex is now the 140-acre Simcoe State Park.

FORT SLAUGHTER (*Camp Muckleshoot Prairie*). A two-bastioned stockade located on Muckleshoot Prairie on the White River close to its junction with the Green River, six miles southeast of Auburn in Pierce County, Fort Slaughter was erected on March 20, 1856, by 9th Infantry troops commanded by Captain Erasmus Darwin, 3rd Artillery. The post was named in honor of 1st Lieutenant William A. Slaughter, 4th Infantry, who was killed by Indians on December 4, 1855. The post was first known as Camp Muckleshoot Prairie and official reports often

referred to it by that name. The post's troops were withdrawn in late July or early August 1857.

SPANISH FORT AT NEAH BAY. The Spanish in March 1792 established a settlement protected by a fort at Neah Bay, just north of the main part of today's town of Neah Bay, at the extreme northwestern tip of present Clallam County. The fortified settlement was called Nuñez Gaona by the Spaniards. Its site is most probably located on the present Makah Indian Reservation.

FORT SPOKANE. SPOKANE HOUSE I.

FORT SPOKANE. A military post located on the south side of the Spokane River, about a mile from its junction with the Columbia, some 50 miles northwest of the city of Spokane, it was established on October 21, 1880, by Major Leslie Smith, 2nd Infantry, and designed to foster peace between the whites and Indians in the area. Originally known as Camp Spokane, the post was designated a fort in late 1881 and its name changed to Fort Spokane on February 11, 1882. Its last garrison withdrawn in 1898 during the Spanish-American War, the post was abandoned by the Army on August 26, 1899. The reservation was officially turned over to the Interior Department's Bureau of Indian Affairs two days later to serve as an Indian school.

SPOKANE HOUSE I (*Fort Spokane*). This North West Company trading post was established during the winter of 1810–11 on the east bank of the Spokane River, about 10 miles northwest of the present city of Spokane. In 1812 John Jacob Astor's Pacific Fur Company built Fort Spokane, a competing post in the immediate environs, and the two operated simultaneously until October 1813, when Fort Spokane was sold to the North West Company. In 1821 it was operated by the Hudson's Bay Company after its merger with the North West Company.

SPOKANE HOUSE II. After the merger in 1821 of the North West Company and the Hudson's Bay Company, the original Spokane House was operated by the HBC. The post was then enlarged into a 130-by-122-foot fort, surrounded by a high stockade built of pine logs, enclosing several buildings attached to its inner walls. The trading post was abandoned in 1826 when the Hudson's Bay Company moved its trading operations to newly established Fort Colvile on the east side of the Columbia, near the present town of Kettle Falls.

CAMP (FRED) STEELE. CAMP SAN JUAN ISLAND.

FORT STEILACOOM. Located at the present town of Steilacoom, a short distance from Tacoma and about a mile east of Puget Sound, Fort Steilacoom was established by Captain Bennett H. Hill, 1st Artillery, on August 28, 1849, to protect the area's settlers, particularly those located in the near environs of the Hudson's Bay Company's Fort Nisqually, six miles to the south. The military post first occupied five buildings on the trading company's property. Originally known as Post on Puget Sound or just Steilacoom, it was later designated Fort Steilacoom after the little river near the post.

In 1857 Lieutenant August V. Kautz supervised construction of a number of new buildings at the fort. Despite delays caused by a shortage of carpenters and bad weather, reconstruction of Fort Steilacoom into a 600-foot-square complex was completed by the end of 1858. The Army abandoned the fort on April 22, 1868, when it was determined that the settlers no longer required protection from the Indians. On April 15, 1874, a part of the military reservation was donated to Washington Territory, which established on the ceded property the Western State Hospital for the Insane. The remainder of the reservation was transferred to the Interior Department on July 22, 1884. Today, a row of four officers' quarters, all that remains of the post's original 15 buildings, have been restored on the grounds of the Western State Hospital.

FORT STEVENS. FORT COLUMBIA.

FORT TAYLOR. Used for only six weeks as a base of operations against the hostile Spokane, Coeur d'Alene, and Palouse Indians, Fort Taylor was located on the left bank of the Snake River at the mouth of the Tucannon, two miles east of the present town of Starbuck in Columbia County. Established by Colonel George Wright on August 11, 1858, the post was constructed of basalt rock with hexagonal bastions of alder and named in honor of 1st Lieutenant Oliver Hazard Perry Taylor, 1st Dragoons, who was killed during a fight with Spokane Indians on May 17, 1858. The post was abandoned on October 2, 1858, when the campaign against the Indian hostiles ended.

FORT THOMAS. A temporary Army blockhouse erected in 1855 by elements of the 4th Infantry, Fort Thomas was located on the south bank of the Green River, 6 miles north of Auburn in King County. A 26-foot-square of notched round logs with a shake roof, with its second story offset 45 degrees from the first, it was named for John M. Thomas on whose land claim the fort stood.

FORT TILTON. Located about three miles below the falls of the Snoqualmie River in King County, Fort Taylor was established in 1855 as the headquarters and principal depot of the Northern Battalion of the Washington Territorial Volunteer Regiment. Named for Major James Tilton, surveyor general of the Volunteers, the post included a blockhouse and outbuildings. It was occupied until the end of the Indian war emergency in 1856.

FORT TOWNSEND. Located on the west side of Port Townsend Bay at the entrance to Puget Sound, Fort Townsend was established on October 26, 1856, by Captain Granville O. Haller, 4th Infantry, to protect the area's settlers from Indian hostiles. In the summer of 1859, the entire garrison was dispatched to San Juan Island to reinforce an American post that was established during the Great Britain–United States boundary crisis. Fort Townsend was reestablished on July 1, 1874, when Camp Steele (Camp San Juan Island) was abandoned after the international boundary dispute was resolved. The fort was abandoned in 1895 after it was partially destroyed by fire during the winter of 1894–95.

FORT VANCOUVER. VANCOUVER BARRACKS.

VANCOUVER BARRACKS (*Columbia Barracks; Fort Vancouver*). Originally an important Hudson's Bay Company trading post (1829–46), it was established by the U.S. Army as Columbia Barracks on May 13, 1849. After the Treaty of 1846 between the United States and Great Britain fixed the 49th parallel as the southern boundary of British Columbia, it was determined that the Hudson's Bay Company post stood on American territory, within the present city limits of the city of Vancouver. The military post was renamed Fort Vancouver on July 13, 1853, then officially redesignated Vancouver Barracks on April 5, 1879. The historic post was retired by the Army after World War II in 1947. Today a National Historic Site, the post consisted of some 300 buildings, bounded by Evergreen Highway, 4th Avenue, and East and West Reserve streets in Vancouver.

FORT VANCOUVER. This imposing trading post was the headquarters and principal depot for all Hudson's Bay Company operations in the Northwest from 1824, when the company moved here from Fort Astoria (Fort George), to 1846, when the 49th parallel became the international boundary between the United States and Canada. Standing near the north bank of the Columbia opposite today's Portland, Oregon, the fort was a 325-by-732-foot log stockade, fortified by a single bastion, enclosing some two dozen major buildings, one of which was the impressive residence of chief factor John McLoughlin. (See: VANCOUVER BARRACKS.)

FORT WALLA WALLA. (*Fort Nez Percés*). The North West Company established a trading post at the confluence of the Walla Walla and Columbia rivers, just below today's town of Wallula, in 1818, and named it Fort Nez Percés. When the Hudson's Bay Company took over its operations after its merger with the North West Company in 1821, its name was changed to Fort Walla Walla. Under the Hudson's Bay Company, the post became a 20-foot-high palisaded 200-foot-square enclosure of 6-inch-thick, 30-inch-wide planks, armed with four small cannon and ten swivel guns. Abandoned in 1860, its site is now beneath the Columbia's water impounded by the McNary Dam.

FORT WALLA WALLA. This U.S. Army post occupied three sites, the second and third within the present city limits of Walla Walla. It was first established on September 23, 1856, on the Walla Walla River west of today's city by 9th Infantry troops commanded by Major Edward J. Steptoe,

occupying a small stockaded blockhouse. About a month later, they moved to present Walla Walla and erected another blockhouse surrounded by a collection of huts. This second site is now the intersection of 1st and Main streets in downtown Walla Walla. The expansion of the village of Steptoeville, later renamed Walla Walla, around the post, and the need for water to operate its sawmill, compelled the garrison to move to its final location a mile and a half away to the bank of Mill Creek.

The post was intermittently garrisoned from 1864 to 1867. From 1867 to 1873, it was used as a depot for wintering animals. Reoccupied by troops in August 1873, it became a permanent post, consisting of five double sets of officers' quarters, barracks adequate to accommodate six companies of troops, and a number of other buildings. It was finally abandoned on March 31, 1911. Its site is now occupied by a Veterans Administration hospital.

FORT WARD. Construction of this coast artillery fortification was begun on February 1, 1900, occupying 375 acres on Bainbridge Island (King County) and a like number on the mainland across Rich's Passage, commanding the entrance of Port Townsend Bay, both of which lead to the vital Bremerton Navy Yard. Officially designated Fort Ward on June 12, 1903, it mounted five Endicott-period batteries of three-, five-, and eight-inch guns. Abandoned as a coast defense in 1934, the sites of the fort were turned over to the U.S. Navy four years later.

FORT WATERS. Located six miles west of present Walla Walla, on the site of Waiilatpu Mission, burned by the Indians following the Marcus Whitman massacre in November 1847, Fort Waters was established on March 2, 1848, by Lieutenant Colonel Cornelius Gilliam, Oregon Volunteers, to serve as a base of operations during the Cayuse War. Named for Lieutenant Colonel James Waters of the Volunteers, the post was constructed from the salvageable remains of the mission's structures. Occupied for a short period during the Indian campaign, its site is now the Whitman Mission National Historic Site, administered by the National Park Service.

FORT WHITMAN. Construction of this coast artillery defense located on Goat Island, two miles southwest of La Conner, in Skagit County, was begun in 1909 and completed in 1911. Named in honor of Dr. Marcus Whitman, victim of an Indian massacre in 1847, Fort Whitman included, in addition to its Endicott-period six-inch gun battery, the commanding officer's quarters, administration building, two 20-by-100-foot barracks, kitchen and mess hall, and other utility buildings. The post was transferred to Washington state as a wildlife refuge in 1947.

FORT WILSON. FORT WORDEN.

FORT WORDEN (*Fort Wilson*). Named in honor of Admiral John L. Worden, who commanded the Monitor during its historic battle against the Confederacy's *Merrimac,* Fort Worden was a coast artillery defense located on Wilson Point two miles from Port Townsend on the Olympic Peninsula. Begun in 1898 with the mounting of its first gun batteries, the fort was established in 1900. Its site was first occupied by Fort Wilson, a temporary defense erected in 1855 during the Indian war and abandoned in 1856. Fort Worden consisted of 503 acres of ground, with most of its permanent structures erected and completed during 1904–5. The post served until the end of World War II, by which time all of its Endicott-period guns were removed. In 1947 it was established as a training post for engineers, discontinued in 1953. Fort Worden's remaining buildings and empty gun emplacements now constitute the Fort Worden State Park, named a National Historic Landmark.

FORT (GEORGE) WRIGHT. Originally known as Military Post at Spokane when it was established in 1895, Fort Wright was located at the western edge of the city of Spokane. Practically all of northeast Washington's military operations were consolidated there. The post was named in honor of the Pacific Northwest's noted Indian wars leader during the 1850s and a brigadier general during the Civil War. He was drowned on July 30, 1865, in a shipwreck while en route to take command of the Department of the Columbia. The post's solid-brick buildings were turned over to the Army Air Corps in 1941, using the facilities for a series of different Air Force activities until 1961, when the post was abandoned and sold. The major purchasers of the property were the Fort Wright College of the Holy names, the Spokane Community College of Liberal Arts, and the Spokane Lutheran School, today collectively called the Fort George Wright Historic District.

CAMP ALLEGHENY (*Camp Baldwin*). A fortified Confederate post, also known as Camp Baldwin, was established on October 3, 1861, by Brigadier General Henry R. Jackson, atop an Allegheny Mountains summit astride the important Parkersburg-Staunton Turnpike, about eight miles southeast of present Bartow in Pocahontas County. The well-entrenched post, mounting eight guns, was attacked on the morning of December 13 by Federal forces under Brigadier General Robert H. Milroy. By two o'clock in the afternoon, the battle was over. The Union troops fought stubbornly for a time but, outnumbered by the defenders with the advantage of the mountainous terrain, which precluded the mass movement of troops, were driven back, taking their casualties with them. The fight at Camp Allegheny ended the Confederates' mountain campaign. They occupied the post until April, 1862. (See also: CAMP BARTOW.)

FORT ASHBY. The only remaining French and Indian War fort south of the Potomac River, Fort Ashby was built in 1755 on the east side of Patterson's Creek, Hampshire County, Virginia (now Mineral County, West Virginia), by Lieutenant John Bacon in compliance with an order of Colonel George Washington. Located in the present town of Fort Ashby, the old fort was restored in 1938 by the Works Progress Administration (WPA) and opened to the public on July 4, 1939.

CAMP BALDWIN. CAMP ALLEGHENY.

CAMP BARTOW. A fortified Confederate encampment commanded by Brigadier General Henry R. Jackson and located at present Bartow in Pocahontas County, Camp Bartow was attacked on October 3, 1861, by Federal forces under Brigadier General Joseph J. Reynolds in an attempt to clear the vital Parkersburg-Staunton Turnpike on which the post was situated. The Union troops were repulsed and returned to their fortified post on Cheat Summit, about 12 miles distant. Shortly after the battle, the Confederates abandoned Camp Bartow and established Camp Allegheny about 8 miles to the southeast. Union forces then moved in and occupied the deserted Confederate post. (See also: CAMP ALLEGHENY.)

BAUGHMAN'S FORT. A "private" fort erected by Henry Baughman shortly after the outbreak of the French and Indian War, it was located on the south side of the Greenbrier River, just west of the present town of Alderson in Monroe County. On August 12, 1855, the fort was at-

West Virginia

tacked and destroyed by a large party of Indians, massacring all its 10 occupants, including Henry Baughman.

BEECH FORT. WEST'S FORT.

BEECH BOTTOM FORT. A stockaded blockhouse erected in 1772, it stood on the east bank of the Ohio River, 12 miles above Wheeling, in Brooke County. A number of men from its garrison went to the aid of Fort Henry when it was first besieged in 1777. Beech Bottom Fort survived until at least 1789.

FORT BELLEVILLE. A substantial fort located at the present town of Belleville, southwest of Parkersburg, in Wood County, it was erected in the fall of 1785 and spring of 1786 by Captain Joseph Wood and a group of hired Pittsburgh laborers. At first a two-storied 20-by-40-foot, portholed structure, the fort was soon after significantly enlarged into a regular 10-foot-high palisaded 100-by-300-foot square, with a blockhouse at each of its angles, enclosing the original fort and several cabins. Fort Belleville was continually garrisoned as late as 1791.

FORT BLAIR. FORT RANDOLPH.

FORT BLIZZARD. FORT SEYBERT.

FORT BOREMAN. Nemesis Park, on the summit of a hill, originally known as Mount Logan, located just south of the mouth of the Little Kanawha River at Parkersburg, Wood County, occupies the site of Fort Boreman, erected by Union troops in 1863 to protect the city from Confederate invasion. The defense was named in honor of Arthur Ingram Boreman, first governor of West Virginia, elected in 1863; after being twice reelected, he was sent to the U.S. Senate. After the war, the fort was converted into a private residence and stood until 1916, when it was destroyed by fire.

FORT BUCKHANNON. This small Revolutionary War fort was situated near the site of the present town of Buckhannon in Upshur County. On March 8, 1781, as William White, Timothy Dorman, and his wife were approaching the fort, they were attacked by Indians. White was killed and scalped, and Dorman and his wife taken prisoners. Dorman became a renegade and accompanied the Indians on their raids. Sometime after April of the same year, the fort's occupants, fearful of an incursion by Dorman and his Indians, abandoned their defense and removed elsewhere. A few days later, Dorman and an Indian war party burned Fort Buckhannon.

FORT BURRIS. A small blockhouse, possibly two-storied, was built in 1774 by John and Alex Burris on their land grant on the present site of the Summers Masonic Lodge at the intersection of Burroughs and Windsor streets in Morgantown, Monongalia County.

FORT BUSH. One of the strongest Revolutionary War forts on the Monongahela River frontier, it was erected by John Bush in 1773 at present Buckhannon, almost adjoining today's Heavener Cemetery, in Upshur County. Probably intermittently garrisoned by local militia led by Captain William White who used the fort as his headquarters, Fort Bush was destroyed by Indians in 1782.

FORT BUTTERMILK (*Fort Waggener*). A French and Indian War stockaded defense situated on the South Branch of the Potomac, between the present towns of Old Fields and Moorefield in Hardy County, Fort Buttermilk was erected in 1756 by Captain Thomas Waggener in compliance with orders of Colonel George Washington. On May 16, 1757, Governor Robert Dinwiddie ordered Colonel Washington to post 70 men under Captain Waggener at the fort, which was referred to by some historians as Fort Waggener.

CAMP CHARLOTTE. A short-duration camp established just after the Battle of Point Pleasant on October 10, 1774, marking the end of Lord Dunmore's War, it was located near the present town of Point Pleasant, at the confluence of the Ohio and Kanawha rivers, in Mason County. At Point Pleasant, forces led by Colonel Andrew Lewis decisively defeated the Shawnee commanded by Chief Cornstalk. By the Treaty of Camp Charlotte, the Indians agreed to give up hunting rights in the Kentucky-Virginia region and permit unmolested transportation on the Ohio River.

CHEAT MOUNTAIN SUMMIT CAMP. FORT MILROY.

CLENDENIN'S FORT. FORT LEE.

COOK'S FORT. A substantial Revolutionary War period defense, probably erected in 1770, Cook's Fort was an oblong structure occupying one and a half acres, with cabins joined by its palisades and a blockhouse in each of its four angles, constructed under the direction of Captain John Cook. It was reported that in 1778, it sheltered more than 300 settlers. Cook's Fort was located on Indian Creek, just below Greenville, in Monroe County.

COON'S FORT. A Revolutionary War defense designed to protect the valley's settlers, Joseph Coon (Koon) in 1777 built this large stockaded two-storied blockhouse, under the direction of Captain James Booth, on the West Fork River, about four miles upstream from the present town of Everettville, on U.S. 19, in Marion County. The fort underwent many attacks, in some of which sons, daughters, and grandchildren of the builder were killed. Joseph Coon died in 1798 and was buried near the site of the fort.

COURT HOUSE FORT. FORT LIBERTY.

FORT COX. A French and Indian War stockaded defense, it was erected in 1756 on the 240-acre tract of land owned by Captain Friend Cox. Located at the confluence of the Little Cacapon and Potomac rivers, in present Hampshire County, it is shown in Colonel Washington's 1756 map of the Upper Potomac. A letter written on May 5, 1756, by the young colonel recommended that Fort Cox be designated the principal depot of supplies for the Upper Potomac defenses. During his journey to the Ohio in 1770, George Washington visited its site, but Fort Cox had disappeared.

FORT CULBERTSON. According to the *West Virginia Highway Markers* publication, Fort Culbertson was erected in 1774 at the outbreak of Lord Dunmore's War by Captain James Robertson in compliance with an order of Lieutenant Colonel William Preston. Continually garrisoned during the war, the fort was located on the "New River at Crump's Bottom," south of "Bellepoint," on S.R. 3, in Summers County.

FORT DINWIDDIE. (*Fort Rogers*). Named for Governor Robert Dinwiddie of Virginia during the French and Indian War, it was remembered as having been a fort of "considerable size" erected in 1772 on property owned by Jacob Rogers and located at the present village of Stewartstown, near the Forks of Cheat Baptist Church, on the west side of the Monongahela, in Monongalia County. It served as an important river defense during the Revolution.

FORT DONNALLY. This Revolutionary War period fort was erected by Colonel Andrew Donnally in 1771 near the present town of Frankford,

10 miles north of Lewisburg, while the locality was still in Botetourt County, now in Greenbrier County. A large palisaded two-story double-log structure, it served as a valuable defense during the war, heavily attacked by a large party of British-allied Indians in 1778. The fort was razed in 1825.

FORT EDWARDS. A French and Indian War period defense erected about the year 1750 on a large tract of land owned by the three Edwards brothers, it was located at the present town of Capon Bridge, on the Cacapon River, in Hampshire County. A large body of troops from Fort Edwards, garrisoned in 1756 by command of Colonel George Washington, was ambushed near the fort, with most of the men slaughtered. Later in the same year, a large party of French and Indians attacked the fort itself, but its small remaining garrison was reinforced by Daniel Morgan (a first cousin of Daniel Boone) and other frontiersmen and repulsed the assault.

FORT FINCASTLE. FORT HENRY.

FORT FULLER. Between 1861–65, the town of Keyser, then called New Creek, in Mineral County, was a battleground for Union and Confederate armies. It changed hands 14 times. The site of the strong Federal defense known as Fort Fuller, supported by a series of forts girding the town, is today occupied by the Potomac State College of West Virginia University.

FORT GARNETT. A temporary Confederate post named in honor of Brigadier General Robert Selden Garnett, later killed on July 13, 1861, at Carrick's Ford in Virginia, fortified Camp Garnett was established on June 16, 1861, on the vital Parkersburg-Staunton Turnpike, at the western base of Rich Mountain, seven miles west of Beverly in Randolph County. The Confederates abandoned the post on July 12, 1861.

HARPERS FERRY ARSENAL (*John Brown's Fort*). Provided for in the Armor Act of 1794, a U.S. Armory was located at Harpers Ferry through the persistent efforts of George Washington. President Washington chose Harpers Ferry because of its convenient access to water power and raw materials, its secure position, and, more importantly, its proximity to the new capital of the Nation. Construction of the armory buildings and canal got under way in 1796. By 1801 the armory was producing its first weapons. Arms produced here were used by Lewis and Clark on their famous expedition of 1804–6.

The armory eventually expanded into three sections. The main component, a 20-building complex where weapons were fabricated, was located along the Potomac River. Across the street from the entrance of the armory along Shenandoah Street stood the arsenal where completed arms were stored and displayed. The third portion, the Hall Rifle Works, was located at the upper end of Virginius Island along the Shenandoah River. The one armory building destined for lasting fame was the fire engine and guardhouse, built in 1848 during a period of major renovation of the arsenal. It is now known to many as John Brown's Fort.

John Brown, whose raid brought Harpers Ferry into national prominence, was a native of Connecticut and an abolitionist all his life. Of stern religious bent, ardent to the point of fanaticism, he had conceived a plan to liberate slaves by violence. He fixed upon Harpers Ferry as the starting point for the insurrection. Capture of the thousands of arms stored in the arsenal of the U.S. Armory at the ferry could equip a formidable army. Brown and his 22-man "army of liberation" attacked Harpers Ferry on the night of October 16, 1859, seizing the armory and several other strategic points before the startled townspeople realized their purpose. When the alarm spread and local citizens and state militia converged on the town, the raiders barricaded themselves in the armory fire engine and guardhouse ("John Brown's Fort"). They were captured when a contingent of marines commanded by Colonel Robert E. Lee and Lieutenant J. E. B. Stuart stormed the building on the morning of October 18. Brought to trial for murder, treason, and conspiring with slaves to create insurrection, Brown was found guilty and subsequently hanged at nearby Charles Town on December 2, 1859.

Sixteen months later, on April 12, 1861, the war that John Brown seemed to foretell began at a place called Fort Sumter in Charleston Harbor, South Carolina. The Civil War wrecked the town of Harpers Ferry's economy. The arsenal and armory buildings were burned in 1861 to keep them from falling into Confederate hands. Because of the town's geographical location and its railway system, Union and Confederate troop movements through Harpers Ferry were frequent, and soldiers of both armies occupied the town intermittently throughout the war. Today, the site of Harpers Ferry Arsenal and "John Brown's Fort" is a National Historical Park, established and maintained by the National Park Service.

FORT HENRY (*Fort Fincastle*). When the treacherous murder of a small number of unsuspecting Indians, including members of Mingo Chief Logan's family, took place on April 30, 1774, by white frontiersmen, it precipitated a general Indian uprising. Lord Dunmore, Viscount Fincastle, royal governor of Virginia, ordered a strong fort built on an Ohio River bluff, just north of the mouth of Wheeling Creek, in the present-day city of Wheeling, Ohio County. Constructed by Major (later Colonel) William Crawford and soldiers from Fort Pitt and named in honor of the governor, the fort occupied a half-acre and consisted of a log barracks, officers' quarters, storeroom, and cabins, enclosed by a strong palisade of heavy logs.

In 1776 the post was renamed Fort Henry in honor of Patrick Henry, first governor of Virginia. Garrisoned by the Zanes—Colonel Ebenezer, Jonathan, and Silas—and other pioneers, Fort Henry was an important military outpost during the Revolution. In 1777 the fort withstood a prolonged attack by a large band of Delaware, Shawnee, and Wyandot Indians. On September 11–13, 1782, although peace had been declared, about 300 British and Indians unsuccessfully besieged Fort Henry in what is known as the last battle of the Revolution. During the siege, the fort ran short of powder. Betty Zane, sister of the Zane brothers, heroically brought a precious barrel of powder from Colonel Zane's cabin to the fort, rescuing the garrison from defeat. Fort Henry's site is located on Main Street, between 11th and Ohio streets.

FORT HILL. FORT SCAMMON.

HOLLIDAY'S BLOCKHOUSE. Located in present Weirton, in the southern section of the city known as Holliday's Cove, in Hancock County, this large blockhouse was erected in 1776 by John Holliday and served as a supply depot in the Revolution. It was still a major regional fort in 1793.

JOHN BROWN'S FORT. HARPERS FERRY ARSENAL.

FORT LEE (*Clendenin's Fort*). An important military post, erected in April 1788 by a company of Virginia Rangers under Colonel George Clendenin, Fort Lee (also known as Clendenin's Fort) was named for Governor of Virginia General Henry "Light Horse Harry" Lee and stood at the present intersection of Kanawha Boulevard and Brooks Street in Charleston. The city was founded in 1794 by Colonel Clendenin who named it in honor of his father.

FORT LIBERTY (*Court House Fort*). A Revolutionary War blockhouse erected sometime during the middle 1770s, Fort Liberty was located in the present town of West Liberty, north of Wheeling, in Ohio County. Having served as the county's first courthouse, the blockhouse was later often referred to as Court House Fort.

LOWTHER'S FORT. FORT RICHARDS.

CAMP MCCLELLAN. FORT MILROY.

FORT MAIDSTONE. This was a French and Indian War stockaded fort built in 1756 on a bluff at the mouth of the Cacapon River, just east of today's town of Great Cacapon, Morgan County. An important link in Colonel George Washington's line of defenses, it is marked on his 1756 map of the Upper Potomac. Governor Robert Dinwiddie on May 16, 1757, directed Colonel Washington to post Captain Robert Stewart with a 70-man garrison at Fort Maidstone. Captain Stewart was at Braddock's defeat in 1755, assisted in carrying the mortally wounded general off the field of battle, and was with him when he died.

A short-lived mutiny of a part of the fort's garrison gave Washington the opportunity to realign the system of frontier defenses more to his liking. He moved Fort Maidstone east and relocated it at Williams Ferry (present Williamsport), on the east side of the Potomac in today's Washington County, Maryland. Williams Ferry's location, a principal crossing of the Potomac on the old "Philadelphia Road," was more important to Washington's center of activity at Winchester.

FORT MILROY (*Cheat Mountain Summit Camp; Camp McClellan*). Also known as Cheat Mountain Summit Camp and Camp McClellan (for Major General George B. McClellan), Fort Milroy was a Union-built fortified post situated in a gap at the crest of White Top Mountain, part of the Cheat Mountain range, and occupied by Federal troops during the fall and winter of 1861–62. Above the 4,000-foot level, it was the highest placed military post in the Civil War, located between Huttonsville and Valley Head in Randolph County. Established by General Joseph Jones Reynolds and named in honor of Major General Robert Huston Milroy, the post's command of the crucial Parkersburg-Staunton

Turnpike prevented General Lee's Confederate troops from advancing inland.

MINEAR'S FORT. A Revolutionary War defense, this two-story stockade was erected by John Minear in late 1776 and early 1777 on the east side of the Cheat River, at present-day St. George in Tucker County. The fort withstood a number of Indian attacks, the last of which in 1781 claimed Minear's life and that of his son Jonathan.

FORT MOORE. A Union 30-by-30-foot log fort built in the spring of 1864 by the Gilmer County Home Guards, Fort Moore stood on a hill behind today's Glenville State College in the town of Glenville, Gilmer County. Occupied until sometime in December 1864 when it was evacuated, it was burned several days later by Confederate troops under Captain Sida Campbell.

FORT MULLEGAN. A Union defense constructed by troops under the overall command of Brigadier General (later Major General) William S. Starke, Fort Mullegan was located at Petersburg on U.S. 220 (S.R. 28), Grant County. Fort Mullegan was probably named for an artillery officer who was active in the vicinity at the time. Preserved extensive breastworks and trenches remain.

FORT NEALLY. A French and Indian War stockaded defense, Fort Neally was located two miles north of present Martinsburg, Berkeley County. It was captured and its garrison massacred by a large band of Indians on September 17, 1756. Many settlers in the vicinity were also killed, in addition to a number carried off as prisoners.

NUTTER'S FORT. A Revolutionary War period defense erected by Thomas Nutter on his 1,400-acre tract of land in 1772 or 1773, Nutter's Fort stood on the southeast bank of Elk Creek in the present town of Nutter Fort, just south of the city of Clarksburg, Harrison County. It often served as a refuge for the area's early settlers before and during the Revolution and the subsequent Indian wars.

FORT OGDEN. A French and Indian War defense erected in 1755, it was one of the chain of forts established by order of Colonel George Washington. Consisting of a blockhouse and a number of cabins, surrounded by a strong stockade, Fort Ogden was located close to today's U.S. 50, six miles east of present-day Gormania, Grant County.

FORT OHIO. This was a fortified blockhouse established as a trading post and depot for the Indian trade, erected in 1750 by the Ohio Company. It stood on the south bank of the Potomac in the present town of Ridgeley (originally named St. Clairsville for Captain [later General] Arthur St. Clair in Mineral County. The trading post was later abandoned, and a stronger fort, Fort Cumberland, was constructed at Wills Creek, across the river at the present city of Cumberland in Maryland.

CAMP PAU PAU. A large Civil War encampment located 22 miles west of Berkeley Springs, Morgan County, it served as a concentration point for Union troops, holding as many as 16,000 men at one time.

FORT PAW PAW. A Revolutionary War defense erected in 1781, Fort Paw Paw was a 90-foot-square stockade garrisoned by Rangers commanded by Captain John (Jack) Evans. It was situated on a high, flat area overlooking the junction of Paw Paw Creek and the Monongahela, near present Rivesville in Marion County.

FORT PEARSALL. In 1753 the Shawnee and allied tribes along the Ohio, led by Chief Killbuck, threatened a war against the region's settlers. Job Pearsall stockaded his cabin home located on the right (east) bank of the South Branch of the Potomac River, just below the present city of Romney in Hampshire County. In 1756, during the French and Indian War, the stockade was greatly enlarged to encompass a number of cabins that served as barracks for a garrison numbering up to 100 troops. It is shown on the Map of Operations in Virginia in 1756, drawn by Colonel George Washington, who ordered the fort continuously garrisoned. For the next three years, Fort Pearsall was one of the principal supply depots in Virginia.

FORT PICKENS. A Union defense built during the fall and winter of 1861 by Company A, 10th West Virginia Infantry Volunteers, Fort Pickens was located at the present town of Duffy, two miles east of Ireland in Lewis County and named for James Pickens, Sr., who owned the land on which the fort stood. Fort Pickens was burned by "bushwhackers" (Confederate guerrillas) in December 1864.

FORT PLEASANT (*Fort Van Meter; Town Fort*). A substantial French and Indian War palisaded defense enclosing portholed blockhouses, probably in its angles, and cabins, it was located about a mile and a half above the Trough on the South Branch of the Potomac, at the present town of Old Fields, about five miles north of Moorefield, in Hardy County. It was erected in 1756 by Captain Thomas Waggener under orders from Colonel George Washington. During its earlier years, it was called Fort Van Meter for its builders, and later, after the founding of Moorefield, often referred to as the Town Fort, because of its proximity to it. Fort Pleasant is shown on Colonel Washington's Map of the Operations in Virginia in 1756. Later, during the same year, the so-called Battle of the Trough took place a short distance below the fort, the bloodiest battle ever fought in the valley. The garrison from Fort Pleasant was virtually annihilated by the Indians. When General Washington visited the site in 1784, Fort Pleasant was apparently still standing.

CAMP POINT PLEASANT. FORT RANDOLPH.

FORT PRICKETT. One of the strongest Revolutionary War period forts in the Monongahela Valley, Fort Prickett was erected in 1774 at the mouth of Prickett's Creek, five miles north of the present town of Fairmont in Marion County. Standing on land owned by Jacob Prickett, the county's first settler, the palisaded fort was located on the east side of the Monongahela and consisted of a substantial blockhouse in each of its four angles and at least 10 log cabins. During the Revolution it was occupied by a military garrison. Dismantled late in the eighteenth century, the fort was reconstructed beginning in 1974, its bicentennial, and completed in 1976 as a state park, including Jacob Prickett's brick home and a living history museum.

FORT RANDOLPH (*Camp Point Pleasant; Fort Blair*). Erected on the east side of the Ohio River, near the present town of Point Pleasant in Mason County, shortly after the Battle of Point Pleasant on October 10, 1774, ending Lord Dunmore's War, Fort Blair was built by Captain Matthew Arbuckle. It stood on the site of Camp Point Pleasant, the headquarters of General Andrew Lewis during the battle. A primitive rectangular stockade, Fort Blair was evacuated and apparently abandoned in June 1775. In May 1776 it was replaced by Fort Randolph, a much stronger defense, also constructed by Captain Arbuckle. The fort was evacuated and burned in 1779 when Point Pleasant was abandoned. The first stage of its reconstruction, one mile east of Point Pleasant, was completed in October 1974, to mark the 200th anniversary of the Battle of Point

Pleasant. Today, it appears as a true replica of the 1776 Fort Randolph.

FORT RICHARDS (*Lowther's Fort*). A Revolutionary War period stockaded defense built in 1774 by Arnold and Jacob Richards, it was located about six and a half miles south of Clarksburg, near the present town of West Milford, Harrison County. Fort Richards was also known as Lowther's Fort, for Colonel William Lowther, because of his activities there during the 1778–82 period, protecting the Monongahela settlements.

FORT ROGERS. FORT DINWIDDIE.

FORT SAVANNAH. FORT UNION.

FORT SCAMMON (*Fort Toland*). Civil War defenses were built by Union troops over the winter of 1862–63 on the prominent hills in the town of Fayetteville, Fayette County. The one on the southeast edge of town was later known as Fort Toland, and there were two on its northeast end. This complex was ultimately called Fort Scammon for General Eliakim Parker Scammon. The first use of indirect artillery fire was initiated here on May 19, 1863, by a Confederate artillery battery hidden in a clump of trees, arching shells over a hill into Fort Scammon.

FORT SCAMMON (*Camp White; Fort Hill*). The city of Charleston was intermittently occupied by Confederate forces during 1861 and 1862. By March of 1863, however, Union troops returned to defend the city and established what was called Camp White, located in the Fort Hill section on the south side of the city, on the 1,000-foot-high elevation overlooking the Kanawha River, a quarter of a mile from the south bank of the river. By early May troops were fortifying the heights to be named Fort Scammon, also known as Fort Hill, in honor of General Eliakim P. Scammon, commander of the 3rd Division, Department of West Virginia, district of Kanawha. Extensive earthworks elliptical in outline, it was surrounded by deep ditches and enclosed a number of heavy artillery emplacements.

As the command was sent on to the battlefronts in eastern Virginia, by April of 1864 Fort Scammon fell into disrepair, and in time became covered over with grasses and trees. Its earthworks and trenches were restored and preserved in the early 1970s. Placed on the National Register of Historic Places, the site was purchased by the city to be used as a park.

FORT SEYBERT (*Fort Blizzard*). A French and Indian War defense, probably erected soon after Captain Jacob Seybert purchased the 210-acre property on May 21, 1755, Fort Seybert was a strong palisaded fortification enclosing at least two blockhouses and a number of cabins. It stood on the South Fork of the South Branch of the Potomac, at the present town of Fort Seybert, 12 miles northeast of Franklin, in Pendleton County. Fort Seybert (occasionally referred to as Fort Blizzard) was besieged by Indians on April 28,1758, the attack continuing for three days. Its garrison of 30 men surrendered when it was promised no harm. But the Indians rushed in and 20 of the men seated in a row were tomahawked from behind; the other 10 men were carried off as prisoners. The Indians burned the fort but it was rebuilt by order of the Colonial Assembly.

FORT TOLAND. FORT SCAMMON.

TOWN FORT. FORT PLEASANT.

FORT UNION (*Fort Savannah*). Standing on the site of the present town of Lewisburg, Greenbrier County, Fort Savannah was a French and Indian War defense erected by Andrew Lewis in 1755. In 1774 General Lewis congregated 1,000 militiamen at the fort, naming the concentration point Camp Union, and marched the men against the Indians in the campaign that culminated in the Battle of Point Pleasant, October 10, 1774. The battle marked the end of Lord Dunmore's War, compelling the Indians to sue for peace. Later, in 1776, a fort was built on the site of Camp Union, on the Savannah or Big Levels of Greenbrier, and renamed Fort Union. The two-story structure was used for enlistment purposes during the War of 1812. The still-standing fort has been restored as "Fort Savannah Barracks," housing the Fort Savannah Museum, on Jefferson Street, in Lewisburg, opposite Andrew Lewis Park.

FORT UPPER TRACT. This French and Indian War defense, a stockade, was built in early 1756 by Captain Thomas Waggener in compliance with orders of Colonel George Washington. It stood a short distance west of the South Branch of the Potomac, at what is today the town of Upper Tract in Pendleton County. The fort, commanded by Captain James Dunlap, was left at peace until April 27, 1758, when it was attacked by a party of French and Indians who took it by assault and burned the defense. Captain Dunlap and 22 others were killed. The next day, the same enemy destructives laid siege to Fort

Seybert, about 10 miles to the southeast, and massacred its occupants. About 60 were killed and missing at the two forts.

FORT VAN METER. FORT PLEASANT.

FORT VAN METER. A Revolutionary War period stockaded fort, erected in 1774 at the beginning of Dunmore's War, Fort Van Meter (or Vanmeter's Fort) was situated on the north side of Short Creek, about five miles from its confluence with the Ohio, at the present town of Short Creek in Ohio County. Its commandant, noted frontiersman Major Samuel McCulloch, was killed on July 30, 1782, while reconnoitering the country in the fort's environs with his brother John. They were fired upon by Indians in ambush. The major was killed but his brother escaped to the fort and raised the alarm. Men of the garrison went out, retrieved the body, and buried it within the walls of Fort Van Meter.

FORT WAGGENER. FORT BUTTERMILK.

WEST'S FORT (*Beech Fort*). A Revolutionary War period stockaded fort erected sometime between 1770 and 1773 by Edmund West and members of his family, it stood on the bank of Hacker's Creek, near the present town of Jane Lew in Lewis County. It was attacked and burned in 1779 by Indians. Some of the area's settlers returned in 1780 and rebuilt the fort about a half-mile downstream and named it Beech Fort because beech logs were used in its construction. It was still intermittently used until at least 1793.

CAMP WHITE. FORT SCAMMON.

WILSON'S FORT. Possibly the most important early frontier fort in Randolph County, this large Revolutionary War period defense was built in 1774 by Colonel Benjamin Wilson, noted French and Indian War veteran who had accompanied General Braddock on his ill-fated campaign in 1755 against Fort Duquesne at present Pittsburgh, Pennsylvania. Wilson's Fort stood about a half-mile above the mouth of Chenoweth Creek on the east side of Tygart's Valley River, about four miles north of the present town of Beverly.

FORT ATKINSON (*Fort Koshkonong*). In General Henry Atkinson's report of July 17, 1832, to General Winfield Scott, he stated that "whilst lying here we have thrown up a stockade work flanked by four blockhouses for the security of our supplies and the accommodations of the sick." With more than 4,000 regular Army cavalrymen and some independent Illinois companies, Atkinson had pursued Sauk Chief Black Hawk and his army of warriors up the east side of the Rock River in an attempt to end the Black Hawk War against the white settlements in Illinois and Wisconsin. After an unsuccessful sortie up the Bark River, the general returned to the Rock River and built temporary Fort Koshkonong, later known as Fort Atkinson.

The site of the fort is located at the present town of Fort Atkinson, just northeast of Lake Koshkonong, in Jefferson County. The fort, with its palisades constructed of eight-foot-long oak logs, was abandoned when Atkinson and his army finally caught up with the Indians and defeated Black Hawk at the Battle of Bad Axe in August 1832. So ended the Sauk's last major fight against continued encroachment of white settlers into their ancestral lands. In September 1836 Dwight Foster arrived at the site of the fort and there erected the first cabin on property close by. He and other settlers used logs from the stockade to build cabin homes, river rafts, and for firewood. By 1840 little of the fort remained. In 1908 the Fort Atkinson D.A.R. erected and dedicated a memorial near the site of the fort.

FORT BARBOUR. The Columbia Fur Company's trading post at St. Croix Falls on the Mississippi River, in present Polk County, was designated Fort Barbour by Lawrence Taliaferro, in the 1820s. Several other traders, independents, had trading houses there from time to time, notably Joseph R. Brown, as late as 1832.

CAMP BARSTOW. A temporary Civil War encampment, located at or near Janesville in Polk County, Camp Barstow was established in October 1861 as the recruiting point and training camp for the 3rd Wisconsin Cavalry Regiment. William A. Barstow, exgovernor of the state, was the colonel of the Regiment.

BELOIT POST. Independent fur-trader Joseph Thibault in 1824 established a trading post at the present city of Beloit on the Rock River, Rock County. Permanent settlers arrived in 1837.

FORT BLUE MOUNDS. One of the numerous fortified mining settlements in southwestern Wis-

Wisconsin

consin during the 1832 Black Hawk War, Fort Blue Mounds was located one and a half miles south of the Blue Mound, a prominent hill almost on the Dane-Iowa county border. The site today lies just south of the present town of Blue Mounds in Iowa County.

CAMP BRAGG. A temporary Civil War organization point and training center for the 21st and 32nd Wisconsin Regiments, it was named in honor of Brigadier General Edward S. Bragg of the "Iron Brigade" (6th Wisconsin Infantry). The site of the post is now within the Camp Bragg Memorial Park on the northeast corner of Hazel and Cleveland streets in the city of Oshkosh, Winnebago County.

BRISBOIS HOUSE. Still standing, well-preserved and maintained, on North 1st Street in Prairie du Chien, Brisbois House was a stone-built trading post and warehouse constructed in 1815 by fur-trader Michael Brisbois for the American Fur Company.

FORT CASSVILLE. A temporary "public" fortification erected during the 1832 Black Hawk War, it was located in or near the present town of Cassville in Grant County.

FORT CRAWFORD (*Fort Shelby; Fort McKay*). In June 1814, soon after Governor William Clark, governor of Missouri Territory, occupied Prairie du Chien during the War of 1812, 60 regulars of the 7th Infantry commanded by Lieutenant Joseph Perkins erected a double-blockhouse that he named Fort Shelby in honor of Isaac Shelby, governor of Kentucky. In mid-July of the same year, a force of British and Indians arrived on the bluffs overlooking Prairie du Chien and began a bombardment with a three-pounder cannon. For three days, Fort Shelby withstood the siege. Finally, on July 20, realizing that he was out-numbered ten to one, Lieutenant Perkins surrendered his garrison. The American flag was lowered to be replaced by the British Union Jack. The fort, renamed Fort McKay for Major William McKay, was burned by the British when they evacuated the area at the end of the war. Its site is now occupied by Villa Louis, a mansion built in 1843 by Hercules L. Dousman, agent for John Jacob Astor's American Fur Company, and now enclosed within present Dousman Park.

In June 1816, a new fort was established by Brigadier General Thomas A. Smith at Prairie du Chien, on the left bank of the Mississippi, about two miles above the mouth of the Wisconsin River, to protect the settlers and traders moving into the Northwest and to put an end to British influence in the region. The fort was named in honor of William H. Crawford, secretary of war. In 1829 the fort was abandoned because of flooding and replaced by a new defense on higher ground one mile to the southeast. It was a major treaty ground, the location of a government-operated trading post, and important in the Black Hawk War of 1832 as an Army concentration point. Fort Crawford was abandoned on April 29, 1849, reoccupied on October 19, 1855, and permanently abandoned on June 9, 1856. The site of the first Fort Crawford is today occupied by St. Mary's College.

FORT DEFIANCE. One of the numerous temporary "public" defenses erected in southwestern Wisconsin during the Black Hawk War of 1832, Fort Defiance was a stockaded area located about five miles southeast of Mineral Point in Lafayette County. It stood on a farm then owned by William Parkinson and was garrisoned by lead miners and local settlers.

CAMP DOUGLAS. This military reservation in Juneau County was first established in 1864 as a wooding camp for the Milwaukee Railroad. In 1888 it was taken over as a National Guard post and rifle range. Named Camp Douglas, it was developed by the state of Wisconsin during the administration of Governor William D. Hoard. Actively in use by the Wisconsin National Guard for many years, it became a training center for the state's World War I troops. Its name is still retained by the nearby town of Camp Douglas.

DU BAY POST. In 1834 John Baptiste Du Bay established a fur-trading post for the American Fur Company on the Wisconsin River, one mile west of the present town of Knowlton in Portage County. His wife was Princess Madeline, daughter of Oshkosh, chief of the Menominee Indians. According to tradition, Du Bay's father, John Lewis Du Bay, a French-Canadian voyageur, spent the winter of 1790 on the same site. Lake Du Bay, created in 1942, covers the original site of the trading post. A monument marks Du Bay's grave in Knowlton Cemetery.

FORT EDWARD AUGUSTUS (*Fort La Baye; Fort St. Francis*). Green Bay, located along the banks of the Fox River in present Brown County, is the oldest settlement in Wisconsin. Very early French voyageurs and *coureurs de bois* knew the site and named it Baye de Puants because the Puant, a Winnebago tribe, lived there. Not until 1624, however, did Jean Nicolet, commissioned by Samuel de Champlain, arrive at La Baye and claim the region for France. For more than 30 years, little occurred there, but in 1669 Father Claude Allouez, a Jesuit missionary, founded a mission at La Baye to convert the Indians to Christianity. In 1673 Marquette and Jolliet left St. Ignace to open up a water route to the Mississippi. They canoed from Lake Michigan to Green Bay and then went down the Fox and Wisconsin rivers to the Mississippi. Subsequent to this exploration, because of its strategic position on the water route, La Baye became an important fur trading center and rendezvous. In 1684 Nicolas Perrot, appointed commandant of the region, built a crude frontier fort and trading post known as Fort La Baye. Within the next few years, many traders, trappers, Indians, missionaries, and French soldiers settled there.

During the first half of the eighteenth century, the settlement was involved in constant warfare with the Fox Indians. The French rebuilt Fort La Baye in 1717, renaming it Fort St. François (Francis). In 1728 the Indians destroyed the fort, but the French rebuilt it five years later. In 1760 Fort St. Francis was evacuated. In 1761 after the British conquest of Canada virtually ended the French and Indian War, troops commanded by Lieutenant James Gorrell occupied the town, calling the settlement Green Bay (La Baye Verte) because of the coloration of its offshore waters, reconstructed the old French fort, and renamed it Fort Edward Augustus after the Duke of Kent. The fort was abandoned during the Pontiac Uprising. In 1816 because of the insistence of John Jacob Astor's American Fur Company, the American government built Fort Howard on the site of the old French (and later British) fort, at the foot of the Dousman Street Bridge. (See also: FORT HOWARD.)

FORT ELK GROVE. One of the temporary defenses built in southwestern Wisconsin during the Black Hawk War of 1832, it was a stockaded area, intermittently garrisoned by lead miners and settlers, at or near the town of Elk Grove in present Lafayette County.

FORT HAMILTON. The Diggings (lead smelter) and the fort established by William Stephen Hamilton, a son of Alexander Hamilton, were located on the Pecatonica River, near the town of Wiota, 15 miles above the Illinois border, in what was then Michigan Territory, now in eastern Lafayette County, Wisconsin. The blockhouse fort, completed in May 1832, was principally used during Black Hawk's War of 1832, when it was garrisoned by 69 well-armed men.

CAMP HARVEY. A temporary Civil War training camp, Camp Harvey occupied ground south of the city of Kenosha, now a part of Green Ridge Cemetery. The post was named in honor of Wisconsin's Governor Louis Powell Harvey, who was killed while on a trip to the South to inspect Wisconsin troops.

FORT HOWARD. At the close of the War of 1812, American occupation of the Northwest began, accompanied by John Jacob Astor's American Fur Company gaining control of the major share of the fur trade in the region. In 1816, partially because of Astor's demands for

FORT HOWARD. Lithograph. (From Vues et Souvenirs de l'Amerique du Nord, *by Francis de Castelnau, 1842. Courtesy of the State Historical Society of Wisconsin.)*

military protection, forts were built at the two ends of the Fox-Wisconsin waterway route—Fort Howard at Green Bay and Fort Crawford at Prairie du Chien. The site of Fort Howard, on the west side of the Fox River at the foot of the Dousman Street Bridge in Green Bay, is commemorated by a white flagpole. The site of the French's first fort erected in 1684 and rebuilt in 1717, it was reoccupied by American troops in August 1816. By the spring of 1817, Fort Howard, named for General Benjamin Howard, was completed. The soldiers cut the logs, and erected the buildings, stockading the complex with a blockhouse in all four angles, each mounting a small cannon. Later in the same year, General Zachary Taylor took command of Fort Howard, which rapidly became the focal point for settlement by homesteaders from the East. The garrison was withdrawn in 1841 but regarrisoned after the War with Mexico. The post was finally abandoned on June 8, 1852. The old Fort Howard hospital, built in 1816–17 as the post sergeant's residence and office outside the fort's stockade, is all that remains of a dozen or more buildings. The story-and-a-half structure, no longer on its original site, stands at the corner of Chestnut and Kellogg streets to which it was moved in 1868. (See also: FORT EDWARD AUGUSTUS.)

FORT JACKSON. In mid-may 1832 Black Hawk and his army of some 400 warriors crossed the Illinois bordered and invaded southwestern Wisconsin, then in Michigan Territory. Mineral Point, then the county seat and capital of the lead region, in present Lafayette County, was soon surrounded by about 15 forts and blockhouses. The town's miners and militia at once prepared for Indian warfare and began erecting Fort Jackson, named in honor of President Andrew Jackson. It stood at the intersection of Commerce and Jerusalem (now Fountain) streets. Lumber being in short supply, the citizens dismantled the town jail, sharpened the ends of its logs, and embedded them upright in a trench around an outlined area. Blockhouses and gateways were constructed at two diagonal corners. Within the stockade the settlers built several large cabins for the garrison and their families. When all was completed, Mineral Point was leveled to the ground except for three buildings—all the wood had been used to construct Fort Jackson.

During the five-month-long war—April to August 1832, ending in a battle on the banks of the Mississippi—Mineral Point was unmolested. About 250 white people were killed in massacres and various pitched battles. Additional lives were lost in an epidemic of cholera. Black Hawk's total band of about 1,000 was almost entirely annihilated.

FORT KOSHKONONG. FORT ATKINSON.

FORT LA BAYE. FORT EDWARD AUGUSTUS.

FORT LA POINTE (*Le Sueur's Fort*). At the southwestern tip of Madeline Island, at present Grant's Point on Chequamegon Bay in Lake Superior, about 14 miles north of Ashland in Ashland County, is the historic town of La Pointe. In 1693 Governor Frontenac of New France sent soldier Pierre Le Sueur to La Pointe to erect a fort and garrison it with a company of traders and 30 soldiers under the command of La Gardeur de St. Pierre, as well as other posts at points further west for conducting trade with the Indians. At this time, the French named the island St. Esprit for the first mission established there in 1660. Le Sueur's Fort, however, was abandoned in 1698. In 1718 the island was reoccupied by the French and Fort La Pointe was built, possibly on or near the same site. It was New France's principal fur-trading post on Lake Superior until Canada fell to the British in 1760, ending France's colonial empire in North America. In the early 1800s, the American Fur Company had a post there, and in 1834 it established its inland headquarters on Madeline Island, erecting extensive warehouses and other structures.

LE SUEUR'S FORT. FORT LA POINTE.

CAMP MCCOY (*Camp Robinson*). Located seven miles east of Sparta, Monroe County, this military post was established in 1909 as Camp Robinson, occupying about 14,000 acres. During World War I, it was principally used by field artillery units. From 1919 until 1923, the camp was known as the Sparta Ordnance Depot. In 1926 the post was renamed in honor of Wisconsin National Guard Major Robert Bruce McCoy, World War I veteran, who died on January 5, 1926. In 1941–42 the post was expanded, opening officially in August 1942. During the camp's World War II peak, about 35,000 troops were stationed here. In 1945 Camp McCoy was a separation center, and in 1946 all training there ended. Decision to close Camp McCoy was announced in November 1952. It was officially inactivated in January 1953. Since then, it has been used as a summer camp for Reserve and National Guard troops.

FORT MCKAY. FORT CRAWFORD.

CAMP MCKOWN. A temporary U.S. Army post located at Portage, Columbia County, during the Winnebago Indian troubles, Camp McKown was established in 1840 by eight companies of the 8th Infantry. The post was apparently named for Lieutenant (later Major) James McKown of the New York Infantry.

CAMP RANDALL. A Civil War training post located on the grounds of the University of Wisconsin at Madison, Camp Randall was named in honor of Governor Alexander W. Randall. Occupying 42 acres extending from University Avenue to Monroe Street, between Breese Terrace and Randall Avenue, the acreage was donated in 1861 by the Wisconsin State Agricultural Society to the state legislature as a drill ground for Union troops. The camp became the center of Wisconsin military activities, and more than 70,000 men were quartered and trained here. After the war, the property became the State Fairgrounds, but in 1893 it was acquired by the university as an athletic field. In 1911 a section of the property was set aside as the Camp Randall Memorial Park, with a Memorial Arch completed in 1912 to honor Wisconsin's Civil War soldiers. During World War I, the camp was temporarily reactivated as a drill ground for troops destined for overseas, many of them university students.

CAMP RENO. In 1861, shortly after the outbreak of the Civil War, Camp Reno was established on rented land as a reception center and training post in the city of Milwaukee. The property was leased to the government for the nominal sum of $1.00, for a term expiring August 23, 1865, by Colonel George H. Walker, a former mayor of the city. The camp's eastern boundary was North Prospect Avenue on Lake Michigan. Sometime in early 1866, the post's buildings were auctioned off by the government. The only remaining structure is the camp's two-story guardhouse, moved several years after the war from the Camp Reno site to Albion Street, and used as a dwelling since then.

CAMP ROBINSON. CAMP MCCOY.

ROUNTREE'S FORT. A temporary "public" defense established in early April 1832, shortly after the outbreak of Black Hawk's War, it was erected at Platteville, Grant County, by a company of local militia organized by J. H. Rountree. It consisted of a circular stockade about 100 feet in diameter, enclosing a 20-foot-square blockhouse.

FORT ST. ANTOINE. French fur trader and diplomat Nicolas Perrot was appointed commandant of the Wisconsin territory by Governor Frontenac in 1685. In 1686 he erected Fort St. Antoine on a bluff on the northeast shore of Lake Pepin. Its site is a short distance east of the present town of Pepin.

FORT ST. FRANCIS. FORT EDWARD AUGUSTUS.

FORT ST. NICHOLAS. One of Nicolas Perrot's fur-trading posts, it was built about 1686 at the mouth of the Wisconsin River at or near the present city of Prairie du Chien in Crawford County.

CAMP SCOTT. A Civil War reception center and training camp established in 1861 at Milwaukee, Camp Scott was located on Spring Street (now Wisconsin Avenue), west of 12th Street. Wells Street and Kilbourn Avenue are the thoroughfares that cross the Camp Scott area today.

FORT SHELBY. FORT CRAWFORD.

CAMP SIGEL. A Civil War training post established in 1861 at Milwaukee, Camp Sigel's former site is today intersected from north to south by Oakland and Farwell avenues.

SUPERIOR STOCKADE. The Sioux uprisings in Minnesota during the summer of 1862, culminating in the New Ulm Massacre, caused great alarm in Superior in Douglas County. A Committee of Safety was chosen, a Home Guard organized, and a stockade built on the bay shore here. An inventory of all firearms in the town revealed a total of 60 shotguns, rifles, and pistols. The state sent 192 muskets and 2 cannon. To assist the Home Guard, Wisconsin's governor sent a company of Wisconsin soldiers that had been captured by the Confederates at Shiloh and paroled. This company was called back for Civil War duty in the summer of 1863 and was replaced by other Wisconsin paroled troops. The Chippewa residing in Superior's environs, however, remained friendly to the whites. By August 1863, the Sioux in Minnesota had been overcome and most of the soldiers left Superior. Eventually the stockade was abandoned.

TREMPEALEAU POST. In 1685 fur-trader Nicolas Perrot wintered at his post at the base of Mount Trempealeau at the present-day town of Trempealeau on the Mississippi River. In 1731 French officer Godefroy de Linctot built a fort

FORT WINNEBAGO. Oil painting of the fort as it looked in 1834. (Courtesy of the State Historical Society of Wisconsin.)

among the Sioux on the site and maintained it for five years. In later years, John Jacob Astor's American Fur Company also had a post on this site, set aside in recent years as the Perrot State Park.

CAMP WASHBURN. A Civil War reception center and training post established in October 1861, Camp Washburn was located on the old Cold Spring racetrack west of 27th Street, which at the time of the war was outside of the city limits of Milwaukee.

FORT WINNEBAGO. Established on October 7, 1828, by troops of the 1st Infantry under the command of Major David E. Twiggs (later a Confederate general), Fort Winnebago was situated on the right bank of the Fox River at the portage between the Fox and Wisconsin rivers near the present-day city of Portage in Columbia County. The post was primarily intended to control the important portage and to protect American traders in the area. Fort Winnebago was abandoned on September 10, 1845 and destroyed by fire in 1856.

FORT ANTONIO. PORTUGUESE HOUSES.

CAMP AUGUR. FORT WASHAKIE.

CAMP BETTENS. A temporary intermittently occupied Army Camp of Instruction, Camp Bettens was located on the Powder River, north of the present town of Arvada, Sheridan County. The post was first established on June 21, 1892, during the so-called Johnson County War (April–November 1892), by six companies of the 9th Cavalry, commanded by Colonel James Biddle, commanding officer of Fort Robinson, Nebraska. The six companies remained there until about the end of October of the same year. The post was reoccupied during the next three summers by Fort Robinson troops when the site served as a Camp of Instruction.

FORT BONNEVILLE (*Fort Nonsense*). Although the mountains of the Northwest literally swarmed with rival fur-trading companies and independent outfits in 1832, another organization, heavily financed and equipped, entered the field. Captain Benjamin L. E. Bonneville, French-born and a West Point graduate, had been granted a leave of absence from the U.S. Army. Gaining the financial backing of several officers of John Jacob Astor's American Fur Company in New York City, Bonneville organized a company of his own. A competitive venture in appearance, it was most probably designed as a subsidiary of Astor's enterprise.

On May 1, 1832, with 110 men and 28 loaded wagons, he set out from Fort Osage on the Missouri, took a route that later became the Oregon Trail, crossed South Pass, and reached the Green River in the first week of August. Here, a few miles from the mouth of Horse Creek, in the environs of the present-day town of Daniel in what is now Sublette County, he and his men spent several weeks constructing Fort Bonneville, a strong stockade, with blockhouses at two diagonally opposite angles, to enclose a few cabins. Shortly after the post was completed, he evacuated it and moved his outfit to a succession of fur-trade rendezvous sites within the same area. Because of his waste of considerable effort building short-lived Fort Bonneville, opposition traders and trappers derisively called the post Fort Nonsense and "Bonneville's Folly."

FORT BRIDGER. With the decline of the Rocky Mountain fur trade in the late 1830s, the "mountain men" who remained on the frontier were forced to find new occupations. Jim Bridger, ultimately the most famous of this group of early

Wyoming

FORT BRIDGER. Portrait of Jim Bridger. (Courtesy of the Wyoming State Archives and Historical Department.)

trappers, along with his partner, Louis Vasquez, chose to establish a trading post in the valley of Black's Fork of the Green River, on a site in the southwest corner of the present State of Wyoming, at today's town of Fort Bridger, Uinta County.

I have established a small fort, with a blacksmith shop and a supply of iron on the road of the emigrants on Black Fork of Green River, which promises fairly. In coming out here they are generally well supplied with money, but by the time they get here they are in need of all kinds of supplies, horses, provisions, smithwork, etc. They bring ready cash from the states, and should I receive the goods ordered, will have considerable business in that way with them, and establish trade with the Indians in the neighborhood who have a good number of beaver among them. (Kent Ruth, *Great Day in the West* [1963], p. 290)

Travelers observed the post as consisting of two adjoining log houses with dirt roofs and a small picket yard of logs set in the ground about eight feet high. The loading apartments, trading offices, and blacksmith shop opened into a square protected from attack by a strong gate of timber. Adjacent and continuous with these walls was another picket fence enclosing a large yard for animals.

Because of its convenient location on the overland route, Fort Bridger became the second important outfitting point for the emigrants between the Missouri River and the Pacific Coast—Fort Laramie being the first, and Fort Hall in

Idaho, the third. Fort Bridger hosted numerous parties of Indians, emigrants, gold seekers, adventurers, travelers, and the 1849 military expedition of Captain Howard Stansbury. After 1847 the growing influence of the Mormon settlement to the south and west began to be felt. A controversy arose in 1853 when the Mormons claimed to have purchased Fort Bridger from its owners. Bridger denied such a transaction had occurred. That fall two parties of Mormons sent out from Salt Lake City came to the vicinity, took over Fort Bridger, and established Fort Supply about 12 miles to the southwest. The two forts were then used to aid the converts to the Church as they traveled over the trail to Salt Lake City; to establish trade with the other emigrants; and to check the threat of Indian hostilities the Mormons claimed Bridger was promoting.

In the late 1850s, friction developed between the newly established Mormon state and the Federal government. As a result, President Buchanan dispatched U.S. troops to the area in 1857 under the command of Colonel Albert Sidney Johnston, 2nd U.S. Cavalry. This action precipitated the so-called "Mormon War." Upon the approach of Johnston's army, the Mormons deserted and burned both Fort Bridger and Fort Supply. Johnston immediately took over the site and declared Fort Bridger to be a military reservation. In 1858 it was officially made a military post, and a building program was started.

At the beginning of the Civil War, the post was, for a year, without a garrison, and a company of mountain men was organized by W. A. Carter, post sutler, for protection. Next a group of Nevada and California volunteers were garrisoned there at short intervals. By midsummer of 1866, the last of the volunteers were mustered out, and Fort Bridger was garrisoned by two companies of regular infantry under Brevet Major A. S. Burt. During the early 1860s the fort served as a station on the Pony Express and the Overland Stage routes and its troops helped keep the trails open when constant Indian depredations made travel extremely hazardous.

From 1867 to 1869, new life and excitement was brought into the life at Fort Bridger. To the northwest around the South pass and Sweetwater River region, the discovery of gold precipitated a "rush," and the advancing construction of the Union Pacific Railroad made the fort a strategic supply center. The troops from the fort were again called upon for protection from the Indians. A period of relative peace settled upon the valley in the 1870s despite the Indian Wars taking place on the Northern Plains. The post was abandoned in 1878 but reactivated on June

FORT BRIDGER. 1858 newspaper sketch. (Courtesy of the Wyoming State Archives.)

28, 1880. Additional barracks and officers' quarters were erected and general improvements made. But as the frontier continued to be settled, the military significance of Fort Bridger waned. On October 1, 1890, it was permanently abandoned by the military.

After its abandonment, the fort remained a community center and the home of the family of Judge W. A. Carter, long-time resident and post trader. In the late 1920s, the state of Wyoming acquired the site through the efforts of the Wyoming Historical Landmark Commission. Since that time, the state has preserved and maintained Fort Bridger as a lasting reminder of Wyoming's past. Fort Bridger Historic Site is located on U.S. 30 (Interstate 80) nine miles east of Evanston. The fort's museum features displays and interpretive devices to provide a better understanding of the post's history.

CAMP BROWN. FORT WASHAKIE.

CAMP CARLIN. FORT FRANCIS E. WARREN.

FORT CASPAR (*Fort Clay; Camp Davis; Platte Bridge Station*). One of the important posts guarding the overland emigrant trail, it was located at a natural river crossing, on the south side of the North Platte River, a mile from the present town of Casper (named for the fort but with a slightly altered spelling, used in official reports), in Natrona County. The site was first occupied by a camp established on October 27, 1855, by a detachment of troops from Fort Laramie. Early post returns referred to the camp as Fort Clay and Camp Davis. The campsite was first officially established as Platte Bridge Station in 1858, consisting of several adobe-built structures. From July 29, 1858, to April 20, 1859, two companies of the 4th Artillery, commanded by Captains Joseph Roberts and George W. Getty, were posted there to primarily safeguard the emigrant travel route. The post later served to facilitate the transport of supplies for General Albert Sidney Johnston's Utah expeditionary force destined for Salt Lake City in the self-proclaimed state founded by the Mormons.

In 1859 a 1,000-foot-long bridge across the river was completed by Louis Guinard. In May 1862 6th U.S. Volunteer troops were stationed there to continue protection of the crossing and the newly established militarily vital telegraph

FORT CASPAR. Reconstruction. (Courtesy of the Wyoming Travel Commission.)

line from marauding Indians. In the spring of 1865, Platte Bridge Station was declared a permanent post. In November of the same year, Major General John Pope, commanding the department, officially renamed the post Fort Caspar in honor of 1st Lieutenant Caspar W. Collins, 11th Ohio Cavalry, killed during the Platte Bridge Battle on July 28, 1865.

Fort Caspar was first garrisoned by Army regulars on June 28, 1866, commanded by Captain Richard L. Morris, 18th Infantry. Although the post was rebuilt and enlarged in 1866, it was abandoned a year later, on October 19, 1867, at which time it was replaced by Fort Fetterman, also on the river, near the present town of Douglas in Converse County. Immediately after the garrison evacuated Fort Caspar, its buildings and the bridge across the river were burned by the Indians. Portions of the old fort have been reconstructed on its original foundations within a park, maintained by the city of Casper.

FORT CLAY. FORT CASPAR.

FORT CONNOR. FORT RENO.

POST ON CROW CREEK. FORT FRANCIS E. WARREN.

FORT D. A. RUSSELL. FORT FRANCIS E. WARREN.

CAMP DAVIS. FORT CASPAR.

CAMP ELKINS. As a result of the so-called Johnson County War (April–November, 1892), a civil disturbance created by the overall plan by Wyoming cattle barons to drive out the small independent ranchers, this temporary field encampment, officially designated Camp Elkins, was established by six companies of the 6th Cavalry, permanently stationed at Fort Niobrara, Nebraska, on June 20, 1892. The post, located near the site of Fort Fetterman in Converse County, was permanently abandoned in late October or early November of the same year, when its garrison returned to Fort Niobrara. (See also: CAMP BETTENS.)

FORT FETTERMAN. Located on a plateau on the south bank of the North Platte River, close to the mouth of La Prele Creek, at the place where the Bozeman Trail turned north from the river, Fort Fetterman was established on July 19, 1867, by Major William McEntyre Dye, 4th Infantry. The post was named in honor of Captain William J. Fetterman, 27th Infantry, killed by Sioux Indians during the so-called Fetterman Massacre

on December 21, 1866, near Fort Phil Kearny. Consisting of four barracks and seven officers' quarters, located about eight miles northwest of present-day Douglas in Converse County, the post was designed to protect the emigrant travel routes in the area. Abandoned on May 20, 1882, the post's buildings were sold on September 29, 1882. The reservation was transferred to the Interior Department for disposition on July 22, 1884. Several preserved buildings still stand in a state park, including a small museum occupying the former officers' quarters.

FORT FRANCIS E. WARREN (*Post on Crow Creek; Fort D. A. Russell; Camp Carlin*). Located three miles west of the present city of Cheyenne on the north bank of Crow Creek, a branch of the South Platte, this post was originally established by Brevet Brigadier General John D. Stevenson of the 30th Infantry, at the point where the Union Pacific Railroad would cross Crow Creek. Designed to protect the railroad construction crews, the post was first known as the Post on Crow Creek, then officially designated Fort D. A. Russell on September 8, 1867, in honor of Brigadier General David A. Russell, who was killed on September 19, 1864, in the Battle of Opequon, Virginia.

The history of nearby Camp Carlin is intimately connected to that of the fort since August 1867, when Colonel E. B. Carlin arrived and began the construction of a quartermaster depot on Crow Creek very near Fort D. A. Russell. When finally completed about March 1871, its name was changed to Cheyenne Depot or the Quartermaster Depot at Cheyenne.

A few years after its establishment, Fort D. A. Russell was determined to be of such importance, because of its location, that it was made a permanent installation, frequently enlarged and improved. Effective January 1, 1930, the name of Fort D. A. Russell was changed to Fort Francis E. Warren, in honor of a Civil War veteran who was the first governor of the state of Wyoming. The post was transferred to the Department of the Air Force on April 1, 1948, and is now the Francis E. Warren Air Force Base.

FORT FRED STEELE. Located on the left bank of the North Platte River, about 15 miles east of the present town of Rawlins, where the Union Pacific Railroad crossed the river, in Carbon County, Fort Fred Steele was established on June 30, 1868, by Major Richard I. Dodge, 30th Infantry. Designed as a part of the line of Army posts to protect the Overland Trail and the railroad's construction crews, the post was named

in honor of Colonel Frederick Steele, 20th Infantry, who died on January 12, 1868. Although the military reservation was officially abandoned and transferred to the Interior Department on August 9, 1886, the last of the garrison's troops left the post on November 3. The site of the post is now a state park.

CAMP GUERNSEY. Located near the town of Guernsey in Platte County, this post was first used for summer maneuvers by Fort Francis E. Warren's cavalry troops, occupying temporary tent facilities in the early 1930s. In the late 1930s permanent buildings were erected by construction crews of the Works Progress Administration (WPA). During World War II, Camp Guernsey served as a training post for quartermaster troops. Since the war, the post was used for summer training maneuvers by the Wyoming National Guard.

FORT HALLECK. Located at the north base of Elk Mountain, west of the Medicine Bow River, and near the present town of Elk Mountain in Carbon County, Fort Halleck was established on July 20, 1862, by Major John O'Ferrall, 11th Ohio Cavalry, and named for Major General Henry Wager Halleck, United States Military Academy graduate and author of *Elements of Military Art and Science.* The post was established primarily to protect the Overland Trail and the important telegraph line from the Indians. Abandoned on July 4, 1866, the reservation was later transferred to the Interior Department for disposition. The site and several of the post's original buildings are presently owned and occupied by the Quealy Ranch.

FORT JOHN. FORT LARAMIE.

FORT JOHN BUFORD. FORT SANDERS.

LA BONTE STATION. CAMP MARSHALL.

FORT LARAMIE (*Fort William; Fort John*). Fort Laramie, on the eastern Wyoming prairies, was a private fur-trading post from 1834 to 1849 and a military post from 1849 to 1890. It figured prominently in the covered-wagon migrations to Oregon and California, in a series of bloody Indian campaigns, and in many other pioneer events.

After the purchase of the Louisiana Territory from France in 1803, American trappers and traders pushed boldly up the Missouri River, anxious to exploit the great fur resources of the Rocky Mountains and Great Plains. Fur companies large and small battled each other, often unscrupulously, for control of the region's trade. In the early part of the nineteenth century, beaver fur was in great demand for wearing apparel—the Laramie River country was abundant with the prized beaver. In 1834 two experienced and enterprising traders, William Sublette and Robert Campbell, realized the lucrative potential of the region and built a crude stockade fort near the confluence of the Laramie and the North Platte. It was named Fort William, after the senior partner, but it was more commonly called Fort Laramie.

When John Jacob Astor's American Fur Company purchased the post in 1836, Fort Laramie became one of the major trading centers in the Rockies. Fur traders and Indians came to barter, and depended on the fort for supplies and protection in time of trouble. Bands of Sioux, Cheyenne, and Arapaho camped nearby, eager to trade pelts and robes for dry goods, tobacco, beads, and whiskey. In 1841 when the second Fort Laramie was built (as Fort John), the fur trade was on the decline and the first covered-wagon emigrants (the Bidwell-Bartleson expedition) had passed by. The Marcus Whitman party, en route to Oregon, visited the fort in 1843, followed four years later by the initial Mormon emigration to Utah. By 1849 hundreds of covered wagons were on their westward trek, spurred on by the discovery of gold in California. The following year the high tide of westward migration began, with

FORT LARAMIE. Southern view facing the parade ground, with three ruined walls of officers' quarters on the right. (Courtesy of the National Park Service.)

thousands of travelers stopping at the fort, some only long enough to have broken equipment repaired or to take on supplies.

The U.S. government bought Fort Laramie in 1849, after recognizing that an Army post here would help to protect emigrants using the Oregon Trail from Indian hostiles. A building campaign was initiated, and within a decade Fort Laramie became a sprawling military reservation. In 1851 and again in 1868 important treaties were drawn up at Fort Laramie, by which the Sioux, Cheyenne, and other tribes of the Great Plains surrendered most of their claims to the region. For a while, the fort served as a station for the Pony Express and the Overland Stage, and later it was a supply base for long, costly wars with the Plains Indians. The last major Indian engagements in which Fort Laramie played a significant role were in connection with the Sioux and Cheyenne campaigns of 1876, directed against Sitting Bull and other Sioux chiefs as an aftermath of the Black Hills gold rush.

Beginning in the late 1870s, ranchers and homesteaders moved into the Fort Laramie region. The fort served for a time as a supply center for many of these settlers and afforded them protection against Indians and outlaws. But its importance eventually waned. In 1890, four years after recommendations had been made to abandon the old post, the troops marched away from Fort Laramie for the last time. Later, some structures were dismantled; other buildings and fixtures were auctioned off.

For nearly 50 years, Fort Laramie was allowed to fall into decay. Although the fort's historic importance was recognized earlier, it was not until 1937 that Wyoming appropriated funds for the purchase and donation to the Federal government of 214 acres of the former military reservation. By presidential proclamation in 1938, Fort Laramie National Historic Site became a unit of the National Park System. Maintained and operated by the National Park Service, the site is three miles southwest of the town of Fort Laramie on U.S. 26.

FORT MCGRAW (*Fort Thompson*). Congress in 1856 provided for a road branching northward from the Oregon Trail to deliberately bypass Utah Territory and avoid trouble with the Mormons. Surveyors and troops from Fort Kearny on October 3, 1857, established winter quarters, first known as Fort Thompson (soon renamed Fort McGraw), for working on the Fort Kearny, South Pass, and Honey Lake Wagon Road to Oregon. Located two miles northeast of present Lander, in the Popo Agie Valley, in Fremont County, the post was apparently abandoned on February 25, 1858.

FORT MACKENZIE. A major fortification located two miles northwest of the town of Sheridan, established because of the 23,000 Indians adjacent to the fort site, Fort Mackenzie was first garrisoned on May 11, 1899, by troops of the 25th Infantry. The post was named in honor of Civil War Major General Ranald Slidell Mackenzie. By 1905 it was a well-equipped installation, the second most important fort in the state. Although discontinued by the Army on November 3, 1918, during the final days of World War I, the reservation continues as a Veterans Administration psychiatric hospital.

FORT MCKINNEY (*Cantonment Reno*). After the Big Horn Expedition headed by Brigadier General George Crook had been stopped by Chief Crazy Horse and his warriors at the bank of the Rosebud, another column known as the Powder River Expedition was organized under the command of Colonel (later Major General) Ranald S. Mackenzie, 4th Cavalry, using Fort Fetterman as a base of operations. One of the campaign's series of depots, Cantonment Reno was established on October 12, 1876, by Captain Edwin Pollock, 9th Infantry, located three miles south of abandoned Fort Reno (1865–68). However, when the site of the cantonment proved to be unhealthful, the post was reestablished on July 18,1877, on the right bank of Clear Creek, a tributary of the Powder River, near the present town of Buffalo, two miles above the old Bozeman Trail, in Johnson County.

Used as a supply base for the campaign, the post included 7 two-story barracks, 14 officers' quarters, kitchens, a hospital, and a guardhouse. On August 30, 1877, the post was officially designated Fort McKinney in honor of 1st Lieutenant John A. McKinney, 4th Cavalry, killed by Indians on November 25, 1876, and became the military center for control of the Indians in the cattle-raising country east of the Big Horn Mountains. Abandoned on November 7, 1894, the post's buildings and a portion of the reservation were transferred to the state of Wyoming. In 1905 the old post became the State Soldiers and Sailors Home, three miles west of Buffalo.

CAMP MARSHALL (*La Bonte Station*). A guard post established in 1862 by detachments of troops to protect an important telegraph station on the Oregon Trail, it was originally known as Detachment at La Bonte Station and located on the North Platte River, at the mouth of La

Bonte Creek (so-named for an old French fur trapper), about 10 miles south of the present city of Douglas, Converse County. In 1863 when a company of the 11th Ohio Cavalry commanded by Captain Levi G. Marshall constructed more permanent quarters, the post was renamed Camp Marshall, a stockaded square of barracks and stables surrounding the telegraph station and defended by two mountain howitzers. Camp Marshall was abandoned in 1866 after the troubles of the 1864 Indian War were finally resolved.

NEW FORT RENO. FORT PHIL KEARNY.

FORT NONSENSE. FORT BONNEVILLE.

FORT PHIL KEARNY (*New Fort Reno*). The most important military post on the Bozeman Trail, Fort Phil Kearny was established by Colonel Henry B. Carrington on July 13, 1866. Intended to be a replacement for Fort Reno, it instead became the headquarters for its two other Bozeman Trail forts, Reno on the Powder River and C. F. Smith in Montana. It was located on Piney Creek, a branch of the Powder River, in the foothills of the Big Horn Mountains, about 12 miles northwest of the present town of Buffalo, Johnson County. The post was known as New Fort Reno until official orders, dated June 28, 1866, were received, designating it Fort Phil Kearny, in honor of the general who was killed on September 1, 1862, during the Battle of Chantilly, Virginia.

A palisaded complex of 42 log buildings, almost continually besieged by Indians, the fort was defended by a 500-man garrison with four pieces of artillery. It was from this fort that Brevet Lieutenant Colonel William J. Fetterman recklessly led 79 troops and 2 civilian teamsters to their deaths in the Fetterman Massacre on December 31, 1866, decoyed by a band of Sioux under Chief Crazy Horse into an ambush. A year later, the fort's troops, armed with new breech-loading rifles, avenged the massacre by nearly annihilating an ambush-hidden force of Indians in what became known as the Wagon Box Fight. Fort Phil Kearny was abandoned on July 31, 1868, as a result of the Fort Laramie Treaty of April 29, 1868.

CAMP PILOT BUTTE (*Camp Rock Springs*). A post was established by troops on September 5, 1885, at Rock Springs, on present I-80 between Evanston and Rawlins, Sweetwater County, to restore civil order after an anti-Chinese miners' riot erupted on September 2, killing about 20 of the foreign laborers. Two companies remained as a garrison when the major part of the force was withdrawn on October 20, 1885, when the post was officially designated Camp Pilot Butte. The post was continually garrisoned until 1899. Several of the post's buildings are still in use, with the former barracks converted as a parochial school operated by the Church of Saints Cyril and Methodius.

FORT PLATTE. A large strongly constructed trading post, located on the bank of the North Platte River, directly on the Oregon Trail, it was established in 1841 by independent trader Lancaster P. Lupton in opposition to Fort Laramie about a mile and a half away. The construction of the 103-by-144-foot post stimulated the American Fur Company to rebuild Fort Laramie. A year later, Lupton sold out to another opposition firm, Sybille, Adams and Company, and later still to Pratte, Cabanne and Company. Fort Platte was abandoned apparently sometime in 1847.

PLATTE BRIDGE STATION. FORT CASPAR.

FORT PHIL KEARNY. Artist's rendition. (Courtesy of the National Archives.)

PORTUGUESE HOUSES (*Fort Antonio*). One of the earliest trading posts in the Wyoming country, it was established in the fall of 1834 by Antonio Montero near the confluence of the North and South Forks of the Powder River in the southern part of today's Johnson County, 12 miles east of the present-day town of Kaycee. A small complex of several log cabins enclosed by a palisade constructed of large hewn timbers, occasionally known as Fort Antonio, it was usually referred to as Portuguese Houses. Although attacked and besieged by Blackfeet Indians at various times, Montero developed a strong trade with the Crow Indians who had several villages in the near environs of the fort. During the winter of 1836–37, the area was invaded by some 300 competitive fur-hungry trappers, ultimately forcing Montero to abandon his post, probably sometime in 1840.

CANTONMENT RENO. FORT McKINNEY.

FORT RENO (*Fort Connor*). A Bozeman Trail post located on a plateau about 100 feet above the east bank of the Powder River, about two miles north of the present town of Sussex in Johnson County, Fort Connor was established on August 14, 1865, by Brigadier General Patrick E. Connor as a temporary base of supplies during his Powder River campaign against the Sioux. On November 11, 1866, when the open post was rebuilt with blockhouses enclosed by a stockade by Colonel Henry B. Carrington, it was renamed Fort Reno in honor of Major General Jesse Lee Reno, killed on September 14, 1862, in the Battle of South Mountain, Virginia. Fort Reno was abandoned on August 18, 1868, when the Army was compelled to withdraw its garrisons in the area, in accordance with the Fort Laramie Treaty of April 29, 1868.

CAMP ROCK SPRINGS. CAMP PILOT BUTTE.

FORT SANDERS (*Fort John Buford*). Located about two miles east of the Laramie River and three miles south of the present city of Laramie in Albany County, this post on the Overland Trail was designed to protect the emigrant route, the stage line between Denver and Salt Lake City, and the construction crews of the Union Pacific Railroad. Established on July 10, 1866, by Captain Henry R. Mizner, 18th Infantry, it was originally named Fort John Buford in honor of Civil War Major General John Buford who died on December 16, 1863. The post was officially designated Fort Sanders a month later in honor of Brigadier General William P. Sanders, who died on November 19, 1863, of mortal wounds suffered at Knoxville, Tennessee.

When first constructed, Fort Sanders was a four-company post arranged around a 223-by-400-foot parade ground. It was later enlarged to a 500-by-600-foot parade with additional barracks to accommodate six companies, officers' quarters, magazine and guardhouse. Abandoned on May 18, 1882, the military reservation was transferred to the Interior Department on August 22, 1882, for disposition. Two stone-built structures, the magazine and the guardhouse, still stand on the site of the fort.

CAMPS SCOTT. When Colonel Albert Sidney Johnston's Utah Expedition of cavalry troops arrived at Fort Bridger in the late fall of 1857, they found that both it and Fort Supply, a short distance to the south, had been burned by the Mormons. Forced to improvise winter quarters, the troops on November 17, 1857, established Camp Scott two miles form Fort Bridger's ruins. Here they suffered through a harsh winter in a shabby complex of tents and dugouts, and crudely

FORT RENO. Artist's rendition. (Courtesy of the National Archives.)

built huts and lean-tos. The post was abandoned on June 18, 1858.

CAMP SHERIDAN. FORT YELLOWSTONE.

CAMP STAMBAUGH.

Located in Smith's Gulch, about three miles east of the present town of Atlantic City, Fremont County, in the Sweetwater mining district, Camp Stambaugh was established on June 20, 1870, by Major James S. Brisbin with Company B of the 2nd Cavalry, and named in honor of Lieutenant Charles B. Stambaugh, 2nd Cavalry, killed by Indians on May 4, 1870, near the former town of Miner's Delight, near Atlantic City. At first a subpost of Fort Bridger, then declared an independent post on August 20, 1870, it was established in response to demands by the district's miners for protection from the almost adjoining Shoshoni Indian Reservation. Camp Stambaugh consisted of two 80-by-32-foot hewn-log barracks, four sets of married soldiers' lodgings, four officers' quarters, and other auxiliary structures. The post was abandoned on May 16, 1878.

FORT SUPPLY.

An experiment in the Mormons' religious practicality, representing a part of the second phase of the Church's long-range colonization plan "beyond Utah's cultivatable valleys," Fort Supply was established in the fall of 1853 in Black's Fort Valley in southwestern Wyoming, twelve miles south of Fort Bridger and one mile west of the present town of Robertson in Uinta County. A cluster of buildings surrounded by a high stockade, it was an attempt to establish a supply base and a farm, the first in Wyoming territory, to support emigrating Mormon wagon trains moving west to Utah. The fort was burned by the Mormons in 1857 in advance of General Albert Sidney Johnston's Utah Expedition.

FORT THOMPSON. FORT McGRAW.

CAMP WALBACH.

Established by two companies of the 4th Artillery on September 30, 1858, to protect the Lodgepole Creek emigrant route, particularly the dangerous crossing through Cheyenne Pass, Camp Walbach was located on the creek, about four miles west of the present town of Federal in Laramie County. The post was named in honor of Colonel John De Barth Walbach, 4th Artillery, who died on June 10, 1857. Camp Walbach was abandoned on April 19, 1859.

FORT WASHAKIE (*Camp Augur; Camp Brown*).

Located in the Popo Agie River valley at the present town of Lander in Fremont County, Camp Augur was established on June 28, 1869, by 1st Lieutenant Patrick Henry Breslin, 4th Infantry, and named for Brigadier General Christopher C. Augur. Designed to protect the Bannock and Shoshoni Indians against other hostile Indians, particularly the Sioux and the Cheyenne, the name of the post was changed on March 28, 1870, to Camp Brown in honor of Captain Frederick H. Brown, 18th Infantry, who was killed on December 21, 1866, in the Fetterman Massacre. In June 1871 a new site was selected on the south bank of the South Fork of the Little Wind River at its confluence with the North Fork of the river, about 15 miles northwest of Lander.

The new post was reestablished by Captain Robert A. Torrey, 13th Infantry. On December 30, 1878, the post was officially designated Fort Washakie in honor of Shoshoni Chief Washakie. In 1899 the War Department ordered the post abandoned, but Chief Washakie, then more than 90 years old, objected so vehemently that the order was rescinded. Evacuated on May 1, 1907, but reoccupied a month later, it was declared a permanent post. Fort Washakie was permanently

FORT SUPPLY. Artist's rendition. (Courtesy of the Wyoming State Archives and Historical Department.)

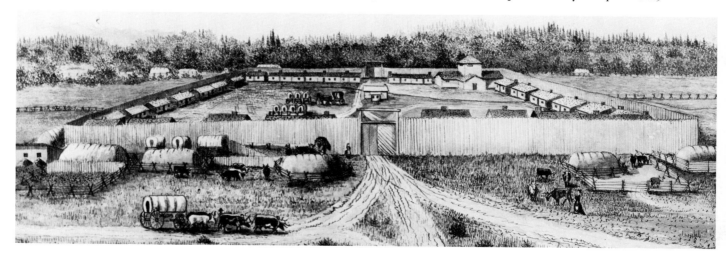

abandoned on March 30, 1909. The post's buildings and military reservation property, transferred to the Interior Department, became the headquarters of the Wind River (Shoshoni and Arapaho) Indian Reservation, at today's town of Fort Washakie.

FORT WILLIAM. FORT LARAMIE.

FORT YELLOWSTONE (*Camp Sheridan*). Yellowstone National Park was created in 1872 and placed under the jurisdiction of the Interior Department. In 1886 when Congress failed to make an appropriation for the continuance of the Park, the Interior Department requested the War Department to send troops to protect the area from vandalism and to preserve its natural wonders. Captain Moses Harris and Company M, 1st Cavalry, arrived on August 17, 1886, at Mammoth Hot Springs, and established Camp Sheridan, named in honor of Lieutenant General Philip Sheridan, in what is now Yellowstone National Park County. A small temporary complex of wooden buildings, adequate for just one troop of cavalry, Camp Sheridan was abandoned in 1891 when the permanent buildings for Fort Yellowstone were completed. The site of the camp is located south of the Park's headquarters. Camp Sheridan's last remaining building burned down in 1964. At least four troops of cavalry occupied the new post, officially designated Fort Yellowstone on May 11, 1891. Abandoned by the Army in 1918, the fort's buildings are now occupied by the National Park Service's administrative staff.

General Bibliography

Athearn, Robert G. *Forts of the Upper Missouri*. Englewood Cliffs, N.J., 1967.

Barnett, Correlli. *Britain and Her Army, 1509–1970*. New York, 1970.

Barrett, Arrie. "Western Frontier Forts in Texas, 1845–1861," in West Texas Historical Association *Year Book*, 7:115–139 (June, 1931).

Beers, Henry Putney. *The Western Military Frontier, 1815–1846*. Philadelphia, 1935.

Bertsch, W.H. "The Defenses of Oswego," in *Proceedings of the New York State Historical Association*.

Boatner III, Mark Mayo. *The Civil War Dictionary*. New York, 1959.

————. *Encyclopedia of the American Revolution*.

————. *Landmarks of the American Revolution*. Harrisburg, Pa., 1973.

Boorstin, Daniel J. *The Americans: The Colonial Experience*. New York, 1958.

Boynton, Edward C. *History of West Point*. New York, 1863.

Brandes, Ray. *Frontier Military Posts of Arizona*. Globe, Ariz., 1960.

Brown, Dee. *Fort Phil Kearny: An American Saga*. New York, 1962.

Burlingame, Merrill G. *The Montana Frontier*. Helena, Mont., 1942.

Casey, Powell A. *Encyclopedia of Forts, Posts, Named Camps and Other Military Installations in Louisiana, 1700–1981*. Baton Rouge, La., 1983.

Commager, Henry Steele, and Richard B. Morris. *The Spirit of 'Seventy-Six*. 2 vols. Indianapolis, Ind., 1958.

Dunnack, Henry E. *Maine Forts*. Augusta, Me., 1924.

Ellison, Robert S. *Fort Bridger, Wyoming: A Brief History*. Casper, Wyo., 1931.

Emmett, Chris. *Fort Union and the Winning of the Southwest*. Norman, Okla., 1965.

Foote, Shelby. *The Civil War: A Narrative (Fort Sumter to Perryville)*. New York, 1958.

————. *The Civil War: A Narrative (Fredericksburg to Meridian)*. New York, 1963.

————. *The Civil War: A Narrative (Red River to Appomattox)*. New York, 1974.

Frazer, Robert W. *Forts of the West*. Norman, Okla., 1965.

Foreman, Grant. *Advancing the Frontier, 1830–1860*. Norman, Okla., 1933.

Frontier Forts of Pennsylvania, Report of the Commission to Locate the Site of the. Vol. I: "The Indian Forts of the Blue Mountains" by H.M.M. Richards; Vol. II: "The Frontier Forts of Western Pennsylvania" by George Dallas Albert. Harrisburg, Pa., 1916.

Grant, Bruce. *American Forts Yesterday and Today*. New York, 1965.

Grismer, Karl H. *The Story of Fort Myers: The History of the Land of the Caloosahatchee and Southwest Florida*. St. Petersburg, Fla., 1949.

Hafen, LeRoy R., and Francis Marion Young. *Fort Laramie and the Pageant of the West, 1834–1890*. Glendale, Calif., 1938.

Hameraly, Thomas H.S. *Complete Regular Army Register of the United States for One Hundred Years (1779–1879)*. Washington, D.C., 1890.

Hammond, John M. *Quaint and Historic Forts*. Philadelphia, 1915.

Handy, Mary Olivia. *History of Fort Sam Houston*. San Antonio, Tex., 1951.

Hart, Herbert M. *Old Forts of the Far West*. Seattle, Wash., 1964.

————. *Old Forts of the Northwest*. Seattle, Wash., 1963.

_____. *Old Forts of the Southwest.* Seattle, Wash., 1964.

_____. *Pioneer Forts of the West.* Seattle, Wash., 1967.

Havinghurst, Walter. *Three Flags at the Straits: The Forts of Mackinac.* Englewood Cliffs, N.J., 1966.

Heitman, Francis B. *Historical Register and Dictionary of the United States Army, from Its Organization, September 29, 1789, to March 2, 1903.* 2 vols. Washington, D.C., 1903.

Hunt, Elvid. *History of Fort Leavenworth.* Fort Leavenworth, Kans., 1926.

James, Alfred Procter, and Charles Morse Stotz. *Drums in the Forest.* Pittsburgh, Pa., 1958.

Jones, Robert Ralston. *Fort Washington at Cincinnati, Ohio.* Cincinnati, Ohio, 1902.

Lavender, David. *Bent's Fort.* Garden City, N.Y., 1954.

Lewis, Emanuel Raymond. *Seacoast Fortifications of the United States: Introductory History.* Washington, D.C., Smithsonian Institution Press, 1970.

Long, E.B., with Barbara Long. *The Civil War Day by Day: An Almanac, 1861–1865.* Garden City, N.Y., 1971.

Lossing, Benson J. *The Pictorial Field-Book of the Revolution.* 2 vols. New York, 1869.

_____. *The Pictorial Field-Book of the War of 1812.* New York, 1869.

Mansfield, Joseph K.F. *On the Condition of Western Forts, 1853–54.* Edited by Robert W. Frazer, Norman, Okla., 1963.

Meredith, Roy. *Storm Over Sumter: The Opening Engagement of the Civil War.* New York, 1957.

Miller, Don, and Stan Cohen. *Military & Trading Posts of Montana.* Missoula, Mont., 1978.

Monaghan, Jay. *Civil War on the Western Border, 1854–1865.* New York, 1955.

Moorhead, Max L. *The Presidio: Bastion of the Spanish Borderlands.* Norman, Okla., 1975.

Morrison, William Brown. *Military Posts and Camps in Oklahoma.* Oklahoma City, Okla., 1936.

Palmer, Dave Richard. *The River and the Rock: The History of Fortress West Point, 1775–1783.* New York, 1969.

Pargellis, Stanley, ed. *Military Affairs in North America 1748–1765.* Hamden, Conn., 1969.

Peckham, Howard H. *The Colonial Wars: 1689–1762.* Chicago, 1964.

_____. *Pontiac and the Indian Uprising.* Chicago, 1947.

Pell, Stephen H.P. *Fort Ticonderoga: A Short History.* Ticonderoga, N.Y., 1935.

Peterson, Harold L. *Forts in America.* New York, 1964.

Phillips, Paul Chrisler. *The Fur Trade.* 2 vols. Norman, Okla., 1961.

Pride, Woodbury Freeman. *The History of Fort Riley.* Fort Riley, Kans., 1926.

Prucha, Francis Paul. *Broadax and Bayonet.* Madison, Wis., 1953.

_____. *A Guide to the Military Posts of the United States.* Madison, Wis., 1964.

_____. *The Sword of the Republic: The United States Army on the Frontier, 1783–1846.* New York, 1969.

Quaife, Milo M. *Chicago and the Old Northwest, 1673–1835.* Chicago, 1913.

Roberts, Robert B. *New York's Forts in the Revolution.* Rutherford, N.J., 1980.

Ruth, Kent. *Great Day in the West: Forts, Posts, and Rendezvous Beyond the Mississippi.* Norman, Okla., 1963.

Scanlan, Tom, ed. *Army Times Guide to Army Posts.* Harrisburg, Pa., 1963.

Smith, Justin H. *Arnold's March to Quebec.* New York, 1903.

Sosin, Jack. *The Revolutionary Frontier, 1763–1783.* New York, 1967.

Stember, Sol. *The Bicentennial Guide to the American Revolution.* 3 vols. New York, 1974.

Swiggett, Howard. *War Out of Niagara.* New York, 1933.

Thum, Marcella, and Gladys Thum. *Exploring Military America.* New York, 1982. United States. Department of the Army Headquarters. *American Military History 1607–1958.* Washington, D.C., 1959.

_____. Department of the Army Headquarters. *United States Army Installations and Major Activities.* Washington, D.C., February, 1980.

_____. Department of the Interior, National Park Service. *Colonials and Patriots.* Washington, D.C., 1964.

_____. Department of the Interior, National Park Service. *Soldier and Brave.* Introduction by Ray Allen Billington. New York, 1963.

_____. War Department. *The War of the Rebellion: A Compilation of the Official Records of the Union and Confederate Armies.* 128 vols. Washington, D.C., 1880–1891.

_____. Army Corps of Engineers. *United States Coast Defense, 1775–1950: A Bibliography* by Dale E. Floyd. Washington, D.C., 1985.

_____. War Department, Adjutant General's Office. *Army Posts, Camps, Cantonments, Etc., in the United States, November 15, 1918.* Washington, D.C., 1918.

————. War Department, Adjutant General's Office. *List of Military Posts, Etc., Established in the United States from Its Earliest Settlements to the Present Time.* Washington, D.C., 1902.

————. War Department, Adjutant General's Office. *List of Military Posts, Camps, and Stations in the Continental United States, 1941–1946.*

————. War Department, Adjutant General's Office. *Military Posts, Camps, and Stations in the Continental United States, 1947–March 1953.*

————. War Department, Inspector General's Office. *Outline Descriptions of the Posts and Stations of Troops in the Geographical Divisions and Departments of the United States.* Compiled by R.B. Marcy. Washington, D.C., 1872.

————. War Department. *A Report on the Hygiene of the United States Army, with Descriptions of Military Posts.* Circular No. 8. Washington, D.C., 1875.

————. War Department. *Annual Reports of the Secretary of War.* Washington, D.C., 1823–1941.

————. War Department, Surgeon General's Office. *A Report on Barracks, and Hospitals, with Descriptions of Military Posts.* Circular No. 4. Washington, D.C., 1870.

Utley, Robert M. *Frontier Regulars: The United States Army and the Indian, 1866–1891.* New York, 1973.

Vauban, Sebastien LePrestre de. *A Manual of Siegecraft and Fortification.* Translated, with an Introduction, by George A. Rothrock. Ann Arbor, Mich., 1968.

Vrooman, John. *Forts and Firesides of the Mohawk Country.* Philadelphia, 1943.

Ward, Christopher. *The War of the Revolution.* 2 vols. New York, 1952.

Ware, Captain Eugene F. *The Indian War of 1864.* New York, 1960.

Weigley, Russell F. *History of the United States Army.* New York, 1967.

West Point Atlas of American Wars, The. Compiled by the Department of Military Art and Engineering, United States Military Academy. Chief Editor, Brig. Gen. Vincent J. Esposito (Ret.). Volume I: 1689–1900; Volume II: 1900–1953. New York, 1959.

Whiting, J.S. *Forts of the State of Washington.* Seattle, Wash., 1951.

————, and Richard J. Whiting. *Forts of the State of California.* Seattle, Wash., 1960.

Young, Rigers W. "Fort Marion During the Seminole War, 1835–1842," in *Florida Historical Society Quarterly,* 12:193–223 (April, 1935).

State Archives and Libraries

Alabama Department of Archives and History
  624 Washington Avenue
  Montgomery, AL 36104

Alaska Historical Library
  Pouch G, State Capitol
  Juneau, AK 99801

Arizona State Department of Library, Archives and Public Records
  State Capitol
  Phoeniz, AZ 85007

Arkansas History Commission
  One Capitol Mall
  Little Rock, AR 72201

California Historical Society
  2090 Jackson Street
  San Francisco, CA 94109

California Department of Parks and Recreation
  1416 9th Street
  Sacramento, CA 95814

Colorado Division of State Archives and Public Records
  1530 Sherman Street
  Denver, CO 80203

State Historical Society of Colorado
  200 14th Avenue
  Denver, CO 80203

Connecticut Historical Society
  1 Elizabeth Street
  Hartford, CT 06105

Connecticut State Library
  231 Capitol Avenue
  Hartford, CT 06115

Historical Society of Delaware
  505 Market Street
  Wilmington, DE 19801

Library of Congress
  Washington, DC 20540

National Archives
  Constitution Avenue
  Washington, DC 20408

Smithsonian Institute
  1000 Jefferson Drive, S.W.
  Washington, DC 20560

Florida Division of Archives, History and Records Management
  The Capitol
  Tallahassee, FL 32301

Georgia Department of Archives and History
  330 Capitol Avenue
  Atlanta, GA 30334

Hawaiian Historical Society
  560 Kawaiahao Street
  Honolulu, HI 96813

Idaho State Historical Society
  610 North Julia Davis Drive
  Boise, ID 83706

Illinois State Archives
  Spring Street
  Springfield, IL 62706

Illinois State Historical Library
  Old State Capitol
  Springfield, IL 62706

Indiana Division, Indiana State Library
  140 North Senate Avenue
  Indianapolis, IN 46204

Indiana Historical Society
140 North Senate Avenue
Indianapolis, IN 46204

Iowa Department of History and Archives
East 12th Street and Grand Avenue
Des Moines, IA 50319

Kansas State Historical Society
Memorial Building, 120 West 10th Street
Topeka, KS 66612

Filson Club
118 West Breckinridge Street
Louisville, KY 40203

Kentucky Historical Society
Old State House
Frankfort, KY 40601

Louisiana Historical Society
231 Carondelet Street
New Orleans, LA 70130

Maine State Archives
Archives Building
Augusta, ME 04330

Maine State Museum
State House
Augusta, ME 04330

Maine Historical Society
485 Congress Street
Portland, ME 04111

Maryland Hall of Records
College Avenue and St. John's Street
Annapolis, MD 21404

Maryland Historical Trust
21 State Circle
Annapolis, MD 21401

Massachusetts Historical Society
1154 Boylston Street
Boston, MA 02215

Michigan Historical Collections
Bentley Historical Library
1150 Beal Avenue
Ann Arbor, MI 48105

Minnesota Historical Society
690 Cedar Street
St. Paul, MN 55101

Mississippi Department of Archives and History
100 South State Street
Jackson, MS 39201

Mississippi Historical Society
P.O. Box 571
Jackson, MS 39205

State Historical Society of Missouri
Hitt and Lowry Streets
Columbia, MO 65201

Montana Historical Society
225 North Roberts Street
Helena, MT 59601

Nebraska State Historical Society
512 East Avenue
Lincoln, NE 68508

Nevada State, County and Municipal Archives
Capitol Building Annex
Carson City, NV 89701

New Hampshire Historical Society
30 Park Street
Concord, NH 03301

New Jersey Bureau of Archives and History
State Library
185 West State Street
Trenton, NJ 08618

Museum of New Mexico
113 Lincoln Street
Santa Fe, NM 87501

Albany Institute of History and Art
124 Washington Avenue
Albany, NY 12210

New York Historical Society
170 Central Park West
New York, NY 10024

North Carolina State Archives
109 East Jones Street
Raleigh, NC 27611

North Dakota State Historical Society
Liberty Memorial Building
Bismarck, ND 58501

Cincinnati Historical Society
Eden Park
Cincinnati, OH 45202

Oklahoma Historical Society
2100 North Lincoln Boulevard
Oklahoma City, OK 73105

Oregon Historical Society
1230 S.W. Park Avenue
Portland, OR 97205

Historical Society of Pennsylvania
1300 Locust Street
Philadelphia, PA 19107

U.S. Army Military History Institute
Carlisle Barracks, PA 17013

Rhode Island Historical Society
52 Power Street
Providence, RI 02906

South Carolina Historical Society
100 Meeting Street
Charleston, SC 29401

South Dakota State Historical Society
East Capitol Avenue
Pierre, SD 57501

Tennessee Historical Society
403 7th Avenue North
Nashville, TN 37219

Tennessee State Library and Archives
411 7th Avenue North
Nashville, TN 37219

Texas Library and Historical Commission
1201 Brazos Street
Austin, TX 78701

Utah State Historical Society
603 East South Temple
Salt Lake City, UT 84102

Vermont Historical Society
State Street
Montpelier, VT 05602

Virginia Historical Society
428 North Boulevard
Richmond, VA 23220

Seattle Historical Society
2161 East Hamlin Street
Seattle, WA 98112

Washington State Historical Society
315 North Stadium Way
Tacoma, WA 98403

West Virginia Department of Archives and
History
400 East Wing, State Capitol
Charleston, WV 25305

State Historical Society of Wisconsin
816 State Street
Madison, WI 53706

Wyoming State Archives and Historical Department
State Office Building
Cheyenne, WY 82001

Index to Forts

A

Fort A. *See* Fort Girardeau (MO)
Camp Abbot (OR), 661
Fort Abbot (VA), 801
Fort Abercrombie. *See* Fort Greely (Kodiak Island) (AK)
Fort Abercrombie (ND), 627
Aberdeen Post (MS), 441
Aberdeen Proving Ground (MD), 375–376
Abiquiu Post (NM), 521
Abó Pass Post (NM), 521
Abó Station. *See* Abó Pass Post (NM)
Camp Abraham Lincoln. *See* Camp Berry (ME)
Fort Abraham Lincoln (ND), 627–628
Acushnet Fort (MA), 393
Presidio de los Adaes (Adais) (LA), 325
Camp Adair (OR), 661
Fort Adair (TN), 737
Fort Adams (AK), 19
Camp Adams (CO), 101
Camp near Adams (FL), 143
Fort (T.B.) Adams (FL), 143
Camp Adams (MA), 393
Fort Adams (MN), 427
Camp Adams. *See* Jefferson Barracks (MO)
Cantonment Adams. *See* Jefferson Barracks (MO)
Fort Adams (MS), 441
Fort Adams (OH), 635
Fort Adams (RI), 697–698
Fort Adams. *See* Fort Pickering (TN)
Camp Adams (TX), 749
Addison Blockhouse. *See* Fort Duncan McRae (FL)
Adobe Camp (OR), 661
Fort Adobe (Walls) (TX), 749
Adobe Meadows Camp (CA), 59
Fort Advance (GA), 215
Camp Advance (NC), 607
Advanced Redoubt (FL), 143–144
Camp A. E. Wood. *See* Camp Yosemite (CA)
Fort Aikman (IN), 273
Aitken's Post (MN), 427
Camp Ajo (AZ), 33
Fort Alabama. *See* Fort Jackson (AL)
Fort Alabama. *See* Fort Foster (FL)
Fort Alafia (FL), 144
Camp Alamance (NC), 607
The Alamo (TX), 749–750
Fort Alaqua (FL), 144
Fort Albany. *See* Fort Frederick (NY)
Fort Albany (VA), 801
Camp Albert (CA), 60

Camp Albert. *See* Fort Larnes (KS)
Camp Albert C. Ritchie. *See* Fort Ritchie (MD)
Fort Albert Sidney Johnston (KY), 303
Post of Albuquerque (NM), 521
Alcatraz Island (CA), 59–60
Fort Alden (NY), 537
Camp Alden (OR), 661
Fort Alden (WA), 829
Fort Alert (GA), 215
Fort Alexander (AK), 19
Alexander Redout. *See* Fort Alexander (Cook Inlet) (AK)
Battery Alexander (DC), 133
Alexander Redoubt. *See* Fort Elizabeth (HI)
Fort Alexander. *See* Fort Sumner (MD)
Alexander Barracks. *See* Schofield Barracks (MO)
Fort Alexander (MT), 467
Camp Alexander (VA), 801
Fort Alexander (VA), 801
Alexander's Blockhouse (WA), 829
Fort Alexandria (AL), 1
Cantonment Alexandria. *See* Camp Beauregard (LA)
Post of Alexandria (LA)
Alexandria Defenses (VA), 801–802
Fort Alexandrovsk. *See* Fort Alexander (Nushagak) (AK)
Fort Alexis. *See* Spanish Fort (AL)
Camp Alfred Vail. *See* Fort Monmouth (NJ)
Alger Garrison (ME), 357
Camp (Russell A.) Alger (VA), 802
Fort Algernourne. *See* Fort Monroe (VA)
Algiers Barracks. *See* Powder Magazine Barracks (LA)
Algodones Quartermaster Depot (NM), 521
Alkali Station (NE), 481
Fort Allatoona (GA), 215
Allatoona Pass Fort (GA), 215
Allegheny Arsenal (PA), 671
Camp Allegheny (WV), 841
Camp Allen (CA), 60
Camp Allen (IN), 273
Camp Allen (KY), 303
Fort Allen. *See* Fort Gloucester (MA)
Fort Allen (ME), 357
Fort Allen (NC), 607
Fort Allen (PA), 671
Allentown Camp. *See* Camp Crane (PA)
Allerton Battery. *See* Fort Revere (MD)
Fort Alligator (FL), 144
Fort Allison (IL), 255
Alstead's Forts (NH), 497

Fort Altena. *See* Fort Christina (DE)
Altes Fort. *See* Fort la Fourche (IL)
Alton (Camp) Post (IL), 255
Alum Creek Blockhouse (OH), 635
Camp Alvin Saunders (NE), 481
Camp Alvord (OR), 661–662
Fort Amanda (OH), 635
Amatol Arsenal (NJ), 505
Amboy Ferry Post (NYC), 605
Amchitka Post (AK), 19
Camp Amelia (FL), 144
Amelia Island Blockhouse (FL), 144
American Camp. *See* Camp San Juan Island (WA)
Amersfort Blockhouse (NY), 537
Fort Amherst (NY), 537–538. *See also* Fort Crown Point
Amite Barracks (LA), 326
Amite Post (LA), 326
Camp Ammen (OH), 635
Fort Ammen (TN), 737
Camp Amory (NC), 607
Fort Amory. *See* Camp Amory (NC)
Fort Anáhuac (TX), 750
Fort Anawagon (ME), 357
Camp Anchorage. *See* Fort Richardson (AK)
Fort Anchusa (FL), 144
Camp Anderson (CA), 60
Fort Anderson (CA), 60
Camp Anderson (DC), 133
Camp Anderson (IN), 273. *See also* Camp Stilwell (IN)
Fort Anderson (KY), 303
Camp Anderson (NC), 607
Fort Anderson (NC), 607–608
Fort Anderson. *See* Thicketty Fort (SC)
Anderson Blockhouse (VA), 802
Redoubt (Battery) Anderson (VA), 802
Andersonville Prison. *See* Camp Sumter (GA)
Andover Garrisons (MA), 393
Camp Andrade (CA), 60
Fort Andreavsky (AK), 19–20
Fort Andrew (MA), 393
Camp Andrew. *See* Camp Wool (MD)
Camp Andrew (MT), 467
Camp Andrew (VA), 802
Camp Andrew Jackson (TN), 737
Camp Andrews (DE), 127
Fort Andrews (FL), 144
Fort Andrews (MA), 394
Fort Andrews (ME), 357
Camp Andrews (OH), 635–636
Fort Andros. *See* Fort George (Brunswick) (ME)
Camp Andy Johnson (IN), 273
Camp Andy Johnson (KY), 303–304

Camp Andy Johnson. *See* Fort Johnson (TN)
Post of Angel Island. *See* Fort McDowell (CA)
Fort Ann (FL), 144–145
Fort Ann. *See* Fort Pickering (MA)
Fort Ann (MS), 441
Camp Anna (IL), 255
Fort Anne (ME), 357
Fort Anne (NY), 538
Fort Anne. *See* Fort Wolcott (RI)
Annette Island Post (AK), 20
Camp Anniston (AL), 1
Annunciation Square Camp (LA), 326
Fort Annutteeliga (FL), 145
Fort Anson (MA), 394
Antelope Station Post (NV), 489
Fort Antes (PA), 672
Camp Anthony Wayne (PA), 672
Fort Antoine (MN), 427
Camp Anton Chico (NM), 521–522
Fort Antonio. *See* Portuguese Houses (WY)
Camp Anza (CA), 60
Camp Apache. *See* Fort Apache (AZ)
Fort Apache (AZ), 33
Apalachicola Fort (AL), 1
Apalachicola Arsenal (FL), 145–146
Camp Apalachicola (FL), 145
Fort Apalachicola. *See* Fort Gadsden (FL)
Fort Apple River (IL), 255
Aptuxet Trading Post (MA), 394
Fort Aransas (TX), 750. *See also* Fort Shell Bank
Fort Aravaipa. *See* Fort Grant No. 1 (AZ)
Fort Arbuckle (FL), 146
Camp Arbuckle (OK), 651
Camp (Old Fort) Arbuckle (OK), 651
Fort Arbuckle (OK), 651–652
Fort Arbuthnot. *See* Fort Moultrie (SC)
Camp Arcadia (CA), 60
Fort Archangel Gabriel. *See* Fort St. Michael (AK)
Fort Archangel Michael. *See* Fort St. Michael (AK)
Fort Argyle (GA), 215–216
Camp Argyle (NC), 608
Arikara Post. *See* Fort Manuel Lisa (ND)
Camp Arivaca (AZ), 33
Camp Arivaca Junction (AZ), 33
Fort Arkansas. *See* Arkansas Post (AR)
Arkansas Post (AR), 51–52
Camp Arlington (VA), 802
Arlington Cantonment (VA), 802
Camp Armistead (FL), 146
Fort Armistead (FL), 146
Fort Armistead (MD), 376

M

U

V

W